GEMINATION IN THE AKKADIAN VERB

STUDIA SEMITICA NEERLANDICA

edited by

prof.dr. W.J. van Bekkum, prof.dr. W.A.M. Beuken s.j., prof.dr. H.Daiber, dr. C.H.J. de Geus, prof.dr. J. Hoftijzer, prof.dr. T. Muraoka, prof.dr. W.S. Prinsloo, prof.dr. K.A.D. Smelik, prof.dr. K. van der Toorn and prof.dr. K.R. Veenhof

For publications in the series see page 495.

Submission of manuscripts

- Manuscripts should be submitted to the senior editor of Van Gorcum Publishers, P.O. Box 43, 9400 AA Assen, The Netherlands.

- Each manuscript submitted is reviewed by two reviewers.

- The reviewers will not be identified to the authors.

N.J.C. Kouwenberg

GEMINATION IN THE AKKADIAN VERB

1997
Van Gorcum

ISBN 90 232 3255 0

Printed by Van Gorcum & Comp. B.V.

ACKNOWLEDGEMENTS

The completion of this book has been greatly expedited by a grant from the Research School CNWS of Leiden University, for which I would like to express my gratitude.

I am also grateful to Prof. Dr. K. R. Veenhof, who suggested the Akkadian D-stem as a fruitful field of research and who supplied useful material on which I have drawn, especially from Old Assyrian.

Finally, I would like to thank my wife Yvonne for her support and patience during the writing of the book and, above all, for correcting the English.

TABLE OF CONTENTS

Introduction ---------- 1

CHAPTER ONE Earlier approaches to the D-stem---------- 4

1.1. Views on the D-stem up to 1942---------- 4
1.2. Views on the D-stem since 1942---------- 5
1.3. Problems raised by the D-stem---------- 6
1.4. Solutions proposed up to 1942---------- 7
1.5. The inadequacy of these solutions---------- 8
1.6. Goetze's solution---------- 10
1.7. Positive points of Goetze's solution---------- 11
1.8. Criticism of Goetze---------- 12
1.9. Conclusions---------- 15
Notes to Chapter One---------- 16

CHAPTER TWO Iconicity and grammaticalization ---------- 19

2.1. Iconicity---------- 19
2.1.1. Iconicity and arbitrariness---------- 19
2.1.2. Motivation---------- 21
2.1.3. Root extensions in Semitic---------- 22
2.1.4. Gemination in Akkadian---------- 23
2.1.5. Gemination and plurality---------- 24
2.2. Grammaticalization---------- 26
2.2.1. The development of grammatical elements---------- 26
2.2.2. Renewal---------- 28
2.2.3. Weakening and renewal in Semitic---------- 31
2.2.4. The nature of gemination---------- 33
2.2.4.1. Gemination as an expressive device in Semitic---------- 34
2.2.4.2. The functional erosion of gemination---------- 35
2.2.4.3. Lexicalization---------- 37
2.2.4.4. Gemination and reduplication---------- 38
2.3. Excursus on reduplication in Semitic---------- 39
Notes to Chapter Two---------- 45

CHAPTER THREE The patterns *parras, parris* and *parrās*---------- 49

3.1. The pattern *parras*---------- 49
3.1.1. *Parras* for agent nouns derived from fientive verbs---------- 49
3.1.2. *Parras* for (mainly) literary adjectives---------- 51
3.1.3. *Parras* forms of adjectives denoting dimensions---------- 52
3.1.3.1. The evidence---------- 52
3.1.3.2. Conclusions about the plural function of *parras*---------- 55
3.1.3.3. *Parras* and *purrus* of the same adjective---------- 58
3.2. The pattern *parris*---------- 58
3.2.1. The evidence---------- 59

3.2.2. Conclusions on the nature of *parris*-59
3.3. The pattern *parrās*- 61
3.3.1. The evidence- 63
3.3.2. Conclusions-64
3.4. The role of gemination in the patterns *parras, parris* and *parrās*-64
Notes to Chapter Three-66

CHAPTER FOUR The Gtn-stem- 69
4.1. The formal analysis of the Gtn-stem-69
4.1.1. The debate- 69
4.1.2. An alternative analysis-71
4.1.2.1. The origin of the Gtn-stem- 72
4.1.2.2. The Dtn-, Štn- and Ntn-stems-75
4.1.2.3. The origin of the nasal- 77
4.1.3. Conclusions-79
4.2. Function and use of the *-tan-* stems-79
4.2.1. Iterativity- 80
4.2.2. Frequentativity-80
4.2.3. Plurality- 81
4.3. The role of gemination in the Gtn-stem- 84
Notes to Chapter Four-85

CHAPTER FIVE The D-stem and transitivity-89
5.1. A preliminary classification of D-stems- 89
5.1.1. *Purrus* adjectives- 89
5.1.2. D tantum verbs-90
5.1.3. Verbal D-stems-91
5.2. The four types of verbal D-stems- 91
5.3. High and low transitivity- 92
5.4. High transitivity and salience- 94
5.5. The role of high transitivity in Akkadian-95
5.5.1. The distinction between transitive and intransitive-95
5.5.2. The classification of D-stems of Type IV-98
5.5.3. The verbs *dabābu* and *kašādu*- 100
5.5.4. Conclusion- 101
5.6. The association between the D-stem and high transitivity- 101
5.6.1. High transitivity in factitive D-stems-102
5.6.2. High transitivity and D-stems of transitive verbs-102
5.6.2.1. Low transitivity verbs without a D-stem-102
5.6.2.2. High transitivity verbs with a D-stem- 103
5.6.3. The contrast G - D as a contrast in transitivity- 104
5.6.4. D-stems of transitive verbs and prototypical transitivity-106
5.6.5. Some final remarks-109
Notes to Chapter Five- 110

CONTENTS

CHAPTER SIX The D-stems of transitive verbs - - - 114

6.1. General premises - - - 115
6.2. The functions of the D-stems of Type I - - - 116
6.3. The D-stems of Type I and plurality - - - 117
6.4. Plurality of the direct object - - - 119
6.4.1. Verbs of destruction - - - 121
6.4.2. Verbs for actions which have a violent impact on the object - - - 128
6.4.3. Verbs of closing and opening, binding and loosening and related notions - - - 131
6.4.4. Verbs of seizing and controlling - - - 135
6.4.5. Verbs of collecting - - - 137
6.4.6. Verbs of creating - - - 139
6.4.7. Verbs of giving taking and carrying - - - 140
6.4.8. Remaining verbs - - - 142
6.4.9. Conclusions about the use of D for plurality of the direct object - - - 143
6.5. Plurality of other constituents than the direct object - - - 147
6.5.1. Plurality of the subject - - - 148
6.5.2. Plurality of the indirect object - - - 149
6.5.3. Plurality of the adjunct accusative - - - 151
6.6. The D-stem for plurality of action - - - 153
6.6.1. D-stems in the present tense in *šumma* clauses - - - 154
6.6.2. Absolute use of participles - - - 160
6.6.3. Plurality of action in some individual verbs - - - 162
6.6.3.1. D-stems for plurality of action in Old Assyrian - - - 162
6.6.3.2. D-stems for plurality of action in Old Babylonian - - - 164
6.6.3.3. D-stems for plurality of action in Standard Babylonian - - - 167
6.7. Conclusions about the D-stem and plurality - - - 168
6.7.1. General characteristics of the association of the D-stem with plurality - - - 168
6.7.2. Long constituents - - - 170
6.7.3. The D-stems for plural action compared to the Gtn-stem - - - 171
6.8. D-stems of Type I with other functions than plurality - - - 175
6.8.1. Idiomatic D-stems - - - 175
6.8.2. The "intensive" function of the D-stem - - - 178
6.8.3. Lexicalized D-stems - - - 179
6.8.4. D-stems of unknown function - - - 180
6.8.5. The verb *(w)aṣābu* - - - 182
6.9. Various remaining issues - - - 183
6.9.1. Dialect differences - - - 183
6.9.1.1. Old Babylonian - - - 183
6.9.1.2. Old Assyrian - - - 184
6.9.2. Standard Babylonian - - - 185
6.9.2.1. D versus G in scholarly texts - - - 186
6.9.2.2. Literary texts - - - 187
6.9.3. The role of convention - - - 189
6.9.4. The use of D for stylistic variation - - - 191
6.9.5. Some problematic passages - - - 192

6.10. Conclusions - 196
Notes to Chapter Six - 197
Appendix to Chapter Six: transitive verbs with a D-stem of Type I - 200

CHAPTER SEVEN The factitive D-stem - 237

7.1. Factitive and causative - 237
7.1.1. Goetze's definition of factitive versus causative - 238
7.1.2. A definition of "causative" - 239
7.1.3. Bivalent versus trivalent causatives - 240
7.1.4. Causatives that are not formally distinguished from non-causatives - 241
7.1.5. Fixed and alternating valency - 242
7.1.6. The difference between causative and factitive - 243
7.1.7. The language-specific nature of alternating valency - 244
7.2. The connection between the D-stem and alternating valency - 244
7.2.1. Causative, factitive and the four Types of D-stems - 245
7.2.2. Causative, factitive and the nature of the subject - 246
7.2.3. The factitive D-stem and adjectives - 247
7.2.4. The virtual absence of causative D-stems - 248
7.2.5. Factitive G-stems in Akkadian - 249
7.2.6. Factitive D versus causative Š - 250
7.2.7. Conclusions - 251
7.3. The nature of factitivity - 251
7.3.1. Factitive and agentive: the case of *malû* - 252
7.3.2. Agentivity in other factitive D-stems - 254
7.3.3. Factitive and intensive - 256
7.3.4. Concluding remarks - 257
7.4. The intransitive use of factitive D-stems - 258
7.4.1. Factitive D-stems in hendiadys constructions - 259
7.4.2. The intransitive use of *damāqu* D - 261
7.4.3. Other factitive D-stems without object - 262
7.5. The relationship between the D- and the Š-stem - 265
7.5.1. Formal aspects of the relationship between D and Š - 265
7.5.2. Functional aspects of the relationship between D and Š - 266
7.5.3. Causative Š versus factitive D of the same verb - 267
7.5.4. Dialectal and semantic differentiation between D and Š - 270
7.5.5. Stylistic differentiation between D and Š - 271
7.5.6. D- and Š-stems with no apparent difference in use - 277
7.5.7. Conclusions on the relationship between D and Š - 279
7.6. Non-factitive D-stems of intransitive verbs: the D-stems of Type II - 281
Notes to Chapter Seven - 286
Appendix to Chapter Seven: list of factitive D-stems - 292

CHAPTER EIGHT D tantum verbs and denominative D-stems - 301

8.1. Problems of classification - 301
8.2. General features - 303
8.3. Denominative D-stems - 304

8.3.1. The term "denominative"- - - 304
8.3.2. The denominative function of the D-stem- - - 305
8.3.3. How to distinguish denominatives from ordinary verbs- - - 307
8.4. List of denominative D-stems- - - 309
8.4.1. Denominative D-stems derived from adjectives- - - 309
8.4.2. Denominative D-stems derived from substantives- - - 310
8.5. Conclusions- - - 312
8.6. D tantum verbs- - - 312
8.7. Some final observations on the D tantum verbs- - - 316
Notes to Chapter Eight- - - 317

CHAPTER NINE The secondary stems of the D-stem- - - 318
9.1. The Dt-stem- - - 318
9.1.1. The general passive/intransitive use of the Dt-stem- - - 319
9.1.2. Dt forms with a reflexive translation- - - 324
9.1.3. Reciprocal Dt forms- - - 325
9.1.4. Dt forms contrasting with *purrus* forms- - - 328
9.1.5. Dt versus Gt- - - 329
9.1.6. Dt to underline low transitivity- - - 331
9.1.7. Varia- - - 332
9.2. The Dtn-stem- - - 334
9.2.1. How to distinguish the Dtn-stem from the Dt-stem- - - 334
9.2.2. The use of the Dtn-stem- - - 335
9.3. The ŠD-stem- - - 336
Notes to Chapter Nine- - - 339

CHAPTER TEN The pattern *purrus*- - - 342
10.1. *Purrus* as a nominal pattern- - - 343
10.2. The inflectional function of *purrus*- - - 343
10.3. The lexical function of *purrus*- - - 346
10.3.1. Isolated lexical *purrus* forms- - - 348
10.3.2. Lexical *purrus* forms related to transitive verbs- - - 348
10.3.3. Lexical *purrus* forms related to intransitive verbs- - - 349
10.4. *Purrus* forms derived from adjectives- - - 350
10.4.1. "Pure" versus resultative states- - - 351
10.4.2. Stative D versus stative G- - - 352
10.4.3. Conclusions about *purrus* forms of adjectives- - - 357
10.5. General conclusions about the lexical and inflectional functions of *purrus*- - - 357
10.6. The lexical use of *purrus*- - - 359
10.6.1. *Purrus* for plurality- - - 359
10.6.1.1. Contrasting pairs of *purrus* and *parVs*- - - 361
10.6.1.2. Other indications for the association of *purrus* with plurality- - - 364
10.6.1.3. Conclusions- - - 370
10.6.2. *Purrus* forms for salient bodily characteristics- - - 371
10.6.3. *Purrus* names- - - 374
10.6.3.1. Introductory remarks- - - 374

10.6.3.2. Lists of *purrus* names- - - 375
10.6.3.3. Conclusions about the *purrus* names- - - 377
10.6.4. Conclusions about *purrus* for salient bodily characteristics- - - 378
10.7. Lexicalized *purrus* forms in omens and literary texts- - - 378
10.7.1. Lexicalized *purrus* forms in omen texts- - - 379
10.7.2. Lexicalized *purrus* forms in literary texts- - - 386
10.7.3. Conclusions on lexicalized *purrus* forms in omens and literary texts- - - 387
10.8. The alleged intensive function of *purrus*- - - 388
10.9. A general characterization of *purrus*- - - 393
10.10. The shift from lexical to inflectional- - - 398
10.11. Conclusions- - - 401
Notes to Chapter Ten- - - 402
Appendix to Chapter Ten: list of *purrus* forms- - - 406

CHAPTER ELEVEN The development of the D-stem- - - 429
11.1. The rise of the D-stem- - - 429
11.2. The spread of the D-stem- - - 432
11.2.1. D-stems from *purrus* adjectives- - - 433
11.2.2. D-stems from simple adjectives- - - 433
11.2.3. D-stems from verbal adjectives- - - 434
11.2.4. D-stems derived from all kinds of verbs- - - 434
11.3. The functional differentiation of the D-stem- - - 435
11.4. Additional evidence: the "factitive G-stems"- - - 438
11.4.1. Evidence from Semitic- - - 438
11.4.2. Evidence from Akkadian: factitive G-stems in Akkadian- - - 438
11.5. Conclusions- - - 441
Notes to Chapter Eleven- - - 443

CHAPTER TWELVE Gemination: from iconic to grammatical- - - 445
Abbreviations and Bibliography- - - 451
Index of Akkadian words- - - 463
Index of Akkadian texts- - - 479

INTRODUCTION

The aim of this study on gemination[1] in the Akkadian verb is twofold. First, it intends to describe the use of the grammatical categories which are characterized by gemination of the second radical; second, it formulates a hypothesis concerning the functional relationship between these categories and the general nature of gemination in Akkadian from a diachronic perspective.

By far the most important of these categories is the D-stem,[2] the verbal stem with gemination of the second radical: it is the most frequent of the derived verbal stems of Akkadian, and also the most controversial, since it has a variety of functions which seem difficult to reconcile; this sets it apart from other derived stems, such as the N-stem and the Š-stem, which generally have a rather straightforward function.

Moreover, the D-stem in Akkadian is the subject of a very influential article by A. Goetze (Goetze 1942, cf. 1.6), which has inspired scholars of other Semitic languages to describe the corresponding verbal stem in these languages on the basis of Goetze's ideas (cf. 1.7). This article is, however, extremely sketchy as regards the actual use of the D-stem and highly disputable on several points.

Consequently, a detailed description of the D-stem - which has not been undertaken so far - seems to fill an urgent need, both for our knowledge of Akkadian itself, and for Semitic studies in general. Therefore, a large part of this study is taken up by a detailed study of the different functions of the D-stem, including those of the partly nominal, partly verbal pattern *purrus*.

Other categories with gemination will be discussed less extensively: the Gtn-stem and the nominal patterns *parras, parris* and *parrās*. They are less productive and less controversial than the D-stem. On some points, however, they offer important parallels that clarify several aspects of the D-stem, and on other points their use is complementary to it.

A further category with gemination of the second radical is the present tense (*iparras*). The only aspect of *iparras* that will be examined here is the relationship between its geminate and the overall function of gemination. The general use of the present tense, in contrast to other verbal categories such as the preterite, the perfect and the stative, falls outside the scope of this study.

This study is primarily concerned with the grammatical functions of the categories with gemination, not with the lexical meaning of individual words, although many words are examined in detail in order to establish these functions accurately. It is not concerned with the phonological aspects of gemination either: it is based on the assumption that there exists a phonologically relevant contrast between geminate and "simple" consonants in Akkadian. Nor is it concerned with morphological issues such as the paradigm of the D-stem in general (for which see GAG § 88a/b and the Verbalparadigmen on p. 10*ff), the D forms of hollow roots, and the question whether Assyrian *parrus* or Babylonian *purrus* is the more original form. Section 4.1, however, contains a morphological analysis of the Gtn-stem, since this bears on the very nature of the geminate in this verbal stem, and is therefore directly relevant to the argument.

The description of the categories with gemination is based on a corpus of Akkadian which basically comprises the two major dictionaries, the Chicago Assyrian Dictionary (CAD) - the latest volume available to me is 17/3 (Š/3) - and Von Soden's Akkadisches Handwörterbuch (AHw). In fact, it is only the completion or near-completion of these works that has made a study of this kind possible.

In addition, I have examined several important text editions which have appeared since the publication of these dictionaries for relevant forms. These mainly include editions of Old Babylonian letters from Mari, AbB 12 and 13, and SB texts from Uruk (SpTU).

It could be argued that this corpus, which I assume to be representative of the whole of Akkadian, is too large and too diverse to offer an acceptable basis for description. It will transpire from this study, however, that the grammatical functions of the categories involved have been remarkably constant over the long period in which Akkadian is attested. It is mainly the frequency with which they occur and the behaviour of individual verbs which vary according to dialect, period and genre. Besides, most dialects that are traditionally distinguished offer far too little material for a study as the present one, and none of them seems to be representative of Akkadian in its entirety.

My indebtedness to the dictionaries mentioned above is obvious and can hardly be overrated. This applies in particular to CAD, which is the more suitable for the subject at hand, because it gives extensive quotations and translations of whole passages. Whenever I quote these verbatim, this is indicated by the remark "(tr. CAD)"; however, in my rendering of the meanings of Akkadian verbs, too, I have relied heavily on the glosses of CAD without acknowledging this explicitly on each occasion.

Apart from describing the grammatical functions of the categories with gemination, I will also formulate a hypothesis concerning the relationship between these categories and the general nature of gemination from a functional perspective, with the aid of the phenomena of iconicity and grammaticalization. For reasons of convenience, this is not strictly separated from the descriptive part, but mainly comprises Chapters II, XI and XII.

The structure of the argument is as follows. After a summary discussion in Chapter I of earlier views that have been expressed on the D-stem - on which almost all research into the nature of gemination has concentrated - Chapter II deals with iconicity and grammaticalization, which in my view are of vital importance in order to understand the role of gemination in Akkadian and the relationship between the various categories with gemination.

In the next chapters two of these categories are discussed: the nominal patterns *parras*, *parris* and *parrās* in III and the Gtn-stem in IV.

Chapters V to IX give a detailed description of the use of the verbal D-stem: V discusses the fundamental relationship between the D-stem and high transitivity; VI deals with the D-stems of transitive verbs, VII with those of intransitive verbs (the "factitive" D-stems), VIII with the D-stems which do not have a regular relationship to the G-stem, and IX with the secondary stems which are derived from the D-stem (Dt, Dtn, ŠD).

Chapter X offers an extensive discussion of the pattern *purrus*, which is partly a nominal, adjectival pattern complementary with *parras*, and partly incorporated into the verbal D-stem as stative and verbal adjective.

Finally, Chapter XI gives an account of the historical development of the D-stem and of the relationship between its functions, whereas Chapter XII does the same for gemination in Akkadian in general.

Notes to the Introduction

1 I will use the terms "gemination" and "geminate" for the phenomenon in question, in accordance with the practice in general linguistics: Catford (1977: 210) states that geminates are strictly speaking "sequences of two identical articulations", but that many geminates in fact involve continuity of articulation (as in [*zz*], [*nn*], [*ll*], etc.). According to him, "the term "geminate" is most commonly used when, in spite of the continuity of articulation the bi-segmental nature of the sequence is made clear by the presence of a syllable division within the period of maintained articulation. (...) The term "geminate" is, however, applied only to those cases where the sequence occurs within one and the same morpheme." Both these conditions are fulfilled for the D-stem (for the syllable in Akkadian see Greenstein 1984: 11), but not for other geminates, such as those which result from assimilation on a morpheme boundary.

Other terms used among Semitists are "doubled" (e.g., Moscati 1969: 78f and 124 (but "gemination" on p. 78)), and "long" (Reiner 1966: 43); Brockelmann (1908: 66), speaks of "verdoppelt oder geminiert"; GAG § 20a of "betonte Längung".

2 For the names of the Akkadian verbal stems I will conform to the system used by GAG and AHw (G for the basic stem, D for the stem with geminate second radical, Š for the stem with prefixed *š*-, N for the stem with prefixed *n*-, and R for the occasional verb forms with reduplication, if necessary with added t or tn for the forms with infixed *-t-* or *-tan-*). This notation is objective (because it refers solely to the formal characteristics of the stems) and more transparent than the use of Roman and Arab numerals (as in CAD). I will also use the Akkadian terms when referring to a verbal stem in Semitic in general.

CHAPTER ONE

EARLIER APPROACHES TO THE D-STEM

1.0. The study of gemination in Akkadian has always strongly focused on the D-stem. A striking characteristic of this stem, not only in Akkadian, but also in Semitic in general, is the discrepancy between its obvious formal unity and the diversity of its functions. Since the beginning of Semitic studies in the Western world in the nineteenth century this discrepancy has been felt to be problematical and a whole array of ideas has been proposed to explain it. In this introductory chapter we will discuss the various functions which the main grammars and handbooks of Semitic assign to the D-stem, and the claims they make concerning the relationship of these functions, with due emphasis on the situation in Akkadian.

1.1. Views on the D-stem up to 1942

An important dividing line in the history of the study of the D-stem is the year 1942, when Albrecht Goetze published his influential article *The So-called Intensive of the Semitic Languages*. Goetze's ideas found their way into the current standard grammar of Akkadian, Von Soden's *Grundriss der akkadischen Grammatik* (GAG), which dates from 1952, and subsequently into almost all later accounts.

The description of the D-stem in the older grammars of Akkadian which date from before 1952 is largely based on the then current views about the corresponding verbal stem in other Semitic languages, which have a much longer tradition of grammatical and philological studies, notably Stem II in Arabic and Ethiopic, and the Pi^{c}el in Hebrew.

It was customary to ascribe three principal functions to these stems: an intensive, a causative and a denominative function; in intensive D-stems the action is performed with greater care, force or intensity, or it takes place during a longer period; it may also involve a plurality of subjects or objects. Causative D-stems serve to derive transitive forms from intransitive G-stems, or double transitive forms from transitive ones; then there are denominative D-stems, about which little was said, except that they often lack a corresponding G-stem (Brockelmann 1908: 508ff; Wright 1896/98: I 31f; Reckendorf 1967: 44f; Gesenius-Kautzsch 1985: 148f; Dillmann-Bezold 1907: 145). Cf., by way of example, the following quotation from Brockelmann:

> Die durch den Stamm ausgedrückte Intensität kann sich auf sehr verschiedene Seiten der Tätigkeit beziehn, auf eine besondere physische Kraftentfaltung, (....) auf längere Dauer oder häufige Wiederholung, (...) oder auf die Teilnahme vieler Subjekte (...) oder auf viele Objekte (...) oder endlich auf den Eifer und die Sorgfalt, die auf die Handlung verwandt werden (...). Diese Bemühung um das

> Zustandekommen einer Handlung führt, wie schon der Grundstamm nicht selten bedeutet, daß man eine Handlung als intellektueller Urheber durch einen andern ausführen läßt (...) oft zur kausativen Bedeutung, der aber meist noch der Nebensinn der Sorge und des Eifers anhaftet (...). Sehr häufig dient der Intensivstamm zur Bildung von Denominativen, zunächst in der ganz allgemeinen Bedeutung "sich mit etwas beschäftigen" (1908: 508f).

Sometimes other functions of less importance were added: a declarative function, e.g., Arabic *kaððaba* "to call sb a liar" (cf. *kaðaba* "to lie"); Hebrew *qiddaš* "to declare sb holy (*qādōš*)"; and an estimative one, e.g., Arabic *ṣaddaqa* "to believe sb" (lit. "to think that he tells the truth"), from *ṣadaqa* "to tell the truth". They were usually regarded as subtypes of the causative function (Brockelmann 1908: 509; Gesenius-Kautzsch 1985: 149; Bauer-Leander 1922: 292; Wright 1896/98: I 31; cf. also Joüon-Muraoka 1991: 155). Finally, with regard to the denominative D-stems special mention was often made of the privative function (Gesenius-Kautzsch 1985: 149; Bauer-Leander 1922: 291; Reckendorf 1967: 45), e.g., Hebrew *šẹrẹš* "to uproot", from *šōreš* "root" (see 8.3.3).

On the basis of such descriptions the older grammars of Akkadian tend to mention the intensive function first (Delitzsch 1889: 230; Scheil-Fossey 1901: 37; Ryckmans 1938: 62; Ungnad 1926: 49 (Ungnad does not use the term intensive but states that "D bezeichnet eine besondere Stärke der Handlung"); Furlani 1949: 60f (adding "plurality of action" to intensity)). In the second place they mention the transitivizing function, which they call "causative", "factitive", or simply "transitive" (Delitzsch 1889: 230; Scheil-Fossey 1901: 37; Ungnad 1926: 49; Ryckmans 1938: 62; Furlani 1949: 61). Lipin (1964: 105) follows this description, although it dates from after the publication of GAG in 1952 (see below). As an example it may suffice to quote Delitzsch 1889: 230f:

> [The D-stem] hat intensive Bedeutung: *nabû* "kund thun", *nubbû* (*numbû*) "laut rufen, laut jammern", *ḳibû* "sprechen", *ḳubbû* "laut schreien", *šarâṭu* "zerreissen", *šurruṭu* "zerfetzen"; und macht intransitive Verba transitiv: *ruppušu* "erweitern", *ṣahâru, arâku* "klein, lang sein", *ṣuhhuru, urruku* "verkleinern, verlängern".

1.2. Views on the D-stem since 1942

The publication of Goetze (1942), which will be discussed in detail in sections 1.6 to 1.8, represents a turning point in the study of the D-stem. Goetze's ideas have strongly influenced the account of the D-stem in GAG.

In accordance with Goetze's proposals, GAG and other grammars which were published after its appearance, such as Lancellotti (1962), Ungnad-Matouš (1964) and Caplice (1980), claim that the main function of the D-stem is to bring about the state denoted by the stative of the G-stem, e.g., *dummuqu* "to make good" from *damiq* "he/it is good". This is especially clear in "stative" verbs, i.e., those which are associated with adjectives, in this case *damqu* "good", but also applies to intransitive fientive verbs, where the D-stem typically denotes the transitive counterpart of the process denoted by the G-stem, e.g., *pahāru* "to come together" versus *puhhuru* "to bring together". This roughly corresponds to the transitivizing function of the older grammars, and is now generally known as the factitive function of the D-stem (GAG § 88c/e, Lancellotti 1962: 113; Ungnad-Matouš 1964: 75; Caplice 1980: 58).

More problematic are the D-stems of transitive fientive verbs; in earlier accounts they were usually described as intensive (cf. the quotation of Delitzsch above), but Goetze rejects any such nuance in the D-stem (see 1.6). Accordingly, GAG § 88f/h passes over the intensive function in silence and lists the following possibilities:

1) resultative, e.g., *ṣabātum* "packen" vs. *ṣubbutum* "gepackt halten", *paṭārum* "(ab)lösen" vs. *puṭṭurum* "auflösen", *zâzum* "teilen" vs. *zu''uzu* "verteilen", and *ṭarādum* "schicken" vs. *ṭurrudum* "verjagen";

2) plurality of the object, e.g., *nakāsum* "abschneiden", *nukkusum* "vieles abschneiden";

3) same meaning as G, e.g., *rasāpu* and *russupu* "erschlagen";

4) possibly a stylistic difference (§ 88f Anm.: "Bisweilen scheint nur der vollere Klang zum Gebrauch des D-Stammes verleitet zu haben.").

Lancellotti (1962: 113f) closely follows GAG. Ungnad-Matouš (1964: 75) state that such D-stems indicate an action which contains a plural element, e.g., *išber* "er zerbrach", *ušebber* "er zerbrach viele", or that they are resultative, clearly in imitation of GAG; Caplice (1980: 58) only mentions plurality: "with action-verbs the D may express multiplicity of action or its object (the so-called Poebel Piel)".

Apart from these two types, there are a considerable number of D-stems with a wide range of meanings, which do not have a corresponding G-stem, the "D tantum verbs", such as *kullu* "to hold", *kullumu* "to show" and *duppuru* "to remove, go away". Some of these can be explained as denominative verbs (GAG § 88g; Lancellotti 1962: 113f; Ungnad-Matouš 1964: 75), e.g., *kullulu* "to crown" from *kulūlu* "crown", and *ṣullulu* "to roof over, to shade", from *ṣulūlu* "roof" (ultimately from *ṣillu* "shade"). For others, GAG § 88h points to their clearly durative meaning, suggesting that this is the reason for their D form, e.g., *bu''û* "to look for" or *sullû* "to pray" (see further Chapter VIII).

1.3. Problems raised by the D-stem

If we sum up these accounts and try to give a definition of the D-stem as it is currently described, we find at least three different kinds of D-stems: factitives, D-stems of transitive verbs, which are usually called intensives, and D tantum verbs. This functional diversity not only contrasts with its formal unity, but also marks it off from other verbal stems, such as the passive N-stem and the causative Š-stem, which have a more or less uniform function. This contrast between the D-stem on the one hand, and most other verbal stems on the other, is found in other Semitic languages as well, cf. Goshen-Gottstein 1969: 82ff; Goetze 1942: 2b.

It may also be clear from the preceding survey that it is not primarily the meaning of individual D-stems which is problematical. In fact, once we know the meaning of the G-stem, that of the corresponding D-stem is largely predictable: if the G-stem is intransitive we expect the D-stem to be factitive (i.e., transitive), and if it is transitive we assume that the D-stem is also transitive, and probably has more or less the same meaning, unless the context belies this; in that case we assign a different meaning to it, which fits the context, and we say that it is "lexicalized". Usually this procedure leads to a satisfactory translation, and, even though we may not be able to explain what the difference is - if any - between G and D of, for instance, *katāmu* "to cover, close" or *gamāru* "to bring to an end, do completely, use up, control" - to mention only two striking cases of apparently interchangeable G- and D-stems (see 6.8.4) - in most contexts there can be little doubt about the general meaning of the D-stems of these two verbs.

The problems presented by the D-stem, which will be discussed in the course of this study, relate to a deeper level of interpretation than the simple meaning of individual D-stems and are of a more theoretical nature. The interpretational problems concern the difference between G- and D-stems which have no obvious difference in meaning; this applies mainly to two categories: D-stems of transitive verbs, such as *ṣubbutu* "to seize" or *puttû* "to open" versus the G-stems *ṣabātu* and *petû*, and (verbal) adjectives of the pattern *purrus*, such as *burrumu* "multicoloured" versus the simple adjective *barmu*.

The more theoretical problems concern the interrelationship between the various functions of the D-stem, more specifically whether or not they can be derived from a common source, and, if so, how their divergent development is to be explained.

1.4. Solutions proposed up to 1942

These problems also apply to the D-stem in other Semitic languages. The debate concerning them concentrated, in particular, on two issues: the origin of gemination and the relationship between the intensive and the causative. The first issue will not be a central concern of this study (but see the Excursus to Chapter II); for a discussion of various proposals to derive gemination from assimilation of the second radical to a neighbouring consonant or from the reduction of a reduplicated syllable, see Ryder 1974: 29ff.

The debate started from the implicit assumptions that the D-stem is a derivation of the G-stem and that it should be semantically homogeneous, since it clearly forms a morphologically uniform category (cf. Ryder 1974: 11). The most common view was that the original function must be the intensive, because the geminate second radical was supposed to symbolize the intensification of the action expressed by the G-stem. Consequently, many scholars considered the causative to be derived from the intensive, arguing that the intensity could imply that the agent made someone else perform the action (Brockelmann 1908: 509 (quoted above on p. 4f); Gesenius-Kautzsch 1985: 149; Reckendorf 1967: 44; Dillmann-Bezold 1907:

145), and also Wright 1896/98: I 31, but without argumentation).

Exactly the same reasoning led Poebel (1939: 65ff) to a different view, namely, that the basic function of the D-stem is not to express intensity but plurality (1939: 66). He claims that gemination of the second radical is not a strengthening ("Verstärkung") but the last remnant of reduplication of the whole root. In many languages reduplication is a means of expressing plurality, e.g., in Sumerian. Such reduplicated forms are often shortened, and this happened in Semitic, too: a form like Arabic *yuqattilu* "he kills many" goes back to an original *y-qtl-qtl*, cf. Hebrew forms like *kilkẹl* (< *kwl-kwl*) from *kwl* and *gilgẹl* (< *gll-gll*) from *gll* (1939: 66f). He concludes from this that the D-stem, too, expresses plurality.

Poebel explaines the causative function of the D-stem, by positing (1939: 68) the original existence of an intransitive *qatil*, with *qattil* for plurality, and a transitive *qatal*, with *qattal* for plurality; the causative function of the D-stem arose out of this configuration by the elimination of *qatal* and *qattil*; this entailed the direct opposition *qatil* (intrans.) vs. *qattal* (trans.) which is historically attested.

Another interesting minority view is that of Christian (1935: 41ff). Chistian agrees with the majority of scholars in regarding the intensive function of the D-stem as basic. However, he rejects the claim that the causative function can be directly derived from it in the way they propose, but explains it as one of the possible realizations of the denominative function, depending on the presence of a direct object and the semantic relationship between the noun in question and the verb derived from it. In his view, a denominative D-stem is intransitive if it denotes the activity implied in the source noun, such as Hebrew *kihhẹn* "to serve as priest (*kōhẹn*)" or if the source noun is the result of the action, such as Arabic *xayyama* "to pitch a tent" (*xaymah*); in the latter case the verb is only seemingly ("nur scheinbar") transitive. However, if it has an object to which the activity implied in the noun is ascribed, it is really transitive, namely a declarative or an estimative D-stem, e.g., Arabic *kaððaba* "to call sb a liar", or Hebrew *ṣiddẹq* "to regard sb as just" (Christian evidently derives these verbs from the nouns *kaððāb* "liar" and *ṣaddīq* "just", respectively, rather than from the corresponding G-stems *kaðaba* "to lie" and *ṣādẹq* "to be just"). If the activity is aimed at the realization of a verbal concept, the D-stem becomes a causative, e.g., Arabic *ᶜallama* "wissen machen, lehren" (1935: 43).

Christian (1935: 43) concludes that the causative function is not an isolated phenomenon, but is on a par with the other functions of the D-stem, and that the decisive factor for it to be realized is the presence of an object to which the activity in question can be ascribed; without an object there can be no causative.

1.5. The inadequacy of these solutions

The views outlined above about the origin of the gemination, the various functions of the D-stem and their mutual relationship contain many sound ideas and observations, but as a whole they are inadequate on two points: the lack of textual evidence and their a priori character.

As to the first point, most scholars limit themselves to adducing a few examples of a given function, and on the basis of these extrapolate an overall function. Moreover, the examples are often quoted without context, and systematic surveys of the relevant verbs are not given, so that it is difficult to get a clear idea of the extent and the importance of the function under discussion.

A conspicuous example of this procedure concerns the intensive function of the D-stem. In the works mentioned above it is illustrated by means of a very small number of verbs which crop up in every new discussion of the topic. Most of these belong to a few well-defined semantic types:[1]

1. Transitive verbs of hitting and breaking: Arabic *ḍarraba* "to beat violently" (Br, Sd); *kassara* "to break into many pieces" (Sd) but "to continue breaking" (R); *jarraḥa* "to inflict many wounds" (Fl); *qattala* "to massacre" (Sd); *qaṭṭa*^{c}*a* "to cut into many pieces" (Sd); Hebrew *šibbar* "to break into many pieces"; Syriac *paqqa*^{c} "spalten" (Brockelmann); Ethiopic *daqqaqa* "ganz zerstoßen" (id.); Akkadian *šarraṭ* (sic) "zerfetzen" (all Br).

2. Intransitive verbs indicating a (mostly repetitive) movement: Arabic *jawwala* and *ṭawwafa* "hin- und hergehen", Hebrew *hillẹk* and Syriac *hallek* "wandern"; Ethiopic *šaggara* "schnelle Schritte machen"; *xallaja* "hin- und herreden, nachdenken" (all Br).

3. A somewhat wider range of verbs can be used in the D-stem if their subject or object is plural (this condition plays an important role in type 1. as well): a) intransitive verbs (plural subject): only in Arabic: *barraka* "to kneel"; *rabbaḍa* "to lie down" (Br); *mawwata* "to die" (Br, Sd); *qawwama* "to stand up" (R); *rawwaḥa* "to go"; *nawwama* "to sleep" (Sd); b) transitive verbs (plural object): Arabic *fajjara* "to pour forth" (R); *ġallaqa* "to close" (Br); Hebrew *šillẹ*^{a}*ḥ* "to send" (JM); *qibbẹr* "to bury"; Syriac *fattaḥ* "to open"; Akkadian *uddulu* "to close" (all Br); c) transitive verbs (plural subject): Hebrew *ši'ẹl* "to ask" (JM).

4. Apart from these three types some other words are quoted which do not belong to any of them: Arabic *bakkā* "to weep much" (Sd); Hebrew *rinnẹn* "to jubilate", *riqqẹd* "to dance", *niggẹn* "to make music" (all G), *sippẹr* "to tell, to recount" (from *sāfar* "to count") (JM); *śiḥḥẹq* "to mock at" (from *śāḥaq* "to laugh") (JM); *ši'ẹl* "to beg" (from *šā'al* "to ask") (GK, JM); *pittaḥ* "to untie" (from *pātaḥ* "to open") (JM).

Virtually all of them are quoted without context. Often we are kept completely in the dark as to whether a verb is meant to be an example of a wide-spread use, or is quoted as a grammatical oddity. The general impression is that the intensive D-stems are very limited in number and in frequency, and constitute a marginal group compared with the mass of "causative" D-stems.[2]

Some claims are not supported by any evidence at all, for instance Brockelmann's remark (1908: 509, quoted above p. 1) that if a D-stem is causative it also implies that the action is performed with care or zeal, and Poebel's explanation (1939: 68) of the rise of the causative function, outlined in section 1.4.[3]

Concerning the second point, the discussion was dominated by implicit assumptions of an a priori nature, which were not supported by arguments. They comprise the idea that the presence of gemination proves that the intensive function of the D-stem is primary; that the D-stem must be functionally uniform because it is morphologically uniform; and that difference in form must entail difference in meaning. A striking illustration of this way of thinking is provided by Poebel's vigorous denial of the intensive function of the D-stem (1939: 65f): in his view, the fact that gemination does not represent a strengthening of the consonant but a reduction of a reduplicated syllable, automatically entails that it cannot express intensity but only plurality. Apparently, it did not occur to him to verify these claims from the actual use of the D-stem in texts.

Christian's contribution to the debate (1935) deserves special mention because of his insistence on the relevance of the object for the realization of the causative function. This shows his awareness of the fact that such concepts as causative often do not depend on the formal characteristics of a verb form, but on the structure of the predicate. On the other hand, his explanation of the causative function as arising from the denominative one is untenable: if an activity is aimed at the realization of a verbal concept ("ein Verbalbegriff" (1935: 43)), it can hardly be called a denominative, as his example, Arabic *ᶜallama* "to cause to know, to teach", shows: synchronically, at least, this verb is not based on a noun, but on the verb *ᶜalima* "to know".[4]

1.6. Goetze's solution

The inadequacies in what can be called the traditional view of the D-stem prompted Goetze (1942) to adopt a completely different approach. In his opinion it is unsatisfactory to regard the D-stem as an intensive derivation - or "modification" in his terminology - of the G-stem, for three reasons: firstly, this view is an a priori based not on a "broad enough survey of actual occurrences", but on the "romantic notion" that the gemination "symbolizes a corresponding intensification of the form" (1942: 2b); moreover, it only concerns a small group of verbs (1942: 2f); and, finally, nobody has been able to give a satisfactory explanation of the development of a causative-factitive meaning from the intensive (1942: 3b).

For a solution he points to the special situation created by the existence of the stative in Akkadian, a form "obviously" of nominal origin, the predicative state of an adjective. It describes a condition "outside any system that makes action and tense its basic categories" (1942: 4b). He distinguishes three kinds of statives: a durative stative which "denotes an inherent quality of a person or a thing", e.g., *ṭāb* "is good"; a perfect stative which "denotes a condition which results from the subject's own action with reference to a person or a thing", e.g., *ahiz* "holds", or with intransitive verbs "the rest after some movement", e.g., *wašib* "is seated, staying"; and finally, a passive stative denoting "a state of affairs which results from another person's action, e.g., *ahiz* "(is) held" (1942: 5).

He claims - and this is essential for his theory - that there is a close correspondence between the stative and the D-stem of a verb: "To every one of the statives which have been posited a D stem corresponds" (1942: 5b). If a stative has a double meaning, as for instance in *ahiz* ("holds" and "(is) held"), there is also a double D-stem: according to Goetze, *uhhuzu* means both "make (somebody) hold (something)" and "make (something) fitted" (1942: 6b).

His conclusion is that "all D stems [except a few "apparent D forms", see below] are in parallelism with statives". Thus

> "the D stem is derived from B [i.e., G] stative. As has been shown above, the stative is basically a nominal form. Hence, one can say that the denominative function of the D form (...) is the primary force of the form. If derived from adjectives, it denotes "make a person or a thing what the adjective indicates", i.e. it is a factitive." (1942: 6b).

In transitive verbs

> "the difference in meaning between D and B is very slight. With B the emphasis is laid on the action performed, with D, however, on the effect of the action." (1942: 6a).

1.7. Positive points of Goetze's solution.

This theory has met with wide acclaim, and has had an impact on almost every subsequent treatment of the D-stem. Some scholars took over Goetze's claim that it is a factitive rather than a causative, without discarding the intensive and/or pluralizing function (e.g., Moscati 1969: 124; Castellino 1962: 128ff; Caplice 1980: 58; Segert 1975: 366; Joüon-Muraoka 1991: 155). Others went much further and accepted the whole theory with all its implications: Von Soden did so in his description of the D-stem in Akkadian (GAG § 88, see 1.2). Ryder (1974: 165) took over Goetze's conclusions in their entirety, after a lengthy discussion of all aspects of the problem. In the studies of Jenni (1968) and, in his wake, Leemhuis (1977) they form the basis for far-reaching conclusions about the semantic differences between G and D on the one hand, and D and Š on the other, in Hebrew and Arabic, respectively.[5]

Without any doubt the solution Goetze offers for the problems raised by the D-stem is in some respects an important step forward, but on other points his views are open to serious criticism. We will first turn to the positive elements.

Goetze rightly exposes the weak points in the older views, especially the lack of argumentation and textual evidence, and he points to two facts which are crucial to a correct understanding of the D-stem. The first of these is the association between the D-stem and adjectives. Of the three kinds of statives Goetze distinguishes (1942: 5), the first kind, the "durative" stative, usually has a factitive D-stem, in clear contrast to the other two kinds, the "perfect" and the "passive" stative, in which the correlation between the stative and the D-stem is far from perfect, in spite of Goetze's claim to the contrary (see 1.8 below). This "durative" stative is nothing but the predicate form of an adjective. In fact, a survey of Akkadian adjectives shows that a large majority of them have a factitive D-stem, or at least a *purrus* form (see 11.1).

The second fact pointed out by Goetze is the importance of a distinction between the notions of "causative" and "factitive". He defines the function of the former as "[to] cause someone to act in the way which the basic verb indicates" (1942: 4b); the function of the latter as "[to] make a person or a thing what the adjective indicates" if the D-stem is derived from an adjective (1942: 6b), or "[to] put a person or a thing in the state which the stative describes" for other D-stems (1942: 6a).

It will become clear from our discussion of factitive D-stems in Chapter VII that the terms causative and factitive refer each to a specific semantic relationship between a derived verb and the corresponding G-stem, which it is of crucial importance to distinguish, in spite of the fact that there is not a neat opposition between causative Š-stems and factitive D-stems: Akkadian has also a few causative D-stems and a fair number of factitive Š-stems, regardless of whether we apply Goetze's definition or the one adopted here (see 7.2.4 and 7.5.5).

1.8. Criticism of Goetze

On other points, however, Goetze's solution of the problems raised by the D-stem is inadequate and does not stand up under scrutiny. The main points of criticism are the following.

First, the parallelism Goetze claims to exist between the D-stem and the stative can only be demonstrated for the first kind, the durative stative, which is derived from adjectives (see 1.7). The two other kinds, the perfect and the passive stative, are derived from fientive verbs; there are no indications that the D-stem of a fientive verb - if it has one - is more closely connected with the stative than with any other form of its paradigm. In fact, six of the sixteen statives Goetze mentions as examples (1942: 5) do not even have a regular factitive D-stem.[6]

Many statives which come from transitive verbs can be given both an active and a passive translation; in Goetze's terminology: they can be both perfect and passive statives. They are the cornerstone of his theory since they are supposed to have a double D-stem as well: "It is of particular interest that those verbs which have two statives (a perfect and a passive one) likewise possess a double D-stem" (1942: 6). Goetze mentions the following eight forms:

ahiz	"holds" and "(is) held"	*šakin*	"has placed" and "(is) placed"
ṣabit	"possesses" and "(is) seized"	*šaṭer*	"has by written deed" and "(is) deeded"
maher	"has received" and "(is) received"	*zīz*	"has divided" and "(is) divided"
naši	"has (for carriage)" and "(is) lifted"	*waldat*	"has born (children)"/*walid* "(is) born"

However, none of these eight statives have such a double D-stem. Apart from the fact that *naši* and *šakin* do not have a D-stem at all (see note 6), factitive D-stems corresponding to the perfect stative - which for these verbs would mean "to make somebody hold, possess, receive, have, place, write, divide and give birth" - do not exist in Akkadian.[7]

In fact, it is for only three of these statives (*ahiz*, *zīz* and *walid*) that Goetze claims the existence of a double D-stem, which he translates as follows (1942: 6b): *uhhuzum* "make (somebody) hold (something)" and "make (something) fitted"; *zuzzum* "make (somebody) divide (an estate)" and "make (an estate) divided"; *wulludum* "make (a woman) give birth (to a child)" and "make (a child) borne".

However, the dictionaries do not mention the first of the two meanings of *uhhuzum* and *zuzzum*. Neither does *uhhuzum* mean "make (something) fitted", unless we assume that its usual meaning "to mount an object in precious materials" (CAD sv *ahāzu* 8a, for the only exception see note 6) goes back to such a literal meaning. This is improbable because of the very specialized nature of this verb; it rather suggests that *uhhuzum* is not a regular derivation of *ahāzu* "to take, marry, learn", but a denominative of *ihzū* "mountings (for setting stones and decorating costly objects)" (tr. CAD sv), as GAG § 88g suggests (see also 8.3.3). The same applies to *wulludum* in the first meaning; it is also restricted to a single context, viz., "to deliver", with the midwife as subject and the child or the mother as object (CAD sv *alādu* 2b). Therefore, it is a technical term, just as *uhhuzum,* and probably a denominative; since this meaning also occurs in Hebrew and Arabic (Gesenius-Buhl 1915: 300b; Wehr-Cowan 1966: 1097a), it is likely to date back to Common Semitic. Finally, it is only for the sake of the theory if one translates *zuzzum* as "make (an estate) divided" rather than simply "divide (an estate)", and *wulludum* as "make (a child) borne" rather than "give birth to" or "beget". Moreover, this ignores the actual use of these forms, which is mainly connected with plurality (see 6.5.2 for *zâzu* D and 6.4.6 for *(w)alādu* D).

Thus there is no significant degree of parallelism between the "perfect" and the "passive" stative on the one hand and the D-stem on the other, and the alleged double D-stem cannot be demonstrated with certainty for a single verb. This leads to the conclusion that there is no reason to assume that the D-stem is more closely connected with the stative than with any other member of the paradigm of the G-stem, and that Goetze's theory has no factual basis. It is only for the durative stative that his claim that "to every one of the statives which have been posited a D stem corresponds" (1942: 5b) holds (see 1.7). The major fallacy in Goetze's argument is that he also applies this to other statives which belong to the paradigm of the fientive verb and have a different status.

Second, there are a number of verbs which lack a stative, but nevertheless have a D-stem; Goetze admits that they remain unaccounted for (1942: 6b); as examples he quotes such cases as *uhhurum* "lag behind", *lupputum* "loiter", *qubbûm* "shout", and *ruqqudum* "dance" (his translations), and points out that, semantically, such verbs are "cursive, i.e. they denote a state of continuous action" (sic!), and that they cannot be derived from the stative since "their very nature is irreconcilable with the basic meaning of the stative" (1942: 7a.).[8] Instead, he associates them with West Semitic verb forms like Hebrew *hillęk* "walk continuously, habitually" and the *-tan-* stems of Akkadian which express the same semantic notions, and concludes that in these cases the geminate originates from the assimilation of the *n*-infix which also occurs in the Akkadian *-tan-* forms: *uraqqid* ← **yu-ra-n-qid*. Therefore, the D-stems of these verbs are only "apparent D forms" (1942: 6b).

It goes without saying that this solution is arbitrary: there is no reason to set apart these D-stems, except that they do not fit in with his theory. Moreover, in 4.1 I will argue that also in the *-tan-* forms the geminate is "real", i.e., not the result of assimilation of a nasal infix.

Third, Goetze cannot account for the meaning of the D-stems of transitive verbs (those which are traditionally described as "intensive"). He makes the following claim about them (1942: 6a, already quoted in 1.6 above): (in transitive verbs) "the difference in meaning between D and B [i.e., G] is very slight. With B the emphasis is laid on the action performed, with D, however, on the effect of the action.". However, he does not give a single example to prove his point, and the paraphrase he uses to indicate the basic meaning of such D-stems, "to make something buried, written, divided", etc., does not contribute at all to the clarification of how these forms are actually used.[9]

Fourth, Goetze leaves the source of the primary morphological characteristic of the D-stem, the geminate second radical, unexplained. If the D-stem is derived from the stative G (1942: 6b), for instance, *udannan* "he makes strong" from *dān* "he is strong", it remains unclear where the geminate comes from. Moreover, it also remains unclear why *udannan* means "he makes strong" rather than "he becomes strong" or some other fientive meaning; in other words, why the D-stem is factitive in the first place. By asserting that the D-stem has factitive meaning Goetze merely states a fact and does not give an explanation.

Finally, it would take us too far afield to examine in detail some basic assumptions Goetze makes concerning the nature of the stative, viz., that there are three different kinds of statives and that sentences with a stative as predicate are nominal sentences.

Suffice it to say that, first, the distinction which Goetze makes between three types of statives reflects a semantic distinction between different types of verbs which has no grammatical relevance for Akkadian. From the point of view of Akkadian, the stative has a completely uniform grammatical function, namely, to denote a state, i.e., the absence of any action or change. All differences between individual statives, such as whether a stative expresses a "pure" state (e.g., *šalmāku* "I am well"), or a state resulting from a previous event (e.g., *halqat* "she (has escaped and) is (now) on the run" (ARM 1, 89: 6) or whether it qualifies the subject or the object of the corresponding transitive sentence (as in ARM 2, 133: 10 *awīlī kalêku* "I have been detaining the men", and in *kaliāku* "I have been (and therefore am now) detained (e.g., AbB 1, 132: 10, Kraus: "ich sitze fest"), respectively, cf. CAD sv *kalû* v. 1a-1') are determined by the lexical meaning of the verb and by the context, cf. Rowton 1962: 234; Rundgren 1963a: 109; 1963b: 63f, 100f. Therefore, there are no differences between D-stems discernible which correlate with the three kinds of statives distinguished by Goetze. The differences that do exist are not related to the stative, but to the valency of the basic verb, cf. 5.2.

As to the second point, it has been a matter of dispute whether sentences with a stative are to be considered nominal or verbal. Goetze's position that such sentences are nominal

(1942: 4b) represents a minority view, put forward especially by Buccellati and Huehnergard.[10] Most scholars, however, regard such sentences as verbal: Rundgren (1964: 61f), Illingworth (1990: 333ff), Kuryłowicz (1972: 92f), Ravn (1949: 303f), and, last but not least, Von Soden, who explicitly states in his grammar that a verbal sentence is a sentence "mit einer finiten Verbalform als Prädikat, die auch ein im Stativ konjugiertes Nomen sein kann." (GAG § 125c). The fact that the stative is undoubtedly etymologically derived from a nominal category is irrelevant in this context (cf. 8.3.1).

1.9. Conclusions

This review of Goetze's article leads us to the conclusion that most questions concerning the D-stem are still unsolved, including the most controversial ones formulated in 1.3: first, the difference between the G- and the D-stem of transitive verbs and that between a *purrus* form and the corresponding simple adjective, and, second, the relationship between the various functions of the D-stem, and whether or not they can be derived from a common source. Further problems awaiting a solution are the relationship between the D-stem and other grammatical categories with gemination and the overall role of gemination in Akkadian.

The aim of this study is to formulate an answer to these questions. It will be argued that by disparaging the intensive function of the D-stem (1942: 2b),[11] Goetze has cut off the way to a correct understanding of it, and that we have to rehabilitate the "traditional" views outlined in sections 1.1 and 1.4, which were in vogue before the publication of Goetze's article, if we want to attain a satisfactory account of the diverse and complicated ways in which the D-stem is used. These traditional views are, in short, that gemination of the second radical symbolizes an intensification of the action; that the D-stem can be characterized as basically intensive, and, finally, that the "causative" function of the D-stem is an offshoot of that intensive character. However, I will use a different terminology and provide a detailed argumentation for these claims, in contrast to the practice of the original adherents of these views (cf. 1.5).

The basic claims I will put forward are the following. First, the relationship which in the traditional view exists between gemination and intensity is not, as Goetze would have us believe, a "romantic notion", but a correct intuition about the nature of language: although the use of gemination for intensity is difficult to prove and marginal at the most, there is a clear association between gemination and nominal and verbal plurality (habituality, durativity, plurality of subject and object, etc.) in Akkadian. This suggests that there is an *iconic* relationship between form and function of gemination; in other words, the presence of a geminate in a motivated word reflects, or used to reflect, some kind of extension in its meaning compared to the meaning of the corresponding word without gemination; this extension is usually realized as an increase in number (plurality), in duration (permanence, habituality) or in salience.

Second, those categories with gemination of Akkadian in which this association between gemination and nominal or verbal plurality is less obvious or perhaps completely absent can be explained by means of the phenomenon of *grammaticalization*. In the course of time grammaticalization has led to erosion of the iconic nature of gemination; as a result iconicity has partly lost its association with notions such as plurality and salience and acquired various grammatical functions in which its extensional nature vis-à-vis the corresponding simple forms is less obvious and more abstract; the most important of these functions as far as verbal forms are concerned are those of underlining a high degree of transitivity in the D-stem and of expressing the present tense in the G-stem and several derived stems.

Third, different processes of grammaticalization have led to a disintegration of the function of gemination into separate categories, each with its own function. These functions, however, are sufficiently similar to enable us to glimpse a common background and a single denominator for all of them, not only for the D-stem itself, but for all motivated categories with gemination of the second radical. In the next chapter we will start with a short discussion of iconicity and grammaticalization in general and their relevance to Akkadian.

Notes to Chapter One

1 The examples quoted come from Brockelmann 1908: 508 and 1913: 141f (Br); Wright 1896/98: I 31 (Wr); Fleisch 1979: 288 (Fl); Saad 1982: 74f (Sd); Gesenius-Kautzsch 1985: 148 (GK); Joüon-Muraoka 1991: 155 (JM); Ryder 1974: 13f (R) and Goetze 1942: 2f (G).

2 Cf. Beeston (1970: 75 note 1): "The frequently repeated statement that this stem has an "intensifying" value is, as a generalization, totally false. The two examples invariably quoted, *kassara-hu* "he smashed it" versus *kasara-hu* "he broke it" and *qattala-hum* "he massacred them" versus *qatala-hum* "he killed them" are rarities with hardly any parallel in the whole lexicon."

3 I will demonstrate in Chapter XI that the development which Poebel posits in order to account for the causative function of the D-stem is precisely what actually happened, but since he does not give any argumentation it is not surprising that his explanation did not enjoy wide acclaim.

4 The fact that the D-stem is denominative in origin, as is generally acknowledged (see 11.1), is irrelevant in this context. However, if we apply Christian's solution to Akkadian, it becomes much more attractive because the Akkadian stative, although it is basically a verbal category (see 1.8), has more nominal characteristics than any Arabic finite verb form. Therefore, it is possible that Christian's views have influenced Goetze, who also explaines all functions of the D-stem from the denominative function, but on the basis of the Akkadian evidence (see 1.6).

5 See especially Jenni 1968: 12ff, 275f, Leemhuis 1977: 125f; cf. also Whiting 1981: 26f note 101. For a recent discussion of Jenni's view about the Piᶜel in Hebrew, see Siebesma 1991; for a review of Leemhuis 1977, see Goshen-Gottstein 1985 and Justice 1987: 386ff.

6 This is true of *ahiz, naši, šakin, wašib, ṣalil* and *maqit*. However, a D-stem corresponding to *ahiz* "is held" is found once in MA, cf. App. to Ch. VI sv *ahāzu*; for *uhhuzu* in the technical meaning of "to mount an object in precious materials" see 1.8 below; for the denominative verb *šukkunu* "to appoint sb governor or commander (*šaknu*)" see 8.4.2; a D-stem *ṣullulu* as a factitive of *ṣalil* "he is asleep" is also attested once (SKS p. 54: 147), instead of the usual Š-stem; *maqit* "he has fallen, is on the ground" does not have a corresponding factitive D: a *purrus* form *muqqut* "ailing, sick" is attested in LL and medical texts (CAD sv 6; AHw sv D 2, and see 10.3.3 and 10.7.1.2), but there is no verb *muqqutu* in the meaning "to put on the ground"; this notion is expressed by the Š-stem. The OA instances of *maqātu* D quoted in CAD sv 5 and AHw sv D 1 are quite uncertain: TC 3, 137: 3 *ma-qí-ta-ma* (in fragmentary context) might be an imperative pl. parallel with *epšā*, but may also qualify the preceding noun *a-mu-ra-am*; in CCT 2, 42: 8 the text has *ma-BA-ta-am* rather than *ma-qú-ta-am*, as read by AHw, but the context is quite obscure; cf. also CAD sv *le'û* 1a-1' for a different solution in order to make sense of this passage (K.R. Veenhof, personal communication).

7 An exception might be *maher*, whose D-stem *muhhuru*, if it means "to present sb with sth, offer" (cf. App. to Ch. VI sv *mahāru* 1.), could be interpreted as a factitive ("he made receive") of a perfect stative *maher* "he has received". However, it seems more likely that *muhhuru* in most of its meanings is a denominative of a noun *mahru* "front side", or something similar, and that its literal meaning is "to confront sb with sth", cf. 6.8.3 sv.

8 Most verbs of this type are atelic verbs denoting sounds (*habābu* "to whisper, murmur", *nabāhu* "to bark", *sa'ālu* "to cough") and movements (*akāšu* "to go, move", *namāšu* "to move, depart", *narāṭu* "to tremble, shake", *rapādu* "to walk around"). The D-stems of the former group are usually intransitive just as the G-stem; they will be discussed in 7.6. Those of the latter group are mostly factitives, see Chapter VII.

9 See the discussion of these verbs in Chapter VI. Von Soden's claim that the D-stems of some transitive fientive verbs have a kind of resultative meaning (GAG § 88f) is presumably inspired by this definition of the difference between G and D (although he does not define the term "resultative"). It will become clear from the discussion of the D-stems mentioned as examples (*ṣubbutu, puṭṭuru, zu''uzu* and *ṭurrudu*, see 1.2) that they have to be interpreted otherwise (see 6.4.4.1, 6.4.3.1, 6.5.2 and 6.8.1 ssvv., respectively).

10 The most uncompromising statement that a sentence with a stative as predicate is a nominal sentence is made by Buccellati (1968) and (1988). His arguments were refuted by Kraus (1984: 16f), who concludes (1984: 13) that the stative of stative verbs constitutes a nominal sentence, the stative of other verbs a verbal sentence. Huehnergard (1987: 218f), rightly finds this unsatisfactory, but he makes things even worse: he considers sentences with a stative to be nominal - while admitting that syntactically they frequently function verbally (1987: 231f), but makes an exception for the "active" statives, which he calls "pseudo-verbal", as a kind of intermediate category between nominal and verbal.

In fact, it is a typical characteristic of a category like the stative - which expresses a state and is therefore less verbal than categories which express actions or processes, such as the prefix conjugations of Akkadian - that typically verbal distinctions, for instance, between different tenses and between active and passive, are neutralized, just as in the infinitive, which is also more nominal than the prefix forms (cf. GAG § 85b). Grammatically, there is no difference between "active" and "passive" statives, just as there is no difference between "active" and "passive" infinitives. For this phenomenon in general see Givón 1984: 51ff.

[11] Goetze does not deny the existence of intensive D-stems, but he tries to belittle their relevance. About those which are mentioned by earlier scholars (see 1.3) he states that "Arabic-Hebrew grammarians claimed intensive-frequentative force for only one group of pi^{c}el forms" (1942: 2b). Some of these he explains as "apparent D forms" (1942: 6f). At the very end of his article (1942: 8b) he suggests that perhaps the loss of the stative in the West Semitic languages, which "cut the D form loose from the ground on which it was grown" is responsible for the rise of intensive D-stems under the influence of "apparent D forms". Thus he tries to dispose of them as secondary formations. He apparently recognizes no intensive D-stems in Akkadian.

CHAPTER TWO

ICONICITY AND GRAMMATICALIZATION

2.0. This chapter discusses the phenomena of iconicity - a concept originating from semiotics - and grammaticalization, and their relevance to Akkadian. It argues that in Akkadian gemination has an iconic nature, i.e., it reflects an extension in the meaning of the word as compared to the meaning of the corresponding simple word, and that where this is not readily observable this iconic nature has been eroded by a process of grammaticalization. Thus these two concepts are of fundamental importance to a correct understanding of the role of gemination in Akkadian.

2.1. Iconicity

2.1.1. Iconicity and arbitrariness

In semiotics[1] an icon is a non-arbitrary sign which expresses a formal or factual similarity between the shape of the sign and what it stands for (the *signans* and the *signatum*). As such it is opposed to an index and a symbol. An index is based on a material relation (factual, existential contiguity) between signans and signatum (e.g. smoke is an index of fire). Examples of indexes in language are deictic elements and the expressive extensions to be discussed in 2.2.3 (see Lyons 1977: 106ff; Jakobson 1990: 386ff). A symbol is based on a conventional relation between signans and signatum, which has to be learned; a symbol is by definition arbitrary (see below). This triple division of the sign goes back to the founder of semiotics, C.S. Peirce, cf. Jakobson 1990: 408ff.

On the basis of this, elements in language which reflect in their form or structure the form or structure of their referents can be called iconic.

There are three kinds of icons, each of which plays a different role in language (cf. Ullmann 1962: 81ff). The first kind is the *image*: an image is an icon in which the "signans represents the 'simple qualities' of the signatum" (Jakobson 1990: 412). A picture, for instance, is an image of what it represents. In language onomatopoeic words are images: they represent natural sounds (phonetic iconicity), but are not exact reproductions of them: Anttila (1989: 14f) insists that onomatopoeic words are not completely iconic: their partly symbolic character is apparent from the fact that the same sound is rendered differently in different languages. The second kind is the *metaphor*, in which the similarity is based on a parallelism in meaning (semantic iconicity).

The third and for language most important kind of icon is the *diagram*: a diagram is a complex sign, in which there is a correspondence between the different parts of the sign and those of the concept it represents (Haiman 1985: 9ff), or in which "the relations in the signans correspond to the relations in the signatum" (Jakobson 1990: 412). The different parts of the diagram themselves may be, and indeed usually are, symbolic. A stock example quoted by Jakobson (1990: 412) is "two rectangles of different size which illustrate a quantitative comparison of steel production in the United States and the USSR (cf. Anttila 1989: 16)."

Since language is a network of relations on different levels (between words in syntax, between morphemes in morphology, between phonemes in phonology) diagrams play an essential role in it. Especially syntax and morphology abound in diagrammatic relations. Those in syntax mostly concern word order, such as the fact that events tend to be described in the order in which they occur, that what is more important or less predictable tends to be expressed with more coding material, and that elements which belong together tend to be placed together (cf. Haiman 1985; Givón 1990: 966ff).

Diagrammatic relations also play an important role in morphology. A very general diagrammatic phenomenon is the tendency to assign zero morphemes to basic, unmarked categories and explicit morphemes to marked ones (Matthews 1991: 234ff). Thus, plural forms tend to be longer than the corresponding singulars; in many Indo-European languages the superlative consists of more morphemes than the comparative, and the comparative of more morphemes than the positive: *high-higher-highest, altus-altior-altissimus, haut-plus haut-le plus haut* (Jakobson 1990: 414f; Haiman 1985: 4ff; Anttila 1989: 17).

It is evident that iconicity clashes with the arbitrariness of language, which, since Saussure, has been regarded as one of its "design features" (Lyons 1977: 70f). However, even Saussure himself, while advocating the fundamental arbitrariness of the linguistic sign, acknowledges signs which are "*relativement motivé*" (1964: 180ff; cf. also Ullmann 1962: 80ff; Lyons 1977: 105; Jakobson 1990: 415ff; Haiman 1985: 14f). These signs can be analysed, and to a certain extent their meaning can be inferred from their constituent parts. For instance, whereas a numeral like *vingt* "twenty" is unmotivated (arbitrary), *dix-neuf* "nineteen" is motivated since it consists of the (in themselves arbitrary) elements *dix* and *neuf; berger* "shepherd" is unmotivated, but *vacher* "cowherd" is motivated by its association with *vache* "cow". Likewise, plural forms as English *ships* or *houses* are also motivated in so far as the suffix *-s* is for speakers of English easily identifiable as a plural marker.

Such motivated words show diagrammatic iconicity: although their constituent parts are arbitrary, their combination makes them analysable and, to a certain extent, predictable in meaning.

The examples given above show how important the role of motivation is, especially in morphology. A regular morphological rule results in motivated words; such words are more economic and more transparent than unmotivated ones: more economic because they do not have to be learned and stored in memory as separate entities, but can be derived by means of a grammatical rule; more transparent because they are analysable and therefore to a large extent predictable as to their meaning, their grammatical function and/or the category they belong to; in short, motivation causes a more regular relationship between form and meaning. Therefore, Ullmann (1973: 16) calls it "one of the great creative devices in language".

Arbitrariness and iconicity are complementary rather than contradictory. Linguistic signs are basically symbolic (arbitrary), but this symbolic character is accompanied, mainly in syntax and morphology, by varying degrees of iconicity: "vocabulary is predominantly symbolic, and the rules of the language, iconic or diagrammatic (e.g., word order)" (Anttila 1889: 17; cf. also Haiman 1985: 10; Jakobson 1990: 412ff). This twofold, or even threefold nature of the sign (if it also has indexical elements) makes it more effective than a pure symbol, because "the most perfect of signs are those in which the iconic, indexical, and symbolic characters are blended as equally as possible" (Peirce, as quoted by Jakobson 1990: 412).

The two phenomena are complementary also in a diachronic perspective. Whereas sound change tends to diminish iconicity and to increase arbitrariness, because it makes words less transparent, morphological change (analogy) tends to lead to an increase in iconicity, and ultimately toward *isomorphism*: a one-to-one relation between form and meaning, between the "expression level" and the "content level" (Shapiro 1991: 12f; Mayerthaler 1988). The ideal of isomorphism is, however, hardly ever reached in natural languages; rather, the history of language is characterized by a continuous fluctuation between different degrees of isomorphism, because the expression level tries to destroy it (mainly by sound change), whereas the content level tries to maintain or restore it (by analogy) (cf. also Anttila 1989: 181f and 407).

2.1.2. Motivation

Saussure (1964: 183f), distinguishes two types of language according to the degree of relative motivation of their vocabulary: languages with a low degree of motivation, which he calls "*lexicologiques*", e.g., Chinese and French, and languages with a high degree of motivation, which he calls "*grammaticales*", e.g., Sanskrit and many other "classical" Indo-European languages. Languages may shift from one type to the other (as happened with French), because motivation can be abolished by sound change; the Latin word *inimicus*, for instance, is a motivated compound of *in* + *amicus* "not-friend"; its French offshoot *ennemi* (and English *enemy*) has lost its motivated character: it is unanalysable for speakers of the language.

It will be clear that the Semitic languages are outspoken examples of "langues grammaticales", cf. D. Cohen (1970: 31): "tout mot sémitique est relativement motivé, toute forme sémitique est en quelque sorte une forme dérivée." Accordingly, they show numerous diagrammatic features.

In fact, the whole morphological structure of Semitic, with its characteristic "root-and-pattern derivation" (cf. Cantineau 1950: 73ff.) is characterized by a high degree of diagrammatic iconicity: the lexical meaning of many words resides in the consonantal skeleton (the "root"), whereas the vowel pattern, sometimes in combination with consonantal affixes, indicates the category to which they belong or their grammatical function.[2]

For example, if we encounter an Akkadian word of the pattern *pāris*, we can predict with a high degree of certainty that it will be a participle (or rather an agent noun, see note 11 to Ch. III). In this way we can assign rather precise functions to most patterns, not only in nominal categories (e.g., *taprist* for verbal nouns of the D-stem, *maprast* for instruments, *purs* for abstract nouns derived from adjectives, *paris* for verbal adjectives, etc., cf. GAG § 54ff), but also in the paradigm of the verb: a form such as *iprus* can only be a third person preterite singular of the G-stem, *parās* only an infinitive, etc. The same applies to other Semitic languages, cf. Moscati 1969: 76ff. Thus Semitic shows a high degree of isomorphism.

Moreover, Semitic conforms to the widespread tendency to use zero morphemes for unmarked categories: in the noun, masculine is unmarked versus feminine, which is usually indicated by a suffix *-(a)t*, and singular is unmarked versus dual and plural. In the verb, the basic stem, the G-stem, which is morphologically unmarked, also expresses basic, unmarked concepts, whereas the derived stems stand for complex concepts such as passive, reciprocal, causative and iterative.

There is also a diagrammatic relationship between the length of a pattern, i.e., its formal complexity, and its semantic complexity. The short, unextended patterns (*qatl, qitl, qutl, qatal, qatil, qatul*, etc.) usually denote basic concepts of a general nature, have a broad range of application, and their function can therefore be described only in rather vague terms (see, for instance, Brockelmann 1908: 335ff). The longer a pattern, however, the more specialized and complex its meaning. This is especially manifest in the verbal paradigm, where we find the longest patterns, such as the participles and verbal nouns of the derived stems, e.g., *pašqu* "narrow, difficult", *pušqu* "narrowness, distress", versus *muštapšiqtu* "woman who has difficulty in childbirth".

2.1.3. Root extensions in Semitic

The type of diagrammatic iconicity in Semitic which is most relevant for our purpose concerns the use of several types of root extensions. A Semitic root can be extended by means of various procedures, among which we can distinguish two types: one of these involves the addition of one or more affixes (pre-, in-, or suffixes); the other consists of an extension by means of either gemination of one of the radicals, reduplication of (part of) the root, or lengthening of one of the vowels of a specific pattern. In this study, we will be concerned with the latter type of extension.

It is claimed here that extensions consisting of gemination, reduplication or vowel lengthening (or a combination of them) are iconic (diagrammatic) in nature; in other words, they typically express meanings which also represent (or represented) some kind of extension as compared with the corresponding simple form (cf. Rundgren 1959a: 271f). However, this is not equally clear in all three of them: it is most evident for reduplication, and least evident for vowel lengthening, with gemination taking a middle position.

Cross-linguistically, reduplication is one of the most indisputably iconic phenomena in language. In many languages there is a clear diagrammatic relationship between the repetition of (mostly) consonants and the semantic categories commonly expressed by total or partial reduplication, such as iterative, habitual, plural and intensive; for examples and references see 2.3, where reduplication in Semitic will be discussed more extensively.

The phenomenon which has the weakest iconic force of the three is vowel lengthening: in many cases the lengthening does not correspond to a semantic extension, but has acquired a grammatical function, i.e., it is grammaticalized (see 2.2). An iconically motivated case of vowel lengthening is that which accompanies substantivation of adjectives, such as the replacement of *parras* by *parrās* in substantival agent nouns, and that of the verbal adjective *paris* by *parīs* when it is substantivized (see 3.3). Another case may be the active participle *pāris*, if we assume, with Rundgren (1959a: 39), that the long *ā* represents "grammatikalisierte Durativität".

The iconic phenomenon which is most important for our purpose and which will be dealt with in the following sections is gemination.

2.1.4. Gemination in Akkadian

The phonological opposition between geminate and simple consonants is one of the typical features of Semitic, and plays a prominent role in the derivational procedures of many Semitic languages (cf. Brockelmann 1908: 66; Kuryłowicz 1972: 113ff; Ullendorff 1955: 216ff; Fleisch 1961: 250f). We will concentrate on gemination of the second radical, which is by far the most common type, and represents the main formal characteristic of the D-stem and other grammatical categories, both nominal and verbal; the marginal cases of gemination of the third radical will be discussed briefly in 2.2.4.1.

If we want to assess the role of gemination as a grammatical device, we have to concentrate on categories in which gemination is grammatically relevant, i.e., in which it serves to contrast the category in question with a corresponding one without gemination. Such words are *motivated* in the Saussurean sense of the word (see 2.1.2), i.e., they can be derived from a consonantal root which also occurs in other words with a related meaning (among which is usually a verb). Akkadian examples are *kabbaru* "thick" (mostly plural) versus *kabru* "thick", from the adjectival pattern *parras* (see 3.1.3), and *šaggišu* "murderer" versus *šāgišu* "murdering, murderer", from the pattern *parris* which usually denotes agent nouns (see 3.2).

Not all motivated words with gemination, however, are directly relevant. In some words gemination has no distinctive function, but is simply copied from the (relatively) basic word it is derived from. An Akkadian example is *dubbubtu* "complaint", a verbal noun derived from *dubbubu* "to complain", in which *-bb-* is a repetition of the geminate of the verb. Such words provide no independent evidence for the role of gemination (but, of course, *dubbubu* itself does, since it contrasts with *dabābu* "to talk"). An important group of these are nouns which serve as abstract nouns or infinitives of the D-stem.[3]

Gemination in unmotivated words is not contrastive, and therefore not directly of use in establishing its grammatical function. If such words refer to persons, animals or concrete objects (such as *immeru* "sheep", *haṣṣīnu* "axe"), however, it is possible that their geminate has an "expressive" background, cf. 2.2.4.1.

Two kinds of gemination completely fall outside the scope of this study, namely, that which is caused by assimilation (Brockelmann 1908: 157ff, 170ff; Gesenius-Kautzsch 1985: 74ff; GAG § 20c, 33d) - note, however, that according to the definition of Catford (1977: 210), quoted in note 1 to the Introduction, such cases do not fall under the term gemination - and that which serves to protect a preceding short vowel: "secondary gemination" (Speiser 1967: 396ff; Joüon-Muraoka 1991: 79ff (who call it "spontaneous gemination"); Segert 1975: 115). It is rather frequent in the later stages of Akkadian (MA and NA: GAG § 20e/g and Mayer, Or. 61, 47 note 34).[4] These kinds of gemination are not motivated by semantic reasons, but are the result of purely phonological processes.

2.1.5. Gemination and plurality

Apart from a few words with gemination of the second or the third radical which are motivated in so far as they are from a well-known root but do not belong to a productive pattern (to be discussed in 2.2.4.1), most motivated words with gemination in Akkadian belong to a small number of categories with rather specific functions; these are, in approximate order of importance (the section numbers refer to GAG):

1. the present tense (§ 78a) of the G-stem (*iparra/i/us* § 87c), of several derived stems (Gt *iptarras* § 92a, N *ipparras* § 90a, Št$_2$ *uštaparras* § 94c) and of the quadriliteral verbs (e.g., N *ibbalakkat*, Š *ušbalakkat*, cf. GAG Verbalparadigma 39);
2. the verbal D-stem (§ 88) and its secondary derived stems Dt (§ 93), Dtn (§ 91) and ŠD (§ 95a);
3. the Gtn-stem (§ 91a/b, see 4.1 for its inclusion here);
4. the pattern *purrus* in its nominal function of denoting adjectives (§ 55n);
5. the nominal patterns *parris* (§ 55m) and *parrās* (§ 55o), which are derived from fientive verbs and denote professions and habitual activities;
6. the nominal pattern *parras* (§ 55m), which forms adjectives with gemination from simple adjectives.

The function(s) of most of these categories will be discussed in detail in the course of this study. If we anticipate the results of this discussion in some respects and base ourselves on the functions which are currently ascribed to them (as, for instance, in GAG), it turns out that many categories with gemination serve to express plurality.

As for the nominal categories, it will be shown in 3.1.3 that the main function of *parras* is to serve as a plural formation of simple adjectives denoting dimensions, and in 10.6.1 that the same holds for a number of *purrus* forms. Gemination is also associated with plurality in a few underived biradical substantives of Common Semitic stock, which have not only the regular long vowel in the plural (*šarru* "king", *šarrū* "kings"), but also gemination of the second radical: *abbū* "fathers" (OA/MA *abbā'ū*), *ahhū* "brothers", *ahhātu* "sisters" and *e/iṣṣū* "trees", from the singulars *abu, ahu, ahātu* and *iṣu,* respectively.[5]

In the verbal categories we find a number of different realizations of "verbal plurality". This term was introduced by Jespersen (1924: 210f) and elaborated by Dressler (1968: 51ff). On the basis of material collected from over 40 languages (1968: 91) Dressler establishes that in the Amerindian languages the typical formal procedure for the expression of verbal plurality is partial or total reduplication or repetition of a whole word, and that the Indo-European languages mostly use preverbs and suffixes for the same purpose. As to the semantic aspect of these formations, he shows that the general idea of plurality is realized in many different but closely related ways, the most important of which are iterative (1968: 62ff), distributive, i.e. more subjects perform, or more objects undergo the action simultaneously or successively - in general this applies to subjects of intransitive and objects of transitive sentences - (1968: 66ff), continuous (1968: 74ff), and intensive (1968: 77ff). Each of these notions can be subdivided into more subtle nuances, and every language makes its own choice from these possibilities.

Dressler draws two important conclusions from his study of categories which can express verbal plurality. In the first place, he claims (1968: 58) that polysemy ("Mehrdeutigkeit") is a fundamental feature of verbal plurality, because the verbal predicate interacts with many other constituents of the sentence at the same time, and is not only characterized by an extension in space (as most nouns are), but also in time. Therefore, the verb forms in question are often not restricted to expressing a single aspect of verbal plurality, but can express several or all of the aspects mentioned above, depending on the context.[6]

His second conclusion (1968: 92ff) is that it is an essential feature of verbal plurality to have a "Globalbedeutung", i.e., it gives a plural meaning to the whole sentence, and sometimes even beyond that, to the wider context, rather than indicating plurality of a single part of it.

Many of the categories with gemination enumerated above are used to express various types of verbal plurality: the Gtn-stem, which is used for iterativity, frequentativity and plurality (see 4.2), the verbal D-stems of transitive verbs, which are frequently used to underline plurality, most often plurality of the object (see 6.4), and sometimes for durativity (see especially 6.6.1).

The nominal patterns with gemination *parris* (see 3.2) and *parrās* (see 3.3) also represent verbal plurality, because they are nominalizations of the corresponding verbs. They typically denote agent nouns, more specifically, names of professions or habitual activities, so that their geminate second radical can be explained on the basis of the permanence and habituality which is inherent in this meaning (see further 3.4).

Consequently, four out of six categories with gemination are associated with plurality, either in their entirety (numbers 3 and 5) or as their main function (number 6), or in part of their functions (numbers 2 and 4). In these cases the iconic nature of the geminate is demonstrated beyond a doubt by the fact that it reflects a concrete and palpable extension in meaning as compared to that of the corresponding simple words.

In the remaining categories with gemination, however, the association of the geminate with a semantic extension is far less obvious. This applies first and foremost to the present tense gemination, but also to the numerically very important group of factitive D-stems, and to a large number of individual nouns and verbs, in particular many "D tantum verbs" (cf. especially 8.6) and many *purrus* adjectives (see Chapter X).

In these cases, however, gemination can be explained as iconic, too, but for two reasons this is less clear than in the categories just mentioned. First of all, in some cases the semantic extension which we expect to find in their meaning is realized in a way which is less readily observable and more abstract than in the case of plurality: it has acquired the function of underlining an increase in salience and/or in transitivity, the former especially in many *purrus* forms (see 10.6.2) and D-stems of transitive verbs (see 5.6.4); the latter in the verbal D-stem in general (see, in particular 5.6.4 and 6.1). This claim will be illustrated and elaborated throughout the present study.

Second, it can plausibly be argued that gemination has undergone a historical development in which its iconic nature was reduced and the geminate either acquired a grammatical function instead of a semantic one (grammaticalization), or was subject to erosion so that forms with gemination became synonymous with simple forms (lexicalization); the former explains the geminate of the present tense (*iparras*), the latter the large number of individual words (especially verbs and adjectives) in which the iconic nature of the geminate is far from obvious. In the following sections we will discuss the phenomena of grammaticalization and lexicalization and their impact on the role of gemination.

2.2. Grammaticalization

2.2.1. The development of grammatical elements

Grammaticalization[7] is an evolutionary process in language "through which a lexical item in certain uses becomes a grammatical item, or through which a grammatical item becomes more grammatical" (Hopper-Traugott 1993: 2).

In recent years much work has been done on grammaticalization (Hopper-Traugott 1993: 24ff) in which a strong emphasis has been laid on the first part of the definition, the development of full words into grammatical elements. It is in this sense that the term was introduced by Meillet (1912: 133), who defines it as "le passage d'un mot autonome au rôle d'élément grammatical" (1912: 131). However, the ideas involved are found much earlier, in the works of Wilhelm von Humboldt (1767-1835) (Hopper-Traugott 1993: 18ff).

A well-known example of this type of grammaticalization, of which many instances can be found in West-European languages, is the widespread development of main verbs into auxiliary verbs, which are sometimes further reduced to affixes or particles. Latin *habere* "to have", for instance, ended up as an auxiliary verb of the perfect tense and as an affix of the future tense of Romance (beside maintaining its status as an independent verb), cf. Italian *canteremo* "we will sing" from *cantare habemus*, which is itself a replacement of Latin *cantabimus* (Hopper-Traugott 1993: 42ff); ancient Greek θέλειν "to wish" gave rise to the modern Greek future particle θα < θέλω ἵνα "I wish that" (Meillet 1912: 145).

Grammaticalization also involves the reduction of nouns to prepositions (French *chez* "at" from Latin *casa* "house"), to adverbs (German *weg* "away" from *Weg* "way") and to negations (French *pas* "not" from *pas* "step", cf. Hopper-Traugott 1993: 114ff). Other nouns developed into suffixes with a grammatical function: the Latin noun *mens, -ntis* "mind" became an adverbial suffix in Romance languages (French *-ment,* Italian *-mente*, etc., cf. Hopper-Traugott 1993: 130f); the English suffixes *-ly* and *-hood* are derived from nouns meaning "body, form" and "state, quality", respectively (Hopper-Traugott 1993: 40f; Anttila 1989: 150).

Not only full words with a lexical meaning, but also grammatical words (pronouns, etc.) and morphemes can undergo this process. Grammaticalization of pronouns can be found in the frequent development of demonstratives into personal pronouns or articles, e.g. Latin *ille* "that", which gave rise to both *il* "he" and the article *le* in French (Hopper-Traugott 1993: 16).

In recent literature on grammaticalization much less attention has been paid to the fact that also morphemes may undergo grammaticalization. In this case it represents "the increase of the range of a morpheme advancing from a lexical to a grammatical or from a less grammatical to a more grammatical status" (Kuryłowicz 1975: 52). A case in point is the tendency of concrete cases (i.e., those which denote spatial relations) in Indo-European languages to develop into grammatical cases with a syntactic function. The accusative, for instance, became a means of denoting the direct object instead of a direction, as in Latin, where the latter use is vestigial (*domum/Romam ire* "to go home/to Rome"), cf. Kuryłowicz 1964: 201ff; 1975: 48f.

This type of grammaticalization applies in particular to morphemes which undergo a shift in status from derivational to inflectional (Kuryłowicz 1964: 35ff). Generally speaking, derivational morphemes have a semantic content since they serve to create new words which differ in meaning from their basic words. Typical categories they express are iteratives, intensives, collectives, verbal nouns and agent nouns. Inflectional morphemes, on the other hand, do not change the semantic content of a word, but only specify such categories as case, number, person, tense, etc.[8] The shift referred to above, therefore, entails a loss of semantic content and an increase in grammatical function. As examples Kuryłowicz mentions the development of verbal nouns into infinitives in Sanskrit and of verb forms with iterative meaning to inflectional forms which express the imperfective aspect in Slavonic languages (1964: 36). The latter example is exactly parallel to the development of the Akkadian present *iparras* out of an earlier iterative formation (1972: 53f, 57ff, and see 2.2.4.2).

In fact, the various kinds of grammaticalization distinguished here represent a continuous development: once a lexical word has acquired a grammatical function, it tends to become a derivational morpheme in the first instance, after which it may further develop into an inflectional one. In the course of this process it becomes applicable to an increasing number of contexts, but loses more and more of its semantic content ("bleaching", Hopper-Traugott 1993: 87f, or"generalization", Bybee-Perkins-Pagliuca 1994: 289ff). This process is often accompanied by other features, such as the attrition of its form, the reduction of its paradigm to a single or a few forms, and its fixation in a specific place in the sentence (Hopper-Traugott 1993: 145ff; Lehmann 1985: 306ff).

2.2.2. Renewal

Grammaticalization, then, is basically a process of erosion which leads to loss of semantic content and reduction of form. It is counterbalanced, however, by a reverse process of renewal, which is caused by the urge of speakers to use innovative ways of saying things. This results in the rise of new expressions, which are usually periphrastic and therefore transparent and more expressive than the older ones they replace.

Meillet (1912: 131ff) strongly emphasizes the importance of grammaticalization as being the only process in language capable of creating new grammatical categories, whereas analogy, the other creative procedure in language, can do no more than transform and rearrange existing categories. However, it is only in a part of the documented cases of grammaticalization that the process leads to the rise of a new grammatical category, which expresses a meaning which could not be expressed by grammatical means in the language beforehand. In many cases the categories which have come into being by means of grammaticalization compete - often for a very long time - with existing ones which have approximately the same function, and subsequently replace them, so that the net result is ultimately zero (Lehmann 1985: 312ff). This applies to many of the examples mentioned above, especially to those which involve grammatical categories.

The question is, therefore, what the *raison d'être* of grammaticalization is. Meillet is quite definite in his answer: grammaticalization is set in motion by the urge of speakers to be *expressive*: "le besoin de parler avec force, le désir d'être expressif" (1912: 139). Frequently used words and constructions tend to weaken both in form and in content; to remedy this they have to be constantly renewed (1912: 135ff). Therefore, grammaticalization is a cyclical process (1912: 140f).

A similar claim is made by Lehmann (1985). In his view, speakers of a language strive for originality and expressiveness, because they "do not want to express themselves the same way they did yesterday, and in particular not the same way as somebody else did yesterday." (1985: 315).

It is doubtful whether this answer is valid as an overall solution (cf. Hopper-Traugott 1993: 23f). There can be no doubt, however, that in many areas of language, both in grammar and in vocabulary, the urge to be clear, original and emphatic leads to the creation of new ways of expression, which, if they take on, start to compete with existing expressions.

Well known examples of such areas, taken from vocabulary, are negatives, intensifiers, deictic elements and diminutives. Speakers often feel a need to reinforce such words, so that we can observe their constant renewal in a cyclical process (Meillet 1912: 140; Kuryłowicz 1964: 52f; 1977: 27f; Hopper-Traugott 1993: 89, 121f).

An example from grammar is the development of case functions in Indo-European, which is also cyclical: cases arise primarily to denote spatial relationships, and only secondarily do they acquire grammatical functions. As soon as the latter process starts, there is a tendency to renew the expression of spatial relations by means of prepositional clauses, which in their turn come to express grammatical relations, too (cf. Kuryłowicz 1977: 141ff; Blake 1994: 172ff).

Similar processes of renewal can be observed in verbal categories, as has been shown by Kuryłowicz in many publications. Such a phenomenon, which is of prime importance - not only in Indo-European but also in Semitic - concerns the rise of new formations to express the present tense, and the subsequent relegation of the old present to secondary, often modal, functions:

> "The most important phenomenon which has repeated itself over and over again and has left numerous traces in the old I.E. languages, is the renewal of the *durative* character of the verbal forms denoting the moment of speaking (present-imperfect system). The durative form may easily invade other semantic spheres: general ("timeless") present, futurity, modality ("capability", "eventuality"), etc. This expansion, involving the loss of expressiveness (i.e. of concentration on durativity), is the cause of drawing upon derived forms designed to renew the durative function. A formal split is likely to ensue: durative present (new form) and general or indetermined present (old form), present (new form) and future (old form), indicative (new form) and subjunctive (old form)." (Kuryłowicz 1975: 104).

Kuryłowicz's claim is confirmed by the findings of Bybee, Perkins and Pagliuca: on the basis of a stratified probability sample of 76 languages they conclude that durative presents (which they call "progressives") are often relatively young formations whose origins are still transparent (1994: 127ff), and that many present tense categories originate from the grammaticalization of such progressives (1994: 140ff). Semitic offers a number of instances of this development, in the first place the Akkadian present *iparras*, see below 2.2.4.2. Other cases are the rise of present forms with a prefix *bi-* in several modern Arabic dialects, which has restricted the old imperfective without *bi-* to modal use (Fischer-Jastrow 1980: 182; D. Cohen 1984: 289ff; Bybee-Perkins-Pagliuca 1994: 233f)[9], and the introduction of *kotẹv* as a present tense, with the older form *jixtov* surviving as a future, in post-biblical Hebrew; for similar processes in modern Ethiopic dialects and in Neo-Aramaic, see Rundgren 1963b: 64ff.

A corresponding process for past tenses concerns the perfect:

> "As regards the so-called *perfect* the normal evolution seems to be: *derived form* (or verbal noun + auxiliary verb) > *perfect* > *indetermined past* ("passé indéfini") > *narrative* tense. The derivative is adopted as a regular member of the conjugation in order to replace the old form of the perfect, which, having been additionally charged with the narrative function, has lost its expressiveness." (Kuryłowicz 1975: 106; cf. also 128).

The correctness of this claim is also confirmed by the study of Bybee, Perkins and Pagliuca mentioned above. In their sample the main path of development in past tense morphology is that of "resultative or completive leading to anterior [more commonly called perfect] and then to perfective or simple past" (1994: 104).

Examples of this development are the periphrastic past tenses of Romance and Germanic languages (1994: 85). It is likely that the gradual replacement of the preterite *iprus* by *iptaras* in affirmative declarative main clauses, which starts in OB and can be observed throughout the history of Akkadian, is caused by the same phenomenon, although the details of this process are still to be established, cf. Streck 1995: 207. Moreover, the relationship between the Akkadian stative and the West Semitic perfect *qatala* can be explained along the same lines, see 4.1.2.1 and Rundgren 1963b: 85ff.

These two processes concerning the development of present and past tense morphology can be related to the renewal of categories such as intensifiers mentioned above. The main function of the durative present is to refer to the actual "*hic-et-nunc*" situation, i.e. to what is going on at the moment of speaking. Likewise, the general function of the perfect is to denote a past event which is still actual, or relevant for the present moment. It seems plausible that it is this actuality which speakers wish to underline by using an innovative, more strongly characterized and therefore more expressive form or construction.

This leads to the conclusion that certain categories have a tendency to undergo a process of renewal, which is relatively fast in the case of lexical categories such as intensifiers, etc., but - at a slower pace - also occurs in grammatical categories. Whether this renewal is caused by the preceding weakening of the older category or whether this weakening is the result of the preceding rise of the new category is often difficult to determine. This seems to be of secondary importance, however.

2.2.3. Weakening and renewal in Semitic

The history of Semitic offers many examples of weakening and renewal of forms. Several cases of renewal of verbal categories have been mentioned above: that of the present tense in Akkadian, modern spoken Arabic and modern Hebrew (2.2.2), the replacement of Akkadian *iptaras* with durative function by the geminated form *iptarras* (4.1.2.1), and that of *iprus* by the perfect *iptaras* (if the assumption made in 2.2.2 is correct).

In the domain of word formation we also find many examples of the replacement of shorter patterns by longer ones. It can be studied most fruitfully in Arabic with its proliferation of words, which were recorded and studied by the Arab grammarians, almost from the beginning of Arab civilisation.

In several of his works H. Fleisch stresses the important role of expressivity for Arabic word formation and derivation (e.g., 1961: 362ff, 377ff; 1968: 52ff, 68ff). He mentions many cases in which the expressive force of a word is repeatedly renewed by means of some morphological extension. Well-known examples of this development are the adjectives of the patterns *qatīl*, *qatūl*, *qutāl* and *qi/atāl*: they originate as variants of the simple patterns with one or two short vowels (*qVtl* or *qVtVl*) (Fleisch 1968: 68f; Wright 1896/98: I 136; Fisher 1965: 192ff, 197f; Kuryłowicz 1972: 111ff, 149.). The expressive character of *qutāl* is supported by Akkadian, where *purās* is especially common for personal names, in close parallelism with *purrus*, for instance in word pairs such as *Kuzzubu/Kuzābu*, *Hunnubu/Hunābu*, *Buqqušu/Buqāšu*, *Huzzulu/Huzālu*, etc., see 10.6.3 for these *purrus* names. Therefore, Diem's scepticism (1970: 61ff) about the (originally) intensive nuance in words of this pattern is unwarranted.

Because of the erosion of their expressive character, however, these patterns were reinforced by means of gemination and vowel lengthening, which resulted in patterns such as *qattāl*, *quttāl* and *qittīl*, which are still strongly expressive in written Arabic (Fleisch 1961: 358r, 379f, and see 2.2.4.1 below). In its function of passive participle, *qatūl* was replaced by *maqtūl* (Kuryłowicz 1972: 119f); in the same way *qitāl*, which was mainly used for instrument nouns, was reinforced by means of affixation, resulting in *miqtāl* (Kuryłowicz 1972: 118). According to Ambros (1969: 103), this pattern, although very common, is no longer productive in Modern Standard Arabic and in spoken Arabic; its successor is the ancient agent noun pattern *qattāl*, mainly in its feminine form *qattālat* (1969: 95ff). Ambros attributes the spread of *qattāl(at)* at the expense of *miqtāl* for the expression of instrument nouns in particular to "die Unanschaulichkeit, der abstrakte Charakter" of the latter, as opposed to the "affektiv-anschauliche Bildung" *qattāl(at)* (1969: 102f). In this process of renewal, reinforcement and functional differentiation go hand in hand.

The frequent and continuous renewal of words is especially common in that part of vocabulary which refers to spheres of life that arouse a special interest and involvement in people, i.e. that are highly salient. This applies in the first place to their fellow men - hence the large variety of expressive words denoting or describing human beings, especially if they deviate in one way or another from what is considered proper or normal; secondly, those aspects of their surroundings which have a special importance for them: the animals they like or fear, the flocks and plants they need for their subsistence; and, thirdly, other objects they fear or cherish and phenomena that catch their eye or imagination (e.g., colours, diseases).[10]

Words belonging to these semantic categories are often extended by means of morphological procedures which iconically express this heightened interest or emotional involvement. Such extended forms have the same referential meaning as the unextended ones, but have in addition an "emotive" or "affective" meaning (cf. Lyons 1977: 175) which expresses the speaker's attitude, either positive or negative, towards the person, object, action or quality he is speaking about (Stankiewicz 1954: 457). In this sense they are "expressive", and not only iconic, but also indexical, because they "indicate" the emotional condition of the speaker, cf. 2.1.1 and Lyons 1977: 106ff.[11] A useful characterization of expressive elements in language is given by Pfister 1969: 78f:[12]

> "Als expressiv bezeichne ich alle Spracherscheinungen, bei denen die Natur der Laute und Lautfolgen in einem wesentlichen, nicht rein konventionellen Zusammenhang mit dem Ausgedrückten steht. Expressive Wörter zeigen (..........) bestimmte Lauterscheinungen wie Konsonantendehnung oder -verdoppelung, Reduplikation und gebrochene Reduplikation, Verwendung von Lauten oder Lautfolgen, die in normalen Wörtern selten oder gar nicht vorkommen, sowie Abweichungen von Lautgesetzen, manchmal auch Schwankungen in der lautlichen Form. Die Wörter gehören vielfach nicht der Schrift-, sondern der Volks- und Umgangssprache an. Schließlich gehören sie meist zu bestimmten Bedeutungsgruppen."

The morphological extensions of these words can take any form, but a very popular device in languages all over the world is reduplication (see note 20 for references). For Semitic, we will once more take Arabic as example. Apart from reduplication, Arabic has the following procedures:

1. suffixation, e.g., with *-ān,* which according to Wright (1896/98: I 113) denotes "violent or continuous motion", cf. also Wehr 1952: 611; with *-ah* (Wright 1896/98: I 139f; Fleisch 1961: 460ff, especially 462f § 98k/l; Brockelmann 1928: 130f); and sporadically with *-n* and *-l* (1928: 124ff) and with *-m* (Fleisch 1961: 465ff; for *-m* in colour names, cf. Fisher 1965: 203);
2. prefixation of *t-* (Fleisch 1961: 421f), of *m-* (Wright 1896/98: I 138, 186; Fleisch 1961: 433f) and of *y-* (418f). The pattern *'aqtal* for elatives and (mostly) physical characteristics, which is sometimes strengthened to *ᶜaqtal* (Fisher 1965: 201f), goes back to the same source. This is indicated by the semantic range of its members (colours, physical characteristics and elatives), and is consistent with its origin as proposed by Wehr (1952: 604ff) and Fisher (1965: 149).
3. dissimilation of geminates (Fleisch 1968: 128f; 1979: 428ff);
4. addition of a fourth radical (*ibidem*);
5. insertion of a semivowel (*ibidem*).

The last three procedures are mainly verbal and result in the creation of quadriliteral verbs. According to Nyberg (1954: 136), these have expanded enormously in the modern Arabic dialects and in the modern languages of Ethiopia, and now coexist with or replace many triliteral verbs. Their expressive character is indicated by Nyberg's observation (1954: 136) that "[f]ast alle lautmalenden oder in irgendeiner Weise konkret veranschaulichenden Verba, fast alle irgendwie expressiven Benennungen werden vierkonsonantisch gebildet, während die dreikonsonantischen Bildungen mehr dem abstrakten Wortschatz angehören." (cf. also Kamil 1956; Joly 1907). Another characteristic of expressive words is that they occur more often in informal language than in formal style.[13]

The expressive force of a word wears out quickly and has to be constantly renewed: the more original and striking such a word is, the stronger its impact is. This explains why many of them appear in more than one form (cf. Fleisch 1961: 363 and 391 note 3; 1968: 60), and why they seldom have exact counterparts in cognate languages: they are, almost by definition, recent formations, cf. Nyberg's claim (1954: 129) that in reduplication "nur das Bildungsprinzip ursemitisch ist"). A comparable phenomenon in English is the proliferation of adverbs as *awfully, terribly, dreadfully, horribly*, when they are used as intensifiers, cf. Palmer 1972: 326ff; Hopper-Traugott 1993: 121.

The urge to use expressive forms is a driving force behind the development of the Semitic languages. It caused the continuous creation of new and longer patterns. Because these had a stronger morphological marking, they tended to spread at the cost of the older ones with which they competed.[14] This spread may eventually lead to a total replacement. More often, however, the formal relationship between simple and expressive forms is copied by other words of the same category and becomes productive. Thus words with extensions are created which have the same semantic relationship to the simple word as the original pair(s), and a pattern arises whose members have a predictable meaning; in other words, it acquires a specific semantic or grammatical function in opposition to the simple pattern.

This process is accompanied by a weakening of the expressive nature of the words in question. This weakening is a paradoxical process. On the one hand, the productivity of such forms is caused by their expressive nature; on the other hand, the increase in frequency automatically results in a decrease of expressivity, since the impact of an expressive form depends largely on its original and unexpected nature. This can lead to the beginning of a new cycle of weakening and renewal (McMahon 1994: 172). In the next sections we will discuss various patterns with gemination in order to illustrate these possibilities.

2.2.4. The nature of gemination

On the basis of the facts presented in the previous sections, it seems plausible to hypothesize that gemination arose as a formal extension which served to make words more expressive, intensive, emphatic, etc., and was largely grammaticalized in the course of time. This assumption enables us to posit a common background for its various functions. There are three arguments to support such a hypothesis: first, the fact that a number of words with gemination have preserved some typical features of expressive categories (2.2.4.1); second, the fact that in several patterns with gemination we can discern different stages of the process of grammaticalization (2.2.4.2); and, third, the close relationship between gemination and reduplication, which is by far the strongest iconic and expressive device of Semitic. The third point will be discussed in 2.2.4.4 and in the Excursus to this chapter.

2.2.4.1. Gemination as an expressive device in Semitic

The use of gemination as an expressive device is mainly preserved in nouns which generally belong to unproductive patterns.[15] Such nouns are extremely rare in Akkadian. I can only mention *šakkūru* (see AHw sv, CAD: *šakkurû*) "drunkard", *habbūbu* "lover" and *hattītu* "person infested with vermin" (cf. CAD sv, restored and uncertain), which refer to persons. Besides, there are a few cases like *muttāqu* "sweetmeats" and *(w)urrīqu,* a yellow or green mineral or a yellow stone, which are substantivations of intensive adjectives derived from *matqu* "sweet" and *(w)arqu* "yellow, green", respectively. A motivated word with gemination of both the second and the third radical is *ziqqurratu* "ziggurat, temple tower", which is related to *zaqāru* "to build high".

Arabic has more instances: it has a number of sporadic patterns with gemination of the second radical and (usually) a long vowel in the second syllable; most of them comprise only a very small number of words; a few examples of such words are *farrūq* "very fearful", *kubbār* "very great" and *quddūs* "very holy", cf. Fleisch 1961: 358f; Wright 1896/98: 137f. They typically denote qualities of persons and colours; Moscati (1969: 78f) describes them as "adjectives with intensive meaning", and similar qualifications are found in Fleisch and Wright. In Hebrew we find the patterns *qattīl* and *qattūl*, which Joüon-Muraoka (1991: 253) describe as intensives of *qatīl* and *qatūl*, and a small group of adjectives referring to mental and physical characteristics with the pattern *qittẹl* (Gesenius-Kautzsch 1985: 243; Joüon-Muraoka 1991: 253).

A small number of motivated words with gemination of the third radical can also be added to this group. If we omit words of unknown derivation, adjectives of this type mainly occur in Arabic and Akkadian (Brockelmann 1908: 364f; Barth 1894: 26f, 164ff, 167f; Moscati 1969: 79; Fleisch 1961: 356ff; Kuryłowicz 1972: 115f; for the possible existence of such words in Hebrew see note 4). They fall into the same semantic categories as the words with gemination of the second radical just mentioned. In Arabic they denote expressive qualities of persons, e.g., *hizaff* or *hijaff* "fat", *nixibb* "timid", *ġuḍubb* "quick-tempered". According to Fleisch (1961: 358) "cette (...) classe a donné du vocabulaire bédouin, expressif".

In Akkadian only a few instances occur, which are characterized by GAG § 55p as "Steigerungsadjektive mit numinösem Bedeutungsgehalt": *namurru* "furchtbar glänzend", *rašubbu* "rot gleissend" (rather "awe-inspiring", cf. AHw sv), *da'ummu* "unheimlich dunkel", *šaqummu* "totenstill" and *šahurru* "ganz starr". However, *da'ummu* almost always appears in the forms *du'ummu* and *du'ūmu*, which are used interchangeably with the simple adjective *da'mu* "dark" and have the same function as the pattern *purrus* for other adjectives, see 10.7.1.2 sv. A second instance of the pattern *puruss* is *burummu*, which is found in LL as a bird name and in the plural (*burummū*, but also *burūmū*) as a poetic word for the sky, cf. CAD sv; both are derived from *barmu* "multicoloured". The semantic range of these words with gemination of the third radical leaves little doubt about their expressive background.[16] This also applies to gemination of the third radical in verbal categories of Arabic, which will be discussed in 2.2.4.2.[17]

The words mentioned in this section are generally infrequent, have patterns which are not productive, and typically belong to the semantic range in which we expect expressive extensions as defined in 2.2.3. This suggests that they are expressive in origin and have preserved this expressive nature. Therefore, they represent the type which is the least grammaticalized among the words and patterns with gemination in Semitic.

2.2.4.2. The functional erosion of gemination

Most motivated nouns with gemination belong to patterns which are more productive and less evidently expressive than those of the previous section. This is due to the process of weakening to which expressive categories are typically susceptible. For some of them, however, there are indications that they have originated from a nucleus of similar expressive adjectives. This applies in particular to the Akkadian pattern *purrus*. Its most typical function is to denote salient physical characteristics, such as *huppudu* "blind", *gullubu* "bald" and *kubbulu* "paralyzed", cf. 10.6.2. This function connects it with the sporadic patterns mentioned above, and suggests that it owes its geminate to the highly salient nature of these characteristics. It has a precise parallel in the Hebrew pattern *qittẹl* mentioned in the previous section. However, *purrus* has become very productive in Akkadian: it has acquired a purely grammatical function, viz., that of serving as stative and verbal adjective of the D-stem; on the other hand, it is to a large extent lexicalized. It will be discussed in detail in Chapter X.

A similar case is the pattern *qattāl* in Arabic. We can roughly distinguish three stages in its development. Originally, it is a pattern for intensive agent nouns (Ambros 1969: 89ff) and, according to Fleisch (1955 and 1961: 365f), an extension of an ancient agentive pattern *qatal* (cf. also note 18 to Ch. III). This use is found in cases such as Arabic *ᶜallām* "very learned", *ṭammāᶜ* "very eager" (Fleisch 1961: 358r; Wright 1896/98: I 137). It is sporadically attested in other Semitic languages, but there it is used for intensive adjectives rather than agent nouns: Hebrew *qannō* "jealous" (cf. Aartun 1975: 7), and *keḥḥāš* "mendacious" (for forms as *rakkāḇ*, which may also go back to *qattal*, see Aartun 1975: 5f and note 14 to Ch. III). Akkadian *qar-*

rādu "hero", *dappānu* "heroic, martial" and *hassā'u*, which denotes a bodily defect, can be assigned to this type as well (cf. 3.3.2).

The second stage is represented by a much more prominent function of *qattāl*, namely, that of denoting occupations, just as *parrās* in Akkadian (cf. 3.3), cf. Brockelmann 1908: 360f; Wright 1896/98: I 137; Loretz 1960: 411ff. According to Fleisch (1961: 365f), following Nöldeke (1875: 120) and Brockelmann (1908: 361), Arabic has borrowed this usage from Aramaic. Ambros, however, points out (1969: 90) that there is no positive evidence for this assumption, and that already in Quranic Arabic *qattāl* forms are found which denote occupations and have not been borrowed from Aramaic. Whichever of these views is correct, the essential point is that in this function the use of *qattāl* is no longer motivated by the expressive character of the geminate and/or the long vowel, but results from the analogical application of a grammatical rule (cf. Fleisch 1968: 55). It has become a conventional pattern for the expression of occupations.

The next stage in the development of *qattāl* occurs in Modern Standard Arabic and spoken Arabic, where according to Ambros (1969: 95f) *qattāl*, especially in its feminine form *qattālat*, has become a productive pattern for instrument nouns, replacing the older instrument noun pattern *miqtāl* (cf. 2.2.3 above). Instrument nouns often originate as agent nouns (Ambros 1969: 98; Kuryłowicz 1975: 26; Eilers 1964/66: 144; Panagl 1975), and the spread of *qattāl* from agent noun (animate) to instrument noun (inanimate) removes it one more step from its expressive origin.

Thus *purrus* and *qattāl* are good examples of originally intensive and expressive categories which have been grammaticalized: they have acquired grammatical functions, the former that of serving as stative/VA of the D-stem (cf. 10.2), the latter that of denoting agent nouns which refer to occupations and habitual actions. However, both have preserved clear traces of their original nature: *purrus* does not only serve as stative/VA of the D-stem, but has also preserved its function of forming adjectives that refer to salient inherent qualities and of underlining plurality. In *qattāl* the geminate preserves its iconic nature, in so far as it underlines the permanence and habituality which are inherent in agent nouns used for occupations and habitual actions, just as in the corresponding Akkadian patterns *parris* and *parrās*, cf. 3.2 and 3.3.

A third category with gemination which has undergone a similar development is the present tense in Akkadian, symbolized here by *iparras*. The rise of the present formation *iparras*, which, mainly in a prehistoric stage of Akkadian, replaced an older present *iprusu*, corresponding to Common Semitic *yaqtulu*,[18] is a prime example of the process of renewal which is typical of present formations; this process was first pointed out by Kuryłowicz and confirmed by the cross-linguistic research of Bybee, Perkins and Pagliuca (see 2.2.2 above). The overall function of gemination strongly suggests that *iparras* originally had durative, iterative, or similar meaning, a view which has been maintained by Rundgren on many occasions ("*réemploi de l'intensif*", e.g., 1955: 323ff: 1959a: 44f, and elsewhere). The introduction of *iparras* relegated *iprusu* to subordinate clauses, which is comparable to a modal use, and to the reanalysis of *-u* as a marker of subordination (Kuryłowicz 1972: 60; Bybee-Perkins-Pagliuca 1994: 230ff). The use of the same verb forms in oaths is also a residue of its former use, surviving in a specific context, comparable to the survival of Arabic *yaqtul* as a past tense after the negation *lam*.

The development of *iparras* is a typical instance of grammaticalization. Originally, it differed semantically from the forms without gemination in expressing durativity or a similar notion. In the historical stage of Akkadian, however, there is no longer a semantic difference, and *iparras* differs only in tense, i.e., grammatically, from the other forms of the G-stem. In contrast to the geminate of *purrus* and *qattāl,* that of *iparras* shows few traces of its original iconic nature, apart from the fact that there is generally a close relationship between present formations of the kind of *iparras* - which basically denotes a non-completed action - and durative Aktionsart (Comrie 1976: 24ff; Dressler 1968: 60ff).

Thus the Akkadian present tense *iparras* represents an advanced stage of grammaticalization of the geminate second radical. Moreover, it shows the overall correlation between the frequency of a category and the degree to which the iconic nature of gemination is still perceptible: it is most clearly perceptible in the sporadic patterns discussed above, and it is least obvious in the present *iparras*.

The developments of *purrus, qattāl* and *iparras* are examples of grammaticalization, in which the opposition between a neutral and an expressive form has been exploited for the expression of a grammatical contrast between a basic and a derived form. At this stage grammaticalization has caused an important change in the status of gemination as a sign: instead of an icon it has become a symbol. This is a very common process, cf. McMahon 1994: 172 and in particular Peirce 1960: II 169: "Symbols grow. They come into being by development out of other signs, particularly from icons".

2.2.4.3. Lexicalization

If we want to explain the functional relations between different categories with gemination in Akkadian, grammaticalization is, of all possible developments, the most important one. It enables us to explain not only the introduction of gemination to characterize the present tense, but also the rise of the Gtn-stem and the factitive function of the D-stem.

In many cases, however, weakening of an expressive category leads to a different outcome, in which there is no question of grammaticalization, but of lexicalization. First of all, words with gemination can become variants of the corresponding simple word, without a noticeable difference in meaning, but sometimes with a stylistic or dialectal difference. As will become apparent in the course of this study, the coexistence of forms with and without gemination which are more or less synonymous is widespread in Akkadian, especially in the *purrus* forms to be discussed in 10.7, in literary *parras* forms (cf. 3.1.2) and in D-stems of transitive verbs (cf. especially 6.8.4).

Secondly, such words with gemination, favoured because of their expressive character and their formal extension, can replace the simple word and can themselves become the standard form for the expression of the concept in question. This happened in many Semitic languages to colour terms with expressive extensions (Fisher 1965: 7f; Kuryłowicz 1972: 153), though not in Akkadian, where most colour terms are usually expressed by the simple adjective.[19] The same development can be observed in Arabic with regard to the verbs of Stems IX (*iqtalla*) and XI (*iqtālla*), which show gemination of the third radical. The verbs that occur in these stems typically refer to colours and defects (Wright 1896/98: I 43f; Fleisch 1979: 316ff), which points to an originally expressive character. However, since they have largely replaced the corresponding simple verbs, they do not show significant traces of greater expressivity or intensity in their actual use, according to Fleisch (1979: 318).

In Ethiopic many Stem II verbs are variants of the corresponding simple verbs or have replaced them (M. Cohen 1936: 201; D. Cohen 1984: 62; Ullendorff 1955: 218; Dillmann-Bezold 1907: 145f). According to Rundgren (1959a: 174; 1959b: 369), gemination was renewed by means of a reduplicated form with the pattern *qatātala* (*sabābara*).

In Akkadian this has happened to many *purrus* forms for physical defects: most of these do not have a corresponding simple form or they have one that is extremely rare (see 10.6.2 for details), so that they themselves have become the neutral way of expressing the quality in question.

These cases are instances of lexicalization: the words in question have become more or less independent lexemes with their own specific and largely unpredictable range of use which is not determined by a grammatical rule.

The complex situation we find in Akkadian with regard to the function of gemination is due to the fact that it is in the midst of a process of grammaticalization and lexicalization. This has led to its disintegration into different categories, each with its own function, so that its formerly uniform character was obscured. The various categories with gemination represent different stages in this continuous process. But even within a specific category the status of gemination may vary widely; the pattern *purrus*, for instance, spans the whole continuum from clearly iconic and expressive if it denotes striking physical characteristics, to completely grammaticalized if it functions as stative and verbal adjective of the D-stem (cf. 10.2). In Chapters III to XI we will substantiate this claim by means of a detailed discussion of the way they are used and their relationship to the basic category.

2.2.4.4. Gemination and reduplication

Another argument for the claim that gemination is originally expressive is provided by the relationship between gemination and reduplication in Semitic. The Excursus on reduplication which follows this section aims to show that gemination and reduplication are closely related, and perhaps even have a common origin, although they have undergone a completely different development: the former has been strongly grammaticalized, the latter has kept its expressive character almost intact. The fact that reduplication is a clearly iconic and highly expressive category supports the claim that gemination has an expressive background as well.

EXCURSUS ON REDUPLICATION IN SEMITIC

2.3. Introduction

The best way to illustrate the impact of grammaticalization on gemination in Akkadian is by comparing it to the related phenomenon of reduplication. It will transpire that there was originally a close similarity between the two phenomena, which was, however, for the most part undone by their opposite development: whereas gemination was to a large extent grammaticalized, reduplication preserved its iconic and expressive nature. Moreover, on the basis of this comparison we can set up a hypothesis about the rise of gemination as a phonologically relevant category.

Reduplication is one of the most undisputedly iconic phenomena in language.[20] In languages all over the world it has a very specific function, cf. Mayerthaler 1988: 85f: "reduplication generally codes plural(ity), abundance, iteratives, habituatives, frequentatives, distributives, augmentatives, intensives and emphasis. It codes diminution relatively less frequently". There is a clear iconic relationship between this range of functions and their expression by means of a repetition of consonants (Jakobson-Waugh 1987: 199).

In Semitic, however, the use of reduplication is rather more restricted than this description would lead us to expect. It is very restricted in Akkadian, especially if we only consider motivated words (cf. 2.1.2; for a possible reason see note 13). Therefore, I will also adduce cases from other Semitic languages, notably Arabic, which offers a remarkable wealth of material, and Hebrew. It is not the aim of this excursus to give an exhaustive account of reduplication; I will only deal with its typical manifestations on the basis of a sufficient number of examples to compare it with gemination (for general literature on reduplication in Semitic see note 20).

A fundamental distinction can be made between two types of words with reduplication: the first type (2.3.1) has phonetic iconicity, i.e., onomatopoeia (see 2.1.1), the second type (2.3.2) consists of words which are iconic extensions of simple words through reduplication of one or two radicals.

2.3.1. Onomatopoeic words

Many words with reduplication are not motivated in the grammatical sense described in 2.1 and cannot be derived from a verbal root (as far as we know), but are motivated by onomatopoeia. This is especially frequent in words which consist of the total reduplication of a biconsonantal base (*qalqal* etc.) (Brockelmann 1908: 368ff; Barth 1894: 204ff; Moscati 1969: 84; Dillmann-Bezold 1907: 131f; Nyberg 1954: 128f; Fleisch 1968: 78f and 130f). Many Hebrew examples can be found in Yannay 1974. Much Arabic material has been collected and studied by Joüon 1926: 24ff and Procházka 1995. Procházka (1995: 46) describes their overall semantic range as "Wiederholung und Intensivierung im weitesten Sinne"; Fleisch (1968: 78) characterizes them as "des vocables expressifs, figurant des mouvements, des sons, des bruits particuliers ou caractéristiques".

I will follow the distinction made by Ullmann (1973: 13f, cf. also 1962: 84), between primary and secondary onomatopoeia. The former refers to "some sound or noise which is imitated by the phonetic structure of the name" (1973: 13); the latter applies if "the experience thus depicted [is] not an acoustic phenomenon but something belonging to a different sense such as touch or sight" (1973: 14).

2.3.1.1. Primary onomatopoeia

Primary onomatopoeia is found in both nouns and verbs. The nouns comprise bird names as *hudhud* "hoopoe", *^{c}aq^{c}aq* "magpie" and *qa^{c}qa^c* "raven"; verbs of this type are more numerous, e.g., *waswasa* "to whisper, to suggest (evil)" with the abstract nouns *waswās* and *waswasah*, and *baqbaqa* "to gurgle, to prattle" with *baqbaqah* "gurgling, prattling" and *baqbāq* "garrulous, chatterbox" (Procházka 1995: 51/54). Some verbs are denominative: *sa'sa'a* "to call a donkey by shouting *sa'sa'*" (Fleisch 1968: 130). Akkadian instances are *raqraqqu* or *laqlaqqu* "ostrich" (that says *rīqa rīqa* acc. to AnSt. 20, 112: 8) and *puhpuhhu/ū*, if AHw's interpretation "Kampfschnauben, Streit" and etymology (from *napāhu* "to blow") are correct. Some other Akkadian instances are mentioned by Livingstone, NABU 88/65: *damdammu*, a kind of donkey, cf. *damāmu* "to wail, to bray"; *halhallatu*, a musical instrument, cf. *halālu* "to whistle", and *haphappu*, the lower part of a door, from *hapāpu* "to batter, to knock". If AHw's tentative suggestion (628a sv) that *mašmaš(š)u* "exorcist" is onomatopoeic ("lautmalend?"), is correct, it belongs here, too. Livingstone, however, connects it with *mašāšu* "to wipe, to clean"; in that case it belongs to 2.3.2.

2.3.1.2. Secondary onomatopoeia

Cases of secondary onomatopoeia with the pattern *qalqal* are much more frequent. Here the word form is related to the visual effect of an action, an object or a phenomenon: e.g., in Akkadian we have *birbirrū* "luminosity" from *barāru* "to glitter" (cf. AHw sv: "flimmern"); in Arabic *ša'ša'a* "to glitter, to shine" and *zalzala* "to shake" with *zalzalah*, *zalzāl* and *zilzāl* "shock, earthquake", and many others, cf. Procházka 1995: 54f. It is often found in the names of animals or objects which tend to be seen in large groups: Akkadian *paspasu* "duck", *wazwazu* "goose" (Black-Al-Rawi 1987: 122), *ṣarṣar* "locusts" (ARM 27, 27: 6 and elsewhere, cf. p. 10 § 6), *zunzunu* or *zirzirru* "small locust" (also *zīru*, *zizru* and *ziruziru*, cf. CAD ssvv), *p/bilp/billu* "wasp", *baqbaqqu* "small gnat" (besides *baqqu* and *buqāqu*) and *duqduqqu* or *diqdiqqu*, a small bird (a wren, according to Stol (RA 65, 180), perhaps from *daqāqu* "to be very small". Arabic instances are *waṭwāṭ* "bat", *ṣurṣūr* "cricket", *zurzūr* "starling", *lu'lu'* "pearl" and Common Semitic **kabkab* "star" (cf. Brockelmann 1908: 369). It is also used for objects which consist of many small parts: Arabic *sinsinah* "spinal column", *silsilah* "chain", cf. Akkadian *šeršerru* "chain" and *šeršerratu* "chain, fetters, shackles (CAD sv), which are connected with *šertu* "ring", cf. Livingstone, NABU 88/65.

Hebrew has a few verbs of the type Pilpel which, according to Joüon-Muraoka (1991: 169), "signify repetition of an action, often in quick succession", e.g., *gilgẹl* "to roll" (trans.). In some Hebrew nouns the plural idea is made explicit by a plural ending: *gargĕrīm* "berries", *zalzallīm* "vines".

The form of these words is largely determined by the visual or auditive impression that the corresponding entities make. But there are also words of the pattern *qalqal* which cannot be explained as onomatopoeic, e.g., the Common Semitic words for "head" (**qadqad*) and "skull" (**gulgul-t*), cf. Nyberg 1954: 128.

Some verbs II/gem. resemble these *qalqal* forms with secondary onomatopoeia in that they denote actions with a repetitive character ("Kettendurative" GAG § 101b): Akkadian *dabābu* "to talk", *arāru* "to tremble", *baṣāṣu* "to drip", *ṣabābu* "to flap (wings)", cf. also Moscati 1969: 169, Gesenius-Kautzsch 1985: 160 note 1; Whiting 1981: 23 with notes 88f. In other verbs of this type, however, the repetition of the second radical has a purely grammatical cause, viz. the tendency to adapt these roots to the prevailing triliteral root pattern. This is demonstrated by the numerous cases where the same root has also other extensions (e.g., a long vowel or a weak third radical). See Kuryłowicz 1972: 8ff, for an explanation of the mechanism involved and many examples; for Akkadian GAG³ § 105a mentions *herû* and *harāru* "to dig", *redû* and *radādu* "to follow", *kepû* and *kapāpu* "to bend"; other examples are *dâku* "to kill" and *dakāku* "to crush" (cf. AHw sv *dakāku* I) and *rašû* "to be red" beside *rašāšu* "to glow red" (cf. Oppenheim *et al.* 1970: 73).

2.3.2. Root extensions by means of reduplication

In many other words reduplication is not onomatopoeic, but an extension of a verb or a noun, which makes it more expressive or intensive. There is no formal difference between this and the preceding type; we find the pattern *qalqal* again, in Arabic verbs like *kabkaba* "to topple, to overturn" from *kabba* (id.), *ṣarṣara* "to shout" from *ṣarra* (id.) (Fleisch 1968: 131), and in extended triliteral roots, e.g. *faxfaxa* "to be a braggart" from *faxara* "to boast". Procházka's claim (1995: 64f) that in such cases the reduplicated form is original and the simple form the result of adaptation to the prevailing triliteral system seems to be unlikely in view of the general tendency in Arabic to extend roots rather than to reduce them, as argued in 2.2.3.

Adjectives of the same type are, e.g., Arabic *maðmāð* "always crying" and *ṭurṭūr* "stupid" with intensive meaning (Brockelmann 1908: 370). We also find it in later Akkadian: *dandannu* "strong", *babbanû* "beautiful", *kaškaššu* "overpowering" and *lašlašu* "nichtswürdig" (AHw 1571a sv), which are strengthened forms of *dannu*, *banû*, *kaššu* and *laššu* respectively. A substantive to be listed here is Akkadian *ziqziqqu* "storm" from *zâqu* "to blow" (of the wind).

Of a similar nature are some of the words which contain reduplication of the second syllable of a triconsonantal root (*qataltal*, etc.) (cf. Barth 1894: 216ff; Brockelmann 1908: 367f; Nyberg 1954: 132; Fisher 1965: 200; Fleisch 1968: 77). They are represented in all Semitic languages except Akkadian. Arabic has a number of substantivized adjectives of this type: *ᶜarakrak* "a (strong) camel"; *barahrahah* "a fat woman". Classical Ethiopic. has adjectives of this kind for colours and physical defects: *ḥamalmīl* "green" (Brockelmann 1908: 368; Nyberg 1954: 132). Hebrew also has colour names (*yraqraq* "greenish", *'ădamdam* "reddish" and a few other adjectives, e.g., *hăfakpak* "tortuous" (Bauer-Leander 1922: 482f; Gesenius-Kautzsch 1985: 224f). In Ethiopic this pattern characterizes abstract nouns derived from verbs denoting "rhythmisch-iterative Handlungen und Zustände (Brockelmann 1908: 367f; Nyberg 1954: 132).

As to the verbal formations, Hebrew has a verb *sḥarḥar* "to palpitate", cf. Joüon-Muraoka 1991: 169. Many of the "rare stems" in Arabic (Stems XI-XV) are based on this type of reduplication, e.g., *iḫlawlaka* "to be pitch-black", *iḥdawdaba* "to be hunch-backed". All these stems are characterized by Fleisch (1979: 334), as "des formations intensives, expressives"; cf. also 1968: 126f.[21]

2.3.3. Reduplication of a single consonant

Apart from the types *qalqal* and *qataltal*, there are many words with reduplication of a single consonant: either the second or the third radical. Reduplication of the second radical is frequent only in Ethiopic in order to form iterative and frequentative verbal patterns, e.g., *sabābara* "to break into small pieces". They replace the pattern with gemination, which has become a variant of the basic stem (Rundgren 1959a: 174; 1959b: 364f, 369).

Akkadian has a few nouns of this type, cf. GAG § 55r: *zuqaqīpu* (with variants) "scorpion", from *zaqāpu* "rear up", *dababābu* "Rederei" (AHw sv; but CAD sv translates "case" and comments: "possible scribal error for *da-ba-bu-um*"), and *hananābu* "a sweet fruit" from *hanābu* "grow abundantly".[22] In other cases mentioned by GAG § 55r the reduplication is not contrastive, but copied from a verbal root II/gem., e.g., *ṣurarû* (with variants) "lizard", which is to be connected with *ṣarāru* B "to flash" (said mainly of shooting stars), "to flit" (said of demons), cf. CAD sv) and *hibabîtu* "bride" (1x LL, not in GAG) with the abstract noun *hibibātu* "virginity", which CAD sv derives from *habābu* "to caress". In order to explain the abstract nouns *tumāmîtu* or *tammāmîtu* "oath" and *ṣumāmu* and *ṣumāmîtu* "thirst" we probably have to presuppose the existence of the root variants *t-m-m* and *ṣ-m-m* beside *t-m-ā* and *ṣ-m-'*: cf. *tammamû* "der oft schwört", cf. AHw sv and 3.1.1. The other nouns mentioned in GAG § 55r are of Sumerian or unknown origin.

Reduplication of the third radical (cf. Barth 1894: 214ff; Brockelmann 1908: 365ff; Fleisch 1968: 75ff; Nyberg 1954: 130; Fisher 1965: 200f) occurs sporadically in Arabic nouns, often with a diminutive or pejorative meaning, e.g., *quᶜdud* "ignoble", *riᶜdīd* "cowardly", *siktīt* "very silent", comparable with Hebrew adjectives such as *raᶜănān* "green", *'umlāl* "languishing" (Joüon-Muraoka 1991: 254).

Akkadian has *išbabtu* "a grass or a weed" (CAD sv), from *ešēbu* "to grow luxuriantly", *za/iqīqu* (or *zā/īqīqu*) "phantom, ghost, soul, dream god", from *zâqu* "to blow" of the wind (cf. CAD Z 60b), *kulbābu* "ant" (from *kalbu* "little dog" (??)), *burmāmu* "porcupine" from *barmu* "multicoloured", *nam(m)ušīšu*, a derivation from *namāšu* to go": "etwa 'beweglich'" acc. to AHw sv, but a euphemism for "dead" acc. to CAD sv, and a few plural nouns: *a/ilkakātu* from *alaktu* "gait, movement, behaviour", *namrirrū/namrīrū* "supernatural, awe-inspiring luminosity" (CAD sv) from *naw/māru* "shine brightly". GAG² § 56o posits a pattern *pursāsī* with diminutive/pejorative meaning on the basis of *bun(n)annû* "appearance, features", *hubšāšû*, a type of cup, *sūqāqû* "alley" (cf. *sūqu* "street"), and *upšašū* "witchcraft" from *epēšu* in the technical sense "to practise witchcraft" (CAD E 228f sv 2f-1').

Verbs of the pattern *qatlala* are frequent in Ethiopic, e.g. *ḥanqaqa* "to worry", *damsasa* "to destroy" (Dillmann-Bezold 1907: 133f; Fleisch 1979: 335). Hebrew has a few Paᶜlel or Piᶜlel verbs, which Gesenius-Kautzsch (1985: 159) compare with the Arabic Stems IX and XI (cf. also Joüon-Muraoka 1991: 169). Arabic has a few denominative verbs of this type: *šamlala* "to be agile, nimble" from *šimlāl*, *jalbaba* "to wear a *jilbāb*" (Fleisch 1968: 148f). In Akkadian we find the quadriliteral verb *šuqallulu* "to be suspended, to hang" (later also transitive), which looks like an extension of *šaqālu* "to hang" (trans.), to weigh, to pay". The analysis of other verbs with this pattern (*šuqammumu* "to be(come) silent" and *šuharruru* "to be(come) numb with fear") is unclear since we do not know from which root they are derived, cf. Whiting 1981: 5ff.

It is possible that the Arabic Stem IX *iqtalla*, which mainly denotes colours and physical defects, goes back to **iqtalala* and also belongs here (see 2.3.6 below); it can be reinforced by lengthening of the vowel: *iqtālla* (Stem XI). The overlong syllable of this form can be replaced by *hamza* or another consonant: *iqta'alla, iqtahalla, iqtaᶜalla*; these forms constitute Stem IV of the quadriliteral verb (Fleisch 1979: 315ff, 453f; Nyberg 1954: 130). According to Wright (1896/98: I 49), this stem "expresses an extensively or intensively high degree of an intransitive act, state or quality".

2.3.4. Other words with reduplication in Akkadian

Akkadian has many other words with reduplication, which cannot be derived from a verbal root which recurs in other words. They usually denote concrete entities: persons, animals, body parts and plants. I will restrict myself to mentioning a selection of typical cases of reduplication of a biconsonantal base, which can be considered representative.

1. Persons: *durduru* (denoting a human quality), *harharu* "scoundrel", *hašhašu* (a person with a physical defect), *pilpilû* "male prostitute", *qumqummatu* (designation of a witch);

2. Birds (apart from those already mentioned in previous sections): *gamgammu*, *kipkippu*, *kurkurru*, *naṣnāṣu*, *terterru* (all unidentified); cf. Black-Al-Rawi 1987: 120ff.
3. Other animals: *barbaru* "wolf";
4. Plants: *gabgabu* (a kind of brier), *galgaltu* (a drug), *gurgurru* (a plant), *hinhinu* (a kind of reed), *kudkudu* (unidentified), *puhpuhu* "purslane", *rušruššu* (unidentified), *zimzimmu* (a kind of onion);
5. Parts of the body: *gulgul(la)tu* "skull", *kaskasu* "soft part of the sheep's breastbone", *kimkimmu* "wrist(?)", *nahnahatu* "cartilage", *qaqqadu* < **qadqadu* "head", *sapsapu* "moustache" (cf. George, NABU 96/60), *gubgubu* (unidentified).

Many other words for concrete objects with reduplication occur in Akkadian. Abstract words with reduplication, however, are very rare: AHw has only *kiskīsu* (a month name), *derderru* "battle", *galgal(la)tu* or *kalkaltu* "hunger", and *laplaptu* "parching thirst(?)". These last three words presumably denote some salient physical feature of thirst or starvation, or of the general conditions prevailing in times of draught or famine, rather than simply "lack of food or drink"; it is perhaps not accidental that also more common words for these concepts show reduplication: of the first consonant in *bubūtu* "hunger", of the second one in *ṣumāmu* and *ṣumāmītu* "thirst", cf. *ṣūmu* and 2.3.3.

2.3.5. Conclusions

This survey may suffice to bring out two remarkable features of reduplication in Semitic. In the first place, its use is largely restricted to words of a specific semantic range, such as onomatopoeics, terms for repetitive actions, colours and striking qualities of persons; the reduplication iconically reflects and underlines their expressive character. Since they generally refer to very specific entities, qualities or events, the majority of these words are very rare.

In the second place, the words with reduplication differ from the rest of Semitic vocabulary in that they do not easily fit in with the predominating root-and-pattern structure (cf. 2.1.2). If we try to arrange them into patterns with a more or less consistent function, we end up with a large amount of patterns - each of them comprising a very small number of words - which are poorly differentiated in function. Moreover, many words with reduplication do not even belong to a verbal root.

This leads us to the conclusion that gemination and reduplication are both expressive in origin (cf. 2.2.4.1 with regard to gemination), but have undergone completely different historical developments. The former has been strongly grammaticalized, but the latter has largely maintained its iconic and expressive character; apparently, it was so strongly tied up with it that it could not spread to other contexts. Therefore, it has not become a productive means of marking grammatical categories and hardly plays a role in nominal and verbal derivation in Semitic (with the exception of Ethiopic, cf. Dillmann-Bezold 1907: 131ff). In other words, reduplication - in contrast to gemination - has not been grammaticalized.

Both reduplication and gemination, then, can be regarded as iconic phenomena in Semitic. Since gemination is not only formally, but also functionally weaker (less salient) than reduplication, since it is largely grammaticalized, the relationship between the two phenomena is iconic as well.

2.3.6. The formal relationship between gemination and reduplication

If we compare the use of reduplication in Semitic with its general use as defined by Mayerthaler (cf. 2.3), we find an important difference. Except in Ethiopic, reduplication is conspicuously absent as a means of characterizing the semantic categories that Mayerthaler mentions; in Semitic it is gemination which typically performs these functions. This suggests a possible origin for gemination as a phonologically contrastive phenomenon in Semitic, namely, that it results from a reduction of reduplication.

Several scholars of Semitic have in fact expressed this idea. Poebel (1939: 65ff) claims that gemination is a remnant of the total reduplication of a root and that it denotes plurality (cf. 1.4). Christian (1929: 209) derives a form such as *qattala* from *qatlala.* Halévy (JA, 9ème série, t. 9 (1902), 136f) suggests on the basis of Ethiopic pairs as *qabbala* "to receive" versus *qabbābala* "to receive frequently" that the D-stem arose through contraction of *qababala,* which itself stands for *qabalbala.* None of these claims is supported by conclusive arguments, see the detailed discussion in Ryder 1974: 31ff, and cf. note 6.

On the basis of the following considerations, however, one is tempted to hypothesize that gemination of the second radical originally represents a realization of a pattern *qatatal*, with reduplication of the second radical and short vowels.

First, this hypothesis is in line with the claims made by Bybee, Perkins and Pagliuca (1994: 166ff) about the grammaticalization of reduplication. The authors claim that the typical path of grammaticalization of reduplication is from iterative via continuative to progressive, or via frequentative to habitual, both paths leading to imperfective or occasionally to intransitive; and that this functional development correlates with a reduction in form: whereas iterativity is more often expressed by means of total reduplication, the more grammaticalized functions tend to be more commonly expressed by partial reduplication.

Although these claims are based on a rather limited number of languages - only 16 languages out of their sample of 76 (cf. 2.2.2) contain verb forms with reduplication, cf. 1994: 168 table 5.10 - they seem to be valid for Semitic, if we replace "partial reduplication" by "gemination". The functions of gemination in Semitic largely agree with the more grammaticalized functions which the authors claim to be typical of partial reduplication. This supports the idea that gemination is a reduction of reduplication.

On the other hand, there are some obvious difficulties in the application of this hypothesis to Semitic. First of all, although iterativity is occasionally expressed by means of the repetition of a whole word - an example from Akkadian is NABU 88/17 p. 14 no. 34 *kajjān[um têrētim]* (....) *[ušē]pišma* (...) *la-ap-ta la-ap-ta* "I have had extispicies made regularly, (but) they are unfavourable each time" - total reduplication is not a regular grammatical device in Semitic, and it is a matter of speculation whether it ever was. Secondly, it cannot be shown that in Semitic partial reduplication arose out of total reduplication, in spite of Poebel's claim to the contrary; in fact, plurality can be expressed equally well by partial reduplication, just as any other realization of "verbal plurality", cf. Dressler 1968: 56ff. Therefore, the first stage of the grammaticalization process in question remains hypothetical.

Second, among the various words and patterns with reduplication of the second radical, there are no definite instances of *qatatal,* whereas we find numerous cases in which one or more of its constituents are lengthened or geminated (see 2.3.3). This suggests that *qatatal* could not be realized as such, but that it was either strengthened to *qatātal* or *qatattal* - cf. Ethiopic forms such as *sabābara* - or automatically realized as *qattal.* Such a rule would represent a restricted version of the vowel deletion rule of Akkadian, which deletes a short vowel in the environment VC_CV (Greenstein 1984: 13ff), i.e., it reduces a form as **parisu* to *parsu*; it would be restricted in that it only applies if the consonants surrounding the vowel are identical.

The existence of such a rule is suggested by the conjugation of verba II/gem. in Arabic and Hebrew and of the verbs of Stem IX in Arabic: compare the 3rd p. sg. masc. *ᶜadda* "he counted" < **ᶜadada*, cf. *ᶜadadtu* "I counted", and *farra* "he fled" < **farira*, cf. *farirtu* "I fled". Likewise in Stem IX: *iqtalla* < **iqtalala* (1st p. sg. *iqtalaltu* (Fleisch 1979: 343ff). It leads to a situation in which gemination and reduplication are in complementary distribution: reduplication before a suffix beginning with a consonant, gemination when the suffix begins with a vowel. A similar phenomenon is found in Hebr.: *sāḇaḇ* "he surrounded" vs. *sabbōtā* "you surrounded", cf. Joüon-Muraoka 1991: 224f.

On the basis of these facts we may speculate that gemination as a phonologically contrastive phenomenon arose from a reduction of reduplication by means of a vowel deletion rule which only applied to identical successive consonants followed by short vowels, i.e., which reduced *qatatal* to *qattal.*

Recently Whiting (1981: 28ff) has presented a similar idea about a possible development of the Akkadian D-stem *uparras* from **upararas*. He was inspired by Givón 1976: 493f, who took up Poebel's idea described in 1.4, and proposed a scheme for the reduction of the reduplicated root; as one of the stages of this he assumed the existence of a form *sababara* (his example), which could be accented either *sábabara* or *sabábara*. From these forms Whiting (1981: 30 n. 109) tentatively derives the D-stem *uparras* and the R-stem *upararras* respectively.

The main objections against this view are, first, that we find all kinds of reduplication in Semitic (see above), but no cases of the reduplication that Givón and Whiting presume, i.e. *qatatala*; second, that everything seems to indicate that stress in Proto-Semitic was not phonological, but assigned on the basis of syllable structure (cf. Moscati 1969: 65f; Knudsen 1980: 15), so that contrasting pairs as *sábabara* and *sabábara* were not possible; third, the Akkadian reduplicated verbal forms which Whiting puts on a par with the D-stem are rare and marginal and have no exact equivalents in other Semitic languages. It is likely, therefore, that their existence is dependent upon internal developments in Akkadian.

Moreover, the existence of gemination with phonological status in common Semitic is well established, since it occurs in all older Semitic languages. Therefore, the process assumed here to explain its origin must have taken place in a remote period of Proto-Semitic and should not be made directly responsible for historically attested cases of gemination.

If the hypothesis that gemination of the second radical is a reduced form of reduplication is correct, the two phenomena have a common origin not only semantically, but also formally, and are different realizations of a single phenomenon, which, in the course of time, developed in opposite directions.

Notes to Chapter Two

1 The following ismainly based on Anttila 1989: 12ff and Jakobson 1990: 407ff. For iconicity in language see, in general, Lyons 1977: 99ff; Haiman 1985; Croft 1990: 164ff; Matthews 1991: 223ff; McMahon 1994: 84ff.

2 Dressler 1985: 331, claims that the typical relationship between consonants and vowels of Semitic is also a case of (diagrammatic) iconicity: "Syllable onset consonants are more salient than vowels (....) and more distinguishable consonants can be articulated and perceived than vowels, so that almost all languages have more phonemic consonants than vowels. Since there are many more lexical than grammatical morphemes, it is both economical and diagrammatic to concentrate lexical meaning in consonants, grammatical meaning in vowels, as in Semitic languages and in Proto-Indo-European."

3 See Kuryłowicz 1972: 115; examples are *qittūl* in Hebrew (abstract noun, cf. Bauer-Leander 1922: 480f); *qattālā* in Aramaic (inf. Paᶜel, cf. Segert 1975: 152); in Akkadian the inf. D *purrus* and the verbal noun *purrust* derived from it (GAG § 55n). Some concrete nouns may also go back to verbal forms, e.g., Akkadian *sikkūru* "bolt" and *ma/ihhūru* "sacrifice" (GAG § 55o: "deverbale Gegenstandsbezeichnungen").

4 In some cases it is difficult to determine the status of the geminate of a word with certainty: for instance, for Hebrew colour terms such as *'ādōm* "red" or *bārōd* "speckled" Gesenius-Kautzsch (1985: 240), Bauer-Leander (1922: 466f) and Joüon-Muraoka (1991: 79) posit a pattern *qatul*, with secondary gemination if a vocalic suffix follows. Fisher (1965: 199f), however, posits *qatull*, in accordance with the ten-

dency of Semitic to use gemination or reduplication in colour terms, and because of the parallelism with Akkadian words such as *da'ummu* "dark".

5 The use of gemination in the plural of substantives is also found in *bakru*, pl. *bakkarū* "young of a camel or donkey", *zikru*, pl. *zikkarū* "man, male", see CAD ssvv; and also in the OA pl. *e-ba-ru-tim* "fellow merchants", from *e/ibru* "friend, colleague" according to CAD sv *ibru* and Reiner 1966: 64f.

6 The importance of this polysemous nature of verbal plurality with regard to the D-stem concerns two points in particular. First, it shows that it is futile to regard any of the meanings listed by Dressler as applying to the D-stem, while at the same time rejecting the relevance of others; second, it shows that all theories which claim that the D-stem has a multiple origin on *semantic* grounds are superfluous. The first point applies to Ryder, who assigns an "extensive" function to the D-stem (i.e., "the "extension" of an action, either in time or in physical extent" (1974: 166), but denies an intensive function, and to Poebel, who vigorously denies the existence of an intensive D, but regards plurality as its primary function (1939: 65ff, see 1.4). The second point applies to Goetze, who assumes that in some verbs gemination results from assimilation of a nasal to the second radical (1942: 7b, cf. 1.8), to Speiser's proposal (1967: 506ff) to explain some Hebrew verb forms in the same way (see also 4.1), and to the ideas of Christian (1929: 209), who distinguishes an original intensive *qatlal* from a durative *qantal*, both of which eventually merged into *qattal*.

7 A general introduction is Hopper-Traugott 1993; see also Bybee-Perkins-Pagliuca 1994: 4ff; Croft 1990: 230ff; McMahon 1994: 160ff.

8 It goes without saying that this is a rather simplistic account of this controversial and much debated issue, see the discussions in Matthews 1991: 42ff and Bybee 1985: 81ff.

9 The authors claim (1994: 129ff) that locative elements are the most important source for the creation of progressives; the use of the preposition *bi-* for this purpose in Modern Arabic is another example of this phenomenon.

10 The overall predilection of Semitic for expressive forms is especially striking with regard to colours and physical characteristics, cf. Rundgren 1959a: 272f; Fisher 1965: 199; Kuryłowicz 1972: 152ff (who claims (153) that it is the permanence of the qualities expressed which accounts for the formal extension). A typical area which also abounds in expressive forms is that of augmentatives and diminutives, not only in Semitic (especially Arabic: Fleisch 1961: 390ff), but also in other language types (Brockelmann 1928: 131ff); what they have in common is the emotional involvement both categories imply.

11 The term "expressive" is also used by Martinet 1937; Stankiewicz 1954; Kuryłowicz 1973: 260. As to Semitics, Fleisch (e.g. 1968: 68ff) speaks of "expressivité", belonging to the "langage affectif". Other terms for this phenomenon include "evaluative" (Worth 1967: 2272) and "emotive" (Jakobson 1990: 69ff). Fisher (1965: 6), speaks of "bedeutungswertende" (versus bedeutungsinhaltliche) Ableitungsmorpheme", which he defines as follows: [such morphemes] "kennzeichnen ihrem Bedeutungsinhalt nach synonyme Wörter über den konstatierenden Inhalt hinaus, das betreffende Wort aufwertend oder abwertend." "Expressive" has, however, the disadvantage that it is often used in a wider sense than is meant here, cf. Lyons 1977: 50ff, 107.

12 There seems to be no general study of this phenomenon. The semantic categories which offer many expressive words are listed by Martinet 1937: 40; Wissmann 1932: 162ff; Kuryłowicz 1973: 260 (but cf. the critical assessment of these three authors in Lühr 1988: 66ff).

13 This is perhaps the reason why expressive forms are so rare in Akkadian: the majority of the preserved texts contain the rather stylized language of literary, legal, economic and scientific works; in letters we might expect a more informal style, but even these are rather stylized ("Kanzlei-Sprache", cf. Kraus 1973: 34 and 41f). The fact that expressive words did exist can be glimpsed from lexical texts, which contain a fair number of words with expressive features, such as reduplication.

14 Cf. Kuryłowicz's first law of analogy: "un morphème biparti tend à s'assimiler un morphème isofonctionnel consistant uniquement en un des deux éléments, c.-à.-d. le morphème composé remplace le morphème simple" (1973: 70).

15 A general survey is found in Brockelmann 1908: 360ff; Barth 1894: 23ff, 48ff, 65, 139, 145f, 168f, 196ff; Moscati 1969: 78f; Kuryłowicz 1972: 113ff. For specific languages see GAG § 55m/q, 56o; Fleisch 1961: 358f; Segert 1975: 152f; Gesenius-Kautzsch 1985: 242ff; Bauer-Leander 1922: 476ff; Dillmann-Bezold 1907: 231f. For gemination as an expressive device in Indo-European languages see Martinet 1937 and Meillet 1931: 166ff.

16 It is difficult to account for the geminate third radical of motivated nouns such as *gimillu* "favour", *hubullu* "debt" and *kunukku* "seal". The latter two can be explained as occasional replacements of the more common pattern *purūs*, which forms "deverbale Gegenstandsbezeichnungen" (GAG § 55l), e.g., *rukūbu* "boat, chariot" and *lubūšu* "garment" (doubtless originally abstract nouns, cf. *buqūmu* "wool plucking", *hubūru* "noise"), on the basis of the interchangeability of long vowel plus simple consonant and short vowel plus geminate (GAG § 20d; Reiner 1966: 45f). This will not do, however, for *gimillu*, since a pattern *pirīsu* is hardly attested (GAG § 55j), and neither for the extended pattern *purussā'u* (GAG § 56o), which mainly forms legal terms (e.g., *purussā'u* "judicial decision"), cf. Von Soden 1989: 69ff.

17 Akkadian does not have a verbal stem with gemination of the third radical. However, this kind of gemination occurs rather systematically in the Ntn-stem of verbs II/gem., cf. GAG[3] § 101g/h. Additional forms are mentioned in NABU 88/17 nos. 13-15; cf. also OBTR 147: 28 *lā ta-ta-na-aš-ša-aš-ši* "do not keep fretting" (tr. Dalley) from *ašāšu* "to be worried" (imp. fem. sg.), and *i-ta-aš-mu-um-mu* from *šamāmu* "to paralyze", quoted in CAD sv lex. sect. Sporadically, it also occurs in the Gt-stem: BRM 4, 16: 16 *iš-ta-an-na-an-nu* and KUB 37, 168: III 8' *ta-aš-ta-an-na-an-na* from *šanānu* Gt "to rival each other" and in the Gtn-stem: MARI 7, 199: 39 *ta-ah-ta-na-as-sà-as-sà* (cf. also 35) and BBS 6: II 52 *li-ih-ta-sa-as-su-šu* from *hasāsu* "to think of, to mention". Moreover, there are a few participles with a *-t-* infix and gemination of both the second and the third radical, also from verbs II/gem.: *muktaššaššu* "overpowering" from *kašāšu* "to overpower" and *muštabbabbu* "flasher" (name of a demon) from *šabābu* "to burn" (?). They are most likely to be "reinforced" Gtn participles (*muptarrisu*). Note that the forms discussed in this note cannot be classified as "R-stems": they do not contain reduplication, as maintained by Kienast 1957b, Gröneberg 1989: 33f, Whiting 1981: 35 note 125, and GAG[2] § 101f, but gemination of two radicals; it is only the verbal root from which they are derived which contains a reduplicated radical.

18 The rise of *iparras*, its relationship with Eth. *yeqattel* and the question whether it also occurs in West Semitic, is one of the most controversial issues of comparative Semitic studies, cf. the bibliography collected by Knudsen (1982: 9 note 24; 1984/86: 238 note 1). There can be no doubt that the view advocated by Kuryłowicz 1972: 59f, Rundgren 1959a: 37 (and passim), and many others, that *iparras* originates as a derivational iterative which has become an inflectional member of the G-stem with the function of expressing the present is correct. The hotly debated question whether this process dates from the period of common Semitic (so that there may be traces of a similar category in West Semitic), or whether it is an internal Akkadian development, need not concern us here.

19 For the basic colour names Akkadian almost always uses the simple adjective (cf., in general, Landsberger 1967b); only exceptionally do we find a *purrus* form, cf. App. to Ch. X ssvv *puṣṣû, summu, ṣullumu* and *(w)urruqu*. However, *purrus* is frequently used in words which are semantically related to colour names, such as *burrumu* "multicoloured", cf. 10.6.2; in particular in words which denote various shades of dark: *ukkulu, turruku, urrupu* and the "pseudo-*purrus* form" (cf. 10.7.1.2 sv) *du'ummu/du'ūmu*, cf. App. to Ch. X ssvv. *Ruššû* "red" only occurs as a *purrus* form, but may be a byform of *huššû*, which is a Sumerian loanword, cf. note 20 to Ch. X.

20 Cf. Sapir 1921: 79ff; Key 1965: 89ff; Moravcsik 1978: 316ff; Jakobson-Waugh 1987: 198ff; Mayerthaler 1988: 85f. For Indo-European languages see Tischler 1976; Martinet 1937; Stankiewicz 1954: 457f; Schwyzer-Debrunner 1939/53: I 315. General surveys of reduplicated forms in Semitic are found in Barth 1894: 202f; Brockelmann 1908: 365ff; Botterweck 1952: 45ff; Nyberg 1954: 131f; Castellino 1962: 121ff; Moscati 1969: 79.

21 See further Wright 1890: 220f; 1896/98: I 46f (with many examples); Nyberg 1954: 128; Whiting 1981: 22 note 83; Fisher 1965: 230. For the verbal forms with reduplication in Akkadian see Whiting 1981, Gröneberg's sceptical assessment (1989: 27ff), note 17 to this chapter and note 1 to Ch. IX.

22 I have listed these words in the form given by the dictionaries. However, the vowel elision rule of Akkadian (Greenstein 1984: 13ff) requires the first and/or the second syllable of these words to be long (cf. **parisūtu* > *parsūtu*), so that it is rather *zuqaqqīpu* (which is also attested, cf. CAD sv lex. sect.) or something similar.

CHAPTER THREE

THE PATTERNS *PARRAS, PARRIS* AND *PARRĀS*

3.0. In this chapter we will discuss the use of nouns of the patterns *parras, parris* and *parrās*. More specifically, we will be concerned with, first, the nature of the contrast between these nouns and the corresponding simple nouns without gemination, and, second, the differences in function between these patterns themselves, in order to establish the function of gemination as accurately as possible.

Therefore, we will concentrate on words in which the formal differences between these patterns are immediately observable, i.e., on nouns which are derived from strong roots and do not have *e*-colouring. Generally speaking, these can be assigned to a specific pattern with a reasonable degree of certainty, in spite of the fact that cuneiform writing does not consistently distinguish between simple and geminate consonants on the one hand, and short and long vowels on the other (cf. GAG § 7d/e). The former feature makes it often difficult to decide whether a given form belongs to *pāris* or *parris* (see 3.2); the latter whether it belongs to *parras* or *parrās* (see 3.3).

It is not the purpose of this chapter to give an exhaustive account of these patterns. Poorly attested and uncertain cases are generally not considered, unless they are interesting for some specific reason.

3.1. The pattern *parras*

The pattern *parras* has a double function: it is used to form agent nouns from fientive verbs for the expression of activities, and to form derived adjectives from basic adjectives for the expression of states and qualities (GAG § 55m). We will deal with the former function in 3.1.1. The latter function is by far the most common. The *parras* forms in question can be divided into two types. The first type, to be discussed in 3.1.2, are *parras* forms which for the most part are very rare and mainly restricted to literary and lexical texts. The second type, to be discussed in 3.1.3, consists of a group of adjectives - some of which occur quite frequently - which are mostly used as plural formations of simple adjectives denoting dimensions. It is mainly this type which has a special relevance for our purpose.[1]

3.1.1. *Parras* for agent nouns derived from fientive verbs

Agent nouns are almost always expressed by *parris* and *parrās*, and by the pattern *pāris*, which represents the simple, neutral form with which *parris* and *parrās* contrast. The use of *parras* for agent nouns is marginal; only the following three types are found.

First, the only certain *parras* substantive derived from a fientive verb with a strong root is OA *šarruqum* "thief", in which the presence of vowel harmony guarantees the short *ă* (cf. GAG § 10e; Hecker 1968: 19ff). Hecker's examples for his claim that occasionally also long vowels are subject to vowel harmony (1968: 20f) are unconvincing: in none of them is the long vowel based on independent evidence. It will be argued in 3.3 that in all probability fientive *parras*, in so far as it has substantival function, has usually been replaced by *parrās*.

Second, there are a few more agent nouns with the pattern *parras* that are used as adjectives (for the reason why these nouns are interpreted as *parras* rather than *parrās* forms, see 3.3), such as *aššaru* "expert" in *áš-šá-ru ṭênga* "your expert mind" (BWL 80: 167, tr. CAD sv), *gammalu* "merciful", cf. AHw sv (also *gammalû*, see below) and *šallaṭu* "domineering" in SpTU 4, 149: II 20' *[š]á-al-la-ṭa-at* "sie ist tatkräftig" (tr. Von Weiher). In some other cases the *parras* form has been extended with a suffix *-i*, which coalesces with the case ending into *-û*, and possibly serves to underline their adjectival character: *nakkapû* "prone to goring", *šaggašû* "murderous", *tammamû* "often swearing" and *gammalû* "merciful" (quoted AHw sv *gammalu/û* I).

Third, a small but remarkable group of *parras* forms which are also derived from fientive verbs and used as adjectives consist of plural forms of *pāris* participles:

Allaku "going, moving" in *al-la-ka birkāja* "my knees are moving" BWL 242: 21; *šēpēki al-la-ka-a-ti* Maqlû III 96 and II 33 (with *šēpēja*). [The other instance mentioned in CAD sv (BWL 134: 139) is a substantive, and more likely to represent *allāku* "traveller", cf. 3.3.1 and CAD sv *šamallû* 1c].

Ebberu "marching" in *birkēja eb-bé-re-e-ti* "my marching knees" Maqlû II 34 (but III 97 *birkēki e-bi-re-e-ti*). [The other instances mentioned by CAD and AHw sv are to be cancelled: Ee VII 125 *lā eb-bi-ru* is a present 3rd p. pl. and Tn-Ep. IV 25 *eb!-be-ri* (AHw) is more likely to contain the word *bēru* "mile", cf. CAD sv *bēru* A 1a 2' and sv *nesû* 1b-1'].

Lassamu "running" in *ina šēpēja la-sa-ma-t[e]* "on my swift feet" RIMA 2/I, 135: 70 (beside *la-as-ma-te* 154: 124).

Sahharu "turning" in *errī sah-ha-ru-tu* MSL 9, 10: 109, a unique variant of *errū sāhirūtu* "convoluted intestines" (cf. CAD sv *sāhiru* B adj. lex. sect.).

Ṣarraru "blazing" in *[ṣa-a]r-ra-ra* (Var. of *ṣa-ri-ir*) *niši īnīšu* "his (Marduk's) eyes, when they look, are frightening" Ee I 87 (restored and tr. CAD sv), but "blazing" seems a better translation, cf. AHw sv *ṣarāru* I G 4a "funkeln"; *ṣarir* is the grammatically correct form, *ṣarrarā* is a constructio ad sensum.

Maššû "forgetful in *uznēja m[a-á]š-šá-a-tú* "my forgetful ears" STT 66: 35, cf. AHw 1574a sv, is an exact parallel of the preceding cases; therefore it is likely to represent *parras*, although the fact that it comes from a weak root does not allow us to classify it on the basis of its form.

The similarity in the use of these words is striking: they qualify parts of the body as variants or parallels of *pāris* forms in literary - in one case (*sahharu*) lexical - texts. This suggests that, in spite of the fact that they are extremely rare, they are a definite subgroup of *parras* in its function of forming the plural of adjectives (see 3.1.3). They have a parallel in Arabic, where *qātil* participles often have a broken plural with gemination: the patterns *quttal* or *quttāl* (Wright 1896/98: I 206f; Fleisch 1961: 483).

Finally, the most numerous group of agent nouns with the pattern *parras* are derived from hollow roots, e.g., *bajjašu/û* "decent, modest", *qajjalu* "attentive", *qajjašu* "generous", *ṣajjadu* "roaming about" and *ṣajjahu* "laughing, delightful", and some others. The relatively large number of such *parras* forms is remarkable and suggests that in this type of weak roots *parras* takes the place of *parris*: just as in the strong roots we find *pāris* → *parris* to underline the more nominal character of the word (cf. 3.2.2), we here find *pāris* → *parras*, presumably for a phonological reason, viz., dissimilation of the glide and the following *i*.

3.1.2. *Parras* for (mainly) literary adjectives

Parras is much more important as a pattern to form adjectives with gemination derived from simple adjectives. The first of the two types to be discussed (cf. 3.1) are *parras* forms which - in contrast to the second type - occur both in the singular and the plural, and are for the most part very rare and restricted to literary and lexical texts. The reason for assigning them to *parras* rather than *parrās* is their clearly adjectival character and the fact that they are not agent nouns, cf. 3.3. Just as some of the agent nouns discussed in 3.1.1, they can be extended with the suffix *-i*; in one case we find a suffix *-āni* (*šakkarānû*).[2]

The following list presents *parras* forms of strong roots whose geminate second radical is explicitly written in at least one instance. They are SB unless indicated otherwise; to give an idea of their frequency I have added "1x" for unique forms; most of the other ones occur two to four times. If no references are given, see the dictionaries.

Aggagû[a]	angry 1x	**Lappanu**[h]	poor 1x	**Šammahu**	luxuriant
***Dallapu**[b]	awake 1x	**Marraṣu**[i]	sickly	**Šammaru**	impetuous
Hannamu	blooming 1x	**Nakkaru**[j]	hostile OB 1x	**Šappalu**	low OB+[o]
Hannaqu[c]	furious NB	**Pallahû**[k]	fearsome OB LL 1x	**Šarrahu**	proud, noble MB, SB
Haššaʼu[d]	crippled OB LL 1x	**Passalu**[l]	crippled 1x	**(W)aqqaru**	precious
Innabu[e]	luxuriant LL/PN	**Ṣallamu**[m]	black	**(W)arraqu**	green 1x
Kammalu[f]	adversary OB+	**Š/sabbasû**	angry MB, SB	**(W)attaru**[p]	replacement OB+
Labbabu[g]	raging 1x	**Šakkarû**[n]	drunkard OB+ LL		

NOTES: a) in *ag-ga-gi* PR 437: 26, stative 3rd sg. masc; b) only in *dal/da-la-piš/pi-[iš]* "awake" Ee I 66 (Var.) acc. to AHw sv *dalapiš*; c) from NB *hanāqu* "to be annoyed", CAD sv *hanāqu* 3; d) MSL 12, 160: 89, spelled *ha-aš-ša-a-ú*, cf. note 17; e) related to *inbu* "fruit" and *unnubu* "fruitful" (10.6.2) with *inn-* influenced by *inbu*?; also OB PN: *in-na-ba-tum* OBRED 2, 260: 17; f) from *kamālu* "to be angry"?; listed as *kammālu* in AHw and CAD; g) ZA 16, 180: 31 *lab-ba-bat*, variant of *labbat* (said of Lamaštu); h) STT 65: 16 acc. to AHw 1570b sv, but cf. Lambert, RA 53, 129f; i) also SpTU 1, 82: 11'; 17'; 41'; j) YOS 10, 33: V 29 *na-ak-ka-ra-am*; possibly, there are also other instances belonging to this form where the consonant is not written as a geminate, cf. CAD sv *nakru*; k) cf. MSL 12, 185: 47f lú.ní.te = *pa-al-hu*, lú.ní.te.te = *pa-a[l]-la-hu* (also 162: 155); l) Izbu 223: 416 *pa-sa-lum* = *kub-bu-[lu]*; the geminate is shown by the OB PN *pa-as-sà-lum*, cf. AHw sv; m) also *ṣallāmu*, cf. 3.3.2; n) also *šakkarānû* (JCS 29, 66: 8 *šak-ka-ra-ni* (stative

3rd sg. masc.) and *šakkūru*, cf. 2.2.4.1; o) in OB/SB omen texts; p) usually substantive, see below.

A few geminated adjectives with a weak root and/or *e*-colouring which are derived from simple adjectives can be added to this group: *deššû* "abundant" (1x SB: BWL 60: 98), *eddešû* "new" (SB, mostly used as an epithet of gods: CAD sv: "constantly renewing itself, ever brillant"), *lemmenu* "bad" (1x SB: BWL 32: 56 *lem-mèn* acc. to AHw 1571a sv), and *zenne'u* "angry (1x OB LL *ze-ne/né-e-ú* MSL 12, 197: 20, cf. note 17); for *ṣehheru* see 3.1.3.1; for **ebbû* see note 3.

The list clearly demonstrates the rarity and the predominantly literary character of these words. The main exception in both respects is *(w)attaru* "replacement", which also differs from the rest in that it has acquired a specialized meaning (cf. *watru* "extra, additional, excellent") and is mainly used as a substantive (possibly as an adjective in AND 120: 8 *amātum wa-ta-ra-tum* "slave girls (as) replacements" (OB), which, however, may also be explained as a plural of *watru,* cf. note 6).

The overall rarity of these adjectives makes it difficult to establish in what respect they differ from the corresponding simple adjectives, but their actual use suggests that most of them are stylistic variants of the latter. In this respect they resemble the literary *purrus* forms to be discussed in 10.7.2. For a discussion of the alleged "intensive" function of such adjectives which gemination see 10.8.

3.1.3. *Parras* forms of adjectives denoting dimensions

3.1.3.1. The evidence

The most common type of *parras* forms are those which serve as a plural formation to adjectives denoting dimensions. It concerns the following words:[3]

Arraku	long, tall	**Qattanu**	thin, fine	**Raqqaqu**	thin, small
Daqqaqu	small, tiny	**Rabbû**	big	**Ṣehheru**	small, young
Kabbaru	thick	**Rappašu**	broad	(Ass. *ṣahharu*)	
Qallalu	small				

The main function of these words is to serve as plural forms of the corresponding simple adjectives. This pluralizing function is explicitly stated by CAD under the words in question - cf. especially the remark concerning *arraku* (A/2 304a) - and by Reiner (1966: 64), and is only one instance of the common association of gemination with plurality in Akkadian (see 2.1.5). As such they coexist with plural forms without gemination; we find, for instance, *arkūtu* beside *arrakūtu, ṣehrūtu* beside *ṣehherūtu,* etc. We will take a closer look at the use of these *parras* forms in order to establish the difference between the plural forms with and those without gemination.

The following survey contains the attested cases of the *parras* forms enumerated above. Since, however, the use of these adjectives with a noun in the plural is amply documented in the dictionaries, it will not be repeated here; instead, emphasis will be on cases which are exceptional or otherwise interesting or illuminating. A point which should be mentioned in advance is that plurality should be taken to include mass nouns, and also cases which are grammatically singular, but logically plural, cf. 6.3.

Arraku is used in the plural to qualify persons, body parts, large objects such as beams and columns (cf. (03), (09) and (10)), sesame stalks (1x) and daggers (1x), cf. CAD sv. Additional instances include loaves (ninda.meš VS 19, 7: l. 6) and pock marks on the spleen ([*zi*]*qtī* RA 67, 42: 17'). It is grammatically singular, but logically plural in:

(01) (= (15A)) CT 41, 9a: 1 *šumma immeru uznī ar-ra-ak* "if a sheep is long as regards the ears", i.e., "has long ears";

(02) Or. 23, 338: 3ff (Lamaštu) [*a*]?-*ra-ka-at ubānātim ṣuprātim ar-ra-ka-at* "she has long (?) fingers (and) long claws".

The plural function of *arraku* is apparent from the following case where forms with and without gemination are opposed as singular versus plural:

(03A) AfO 17, 146: 6 *4* (or *5*) *timmū* 10.ta.àm *ina ammete malla eṣemte ar-ru-ku* "4 (or 5) columns (which) are each ten cubits and one *eṣemtu* long" (see note 9);

(03B) *ib.* 3 and 7f *1 timmu 10 ina ammete a-ri-ik* "one column ten cubits long."

Cf. also UM 2/2, 69: 3 with plural *ar-ra-ku* versus *ib.* 16 and 26 *a-ri-ik*, which is grammatically singular, although the number of beams is plural in all three lines.

In most of the contexts mentioned above the simple plural *arkūtu* is also used regularly (cf. CAD sv).

Daqqaqu occurs once in context: SpTU 1, 83: r.4 *īnāšu daq-qa-qa* "his eyes are small", glossed as *ša īnāšu ṣah-ha-ra*, and twice as a plural in LL, quoted CAD sv (considered by AHw sv to be an abstract noun "Winzigkeit", which is possible (cf. *rabbûtu* below), but less probable in the light of the other *parras* forms). Elsewhere *daqqūtu* is used.

Kabbaru is used in the plural to qualify animals, body parts and large objects, cf. CAD sv [cancel STT 87: 29 [...*k*]*ab-ba-ra*, quoted CAD sv *kabāru* 1e, cf. SAA 3, 10: 29]; it is logically plural in:

(04) (= (16A) OEC 6, 7: 20 *būru ekdu ša qarnī kab-ba-ru* "impetuous calf with thick horns".

A contrasting pair with singular versus plural is:

(05A) SAA 5, 294: 12'f (ten *musukannu* trees) *ša 2 qa-a-a kab-ba-ru-u-ni* "each of which are two *qû* measures thick." (tr. Lanfranchi-Parpola).

(05B) *ib.* 14'f (one good box-tree) *2 qa lū kab-ra* "it should be two *qû* measures thick."

In addition, *kabbaru* often qualifies mass nouns: reed (MSL 7, 13: 82), linen (Nbn 163: 2; 164: 12; GC 1, 388: 16, all NB), hair (MVAeG 40/2, 82: 90 *šumma šārat qaqqadi ka-ab-bar* "if he has a thick growth of hair on his head" (tr. CAD sv b-4'), cf. *qattan* in 91).[4] As singular objects we find a carnelian stone (BIN 1, 124: 2 (NB)), the *bisru*-plant (AMT 85, 1: II g), a poplar tree (or poplar wood) (Glass p. 32: A 10 and B 17), and BWL 34: 74 *libbī kab-ba-ra-a* "my robust heart" (tr. Lambert). As indicated, many of these cases are NB, so that the geminate may only be graphic, cf. GAG § 7d and *qallalu* below. Another possibility is that in NB the form with gemination has spread to singular contexts as well.

The simple plural *kabrūtu* has a much wider range; it is especially popular as an attribute of animals ("fattened") and grain ("plump"), and it is also used with pluralia tantum (CAD sv); with textiles both forms are found.

Qallalu (only NA and NB) is rare compared to the normal pl. *qallūtu* (CAD sv); in the plural it qualifies persons (ABL 494: r.2 SAL *qa-al-lal-a-te*), shoes and some unidentified objects; in the singular it occurs with the mass noun *kaspu* in *kaspu qallalu* "silver of inferior quality" (CAD sv 2a). *Qa-lál* in é *qa-lál* (versus é sig_5) in a NA letter quoted CAD sv *qallalu* 2b and SAA 3, 29: r.10' *qa-lál* are exceptions (cf. the remark on NB *kabbaru* in the singular sv *kabbaru* above)? ABL 1132: 7 (= SAA 10, 72: 9) [...] *qal-lu-lu* (quoted AHw sv *qallalu* 1) belongs to *qalālu* D, cf. CAD sv *qullulu* and Parpola, SAA 10 *ad l.* (they restore [lú]: "a vile man"); see also note 9.

Qattanu refers to body parts (also Emar VI/4 p. 255 no. 651: 23 (= (12A)), logs (1x, but also ARM 23, p. 547 no. 581: 7. 9. 10. 11. 24) and palm fibers (1x LL), cf. CAD sv b, all in the plural. In the singular, it is only found with hair in MVAeG 40/2, 82: 91 *šumma* [*šā*]*ra*[*t qa*]*qqadi qa-at-ta-an* "if he has a thin growth of hair on his head" (tr. CAD sv a), versus the opposite *kabbar* in 90, which is also exceptional (see above sv *kabbaru*). The simple plural *qatnūtu* is mainly used for textiles and wool (CAD sv b/c and Veenhof 1972: 214ff).

AMT 25, 6: II 7 *lubārē qa-tu-nu-ti* "thin rags" is an Assyrianism either for *qattanūti* (vowel harmony), or for *quttunūti* (a *parrus* form): it is unusual either way, because *quttunu* occurs only as a PN or a kind of person (cf. CAD sv and App. to Ch. X sv), and for textiles we would expect *qatnūti* without gemination; it is more likely to stand for *qattanūti*, cf. 3.1.3.3 below with note 9.

Rabbû can only be distinguished from *rabû* if the geminate is written explicitly. Instances of the plural form *rabbûtu* where this is the case refer to persons and a wide range of concrete objects (cf. AHw sv), only rarely to abstract nouns. For the contrast singular versus plural, cf. especially:

(06A) ARM 10, 146: 4 *ina kirrēt kaspim ra-ab-bé-e-tim* "among the large *kirru*-jars of silver";
(06B) *ib.* 7 1 *kirri kaspim* [*r*]*a-bi-im-*[*m*]*a* "one large *kirru*-jar of silver".

Notable, however, is the existence of an abstract noun *rabbûtu* "greatness" (of gods), occurring in Mari as "rank" (ARM 26/2, p. 192 no. 380: r.5' and p. 462: 5").

In the singular, *rabbû* is only used to qualify *abnu* "stone":

(07) ARM 14, 7: 6 (DN ...) *abnam ra-ab-bi-tam it-ta-ad-di* "(Adad ...) a renversé une pierre énorme" (tr. Birot).

(08) UET 6, 391: 10 // UM 12/1, 6: r.13 *ab-nu/ab-ni rab-ba-a kīma mê unarrabu* "they (the demons) soften the biggest stone like water" (Sum. na_4.gal.gal.lá/la) (tr. CAD sv *narābu* lex. sect.), cf. Udughul 34: 254. CAD sv *abnu* A lex. sect. emends UM 12/1, 6: r.13 into a plural: *abnī rabbâ*<*ti*>.

These exceptions are remarkable, not only because both of them concern *abnu* "stone", but also because of the Gtn form *ittaddi* in (07), which occurs in a context where no repetition, habit or plurality seems to be implied (cf. 4.2). Possibly, *abnu* is to be interpreted as a mass noun (cf. CAD's translation sv *abnu* A 1 of a similar passage in ARM 6, 5: 5 (qu. as (18) in 6.4.9): "a rock(slide)") or a collective (cf. Stol, BiOr 35, 219a); see for this passage also 4.2.3. *Rabbû* in (08) contrasts with *ṣehheru* in the singular in the previous line, cf. below sv *ṣehheru*.

Rappašu occurs a few times as plural of *rapšu*: AfO 18, 306: IV 13' (parts of a brazier); VAB 2, 14: I 77 (rings); TBP 21: 27 (eyes?); Emar VI/4 p. 255 no. 651: 23 (= (12A) (the horns of the moon), beside the much more common *rapšūtu*. A singular instance is TU 17: r.12 u_4.1.kam tùr nigin-*ma ka-bar u rap-*[*pa*]*-áš* "it (the moon) is surrounded by a halo on the first day (of the month) and it is thick and broad." (restored as AHw sv; translation partially from CAD sv *kabāru* 1f).

Raqqaqu is found in the plural in SAA 5, 295 (= ABL 467): 28 (beams), and twice in the singular with a collective as subject: BRM 4, 32: 12 (herbs) and SAA 10, 21: r.8' (*am-mar eš-šú-un-ni* "all the new stuff" (tr. Parpola).

Ṣehheru is mainly used as a plural of *ṣehru* "young, small" (adjective), or "child" (substantive), apart from a few specialized, and therefore probably secondary, meanings (see below). It usually refers to animate beings, cf. AHw sv 2; more rarely to concrete objects: body parts, cities, jars, doors, textiles, trees (ARM 23 p. 547 no. 581: 29), stones, floods, oil bubbles, offshoots (MSL 5, 116: 272), cf. AHw sv 1a/e. It refers to mass nouns in giš.hi.a *ṣé-eh-he-er-tim/tum* (ARM 13, 13: 5f) "small timber" or the like, and MSL 7, 112: 112 *haṣbu ṣa-ah-ha-ru* "small potsherds".

In its regular meaning *ṣehheru* is exceptional in the singular: UET 6, 391: 9 *ab-nu ṣe-eh-he-ru upassasū* "they (the demons) destroy a small stone" (Sum. na_4.di_4.di_4.lá) contrasts with *abnu rab-ba-a*, which is also unusual, see (08) sv *rabbû* above; AbB 3, 16/7: 13 *ištu ṣe-eh-he-re-ku* "Seitdem ich sehr jung war" (tr. Frankena), contrasts with the common idiom *ištu ṣehrēku, -ēta,* etc. (cf. CAD sv *ṣihru* 2b). In OA we find *ištu ṣa-ah-ra-ku-ni* "since I was a child" (BIN 6, 24: 3) versus *ištu ṣa-ha-ra-ni-ni* (i.e., /*ṣahharānīni*/) "since we were children" (kt n/k 404: 4). Finally, *ṣehheru* occurs in the singular as a citation form in LL: $^{tu\text{-}ur\text{-}tu\text{-}ur}$TUR.TUR = *ṣe-eh-he-rum* (CAD sv *ṣihhiru* lex. sect.).

In the plural we find both *ṣehrūtu* and *ṣehherūtu*. There is a difference between them depending on whether the word is used as an attributive adjective or as a substantive. In the former case it is almost always the form with gemination which is used;[5] exceptions are YOS 10, 47: 47 (= (14C)), RA 35, 49 no. 28: 2 (= (14A) (OAk), and Izbu 124: 36' (= (11)). In the other cases mentioned by AHw and CAD *ṣehrūtu* is substantivized ("youngsters, servants, retainers"). Used as substantives, *ṣehrūtu* and *ṣehherūtu* seem to be interchangeable; the latter form is more common, but there is no observable difference in meaning; cf., for instance, the expression "old and young", which is *šībūtu u ṣehrūtu*, but also *šībūtu u ṣehherūtu* (CAD sv *ṣihru* 2c-2'), and the variants *ṣe-he-ra-a-ti* and *ṣe-eh-ra-a-ti* in parallel sentences in AnSt. 10, 122: 4'. 20'.

Moreover, *ṣehheru* has acquired a few specialized uses as a substantive. The most important ones are *ṣehhertu* "minor crop" and "scraps, small items" (LL only, cf. CAD sv *ṣihhirtu* and AHw sv *ṣehhertu* 2) and *ṣahharu* "mottled barley" (SB) or "minor crop" (LB), cf. CAD/AHw sv. In addition, CAD has *ṣehheru* "finely ground flour" (MB), which AHw sv *ṣehheru* 1g takes to be a variant of *ṣahharu*. These meanings are based on the use of the *parras* adjectives for qualifying mass nouns and collectives. AHw's *ṣehhertu* "kleines Mädchen" should rather be interpreted as sg. *ṣehertu*, pl. *ṣehherētu*, just like masc. sg. *ṣehru*, pl. *ṣehherūtu*.

3.1.3.2. Conclusions about the plural function of *parras*

The following conclusions about the use of these *parras* forms can be drawn from this survey. First of all, the overall association of these *parras* forms with plurality is demonstrated by the fact that a large majority of the attested instances is plural, and by the contrasting pairs (03), (05) and (06), where the use of *parVs* versus *parras* directly correlates with the opposition singular versus plural. In so far as *parras* forms are found in the singular, they are logically plural, such as (01), (02) and (04), or they qualify mass nouns (hair, linen, barley, etc., quoted under *kabbaru, qattanu* and *ṣehheru*). The description of the verbal D-stem in Chapter VI and of the nominal pattern *purrus* in Chapter X will show that it is a general feature of Akkadian to treat mass nouns and collectives on a par with plural forms as far as the use of gemination is concerned.

In spite of this clear association with plurality, GAG § 55m defines *parras* forms as intensive adjectives ("Steigerungsadjektiven") and AHw ssvv consistently translates them with "sehr ...". The contexts in which they are used, however, do not support this view (although in general it is difficult to determine differences in intensity between contrasting forms, see 10.8). A case in point is the use of *arraku* and *kabbaru* with measurements, where an intensive meaning seems just as implausible in Akkadian as it would be in English. It is illustrated by (03A), and (05A) above; cf. also:

(09) SAA 5, 294: 16'f *20 šaššūgu*-trees *ana tallī 10-a-a ina* 1 kùš *lū ár-ru-ku* "20 *šaššūgu* trees for the shafts; they should each be 10 cubits long" (tr. Lanfranchi-Parpola).

(10) TCL 9, 121: 10f (beams?) *ša 20.*àm *u 15.*àm *a-ra-ku* "which are 20 and 15 cubits long" (tr. CAD sv 2'); see further CAD sv *arraku* a, *kabbaru* a-4'.

Second, the entries of *parras* forms in the dictionaries and the indications given in the survey show that they are predominantly used to qualify concrete nouns, in particular those referring to persons, animals and body parts; if they qualify objects, these are usually large (parts of buildings, trees, etc.). In all these cases the quality denoted by the adjective is immediately perceptible to the senses; in other words, it has a high degree of salience. On the other hand, we do not find gemination if there is no salience, for instance in combination with abstract nouns, and it is only rarely found with small unimpressive objects. It is significant in this context that in the frequent expression *ūmū arkūtu* "long days", i.e., "a long life", the plural with gemination is never found, cf. CAD sv *arku* 1b-1' and sv *arraku.*

The relevance of salience for the use of gemination does not only explain the fact that the plural with gemination is often preferred for the description of animate beings and body parts, entities which have a high intrinsic salience (see 5.6.4), but also the fact that this plural formation is only common for adjectives denoting dimensions, since dimensions also have a high intrinsic salience. In this respect the pattern *parras* is similar to *purrus*, the use of which is often motivated by another kind of salience, namely, that of more or less unusual characteristics of persons, in particular physical defects (see 10.6.2).[6]

Third, there are numerous instances where the plural without gemination is used in precisely the same contexts, also in combination with persons, animals, body parts, etc. The proportional frequency of the two competing forms varies considerably from word to word and from dialect to dialect. The indications given above for the individual *parras* forms show that some of them are very rare, no more than exceptional variants of the simple plural, whereas others are more common than the simple plural.

There are some striking cases in which plural forms with and without gemination occur side by side in the same text, even in the same sentence:

(11) Izbu 124: 35'/36' *šumma izbu īnāšu ra-ab-bi-a* / *ṣa-ah-ra-a* "if the *izbu*'s eyes are big / small";

(12A) Emar VI/4, p. 255 no. 651: 23 *šumma Sîn qarnāšu ra-ap-pa-š[a]* (....) *u šumma qarnāšu qa-at-ta-na* "If the horns of the moon are wide (...) and if his horns are thin";

(12B) *ib.* 24 *šumma Sîn qarnāšu kīma qablîtišu ka-ab-ra* "if the horns of the moon are as thick as its middle part";

(13) RA 65, 71: 16f *šumma qerbū kab-ba-ru-tu qá-at-ta-nu-ti altū,* (...) / *šumma qerbū qá-at-ta-nu-tu kab-ru-ti altū* (...) "if the thick intestines have swallowed the thin ones, (...) / if the thin intestines have swallowed the thick ones, (...)". The presence of *kabbarūtu* in 16 suggests an emendation *kab-<ba>-ru-ti* in 17, as proposed by Nougayrol, which is adopted by CAD sv *qattanu* b. The parallels adduced here, however, leave the possibility open that the text is correct as it stands.

(14A) RA 35, 49 no. 28: 2 *šahluqti ālī ṣa-ah-ru-tí* "destruction of small towns";

(14B) *ib.* 46 no. 18: 3 *na-qá-ar ālī ṣa-ha-ru-tí* "(an omen concerning) the destruction of small towns";

(14C) YOS 10, 47: 47 *na-ka-ar ālī ṣe-eh-ru-tim* "the estrangement of small towns" (apodosis, tr. CAD sv *nakāru* 1b-3') (or read *na-qà-ar* as in (14B) ?).

Summarizing, we can establish the following characteristics pertaining to the use of these *parras* forms as against that of the corresponding simple adjectives. First, the use of gemination is determined by two factors: by plurality (including collectives and mass nouns), and by the high degree of salience inherent in the clause or the word group, i.e., in the nature of the quality that is ascribed to an entity (a dimension), and in the entity itself. Second, gemination is an optional feature, which is added to the primary plural morpheme for adjectives, the ending *-ūtu/-ātu*, which is obligatory for the expression of plurality. Third, the contexts in which corresponding *parVs* and *parras* forms are used do not point to a significant difference in meaning between them.

This state of affairs seems to be best accounted for by means of the following hypothesis concerning the function of gemination in these adjectives: gemination does not in itself denote plurality, but merely *underlines* the plurality and salience which is inherent in the word group to which it belongs. By using the form with gemination the speaker makes this plural and salient nature explicit; if he uses the simple form he leaves it implied in the context. In this way we can explain why *parras* is restricted to specific contexts, and at the same time alternates with the simple adjective in these contexts, apparently without any difference in meaning.

This implies that, from a *functional* point of view, gemination is not contrastive here. Forms with and without gemination of the same word cannot be used to express a contrast between two different meanings, for instance, between a normal and an intensive degree of a quality, as is assumed by AHw (see above). If such forms occur side by side, it is either concomitant with another difference between the respective clauses, typically that of singular versus plural, as in (03), (05) and (06) above, or else, if there is no such concomitant difference, the two forms are alternatives referring to the same quality, as in (13) and (14). It is, however, difficult to demonstrate this on the basis of these *parras* adjectives. Therefore, we will leave this point until we have discussed the D-stems of transitive verbs in Chapter VI and the *purrus* adjectives in Chapter X. These two categories show the same type of relationship between geminate and simple forms as the *parras* adjectives under discussion.

3.1.3.3. *Parras* and *purrus* forms of the same adjective

The use of *parras* for underlining plurality is largely restricted to adjectives denoting dimensions (see note 6, however). Gemination can also be used in adjectives of other semantic categories to underline plurality; in that case the pattern *purrus* is normally used, which will be discussed extensively in Chapter X, see especially 10.6.1. Thus for this particular function the two patterns are complementary.

The adjectives denoting dimensions also have *purrus* forms, but these are relatively rare compared to the *parras* forms. We find a very small number of cases in which they interchange with *parras* to underline plurality, such as the following:

(15A) (= 01) CT 41, 9a: 1 *šumma immeru uznī ar-ra-ak* "if a sheep has long ears";
(15B) BiOr 11, 82a: 7 (a dog) *ur-ru-uk birkāšu* "with long legs" (lit. "knees").[7]
(16A) (= 04) OEC 6, 7: 20 *būru ekdu ša qarnī kab-ba-ru* "impetuous calf with thick horns";
(16B) LKU 16: 12 *rīmu rabû ša mešrêti kub-bu-ru* "great wild bull with massive limbs".

In general, however, the *purrus* forms of these adjectives have been differentiated in use from the *parras* form and are not associated with plurality.[8] Some of them are mainly used as stative and verbal adjective of the D-stem (cf. 10.2 and 10.4.2). This applies to *qullulu*, which is only found as stative/VA of the verb *qullulu* "to despise, discredit" (cf. CAD sv *qalālu* 4 and *qullulu* adj., and 10.4.2), and to *ṣuhhuru*, which serves in OA and OB as stative of *ṣuhhuru* in the specialized meaning of "to debit (an amount), to deduct" (cf. CAD sv *ṣehēru* 2c and 10.4.2).

Others are used as proper names (*Kubburu* and *Quttunu*, see 10.6.3). The remaining ones (*duqququ, rubbû, ruppušu, ruqququ, kubburu* (when it is not a proper name), *quttunu, urruku* (but see note 7), and *ṣuhhuru* (in other contexts than the one just mentioned)) alternate with simple adjectives for reasons which are difficult to determine, especially because most of them are very rare.[9]

3.2. The pattern *parris*

The second nominal pattern with gemination which can shed light on the role of gemination in Akkadian is *parris*. A major problem, however, is the fact that a *parris* form whose second radical is not written as a geminate cannot be distinguished from the *pāris* participle of the same root. To determine the function of *parris*, therefore, we can only use instances in which the gemination is explicitly written. Thus our knowledge of the extent of the use of *parris* will inevitably be incomplete, since there can be no doubt that a considerable number of apparent *pāris* forms are in fact *parris* forms whose geminate is left unexpressed. On the other hand, there are enough attested *parris* forms to get a general idea of the character of *parris*.

3.2.1. The evidence

The dictionaries mention about 60 to 70 *parris* forms, but most of them are very rare: many occur only once and/or are restricted to lexical texts. For the purpose at hand we will concentrate on those which are slightly more common, and are attested in context. They are contained in the following list. For more detailed information and references see the dictionaries; in the notes following the list references are given which are not in CAD and/or AHw.

Akkilu	eater, voracious[a] OB+	**Sahhiru**	roaming, a priest[e] SB
Babbilu	carrier OB	**Ṣarrišu**	proliferating[f] MB
Dabbibu	gossiper, gossiping SB	**Ṣarritu**	farter[g] SB
Habbilu	evil(doer) SB	**Šaddidu**	boat-tower[h] OB
Haṭṭi'u[b]	sinner SB	**Šaddihu**	far-extending SB
Maššī'u	robber, robbing OB+	**Šaggišu**[i]	murderer SB
Parriku	lying crosswise[c] SB	**Šakkinu**	contractor[j] OB
Parriṣu	mendacious[d] SB/NA	**Ṭabbihu**	butcher MB
Raggimu	"caller" (a priest) SB+, NA	**Zabbilu**	carrier, carrying OB+
Rahhiṣu	runner SB	**Zammeru**[k]	singer SB

Notes: a) OB: ARM 14, 2: 20 quoted below as (17); b) also *haṭṭû* and perhaps *haṭṭā'u*; c) metaphorically: "self-willed", epithet of gods and kings; d) in NA "Rechtsbrecher" (AHw sv), but with an adjectival plural *parriṣūte*); e) often adj., for the meaning see George, RA 85, 158f; f) an adj. qualifying *simmu* "disease", cf. CAD sv; g) SAA 3, 29: r.4; 30: 2; h) said of persons and animals; i) also *šaggāšu*, cf. 3.3.1; j) more precisely "seasonal contractor for date harvesting and delivery" (CAD sv *šākinu*); k) also *zammāru* (Ass., cf. 3.3.1).

3.2.2. Conclusions on the nature of *parris*

This enumeration of the most common *parris* forms may suffice to demonstrate the following points. First, the typical function of *parris* is to form agent nouns from fientive verbs. This also applies to the many instances of *parris* not mentioned here, with one important exception, viz. *z/sarriqu* "with speckled eyes" (CAD) or "etwa 'schillernd'" (AHw), which has no corresponding verb, and is one of the few adjectives for physical characteristics outside the pattern *purrus* (see 10.6.2).[10]

As agent nouns they almost always refer to animate beings, or objects which can be personified, such as body parts; see, for instance, (18) and (22) below. Syntactically, they are used both as substantives and as adjectives; a few typical cases of adjectival use are:

(17) ARM 14, 2: 20 *nēšum ak-ki-lum* "a voracious lion";

(18) Maqlû III 186 acc. to AHw 1549a sv *aššu pîki da(-ab)-bi-bu* "because of your talkative mouth";

(19) II R 47: I 13 <u>lugal</u> *za-ab-bi-lu* "a king laden (with gifts)" (tr. CAD sv *zabbilu* adj.);

(20) CT 16, 13: III 17 *sebet ilāni maš-ši-'u-ú-ti* "seven rapacious gods";

(21) Šurpu III 86 *māmīt eṭemmī sah-hi-ru-ti* (var. *sa-hi-ru-ú-te*) "an oath by the ghosts who roam about".

Note especially the adjectival plural forms of (20) and (21), and also the use of a *parris* form as a stative in:

(22) MSL 4, 72: 171f *qātāšu za-an-bi-la* "his hands are used to carrying (gifts)" (tr. CAD sv *zabbilu* adj.).

The simple form with which *parris* directly contrasts is the participle (or rather agent noun, cf. note 11) *pāris* (GAG § 85d). The functional similarity between these two patterns is striking: both are agent nouns derived from fientive verbs, typically denoting habitual and/or professional activities.[11] This raises the question of what is the exact difference between them (if any).

If we compare the use of some of the more common *parris* forms with that of the corresponding *pāris* forms, it turns out that the *parris* forms are excluded from typically verbal syntagms, i.e., constructions which are transformations of a verbal sentence; in such syntagms only *pāris* seems to be allowed whereas *parris* seems to be avoided, even when it does occur in other contexts.

There are two such verbal syntagms. The first is a combination of a participle in the construct state and a noun in the genitive, which results from a transformation of the corresponding finite verb form plus an object. In such a construction a word belonging to either *pāris* or *parris* is almost always written with a single second radical. If there is no genitive following, the second radical is written either as a single consonant or as a geminate.

Thus we find *babbilu/bābilu* "carrier" written with *-b-* or *-bb-* if it is used as an independent noun, but only with *-b-* in syntagms as *lā bābil hiṭīti* "not guilty, innocent", *lā bābil panī* "merciless", *lā bābil šipri* "shirker" (CAD B 9 ssvv). The same is true of *zabbilu* "carrier" vs. *zābil* if it qualifies *ereqqu, iṣu, kudurru, libittu, šaharru, ṭupšikku* and *uṭṭatu* (CAD sv *zabbilu* B and *zābilu*); of *šaddidu* "draft animal, boat tower" vs. *šādid ašli* and *šādid eqli*, always written with a single *-d-* (CAD sv *šādidu*); of *akkilu* "eater, glutton" vs. *ākil karṣī-* "maligner" with *-k-* (CAD A/1 266 sv) (all other examples of *ākil* + gen. quoted sv *akālu* 1/7 (*ib.* p. 247-256) are written with a single *-k-*, too); of *šaggišu* "murderer" vs. *šāgišu*: none of the instances written with *-gg-* have a following genitive (CAD sv *šaggišu*); whenever the word is used as an epithet in the construct state with a genitive a single *-g-* appears (CAD sv *šagāšu* 1a/b).

Secondly, the verbal character of *šāgišu* is also indicated by an other syntagm, which can be found, for instance, in the common omen apodosis *šāgišu išaggassu* "someone will murder him", always written with a single *-g-*, according to CAD sv *šagāšu* 2a. This paronomastic construction of a finite verb preceded by a *pāris* form of the same verb is a syntactic means of expressing an indefinite subject and a typically verbal use of the *pāris* form.[12]

If we consider these words individually, the evidence is too meagre to be conclusive, but taken together, they lead to the conclusion that if *pāris* and *parris* exist side by side, the first form is selected in syntagms where the participle is felt to be the result of a transformation of a finite verb (e.g., *ākil karṣī-* from *ša karṣī ikkalu/īkulu*), whereas the latter may be used in order to stress the nominal character of the word in question.

This speaks against the claim advanced by Reiner (1966: 45f) that nouns of the pattern *parris* are to be considered variants of the corresponding *pāris* nouns and can be listed in the dictionary under the same entry. Reiner's claim is based on the fact that in Akkadian the sequences long vowel + consonant and vowel + long consonant are in phonotactic free variation, a fact which explains the coexistence of nouns such as *šarrūtu* and *šarruttu* "kingship" or *kūṣu* and *kuṣṣu* "cold, winter" (GAG § 20d).

However, Reiner (1966: 87 and 90) admits that this free variation can be suppressed if it has a functional load in contrasting pairs of present and preterite verb forms, as in *irrub* "he enters" vs. *īrub* "he entered" or *ikunnū* "they become stable" vs. *ikūnū* "they became stable". It is plausible that the contrast between *parris* and *pāris* is another instance of this phenomenon.

Since a substantival noun typically expresses a more permanent quality than an adjective or a participle with a verbal background (cf. English *he is a writer* versus *he is writing*), the difference between a more permanent and a more accidental quality entails a difference between a more nominal (*parris*) and more verbal character (*pāris*), cf. Givón 1984: 51ff. It is this permanence which is underlined by the geminate second radical.

It is probable that *parris* forms are directly derived from *pāris* by the insertion of gemination in a *pāris* form (which automatically leads to the shortening of the long vowel, cf. Reiner 1966: 44 and 52, and that the *i* of *parris* copies the *i* of *pāris*.

3.3. The pattern *parrās*

The third nominal pattern with gemination to be discussed is *parrās*. Since cuneiform writing does not always indicate vowel length explicitly (GAG § 7e), it is often doubtful whether a given word belongs to *parrās* or *parras*. There is only a small number of cases which can be assigned to *parrās* with certainty, either because a plene writing is attested, or because the absence of vowel harmony in Assyrian shows the vowel following the geminate to be long; these cases are listed below as Group A. However, since plene writings are rather unusual - even for very common *parrās* forms we find no more than one or two cases, cf. the indications which follow the list of Group A below - it is plausible to assume that many other words belong to *parrās*, too, even though it cannot be proved that they have a long vowel. This assumption is based on the following considerations.

In the first place, the *parrās* forms which have a demonstrably long vowel are typically agent nouns denoting occupations or occupation-like activities, used as substantives (see group A below). Second, words of the pattern *parras* whose short vowel is guaranteed because it is subject to vowel harmony in Assyrian are adjectives derived from simple adjectives (such as *arraku* "long", *kabbaru* "thick", *qattanu* "thin" and *ṣehheru* (Ass. *ṣahharu*) "small" (see 3.1.3).

Third, there is at least one *parras* form which is an agent noun derived from a fientive verb, namely, OA *šarruqum* "thief", which vowel harmony shows to be a *parras* form **šarraqum* (cf. AHw sv 1), and which contrasts with Bab. *šarrāqu* (cf. BWL 192: 25 *ša-ar-ra-a-qu*).

Thus *parras* is used both to derive agent nouns from fientive verbs denoting activities, and adjectives with gemination from simple adjectives (denoting qualities), in contrast to *parris* and *parrās* which, but for a few exceptional cases, are only used to forms agent nouns.

The fact that the adjectives in question have a short vowel in so far as they are attested in Assyrian suggests that similar adjectives, which are attested only in Babylonian, such as *šammaru* "impetuous" and *šarrahu* "proud" (see 3.1.2), also belong to *parras* rather than to *parrās*. The problematic group then are the agent nouns derived from fientive verbs whose long vowel cannot be proved: are they *parras* or *parrās* forms?

The solution adopted here by way of hypothesis is that they are *parrās* forms in so far as they are typically used as substantives. This is based on the consideration that the distribution of *parras* and *parrās* forms we find in Akkadian points to a historical development in which at a certain moment - possibly already in the Common Semitic period, cf. note 14 - the pattern *parras* was split in two by the introduction of a long *ā* in those *parras* forms which were agent nouns and used predominantly as substantives, whereas the other *parras* forms remained unchanged.[13] The feminine forms in which the suffix *-t-* immediately followed the third radical, as in *kaššaptu* "sorceress", did not change either, since a long vowel is not allowed before a consonant cluster, cf. Reiner 1966: 44; 120f; Greenstein 1984: 42f.

The lengthening of the vowel was motivated by the more substantival nature of such agent nouns in comparison to the more adjectival nature of the other *parras* forms (cf. 3.2.2 end). A similar process of vowel lengthening is found in the pattern *parīs,* which denotes "substantivierte Verbaladjektive des Typs *paris*", according to GAG § 55i (cf. also Kuryłowicz 1972: 112); examples are *kanīku* "seal" from *kanāku* "to seal", *zaqīpu* "stake" from *zaqāpu* "to plant, set up", *ṭarīdu* "exile" from *ṭarādu* "to drive out, banish", *asīru* "prisoner (of war)" (AHw sv), cf. *esēru* "to confine", and *pašīšu,* a kind of priest, lit. "the anointed one" (Eilers 1964/66: 85). This vowel lengthening is an iconic phenomenon, comparable to gemination, because the difference between the short and the long vowel, as in **pašišu* "anointed" (> *paššu*) vs. *pašīšu,* corresponds to the difference between a temporary or accidental, and a permanent characteristic of the person described, so that it is diagrammatic (cf. 2.1.2).

This process may have taken place over a long period of time, in which the *parras* agent nouns were gradually replaced by *parrās* forms.[14] OA *šarruqum* shows that it was still going on in the historical period of Akkadian, but because of the deficient writing of long vowels it is impossible to establish in detail how far it had proceeded at a given moment. This leaves the possibility open that some of the words classified below in Group B as *parrās* forms were actually (still) *parras* forms.

Consequently, substantival agent nouns will be classified as *parrās* forms even though they cannot be proved to have a long vowel (in group B below). On the other hand, those which are mainly used as adjectives will be regarded as *parras* forms.[15] Some of these were discussed in 3.1.1.

3.3.1. The evidence

The two lists below comprise the most common agent nouns of the pattern *parrās* which are predominantly used as substantives, in Group A the words whose *ā* is guaranteed by Assyrian vowel harmony or plausible because of one or more plene writings (references are added in the notes),[16] and group B with *parrās* forms which are listed here by way of hypothesis on the basis of the considerations expounded above. Some words derived from weak roots or with *e*-colouring which can plausibly be regarded as *parrās* forms have also been included. If no indication of dialect is given, the word is attested more or less throughout Akkadian; where no references are given see the dictionaries.

GROUP A

Bakkā'u[a]	wailer OB LL	**Kaṣṣāru**[i]	donkey driver OA
Dajjālu[b]	scout, inspector SB+, NA	**Najjālu**[j]	a kind of tenant MA+, NB
Dajjānu[c]	judge	**Nappāhu**[k]	smith
Ekkēmu[d]	robber SB	**Sarrāru**[l]	robber, criminal OB+
Errēšu[e]	cultivator	**Šaggāšu**[m]	murderer OB+
Eṭṭēru[f]	deserter SB	**Šarrāqu**[n]	thief
Gallābu[g]	barber	**(W)aššābu**[o]	tenant, resident
Habbātu[h]	robber	**Zammāru**[p]	singer MA+, NB

Notes: a) *ba-ka-a-a-ú*[17] MSL 12, 161: 129; also adj. *bakkû* and fem. *bakkîtu*; b) *da-ja-a-li* SAA 5, 105: 17; c) *da-ja-a-nu* VAB 4, 102: II 29; d) *ek-ke-e-ma* Maqlû II 119; but there is also a corresponding adjective "rapacious" which shows no plene spellings, cf. CAD sv *ekkēmu*; therefore, I interpret it as *ekkimu* (cf. AHw sv); e) *er-re-e-ši-im, -š[u]* AbB 9, 190: 16 and 18; *er-re-e-ši* TCL 17, 7: 10; it is impossible to decide whether variant spellings as *e-ri-ši-im* for *er-re-ši-im* (KH r.XV: 4) represent a *pāris* form *ērišu* (as claimed by CAD sv *errēšu*) or a defective spelling for *errēšu*; f) *eṭ-ṭe-e-rù* MSL 16, 159: 178; cf. *eṭṭiru* "saver, saving"; g) no vowel harmony in OA *ga-la-bu-tim* Gol. 20: 24 (abstract noun), MA *mār gal-la-be* AfO 10, 35 no. 61: 7; h) *hab-ba-a-tú* MSL 16, 156: 90 Var., *hab-ba-a-ti* BRM 4, 12: 27, *ha-ab-ba-a-tim* VAB 4, 84: no. 5 II 2, cf. also SAA 8 gloss. p. 319b sv; i) no vowel harmony in OA, cf. CAD sv b (also *kaṣṣārūtu*) (but cf. CCT 5, 32b: 3 (the wagon) *ša kà-ṣí-ri-im* "of the donkey driver": this may stand for a *pāris* form */kāṣirim/* - which, however, has a different meaning outside OA (a kind of textile worker) - or for a *parras* form */kaṣṣirim/* with vowel harmony, like *šarruqum*); j) *na-ja-a-li* KAJ 160: 7, 162: 4; k) no vowel harmony in OA, cf. CAD sv a-2'; l) *sa-ra-a-ar* SpTU 1, 72: 17; m) *ša-ag-ga-a-šum/šu* TLB 2, 21: 10; CT 51, 142: 6; also *šaggišu*, cf. 3.2.1 and 3.2.2; n) *ša-ar-ra-a-qu* BWL 192: 25, but OA *šarruqum*, see 3.1.1 and 3.3; o) if we accept OA *ú-ša-bí* BIN 6, 20: 22 as a form of this word (thus CAD sv a-1'; also AHw sv 1a with a question mark; I have found no plene writings of this rather common word; p) no vowel harmony in Ass., cf. CAD/AHw sv; also *zammeru*, cf. 3.2.1. [Cancel *makkāru* "merchant" (CAD/AHw sv), cf. Veenhof, NABU 92/5].

GROUP B: *parrās* forms with a hypothetical *ā*:

Ahhāzu	catcher[a] SB	**Kaššāpu**	sorcerer OB+
Allāku[b]	traveller Bab.	**Qabbā'u**	an official[e] OB
Ammāru	overseer[c] NB	**Rakkābu**	sailor OB+
Hannāqu	strangler[d] SB LL	**Šassā'u**[f]	caller, wailer SB

Notes: a) a demon causing jaundice and the illness itself (cf. Adamson, RA 87, 157), but in OB Mari an official?, cf. ARM 27, p. 124 no. 61: 10 with n. b; b) also *allaku* (adj.), cf. 3.1.1; c) also SB in the fem. as an epithet of Ištar, cf. CAD sv b; d) a person (LL) and an instrument, cf. CAD/AHw sv, beside *hannaqu* "furious", cf. 3.1.2; e) acc. to Charpin, NABU 93/23, a kind of official informant; f) Written *ša-ás-sà-a-ú* MSL 12, 162: 139; 183: 9, but *ša-sà-ú ib.* 209: 313, cf. note 17; often fem. *šassā'ītu* (or *šassa'ītu*?).

3.3.2. Conclusions

These lists show that the regular use of *parrās* is to form substantival agent nouns derived from fientive verbs, in particular for denoting professions and profession-like activities. Therefore, *parrās* has the same function as *parris* (cf. 3.2.2) and as the simple pattern for agent nouns *pāris*. Both *parris* and *parrās* contrast with *pāris* as agent nouns with and without gemination, respectively.

The relationship between *pāris* and *parrās* is doubtless similar to that between *pāris* and *parris* as expounded in 3.2.2, but there are two differences. First, whereas *parris* can be derived directly from *pāris* by the insertion of a geminate, the formal relationship between *pāris* and *parrās* can only be indirect, resulting from a secondary association of two categories which were independent in form but closely related in function.[18]

Second, according to the words of group A, whose long vowel is certain, *parrās* is more often used for substantives than *parris*. This agrees with the fact that *parrās* also has a stronger marking than *parris*: it has not only gemination but also a long vowel. Both features add up to underline the permanent and therefore substantival character.

A few *parrās* forms are exceptional in that they are derived from adjectives; the most important are *kajjānu* "constant, regular, normal" and *tajjāru* "merciful"[19], which doubtless owe their special status to the fact that they are derived from hollow roots. Instances derived from strong roots are *dappānu* "warlike, martial", *qarrādu* "hero", and *ṣallāmu* "black"; parallel to a form such as *bakkā'u* (group A) is *hassā'u* (OB LL), which doubtless refers to a bodily defect (cf. 10.6.2).[20] In so far as we can establish their use, they seem to serve predominantly as substantives, too.

3.4. The role of gemination in the patterns *parras, parris* and *parrās*

The three patterns discussed in this chapter have in common that the forms with and without gemination basically have the same function. It was argued in 3.1.3 that the *parras* forms denoting dimensions are optional alternatives to the simple forms and serve to underline the plural and salient nature of the word group. In contexts which meet the conditions of plurality and salience, they are interchangeable with the simple forms.

In the agent nouns discussed in 3.2 and 3.3 we find a similar situation: *pāris* is the simple pattern for agent nouns and the use of gemination in *parris* and *parrās* can be regarded as basically optional, too. In this case gemination serves to underline the more nominal and permanent character of the activity as against the more verbal character of *pāris*.

In the relationship between *pāris* and *parrās*, however, this state of affairs is obscured by the fact that the use of these patterns is more lexicalized than that of *parras*: for some concepts both patterns can be used (e.g., *āliku* and *allāku* in the meaning "messenger"), for others one or the other pattern has become obligatory, such as *nappāhu* for "smith" (never **nāpihu*) or *šarrāqu* for "thief" in Babylonian, or, conversely, *rābiṣu* "guard" and *māhiṣu* "weaver" (cf. note 11), never **rabbāṣu* or **mahhāṣu*. In individual cases this may lead to differentiation in meaning, as in *rākibu* "rider" and *rakkābu* "sailor" (although not quite consistently in this pair, cf. AHw ssvv). What is most important in this context is the general function of *parrās* and *pāris* as categories, not the use of individual members.

A final point concerns the relationship of *parras, parris* and *parrās* to the D-stem. As noted in 3.1.3.3, *parras* in its most common function is complementary to, and therefore closely connected with, the pattern *purrus*. In this way *parras* is indirectly connected with the D-stem, but not derived from it, no more than *purrus* is derived from it; it will be argued in 11.1 that the verbal D-stem is derived from *purrus* adjectives, and in some cases possibly from *parras* forms, rather than the other way round.

In their function of agent nouns the patterns *parras, parris* and *parrās* are clearly associated with the G-stem, not with the D-stem. This follows from two facts. First, the existence of a D-stem is not a prerequisite for the existence of a *parris, parrās* or *parras* form, cf. *šarruqu* (OA) and *šarrāqu* "thief", *allāku* "traveller, messenger", *najjālu* "tenant", *zajjāru* "enemy", *akkilu* "voracious", and many other nouns which are derived from verbs without a D-stem (cf. also Loretz 1960: 415).

Second, when the D- and the G-stem of a verb have a clear difference in meaning these nouns agree with the G-stem; e.g., *ahhāzu* "catcher" is derived from *ahāzu* "to take", not from *uhhuzu* "to mount" (an object in precious materials), *rakkābu* "sailor" from *rakābu* "to ride, to sail", not from *rukkubu* "to fertilize" (a date palm), *zabbilu* "carrier" from *zabālu* "to carry", not from *zubbulu* "to keep waiting, to linger". The same applies to factitive D-stems: *sahhiru* "roaming" corresponds to intransitive *sahāru* "to turn, to go around", not to transitive *suhhuru* "to turn" (trans.).

Admittedly, there are a few cases where such nouns serve as agent nouns of a D-stem: *gallābu* "barber", *raqqû* "oil-presser" and *karrištu* "slanderer" (fem.). For the first two there is no G-stem (but see 8.2 for *gallābu*); *karrištu* goes against the rule stated above (cf. *karāṣu* "to pinch off, break", *kurruṣu* "to accuse, slander", cf. 8.4.2 sv), but occurs only once. The regular agent noun of the D-stem is the participle *muparris*, cf. GAG § 56e and 6.6.2.

Consequently, the two categories are grammatically independent of each other, although they share the feature of gemination of the second radical, and thus ultimately have the same background (cf. Chapter XII). The fact that many roots show both a D-stem and one or more nouns of these patterns is certainly an accidental result of the high productivity of the D-stem.

Notes to Chapter Three

1 In NA some apparent *parras* forms are found - listed as such in the dictionaries - which in reality are *purrus* forms (Assyrian *parrus*), such as *haṣṣaṣu* "broken", *labbašu* "dressed" and *rakkasu* "bound"; they occur only in the plural (see the dictionaries) and have undergone the sound change *u* > *a*, which occurred in NA before endings with *ū* (GAG § 15f; Borger 1979: 150; Deller 1959: 71). Cf., for instance, the parallel occurrence of *haṣṣuṣu* and *haṣṣaṣu* in KADP 12: I 13 *qanê ha-ṣu-ṣu-te* vs. *ib.* 11: II 69 *qanê ha-ṣa-ṣu-ti* "broken reeds". Other cases include SAA 1, 77: r.7 *ka-sa-pu-ni* (i.e., */kassapūni/* for */kassupūni/*, cf. App. to Ch. VI sv) and SAA 11, 219: II 28' *ka-ṣar-u-ni* (i.e., */kaṣṣarūni/* for */kaṣṣurūni/*). They differ from the *parras* adjectives to be discussed in 3.1.3 in that they are verbal adjectives derived from fientive verbs, and simple adjectives other than those which denote dimensions (for the latter type, cf., for instance, ABL 1009: 11 lú *dam-ma-qu-te*), and that they are restricted to NA.

2 This group of *parras* forms also comprises a few proper names: *Hannabu* "luxurious" and **Massaku* "inferior" (?), cf. Saporetti, OMA 321f and CAD sv *mussuku*. Other *parras* forms used as proper names are **Innabu* (in *Innabātum*), *Passalu* and *Šammahu*, quoted in the list of this section. They are parallel to the corresponding *purrus* names *Hunnubu, Pussulu, Šummuhu* and *Unnubu*, which are far more common, cf. 10.6.3 (but *mussuku* is not attested as a proper name, as far as I am aware).

3 Strictly speaking, *rabbû* is not a *parras* form, cf. uncontracted forms as *ra-ab-bi-a* (stative dual, AfO 18, 64: 23) and Mari forms as *ra-ab-bé-e-tim* (fem. pl. < *rabbiātim*, ARM 10, 146: 4 = (06A)), but clearly belongs to this group on the basis of its meaning. Its deviant form is due to the fact that in verbs whose third radical is weak, the three patterns *parras, parris and parrās* fall together into a single pattern *parrû*, fem. *parrîtu*. The same applies to **ebbû* "thick" which is only attested in substantivized form in NA *ebbiāte* "thick loaves", cf. CAD sv **ebû* adj. Another word which in spite of its different pattern belongs here semantically is **kurrû* "short", which is only attested in the plural and refers to body parts and horses, acc. to CAD sv. According to AHw sv, the sg. *kurû* is a *purîs* form < **purais*, which is frequent for diminutives in Arabic (*qutayl*), cf. Fleisch 1961: 366ff, 380ff and GAG^{2} § 55k.

4 Omen texts like TBP and many other comparable texts have a striking predilection for nouns with gemination in the protasis, especially when the subject is personal. Many of these occur only in this context.

5 A number of such cases, however, are listed by CAD under *ṣihru*, instead of under *ṣihhiru*, where they belong: Erra IV 111 *ardāti ṣa-har-a-ti* "small girls", 122 *nārāti ṣa-har-a-ti* "small canals"; likewise VAB 4, 76: 13 (plural acc. to CAD sv *ṣihru* 1a); YOS 6, 154: 8; Camb. 273: 7; BE 14, 128a: 19; STT 28: V 4' (= AnSt. 10, 122: 4'). Some of the spellings used in these cases are ambiguous: the late spelling *ṣa-har-a-ti*, for instance, can be interpreted as */ṣahrāti/* or as */ṣahharāti/*, but the usual association of the form with gemination with plurality strongly favours the latter interpretation.

6 There are some indications that the use of *parras* for plurality also spread to adjectives with other meanings. This is suggested by cases such as TBP 38a: r.21 // BRM 4, 23: 16 *pindū ka-ṣa-ru-ti/tú*

"concentrated coloured spots" (cf. CAD sv *kaṣru* b), Nbn 441: 5f *gušūrū a-ba!-lu-tu₄ pe-ti-nu-tu* "strong dry beams", and VS 5, 11: 9f *huṣābī a-ba-lu-tú* "dry poles". These cases are similar to the *parras* forms discussed in this section in that they refer to concrete salient objects in the plural. However, since they come from late texts and the geminate is not explicitly written, they may be just irregular spellings of the normal plural forms */kaṣrūtu/*, */ablūtu/* and */petnūtu/*, or incidental cases of vowel epenthesis.

7 An unusual instance of *arruku* (i.e., *urruku*) instead of *arraku* from OA is CCT 4, 6c: 18ff *hu-ra-tim ša adi šamā'im a-ru-k*[*à*]*-ni* "(objects) which were so long (that they reached) up to the sky", where we would rather expect the *parras* form *arrakāni*.

8 Cf., for instance, the use of *kabbaru*, rather than *kubburu*, among a series of plural *purrus* forms qualifying the finger nails (SpTU 4, 149: II 24'-33'); this shows that for the author of this text *kabbaru* was a more obvious choice for the plural of *kabru* than *kubburu*.

9 This functional differentiation helps us to distinguish *parras* from *purrus* forms in Assyrian. Owing to the rules for vowel harmony and the fact that Assyrian uses *parrus* instead of Babylonian *purrus*, the Assyrian nom. masc. sg. *parrusu* and the masc. pl. forms *parrusūtu/i* and *parrusū* (stative) can represent both *purrus* and *parrus*. The fact that, in contrast to the *purrus* forms of these adjectives, the *parras* forms are associated with plurality, indicates that plural forms are more likely to belong to *parras*, and singular forms to *purrus* (although we cannot be absolutely certain, cf. note 7). Therefore, AfO 17, 146: 6 and 11 *ar-ru-ku* and *kab-bu-rù* (said of columns) are from *arraku* and *kabbaru* (*pace* AHw sv *arāku* D 1 and *kabāru* D 1); ABL 1132: 7 *qal-lu-lu* (of a man) is from *qullulu* "to despise" (*pace* AHw sv *qallalu*, and cf. 3.1.3.1 sv *qallalu*)*;* AMT 25, 6: II 7 *lubārē qa-tu-nu-ti* belongs to *qattanu* (*pace* AHw sv *quttunu* 2, see 3.1.3.1 sv *qattanu*); and AfO 18, 306: IV 13' *mussirūšunu rap-pu-šu* to *rappašu* (*pace* AHw sv *mussiru* 1). As to OA, BIN 4, 10: 14 *ṣa-hu-ru* (of textiles) and EL 290: 15' *ṣa-hu-ru-tim* (of persons) belong to *ṣahharu*, according to the same criterion (*pace* Veenhof 1972: 185 note 297).

10 Some other, very rare exceptions are the PN *zaqqinu* quoted AHw sv "mit vollem Bart" (OB 1x), *dappinu* "heroic, martial", a rare variant of *dappānu*, cf. AHw/CAD sv *dāpinu*, and *daqqiqu*, cf. AHw sv (not in CAD).

11 Frequent *pāris* forms denoting professions are *kāṣiru* (a kind of textile maker), *māhiṣu* "weaver", *māliku* "counselor", *rābiṣu* "guard", *šāpiru* "overseer"; the fact that in spite of their frequency these words are never spelled with a double consonant, strongly suggests that they are *pāris* rather than *parris* forms, as would be theoretically conceivable. The participial use of *pāris* is much less common than its use as an agent noun; typical instances of it are *āliku* in the meaning "appropriate" (CAD sv *āliku* adj. f) and *ēribu* in *warhum ēribum* "the coming month" (CAD sv *ēribu* 1a), both from OB Mari.

12 Nevertheless, CAD *l.c.* writes *šaggišu*, and gives the improbable translation "a murderer will murder him". A few examples of this paronomastic construction are *bāqir ibaqqarūšu* "anyone who will claim from him" (ARM 8, 1: 27, cf. also YOS 14, 42: 4 and elsewhere); *āmirum i-im-ma-ru-šu* "(and if) someone sees him" (in a relative sentence, BagM 2, 78: 13); *še-mu-um [š]a išemmû* "someone who will hear (this), (what will he say)" (ARM 26/2 p. 398 no. 471: r.4').

13 The starting point of the spread of *ā* was probably the fem. *parrastu*, where *a*, realized as a short vowel because of the following consonant cluster (Reiner 1966: 44), was ambiguous as to its phonological quantity and could be interpreted as standing for *ā*. This could entail the introduction of *ā* in the corresponding masc. (see for this mechanism Kuryłowicz 1975: 62f).

14 *Parras* as a pattern for agent nouns may also be behind the Hebrew pattern *qaṭṭāl*. Since an original *ā* becomes *ō* in Hebrew, the preservation of *ā* in agent nouns as *gallāḇ* "barber" or *rakkāḇ* "charioteer" may indicate that these words are derived from a pattern with a short vowel, which was lengthened in accordance with a rule of vowel lengthening in stressed closed syllables. This view is taken by Aartun 1975: 5ff, and is considered possible by Joüon-Muraoka 1991: 252f and Landsberger, OLZ 29 (1926) Sp. 975 note 3. Moreover, the existence of agent nouns of the pattern *parras* in Akkadian is presupposed by the present tense form *iparras* of verbs of the vowel class *a/u*, which is derived from *parras*, just as *iparris* (vowel class *i/i*) is derived from *parris*, cf. Kuryłowicz 1972: 57 and 113f.

15 It cannot always be established with certainty whether a word is used as a substantive or an adjective, in particular if it occurs in the stative, where the distinction between substantive and adjective is neutralized. In such cases I have considered the meaning: most of the words in question denote qualities; these have been classified as adjectives. Only if they clearly refer to occupations they have been listed as substantives.

16 I have not listed some *parrās* forms which cannot be derived from an Akkadian root; the most common is *naggāru* "carpenter", with *ā* guaranteed by Assyrian and the geminate by syllabic spellings in LL, cf. CAD sv lex. sect. (elsewhere it is almost always spelled ideographically). It was borrowed from Sumerian nagar and adapted to the pattern *parrās* to which it belongs semantically, cf. Lieberman 1977: 22f note 55.

17 I assume that the sequence *-a-a-ú* unambiguously indicates a long *ā*, as in this word and *ha-sà-a-a-ú* (cf. 3.3.2 and note 20), but that the sequence *-a-ú*, as in *ša-ás-sà-a-ú* (group B), does not do so, because of such writings as *i-ma-(aš-)ša-a-ú* "they plunder" (RA 65, 71: 19; AbB 8, 18: 8) where *a* is certainly short.

18 It is possible that *parrās* is an extension of an ancient agent noun *paras* (*qatal*), similar to the basic adjectival patterns *paris* and *parus*. Traces of such a function of *paras* are extant in Arabic. After its replacement by *pāris*, *parrās* became opposed to the latter. Cf. Bauer 1910: 12ff; Fleisch 1955 (summarized in 1961: 365f; 1968: 54f); Rundgren 1959a: 43ff; 1963b: 101ff.

19 For the long *ā* cf. *ka-ja-a-na* Tn-Ep. IIIa 7 and 45, OB *ka-ja-à-ni-iš* RA 75 109: III 24, and *ta-ja-a-ru* Tn-Ep. V 19; *ti-ja-a-rat* BAL II 86: Ass. 3.

20 For the long *ā* of *dappānu*, see *dáp-pa-a-nu* LTBA 2, 1: VI 39; AfO 18, 349: 11; translation from CAD, AHw: "sehr gewaltig(?)", also *dapnu*, *dapinu* and *dappinu*. If it is derived from *dapānu* "to knock down" (CAD) or "etwa 'zügeln'" (AHw), it is an agent noun. For *qarrādu* see KUB 37, 139: 6 *qar-ra-a-ti-*[*šu*] (cf. 7 *qar-ra-ti-ja-ma*), MA *qar-ra-de* (Iraq 30, 159: 16), NA *qar-ra-di* (Iraq 17, 40 no. 9: 18). For *ṣallāmu* see CAD sv a, and Veenhof 1972: 1, esp. note 3; its status is ambiguous: it is used as an attribute of donkeys and copper, but has a substantival plural. *Hassā'u* only occurs in MSL 12, 169: 394 *ha-sà-a-a-ú* (cf. note 17 for *ā*); for its meaning cf. AHw sv *hassûm* "an Haarausfall leidend?"; CAD sv *hazāju* gives no meaning, but refers "possibly" to *hesû* B "be bushy" (said of hair). Compare, however, MSL 12, 169: 394 lú.zé.zé = *ha-sà-a-a-ú* and *ib.* 162: 138 and 183: 8 lú.zé.za = *ha-su-ú*, on the one hand, and, on the other hand, a case such as *ib.* 160: 85f lú.al.sig.sig = *qù-tu-nu-ú*, lú.al.sig.ga = *qá-at-nu-ú*, or sal.la = *raqqu* "thin" (passim) and MSL 13, 213: 26 sal.sal = *ru-uq-qu-qu*. These Sumerian equivalents suggest that *hassā'u* and *hasû* have the same relationship to each other as a *purrus* form and a simple adjective, which pleads against AHw's interpreting *ha-su-ú* as *hassûm* with a geminate and against CAD's separating *hazāju* (see above) from *hasû* "a person with a speech defect".

CHAPTER FOUR

THE Gtn-STEM

4.0. The second of the grammatical categories with gemination to be discussed is the Gtn-stem. It is not particularly problematic as regards its function: it usually expresses various aspects of verbal plurality, such as iterativity, habituality and plurality. In 4.2 we will examine these functions more precisely, offer some illustrative examples and discuss some specially interesting cases.

The controversial aspect of the Gtn-stem, and also of the other *-tan-* stems (Dtn, Štn and Ntn) concerns their form. The question is whether the geminate of the Gtn-stem is a "real" geminate, or the result of assimilation of a nasal to the second radical. The latter view prevails at the moment; if it is correct, the Gtn-stem does not have a "real" geminate and does not belong to the categories with gemination of the second radical. An important part of this chapter consists of a refutation of this view and an alternative analysis which implies that the Gtn-stem does have a real geminate and is therefore to be included among the categories which are examined in this study (4.1).

4.1. The formal analysis of the Gtn-stem

4.1.1. The debate

The most striking feature of the paradigm of the *-tan-* stems is the fact that the present tense is consistently characterized by an infix *-tan(a)-* (Gtn *iptanarras*, Dtn *uptanarras*, Štn *uštanapras*, Ntn *ittanapras*), whereas in all other forms the infix lacks its ultimate *-n-* (e.g., preterite *iptarras, uptarris, uštapris, ittapras*; stative *pitarrus, putarrus, šutaprus, itaprus*). This discrepancy is generally explained by assuming that in the latter forms *-n-* has been assimilated to the following consonant: in the Gtn-stem **ip-tan-ras* > *iptarras*; in the other stems, e.g., the Dtn-stem **up-tan-rris* > **uptarrris* > *uptarris*, with assimilation of the nasal and subsequent reduction of the triple cluster. This solution was first proposed by Poebel (1939: 41ff) and canonized by GAG § 91a (cf. also § 20i and § 33j).

However, Steiner (1981) has demonstrated that the analysis of the *-tan-* stems adopted by Poebel and GAG has serious shortcomings. His criticism boils down to two main points. The first is that the phonological development assumed for the non-present forms of the Dtn-, Štn- and Ntn-stems, viz. assimilation of *-n-* and subsequent reduction of the triple consonant cluster (**up-tan-rris* > **uptarrris* > *uptarris*), is unparalleled in Akkadian. Such clusters of three consonants are resolved by insertion of a vowel, not by elision of one of the consonants (1981: 11; Reiner 1966: 52).

The second point is that the application of the "assimilation plus reduction" rule to quadriliteral verbs and hollow roots results in other forms than are actually attested. In the *-tan-* stems of quadriliteral verbs the analysis of Poebel and GAG presupposes a preterite Ntn **in-tan-balkat* (cf. preterite N *in-balkit* > *ibbalkit*), which would become **ittabbalkat*. The actual form, however, is *ittabalakkat*, with the infix *-t-* after the prefix *n-* and gemination of the third radical; this would force us to assume that *-tan-* was split up into two morphemes, *-ta-* and *-n-*, separated by the first and second radical of the root (1981: 13f).

In the hollow roots (type *kânu* "to be(come) stable, firm") we would expect the *-n-* of *-tan-* to be visible in all forms, since there is no consonant following to which it could be assimilated. We would also expect a preterite **iktanūn* < *ik-tan-ūn* corresponding to the present *iktanân* (< *ik-tan-ân*) (cf. pret. G *ikûn*), but the actual form is *iktūn*; likewise, the preterite Dtn is *uktīn*, rather than **uktanīn*. Moreover, in cases in which the weak radical is realized as a glide, in such forms as *šita"im* (imperative Gtn of *šâmu* "to buy") we would expect the *-n-* to be visible, since according to the usual procedure the clusters */n'/* and */nj/* become */nn/* (GAG § 24c, but see § 33e for exceptions) (1981: 14). Accordingly, we can only account for the correct Gtn forms of quadriliteral verbs and hollow roots by introducing special *ad hoc* rules for each type, which is clearly an unsatisfactory procedure.

Steiner's conclusion is that the existence of *-n-* as the final element of the morpheme *-tan-* cannot be proved outside the present, and that the actual iterative morpheme is *-t-*, which is common to all forms of the *-tan-* stems (1981: 15) and has parallels in Berber languages (1981: 21ff, 26). In the preterite this morpheme occurs in its simplest form (*iptarras*); in the present a nasal is added (*iptanarras*) in the same way as a *-t-* is added in the perfect (*iptatarras*): just as *-t-* is the perfect morpheme (1981: 16) of the iterative, *-n-* is its present morpheme.

The Gtn-stem differs from the other *-tan-* stems in that it has a geminate in all its forms and that it differs from the Gt-stem in its entire paradigm, whereas the other *-tan-* stems only differ from the corresponding *-ta-* stems in the present (1981: 18). This shows the special position of the Gtn-stem vis-à-vis the other *-tan-* stems, which is corroborated by the fact that the latter are far less frequent and mainly attested in the later stages of Akkadian (1981: 19).

In reaction to Steiner's article, Voigt (1987b) defends and, on several points, refines the analysis adopted by Poebel and GAG. He strongly emphasizes the systematic nature of the relationships between verbal categories (1987b: 249ff) and the basic position of the strong verbs which are the model to which other types adapt (1987b: 252ff). For instance, in order to refute Steiner's argument concerning the absence of *-n-* in the preterite of hollow roots (*iktūn* instead of **ik-tan-ūn*, see above), Voigt points out (1987b: 259f) that the paradigm of the weak verbs is modelled on that of the strong verbs: the former do not have *-n-* if the preterite Gtn of the latter (*iptarras*) does not have it either.

Nevertheless, Voigt's account is not sufficient to save Poebel's and GAG's analysis. Firstly, without providing additional arguments, he repeats the "assimilation plus reduction" rule of triple consonant clusters, which Steiner quite justifiably argues to be untenable. Secondly, the systematic nature of the verbal system is not in itself a sufficient argument to assume the original presence of *-n-* in the non-present forms; the next section will show that an equally systematic structure can be attained without the "assimilation plus reduction" rule.

The most important objection, however, is that this rule implies an extremely unlikely development: it causes the elision of the very element which distinguishes the iterative from the corresponding non-iterative forms, because, according to Poebel's analysis, it is only the presence of *-n-* which distinguishes the Dtn-, Štn- and Ntn-stems from the Dt-, Št- and Nt-stems outside the present (Steiner 1981: 12). In this situation we would rather expect the *-n-* to be preserved, even if that would be in conflict with a phonological rule.[1] The fact that the iterative meaning is not overtly expressed in the Dtn-, Štn- and Ntn-stems outside the present can only mean that it was never overtly expressed in the first place, i.e., that it was always contextually determined, as I will argue below.

Finally, neither Steiner's nor Voigt's analysis accounts for some Štn forms of verbs I/*aleph*, in particular the OB participle *mu-uš-ta-ah-hi-iz* (stative 3rd p. sg. masc.) "(that illness) is contagious" (ARM 10, 129: 20), where the geminate is problematic: we would expect *muštāhiz* < **mušta'hiz* in accordance with the paradigm form of the participle Štn *muštapris* (GAG Verbalpar. 13 and 15).[2] Steiner (1981: 14f) posits a special "ŠDtn-stem" to explain this form, which is a completely *ad hoc* solution. Voigt, using *uštakkil* as paradigm form, assumes a development *uš^tan'kil* > *uštankil* > *uštakkil*, in accordance with the "assimilation plus reduction" rule (1987b: 264). This is open to the same criticism as the reduction of a triple consonant cluster in the strong verbs, and also an *ad hoc* solution. The next section will show that also without assuming an assimilated nasal these forms are completely regular within the paradigm of the *-tan-* stems.

In fact, the assumption that in the non-present forms of the *-tan-* stems a nasal was assimilated to the consonant following it, and that the resulting triple cluster was reduced, is completely superfluous, since we can obtain a satisfactory analysis of the *-tan-* stems without it, namely, by considering these forms in a diachronical perspective and by taking into account the special relationship which holds between the Gtn-stem and the other *-tan-* stems.

4.1.2. An alternative analysis

We will propose an alternative analysis of the *-tan-* stems, which accounts for all their peculiarities without resorting to unparalleled phonological rules or *ad hoc* explanations, and which implies that the Gtn-stem contains a real geminate. This analysis basically consists of three claims: first, that the gemination of the Gtn-stem has arisen as a means to reinforce or to renew the durative meaning, which was a secondary, contextually determined function of the infix *-ta-*; second, that we have to separate the Gtn-stem as (relatively) basic from the other *-tan-* stems which are derived from it; and, third, that the nasal is restricted to the present where it was introduced as a consequence of the replacement of an old present form without gemination *iprusu* by the new present formation *iparras*.

4.1.2.1. The origin of the Gtn-stem

The function of the Akkadian infix *-ta-*, which primarily characterizes the perfect (*iptaras, uptarris, uštapris,* etc) and the *-ta-* stems (Gt, Dt, Št), is complex and controversial, and requires a much more detailed study than can be undertaken here.[3] In my view, the following account provides a succinct, but plausible description of its function and historical development, which explains a maximum number of facts on the basis of a minimum number of hypothetical assumptions.

The basic function of *-ta-* in Akkadian is doubtless that of detransitivization, i.e., it denotes a reduction in the degree of transitivity which is inherent in the corresponding form without *ta-* (see 5.3 about transitivity as a gradual rather than a binary phenomenon and the difference between high and low transitivity). Depending on the context and the verb in question, this function can be realized in various ways, most commonly as intransitive, passive, reflexive, reciprocal, etc., cf. GAG § 92-94, and see, for instance, the discussion of the Dt-stem in 9.1.

In these cases detransitivization entails a reduction in valency: in general, the forms with infixed *-ta-* are intransitive derivations of transitive forms without *-ta-*. However, a reduction in transitivity can also be realized without a reduction in valency; this is the case if *-ta-* has a resultative function, i.e., if it denotes a state which results from a preceding event (cf. Nedjalkov-Jaxontov 1988: 6). Since the degree of transitivity is in particular related to the salience of the action involved and the agentive nature of the subject (cf. 5.4), the absence of action and the resulting non-agentive nature of the subject entail a drastic reduction in transitivity. A prime example of such a resultative is the Akkadian stative, see below.

This suggests that *-ta-*, if combined with a past tense form, could also have a resultative function, as already claimed by Kuryłowicz 1972: 61. Categories with a resultative function have a natural and widespread tendency to shift to the expression of the previous event itself and thus come to express a perfect (Jespersen 1924: 269ff; Kuryłowicz 1975: 109f; Voigt 1987a: 88ff; Nedjalkov-Jaxontov 1988: 41ff; Bybee-Dahl 1989: 68ff; Bybee-Perkins-Pagliuca 1994: 104). This is what happened to intransitive verbs in Akkadian (GAG § 80b): *imtaqut* "he has fallen". In transitive verbs there were two ways in which the resultative function could be realized: it could describe either the state of the subject of the preceding event: *iṣṣabat* "he has seized (and now possesses)", or the state of its object: *iṣṣabat* *"he/it has been seized (and is now in someone's possession)" (cf. Nedjalkov-Jaxontov 1988: 9f).

The first of these two realizations has been generalized in Akkadian as the well-known perfect *iptaras*, which has become extremely productive and developed from a derived stem into an inflectional member of the paradigm of the G-stem (Kuryłowicz 1972: 61f).

The second one, *iṣṣabat* in the meaning *"he/it has been seized" is not attested in Akkadian, but it is common in other Semitic languages where *-ta-* serves as a passive marker (Moscati 1969: 127ff). The shift from resultative to passive is also a very common development, which accounts for the fact that in many languages (in Romance and Germanic, for instance) states and passives are expressed by the same or similar categories (Kuryłowicz 1964: 56ff; Nedjalkov-Jaxontov 1988: 45ff; Voigt 1987a: 90ff note 15).

That *iptaras* had this double meaning at a prehistoric stage of Akkadian is indicated by two further circumstances. In the first place, it has a precise parallel in the use of the stative in historical Akkadian. A stative of a fientive verb is in fact a resultative (GAG § 77e/f); if derived from a transitive verb it can require an active or a passive translation depending on the context: *ṣabit* can mean either "he/it has been seized" or "he has seized (and now possesses)", cf. 1.8 and Rowton 1962). In the light of the subsequent development to be discussed below, it seems a plausible assumption that in this respect the stative is the successor of *iptaras* in its resultative function.

Secondly, the double meaning of *-ta-* is preserved in the derived stems, where a form as *uptarris* (from *parāsu* G and D "to separate") is used both as a perfect D "he has separated" (active) and as a pret. Dt "he was separated" (passive/intrans), again with the shift "result of previous event → previous event". The same applies to the Š-stem, e.g., *uštaddin* "he collected" (lit. "he caused to give" (taxes)) and "it was collected" (cf. CAD sv *nadānu* 3 and 5).

There is a close connection between stativity and durativity, because a state implies a certain duration. Therefore, a change from event to state implies a change from momentaneous to durative. For instance, the action expressed by Akkadian *eqlam iṣbat* "he seized (took possession of) the field" is momentaneous, but its resultative counterparts, both *eqlum ṣabit* "the field has been seized (and is now in someone's possession)" and *eqlam ṣabit* "he has seized (and is now in possession of) the field" are clearly durative.[4] Likewise, *iptaras* could have a secondary, contextually determined, durative meaning. This theoretical assumption is confirmed not only by the parallel use of the stative, but also by some lexicalized remnants of this use of *iptaras*, which will be mentioned below.

At this stage a verb form of the category *iptaras* could have at least three different meanings depending on the context: it could be a perfect, a passive or a durative. This state of affairs survives in the derived stems (see the next section). In addition, it may have retained (part of) its original resultative function. In the G-stem, however, a development took place consisting in the renewal of two of its three functions: the passive and the durative one. This process was undoubtedly caused, or at least facilitated, by the productivity of its third function, viz., that of denoting the perfect, and by its change from a derivational into an inflectional form of the G-stem (Kuryłowicz 1972: 61). The passive function was taken over by the N-stem (1972: 62f). It is, however, the renewal of the durative function which is especially relevant to the subject at hand.

This durative function was reinforced and made explicit by the insertion of a geminate as second radical; in this way the Gtn form *iptarras* (later exclusively preterite, see below) arose, formally based on the Gt-stem, cf. *iptaras* → *iptarras, imtaqut* → *imtaqqut, iptaqid* → *iptaqqid.*

The extant use of the Gt-stem reflects this development. Among the verbal stems of Akkadian the Gt-stem is one of the most problematical, in that it has a number of apparently unrelated functions. GAG § 92 mentions three groups of Gt verbs: reciprocal ones (e.g., *mahāru* Gt "to meet or confront each other"), separative ones (e.g., *alāku* Gt "to go away, to depart"), and a third group consisting of verbs whose meaning is hard to distinguish from that of the corresponding G-stem, but which GAG § 92f claims to be sometimes ("*mehrfach*") durative or habitual. It is difficult to detect a common ground in these three uses, cf. GAG § 92c.[5]

The character of the Gt-stem becomes less enigmatic if we consider the development outlined above, viz., the renewal of the passive function of *iptaras* by means of the N-stem and that of its durative function by the insertion of gemination. Such a process is a gradual one and tends to leave behind a residue of words which retain their old form, usually as more or less isolated, lexicalized entities. The diverse use of the Gt-stem, then, is caused by the fact that it is a typical example of such a residual category. The reciprocal and reflexive Gt verbs are remnants of its older function, after the latter was taken over by the N-stem.[6]

Likewise, after the durative function had been taken over by the Gtn-stem, the older forms without gemination, with their contextually determined durative character, did not disappear altogether, but could survive in favourable circumstances. This is the explanation for the third group of Gt-stems verbs in GAG § 92f γ), those which are neither reciprocal nor separative. Most of them occur in literary texts and many of them are statives (GAG *l.c.*). The first fact suggests that they owe their survival to their stylistic value, the second one supports the original stative meaning of the *-ta-* infix.[7] GAG (*l.c.*) claims that they mean "etwas für die Dauer tun" and sometimes have habitual meaning; in other words, they convey meanings for which the Gtn-stem is the regular and productive category.

A second group of residual forms which support the idea that the Gtn-stem has replaced the Gt-stem in its durative function, consists of a small number of Gt participles (*muptarsu*) which alternate with Gtn participles (*muptarrisu*) without a noticeable difference in meaning: *mundahṣu* and *mundahhiṣu* "fighter", *murtapdu* and *murtappidu* "roving", *muštaptu* and *muštappitu* "treacherous", *muštarhu* and *muštarrihu* "vainglorious", *muštarqu* and *muštarriqu* "secret lover", *mūtaplu* and *mūtappilu* "requiter" and *muttakpu* and *muttakkipu* "goring". They were pointed out by Reiner and Renger (1974/77: 185), from which the translations have been taken.[8]

The insertion of gemination made the Gtn-stem into a full-fledged iconic category and broadened its scope to a wider range than only durativity, to include additional manifestations of verbal plurality, such as iterativity, habituality, plurality of subject, etc., see 4.2.

Such is the process which gave rise to the Gtn-stem; now we will turn to the rise of the other *-tan-* stems, which presupposes the prior existence of the Gtn-stem.

4.1.2.2. The Dtn-, Štn- and Ntn-stems

The relationship between the Gtn-stem and the other *-tan-* stems (Dtn, Štn and Ntn) is determined by two factors: the first of these is the overall basic nature of the G-stem as opposed to the derived nature of the other verbal stems; in the same way the Gtn-stem is "relatively basic" versus Dtn, Štn and Ntn; the second factor is the much higher frequency of Gtn compared to that of the other *-tan-* stems.

The basic position of the G-stem versus the derived stems in general is due to the fact that it is formally and functionally unmarked, i.e., it has no explicit morpheme to characterize it and no semantic restrictions. Accordingly, it also has the highest frequency (for the relationship between markedness and frequency see Greenberg 1966 and Croft 1990: 84ff). Moreover, the paradigm of the derived stems is completely predictable from that of the G-stem, whereas the reverse is not true, and the G-stem has the highest number of distinctions in its paradigm.[9]

The consequence of this relationship between the G-stem and the rest of the verbal stems is that the paradigm of the latter is modelled on that of the G-stem, which tends to impose its paradigm on the other stems. This can be illustrated by numerous phenomena in the verbal system of Akkadian. We will give only one example, which is especially interesting because it is relevant to the issue under discussion, namely the gemination in the present tense of the Š-stem of the verbs I/*aleph* and I/w (*ušakkal* "he feeds", *ušabbal* "he causes to bring, sends". On the basis of the paradigm of the strong roots we would expect these forms to be **ušākal* and **ušābal*, originating from *uša'kal, uša'bal,* like *ušapras*. The actual form, however, is *ušakkal,* etc., because the presence of a geminate in the present tense of the G-stem (*iparrVs*) has caused its introduction in the corresponding forms of the derived stems wherever possible. Thus we find *ušapras* in strong roots, because a consonant cluster cannot be geminated, but *ušakkal* rather than **ušākal*, since nothing prevents the insertion of a geminate here.[10] The geminate automatically entails a shortening of the preceding vowel (Reiner 1966: 44; Greenstein 1984: 42f).

Just as the G-stem is basic in an absolute sense, the Gtn-stem is relatively basic versus the other *-tan-* stems; this implies a similar formal domination. Before discussing the consequences of this fact in detail, we will first turn to the second factor which determines the relationship between Gtn and the other *-tan-* stems, i.e., their relative frequency.

The Gtn-stem is by far the most frequent of the *-tan-* stems. As regards its type frequency, the number of each of the *-tan-* stems listed in AHw clearly indicates this: AHw has 312 verbs with a Gtn-stem, as against 88 with a Dtn-, 53 with a Štn- and 88 with an Ntn-stem.[11] The real number may well be even lower, because outside the present the Dtn-, Štn- and Ntn-stems have the same form as the corresponding *-ta-* stems, so that it is not always possible to determine to which stem a given form belongs.[12]

If we consider the token frequency, i.e., the number of times a *-tan-* stem of a specific verb is attested, the predominance of the Gtn-stem is overwhelming: it is not only attested for more verbs than the other *-tan-* stems, but most of the latter are extremely rare,[13] whereas the Gtn-stem of many verbs is quite common (see 6.7.3 for details).

Therefore, Steiner (1981: 19) is doubtless correct in describing the Gtn-stem as "der primäre und somit eigentliche 'Iterativstamm' des akkadischen Verbums". The dominant position of the Gtn-stem versus the other *-tan-* stems, caused by its relatively basic nature and its much higher frequency, explains the formal structure of the latter stems in general, and the fact that they have an incomplete paradigm, in so far as only their present forms have an explicit morpheme to distinguish them from the corresponding *-ta-* stems.

We will take up the second point first. In a diachronic perspective structural changes tend to originate in basic categories, in our case the G-stem, and may, but need not, spread from these to other categories. This offers a historical explanation for the fact mentioned above, that the basic category shows the greatest number of distinctions, since it may have distinctions which have not (yet) spread to the derived categories.

This tendency explains why the Dtn-, Štn- and Ntn-stems show no trace of a nasal before the second radical in their non-present forms. The renewal of *iptaras* by means of the N-stem for the passive and by the insertion of a geminate for its durative function took place only in the G-stem and never spread to the derived stems. In the latter, therefore, the original situation in which the infix *-ta-* expressed both the perfect and the passive and also had a secondary durative meaning, is preserved, so that a form like *uptarris* has three meanings: 1) he has separated (perfect D), 2) he was separated (preterite Dt) and 3) he separated (much, often, constantly, etc.) (preterite Dtn).

Our next concern is the paradigm of the Dtn-, Štn- and Ntn-stems in general. Just as the paradigm of the Gtn-stem is based on that of the G-stem, the paradigms of the Dtn-, the Štn- and the Ntn-stems are based on that of the Gtn-stem. We will first consider the non-present forms; the present forms will be dealt with in 4.1.2.3.

In 4.1.2.1 we saw that the primary form of the Gtn-stem is *iptarras*, which arose from *iptaras* by the insertion of a geminate. The category which is functionally opposed to *iptarras* is the corresponding non-iterative present *iparras*. The rule deriving *iptarras* from *iparras* simply says: "insert *-ta-* after the first consonant". In addition, the other *-tan-* stems will have gemination whenever possible, since the Gtn-stem always has gemination. Accordingly, for the preterite Dtn and Štn we find *uparris* → *uptarris* and *ušapris* → *uštapris* respectively, without gemination, since gemination of a geminate and of a cluster is impossible. The rule for the preterite Ntn includes an additional rearrangement of the pattern: *in-paris* → *in-ta-pras* > *ittapras*.

In the stative this rule gives rise to (*purrus* (Ass. *parrus*)) → *putarrus*, (*šuprus* (Ass. *ša-prus*)) → *šutaprus* and (*naprus* →) **nitaprus*, which becomes *itaprus* by dissimilation of the two consecutive dentals *n* and *t* (GAG § 33b); cf. the same process in MA *da'ānu* < *danānu* "strength" (GAG § 33c) and in a form such as SB *iṣbatū'inni* < *iṣbatūninni* "they seized me", GAG § 84d). The vowels *u* and *i* in the first syllable are copied from the corresponding prefix conjugations: D *uparras* and Š *ušapras* versus N *ipparras*.

In hollow roots this rule results only in the insertion of *-t-* after the first consonant: pret. D *ukīn* → Dtn **uktinn* > *uktīn*, in the plural D *ukinnū* → Dtn *uktinnū*, with gemination of the final radical in all cases in which the strong verbs have gemination of the second radical.

The same rule also explains the Štn forms of verbs I/*aleph* and I/w, which have been adduced to support the claim that the nasal of *-tan-* is also found outside the present (cf. Voigt 1987b: 264; Edzard 1962: 116b note 30) and for which Steiner has no satisfactory explanation (1981: 14f; see above section 4.1.1). On the model of the strong roots (*ušapras*), the Š forms of these verbs would have a single consonant: present **ušākal*, **ušābal*, preterite *ušākil*, *ušābil* (or *ušēbil*). According to the rule formulated above gemination should therefore occur in the corresponding Štn forms: **uštakkal*, *uštakkil*, *šutakkil*, etc. In fact, only two or three of such forms have been found in Akkadian. (see 4.1.1 and note 2). The important thing is that they do not support the claim that there is assimilation of a nasal in the non-present forms of the Dtn-, Štn- and Ntn-stems.

4.1.2.3. The origin of the nasal

The present forms with the infix *-tan-* of both the Gtn-stem and the other *-tan-* stems owe their existence to the replacement of an older present formation *iprusu* by *iparras*, which largely took place at a prehistorical stage of Akkadian (see 2.2.4.2). Knudsen (1984/86) has demonstrated that the spread of the new present can still be observed in historical Akkadian, where two present formations coexist: an older one, consisting of an apophony *i/a* for the preterite and the present respectively, and a more recent one, with gemination of the second radical. The former is used in the D- and the Š-stems and some weak verbs; the latter has penetrated into all categories in which this kind of gemination is possible (1984/86: 231ff, esp. 236).

The development of the old derivational durative or iterative *iparras* into an inflectional part of the verbal paradigm in order to denote the present necessitated the creation of such a present for all verbs and all stems on the basis of the old form without gemination. The model of the G-stem *iprus(u)* → *iparras* was imposed on the derived stems. For the Gtn-stem a new present was created on the basis of the proportion *iprus(u)* : *iparras* = *iptarras* : x, in which, apart from minor changes, x has to be one syllable longer in order to preserve the heterosyllabic contrast with the preterite (cf. Reiner 1966: 75f, 95): **ipta-arras*. From then on *iptarras* itself was restricted to the past.

The question why this form ended up as *iptanarras*, with an infixed *-n-*, has been answered convincingly by Kuryłowicz 1961: 63f, repeated in 1972: 63. Since it is a general rule of Akkadian that *n* assimilates to a following consonant (GAG § 33d), a geminate can be interpreted as consisting of *n* + consonant. This also applies to the geminate of the Gtn-stem: it is possible to reanalyse *iptarras* as representing an underlying form **iptanras*. This reanalysis led to the introduction of *n* in the present on the basis of the proportion *iprus(u)* : *iparras* = **iptanras* : *iptanarras*.[14]

The correctness of Kuryłowicz's explanation is confirmed by the fact that the same procedure was used to create present forms for the quadriliteral verbs of the type *nabalkutu* (cf. GAG Verbalpar. 39). In these verbs the present was formed by splitting up the consonant cluster of the old present **ibbalkat* (which contrasted with the preterite *ibbalkit* by the *a/i* apophony, cf. Knudsen 1984/86: 232, type B) and by geminating the third consonant: **ibbalkat* → *ibbalakkat*, which is precisely the same derivation as **iptanras* → *iptanarras*.[15]

After the proportion *iptarras* → *iptanarras* had thus arisen in the Gtn-stem, it became a model for the creation of similar present forms in the other *-tan-* stems, which replaced older apophonic present forms: **uptarras* → *uptanarras*, **uštapras* → *uštanapras*, *ittapras* → *ittanapras*, and in the verbs I/*aleph* and I/w: **uštakkal* → *uštanakkal*.

However, this spread of the nasal in the present only took place in those forms which serve to express verbal plurality, not in the purely passive/intransitive use of these presents. Thus the passive/intransitive Dt- and Št-stems have retained their old present forms *uptarras* and *uštapras*, without *-na-*. This is doubtless related to the fact that derived passive/intransitive forms are generally backgrounding, whereas innovative forms tend to be introduced first in foregrounding contexts, such as main clauses, cf. Givón 1979: 45ff and 121.

Parallel to the splitting of *uptarras* into a foregrounding form *uptanarras* and a backgrounding form *uptarras* is the difference in present forms between the passive Št-stem (*uštapras*) and the "lexical" Št-stem (*uštaparras*): the geminate of the latter and the absence of gemination in the former can be explained by the fact that the "lexical" Št-stem is generally active and transitive, and thus foregrounding, whereas the passive Št-stem is generally backgrounding because of its passive meaning.

The fact that the nasal did spread to the Ntn-stem cannot be considered a counter-argument, because the Ntn-stem is not simply a derivation of the passive N-stem with meanings such as iterative and habitual. It is, on the contrary, a highly expressive category with idiosyncratic uses, which often strongly differ from those of the N-stem; many Ntn-stems do not have a corresponding N-stem. Moreover, it is closely related in form and use to the quadriliteral verbs, many of which are also expressive in nature. However, a detailed study of these verbs and the Ntn-stem cannot be undertaken here; see GAG³ § 91g, 101g and 110.

4.1.3. Conclusions

This lengthy discussion of the formal structure of the *-tan-* stems leads to two important conclusions. First, the geminate which characterizes the Gtn-stem is a real geminate, not the outcome of assimilation of a nasal, and belongs to the categories with gemination enumerated in 2.1.5. Second, it is this geminate which lies at the root of the iterative function of the *tan-* stems, not the infix *-tan-* itself, as is usually assumed, nor *-t-*, as Steiner (1981: 15f) claims. The fact that there is no gemination in the Štn- and the Ntn-stems, and no additional gemination in the Dtn-stem, does not speak against this, since it follows naturally from the way these forms have originated. Synchronically, however, it is the infix *-na-*, the only element which distinguishes the *-tan-* forms from the neutral forms in the present, which carries the iterative function.

These conclusions are confirmed by the fact that from a functional point of view the Gtn-stem clearly belongs to the categories with gemination, as enumerated in 2.1.5. Since many of these are associated with plurality, it is extremely far-fetched to claim that the geminate of the Gtn-stem, which is also clearly associated with plurality, has a different origin and is to be explained on the basis of an unparalleled and highly improbable phonological rule.

Finally, the presence of *-na-* in the present forms of the *-tan-* stems proves to be dependent on two conditions: the rise of the new present *iparras,* and the presence of an overall assimilation rule of *n* to a following consonant. This explains why in other Semitic languages, where these conditions are not met, there are no convincing traces of categories which can be related to the Akkadian *-tan-* stems, in spite of all efforts to find them.[16]

4.2. The function and use of the *-tan-* stems

The Gtn-stem is a productive category which can in principle be derived from any G-stem. The same applies to the other *-tan-* stems, but, as already stated in 4.1.2.2, these are considerably less productive. Most examples in the following sections will therefore be Gtn forms; the Ntn-stem is largely left out of account, since many Ntn-stems deviate semantically from the corresponding N-stem, cf. 4.1.2.3.

As already stated in the introduction to this chapter, the general function of the *-tan-* stems is well-established. GAG § 91e/f describes them as iterative, habitual and distributive, and the other grammars of Akkadian use practically the same terms; cf., for instance, Ungnad-Matouš 1964: 80 and Caplice 1980: 67; note especially the unusually detailed description in Hecker 1968: 143ff; see also Steiner 1981: 24f and Von Soden 1973. Therefore, I will refrain from quoting extensive examples of their normal use and mainly concentrate on some interesting aspects.

In describing the use of the *-tan-* stems it is convenient to distinguish semantic notions such as iterative, habitual, distributive, etc., but it is important to recall that they are contextually determined realizations of a single basic function, viz., that of expressing verbal plurality, as defined by Dressler (1968: 51ff), cf. 2.1.5. Which of these realizations applies in a given case is determined by the meaning of the verb and the context. Therefore, it is often difficult to distinguish them in practice and in many contexts more than one realization may be involved at the same time. This is in accordance with Dressler's claim that it is typical of verbal plurality to be polysemous (1968: 58), and to have a "global meaning" extending over the whole sentence or even further (1968: 92ff), cf. 2.1.5.

I will use the traditional term "iterative" as the general designation of the function of the Gtn-stem. In the following sections three concrete realizations of verbal plurality are distinguished: iterative in the strict sense of the word (4.2.1), frequentative (which includes habitual and continuous) (4.2.2) and plurality (4.2.3).

4.2.1. Iterativity

The term iterative is used here, following Bybee, Perkins and Pagliuca 1994: 160ff, and Schaefer 1994: 80ff, to refer to a situation in which the subject performs a series of actions which together can be seen as comprising a single occasion. For this kind of verbal plurality Akkadian uses the Gtn-stem mainly in verbs of movement: the G-stem denotes a single movement, the Gtn-stem a movement in different directions. This function is especially common in *alāku* Gtn "to walk about", cf. CAD sv 6a; other common examples are the Gtn-stems of *nagāšu* and *rapādu* with the same meaning, *lasāmu* "to run around" (e.g., FM 2 p. 106 no. 66: 8f), *raqādu* "to jump around", *ṣâdu* "to turn about, to prowl, to whirl", *šahāṭu* "to leap up and down, to move back and forth", and *ša'û* "to fly about, to circle". A transitive Gtn-stem with this meaning is *mašāru* "to drag around". A randomly selected example is:

(01) AfO 27, 70: 20f (If a male donkey has taken a horse's tail in its mouth or in [...] and) *ina libbi ālim u ṣērim il-ta-na-as-su-um* "keeps running around in the city or the plain".

In other contexts these Gtn-stems can also convey other notions; for instance, *alāku* Gtn can also mean "to go or come repeatedly" (to a specific goal), cf. CAD sv 6d, as in:

(02) TC 2, 44: 31ff *ahī atta têrtaka išti ālikim ālikimma li-ta-lá-kà-ma* "my dear brother, your report should come to me with every person passing through" (tr. CAD sv 6d).

4.2.2. Frequentativity

Frequentative (referring to an action or process which is repeated by the same subject on more than one occasion), habitual (used for a habit, only with animate beings as subject), and continuous (referring to an activity or process which is prolonged beyond its normal duration) are three aspects of verbal plurality which in practice are difficult to distinguish and partly overlap. The difference between frequentative and continuous concerns the meaning of the verb: punctual, telic verbs are typically frequentative; durative, atelic ones are typically continuous. Habitual forms occur in both types. Common examples of frequentative Gtn-stems are telic verbs such as *nadû* "to leave, to put down", *šapāru* "to send", *šakānu* "to place", *leqû* "to receive", and *petû* "to open". Continuous ones are *bakû* "to cry", *dagālu* "to watch", *damāmu* "to mourn", and *še'û* "to look for". It is often difficult to establish - and rather inconsequential for the interpretation - whether a Gtn form refers to a repeated or a prolonged action, as in:

(03) YOS 10, 41: 55f *wāšib mahrika [kar]ṣīka i-ta-na-ka-al* "a personal servant of yours will constantly (or repeatedly) slander you".

(04) ACh. Ad. 9: 4 *šumma Adad iš-ta-na-as-si* "if Adad thunders constantly (or repeatedly)".

The precise meaning of such forms is often specified by temporal adverbs such as *ūmišam* "daily", *warhišam* "monthly", *šanassu* or *šattišam* "annually" *ginâ* "regularly", by pronominal elements such as *mala* or *mimma ša* "everything which", or by repetition of a constituent of the sentence, as in (02) above and in:

(05) CT 6, 2: case 1 *āl pāṭija ana nakrim awātim awātim i-za-na-bi-il* "a city near my border will constantly carry news to the enemy" (reading and tr. CAD sv *zabālu* 1e)

On the other hand, *-tan-* forms are generally not used if an exact (real or conventional) number of occurrences is specified; cf. the following examples of expressions frequently found in OB letters:

(06) Ét. Garelli 153: 40f *1-šu 2-šu aš-pu-ra-kum-ma* "I wrote to you once and twice" (idem ARM 5, 54: 5ff; cf. also 27, 57: 4f with *bakû* "to complain"; 10, 173: 13 with *qabû* "to say";

(07) AbB 13, 155: 6 During the last ten days *hamšīšu aš-tap-ra-kum* "I have written to you five times" (also 10, 77: 10f with *qabû* "to say");

(08) ARM 18, 8: 6 *1 šu-š[i]-šu aq-bé-ek-kum* "I told you sixty times"

The combination of Gtn forms with such numerals is very unusual (e.g., AbB 3, 15: 10f), cf. CAD ssvv *šinīšu, šalāšīšu, erbēšu, hamšīšu, šeššīšu,* and *ešrīšu.*

4.2.3. Plurality

In the instances mentioned so far in 4.2.2 the plural element lies in the action itself, since the clauses in question - apart from (05) - do not contain other plural elements. However, numerous Gtn forms occur in sentences which contain one or more plural participants. In that case the Gtn-stem may still refer to a repeated or prolonged action, but it can also refer to an action which is, on a single occasion, performed by more subjects, undergone by more objects or directed at more persons or entities. This makes the plural nature of the action a corollary of the plural nature of one of those constituents.

Thus if one of the constituents of the sentence is plural, the Gtn-stem does not automatically refer to a repeated or prolonged action, but may also be distributive (cf. Dressler 1968: 70; Hecker 1968: 144), i.e., it may indicate that a plurality of subjects perform an action individually and/or successively:

(09) RA 65, 74: 68' *ṣehherūtu ina nārim im-ta-nu-ut-tu* "children will die one after the other in the river" (tr. CAD sv *mâtu* 1a-o'; more examples *ib.* p. 425a bottom);

(10) Slm.Mon. II 73 *ma'dūtīšu ana kāpi ša šadê i-ta-na-qu-tu-ni* "many of them hurled themselves off the cliff of the mountain" (tr. CAD sv *mādu* d) 3' a');

(11) KAV 1: II 67f (If a man has said to another man:) *aššatka it-ti-ni-ik-ku* "everybody has sex with your wife";

(12) MVAeG 41/3, 14: 4f *šulmānāte [ana] šarri uq-ṭa-na-ru-bu* "(the officials) offer presents to the king", i.e., on a single occasion, but, presumably, one by one, each one individually; cf. *ib.* 5f *šulmāna pānīa ša ana šarri [ú]-qar-ri-bu-ni* "the former present which they offered to the king" (they shall bring to the temple of Assur), and *ib.* 7f *ištu nāmurāte ana šarri ú-qar-ri-bu-ni* "after they have offered presents to the king", where the distributive character of the action - which lies in the past - is irrelevant and thus left unexpressed.

or that an action is aimed at a plurality of persons (often with *šapāru* "to send"):

(13) AbB 13, 8: 5ff (as soon as you have read this letter of mine) *ana šāpir mātim ša lītim šapiltim ša qātika [š]i-ta-ap-pa-ar* "issue a written order to all the governors of the lower district who are under your authority" (tr. Van Soldt); cf. also *ib.* 9: 11;

(14) MARI 5, 165: 39ff *ši-ta-ap-pa-ar* <<X>> *warkat mê ša ina harrānātim šināti ibaššû [da]mqiš li-pa-ri-su-ni-kum-ma* "send (messengers) (everywhere, cf. Durand: "partout") in order that they thoroughly investigate for you the water (supplies) which are along those roads" (with the indirect object or a directional element implied in the context; note the connection between the use of Gtn and the unusual D form of (*warkatam*) *parāsu*, cf. 6.4.1.1 sv *parāsu*); also ARM 14, 121: 29;

(15) RA 74, 117: 10ff x silver PN *abbābātīšu i-ta-na-di-in* "PN will give x silver for his debts" (to three creditors, cf. Charpin's note on p. 118);

(16A) ARM 27, 107: 6ff PN_1 paid (*iš-ta-qa-al*) x silver to PN_2 and last year PN_1 paid (*iš-qú-la-am*) that silver to me";

(16B) *ib.* 11ff x silver *ša* PN_1 *ana* PN_2 *u ajjâšim iš-ta-aq-qa-al* (sic) "x silver that PN_1 paid to PN_2 and me" (with G plus a dative singular versus Gtn plus a dative plural).

or that an action occurs in several places or on several occasions in succession;

(17) YOS 10, 31: IX 51ff *išātum ina mātim it-ta-na-an-pa-ah* "Fire will be lighted (everywhere) in the land" (Ntn);

(18) BE 15, 7: 1f (Barley) *ša ina qāt* PN_1 *ṭupš[arri]* PN_2 *li-te-eq-qu-ú* "which PN_2 has received (on various occasions) from PN_1, the scribe"; cf. also *ib.* 48: 3 with *mahāru* Gtn;

(19) KAR 4: r.12 *šumēšunu ta-za-na-kà[r]* "you name them one after the other" (tr. CAD sv *zakāru* A 4a);

(20) Gilg. XI 211 (Bake bread for him and) *ši-tak-ka-ni ina rēšīšu* "place one (loaf) after another at his head" (tr. CAD sv *šakānu* 1a-13' (p. 120f);

This nuance is also prominent in verbs such as *šâmu* Gtn "to buy one by one, here and there" (CAD sv *š*. A 2) and *mahāru* Gtn "to receive (tribute) regularly", which is common in RIs (CAD sv 6b).

Very common is the use of the Gtn-stem with a plural object in those verbs which do not have a D-stem, such as *apālu* "to pay" (cf. CAD sv a. A 2d-2'), *leqû* "to receive", *nadû* "to leave, to put down", *šemû* "to hear" and *šakānu* "to place". This is especially common in SB, where we often meet expressions such as *(mimma) epšēt ēteppušu* "(all) the deeds which I have done" (discussed by Poebel 1939: 32f). It is one of the points on which the Gtn- and the D-stem are complementary, since many D-stems of transitive verbs are also used to underline plurality of the direct object, cf. 6.4, and especially 6.7.3 about *retû* D versus Gtn. A few randomly selected examples are:

(21) Gilg. X v 26f *e-te-et-ti-qa šadê marṣūti e-te-te-bi-ra kalīšina tâmātum* "I passed through inaccessible mountains and crossed all the seas";

(22) AfO 25, 39: 12 *dalpāte mal a-tam-ma-ru* "(all) the troubles which I have experienced";

(23) SpTU 3, 80: 32 *šunātu pardāta ša at-ta-aṭ-ṭa-lu* "the terrifying dreams I have seen";

(24) RIMA 1, 64f: III' 7ff *ālāni dannāti ša māt GN kalāšunu ina Magrānim ú-ṣa-ab-bi-it-ma bīrātīja lū aš-ta-ak-ka-an* "in the month of Magrānum I captured all the fortified cities of the land of GN. I established my garrisons everywhere" (tr. Grayson) (with *ṣabātu* D beside *šakānu* Gtn, cf. 6.7.3).

In these cases plurality of action and plurality of object are mutually implicit; strictly speaking the Gtn is redundant, but it doubtless contains a nuance of emphasis and/or totality, as compared to the corresponding G-stem, cf. especially:

(25) ABRT 1, 4: I 12f (If so-and-so's wife) SAL.meš *it-ta-na-al-la-du*(! sign IŠ)*-ma* [...] *zikaru ja'nūma* "gives birth to one girl after another, but there is no boy" (tr. CAD sv *alādu* 1a-2').

If the Gtn-stem is accompanied by one or more plural constituents, it is sometimes difficult to determine whether the action itself is repeated, i.e., whether it is frequentative or continuous, or whether plurality only lies in the participants. Consider the following examples, where several options are mentioned in the translation:

(26) ARM 27, 89: 20ff PN *ana GN illikamma ana šarrāni iš-ta-ap-pa-ar-ma mamm*[*an*] *ina šarrāni ul illikšumma* "as soon as PN arrived in GN, he sent (or: kept sending) (messengers) to the kings, but none of the kings has come to him"; comparable instances of *šapāru* suggest that Gtn does not imply a repeated action but the action of sending persons to different places, cf. (13) and (14).

(27) ARM 4, 24: 24f lú.meš *tu-ru-ku-ú bi-te-ru-ú mākalam ul išû* "The Turukkaeans are constantly hungry; they have no food" (tr. CAD sv *berû* B v. 1a-3'); or: "all the Turukkaeans" ?;

(28) FM 1 p. 63: 32ff *annêtim* PN_1 [...] PN_2 *u* PN_3 [...] *war*<*ki*> giš.ig.t[ab.ba] *iš*$_7$*-te-né-mu-ú* "all these things, from beginning to end, PN_1, PN_2 and PN_3 (over)heard (hidden) behind the double doors"; or: "each one of them"? (Ghouti: "Cela, PN_1 (... etc.) l'ont parfaitement entendu".

(29) CT 38, 1: 18 *šumma ālānu ekurrātu qaqqassunu* (sic) *ana šamê it-ta-na-aš-ša-a* "if the cities' sanctuaries raise their tops to the sky everywhere"; or: "all the sanctuaries" ? Contrast *ib.* 15 *šumma ālu qaqqassu ana libbi šamê* íl (= probably *naši*, cf. CAD sv *n.* A 2a-2' a') "if the city raises its top to the sky".

There are some other Gtn forms which are difficult to interpret as to the nuance of plurality they convey:

(30) AfO 18, 67: 28 and 31f *šumma awīlum inūma ṣallu ālum im-ta-na-qú-ta-šum* "if a man, when he sleeps, (dreams that) the entire city is falling upon him" (tr. CAD sv 1a); possibly "that the city constantly threatens to fall upon him", cf. (33) below and ARM 27, 59: 22, where the same nuance fits the context quite well (cf. *ib.* 29);

(31) ARM 14, 7: 6 *DN* (...) *rigimšu udannin abnam ra-ab-bi-tam it-ta-ad-di* "Adad (i.e., a thunderstorm) has raged violently (lit. "Adad has made his thunder strong") and has deposited an enormous rock" (Birot: "Addu (...) a renversé une pierre énorme".

The use of the Gtn form in (31) is remarkable because the sentence does not seem to imply any nuance of plurality. Moreover, it contains another irregularity, namely the use of *rabbû* with a singular noun, cf. 3.1.3.1 sv. Possibly, both the Gtn form and the adjective with gemination underline the enormity of the stone(mass); a parallel of this use may be found in ARM 6, 5: 12f, quoted as (18) in Chapter VI, where, by way of exception, the D-stem of *hepû* is used with a singular object, also *abnum,* cf. 6.4.9.

Sometimes it is claimed that the Gtn-stem can also have an intensive meaning (Hecker 1968: 142). This may be the case in lexicalized expressions such as *lamādu* Gtn "gründlich studieren" acc. to AHw sv Gtn 2 (OA) (but CAD sv 6: "referring to a plurality of objects"), *šemû* Gtn "immer wieder genau anhören" acc. to AHw sv Gtn 1d, and *amāru* in the stative Gtn "genau kennen" acc. to AHw sv Gtn 2, doubtless literally "to have frequently seen"; cf. also *šasû* Gtn "immer wieder (vor)lesen, studieren", acc. to AHw sv Gtn 13. However, convincing examples of non-lexicalized intensive Gtn forms do not seem to be attested.[17]

4.3. The role of gemination in the Gtn-stem

There is an important difference between the Gtn-stem and the nominal patterns *parras, parris* and *parrās* with regard to the role of gemination. As we saw in 3.4, in the latter categories the forms with and without gemination basically have the same function, but the geminate can be used to underline either the salient and plural nature of the word group (in *parras* forms of adjectives denoting dimensions), or the more nominal character of the word, as opposed to the more verbal character of *pāris* (in the agent nouns derived from fientive verbs).

The relationship between the Gtn-stem and the corresponding simple pattern, the G-stem, is quite different. As argued in 4.1.2.1, the Gtn-stem arose as a result of the insertion of a geminate in a form with infixed *-ta-* with resultative meaning (*iptaras*), which had the secondary, contextually determined function of expressing durativity. Since the creation of the Gtn-stem, this latter function has become obsolete, and *iptaras* predominantly serves to express a perfect. Therefore, apart from a few residual cases (the Gt-stems mentioned in 4.1.2.1), the Gtn-stem is no longer an optional alternative to *iptaras*, but contrasts with the G-stem both in form and in function, as a fully independent category, which is not restricted to underlining a feature which is already present in the context, but can express verbal plurality by itself, independent of the context. In this respect it differs from the nominal patterns discussed in Chapter III, especially from the *parras* forms of 3.1.3, cf. 3.4.

In contrast to these patterns, therefore, and also to the D-stems of transitive verbs to be discussed in Chapter VI and the *purrus* forms to be discussed in Chapter XI, we find contrasting pairs of G- and Gtn-stems which do not differ in any other respect from each other, such as the following:

(32) CT 40, 12: 7/8 *šumma sikkat namzaqi ša bīt ištari is-ki-il* / *is-sà-na-ki-il* "if the lock pin of the temple of a goddess has got stuck / gets stuck all the time" (cf. 6.6.1);

(33) TDP 8: 20f *šumma ṣēru ana muhhi marṣi imqut* (šub) (...) / *šumma ṣēru ana muhhi marṣi imtanaqqut* (šub.šub-*ut*) "if a snake has fallen on a sick man, (he will die on the third day) / if a snake constantly threatens to fall on a sick man, (his illness wil be long, but he will recover)" (for the translation cf. (30) above);

(34A) ÖB 2, 65: 52 *šumma ina libbi ummatim šulmū mādūtum ú-ṣú-nim-ma* "if many bubbles have appeared from the mass (of oil)";

(34B) *ib.* 66: 61 *šumma ina libbi ummatim šulmū mādūtum it-ta-na-ṣú-nim* "if many bubbles keep appearing from the mass (of oil)".

Other instances are BagF. 16, 261: 65f; TDP 10: 31f; 48 C II: 6ff; Dreams 330: 56f; CT 38, 1: 15ff (= (29)); 39, 44: 10f; Izbu 172: 100'f; MSL 11, 28: 10'f; cf. also an expression such as AbB 13, 149: 25f *kīma ta-ag-da-na-am-mi-la-an-ni gi-im-la-an-ni* "oblige me as you have always obliged me" (tr. Van Soldt). In this respect the Gtn-stem represents a more advanced stage in the process of grammaticalization than the patterns *parras, parris* and *parrās* (see further Chapter XII).

Notes to Chapter Four

1 A well-known case of the preservation of a morpheme which carries an important grammatical contrast against the workings of sound change is the -σ- which characterizes the future tense in Classical Greek. Normally, a -σ- is lost between vowels, but in the future it was preserved to prevent the future from becoming indistinguishable from the present, cf. Anttila 1989: 98f.

2 Edzard (1962: 116b note 30) quotes two similar cases: Ee VII 46 *liš-tal-li-lu* "may they (the gods) keep making ovations", from *alālu* Štn, and AbB 9, 66: 11 *šu-ta-ar-ri-ih*; the latter form is, however, a Dt of *šarāhu* rather than a Štn of *arāhu*, as assumed by Stol ("hurry!") and the dictionaries, see 9.1.1 with note 3.

3 See GAG § 92-94 for the basic facts; I will generally adhere to the views of Kuryłowicz (1972: 61f); other, often more speculative, proposals have been made by Von Soden (1962); Loprieno (1986: 124ff), and Voigt (1987a: 88f). Diem (1982: 73ff) is mainly concerned with formal matters.

4 Cf. Rundgren 1963b: 64; D. Cohen 1984: 265. This feature of the stative is discussed and documented in great detail by Rowton 1962. It is perhaps most strikingly illustrated by the fact that many scholars call the stative "permansive". However, this durative nuance of the stative is a typical "secondary function" in the sense in which this term is used by Kuryłowicz (for instance, 1964: 14ff), i.e., a function which is determined by the context and the lexical meaning of the word in question.

5 The claim made by Von Soden in GAG § 92c that "die Grundfunktion des *ta*-Infixes von Gt, Dt und Št ist gewiss eine richtungsändernde" does not help us any further to understand the Gt-stem, even though it may superficially apply to two (not all!) of its uses, the passive/reciprocal and the separative one. It is an attempt to formulate a common denominator to cover the various meanings of Gt verbs and does not say anything about the function of the Gt-stem as a grammatical category. Functions of grammatical categories should be formulated in grammatical terms, which "change of direction" is obviously not (cf. also Streck 1995: 217f).

6 The fact that these remnants largely consist of reciprocal and reflexive verbs and not of passives, is not due to semantic reasons, as is clear from the existence of reciprocal and reflexive N-stems (GAG[2] § 90f), but to the relatively high degree of lexicalization of such verbs: they were less dependent on the corresponding G-stem than ordinary passive forms and therefore had more chance to survive as more or less isolated entities.

7 The separative Gt-stems (GAG § 92e) should be in a class of their own, because they represent a semantic function of the infix, which is quite different from grammatical functions as reciprocal or durative. Moreover, there is a fundamental difference between the real separative Gt-stems *atluku* "to depart" and **etlû* "to lose" (+ *ina*) on the one hand, and cases as *(w)aṣû* vs. *taṣû*, "go out", or *(w)abālu* vs. *tabālu* "to carry (away)" on the other hand, which are the result of an accidental phonological circumstance, namely, the fact that *w* assimilates to a following *t*, so that the cluster *-tt-* is ambiguous (already in Proto-Semitic, cf. Diem 1982: 39f); this allowed a form as *ittaṣi* < *iwtaṣi* to be reanalysed as resulting from *ittaṣi*, which led to a secondary verb stem with *t* as first radical. The semantic differentiation found in *(w)abālu* "to bring" vs. *tabālu* "to take away" is also secondary; it is absent from other pairs as *(w)aṣû* and *taṣû*, *(w)ašābu* and **tašābu* (only imperative *ti/ašab* attested) "sit (down)" and OAk *wamā'um* vs. later *tamû* "to swear". The fact that *-tt-* can also be the result of assimilation of *-nt-* gave rise to the Assyrian variant *tadānu* of *nadānu* "to give" through the same process. Cf. Kuryłowicz 1972: 8 note 5, for similar cases in Arabic.

8 The *muptarrisu* participles are either Gtn, Dt or Dtn forms; Reiner and Renger opt for Dt, since they see no functional opposition between Gt and either Gtn or Dtn which could account for the coexistence of such pairs of near-synonymous forms, and claim a Gt : Dt opposition with Dt for plurality, such as exists between G and D (1974/77: 184f). This, however, gives rise to the following objections: 1) such a Gt : Dt opposition is attested for only one verb (*kaṣāru*) on the authority of Edzard 1962: 116f (but see 9.1.5 for additional instances; 2) the association of the *muptarrisu* participles with plurality is very tenuous, cf. the comments of the authors on p. 185; 3) Most of the verbs involved have a common Gtn- stem (except *mahāṣu* and the very obscure verb *šapātu*), but only a few of them have a common D-stem (*mahāṣu*, *šarāhu* and *nakāpu*, apart from *rapādu*, whose D-stem has quite a different meaning).

An unbiased consideration of these participles leads to the conclusion that they are more likely to be Gtn forms. In fact, it is the Gt participles which are problematical, since they do not conform to the usual reciprocal or separative function of the Gt-stem. The relationship between Gt- and Gtn-stem assumed here offers a straightforward solution: they are remnants of a use of the Gt-stem which was almost completely replaced by its successor, the Gtn-stem.

9 The former characteristic is caused by the different vowel classes of the fientive forms of the verb (GAG § 87a/d) and the three different patterns of the stative G (*paris*, *parus* and *paras*). The second can be exemplified by the fact that in the G-stem the infinitive and the verbal adjective both have a separate form (*parāsu* and *parsu*, respectively), whereas in the derived stems they have the same form (*purrusu*, *šuprusu*, *naprusu*, etc.). For other examples see below.

10 The explanation of *ušakkal* proposed by Voigt 1987b: 251f, viz., that it is derived from **uša'kal* by "die einfache Regel (*'k*): → *kk*", has to be rejected because such a simple rule does not exist in Akkadian. The rule is that in the cluster /*'k*/ the *aleph* is lost after a vowel, and the vowel itself is lengthened (cf. GAG § 24e).

11 See note 1 to Chapter V. The number of 88 Ntn-stems does not include 10 cases derived from quadriliteral verbs, which have to be regarded as a separate class. This accounts for the different number mentioned in the note.

12 For the Dtn-stem the problem is whether *uptarris* is a perfect D or a preterite Dtn (the pret. Dt is usually easy to identify because of its passive or intransitive meaning), cf. 9.2.1. Even more ambiguous is *uštapris*, which can be perfect Š, preterite Štn and preterite of the "lexical" Št, which is often transitive. The only safe criterion to ascertain whether a Dtn-, Štn- or Ntn-stem of a specific verb is actually attested is the existence of a present form with the infix *-tana-*. A considerable number of those listed in AHw do not meet this criterion.

13 According to the references of AHw (cf. note 1 to Chapter V), 49 out of 88 Dtn-stems, 30 out of 53 Štn-stems and 45 out of 98 Ntn-stems are hapax legomena. Only a handful of Dtn-stems occur more than a few times (*kullu*, *nâdu*, *nakāru*, *parādu*, *šanû* "to repeat, to narrate", *šarāhu* "to praise", *šurru*, *târu* and *(w)âru*), cf. 9.2. The only common Štn-stems are those of *(w)abālu* "to bring" and of *(w)aṣû* "to go out". The Ntn-stem, on the other hand, is more frequent: there are about 25 Ntn-stems which occur occasionally, although they are not really common. There are some indications that the Ntn-stem is not simply an iterative of the passive N-stem, but has other uses as well, cf. 4.1.2.3.

14 The same derivational rule is posited by Voigt (1987b: 249f) to account for the Gtn forms. Voigt, however, regards **iptanras* as the real underlying form, characterized by an infix *-tan-*, whereas in Kuryłowicz's view it is a form which does not actually exist, but results from an analysis of *iptarras* which is strictly speaking unetymological.

15 Another instance of this procedure is the creation of a present *inaddin* or *inaddan* beside the preterite *iddin* "he gave". These forms replace (and in Assyrian coexist with) the older apophonic present *iddan*: **indin* → *inaddin*. The form *inaddan* with both apophony and gemination is a blend of the old and the new form, comparable to the "mixed type presents" discussed by Knudsen 1984/86: 233f. See CAD N/1 43f for the distribution of these present forms over the dialects. The fact that the preterite is always *iddin*, whereas the form of the present fluctuates, testifies to the relatively recent origin of the present *i-parras*.

16 Well-known instances are Speiser's claim about the Hitpa^cel in Hebrew (1967: 506ff), and Goetze's analysis, discussed in 1.8, of the "apparent D forms" (1942: 6b). These and similar claims are superfluous in the light of the typically polysemous nature of "verbal plurality", cf. 2.1.5 with note 6 to Chapter II.

17 It seems doubtful whether the OA instance CCT 3, 20: 17f *kīma ṣuhartum i-ir-ta-bi-ú-ni* contains a preterite Gtn, as Hecker (1968: 144) claims ("weil die Kleine sehr groß geworden ist"); it rather looks like a perfect G even though the notion of intensity is expressed later in the same letter (38f) with *ṣuhartum danniš ir-tí-bi* "the girl has fully grown up". The rules of Assyrian vowel harmony do not seem to exclude the possibility that *-b-* is a single consonant, cf. Hecker 1968: 19f, against 72 (§ 47c) and 135 (§ 79g).

CHAPTER FIVE

THE D-STEM AND TRANSITIVITY

5.0. This chapter serves as an introduction to the detailed discussion of the D-stem in Chapters VI to VIII. The D-stem is not only by far the most important category with gemination of the second radical in Akkadian, but also the most frequent among the derived verbal stems. About 935 roots exhibit D forms, ranging from a single form - usually a *purrus* adjective or stative, e.g., *šu"uru* "hairy", sometimes a participle, e.g., *muna"išu* "veterinarian", lit. "healer" - to a complete verbal paradigm.[1]

Because of this enormous number of words to be discussed and the variety of functions the D-stem can have, it is convenient to make a twofold division. We will first divide the total range of forms which are traditionally assigned to the D-stem into into three categories: *purrus* adjectives, D tantum verbs and verbal D-stems; next we will concentrate on the verbal D-stems, and divide them into four types depending on their relationship to the corresponding G-stem. Each of these categories represents a different aspect of the D-stem and gives rise to specific problems. The main part of this chapter will be concerned with the relationship between the verbal D-stem and high transitivity.

5.1. A preliminary classification of D forms

5.1.1. *Purrus* adjectives

The first distinction we will make is that between the nominal pattern *purrus* and the verbal D-stem. The former is an adjectival pattern which is traditionally defined as intensive (e.g., GAG § 55n). It is closely related to the adjectival *parras* forms discussed in 3.1.3, a relationship which is more evident from its Assyrian form *parrus*. Both patterns serve to derive adjectives with gemination from simple adjectives and are partly complementary (cf. 3.1.3.3).

For a D-stem to qualify as verbal, at least one unambiguous verbal form should be attested. The forms which demonstrate the existence of a verbal paradigm (cf. Bybee 1985: 49) are the prefix conjugations, the imperative, the infinitive and the participle, i.e., all forms apart from the stative and the verbal adjective (VA). We cannot deduce the existence of a verbal paradigm from a stative or a VA, because it has an ambiguous position: in a fientive verb, it is dependent on, and derived from, the verbal paradigm, since it denotes the result of the action expressed by that paradigm (e.g., *nadānu* "give" → *nadin* "he/it has (been) given"). In other cases, however, it is the predicative form of an adjective and may exist without any corresponding verbal paradigm (e.g., *zaqin* "he has a beard"). A VA is by definition derived from a verbal paradigm, but there is no consistent formal difference between VAs and basic adjectives in Akkadian, so that often we cannot determine which of the two a given word is.

However, the pattern *purrus* has two functions: it is not only a nominal pattern for adjectives, but also serves as the stative and VA of the D-stem. Thus we find, on the one hand, adjectives like *gubbuhu* "bald" and *šu''uru* "hairy", and, on the other hand, statives like *(w)uššur* "he has been released" (with the VA *(w)uššuru* "released", cf. AHw sv) and *buzzu'āku* "I have been treated unjustly" (e.g., AbB 9, 104: 20), which belong to the verbal D-stems *(w)uššuru* "to release" and *buzzu'u* "to treat unjustly". It is not always possible to establish to which type a given *purrus* form belongs; this makes the distinction proposed here somewhat problematical. In Chapter X, which is concerned with the nominal *purrus* forms, additional criteria and a more detailed argumentation will be given.

In the remainder of this study, the adjectives will be called "*purrus* adjectives" or "*purrus* forms" and the verbs "verbal D-stems" or simply "D-stems".

5.1.2. D tantum verbs

Next we will divide the verbal D-stems into two types, according to whether or not they are dependent upon a corresponding verbal G-stem of the same root.[2] D-stems which are not dependent upon a G-stem - either because it does not exist or because it differs so strongly in meaning that it is likely to belong to a homonymous root rather than to the same root - will be called "D tantum verbs".

This classification is motivated by the fact that the presence or absence of a contrasting verbal stem results in a different status for the derived stem. If a G- and a D-stem of the same root coexist, the D-stem usually denotes some predictable modification of the G-stem. For instance, if the G-stem denotes an intransitive event, the corresponding D-stem denotes its transitive counterpart (*pahāru* "to come together" vs. *puhhuru* "to bring together"). This makes it possible to assign one or more grammatical functions to the D-stem, such as "factitive" for the relationship between *pahāru* and *puhhuru*. The existence of such a function depends on its contrast with the G-stem.

The D tantum verbs, however, do not enter into such a contrast and, therefore, do not have a grammatical function. They are independent verbs with the same grammatical status as G-stems. The question they raise is not what their function is, but why they have the formal characteristics of the D-stem rather than those of the neutral (unmarked) G-stem. The answer must be sought in their etymological background or in their semantic nature. The D tantum verbs will be discussed in Chapter VIII.

Sometimes it is uncertain whether a D-stem is a D tantum verb or not; it is debatable, for instance, whether *lupputu* "to tarry, to be delayed" is a D-stem of *lapātu* "to touch, to smear, to affect", or whether it belongs to a homonymous root without a G-stem. As a general rule, cases in which the semantic connection between G and D is not obvious, have been classified as D tantum verbs.

5.1.3. Verbal D-stems

Now that we have made separate categories for the *purrus* adjectives and the D tantum verbs, we are only left with verbal D-stems which are dependent upon a verbal G-stem of the same root. The criterion for qualifying as a verbal D-stem was discussed in 5.1.1: it must be attested in a form which unambiguously belongs to the verbal paradigm, i.e., not exclusively as a stative or VA. If, however, such a form denotes a state which can only be the result of an action, it is plausible to assume that the stative in question belongs to a verbal paradigm, of which accidentally no forms are attested that are unambiguously verbal. Thus some of the verbal D-stems to be listed in the next chapter occur only in the stative, or even as a VA; they are all very rare and/or restricted to a single context, cf. the Appendix to Chapter VI sv *(h)alālu, puāgu, šapāṣu* and *šatāqu.*

The rest of this chapter and the Chapters VI and VII will deal exclusively with the verbal D-stems which are dependent upon a corresponding G-stem.

5.2. The four Types of verbal D-stems

The use of the verbal D-stems must be described in terms of their contrast with the corresponding G-stems. Since this contrast involves either a change in valency or the absence of such a change, four types of verbal D-stems will be distinguished on the basis of their valency relationship to the G-stem. Taking the G-stem as a starting point seems the best procedure.

Type I are the transitive G-stems whose D-stem is also transitive, e.g., *petû* and *puttû*, both of them meaning "to open" (trans.).

Type II are the intransitive G-stems whose D is also intransitive, e.g., *sa'ālu* and *su''ulu* "to cough".

Type III are the intransitive G-stems with a transitive D-stem, e.g., *pahāru* "to come together" versus *puhhuru* "to bring together". This is the well-known factitive function of the D-stem (GAG § 88c).

Type IV are the transitive G-stems whose D-stem is claimed to be doubly transitive, e.g., *lamādu* "to know, learn" versus *lummudu* "to inform, teach".

Most verbs can be assigned to one of these four types without difficulty. A few verbs, however, raise problems because they are borderline cases between transitive and intransitive. They will be discussed in 5.5.1 and 5.5.3.

A common feature of Types I and II is that their D-stem has the same valency as the G-stem; I will call such D-stems "valency-preserving". As such they contrast with the verbs of Types III and IV, which have as a common feature that the D-stem indicates a higher valency than the G-stem. I will call these D-stems "valency-extending".

Another important distinction contrasts Types II and IV, on the one hand, with Types I and III, on the other; this contrast concerns the number of verbs falling under them: Types I and III are very numerous and therefore represent the "regular" cases, whereas Types II and IV comprise only a small number of verbs and can be considered "marginal". Type II mainly consists of verbs denoting sounds and bodily functions, and will be discussed in 7.6. Type IV comprises a few verbs which usually have an accusative complement and as such qualify as transitive, and whose D-stem appears to involve the addition of an extra participant. Apart from *lamādu,* the most prominent example is *labāšu* G "to put on (clothes)", D "to clothe sb else, to provide sb with clothes". I will argue in 5.5.2 that these verbs are a subtype of the intransitive G-stems of type III.

If we do not consider the marginal types, it can be stated as a general rule that of the two grammatical functions the D-stem has,[3] the valency-preserving function applies to transitive, and the valency-extending function to intransitive verbs, a state of affairs which was already established by Poebel (1939: 5 note 1, unjustifiably criticized by Goetze 1942: 2 note 26). Each of the two functions gives rise to different problems: the main problem of the valency-preserving D-stems to be discussed in Chapter VI concerns the difference between G and D (if any), in view of the fact that there is no difference in valency. The problem with the valency-extending or factitive function of the D-stem lies in its relationship to its other uses (cf. 1.4 and 1.5); this problem will be discussed in Chapter VII.

The fact that the D-stems of intransitive verbs are valency extending and those of transitive verbs valency preserving leads to the situation that almost all D-stems are transitive; this is true of all types except the marginal Type II, the intransitive D-stems of intransitive G-stems. In addition, some D tantum verbs are intransitive, such as *uhhuru* "to be delayed", and *šurru* "to bend, lean or go down", or can be intransitive, such as those meaning "to pray" (see 5.5.1, 8.6 and 8.7), and *duppuru* "to go away" or "to drive away". All other D-stems are basically transitive.

5.3. High and low transitivity

Transitivity, then, is an important overall characteristic of the verbal D-stem. In fact, we can be even more specific, and establish a close association between the use of the D-stem and the concept of high transitivity, as it is defined by Hopper and Thompson (1980).

They consider transitivity to be "a global property of an entire clause" and suggest that the opposition transitive vs. intransitive is not binary, but gradual, in other words, clauses should be considered more or less transitive, rather than transitive or intransitive. They establish a scale from high to low transitivity, in which the clauses with high transitivity typically show the following properties (1980: 252):

1. they have two or more participants;
2. they describe actions rather than states;
3. these actions are telic, i.e., they are viewed from their endpoint and it is suggested that they are carried out in their entirety (e.g., *I ate it up* is more transitive than *I am eating it*);
4. they are punctual because "actions carried out with no obvious transitional phase between inception and completion have a more marked effect on their patients than actions which are inherently on-going." (e.g., a clause with *kick* (punctual) is ceteris paribus more transitive than one with *carry* (non-punctual));
5. they are volitional, i.e., they describe actions which are carried out purposefully (e.g., *I wrote your name* is more transitive than *I forgot your name*);
6. they are affirmative rather than negative;
7. they are real rather than non-real;
8. they have an agent which is high in potency;
9. their object is totally affected,
10. and highly individuated, i.e., it comprises nouns which are proper, human or animate, concrete, singular, count, referential and definite rather than common, inanimate, abstract, plural, non-count and non-referential.

On the other hand, clauses with a low transitivity have characteristically one participant, describe a non-action, are atelic, non-punctual, non-volitional, negative and non-real, have an agent low in potency and an object which is not affected and non-individuated.

Each of these properties involves a different facet of the effectiveness with which the action is transferred from one participant to another; taken together they allow clauses to be characterized as more or less transitive (1980: 253): the more features they have which belong to "high transitivity", the more transitive they are.

Hopper and Thompson claim (1980: 254) that all these features co-vary extensively and systematically within a clause, and this leads them to "a claim about a universal property of grammars" formulated as the Transitivity Hypothesis (1980: 255):

> "If two clauses (a) and (b) in a language differ in that (a) is higher in Transitivity according to any of the features 1A-J [i.e. 1. to 10. above], then, if a concomitant grammatical or semantic difference appears elsewhere in the clause, that difference will also show (a) to be higher in Transitivity."

The correctness of this hypothesis is illustrated with evidence from a wide range of languages (1980: 256ff), cf. also Hopper and Thompson (1982).

The authors claim that, ultimately, the explanation of the salience of those features which combine to cause high or low transitivity is to be found in discourse, more specifically in the distinction between foregrounding and backgrounding: high transitivity correlates with foregrounding, low transitivity with backgrounding (1980: 284ff; 294f).

5.4. High transitivity and salience

In this view, the question whether a clause is transitive or not, is not determined by a single criterion - in this case, the presence of an object - but by the presence or absence of a number of properties; the more of these properties are found, the higher the degree of transitivity; therefore, transitivity is a *prototype category*.[4] If all, or almost all, criterial properties are present, we can speak of *prototypical transitivity*.

Givón (1990: 565f), defines a prototypical transitive clause as involving, first, "a volitional, controlling, initiating, active agent, one that is responsible for the event, i.e. its salient cause"; second, "an inactive, non-volitional, non-controlling patient, one that registers the changes-of-state associated with the event, i.e. its salient effect"; and, third, "a compact (non-durative), bounded (non-lingering), realis (non-hypothetical) verb and tense-aspect-modality", representing "an event that is fast-moving, completed and real, i.e. perceptually and cognitively salient."

If a clause deviates in some respect from the prototype, this results in a reduced degree of transitivity, for example, if the object is inanimate (*Liquor killed him*), if it is omitted, or if it is only partly affected by the action. The degree of transitivity is also reduced when the sentence is, for instance, passive rather than active, negative rather than affirmative, or non-real rather than real (Givón 1984: 20ff; 98ff).

Givón, then, emphasizes the strong correlation between high transitivity and *salience*: in his definition of the "prototypical transitive clause" quoted above, the agent is the "salient cause", and the object the "salient effect" of the clause, and also the verb is "perceptually and cognitively salient" (cf. also 1984: 96ff). Generally speaking, the more salient the agent, the effect of the action on the patient and the event itself are, the higher the degree of transitivity of the clause in which they occur. In this respect, Givón's views differ from those of Hopper and Thompson, who lay more emphasis on the correlation of high transitivity with foregrounding and backgrounding; the two views seem to be complementary rather than contrasting, however. Wallace (1982: 211ff), suggests that the transitivity scale is part of a larger hierarchy of salience, which is ultimately based on the distinction between "figure" and "ground" of Gestalt psychology: the "figure" is that part of a visual phenomenon "which stands out distinctly from the rest (the "ground")". The importance of these views on transitivity lies in the fact that they offer a pragmatic motivation for the role of transitivity in language.

Although the degree of transitivity is principally bound to the clause as a whole and is influenced by the nature of the participants and other modalities, the meaning of the verb is the predominant factor in determining the degree of transitivity of a clause.[5] Therefore, we can define verbs which typically occur in sentences exhibiting many of the features of high transitivity as "prototypical transitive verbs".

On the other hand, there are also verbs which typically occur in sentences with a low degree of transitivity and can, therefore, be defined as "verbs of low transitivity". To this type belong, in the first place, the verbs which the traditional view classifies as intransitive. More consequential, however, is that it also comprises verbs which normally have an object, but fail to meet most other conditions for high transitivity. This applies in particular to verbs which have one or more of the following properties: an atelic or stative character, a non-agentive subject and an object which is not affected by the event: for instance, verbs of perception (*to see, to hear, to watch*), cognition (*to know, to understand*), verbs denoting feelings (*to love, to hate*) and verbs of movement which normally occur with an object (*to pass, to enter, to leave*).

Adopting Hopper and Thompson's view on transitivity leads to a division between types of verbs which is different from, and more meaningful than, the traditional one. The dividing line is not between transitive verbs (with an object) and intransitive verbs (without an object), but between verbs denoting actions which affect the object, and the rest of the verbs, whether they have an object or not. It will be shown in the following sections that the latter classification solves a number of problems related to the nature of transitivity in Akkadian.

5.5. The role of high transitivity in Akkadian

The notion of transitivity as outlined in the previous sections is of fundamental importance to a correct understanding of the D-stem. First, it enables us to solve some practical problems concerning the classification of verbs as transitive and intransitive (see 5.5.1). Second, it clarifies the status of the verbs of type IV, which have an object - and are therefore transitive according to the traditional criteria - but nevertheless, against the general rule, have a valency-extending D-stem (see 5.5.2). The third and most important point is that it enables us to formulate a general characteristic of the D-stem, which encompasses the various grammatical functions ascribed to it, and therefore clarifies the relationship between its two main functions: the valency-extending or factitive function and the valency-preserving function (see 5.6).

5.5.1. The distinction between transitive and intransitive

Generally speaking, it is not difficult to establish the basic valency of an Akkadian verb. Most verbs are clearly transitive or intransitive (in the traditional sense of the word),[6] in spite of the fact that some intransitive verbs are used transitively in specific circumstances (see below), and that almost all transitive verbs are occasionally used without an object. Examples of the latter are idiomatic expressions, such as *nadû* "to stop working" (CAD sv 1c-5' (p. 78b)), *napāhu* "to rise, brighten" (of celestial bodies, CAD sv 4), *našû* "to rise" (of water), proceed" (CAD sv *n.* A 5), *paṭāru* "to leave" (AHw sv G 14), and *tabālu* "to disappear" (of stars) (AHw sv G 7).[7] Many of such cases are restricted to a more or less technical context.[8]

For some verbs, however, a classification as either transitive or intransitive is somewhat problematical.[9] They can be broadly divided into four groups. The first group comprises a few verbs which have the same peculiarity as English verbs as *to break, to change, to open* and *to lengthen*: if an agent is present, they denote an action; otherwise they denote the corresponding process. Accordingly, they can have either an agentive or a non-agentive subject. The most common example is *emēdu* intrans.: "to come into contact with, to lean against" (with accusative (*sic!*) or *ana*, see below), trans.: "to place, to lean, to impose" (CAD sv 1 and 2/3). Although insignificant in number, they are important because they throw light on the nature of factitivity, as defined in Chapter VII. They will be listed and discussed in 11.4.2.

The second group comprises a few verbs which in the G-stem can be both transitive and intransitive, but always have a non-agentive subject: *malû* "to be(come) full" (intrans.), "to fill, cover" (trans.), and *hamāṭu* and *kabābu,* which both mean "to burn" (trans. and intrans.). These verbs will be examined in 7.3.1 and 7.3.2.

The third group consists of *dabābu* "to talk" and "to speak (words, etc.)", and *kašādu* "to reach, to arrive" and "to take possession of". For reasons to be explained below, these verbs are subsumed under Type IV and discussed in 5.5.3.

The fourth group consists of verbs which denote a movement or a location and are, therefore, regularly qualified by directional or locational elements, specifying the place of the action, its aim or source, or the path along which the movement takes place.

In this section we will concentrate on this fourth group. It is typical of movement verbs in Akkadian that such elements can be expressed both by a direct object and by a prepositional phrase, cf. GAG § 143c. Some examples are:

Alāku "to go": we find *sūqa* or *ṣēra alāku* "to walk along the street, in the open country" (AHw sv G III 2a/b), beside *ina sūqi alāku* (Atr. 112: 6 (Gtn)) and *ina/eli ṣēri alāku* (CT 16, 37: 15; Gilg. M I 10 (Gtn)). Moreover, we find both *harrāna alāku* (AHw sv G III 2a) and *ana harrāni alāku* (RA 8, 67: II 7/9; VS 8, 71: 8f; Iraq 21, 52: 42) "set out for a journey, an expedition"; cf. also *(w)aṣû* below.

Emēdu "to come in contact with, lean against" (intr.) is used either with an acc. (AHw sv G 1a, CAD sv 1a-1') or with a preposition, usually *ana* (*ib.* sv 1b, and 1a-2', respectively);

Erēbu "to enter" regularly has a preposition (mostly *ana*) but an acc. is also found (typically *bābu* "door" (CT 39, 33: 51 // 40, 46: 11; BAL II 89: 42, 45, etc. (Š)), *abullu* "gate" (LE A IV 11 // B IV 15: Maqlû V 135), *bītu* "house" (RA 33, 106: 24; BRM 4, 9: 40; AfO 14, 146: 120), and elsewhere.

(W)aṣû "to go out" is almost always used with *ina, ištu,* etc.; a few times we find an acc., usually *bāba* "door" or *abulla* "gate" (AHw sv G I 1c β, e.g., Maqlû VII 154, with *ālam* KH r.IX 71 (Š)) (cf. *erēbu*); but *ina bābi aṣû* BBR 26: III 19 (CAD sv *aṣû* 1k) and RA 48, 180: 14. In OB Mari we find *ana harrānim waṣûm* (ARM 2, 20: 7) beside *harrānam waṣûm* (2, 138: 7), and *ana gerrim waṣûm* (FM 2 p. 34 no. 10: 5) beside *gerram waṣûm* (MARI 7, 45: 12'. 15'), cf. *alāku* above.

(W)ašābu "to sit, settle down" occasionally has an acc. instead of the usual preposition: cf. AbB 7, 42: 13 *kīma ālam lā wašbāta aqbi* "I said that you were not staying in the city", and 5, 232: 9 *inūma* (...) *ina ālim wašbāti* "when ... you are staying in the city". Also ARM 2, 100: r.5' (*mātam*, according to AHw sv G 2c α); Kisurra 153: 24; EL 7: 8; 286: 1 (with *eqlam*).

A group of verbs semantically related to verbs of movement are those which denote the addressing of persons; here, too, we frequently find a direct object interchangeable with a prepositional phrase, mostly with *ana*:

Kašādu "to reach, arrive" has an acc., a dative, or a prep. (*ana, adi* or *ana ṣēr*) to indicate the person reached or the place of arrival (CAD sv 1a); it is also used with a prep. or an acc. in the meaning "to turn to, approach" a person (CAD sv 1d).

Mahāru "to turn to, approach (an authority)" generally takes an acc., but *ana* is found in Asb. A II 117; VAB 7, 348: 1; SAA 1, 190: 10, and elsewhere in NA (CAD sv 2a-4' (but cf. GAG § 114e?)) [TIM 2, 129: 23f (= Sumer 15, pl. 8: 23f), mentioned as taking an acc. in AHw sv Gtn 1, is interpreted differently by CAD sv 6e].

Sahāru "to turn to" has an acc. or *ana*, cf. CAD sv 2b/c and 2a respectively (apart from transitive *sahāru* "to look for").

The same interchangeability of an accusative and a prepositional phrase is found in verbs of praying: *karābu, sullû, suppû, surruru, ṣullû*; verbs of waiting: *qu''û* and *(w)aqû* (cf. GAG § 143c); and some other verbs, such as *kapādu* "to plan, devise" (CAD sv 1a (+ acc.) and 1b (+ *ana*)), *naṭālu* "to see, look at", usually with acc., but with *ana* "to look for support, to wait" (CAD sv 3), and *šalāṭu* "to dominate, control", with acc. (CAD sv *š.* A 1a) or *ana*/*ina muhhi* (*ib.* 1b). An interesting case is *tamû* "to swear", which has an acc. (AHw sv G I 2) or *ina* (*ib.* II 1) for the object sworn by, e.g., OA *patram* or *ina patrim ša Aššur tamā'um* "to swear by the dagger of Aššur" (Hirsch, AfO Beiheft 13/14, 65a, and similarly with *šugarriā'um* 66a); likewise we find *mamītam tamā'um* "to swear an oath" in OA (AHw sv G I 2), but *ina mamītim tamûm* in OB (*ib.* II 1, e.g., AbB 9, 216: 10f).

This need not imply that both constructions always have precisely the same meaning: there may be subtle differences in meaning between the construction with an accusative and that with a preposition. This is the case in comparable cases from English mentioned by Givón (1984: 98f): *to ride a horse* or *to ride* on *a horse, to swim the Channel* or *to swim* across *the Channel* (cf. also Taylor 1995: 211f). As for Akkadian, a similar differentiation may be posited for *emēdu* and *alāku*. A global survey of the CAD entry of "intransitive" *emēdu* shows that, if an accusative is used, the verb denotes immediate contact, is mostly stative, and the object is inanimate (a typical example is *šamê emid* "he/it reaches the sky", CAD sv 1c); with a preposition, the object is often personal, the verb is usually non-stative and denotes nearness or approach, cf. the OB and MB PNs of the type *ana-DN-ēmid* "I took refuge with DN" (CAD sv 1d-2'). The difference between the two constructions is iconic: the absence of the preposition from the sentence reflects a greater proximity in reality, its presence a greater distance.

In *alāku,* an accusative seems to be more common with the G-stem, a preposition with the Gtn-stem; this can be explained from the fact that in *ṣēra alāku* the accusative and the verb are a single concept, with *ṣēra* as a kind of cognate object (cf. AHw sv G III 2), whereas in *ina ṣēri atalluku* the two concepts of roaming around and the location are more independent of each other. Here, too, this greater independence is iconically reflected in the greater distance between the verb and the noun caused by the presence of the preposition.

The traditional notion of transitivity cannot easily account for these verbs. In spite of the fact that there is usually little difference in meaning between their transitive and intransitive use, they must be classified as both transitive and intransitive. This is somewhat embarrassing, if we claim that the distinction between transitive and intransitive is grammatically meaningful. If, on the other hand, we view transitivity as a matter of degree, determined by a number of features, the relationship between the two possible constructions becomes clear: since the constituent in the accusative or the prepositional phrase is not directly affected by the actions in question, these verbs have a low degree of transitivity, regardless of whether they contain a direct object or a prepositional phrase. The difference in construction is superficial and subordinate to the similarity in meaning.

Consequently, the Akkadian verbs mentioned above belong typologically to the intransitive verbs (in the traditional sense), in spite of the fact that they can take an accusative.

5.5.2. The classification of the D-stems of Type IV

The second point on which the notion of high transitivity is relevant to the classification into four types of verbal D-stems (cf. 5.2.) concerns the verbs of Type IV, the transitive verbs whose D-stem is valency-extending, such as *lamādu* "to learn, know", *lummudu* "to inform". As pointed out in 5.2, these D-stems are unusual, since D-stems of transitive verbs are normally valency-preserving. The main verbs belonging to the marginal Type IV are the following, in approximate order of frequency:

Lamādu	"to know, learn", D "to inform";
Labāšu	"to wear, put on", D "to dress sb, provide sb with clothes";
Edû	"to know", D *(w)uddû* "to identify, inform, assign";
Hasāsu	"to think of, heed, mention", D "to remind" (also "to study, investigate", see 7.6.3);
Tamû	"to swear" (with *nīšu* or *mamītu* "oath", or the god sworn by as object), D "to make sb swear";
Palāhu	"to fear, respect", D "to frighten"[a];
Šahātu	"to fear, respect", D "to frighten"[a];
Habālu	"to become indebted to (dat.) for an amount (acc.)", D "to make indebted to";
Apāru	"to have or put sth on the head", D "to put sth on somebody else's head"[b];
Magāru	"to agree, grant", D "to make someone agree";
Mašû	"to forget", D "to make forget"[c]
Harādu	"to watch over, guard", D "to put on the alert" (NA);

Notes:

a) Other verbs of fear could be added: *arāru* "to fear" (AHw "zittern") and *galātu* "to start, fear", but they differ from *palāhu* and *šahātu* in the fact that they are only exceptionally found with an object: *arāru* only UET 6, 392: 5 and Gilg. XII 21; *galātu* only Erra IIId: 10 and Sg. 8: 17. It is typical for verbs of fear to be used both with and without an object. The very common verb *adāru* "to fear" often has an object, but, according to the dictionaries, uses only the Š-stem in the meaning "to frighten", whereas *adāru* D is interpreted as "to annoy, make restless" (CAD sv *a.* A 3/5) or "verfinstern" (AHw sv D/Dt);

b) Occasionally, however, G has the meaning of D, cf. 11.4.2 sv.

c) Although the dictionaries give this as the meaning of D, these is no unambiguous evidence for it (such evidence would consist of a sentence with *mašû* D and a double accusative), cf. CAD sv *m.* A lex. sect. and 2; AHw sv *m.* II D. Therefore, it is possible that *mašû* belongs to the verbs of Type II listed in 7.6.3.

Some other verbs of the same nature which are very rare or uncertain are: *bêlu* "to rule, have at one's disposal", D "to let sb rule" (only OBTA 31: 9; the other instance of D mentioned in CAD sv 2 (AfK 1, 28: II 1 (= St. Kraus 198: 52)) is likely to be a factitive of the related *ba'ālu* "to be strong", cf. AHw sv *ba'ālu* D); *hašāhu* "to need, require", D "to deprive of", lit. "to cause to need" (only CT 39, 44: 15 (cf. Lambert 1992: 151), and CT 27, 3: 10 // 14: 31 (Dt); *šemû* "hear", D only ABL 896: 13 *šummu šam-mu-a-ku-u-ni* "(I swear that) I have not been informed", cf. CAD sv *šemû* 5; *amāru* "see", if we may interpret MA *mummirtu* "procuress" (cf. CAD sv) as "a woman who shows" (women to prospective lovers). Moreover, the idiomatic D-stems *burrû* "to usher, announce" and *ruddû* "to add" can be plausibly explained as basically meaning "to let see" (from *barû* "to look at") and "to let follow" (from *redû* "to follow"), so that they also belong to this type.

What these verbs have in common is that, although they usually have an object, also in the G-stem, they typically show a low degree of transitivity, since they do not have an agentive subject, and their object is not strongly affected by the action of the verb. Their general meaning and the way they are glossed in English suggest that most of them are basically stative verbs, which do not denote any action at all.

Thus typologically they belong more closely to the verbs which are traditionally regarded as intransitive. Some of these verbs resemble intransitive verbs in other respects, too: in belonging to a vowel class which is typical of intransitive verbs, and/or in the fact that their N-stem is translated as an ingressive rather than as a passive. The former applies to *labāšu, lamādu, palāhu* and *tamû,* which belong to the *a/a* class, and *šahātu,* which belongs to the *u/u* class; *magāru* has in OB and OA *a/u,* but later switches to *u/u* (cf. CAD, AHw sv). For the association of the classes *a/a* and *u/u* with intransitive verbs, see Kienast 1967: 81.

The ingressive use of the N-stem is found in *labāšu* (cf. AHw sv N), *habālu* (cf. AHw sv *h.* III N) and *harādu* (in spite of CAD's translation "to be alerted" (sv 3)). Both functions coexist in *magāru*: it is usually ingressive: "to come to an agreement" (cf. CAD sv 10a/b, AHw sv N 1/3), but may also serve as a passive (*ll.cc.* 10c and N 4), e.g., AbB 2, 86: 15 *ašar taqabbû ta-am-ma-ag-ga-ar* "where you give orders, you will be obeyed". Of the N-stem of *edû* mainly some rather artificial-looking forms are found in bilingual texts as translation of Sum. zu (cf. CAD sv *idû* 8); *palāhu* N is attested once as a variant of G (AHw sv N). An N-stem of *šahātu* and *tamû* is not attested. In addition, *tamû* shows the wavering between having a direct object and a prepositional phrase, which is typical of this kind of verbs, as we have seen in 5.5.1.

Thus, rather than being an exception to the rule stated in 5.2, these verbs show that the main factor which decides whether their D-stem will be valency-preserving or valency-extending is not the transitive or intransitive character of the G-stem, but the degree of transitivity with which it is associated. What Types III and IV have in common is that the verbs belonging to both of them typically have a low degree of transitivity. That those of Type IV regularly take a direct object, makes no difference in this respect.

In such verbs the D-stem denotes a valency increase; in verbs which typically occur in sentences with a high degree of transitivity, it preserves the valency of the G-stem. Consequently, the verbs of Type IV are a subtype of III and are also factitive. They will be discussed together with the verbs of Type III in Chapter VII.

5.5.3. The verbs *dabābu* and *kašādu*

There are two other verbs which are similar to the verbs of 5.5.2 in that they can be transitive in the traditional sense, but typically have a low degree of transitivity: *dabābu* "to speak, to speak to/with", and *kašādu* "to lay hands on, to take possession of":

Dabābu "to speak, speak to/with" can be intransitive and transitive; in the latter case it has a cognate object (words, or other kinds of utterances, cf. CAD sv *d.* v. 1c/2, AHw sv *d.* II G 1c/e), and therefore a very low degree of transitivity according to the criteria defined in 5.3 and 5.4 above, cf. also Givón 1984: 105f. The D-stem *dubbubu,* on the other hand, is often used with a personal object in the meaning "to pester, harass" or "to entreat" (CAD sv 8b/c), which involves a more agentive subject and a strongly affected object, and therefore a sharp increase in transitivity. In addition, the D-stem can also be intransitive; "to complain, grumble" (CAD sv 8a); in this use it belongs to the intransitive D-stems denoting sounds, which will be discussed in 7.6.1 (G is also found in this meaning, cf. CAD sv 5, AHw sv G 3). It seems a plausible assumption that both usages are lexicalizations of an original iconic meaning "to talk much, loud, etc." (cf. AHw sv D "viel reden"); this meaning is perhaps attested in ARM 2, 24: 12f *annêtim u mādātim ú-da-ab-bi-ib-šu-ma* "these and many (other) things I spoke to him", where *dubbubu* does not seem to have its usual meaning.

Kašādu has an extensive range of use. It was already discussed in 5.5.1, because it can have a direct object or a prepositional phrase when it means "to turn to, reach, arrive". It can also mean "to lay hands on, to take possession of"; in that case it has a direct object, and often "hand(s)" as subject (CAD sv 2a/h); as such it is akin to verbs of possession, which typically have a low degree of transitivity, cf. Givón 1984: 103ff. *Kuššudu*, on the other hand, normally means "to pursue, to (try to) catch" or "to drive away, expel, remove" (cf. the Appendix to Chapter VI sv, CAD sv 4/5). This semantic development has an exact parallel in French *chasser* "to hunt" and "to chase away", from Vulgar Latin *captiare* "to try to catch" (cf. *capere* "to take, to catch"), cf. Jongen 1985: 131f. It has a personal object which is strongly affected and denotes a highly salient action, and therefore typically has a high degree of transitivity.[10] Moreover, *kuššudu* always refers to a conscious volitional action and has an agentive subject; *kašādu* can be used either with an agentive or a non-agentive subject.

In these verbs the G- and D-stem have been differentiated in meaning on the basis of the degree of transitivity which they typically show. The G-stem of these verbs can be both transitive and intransitive, but always has a low degree of transitivity, whereas the D-stem has a high degree of transitivity, which is mainly caused by the more agentive nature of the subject (see further 7.3). In this respect these verbs are similar to the factitive D-stems of the previous section - which are also mostly transitive - but differ from them in that their D-stem is not factitive. Instead, the difference in transitivity between their G- and D-stems is realized in an idiosyncratic way, depending on their lexical meaning. They take an intermediate position between the verbs of Type IV and the "real" transitive verbs of Type I.

5.5.4. Conclusion

A more general conclusion which can be drawn from this state of affairs is that the distinction between high and low transitivity is grammatically more relevant and more meaningful than the traditional one between transitive and intransitive, as far as Akkadian is concerned. The major dividing line between Akkadian verbs runs between those which are typically associated with high and those which are typically associated with low transitivity. Verbs positioned above that line have a D-stem which retains the valency of the G-stem, can only use a Š-stem to indicate a valency increase (i.e., a causative, see 7.2) and if they have an N-stem, it has a passive meaning. Verbs positioned below that line have a D-stem with increased valency (but can also use the Š-stem in the same function, see 7.5), and their N-stem, if used at all, more often has an ingressive than a passive meaning.

5.6. The association between the D-stem and high transitivity

The most important contribution which Hopper and Thompson's view on transitivity makes to the clarification of the nature of the D-stem is that it enables us to discern a common background behind the various functions which are traditionally assigned to the D-stem. This common background is the overall association between the verbal D-stem and high transitivity. We saw in section 5.2 that from the four types of D-stems three are transitive, and that the only non-transitive type (Type II) is marginal. We can make an even stronger claim, namely, that the D-stem is not simply transitive in the sense that it normally has an object, but that it is closely associated with, and motivated by, a high, or even prototypical, degree of transitivity.

This claim is based upon three characteristic features of the D-stem: first, its factitive function; second, the fact that many transitive verbs which typically denote a relatively low degree of transitivity do not or only rarely occur in the D-stem, whereas those which do have a frequent D-stem typically have a meaning which implies a high degree of transitivity; and, third, the fact that the D-stems of the latter verbs, in so far as they have approximately the same meaning, are generally preferred in sentences which rank in the topmost part of the transitivity scale because of the highly salient nature of the subject, the object and the action itself. These three characteristics will be discussed in the next sections.

5.6.1. High transitivity in factitive D-stems

As to the first point, the factitive function of the D-stem (Types III and IV) results from the fact that a transition from a process to an action through the addition of an agent entails a sharp increase in transitivity: whereas the G-stems in question have a very low degree of transitivity if they are intransitive, or even zero transitivity if they are stative verbs, factitive clauses have a high degree of transitivity by definition, because they denote that a person or a thing is brought into a specific condition (see 7.1). Thus they have an agentive subject, a strongly affected patient object and a telic (bounded) verb, three features which, as we have seen, determine high transitivity (see 5.3 and 5.4). It will be argued in Chapter VII, where we will examine the factitive function of the D-stem, that it is this property which motivates the use of the D-stem in such clauses.

5.6.2. High transitivity and D-stems of transitive verbs

The connection between the D-stem and high transitivity is also demonstrated by the fact that most transitive verbs which have a common D-stem are typically associated with a high degree of transitivity, whereas verbs which are not or only very rarely found in the D-stem generally belong to semantic classes with a relatively low degree of transitivity.

5.6.2.1. Low transitivity verbs without a D-stem

The most striking evidence for this claim is the fact that Akkadian has a number of very common transitive verbs of which a D-stem is either not attested or very rare. The frequency of these verbs and the fact that they are semantically homogeneous show that the absence of a D-stem is not accidental. The verbs referred to can be divided into the following groups:

1. Verbs of giving, taking, sending and placing: *nadānu* "to give, sell", *nadû* "to put down, to leave", *našû* "to carry", *šakānu* "to place" (for CT 34, 41: 24 (= TCS 5, 169: 24) *ú-šá-ka-nu-šu* see 8.4.2 sv *šukkunu*), *šâmu* "to buy", *šapāru* "to send", *šarāku* "to grant, dedicate", *šarāqu* "to steal", *tarû* "to take, bring", *(w)abālu* "to bring" (the D/Dtn forms fom EA are doubtless incorrect, cf. AHw sv (D) and (Dtn)); for *bubbulu* "to parade" see 8.6 sv), *(w)arû* "to bring, lead". Less frequent cases are *bêru* "to select", *eṭēru* "to take away", *hâru* "to choose", *karāru* "to place", *râmu* "to bestow", *ṣalā'u* "to put down", *ṣênu* "to load", *z/ṣarāpu* "to buy". The relatively low or less than prototypical degree of transitivity of these verbs is caused by the fact that they do not involve a "physical, discernible change" (Givón 1984: 97) in the condition of the object, but only a change in location or in ownership.

2. Verbs of eating and drinking: *akālu* "to eat, *šatû* "to drink", and the less frequent verbs *patānu* "to eat", *lêmu* or *lemû* "to take" (food or drink). In these verbs the less than prototypical transitivity is related to the fact that in many contexts the activity of eating and drinking is more prominent than the substance which is eaten or drunk; therefore the object of these verbs is often less relevant and frequently omitted.

3. Verbs of observing and watching: *amāru* "to see" (but see 5.5.2 for *mummirtu*), *dagālu* "to see", *naṣāru* "to guard, watch" (the D forms from EA and Alalakh are doubtless incorrect, cf. AHw sv D, CAD sv

14), *re'û* "to watch" (the sheep), i.e., "to tend". The object of these verbs is not affected by the action, the agentive nature of the subject is less outspoken than in most types of transitive verbs, and the action is often atelic and protracted rather than telic.

4. Verbs denoting possession, control, care and love/hate: *ašāru* "to take care of", *gamālu* "to spare, oblige", *kalû* "to detain, withhold" (the instances of *kalû* D mentioned CAD sv 7/8 belong to *kullu*, cf. AHw sv *kalû* V (D)), *kašāšu* "to dominate", *rašû* "to get", *rêmu* "to have compassion", *zêru* "to hate" (for *râmu* "to love" see below). Most of these verbs are basically stative and have a less agentive subject and an object which is not affected.

5. Verbs of movement which are regularly used with a direct object: *bâ'u* "to walk along, pass over", *ebēru* "to cross", *etēqu* "to pass along, cross". These verbs belong semantically to the verbs of movement discussed in 5.5.1, but differ from them in that they usually have a direct object, rather than a prepositional phrase; what was said there about their typical degree of transitivity also applies to this group of verbs.

To these verbs a number of others can be added which belong to the same semantic types but are found in the D-stem by way of exception; since they are listed in the Appendix to Chapter VI, we mention them here without references.

To group 1 can be added *abāku* A "to send, lead, dispatch" (D 1x ("to drive away")), *aḫāzu* "to take, marry" (D 1x); *ekēmu* "to take away" (D 1x), *leqû* "to take, receive" (D 3x OA), and *tabālu* "to take away" (D 1x). To group 3 can be added *ḫâṭu* "to watch, examine" (D 3x), *naṭālu* "to look at, watch" (D 2x), and *šemû* "to hear" (D 1x, factitive, quoted in 5.5.2); to group 4 *râmu* "to love" (D 1x, and 1x reciprocal Dt, see 9.1.3 sv), *bêlu* "to rule, control" (D 1x, see 5.5.2); to group 5 *ezēbu* "to abandon, leave" (D 1x).

A small number of verbs of the types considered, however, are incongruous in that they have a D-stem which is less rare. This applies to the following verbs of group 1: *apālu* "to pay" (4x OB, see 6.4.7.1 sv), *paqādu* "to entrust" (very common, see 6.4.7.1 sv); *esēku* "to assign", *eṭēru* "to pay", *qâšu* "to give" (as a present) (see 6.4.7.1 sv, and *šaqālu* "to pay" (OA, see 6.6.3.1). In other cases a D-stem is attested, but in a different meaning: *maḫāru* "to receive" (see 6.8.3), *ṭarādu* "to send" (see 6.8.1).

5.6.2.2. High transitivity verbs with a D-stem

There is a marked contrast between the non-existence or extreme rarity of the D-stems of the verbs mentioned so far, and the relatively frequent use of the D-stem of transitive verbs which belong to different semantic types. The D-stem of transitive verbs will be examined in detail in the next chapter; it will become evident from the verbs listed and discussed there that the D-stem occurs with the highest frequency in verbs which have prototypical transitivity. Among the verbs which frequently occur in the D-stem we can distinguish the following semantic types (only common verbs with a frequent D-stem are mentioned here; for all references see the Appendix to Chapter VI):

1. Verbs which entail a partial or total destruction of the object: *abātu* "to destroy, ruin", *batāqu* "to cut off, pierce, break", *hamāṣu* "to strip, skin, tear off", *hepû* "to break, demolish", *nakāsu* "to cut off, fell", *nasāhu* "to tear out, remove", *palāq/ku* "to slaughter", *parāsu* "to cut off, cut into pieces, separate", *pasāsu* "to cancel, destroy", *pašāṭu* "to erase", *šarāṭu* "to tear", *šebēru* "to break", *ṭabāhu* "to slaughter".

2. Verbs which entail a more or less violent impact on the object: *kabāsu* "to step upon, trample", *mahāṣu* "to hit, smash, wound", *našāku* "to bite", *palāšu* "to pierce", *sapāhu* "to disperse, scatter, ruin".

3. Verbs which entail a change in the condition of the object, which is less drastic or permanent than in the verbs of group 2: verbs of closing and opening: *edēlu* "to close", *petû* "to open"; of binding and loosening: *e'ēlu, kasû, kaṣāru, rakāsu* "to bind", *retû* "to fix", *pašāru, paṭāru* "to loosen"; of covering and smearing: *katāmu* "to cover", *lapātu* "to affect, smear", *salā'/hu* "to sprinkle"; of bringing together: *kamāsu* "to collect, assemble", *qarānu, kamāru* "to pile up", *šapāku, tabāku* "to heap up, pour out"; verbs of washing and cleaning: *kapāru* "to clean, purify", *mesû* "to wash";

4. Verbs which refer to an oppressive treatment of people: *esēru* "to put under pressure", *sanāqu* "to interrogate, harass, keep under control", *ṣabātu* "to seize".

5. Verbs of creating: *eṣēru* "to draw, design", *(w)alādu* "to give birth to, produce".

This enumeration comprises only the most common verbs of the types in question, and could easily be extended. The Appendix to Chapter VI gives a more complete survey, but for the issue at hand these verbs may suffice to demonstrate the correlation between the frequency of the D-stem and a high degree of inherent transitivity.

This correlation, however, is not absolute: just as there are some exceptions in the verbs of low transitivity (notably *paqādu*), there are also verbs belonging to one of the semantic types listed here which do not have a D-stem, such as *nasāku* "to throw down", and *enû* "to change", or one that is very rare, such as that of *dâku* "to kill", *naqāru* "to tear down, destroy", *šarāpu* "to burn" (trans.), and *šagāšu* "to murder". Moreover, many of the transitive verbs do not belong to one of the two prototypical classes of high and low transitivity, but are situated somewhere in the middle of the continuum between the prototypes; there is little uniformity in the way they behave.

The contrast between the rare occurrence of the D-stem in verbs of low transitivity and its frequent occurrence in the opposite type clearly shows that the degree of transitivity which a verb typically has is an important factor in the use of the D-stem. At the same time it offers an explanation for the remarkable fact that a number of very common verbs lack a D-stem.

5.6.3. The contrast G - D as a contrast in transitivity

Finally, we come to the D-stems of Type I, which are derived from transitive G-stems. As we have seen in the previous sections, the transitive verbs which have a common D-stem, generally have a high degree of transitivity themselves; the same holds for the D-stems derived from them. The latter confirm, therefore, the overall association of the D-stem with high transitivity.

There is, however, a fundamental difference between the D-stems of Type I, which are derived from transitive verbs, and the factitive D-stems of Types III and IV, which are derived from intransitive (or lowly transitive) verbs. This difference concerns the relationship to the G-stem. If the G-stem itself is intransitive, there is a sharp contrast in transitivity between G and D; they occupy opposite positions on either end of the transitivity scale; if it is transitive, the difference in transitivity is small, and their positions on the transitivity scale are more or less contiguous. This explains why the relationship between the G- and D-stems of transitive verbs is quite different from that of intransitive verbs.

In intransitive verbs (Types III and IV) the existence of a verbal stem with gemination beside the basic stem enables a speaker of Akkadian to make a formal distinction between the expression of a process (lowly transitive) and that of the corresponding action (highly transitive). The former is rendered by the G-stem, e.g., *pahāru* "to come together", or *danānu* "to become strong(er)"; for the action the D-stem is used: *puhhuru* "to bring together", *dunnunu* "to make strong(er)". The geminate underlines the significantly higher degree of transitivity caused by the addition of an agent and the transition from monovalent to bivalent, that usually accompanies this addition.

This sharp contrast in transitivity has been grammaticalized as the factitive function of the D-stem. The enormous productivity of this function and the consistency with which the formal differentiation between the expression of actions and processes has been implemented show that this distinction was a welcome addition, and filled a gap in the system. As a result, the relationship between D and G is completely regular, the meaning of D is predictable, and for the expression of an action (in so far as it is opposed to a process) its use is obligatory (see 11.4.2 for exceptions). We can study these verbs as a class without considering each verb individually (see further Chapter VII).

For the D-stems of transitive verbs (Type I) the situation is quite different. Since the corresponding G-stems themselves tend to have a high degree of inherent transitivity, it is generally impossible for this type of D-stem to denote an increase in transitivity comparable to that of the intransitive G-stems. Moreover, there is no gap in the system which they could fill, and no obvious grammatical function which could be assigned to them (the question why such D-stems of transitive (bivalent) G-stems cannot be trivalent, i.e., why they are not used as causatives of the G-stem, will be dealt with in detail in Chapter VII).

This is the reason why the clear division of tasks between the G- and the D-stem which is typical of Types III and IV is absent in the verbs of Type I, and why the coexistence of a G- and a D-stem in transitive verbs has not led to a consistent grammatical differentiation. The relationship of the D-stems of Type I to the G-stem cannot be formulated as a grammatical rule; it depends on the meaning of each individual verb, and is determined by non-grammatical factors such as style, convention, and personal preferences of speakers; to a large extent it is unpredictable and idiosyncratic (see further Chapter VI).

Thus instead of having acquired grammatical status, the contrast between the D- and G-stems of transitive verbs has preserved the predominantly semantic character which we generally find between simple forms and forms with an iconic extension of the kind discussed in 2.2.4.

5.6.4. D-stems of transitive verbs and prototypical transitivity

The fact that the D-stems of Type I do not differ grammatically from the corresponding G-stems makes it possible to use them - even to a larger extent than the other types - as the category *par excellence* to underline prototypical transitivity. They are typically used in sentences with an agentive, usually human, subject, with a salient action, and with a direct object which is concrete and strongly affected; these are the features which constitute what Givón (1990: 565f) defines as "prototypical transitive sentences" (cf. 5.4).

As far as the nature of the action and the direct object is concerned, this statement can be ascertained from the Appendix to Chapter VI, which represents the corpus of D-stems of Type I on which the discussion in Chapter VI is based. It comprises all relevant verbs whose meaning can be established beyond doubt, and the direct objects they are attested with. This corpus clearly demonstrates the preponderance - already noted in 5.6.2.2 - of verbs denoting actions which strongly affect the object.

On the other hand, the G-stems of these verbs also tend to have a basic meaning which refers to some salient action with a high degree of inherent transitivity. Many of them, however, especially those which occur frequently, are not only used in this basic meaning, but also in a number of secondary meanings and idiomatic expressions. Since the normal development in language goes from concrete to abstract, such secondary meanings are often more abstract and less salient than the basic meaning. This often implies that they have more abstract and therefore less salient nouns as direct object. Thus they do not always share the high degree of transitivity which characterizes the verb in its literal meaning; in some cases they can even be intransitive.

Examples of this situation are the following verbs with a frequent D-stem: *batāqu* "to cut off, pierce" can also mean "to accuse, denounce" (CAD sv 6) or "to stop work" and "to become cheap" (*ib.* sv 5); *kabāsu* "to step upon, trample", can also mean "to exert oneself", "to drop a claim", "to pardon" (a sin), and other idiomatic expressions (CAD sv 4); *mahāṣu* "to hit, smash", but also "to weave", "to play" (an instrument), "to stir" (powder into a liquid), "to coat", and a host of other expressions (CAD sv 3/4); *parāsu* basically means "to cut off, cut into pieces, sever", but also in metaphorical sense "to decide" (AHw sv G 9), "to prevent", "to keep away", "to interrupt" (G 1, 6), or - (with *(w)arkata(m)*) - "to investigate (a matter)" (G 8); *ṣabātu* "to seize, arrest", also means "to begin", "to be busy with", "to contain", etc. (CAD sv 4/5/6); *tabāku* lit. "to pour out" substances, but also, metaphorically, abstract concepts as life, fear, etc (AHw sv G 6/7). Examples of intransitive use are *paṭāru* "to take leave, go away" (AHw sv G 14) (normally "to loosen"), and *napāṣu* "to flop about, thrash around", versus transitive "to strike, kill" (CAD sv 1). *Nasāhu,* lit. "to tear out, remove", has secondary transitive meanings, such as "to transfer, deduct (CAD sv 4/5), beside being used intransitively "to displace oneself" or "to pass" (of time) (*ib.* sv 7/8).

The D-stems of these verbs, however, tend to be more or less restricted to the basic and most salient meanings, and are only rarely found in secondary meanings, unless these also denote salient actions (see 6.4.9).

This restriction leads us to the second point: the preference for D forms if the direct object is concrete rather than abstract. This is a pervasive characteristic of the D-stems of Type I, and will be illustrated extensively in Chapter VI, see especially 6.4.1.2, 6.4.2.2 and 6.4.9. The D-stem is predominantly used with the following types of objects: first, animate beings (mostly humans) and large salient aspects of the environment (houses and other buildings, fields, mountains, land), irrespective of whether they are singular or plural; second, mass nouns and collectives, both of animate beings and objects; third, all other concrete objects, but mainly when they are plural. Special mention should be made of body parts which - because of their highly salient character - have a strong predilection for the D-stem, in particular when they are plural, but often in the singular, too. Thus the typical direct objects occurring with D-stems of Type I belong to the categories which are cross-linguistically most salient: persons, animals and concrete objects (cf. Wallace 1982: 211f; Croft 1990: 111ff).

In some verbs this process has led to a partial differentiation in use between G and D consisting in a restriction of G to abstract objects, or of D to concrete objects. The first type is represented by *pasāsu* "to cancel, to destroy", which uses G only with abstract objects, cf. AHw sv G 1/4 (order, judgment, oath, agreement, a kind of status (*kidinnūtu*), evil omens, sin, punishment). D is more frequent and used for the same abstract concepts (*ib.* D 3/5, Dt 3/4 and App. to Ch. VI sv **3.**), but it is the only form which is found with concrete objects (*ib.* D 1/2, Dt 1/2, and App. to Ch. VI sv **1.-2.**).

A restriction of D to concrete objects is found in *letû* and *ṭarādu. Letû* "to split, to divide" uses D in its basic, most literal meaning ("to cleave") with a concrete object, cf. App. to Ch. VI sv (persons, body parts, stones and mountains, both sg. and pl.). G is also occasionally found with a concrete object (ZA 16, 154: 3 // D in RA 18, 198: 3 (head); ZA 53, 216: 5 (ground)), but mostly occurs in the stative in omen texts (CAD sv 1a), i.e., in a typical context of low transitivity, cf. 5.6.5 (the unique instance of D in this context (AMT 75, 1: IV 19 (heels)) is doubtless caused by its plural subject, cf. 10.6.1). The few other instances which occur in a transitive sentence, have a more abstract and therefore less salient meaning: "to divide" (an army, a field, cf. CAD sv 1b).

Ṭarādu "to drive away, banish" (for G "to send" see 6.8.1) only uses D with concrete objects: persons, animals, demons, cf. App. sv and AHw sv D 1/3 and Dt, with one exception: BWL 82: 213 (wisdom). G is used with both concrete and abstract objects, cf. AHw sv G

3a/c and part of 3d (concrete) and G 3d (rest) (abstract: illness, sorcery, evil, trouble, etc.).

The same type of differentiation is shown by *emēdu* in its transitive meaning "to place upon, to impose": D typically has concrete objects (beams, body parts), whereas G is mostly used for imposing taxes, punishments and similar concepts, but in OB and in literary texts G is also found with concrete objects; see 11.4.2 for details and references.

In many other verbs to be discussed in Chapter VI the same tendency is observable, but usually it is less consistent, and hard to distinguish from other tendencies in the use of D, such as its association with plurality.

The third characteristic of prototypical transitivity is the presence of an agentive subject. This holds for almost all instances in the corpus (in so far as they occur in transitive sentences with an object; it does not apply to passive/intransitive Dt forms, nor to stative forms, cf. 5.6.5). It is difficult, however, to make a clear-cut distinction between agentive and non-agentive subjects. In the first place, we have to allow for the fact that the range of entities falling into the category "animate", and therefore potentially agentive, was larger in ancient Mesopotamia than it is in the modern world: apart from gods and demons, it comprises also many natural phenomena, such as flood, wind, storm, and celestial bodies (which are often deified). It also includes illnesses, and concepts and objects belonging to the sphere of magic and sorcery. Moreover, we occasionally find personified instruments and manifestations of divine and royal power as subjects of D-stems.[11]

The subjects belonging to these categories can be seen as animate, and therefore as agentive. If we leave them out, only a small number of positively non-agentive subjects remain. There is one systematic exception: in medical texts several D-stems are used with body parts as subject and a personal object meaning "to cause pain", in sentences such as BKBM 2: 26 *šumma amēlu* (...) *takaltašu ú-sa-hal-šú* "if the stomach of a man "pierces" him", i.e., "if he has a piercing pain in his stomach."; they underline the durative character of the process. Such idioms will be discussed more thoroughly in 6.2.1.2.[12]

Apart from this medical idiom, the number of subjects which are positively non-agentive is extremely small: 13 cases occur in the corpus. In the Appendix to Chapter VI they are indicated by "non-ag." They comprise, first, a few abstract subjects: *edēpu* **2**.: SAA 3, 32: r.20f ("distress, acts of violence and rebellion" (tr. Livingstone)); *hatû*: HGŠ 114: 17 ("curse, illness (and) suffering"); *našāru* **2**.: HGŠ 96: 13 (misery, cf. tr. CAD sv *n.* A 4b); *(w)alādu* **4**.: BWL 252: 19ff ("long life, secretive behaviour (and) wealth"), all from texts of a highly literary nature; and, second, the following cases: *batāqu* **6**.: AbB 1, 27: 2ff (= (22) in Ch. VI) (fetters); *pehû* : BRM 4, 13: 21 (snow); *qalāpu* **1**.: Gilg. Iraq 28, 110: 26 ("thorn and bramble"); *sahālu* **1**.: Gilg. XI 269 (thorn); AnSt. 30, 105: 21 (= (85) in Ch. VI) (beatings); BWL 44: 101 (= (86) in Ch. VI) (goad); *ṣabātu* **7**.: SAA 5, 146: 7f (snow, quoted below); *šebēru* **1**.: RA 77, 20: 22 (tablet); *tarāṣu* **2**.: CT 41, 10b: 13 // 31, 33: 31 (head of a sheep).

The usual state of affairs is that the corresponding G-stem is combined with all types of relevant subjects, although animate subjects are far more common, as is to be expected for verbs which basically denote actions. A G-stem as *ṣabātu* "to seize", for instance, is found rather often with an inanimate subject, cf. CAD sv *ṣabātu* 1b/c/d; the use of *ṣabātu* D with these subjects is exceptional: the corpus only contains SAA 5, 146: 7f *kuppû* kaskal.meš *ú-ṣa-bi-it* "snow has blocked the roads".

In other verbs, which often have an inanimate subject, such as *katāmu* (CAD sv 2) and *sahāpu* (CAD sv 1), the situation is less clear, since these verbs are often found in literary texts, where the D-stem is more widespread than elsewhere and often seems to be used more or less interchangeably with the G-stem (cf. 6.9.2.2).

This leads to the conclusion that, if we view transitivity as a continuum from high to low (see 5.3), the G-stem occupies a very wide range, depending on its meaning and the context. The corresponding D-stem, however, has a strong connection with the topmost part of the continuum.

5.6.5. Some final remarks

Strictly speaking, the association of the D-stem with high transitivity only applies to those forms which occur in transitive sentences with a direct object, i.e., to the prefix conjugations, the infinitive and the imperative of the verbal D- and Dtn-stems. It does not apply to the forms of the passive/intransitive Dt-stem, nor to the stative D with its resultative meaning, nor to the participle D, which is active, but typically expresses a quality rather than an action. It is especially true of the stative, which explicitly denotes the absence of action and therefore has zero transitivity, regardless of whether it has an object or not. The same applies to the verbal adjective, which, in a fientive verb, is a nominalization of the stative.

The fact that, in spite of this, D forms of these categories are not uncommon is due to the following two factors. First, the sentences in which they occur are transformations of active, transitive sentences, and the D forms in question are productive derivations dependent upon the active paradigm of the D-stem (the stative only in so far as it is derived from a verbal paradigm, see 10.2). Therefore, there is a tendency to preserve the same stem form in such transformations. Thus the association of the Dt-stem and the stative, verbal adjective and participle D with high transitivity is indirect.

The second fact which explains why the D-stem is not restricted to transitive sentences is that gemination is not only used to underline high transitivity. In other contexts it underlines plurality or salience, cf. the discussion of the pattern *parras* in 3.1.3. A considerable part of the instances of the stative D, and to a lesser extent, of the Dt-stem, can be explained by the fact that they have a plural subject. In transitive sentences with a direct object in the plural both functions of gemination reinforce each other.

This situation accounts for the predominance of transitive sentences with a plural object in the use of the D-stems of Type I, and the rare occurrence of Dt-stems, in so far as they serve to denote the corresponding passive or intransitive. The Dt-stem will be discussed in greater detail in Chapter IX; let it suffice here to point to the almost complete absence of Dt forms of frequent D-stems as *kaṣāru* "to bind together, join, collect, organize", *nakāsu* "to cut off, fell", *paqādu* "to entrust, appoint, take care of, inspect", *rakāsu* "to bind", and *ṣabātu* "to seize", cf. the respective entries of AHw sv Dt (note that the claim made here does not apply to the reflexive and reciprocal function of Dt, see 9.1.2 and 9.1.3).

This rare occurrence of the Dt-stem as intransitive equivalent of the D-stem suggests that normally the N-stem is used instead; this situation is found, for instance, in *sapāhu* if it means "to waste, squander"; this meaning is almost always expressed by D (cf. 6.4.2.1 sv, 1x G), but in the passive the N-stem is usual (cf. also CAD sv 6 for D, 7 for Dt, 10 for N). It is, however, difficult to find passages where a passive N-stem is used beside a transitive D-stem, as in ARM 6, 37: r.4'-14', cf. CAD sv *qebēru* 4.

Of the four types distinguished in 5.2, then, it is only in Type II, the intransitive D-stems derived from intransitive G-stems, that the D-stem is not associated with high transitivity. This leads to the conclusion that, as far as the verbal D-stem is concerned, this association is the most important way in which the iconic force of the geminate second radical has been grammaticalized. It provides the link between the two main types of D-stems traditionally distinguished, the intensive and the causative or factitive one, a link which Goetze (1942: 3b, claimes to be inexplicable. The difference between the former and the latter, i.e., between the valency-preserving and valency-extending D-stems, concerns their relationship to the corresponding G-stems; it does not reflect a division in the D-stem itself, which is basically homogeneous in function.

In this chapter only the general background of the verbal D-stem has been outlined. The details will be supplied in the next chapters: Chapter VI will deal with the D-stems of Type I, Chapter VII with those of Types II, III and IV, and Chapter VII with the D-stems which are not dependent upon a G-stem.

Notes to Chapter Five

1 It is pointless to give exact figures, because of the numerous uncertainties in the interpretation of specific verb forms, and, especially, because of the subjective judgements involved in deciding to what extent verb forms which appear to have the same root consonants but have a divergent meaning belong to a single verb or to two or more homonymous verbs. The dictionaries AHw and CAD show striking differences in their handling of such cases; to mention only one extreme example, AHw lists one verb *hesû(m), hasû(m)* "zudecken", which CAD H 176ff splits up into seven verbs.

Nevertheless, we can get a rough impression of the numerical proportions among the verbal stems by taking AHw as a corpus and by simply counting how many times a specific stem is listed in the verbal entries. In doing so, I have adopted the classification of AHw without any critical assessment, and ignoring any forms which have come to light since its publication (but including the Addenda on p. 1541ff). Whenever AHw gives two possibilities for a specific verb form (e.g., sv *ekēpu* "Ntn od Nt") I have counted the first one.

For the D-stem this results in 903 D-stems listed in verbal entries, and another 32 nominal forms with the pattern *purrus* without a corresponding verb or belonging to verbal entries which do not comprise a D-stem. The figures pertaining to the other stems are as follows: G: 1316, Gt: 167, Gtn: 312, N: 395, Nt: 6, Ntn: 98, Š: 369, Št$_1$ (i.e., passive or intransitive forms of Š): 36, Št$_2$: 94, Štn: 53, ŠD: 25, ŠDt: 1 (*raqādu*), Dt: 237, Dtt: 17, Dtn: 88, stems with reduplication: 6. The total number of verbal stems listed in AHw is 1546.

2 The criterion for the existence of a verbal G-stem is the same as that of a verbal D-stem, i.e., that at least one member of the verbal paradigm is attested (see 5.1.1). Thus the occurrence of only a stative, a quite common situation, is not sufficient to prove the existence of a verbal G-stem. Therefore, I have listed D-stems such as *buhhuru* "to make hot" and *quddušu* "to purify" as D tantum verbs (cf. 8.4.1), in spite of the existence of a stative G, in accordance with CAD ssvv, whereas AHw lists them under *bahāru* and *qadāšu*. However, the derivation of verbal forms from adjectives is doubtless a productive procedure, so that it may be merely accidental that no verbal forms are attested.

The usefulness of this criterion is somewhat compromised by the fact that in lexical lists the infinitive is used as a citation form. I assume that, if we find of a specific adjective only adjectival or stative forms and an infinitive in LL, this is not a sufficient criterion to qualify as a verbal G-stem either. Examples are the adjective *dašpu* "sweet", and the stative *zaqin* "he has a beard", from *zaqnu* "bearded", cf. AHw ssvv *dašāpu* and *zaqānu.*

3 The D-stem may have other functions as well, in particular that of forming denominative verbs (GAG § 88g), but this function cannot be considered grammatical since it refers to the etymological background of a verb, not to its use within a system of oppositions determined by grammatical rules, cf. 8.2.

4 For the terms "prototype" and "prototypical" and their use in linguistics, see Taylor 1995, esp. 206ff; Givón 1984: 11ff; Croft 1990: 124ff (in general), 130ff (in relation to transitivity). The prototype or the prototypical member of a category is "the one displaying the greatest number of the most important properties/features" which define the category (Givón 1984: 17). As such it differs from a more peripheral member of the category, which lacks one or more of the relevant properties/features.

5 Cf. Saad and Bolozky 1984: 31. They restrict the number of features that determine the degree of transitivity to two: the number of participants and the degree of affectedness of the object, and claim that "[a]t least as far as Arabic and Hebrew are concerned, these two are sufficient for the purpose of accounting for all or most morphological processes applying to the verb."

6 I will use the terms "transitive verb" and "intransitive verb" in their traditional meaning to indicate the way in which a verb behaves syntactically, i.e., whether it normally has an object or not. There is only an indirect relationship between this syntactic feature of a verb and the degree of transitivity of the sentence in which it occurs, since this degree is determined by other factors, too. I will only distinguish between different degrees of transitivity when it is relevant to the argument.

7 The intransitive use of basically transitive verbs in specialized meanings is widespread in many languages. GAG § 144c and 184d and AHw (e.g., sv *nasāhu* I G 23/24, *našû* II G I 6, *paṭāru* G 14, *tabālu* G 7) explain such cases as elliptic. However, the term "ellipse" implies that something has been omitted; it is only appropriate if we can point out some specific word which has been omitted from the surface structure of the sentence, but is present in the underlying structure and has to be understood to make the sentence complete. Ideally, both the full and the elliptic construction should be attested for a specific expression to qualify as an ellipse. Most cases glossed as elliptic by GAG and AHw do not meet these conditions.

Examples of elliptic constructions in Akkadian are *nadû* "to cast the net" (to catch fish) AbB 2, 169:

12. 16 (ellipse of *šētum*, cf. CAD sv *nadû* v. 1f (p. 80a)); *gamāru* "to render final judgment" AbB 11, 72: 31 (ellipse of *dīnum*, cf. CAD sv 1d-3', AHw sv G 4c); *amāru* "to have a dream" ARM 26/1 p. 477 no. 236: 6f (ellipse of *šuttum*), and *šutēšuru* "to proceed, march on", with ellipse of *urha* or *harrāna* (CAD sv *ešēru* 8a/b; AHw sv *ešēru* St[2] 8). Instances involving D-stems are *ṣubbutum* "to take action" (ARM 26/1 p. 159 no. 27: 37) for normal *ṭêmam ṣubbutum* (OB Mari); *ummudu* "to start work" for *qāta* or *idī ummudu*, cf. CAD sv *emēdu* 4c 3'-a' (NA); *puttû* "to inform" for *uznī puttû* "to open the ears" (OA, see App. to Ch. VI sv **8.**); *nuppulu* "to gouge out (eyes)", to blind" (also with *īnī*, see App. to Ch. VI sv **1.**), and *tubbuku* "to discharge (faeces), to defecate" SpTU 1, 44: 13 (SB).

8 This intransitive use of basically transitive verbs is especially common in the technical language of omens, for instance, *(h)alālu* "to hang" (intr.) (CAD sv *alālu* A 1a-3'); *hepû* "to split" (intr.) (CAD sv 5c); *kaṣāru* "to cluster" (CAD sv 3a); *parāsu* "sich teilen" (AHw sv *p.* I G 7b); *paṭāru* "sich auflösen" (AHw sv G 14f); *petû* "sich entfernen" (of celestial bodies, AHw sv G 22), and *zâzu* "to divide" (intrans.) (CAD sv 1a, AHw sv G II 3a, 3d).

9 We will ignore here verbs which have a different meaning depending on whether they are transitive or intransitive, such as *sanāqu* "to arrive" versus "to check, to interrogate", *sadāru* "to array, set in a row", versus "to do/occur regularly", and *sahāru* "to seek", versus "to turn" (intr.). Such verbs must be classified both as transitive and as intransitive.

10 An exception is the OA idiom *harrānam kuššudum* "to join a caravan" (CAD sv 5a); possibly, *harrānum* can be taken here as a collective noun referring to the people partaking in the caravan. Other usages such as those mentioned by CAD sv 5c and 6, and AHw sv D 1e/f represent peripheral Akkadian and are ignored here.

11 A selection of typical examples from the corpus comprises the following:
A) natural phenomena: wind (e.g., *abāku* B (all instances); *našāpu*: BagF. 16, 262: 86); storm (e.g., *kapāru* B: ZA 83, 5: 24; *pasāsu* **1.**: AbB 3, 34: 14; *rakāsu* **4.**: SBH 4: 37 + 9/10: 35); flood (e.g., *abātu* **2.**: Sg. 8: 90), the river (*abātu* **2.**: Sn. 99: 46), and the sea (*gamāru* **10.**); possibly also *našāru* **2.**: UET 6, 392: 14 // CT 16, 12: I 3 (freezing and frost). Fire also belongs to this category, but since it is regularly deified, it falls directly under the animate beings; this also applies to stars and planets.
B) manifestations of divine or royal power comprise concepts as the "word" of a god (*abātu* **1.**: ASKT p. 127: 34; *ṣarāpu* **1.**: LSS 1/6, 34 note 10); numinous phenomena as *melammū*, the awe-inspiring radiance of gods and kings (*sahāpu* **1.**); divine weapons which represent their power: a sword (*sahāpu* **4.**: IV R 21b: r.19; *letû* **2.**: RA 18, 198: 3); a *miṭṭu* (*kamāru* **2.**: Lugal 257); a weapon in general: *kakku* (*râs/šu*: Ee IV 16; *abātu* **1.**: Angim 165); furthermore, instruments used by kings to defeat or kill enemies: the *rappu* "bridle" and the *nīru* "yoke" (both *lâṭu* **2.**, **3.**), and an arrow (*šaqāru*: ArOr 37, 488: 2). Such cases are difficult to distinguish from cases of personification: of a wall (*katāmu* **4.**: BWL 100: 39); a bolt (*katāmu* **6.**: MAOG 5/3, 17: 14 var.); a net (*sahāšu*: Ét. de Meyer 85: 2); a shoe (*našāku* **2.**: Gilg. VI 41 acc. to CAD sv *šēnu* A 1d: "(You, Ištar, are a shoe) *mu-na-ši-kat bēliša* "that pinches its owner").
C) words referring to magic and sorcery (*kišpū*, *ruhû*, *rusû*), or substances which can contravene sorcery: the *hašû*-plant (*hašû*: Maqlû V 35); the *tiskur*-plant (*sekēru*: RA 18, 165: 20); the tamarisk (*paṭāru* **3.**: BagF. 18, 272: 17'); water (*mesû* **1.**: BW 15: 16b); herb (*pašāru* **2.**: KAR 165: 17).
D) illnesses: headache (*haṣāṣu* **3.**: SpTU 2, 2: I 6 // CT 17, 19: 6; *salātu* **1.**: *ib.* 8); the *šimmatu* disease (*zaqātu* **2.**: JNES 33, 342: 20); the *urbatu* disease (*abātu* **4.**: RA 41, 41: 7); an unknown illness (*katāmu* **5.**: Iraq 31, 87: 50); to these concepts one could add sleep, which "overwhelms" persons (*katāmu* **5.**: BWL 42: 72).

Sometimes it is difficult to determine whether a specific concept which is mentioned as subject of an action verb should be regarded as agentive or not, first, because of the possibility of personification, and, second, because it is quite common to say in Akkadian that misfortune or a part of the body has "seized" a man (cf. CAD sv *ṣabātu* 1b/c), that fear or sleep has "covered" him (CAD sv *katāmu* 2): it is not always obvious whether the subject in question is seen as an entity endowed with power, or whether the expression in question has become purely conventional.

12 It might be argued that participles used as instrument nouns, such as *mušaqqiltu* "balance" (App. sv **3**.), also have an inanimate subject ("a thing which weighs"). The relevant words occurring in the corpus are enumerated in note 18 to Ch. VI. However, such cases are clearly secondary developments: starting as participles used as agents noun referring to persons, they extended their semantic range to include instruments and were subsequently lexicalized. The development from agent noun to instrument noun is well known in language, cf. the literature cited in 2.2.4.2.

CHAPTER SIX

THE D-STEMS OF TRANSITIVE VERBS

6.0. This chapter deals with the D-stems of Type I according to the classification adopted in 5.2, i.e., the D-stems of transitive G-stems which preserve the valency of the G-stem. The general character of these D-stems and the way they are related to other types have already been expounded in 5.6. In this chapter a more detailed description is given of the most important D-stems of type I.

Two kinds of D-stems, however, which would seem to belong to this type, will not be discussed here. The first kind are D-stems which differ so markedly in meaning from their corresponding G-stems that it is doubtful whether they are derived from the same root. Well-known cases are *upputu* "to tarry, be delayed" (cf. *lapātu* "to touch, smear, affect") and *zubbulu* "to linger, keep waiting" (cf. *zabālu* "to carry"). Since this study is not concerned with etymological speculations or lexical aspects of individual D-stems, but with the nature of the D-stem as a grammatical category, I will regard the D-stem in all such cases as independent of the G-stem, i.e., as a D tantum verb. Thus *lupputu* and *zubbulu* in the meanings specified above are listed as D tantum verbs in Chapter VIII.

The second kind consists of D-stems which, for various reasons, are likely to be denominatives of nouns derived from the corresponding G-stems. In this case the relationship between G and D is indirect. Examples are *uhhuzu* "to mount (an object) in precious materials", from *ihzū* "mountings"; and *muhhuru* "to go or send upstream", probably from *māhirtu* "upstream direction" (CAD sv *māhiru* 2). The main argument for regarding these examples as denominatives is their close semantic association with a noun in combination with their specialized meaning. There is, however, no clear-cut distinction between the denominative D-stems to be discussed in Chapter VIII, and some idiomatic and lexicalized meanings of D-stems discussed in this chapter. This problem will be dealt with in greater detail in Chapter VIII.

The description of the D-stems of Type I is based on a corpus of D-stems which is found in the Appendix to this chapter (pp. 200-236). It basically comprises all transitive verbs whose meaning can be established beyond a doubt, and all D forms of these verbs which are registered in the dictionaries, except those which - for whatever reason - are uncertain, or belong to peripheral dialects of Akkadian. A more detailed account of the criteria for inclusion is to be found in the Introduction to the Appendix on p. 200f.

The large number of D-stems of Type I and the enormous variety in the way in which they are used necessitates a rather detailed description of many individual verbs. So as not to clog the argument and make this chapter even longer than it is, only a limited number of verbs will be discussed in the main text.

6.1. General premises

In the previous chapter (especially 5.6.4) the general nature of the relationship between the D-stems of Type I and the corresponding G-stems was described. It can be summarized in the following way.

The contrast between verb forms with and without gemination is basically realized as a contrast in transitivity: forms with gemination are generally associated with a high degree of transitivity. In intransitive verbs, therefore, there is a sharp contrast in transitivity between D and G, which has been grammaticalized as the factitive function of the D-stem. In transitive verbs such a sharp contrast does not exist, because only highly transitive G-stems have a frequently used D-stem; this precludes a grammaticalization process of the kind which took place in the factitive D-stems. This situation has two important consequences.

First, the coexistence of D and G forms with a closely similar function has made it possible to reserve the D-stem primarily for sentences with prototypical transitivity, i.e., those which have an agentive subject, denote a salient action - such as the verbs listed in 5.6.2.2 - and have an object which is concrete and affected by the action.

The corresponding G-stem can be used in the same circumstances, but to a much larger extent than the D-stem it is also used in a wider range of contexts, e.g., in secondary meanings, with abstract objects, or without object, irrespective of the degree of transitivity they imply, cf. 5.6.4. By using a D form, a speaker can emphasize that the action denoted by the verb should be viewed in its concrete, literal sense, rather than in some secondary metaphorical meaning; that it has a visible effect on the object; and that the direct object (the "patient" in the literal sense) is actually and visibly affected by the action.

Second, in the verbs of Type I the original semantic contrast which tends to exist between iconic categories and the corresponding neutral ones has been preserved. As we have seen in the previous chapters, gemination of the second radical in Akkadian has a strong association with plurality and salience. This also applies to the D-stems of Type I.

Thus gemination has a wider use than underlining high transitivity alone, which, strictly speaking, only applies to the verbal D-stem used in the predicate of transitive sentences. In transitive sentences with a plural object, the association with high transitivity and with plurality reinforce each other. Accordingly, the great majority of the instances of the D-stems of Type I consist of active sentences with a plural element, usually the direct object.

Because the difference in transitivity between the G- and the D-stems of Type I is too small to lead to a grammaticalization of the forms with gemination and, consequently, to a clearcut distinction in use, it is generally unpredictable how the D-stem of a specific transitive G-stem will be used, apart from the limitations imposed upon it by its association with high transitivity, salience and plurality.

This explains the striking differences between verbs of similar meaning and between different dialects with regard to the use of the D-stem. The first point was already touched on in 5.6.2.2, where it was pointed out that even verbs with closely similar meanings may behave quite differently. For example, Edzard (1962: 116a) points to the striking contrast between *dâku* "to kill", which is hardly found in the D-stem (see App. sv), and *ṭabāhu* "to slaughter", which is almost always D if its object is plural (see 6.4.1.1 sv).

The differences between dialects are even more evident. If we compare the three most important dialects, OB, OA and SB, we find striking differences as to which D-stems are used, and in which way. Each dialect has made its own selection, and has used the forms selected for its own ends. Since the use of D in these three dialects is to be compared in 6.9.1 and 6.9.2, no examples will be given here.

The best way to characterize the relationship between a D-stem of Type I and the corresponding G-stem is to view them as basically separate verbs, which have their own typical range of uses, but are also closely associated through their common root and the ensuing common meaning. The former characteristic explains the overall unpredictability of their relationship, the latter explains the large overlap in meaning between D and G that we see in many verbs of Type I.

It will be argued in Chapter XI that such a characterization agrees with the actual way in which the verbal D-stem has originated: not through direct derivation, but through a secondary association between verb forms with gemination and corresponding simple forms (see 11.1 and 11.2). The much more regular relationship existing between factitive D-stems and the corresponding G-stems represents a more advanced stage of development.

6.2. The functions of the D-stems of Type I

The association of the D-stem with high transitivity, salience and plurality provides a general framework which determines to a large extent how it is used. Within that framework we can distinguish three functions for which the D-stems of Type I are used. By far the most important function is that of underlining the presence of a plural element in the sentence; it will be designated briefly as "D for plurality". A large part of this chapter (6.3 - 6.7) is taken up by an examination of which types of plurality play a role in the use of D, in which verbs they occur and in which circumstances these D-stems are used. The second function, which will be called "idiomatic" or "lexicalized", is to convey another meaning than that of the G-stem, often in such a way that D implies an increase in the salience of the action or its participants. It has a rather marginal position as compared to plurality and will be examined in 6.8.1 - 6.8.3.

These two functions cannot, however, account for all D-stems of Type I. A considerable number of them show neither an association with plurality nor a differentiation in meaning. In that case it usually remains unclear what the difference between G and D is (if any). Most of these verbs are too rare to give us a clear notion of the way they are used (and will therefore not be discussed in detail), but there are also a few very common D-stems to which this applies, such as *gamāru* "to bring to an end, do completely, use up" and *katāmu* "to cover, close" (see 6.8.4).

In the following sections the use of the D-stems of Type I will be described in detail, in its three main categories: plurality (6.3 - 6.7), idiomatic use (6.8.1 - 6.8.3), and the unclear cases (6.8.4), a classification which is convenient in view of the large amount of material to be included and discussed, but rather artificial, because many D-stems fall under more than one category. This description necessitates a rather lengthy exposition of many individual verbs; we will concentrate in particular on those which occur with sufficient frequency to permit meaningful conclusions.

6.3. The D-stems of Type I and plurality

The most important function of the D-stems of Type I is that of underlining plurality. Before enumerating the relevant verbs and discussing the general nature of this function, we have to make the following preliminary remarks.

First of all, this function is a typical representative of verbal plurality with its "global" meaning (cf. Dressler 1968: 92ff and 2.1.5): it can underline plurality of various constituents of the sentence, depending on the context and the meaning of the verb. In this chapter evidence is provided for plurality of the action itself, the subject, the direct object, the indirect object, and the accusative used to qualify a passive verb form, mostly a "passive" stative (cf. GAG § 145c/d/h), which is henceforth called an "adjunct accusative". However, plurality of the direct object is the only kind of verbal plurality which is frequently expressed by the D-stem; for the other kinds its use is marginal, restricted to a specific context (such as durativity in *šumma*-clauses, see 6.6.1) or more or less hypothetical. The form that is normally used for the expression of verbal plurality in these cases is the Gtn-stem, which is in this respect complementary to the D-stems of Type I (cf. 6.7.3).

Second, it was argued in 5.6.3 that the relationship between the D-stems of Type I and the G-stem has not been grammaticalized but has preserved its original semantic nature. Therefore, the use of D forms in plural contexts is not a grammatical rule, but a tendency based on semantic factors. This implies that it is optional: this tendency need not be realized, and the G-stem can also be used in the same circumstances. On the other hand, this state of affairs allows a speaker of Akkadian to deviate from the norm and to use D forms in contexts which are not strictly plural, in order to convey some special nuance; see further 6.4.9 and 6.9.2.2.

Moreover, the kind of plurality involved is not grammatical but semantic plurality. The constituent in question may be singular in form, provided that it is semantically equivalent to a plural. This applies in particular to two kinds of substantives which take an intermediate position between singular and plural: collectives, i.e., "lexemes which denote collections or groups, of persons or objects" (Lyons 1977: 315), and mass nouns, or "non-count nouns", which refer to substances that are normally not seen as consisting of individual entities.

Examples of collectives found in combination with D-stems which normally have a plural object are *ṣābu* "troop of workers or soldiers, army, people",[1] and *awīlūtu* "mankind, people, men", which refer to persons, and *makkūru* "possessions", *enūtu* or *unūtu* "tools, equipment" and *luqūtu* "goods, merchandise", which refer to inanimate objects. Just as *ṣābu,* other words which can refer to groups of people are used as collectives, too: the words *mātu* "land, people" (cf. CAD sv 4), *ummānu* "army", *emūqu* "military forces", and *puhru* "assembly" are also qualified by D-stems which regularly or often have a plural object.[2]

A peculiar feature of the D-stems associated with plurality is that they often occur with mass nouns, too. In OB and SB, for instance, we find many D forms which normally have a plural object, qualifying words such as *še'u* "barley", *qanû* "reed" and metals. Especially in OA, metals are often qualified by D-stems and in particular by *purrus* forms.[3]

This is consistent with the fact that in Akkadian mass nouns are also frequently plural in form, cf. the pluralia tantum *mû* "water", *šūmū* "garlic", and *šamaššammū* "sesame", possibly also *sahlû* "cress", cf. AHw sv ("meist Pl."). GAG § 61h observes that in later Akkadian, especially in NA, words for metals and produce are often written with a plural determinative, and may possibly represent pluralia tantum, too. A word which also behaves like a mass noun is *šīru* "meat, flesh, body";[4] this is in line with the apparently indiscriminate use of singular *šīru* and plural *šīrū* "flesh", cf. CAD sv.

The use of gemination in combination with mass nouns and collectives was already pointed out in 3.1.3.2 with regard to the plural forms of the pattern *parras.* Yet such concepts seem to be less consistently accompanied by D forms than real plurals; this is in accordance with their intermediate status between singular and plural. The same applies to a noun as *panû* "face", which is a plurale tantum. Moreover, a number of exceptions noted in the following sections can be explained by assuming that words for "everything" (*napharu, kalû, mimma,* etc.), generalizing relative sentences with *mala* "everything which", *ša* "whosoever", etc., and generic singulars ("each man", etc.) can also be treated on a par with plurals.[5]

A certain ambiguity arises from the fact that plural nouns in the construct state are often not explicitly marked as such, cf. GAG § 64l and Mayer, Or. 59, 452f. If they form an exception as singulars, such cases are classified as plural here, unless this is contradicted by the context. Cases in point are the expressions *ṣubāt rubûtija* "my princely garments" (Ash. Nin. A I 56) and *ṣubāt* (túg) *kabrūtini* "our heavy garments" (tr. CAD sv *kabru* d), which, if interpreted as singular, form an exception to the otherwise strong association of *šarāṭu* with plurality (cf. App. sv). In many cases, however, the plural nature of such construct states is made unambiguous by means of a following genitive in the plural, as in *pa-gar gērîšu* "the bodies of his enemies" (RIMA 2/I, 195: 29, alternating with *pa-ag-ri gērîšu* in 308: 18), or an attributive adjective, e.g., *halqūtum e-pí-iš haṭîtim* "runaway evildoers" (AbB 13, 60: 69, tr. Van Soldt). If they form the subject of the sentence, the agreement in number between subject and finite verb shows whether they are plural or not: for instance, AGH 80: 83 *lip-ta-aṭ-ṭi-ru ki-ṣir lemnūtija* "let the knots of my enemies be untied", and OEC 1, 33: 60 *pu-uṭ-ṭu-ru ri-ki-is bābāti* "the joints of the doors are loose".

In the next sections the various types of plurality expressed by the D-stem of Type I will be listed and discussed. Because the material is so extensive, the verbs in question will be divided into several groups and subgroups. The first main group (6.4 - 6.5) concerns the use of D in sentences which contain an explicit plural element: this is usually the direct object (6.4), but may also be another constituent, namely, the subject (6.5.1), the indirect object (6.5.2), or an adjunct accusative (6.5.3). The instances with a plural object (6.4) have in their turn been divided into subgroups on the basis of their meaning and frequency.

The second main group (6.6) concerns the use of D in sentences which do not contain an explicit plural element; in this case plurality refers to the action itself. This group will be divided into three subgroups: the present D in *šumma*-clauses (6.6.1), the absolute use of D in participles (6.6.2) and some individual verbs arranged according to dialect (6.6.3).

This classification is convenient for the presentation of the material, but in view of the global nature of verbal plurality (see 2.1.5) it is rather artificial. Many verbs have to be assigned to more than one group.

A final remark should be made concerning the purpose of the lists in the following sections. They are first and foremost descriptive. It cannot be proved for every individual instance, that the presence of the plural element in question is the actual motivation for the use of D, because that use is influenced by other factors, too. However, the fact that most of these D-stems correlate rather consistently with a plural object (in the case of plurality of the object), and/or are used in contrast to the corresponding G-stems in passages where a plural element contrasts with a singular element, shows that it is plurality which causes the use of the D-stem in these cases. As such they contrast with many other D-stems which are also found in sentences with a plural element, but for which it is difficult to prove that plurality is the motivating factor.

6.4. Plurality of the direct object

The most important and best known aspect of verbal plurality expressed by the D-stem is its use in sentences with a plural object. This use is recorded in many grammatical studies of Akkadian.[6] It is explicitly indicated for a number of verbs in CAD and AHw[7] and corresponds to a similar use in other Semitic languages.[8]

There is twofold evidence to show that plurality of the object can cause the use of D. Firstly, there is the fact that there are a number of very common verbs whose D-stem is largely restricted to sentences with a plural object. Secondly, there are contrasting pairs of G and D correlating with a singular and a plural object, respectively, in the same sentence or in the same text; cf., for instance, the following cases of *petû* G and D:

(01A) RIME 4, 603: 26f *nārātim ú-pé-et-ti* "I dug (lit. opened) (D) canals";
(01B) *ib.* 47 *nāram ep-te-šum-ma* "I dug (G) a canal for it (GN)";

(02) RitDiv. 32: 47f *abullaša lū pe-ti-a-at* (...) *padānāt imittim lū pu-ut-ta-a* "Let its gate (i.e., of the *bāb ekallim* of the liver) be open (G) (...), let the paths of the right be open (D)."

Compare also the following duplicate versions of the same text, which differ, however, in that one of them has a singular object with a G-stem, the other the corresponding plural object with a D-stem:

(03A) ZA 16, 180: III 33f *i-lap-pat libbu* (*šà-bu*) *ša haršā[ti]* / *i-šal-lip šèr-ru ša tarâ[ti]* "(Lamaštu) touches (G) the belly of the women in labour, she snatches (G) the infant from the nurses";
(03B) UM 1/2, 113: III 18f *ú-lap-pat libbī* (*šà-bi*) *ša haršā[ti]* / *ú-šal-lap šèr-ri ša tarâti* (same translation, but with "bellies" and "infants" and 2x D (cf. CAD sv *šalāpu* 1c);

Although such contexts are comparatively rare, they form important evidence for the association of the D-stem with plurality. Not all contrasting pairs of G and D, however, can be used to demonstrate the connection between the use of D and a plural object. There are also passages in which G and D occur side by side, where both stems have a plural or singular object, for instance:

(04) AfO 18, 290: 18 *libbī unnišū idīja ik-su-ú birkīja ik-su-ú šēpīja ālikāt[i] ú-ka-su-u* "(the demons) have weakened my heart, have bound (G) my arms, have bound (G) my knees, have bound (D) my running feet." (Also quoted as (122) in 6.9.4);

(05) SKS p. 42: 45 *e-dil*$_x$(TIL) *bītu ud-du-lu bābu nadû har-gul-lim* "the house is closed (G), the door is shut (D), the bolts are put in place." (Also quoted as (127) in 6.9.4).

Such passages are especially common in literary texts, where many D-stems are used as stylistic variants of the G-stem. Thus the use of a D-stem with a plural object and a G-stem with a singular object in the same passage is especially meaningful if it occurs in stylistically neutral (i.e., non-literary) texts, such as letters, legal and administrative documents, and in scholarly texts such as omens and prescriptions. It is also significant that the fourth combination which is theoretically possible, i.e., a G-stem with plural object beside a D-stem with the same object in the singular, does not seem to be attested.

The D-stems which are predominantly used with a plural object will be listed in the following groups on the basis of their meaning: 1. verbs of destruction (6.4.1); 2. verbs which have a violent impact on the object (6.4.2); 3. verbs of closing, opening, binding and loosening (6.4.3); 4. verbs of seizing and controlling (6.4.4); 5. verbs of collecting (6.4.5); 6. verbs of creating (6.4.6); 7. verbs of giving, taking and carrying (6.4.7), and 8. verbs which have a marginal association with plurality of the direct object (6.4.8).

This division is mainly for practical purposes; the boundaries between the groups are not clear-cut, and the classification of some verbs, especially those which have a wide range of uses, is to some extent subjective and disputable.

Of each group the most important, typical and/or remarkable verbs will be discussed in the main text of this chapter; the rest is briefly discussed in the Appendix. The entry for each verb begins with a survey of the direct objects with which it is combined; this is a condensed version of the corresponding entry in the Appendix. Subsequently, the general nature of the use of the D-stem is discussed, some relevant passages are quoted, and a characterization of the use of the corresponding G-stem is given in the shortest way possible, mostly by means of a reference to one of the dictionaries, preferably CAD, which often quotes a fuller context and thus gives a better idea of the way a verb is used.

The verbal adjective of the verbs discussed here is largely omitted; the reason for this is stated in the introduction to the Appendix. If it were not omitted, there would be a remarkable increase in the number of exceptions; this also applies to the stative in so far as it is used in omen texts in a specialized meaning. All cases which are not included here will be discussed in Chapter X, which deals with the pattern *purrus*.

For the symbols and abbreviations used here and in the Appendix, see the Abbreviations on p. 451. An additional symbol is ↔, which denotes contrasting pairs of a G form with a singular object versus a D form with a plural object. Note that in this chapter the term "plural" includes the dual, and that "plural object" also comprises plurality of the subject of passive Dt forms and of statives which require a passive translation, and plurality of nouns in the genitive which follow a participle.

6.4.1. Group I: verbs of destruction

The first group to be discussed consists of verbs denoting actions that result in a destruction of the object. Semantically they belong to the most typical high transitivity verbs (cf. 5.4 and 5.6). Their meaning entails that the action can be performed only once for a specific object: one can only once fell a single tree, slaughter a single sheep or sever a single body part. Conversely, each tree to be felled, each sheep to be slaughtered and each body part to be severed normally requires a separate act of felling, slaughtering and severing. Thus plurality of such objects typically entails plurality of the action. This is the main criterion for inclusion in this group. It explains the remarkably consistent correlation that these verbs show between the use of D and plurality of the direct object, and it contrasts them with other verbs that are similar in meaning, but can also refer to actions that can be performed repeatedly for the same object, such as ***našāku*** "to bite", ***kabāsu*** "to trample" and ***sahālu*** "to pierce" (see 6.4.2).

The following list enumerates the D-stems of this class, classified according to frequency: group Ia occurs more than ten times in the corpus, group Ib from three to ten times, group Ic less than three times. The verbs under C have been included mainly for the sake of completeness; the evidential value of such a small number of instances is obviously insubstantial.[9] As examples of this group the verbs of Ia will be discusssed.

Group Ia: D-stems occurring more than ten times in the corpus:

Abātu	to destroy, ruin	**Palāq/ku**	to slaughter, massacre
Batāqu	to cut off, pierce, break	**Parāsu**	to cut off/into pieces, separate
Hepû	to break, demolish	**Rasāp/bu**	to strike, cut down
Nakāsu	to cut off, fell	**Salātu**	to split off, cut
Napālu	to tear out, dig up, demolish	**Šebēru**	to break, smash
Napāṣu	to strike, smite	**Ṭabāhu**	to slaughter
Nasāhu	to tear out, remove		

Group Ib: D-stems occurring from three to ten times in the corpus:

Alātu	to swallow	**Qamû**	to burn
Hanāqu	to strangle	**Qatāpu**	to pluck, cut off
Haṣāṣu	to break (reeds)	**Râs/šu**	to strike
Kapāru B	to uproot, cut down	**Šahāṭu**	to strip, remove
Karātu	to break off, cut off	**Šalāpu**	to tear out, draw (weapon)
Kaṣāṣu	to trim, cut, mutilate	**Šalāqu**	to cut open, slit
Marāqu	to crush	**Šamāṭu**	to strip off, tear loose
Parā'u	to cut off, sever	**Šarāṭu**	to tear to pieces, shred
Pašāṭu	to erase	**Šatāqu**	to split, fissure
Qalāpu	to peel, skin		

Group Ic: D-stems occurring less than three times in the corpus:

Abāku B	to uproot, overturn	**Pâšu**	to crush
Haṣābu	to break, cut off, cut down	**Šarāmu**	to trim
Kasāpu	to chip, break off	**Šarāpu**	to burn
Kasāsu	to gnaw, consume	**Šaṭāṭu**	to tear open
Kâṣu	to flay, skin		

6.4.1.1. Discussion of the most important verbs

Abātu "to destroy, ruin"; D mostly has a pl. obj.: **1.** places, mountain(s), land, city/cities, etc.; **2.** (parts of) buildings (also sg.); **3.** persons (118), mostly part. + gen. pl., rarely with sg. obj.; **4.** body (parts); **5.** boundary stone (sg.).

Abātu D is a purely literary D-stem restricted to SB (1x literary OB); a large part of the instances are participles, used as epithets of gods and kings, in which the use of D seems to be stereotyped, cf. 6.9.3. The distinction AHw sv D makes between G "vernichten" and D "ganz vernichten, zerstören" is difficult to ascertain. Most objects of D are plurals, collectives or mass nouns. Moreover, the sg. objects mostly concern large buildings, so that what is said in 6.4.9 may be relevant here. The main exception to this is 5., which comprises instances of a single clause from the curse formula of boundary stones, for instance BBS 34: 9ff *mannu arkû ša ṣalmu u narâ annâ ub-ba-tu* "whoever in the future will (wants to, tries to, etc.) destroy this statue and stela"; perhaps D is caused by the generic character of the clause. That it is also a stereotyped expression is suggested by the fact that a similar clause also occurs in RIs, and always has G there, acc. to CAD sv 1b [cancel AKA 251: 85, cf. RIMA 2/I, 254: 85]. As to the other exceptions, for

Maqlû III 110 see (118) in 6.9.2.2; KAR 350: 19 *ub-bu-ta-ku* "I am destroyed" is obviously metaphoric and quite atypical; for RA 41, 41: 7 (the *urbatu* disease) *mu-ab-bi-ṭat kalla zumur amēli* "that destroys the whole body of a man", see the remark on the part. D above.

Most instances of G listed in CAD have a sg. obj. (pl. only Maqlû II 174 (persons), VAB 7, 184: 53 (armies), Ee VII 90 (gods, part.), BA 5, 618: 26 (houses), CT 39, 18: 74 (walls), cf. CAD sv lex. sect. and 1a-d). Thus there is a correlation between D + pl. obj. versus G + sg. obj., although it is not quite consistently observed, cf. 6.9.2.2.

Batāqu "to cut off, pierce (dykes), break"; D almost always has a pl. obj.: **1.** body parts; **2.** persons (1x); **3.** various objects: trees, stones, pieces of clothing, causeways, ropes, rings, *but(t)uqātu* "breaches" (qu. below); **4.** water(ways); **5.** abstract object: *bit[qū'a]* "allegations against me" (1x); **6.** exceptions: see below.

The use of D + pl. obj. is explicitly indicated by AHw sv D 1: "(in großer Zahl) abschneiden". For the contrast G ↔ D cf. especially **1.** versus *qaqqada batāqu* "to cut off the head" (CAD sv 1a), and the parallel contrast N/Dt in the recurring omen apodosis *but(t)uqtum ibbattaq* vs. *but(t)uqātu ub-ta-at-ta-qá* "the dyke/dykes will be burst" (RA 65, 74: 74'; also YOS 10, 26: III 29). For the restriction of D to the literal meaning of *batāqu,* and to concrete objects see 5.6.4.

If the objects listed above occur in the sg., G is mostly used, cf. CAD sv 1-3, AHw sv G, but with *mê* "water" both D (**4.**) and G (CAD sv 2b, AHw sv G 4d) are found. Otherwise, G + pl. obj. is rare (VAB 4, 174: 34 "to cut through" (mountains)); a remarkable exception is the consistent use of G, also with a plural object, for the productive rather than destructive act of cutting stones to make statues: "to roughhew", cf. CAD sv 4, AHw sv G 2, also SAA 1, 110: 12ff and possibly 229: 10 ("to trim" trunks (?)).

Exceptional cases of D + sg. obj.: AbB 1, 27: 28 = (22), see 6.4.9; TuL 74: 7 ${}^{\text{GIŠ}}$*lammu ištu kirê ú-bat-ta-qu-u-ni* "they cut an almond tree from the garden", see possibly CAD sv 8c ("they cut branches off the nut trees in the garden", a logical plural ?).

Hepû "to break, demolish"; D usually has a pl. obj.: **1.** tablets and the like; **2.** other concrete objects; **3.** "to destroy": wells, houses, cities, lands (06B), mountains, etc.; **4.** "to destroy, mutilate" animate beings and body parts; **5.** "to cut" (planks), "to prune" (trees); **6.** exceptions: see below.

For the use of D + pl. obj., cf. CAD 170b sv ("with object in plural"); for G + sg. obj. ↔ D + pl. obj., cf.:

> (06A) Sg. Wi. 112: 80 *āl šarrūtišu* (...) *karpāniš ah-pi* "I destroyed his royal city like a pot";
> (06B) *ib.* 98: 14 *mātāti nākirī kalīšin karpāniš u-hap-pi-ma* "I destroyed all lands of the enemies like pots"; similarly BiOr. 28, 11f: 22'f (but written ideographically: gaz vs. gaz.meš).

G mostly has a sg. obj., but G + pl. obj. is common, too; cf., for instance, OB *kunukkātim huppûm* in VAB 6, 207: 19, but *kunukkātim hepûm* in VAB 5, 23a: 47 and BIN 7, 75: 14, and *ṭuppātim huppûm* in AbB 7, 153: 9, but *ṭuppātim hepûm ib.* 39 and 48 (= (131BC) in 6.9.5), and also in 2, 162: 7. The polysemy of the sign AH (for *ah, ih* and *uh*) makes some forms ambiguous, e.g., *AH-te-pi-šu-nu-ti* UM 1/2, 56: 8.

Exceptional cases of D + sg. obj.: AbB 1, 27: 20 = (22); ARM 6, 5: 13 = (18); BWL 146: 38 = (23); ABL 892: r.25 = (24), all discussed in 6.4.9; ARM 27, 12: 10 ${}^{\text{GIŠ}}$m[á] *hu-up-pa-at* "the ship is broken", see 10.2; NESA 345: r.2 var. (obj. *šá-da-a*, prob. to be explained as a collective; AMT 105: 19 *tultu* (...) [*ina*] *muhhi appišu ú-hap-pa* "he will crush a worm (...) upon his nose" (influenced by *ib.* 15 where the object is plural ?); Tn.-Ep. VIa 21 *ša kippassu hup-pa-at* (cf. CAD sv 1 end, meaning unclear).

Nakāsu "to cut off, fell"; D almost always has a pl. obj.: **1.** "to cut off" body parts; **2.** "to slaughter" animals and people "like animals"; **3.** "to cut, fell" trees and other wooden objects (132A); **4.** various other pl. objects; **5.** exceptions: see below.

For the use of D + pl. obj., cf. CAD sv 6 "with pl. object"; the contrast G ↔ D is particularly evident in the MA laws where the cutting off of parts of the body as a punishment is expressed by D for paired limbs as ears (KAV 1: I 52. 54. 65; III 57; V 92; also nose plus ears: I 50), but by G for single limbs: a finger (I 80, 92, 96; 2: IV 17), a lip (1: I 96), the nose (1: II 53). In the apparent exception KAV 1: III 79 *šumma a'īlu* (...) *ašassu lā ú-na-ak-ki-iš* "If a man (whose wife has run away from him) does not mutilate his wife" (thus CAD sv 6b; cf. AHw sv D 3 (sic)), the mutilation consists in the cutting off of her ears (cf. *ib.* 57); the ears form the logical object which causes the use of D (cf. Driver-Miles 1935: 468).

If the objects specified above are sg., G is normally used, but G + pl. obj. is also found, cf. CAD sv 1-4, AHw sv G, and note esp. D // G in Sn. 46: 12 = (20), and - in contrast to the situation in MA pointed out above - AfO 17, 273: 36 "they will cut off (*i-na-ki-su*) his nose and ears", from a MA harem edict.

For the remarkable difference in the use of *nakāsu* D between OB and SB see 6.9.3.

Exceptional cases of D + sg. obj.: TDP 182: 44f, see 6.6.1.1 sv; KAV 1: III 79 (see above); BWL 78: 136 *bēra lu-na-ak-kis* "I will slaughter a calf"; IV R 25: II 22 (hand, context broken), see 6.9.2.2.

Napālu "to tear out, dig up, demolish"; D mostly has a pl. obj.: **1.** "to gouge out (eyes), to blind", + *īnī*, elliptically without *īnī*, with sg. and pl. obj., and without overt obj. (08); **2.** teeth: "to pick" (?) (prot.); **3.** "to dig up" *eperē* "dust, earth" (prot.); no overt obj.: part. *munappi[lum]* "digger" → 6.6.2 and "to search" (80) → 6.6.3.2; **4.** rest: "to turn upside down" a city (79), a house (prot. → 6.6.1); "to destroy" a temple (1x).

D shows a wide variation in its association with plurality: pl. obj. in **1.** and **2.**, different types of pl. action in **3.** and **4.** Most instances are discussed in 6.6.1.1 sv, 6.6.2, and 6.6.3.2.

G is used in similar contexts (CAD sv *n.* A 1: "to dig out, dig up, quarry, gouge out (eyes, nipples)"), but far more often means "to tear down, demolish" (*ib.* 2, AHw sv *n.* I G 3). It is remarkable that D is not found in this meaning, apart from the one instance mentioned under **4.**; cf. *naqāru* (often coordinated with *napālu*, cf. CAD sv *napālu* A 2a-1' a'), which has the same peculiarity.

Napāṣu "to strike, smite"; D mostly has a pl. obj.: **1.** people and animals; **2.** "to break" doors; **3.** of substances (cf. 6.3): dough ("to break"), barley ("to crush", also G: AbB 13, 49: 11 + note); VA LL, said of malt, beerwort and sesame (all pl.); **4.** accounts: "to clear" (OA).

Apart from **4.**, D is restricted to the most salient nuances of the verb, which involve a destruction of the direct object, esp. **1.** and **2.**, cf. 5.6.4. G is often intrans., cf. CAD sv *n.* A 1; if it is trans., the object is sg. (*ib.* 2a/b, 4), except BA 5, 533: 17 (people) and Šurpu III 70 (door+bolt), or a mass noun (*ib.* 3) (flax, bitumen, etc.). G is also common in OB in the idiomatic expression *qātam napāṣum* "to reject, refuse", cf. CAD sv 2c, and with *nikkassu* "to clear" (accounts), cf. CAD sv 5 (versus D in OA (**4.**)).

Nasāhu "to tear out, remove"; D mostly has a pl. obj.: **1.** "to remove, uproot" persons; **2.** body parts; **3.** other concrete objects; **4.** idiomatic (obj. also sg.): + *awātim* "to conclude", of silver: "to cash"?, + *šīmam*: "to deduct", "to excerpt" (tablet(s), both sg. and pl.?); **5.** exceptions: see below.

D has a strong association with pl. obj. in so far as the direct obj. is concrete and inanimate, and the verb has its literal meaning of "to tear out" (**2.** and **3.**), cf. 5.6.4. With a personal object (**1.**) D is rare, compared to the very common use of G, cf. CAD sv 4 "to transfer, remove", also with pl. obj. Apart from the combination with tablets (more often G, cf. CAD sv 6), D is not used or exceptional in such meanings as "to expel" (sickness, etc.), and "to deduct", cf. CAD sv 3 and 5, but see **4.**). In all contexts G + pl. obj. is much more common than D + pl. obj., cf. CAD sv 1-6.

As to **5.**, ARM 27, 36: 37 = (138) and TuL 88: 4 may be due to the more or less idiomatic meaning "to evict" in combination with the personal object, cf. 6.4.9; for the other exceptions see App.

Palāq/ku "to slaughter, massacre"; D always with pl. obj.: **1.** sacrificial animals; **2.** enemies "like animals".

All comparable instances of G listed in AHw (sv G 1/2 and sv *naplaqtu* 2) have a sg. obj.; remarkable is ABL 210: 17 *ip-tál-li-iq* (obj. people): Gtn, cf. *retû* Gtn in 6.7.3? or standing for */iptaliq/*? Note that it differs in genre and period (NB letter) from the other instances (MB, SB).

Parāsu "to cut off, cut into pieces, separate, decide"; D mostly has a pl. obj.: **1.** "to cut off, cut into pieces" animals and body parts (pl.); **2.** "to separate" people and animals; **3.** with abstract pl. obj.: sins (124), accounts; **4.** "to cut or split into many parts"; **5.** + *(w)arka/ātu* "to investigate a matter/ matters".

D is mainly associated with the literal and salient meanings "to cut off, cut into pieces" (**1.**, cf. 5.6.4); in this meaning G is not attested, acc. to AHw sv *p.* I G, except for the stative G in protases qualifying parts of the liver (G 7a), all sg., versus D + pl. subj. in MVAeG 40/2, 64: 9 (toes). It seems that D with body parts as object means "to cut off", with whole objects "to cut into pieces", also in the sg., probably because of the idea of plurality inherent in the meaning of *parāsu*: the result of the action is plural (cf. AHw sv *p.* I D 3b "zerstückeln"); this is explicitly indicated in YOS 10, 11: I 14f *šumma padānum adi šalāšīšu pu-ru-us* "if the "path" is split in three (parts)"; cf. the same situation for *puṭṭur*, *šulluq* and *šuttuq*, see 10.6.1.1.3.

The use of D with abstract objects (**3.**) comprises only two instances. As to **5.**, G is the normal form in this expression, D is rather unusual (OB Mari and SB LL), but shows some interesting aspects. First, of the OB instances two (ARM 27, 85: 9f and Ét. Garelli 55 M.7322: 25') have a pl. obj. *warkātim*; in 10, 124: 10f the matter is undecided since the word is in the construct state; especially interesting is MARI 5, 165: 39ff *šitappar* (...) *wa-ar-ka-at mê* (...) *[da]mqiš li-pa-ri-su-ni-kum-ma* "send (people to various places) that they thoroughly investigate for you the problem of the water (supplies)" (= (137A) in this chapter and (14) in Ch. IV), where D doubtless underlines the distributive nature of the subject (see 6.5.1), correlates with the distributive imp. Gtn *šitappar* (cf. 4.2.3), and underlines that different (groups of) people have to carry out the order in different places; the same applies to *ib.* 164: 24f: if the restoration of 20 is correct, D is undoubtedly caused by the plurality of the "logical object" of the sentence, *harrānātim*. Second, in SB (MSL 1, 80: 33f) we find the present D alternating with the inf., pret. and stative G (*ib.* 81: 35/38; 93: 36f), all with obj. *arkassu*); see note 19 for a tentative explanation.

In meaning **1.** G is only found with sg. obj., mainly in the stative in omens (see above); this accords with the tendency noted in 5.6.4 and 6.4.1.2, that the use of D is especially associated with notions such as cutting, breaking and tearing. For **2.**, G is more common than D, cf. *ib.* sv G 3. G is the only form attested in various secondary meanings as "to cut off" (food supplies and roads), "to stop" (trans.), "to prevent", cf. AHw sv 1a, 6a/e/f, and 5.6.4.

Rasāb/pu "to strike, cut down"; D: **1.** enemies, soldiers, etc.; **2.** rarely sg., in RIs and elsewhere; **3.** "to beat up" (obj.: limbs, body (?)), cf. similar cases in 6.6.3 (plural action).

Both G and D of *rasāb/pu* are hardly found outside literary texts; G is much rarer than D and typically has a sg. obj. (apart from the expression *ana rasāb nakrūti/nākirē*, cf. AHw sv G 2). This weak correlation between D and plurality is also found in other literary verbs such as *abātu* and *sahāpu*.

Salātu "to split off, cut"; D mostly has a pl. obj.: **1.** body parts (pl.); **2.** other obj. (pl.) and mass noun (wood); **3.** "to cut through": places, mountains, river bank(s); **4.** occasionally with sg. obj.: belly, liver, cord of evil, stone. For D + pl. obj. ↔ G + sg. obj. cf.:

> (07A) CT 17, 19: 8 // SpTU 2, 2: I 8 (the headache) *šer'ānīšu kīma gihinni ú-sal-lit* (// *us-sa-lit*) "slit his sinews as (effortlessly as one slits) a *gihinnu*-basket" (tr. CAD sv *gihinnu* b);
>
> (07B) CT 17, 25: 31 // KAR 368: 3 (the headache) *irtum kīma gihinnu i-šal-lat* "slits his breast, etc.".

For the exceptions see perhaps 6.9.2.2. Comparable instances of G listed in CAD sv lex. sect. and 1. have a sg. obj.

Šebēru "to break, smash"; D usually has a pl. obj. (including substances): **1.** body parts; **2.** weapons (*kakkū*); **3.** other concrete objects; **4.** remaining cases: army (?) (qu. below), barley (1x), copper, cf. 6.3.

For D + pl. obj., cf. the contrast between *kakka šebēru* (CAD sv 1a) and *kakkī šubburu* (3a) "to break the weapon(s)" (but G + *kakkī* in RIME 4, 604: 67; RIMA 1, 51: 131). G typically has a sg. obj., cf. CAD sv 1b/c (but BWL 144: 26 (teeth, cf. **1.**). RA 65, 73: 40' *ina* GIŠtukul *ummānī uš-ta-ab-ba-ar* "my army will be broken in battle" (?) is quite atypical and uncertain. D with obj. copper (OA) is paralleled by the more frequent use of the VA *šabburum* with copper, see 10.6.1.2.4.

Ṭabāhu "to slaughter"; D mostly has a pl. object: **1.** literally, animals; **2.** persons (esp. enemy soldiers and peoples) "like animals"; **3.** exc. sg. obj.: person (1x), sheep (1x).

Acc. to AHw sv G, the G-stem usually has a sg. object; exceptions are: ARM 14, 79: 30 (OB, restored); BIN 4, 157: 9. 23 (OA); other exceptions stem from peripheral Akkadian: Nuzi, Emar (Emar VI/3 p. 421 no. 446: 41) (all with obj. sheep (pl.)).

6.4.1.2. General characteristics of Group I

According to the definition of high transitivity given in 5.3 and 5.4, the verbs of Group I can be regarded as the prototypes of highly transitive verbs. It is not surprising therefore that this group surpasses the other groups to be discussed below in number, in the overall proportional frequency of the D forms involved, and in the consistency of their association with plurality of the object.

As to the first point, most verbs that imply a destruction of the object are often used in the D-stem. There are, however, a few counter-examples. No D-stem at all is attested for *kasāmu* "to cut, chop", *kašāṭu* "to cut down, cut off" (but see App. sv *karātu*) and *sapānu* "to level, devastate". It is very rare for *dâku* "to kill", *šagāšu* "to murder", *šarāpu* "to burn" and *naqāru* "to tear down" (see App. ssvv).

As to the second point, for the reason mentioned in 6.4.1, most D-stems of verbs of destruction are associated with plurality of the direct object. Counter-examples are those of *letû* "to split, divide" and *pasāsu* "to cancel, destroy", which show no correlation with plurality (see 5.6.4), and that of *hamāṣu* "to strip, tear off", which is associated with plurality only in a part of its meaning (see 6.4.8 and 6.8.1).

Moreover, although the use of D to underline plurality is optional (see 6.4.9), many of the verbs of this group show a strong tendency to use it if they have a plural object, cf. the remarks concerning the rarity of the G-stem with plural object of *batāqu, napāṣu, palāq/ku, šebēru* and *ṭabāhu* in 6.4.1.1 and about *alātu, hanāqu, karātu, pašāṭu, qalāpu, šalāpu,* and *šarāṭu* in App. ssvv.

However, a fully consistent correlation between D and plurality of the object is unusual even in the verbs of this group; in all of them the G-stem is also used with a plural object (except *palāq/ku*, but that is doubtless accidental and mainly caused by the highly stereotyped nature of the texts in which it is used, cf. 6.9.3), and in most of them we also find a small number of D forms with a singular object (see below).

The semantic nature of these verbs entails that they normally have concrete entities as direct objects; they can only have abstract objects when used metaphorically. Most of the verbs of this group have hardly any metaphorical meanings. Accordingly, we find very few abstract objects: *batāqu* **5.** (allegations), *napāṣu* **4.** (accounts), *nasāhu* **4.** (in various expressions), *pašāṭu* **1.** (spoken words, quoted in 6.6.1.1 sv), *parāsu* **3.** (sins (= (124) in 6.9.4), accounts) and **4.** (*(w)arkata parāsu*, see above sv), and *šahāṭu* **2.** (misfortune and evil (= (125) in 6.9.4)). Most of these cases are more or less unique; besides, the objects involved are mostly plural, so that they are no exception to the association of these D-stems with plurality.

The final point to be discussed are the D forms of Group I which do not have a plural object, but instead have either no overt object or a singular object. We can distinguish three cases: first, those in which another kind of verbal plurality is involved; second, instances of metaphorical expressions, and, third, real exceptions.

As to the first case, in spite of the claim made in 6.4.1, there are a few instances in which D underlines other kinds of plurality than that of the direct object. One of these is the generic use of these verbs without an overt object in:

(08) AfO 8, 28: 9 (The king commanded) *du-ú-[ku] nu-up-píl* "kill, blind!";

(09) BKBM 30: 43 *adi šibîšu ú-al-lat* "he swallows seven times" (also qu. as (89) in 6.6.3.3).

It is more common in the participles of these verbs: *munappilu, muqallipu, mušaggišu* (see note 9) and *mušarriṭu*, which are discussed in 6.6.2.

Some of these D-stems can also be used for plural action: *kapāru* B (= (75) in 6.6.3.2), *napālu* **3.** and **4.** (= (80) and (79) in 6.6.3.2); *nakāsu* **5.** (quoted in 6.6.1.1 sv). A distributive subject is involved in *parāsu* **5.**, cf. also 6.5.1. The D-stems of *parāsu* (**5.**), *salātu* (**4.**) and *šatāqu* can be used for "to split into many parts", especially in omen texts, cf. 10.6.1.1.3.

Second, if a verb is used in a metaphorical meaning, the association between D and plurality is sometimes abandoned (see 6.4.9). Although metaphorical meanings are unusual in the verbs of Group I, a few singular objects can be explained in this way: AbB 1, 27: 28 = (22) (*batāqu* **6.**); *ib.* 20 = (22) (*hepû* **6.**); KAR 350: 19 (*abātu* **3.**), SpTU 2, 24: 2 and CT 17, 19: 6 // SpTU 2, 2: I 6 (*haṣāṣu* **3.**); ARM 27, 36: 37 = (138) and TuL 88: 4 (*nasāhu* **5.**). All these cases involve persons as direct object of verbs which do not normally have a personal object. Other cases involve abstract objects; apart from the plural instances quoted above, this applies to CCT 3, 16b: 10 (*nasāhu* **4.**).

Finally, there are a number of real exceptions, i.e., singular forms of nouns which normally occur in the plural with the verbs of this group. They are mainly found in literary texts (cf. 6.9.2.2), and thus in typically literary verbs; see especially *abātu* (in almost all its uses: **1.** to **4.**, and especially **5.**), *haṣāṣu* **3.**, *rasāp/bu* **2.** and *salātu* **5.** In non-literary verbs the number of exceptions for which no explanation seems to be at hand is surprisingly small, in view of the semantic rather than grammatical relationship between G and D in these verbs and the overall elusive nature of the D-stems of Type I (cf. 6.1).[10]

A final point which will be discussed later on, but should be touched on here, is the stereotyped character of the use of many D-stems of Type I, especially in RIs. The most striking cases in this group are *abātu* "to destroy, ruin" (often as a participle), *napāṣu* "to kill" enemies, *palāq/ku* and *ṭabāhu* "to slaughter" sacrificial animals and enemies, *rasāp/bu* "to strike, cut down" (enemies) and *šebēru* "to break" (weapons). Many D-stems to be discussed later on are also stereotyped and/or restricted to a narrow range of contexts. Therefore, the discussion of this phenomenon will be deferred until after the presentation of all relevant D-stems, see 6.9.3.

6.4.2. Group II: verbs for actions which have a violent impact on the object

The second semantic group which offers many D-stems associated with plurality is that of verbs denoting actions which have a violent impact on the object. Since they do not necessarily imply the destruction of the object involved, the same object can undergo the action more than once. Therefore, the D-stems of these verbs are used for plurality of the object and of the action. In this section only the former is systematically explored. Plural action will be examined in 6.6.

There is, however, no clear-cut distinction between this group and the previous one, mainly because some of the verbs involved can imply the destruction of the object, but need not do so; *kabāsu*, for instance, can mean "to tread or step upon", but also "to crush"; in the former meaning it belongs to this group, in the latter to Group I. Likewise, *rasāpu* normally means "to strike, cut down" in RIs, but can also refer to an action with a non-lethal result, apparently meaning "to beat up", cf. App. sv **3**.

The verbs selected for discussion are those of IIa, except *dâšu*, which mainly occurs with mass nouns and is therefore not a typical member of this class; for the other verbs see App.

Group IIa (> 10 instances):

Dâšu	to thresh, trample	**Palāšu**	to pierce, perforate
Kabāsu	to step or walk upon, trample	**Sahālu**	to pierce, stab
K/qanānu	to twist, coil	**Sapāhu**	to disperse, scatter, ruin
Nakāpu	to butt, gore	**Šêlu**	to sharpen
Našāku	to bite		

Group IIb (3 to 10 instances):

Egēru	to twist	**Patāhu**	to pierce, perforate
Ešû	to confuse	**Sekēru**	to dam, block
Makāru	to flood, irrigate	**Šaqāru**	to pierce

Group IIc (< 3 instances):

Eṣēlu	to paralyze	**Mazā'u**	to squeeze
Haṭāmu	to block	**Zâru**	to twist
Magāgu	to spread out		

6.4.2.1. Discussion of the most important verbs

Kabāsu "to step or walk upon, trample"; D: **1.** "to step upon" objects and persons (sg.) compared to objects: threshold (74), thorn bush (84) // G, figurines (83), *ša* "whatever" (82), *lahmu*'s; in obscure context: person; **2.** "to tread down" (necks of) enemies; **3.** "to trample, crush with the foot" person, bodies, corpses on the battlefield, parts of fields, etc.; **4.** "to walk across, over" mountains; **5.** *anzilla kubbusu* "to infringe a taboo, commit a sacrilege"; **6.** metaph.: "to trample on" rites, "to pardon" sin(s); **7. OA** "to drop a claim" (64) - (66) → 6.6.3.1; 1x reciprocal Dt qu. in 9.1.3 sv.

The rather wide range of meanings expressed by *kabāsu* and its frequent occurrence in literary texts makes the use of its D-stem particularly diverse and complicated. It is mainly restricted to the more literal meanings of the verb, i.e., **1.**-**5.**, cf. 5.6.4 (assuming that **5.** has to be taken literally, at least in origin, cf. the remark of CAD sv *anzillu* end). Most instances of D have a pl. obj., some others can be accounted for by assuming that D is also used for pl. action (**1.**), cf. 6.6.3.2 and 6.6.3.3; other instances, including several with a pl. obj., seem to denote a more violent action "to trample, crush with the foot" (**3.**), cf. 6.8.1; in many contexts, however, both meanings are possible. G is mainly used with sg. obj. or a substance (often water) (CAD sv 1/2a), implying a single action, except in RIs where G often has pl. obj., cf. CAD sv 2b-2'. An atypical exception is Iraq 30, 101: 17 (**6.**): sg. obj. *and* metaphorical); for ABL 1022: 8 (obj. *mātu*) see 6.3.

K/qanānu "to twist, coil"; D: **1.** body parts and other objects in the pl. (strings (113A)); **2.** sg. obj.: foot (in a *šumma* clause (TDP 20: 26f, cf. 6.6.1.1 sv); AMT 9, 1: II 26f *šer'ānu šer'ānu ú-qa-an-na-an* "sinew twists sinew", reciprocal, cf. 9.1.3, and CT 16, 23: 334 (obj. snake, cf. CAD sv lex. sect.).

G has a sg. obj., cf. CAD sv *kanānu* 1a/b, except in ZA 16, 186: 26 = (113B) and 176: 58. There can be little doubt that the alleged preterite Gtn forms quoted in CAD sv 2 and in AHw sv Gtn are perfect G forms rather than preterite Gtn, cf. 6.6.1.

Nakāpu "to butt, gore"; D: **1.** literally, with animals as subj. and personal obj. or no obj., all quoted in 6.6.1 sv, 6.6.3.2 (76) or 6.6.3.3 (87) as instances of pl. action; **2.** metaph. with gods as subj., obj. enemies, etc.; **3.** idiomatic: "to invade" hostile country, in omen apodoses, similar to *palāšu* **4.**, and replacing it after OB.

D is used with pl. obj. (**2.**), pl. action (**1.**) and in an idiomatic expression similar to those discussed in 6.4.9 (**3.**). G has a sg. obj., acc. to CAD sv 1, unless it is stative in a metaphorical meaning.

Našāku "to bite, gnaw"; D: **1.** outside omen protases, with animate beings and body parts as object, mostly pl.; **2.** part. *munaššiku* → 6.6.2; **3.** often in prot. → 6.6.1 and 6.6.1.1 sv.

D either has a pl. obj., or it is used for plurality of action in protases or participles, such as Gilg. VI 41, qu. in note 11 to Ch. V *sub* B, doubtless to be explained as habitual, cf. 6.6.2; G mostly has sg. obj. (person or body part), cf. CAD sv 1/2 (G + pl. obj.: TBP 55: 5 (lips). Thus D basically refers to a series of bites, or biting as a habit or a possibility, G to a single bite.

Palāšu "to pierce, perforate, burgle"; D: **1.** bodies and body parts; **2.** other objects: houses, blocks, holes ("to make"); **3.** with abstract object: *awātim*: "to see through"); **4.** + *mātam* "to invade" (OB omens).

D mostly has a pl. obj.; for the contrast D vs. G cf. the use of G + *bīta* (AHw sv G 1a) versus D + *bītāti* (**2.**); for stative *pulluš* "having many holes" in omen texts see (46) in 10.6.1.1.3; the expression *mātam pullušum* in OB omens is only used if the protasis contains the stative *pališ* or refers to sharp or pointed features of the entrails; this suggests that it is an artifical combination coined expressly with the purpose of matching protasis and apodosis of these omens. The D-stem may be explained according to 6.3 (collective) or 6.4.9 (a metaphorical expression). G usually has a sg. object, cf. AHw sv G 1/3, except for the stative in protases of omens, which often has a pl. subject (*ib.* sv 4).

Sahālu "to pierce, stab"; D: **1.** body parts (pl.); **2.** body (sg.) and person (sg.); **3.** "to cause a piercing pain" with pers. obj. and a body part as subject → 6.6.1.2 sv.

The pl. objects of **1.** and the idiom of **3.** point to a basic association with plurality. The instances of **2.** with sg. obj. probably underline pl. action, see (85) and (86) in 6.6.3.3. Thus D seems to be generally used for inflicting a plurality of stabs. G, on the other hand, usually has a sg. obj., and refers to a singular stab or prick, cf. CAD sv 1a/b (it has a pl. obj. in RA 28, 161: 30, AnSt. 5, 102: 71, RA 33, 106: 32, and Gilg. XI 274 (if the restoration is correct).

Sapāhu "to disperse, scatter, ruin"; D: **1.** "to disperse" persons and groups, both pl. and collectives; **2.** "to scatter" animals, objects and substances; note with abstract obj.: matter(s): "to divulge"; **3.** "to sprinkle" or "to spill" water; **4.** "to waste, squander" (money, barley, and other commodities, often + *bīta* "the estate"); **5.** "to ruin" a district; **6.** "to thwart, to bring to nought" (plan(s), deeds, activity, sorceries, *rikista* "what is tied", sin (AGH 74: 37 // G, cf. Iraq 31, 83 *ad* l. 37), words, advice.

In its literal meaning D mostly occurs with pl. obj. When used idiomatically, D is not restricted to plural objects (see 6.4.9 for other instances of this phenomenon): "to waste, squander" (**4.**), "to ruin" a district (**5.**) and "to thwart, to bring to nought" (**6.**). **4.** is more or less consistently expressed by D (CAD sv 4 has one case of G: CT 28, 40b: 16). **6.** alternates with G, cf. CAD sv 2; it is a remarkable exception to the restriction of D to concrete objects.

Šêlu "to sharpen, whet"; D always has a pl. obj., usually "weapons" (*kakkū*), 1x arrows. G is also found with "weapons" and "teeth" as obj., cf. CAD sv *š*. A 1, AHw sv G 1/2).

6.4.2.2. General remarks concerning Group II

The remarks on the D-stems of Group I in 6.4.1.2 basically apply to this group as well. These verbs are also typical high transitivity verbs with a D-stem that is relatively frequent. In their literal meaning most of the D-stems show the same rather consistent correlation with plurality of the object as Group I; this applies to those of *dâšu* (mainly mass nouns), *palāšu* and *šêlu* of IIa and all D-stems of IIb/c. There seem to be hardly any exceptions. *Šêlu* D, which is almost only attested in RIs in the expression *kakkī šullu* "to sharpen the weapons" (App. sv), is one of the most striking illustrations of the highly stereotyped and conventional nature of the use of many D-stems of Type I, see further 6.9.3.

The use of D for plural action, irrespective of whether the object is singular or plural, is especially prominent in *kabāsu, nakāpu, našāku* and *sahālu*. The relevant instances will be discussed in 6.6.1 (if they occur in *šumma* clauses) and in 6.6.3. In addition, *kabāsu* is also used to convey a more forceful nuance of the actions expressed by the G-stem: "to crush" instead of "to walk or tread upon", cf. 6.8.1.

In accordance with their basic meaning, these verbs generally have concrete entities as direct object, and can only have abstract objects only when used metaphorically, as in *kabāsu* said of rites: "to trample", of sins: "to pardon" (**6.**) and of claims in OA: "to drop" (**7.**), *sapāhu* said of plans and actions (**6.**) and *palāšu* said of words: "to see through" (**3.**). Another kind of metaphor is the use of *nakāpu* (**3.**) and *palāšu* (**4.**) in the meaning "to invade" (hostile country), for which see 6.4.9.

6.4.3. Group III: verbs of closing and opening, binding and loosening, and related notions

What the verbs of this group have in common is that they are change-of-state verbs and thus have a high degree of inherent transitivity, but less so than the preceding groups, since they lead to a state which is not principally abnormal, but transient and reversible, and thus less salient. This is the reason for the inclusion of *tarāṣu*, which shows the same characteristic, although it deviates semantically from the other verbs.

It is typical of many of these verbs that they are often used in secondary metaphorical meanings. Such deviations from the basic meaning often result in a different use of the D-stem, cf. 6.4.9. Therefore, the entries of these verbs in the Appendix have been subdivided, if necessary, into three sections: A for the literal meaning(s) of the verb in which D correlates with plurality of the object, B for idiomatic uses of the D-stem, in which it does not, and C for exceptions. The verbs of Group IIIa and *edēlu* and *e'ēlu* from IIIb will be discussed here.

Group IIIa (> 10 instances):

(H)arāmu	to cover	**Rakāsu**	to bind, fix
Kanāku	to seal, put under seal	**Retû**	to fix
Kaṣāru	to bind, join, collect, organize	**Sahāpu**	to cover, overwhelm, lay flat
Paṭāru	to loosen, release, redeem	**Tarāṣu**	to direct, stretch, straighten
Petû	to open	**Zaqāpu**	to erect, plant

Group IIIb (3-10 instances):

Edēlu	to close	**Temēru**	to bury
E'ēlu	to hang up, bind		

Group IIIc (< 3 instances):

Barāmu	to seal	**Šâlu**	to coat, smear
(H)apû	to cover, pack		

6.4.3.1. Discussion of the most important verbs

Edēlu "to close"; D usually has a pl. obj.: **1.** doors and gates; **2.** affairs (1x). Exceptional cases of D with sg. obj. are SKS p. 42: 45 (house), qu. as (05) in 6.4. and as (127) in 6.9.4, and (3x in the same text) Racc. 92: r.9; 93: 14; 119: 13 *bābu (ul) ut-ta-dal* "the door should (not) be closed", for which no easy explanation is at hand.

G typically has a sg. obj. (*daltu, bābu, abullu*, cf. CAD sv a-1', and various other nouns (*ib.* sv. b), except in Gilg. X I 16. 21 (bolts, restored), in a metaphorical use with obj. *pānī* (*ib.* b-1'), in the stative with hands as subject (TBP 11c: VI 37'), and in LKA 141: 18 *e-di-lu petâti* "who closes what is open".

E'ēlu "to hang up, bind"; D has a pl. obj.: **1.** concrete: donkeys, severed heads; **2.** abstract: agreements; **3.** idiomatic: fluids → 9.1.4. For the use of D with pl. obj., cf. AHw sv D 1 "zahlreich aufhängen"; as for **1.**, cf. G for one head, CAD sv 1b (but cf. RIMA 2/I, 207: 71 "I cut off their heads and *ina gupnī ša tarbaṣ ekallišu e-'i-il* (var. *ú-'i-il*, cf. p. 407a bottom) "hung (them) on trees of the courtyard of his palace"; same expression with D: *ib.* 201: 118; 248: 86; with G: 245: 13); with other objects G + pl. obj. is also found, CAD sv 1a, 2b; as for **2.**, cf. G for one contract, CAD sv 2a, AHw sv G 4.

(H)arāmu "to cover"; D has a pl. obj.: **1.** "tablets" in OA, often VA; **2.** "matters" (*awātum*), 1x OB. The association of G and D of this verb and its VA with the sg. and pl. of *ṭuppu* "tablet", respectively, is very strong in OA; for G + sg. obj. cf. CAD sv *arāmu* 3 and *armu* adj. An exceptional case of G + pl. obj. is BIN 6, 54: r.9'; an exceptional case of the VA *ha-ar-ru-mu-um* in the sg. is AKT 3, 38: 15 (a scribal error? cf. *ha-ar-mu-um* in 27). In the expression *šībī harāmum* "to put down the names of witnesses on a sealed tablet" G is used (e.g., CCT 5, 2a: 20; TC 3, 62: 23). Here G apparently correlates with the implied object "tablet". Outside OA, and in combination with other objects, only G is used, apart from the unique case mentioned under **2.**

Kanāku "to seal, put under seal"; D: A. with pl. obj.: **1.** "to seal" objects (pl., collectives and mass nouns);
B. idiomatic: **2.** "to put under seal" houses and storehouses, both sg. and pl. (130A);
C. **3.** exceptions: see below.

Kanāku shows a gradation in its use of D: only G is used for the basic meaning "to seal" a tablet or document; if other (larger) concrete objects are involved, D can be used, if they are plural or a substance (**1.**), but instances of D + pl. obj. are rare compared to G + pl. obj., cf. CAD sv 1a and 3. If the direct object represents large entities such as buildings (**2.**), D can be used irrespective of number, see 6.4.9; for G cf. CAD sv 1b (almost all instances have a sg. obj. (exc.: CCT 3, 14: 11; KAV 98: 37, and two cases from Nuzi)). As to the exceptions, for ARM 26/2 p. 420 no. 483: 38 a tentative explanation is offered in note 23; for Maqlû III 109 = (118) see 6.9.2.2.

Kaṣāru "to bind together, join, collect, organize"; D: A. with pl. obj.: **1.** "to tie, bind" concrete objects; **2.** id., persons and body parts; **3.** in military contexts: "to concentrate, prepare for battle", mostly with collectives; **4.** Dt "to gather" (intrans.): armies, clouds → 9.1.5.
B. **5.** idiomatic: "to build, fortify, restore" town(s) and buildings (sg. and pl.).
C. **6.** Exceptions: see below.

The clearest evidence of the relevance of plurality is the use of Dt for clouds (**4.**), vs. G for a single cloud, cf. CAD sv 3a. In most contexts G is more common than D: compare CAD sv 1a with **1.**, and *ib.* 2a with **3.** (esp. in SB). With persons and body parts, G + pl. obj. is rare, except in the stative, cf. *ib.* 3b. For the idiomatic use **B5.** see 6.4.9; it is restricted to OB Mari and SB, and expressed by G elsewhere, cf. CAD sv 1b (mainly SB), cf. esp. Sg. 8: 254 *ú-ka-ṣi-ra* [*ušmannī*] "I pitched my camp" with *ib.* 27 *ak-ṣu-ra ušmannī*.

As to the exceptions, for SpTU 3, 74: 112 = (118) see 6.9.2.2; for BAM 237: IV 39 (person: "to attach stones to"?, see 6.5.3? cf. G in 41 with obj. "knots"). Difficult to explain are ARM 26/1 p. 424 no. 197: 15 *ana šētim ša ú-kà-aṣ-ṣa-ru akammissu* "I will trap him in the net I am (? or: he is?) making", and Atr. 110: 61 *rēmu ku-ṣur-ma ul ušēšir šerra* "the womb was tied up, did not allow the child to pass" (tr. CAD sv 6a, cf. also 108: 51) (idiomatic, underlining the permanent nature of the quality ? (see 10.3)).

Paṭāru "to loosen, release, redeem": D: A. with pl. obj.: **1.** "to loosen" knots, ties and bonds; **2.** id. with other concrete objects: hems of a garment, combs, mountings, hides, limbs, wells ("to open"); **3.** "to undo" abstract objects: sins, ordinances, sighs, fears, portents, *namburbi*s, calculations ("to do");
B. idiomatic (obj. both sg. and pl.): **4.** "to release, let go" persons; **5.** "to clear, demolish" buildings; **6.** intrans. Dt "to decay, disintegrate" (of buildings, cf. (06) in Ch. IX); **7.** "wehrlos machen" (AHw) (enemy, 1x);
C. **8.** for other idioms, deviations from normal use and exceptions, see below.

Paṭāru D has a rather strong correlation with plurality (which is also apparent from the use of *paṭer* vs. *puṭṭur* in omens, cf. 10.6.1.1.3), but this correlation is largely restricted to the basic meaning "to untie, undo", and to inanimate objects, both concrete (**1.-2.**), and abstract (**3.**). With these objects G + pl. obj. is also common, esp. in **3.**, cf. AHw sv G 8; both D and G are frequent in prayers, incantations and litanies, often coordinated with *pašāru* (**2.**) and *pasāsu* (**4.**) in the highly repetitive style which characterizes such texts (cf. 6.9.4).

In the idiomatic meanings **4.**, **5.** and **6.** D has no correlation with plurality, see 6.4.9. As to **4.**, there may be a semantic difference between G and D, in that D mostly means "to release, let go" (cf. AHw sv D 13 "freistellen"), and only rarely "to redeem, ransom", whereas G can express both nuances (*ib.* sv G 9 ("lösen"), 11 "auslösen"), although many contexts are ambiguous.[11] Possibly, *paṭāru* D "to release" is a factitive of intransitive *paṭāru* "to go away, depart" (see Ch. VII). It is rare after OB (CT 22, 74: 27; ABL 460: r.2; 702: r.2, Nbn. 1113: 1. 19, all NB). For **6.**, compare the similar use of the Dt-stems of *hepû* (qu. as (23) in 6.4.9), *pasāsu* **1.**, *paṣādu* and *tabāku* **5.**, discussed in 9.1.1, see esp. (06).

There are many instances of D + sg. obj. in various secondary meanings, of which it is often difficult to explain why G or D is used. Erra I 133. 136. 170 (the order (*šipṭu*) of heaven and earth) and SpTU 3, 82: I 28 (the structure (*šiknu*) of heaven and earth) are possibly modelled on **5./6.**; ABRT 1, 57: 27 *mu-paṭ-ṭer ennitti* "who removes punishment", may be a reinterpretation of an earlier expression *mupaṭṭer ennēti* (**3.**, RA 16, 89 no. 45: 7; SpTU 2, 18: 24); MSL 5, 37: 353 (no obj.) probably belongs to **4.** Two cases of D (Šurpu II 167 = (92) in 6.7.2, and AGH 14: 23 *ikkibkunu pu-ṭí-ra* "release your taboo" might be caused by plurality of the subject, cf. 6.5.1. Exceptions for which no explanation seems to be available are AbB 2, 98: 17 (ship: "to untie", cf. G in Atr. 92: 55 "to set adrift"); AbB 6, 135: r.15' (yoke, cf. G in Atr. 60: 243; 80: V 19; 84: 28); ARM 13, 24: 6, cf. MARI 2, 145 (table: "to remove"?).

Petû "to open"; D: A. with pl. obj.: **1.** doors, gates, locks, seals (02); **2.** houses, rooms, storerooms, graves; **3.** roads, mountains (145A) and mountain passes); **4.** waterways, cf. esp. (01A) and Iraq 55, 129: I 4' (RN) *mu-pat-tu-ú nārāti* vs. *pe-ti nārātim* RIME 4, 603: 47; **5.** other concrete objects; **6.** abstract objects: hardships: "to relieve", words: "to make known"; **7.** part. *mupettû* "a person who opens sleuce-gates", an instrument and a PN, → 6.6.2; **8.** "to open sb's ears, to inform";
B.: idiomatic: **9.** "to reclaim" uncultivated land; **10.** "to expose" body parts (MA);
C. **11.** Exceptions: see below.

For the correlation between D and pl. obj., cf. the two contrasting pairs quoted in 6.3 as (01) and (02). The use of G + pl. obj. is also very common, cf. AHw sv G, and compare, for instance, AGH 48: 107 *edlūti sikkūr šamê tu-pat-ti* "you have opened the closed bolts of the sky" (SB) with RA 38, 87: 10 // RitDiv. 30: 9 *te-ep-te-a-am sikkūrī dalāt šamê* "you have opened the bolts of the doors of the sky for me" (OB).

In the idiomatic expression **9.** D and G interchange without observable difference (for G cf. AHw sv G 10); in **10.** D is only MA, elsewhere G is used, cf. AHw sv G 17c (OB/SB).

Exceptions: EL 326: 34; Ee V 54 (well, cf. 6.9.2.2); Kish I pl. 34b: II 3 ([*ša*] *kimahha* [*an*]*nâ ú-pe-tu-ú* "whoever opens this tomb": D because of the generalizing relative sentence (cf. 6.3))?

Rakāsu "bind, fix"; D: A. with pl. obj.: **1.** "to bind" persons, animals (horses) and body parts; **2.** "to fasten" parts of buildings (cf. (120) in 6.9.3); **3.** "to erect" (parts of) buildings; **4.** other concrete objects; **5.** + *riksātu*: "to make a binding agreement", or "to draw up regulations"; **6.** intrans. Dt: rains: "to concentrate" → 9.15; **7.** part. *murakkisu* "binder of sheaves" → 6.6.2.
B: idiomatic (obj. sg. and pl.): **8.** "to bandage": person, foot, bandage ("to apply"), also without overt obj.; **9.** "to bind sb by contract".
C. **10.** Exceptions: see below.

In its literal meaning D regularly has a pl. obj. Cases of G + sg. obj. ↔ D + pl. obj. are SpTU 2, 2: 82. 84 *qaqqad marṣa ru-ku-us-ma* (...) *napištašu ru-ku-u*[*s-ma*] "bind the head of the patient (with magical threads), (...) bind his throat." (cf. also *ib.* 44. 46 (G with object "hair")), versus *ib.* 86 *mešrêtīšu ru-u*[*k-kis-ma*] "bind his limbs", and AfO 8, 182: 52 vs. Asb. A VIII 12 with D and G respectively in exactly the same context. Corresponding instances of G + pl. obj. are very common for **1.** and **4.**, cf. AHw sv G, but very rare for **2.** and **3.**, cf. *ib.* sv 11 (only Sg. Lie 52: 15 (*halṣē*)).

In the idiomatic meaning **8.** both G and D occur (G: ARM 7, 23: 2; BiOr 18, 71: 8) with sg. obj. In meaning **9.** G does not seem to be attested.

Exceptions: Ee V 59 = (38) (tail with ropes), see 6.5.3; TCS 2 p. 33 no. 14: 5f *lu-ra-ki-is*, var. *lu-ú ú-ra-ki-is* (obj. buck, ram) may be explained as a misinterpretation of a stative with precative *lū rakis*.

Retû "to fix"; D always has a pl. obj.: **1.** "to fasten" doors (cf. (120) in 6.9.3); **2.** "to fix" various objects: corpses on stakes, pegs, stelae, etc.; **3.** "to fix" eyes. G usually has a sg. object, typically "peg" (AHw sv G 1), *išdu* "fundament" (but also *uššû* (pl. tantum), and *temmēnu* "foundation terrace" (*ib.* G 4a); G + pl. obj. is found in RIME 4, 700: 8 (doors), AnSt. 6, 156: 132 (five pegs), and VAB 4, 216: 25 (doors). It is remarkable that a few RIs of Nebuchadnezzar in VAB 4 use the Gtn-stem in meaning **1.**, cf. AHw sv Gtn, and see 6.7.3.

Sahāpu "to cover, overwhelm, lay flat"; D: **1.** "to overwhelm" enemies, *mātu* "the land", mountains, in RIs often with subject *melammū*; **2.** "to cover" persons with dust; **3.** part., **SB**: *musahhiptu* "a net for gazelle hunting" → 6.6.2; **4.** occasionally with sg. obj.: mountain, demon, a person with diseases (= (41) in 6.5.3).

A typically literary D-stem (but not exclusively, cf. OB ARM 26/2 p. 393 no. 469: 7 in uncertain meaning); esp. in RIs it alternates with G without observable difference; compare, for instance, the cases with subject *melammū* (**1.**) with the corresponding use of G in CAD sv 1c. Like other literary verbs, D is mostly associated with plurality, but shows a few exceptions which are difficult to explain.

Tarāṣu "to direct, stretch, straighten"; D mostly has a pl. obj.: **1.** body parts; **2.** id. in prot. → 6.6.1.1 sv (eyes, lips); **3.** occasionally other objects; **4.** a process performed on metal (= (133) in 6.9.5).

G usually has a sg. obj., esp. "hand" (AHw sv *t.* I G 1c) and "finger" (*ib.* 1d); occasionally G + pl. obj. is also found with body parts, esp. in the stative (*ib.* 2). For **4.** see 6.9.5; it is remarkable because in the text in question a G form alternates with D forms with the same pl. obj.

Zaqāpu "to erect, plant": D: **1.** "to impale" enemies; **2.** "to erect" standard(s) (*urigallu*), usually pl. but also sg.; **3.** id., with other concrete objects; **4.** with body parts: eyes (often in prot. → 6.6.1.1 sv, also sg.), hair, penis; 5. part. *muzaqqi[pu]* (an agricultural worker) → 6.6.2.

D has a rather strong association with plurality, usually a pl. obj.; a few cases fall under plurality of action (in *šumma* clauses). The exceptions mostly concern the obj. *urigallu* (**2.**), 2x a body part (penis); the use of D with obj. hair (mostly in the stative) is probably to be explained by the fact that it is mass noun, cf. *kabbaru* and *qattanu* (cf. 3.1.3.1 ssvv),

G + pl. obj. is also frequent, esp. in RIs, said of standards (*šurinnī*), doors and trees, cf. CAD sv 1a,1c.

6.4.3.2. General remarks concerning Group III

The use of the D-stems of this group is much more complex than that of the two previous groups. This is mainly caused by the semantic nature of these verbs, which are particularly susceptible to acquiring secondary metaphorical meanings. Verbs meaning "to bind" have a natural tendency to develop meanings such as "to bind" by magic or by legal obligations; their antonyms for "to untie" are naturally extended to "to free, release" from captivity, "to undo" sins and guilt, etc.

Such secondary meanings tend to influence the use of the D-stem. If the verbs of group III have their literal meaning and are combined with such objects as are most typically associated with that meaning, their D-stems tend to correlate rather consistently with plurality of the object. This applies to *petû* with doors, houses, roads, etc., to *kaṣāru, paṭāru* and *rakāsu* wih relatively small objects and body parts (hands and feet), which are the typical entities to be tied and untied in the literal sense.

If, on the other hand, these verbs are used in secondary meanings, it basically depends on the transitivity inherent in the expression in question whether a D-stem is used. If it entails a reduction in transitivity, the D-stem tends not to be used or only rarely (cf. 5.6.4). Otherwise, it may be used, but in that case there is often no correlation with plurality. It may be the only form in use, or else G and D may be used indiscriminately.

Accordingly, if these verbs have a metaphorical meaning which entails a personal object (*paṭāru* **4**. and *rakāsu* **8**. and **9**.), or an other type of salient object, such as buildings (*kanāku* **2**., *kaṣāru* **5**., *paṭāru* **5**. and **6**.), land (*petû* **9**.) or body parts (*petû* **10**.), the association of D with plurality may be abandoned so that D can also be used if the object is singular; what the difference is between G and D in that situation is usually difficult to infer from the context, but it is doubtless the same as that between G and D if they alternate in a plural context (see 6.7.1). This state of affairs is also found in some other verbs (*sapāhu*, see 6.4.2.1 sv, and *ṣabātu*, see 6.4.4.1 sv). We will discuss this phenomenon in more detail in 6.4.9.

There are some other verbs which belong to this group semantically and have a frequent D-stem, in particular *kasû* "to bind", *katāmu* "to cover, close" and *pašāru* "to untie, release". These D-stems are not clearly associated with plurality and do not show any other consistent pattern; therefore, they are included among the "D-stems of unknown function" in 6.8.4. This can also be said of some less common verbs of the semantic type under discussion: *qebēru* "to bury", *pehû* "to lock" and *ṣamādu* "to prepare, harness, bandage" (rare and mainly idiomatic), cf. App. ssvv.

6.4.4. Group IV: verbs of seizing and controlling

This group comprises a small number of D-stems with plural object, of which only *ṣabātu* D is very common in all periods and dialects. *Ṣabātu* and *lâṭu* will be discussed as examples.

Group IVa (> 10 instances):

Ṣabātu	to seize	**Lâṭu**	to confine, keep in check

Group IVb (3-10 instances):

Pâdu	to imprison	**Tamāhu**	to seize, control

Group IVc (< 3 instances):

Ekēmu	to take away	**Habātu**	to rob, loot

6.4.4.1 Discussion of the most important verbs

Lâṭu "to confine, keep in check"; D normally has a pl. obj.: **1.** lands and kings; **2.** recalcitrant enemies (all part.); **3.** rest: *kiššatu* "the whole world", land (cf. 6.3); **4.** exc. with sg. obj.: Sg. Cyl. 22 (king).

D is only used in literary texts, always in the same context. G is also found in this context, but, apart from VAB 4, 216: 1 *a-lu-uṭ* (obj. enemies), only as a part. *lā'iṭ*, interchanging with *mula''iṭ*, cf. CAD sv *lâṭu* A 1, AHw sv G; e.g., RIMA 1, 310: 5 *rappu dannu mu-la-iṭ lā māgirī* (RN), the strong bridle that keeps in check the insubmissive", vs. Sn. 23: 8f (and elsewhere) *rappu la-'i-iṭ lā māgirī*; note AGH 96: 19 (G // D). Instances of G from other contexts are rare and dubious (*lâṭu* or *la'ātu* "to swallow"?). *Lâṭu* is a prominent example of a stereotyped D-stem which is almost exclusively found in RIs with a very small range of objects, see further 6.9.3.

Ṣabātu "to seize"; D: A. with pl. obj.: **1.** "to seize, arrest" persons, "to capture" enemies; **2.** "to bring" persons as witnesses; **3.** "to seize, capture" animals (141); **4.** "to seize, occupy" cities and forts; **5.** "to seize" produce, merchandise, etc.; **6.** "to install, fasten, adorn" parts of buildings and garments; **7.** various other idioms with pl. obj.; **8.** stat. with pl. adjunct acc. in *qê ṣubbut* in omen prot. → 6.5.3; **9.** part. → 6.6.2.
B. idiomatic: **10.** "to seize" with sorcery (obj. sg. and pl.): person(s) (= (10A) and (53)), *amēlutu* "mankind", body parts, features (*bunnannû* and *šikin pānī*), tracks; **11.** in med.: "to paralyze": person (VA), mouth (11A); "to hold" one's breath (= (13), prot. → 6.6.1); **12.** + *ṭêmam* "to take action" (1x with ellipse of *ṭêmum*, cf. note 7 to Ch. V); **13.** other idiomatic expressions, see under C.
C. Exceptions: see below.

For the association of D with pl. obj., cf. D + pl. obj. ↔ G + sg. obj. in:

(09A) ZA 73, 77: 6ff 1 eme₅ *ša* anše *adi 3* anše.meš *ṣīt libbiša uṣ-ṣa-bi-it iltēšu* "One mare of a donkey together with three donkeys, her offspring, I caught (D) in his possession";
(09B) *ib.* 78: 18 *ūma* 1 eme₅ *ātamar ina qāt aššurājê aṣ-ṣa-bat* "Today I saw one she-ass and caught (G) (her) in the hand of an Assyrian" (tr. M. Hall);

Cf. also the interchanging of D and G in *qê ṣubbut* vs. *qû ṣabit* in omen texts (see 6.5.3). The G-stem of *ṣabātu* is often used with pl. obj., too (see, e.g., (141) in 6.9.5), especially in OB and OA, where D is relatively rare in its literal use (cf. App. **1.-6.**).

Ṣabātu shows the same feature as some verbs of the previous group in that the use of its D-stem differs, depending on its meaning. It clearly correlates with plurality in **1.-8.**; it is rare in meanings which do not involve a literal act of seizing, and are therefore less salient, such as those listed in CAD sv 7 (*ina qāti ṣabātu*) and sv 8 in many idiomatic expressions, cf. 5.6.4. The idiomatic expression *ṭêmam ṣubbutum* in OB Mari (**12.**), beside *ṭêmam ṣabātum* in OB Mari and elsewhere, cf. CAD sv 8 *ṭêmu*), is an exception to this. If, on the other hand, it has an idiomatic meaning involving a salient direct object, D occurs irrespective of the number of the object; this applies in particular to **10.** and **11.**

The idiomatic meanings **10.** and **11.** occur in contexts of magic and sorcery and in medical texts. They owe their use of D doubtless to the fact that being seized by supernatural powers or by disease was seen as a more terrifying experience and thought to be more permanent than being seized by humans. A suitable translation is usually "to overpower" or "to paralyze". However, just as the use of D with plurality of the object is optional, its use in **10.** and **11.** is also optional. Thus we also find G in that meaning, cf. CAD sv 1a/b, AHw sv G II 2/3, and compare, for instance:

(10A) Maqlû VI 115 *ša kišpī ṣu-ub-bu-tu-in-ni* "(Me), whom witchcraft holds (D) in its power";
(10B) YOS 10, 26: I 35 *kišpū awīlam ṣa-ab-tu* "witchcraft holds (G) the man in its power";

(11A) TDP 220: 22f ka-*šú ṣu-ub-bu-ut-ma dabāba lā ile"e* "Its (the child's) mouth is paralyzed (D), so that he cannot speak";

(11B) TCS 5, 80: 21 (The king of Elam had a stroke and) ka-*šú ṣa-bit-ma atmâ lā le'i* "his mouth was paralyzed (G), so that he could not speak."

It is doubtless this use of D which GAG § 88f calls resultative and refers to as "gepackt halten". However, it is more likely the greater force and/or permanence of the action which are underlined by D; these factors lead to an increase in salience, which is responsible for the use of D in other than plural contexts. This is confirmed by some other cases where D has a durative nuance "to hold", whereas G - apart from the stative - typically denotes a punctual action "to seize":

(12) JCS 15, 6: 22 (listed under **13.**) *ú-ṣa-ab-ba-at-ka-ma* "I cling to you" (tr. Held);

(13) SpTU 3, 86: 4 *šumma* (...) *napassu ina appišu ú-ṣab-bat* "if (the patient) (...) holds his breath in his nose" (idem *ib.* 10 with *ištēniš* added).

In **13.** some atypical idiomatic cases are lumped together: for JCS 15, 6: 22 see (12) above; BIN 4, 72: 1 *ramakka ṣa-bi-it-ma* is translated as "make a decision(?)" by CAD sv 10b end, and as "nimm dich zusammen!" by AHw sv D I 5. In view of the preceding remarks, it is rather some durative action which seems to be referred to ("keep it up!"?); ABL 1203: r.4 (a basin) *ša hurāṣi ṣab-bu-ta-tu-ú-ni* "which is inlaid with gold" may be modelled on *uhhuzu*, the normal term for this process.

Other exceptional cases of D + sg. obj. are ARM 26/2 p. 227 no. 394: 8 (obj. *rēš awātim*, cf. note 23); AfO 10, 40 no. 89: 11 (one person, seized by a lion); RIMA 2/I, 291: 70 (room or rooms ?, or cf. 6.5.3?); Asb. A III 132 (cf. G in II 26); VAB 7, 328: 41 (both obj. *mūṣû* "to block" the exit); Or. 61, 24: 25 (id. (or plural?)); Dreams 332 c 3 (string).

6.4.5. Group V: verbs of collecting

Verbs of collecting tend to occur rather often in the D-stem, doubtless because plurality is an inherent part of their meaning: their objects must be plural or substances. The verbs to be discussed are those of Va except for *balālu* (for which see 6.8.1). There are no instances in Group Vc.

Group Va: (> 10 instances):

Balālu	to mix	**Nakāmu**	to stock, heap up
Kamāru	to heap, pile up	**Qarānu**	to store, pile up
Kamāsu	to collect, bring in, finish	**Šapāku**	to heap up, pour out
Laqātu	to collect, scrape together	**Tabāku**	to pour out

Group Vb: (3 to 10 instances):

Hamāmu	to collect, gather	**Šabāšu**	to collect, gather in

6.4.5.1. Discussion of the most important verbs

Kamāru "to heap, pile up"; D: **1.** property and abundance; **2.** other objects: corpses, walls or cities; **3.** exc. of persons: "to assemble", Dt intrans. → 9.1.5; **4.** exc. with abstract object.

The objects of D are either plural or abstract nouns which serve as mass nouns with a concrete meaning, except **4.**, which is a pure abstract noun with a quite different meaning: SAA 10, 294: r.4 *muruṣ* *libbija uk-tam-me-ra* "I (only) heaped up the grief of my heart" (tr. Parpola). G is used in the same contexts in literary texts (CAD lex. sect., 1b/1d), but is mainly used in several metaphorical meanings elsewhere (*ib.* 1a/1c/1e, esp. as a mathematical term "to add" (*ib.* sv 2).

Kamāsu "to finish, collect, bring in"; D: **1.** persons and animals; **2.** obj. "barley" or "field"; **3.** ingredients; **4.** "to gather" (animals); "to lay out" (corpse).

D is especially common in OB Mari, where it occurs mainly with personal obj., typically *ṣābu* "troops, work force" and *halṣu* "(people of the) district", rarely animals (ARM 6, 57: r.15'), alternating with G without any observable difference in meaning. However, with <u>še</u> "barley" or *ebūru* "harvest" as object, G is normal in Mari and D rare, cf. App. **2.**; this contrast can be explained by the difference in salience between persons and produce, cf. 5.6.4. Outside Mari, D is rare and not used with personal object (**2.**, **3.** and **4.**); note esp. the interchange of D and G with ingredients as objects in YOS 11, 25-27: D is found in 25: 63. 66. 70; 26: I 10. 66; IV 19 versus G in 25: 54; 27: 47). All objects are plural, mass nouns or collectives, except AnSt. 8, 50: 10, which also differs from the rest semantically.

Laqātu "to pick up, collect, take away"; D: **1.** "to collect, scrape together" objects in the pl., collectives and mass nouns (129), "everything available"; 1x without overt obj.; **2.** idiomatic: + *bīta* "to strip bare a house" → 6.4.9.

D occurs more often with substances and collectives as object than with countable plurals; for the meaning of D cf. AHw sv D "eilig zusammensuchen"; the contexts of D rather suggest a nuance of "to bring together everything possible", cf. also ARM 1, 42: 33, quoted as (129) in 6.9.5. G with pl. obj. and with mass nouns is also common (CAD sv 1b); a typical use of G is with seed as object (<u>še</u> and *zēru*), esp. in curse formulas: *zēra laqātu* "to destroy sb's progeny", cf. CAD sv 1a-b'.

Nakāmu "to stock, heap up"; D: **1.** treasures and possessions, all in RIs; **2.** sorceries (143A).

All objects of D are collectives or mass nouns, except **2.**, which is atypical. Apart from **2.**, D is found only in late RIs (of Assurbanipal and Nebuchadnezzar II); earlier RIs use only G; G is also rather common in OB letters, cf. CAD sv a).

Qarānu (CAD: *garānu*) "to store, pile up"; D: **1.** often *karû* (1x *binût karê*) "barley pile(s)", property and produce; **2.** corpses.

G and D are largely restricted to literary texts (OB and SB). G is found with the same objects, cf. CAD sv *garānu* a), but D is more common; GAG § 88f mentions *qarānu* as an example of a verb in which the difference between G and D is "hardly perceptible" ("kaum bemerkbar").

Šapāku "to heap up, pour out"; D: **1.** "to heap up" produce (grain, *karû* or *tabkāni* "piles of grain" and loaves, note esp. Gilg. VI 59 var. *šup-pu-kak-ki* // *iš-pu-kak-ki* acc. to CAD sv 2c-1', AHw sv D 3 (loaves); **2.** id., other objects (mountains, heads/corpses "like grain piles"); **3.** "to pour out" (oil, ice), "to cast" (pillars of bronze); part. *mušappiktu* "pitcher" → 6.6.2; **4.** a process performed on wool.

D is much less common than G and, apart from the technical use **4.**, restricted to SB literary texts. The objects are plural or substances, just as in the other verbs of this group. A remarkable feature of *šapāku* is the large overlap of D and Gtn, cf. the use of D in *mu-šap-pi-ku kar*[*ê*] "who heaps up piles of grain" (BM 41255a: 3 qu. CAD sv 7a) and *mu-šap-pi-ku hursānū* "who heaps up the mountains" (SBM 52a: 12+D) vs. *muš-tap-pi-ki karê* (LSS 3/4, 25: 14) and [*mu*]*š-tap-pik hurš*[*ānī*] (VAT 14051: 4 qu. AHw sv Gtn 2), which doubtless have the same meaning, and cf. also the use of Gtn instead of D in RIs of Nebuchadnezzar II described in 6.7.3.

Tabāku "to pour out"; D: **1.** substances and fluids from the body; without object: "to defecate"; **2.** other substances into water or a container; **3.** metaph.: *hurbāšu* "hoarfrost" (JRAS CSpl. 71: 14 (part.), cf. G in St.

Kraus 194: 21), death, *epēšu* "evil magic"; **4**. persons and body parts: "to weaken, render limp"; **5**. "to crumble", of a building, Dt → 9.1.1).

For the meaning of D cf. AHw sv D: "viel, in Menge hin-, ausschütten". The proper domain of D is SB medical texts, in which it is used in its literal meaning, alternating with G, without observable difference (for G cf. AHw sv G 4). *Tabāku* mainly occurs with mass nouns as object, like the other verbs of this group. AHw's claim that D refers to (relatively) large quantities is possible, and perhaps supported by YOS 10, 47: 24, quoted in 6.6.1.1 sv. D is rare in other periods and in metaphorical uses; also with barley only G is used, cf. AHw sv G 1.

4. is probably a denominative D-stem (listed in 8.4.1) derived from the adjective *ṭubbuku* (cf. 10.3.2), which alternates with *ṭabku* "limp", probably a lexicalized use of the VA of *ṭabāku*, cf. perhaps the similar idiomatic use of *šapāku* "to render limp (?), powerless (?)" acc. to CAD sv 3.

6.4.5.2. Concluding remarks

The inherent plurality of these verbs makes it difficult to detect an overall difference in use between G and D, especially in those verbs which typically occur in literary texts (*kamāru, nakāmu, qarānu* and *šapāku*) and prescriptions (*ṭabāku*). However, most of them show subtle differences which vary according to verb and dialect.

They are typically combined with objects such as *makkūru* and *bušû* "property", and abstract nouns such as *hiṣbu, ṭuhdu, hegallu and nuhšu*, all meaning "abundance, prosperity", which have a concrete meaning in this context.

6.4.6. Group VI: verbs of creating

Three verbs can be assigned to this group: the very common verbs *eṣēru* "to draw, design" and *(w)alādu* "to give birth, beget, produce" (Group VIa: > 10), and the literary variant of the latter *bašāmu* (Group VIb: 3 to 10). The first two will be discussed here.

Eṣēru "to draw, design": D usually has a pl. obj.: **1**. *uṣurātu* "drawings, plans", passim; **2**. other pl. objects: (drawings of) fishes, statues, rites, decorations, lines, nets, kings, days (qu. below); **3**. exceptions: see below.

For the contrast G + sg. obj. ↔ D + pl. obj. cf. especially the use of D with *uṣurātu*, versus G with *uṣurtu* (CAD sv *e*. A 1a-2', 1b-2', AHw sv G 1b, 2c, 3). Note also SpTU 3, 74: 181 (// Maqlû III 181), a stative with pl. acc., quoted as (39) in 6.5.3. Typically, G also occurs with *uṣurātu*: BagF. 18, 305: 19; ACh. 2. Spl. 20: 39; Sg. Cyl. 76, and elsewhere in the RIs of Sargon. Other cases of G + pl. obj. include Gilg. XI 212 *ūmī ša ittīlu ina igāri iṣ-ri* "mark (G) on the wall the days he has slept" (cf. LKU 33: 15 *ūmīšina ina igāra uṣ-ṣar* "(Lamaštu) marks (D) their (the pregnant women's) days on the wall"), and many cases of *eṣrū* with pl. subject in protases of omens (CAD sv 1c, AHw sv G 2c).

Exceptions: Ee VII 63 = (88) in 6.6.3.3; Racc. 28: 21 *bēlum mu-uṣ-ṣir mātiš[u]* "the lord who designed his country", see possibly 6.9.2.2 or 6.9.3.

It seems likely that the original meaning of *eṣēru* is "to scratch", so that it belonged semantically to the verbs of Group II. In OB this meaning is still attested sporadically, cf. Veenhof 1995: 318ff ("to cross out, make invalid").

(W)alādu "to give birth, beget, produce"; D mostly has a pl. obj.: **1**. said of human offspring (14A); **2**.

of sheep: "to breed"; **3.** with gods as subject and as objects gods, winds, mankind, grain, vegetation, "everything"; **4.** metaph., with abstract subj. and obj. (1x); **5.** exc. with sg. obj. (demon).

For the use of D + pl. obj. cf. CAD sv *alādu* 2a-1' "to give birth (to many)", and *ib.* 2' "to beget (many)", AHw sv *w.* D "(viele) zeugen, gebären, schaffen".

In OB G + pl. obj. is much more common than D, which seems to be used only with the father as subject; compare the 3 OB instances of **1.** with the very similar phrases in law codes, where the mother is subject and G is used, for instance:

> (14A) LE § 59 A IV 29f *šumma awīlum mārī wu-ul-lu-ud-ma aššassu īzimma [ša]nītam ītahaz* "if a man who has children has left his wife and has married someone else";
> (14B) KH r.X 24ff (§ 158) *šumma awīlum warki abīšu ina sūn ra-bi-ti-šu ša mārī wa-al-da-at ittaṣbat* "if, after his father's death, a man is caught having intercourse with his (i.e., his father's) chief wife (?), who is the mother of children" (cf. also *ib.* r.VIII 47. 52. 61; r.XII 39. 41. 44).

The question is whether G or D would be used with the father as subject and a *singular* obj.; as far as legal texts are concerned the dictionaries have no such instances; an OB literary text has G: VS 10, 213: 14 DN *ú-ul-da-an-ni-ma* "Sin begot me".

In SB D is only used of gods, often as epithet (*mu'allid* + gen., beside *ālid* + gen, cf. 6.9.3 and St.Or. 7, 87), and metaphorically, with the exception of ACh. 2. Spl. 51: 17. The technical use of D (**2.**) is restricted to OB.

6.4.7. Group VII: verbs of giving, taking and carrying

As was argued in 5.6.2.1, verbs of giving, taking and carrying do not belong to the typical high transitivity verbs and thus do not in general have a frequent D-stem. A few of them, however, are occasionally found in the D-stem; *paqādu* even rather frequently. Part of these D-stems are used to underline plurality of the object. *Naqû* and *nasāqu* have been included here for lack of a better place, although they are not typical verbs of giving or taking. The verbs selected for discussion are those of VIIa, and *apālu* and *nasāqu* of VIIb.

Group VIIa (> 10):

Naqû	to pour out, sacrifice	**Qâšu**	to grant, donate
Paqādu	to entrust, appoint, inspect		

Group VIIb (3 to 10):

Apālu	to pay	**Zabālu**	to carry
Nasāqu	to choose, select		

Group VIIc (< 3):

Ahāzu	to marry	**Katā'u**	to take as security
Esēhu	to assign	**Puāgu**	to take away

6.4.7.1. Discussion of the most important verbs

Apālu "to pay, satisfy"; D occurs only with obj. *hu-bu-li-....* "debt(s)", or "additional costs" (*ahiātu*). G is the normal form with the creditor and/or the debt as object, cf. CAD sv *a.* A 1; for ***hubullu*** with G see, e.g.,

BDHP 66: 6. There are two cases with G and D in the same sentence: TCL 1, 195: 14 quoted as (135) in 6.9.5, and TSifr. 37a: 10f *ummeānam i-pu-lu-ú-ma ahiātīšunu ú-up-pi-lu-ú-ma* "they paid the creditor and paid their additional costs".

Paqādu "to entrust, appoint, take care of, inspect"; D mostly has a pl. obj.: **1.** "to entrust (to)": animals, "everything" (note esp. RA 59, 151ff: 11. 14. 23. 63 with D, but G in 152: 37, see 5.6.5?) and "everybody (cf. 6.3), silver, persons (16); **2.** id. in **MA** with pl. *indirect* obj. (sheep to persons) → 6.5.2; **3.** "to inspect, muster": oracles, figurines, gods, bonds of heaven, limbs; **4.** "to take care of": houses, sanctuaries, persons (?); **5.** "to provide": bribe(s), sheep (pl.); **6.** "to appoint" persons (15), note esp. Asb. A I 111 vs. G in 113 with the same object; **7.** exceptions: see below.

For D with pl. obj. cf. AHw sv D 1 "(vieles) übergeben, anvertrauen"; instances of D + pl. obj. ↔ G + sg. obj. side by side are:

(15) ABL 885: 10f a.sig$_5$ *ša abīja ša ina muhhi <dul>li pa-qu-du-u-ni qanni išmûni mā* lú.a.ba *pa-qi-id dullu ittaṣû* "As soon as my father's ...-men, who had been put in charge (D) of the work, heard "a new man has been appointed (G)", they left the work." (tr. CAD sv *qannu* 3b);

(16) ABL 530: r.9'/13' (*šarru* ...) *napšātīšunu irēnšunūtīma šuglû pu-uq-qud(u) ana bulṭu* (...) *bēl šarrāni lip-qí-dan-nu ana bulṭu* "the king showed mercy to them (i.e., those who sinned against him) and those who were deported were pardoned (lit. entrusted for living) (D); (...) may the lord of kings pardon (G) me, too!" (tr. of r.9' CAD sv *šuglû* adj.)

Paqādu is semantically out of tune with most verbs that have a D-stem for plurality (cf. 5.6.2.1), but its association with plurality is quite strong. On the other hand, the use of G + pl. obj. is at least as frequent as that of D + pl. obj., cf. AHw sv G passim.

Exceptions: ARM 27, 1: 4. 7 may be an idiomatic usage comparable to those discussed in 6.4.9; for Maqlû II 50 = (93) and AfO 18, 298: 34 = (94) see 6.7.2; for SAA 3, 3: 17 = (34A) a possible explanation is offered in 6.5.2.

Qâšu "to donate, grant"; D: **1.** normally with obj. *qīšāti* "presents"; **2.** 1x Dt with subj. broken but sg. (?) (Racc. 26: 25); **3.** 1x no obj. (MSL 1, 4: 38). For the association of D with pl. obj., cf. CAD sv 3 "to bestow many gifts", AHw sv *qiāšum* D "viel schenken, beschenken"; it mostly occurs in the stereotyped expression *qīšāti quššu* "to offer presents" in RIs, which contrasts with the usual G + sg. obj. in *qīšta qâšu*, e.g., Angim 90f; LKA 73: r.9 (G + pl. obj. is also found: Syr. 19, 109: 28 (OB); VS 1, 37: III 34; WO 2, 150: 83). For MSL 1, 4: 38 *ú-qa-as-su*, contrasting with G in 3: 35, see note 19.

Naqû "to pour out, sacrifice"; D: **1.** various combinations of liquids, beer (cf. (110) and (114) in 6.9.2.1), water; part. *munaqqîtu* "libation bowl" → 6.6.2; **2.** substances: grain, flour; **3.** obj. *niqû*; **4.** "to shed" blood.

D is rare compared to the very common G-stem, with which it alternates in ritual texts (cf. 6.9.2.1) with substances as object (cf. also CAD sv 1), but it is not used with sacrificial animals, whether pl. or sg. (CAD sv 3b), except **3.** (1x); this is remarkable in view of the use of D with similar verbs as *palāq/ku* and *ṭabāhu*, if they have a pl. obj. For KAR 16: r.26, Racc. 42: 19 and 46: 22 → 6.7.2?

Nasāqu "to select, choose"; D: **1.** literally: workmen, copper ingots, textiles, young men, days; with a mass noun: wool; **2.** id. with sg. obj.: an expert (ARM 13, 44: 9 = (78) in 6.6.3.2); **3.** idiomatic: + *dabābam* "to look for trouble"; + *ramanka* "yourself" (BSOAS 20, 265: 9, cf. G with negation in 264: r.3 (context fragmentary)). G is the normal form both with sg. and pl. obj., cf. esp. CAD sv 1a-2'/3' (objects and persons).

6.4.8. Remaining verbs

This category comprises verbs whose D-stem is mainly used for another purpose than that of underlining plurality, but can also be used for plurality of the direct object. In most cases the latter function is restricted to a specific type of object or a specific dialect.

Epēšu "to make, do"; D is mainly used in several lexicalized meanings, varying according to dialect, see 6.8.3. In 6.5.1 evidence will be provided which points to an association of D with plurality of the subject, cf. (25) and (26). A number of other cases scattered over various dialects suggest that D can also underline plurality of the direct object. For an OB instance see (91) in 6.7.2. In OA we find the expression *awātim eppušum* (App. **6.**) "to arrange matters (?)" acc. to CAD sv 2c *amatu* d' (p. 202b bottom), and the isolated instance KTS 57c: 11 (a smith) *ša alî ú-pu-šu* "who makes *alûs*".

Gamāru "to bring to an end, use up, control"; D with pl. obj. is perhaps found in *awātim* (pl.) *gummurum* (App. **6.**, 1x OB, often in OA) "to settle disputes"; this is suggested by the fact that we find G + pl. obj. (e.g., *gāmir awātim*, passim) and G + sg. obj. in this idiom, cf. CAD sv 1d-1', AHw sv *g.* II G 4a, but not D + sg. obj.

Hamāṣu "to strip, skin, tear off"; D usually has the idiomatic meaning of "to skin" an animal, "to tear off" metal from an object (cf. App. **2.** and 6.8.1), and "to rob, ransack" a house or temple (cf. App. **3.** and 6.4.9). With clothes as obj., D goes with a pl. obj. in OB, cf. especially D and G in contrast in:

> (17A) TCL 11, 245: 1ff *aššum* <u>túg.dugud</u> *u* <u>túg.bar.si</u> *ša DN labšat u* [*š*]*a hu-mu-ṣa-at* "concerning the heavy cloak and the headdress in which DN was clothed and of which she has been stripped (D)."
>
> (17B) *ib.* 9f *širiṭ* <u>túg.dugud</u> *annûm* (...) *lū ša DN ha-am-ṣa-at* "this piece of the heavy cloak (...) is that of which DN has been stripped (G)."
>
> (17C) *ib.* 25ff *šurāṭ* <u>túg.dugud</u> [...] (...) *ša ina* [*pag*]*ar DN ha-am-ṣú* "a piece of the heavy cloak which has been stripped (G) off the body of DN."
>
> (17D) *ib.* 32ff *ina* <u>túg.dugud</u> *u* <u>túg.bar.si</u> *ša pagar DN hu-mu-ṣí būr* "he has been convicted of stripping (D) the heavy cloak and the headdress off the body of DN."

where G in (17BC) refers to a sg. noun, D in (17AD) to two coordinated nouns.

Lapātu "to touch, smear, affect"; D mainly serves to underline plural action, cf. 6.6.3.2 with (69) - (73) and 6.6.3.3 with (84) and (90A). There may be an association with plurality of the direct object when it means "to touch, affect" persons and objects (App. **1.**). However, it is very difficult to separate the various tendencies which determine the use of *lapātu* D.

Mahāṣu "to hit, stab or wound"; D is mostly used idiomatically "to strike sb with a weapon" (App. **1.** and 6.8.1 sv), and for plural action in protases (App. **3.** and 6.6.1.1 sv and 6.6.1.2 sv); D with pl. obj. is restricted to inanimate objects (App. **2.**)

Napāhu "to light, set fire to, rise, blow"; D is sometimes used for plurality of object in its transitive meaning "to light, set fire to" (App. **1.**). Note esp. ARM 26/1 p. 159 note a A.2821: 9 *išātātim nu-up-pí-ih* "light fire signals!", versus *ib.* p. 176 no. 40: 25 and p. 414 no. 192: 23 *išātam ap-pu-uh/ú-pu-uh* (but RA 35, 183 note 2: 7 *3 išātātim ap-pu-uh-ma*). G has as objects "fire" (CAD sv 2a), and "brazier, stove, pyre", etc., always sg. acc. to CAD sv 2b, except in RA 35 quoted above. D is also used intransitively, see 7.6.1, and as a lexicalized stative in omens which usually has a pl. subj., see (36) in 10.6.1.1.1 and 10.6.1.2.1 sv.

Parāku "to block, obstruct"; D + pl. obj. mainly applies to App. **3.** "to lay crosswise", with concrete inanimate objects. The other uses listed in App. **1.-2.** and **4.-5.** do not seem to correlate with plurality.

Šaṭāru "to write, register"; D correlates with pl. obj. in the meanings "to write down" words and deeds (**1.**) and "to register, record" (mainly persons) (**2.**). Its most frequent use is in OB Mari in the idiomatic meaning "to write (a letter, report, etc.) *to* (a person), with sg. or pl. obj., cf. 6.8.1. sv.

6.4.9. Conclusions about the use of D for plurality of the direct object

Plurality of the direct object is by far the most common type of verbal plurality expressed by the D-stems of Type I. It is also the only type which is frequent enough to enable us to establish in broad outline the conditions of its use. Before continuing, therefore, with the other, more marginal, kinds of verbal plurality expressed by the D-stem, I will describe the two major characteristics of the use of D for plurality of the object on the basis of the general relationship between the D-stems of Type I and the corresponding G-stems as described in 6.1. These are, first, the fact that the use of a D-stem in connection with plurality is a semantic tendency, not a grammatical rule, and, second, that there is a tendency to restrict the association between D and plurality to the basic meaning of the verb.

The first of these characteristics, i.e., the semantic rather than grammatical nature of the relationship between D and G, has three important consequences.

First of all, the use of D is determined by the semantic character of the direct object in question, not primarily by whether it is grammatically plural or not (see 6.3). Plurality is an important factor in determining this character, but it is not decisive. The constituent need not be plural in form, provided that it can be interpreted as plural or as resembling a plural in some respect. This explains the use of D with mass nouns, with nouns as *mātu* "land", *ṣābu* "work force, army, people" and *ummānu* "army", which refer to a group of people, and with generic singular nouns (cf. 6.3).

From here it is only a small step to the use of D forms with other objects which, although being singular, are in some respect "more" than the normal object of a verb, in particular, more salient, for instance, because they are unusually large in size. This may be a factor in the exceptional use of D forms with the singular of nouns for mountains and large buildings (cf. *abātu* **1.** and **2.** "to destroy, ruin" (Group Ia), *hepû* **6.** "to break, smash" (Group Ia) and *sahāpu* **4.** "to cover, overwhelm, lay flat" (Group IIIa). It is also possible, however, that some of these objects can be viewed as collectives. Unusual size may also explain the following D form in an OB Mari letter:

(18) ARM 6, 5: 12f (about a stone (mass) ($\underline{na_4}$) which has fallen into a canal) *inanna abnam šâti ú-ha-ap-pa* "now, I am demolishing (or: going to demolish) that stone (mass)."

This exceptional use of *hepû* D with a singular object (see 6.4.1.1 sv) may be motivated by the wish on the part of the sender of this letter to convince the addressee (the king of Mari) of the enormity of the work required to remove it. It is remarkable that also on another occasion a similar situation leads to the use of exceptional forms with gemination, viz., in ARM 14, 7: 5f, quoted and discussed in 4.2.3. as (31).

The second consequence of the semantic nature of the relationship between G and D is that the use of D is optional. This not only applies to all cases in which D underlines plurality of the object, but also to a majority of the idiomatic uses discussed in 6.8.1. It is difficult to prove for each individual instance of D that the use of G would be equally grammatical in the sentence in question and does not entail a significant change in meaning. However, there are two indications which make it plausible.

The first one is that, if we consider the use of frequent D-stems of Type I, we find that there are hardly any instances of D which cannot be paralleled by an instance of G with a similar object in a similar context. This is especially clear in SB. In the numerous more or less stereotyped passages of royal inscriptions and of prayers and incantations, many verbs are used both in the G- and the D-stem without an appreciable difference in meaning. Common examples are *kabāsu* "to tread down" enemies (for D see App. **2.**, for G CAD sv 2b-2'), *ṣabātu* "to capture" enemies (D: App. **1.**, G: CAD sv 2c), and animals (D: App. **3.**, G: CAD sv 3b), *qarānu* "to heap up" tribute and corpses (D: App. **1./2.**, G: CAD sv *garānu* a), and *sahāpu* "to overwhelm" enemies (D: App. **1.**, G: CAD sv 1c). In prayers and incantations, verbs as *paṭāru, pašāru* and *pasāsu,* all used for "to undo, cancel" (sins, curses, etc.) seem to be used indiscriminately in G and D (cf. *paṭāru* **3.** and AHw sv G 8; *pašāru* **2.** and AHw sv G 7; *pasāsu* **3.** and AHw sv G 4). Another context in which we find apparently indiscriminate use of G and D on a rather large scale is in prescriptions, usually in medical or ritual texts, where many verbs occur in the G- and the D-stem without an observable difference; the most striking cases will be enumerated in 6.9.2.1.

The second indication comes from texts of which duplicate versions are extant; they contain a considerable number of cases where one version has a D form, and another version a G form, as in:

(19) Maqlû VII 2 *šī kaššaptu ú-nak-ka-ma* // *i-na-ak-ka-ma kišpīša* "she, the sorceress, piles up her sorceries" (also quoted as (143A) in 6.9.5);

(20) Sn. 46: 12 *ú-na-kis* // *ak-kis qātīšun* "I cut off their hands";

(21) BAM 248: IV 30 // AMT 67, 1: IV 23 *allān Kāniš ina pīša i-mar-raq-ma* // *ú-mar-raq-ma* "she crushes a piece of Kaniš oak in her mouth".

Such cases are indicated by means of the symbol D // G in the presentation of the verb in question in this chapter, or, for verbs which are not discussed, in the Appendix.

The only exceptions to the optional nature of D are idiomatic and lexicalized expressions in which the use of D has become stereotyped, such as *bīta luqqutu* "to strip a house bare", or *uppušu* "to calculate" (see below in this section and in 6.8.3 respectively). However, in 6.9.5 some passages will be discussed which suggest that in contexts where both G and D are possible there can be a subtle semantic difference between them, at least if they are used side by side in the same passage.

The alternation of G and D in the same contexts and as variants in duplicate texts shows that there is no essential difference between the use of G and D: both forms can refer to the same situation. Consequently, such D and G forms are not contrastive: if they contrast with each other in the same passage, this is either concomitant with another difference between the two clauses in which they occur (usually plural versus singular); or else, if these clauses differ only in that one has a G form and the other one the corresponding D form, they are variants of a single clause. This situation is found almost exclusively in literary texts, where G and D forms are sometimes juxtaposed for stylistic variation, cf. 6.9.4.

The relationship obtaining here between corresponding D and G forms is doubtless comparable to that between corresponding forms with and without gemination of the adjectives denoting dimensions. It was shown in 3.1.3.2 that the use of the pattern *parras* to form the plural of adjectives is determined by the salience of the adjective itself and of the entity it qualifies. As to the difference between the two forms, it was further hypothesized that in this situation a speaker of Akkadian can either make this high degree of salience in combination with plurality explicit by using a form with gemination, or leave it implicit in the context by using a simple form. The characteristic features of the use of D with a plural object suggest that the same mechanism applies to the relationship between corresponding D and G forms. It will be argued in 10.8 that it also applies to the relationship between many *purrus* adjectives and the corresponding simple adjectives.

The third consequence of the semantic nature of the relationship between G and D is that it accounts for many cases - mentioned in the previous sections - where a D-stem is used with a singular object. Apart from a number of real exceptions which cannot be explained away, most of these cases result from other tendencies which interfere with the use of D for plurality of the object, such as the fact that the D-stem is not restricted to plurality of the object alone, but also serves to underline plurality of action and of other constituents of the sentence (see 6.5 and 6.6), and the fact that frequently the association of D with plurality only applies to a part of the meanings of the D-stem.

The latter fact brings us to the second of the two major characteristics of the use of D for plurality of the direct object to be discussed in this section, viz., that there is a tendency to restrict the association between D and plurality to the basic ("prototypical", see 5.4) meaning of the verb. This tendency explains numerous deviations noted in the previous sections in cases where metaphorical expressions are involved. It is especially clear in some verbs of Groups III and IV: *kaṣāru, paṭāru, petû, rakāsu* and *ṣabātu.*

The way the D-stems of these verbs behave depends on whether they have a direct object which can be regarded as one of the prototypical objects of the verb in question (normally a concrete entity), or a direct object which gives the verb a non-prototypical, more or less metaphorical meaning. In the former case we tend to find D forms only when that object is plural. In the latter case there is often no correlation between the use of D and plurality.

As prototypical objects of the verbs mentioned above can be regarded entities such as relatively small objects and body parts for *kaṣāru* "to bind together, etc." (cf. **1**.-**2**.), ties, knots and other small objects for *paṭāru* "to loosen" (cf. **1**.-**2**.), doors, roads, canals, etc., for *petû* "to open" (cf. **1**.-**5**.), animate beings and body parts for *rakāsu* "to bind" in its literal meaning (cf. **1**.), and persons, animals or objects for *ṣabātu* "to seize" in its literal sense (cf. **1**.-**6**.). In these combinations (listed under A̲ in the presentation of the respective verbs in 6.4.3.1 and 6.4.4.1) singular objects are exceptional (they are listed under C̲).

The expressions in which D-stems do not show a correlation with plurality are the following: *kaṣāru* **5**. "to build, fortify, restore" (a city, a wall, a house, a camp); *paṭāru* **4**. "to release" (a person), and **5**./**6**. "to clear away" (ruins from a building site), with the intransitive Dt "to decay, disintegrate"; *petû* **9**. "to reclaim" (uncultivated land) and **10**. "to expose" (a part of the body); *rakāsu* **8**. "to bandage" (a person), and **9**. "to bind by contract" (a person); and *ṣabātu* **10**. "to seize" with sorcery (a person or body part), and **11**. "to paralyze" (a person or body part).

In these cases D and G alternate without an observable difference and irrespective of the grammatical number of the object. Accordingly, both D and G can be used for *kaṣāru* **5**. (cf. CAD sv 1b (but G in OB Mari acc. to CAD and AHw sv G 5), *paṭāru* **4**. (cf. AHw sv G 9, 11) and **5**./**6**. (cf. AHw sv G 4), *petû* **9**. (cf. AHw sv *p.* II G 10), *rakāsu* **8**. (cf. AHw sv G 3d) and *ṣabātu* **10**., **11**. and **12**. (cf. CAD sv 1a/b, 8 *ṭēmu*, AHw sv G II 2/3, IV 5b); for *rakāsu* **9**. there are no exact parallels with G, cf. AHw sv G 17.

A typical feature of many of these objects is that they often involve an action which requires more energy, more time, etc., than the action associated with the "normal" object, and often denote entities which are larger in size, and/or more salient than the "average" object associated with the verb (buildings, fields, and persons (for verbs which basically do not have a personal object)). This is particularly clear in *kaṣāru* **5**. "to build, fortify, restore" (a building), in *petû* **9**. "to reclaim" (uncultivated land) and in *paṭāru* **5**. "to clear away" (a building), as compared to "to bind a knot", "to open a door" and "to loosen a knot", respectively; this also applies to *ṣabātu* D "to seize" (by magic means) or "to paralyze" versus G "to seize" (by humans), see 6.4.4.1 sv.

The same tendency explains the use of D with a singular object in a few other expressions: *hamāṣu* **3**. "to ransack" (a house), *kanāku* **2**. "to put under seal" (a building), *laqātu* **2**. "to strip bare" (a house), *nakāpu* **3**. and *palāšu* **4**. "to invade" (a country, always D), *nasāhu* **5**. "to evict" (a person), *sapāhu* **4**. "to waste, squander" (money, barley, an estate, etc., almost always D) and **5**. "to ruin" (a district"), and *ṣamādu* **3**. "to bandage" (a person or a wound). It may also be responsible for some abstract objects in the singular: *sapāhu* **6**. "to thwart, bring to nought" and *ṣabātu* **12**, in OB *ṭēmam ṣubbutum* "to take action".

A more general conclusion which can be drawn from the behaviour of these D-stems is that there is a gradation in the tendency to use the D-stem: as a general rule, D tends to be absent if the verb in question has a secondary meaning which entails a decrease in transitivity and a less salient object or no object at all (cf. 5.6.4); it tends to correlate with plurality if the verb has its basic meaning and the kind of object which is most typical of it; and it tends to be used both with singular and plural objects, if the direct object is more salient, or personal in cases in which the typical object is non-personal.

The characteristic behaviour of the D-stem observed here suggests an explanation for a number of apparent exceptions which have been noted so far. If we find an exceptional singular object belonging to a salient category, and it is atypical of the verb in question, it can be explained as an idiomatic expression. A good example is provided by the use of *batāqu* and *hepû* in the same OB letter:

(22) AbB 1, 27: 20ff (about a slave girl) [20]*ú-ha-ap-pí-ši-ma* (...) [24](...) *maškana* [25]*ša 5 mana idīšīma kilēši* [26]*amtum uznāša annî[š]ma* [27]*ihalliqki* (or *ihalliqqi* ?) *maškanu* [28]*li-ba-at-ti-iq-ši* "I have beaten her up (?)" (...) "chain her with a chain of 5 minas and lock her up! The slave girl has set her mind on escaping (from you?); let the chain prevent (??) her" (cf. Kraus's translation).

Whatever the precise meaning of these two D-stems, they obviously do not have their usual meaning of "to break" and "to cut off", respectively. Therefore, they can be classified as idiomatic, even though no other cases of such idioms are extant. Note that a personal object is involved, which is very unusual with both *batāqu* and *hepû*.

Another exception which may be explained in the same way is *bīta huppû* (cf. *hepû* **6.** in 6.4.1.1 sv); the contexts suggest that it means "to ruin a household, a family or an estate", rather than literally "to destroy a house":

(23) BWL 146: 38 *bīt abīšu uh-te-pe* (thus AHw sv Dt 1, against Lambert (*ad l.*) *ih-te-pi*) "his father's house will fall into ruin" (cf. also (05) and (06) in 9.1.1);

(24) ABL 892: r.24f *bīta ša ardi ša šarri lā ú-he-ep-pe* "may he (the king) not ruin the "house" of the king's servant".

Because of the more or less idiomatic nature of the meanings involved, these D-stems are related to the idiomatic D-stems which will be discussed in greater detail in 6.8.

6.5. Plurality of other constituents than the direct object

Plurality of the object is by far the most common, but not the only way in which the association of the D-stems of Type I with plurality can be realized. Occasionally, we find D forms which are motivated by plurality of other constituents of the sentence, namely the subject, the indirect object and the adjunct accusative. We will examine these cases one by one. Note that subjects of passive sentences are subsumed under the cases of plural object of the corresponding active in 6.4.

6.5.1. Plurality of the subject

A few contrasting cases of G and D suggest that plurality of the subject can also lead to the use of a D-stem. Two of them concern the verb *epēšu* "to make, do" (cf. CAD sv 4f-1'):

(25) RIMA 1, 101f: 5ff *dūrum ša RN_1 RN_2 RN_3 RN_4 RN_5 mār RN_6 abbāja ú-up-pí-šu-ni ēnahma* (...) *e-pu-uš* (...) *rubā'u urkiu enūma dūrum šūt ēnuhūma e-ep-pu-šu DN_1 u DN_2 ikribīšu išamme'ūšu* "the wall which RN_1, RN_2, RN_3, RN_4 and RN_5, the son of RN_6, my forefathers, had built (D), had become dilapidated and I rebuilt (G) (it) (...); (as for) a future prince, when that wall becomes dilapidated and he rebuilds (G) (it), DN_1 and DN_2 will listen to his prayers";

(26) ABL 511: 18 *li-pu-uš abī u* lú.erim.meš-*šú gabbi lu-up-pu-šú* "may my father work (G) and may all his workmen work (D)."

These two instances contrast with scores of cases where *epēšu* has a plural subject, but no D-stem; with regard to (25), there can be little doubt that this exceptional instance is connected with the remarkable structure of the subject, a series of five coordinated nouns, and has distributive meaning: it underlines that the action is performed by different subjects on successive occasions (cf. also AHw sv D 3b: "nacheinander(?)"; see further 6.7.2).

The following OB case of G and D in the same letter may also be explained by the contrast between a singular and a plural subject:

(27) ARM 14, 3: 10 vs. 19 (A servant who is with me is ill) [10]*2 asû ša mahrija ú-ṣa-ma-du-šu-ma* "two physicians who are with me are bandaging (D) him, (but his illness does not change; now let my lord send another physician (...)) *simmam ša ṣuhārim līmurma* [19]*u li-iṣ-mi-is-sú* "in order to examine the sore of the servant and bandage (G) him." (Comparable, but partly broken and therefore uncertain, is *latāku* G and D in AIPO 14, 135: 17 and 20 (G), versus 22 (D, restored).

It is, however, also possible that the sender of this letter attempts to make his request more urgent by emphasizing the persistent and frantic efforts of the two physicians by means of the D form in 10 (cf. 6.6.3.2), as opposed to the neutral, more factual nature of G in 19.

There is also a contrasting pair, although not in the same text, of G and D of *lapātu* "to touch, smear, affect", correlating with the singular and plural of *ittu* "(ominous) sign", in an idiomatic expression of which the meaning is not quite clear:

(28A) AbB 6, 22: 6 *ittī i-la-pa-ta-ni* "(...) juckt mich mein Schönheitsfleck" (tr. Frankena, cf. p. 17 n. 22a: "Ich sorge mich um dich" or the like);
(28B) MSL 4, 119: 19f *ittātūja ú-la-pa-ta-ni-in-ni* "I feel my beauty spots (= I think of you)" (tr. Landsberger);
(28C) JCS 15, 7: 20 *ittātūja ú-la-ap-<pa>-ta-ni-[in-ni]* "I sense my beauty spots" (tr. Held).

In (28) the contrast between G and D suggests that the use of D is related to plurality of the subject. In addition, this plural subject may imply that the direct object is affected more completely or perhaps repeatedly by the subject; in this respect, the use of *lapātu* D here is comparable to that illustrated by (69) to (73) in 6.6.3.2 and (90A) in 6.6.3.3.

Other cases of D-stems which may be explained - more or less tentatively - by plurality of the subject concern *madādu* in OA (see (67) and (68) in 6.6.3.1), *parāsu* in OB Mari (see 6.4.1.1 sv), *paqādu* in Maqlû II 37ff and AfO 18, 298: 29ff (= (93) and (94) in 6.7.2), and *paṭāru* in Šurpu II 167 (= (92) in 6.7.2) and AGH 14: 23 (quoted in 6.4.3.1 sv).

There can be little doubt that there are many more cases where plurality of the subject leads to the use of a D form. Without a contrasting G-stem with a singular subject, however, it is difficult to determine whether the plural subject is the actual motive for the use of D.

There are no D-stems which are exclusively motivated by plurality of the subject, but for *našāqu* "to kiss" it seems to be the most important factor:

Našāqu "to kiss"; D: **1.** person (sg.); **2.** feet, 1x knees+feet; **3.** *qaqqara* "the ground". D is mainly used in plural contexts, but the details are rather complicated. With pers. obj., only instances with a sg. obj. are attested; in this case G typically refers to a single kiss and has a single subject, cf. CAD sv 1a. Of the rare cases of D with pers. obj. (App. **1.**, cf. CAD sv 3a), three are used in a context of tenderness (rather than submission, as in **2.** and **3.**) and suggest a meaning "to cuddle, fondle" (between brother and sister in VAB 2, 357: 86, son and father in Ee I 54; mother (?) and child in SAA 3, 37: 8'), rather than "to give a kiss"; thus it underlines plurality of the action, cf. 6.6.3); note that "to kiss sb's lips" is always expressed by G (CAD sv lex. sect. and 1b), in spite of the dual object, since this act requires no more than a single kiss.

D is most frequently used with the objects "feet"[12] and *qaqqaru* "the ground". Outside RIs, it always has a pl. *subject* (with two exceptions, see below), whereas G usually has a sg. subj., cf. CAD sv 1b/c/d (G + pl. subj.: OB: RA 46, 90: 42 (OB Anzû, cf. D in SB parallel *ib.* 48, 146: 109); SB: AGH 142a: 3; AnSt. 33, 148: 13. 15. 18; Or. 17, pl. 22: 4. 9; NB: ABL 283: r.17; 793: r.19). The two exceptions (MB: BE 17, 5: 18, and NA: SAA 1, 133: r.3') can be explained as being due to plurality of the object, which implies a plural action: in BE 17, 5: 18 knees and feet are the object, in SAA 1, 133: r.3' the feet of several gods.

In SB RIs G and D seem to be used indiscriminately: both occur with sg. and pl. subj.; note esp. Sn. 30: 60 with a long list of kings as subject but still a G-stem (contrary to the claim made in 6.7.2); D, however, is much more frequent, for G cf. CAD sv 1c-1'. Caplice's claim (1980: 45) that D is iterative (*šēpīja unaššiq* = "he kissed my feet (repeatedly)", vs. *šēpīja iššiq* = "he kissed my feet"), is probably correct, but is difficult to verify from the respective contexts.

It is not surprising that in this verb plurality of the subject should be more prominent than that of the object: although it is formally a transitive verb, it is the action of kissing which is focused on, and which is therefore most salient, not the direct objects "feet" or "ground". In this respect *našāqu* resembles the verbs of eating and drinking (cf. 5.6.2.1).

6.5.2. Plurality of the indirect object

Evidence for plurality of the indirect object as a motive for using the D-stem is scarce; it may be provided by the following instances of *paqādu* "to entrust" in MA:

(29A) AfO 10, 34ff passim *x sheep ana PN pa-qi-id* or *pa-aq-du* "x sheep has/have been entrusted to PN (for fattening)";
(29B) *ib.* 43 no. 102: 9 (1 sheep for PN_1, 1 sheep for PN_2, 2 sheep in total), *ša <ana> abullāte pa-qu-du-ni* "which have been entrusted to (the men of) the gates." (also elsewhere in MA, see App. sv 2.).

Here a single person as indirect object correlates with a stative G, and a plurality of persons with the stative D. Note that the use of *paqādu* D is more frequently caused by plurality of the direct object, cf. 6.4.7.1 sv.

Just as in the preceding section, D seems to be distributive here, and underlines that the action is directed at various people. The occurrence of (29) suggests that in other verbs, too, plurality of the indirect object may be responsible for the use of a D-stem, but usually it is difficult to determine whether in a given context this kind of plurality is the actual factor which causes the use of a D-stem, or whether some other factor should be held responsible.

A good candidate for a D-stem which is determined by plurality of the indirect object seems to be *zâzu* in SB in the meaning "to distribute, to apportion", which has an inherently plural dative:

Zâzu "to divide, distribute" uses G and D differently in different periods. In OB D is too rare to draw meaningful conclusions, cf. App. sv **1**. In MB, NB and (rarely) NA D spreads at the expense of G, without replacing it completely, and no difference in use is observable, cf. CAD sv 5c, AHw sv D 4.

What is relevant here is the use of D and G in SB (**2.**). In SB a difference can be observed - although it is not quite consistent - between D "to distribute, apportion" and G "to divide". D mostly refers to the distribution of portions, positions (*manzāzu*), ordinances and courses (*harrānī*) to gods, and that of goods, animals and people, etc., to a plurality of people, cf. CAD sv 5a/b and 6, AHw sv D 2c/d/e. It is often accompanied by *ana*; sometimes the dative is implied, for instance, in Ee VII 60 (water in abundance), Racc. 129: 14 (portions, part.); ArOr 37, 484: 50 (portions). A variant of this construction is used in Ee VI 39 "(Marduk distributed (*ú-za-'i-iz*) all the Annunaki) *eliš u šapliš* "above and below", i.e., "over the upper and lower regions".

G, on the other hand, is mostly used in SB without mentioning a beneficiary in the meaning "to divide", cf. CAD sv 2a-d. Occasionally, however, D is also used for "to divide" in SB: Ee IV 136 (*kūbu* "monster"); BAM 74: IV 3 (herbs); RA 33, 106: 23 (*kīma būšê šaknūti zu-'u-ú-za-ku* "I (Ištar) have been divided (or distributed?) like heaped up goods", quite atypical). An exceptional instance with a sg. indirect object is MSL 1, 4: 39 *ú-za-as-su* "he will apportion to him" (no obj., no context), a present D contrasting with a preterite G in 3: 36; for parallels and a tentative explanation see note 19.

In other periods, G means both "to distribute" and "to divide", cf. CAD sv 4a (OA), 4b (OB), 4c (Elam), 4d (lit. and omen texts, only OB!), 4e (NB).

Plurality of the indirect object may be responsible for the use of a D form in cases such as the following:

(30) Sn. 97: 88 (= 101: 58) *ana mārē GN pilku ú-pal-lik* "I marked out a plot of land for the citizens of Niniveh";

(31) "C 18": 33 (qu. by Veenhof 1987: 67 note 18) (tin ...) *ana ahim u ebrim za-ri-šu-ma* "scatter it among friends and colleagues" (cf. Veenhof 1987: 45f);

(32) Tn.-Ep. II 10 [*ana m*]*ahar DN ana rēšīšunu ú-še-pi-ik šamna* "in the presence of DN I poured oil over their heads" (cf. also AnSt. 8, 52: III 39);

(33) ARM 3, 17: 17ff *kajjantam* lú.meš *šībūt ālim ana mahar DN errubūma ana bēlija u ummānātim ša bēlija ú-ka-ar-ra-bu* "the elders of the city regularly enter into the presence of DN and pray for my lord and the troops of my lord." (cf. Edzard 1962: 112b).

The verbs *palāku* and *zarû*, literally "to sow", are hardly found in the D-stem; it is probably no accident that it is used here: in (30) it doubtless serves to emphasize the large number of people who benefit from the activities of the king, and in (31) the context suggests a similar nuance, cf. Veenhof 1987: 46. The two instances of *šapāku* D contrast with numerous cases of G where *ana* is followed by a singular noun (either a dative or a directional element), cf. CAD sv 2a/b. For a possible explanation of (33), a unique instance of *karābu* D, see 6.7.2.

It is possible that the use of *paqādu* D illustrated above also explains the exceptional occurrence of this verb with a singular object which was listed in 6.4.7.1 sv, as appears from a comparison between (34A) and (34B):

(34A) SAA 3, 3: 17 *ana maṣṣārī šulme u balāṭi ú-paq-qí-du napištī* "(the gods) assigned my life to guardians of well-being and health" (tr. Livingstone);
(34B) ABL 113: 13 *maṣṣār šulmi balāṭi ana šarri bēlija lip-qi-du* "May (the gods) assign to the king, my lord, a guardian (or: guardians ?) of well-being and health" (also elsewhere, cf. CAD sv *maṣṣaru* 1c).

This is another instance of D with a dative plural versus G with a dative singular, as in (29). However, the distributive character of the dative in (34A) is not very clear; it is also conceivable that the use of D is due to the more literary character of the text in which (34A) occurs, cf. 6.9.2.2.

6.5.3. Plurality of the adjunct accusative

The use of the D-stem motivated by an adjunct accusative (i.e., an accusative which qualifies a verb form with passive meaning, cf. 6.3) in the plural is mostly found with statives in protases of omen texts. The most common instance is the expression *qê ṣubbut* in liver omens (App. sv *ṣabātu* **8.**); cf. especially the contrast between G and D in:

(35A) YOS 10, 42: II 33 *šumma rēš libbi qê ṣú-bu-ut* (...) "if the epigastrium is held by filaments (the anger of the god towards the man is not (yet) appeased)";
(35B) *ib.* 35 *šumma rēš libbi qû[m] ṣa-bi-it* (...) "if a filament holds the epigastrium (the commander of the army will be taken captive)" (cf. also OBE 1: 12ff).[13]

Both constructions are very common in extispicy omens, cf. CAD sv *ṣabātu* 10i-2' and sv *qû* A 3a; a few times *qê ṣubbut* is replaced by the apparently more or less synonymous *qê šuppuṣ*, cf. App. sv **2.** and CAD sv *šapāṣu* 3.

Two D-stems almost exclusively occur with a plural adjunct accusative: *edēhu* and *(h)alālu*:

With a single exception (App. sv **1.**), **edēhu** "to cover with patches" is used in the stative accompanied by a pl. adj. acc., mostly in omens, with parts of the liver as subject: (covered with) veins, red or white *kasû*-seeds, green threads; also with mass nouns: *šīram* "tissue" (36B), *mēdehti ša urqi* "patches of green"; elsewhere, said of stones, (covered with) patches of several colours (37).

A remarkable contrasting pair of *edēhu* G versus D qualifying the mass noun *šīrum* "flesh, tissue", which shows the same peculiarity as *qê ṣubbut* versus *qû ṣabit*, is the following:

(36A) YOS 10, 24: 33 *šumma bāb ekallim ši-rum e-di-ih* "if a piece of tissue (? see note 14) covers (lit. "has covered") the "palace gate" (the city will rebell and kill its lord)" (cf. also *ib.* 34);
(36B) *ib.* 35 *šumma bāb ekallim ši-ra-am ú-du-uh* "if the "palace gate" is covered with tissue ((it is) the omen of Šulgi, who captured Tabbadarah)."

In (36A) *šīrum* is treated as a singular, on a par with *qû* in (35B), but in (36B) the stative D suggests that it is on a par with a plural, as *qê* in (35A). This testifies to the ambiguous status of a mass noun as *šīrum*, which fluctuates between singular and plural (cf. 6.3). The equivalence of *šīrum* to a plural is confirmed by the fact that all other instances of *udduh*, apart from MDP 57, 167: 30 (with *mēdehtu*, also a mass noun), are accompanied by an accusative plural (cf. App. sv **2**). It is unclear, however, what the semantic difference between the two protases is.[14]

A particularly interesting case of contrasting *edih* and *udduh* is:

(37) STT 108: 15/18 and 22 [15]*[abnu šikinš]u sūma* (sa$_5$) *pūṣa* (babbar) *u ṣulma* (mi) *[ud-d]u-uh*[15] *luludānītu šumšu* / [16]*a. š. pūṣa u ṣulma* [ ]*-AH* (= *edih* or *udduh*) *hulālu šumšu* / [17]*a. š.* [*ṣal*]*imma 1* [*pūṣa*] *e-di-ih pappardilû šumšu* / [18]*a. š.* [*ṣal*]*imma 2 pūṣī e-di-ih papparminû šumšu* / (...) / [22]*a. š. pūṣa ṣulma u urqa* (sig$_7$) *ud*[*-d*]*u-uh* [*ma*]*r-hal-lum šumšu* "The stone whose surface (lit. appearance) is čovered (D) with red, white and black patches is a *luludānītu*; ... whose surface is covered (G or D) with white and black patches is a *hulālu*; ... whose surface is black and covered (G) with one white patch is a *pappardilû*; ... whose surface is black and covered (G) with two white patches is a *papparminû*; ... whose surface is covered (D) with white, black and green patches is a *marhallum*".

Here it is apparently the number of different colours of the stone which decides whether G or D is used: D for three different colours (in 15 and 22), but not for two patches of the same colour (in 18). Unfortunately, it remains unclear which form has to be restored in 16, with two different colours. In this instance it is particularly clear that the preference for D is not determined by a grammatical rule of agreement, but by semantic factors.

The instances of G (*edih*) with an adjunct acc. quoted by CAD sv a all have a sg. acc. (but see STT 108: 18 quoted above in (37)).

(H)alālu "to hang" is once found as stative D with pl. subj. (App. sv **1.**); elsewhere as stative D with pl. adjunct acc. (**2.**) in protases with parts of the liver as subj. and acc. *zihhī* "hung with pustules", but 1x with *ishunnātu* "bunches of grapes".

Contrasting cases of G with sg. *zihha* are not attested; neither are there any certain instances of *(h)ullul* with a sg. acc. or sg. subject (but see SAA 4, 45: r.11' in a fragmentary context). An isolated example of stative G with a pl. subj. (not an omen protasis) is Spirits p. 10: 96.

A comparable case, also from the technical jargon of extispicy omens, is the expression *lipiam* (later *lipâ*) *kussu* "enveloped with fat" (App. **4.** and CAD sv *kasû* A 5b), which has a mass noun instead of a plural (for *kasû* in general see 6.8.4 sv).

The fact that these instances of the use of D for plurality are all more or less restricted to one specialized context is a strong argument for the highly conventional and stereotyped nature of the D-stems of Type I (cf. 6.9.3).

It is a plausible assumption that a plural adjunct accusative can also cause the use of a D-stem in other contexts. Likely candidates are cases in which a D-stem which normally has a plural object has a singular object but is accompanied by a plural adjunct accusative:

(38) Ee V 59 *ēgir zibbassa durmāhī ú-rak-kis-ma* "he (Marduk) twisted her (Tiamat's) tail and tied it with strong ropes";

(39) SpTU 3, 74: 181 (// Maqlû III 181) *uṣurāt balāṭi ú-ṣu-rak anāku* "I am marked by the designs of life";

(40) MSL 7, 161: 49 (a knife) *ša sikkātu muh-hu-ṣu* "which is studded with pegs";

(41) Maqlû VIII 41 [DN (...) *li-s*]*a-hi-ip-ši benna tēšâ ra'ība* "[may Ea] cover her with epilepsy, vertigo, and trembling" (tr. CAD sv *sahāpu* 4a) (cf. also 6.7.2?).

Judging by the evidence presented in these sections, there is a tendency to correlate the use of the D-stem with other constituents than the object; how strong this tendency is, however, is is very difficult to determine, since in most contexts where we find a subject or a dative in the plural in combination with a D form, it is not certain whether there is a causal relationship between the two, since the D-stem can also be determined by other factors. A more common way of underlining plurality of other constituents than the direct object is the Gtn-stem, for which see 4.2.3 and 6.7.3.

6.6. The D-stem for plurality of action

The evidence presented in the preceding sections for the relevance of plurality in the use of the D-stems of Type I is based on the presence of an explicit plural element in the sentence. Also without the presence of such a plural element some instances of the D-stem serve to underline that the verb in question does not refer to a single action, but to a habit, an ongoing activity or process, or that the action is referred to in a general sense, without being aimed at a specific object. These nuances will be referred to briefly as "plural action" or "plurality of action" in the strict sense of the word, as opposed to plurality of one or more of the participants in the sentence, as discusssed in 6.4 and 6.5.

The use of D for plural action is harder to identify than its use for plurality of an explicit constituent of the sentence. In many contexts it is not easy to prove, first, that the action should be interpreted as plural, and second, that there actually is a causal relationship between this plural action and the use of D. For instance, it could be argued that plurality is merely implied by the context, and that in fact the D-stem has nothing to do with it, but is motivated by some other factor. In the case of plurality of the object this argument can be refuted by the fact that the high degree of consistency with which some verbs occur with a plural object can hardly be accidental, and by means of contexts in which G with a singular, and D with a plural object are in immediate contrast. Comparable arguments for the correlation between D and plural action are scarce.

Accordingly, in many instances of D-stems used in contexts which imply a plural action, we cannot be certain that the use of D is actually motivated by the tendency to make this plural character explicit. However, if it concerns a verb which is predominantly associated with plurality in other contexts, it seems more plausible to assume that the D-stem can also serve to underline plurality of action, than to regard the cases in question as exceptions.

Moreover, there are a few contexts which are particularly suitable to show that the use of D can be caused by plurality of action. They comprise the use of present tense forms of some D-stems in conditional sentences introduced by *šumma* "if" (cf. 6.6.1), and the use of participles of D-stems which normally have a plural object (cf. 6.6.2). In 6.6.3 I will discuss some individual verbs which offer interesting evidence with regard to plurality of action, arranged according to dialect: OA in 6.6.3.1, OB in 6.6.3.2 and SB in 6.6.3.3.

6.6.1. D-stems in the present tense in *šumma* clauses

One type of context which shows that some D-stems can be used to underline plurality of action is the conditional clause introduced by *šumma* "if". We will only concern ourselves with *šumma*-clauses which contain a verb form in the present, preterite or perfect and refer to an action, an activity or a process, not with *šumma*-clauses with a stative (some of the latter will be dealt with in Chapter X, in so far as they contain a *purrus* form).

As a general rule, *šumma* is followed by a past tense (preterite or perfect), cf. GAG § 161d/f. This is especially common in legal texts, such as the Codex of Hammurabi, the Laws of Ešnunna and the Middle Assyrian Laws; in such texts the condition has to be fulfilled - i.e., the unlawful act must have been committed - before the specified sanction can apply (cf. Hirsch 1969: 125). The use of the preterite and perfect in such conditional clauses is in accordance with their basic function of denoting actions which are completed at the moment of reference. In translating such preterites and perfects into modern European languages the present tense is often used, cf. GAG § 161d, and the practice of CAD. A serious disadvantage of this practice is, however, that it obscures the difference in meaning between a protasis with a past tense and one with a present tense.

The present tense is less common in *šumma*-clauses. According to GAG § 161i, it usually expresses intent, more rarely obligation ("Tun-Wollen oder seltener -Sollen"), or refers to the future. GAG (*ib.*) also claims that it is only very rarely ("nur ganz selten") used to refer to the present, and then denotes habitual activities. Actually, this use is quite common in a few specific types of texts. These texts are, first, omen texts which refer to particular activities or behaviour of people and animals - sometimes also other phenomena - which were regarded as ominous, i.e., especially omens from the series *Šumma Ālu* (cf. Oppenheim 1964: 220f). The second type are medical texts, where we find protases in which symptoms of patients are described; in so far as these symptoms are activities rather than conditions of the patient, the present tense is often used. Typical are the following examples from medical texts:

(42) Epilepsy p. 91: 104f *šumma* (...) *pâšu iptenette* (bad.bad-*te*) *lišānšu* / *ú-na-šak* "if he (the patient) (...) constantly opens his mouth and bites his tongue (Lugalgirra has seized him)";

(43) *ib.* p. 69: r.13 *šumma minâtūšu išammamāšu ú-zaq-qa-ta-šú* "if his limbs are paralyzed (and) give him sharp pains" (tr. Stol) (followed by a further symptom and a diagnosis).

These protases clearly do not refer to a single action, but to an activity which stretches over a certain period of time (cf. the coordination of D with Gtn in (42)), and is not necessarily completed before the apodosis applies (cf. also the remarks of Kraus, AfO 11, 220). As such, they can be opposed to *šumma*-clauses with the same verbs in the preterite G:

(44) LE § 56/57 A IV 20ff *šumma kalbum šegîma* (...) *awīlam iš-šu-uk-ma uštamīt* "if a dog is rabid (...), has bitten a man, and thereby has caused his death", and:

(45) TDP 4: 31 (When the exorcist is on his way to the house of a patient) *šumma idi imittišu iz-qut-su* "if (then) his right side hurt him" (cf. CAD sv 1b: "if he has a sudden pain in his right side"),

which clearly refer to a once-only event. In contrast to (43), there is no question of a symptom of an illness in (45), but of an accidental event, on a par with other events which might happen "when the exorcist is on his way to the house of a patient" (and which are also in the preterite), cf. TDP p. 2ff. A further example of this contrast is:

(46) BAM 152: IV 16 *šumma amēlu šēpāšu kinṣāšu kabtāšumma ú-sah-ha-la-šú* "if a man's feet and shins feel heavy and cause him piercing pain" (tr. CAD sv 2b, lit. "pierce him");

(47) Dreams 329 a 62 *šumma* giš.igi.dù *gišimmari is-hul*(! sign NIN)-*šú* "if (in his dream) the thorn of a date palm has stung him".

Thus between (42), (43) and (46) on the one hand, and (44), (45) and (47) on the other, there is a double contrast, both in tense and in verbal stem. Whereas the contrast in tense is essential, the contrast in verbal stem is contingent on the general way in which G and D of the verb in question are used. For instance, beside (43) and (46) with D we also find G:

(48) KAR 157: r. 30 *šumma amēlu* (...) *kinṣāšu i-za-qat(a)-šú* (for /*izaqqatāšu*/ "if a man's shins hurt him" (cf. CAD sv 1b);

(49) BAM 26: 1 *šumma amēlu šinnāšu i-sah-ha-la-šú* "if a man's teeth cause him a stabbing pain" (tr. CAD sv 1a), lit. "pierce him",

but the dictionaries mention no instances of *našāku* G in *šumma*-clauses comparable to (42): either the preterite G *iššuk* is used, or the present D *unaššak*.

This leads to the conclusion that also in other cases - where the context may be less unambiguous - a preterite refers to a single action which is completed before the apodosis is realized, whereas a present can refer to an action which is repeated or stretches over a period of time, in addition to expressing intent, obligation or future (cf. GAG § 161i). Compare, for instance, from the same text:

(50A) CT 40, 34: r.16 *šumma sīsû ana bīt amēli īrubma lū imēra lū amēla iš-šuk* "if a horse has entered a man's house and has bitten either a donkey or a person";

(50B) CT 40, 34: r.8 // TU 8: r.5 [*šumma sīs*]*û iššegûma lū tappâšu lū amēlī ú-na-šak* "if a horse has become rabid and bites all the time/wants to bite/tries to bite/is prone to biting either its companion or people".

The preterite in (50A) implies that an actual event has occurred, just as in legal texts (cf.

(44)); the present in (50B) suggests that the biting is not (yet) completed, but is repeated (habitual), or has a nuance of intention (cf. (42)). It is quite natural that the notions of intent, obligation and future go together with that of plural action: both share the feature of being non-completed, and therefore indeterminate, as opposed to the reality of an actual event which has already occurred, and which is expressed by the preterite.[16]

That the present D in protases really serves to underline plurality of the action, is confirmed by the fact that for verbs which do not normally occur in the D-stem, or whose D-stem has another meaning, we find the present Gtn in *šumma*-clauses, in opposition to the preterite G, used in exactly the same way as the present D in the verbs discussed here. Cf., for instance:

(51A) CT 39, 41: 17 *šumma amēlu egerrû ana panīšu 1-šú i-pu-ul-šú* "if a chance word has once answered a man (from) in front of him";

(51B) *ib.* 23 [*šumma amē*]*lu egerrû ana arkišu i-ta-nap-pal-šú* "if a chance word keeps answering a man (from) behind" (cf. CAD sv *a.* A 2a-3'/4').

A similar use of the present Gtn versus the preterite G in *šumma*-clauses is found in most of the verbs which typically occur in omen texts; examples are *bakû* "to cry, moan", *galātu* "to quiver", *maqātu* "to fall", *šasû* "to call", *(w)aṣû* "to come out, to appear".[17] In fact, it is difficult to find an unambiguous preterite Gtn in a protasis; most of the cases claimed to be such in CAD and AHw are more likely to be perfects of the G-stem. Of some verbs both present Gtn and present D are found in *šumma*-clauses, e.g., *ekēku* "to scratch", *tarāṣu* "to stretch", and *zaqāpu* "to erect", cf. 6.7.3.

Just as in some verbs both present D and present G are used, we also find both present G and Gtn in, for instance, *bakû* "to cry, moan" (CAD sv 4), *šasû* "to call" (*ib.* sv 1), and *galātu* (*ib.* sv 1c, even coordinated with Gtn forms in TDP 224: 55).

This leads to the conclusion that in *šumma*-clauses we typically find the D-stem in the present, but the G-stem in the preterite. This double contrast shows that if the D-stem occurs in the present tense in such contexts, it serves to underline plurality of action, more specifically, the durative or habitual nature of the action expressed by the protasis.

If the preterite of a D-stem is used in a *šumma* clause, it usually refers to an action which is completed before the action expressed by the main clause is realized, in accordance with the general meaning of the preterite in such clauses, and is motivated by some other factor, such as plurality of the object. Consider the following examples:

(52) KH r. XXI: 57f (§ 251) (*šumma* ...) *qarnīšu lā ú-šar-*[*r*]*i-im* "if he (the owner) has not trimmed its (the ox's) horns". *Šarāmu* D has a pl. obj., cf. App. sv.

(53) CT 39, 46: 46 (if a man has divorced his wife and) *ina upīšī ú-ṣa-bit-si* "has paralyzed her by means of black magic"; the pret. *uṣabbissi* is parallel with *ihnuqši* "and has strangled her" in the preceding line. D represents the idiomatic meaning discussed in 6.4.4.1 sv, cf. esp. (10A).

(54) CT 39, 27: 20 (if a mungo has given birth in the street and) [...] *ana bīti ú-za-ab-bi-il* "has

carried (its young) into the house" (also *ib.* 21 from the house into the street). The other cases of *zabālu* D "to carry" have a pl. obj., cf. App. sv.

(55A) CT 39, 29: 30 (if a falcon has entered the king's palace, uttered a cry in front of the king,) *kappīšu ú-sa-lil-ma ūṣi* (è) "has flapped his wings and flown away" (pret. for a single event);

(55B) *ib.* 30: 58 (if a falcon sits on the *samītu* of a wall and) *kappīšu ú-sa-lal* "flaps its wings" (tr. CAD sv *samītu* a) (present with a durative nuance); the few cases of *salālu* D have a pl. obj., cf. 6.6.1.2.; G is found in CT 40, 49: 12 (obj. one wing).

Similar preterite forms of D-stems whose function is less clear are JCS 29, 66: 6 (*pašāru*); CT 28, 29: 8 (*kapāru* A); CT 39, 4: 32 (= SAA 10, 42: r.5); CT 40, 46: r.50 (*qalû*); BagF. 16, 262: 86 (*našāpu*); K.11716+: 5 (*labānu,* qu. CAD sv *l.* B 2 (*ú-lab-bi-in* mistake for *i-lab-bin*?)).

The D-stems which are used in the present tense in the protases of *šumma* clauses to convey a durative nuance are indicated in the Appendix by means of "prot." The following list contains an ample selection of them. They have been divided into two groups; the first one consists of protases which refer to an activity of persons or animals; the second one comprises verbs which serve to express a frequent idiom in medical texts in which a body part or body parts are subject and the patient object; these verbs denote different nuances of "to hurt". The symbol "≈ G" introduces instances of present G forms in the same context. The bold numbers refer to the appendix, where full references are found.

6.6.1.1 Group I: activities of persons and animals

Baqāmu "to pluck, tear out": hair; ≈ G: CT 40, 43a: 3 (shoots); D is not attested elsewhere.

Ekēku (*egēgu*) "to scratch", **1.**: in medical texts: a person body parts; in omens: an ox the ground; pres. G 1x with a negation (TDP 192: 34 var.); no pret. G; some texts use the pres. Gtn instead of D, cf. CAD sv a, and see 6.7.3.

Kanānu (*qanānu*) "to twist, coil", **1.**: TDP 20: 26f (foot); ≈ G: TDP 144: 56'; 188: 6 (foot); elsewhere D mostly has a pl. obj., cf. 6.4.2.1 sv; cf. also pret. G referring to a single event in CAD sv 1c (but intrans.).

Karāṣu "to pinch off (clay), to break": CT 38, 45/6: 18 *šumma šahû libitti bīti ú-kàr-ra-ṣú* "if pigs scrape off the brickwork of the house"; the only other case of D has a pl. obj., cf. App. sv; no pret. G in *šumma* clauses.

Karātu "to break off, to cut off": AfO 11, 222 no. 1: 6 (kú.meš, unidentified body parts (lips?); cf. pret. G for a single action in TU 9: 15 acc. to CAD sv 1a.

Kaṣāru "to bind together, join, collect, organize", **2.**: AfO 11, 222 no. 2: 8 (eyebrows: "to contract"); G in *šumma* clauses is said of a cloud or smoke (stative, pret. or perf. (intrans.)), acc. to CAD sv 3a; *kaṣāru* D normally has a pl. obj., cf. 6.4.3.1 sv.

Katāmu "to cover, close", **6a.**: eyes or eye; note esp. CT 31, 33: r. 17/18 (if after the head of the sheep has been cut off) *īn imittišu / šumēlišu ipette u ú-kàt-tam* "it keeps opening and closing its right / left eye", with *katāmu* D beside *petû* G, in accordance with the strong association of *petû* with plurality, cf. 6.4.3.1 sv. Pret. G for a single action occurs in the omen series *Šumma izbu,* e.g., Izbu 149: 93' (if the tongue of an *izbu* is long and) *nahīrīšu ik-tum* "has covered its nostrils" (alternating with the "active" stative).

Lapātu "to touch, smear, affect", **3a.**: "to rub, scratch" (parts of) the body; CAD sv 1n/o has no comparable cases of G pret.; a G pret. from another genre is CT 40, 26: 14 [*šumma zuqaqīpu*] (...) *amēla* t̲a̲g̲-*ut* (= *ilput*) "if a scorpion has stung a man", clearly referring to a single action; cf. also Iraq 30, 230 right: 14, qu. CAD sv 1p. D is also found in astronomical contexts in the present after *šumma*: ZA 52, 248: 62 (stars), cf. 6.6.3.3.

Lêku "to lick": CT 40, 32: r.23 *šumma alpu* s̲u̲.m̲e̲š̲-*šú ú-la-ak u ú-sal-lat* "if an ox licks and rips its skin (?)" (tr. CAD sv *salātu* 3a-1'); no other D forms, no comparable G forms.

Mahāṣu "to hit, smash, weave", **3a.**: with pers. subj. in med.: eyes, lap (cf. CAD sv 7b "to hit repeatedly") [for **3b.**), see group II]; **3c.**: of the sacrificial sheep "to flap" tail/ear; cf. the contrast between pres. D and pres. G in TuL 43: r.11 *šumma immeru* (...) *zibbassu* z̲a̲g̲ *u* g̲ù̲b̲ *ú-ma-ha-aṣ* "if the (sacrificial) sheep flaps its tail to the right and the left", versus YOS 10, 47: 41 *šumma zibbatum ištu šumēlim ana imittim i-ma-ha-aṣ* "if the tail (of the sacrificial animal) flaps from the left to the right" (also *ib.* 40 from the right to the left), where the G form may be due to the inanimate subject, cf. 5.6.4.

For G pret. and perf. cf. CAD sv 1a-1' and 1b, e.g., KH r.XVII 78. 85. 90; r.XVIII 1. 6 (§ 202ff) (all perf.); r.XVIII 11. 25. 46 (§ 206, 209, 213) (all pret.); in SB G pret. is found, for instance, in CT 40, 34: r.17. All these cases clearly refer to a single action. For *mahāṣu* with a body part as subject and a personal object, see group II in the next section.

Marāṭu "to rub, scratch": cheeks, ear, lips, tongue; no other D forms, no pres. G after *šumma*, but cf. pret. G in AMT 15, 3: IV 5 + 75, 1: IV 26 *šumma amēlu* (...) *ina mimma lū šēpšu lū ubānšu im-ru-uṭ-ma* "if a man has scratched either his foot or his finger with something", referring to a single action.

Nakāpu "to butt, gore", **1.**: CT 40, 41a: 8 *šumma rīmu alpa ina āli ú-na-kap* "if a wild bull constantly gores (or: "wants to/tries to gore") an ox in the city"; cf. pret. G for a single event in *ib.* 43a: 4 *šumma ṣabītu ana abulli iqribamma amēla ik-kip* "if a gazelle has come near the city gate and has gored a man", and in OB: LE A IV 13f // B IV 17 *šumma alpum alpam ik-ki-im-ma uštamīt* "if an ox has gored another ox and caused its death"; other examples CAD sv *n.* A 1a.

Nakāsu "to cut off, fell", **5.**: TDP 182: 44f *šumma ṣubassu ú-na-kas*$_4$ "if he (the patient) constantly tears (or rather: "tries to, wants to ...", etc.) his garment", an exceptional case of D + sg. obj. There are no precise parallels with pret. G (CT 39, 38: r.7 k̲u̲d̲-*is* can be pret. or pres.), but pret. G is found with trees (cf. CAD sv 1a-2') and perf. G with body parts (*ib.* 2b-2' and 2d).

Napālu "to tear out, demolish", **2.**: teeth: "to pick" (?); **3.** *eperē* "dust, earth": "to dig up" CT 39, 7b: r.5 (cf. 38, 50: 50f with G (but obj. restored)); a remarkable case of pret. D is CT 38, 47: 42 // 30, 30b: 11 *šumma šahû ana bīt amēli īrubma bīta ú-na-píl/pil* "if a pig has entered a man's house and has turned the (whole) house upside down" (also SpTU 3, 94: 150 with *šahû lā šû* "a pig which is not his own"), doubtless to be explained in the same way as (79) and (80) in 6.6.3.2. Cf. with pret. G for a single action: CT 40, 8c: 11 *šumma parakka īpušma ip-pu-ul* (var. *mārūšu ip-pu-lu*) "if he has built a sanctuary and then has torn (it) down" (var. "his sons have torn (it) down").

Naqāru "to tear down, scrape": CT 39, 25a: 11 *šumma āribū ana pān amēli qaqqara ú-na-qa-ru* "if ravens turn up the ground in front of a man" (tr. CAD sv 4); for pret. G cf., for instance, CBSM p. 64 § 7: 1 *šumma ina Nisanni bīta iq-qur* "if he tore down a house in the month of Nisan".

Naṣābu "to suck, lick": SpTU 1, 37: 3 // 2, 44: 3 *šumma* (...) *ubānātīšu ú-na-ṣab* "if he (...) constantly sucks his fingers" (coordinated with *šakānu* Gtn); no other instances of *naṣābu* are attested in *šumma* clauses (but cf. G + one finger UET 5, 8: 14. 18 (OB)).

Našāku "to bite, gnaw", **3a.**: with a person as subject and (a) body part(s) as objects (42); **3b.**) with an animal, a body part or "the ground" as objects (50A); also dogs each other (cf. 9.1.3). Pret. D and pres. G are not attested in *šumma*-clauses; very frequent is G with pret. or perf., typically referring to a single event, cf. CAD sv 1, and (44) and (50A).

Pašāṭu "to erase"; D usually has a pl. obj, cf. App. sv **1.**; a pres. D in protasis is BKBM 32: 51 "if a man has drunk beer and his head constantly "seizes" him (*iṣṣanabbassu*), (so that) *amātīšu imtanašši ina dabābišu ú-pa-áš-šaṭ* "he constantly forgets his words and mangles (them) (?, lit. "wipes (them) out") while speaking" (note the coordination of Gtn and D). Cf. KH r.XXVI 34 with a pret. G for a single action.

Salāh/'u "to sprinkle, moisten", **1.**: with tears: CT 40, 32: r.16 [*šumma alp*]*u ina bakîšu dimātīšu qaqqara ú-sal-làh* (var. 31a: 11 *i-sal-la-ah*) "if an ox sprinkles the ground with his tears when he moans", where the phrase *ina bakîšu* suggests a durative interpretation (the verb could also be read as a preterite: *ú-sal-lìh*, but the variant makes this unlikely); compare this with Dreams 311 a 2 (= AMT 63, 5: IV 3) *šumma ina šīnātišu ramanšu is-luh* "if he has spattered himself (in his dream) with his own urine".

Tabāku "to pour out" (substances and fluids from the body), **1.**: YOS 10, 47: 24 *šumma* [*immerum*] *paršam mādam ú-ta-ab-ba-ka-am* "if [a sheep] (while being slaughtered) passes a lot of faeces" (OB); passim in SB med., esp. with *dāmu* "blood" as object, cf. AHw sv D 1b; ≈ G TDP 218: 11; 216: 1 (with a negation). Pret. G for a single action is found in Dreams 310 b 13/19; CT 39, 48b: 10; AMT 66, 2: 7f (faeces and urine).

Tarāṣu "to direct, stretch, straighten", **2.**: eyes, lips ≈ pres. G in TDP 144: 57'; 192: 35 and elsewhere; also pres. Gtn, cf. AHw sv *t.* I Gtn; for pret. G cf., for instance, YOS 10, 47: 26 "(if the (sacrificial) sheep has shivered and) *imittašu it-ru-uṣ* "stretched its right (leg?)".

Ṭapālu "to insult, disparage": ZA 43, 102: 29 *šumma ú-ṭa-pa-al*, with a clear habitual nuance (between participles, Gtn forms and statives); cf. 92: 42 (pret. D, but obj. broken).

Zaqāpu "to erect, plant", **4.**: eye or eyes; note TDP 224: 56 with pres. Dtn (≈ pres. Gtn in 50: III 11 (acc. to AHw sv Gtn 1, CAD sv *z.* A 1e-2') *šumma īnīšu iz-za-naq-*[*qap*]); no pres. G or pret. D attested in *šumma*-clauses; for pret. G cf. TDP 190: 20 *šumma* (...) *īnīšu iz-qup*, which probably refers to a single event (in a specific combination of symptoms). For G pret. elsewhere, see, for instance, KAR 392: obv.! 23 *š. kirâ ina libbi āli iz-qup* "if he has planted an orchard in the middle of the city", cf. CAD sv *z.* A 1c-4'.

Many of these D-stems have a body part or body parts as object; if this object is always plural in *šumma* clauses, and the verb in question generally belongs to the D-stems used for plurality of the object or does not occur elsewhere, the two aspects of plurality of object and action go together. This applies to ***karātu, kaṣāru, lêku, naṣābu, pašāṭu*** and ***tarāṣu***. For most verbs, however, we find both plural and singular body parts as objects, so that it is plausible that number is not the decisive factor here.

6.6.1.2. Group II: body parts as subject with personal object in medical texts:

Mahāṣu "to hit, smash", **3b.**) "to hurt, sting", subjects: *kunuk kišādi*, kidney, temples; elsewhere ideogr., cf. CAD sv 7a. No comparable instances of pres. G. [For 3a) and 3c), see group I].

Sahālu "to pierce, stab", **3.**: "to cause a piercing pain", subjects: feet+shins (= (46)), womb (*elân ūri*), stomach; ≈ G, cf. CAD sv 1a and (49), and pret. G for a single action, cf. (47).

Ṣarāpu "to burn", **3.**: "to cause a burning pain", with *rēš libbi* = epigastrium as subj.; no pret. or pres. G, no pret. D in comparable contexts.

Šamāmu "to paralyze", subjects: hands+feet, flesh (uzu.meš), arms; ≈ pres. G (more common), cf. CAD sv 1 and (109) in 6.9.2.1; the three instances of pres. D have a plural subject, cf. 6.5.1 ?; G occurs both with pl. and with sg. subject; no pret. forms attested. Note LKU 85: r.4 (D) // KAR 267: 14 (G) (not in prot.).

Zaqātu "to sting, to hurt", **1.**: subjects: tongue, nose, fingers, anus, penis, *kunuk kišādi*, etc., → CAD sv 2a, AHw sv D 2/Dtn; also SpTU 2, 22: IV 26; Epilepsy p. 69: r.13 = (43); ≈ G: KAR 157: r.30 = (48); STT 89: 58. For pret. G see (45). The pret. is also used with an agentive subject: a scorpion or an insect, cf. CAD sv 1a, e.g., CT 38, 44a: 7 *šumma sassu amēla iz-qut* "if a moth has stung a man".

Other verbs used in this idiom are *lapātu*, lit. "to touch, affect", but apparently always spelled ideographically, cf. CAD sv 1n for G, and 3c for the spellings tag.meš and tag.tag, which may be interpreted as D or Gtn; *hamāṭu* D (and G), cf. CAD sv *h.* B 1b, AHw sv *h.* III D 3b (since this verb is basically intransitive (or rather lowly transitive, see 7.3.2 sv), it is not listed here); and *akālu* and *kasāsu*, but only in the G-stem, cf. CAD sv *k.* B a, AHw sv *k.* III G 3, and CAD sv *akālu* 6, AHw sv *a.* G 7a.

6.6.2. Absolute use of participles

A second group of verbal D forms which may serve to underline plurality of action are participles in the D-stem (*muparris*) which are used without a following genitive and refer to some profession or habitual activity. Especially for participles of D-stems which normally have a plural object, it seems plausible that they are caused by the plurality inherent in such forms. The following participles come from D-stems of Type I which normally have a plural object; they all refer to persons or animals, except *muṣabbit(t)u* and *mupattîtu*, which are instrument nouns; most of them are substantives, one also occurs as an adjective (*munaššiku*):

Munappilu "digger, wrecker" (*napālu* **3.**), OB LL; note esp. MSL 12, 164: 221f lú.du$_6$.ba.al = *na-pi-[lum]* / lú.ki.ba.al = *mu-na-pi-[lum]*.

Munaššik(t)u "biting" (*našāku* **2.**), SB: designation of a dog, both as substantive and as adjective; also metaphorically of a shoe (quoted in note 11 to Ch. V *sub* B).

Mupettû "person opening sluice gates" OB LL, and (in fem.) an instrument: a plug for regulating a sluice gate (?) (*petû* **7.**); cf. *pētû* LL: "doorkeeper, wrestler, thresher", acc. to AHw sv.

Muqallipu "barley husker" (*qalāpu* **2.**), OB LL.

Murakkisu "binder of sheaves" (*rakāsu* **7.**), SB LL.

Muṣabbit(t)u (part of a loom), SB LL; (an instrument), NB (quoted CAD M sv 2) (*ṣabātu* **9.**).

Mušaggišu "murderer" (*šagāšu*), OB LL; normally *šaggišu*, cf. 3.2.1 and 3.2.2, or *šaggāšu*, cf. 3.3.1.

Mušarriṭu "person who tears garments to shreds" (*šarāṭu* **3.**), OB LL.

Muzaqqipu (an agricultural occupation, AHw sv "ein Garbenbinder?") (*zaqāpu* **5.**), OB LL; cf. *zāqipānu* "caretaker of an orchard" (lit. "planter"), NB.

Other D-stems of Type I also have a participle which is used without a genitive to denote an occupation and/or habitual activity. If they denote an activity which is elsewhere expressed by the G-stem, it is possible that they, too, serve to underline the habitual nuance inherent in such words. This applies to the following participles of D-stems of the corpus:

Muha"iṭu "man on the lookout" (*hâṭu* 2.), SB LL (MSL 12, 230: IV 28', equated with lú *ša dagilti*); cf. *hā'iṭu* "night watchman, surveillant" (very common); perhaps D is a literary equivalent of *hā'iṭu*.
Mupattilu "yarn twister" (acc. to CAD M sv) (*patālu*), OB LL (D only as *purrus* form, cf. 10.7.1.1 sv).
Mušaqqû (only ARM 9, 26: 9) "irrigateur" (Birot), "person who gives water to animals" (CAD sv), "Viehtränker" (AHw sv), OB Mari (between *kullizū* = ox drivers and *kāsimū* = weeders); this unique form (in more than one sense: *šaqû* has no other D forms) contrasts with the common *pāris* form *šāqû* "steward, cupbearer" (also in OB Mari, cf. CAD sv *š*. A): a case of semantic differentiation?

If there is no difference in use between the verbal D-stem and the participle, the participle does not have such a special nuance, and need not be discussed separately. Such cases are listed in the Appendix under the respective verbs, with the gloss "part."[18]

By far the most remarkable feature of these D forms is their extreme rarity. Most of them are only found in lexical lists, especially in lú = *ša*, published in MSL 12; the others occur no more than a few times. It seems that not a single one of them functions as a current designation of a particular profession, habit or instrument (unless it were a very unusual one); a fair number of them probably belong to literary style. As a category, they are insignificant compared to the common patterns used for names of professions and habitual activities, which were discussed in Chapter III: *pāris, parris* and *parrās*.

The fact that participles D of the verbs of Type I are so rare is doubtless related to the function of most participles in Akkadian: they are agent nouns which normally do not refer to a single occasion, but imply a habitual nuance; hence their frequent use as names of professions (cf. 3.3). This also applies to participles of the G-stem, and explains why the G-stem participle *pāris* (sometimes strengthened to *parris* or *parrās*, cf. 3.4) serves as the usual agent noun of the verbs of Type I, and why the forms listed above take up such a marginal position: they are in a sense superfluous: they do not add anything to what is already implied by the corresponding participles of the G-stem.

This explanation is indirectly confirmed by the fact that if we find a *muparris* form as an agent noun, it is normally derived from a factitive D-stem or a D tantum verb: cf. cases as *mubannû* "cook", *muma"iru* "commander", *muqerribu* "guide, escort", *mušahhinu* "cooking vessel", from factitive D-stems, and *munaggiru* "informer" from *nugguru* "to inform, denounce". For such verbs the participle of the D-stem is not superfluous, but the only pattern available for forming an agent noun, since the G-stem has a different meaning or does not exist (cf. 3.4). For the D-stems of Type I, in which G and D often have approximately the same meaning, the participle G is apparently preferred under normal circumstances.

The very common use of participles of both D and G as epithets of gods and kings is not considered here; they are almost always followed by a genitive. In so far as they show interesting features, they will be dealt with in 6.9.3, which discusses the stereotyped use of D-stems in literary texts.

6.6.3. Plurality of action in some individual verbs

Finally, there are a few individual verbs whose D-stem can be demonstrated to underline plurality of action in other situations than those described in the previous sections. Some of these verbs show interesting instances of D and G alternating in the same context, not in connection with a plural versus a singular object, but with a difference in the nature of the action. This is especially true of OA *šaqālu* "to pay", with D "to pay (on several occasions)" and OB/SB *lapātu* "to touch, smear, affect", with G used for a specific individual or a limited range of applications, and D referring to a more general situation (also without object). It is convenient to discuss these verbs and some others according to dialect: OA instances in 6.6.3.1, OB ones in 6.6.3.2 and SB ones in 6.6.3.3.

6.6.3.1. D-stems for plurality of action in Old Assyrian

In some OA texts we find *ašqul* and *ušaqqil* ("I paid") side by side: TTK 2 pl. 290 and pl. 291. They are lists of expenses made in a certain place, in which each payment is expressed by *ašqul* "I paid", but each group of items is summed up by *ušaqqil*:

(56) TTK 2, pl. 290: 6ff *x kaspam ana perdim áš-qúl* (...) *x kaspam ana bīt kārim šaddu'atam áš-qúl x* urudu (...) *ana ki-ra-nim áš-qúl* (...) [14]*mimma annim ina GN aššumi perdim ú-ša-qi-il*$_5$ "I paid (G) x silver for a *perdum* (...), "I paid (G) x silver to the *bīt kārim* as a *šaddu'atum*-fee (...), I paid (G) x copper for a .... (...). All this I paid (D) in GN for a *perdum*". Likewise *šaqālu* G in 19, 21, 23, 26f, versus *mimma annim ušaqqil* in 35; in the same way TTK 2, pl. 291 has *šaqālu* G in 7, 9 and 11 for a single payment, summed up in 13 by means of D, and again G in 17 versus D in 22.

In these texts *šaqālu* G is used for a single payment and D for a series of payments. In so far as these payments are made to different persons, this use can be compared to that of *paqādu* D "to entrust" (to a plurality of persons), discussed in 6.5.2. However, in another document, which has exactly the same structure, only *šaqālu* G is used:

(57) kt b/k 176: 17ff From x silver of the capital of PN$_1$ I paid (*áš-qúl*) y to PN$_2$ for the debt of PN$_3$, I paid (*áš-qúl*) y to PN$_4$, the son of PN$_5$, (and) I paid (*áš-qúl*) z to PN$_5$, the son of PN$_7$) [25]*mimma annim* [26]*aššumi* PN$_3$ *áš-qúl* "all this I paid (G) on behalf of PN$_3$" (cf. also RA 58, 127 Sch. 22: 39 and kt 86/k 98: 14).

This eloquently demonstrates the optional nature of the use of D in such circumstances, and the fact that it varies from speaker to speaker, which can already be surmised on the basis of much other evidence, but is particularly clear in this case.

The question is whether *šaqālu* D always refers to a multiple action, or whether it only does so in specific circumstances, for instance, if the D form is in contrast with a G form, as in (56). Among the instances of *šaqālu* D listed in CAD sv 7, there are some other cases in which D refers to a repeated act of payment. Consider, for instance:

(58) EL 245: 7f *kaspam aṣṣērišu ušebbalamma ana tamkār abīja ú-ša-qal-ma u ṭuppīsu harrumūtim ušeṣṣamma* "he used to send silver to him, thus paying (D) the creditor of my father and obtaining his case-enclosed tablets" (tr. CAD *l.c.*) (rather: "creditors"?);

(59A) CCT 5, 6a: 7 (I have lived in Assur for thirty years) *u nikkassī ù-ša-qal* "and I have (always) paid (D) the accounts" (...);

(59B) *ib.* 19f *37* ma.na *nikkassī áš-qúl* "(now, too) I have paid (G) the accounts (to the amount of) 37 minas";

(60) TC 3, 63: 31ff *x annakam ana* PN_1 *u* PN_2 *ša-qí-la-ma* "pay (D) x tin to PN_1 and PN_2";

(61) KUG 26: 11ff "I paid (*áš-qul*) x silver to PN, the miller; I paid (*áš-qul*) x silver for a .... ; I paid (*áš-qul*) x silver for two slave girls; we paid (*ni-iš-qú-ul*) x silver as the price of a prisoner; PN took x silver and paid (*ú-ša-qí-il*$_5$) for sundries and food; x silver for drinks and meat when PN_2 had paid (*iš-qú-lu-ni-a-tí-ni*) us the silver."

The contexts of (58) and (59A) suggest a habitual interpretation; in (60) we find two coordinated indirect objects, which points to two different occasions. *Ušaqqil* in (61), opposed to the G-stems in the same text, is also likely to refer to different purchases.

Other cases which probably refer to payments on different occasions are TuM 1, 22a: 12; BIN 4, 65: 50; Arkeologya Dergisi 4, 7: 24f (all with *mala* "everything which"); CCT 3, 8b: 30. 32 (iterative, cf. Larsen 1967: 164); BIN 4, 65: 39; TC 3, 107: 17 (payments in the G-stem summed up by means of a stative D); KUG 27: 23 (stative with plural subject); ATHE 41: 12 (payment to two creditors, cf. Kienast's note on p. 61); kt 92/k 1050: 9 (loan to two debtors, courtesy K.R. Veenhof), and TC 3, 79: 21 (cf. Gtn in 19). A nuance of completeness may be underlined by D in OIP 27, 57: 25 (*ša ša-qú-lim ú-ša-qí-il*$_5$*-ma* "he paid everything there was to pay".

In other cases it is difficult to establish on the basis of the context whether a D form refers to a single payment or not, for example, in VAT 13459 (= VS 26, 55): 25 (versus G in 13 and 16), BIN 4, 33: 8 (versus G in 6), ATHE 58: 15, and KUG 19: 7. 13.

If we broadly consider the cases of *šaqālu* G listed in CAD sv 3b, it seems plausible that, in so far as this can be established, they typically refer to a single payment. Many of them do not have an object ("to make a payment"), and/or concern a payment made to a single person; it may be relevant in this context that only G seems to be used when a date of payment is specified (CAD sv 3b-3'; none of the instances of D in *ib.* 7 has such a specification).

Some other OA D-stems can be explained in the same way. First of all, the three instances of *našāru* D "to set aside, save" mentioned by CAD sv 4a all refer to a repeated action. In two of them this is clear from the distributive suffix .ta after the amount of silver involved in the transaction; in the third instance it appears from the coordination with a Štn-stem:

(62) CCT 4, 10a: 13ff *a-ni-ma 5* ma.na.ta *kaspam nu-na-ša-ra-kum* "now, we will set aside five minas of silver for you each time" (also BIN 4, 51: 45);

(63) Or. 36, 408 note 1 sub d 2ff *ṣubātī ištēnâ u šanâ ú-na-ša-ar-ma uštenebbalakkum* "each transaction I will set aside one or two garments and send (them) to you." (tr. CAD sv 4a).

However, most of the instances with G mentioned in CAD sv 2a also refer to a repeated action; so the situation is comparable to that of *šaqālu* in (56) versus (57): one speaker uses a D form to underline a repeated action, another speaker leaves it implicit in the context.

A slightly different case is *kabāsu* D. Apart from a reciprocal Dt-stem to be discussed in 9.1.3 sv, there are three OA instances with the same idiomatic meaning as G: "to drop a claim" (CAD sv 4c for G, 5d for D, see App. **7.**). In two of them it concerns a large amount (*mādum*), in the third one the object is *mimma* "everything":

(64) Or. 36, 403 no. 21: 4f *ištu mādātum kà-bu-sà-ni* "after many claims have been dropped";

(65) *ib.* no. 20: 11f *inūmi* (...) *kaspam mādamma ina ṣibātim ú-kà-bi-sà-ku-nu-tí-ni-ma* "when I remitted large amounts of silver from the interest (pl.) in your favor" (tr. CAD sv 5d);

(66) kt 91/k 158: 17f *lū mimma abūša šalṭam habbulu ka-bu-us*$_x$(UŠ)*-ma* "let whatever available goods her father owes be remitted".

A comparison of these cases with the instances of G mentioned *ib.* 4c suggests that the use of D in (64) and (65) is related to the presence of the word *mādum* here; if this is correct, the D-stem is used to underline the large amounts involved. The use of D with *mimma* in (66) is paralleled by other OA verbs (*laqātu* **1.**, *leqû, paqādu* **1.**).

Finally, there are two instances of *madādu* D which may belong here:

(67) St. Güterbock 40 kt c/k 1645: 7ff 1.ta *naruq* še*-am ikkarpatim (i-kà-ar-pá-tim) ša Peruwa ú-ma-du-du* "each time they will measure out one sack of grain with the (measuring) pot of Peruwa";

(68) *ib.* 35, 1A: 14f *uṭṭatam ina karpitim* (dug*-tim*) *ša Peruwa ú-ma-du-du* "they will measure out the grain with the (measuring) pot of Peruwa" (tr. Balkan).

In (67) the action is unambiguously plural because of the distributive .ta. In (68) there is no explicit indication of a repeated action, but it is conceivable that the plural subject causes the use of D here (cf. 6.5.1). The same expression occurs more frequently with the G-stem of *madādu,* cf. Balkan 1974: 39f, both with singular and plural subject.

6.6.3.2. D-stems for plurality of action in Old Babylonian

A verb in which plurality of action is an important factor for the use of D is *lapātu* "to touch, affect, smear", especially in OB. Its D-stem is often used with a plural object, but the instances which do not have a plural object usually refer to a non-single event: an action that implies repetition, a habit, a general statement, or a particularly wide range of application.

Of the many different uses of the D-stem of *lapātu* "to touch, affect, smear" enumerated in the App. sv, especially **2.** and **3.** are relevant here. In **3.**, "to touch" as a repetitive act, plurality is inherent in the meaning and not determined by the context; in this meaning, *lapātu* could be added to the idiomatic D-stems to be discussed in 6.8.1. In **2.** D is used for "to touch, to affect" with a nuance of generality or for a recurring situation. Interesting evidence for this comes from some OB Mari letters with *lapātu* with a disease as subject; compare the following sentences:

(69) ARM 26/1 p. 563 no. 261: 17ff *ilum ina* GN_1 [18]*ú-l[a-a]p-pí-it adīni* [19]*ul inūh u inanna* [20]*ina* GN_2 [21]*ú-la-ap-pa-at-ma* "the god (i.e., an epidemic) has affected (D) (people) in GN_1; he is not yet calmed down, and now he is affecting (D) (people) in GN_2";

(70) *ib.* p. 127 no. 17: 20ff *ilum ina halṣ[im el]îm* [21]*ú-[l]a-ap-pa-at-ma* (.. / ..) [23][dum]u.meš *ālāni ša kīma la-ap-tu* [24]*ana ālāni lā la-ap-tu-tim* [25]*lā irrubū assurri māta[m] kal[ā]ša* [26]*ú-la-ap-pa-tu* "the god is affecting (D) (people) in the upper district (...); the inhabitants of whatever towns are affected (G) must not enter the unaffected (G) towns, lest they affect (D) the whole area";

(71) *ib.* p. 575 no. 276: 22ff [*ina bītika u*]*l tuṣṣē* [23][*ilu*]*m ul i-la-ap-pa-at-ka* [24]*taballuṭ* "if you do not leave [your house], the god will not affect (G) you, and you will stay alive."

In the first place, there is a clear contrast between G referring to a specific single person in (71), and D with its unspecified object in (69) and in (70) (line 20f), and with the object *mātam* in (70) (line 25f). The latter is repeated at the end of the letter:

(72) *ib.* p. 127 no. 17: 30 *mātum lu-up-pu-ta-at* "the (whole) area is affected."

Secondly, this stative D contrasts with the stative and the VA G in (70), which both qualify towns. Thus, the concept "land" leads to the use of D, whereas "towns" does not, even though it is plural. This strongly suggests that it is the wide range of the epidemic which is underlined by D, and that the translation offered here for (72) is more likely than Durand's translation (*ad l.*) "Le pays est très contaminé."

A similar nuance of totality is also suggested by the use of the stative *lupput* in a contrasting pair of OB extispicy omens: YOS 10, 48: 41f // 49: 13f, quoted as (38) in 10.6.1.1.2. Although the use of *lapātu* D is extremely complicated (even if we leave out several idiomatic uses, as we have done in this section, cf. App. sv **6.** and **7.**), it seems that in its more literal meanings we can glimpse an overall unity in that it is used in contexts which involve a plural element, or at least a nuance of generality, rather than referring to a single action.

Some other D forms are found in OB which can be plausibly explained as instances of plurality of action, especially if it concerns verbs which have a clear association with plurality in other contexts. Consider the following instances:

(73) BiMes. 19 p. 16: 4 *DNF ša panīša tu-la-pa-tu* "DNF whose face you touch";

(74) ZA 75, 202/4: 96f *kīma as[k]u[pp]a[t]im lu-ka-bi-is-k[a]* / *kīma qaq[qari]m lūtettiqka* "like a threshold I want to step upon you / like the ground I want to walk over you";

(75) ZA 83, 5: 22ff *mehiam ašamšūtam ša terkullam ú-ka-ap-pa-ru* "the storm, the dust storm, which snaps the mooring pole" (tr. CAD sv *ašamšūtu* lex. sect.);

(76) RA 42, 72: 28f *kīma alpim ša ikullâm šebûma [bēlš]u ú-na-ka-pu* "just as an ox who has had its fill of fodder but still gores its master." (rest. and tr. CAD sv *šebû* v. 1a);

(77) AbB 12, 65: 29 *ina d[ab]ābim ú-ma-ah-hi-ṣú-šu-ma* "during the trial they beat him repeatedly" (tr. Van Soldt).

(73) is part of a greeting formula and can thus be interpreted as habitual (apart from the fact that *panû* is formally plural, so that D can also be regarded as correlating with a plural object). In (74) the D form of *kabāsu* is coordinated with the Gtn form *lūtettiqka*, showing that a repeated action is intended (note that *kabāsu* Gtn is not attested according to the dictionaries, cf. 6.7.3). This interpretation supports, and is in its turn supported by, the SB instances of *kabāsu* D quoted below as (82) and (83). The other possible meaning, namely that it is used to underline that the intended action is "to trample" rather than simply "to step upon" (cf. 6.8.1), seems less appropriate with "threshold" as object. (75) is the only instance of *kapāru* B "to pull out, cut down" with a singular object; it seems to be a general statement: "which (always) snaps ....", "which has the power to snap ...", etc., rather than that it refers to a single specific action; therefore, it resembles the use of the present D in *šumma*-clauses (see 6.6.1). The same applies to (76), which seems a proverbial and thus generic statement. As to (77), *mahāṣu* D with a personal object is normally used of wounding somebody with a weapon, whereas beating someone tends to be expressed by G; in this case it seems to fit in with the context to interpret it as referring to a repeated action; this is the normal meaning of *mahāṣu* D in other contexts, cf. 6.6.1.1 sv and 6.6.1.2 sv.

Some other cases in which the D-stem has a slightly different nuance are the following:

(78) ARM 13, 44: 7ff *šībam* (...) *nu-sú-qú-um-ma nu-na-as-sà-aq* "we will look everywhere to find (lit. select) an expert";

(79) ARM 3, 22: 22ff *PN GN kalāšu ú-na-ap-pí-il-ma mimma* giš.hi.a *ul īmur* "(in search of beams) PN has turned the whole of Terqa upside down, but he has found no beams at all";

(80) ARM 27, 161: 4ff *nu-up-pí-il-ma* na_4.za.gìn (...) *kaspam itti tamkārim leqēma šām* "turn (everything) upside down (to find) lapis lazuli (...) and buy (it) after having borrowed money from a creditor".

The D-stem of *nasāqu* "to choose, select" usually has a plural object, cf. App. sv and 6.4.7.1 sv, but seems to be used in (78) - together with the emphatic paronomastic infinitive - to stress that the author of this letter will exert himself in every possible way to find the person wanted, in order to comply with the order of the king. The same nuance is present in (79) and (80), as opposed to the normal meaning of *napālu* "to tear out, dig up"; compare the use of D without object in (80), and the following case of a paronomastic infinitive without object:

(81) ARM 6, 43: 25ff *ištu* ud.7.kam *ša PN ašpuram sú-un-nu-qú-um-ma ú-sà-an-ni-iq* "ever since I sent PN to you seven days ago, I have been pursuing my investigations."

Other cases which might be added here but which have been discussed earlier on are OB *ṣabātu* D "to hold, cling to" with a durative nuance ((12) in 6.4.4.1 sv), and MB *našāqu* D "to fondle" (also SB), discussed in 6.5.1 sv.

6.6.3.3. D-stems for plurality of action in Standard Babylonian

There are quite a few instances from SB, but here the state of affairs is more complicated. In general the use of the D-stem has considerably expanded in SB, and has come to include many cases in which it serves as a stylistic variant of the G-stem and appears to have no semantic motivation at all (see 6.9.2 below). Some of the more interesting instances in which the use of D seems to be meaningful concern *lapātu, rasāpu* and some verbs of Group II (6.4.2), especially *kabāsu, sahālu, nakāpu*:

(83) Maqlû IV 36 (you (pl.) buried figurines representing me in a causeway) *ummānu ú-kab-bi-su* "(so that) people stepped (upon them)";

(84) *ib.* III 151ff *šamû anāku ul tu-lap-pa-tin-ni* / (...) / *sihil balti anāku ul tu-kab-ba-si-in-ni* (var. *ta-kab-bi-si-in-n*[*i*]) / *ziqit aqrabi anāku ul tu-lap-pa-tin-ni* "I am the heavens, you cannot touch me, (...), I am the thorn of a *baltu*-plant, you cannot step upon me; I am the scorpion's sting, you cannot touch me";

(85) AnSt. 30, 105: 21 *zaqtā niṭātūšu ú-sah-ha-la zumra* "his blows are sharp, they pierce the body";

(86) BWL 44: 101 *paruššu ú-sah-hi-il/la-an-ni ziqāta labšat* "the goad pricked me, it is covered with barb(s)" (cf. CAD sv *sahālu* 2a);

(87) BAM 248: III 55 *erû erākūma nu-uk-ku-pu ú-nak-kap* "I am pregnant, and I am ready to gore" (tr. CAD sv 3, said by a cow);

(88) Ee VII 63 (*DN ša* ...) *ika u palga uštēširu uṣ-ṣi-ru apkīsu* "(DN who ...) regulated ditch and canal, who set out the furrow" (tr. CAD sv *apkīsu*);

(89) (= 09) BKBM 30: 43 *adi sibîšu ú-al-lat* "he swallows seven times".

The use of D in (82) - coordinated with two Gtn-stems - and (83) is an exact parallel of the OB case (74) mentioned above; for (84) compare the parallel use of *lapātu* D in OB discussed in the previous section. In (85) plural action is explicit in the plural subject; (86) is less convincing, but plural action does not seem to be excluded. For *nakāpu* in (87), see also (76) and (81). The exceptional case of *eṣēru* D with a singular object in (88) may be explained either as a collective (cf. 6.3) or as a general statement (but many D forms in Ee are difficult to explain, cf. 6.9.2.2). In (89) the plurality of the action is explicitly mentioned; elsewhere *alātu* has a plural object, cf. App. sv.

The same contrast between *lapātu* G and D which we found in OB ((69) - (72) above) recurs in SB in astrological contexts:

(90A) SAA 10, 26: r.7' *kaqquru bīt ú-la-pat-an-ni* "the region which it (the eclipse) will affect (D)";
(90B) *ib.* 100: 29 the eclipse *kaqqaru ša GN lā il-pu-ut* "did not affect (G) the region of GN",

where the single event which has actually occurred has G, whereas D has the nuance of "the region (whichever it may be)". This contrast is related to the contrast discussed above between present D and preterite G in protases (6.6.1).

6.7. Conclusions about the D-stem and plurality

The discussion of the D-stems which underline plurality of action concludes the description of the use of the D-stem for plurality. There can be no doubt that many instances of D-stems of Type I which were not discussed in the previous sections are also in some way related to plurality. However, whenever this relationship is inconsistent, there must be other factors that also influence the use of D, such as semantic or stylistic differentiation, large scale metaphorical use or lexicalization. This makes it difficult to establish plurality as the motivating factor if we find such a D-stem in a plural context. Therefore, we will refrain here from discussing such cases separately.

A few issues remain to be dealt with in the next sections: a short description of the general characteristics of the association of D with plurality (6.7.1), the use of D with long constituents consisting of a series of coordinated nouns (6.7.2) and the relationship between the D-stems of Type I and the Gtn-stem, both of which are associated with verbal plurality (6.7.3).

6.7.1. General characteristics of the association of the D-stem with plurality

The general characteristics of the use of the D-stem with plurality of the direct object have already been described in 6.4.9 and will not be repeated here. The instances presented in 6.5 and 6.6 show that the association of the D-stem with plurality does not only concern the direct object, but fully conforms to the "global nature" (cf. 2.1.5) of verbal plurality in general. There can be little doubt that the dominant role of the direct object is related to the fact that the direct object is the most salient constituent in a prototypical transitive sentence: it has a profound influence on the exact nature of the action, is affected most by it, and, as part of the predicate, it usually carries an important part of the new information conveyed by the sentence (cf. Givón 1979: 51ff). Therefore, the presence of a direct object in the plural will, generally speaking, be a stronger incentive to use a D-stem than, for instance, a plural subject.

Moreover, it is a typical feature of many high-transitivity verbs that the nature of the action they express is such that it has to be performed for each object separately, so that in normal circumstances the presence of a plural object automatically entails plurality of action. This is especially clear in their most typical representatives, the verbs of destruction (Group I in 6.4.1) and the verbs which entail a drastic effect on the object (Group II in 6.4.2); for the verbs of Group I the reverse is also true: a singular object implies a single action, cf. the pertinent remarks in 6.4.1.

This is in marked contrast to the verbs of low transitivity: for actions of placing, giving, sending, watching, possessing, loving, etc. (cf. 5.6.2.1), the number of objects determines only to a small extent the nature of the action: we can place, give, send, etc., one or more entities without a significant change in the nature of the action (obviously within certain limits). This is one of the reasons why these verbs, as we saw in 5.6.2.1, generally do not have a D-stem.

It seems plausible that the characteristic features of the use of the D-stem with a plural object as established in 6.4.9 are also valid for its association with plurality in general. This means that it is not used to express plurality by itself, independently of the context, but only to underline or emphasize the presence of a plural element in the sentence. This element may be indicated explicitly by one or more plural constituents, or it may be implied by the context. The latter situation is most evident in *šumma*-clauses: here the present tense is used to express a durative or habitual activity or process which is not necessarily completed before the apodosis is realized (cf. 6.6.1); this nuance can be underlined by the use of the D-stem, if the verb in question has a D-stem which belongs to Type I and does not have a clearly different meaning. The other kinds of verbal plurality discussed in the previous sections are too incidental to allow reliable conclusions, but there can be little doubt that they basically represent the same stuation.

As a consequence, sentences which only differ in that one of them has a D- and the other a G-stem, are not semantically opposed, but have more or less the same meaning and can refer to the same action. It is a general feature of a large part of the D-stems discussed in the previous sections that they alternate with G-stems in the same contexts (cf. 6.4.9). The contrasting pairs mentioned in the course of this chapter all owe their contrast in meaning to the fact that they differ on some other point, too, usually the singular versus plural nature of the direct object. The contrast between G and D only underlines this difference and makes it more explicit. In the rare cases that we do find pairs of G and D which only differ in the verb form itself, they do not contrast, but are stylistic variants (see 6.9.4).

Finally, if we consider the use of D for plurality and compare the contexts in which it occurs with contexts in which the corresponding G-stem is used, the general impression is that D can best be described as non-singular, i.e., as underlining that the action in question is not envisaged as a single action referring to a specific occasion, but should be regarded as generic, recurring, ongoing, habitual, repeated or repeatable, etc. This is particularly clear if D is in the present tense; in that case its non-singular nuance and the imperfective function of the present strengthen each other. Cross-linguistically, the imperfective is closely related to notions as habituality, repetition, non-completedness, etc., cf. Dressler 1968: 60ff; Comrie 1976: 24ff.[19]

The G-stem can be used in the same contexts, in line with its unmarked character (cf. 12.4), but there is a tendency to restrict it to events which are single and definite. This is especially clear in SB, in which the use of D for plurality is more widespread than in other dialects (see 6.9.2). A good example is the use of the preterite G for a single action in *šumma*-clauses, which was discussed in 6.6.1, but this tendency can also be observed in other contexts.

6.7.2. Long constituents

A remarkable aspect of the association of the D-stem with plurality is the fact that there seems to be a stronger tendency to use a D form if the plural constituent is not simply a plural noun, but consists of a series of coordinated nouns. This is related to the primarily semantic nature of plurality as underlined by the D-stem: such constituents are more saliently plural than single nouns with a plural ending; moreover, they often imply that the action is performed by or on the constituents individually and/or on different occasions.

The main evidence for this is formed by a number of exceptional D-stems or atypical uses of D-stems in combination with constituents consisting of a series of coordinated nouns. The most striking instance is one of the two exceptional cases of *epēšu* D motivated by a plural subject, quoted as (25) in 6.5.1. It can hardly be accidental that among the many cases of *epēšu* with a plural subject, a D-stem is used precisely in this one, in which five kings who have contributed to the building of the wall in question, obviously on five different occasions, are the subject of the sentence.

Other instances of exceptional or atypical D forms are the following:

(91) ARM 27, 100: 22f *nikkassī* lú.lú.meš *ekallim / u* lú.meš *muškênim ú-up-pí-iš-ma* "I have settled the accounts of the personnel of the palace and of the *muškênu*'s".

(92) Šurpu II 166f (// SpTU 2, 13: 26f) "May from the cardinal points of South, North, East and West *šārū erbetti lizīqūnimma li-paṭ-ṭi-ru māmītsu* "the four winds blow towards him and release his oath" (cf. Reiner *ad l.* and CAD sv *māmîtu* 2b-1').

(93) Maqlû II 37ff *ṣalam siparri itgurūti ša kaššāpija u kaššaptija* .... (followed by an 11 line enumeration of types of hostile sorcerers and sorceresses) [50]*ana mīti pu-qu-du-in-ni* "the bronze figurines, placed crosswise, of my sorcerer and sorceress (...) have delivered me to a dead person."

(94) AfO 18, 298: 29ff [*Šamaš, annûtum*] *ēpišū'a* / [ ] *muštēpišū'a* / *ša* (...) / [34]*ana gulgulli ú-paq-qí-du-in-ni* "Šamaš, these are my sorcerers, [my ......], my bewitchers, who (...) have delivered me to a "skull"" (followed by G in 35).

As for (91), the dictionaries do not have other OB instances of *nikkassī* with *epēšu* D (cf. CAD sv *epēšu* 2c *nikkassū*, and sv *nikkassu* A passim, AHw sv *nikkassu* 3).[20] Therefore, its use here might be caused by the fact that two different actions are involved, one for each category of personnel. (92) is remarkable because it is the only D form among 36 G forms in a long litany of the form DN *lipṭur* "may DN release" (viz. "me from the effects of an oath"), or DN_1, DN_2, etc. *lipṭurū* "may DN_1, DN_2, etc., release (me)", with an enumeration of up to five gods (in 182f). It is apparently not merely the quantity of gods which causes the D-stem (cf. 182f): is it too far-fetched to assume that it emphasizes the distributive nature of the subject, i.e., the fact that the winds blow individually from four different directions? The exceptional instances of *paqādu* D with a singular object (cf. 6.4.7.1 sv) may be caused by the unusually long subject. However, the texts in question (Maqlû) contain many problematic D forms, and it is quite possible that they use the G- and the D-stem of this verb indiscriminately or for stylistic variation, cf. 6.9.4.

Other cases of exceptional D-stems which may be explained in the same way are "C 18": 33 = (31) in 6.5.2 (*zarû*); ARM 3, 17: 20 = (33) in 6.5.2 (*karābu*); HGŠ 114: 17 and SAA 3, 32: r. 21' (*hatû* and *edēpu*, respectively, with a plural subject consisting of three abstract nouns), Gilg. VI 85. 90 (*manû*); Glass p. 63 § III 18 (*marāqu*, with four substances as object), KAR 16: r.26; Racc. 42: 19; 46: 22 (*naqû*, cf. App. **1**.); KAR 202: I 27 (*elēhu* "to sprinkle" three substances, vs. G + flour, cf. CAD sv 1); Or. 40, 148: 51 (*temēru* D with a direct object consisting of seven nouns, vs. G in 141: 31'. 47' (two nouns).

On the other hand, there are numerous other instances of constituents consisting of coordinated nouns where the D-stem is not used. Therefore, the passages quoted in this section suggest the possibility that there is a causal relationship between the use of D and the presence of such a constituent, but the evidence is too scarce to be conclusive.

6.7.3. The D-stems for plural action compared to the Gtn-stem

The frequent use of the D-stems of Type I to underline plurality of action gives rise to the question of what is its relationship to the Gtn-stem. The Gtn-stem also has the function of expressing verbal plurality, and usually has iterative, frequentative, continuous, habitual and distributive function, cf. 4.2. These notions are closely related to the ones expressed by the D-stem, especially in the contexts discussed in 6.5 and 6.6, i.e., if plurality lies in another constituent of the sentence than the direct object. Moreover, it follows from the analysis of the Gtn-stem in 4.1, that also in form the two verbal stems are closely connected: both are built upon gemination of the second radical and thus have the same iconic background.

A global comparison of the verbs which frequently occur in the Gtn-stem and those which have a common D-stem shows that these stems are largely complementary. In general, both the Gtn- and the D-stem are very productive (see note 1 to Ch. V), but if we concentrate on forms with a high frequency, it transpires that the frequent Gtn-stems invariably stem from verbs which do not normally have a D-stem, or which have a D-stem with another meaning than the G-stem (this mostly concerns factitive D-stems). On the other hand, Gtn-stems of transitive verbs which have a common D-stem - which in this type of verbs (Type I) tends to have more or less the same meaning as the corresponding G-stem - are mostly rare or unattested.

This can be inferred from a global survey of the relevant entries in AHw. Assuming that the number of instances quoted by AHw roughly mirrors the actual frequency of a form, we find that two kinds of verbs generally have a frequent Gtn-stem: first, verbs which normally do not have a D-stem, and, second, verbs whose D-stem has a different meaning (verbs which only occur in the D-stem by way of exception are ignored here).

The former kind includes first of all the transitive verbs of the semantic classes enumerated in 5.6.2.1, which typically have a low degree of transitivity. Very frequent are the Gtn-stems of *nadû* "to put down, leave", *šapāru* "to send", *šemû* "to hear", *še'û* "to look for", *(w)abālu* "to bring" (all more than 50 instances quoted in AHw); *leqû* "to take, receive", *našû* "to lift, carry", *šakānu* "to place" (> 40x); *nadānu* "to give", *(w)arû* "to send" (> 30x); *apālu* "to pay", *etēqu* "to cross", *šatû* "to drink" (> 20x); *amāru* "to see", *erēšu* A "to ask", *naṭālu* "to watch", *rašû* "to get" (> 10x).

In the second place, it includes intransitive verbs which do not have a D-stem (most of these have a causative Š-stem, see 7.2.2): *alāku* "to go, come" (> 50x), *ṣâdu* "to whirl" (> 40x), *maqātu* "to fall", *šahāṭu* "to jump" (> 30x), *elû* "to go up", *karābu* "to pray, bless", *rapādu* "to walk around" (> 20x), *bakû* "to cry", *erēbu* "to enter, *izuzzu* "to stand" (> 10x).

The verbs whose D-stem has a different meaning than the G-stem include in the first place those which have a factitive D-stem: *redû* "to follow" (see 5.5.2 for *redû* D) (> 50x), *sahāru* "to turn" (intrans.) (> 30x), *nakāru* "to change" (> 20x), *galātu* "to quiver, become restless" (> 10x); and, secondly, various other verbs: *epēšu* "to make, do" (> 50x) and *mahāru* "to receive, turn to" (> 40x), whose D-stems have various specialized meanings (see 6.8.3), *šasû* "to call" (see 7.2.4 for *šasû* D) (> 50x), *qabû* "to say, speak" (see 6.8.1. for *qabû* D) (> 10x).

The frequency of the Gtn-stem of these verbs forms a marked contrast with the rare occurrence of Gtn forms of the verbs whose D-stems have been discussed in this chapter so far. The number of instances listed in AHw of the Gtn-stems of these verbs of groups I to VIII is as follows (verbs listed under C in 6.4 have been omitted as too rare to be relevant):

Group Ia: no Gtn according to AHw for any of these verbs, except for *nasāhu* "to tear out, remove", *palāq/ku* "to slaughter", *parāsu* "to cut off, separate" and *ṭabāhu* "to slaughter" (all 1x), *nakāsu* "to cut off, fell" (2x) and *napāṣu* "to strike, smite" (4x).

Group Ib: a Gtn-stem is listed for none of the verbs of this group, except *hanāqu* "to strangle" (4x, but only in LL); note that *kapāru* B is listed in AHw under *kapāru* I (≈ A of our list), and *kaṣāṣu* "to trim, cut, mutilate" under *kaṣāṣu* I "to gnash" (the teeth); these entries do not contain instances which semantically belong to *kapāru* B and *kaṣāṣu* "to trim").

Group IIa/b: no Gtn is listed in AHw for any of these verbs, except for *dâšu* (AHw: *diāšum*) "to thresh, trample" and *sapāhu* "to disperse, scatter, ruin" (both 1x); more common are *egēru* "to twist" (3x) and *nakāpu* "to butt, gore" (8x).

Group IIIa/b: no Gtn for *(h)arāmu* "to cover", *kanāku* "to seal", *kaṣāru* "to bind together", *rakāsu* "to bind", *sahāpu* "to cover, overwhelm, lay flat", *edēlu* "to close", *e'ēlu* "to bind" and *temēru* "to bury"; 1x for *paṭāru* "to loosen, release, redeem". However, Gtn is more common in *zaqāpu* "to erect, plant" (3x), *tarāṣu* "to direct, stretch" (5x), *retû* "to fix" (6x, see below) and *petû* "to open" (> 10x, see below).

Group IVa/b: no Gtn for *lâṭu* "to confine", *pâdu* "to imprison" and *tamāhu* "to seize, control", but *ṣabātu* "to seize" Gtn is very common (> 20x, see below).

Group Va/b: no Gtn for any of these verbs, except *tabāku* "to pour out" (2x), but *šapāku* "to heap up, pour out" Gtn is rather common (> 10x, see below).

Group VI: no Gtn for *eṣēru* "to draw, design" and *bašāmu* "to create"; 3x for *(w)alādu* "to give birth".

Group VIIa/b: no Gtn for *nasāqu* "to select, choose" and *paqādu* "to entrust, inspect"; 1x for *qâšu* (AHw: *qiāšum*) "to donate, grant" (LL). The other verbs of group VII, however, have a more frequent Gtn-stem: *apālu* "to pay, satisfy" (> 30x), *naqû* "to pour out, sacrifice" (> 10x) and *zabālu* "to carry, transport" (9x);

these verbs belong to a semantic class of verbs with a low degree of transitivity, which normally do not have a D-stem (cf. 5.6.2.1). The fact that they have a Gtn-stem makes their D-stem all the more atypical, and confirms the correlation between low transitivity and the use of a Gtn-stem.

Verbs not listed in 6.4.1 to 6.4.7: no Gtn is listed for other highly transitive verbs such as *hamāṣu* "to strip, skin, tear off" (6.4.8 and 6.8.1), *katāmu* "to cover, close" (6.8.4), *napāhu* "to light, set fire to" (6.4.8 and 7.6.1) and *našāqu* "to kiss" (6.5.1); 1x for *kasû* "to bind, paralyse" (6.8.4); 3x for *mahāṣu* "to hit, stab, wound" (6.4.8 and 6.8.1). More common are *lapātu* "to touch, smear, affect" (cf. 6.6.1.2) and *parāku* "to block, obstruct".

In spite of the small number of exceptions (on which see below) this survey may suffice to show the rarity of the Gtn-stem in verbs whose D-stem is regularly associated with plurality. This leads to the conclusion that the two stems are complementary formations for the expression of verbal plurality.

This conclusion is corroborated by the fact that in many contexts in which the verbs of Type I use the D-stem, other verbs use the Gtn-stem. One of these was discussed in 6.6.1: the parallelism between D and Gtn in conditional clauses introduced by *šumma*. Another one was signalled in 4.2.3: transitive verbs which do not have a D-stem use the Gtn-stem to underline plurality of the direct object. In general, both D and Gtn can have distributive function; for the D-stem this function is largely restricted to the direct object. A global survey of the Gtn-stem shows that, in addition to its iterative, frequentative, continuous and habitual meaning, it is used for plurality of the subject and the indirect object, and for plurality of the object with verbs which do not have a D-stem with the same meaning.

I will now discuss some specific cases of parallel use of D and Gtn. In the protases of omens the stative Gtn of *nadû* "to put down, leave" is sometimes used in correlation with the stative G in exactly the same way as the stative G and D in other verbs; cf. (95) with singular versus plural subject, and (96) with singular versus plural adjunct accusative:

(95A) YOS 10, 51: IV 3f (and elsewhere) *šumma ša[plānum m]anzaz DN sūmum na-di* "if a red spot lies under the "presence" of DN";
(95B) *ib.* IV 7f *šumma ina imitti irti iṣṣūrim sūmū mādūtum i-ta-ad-du-ú* "if many red spots lie on the right side of the breast of the bird" (also *ib.* 12 and 16);

(96A) OBE 14: 30 and 32 *šumma rēš libbim qâ (qá-a) na-di-ma u peṣi* / (...) / *šumma rēš libbim me-er-a na-di-ma u sām* "if the epigastrium is covered by a thread and this is white / (...) / if the epigastrium is covered by a *mer'u* and this is red" (id. 33 with *tarik* "dark" instead of "white");
(96B) *ib.* 34f *šumma rēš libbim imittam* / *šumēlam qê (qé-e) i-ta-ad-du* "if the epigastrium is covered with threads on the right / left" (also *ib.* 36f with *kasî arqūtim* / *sāmūtim*).

In verbs which have a D-stem the same alternation is found with G and D forms of statives and adjectives, cf. 10.6.1.1 and (35) - (37) in 6.5.3.

A similar case is the Gtn-stem of *retû* "to fix". As indicated above, AHw lists six instances, which is more than of most other verbs of its type; all of them, however, stem from RIs of Nebuchadnezzar II, in a stock phrase which has D forms in earlier inscriptions; cf. (97) with an example of the earlier formulation in (98):

(97) VAB 4, 116: 17f *dalāti erēni* (...) *as-kup-pu u nu-ku-še-e pitiq erî ēma bābānīša er-te-et-ti* "I installed door panels of cedar, thresholds and ....-s cast of bronze in its (the palace's) doors" (Gtn also 118: 10; 132: 15; 134: 38; 136: 9; 138: 16 with Gtn in the same or similar phrases, but D in 84 no. 5: I 24 and CT 37, 10: 2 // UM 15, 79: I 65; other NB kings use only D: VAB 4, 68: 29 (Nabopolassar); 222: 12; 256: 6 acc. to AHw sv D 2; CT 34, 29: 13 (Nabonidus));

(98) RIMA 2/1, 282: 63f *dalāti erēni šurmēni daprāni meskanni ina bābiša ú-re-te* "I hung doors of cedar, cypress, *daprānu*-juniper, (and) *meskannu*-wood in its doorways" (tr. Grayson).

In these cases a frequentative interpretation is unlikely. It is possible that the use of *šapāku* Gtn in the same RIs (and also earlier in those of Sennacherib? (Sn. 109: 17; 123: 29, but 133: 79 G in the same context)) has the same background. This Gtn-stem is also atypical in its frequency, as compared to other verbs of the same type (see above), and is unlikely to be frequentative or continuous in a case as the following:

(99) VAB 4, 134: 47ff *<ana>* (or *<aššum>*) *butuqti qerbašun lā šubšî šipik eperī aš-ta-ap-pa-ak-šú-nu-tim-ma* "in order to prevent a dyke break in them, I heaped up an earthen dyke for them".

Of special interest are the few verbs which have both a frequent D- and a frequent Gtn-stem, such as *ṣabātu* "to seize" and *petû* "to open". The difference in use between the Gtn- and the D-stem of these verbs is rather straightforward: whereas D underlines that the object is plural (which usually entails that the action is plural, too), Gtn specifically refers to the action itself and expressly indicates frequentativity; see, for instance:

(100) TC 2, 34: 16f *ša kīma šuāti sikkī i-ṣa-na-bu-tù* "his representatives constantly seize the hem (of) my (garment)" (i.e., summon me (for a court procedure));

(101) AbB 9, 113: 9ff *nukaribbū* é.ì.dub *suluppī ip-te-né-tu-ú-ma suluppī ilteneqqû* "the gardeners open the date store house continually and take dates continually" (tr. Stol); also LB 1201: 9 and BIN 4, 67: 7 (both OA).

However, for some reason the use of *ṣabātu* and *petû* Gtn is very restricted: it occurs predominantly in *šumma*-clauses (cf. 6.6.1). Almost all instances of *ṣabātu* Gtn come from two contexts: first, from *šumma*-clauses in medical texts (cf. AHw sv Gtn 2), such as:

(102) AMT 86, 1: II 3 *šumma amēlu qaqqassu iṣ-ṣa-na-bat-su* "if a man's head constantly "seizes" him" (also elsewhere, but almost always written ideographically (dib.dib, dib.meš));

(103) AfO 11, 222 no. 1: 8 *šumma ina dabābišu pâšu iṣ-ṣa-na-bat* "if he constantly seizes his mouth while speaking";

and, second, from the OA expression exemplified by (100) (also CCT 2, 14: 7 and 3, 11: 11).[21]

About half of the instances of *petû* "to open" occur after *šumma*, and have "mouth" as object (AHw sv Gtn 3); the remaining cases include protases with ears and eyes as object (*ib.* 4/5), and main clauses with various words for containers as object, and a clearly frequentative or habitual meaning, as in (101) (*ib.* 1/2, and add MARI 5, 258: 7f *kajjānu niṣrēt ilāni ap-ta-na-at-ti-a-ak-kum* "I will constantly reveal to you (all?) the secrets of the gods").

Some verbs of which both present Gtn and present D are found in *šumma*-clauses are *ekē-ku* "to scratch", *tarāṣu* "to stretch", and *zaqāpu* "to erect"; they have the same difference: the Gtn-stem is explicitly frequentative or habitual, the D-stem underlines the durative, non-completed meaning of the protasis (and may also correlate with a plural object).

This leads to the conclusion that on the one hand the Gtn-stem is complementary to the D-stem in that most verbs use either Gtn or D with any frequency, but that on the other hand it has a clearly different function in the few verbs in which it competes with the D-stem. It is also complementary in the sense that the D-stem has a clear association with verbs of high transitivity, whereas the Gtn-stem is used predominantly in verbs of low transitivity.

Another important difference between the D-stems of Type I and the Gtn-stem is that the Gtn-stem can express plurality by itself, also if the context does not imply it, whereas it was argued in 6.7.1 that the D-stem is used to underline only plurality which is explicitly indicated by another element in the sentence or implied in the context. Accordingly, there are some contrasting protases with G versus Gtn (mentioned in 4.3), in which a difference in the apodosis shows that there is a semantic difference in the protasis depending solely on whether a G or a Gtn form is used. As noted in 6.7.1, comparable cases of G versus D are not attested.

6.8. D-stems of Type I with others functions than plurality

In 6.2 we distinguished three kinds of D-stems of Type I on the basis of their function: those which are used to underline plurality, those which have been differentiated in meaning from the G-stem, and those which belong to neither of these two kinds and in which the difference in function between G and D is unclear. In the next sections we will examine the D-stems which cannot be shown to be associated with plurality: those which differ in meaning from the G-stem in 6.8.1 to 6.8.3, and the unclear cases in 6.8.4. In 6.8.5 a single verb is discussed (*(w)aṣābu)*, in which the relationship between D and G is influenced by formal factors.

6.8.1. Idiomatic D-stems

A number of verbs do not (or not only) use the D-stem for underlining plurality, but for expressing a different meaning. In some of these cases D expresses a more "intensive" action than G. To translate such a D-stem we mostly use a different verb; I will refer therefore to them in general as "idiomatic D-stems", in contrast to the D-stems for plurality.

A few idiomatic D-stems have already been discussed, because the difference in meaning they show between G and D correlates with a strong increase in the degree of transitivity: in 5.5.2 *burrû* and *ruddû,* in 5.5.3 *dubbubu* and *kuššudu.*

I will distinguish these idiomatic D-stems from the lexicalized D-stems to be discussed in 6.8.3. The former are used (apart from their other functions) to describe actions which are more forceful and energetic - or, in the traditional terminology, more "intensive" - than the action denoted by the G-stem; thus they underline an increase in salience. The conditions determining this use are similar to the conditions determining the use of D to underline plurality; in other words, the D-stem is optional and the increase in salience need not be made explicit.

In lexicalized D-stems, on the other hand, there is no question of D having a more intensive meaning than G; the only thing we can say is that there is a clear semantic relationship between D and G, but its nature is unpredictable and verb-specific. If there is no clear semantic relationship, the D-stem in question is classified as a D tantum verb, cf. 6.0 and 8.1).

The following idiomatic D-stems can be mentioned:

Balālu D "to pour over, stain, pollute" (with dust, tears, excrement, etc., cf. App. **2.**), versus G "to mix, brew (beer), alloy (metal), sprinkle (with oil, wine, beer)"; D denotes a more drastic action and usually has a personal object. A few times G is found in this meaning: ARM 3, 18: 13; IAsb. 71: 13; TDP 170: 20; SpTU 3, 76: 18 (= (126) in 6.9.4), all stative. In addition, *bullulu* shares the meaning "to mix" with G, probably because of the plurality inherent in the notion of mixing (cf. 6.4.5 and App. sv **1.**).

Edēpu D "to blow away/down, damage by blowing" (App. **2.**, SB), G "to blow into, inflate"; the basic difference between G and D is shown by an interesting case from a lexical list, where G is associated with wind (IM, *šāru*), and D with storm (UD, *ūmu*): MSL 16, 275: 21'-24' [I]M.s[ù], [IM].KÍD, [IM].dib, [IM].ri = *e-de-pu ša* IM, versus *ib.* 26' [ú$_4$.šú].šú.ru = *ud-du-pu ša* UD; cf. ACh. Šam. 1: III 35 *šumma ūmu ú-ta-dip* "if there has been a gale blowing".

Hamāṣu D "to tear off" (mainly said of the tearing loose of metal from objects to which it is fixed and the skinning of animals, cf. App. **2.**), versus G "to strip" (someone of clothing); thus D refers to a more forceful act than G. D can also have the same meaning as G, but then with plural object, cf. App. **1.** and (17) in 6.4.8. Moreover, *bīta hummuṣu* means "to ransack" a house, cf. App. **3.** and 6.4.9.

Kabāsu D "to trample, crush underfoot" (**3.**) seems to be one of the meanings of D, versus G "to step or walk upon"; however, D is also used for plurality of object (see 6.4.2.1 sv) and of action (cf. (74) in 6.6.3.2 and (82) - (84) in 6.6.3.3). In practice, it is often difficult to disentangle these various nuances.

Mahāṣu D usually means "to hit, stab or wound" (persons with a weapon, often in military contexts, cf. App. **1.**), if it has a personal object. G can also be used in such contexts, but more typically refers to hitting or beating somebody with the hand or a stick (CAD sv 1a-d, AHw sv G 1a-h), or it is used metaphorically with gods, diseases, etc., as subject (CAD sv 1d, AHw sv G 1j). The correlation with plurality of D is restricted to inanimate objects (App. **2.** and 6.4.8), and to plural action in protases (App. **3.** and 6.6.1.1 and 6.6.1.2 sv).

Mazā'u D "to rape" (MA) versus G "to squeeze" (cf. CAD sv *mazû*). D can also be used in the same meaning as G, cf. App. sv.

Naṭālu D "to look into, consider, inspect" (AHw sv D: "gründlich betrachten") (App. sv, OB Mari), versus G "to see, to look at".

Šaṭāru D is, mainly in OB Mari, used with a pl. obj. (see 6.4.8), but it is also, and more often, used with *ṭuppum* and comparable words as object in the sg., but only if an addressee is mentioned or at least implied (**1.**): "to write sth *to* a person". In this idiom, it usually has a ventive ending (except in the stative), which shows the directional nuance, and it is followed by a dative or a prepositional phrase with *ana* or *ana ṣēr-*, and often by the corresponding form of *šūbulu* "to send" (sometimes replaced by *šapāru*, e.g., ARM 27, 75: 15).[22] An example is:

(104) ARM 26/2 p. 229 no. 395: 5ff *anumma ṭêmam gamram [i]na ṭuppim ú-ša-aṭ-ṭe₄-ra-am-ma ana ṣēr bēlija ušābilam* "now I have written a complete report on a tablet and sent it to my lord."

In many sentences the use of D for plurality (cf. 6.4.8 and App. sv **1.**/**2.**) and this idiomatic use coincide, as for instance in (105), and are even merged into a single expression in (106):

(105) ARM 1, 7: 19ff (3 lots of wood) (...) *idišam ina ṭuppim šu-uṭ-te₄-ra-am-ma ana ṣērija šūbilam* "write (them) separately on a tablet and send it to me";

(106) ARM 26/2 p. 269 no. 405: r.19'f *ṭuppi awīlim u šumšu u pāṭ[erī] idišam šu-ṭe₄-ra-am-ma ana ṣērija šūbilam* "write a tablet listing (lit. of) each man by name, and the men on leave individually, and send it to me" (also quoted as (140A) in 6.9.5, also *ib.* r.27', but G in 24'.).

This idiom is very common in OB Mari, but rare elsewhere (cf. App. **3.**); outside Mari, G is the usual form (e.g., AS 16, 193: 15; AbB 1, 130: 27; 13, 56: 9'; also MA: KAV 99: 24; 104: 22). On the other hand, *šaṭāru* G + *šūbulu* is rare in Mari texts (ARM 26/2 p. 269 no. 405: r.24' = (140B); p. 274 no. 408: 6 and 39 (cf. note 25); p. 391 no. 468: 19; FM 2 p. 81 no. 46: 15 (or read [*šu-ṭ*]*e₄*- rather than [*šu-u*]*ṭ*- ?)). G in the meanings "to write" or "to register" occurs mainly in the stative (ARM 1, 42: 9. 24; 5, 34: 7. 11; 10, 97: 12; 119: 5; 13, 22: 12; 141: 10; 23, 9: 80; 26/1 p. 430 no. 201: 13; 26/2 p. 391 no. 468: 16, and the VA (ARM 14, 62: 6); active cases, apart from the ones already mentioned, are RIME 4, 607: 128 (RI); ARM 3, 20: 5. 11; 26/2 p. 364 no. 448: 10; p. 391 no. 468: 19 (quoting Hammurabi of Babylon); 27, 80: 23.[23]

(W)atû D "to elect" acc. to GAG² § 106o ("erwählen, ausersehen") (typically said of a god with respect to a king) versus G "to find" (typically with an inanimate object). The paradigm of this verb poses some formal problems: the present G *utta* can only be distinguished from the preterite *uta* (or *ūta*?) (vowel class *a*/*a*, cf. AHw sv G) if the geminate is explicitly written; moreover, *utta* can also be interpreted as a D form. Unambiguous D forms only occur in literary texts from Middle Babylonian times onwards (cf. App.); the oldest one is AfO 23, 47 no. 4: 5 *lu-ut-ti*, from a Kassite seal. D is especially common in RIs from Adad-Nirari III onwards (approx. 800 BC), replacing earlier G forms, such as RIMA 1, 183: 23. 44 (*ú-ta-ni-ma*, Shalmaneser I), 234: I 22 (id., Tukulti-Ninurta I), and 2/I, 13: 20 (*tu-ta-a-šu*, Tiglath-pileser I). In exactly the same contexts, later RIs use forms with gemination as *ut-tu-šu-ma* (Sg. Wi. 168: 2), *ut-ta-an-ni-ma* (Sg. Lie 42: 270), etc., cf. AHw sv *(w)atû* D 3, CAD sv *atû* v. 2a. Since this context requires a preterite, these forms are D rather than G.

The usual meaning of these D forms is "to elect" rather than "to find", cf. GAG *l.c.* The use of D may be related to the higher degree of agentivity implicit in the action of electing, as compared to the non-agentive event of finding, and the fact that it has a personal object. It is, however, also possible that the same process has operated as in *(w)aṣābu* (see 6.8.5), i.e., that the replacement of G by D is purely mechanical, resulting from reanalysis of the present *utta* as a D form, which led to a preterite **utti* on the model of D-stems of other verbs with a weak first radical. It is also possible that both factors have contributed to the rise of these D forms.

For some D forms outside RIs, however, the meaning "to elect" is inappropriate (AfO 23, 47 no. 4: 5; Takultu 126: 166). On the other hand, RIMA 1, 183: 44 *ú-ta-šu-nu-ti* is an unambiguous G form (*pace* GAG² § 106o) with the meaning of D: "I selected them". Since the context requires a preterite, D would be *ut-ti-* or *ú-ti-(šunūti)*. Other forms which mean "to elect", but do not have an explicit geminate are therefore ambiguous, such as KAR 107: 37 (= MVAG 23, 59: 37) *ú-ti-i* (imp. sg. fem.) *migirki* "choose your favourite".

Less certain is *sanāqu* D, when it is used with a personal object:

Sanāqu G and D are both used in the meanings "to check" (weights and measures) and "to question" (persons), with no appreciable difference in meaning, cf. CAD sv 4 and 7 for G, 10 and 12a for D. In addition, D seems to have the specific meaning "to harass, plague" (persons), according to CAD sv 12b (OB). If this is correct (it is not accepted by AHw sv D) the D-stem is associated with a more energetic action and a stronger effect on the object. Elsewhere a meaning "to criticize, reproach", or "to teach sb a lesson" (e.g., Akkadica 25, 3: 6. 9; ARM 26/2 p. 192 no. 380: 11; 27, 57: 28f; 163: 3; Sumer 14 p. 31: 27; cf. also ARM 26/1 p. 90 n. f) seems to be appropriate, although these meanings are so similar that many contexts are ambiguous as to which interpretation is best.

Three D-stems which appear to belong here, but actually have a different background are those of *nabû, qabû* and *ṭarādu*:

Nabû D "to wail, lament" (rarely G with the same meaning, cf. CAD sv *nabû* B a), versus *nabû* "to mention, proclaim", and **qabû** D "to wail, lament", versus *qabû* "to say, speak", The semantic relationship between *nabû* G and D, and *qabû* G and D suggests that they originally denoted the production of certain sounds, but that their G-stems became neutral verbs of speaking or naming through weakening of their meaning.

Ṭarādu D always means "to drive away, banish", cf. App. G can have this meaning, too, cf. AHw sv G 3, but in OB and OA it normally means "to send" (*ib.* G 1/2). The basic meaning of this verb is "to drive away, banish". This is indicated, first, by the fact that it is the meaning of G from OAk onwards in all periods of Babylonian (OAk: RA 35, 48 no. 24b: 2 (Dt); in OB only in literary texts: BiOr. 18, 71f: 1. 21; Atr. 90: 44; Ét. de Meyer 85: 15), whereas "to send" is restricted to OB and OA, and, second, by the meaning of the derived nouns *ṭardu* "driven away, banished, and *ṭarīdu* "exile" (cf. 3.3), with the abstract noun *ṭarīdūtu*. See 5.6.4 about the difference between *ṭarādu* G and D in the meaning "to drive away, banish".

The most likely explanation of this state of affairs is that the meaning "to send" is secondary, probably a result of the weakening of the basic meaning, cf. *nabû* and *qabû* above. If this explanation is correct, the more salient meaning of D is not directly related to the presence of gemination.

It is possible that the same process has taken place in *abāku* A, whose D- and G stem show the same semantic relationship as *ṭarādu* (assuming that the differentiation adopted here between *abāku* A and B is correct).

AHw claims that the use of the D-stem for expressing a more forceful, energetic action also applies to several other verbs. It distinguishes, for instance, *mesû* G "waschen, reinigen" from D "durch und durch reinigen?", *abātu* G "vernichten" from D "ganz vernichten, zerstören", and *laqātu*: G "einsammeln", from D "eilig zusammensuchen". As to *law/mû* "to wrap, surround", the D-stem is claimed to mean "to wrap, to surround completely" by CAD sv *lamû* 7, and "rings umgeben" by AHw sv *lawû* D. Although it is possible on theoretical grounds that such a difference really exists, it is difficult to ascertain from the actual use of these forms in their context.

6.8.2. The "intensive" function of the D-stem

Cases such as those discussed in 6.8.1 have given rise to the traditional view that the D-stem has an intensive function. It follows from Givón's definition of high transitivity (see 5.4) that an increase in intensity entails an increase in transitivity, at least if the verb has an object. Hopper and Thompson (1980: 264) already pointed to the correlation between intensity and high transitivity in their pioneering article about the nature of transitivity, cf. 7.3.3.

The more intensive nature of these D-stems can be established from the fact that they occur in other contexts than the corresponding G-stems, so that the difference in use between G and D is directly observable. If D and G are used in similar contexts, referring to similar actions and/or with similar objects, it is generally very difficult to establish differences between degrees of intensity on independent grounds, since it depends on the subjective state of mind of the speaker, and not on objectively observable circumstances, whether he prefers a neutral or an intensive expression. This problem is even more acute in the adjectives of the pattern *purrus*, which are also reputed to have intensive meaning; it will be discussed more thoroughly in 10.8.

The claim, therefore, that the D-stem can have an intensive meaning *in general*, outside the idiomatic cases listed above, in the sense that a speaker of Akkadian can choose a D form instead of the G-stem if he wants to convey an increase in intensity, force, emphasis, etc., is difficult to prove. The balance of the evidence suggests that this is not the case, and that the D-stem can only indicate such a nuance in fixed, idiomatic expressions such as those presented in 6.8.1.

6.8.3. Lexicalized D-stems

Whereas the idiomatic D-stems typologically belong to the D-stems associated with plurality, because both types are characterized by a semantic extension as compared to the G-stem and usually show the same conditions under which G and D interchange, the semantic relationship between the G- and the D-stem of lexicalized D-stems is unpredictable, and it is not always clear why the D-stem is used to express the meaning in question. The difference in meaning mostly seems to have resulted from lexicalization, but it is also possible that some of these D-stems are actually denominative (cf. 8.1). On the other hand, it is possible that some of those listed in 8.4 as denominatives actually belong here.

A typical feature which lexicalized and denominative D-stems have in common is that they are usually restricted to a specific dialect, and have rather specialized meanings; they typically do not occur in literary texts. Moreover, the distinction between idiomatic and lexicalized D-stems is not clear-cut.

The following lexicalized D-stems can be mentioned:

Darāsu D in OB letters: "to chase away, to scare off" (person(s) (App.), versus G "to trample, oppress", cf. CAD sv 1. The difference between D and G is subtle and may be a matter of dialect and/or genre rather than meaning.

Dekû D "to instigate, prompt" (App., OB/MB/NB), G "to move (tr.), lift up, summon, collect".

Elēhu D "to decorate" (App. **2.**, SB), G "to sprinkle" (1x D in this meaning, App. **1.**).

Epēšu D (G: "to make, do") has at least three different lexicalized meanings in different dialects: (1) "to calculate" in OB, cf. App. **1.**; (2) "to copy (a tablet)", mainly in SB, cf. App. **2.**; (3) "to conclude a sales agreement" in MA/NA, cf. App. **3.** It is a typical lexicalized D-stem, because the lexicalized meanings are restricted to a specific dialect, have a more or less technical character, and occur along with other meanings: *epēšu* D is also occasionally associated with plurality in OA, NA and OB (?) (cf. App. **5.** and **6.**, discussed in 6.5.1 and 6.4.8), it has an idiomatic meaning "to practise witchcraft" (App. **4**), and it sometimes seems a mere variant of the G-stem in MA and NA, cf. App. **7**.

Gamāru D "to bring together" (mostly persons) (App. **9.**, OB); G: "to bring to an end, use up, control". Besides, D shares most meanings of G, cf. 6.8.4 sv.

Habālu A D: "to damage", "to destroy", "to take away illegally" (App. **2.**, MB/SB/NB), versus G: "to wrong, oppress".

Harāšu D "to plant" (trees) (App., SB), cf. G "to bind".

Hesû D "to crush, mince" (plants as ingredients)" (App., SB), cf. G "to press, hide"; listed by CAD sv *hussû*, as a D tantum verb; by AHw sv *hesû* "zudecken" D 2 ("auspressen"). Because of the large variety in meanings of G, the precise semantic relationship between G and D remains obscure.

Madādu D + *ina birīt/birte īnī* "to make something clear" (App. **4.**, NA/NB); G: "to measure, to pay or deliver measured quantities".

Mahāru D is used in several lexicalized meanings: "to present sb with sth, to offer" (App. **1.**), and the various idioms mentioned under **4**. The meaning "to go or send upstream" (**2.**) is doubtless denominative (cf. *māhirtu* "upstream direction", and cf. 8.4.2); for meaning **3.** G is the normal form; it is unclear why in these four cases D/Dtn is used. However, it is possible that all meanings of *mahāru* D are to be explained as denominatives derived from *mahru* in its etymological meaning of "front (side)", or from another form of this root; it seems unlikely that they are derived from the verb *mahāru* "to receive, approach, confront".

Marāqu D "to clear" (from claims) (NB), cf. AHw sv D 2b, CAD sv *murruqu* v.; G "to crush" (CAD sv) or "ab-, zerreiben" (AHw sv G).

Mašādu D "to rub, to massage" (App., SB); G: "to comb" (hair or wool), "to strike with palsy" (*mišittu*).

Rehû D "to bewitch", cf. App. **2.**, SB); G "to pour, beget, have intercourse with".

6.8.4. D-stems of unknown function

The two functions of the D-stems of Type I which have been discussed so far (plurality and semantic differentiation) cover a large part of their total use. On the other hand, we are left with a considerable number of D-stems which cannot be accounted for on the basis of these two functions, because they do not show a significant correlation with plurality, nor a consistent semantic difference from the G-stem. It is difficult to establish in what respect (if any) such D-stems differ from the G-stem. The most likely explanation is that these forms have become more or less synonymous with the basic stem through weakening of their originally iconic nature (cf. 2.2.4.3).

In so far as it concerns verbs which are attested only a few times, it is useless to speculate about the nature of their relationship to the G-stem; these verbs are mentioned in the Appendix, but not discussed in detail. Some other D-stems occur more frequently, but their use is so varied and inconsistent that it does not show any specific tendencies. Such cases are *esēru* A "to put under pressure", *esēru* B "to shut in, enclose", *kapāru* A "to wipe clean, rub", *kašāru* "to repair", *madādu* "to measure, measure out", *manû* "to count, recite, entrust", *našāru* "to cut off, reduce", *parāku* "to block, obstruct", *qebēru* "to bury", *salāh/'u* "to sprinkle, moisten", *sarāqu* "to strew, sprinkle, scatter", *ṣamādu* "to prepare, harness, bandage", *ṣap/bû* "to irrigate, moisten", *ṣarāpu* "to burn" and *ṭapālu* "to insult, disparage". These verbs will not be discussed in full, but the Appendix contains references to sections in which some specific idioms are discussed.

However, there are also some quite frequent D-stems for which it is difficult to establish in what respect they differ from the G-stem. Prominent examples are *gamāru, kasû, katāmu, mesû, and pašāru*:

Gamāru "to bring to an end, do completely, use up, control" has been mentioned in 6.4.8 because of its marginal association with plurality of the object (OA *awātim gummurum*), and in 6.8.3 for its lexicalized OB meaning "to bring together". In practically all of its other meanings (**1.**-**8.**) G and D seem to interchange in a rather arbitrary manner, although in many meanings D is more common than G, esp. in OB and NA. With **1.**, cf. CAD sv 1b/c; with **2.**, cf. *ib.* 1f; with **3.**, cf. *ib.* 1g; with **4.**, cf. *ib.* 1c; with **5.**, cf. *ib.* 1e; with **6.**, cf. *ib.* 1d; with **8.**, cf. *ib.* 1a. Only the combination with *libbu* (**7.**) seems to have no counterpart in G, except MSL 12, 216: 6' (a bad copy of OB Lu from Bo.).

Kasû "to bind, paralyze": with animate beings and body parts as objects D and G interchange without observable difference, both in their literal meaning (App. **1.**, for G cf. CAD sv 1), and in the meaning "to bind magically" (App. **2.**, for G cf. CAD sv 3). Especially in magical contexts the use of *kasû* is similar to that of *ṣabātu* (**10.**), with which it is often coordinated, e.g., KAR 226: I 6 *tu-kàs-si-in-ni tuṣabbitinni* "you (fem.) bound me (and) paralyzed me", cf. 6.4.4.1 sv. The reason proposed there for the fact that *ṣabātu* D is also used with a sg. obj. in this meaning, viz., that it is more terrifying and deemed more permanent to be seized by supernatural powers than by humans, is doubtless also responsible for the rather frequent use of *kasû* D.

It is perhaps significant that the OB and MB instances of D with a personal obj. in the sg. seem to have a distinctly emphatic meaning:

(107) ZA 82, 205: 35ff *māratka ul ahhaz ku-sí-ši-ma ana nārim idīši* "I will not marry your daughter! (For all I care) tie her up and throw her into the river!";

(108) Iraq 50, 85: 6ff *ku-us-sí-šu mamman* <^{GIŠ}>šu.meš-*šu lū lā ipūag* "tie him up! Let nobody release his handcuffs."

If this is the case, *kasû* D also belongs to the idiomatic D-stems listed in 6.8.1. In the later instances of D with a personal obj. in the sg. such a nuance is more difficult to detect; the impression is rather that D and G are more or less synonymous. For *kasû* **4.** see 6.5.3.

Katāmu "to cover, to close"; for D, see App. sv, and cf. CAD sv 1a/b/d (G) with 5a/b/c (D), and 2a/b (G) with 5d (D), where many parallel instances with G and D are quoted; cf. esp. AfO 17, 285: 94 (a woman in the harem) *ana bēliša kat-ma-at* "has to remain covered for her master" (tr. CAD sv 1a) vs. *ib.* 287: 105 (if a woman in the harem) *kindabašše lā ka-at-tu-ma-at* "is not even covered with a loin cloth" (tr. CAD sv 5a). For *katāmu* G and D in Maqlû see (123) in 6.9.4.

Mesû "to wash, clean"; for D, see App. sv; for G, see CAD sv 1-3; cf. especially App. **3.** "to wash (ingredients)" with G in the same texts: YOS 11, 25: 26 (*ba-ri* = "?"); 26: I 16 (flour); 27: 6 (salt); 15 (flour?). It is possible that D means "durch und durch reinigen?" (AHw sv *m.* II D), but this is difficult to deduce from its actual use. For reflexive "to wash oneself" Dt is usually found (cf. CAD sv 6 and 9.1.2 sv), but forms as *lim-te-si* could also be Gt (cf. GAG[2] § 92h for the reflexive Gt-stem).

Pašāru "to untie, release" interchanges with G without observable difference, mostly in relation to the undoing of sorcery, spells, sins, etc. (App. **2.**), and often coordinated with *paṭāru* and/or *pasāsu,* which can refer to the same actions, cf. 6.4.3.1 sv *paṭāru.* The other instances (App. **1.** and **3./4./5.**) are too incidental to establish the motives behind their use (for **5.** see also 6.9.1.1).

Some other D-stems seem to be used interchangeably with the G-stem, but only in one or more specific meanings, for instance, *sanāqu* in the meaning "to check" (weights and measures of houses, amounts of merchandise, tablets, etc.), cf. CAD sv 10a (D) versus 4a/b/c (G); however, D is mainly restricted to OB and OA (for a possible partial difference between *sanāqu* G and D with personal object see 6.8.1). Especially in literary texts D and G are often found in very similar or even identical contexts, see 6.9.2.2.

6.8.5. The verb *(w)aṣābu*

The verb *(w)aṣābu* "to add" deserves special mention, because the relationship between its G- and D-stem is influenced by formal factors: because it is a I/w verb, both G and D have the prefix vowel *u*, which makes some forms ambiguous. This has led to a reanalysis of G forms as D forms and a subsequent spread of D at the expense of G:

(W)aṣābu "to add, enlarge" (later *aṣāb/pu,* cf. GAG § 27d): present G and D are identical in form (*uṣṣab*), preterite G (*uṣib,* also *ūṣib*?) and D (*uṣṣib*) can only be distinguished if the geminate is explicitly written. Unambiguous D forms are not found in OA, but occur occasionally in OAk, OB and MB (see App.); in SB almost all attested forms can be interpreted as D. Unambiguous G forms, on the other hand, are common in OA, OB, MB, but almost disappear in SB: SB G forms are only found in LL and SBH 39: r. 14 (inf.)); therefore, such forms as *lu-ṣib* (e.g., Šurpu V-VI 30), which may be G (*/lūṣib/*), are more likely to stand for D: */luṣṣib/*. In later dialects other than SB the verb is not found anymore (ABL 435: 19 qu. CAD sv 2c is derived from *eṣēpu* "to double" by Parpola, SAA 10, 198: 19, cf. gloss. sv).

The paradigm of *(w)aṣābu* in OA and OB shows that the present *uṣṣab* must be interpreted as a G-stem in those dialects; in later periods it was reanalysed as a D-stem because of its similarity to D forms from verbs with a weak first radical, such as *ullad* from *(w)alādu, uṣṣar* from *eṣēru,* etc. This has led to the introduction of gemination in the preterite: *uṣṣib* instead of *uṣib* (or *ūṣib*), and to assimilation of the paradigm to that of other verbs with a weak first radical (*uṣṣab* → *uṣṣib* like *uṣṣar* → *uṣṣir*). The oldest unambiguous preterite form with gemination listed in the dictionaries is SEM 117: III 8 *ú-AṢ-ṣi-bu* (cf. AHw sv D 1, CAD sv *aṣābu* 2a), which doubtless stands for */uṣṣibū/*, with AZ standing for UZ_4 (cf. Von Soden/Röllig 1991: 18 no. 97), from MB times. Other forms than the present and preterite D are hardly attested in SB (stative: BWL 74: 52; Dt: *ib.* 38: 3; N: MSL 1, 19: 45).

It is possible that the same reanalysis has affected the paradigm of *(w)atû* "to find", but this verb also seems to show a semantic differentiation between G and D; therefore, it is discussed in 6.8.1.

6.9. Various remaining issues

After the survey of the most important functions of the D-stems of Type I, a few issues remain, which will be addressed in the following sections. They concern the differences in the use of the D-stem between OB and OA on the one hand, and SB on the other (6.9.1), some aspects of the use of D in SB (6.9.2), the role of convention (6.9.3), and the use of D for stylistic variation (6.9.4). Finally, in 6.9.5 some problematic passages are discussed in which a D- and a G-stem of the same verb occur side by side.

6.9.1. Dialect differences

With regard to the D-stems of Type I there is a remarkable difference between OB and OA on the one hand, and SB on the other. This can be shown by a global comparison between these three dialects.

Since the relationship of the D-stems of Type I to the corresponding G-stems is semantic rather than grammatical, and therefore largely unpredictable (cf. 6.1), the various dialects of Akkadian show considerable differences as to what D-stems they use, and for what meanings they use them. A comparison of the three most important dialects reveals an important tendency in the historical development of the D-stem, namely, the gradual spread of the use of D for plurality, at the expense of other functions. We will not go into details, but consider only the more common D-stems, since the presence or absence of a rare verb in a particular dialect does not carry any weight.

6.9.1.1. Old Babylonian

If we compare the use of the D-stem of Type I in OB with its total use as represented by the corpus, a number of features stand out. First of all, its use for underlining plurality is restricted in comparison with other, mostly idiomatic, uses, and is only found - with widely varying frequency - in a handful of verbs of the groups I-VII (cf. 6.4): *batāqu, edēlu, hepû, kamāsu, nasāhu, palāšu, paqādu, paṭāru, petû, ṣabātu* and *(w)alādu*. However, for some of these verbs the D-stem is also used without any association with plurality; cf., for instance, the idiomatic use of *palāšu* **4.**, *paṭāru* **4.**, *petû* **9.** and *ṣabātu* **12.** Many other OB D-stems are more often used in an idiomatic meaning than for plurality: *hamāṣu* **2.** and **3.**, *kanāku* **2.**, *kasû* **1./2.**, *kaṣāru* **5.** and *rakāsu* **8./9.** On the other hand, OB has a few D-stems used for plurality which are not or only rarely found elsewhere: *apālu, dâšu* **1.**, and *hanāqu.*

Second, some of the most common OB D-stems of Type I have no relationship with plurality: *epēšu* **1.**, *mahāru* **1.**, *parāku* **4./5.**, *sadāru* **1.** and *sanāqu*; but some of them regularly have mass nouns as object (*gamāru* **9.** and *kamāsu* **1./2.**). Less common are cases such as *darāsu, esēru* A "to put under pressure", *hamāṣu* **2./3.**, *kašāru* (also OAk), *latāku* and *sakāpu.* These verbs are typically found in letters. *Hakāmu* is found in Mari letters and OB recipes. A typically literary OB D-stem is *nâdu* "to praise, extol", which seems to be completely interchangeable with G.

Thirdly, an important aspect of the D-stem in OB is its use for all kinds of more or less specialized or technical activities. This seems to be much more prominent than its use to underline plurality. It applies to many of the verbs mentioned above. Some other cases, less common but more clearly referring to specialized activities, are *napāṣu* **3.** "to crush" (barley), *pašāru* **5.**, *šapāku* **4.** (processes performed on wool), and *(w)alādu* **2.** "to breed" (sheep). Especially Mari letters abound in such D-stems, of which it is often uncertain to what activity they exactly refer (cf. *(h)apû, katāmu* **4.**, *patāqu, paṭāru* **8.**, *tarāṣu* **4.**). Such idioms partly agree with the regular use of the verb in question in that they normally occur only if the object is plural. However, as we have seen in the idiomatic expressions discussed in 6.4.9, a nonliteral meaning often leads to the abandoning of the association with plurality.

The relative importance of this use of the D-stem in OB is no doubt partly caused by the subject matter of the majority of extant OB texts: letters which usually deal with commercial and technical matters, and thus contain many terms which are typically absent from the literary idiom of SB.

Generally speaking, however, the D-stems of Type I in OB are more often used in various idiomatic expressions than for underlining plurality. This confirms the basically semantic nature of the relationship between these D-stems and the corresponding G-stems.

6.9.1.2. Old Assyrian

The situation in OA differs from both OB and SB in many respects. The extant OA material is very one-sided as regards subject matter: it consists almost exclusively of business letters and legal and administrative documents of the Assyrian merchants trading in Anatolia, and reflects the language and the technical jargon they used.

This fact may be largely responsible for the rarity in OA of the most common D-stems associated with plurality in other dialects: of all D-stems enumerated in 6.4, only the following are attested in OA (many of them only once, cf. App. ssvv): *nakāsu* (**1.**), *napāṣu* (**4.**), *nasāhu* (**4.**), and *šebēru* (**4.**) of Group I, *kabāsu* (**7.**) and *sapāhu* (**4.**) of Group II, *e'ēlu* (**1.**), *(h)arāmu, kanāku* (**1.** and **2.**), *paṭāru* (**2.** and **4.**), *petû* (**5.**, **8.** and **11.**) and *rakāsu* (**4.** and **9.**) of Group III, *ṣabātu* (**5.** and **13.**) of Group IV, *laqātu* (**1.** and **2.**) of Group V, *paqādu* (**1.**), *nasāqu* (**1.**), *zabālu* and *katā'u* of Group VII.

In spite of the rarity of the verbs of 6.4 in OA, the association with plurality is an important aspect of the OA D-stems of Type I, but in a different way from OB and SB. First, there is a strong tendency to use D in relation with mass nouns, especially metals (cf. note 3, and for the same phenomenon in *purrus* forms see 10.6.1.2.4). Second, plural action seems to be more important in OA than plural object, cf. 6.6.3.1. Third, we do find D-stems motivated by plurality of the object, but in other verbs than elsewhere: *epēšu* **6.**, *gamāru* **6.**, *katā'u,* and *harāmu,* and occasionally in some other verbs.

Moreover, OA has a number of very common D-stems which are very rare or absent in other dialects: *šaqālu* (**2.**) "to pay", *ša'ālu* "to ask" and *lapātu* in the meaning "to write" (**6a.**); less common, but exclusively OA is *agāru* "to hire". A D-stem which OA shares with OB is *sanāqu* D "to check" (weights and measures) (beside G), but *sanāqu* with a personal object, which is very common in OB (App. **2.** and **4.**), seems to be absent from OA.

Finally, some D-stems have a technical use in OA which is absent from other dialects and goes against the tendency noted in 5.6.4 to restrict the use of D to the literal meaning(s) of the verb and to concrete objects: *kabāsu* **7.**, *kasû* **3.**, *napāṣu* **4.**, *nasāhu* **4.** Moreover, OA and OB share the specialized use of *rakāsu* **9.** "to bind sb by contract".

The overall picture offered by OA is that, more than in OB and SB, the use of D is determined by the semantic nature of the action expressed by the D-stem in question rather than by formal plurality.

6.9.2. Standard Babylonian

A global comparison between the use of D in OB and OA on the one hand, and SB on the other, shows that the D-stems of SB are more frequent and also more uniform in function.

The high frequency of SB D-stems can easily be verified from the corpus: many verbs only occur in SB and in most others SB instances predominate. The preponderance of SB may be partly due to the greater number of texts, but even if we take this into account, the use of D-stems of Type I is more frequent than elsewhere. Only a few D-stems are more numerous in OB and OA; the most important of these were mentioned in the two previous sections.

The relative uniformity in use is caused by the fact that many of the idiomatic and lexicalized meanings of OB and OA D-stems, which tend to make the semantic relationship between G and D irregular and unpredictable, are not found in SB. To a much larger extent than in the earlier dialects, therefore, D has the same meaning as G.

The development of the use of D in SB is determined by two processes. On the one hand, the idiomatic function of D has declined, and its other function, viz., that of underlining plurality, has correspondingly gained in importance: it has become far more prominent than in OB and OA. This development can be seen as the beginning of a process of grammaticalization, leading to a more regular and predictable relationship between G and D, at the expense of the more semantic, unpredictable and verb-specific relationship in OB and OA. It is possible that this process has also been operative in MA, MB, NB and NA: in these dialects plurality seems to be relatively important, too, although the smaller numbert of texts available makes it difficult to be certain.

On the other hand, we observe a tendency for the D-stem to spread also to contexts which do not contain a plural element. We find a number of D-stems used with both singular and plural objects, not, as in OB and OA, with a specific kind of object - usually those objects which involve a higher salience (see 6.4.9) - but indiscriminately. Thus the D-stem is less strongly restricted to plural contexts in SB and there is more overlap with the G-stem than in earlier dialects.

In order to illustrate this, it is convenient to divide the SB material in scholarly texts (see 6.9.2.1) and literary texts proper (see 6.9.2.2).

6.9.2.1. D versus G in scholarly texts

The scholarly texts mainly consist of lexical texts, various kinds of omen texts, and technical texts concerning the preparation of substances such as glass and perfumes, culinary texts, etc. They have a very specialized, technical vocabulary, and are often highly stereotyped in their formulation. Many of them, especially medical and ritual texts, have the form of omen texts, with a protasis introduced by *šumma* (cf. 6.6.1), followed by an apodosis which consists of a prescription or a ritual procedure.

In such contexts there is a remarkable degree of interchangeability between the G- and the D-stems of several verbs. Even with identical objects we find numerous cases where in one text G is used, in another one D, and several cases of D alternating with G in duplicate versions of the same text. There are also verbs, however, which clearly distinguish between G and D, and use the latter only with plural nouns or mass nouns as object, such as *alātu* "to swallow" and *qalāpu* "to peel" (cf. App. ssvv). In many cases one of the stems is usual, the other exceptional; this may point to an error on the part of the scribe. A factor which may play a role here is that all these forms are in the present tense and that, at least in the most frequent vowel class, *a/u,* the present forms of G and D differ only in the prefix vowel: *iparras* versus *uparras.*

Some examples of alternating G and D forms in identical contexts are the following:

(109A) TDP 42: 39 *šumma* (...) *qātāšu u šēpāšu i-šam-ma-ma-šú* "if his hands and feet become paralyzed";
(109B) CT 23, 46: III 26f *šumma* (....) *qātāšu u šēpāšu ú-šam-ma-ma-šú uzaqqatāšu* "if his hands and feet become paralyzed and give him pain" (tr. CAD sv *šamāmu* 2);

(110) AnBi,12, 286: 98 *šikara* (kaš) *tu-naq-qa*, versus *ib.* 100 *šikara* bal-*qí* (= *tanaqqi*) "you sacrifice beer";

(111A) BagF. 18, 357: 19 (In order to let the evil arising from a fungus pass (...) you make seven knives of tamarisk wood and) *ina libbi* ka.tar *tu-hal-la-aš* "you scrape (a piece) off the fungus";
(111B) ib. 361: 87 idem with gazelle (var. goat) bone instead of tamarisk wood and *ta-hal-la-a*[*š*]; cf. also G in 358: 29f (six axes instead of seven knives); 358: 47f and 359: 60f (one axe);

(112) BagF. 18, 130: 16ff 14 kinds of herbs *tu-tab-bak*, versus 133: 82ff 13 (var. 14) kinds of herbs *ta-tab-bak* "you combine (lit. heap up) 13/14 kinds of herbs";

(113A) SKS p. 78: 293f *7 kannāti ṣirpi kalīšunu tu-kan-na-an* "you make (lit. twist) seven threads out of all (these) kinds of coloured wool";

(113B) ZA 16, 184/6: 25f *3 kannāti ša 7 ṣirpāni ta-kan-na-an* you make (lit. twist) three threads out of (these) seven kinds of coloured wool".

Examples of alternating G and D forms in duplicate versions of the same text are:

(114) BagF. 18, 325: 10 *šikara* (kaš.sag) bal-*qí* (= *tanaqqi*) // *tu-naq-qa* "you sacrifice beer";

(115) AMT 74: II 19 // BAM 124: II 46 (you boil a leaf of plantain and) *ana* igi *tu-tab-bak* // *ta-tab-bak* "pour it on the eye";

(116) BAM 122: r.7'f // AMT 68, 1: r.10 (cress and licorice leaf/ves) *ina* kaš *pu-ut-ti ina diqāri kīma rabīki tu-ra-ba-ak* // *tara-bak*; "you stir together with *puttu*-beer in a bowl into a solution";

(117) RA 49, 178: 6 (you crush several kinds of dust, mix them with water and) *šaman šurmēni ina libbi tu-rak* // *ta-rak* "you pour cypress oil onto (the mixture)".

A similar case already quoted previously in 6.4.9 is that of *marāqu* (21). Other prominent instances are, first, *kapāru* A "to rub, wipe, wipe clean", of which G and D occur in exactly the same phrases: cf. CAD sv *k.* A 1 (G) with 3a/b (D) and for D see also App. **1** (in the meaning "to purify magically" (App. **2**.) only D is usual), and, second, *salāh/'u* "to sprinkle, moisten" in *šuluhha salāhu* or *sulluhu* "to perform a sprinkling", cf. CAD sv *salāhu* A 1d (G) and 5c (D).

Such alternating G and D forms in prescriptions without apparent difference in meaning are typically found in the following verbs (all cases are SB, unless indicated otherwise, for references see App.): *be'āšu* "to stir", *hâb/pu* "to cleanse, purify, exorcize" (usually D), *halāšu* "to scrape off" (see (111)), *kanānu* "to twist" (see (113)), *kapāru* A "to rub, wipe, wipe clean" (see above), *kâru* "to rub" (D 1x), *marāqu* "to crush" (see (21)), *na'āsu* "to chew" (D 1x), *naqû* "to pour out, sacrifice" (see (110) and (114)), *pa'āṣu* "to crush, smash" (D 2x), *pâšu* "to crush" (D 1x), *rabāku* "to make an infusion" (D 2x, see (116)), *râku* "to pour out" (see (117)), *salāh/'u* "to sprinkle, moisten" (see above), *sanāšu* "to insert", *sarāqu* "to strew, sprinkle, scatter", *šabāhu* "to sprinkle" (D 1x in SB, but also OB, cf. App.), *šahātu* A "to rinse, clean", (D 1x), *šakāku* "to harrow, string", *tabāku* "to pour out" (see (112)) and *ṭepû* "to spread, plaster".

In so far as these verbs have a plural or mass noun as object, they are in accordance with the normal use of the D-stem; what is remarkable about them is the extent to which G and D are used in the same contexts without observable difference.

6.9.2.2. Literary texts

The literary texts proper comprise the following types: royal inscriptions, epic texts, incantations, litanies, hymns and prayers (including hymnal and laudatory parts of other texts), and most other religious texts such as those collected by Lambert in BWL. They differ from the other genres in that their language is more or less consciously embellished by stylistic devices, such as a special vocabulary, changes in word order and particular morphological forms (cf. GAG § 186e/f; Von Soden 1932/33: II 160ff).

The high frequency of the D-stems of Type I in these literary texts shows that the D-stem has a certain stylistic affinity with such texts. This is doubtless related to its marked character: it is longer in form and less common in use; therefore, it is less ordinary and more expressive than the average G-stem (cf. GAG § 88f Anm.). It may also be more emphatic in meaning, although this is difficult to verify from actual texts. In 6.9.5 some passages are discussed which may suggest that the use of D, in so far as it is an optional equivalent of G, is related to foregrounding.

A characteristic feature of the SB literary idiom is the tendency to use words and grammatical forms which are different from those occurring in ordinary speech (cf. also Edzard 1982: 87f). This also applies to several of the verbal stems of Akkadian, which are used differently, and usually more extensively, in literary texts than in other texts. A well known example is the typically literary nature of the ŠD-stem, which can take the place of the D- or the Š-stem, and is not attested outside literary texts (GAG § 95a, see 9.3). Another case, which is to be examined in detail in Chapter VII, is that of the "factitive Š-stems", which are sometimes used in literary texts instead of the corresponding D-stems, for instance, *šūruku* "to make long", instead of *urruku,* which is the normal factitive of *arāku* "to be(come) long" (see 7.5.5.1 sv). Less exclusively literary, but still largely restricted to literary texts are many Gt-stems (GAG § 92f and 4.1.2.1). Apparently, the fact that these forms are seldom or not used in ordinary speech, makes them suitable for stylistically marked texts. To a certain extent this also holds true of the D-stem, but less so because of its overall frequency in all periods and dialects.

In spite of the strong association with plurality, there is also a tendency to extend the use of D to contexts in which there is no plural element. This can be inferred from the typical situation which we observe in many SB D-stems, namely, that many D-stems which mostly have a plural object, are occasionally found with a similar object in the singular. By way of example many of the typically literary verbs which were discussed in 6.4 can be quoted, such as *abātu* "to destroy", *lâṭu* "to keep in check, confine", *rasāb/pu* "to kill", *sahāpu* "to overwhelm", and *salātu* "to split off, cut". As to the verbs which are not exclusively literary, many exceptions to the association of D with plurality are found in literary texts, e.g., *kabāsu* "to pardon" a sin (1x in a RI, App. **6**., and cf. 6.4.2.1 sv), *nakāsu* D "to cut off, fell" (2x sg. obj.: in BWL (lamb) and in a fragmentary ritual (hand), App. **5**.), *ṭabāhu* D "to slaughter" (1x sg. obj. (person) in a historical text, App. **3**. (but also 1x OB)), *(w)alādu* D "to give birth to, produce (1x sg. obj. (demon) in Lugal, App. **5**.), and *petû* D with object "well" (1x in Ee, App. **11**., versus usually "wells".

The fact that these verbs normally have a plural object, but are occasionally also used with a similar object in the singular suggests that the latter cases are secondary, and result from an extension of the use of D beyond contexts which contain a plural element. Sometimes the context indicates that it is a secondary development. This is the case in the exceptional use of *edēlu* "to lock" with the singular object "door" (App. **3**., quoted as (05) in 6.4 and as (127) in 6.9.4, which is motivated by stylistic variation (see 6.9.4), and in the following remarkable passage from the Maqlû series of incantations:

(118) Maqlû III 104ff (// SpTU 1, 8: 1-10, cf. also SpTU 3, 74: 104ff) *atti e ša tēpušinni* [105]*atti e ša tušēpišinni* [106]*atti e ša tu-kaš-ši-pi-in-ni* [107]*atti e ša tu-hap-pi-pi-in-ni* [108]*atti e ša tu-ṣab-bi-ti-in-ni* [109]*atti e ša tu-kan-ni-ki-in-ni* [110]*atti e ša tu-ab-bi-ti-in-ni* [111]*atti e ša tu-ub-bi-ri-in-ni* [112]*atti e ša tu-ka-si-in-ni* (var. *tu-kaṣ-ṣi-ri-[in-ni]* SpTU 3, 74: 112) [113]*atti e ša tu-la-'i-in-ni* "hey, you there (sorceress), who have practised sorcery against me, ... who have made (somebody else) practise sorcery against me, ... who have bewitched me, ... who have ....-ed me, ... who have seized me, ... who have put me under seal, ... who have destroyed me, ... who have bound (?) me, ... who have fettered me, ... who have defiled me."

The use of the D-stem in this passage is clearly motivated by the author's desire to have a series of formally parallel verbs rather than by the exact meaning of each D-stem separately, although most of them are found elsewhere in the same context. It explains, however, the unique use of *kanāku* D, cf. App. **3.** and 6.4.3.1 sv. *Kaṣāru* D is also unparalleled in this meaning, but it is not surprising because of the close similarity in meaning and use between *kasû* and *kaṣāru* in such contexts, especially in the D-stem with body parts as object, cf. CAD sv *kasû* v. 5c and *kaṣāru* 6a, and App. sv *kasû* **2.** and *kaṣāru* **2.**

In some verbs this process has led to a situation in which it is no longer possible to detect any difference in use between D and G. In 6.8.4 a number of such verbs were mentioned. Many of these mainly occur in literary texts; this offers at least a partial explanation of why their G- and D-stems are used without observable difference.

The ultimate motive behind this development is that if a marked and an unmarked category coexist without a clear contrast in meaning or function, there is a tendency for the marked category to spread at the expense of the unmarked one and, at the same time, to lose its more expressive nature (cf. 2.2.4.2 and 2.2.4.3). It is plausible that this is one of the ways in which the use of D has also spread to contexts which do not contain a plural element.

6.9.3. The role of convention

A particularly striking feature of the D-stems of Type I is the highly stereotyped and conventional nature of their use. Many of them are always found in the same genre of texts and/or in very similar contexts. This is especially clear in RIs, which are highly stereotyped in general and often repeat more or less verbatim passages of earlier inscriptions. The most striking cases are *šêlu* "to sharpen" (weapons) and *lâṭu* "to confine, keep in check" (enemies), which are hardly found elsewhere, but there are also many other verbs which predominantly occur in RIs and are more or less restricted to a single context. Examples are *napāṣu* and *rasāb/pu* "to kill" (enemies), *palāq/ku* and *ṭabāhu* "to slaughter" (sacrificial animals and enemies), and *retû* "to fix", preceded by *rakāsu* "to fasten", often in stock phrases such as:

(119) VAB 7, 264: 8 *aslī ṭu-ub-bu-hu lê pu-ul-lu-ku* "sheep were butchered, bulls were slaughtered";

(120) RIMA 2/I, 252: 16ff "I made high doors of fir, fastened (*ú-ra-ki-si*) (them) with bronze bands, (and) hung (*ú-ra-ti*) (them) in its (the palace's) doorway" (tr. Grayson); this phrase occurs - with many variations - passim in RIs.

Yet other instances from RIs are expressions such as *kakkī šubburu* "to break weapons", *qīšāti quššu* "to offer presents", *našāqu* "to kiss" (the ground or the feet of the king), the various verbs referring to the piling up of the spoils the king has seized from his enemies (*kamāru, nakāmu, qarānu, šapāku*), and the rich vocabulary developed for the various ways in which defeated enemies are treated: *kabāsu* "to tread down", *napālu* "to blind", *sahāpu* "to overwhelm", *zaqāpu* "to impale", etc.

Taken together, such stereotyped expressions take up a considerable part of the total use of the D-stems of Type I. A counterpart of this phenomenon in medical texts is the use of verbs such as *mahāṣu* "to hit", *sahālu* "to pierce", and *zaqātu* "to sting", to denote the workings of pain in the human body; they are listed in 6.6.1.2.

Another argument for the importance of convention is offered by the frequent D-stem of *nakāsu* "to cut off, fell" (6.4.1.1 sv). In OB it is rather rare and used with body parts and trees or wooden objects, cf. App. **1.** and **3.** In SB, however, it is very common to refer to the cutting off of body parts and the killing of animals and people (see App. **1.** and **2.**, CAD sv 6a/c, 7a/b, 8), but it is never used for the felling of trees and the like; in this meaning we always find the G-stem (CAD sv 1a/b). This total absence of *nakāsu* D in one context, and its frequent occurrence in another one, as far as SB is concerned, can best be explained by assuming that the choice between G and D was at least partly based on convention.

The ultimate stage of conventional use is the restriction of a particular form to a single stereotyped context. The D-stems discussed so far show many examples of this. Already mentioned were *šêlu* "to sharpen" weapons, *lâṭu* "to confine, keep in check" enemies, which occur only in RIs, always in the same context. Instances from another genre are the D-stems of *edēhu* "to cover with patches" and *(h)alālu* "to hang" in the protases of extispicy omens, which are also generally highly stereotyped, cf. the use of *ṣubbut* with *qû* "threads" and *lipiam/lipâ kussu* mentioned in 6.5.3.

Another important case of stereotyped usage is that of the participle D in epithets, usually of gods and kings. In some cases the D- and the G-stem are equally common and used indiscriminately, e.g., *mudīšu* and *dā'išu* "trampling" (enemies, App. **2.**), *mula''iṭu* and *lā'iṭu* "keeping in check, controlling" (enemies, App. **2./3.**), *mu'allidu* and *ālidu* "bringing forth" (gods, grain, vegetation, "everything", App. sv *(w)alādu* **3.**). In other verbs there is a strong preference for D, as in *mu'abbitu* "destroying" (mountains, towns, enemies, App. **1.**-**4.**, **6.**, 1x *ābitu* Ee VII 90) and in *mušīmu* in *mušīm šīmāti* "decreeing destinies" (App.), *šā'im* 4x, cf. CAD sv *š.* B 2c-2').

In some verbs there is a subtle (and usually not consistently observed) semantic differentiation between the participles of D and G: *mukabbisu* "trampling" ((necks of) enemies, App.

1.-2., **4.**) versus *kābisu* "walking over or treading upon" (the earth, sea, heaven, meadows, etc., cf. StOr. 7, 106f), and *mupettû* "opening" (roads, mountain passes, waterways, etc. by kings, App. **3.**/**4.**) versus *pētû* "opening" (wells, the doors of heaven by gods, cf. ÉR 224).

The stereotyped nature of these expressions is not only evident from the frequent recurrence of fixed combinations, but also from the rather arbitrary distribution of G and D over the various types of text, such as the fact that *mupa/ettû* is said mainly of kings, and *pētû* mainly of gods, although the objects involved would also permit otherwise. It is also remarkable that of the verb *paqādu* "to entrust, appoint, take care of, inspect" which has a very frequent D-stem, we mostly find *pāqidu* as epithet of gods and kings (StOr. 7, 152f, ÉR 218f), whereas in other forms D is regularly used, cf. App. **4.** (but cf. IAsb. 42: 14 DN *mu-paq-qi-du riksīšun* "who keeps in good order their bonds", in a different combination).

6.9.4. The use of D for stylistic variation

In some types of literary texts we find a number of passages in which a G- and a D-stem of the same verb are used side by side. Unlike most of the contrasting pairs discussed so far, however, they show no concomitant difference in the rest of the sentence, such as the singular versus plural nature of one of the other constituents. They exemplify the use of the D-stem as a means of stylistic variation.

This phenomenon is typical of texts which are characterized by a highly repetitive style, such as hymns, prayers, litanies and incantations. Their repetitive character is due to the desire to drive home the message, and to emphasize the predicament the supplicant is in. A randomly chosen example is:

(121) SpTU 2, 12: II 26ff *mimma lemnu* (...) *lū naškun lū ṭarid lū tabil, lū duppur lū ukkuš ina zumrija* "let everything evil (...) be laid down, expelled, taken away, removed and driven from my body".

Another striking instance from Maqlû was quoted in 6.9.2.2 as (118); this compendium of incantations contains many other examples, such as Maqlû II 172-179; III 94-98; IV 117-130; V 125-131 and 166-180.

In such texts G and D forms of the same verb can be used side by side with the same function as the accumulation of different, (near-)synonymous verbs. Consider the following cases:

(122) AfO 18, 290: 18 *libbī unnišū idīja ik-su-ú birkīja ik-su-ú šēpīja ālikāt[i] ú-ka-su-u* "(the demons) have weakened my heart, have bound (G) my arms, have bound (G) my knees, have bound (D) my running feet." (Already quoted as (04) in 6.4);

(123) Maqlû III 162/4 (the hand which) *kīma šēti ú-kat-ti-mu qarrādu* (...) *kīma gišparri ik-tu-mu danna* "covered (D) the hero like a net, (...) covered (G) the strong one like a *gišparru*-trap" (cf. also II 164 and 175);

(124) SpTU 2, 12: II 12 *lū pár-sa lū pur-ru-sa lū purrurā gillātū'a u maskātū'a* "may my sins and misdeeds be removed (G), erased (D) (lit. "cut off") and dispersed";

(125) SpTU 2, 12: II 18 (// CT 51, 195: 6) *lū šá-ah-ṭu lū šu-uh-hu-ṭu lemnētū'a u maskātū'a* "may my crimes and evil deeds be removed (G) and eradicated (D)" (lit. "torn off");

(126) SpTU 3, 76: 18 *ina dimti bu-ul-lu-la-ku ina eperī bal-la-ku* "I am stained (D) with tears, I am smeared (G) with dust";

(127) SKS p. 42: 45 *e-dil*$_x$(TIL) *bītu ud-du-lu bābu nadû har-gul-lim* "the house is closed (G), the door is shut (D), the bolts are put in place" (also quoted in 6.4 as (05));

(128) SKS p. 102: 2 (var. l) *uprūša up-pu-rat agâša ap-rat* "she (Lamaštu) is covered (D) with her *upru*-headdress, she is crowned (G) with her crown" (*apāru* belongs to Type IV, cf. 5.5.2).

For similar instances with *purrus* adjectives, see (53) - (55) in 10.8.

In most of these cases the use of D corresponds to its normal use; only in (127) is the use of D exceptional, since *edēlu* normally has a plural object (see 6.4.3.1 sv); the relationship between *uppurat* and *aprat* can be compared to that between the statives G and D which are discussed in 10.4.2.

6.9.5. Some problematic passages

A final problem to be dealt with is the existence of a number of passages in which a G- and a D-stem of the same verb occur side by side with the same or almost the same object. Some such passages were discussed in the preceding section and argued to be motivated by stylistic variation. Other cases, however, occur in texts which are not characterized by a repetitive style, and thus should be accounted for in a different way.

The number of relevant passages is rather small; I will enumerate them and discuss what seems to be the most likely motive for the use of the G and the D form. Most of them allow more than one interpretation, and there seems to be no single explanation which is valid for all of them. It should be emphasized that the proposed solutions with regard to why a D- or a G-stem is used in a given case are often extremely tentative. We will start with OB, since in OB the use of interchanging G and D forms generally seems to be more meaningful than in later texts.

Consider first the following case of *kaṣāru* G and D:

(129) ARM 1, 42: 26ff *1 [l]im ṣ[ā]bam birīt* [...] [27]*kilallīn ku-ṣú-ur* [28]*u 1 lim ṣābam ina G*[N_1] (...) [29]*ku-ṣú-ur u 6 me-tim* [*ṣ*]*ābam birīt* [30]GN_2 GN_3 [31]GN_4 *u* GN_5 [32]*ku-ṣú-ur ašar 2 me-tim ašar 3 me-tim* [33]*ana zīmim ṣābam lu-qí-it-ma* [34]*5 me-<tim> ṣābam ku-ṣú-ur* (....) [35]*ina ūmišu 6* (?) *limi ṣābam* [36][*t*]*u-ka-aṣ-ṣa-ar* "assemble (G) 1000 men between both [...], and assemble (G) 1000 men in GN_1 (...), and assemble (G) 600 men among the people of GN_2, GN_3, GN_4 and GN_5; pick up 200 men here, 300 men there, according to circumstances, and assemble (G) 500 men. (...) Then you will be able to assemble (D) (a total of) 6000 men."

Both the D form *tukaṣṣar* in 36 and the G-stem imperatives *kuṣur* in 27, 29, 32 and 34 have a plural object. The most likely explanation for the use of D in line 36 seems to be that it emphasizes the relatively large quantity of the contingents involved as compared to the preceding numbers and/or that it underlines the fact that the assembling has to take place in or from various places, or on various occasions, whereas the imperatives refer to a single action of assembling. This seems to be supported by *luqqit* in 33, which also refers to an action in several places.

A different motive is needed in the following cases:

(130A) FM 2 p. 285 no. 130: 6ff (concerning PN who has been killed) [6]dumu.meš *kārim* [7]*ittija* [8]*erdēma bīssu ú-ka-ni-ik* [9]*ina bītim šāti* [10]*ša ak-nu-ku mimma ul āmur* "I have brought the people of the *kārum* along with me (and) put (D) his house under seal; in that house which I have put (G) under seal I have found nothing (there was neither sesame nor barley, not was there any wool)."

(130B) *ib.* 18ff *ina kunukkija u kunuk* [19]dumu.meš *kārim* [20]*bītam ni-ik-nu-uk* "with my seal and the seal of the people of the *kārum* we have put (G) the house under seal".

(131A) AbB 7, 153: 8f (The judges of Babylon and the judges of Sippar (...) examined the lawsuits of the inhabitants of Sippar and) [8]*ṭuppāt šīmātim ša eqlim bītim u kirîm išmûma* [9]*ša ina mīšari waṣiā ú-he-ep-pu-ú* "they heard the sales documents of fields, houses and orchards and broke (D) those which had become invalid according to the *mīšaru*-promulgation." (cf. Kraus's translation and CAD sv *mīšaru* A 1);

(131B) *ib.* 36ff PN (...) [37]*balumma šaptīja išmû* [38]*ina GN ina bīt napṭari*[*š*]*u* [39]*ṭuppātīja ih-pí-ma* "PN, without asking my consent (lit. hearing my lips), broke (G) my tablets in Sippar in his residence."

(131C) *ib.* 47ff *dīn ṭuppātim ša balum dajjānī* [48]*u bēl awātim he-pé-e-em* [49]*bēlī lidīnannīma* "I hope my lord will pronounce judgement for me in the case about the breaking (G) of the tablets without (the presence of) the judges and the litigants."

(132A) AbB 4, 20: 10 [*ina*] *qīšātim šināti* giš.hi.a *nu-uk-ku-su* "in those forests trees have been felled (D)";

(132B) *ib.* 21ff *u* giš.hi.a *ša in-na-ak-su* [22]*maṣṣār qīšātim* [23]*ik-ki-su-ú* [24]*ina qātim ahītim* [25]*in-na-ak-su-ú* "and did the guardians of the forests fell (G) the trees which were felled (N), or were they felled (N) by outsiders (lit., an alien hand)?"

(133A) ARM 13, 55: 9ff (about a kind of ornament) (The king has instructed me as follows) [9](...) *tu-ru-sú-nu-*[*ti*] [10]*umma anākūma* [11]*tu-ru-ṣú* "fabricate (?) (G) them"; [10]I answered him: "they have (all) been fabricated (D) (already)";

(133B) *ib.* 17 (now, when you hear this tablet of mine, (...)) [17]*arhiš li-ta-ri-ṣú-šu-nu-ti* "let them fabricate (D) them (all) quickly".

What the first three passages have in common is that the writers of these letters begin with a D form, but fall back upon a G form if the same verb recurs. This suggests that these D forms may have a foregrounding function, to introduce the subject matter or to give information with some emphasis; once this has been done, the neutral G-stem is used. In addition, it seems that the focus should be on the action or the object, not on the subject, as in (132B). The D forms in (131A) and (132A) also refer to events which may have occurred in several places or on several occasions; this might be an additional reason to use D; this is, however, not possible for (130A) with its singular object. The interchanging G and D forms in (133) are particularly interesting: the stative D in 11 undoubtedly underlines that the order of the king has already been carried out completely (cf. (69) - (72) in 6.6.3.2) and has the emphasis which typically accompanies an untruth. Line 17 is an urgent order, which must prevent the sender of this letter from being exposed as a liar; the king uses a neutral G form, because he focuses on the action itself and does not need emphasis to be obeyed.

An important argument for the foregrounding character of the D-stems of Type I, as opposed to the neutral G-stem, is the fact that in a number of contrasting pairs the D-stem is restricted to the main verb of the predicate, and replaced by G in subordinate clauses and other peripheral constituents; generally speaking foregrounded actions are expressed by means of main clauses, wheras backgrounded information tends to be expressed by subordinate clauses or by constituents on the periphery of the clause (cf. Givón 1980: 287ff). This is exemplified by (130A) with *ú-ka-ni-ik* in the main clause, versus *ak-nu-ku* in the relative clause. A comparable case is:

(134A) Atr. 58: 211/226 *DN li-ba-al-li-il / ú-ba-li-il ṭiṭṭa* "Let Nintu mix / Nintu mixed (D) clay";
(134B) *ib.* 231: *ištūma ib-lu-la ṭiṭṭa šâti* "after she had mixed (G) that clay".

For similar instances from SB see below (142) - (145). This phenomenon seems to occur in particular with an infinitive, cf. (131C) above and:

(135) TCL 1, 195: 4ff (a field) [4]*aššum hu-bu-li-*[*ša*?] [5]*a-pa-li-im* (...) [6]PNF_1 (...) [8]*ana* PNF_2 (...) [10]*iddiššim* [11]PNF_2 [12]*hu-bu-li ša* PNF_1 [13]5 gur še [14]*ú-pa-al* "PNF_1 gave (a field) to PNF_2 in order to pay (G) [her]? debt(s?); PNF_2 will pay (D) the debts of PNF_1 in the amount of 5 gur of barley".

(136A) ARM 26/2 p. 100 no. 329: 18' *š*[*ê*]*m li-ma-ad-di-i*[*d*] "let him measure out (D) the barley";
(136B) *ib.* 21' *ana* [*ṣ*]*ērika ana šêm* [*ma-d*]*a-di-im iṭrudanni* "he has sent me to you in order to measure out (G) the barley".

(137A) (= (14) in Ch. IV) MARI 5, 165: 39f *wa-ar-ka-at mê* (...) [41][*da*]*mqiš li-pa-ri-su-ni-kum-ma* "let them thoroughly investigate (D) for you the problem of the water (supplies)" (D also in 164: 20 and 25; cf. also 6.4.1.1 sv *parāsu*);
(137B) *ib.* 64 *awīlē ša ana wa-ar-ka-at mê pa-ra-si-*[*im illikū*] *ana ṣērija ṭurdamma* "send the men to me who [have gone] to investigate (G) the problem of the water (supplies)."

(138) ARM 27, 36: 35ff [*š*]*a na-sa-ah* [*aw*]*īlim šêti i*[*na*] *halṣim* (sic) *epuš* [36]*inūma awīlam š*[*êt*]i *ina halṣi* (sic) [*a*]*nnîm* [37]*tu-ta-sí-ih nēbihka* [38]*elija ibašši* "see that that man is expelled (inf. G) from the district. If you have expelled (D) that man from the district, I will have an obligation towards you." (Strictly speaking this D form occurs in a subordinate clause, too, but one that is less backgrounding than the inf. in 35).

Here the contrast D versus G correlates with a contrast between the main verb and an infinitive in a peripheral constituent. Such instances suggest that there is a tendency to use D-stems mainly as part of the predicate, and that if the same D-stem is also needed elsewhere in the sentence, the neutral G-stem is deemed sufficient.[24]

A different situation is represented by the following passage:

(139A) ARM 26/1, p. 198 no. 55: 4ff *šaddagdim* (...) sila$_4$.gub.hi.a ^{6}*[h]arīpī ul ul-da* ^{7}*inanna* (...) ^{10}sila$_4$.gub *harīpī ul ul-la-da* "last year the ewes did not produce (G) autumn lambs (cf. *l.c.* p. 199 note c); now (...), the ewes are not going to produce (G) autumn lambs either";
(139B) *ib.* 19f *[ana m]uškênim* ^{20}[sila$_4$.gub *harī]pī ú-wa-li-da* "(...) but for the private citizens the ewes have produced (D) autumn lambs."

Here the D form can also be explained as foregrounding, since it probably emphasizes the contrast with the "zero production" expressed by the negated G forms in 6 and 10 (cf. Durand's note f on p. 199). A similar case is found for *šaṭāru* G and D, also in OB Mari:

(140A) ARM 26/2 p. 269 no. 405: r.19'f *ṭuppi awīlim u šumšu u pāṭ[erī] idišam šu-ṭe$_4$-ra-am-ma / ana ṣērija šūbilam* "write (D) a tablet listing (lit. of) each man by name and the men on leave individually, and send it to me";
(140B) *ib.* 24'f *ṭuppi awī[lim] u šumšu ul áš-ṭú-ur-ma / ana ṣēr bēlija ul ušābil[am]* "I did not write (G) a tablet listing each man by name and send it to my lord";
(140C) *ib.* 26'f *ṭuppi awīlim u šumšu u pāṭerī / idišam ú-ša-ṭà-ra-am ana ṣērija ušabbalam* "I will write (D) a tablet listing each man by name and the men on leave individually, and send it to my lord",

where we also find D in the affirmative sentences (140A) and (140C), versus G in the negative sentence (140B).[25] Negative sentences are in general backgrounding, since the only new information in them tends to be the negation itself; the rest of the sentence is presupposed (Givón 1979: 91ff).

In later texts, in particular in SB literary texts, we find some additional instances, but in such texts the interchange of D and G may also be stylistically motivated or completely random (cf. 6.9.2.2). Some cases worth considering are the following:

(141) RIMA 2/I, 154: 124ff "I captured (*ú-ṣab-bi-ta*) alive nine strong wild virile bulls with horns. (...); I drove four elephants into an ambush and captured (*aṣ-bat*) (them) alive. I captured (*aṣ-bat*) five (elephants) by means of a snare" (tr. Grayson); cf. also *ib.* 226: 35 (D: tigers(?)) vs. 33 (G: lions), where no difference in method is indicated.

(142) KAV 1: VII 1ff ^{1}*šumma lū a'īlu lū sinniltu* ^{2}*kišpī ú-up-pi-šu-ma* (...) ^{6}*mu-up-pi-ša-na ša kišpī* (...) ^{7}*a'īlu ša kišpī e-pa-a-ša ēmurūni* (...) "If either a man or a woman has practised (D) witchcraft (...); the man who practised (D) witchcraft (...); the man who saw the practising (G) of witchcraft (...).

(143A) Maqlû VII 2 *šī kaššaptu ú-nak-ka-ma kišpīša* "she, the sorceress, piles up (D) her sorceries" (var. *i-na-ak-ka-ma*, cf. (19) in 6.4.9);
(143B) *ib.* 6 *usappah kišpīki ša tak-ki-mi* "I will scatter the sorceries you have piled up (G)".

(144) Sg. 8: 262f *tabkāni rab(b)ûti ša* še.pad.meš *u* še.gig.meš *ša ina ūmē ma'dūti ana balāṭ māti u nišī iš-pu-ku qirâte / naphar ummānija ina sisê parê ibilê imērē ušazbilma ina qereb ušmannija kīma tillāni ú-šap-pak* "the large piles of barley and wheat, which he had been piling up (G) for a long time for the sustenance of the land and the people, I ordered my whole army to transport by means of horses, mules, camels and donkeys, and I piled them up (D) as high as hills in my camp."

(145A) Sg. Wi. 98: 14f *huršānī bērūti* (...) *ú-pat-ti(-i)-ma āmura durugšun* "I opened up (D) the mountain region (...) and saw its remotest sections" (tr. CAD sv *durgu* a);

(145B) Sg. Cyl. 10 (the king who) *huršānī bīrūti* (...) *ip-tu-ma ēmuru durugšun* "opened up (G) the mountain region and saw its remotest sections".

In (141) the context points to a contrast between D for capturing animals one by one, versus G for capturing them as a group after they have been entrapped. If this interpretation is correct, it is a prime example of the use of D for plural action, as examined in 6.6.3. The passages (142) - (145) show the phenomenon discussed above with regard to OB (cf. (134) - (138)), namely, that the D-stem is used in the main clause and replaced by a G-stem in the corresponding subordinate clause.

Another fact which suggests a foregrounding function for these forms in SB is the high frequency of D-stems of Type I in RIs to describe the exploits of the king. The king's actions are typically narrated in series of main verbs in the first or third person, the foregrounding character of which is often underlined by the emphasizing particle *lū* (GAG § 81f: for "Beteuerung").

Generally speaking, there is no ban on the use of D in backgrounding contexts; there are numerous instances of D-stems of Type I used in relative clauses, sentences with a negation, or peripheral constituents. The available evidence does no more than suggest that in such circumstances the tendency to use a marked category as the D-stem may have been less pronounced than in the predicate of a main clause. To what extent the tendency to restrict the use of D to foregrounding contexts also applies outside contexts in which D and G are in immediate opposition is difficult to determine.

Moreover, the tendency to restrict the use of D to foregrounding contexts (if there is such a tendency) is counteracted by the fact that in many contexts the use of D has become conventional or stereotyped; such a process causes any restriction on its use to be abandoned. This process plays an important role in the use of the D-stems of Type I, especially in literary texts, cf. 6.9.3 and 6.9.4.

6.10. Conclusions

We can draw the following conclusions from the findings of this chapter. First of all, the nature of the D-stem of Type I as a category seems to be reasonably clear. It is based on two fundamental characteristics: the association of the verbal D-stem with high transitivity and that of gemination in general with plurality and salience. The former restricts the use of the D-stems of Type I to sentences with a high degree of transitivity, i.e., those which have an agentive subject, a concrete and strongly affected object and refer to a salient action. In contrast to the G-stem - which, as the unmarked form, has a wider use - D is used optionally to underline the actual presence of the specific characteristics of high transitivity.

The second characteristic, the association of gemination with plurality and salience, connects the D-stem of Type I with other categories with gemination, such as the Gtn-stem, and the patterns *parras* and *purrus,* and ultimately with the original iconic force of gemination.

It explains the prominent use of D forms in sentences which contain a plural element, to underline various kinds of verbal plurality. In this area D competes with the Gtn-stem, which also serves to indicate verbal plurality, but without being associated with high transitivity.

On the other hand, if we consider the relationship between individual D-stems of Type I and the corresponding G-stems, we find that there is only a limited possibility of predicting if and how a D-stem will be used (cf. 6.1).

The overriding characteristic of the D-stems of Type I is that each one has its own range of use, which is largely unpredictable, idiosyncratic and dependent upon non-grammatical factors such as style, convention and individual preferences of speakers. It is mainly this fact which renders the D-stem of transitive verbs so problematic a category. A complete understanding of the circumstances in which a specific D-stem is used, and more in particular, of the reason why, in a given context, a G-stem is used in one instance, and a D-stem of the same verb in another instance which seems to be completely equivalent, remains beyond our grasp.

Many of the characteristics of the D-stems of Type I will also be found in the use of the adjectives of the pattern *purrus*, which are examined in Chapter X. This applies especially to the fact that these are also used to underline plurality, have a strong preference for salient entities as persons, body parts and large objects, and are highly stereotyped.

Notes to Chapter Six

1 In OB Mari, *ṣābum* is sometimes treated as a plural noun, cf. the remarks of CAD sv (p. 54f); cf. also ARM 14, 62: 6 *ṣa-bu-um lā ša-aṭ-ru-tum* "people who have not been registered", with a plural adjective, and 26/1 p. 308 no. 144: 16' *[aš]šum ṣa-bi šu-nu-ti* "concerning those people", with a plural pronoun.

2 For *ṣābum* see *gamāru* **9.**, *kamāsu* **1.**, *kaṣāru* **3.**, *laqātu* **1.**, *ṣabātu* **1.**, *šaṭāru* **2.**; for *amīlūtu*: *ṣabātu* **10.**; for *makkūru*: *kamāru* **1.**, *nakāmu* **1.**, *qarānu* **1.**; for *enūtu* or *unūtu*: *kanāku* **1.**, *rakāsu* **4.**, *ṣabātu* **5.**); for *luqūtu*: *ṣabātu* **5.**; for *mātu*: *abātu* **1.**, *eṣēru* **3.**, *kabāsu* **3.**, *kaṣāru* **3.**, *lâṭu* **1.** and **3.**, *palāšu* **4.**, *sahāpu* **1.**, *sapāhu* **1.**; for *ummānu*: *kamāru* **2.**, *kaṣāru* **3.**, *sapāhu* **1.**, *šebēru* **5.** (?); for *emūqu*: *gamāru* **9.**; for *puhru*: *sapāhu* **1.**

3 For barley, see *dâšu* **1.**, *kamāsu* **2.**, *kaṣāru* **1.**, *laqātu* **1.**, *napāṣu* **3.**, *qalāpu* **2.**, *sapāhu* **2.**, *šaṭāru* **4.**, *šebēru* **4.** Barley is often qualified by *purrus* adjectives, too, see 10.6.1.2.4; for reed see *haṣāṣu* **1.**, *retû* **2.**, *zaqāpu* **3.**; for metals in OA see *kanāku* **1.**, *paqādu* **1.**, *ṣabātu* **5.**, *šaqālu* **1.** ("to weigh"), *zarû*). For OA *purrus* forms qualifying metals, see 10.6.1.2.4.

4 D-stems for plurality found with *šīru* include *batāqu* **1.**, *edēhu* **2.**, *nakāsu* **1.**, *našāku* **1.**, and *qamû*.

5 For words denoting "everything" see *kabāsu* **7.**, *kaṣāru* **3.**, *laqātu* **1.**, *leqû*, *paqādu* **1.**, *rakāsu* **4.**, *šaqālu* **2.** (OA, cf. 6.6.3.1), *(w)alādu* **3.**; for generalizing relative sentences with *ša* and *mala*, see *abātu* **5.** (?, cf. 6.4.1.1 sv), *kabāsu* **1.**, *karātu* and *nakāsu* **2.** (SKS p. 104: 14f (text k) *ana na-ak-ku-si ša arkīk[i] / ana kur-ru-ti ša eqbī[ki]* "to slaughter those behind you, to cut to pieces those following you"). Singular nouns with generic reference as object of D-stems used for plurality include the instances of *awīlam* as object of *šaṭāru* in, for instance, ARM 14, 62: 15 lú *azzīmišu šu-uṭ-ṭe₄-ra-am-ma* "register (each) man according to

his quality" (cf. 6.8.1 sv); *manzāzu* "station(s) with *bašāmu* (Ee V 1: "to create a *manzāzu* for each of the gods", cf. also *zâzu* **3.**); *kadrû* "present, bribe" with *paqādu* **5.**, and *urigallu* "standard" with *zaqāpu* **2.** (AMT 44, 4: 5: "an *urigallu* in each direction").

6 GAG § 88f (cf. Gelb 1955: 110a); Furlani 1949: 60f; Ungnad-Matouš 1964: 75; Caplice 1980: 58; Edzard 1962: 112b.

7 See, for instance, in AHw ssvv. *batāqu, nakāsu, palāq/ku, paqādu, qiāšum, tabāku, walādu,* and in CAD ssvv *alādu, arāmu, hepû, katū* A, *nakāsu, qâšu, zabālu,* etc. For other verbs, however, in which the association of D with plurality is equally strong, this indication is lacking, e.g., in AHw sv *hepû* "to break", *petû* "to open", *retû* "to fix, fasten", *šebēru* "to break", etc.

8 Cf. Brockelmann 1908: 508; 1913: 141f; Wright 1896/98: I 31; Fleisch 1979: 288; Gesenius-Kautzsch 1985: 148; Joüon-Muraoka 1991: 155; Poebel 1939: 65ff (cf. 1.4).

9 In Group Ic only those verbs are included whose D-stems have a plural object in all attested cases. There are some other rare verbs which semantically belong to this group, whose D-stems are used (also) for other kinds of plurality, e.g., *baqāmu* "to pluck out, tear" (hair) (2x in a *šumma* clause, cf. 6.6.1.1 sv), *karāṣu* (1x pl. obj., 1x in a *šumma* clause, cf. 6.6.1.1 sv), *naqāru* "to tear down, scrape" (1x pl. obj., 1x in a *šumma* clause, cf. 6.6.1.1 sv) and *šagāšu* "to murder" (1x pl. obj., 2x participle, cf. 6.6.2 sv).

10 The following instances occur in the corpus: first, in literary texts: BWL 78: 136 (calf); IV R 25: II 22 (hand: both *nakāsu* **5.**; Ét. de Meyer 70: 33 (temple: *napālu* **4.**); KB 4, 80: III 5 (stela: *pašāṭu* **2.**) and MVAG 21, 80: 11 (person: *ṭabāhu* **3.**); second, in other kinds of SB texts (omens or ritual texts): TuL 74: 7 (tree: *batāqu* **6.**, but see 6.4.1.1 sv); AMT 105: 19 (worm: *hepû* **6.**) and Dreams 328: 7 (eye: *nasāhu* **5.**); third, in OB letters or administrative documents: StEb. 2, 49: 5 (garment: *šarāṭu* **4.**) and BM 96996: r.19 (sheep: *ṭabāhu* **3.**).

11 In OB letters and legal texts the objects of *paṭāru* G are often slaves or relatives of the sender or the addressee which are in prison because of debts or have been kidnapped (a slave in AbB 11, 119: 8; 130: 16'; KH r.IV 3; r.XXIII 96; a relative in AbB 1, 51: 26; 2, 46: 12. 18; 170: 15; 10, 144: 16; 176: 6; ARM 8, 77: 5. 9; a captured soldier in AbB 9, 32: 10; KH XI 18). Often ransom money is explicitly mentioned. However, the D-stem in this context is found in AbB 1, 13: 19 and CHJ 122: 17 "(Give me 5 shekels of silver) *amatka lu-pa-aṭ-ṭe-ra-ak-kum* "that I redeem your slave girl for you." Cf. also Horn Museum p. 127 no. 91: 4 with G "to redeem", with the price specified, versus p. 125 no. 89: 8 with D in the meaning "to release, to let go".

12 I.e., *šēpī-* + suffix or *šēp* + genitive, cf. GAG § 64l; *šēp-* can stand for the construct state of the dual here, cf. esp. AnSt. 33, 148: 13. 15 *še-pí-šu* vs. 18 *še-ep a-bi-šu*; it is unclear whether all cases of *šēp-* before a genitive as object of *našāqu* should be interpreted as a dual, but the dictionaries sv *našāqu* do not register an unambiguous singular form such as *šēpšu.*

13 *Qê ṣubbut* and *qû ṣabit* differ not only in whether *qû* is singular or plural, but also in their construction: the former is a "passive" stative with *qê* as adjunct acc. and the name of some part of the liver as subject; the latter is an "active" stative with *qû* as subject and a part of the liver as object (cf., e.g., YOS 10, 50: 14 *šumma še*$_{20}$*-pa-am qûm ṣa-bi-it*! (sign BI) "if a filament holds the 'foot mark'". The reason for this difference in construction is unclear to me.

14 A tentative explanation, anticipated in the translation of (36a) is that in (36A) *šīrum* refers to a specific piece of tissue as a countable object, whereas *šīram* in (36B) refers to a mass noun, an unspecified quantity of tissue. This would be parallel to the use of *ṣabit* and *ṣubbut* with the sg. and the pl. of *qû*,

respectively. A further parallel may be provided by the interchanging Gtn and G statives of *nadû* in YOS 10, 52: IV 20f *šumma appi ṣēlim ša imittim sūmam i-ta-du* "if the *appi ṣēlim* of the right is covered with red", versus *ib.* 23 *šumma ina rēš ṣēlim elîm sūmum na-di* "if a red spot lies on the top part of the upper rib". For the parallelism between the use of the stative D in general and the stative Gtn of *nadû*, see also (95) and (96) in 6.7.3.

15 Cf. AHw sv D 1; CAD sv *luludānītu* a reads *edih* against the traces on Gurney's copy.

16 This use of the present is very rare in protases of legal texts, because what is stated there typically precedes what is stated in the apodosis and must be completed before the latter (the sanction) can be realized. An example from the Codex of Hammurabi can be found in § 141 r.VII 33ff: "if a man's wife who lives in the house of the man has set her mind on leaving and (therefore) appropriates (*i-sà-ak-ki-il*) things, squanders (*ú-sà-ap-pa-ah*) her property and treats her husband badly (*ú-ša-am-ṭa*), (they shall prove her guilt and ......") (likewise § 143 r.VIII 6f), cf. Hirsch 1969: 121. Another instance is § 172 KH r.XIII 18 (*sahāmu* D). For the use of the present after *šumma* to denote intention or permission, cf. Hirsch 1969: 120ff.

17 For *bakû* cf. AHw sv G 2 vs. Gtn, CAD sv 4; for *galātu* cf. AHw sv G 1a, 2 vs. Gtn, CAD sv 1a/b/c), esp. CT 39, 44: 10 (pret. G) versus *ib.* 11 (pres. Gtn); for *maqātu* cf. CAD sv 1b and elsewhere (G) vs. 2 and elsewhere (Gtn); for *šasû* cf. AHw sv G 1/2 vs. Gtn 1-5, CAD sv 1 (G) versus 9 (Gtn) passim (note esp. Sumer 34 Arab. sect. 43: 7 with a pres. Gtn, vs. pret. G passim, but *ib.* 42: 5 has a present G with a negation); for *(w)aṣû* cf. AHw sv G II 5b vs. Gtn 4 (note esp. ÖB 2, 66: 61 (pres. Gtn) vs. 65/6 passim (pret. G)).

18 We can distinguish two groups: first, those referring to persons and animals: *mude/akkû* "instigator" (*dekû*, cf. G: *dēkû* "summoner (very common), night watchman (LL)), *mudiṣṣu* "deceiver" (*dâṣu*, cf. *dā'iṣu* "arrogant" acc. to CAD sv (LL); rather an agent noun?), *mugammiru* "arresting officer" (*gamāru* **9.**), *mugammertu* (a poetic word for "see") (*gamāru* **10.**), *munambû* "wailer" (*nabû*), *munappihu* "rumour-monger" (*napāhu* **2.**), *munêrtu* "murderess" (*nêru*), *mupaqqirānu* "claimant" (*baqāru*, 1x for *b/pāqirānu*), *mupašširu* 1) person who processes textiles) (*pašāru* **5.**), 2) as adj. (herb) "dispelling" (witchcraft) (*pašāru* **2.**), *muppiš(ān)u* "practitioner of sorcery" (*epēšu* **4.**, also *ēpišu*), *muqallû* "seller of roast barley" (*qalû*), *muqippu* "guarantor" acc. to CAD sv, "Zuverlässigkeitszeuge?" acc. to AHw sv *qiāpu(m)*, cf. *qā'ipu* "creditor"), *muṣappiu* "dyer" (*ṣap/bû*), cf. *ṣāp/bû* "id.".

Second, those used as instrument nouns (1x as adjective): *mubeššu* (or *mube''išu*) "stirrer" (*be'āšu*), *mukattimtu*, a poetic word for "door" (*katāmu* **9.**, also *kātimtu*, cf. CAD sv *kātimtu* 2), *mulappitu* (a tool) (*lapātu* **5.**), *munappih(t)u* "bellows" (*napāhu* **2.**), *munaqqîtu* "libation bowl" (*naqû* **1.**), *musahhiptu* "net for gazelle hunting" (*sahāpu* **3.**, cf. part. G with "net" ZA 71, 61: 2'), *musahhištu*, adj. qualifying a net (*huhāru*) (*sahāšu*, cf. part. G with *huhāru* ZA 71, 61: 3'), *musallihtu* "sprinkling vessel" (*salāh/'u* **4.**), *mussipu* "scoop" (*esēpu*), *mušappiktu* "pitcher" (*šapāku* **3.**), *mušaqqiltu* "balance" (*šaqālu* **1.**).

19 It is possible that this provides an explanation for the use of the present D, as opposed to other verb forms in the G-stem, of the verbs *qâšu* "to grant, donate", *zâzu* "to divide, distribute" and of the expression *(w)arkata parāsu* "to investigate a matter" in MSL 1 (*Ana ittišu*). There we find the present D of *parāsu* (MSL 1, 80: 33f) alternating with the inf., pret. and stative G (*ib.* 81: 35/38; 93: 36f), all with obj. *arkassu*. A similar contrast is found between the present D and the pret. G of *zâzu* "to divide, distribute": MSL 1, 4: 39 [in.na.a]n.ba.e = *ú-za-as-su* "he will apportion to him" (no obj., no context), versus pret. G [in.na.a]n.ba = *i-zu-us-su* in 3: 36, and between the present D and the pret. G of *qâšu* "to give": MSL 1, 4: 38 [in.na.a]n.ba.e = *ú-qa-as-su*, contrasting with pret. G in 3: 35 [in.na.a]n.ba = *i-qí-is-su* "he gave to him". In all three cases the D form does not agree with the normal use of the D-stems in question (plurality of the object in *qâšu*,

of the indirect object in SB *zâzu*; D forms of the expression *(w)arkata parāsu* are very unusual, cf. 6.4.1.1 sv *parāsu*). A (very tentative) explanation might be that the author of *Ana ittišu* uses these D forms in order to underline that the clause does not refer to a specific occasion which occurred in the past, but to a potential action in some unspecified moment in the future, cf. the parallel contrast between *iššuk* and *unaššak* in (50) in 6.6.1.

20 Nor from other periods, except a single NA instance, quoted by CAD sv *nikkassu* A 1i: ABL 347: 10 níg.šid-*ja issi ṭupšarrē lup-pi-šu* "Let them do my accounting with the scribes". If this is not an example of the indiscriminate use of *epēsu* G and D which is typical of MA and NA (see App. sv **7**.), it may be another case of D with a plural subject ("they together with the scribes").

21 The remaining instances listed in AHw are UM 1/2, 72: 26, which is typologically related to a *šumma*-clause; *ib.* 58: 11 (context broken), and LSC 110f *sup(p)ē aṣ-ṣa-bat/ba-at* (which is more likely to be a perfect G). Not considered is the barbaric form *ti-iṣ-na-bat* from Ugarit (PRU 4, 226 b 9).

22 This use of *šaṭāru* D is exactly parallel to *lapātu* D in OA, cf. AHw 536a sv D 4 "schreiben an". Von Soden, GAG[2] § 88f, points to the similarity with the Arabic Stem III (e.g., *kātaba* "to write to"), but thinks it improbable that the OA form reflects **lāputum* rather than *lapputum*. The existence of OB *šuṭṭuru* with the same meaning and an unambiguous geminate proves that he is right.

23 This idiomatic use of *šaṭāru* may explain some exceptional instances of other D-stems in OB Mari, namely, of *kanāku* "to seal" and *ṣabātu* "to seize": ARM 26/2 p. 420 no. 483: 38f *[i]n[ann]a [šapi]rtam ú-ka-na-k[a-am-ma] ana [ṣēriš]u ašapparam* "now, I will seal a message and send it to him" and *ib.* p. 227 no. 394: 6ff *aššum ina ṭuppim wu''urtum ana šaṭārim lā imiddu rēš awātimma ú-ṣa-ab-bi-tam-ma ana bēli<ja> ašpu[r]am* "In order that the report does not become too long to write on a tablet, I have summarized the essence of its contents and sent it to my lord". Since elsewhere *kanāku* D is only used with a plural object, or a mass noun or building as object (cf. 6.4.3.1 sv), and *ṣabātu* D mainly with a plural object (cf. 6.4.4.1 sv), these irregular instances may be caused by analogy with *šaṭāru* D in its combination with *šūbulu*.

24 This tendency does not apply to the paronomastic infinitive: cf. YOS 11, 20: 10f (*hanāqu*); TCL 17, 59: 20 (*harāmu*); ARM 13, 44: 9 = (78) (*nasāqu*); 6, 43: 27 (= 81) (*sanāqu*).

25 A similar but rather puzzling case is ARM 26/2 p. 274/5 no. 408: 6 with G in a negative sentence, whereas in the corresponding affirmative sentences D is used in 13, but G in 39. Is the use of D in 13 caused by its exceptionally long object (cf. 6.7.2)?

APPENDIX TO CHAPTER SIX: Transitive verbs with a D-stem of Type I

This appendix contains the corpus of transitive verbs with a D-stem of Type I (those which have the same valency as the G-stem, cf. 5.2) on which the discussion of these D-stems in Chapter VI is based.

In principle, this list contains all instances of the verbs in question which are listed in the dictionaries; in addition, it contains instances from most text editions published after their appearance. However, for reasons of space I have chosen not to list all instances of frequent D-stems which are used in a more or less uniform way; for these D-stems the reader is referred to the dictionaries.

Since this is a grammatical study of the D-stem as a whole, not a lexical study of individual D-stems, this corpus basically comprises only instances whose interpretation is uncontroversial. Accordingly, the following cases have been omitted: those which are (partly) broken and cannot be restored with certainty; those whose interpretation is doubtful or controversial; those which cannot be assigned with certainty to a specific verb (such as *nuppušu* of textiles, and cases as MDP 14, 51: 12 and 56: 20 *ú-na-aš-šà-AG*:

from *našāqu* (CAD sv 3c) or *našāku* (AHw sv D 2)?; and those of which it cannot be ascertained that G and D belong together (cf. 6.1), including all cases in which the meaning of either one is uncertain. Partly broken passages which can be restored are quoted only if no unbroken parallels are available.

Moreover, instances from peripheral Akkadian (El-Amarna, Boğazköy, Nuzi, Ugarit, Alalakh, Emar) have also been omitted, except for some literary texts, which appear to be trustworthy copies of "normal" Akkadian and do not share the anomalies typical of a large part of the letters and administrative documents found in these places.

Verbs which are used as both transitives and intransitives because they can denote a process as well as an action, such as *emēdu* "to lean on/against" and *hamāṭu* "to burn" (the "factitive G-stems", cf. 11.4.2) are discussed in Chapters VII and XI, and are not listed here. Instances from LL have been omitted unless they are in some respect remarkable; this applies in particular to the verb forms of V R 45, a list of D and Š forms which are quoted without meaning or context, and are therefore useless for determining the function of the D-stem.

The indications of dialect and period generally follow the traditional classification as used in CAD and AHw. Since, however, for our purpose genre is more important than chronological or geographical factors, the range of the literary idiom (SB) has been somewhat extended. It includes, first, all royal inscriptions from Tukulti-Ninurta I onwards, also those dating date from Neo-Babylonian or later times, and, second, literary texts originating from Neo-Assyrian sources (such as those of SAA 3), even though they are strongly interspersed with Assyrianisms. Moreover, NB and LB have been combined into NB, since there are hardly any grammatical differences between them (cf. Streck, *Zahl und Zeit* p. xxvi).

A difficult point are the statives and VAs of many of the verbs listed here. Some of these occur in sentences or word groups which are transformations of transitive sentences with a verbal D-stem. Thus they belong to the verbal paradigm of the D-stem and are listed here together with the other forms of that paradigm. Other statives and VAs have some specialized meaning which differs from that of the D-stem, and are thus to some extent independent of it. Accordingly, they cause many deviations from what can be defined as the regular use of the verbal D-stem (see 5.1.1 for the status of the stative/VA). Such statives and verbal adjectives will be listed in Chapter X, which deals with the pattern *purrus*. The distinction between the two kinds, however, is far from clear-cut, so that the classification of some cases may be disputable.

The entries consist of the references of the D-stem in question, arranged according to meaning, and the direct objects with which it is attested. Further specifications may also be given, if these are relevant for the argument. Explicitly indicated are a Dt- or Dtn-stem, a stative (stat.), a participle (part.), and a verbal adjective (VA). There are also references to the context in which the form occurs: "prot." for a conditional clause (protasis) introduced by *šumma*, and "non-ag." for sentences with a non-agentive subject (cf. 5.6.4). For other abbreviations used in this Appendix see the list of Abbreviations on p. 451.

References marked with an asterisk are quoted in full in the presentation of the verb in the specified section. A number in brackets (00) refers to the numbered passages which are also quoted in full somewhere in Chapter VI. Note that in this Appendix, just as in the text of this chapter, "plural" includes dual, and that "plural object" also comprises plurality of the subject of passive Dt forms and of statives which require a passive translation, and plurality of nouns in the genitive which follow a participle.

A

Abāku A "to send, lead, dispatch", D "to drive away" → 5.6.2.1 and 6.8.1 sv *ṭarādu*, **SB** apod.: ACh. Šam. 9: 48 // Spl. Šam. 31: 59 (king from throne).

Abāku B "to overturn, uproot", D 2x + pl. obj. (6.4.1 group Ic): **SB** apod: ACh. Sin 35: 43 (houses); ACh. Adad 2: 16; 18: 11 (trees). [Atr. 94: 26; 124: 22 unclear].

Abātu "to destroy, ruin", D mostly + pl. obj. (group Ia) → 6.4.1.1 sv, **SB** (unless indicated otherwise):
1. places, regions (*dadmū*), moutain(s), city/cities, embankment(s), fields: passim in SB, cf. CAD sv *a.* A 2c/e, 3; AHw sv D 1, Dt 1, often part., cf. St.Or. 7, 4 and 6.9.3;
2. (parts of) buildings: wall(s), houses, temple, *gigunû* (temple tower), ziggurat, foundation platform, etc, passim in SB, cf. CAD sv *a.* A 2a; AHw sv D 1, Dt 1;
3. persons, mostly part., cf. St.Or. 7, 4 and 6.9.3: RA 86, 5: IV 12 (OB); RIMA 2/I, 194: 8; Ee VI 154; ABRT 1, 59b: 9; Maqlû I 112; PSBA 20, 156: 16; Iraq 56: 38: r.5'; other cases (sg.): Maqlû III 110 = (118); *KAR 350: 19 (stat.);
4. body (parts): RA 41, 41: 7 ("the whole body", part.); SBH 79: 8; ZA 16, 158: II 1 (limbs); AfO 25, 39: 43 (*lānu* "figure"); KAR 226: I 5 (*bunnannû* "appearance"); LKA 160: 8 (flesh, Dt, prot.);
5. boundary stone, **MB/SB**: Sumer 36 Arab sect. 129: 25; BBS 4: III 4; 7: II 11; 8 p. 48: 4; 9: V 2; RA 16, 129: 25; BBS 10: r.36; *34: 13 (date unknown) (all sg. obj.);
6. remainder: Maqlû II 141 (wood and stone, part.).

Agāru "to hire, rent" worker(s) (sg. and pl.), D not disc., **OA**: TC 3, 246A: 8; BIN 4, 98: 9 (both pl. obj.); TC 3, 265: 17 (no overt object); OIP 27, 50: r.5' (sg. obj.).

Ahāzu "to take, marry, learn", D 1x + pl. obj. (6.4.7 group VIIc), also → 5.6.2.1: **MA** "to marry": AfO 17, 272: 22 [(women ...) *ša*] *kīdānu ah-hu-za-a-ni* "who are married to outsiders"; cf. G + sg. obj. in KAV 1: VI 74f *aššassu ša ana kīdi ah-zu-tu-ú-ni* "his wife who was married to an outsider". Elsewhere *ahāzu* "to marry" is always G (with pl. obj.: KH r.XI 53; SAA 10, 226: 18). For *uhhuzu* "to mount" (an object in precious materials) → 8.3.3 and 8.4.2.

Alātu "to swallow", D mostly + pl. obj. (6.4.1 group Ib), **SB** med.: AMT 45, 5: r.6; 68, 3: II 5 + 50, 2: 4 + 27, 2: 4; BAM 159: II 15; BKBM 16: 22; 22: 16; RA 40, 114: 18 (pills); AMT 80, 1: 12 (liquid: *mêšu ú-al-lat*, cf. LKA 136: r.4 *mêšu i-al-lut*); BAM 575: II 8 (garlic in very small pieces (pl. tantum)); BKBM 30: 43 = (09) and (89) (no overt object). G is used with sg. obj, except RA 65, 71: 16'f (OB, "active" stative in metaphorical meaning).

Anāhu "to sing" (thus CAD sv *a.* B) or "seufzen" (AHw sv *a.* II), D 1x + pl. obj. (not disc.), **SB**: Ištar/Dumuzi 57: 19 (*inhu*-songs); for Dt "to produce a moaning(?) sound" → 7.6.1.

Apālu "to pay, satisfy", D + pl. obj. → 6.4.7.1 sv (group VIIb), **OB**: VAB 5, 62: 14; Iraq 25, 178: 7; TCL 1, 195: 14 = (135), all with obj. *hu-bu-li-*.... "debt(s)"; *TSifr. 37a: 11 (*ahiātu* "additional costs").

Arāmu "to cover" → *(h)arāmu.*

B

Balālu "to mix, brew (beer), alloy (metal), sprinkle (with oil, wine, beer)", D:
1. "to mix", mostly + pl. obj. (6.4.5 group Va), **OB**: Atr. 58: 212 (god and man, Dt); Sumer 13, 113A: 4 (two ingredients for beer); AbB 1, 9: 31 (two kinds of barley, Dt); **MB**: ZA 45, 200: 13 (hair and nail parings with clay); **SB**: LKA 85: r.9 // KAR 267: 18 acc. to Von Soden, ZA 43, 269 (clay and wax); IV R 14 no. 2: r.17 (copper and tin, part.); CT 17, 32: 17 (magic with spittle, stat.); with a substance as obj., **OB**: Atr. 58: 211. 226 = (134A) (clay);
2. idiomatic: "to pour over, stain, pollute" with dust, tears, excrement, etc. → 6.8.1: (pers. obj., unless stated otherwise), a) with excrement, **OB**: MSL 12, 201: I 5 (stat.); **SB**: OEC 6, 45: 19 (stat.); BWL 44: 107 (Dt); BA 10, 44: 6 (obj. broken); b) with semen CT 39, 44; 9; 45: 26 (stat.); c) with tears AfO 19, 52: 145 (stat.); SpTU 3, 76: 18 = (126) (stat.); d) rest: RA 62, 125: 17 (garment with vomit); Lugal 263 (Dt, mace with dust); AfO 18, 74f: 16'/21' (hand, substance unspecified, stat.); for stat. *bullul* said of arms → 10.6.1.2.2.

Baqām/nu "to pluck, tear out" (hair), D → 6.6.1.1 sv, **SB** prot.: TDP 124: 23; 236: 38 (hair); for adj. *buqqumu* → 10.3.2 and 10.6.2.

Baqāru (*paqāru*) "to claim, vindicate", D not disc.: **OB**: AbB 1, 58: 16 (stat.); 12, 166: 13; VAB 5, 280: 49; **MB**: BE 14, 168: 16; ASJ 12, 181: r.6'; **NB**: BBS 36: VI 37; VS 1, 70: II 1. 7; BE 8, 3: 28; UET 4, 192: 4; SpTU 2, 55: r.28; TCL 12, 14: 18; part. *mupaqqirānu* Nbk. 100: 6.

Barāmu "to seal", D 1x + pl. obj. (6.4.3 group IIIc): **SB**: Iraq 22, 222: 18f (tongues and openings (*bābu*)).

Bâru (CAD *ba'āru*) "to catch, hunt", D not disc., no finite forms; but note **SB** LL: MSL 17, 224: 133/5 tag = *ba-a-rum* / (...) / tag.tag = *bu-'u-u-rum*.

Baṣāru "to tear off, tear apart" (LL only), D not disc., cf. **SB** LL: MSL 17, 186: 161f KA^ZU^.ku_5.ru = *ba-ṣa-rum* / KA^ZU^.ku_5.ku_5.ru = *bu-uṣ-ṣu-rum*; further:

1. persons and body parts, **OB**: YOS 11, 26: I 3 (neck and claws); **SB**: Maqlû VIII 87 (pers.); *ib.* 88 (*šīrēki* "your flesh"); SAA 12, 26: r.31; 31: r.31 (corpse); ZA 45, 14: II 7 (breast);
2. garlic, **OB**: A 3528: 20 qu. CAD sv 2 ("to pick off").

Bašāmu "to build, create", D + pl. obj. (6.4.6 group VIb): **SB**: Ash. § 53 r.38 (images); Sn. 109: 7; 122: 26 (bronze castings); Ee V 67 (rites); KB 6/1, 42: 2 (the firmament (pl. tantum)); Ee V 1 (*manzāza* "a position", i.e., one for each of the gods, cf. 6.3). G is found with sg. and pl. obj., cf. CAD sv 1/2. .

Batāqu "to cut off, pierce (dykes), break", D almost always + pl. obj. → 6.4.1.1 sv (group Ia):

1. body parts, **MA**: AfO 17, 286: 101 (feet); **SB**: RIMA 2/I, 201: 117 (several limbs); 211: 115; 260: 82 (arms (*kappu*)); 266: 14'f (tongues, necks); 200: 92 (flesh); Ee IV 102 (intestines); SpTU 4, 121: IV 8 (fingers); IAsb. 88b: 3 (tendons); JSOR 6, 119: obv.! 8' (heads); **NA**: SAA 2 p. 57: 627 (arms+feet);
2. with pers. obj. (pl.) "to cut to pieces, mutilate", **SB**: IV R 61b: 47; **NA**: SAA 11, 144: I 5' (stat.);
3. with other obj., **OB**: Gilg. JNES 16, 256: r.21 (trees); **SB**: Gilg. XI 275 (stones); RA 18, 166: 15 (pieces of clothing, stat.); Sg. Wi. 122: 128 (causeways); SAA 3, 15: 2. 4 (ropes, stat.); **NB**: Nbn 368: 15 (hides: "damaged"); **NA**: ABL 633: r.19f (rings); often with *butuqātu* "breaches", **OB**: YOS 10, 46: IV 46; 26: III 29 (Dt); *RA 65, 74: 74' (Dt); **SB**: ACh. Sin 35: 46; SAA 8, 250: r.7;
4. of water(ways), **OB**: YOS 10, 18: 67; **MB**: BBS 6: I 19 (*mašqû* "((access to) watering places, stat.); **SB**: CT 20, 13: r.3. 5 (*mê*);
5. with abstract obj., **MA**: JCS 7, 135 no. 62: 26 (*bit*[*qū'a*] "allegations against me", stat., cf. CAD sv *bitqu* 4a).
6. with sg. obj. → 6.4.1: **OB**: AbB 1, 27: 28 = (22) (person, non-ag.); **SB**: *TuL 74: 7 (tree).

Be'āšu (CAD **be'ēšu*, AHw sv *bêšu* D 2 (retracted 1547b sv *behāšu*) "to stir" (ingredients in a bowl), D → 6.9.2.1, **MA/SB**: Or. 17, 300: 13; 301f: 4. 17. 21. 23; 18, 408: 5 (cf. G in 3); KAR 188: 11; also part. *mubeššu, mube"išu* "stirrer" (cf. CAD sv), cf. 6.6.2 with note 18.

D

Da'āpu "to press, knock over", D not disc., **SB**: Erra I 140 (jewelry, Dt); **NA**: SAA 10, 322: r.12 (*nahnāhatu* "the cartilage" (of the nose)).

Dabābu "to speak, say", D: "to complain, harass, entreat", with pers. obj. → 5.5.3, or intrans. → 7.6.1.

Dakāšu "to pierce, sting" (CAD sv), or "etwa 'auftreiben, ausbeulen'" (AHw sv), D not disc., 1x **SB** prot.: KAR 182: 31 (pers., non-ag.).

Dâku "to kill, beat", D not disc., 2x **SB**: SBH 54: r. 8. 11 part. fem. *mu-di-ik-ti šadî*, alternating with *dā'ik šadî* "killer in the mountains", cf. CAD sv *dâku* lex. sect.

Dalāhu "to stir up, disturb", D not disc.:

1. **OB**: Syr. 19, 120 top (*mātam*, cf. G + *mātam* MARI 5, 213: 5'; ARM 13, 146: 6; 26/2 p. 68 no. 310: 28;

SB: Ee I 108 (sea, // G, cf. CAD sv 1a); BL 194: 13; SBH 27: r.7 // 54: 2; p. 151 no. 24: r.27 (face by tears, all stat); 37: 15 (pers. by storm, stat.); and stat. with personal subject beside *dalih* "afflicted, disturbed" (cf. (54) in 10.8), cf. CAD sv 3a, AHw sv D 3a;

2. "to hurry" (in hendiadys, also G, cf. 7.4.1), **OB**: RA 46, 94: 67 // **SB**: *ib.* 30: 20; SAA 3, 4: r.II 10'; **NA**: ABL 1149: 6.

Dânu "to judge, to start a lawsuit", D 2x + pl. obj. (not disc.), **OB**: AbB 11, 69: r.3' (*dīnātim* "lawsuits"); RÉS 1937, 106 (*dīnī* id.).

Darāsu "to trample, oppress", D in **OB** letters: "to chase away, to scare off" (pers.) → 6.8.4: AbB 4, 23: 19. 33; 5, 249: 6'; 13, 119: 9; 149: 11f; AoF 10, 63 no. 10: 5'.

Dâṣu "to treat with injustice, deceive", D not disc., **OB**: AbB 5, 41: 16 (pers.); 6, 188: 39' (pers.); **SB**: part. *mudiṣṣu* LL "deceiver" (CAD sv), "streitsüchtig ?" (AHw sv) → 6.6.2 with note 18.

Dâšu "to thresh, trample", D + pl. obj. (often coll. and mass nouns) (6.4.2 group IIa):

1. lit. in **OB** Mari: ARM 27, 92: r.2'; 94: 16 (threshing floors, cf. also 26: 37 (obj. restored)); 38: r.8'; 39: r.15'; 41: 14 (barley, cf. also 38: r.2'. r.4' (obj. restored)); 37: 33. 45 (field(s); 39: 20'f (work assignment (<u>áš.gàr</u>, *iškaru*)); FM 2 p. 34f no. 10: 14 (no object); 42 (threshing floors, stat.);

2. metaph. in **SB**: Sn. 47: 29 (bodies); AAA 19, 108: 6 (criminals, part.); RIMA 2/I, 147: 12 (id.); Or. 36, 116: 10 (enemies) → 6.9.3.

The use of D in **1.** is remarkable, since everywhere else G is used in the literal meaning of *dâšu*, cf. CAD sv 1, AHw sv *diāšum* G 1, and D only in a metaphorical sense (**2.**). It may be caused by fact that the letters deal with large quantities of agricultural workers, plough teams and produce.

Dekû "to move (tr.), lift up, summon, collect", D "to instigate, prompt" → 6.8.3, **OB**: AbB 9, 192: 8; 10, 170: 14; 12, 3: 5; AoF 10, 59 no. 7: 15 (*ramānka* "yourself"); **MB**: AfO 10, 5: 10; **NB**: ABL 328: 11 (all pers. obj.); part. **MB** *mude/akkû* "instigator" CAD sv, "etwa "Unruhestifter"" AHw sv → 6.6.2 with note 18.

E

Edēhu "to cover with patches", D → 6.5.3 sv:

1. **SB**: KAR 26: r.22 (obj. torches);

2. stative with a pl. adjunct acc., mostly in omens, said of parts of the liver, **OB**: YOS 31: IV 41 (with veins); RA 65, 73: 29'f; ZA 57, 128: 3 (with red or white *kasû*-seeds); with mass nouns: YOS 10, 24: 35 = (36B); 26: IV 10 (both + *šīram*); MDP 57, p. 167: 30 (+ *mēdehti ša urqi* "patches of green"); **SB**: BKBM 54: 4 (with green threads); elsewhere, said of stones: STT 108: 15. 22 = (37).

Edēlu "to close", D mostly + pl. obj. → 6.4.3.1 sv (group IIIb):

1. doors and gates, **OB**: Bab. 12, 11: 10 (stat.); ZA 43, 306: 4 // RA 32, 180: 4 (stat.); **SB**: EG 91: 16 (stat.); Sn. 41: 19; Asb. A III 108;

2. metaphorically, affairs, **OB**: ARM 26/1 p. 312 no. 148: r.2' (obj. *awātim*, cf. n. c);

3. exc. sg., **SB**: SKS p. 42: 45 = (05) and (127) (door, stat., see 6.9.4); *Racc. 92: r.9; 93: 14; 119: 13 (door).

Edēpu "to blow into, inflate", D **SB** "to blow away/down, to damage by blowing" → 6.8.1 sv:

1. lit.: *MSL 16, 275: 26'; *ACh. Šam. 1: III 35 (Dt, prot., subj. storm); AMT 11, 1: IV 31 (stat.); KAR 195: r.24/7 (woman, stat.);

2. with pers. obj.: SAA 3, 32: r.21 (pers., non-ag.); SKT 2, 1: 10 *mu-dip gērî* ("(his) adversaries").

Edēqu "to cloth, cover", D not disc., **SB**: VAB 4, 276: 27 (statue); Ee I 68 (splendour, Dt → 10.1.2 sv).

E'ēlu "to hang up, bind", D + pl. obj. → 6.4.3.1 sv (group IIIb):

1. with concrete obj., **OA**: TC 3, 51: 25. 27 (donkeys); **SB**: RIMA 2/I, 201: 118; 248: 86 (severed heads);

2. agreements (cf. *rakāsu*), **NB**: YOS 6, 78: 18 (*ú-il-tim*.<u>meš</u> "agreements");

3. metaph.: stative + Dt in **SB** omens, said of fluids, CAD sv 4c "to coagulate (?)", AHw sv D 3/Dt "zusammengelaufen sein/zus. laufen", stative: CT 39, 14: 9f; 16: 42. 49f (= DA 59: 4); Dt: CT 39, 14: 11f; 15: 33; 16: 41 → 9.1.4. [KAJ 104: 4 read *ṭuppušu ... ú-<še>-e-lu-ni* acc. to CAD sv *bābu* A 1c 4-a')].

Egēru "to twist", D + pl. obj. (6.4.2 group IIb), **SB**: AJSL 35, 141b: 15 (feet); Maqlû II 92; V 96 (figurines). Comparable instances of G have a sg. obj., cf. AHw sv G 1.

Ekēku (*egēgu*) "to scratch", D **SB** med.:

1. prot. → 6.6.1.1 sv: AfO 11, 222 no. 2: 4 (temple); 223: 47ff (ear(s)); AMT 74, 2: 32. 34 (foot and/or testicle, implied); Or. 14, 255: 7ff // CT 40, 32: 3f (an ox the ground);

2. rest: AMT 101, 3: 8. 12 ("to scratch *over* sth", intrans.).

Ekēmu "to take away", D 1x + pl. obj. (6.4.4 group IVc): **SB**: RIMA 1, 235: III 25 (persons). G passim with sg. and pl. obj., cf. CAD and AHw sv. For adj. *ukkumu* → note 4 to Ch. X.

Elēhu "to sprinkle", D **SB** (unless indicated otherwise): **1.** lit.: KAR 202: I 27 (herbs);

2. idiomatic: "to decorate" → 6.8.3: TIM 9, 65: 11 // 66: 22 (snake) *ú-lu-ha-am šarātim* "dotted with hairs" (OB); UM 1/2, 121: r.10; AMT 44, 4: 7 (reed posts); K.3268+6033 qu. CAD sv 2b (torches); RA 11, 149: 41 (the appearance of a god); mostly stative: BagF. 18, 133: 76 (torch); ArOr 21, 376: 49 (a god); AGH 152b: 3; KAR 109: 15 (a goddess). [TBP 23: 3f uncert.].

Epēšu "to make, do", D mainly lexicalized and idiomatic → 6.8.3:

1. "to calculate" (mainly **OB**) → AHw sv D 1, CAD sv 4f-4'; also MARI 5, 605: 2; ARM 26/1, p. 162 no. 29: r.16'; 27, 100: 23 (obj. *nikkassī* "accounts") = (91); 102: 14; OBTR 314: 40; CT 48, 104: 8;

2. "to copy (a tablet)", mainly **SB** → AHw sv D 3b, CAD sv 4f-5';

3. "to conclude a sales agreement" in **MA/NA**, → CAD sv 4a, AHw sv D 4 "erwerben";

4. "to practise witchcraft", **MA**: KAV 1: VII 2ff = (142); **SB**: *muppiš(ān)u* "sorcerer", beside *ēpišu* and *mušēpišu*, all with the corresponding fem. forms, cf. CAD ssvv; normally G, cf. CAD sv 2f-1', 2c *ipšu* b', *kišpū*;

5. with pl. subj. → 6.5.1, **MA**: RIMA 1, 101: 8 = (25); **NA**: ABL 511: 18 = (26);

6. with pl. obj. → 6.4.8 sv, **OA**: CCT 6, 22a: 8 (bundles); KTS 57c: 11 (objects); EL 325a: 9; BIN 4, 83: 16 (matters);

7. In **MA/NA** D is used as an occasional variant of G: in the meaning "to treat (a person)" KAJ 2: 12; 6: 16; KB 6/1, 82: 38 (cf. G: CAD sv 2a-1'); in combination with *nikkassu* (ABL 347: 10, qu. in note 20), *ardūta, pīhatūta, šarrūta, bēlūta, qarābu,* and *kišpū* (*ib.* sv 2c vs. 4b, see **4.** above), without object BagF. 16, 247: 6'; and in some other idioms.

Erēšu A "to ask", D not disc., 1x **MA**: KAV 1: VIII 9 (a woman, Dt), cf. AHw sv *urrušu* II.

Erēšu B "to seed, cultivate, D not disc., 1x **SB**: Racc. 134: 241 (part. + *mēreštu*, a plantation).

Esēhu "to assign", D 1x + pl. obj. (6.4.7 group VIIc): **MB**: UM 1/2, 63: 18, with D + pl. obj ↔ G + sg. obj.: *annâtīma tāmirāti nadâti luṣbatma lu-us-si-ih* / *ammīni annâ harra aṣabbatma es-si-ih* "Shall I start to administer (lit. assign) (D) these neglected irrigation districts? Why should I start to administer (G) this *harru*-region?" (tr. partly from CAD sv *harru* A s. 1a). In OB only G is found; for G in MB cf. CAD sv 1c-3'; in Mari *esēku* (G and D) is used instead, cf. CAD note sv on p. 329b.

Esēku "to assign" (variant of *esēhu*), D not disc.:

1. in **OB** Mari (fields and people (*ṣābu*)) ARM 1, 42: 25 (stat.); 4, 39: 7; 5, 85: 7;

2. in **MA/NA** passim (G not attested), cf. CAD sv *esēhu* 2b, AHw sv *esēku* D 3, and cf. *ussuqu* in 8.4.2.

Esēpu "to collect, scrape together", D not disc., **SB**: SAA 3, 32: r.31 (earth); MSL 1, 53: 27 (no overt obj.); part. *mussipu* "a scoop" → 6.6.2 with note 18, **MA**: AfO 18, 308: 23; Or. 17, 304: 21.

Esēru A "to put under pressure", D not disc., cf. 6.8.4 and 6.9.1.1, **OB**: AbB 3, 2: 24; 6, 219: 16. 30; 7, 139: 13'; ARM 14, 64: r.4'; 26/2 p. 348 no. 438: 25' (all with pers. obj.); AbB 12, 72: 29 (in hendiadys); **OA**: Gol. 15: 10 (pers.); **SB**: MSL 1, 36: 56 (entrusted goods: "to collect").

Esēru B "to shut in, enclose", D not disc., cf. 6.8.4, only in omen apodoses, **OB**: YOS 10, 46: IV 21 (king); 47: 9 (id.); YOS 10, 24: 29 (army); YOS 10, 11: II 8 (country, Dt); RA 65, 71: 22' (id.); *ib.* 73: 50' (country and residence); **SB**: CT 20, 26: 16; 31, 12: obv.! II 15; Izbu 109: 73' (all pers.); CT 20, 35: 8 (land); Izbu 147: 59' (land, Dt) and passim in SB → AHw sv Dt, and SAA 8, 318b glossary sv.

Eṣēlu "to paralyze", D 2x + pl. obj. (6.4.2 group IIc): **SB**: Šurpu VII 24 (hands); KAR 80: r.28 (arms); for *uss/ṣṣulu* and Dt *utass/ṣṣalu* → 9.1.4 sv. G is hardly attested, cf. CAD sv 1 (1x sg., 1x pl. obj.).

Eṣēnu "to smell", D: "to sniff" → 7.3.2.

Eṣēru "to draw, design", D mostly + pl. obj. → 6.4.6.1 sv (group VIa): **SB** (unless indicated otherwise):

1. with *uṣurātu* "drawings, plans", **OB**: TIM 9, 35: 13 (qu. App. sv *pašāṭu*); **SB** passim → CAD sv 2a-2', AHw sv D 1; also SpTU 2, 16: I 19. 21; 3, 74: 181 = (39) // Maqlû III 181 (stat. with pl. adj. acc.;
2. other pl. objects: AAA 22, 52: 41 (bodies of fish); 66: 15; Spirits p. 14: 176; p. 35: 2' (statues); Ee V 67 (rites); CT 17, 42: 16 // MIO 1, 72: 53' (*hinṣū*-decorations, stat.); AAA 22, 64: 6; 68: 44 (*mû* "wavy lines" (as a decoration), stat.); BBR 83: 15 (nets (?, interpreted as sg. by CAD sv 2a-1'), stat.); AAA 20, 82: 36 (kings); *LKU 33: 15 (days); perhaps also Ee V 14 (with ellipse of "days", cf. Landsberger, JNES 20, 156f);
3. with sg. obj.: *Racc. 28: 21 (country); Ee VII 63 = (88) (furrow, cf. 6.6.3.3).

Ešû "to confuse, trouble, D + pl. obj. (6.4.2 group IIb), **OB**: RA 46, 88: 4 (all gods); **SB**: BWL 44: 109 (extispicies); ACh. 2 Spl. 14: 50 (*šiknāt napišti* "living creatures", Dt). G is also found with pl. obj., cf. CAD sv lex. sect. and 1. [Cancel AfO 8, 20: IV 20 acc. to AHw 1555a sv].

Eṭēru "to pay", D not disc.:

1. **NA** stative in *uṭṭuru issu pān ahīš* "they are fully paid, one in respect of the other" → CAD sv 2a.
2. **NB** passim, also prefix forms → AHw sv D 2a/b/Dt "voll bezahlen", CAD sv 2b "to pay in full".

Ezēbu "to leave", D not disc., 1x OB Mari: FM 2 p. 297 note 33: r.14' (pers.). For *uzzubu* LL → 10.3 end.

G

Gamāru "to bring to an end, use up, control", D → 6.8.4:

1. "to use up, consume", passim, esp. **OB** and **NA**, cf. CAD sv 3b; AHw sv *g.* II D 2;
2. "to finish work, to complete", **SB**: MSL 1, 61: 27 (planting a tree); KAR 135: II 14 (prayers); AJSL 36, 81: 49 (no overt obj.); **NA**: Or. 21, 144: IV 13 (rituals), and passim, cf. glossaries of SAA 1, 5 and 10;
3. "to do completely" in hendiadys with another verb, cf. 7.4.1: passim in **OB** and **NA**, rarely elsewhere, cf. CAD sv 3i, AHw sv D 7, also AbB 13, 32: 12; 42: 6; Izbu 163: 69'f (stat.);
4. "to give, pay, assign in full, definitely": mostly **OB**, cf. CAD sv 3c; AHw sv *g.* II D 6; **MB**: ASJ 12, 199: 15 (price); **SB**: AnSt 8, 60: 35 (rites, part.); JAOS 38, 168: 6 (judgment, stat., cf. G in STC 2, 76: 13); **NB**: CT 22, 1: 17 (wisdom);
5. "to encompass, control", **SB**: KAR 32: 28; Ash. § 61: 11 (areas, stat.); BWL 148: 84 (territory); 132: 102 (palace); SAA 8, 312: 2; ACh. 2. Spl. 65: 5 ((part of) the sky, stat.); also "to master" (a skill): RIMA 2/I, 25: 57 (hunting, part.); **NA**: SAA 10, 160: r.6. 8f (skills of a lamentation priest);
6. with other abstract objects: + *ṭêmu* "to give a full report", **OB**: CT 48, 105: 9; RA 68, 30: 13; ARM 26/2 p. 87 no. 321: 11; p. 163 no. 362: 44; p. 41 note 89 A.3000: 15 (stat., different meaning?); + *têrtu* "to carry out an order" UET 5, 385: 9; + *awātim* (pl.) OBTR 25: 16; **OA**: CCT 2, 47b: 20; EL 268: 3; 332: 5; ATHE 24a: 16; BIN 6, 217: 2; kt c/k 101: 12, etc. → 6.4.8 sv;

7. + *libbu* "to be completely devoted", **SB**: Gilg. XI 5 (stat.); **NA**: SAA 10, 118: r.5 (stat.); ABL 917: r.5; or "to be completely frank", **OB**: RA 60, 20: 33, cf. Stol, St. Hallo p. 248;

8. "to destroy", **OAk**: Ni 2760 qu. CAD sv 3a (country, part.);

9. "to bring together" persons → 6.8.3, passim in **OB** letters, cf. AHw sv D 4a/b; also AbB 13, 130: 13; in Mari esp. of soldiers: ARM 1, 6: 17 (Dt). 18 (stat.); 26/2 p. 423 no. 488: 28; 2, 21: r.10' (*emūqšu* "his forces"); Ét. Garelli 149: II 15 (id.); of ships: MARI 6, 574: 28. 37; rarely in **SB**: HBA 36: 36 (stars, Dt); 78: 30 (gods, Dt); and **NA**: Iraq 17, 136: 23 acc. to AHw sv Dt 3 (troops); exc. one person ("to arrest"), **OB**: AbB 6, 171: 12. 15 (part.); VS 7, 118: 6;

10. part. *mugammertu*, a poetic word for "sea" ("the all-encompassing"), **SB**: → AHw 667a sv and 6.6.2 with note 18.

Garānu "to stock, pile up" → *qarānu*

Gaṣāṣu "to trim, cut" → *kaṣāṣu*

Gerû "to proceed against, become hostile to", D not disc., **OB**: AbB 6, 41: 10 (pers.); Gilg. P III 29 (lions: "to chase"); **SB**: Maqlû III 140 (pers., Dtn); UnDiv. 104 BM 41005: III 11 (*ṣalātu* "quarrels", Dtn); also with dat. or *ana* (BWL 194: 19), cf. 5.5.1.; note esp. **SB** LL: MSL 13, 164: 134f ga.ba.al.dù = *ge-ru-ú* / ga.ba.al.dù.dù = *gur-ru-ú*.

H

Habālu "to wrong, oppress", D not disc.:

1. id., **MB**: CT 22, 247: 17; **SB**: LKU p. 9: 30 (girls); API 6: 11ff (person);

2. lexicalized (cf. 6.8.3): "to damage", **MB**: MBTexts 41: 2 (obj. *hibiltu*, denominative?); "to destroy", **SB**: VAB 3, 125: 7 (buildings); "to take away illegally", **NB**: TMH 2, 204: 7 (field and house, Dt).

Habāṣu "to break into pieces" (= AHw *h.* II), D not disc., 1x **OB**: YOS 11, 26: I 20 (dough).

Habāšu "to chop up", D not disc., 1x **SB** LL: [haš.h]aš = *hu-bu-šu* (after *šubburu*), cf. CAD sv lex. sect.

Habātu "to rob, snatch, loot", D 1x + pl. obj. (6.4.4 group IVc): **OB**: YOS 10, 33: V 32 (persons, Dt). G passim with sg. and pl. object.

Hâb/pu "to cleanse, purify, exorcize", D → 6.9.2.1, **SB**, cf. CAD sv *h.* A 2a/b/c, said of cultic objects and localities, persons and body parts. D is the usual form, G only 3x: Racc. 22a: 8 (drum, read *ta-hab* acc. to CAD sv 1); 140f: 340. 356 ((part of) a temple, alternating with D in 345. 364. 366 (all infin.)).

Habû "to hide", D 1x **SB**: BagM 11, 93: 17 *tu-ú[h-t]a-bi* (reflexive Dt, cf. 9.1.2).

Hakāmu "to know, understand", D not disc., **OB**: YOS 11, 25: 12. 34. 42. 56; 26: I 12; IV 22 ("to taste", all infin.); ARM 26/2 p. 530 no. 537: r.7'; ARM 23, 100: 3 (stat.); 26/2 p. 81 no. 316: 14" (stat.).

(H)alālu "to hang", D only stative, exc. YOS 10, 20: 7 (the "path" of the liver, Dt):

1. with pl. subject, **SB**: KAR 152: 24f (kidneys);

2. with pl. adjunct acc. → 6.5.3, **OB**: YOS 10, 16: 1; 18: 55; 31: X 18; 46: IV 45; RA 65, 73: 39'; 74: 81'; TIM 9, 78: 10; **SB**: KAR 153: 16; TU 2: 52 (all prot. with parts of the liver as subj. and acc. *zihhī* "pustules"); Gilg. IX v 49 (with *ishunnātu* "bunches of grapes").

Halāšu "to scrape off", D → 6.9.2.1, 1x **SB**: BagF 18, 357: 19 = (111A) (a fungus from the wall).

Hamāmu "to collect, gather"; D mostly + pl. obj. (6.4.5 group Vb): **OB**: MARI 3, 46: 17 (rituals (*parṣū*), part.); **SB**: Maqlû III 38 // SpTU 3, 74: 38 (sweepings); YOS 1 38: I 23 ((stones from) a foundation, Dt). D is rare compared to the common use of G, esp. with obj. *parṣī* and similar words, cf. CAD sv 2, AHw sv G 2; compare esp. OB Mari (temple) *mu-ha-mi-im parṣī* with the common epithet *hāmim par-ṣī*, cf. CAD sv 2a (SB).

Hamāṣu "to strip, skin, tear off", D **OB**, unless indicated otherwise:
1. with pl. obj. (clothes) → 6.4.8 sv: TCL 11, 245: 3 = (17) (pieces of cloth, stat.). 34 (id., but inf.); UET 5, 26: 23 (garments);
2. idiomatic → 6.8.1 sv: a) "to skin" an animal: ARM 14, 86: 10 (a deer); MBTexts 3: 6 (ox, MB); b) "to tear off" metal from an object: UM 8/2, 194: I 7. 12; II 4. 9. 19; III 13. 20; IV 3 (silver and gold, all stat.); BagM 21, 191: 10 (bronze star); OBTR 109: 8 (copper); MSL 12, 182: 34 (emblems, part.); jewelry: ARM 10, 114: 10. 20; c) "to tear out" eyes: MSL 12, 183: 49 (stat.);
3. "to rob, plunder" (a house or temple) → 6.8.1 sv, cf. also 6.4.9: ŠumAkk. 181: r.17; KAV 168: 7 (stat., MA); AfO 12, 53: N 3 (MA). For adj. *hummuṣu* → 10.3.2 and 10.6.2.

Hamû "to paralyze", D not disc., **OB**: St. Sjöberg p. 327: 114; CT 44, 49: 15 (stat.); **SB**: TuL 130: 16; 139: 21 acc. to Von Soden, ZA 43, 266, cf. CAD sv *h.* A (a) (stat. with pers. obj.).

Hanāqu "to strangle", D + pl. obj. (6.4.1 group Ib): **OB**: YOS 11, 20: 10f (children); ZA 71, 63: 7' (id.); MARI 6 p. 64 n. 135 A.402: 28 (men). The (rather rare) instances of G registered in the dictionaries have a sg. obj. (cf. CAD sv 1/2, AHw sv G 1/5), except SAA 2 p. 55: 607, and statives in omens (CAD sv 2, AHw sv G 1). For stative *hunnuq* (pl.) in omen protases → 10.6.1.2.2 sv.

Hapāpu "to crack, split", D not disc., **SB**: Maqlû III 107 = (118) (pers.); K.9873: II 4' qu. CAD sv *huppupu* 1 (door, stat.). [ARM 2, 34: 36 unclear].

(H)apû "to cover, pack", D 1x + pl. obj. (6.4.3 group IIIc): **OB** Mari: ARM 18, 9: 7 (hides).

(H)arāmu "to cover", D + pl. obj. → 6.4.3.1 sv (group IIIa):
1. tablets (plur.) **OA**: BIN 4, 114: 11 (stat.); 6, 73: 25; EL 319: 8; occasionally names of witnesses: EL 250: 11f +D; VA passim, qualifying "tablets" → AHw sv *harrumum*, CAD sv **arrumu*;
2. **OB**: 1x TCL 17, 59: 20 (*awātum* "matters", stat.).

Harāru "to dig", D not disc., **OB**: a process performed on textiles, cf. Lackenbacher, Syria 59 p. 129ff passim (inf.), cf. p. 142. For the stative *hurrur* in omens → 10.6.1.1.3.

Harāṣu "to cut off, reduce, confiscate", D not disc., **OB**: ARM 5, 73: 10 (field, stat.). 16 (id.). 17, cf. G + field in FM 2 p. 79 no. 45: 11. 18.

Harāšu "to bind", D "to plant" (trees) → 6.8.3, in **SB** RIs: Iraq 16, 197a: 9; Ash. Nin. A VI 31; Sn. 97: 87; 101: 57; 124: 41 (all stat.); Sn. 114: 18 acc. to AHw sv *h.* II D 2; Sumer 9, 170: 25.

Hasāpu "to pluck out, remove", D not disc., **MA**: KAV 205: 20. 27. 35 *ša hassupe* (tweezers) "to remove (hair)" (mass noun as implied object, cf. 6.3?).

Hasāru (CAD *hesēru*) "to trim, chip", D not disc., **OB**: PSBA 33, 193 b 8 acc. to AHw sv D 1 (millstone); Ét. de Meyer p. 82: 36 (river banks: "to erode"); **SB**: BBR no. 43: 8'f acc. to CAD sv (e) (lines on a tablet). For the stative *hussur* in omens → 10.7.1.1.

Haṣābu "to break, cut off, cut down", D 2x + pl. obj. (6.4.1 group Ic): **SB**: AnSt. 10, 112: 27'. 30' (restored from SpTU 1, 1: II 6') (trees). G occurs occasionally with sg. and pl. obj., cf. CAD sv *h.* A a/b. For PN *Huṣṣubu* → 10.6.3.2.

Haṣānu "to protect, shelter", D not disc., 1x **NA**: SAA 10, 68: r.12 ("to embrace" (Parpola)).

Haṣāṣu "to break" (reed(s), D usually + pl. obj. (6.4.1 group Ib):
1. lit., reeds (pl.), **SB**: Erra I 72 (Dt); **NA**: KADP 12: I 13; 11: II 69 (VA, qu. in note 1 to Ch. III); reed as a mass noun, **SB** LL: MSL 7, 23: 256f; ZA 10, 200: 1 acc. to AHw sv *huṣṣuṣu*.
2. metaph. "persons like reed(s)": Erra IV 67 (people); Ash. § 65: 33 (hostile kings); BagF. 16, 241: 9 (persons, cf. 8: obj. broken but sg.?); note RIMA 2/I, 195: 23 (mountains and enemies);
3. without overt obj.: SpTU 2, 24: 2; exc. with sg. obj.: CT 17, 19: 6 // SpTU 2, 2: I 6 (person).

Apart from the instances listed here, the association of D with a pl. obj. is shown by three partly broken instances in bilingual texts where the verb and/or a plural object can be restored on the basis of Sumerian (quoted CAD sv lex. sect. and G 153a sv), and the explicit association of *huṣṣuṣu* with a pl. obj. in a commentary quoted in CAD sv lex. sect. There are no certain instances of *haṣāṣu* G outside LL, exc. in the stative, cf. CAD sv 2 (*huṣṣa haṣāṣu* is probably a different verb, cf. 8.3.2). This suggests that D is the only form used in the literal meaning of the verb, irrespective of whether the object is pl. or sg. (cf. *letû* and *pasāsu* discussed in 5.6.4).

Hašû "to chop up" (vegetables), D not disc., **OB**: YOS 11, 14: r.12 (leeks); **SB**: AMT 105: 18 (garlic); 8, 1: 11 (onion); Maqlû V 35 (person, // G);

Hatāpu "to slaughter", D not disc., **SB**: BA 2, 628: 22 (enemies); **NB**: NBDMich. 63: 9 (one sheep, stat.).

Hatû "to smite, strike down", D not disc., **MB**: BE 17, 21: 24 (a well, AHw sv D 2 "aushauen"); **SB**: LSS 1/6, 33: 12; SBH 2: 21; 4: 63 (houses); Maqlû II 67 (flesh); HGŠ 114: 17 (pers., non-ag.).

Haṭāmu "to block", D 1x + pl. obj. (6.4.2 group IIc): **SB**: Sg. 8: 222 + KAH 2, 141, cf. Laessøe, JCS 5, p. 21b (ditches). G 2x (inf. with obj. "mouth"; stative with *le-ti-šú* "cheeks" (obscure), cf. CAD sv 1.

Hâṭu "to watch, examine, weigh out", D not disc., but cf. 5.6.2.1, **SB**:
1. TI pl. 2: II 32 (persons); SAA 3, 32: 2 (convolutions of the intestines, part.);
2. part., MSL 12, 230: IV 28 *mu-ha-'i-i-ṭù* "man on the lookout" → 6.6.2 sv.

Hepû "to break, demolish", D mostly + pl. obj. → 6.4.1.1 sv (group Ia):
1. "to break", tablets and the like, **OB**: AbB 7, 153: 9 = (131A); VAB 6, 207: 19; YOS 12, 290: 17 (VA); 325: 14; **MB**: UM 2/2, 34: 24 (VA); **NB**: TCL 13, 160: 13 (stat.), and passim in NB contracts, cf. NRVGl p. 62;
2. other objects, **OB**: RA 70, 111: 20 (fetters); YOS 11, 26: III 40 (birds (in a recipe)); Gilg. M IV 1; CT 46, 16: IV 9' (the "*šūt abnim*"); **SB**: Gilg. X III 38f (id.); AfO 14, 146: 115 (wood shavings); LKA 108: 7; SpTU 2, 16: III 7 (pottery, Dt); 4, 128: 56 (id., VA);
3. "to destroy", **OB**: RA 85, 120 note 14 (lands); **SB**: RIMA 2/I, 173: 43 (wells). 48 (id., Dt); Iraq 27, 5: 10 (houses); RA 50, 18: III 43 (cities, Dt); Sg. Wi. 98: 14 = (06B) (lands); BagM. 11, 95: 5 (mountains, Dt); LKA 105: 7 (id.); CT 38, 1: 14 (the igi.meš of a city (= ?), Dt, prot.); **NB**: ABL 880: r.3 (houses, stat.);
4. "to destroy, mutilate", animate beings and body parts, **MA**: KAV 1: VI 45 (ears); **SB**: CT 16, 33: 171. 183 (demons, Dt); AMT 105: 15 (geckoes); SpTU 4, 149: II 32' (finger nails, stat.);
5. "to cut" (planks), **NB**: GC 1, 36: 4; Nbn. 784: 10; "to prune" (trees): TMH 135: 22;
6. with sg. object → 6.4.9, **OB**: AbB 1, 27: 20 = (22) (pers.); ARM 6, 5: 13 = (18) (rock); 27, 12: 10 (= (06) in 10.2) (ship, stat.); **MB**: *Tn-Ep. VIa 21 (*kippatu*, stat., obscure); **SB**: NESA 345: r.2 var. (mountain); BWL 146: 38 acc. to AHw sv Dt 1 = (23) (house); *AMT 105: 19 (worm); **NB**: ABL 892: r.25 = (24) (house).

Herû "to dig", D not disc., **OB**: RA 70, 115: II 4' (pits); Gilg. JNES 16, 256: r.21 (*urmazillī* "tree trunks"? (cf. AHw sv)); **SB**: Gilg I III 9. 36; VI 52 (pits); V II 46 (pit); **NB**: YOS 3, 17: 12 // TCL 9, 129: 12 (canal).

Hesû "to press, hide", D → 6.8.3, **SB**: "to crush, mince" (plants as ingredients), cf. CAD sv *hussû*, AHw sv D 2 ("auspressen").

K

Kabāsu "to step or walk upon, trample", D is used with pl. obj. (**1.**, **2.**, **4.**) → 6.4.2.1 (group IIa), pl. action (**1.**) → 6.6.3.2 and 6.6.3.3, and more salient action (**3.**) → 6.8.1:
1. "to step upon" objects and persons compared to objects, **OB**: ZA 75, 202: 96 = (74) (threshold); **SB**: Maqlû III 153 = (84) (thorn bush, // G); IV 36 = (83) (figurines); VII 127 = (82) (*ša* "whatever"); VII 53,

cf. AfO 21 p. 78b (*lahmu*'s, part.); in obscure context, **OB**: ARM 26/1 p. 415 no. 193: 11 (person); **SB**: Syr. 33, 124: 20 acc. to AHw 1565a sv (person, prot.);

2. "to tread down" (necks of) enemies, **SB**: AGH 134: 97 // SpTU 2, 22: III 20 (pers.); in RIs passim, → CAD sv 5b, often part., cf. ÉR p. 122 and 6.9.3; also SAA 3, 38: 11. 42;

3. "to trample, crush with the foot", **OB**: MLVS 2, 4: 27 (pers., VA); **MB**: BBS 8: IV 6 (parts of fields); KB 4, 82a: 15 (id.); BBS 7: II 28 (*miṣiršu* "his borderline"); **SB**: IAsb. 73c: 3 // 78: 15 (bodies); Šurpu II 93 (*dabdâ* "defeat", but here in concrete sense "corpses on the battlefield"; **NA**: ABL 1022: 8 (land);

4. "to walk across, over", **SB**: WO 1, 456: 15 (mountain tops, part., cf. ÉR p. 123f and 6.9.3); AAA 19, 108: 3 (id.); Tn.II. 13 (id.); BWL 136: 170 (mountains);

5. in *anzilla kubbusu* "to infringe a taboo, commit a sacrilege", **SB**: OEC 6, 41: 35. 47; JNES 33, 282: 140; 284: 18; SAA 3, 32: r.27 (*ša* "whoever"); Šurpu IV 5;

6. metaphorically, **SB**: BWL 78: 135 (rites); JNES 15, 142: 57'. 59'; AfO 19, 51: 71 (sins); note sg. Iraq 30, 101: 17 acc. to CAD sv 5e (*hiṭissu* "his sin": "to pardon").

7. **OA** "to drop a claim" in sentences with *mādum* or *mimma* → 6.6.3.1: Or. 36, 403 no. 21: 5 = (64) (stat.); *ib.* no. 20: 15 = (65); kt 91/k 158: 18 = (66) (stat.); 1x reciprocal Dt: KTH 19: 32 → 9.1.3.

Kadāru "to establish" (a border), D not disc., but see 8.3.2; with obj. *kudurra* "boundary stone", **MA**: KAV 2: VII 21 (prot.); **SB**: Šurpu II 45 (2x); SpTU 1, 49: 24; without object: Šurpu III 54 (inf.); **NA**: SAA 1, 103: 11. r.7 (obj. obscure, cf. Parpola's note 10 vs. AHw sv *kut/dabbiru*).

Kamāru "to heap, pile up", D mostly + pl. obj. → 6.4.5.1 sv (group Va):

1. property (*makkūru*), abundance (*hiṣbu, ṭuhdu, hegallu, nuhšu,* etc.) and comparable words, **OB**: KH I 54 (part.); II 44 (id.); **SB**: passim, cf. CAD sv 4a; AHw sv *k.* III D 1;

2. other objects, **SB**: RIMA 2/I, 14: 79; 17: 25 (corpses); Sg. 8: 90 (walls or cities); Lugal 257 (*ummānu* "the (bodies of the) soldiers", or from *kamāru* "to strike down"? (equated with *hatû*, cf. CAD sv *kamāru* and *hatû* A lex. sect.);

3. exc. of persons, **SB**: Dt intrans. "to assemble" → 9.1.5: Gilg. II II 41; I V 34;

4. exc. with abstract object, **NA**: *SAA 10, 294: r.4 (obj. *muruṣ libbija*).

Kamāsu "to finish, collect, bring in", D mostly + pl. obj. → 6.4.5.1 sv (Va): **OB** (but **4.** SB):

1. with personal obj.: passim **OB** Mari (typically *ṣābu* "troops, work force" and *halṣu* "(people of the) district", rarely animals (ARM 6, 57: r.15'), cf. CAD sv *k.* A 4b, AHw sv *k.* I D 1; also ARM 14, 18: 11'f; 26/1 p. 580 no. 280: r.8'; 27, 37: 15. 17 (102: 24 *li-ka-mi-is* is N rather than D);

2. rarely with obj. "barley" or "field": **OB** Mari: ARM 26/1 p. 308 no. 144: 23' (barley, stat.); outside Mari: AbB 1, 135: 10f (field and barley); 13, 44: 18 (field);

3. ingredients, **OB**: YOS 11, 25: 63. 66. 70; 26: I 10, 66; IV 19;

4. **SB**: "to gather" (animals) BWL 170: 19 acc. to AHw sv Dt; "to lay out" (corpse) AnSt. 8, 50: 10.

Kamû "to capture", D not disc., **OB**: ARM 26/1 p. 165 no. 32: r.3' (persons); Dumuzi 60: 65 (person).

Kanāku "to seal, put under seal", D has a pl. obj. (**1.**) → 6.4.3.1 sv (group IIIa) or is used idiomatically (**2.**) → 6.4.9:

1. "to seal" objects (pl.), **OA**: TC 2, 15: 34 (bags); 3, 67: 21 (garments and tin); **MB**: MARI 3, 187: 41 (stat.); **SB**: TuL 94: 31; **NB**: TCL 9, 106: 13 (doors); with coll. and mass nouns, **OA**: Berytus 3, 82: 29 (silver+copper); **OB**: FM 2, p. 24 no. 3: 8f (*enūtu* "household goods"); MARI 6, p. 294: 19 (fruit);

2. "to put under seal" a building (sg. and pl.), **OA**: CCT 5, 1b: 9 (houses, stat.); **OB**: AbB 3, 52: 36; 4, 146: 7 (stat.); YOS 10, 25: 9; 26: III 49; FM 2 p. 285 no. 130: 8 = (130A) (house); **SB**: UET 6, 394: 56 (storehouses, stat., cf. Lambert 1992: 131);

3. exc., **OB**: ARM 26/2 p. 420 no. 483: 38 (message, for a tentative explanation see note 23); **SB**: Maqlû III 109 = (118) (pers.), see 6.9.2.2.

Kanānu (*qanānu*) "to twist, coil", D mostly + pl. obj. → 6.4.2.1 sv (group IIa), **SB**:

1. body parts: Maqlû VII 65. 72; ZA 16, 158: 2; CT 17, 25: 25; STT 76: 24 (limbs), cf. Bit rimki 39: 23 (all pl.); other pl. objects: SKS p. 78: 294 = (113A) (strings);

2. rarely sg. obj.: TDP 20: 26f (foot, prot. → 6.6.1.1 sv); *AMT 9, 1: II 27 (reciprocal, cf. 9.1.3); CT 16, 23: 334 (obj. a snake). For the stative *kunnun* in omen texts → 10.6.1.2.1 sv.

Kapādu "to plan, take care of", D → 7.6.3, **OB**: AbB 5, 172: 20 (storage basin); **SB**: JNES 17, 137: 5' ([*lemn*]*ēti* "evil"); *MSL 16, 81: 112f (LL).

Kapālu (*qapālu*) "to roll up", D not disc., **SB**: in *mu-qa-píl zê* "who rolls excrement" (a dung beetle) MSL 8/2, 59: 208; Dt: → 9.1.5 sv, of persons, **OB**: "to gather" (intrans.) RA 33, 51: 17; YOS 10, 48: 30 // 49: 2; of water, **SB**: "to churn, whirl"? CT 39, 14: 24 (prot.); Or. 58, 91: 16'b (prot.).

Kapāru A "to rub, wipe, wipe clean", D:

1. persons and body parts, mainly in med. and rit. → 6.9.2.1, **OB**: YOS 11, 19: 4 (child); **SB**: ZA 45, 202: 20; KAR 114: r.8 (pers.); OEC 6, 25: r.9 (body); AMT 25, 6: II 12 (nose and nostrils); CT 23, 1: 4 (foot); AfO 18, 77: 10 (hands); in other texts, **SB**: CT 28, 29: 8 (face); KUB 37, 210: 8 (unident. pl. obj., Dtn, prot.); **NB**: GC 1, 141: 2 (jewelry); 2, 141: 6. 9 (ornaments);

2. "to purify magically" (persons and objects), **SB** passim → CAD sv *k*. A 3d, AHw sv *k*. I D 2.

Kapāru B "to uproot, pull out, cut down", D mostly + pl. obj. (6.4.1 group Ib): **SB**: SBH 9: 33; 52: 34; Erra I 71 (Dt, cf. Lambert, AfO 27, 77); IV 144; Sg. 8: 329 (trees); Asb. A VI 29 ("horns" of a ziggurat, cf. *šebēru* **3**.); 1x pl. action, **OB**: ZA 83, 5: 24 = (75) (mooring pole). G has both sg. and pl. obj., acc. to CAD sv 1 (person, buds of a palm tree, stakes), but AHw assigns these cases to *kapāru* A "abschälen (sv *k*. I G 1).

Karābu "to pray, bless", D 1x **OB**: ARM 3, 17: 20 = (33), cf. 6.5.2.

Karāku "to obstruct, dam" (CAD sv; AHw: "aufwickeln, zusammenfassen"), D not disc., 1x **SB**: ZA 45, 26: 4 acc. to CAD sv lex. sect., AHw sv D (tongue).

Karāṣu "to pinch off (clay), break", D 1x pl. obj., **SB**: Atr. 60: 256 (*kirṣī* "pieces of clay", // G *ib*. 60: 5 + Add. p. XII); 1x pl. action in prot. → 6.6.1.1 sv: CT 38, 45 // 46: 18 (brick work). Elsewhere G has both sg. and pl. obj., cf. CAD sv lex. sect. and 1. For *kurruṣu* "to slander" → 8.4.2 sv.

Karātu "to break off, cut off", D + pl. obj. (6.4.1 group Ib), **SB**: SAA 3, 39: r.13 (horns, see below); VAB 7, 214b: 12 (hands); AfO 11, 222 no. 1: 6 (<u>kú.meš</u>, unidentified body parts (lips?), prot. → 6.6.1.1 sv); SKS p. 104: 15 (*ša* "everyone who", qu. in note 5).

For D + pl. obj. cf. CAD sv 2. A case of D + pl. obj. ↔ G + sg. obj. in the same sentence is SAA 3, 39: r.13f *DN qarnīša ú-ka-rit* / [*šēp*]*īša ikkis zibbassa* [*i*]*k-rit* "Bel cut off her (Tiamat's) horns, clove her [fee]t and docked her tail." (tr. Livingstone, who reads, however, *ú-ka-šiṭ* and [*i*]*k-šiṭ*, from *kašāṭu*, which has a similar meaning, but is normally said of trees; no D-stem attested so far). The few instances of G have a sg. object (man, clay figurine, tail (qu. above)).

Kâru "to rub", D not disc., cf. 6.9.2.1 sv, 1x **SB**: TuL 83: 12 (*šīru* "flesh").

Kasāpu "to chip, break off", D 2x + pl. obj. (6.4.1 group Ic): **SB**: KAR 237: 3 // LKA 105: 9 (Dt) (staffs); NA: SAA 1, 77: r.7 (beams).

Note D + pl. obj. ↔ G + sg. obj. in SAA 1, 77: r.1 *šummu gušūru ka-si-ip* "if a beam is broken" (tr. Parpola) vs. *ib*. r.7 *gušūrēšu ša ka-sa-pu-ni* "its beams which are broken" (for *ka-sa-pu-ni* (= /*kassa-pūni*/) instead of *kassupūni*, see note 1 to Ch. III; both CAD K 241b sv *k*. A 1a and AHw 453a sv *k*. I G

2 erroneously list this form under the G-stem). G occurs a few times with sg. and pl. object (beam (qu. above), piece of bread, wings, nails).

Kasāsu "to gnaw, consume", D 1x + pl. obj. (6.4.1 group Ic), **SB**: ZA 16, 158: 2 (sinews); also VA with a mass noun: MSL 7, 24: 257a (reed). For G cf. AHw sv G (sg. and pl. obj.) CAD assumes two different verbs, cf. *k.* A and B.

Kasû "to bind, paralyze", D → 6.8.4:

1. lit. "to bind" persons, animals and body parts, both sg. and pl., passim, cf. CAD sv *k.* A 5a; AHw sv *k.* III D 1/2a; also ZA 82, 205: 37 = (107); ARM 26/1 p. 524 M. 5001: 11; 26/2 p. 180 no. 372: 33 (Dt) (all OB); Iraq 50, 85: 6 = (108) (MB);

2. metaph. "to bind by magic, paralyze" (sg. and pl., cf. *ṣabātu* D), passim, cf. CAD sv *k.* A 5c; AHw sv *k.* III D 1b, 2b, e.g., Maqlû III 112 = (118); AfO 18, 290: 18 = (04) and (122); *KAR 226: I 6; note esp. CT 17, 12: 13 (oxen, // G); also ZA 75, 198: 15f; OEC 11, 20: 22 (both OB);

3. idiomatic, **OA**: "to demand payment", EL 1: 19; BIN 4, 25: 40; kt a/k 503: 6; stative D in *šīmum kassu* "the price is bound, at a standstill", BIN 4, 39: 8; kt 89/k 237: 3', cf. Veenhof 1972: 376 no. 2;

4. stative in omens: *lipiam* (*lipâ*) *kussu* "enveloped with fat", with parts of the liver as subj. → 6.5.3, **OB**: YOS 10, 31: III 34; X 13; 42: II 44; OBE no. 14, 42/5. r.21); **SB**: Izbu 79: 62f.

Kaṣāru "to bind together, join, collect, organize", D is used with a pl. obj. (**1.**, **2.**) → 6.4.3.1 sv (group IIIa) and is used in various idiomatic expressions (**3.**, **4.**, **5.**) → 6.4.9.

1. "to tie, bind", objects, mostly pl., **OB**: Or. 42, 503: 13 (fetters, VA); **SB**: LKA 159: 15f (knots); Maqlû VII 112 (id., VA); ZA 16, 186: 33 (twigs); AfO 21, 17: 18) (stones); Maqlû V 11. 15 (coll. Geller, Or. 61, p. 382 n. 9) (barley (*uṭṭatu*), Dt);

2. persons and body parts, mostly pl., **SB**: AMT 11, 1: 9 (man+woman); TBP 28: 17' (hands+feet, stat.); Maqlû V 95; UM 1/1, 13: 46; SpTU 2, 11: III 39; 19: r.20 (muscles, etc.); 79-7-8, 168: r.4 (qu. CAD sv 6a) (arms?, stat.); AfO 11, 222 no. 2: 8 (eyebrows, prot. → 6.6.1.1 sv); BKBM p. 6: 21 acc. to CAD sv *karšu* 1a-1' (convolutions of the intestines, stat.);

3. in military contexts "to concentrate, prepare for battle", **OB**: ARM 1, 42: 36 = (129); **SB**: Erra IV 31; BHLT p. 34: 14 (army); Asb. B V 36 (*kali* "the whole (army)", stat.); ABRT 1, 81: 18 ("the land (i.e., the army) of his enemy", stat.); IAsb. 83: r.2 ([troops]); Asb. A IX 82 (*anuntu* "battle array", stat.);

4. Dt "to gather" (intrans.) → 9.1.5, a) armies, etc., **OB**: ARM 6, 57: r.6'; 58: 17 (= (33) in Ch. IX); with additional reduplication ARM 3, 16: 12 and 26/1 p. 287 no. 121: 12 (= (34) in Ch. IX); **SB**: SAA 4, 281: r.5'; Asb. A V 76; K.3467: III 10 (qu. AHw sv Dt 1); **b)** clouds, **SB**: SAA 8, 40: r.2; 41: 3 (= (35) in Ch. IX); 267: r.3; 517: 10; 529: r.3; TCS 2 p. 33 no. 14: 2; p. 37 no. 17: 7';

5. idiomatic: "to build, fortify, restore", **OB**: ARM 2, 3: 20 (towns); 1, 39: 7 (stat.); 26/1 p. 351 no. 172: 19 (stat.); 26/2 p. 278 no. 409: 60 (town); p. 319 no. 424: 28 (*adaššam* "la ville basse"); **SB**: AOF 1, 298: 8 (forts); Ee I 6 var. (*gipāru*, a sanctuary, stat.); *Sg. 8: 254 ([camp]);

6. exceptionally sg. obj., **OB**: *ARM 26/1 p. 424 no. 197: 15 (see 6.4.3.1 sv); *Atr. 108: 51; 110: 61 (see 6.4.3.1 sv); **SB**: BAM 237: IV 39 ("to attach stones to a person", see 6.5.3?); SpTU 3, 74: 112 = (118) (person → 6.9.2.2).

Kaṣāṣu (CAD: *gaṣāṣu*) "to trim, cut, mutilate"; D + pl. obj. (6.4.1 group Ib), **OB**: ARM 26/1 p. 582 no. 282: 21 (persons); **SB**: Maqlû VI 135 acc. to AHw sv D (part.); I 119 (Dt); SpTU 3, 73: 10 (Dt) (all fingers); IAsb. 88: 15 (finger nails); CT 17, 35: 66 (wings).

G is not used in comparable contexts: it is said of teeth ("to gnash, to bare", CAD sv *gaṣāṣu* A 1/2, AHw sv *k.* I G 1a), of parts of the liver in extispicy omens (stative only, *ib. g.* B 1a, G 3 "ist abgeschliffen"), and intr. (*ib. g.* A 3 ("to rage", *k.* I G 1b ("Zähne knirschen") (CAD assumes two different verbs). For adj. *kuṣṣuṣu* → 10.3.2 and 10.6.2.

Kâṣu "to flay, skin", D 1x pl. obj. (6.4.1 group Ic): **SB**: AOTU 1, 117: 20 acc. to AHw sv D 2 (enemies). G occurs both with sg. and pl. obj. (typically persons, animals and *masku* "skin" in sg. or pl.), cf. CAD sv 1. [Cancel ABL 1389: 19 acc. to CAD sv *k.* A].

Kašādu "to reach, turn to, arrive, take possession of", D → 5.5.3 sv:

1. "to chase away", passim → CAD sv 4b/c, AHw sv D 1a-d, Dtn 1 (mostly persons and animals, rarely abstract nouns (sins: JNES 15, 134: 66; AfO 19, 57: 109; courage: BWL 192: 15; evil: NE no. 53: 16);

2. "to pursue, try to catch", passim → CAD sv 4a, AHw sv D 2 (usually persons; otherwise: VOM p. 184: 10 (harvest); **OA** + *harrānam* "to catch up with a caravan", **OA** → CAD sv 5a, AHw sv D 2a ("nachreisen"), also Dtn: WO 5, 34: 22 acc. to AHw 1567a sv; without obj.: ARM 2, 130: 25; FM 2 p. 17 no. 2: 16; and in the omen apodosis *kuššid lā takalla* "set off in pursuit, do not stop!" (CAD sv 5c, AHw sv D 1a). [BIN 6, 41: 11 (obj. *awātim*) obscure].

Kašāpu "to bewitch", D not disc., **OB**: YOS 10, 51: II 36 // 52: II 35 (house, stat.); **SB**: CT 20, 43: 4; Maqlû I 4; III 106 = (118); VI 56; SpTU 3, 74: 118 (all personal obj.).

Kašāru "to repair", D not disc., cf. 6.8.4, **OAk/OB**: VAB 1, 180: 49 (temple); ARM 19 p. 53 no. 64 (chariots); p. 63 no. 114 (obj. broken); p. 112 no. 324 (unident. objects)); AbB 2, 77: 6. 17 (wall); TEBA 51: 18 (ship); BagM. 21, 202: 14 (several objects).

Kašāṭu "to cut down, cut off", D: SAA 3, 39: r. 13 acc. to Livingstone: see *karātu*.

Katāmu "to cover, close", D → 6.8.4:

1. "to cover" persons with clothes, **SB**: *AfO 17, 287: 105 (stat.); Gilg. X I 4 (stat.); **NA**: SAA 10, 226: r.3 (Dt); **NB** passim with *muṣiptu* → CAD sv 5a;

2. obj. body parts, **OB**: AbB 7, 36: 5 (face, stat.); **SB**: Erra IIc: 15 (face); CT 17, 19: 35; SpTU 2, 2: I 32. 34; SBH p. 131: 50; no. 40: 17 (head); Gilg. XII 30. 48 (shoulders, stat.);

3. objects with earth (*ep(e)ru*), **MB**: RIMA 1, 134: 40 (stelas); **SB**: 2/I, 54: 60 (layers of brick); KBo 9, 44: r. 17' (crown of a plant); K. 9471: 10; K. 8954: 3, qu. CAD sv *nadû* 6 *upaṭṭu* (p. 96a) (mucus);

4. various objects, **OB**: YOS 11, 26: I 31 (dough, cf. G in 48); AbB 12, 21: 18 (unident. objects, stat.); ARM 13, 19: 27. 30 (ornaments); 22/1 p. 232 no. 115: r.12' (a kind of garment); r.14' (unident. object(s?); **SB**: Racc. 136: 284 (parts of a sanctuary, stat.); Izbu 61: 67 (intestines, stat.); MSL 4, 114: 17 (ship); BWL 100: 39 acc. to CAD sv 5d, AHw sv D 5c (wall which covers its enemies, part.); KAR 43: 4 // 63: 4 *ana erṣeti mu-ka-tim-ti* "to the all-covering earth";

5. "to cover" like a net, **SB**: BWL 42: 72; Iraq 31, 87: 50; Maqlû III 162 = (123) (all pers. obj.); metaph. "to overwhelm": BWL 72: 27 (stat.);

6. "to close" body parts, a) in prot. → 6.6.1.1 sv, **SB**: AfO 11, 223: 17 (eyes); KAR 400: r.!3 (id.); *CT 31, 33: r.17f (eye); b) rest, **SB**: BWL 52: 24 (Dt); AnSt. 8, 60: II 4 (mouth, Dt, note the parallelism with *petû* N, cf. 6.6.1.1 sv); Iraq 51, 118: 20'; Ee II 89; MAOG 5/3, 17: 14 var. (lips);

7. id., other objects, **MA**: Or. 17, 302: 17. 21; 304: 23; 312: IV 3 (pot); **SB**: RA 60, 31: 13; TuL 81: 10 (a mixture); Glass p. 37a § 4A: 48; p. 38a § 5: 21' (door); **NB**: VS 5, 117: 14 (gates); cf. *mukattimtu* sub **9**;

8. "to cover up, hide", **OB**: AbB 9, 113: 13 (matters, Dtn); **NA**: ABL 1389: r.6 (no overt obj.);

9. part. → 6.6.2 with note 18, **SB** LL: *mukattimtu* a poetic word for "door" CT 18, 4: IV 68.

Katā'u (CAD *katû*) "to take as security", D + pl. obj. (6.4.7 group VIIc): **OA**: TC 1, 25: 16; CCT 3, 24: 42 (slave girls). G occurs with one slave (girl) as obj., but also with other objects, cf. CAD sv a/b. Note also TC 2, 46: 10 with Gtn and "slave girls" as object (cf. 6.7.3).

Kaw/mû "to roast, bake", D not disc., 1x **OB**: AbB 9, 152: 32 (*kakkartam*, a kind of bread).

L

La'ābu "to affect with the *li'bu*-disease, afflict", D not disc., **OB**: UET 5, 246: 5 (pers.); **SB**: BWL 42: 67

(limbs); metaph.: HGŠ 105: 28; AGH 78: 56 stative *lu''ubāku* followed by *lupputāku*; note esp. MSL 16, 268: 147f ([sa]).dih = *la-'a-*[*bu*] / [sa].dih.dih = *lu-'u-*[*bu*].

La'ātu "to swallow", D not disc., 1x **SB** med.: AMT 64, 1: 13 // 26, 4: 10 (medicine).

Labānu "to beg humbly" (+ *appa*), D not disc., 1x **SB**: K.11716+: 5 qu. CAD sv *l*. B 2: mistake for *ilabbin*?, cf. 6.6.1 end).

Lamāmu "to chew", D not disc., 1x **SB** med.: AMT 25, 6: II 6 (alum).

Lapātu "to touch, smear, affect", D is used for pl. obj. (**1.**) → 6.4.8, pl. subj. (**4.**) → 6.5.1, but mostly for pl. action (**2.**) → 6.6.3.2 and 6.6.3.3, and for repetitive actions with inherent plurality (**3.**):

1. with pl. obj.: "to touch, affect" persons, **SB**: Maqlû II 143 (part.); body parts: Ee VI 98 (throats); UM I/2, 113: III 18 = (03B) (wombs); Maqlû II 158 (features); other objects: CT 17, 18: 11 (top and bottom, cf. G in CT 16, 45: 146; cf. also STT 176: 11); Spirits p. 16: 250 (various spots); Maqlû II 141 var. (trees and stones, part.); with stars as subj.: ZA 52, 248: 62 (prot.); ACh. Išt. 20: 52; SAA 8, 327: r.3'. r.6'; 10, 8: r.5 (stars, cf. G + sg. obj. *ib.* 307: edge 6; 377: 6); SAA 10, 347: r.12' (lands (omen quotation));

2. idem, referring to a general situation, rather than a single event, **OB**: ARM 26/1 p. 127 no. 17: 21. 26 = (70); 30 = (72) (stat.); p. 563 no. 261: 18. 21 = (69); BiMes. 19, p. 16: 4 = (73) (face); **SB**: SAA 4, 24: r.4; 53: 3'; 76: 10; 77: 12; (all *mimma lu''û* "anything unclean", mostly written tag.meš, cf. SAA 4 glossary sv); Maqlû III 151. 154 = (84) (pers.); SAA 10, 26: r.7' = (90A) (*kaqquru* "region"); Maqlû III 49 (netherworld, part.);

3. "to touch" as a repetitive act: "to rub, scratch, stroke", mostly body parts: **a**) present D in omen protases → 6.6.1.1 sv, **SB**: Iraq 19, 40: I 2 // TDP 190: 14 (lips and chin); AfO 11, 222 no. 2: 6 (face); 223: 33 (nose); *ib.* 37 (KA.meš-*šu*: teeth?); TDP 232: 17; SpTU 3, 86: 8 (body); **b**) elsewhere, **OB**: St. Reiner 422: 13' (vulva); **SB**: Or. 60, 340: 11 (id., cf. G in Gilg. VI 69 (SB)); "to smear" with various substances (passim, but mostly ideogr. → CAD sv 4b), **OB**: YOS 10, 42: I 15; 47: 32f; 86f; 47: 86ff // 48: 23ff (body parts with blood, all stative); **SB**: CT 16, 37: 33 (body); BAM 156: 44 (temples of the head); Racc. 119: 10; SpTU 2, 4: r.III 7 (door posts); note BWL 58: 26 (reflexive Dt → 9.1.2 sv); "to sprinkle" with water or milk, **OB**: Gilg. P III 22 acc. to AHw sv D 5a; **SB**: Racc. 90: 23; 91: r.4; 102: 18; 103: 12; 115: 8; CT 17, 23: 177 (person(s)); **c**) "to play" a musical instrument, **OB**: AfO 23, 85: 16 (drum(s)); **SB**: KAR 361: r. 8; Maqlû VII 163 (strings); KAR 16: r.15f with *ina* + instr. (cf. G + one string: Iraq 30, 230: right col. 14 (OB));

4. with pl. subject, **OB**: JCS 15, 7: 20 = (28C); **SB**: MSL 4, 119: 20 = (28B) → 6.5.1;

5. *mulappitu*, **NA** a tool, SAA 7, 119: I 9'; II 16" → 6.6.2 with note 18;

6. idiomatic: **a**) "to write (a letter) to (a person), **OA** passim, cf. AHw sv D 4 and GAG^2 § 88f; cf. *šaṭāru* 3. in 6.8.1; **b**) "to recrute" personnel, **OB**: ARM 26/1 p. 196 no. 54: 33 (stat.); possibly also *ib.* 29, normally G, cf. AHw sv G 4 "ausheben", CAD sv 1k "to give a work assignment"; **c**) "to collect" *ib.* p. 136 no. 22: 29 (*hišihtu* "necessities");

7. anomalous cases: a) **OB** Mari *pūtam lupputum* "to touch the forehead" as a symbolic act: ARM 26/1 p. 39 note 174; p. 281 no. 114: 8; p. 357 no. 174: 8, cf. G p. 433 no. 205: 10' (restored) and also G in SB Gilg. XI 192); b) SB stative in *lu''ubāku lupputāku* "I am afflicted and disturbed": HGŠ 105: 28; AGH 78: 56. For *lupputu* "to tarry, delay" → 8.6 sv; for *lupput* in omen protases → 10.7.1.1 sv; for *lupputā* qualifying *têrētum* "extispicies" (OB Mari) → 10.6.1 with (33).

Laqātu "to pick up, collect, take away", D + pl. obj. (often coll. or mass noun) → 6.4.5.1 (group Va):

1. "to collect, scrape together" objects, **OA**: CCT 4, 24: 53 (pectorals); **SB**: Maqlû II 185; III 37 // SpTU 3, 74: 37 (sweepings); of coll. and mass nouns, **OB**: ARM 1, 42: 33 = (129) (troops); 26/1 p. 346 no. 170: r.9' (barley); AbB 13, 162: 14 (wool); **OA**: CCT 3, 23b: 14 (metal); 24: 30 (everything available to me";

TC 1, 15: 19 ("everything I have" ??); **SB**: RA 53, 135: 37 (barley); BWL 236: 17 *ul-ta-aq-qí-tam-ma* (no overt obj.: "he has gathered (everything) for himself" (tr. CAD sv 5));
2. idiomatic + *bīta* "to plunder a house" → 6.4.9, **OB**: AbB 1, 47: 8; LE § 37 A 18/B 1 (stat.); **OA**: Bab. 6, 187: 17 (stat.); CCT 3, 24: 13.

Latāku "to test, examine", D not disc., **OB**: AbB 9, 127: 6 (sesame); JCS 21, 269 A.7535: 10 (no overt obj.); AIPO 14, 135: 22 (restored) (herbs, vs. G in 17. 20. 29, cf. 6.5.1?); FM 2 p. 137 no. 75: 15. 22 (well, vs. G *ib.* p. 142 no. 77: 13. 16. 18 (the water of the well).

Lâṭu "to confine, keep in check", D mostly + pl. obj. → 6.4.4.1 group Va), all **SB** RIs:
1. lands and kings: RIMA 1, 236: 42; 244: 30; 272: 21. 38;
2. recalcitrant enemies (all part. → 6.9.3): *310: 5; 2/I, 41: 2; 148: 17; 195: 19; 222: 126; 225: 18; 276: 12; 281: 34; AGH 96: 19 (// G, cf. note 13 in AGH p. 97); LKA 53: 9; Ash. § 65: 20;
3. rest: RA 16, 167: III 16 (*kiššatu* "the whole world", part.); SKT 2, 4 K.1660: 4 (land, part.);
4. exc. with sg. obj.: Sg. Cyl. 22 (king). [JNES 13, 212: 26 // 213: 25 obscure].

Law/mû "to wrap, surround", D not disc., **OB**: TCL 17, 56: 21 (face); **OA**: HUCA 39, 33: 33 (tablet); **SB**: ZA 16, 172: 48 (pers., stat.).

Lêku "to lick", D: 1x **SB** omen prot. → 6.6.1.1 sv: *CT 40, 32: r.23 (su.meš "skin"?).

Leqû "to take, receive", D not disc., cf. 5.6.2.1: **OA**: BIN 4, 79: 8' (stat. with *mimma*, cf. 6.3); *ib.* 14' (stat.); *ib.* 18' (VA). [Cancel Tn.II: r.48, cf. RIMA 2/I, 178: 130].

Letû "to split, divide", D → 5.6.4, **SB**:
1. persons: Iraq 37, 12: 7 (*šakṣī* "the wicked", part.); body parts: AMT 75: IV 19 (heels, stat.); mountains: SAA 3, 1: 31 (part.); IV R 26: 38a (part.); stones VAB 4, 174: 35 (all pl.);
2. with obj. "head": Ee IV 130; VAB 7, 306 γ 4 (*muhhu*); RA 18, 198: 3 (*qaqqadu*, // G in ZA 16, 154: 3).

M

Madādu "to measure, to pay or deliver measured quantities", D not disc., cf. 6.8.4:
1. dimensions of persons and buildings, **SB**: BWL 211: 13 (stat. with sg. subj.); elsewhere with obj. *mindātu* and the like: AfO 18, 291: 21; SBH 6: r.18; VAB 4, 62: 27; CT 17, 15: 21 (*šumātim*);
2. barley (also G passim, cf. CAD sv *m.* A 1a-1'), **OB**: ARM 26/2 p. 100 no. 329: 18' = (136A); **OA**: ATHE 44: 28 (barley rations); St. Güterbock 35, 1A: 15 = (68); *ib.* 40 kt c/k 1645: 9 = (67) → 6.6.3.1;
3. "to calculate", **OB**: ARM 13, 29: 14 (days); AbB 2, 40: 9 (? no overt obj., cf. CAD sv *m.* A 4c);
4. lexicalized, **NA/NB**: *birīt/birte īnī muddudu* "to make something clear" (CAD sv *m.* A 4d; AHw sv *m.* I D 3 → 6.8.3.

Magāgu "to spread out" (skins of enemies) (CAD: *makāku*), D 2x + pl. obj. (6.4.2 group IIc), **SB**: RIMA 2/I, 199: 90; 207: 72. G is used of soil (*eperī*) and a table (cf. CAD sv *makāku* a; moreover, we find *qāta makāku* "to stretch out the hand" (cf. CAD sv *magāgu* 2, if this belongs to the same verb, as AHw claims sv *magāgu* G 1.

Magāru "to consent, grant" → 5.5.2 (Type IV).

Mahāru "to receive, approach, confront", D → 6.8.3:
1. "to present sb with sth, to offer", **OB**: AbB 2, 143: 17 (unguent); 9, 169: 7 (silver); 10, 105: 8' (payments); 11, 83: r.8' (taxes); JAOS 103, 30: 5 (oil); TIM 4, 5: 10 (property); but YOS 14, 135: 13 (silver): "to accept"?; **OA**: Ass. 4062: 11 qu. AHw sv D 5 (jars); **SB**: VAB 4, 294: 31; elsewhere SB in paronomastic construction with *ma/uhhuru* "to make an offering" Berens no. 110: 5; VAB 7, 304: 3; AGH 58: 33; with *muhru* "to address a *muhru*-prayer" CT 34, 16: 30;
2. "to go or send upstream" (CAD sv 7b, AHw sv D 2) → 8.4.2 sv;

3. "to turn to" (rarely instead of G), **OB**: MDP 28, 431: 8 (king and judge); **MB**: Tn.Ep. IVa: 18 (god); **SB**: HGŠ 59: 12 (id.); LKA 29e: I 2 (id., unique Dtn instead of Gtn);

4. various idioms, **MA**: Glass p. 63 § IV 36f ("to mix"); **SB**: BRM 4, 3: 15. 21 ("to steer" (a boat), cf. **2.**?); Asb. B VI 67; AfO 8, 180: 48 (severed heads, with *ma/uhhuriš*: "to expose", cf. **1.**); ZA 36, 198: 33 (glass: "to expose"); Tigl.III 74: 23 (doors: "to turn towards"); Iraq 21, 46: 5 (dust storm: "to face", // G in Bab. 4, 107: 2); BagF. 18, 357: 20 (ingredients: "to collect", cf. G in 358: 31); STT 331: 13 ("to rise", Dtn, intrans. → 9.2 end); MDP 23 "to oppose, contest" (CAD sv 8c), "in Anspruch nehmen?" (AHw sv D 6).

Mahāṣu "to hit, smash, weave", D is with pl. obj. (**2.**) → 6.4.8, for pl. action (**3.**) → 6.6.1.1 sv and 6.6.1.2 sv, and idiomatically (**1.**) → 6.8.1:

1. with animate obj.: "to hit, wound" (both sg. and pl.) → 6.8.1: **a**) persons (pl.), **OB**: ZA 44, 122: 22; **MB**: CT 22, 247: 21; **SB**: BagM 21, 344: 4; **NB**: ABL 520: r.8. 10; **NA**: ABL 424: r.7 (stat.). r.8; **b**) person (sg.)., **OB**: AbB 12, 65: 29 = (77); **SB**: VAB 7, 312 β 2; 314 δ 2 (both stat.); SAA 3, 34: 15; 35: 23 (both stat. sg. with pl. adj. acc. → 6.5.3); **NA**: SAA 5, 53: r.5; note **SB**: ZA 16, 160: 26; 194: 37 (personified: "to stab" a figurine); **c**) animal(s), **NA**: ABL 241: r.14 (sheep (pl.), stat.); SAA 1, 221: r.3 (locusts (meaning uncert.)); **NB**: YOS 7, 107: 8. 10. 12 (if UD stands for *tú* (AHw sv D 1), not for *tam* (CAD sv 1a-1') (dog with a stone);

2. inanimate objects (all pl. → 6.4.8), **SB**: Sg. 8: 218 (beams, AHw sv. D 5: "behauen", but CAD sv 7d "to smash, destroy"); VS 1, 37: III 22 (boundary stones, stat.); MSL 7, 161: 49 = (40) (pegs → 6.5.3);

3. in prot.: **a**) with pers. subj. → 6.6.1.1 sv, **SB** med: TDP 190: 19 (eyes); 236: 56 (lap); **b**) "to hurt, sting" with pers. obj. and body parts as subj. → 6.6.1.2 sv: LKA 155: 28 (subj. *kunuk kišādi*); BAM 228: 25 // 229: 19; 323: 90 (subj. kidney); TDP 76: 61; 36: 35 // SpTU 3, 88: I 14 (subj. temples), and elsewhere ideogr., cf. CAD sv 7a, AHw sv D 8; **c**) of the sacrificial sheep → 6.6.1.1 sv, **OB**: TuL 42: 6; *43: r. 11 ("to flap" tail or ear).

Makāru "to flood, irrigate", D + pl. obj. (6.4.2 group IIb), **SB**: Tn-Ep. IV 32 (fields with blood); RIMA 1, 244: 44 (id.); 2/I, 290: 38 (fields with water); VAB 4, 104: 18 (part.); 176 no. 20: 18 // UM 15, 79: I 13 // CT 37, 5: 10 (part.); K. 9504 + 10172: 7 qu. CAD sv 3, AHw sv Dt (*ugāru*-fields, Dt); K. 4441: 7 qu. AHw sv D 1 (temple, sg.?). G occurs both with sg. and pl. obj., cf. CAD sv *m.* A 1 (typically *eqlu* and *ugāru* "field").

Manû "to count, recite, entrust", D not disc., cf. 6.8.4:

1. "to enumerate", **SB**: Gilg. VI 85. 90; "to count", **NB**: VS 6, 10: 1 (sheep, stat.); 78: 2 (vats, stat.);

2. "to entrust" (with *ana qāti*), **SB**: Sg. Lie 32: 197 (people, // G [*im*]-*nu* acc. to CAD sv 9e); Or. 36, 116: 21 (*têrētu* "regulations"); 124: 146 (the art of medicine) (cf. G passim);

3. "to charge" in NB contracts → CAD sv 9d, AHw sv D 2b, obj. sheep (vs. G said of work, wages, barley, silver → CAD sv 5b).

Marāqu "to crush", D mostly + pl. obj. (6.4.1 group Ib):

1. substances, **MB/SB**: Glass p. 63 § III 18; AMT 80, 1: 12; 67, 1: IV 23 = (21);

2. objects, **SB**: SAA 3, 13: r. 10 (insects, Dt); CA 128: V 13 (salt containers); CT 53, 151: 14 acc. to AHw 1573b sv (skulls); exc. sg. obj., **NA**: WZKM 57, 37: bottom 10 (document, cf. G qu. CAD sv 2a);

3. **LB** *murruqu* "to clear" (from claims) → 6.8.3. For *murruqu* (adj.) → 10.6.1.2.4.

G is found in the same contexts as **1.** and **2.** with a somewhat higher frequency, cf. CAD sv 1/2.

Marāṭu "to rub, scratch", D in prot. → 6.6.1.1 sv, **SB**: AfO 11, 223: 41 (cheeks); 46 (ear); 54/6 (lips); TDP 62: 14 (tongue).

Mašādu "to strike with palsy, to comb" (wool), D: "to rub?" acc. to CAD sv 4, "massieren" acc. to AHw sv → 6.8.3, **SB** (also SpTU 1, 47: 10 *muš-šu-da* = *muš-šu-'u*).

Mašāšu "to wipe, polish", D not disc., **OB**: BM 13928: 15 qu. CAD sv 2, AHw sv D; **SB**: OEC 6, 54: 29 *lim-ta-ši-iš*, Dt replacing the usual N form *limmašiš*, cf. CAD sv lex. sect. and 3, AHw sv N (person).

Mašā'u "to rob, plunder", D not disc., 1x **OB**: FM 2 p. 112 no. 71: r.11' (person).

Mašû "to forget" → 5.5.2 sv.

Mazāqu "to suck", D: not disc., **SB**: TDP 92: 27 (hands); 96: 36 (fingers), both in prot., cf. 6.6.1); AMT 30, 6: 7. r.3; 52, 1: 17 (medication); RA 36, 3: 10 // AMT 25, 1: I 3 + 2: 26 ("what?", cf. G in RA 36, 3: 3); **NA**: SAA 1, 229: r.5 (water, Dt).

Mazā'u "to squeeze, press", D 2x + pl. obj. (**1.**) (6.4.2 group IIc) or it is used idiomatically (**2.**):

1. pl. obj., **OB**: YOS 11, 26: IV 12 (ingredients); **NA**: SAA 1, 1: r. 50 (persons). Elsewhere G is used for "to squeeze", cf. CAD sv *mazû* 1.

2. idiom., MA *mazzu'u* "to rape" → 6.8.1 sv. For **muzzu'u* (NA) "narrow, difficult" → App. to Ch. X sv.

Mesû "to wash, clean", D → 6.8.4 sv:

1. persons and body parts, **SB**: BW 15: 16b (pers.); CT 16, 11: 35 (Dt pass.); Šurpu VII 82 (Dt pass.); VIII 83 (Dt pass. (?, or refl.?) (all pers.); AfO 19, 54: 234 (arms, stat.); OEC 6, 49: 25 (mouth, stat.); BAM 161: II 14 acc. to AHw sv Dt 2 (mouth, Dt pass.); for reflexive Dt "to wash" (oneself) → 9.1.2 sv;

2. animal, **OB**: AbB 3, 36: 27 (donkey, Dt (but CAD sv 6: obscure);

3. ingredients in recipes, **OB**: YOS 11, 26: I 5; III 40 (birds); II 27 (intestines); I 53; 57; II 23 (bird);

4. "to refine" copper, **OA**: kt c/k 216: 18; ICK 1, 85: 8 (VA, → 10.6.1.2.4 sv).

Mêšu "to despise, treat with contempt", D not disc., **OB**: UET 5, 81: 22. 29. 52 (cf. G in 18) (person); **SB**: Racc. 144: 425 (rites of a temple).

N

Na'āsu "to chew", D not disc., cf. 6.9.2.1. sv, **SB**: BBR p. 112: 6 (cedarwood, // G).

Nabû "to name, call", D **SB**: "to lament" (intr.) → 6.8.1 sv, cf. CAD sv *n.* B b (also UnDiv. 104: II 21).

Nâdu "to praise, extol", D not disc., but cf. 6.9.1.1: **OAk** in PNs → MAD 3, 189; **OB**: VS 10, 214: I 1; RA 15, 181: 11; 22, 172: 2f; HSAO 185: 1f; **SB**: passim → CAD sv lex. sect. and 3/4/5, AHw sv D/Dtn/Dt; note especially Gilg. VI 170 G // D, cf. CAD sv 1a.

Nakāmu "to stock, heap up", D + pl. obj. → 6.4.5.1 sv (group Va), **SB**:

1. treasures and possessions, all in RI: VAB 4, 114: 47; 134: 21 (*bušû* "property"); 116: 21; 136: 18 (*niṣirtu* "treasure(s)); 152: 32 (all kinds of treasures); Asb. A V 134 (*makkūru* "property", stat.); AfO 13, 205: 7 (*simtu* "what is fitting" (for a temple), part.);

2. sorceries: Maqlû VII 2 = (19) and (143A).

Nakāpu "to butt, gore", D is used for pl. obj. and pl. action → 6.4.2.1 sv (group IIa):

1. literally, with animals as subj., **OB**: RA 42, 72: 29 = (76) (obj. person); **SB**: CT 40, 41a: 8 (obj. ox, prot. → 6.8.1.1 sv); BAM 248: III 55 = (87) (no overt obj.);

2. metaph. of gods: obj. enemies, **OB**: KH III 9 (part.); **SB**: Asb. A IX 78; elsewhere part.: AAA 20, 80: 7; BMS 46: 19 (acc. to CAD sv *n.* A 3); PEA p. 32: 5; VAB 4, 222: 14; other objects: RA 13, 107b: 7 (*kibrāti* "the world"); Or. 36, 118: 47 (*ṣuṣû* "reed beds"); RA 27, 19: 23 (*anuntu* "battle array", cf. *kaṣāru* **4.**);

3. idiomatic → 6.4.9: "to invade" hostile country, **OB**: OBE no. 1: r. 19'; **SB**: SAA 8, 331: 5; 362: 3; 389: r.4; 505: 6 (obj. the enemy's land and equivalent expressions), all omen apodoses, cf. *palāšu*.

Nakāsu "to cut off, fell", D almost always + pl. obj → 6.4.1.1 sv (group Ia):

1. "to cut off" (body parts), **OB**: AbB 9, 264: 11 (ears+necks, stat.); **OA**: AMM p. 152 kt k/k 108: 10 (necks); **SB** passim → AHw sv D 3, CAD sv 6a/c; note with *šīrū* "flesh" Asb. B VI 82; IAsb. 95 a 7 // b 5; Asb. A IV 74 (VA); also SpTU 3, 94: 48 (feet); 53 (heads); JAOS 103, 212: 19 (wombs);

2. "to slaughter" animals, lit.: **OAk**: BIN 8, 141: 16 (sheep); **SB**: LKU 51: 9 (sheep, Dt); **NB**: BIN 1, 25: 27. 31. 38; TCL 13, 145: 10. 12; YOS 7, 8: 20; 143: 4 (sheep); metaph., people "like animals", **SB**: RIMA 2/I, 19: 99; Sg. Wi. 122: 131; Iraq 25, 56: 44; SKS p. 104: 14 (*ša* "whoever", qu. in note 5);
3. "to fell", **OB**: AbB 4, 20: 10 = (132A) (trees); 10, 211: 10 (*la-he-e*, wooden objects);
4. other pl. objects, **MB**: UM 1/2, 20: 4 (grain piles, cf. G in WZJ 8, 565: 35); **SB**: garments TuL 95: 44 (VA); **NB**: breaches ABL 1339: 4 (*ni-ka-si* ↔ G + *niksu*, cf. CAD sv 1c); dates CT 22, 78: 10. 13 (stat.);
5. with sg. obj., **MA**: *KAV 1: III 79 (see → 6.4.1.1 sv); **SB**: TDP 182: 44f (garment, prot. → 6.6.1.1 sv); BWL 78: 136 (calf); IV R 25: II 22 (hand). [Iraq 14, 34: 90 read *ú-na-pi-iṣ*, cf. RIMA 2/I, 291: 90].

Napāhu "to light, set fire to, to rise, to blow", D is used with pl. obj. (**1.**) and as a part. (**2.**):
1. "to light", with pl. obj. → 6.4.8, **OB**: *ARM 26/1 p. 159 note a A.2821: 9 (fire signals); **SB**: VAB 7, 264: 10 (piles of brushwood, stat.); HBA 86: II 9 (braziers, Dt);
2. part. *munappihu* "rumor-monger" (CAD sv), "Feueranzünder, Hetzer (?)" (AHw sv), and *munappihtu* "bellows" → 6.6.2 with note 18. For intr. D "to hiss, snort, rattle" → 7.6.1; for *nuppuh* "bloated" or "inflamed" in omens → 10.6.1.2.1 sv and 10.8.

Napālu "to tear out, dig up, demolish", D is used for pl. obj. (**1.**, **2.**) → 6.4.1.1 sv (group Ia) or pl. action (**3.**, **4.**) → 6.6.1.1 sv and 6.6.3.2:
1. "to gouge out (eyes), to blind", + *înīšu*, **SB**: RIMA 2/I, 201: 117; 221: 113; AfO 8, 22; 2; Dreams 328: 5; elliptically without *înīšu*, with pl. obj.: **MB**: RIMA 1, 184: 74; **SB**: RIMA 2/I, 88: 10'; LKA 62: r.3 (all pers.,); exc. with sg. obj. see **5.**;
2. teeth: "to pick" (?), **SB**: AfO 11, 223: 38 (prot. → 6.6.1.1 sv);
3. "to dig up", **SB**: CT 39, 7b: r.5 (*eperē* "dust, earth", prot. → 6.6.1.1 sv); **OB**: part. *munappi[lum]* "digger" MSL 12, 164: 222 (cf. G in 221) → 6.6.2 sv;
4. with sg. obj. or without obj., mostly for pl. action, **OB**: ARM 3, 22: 24 = (79) (town); 27, 161: 4 = (80) (no overt obj.: "to search"); **SB**: AfO 8, 28: 9 = (08) (no overt obj.); CT 38, 47: 42 // 30, 30b: 11 (house: "to turn upside down", prot. → 6.6.1.1 sv); SpTU 3, 94: 150 (id.);
5. Exc. with sg. obj., **SB**: BWL 146: 45 (eye, stat.); Ét. de Meyer 70: 33 (temple: "to destroy").

Napāṣu "to strike, smite", D mostly + pl. obj. → 6.4.1.1 sv (group Ia):
1. people, **SB**: LKU p. 9: 31 // UM 1/2, 113: 16 (children); JNES 17, 138: 11 (heroes); ACh. Ad. 17: 35 // ACh. Spl. 59: 12 // 60: 2 (*ašarēdūtu* "vanguard"); K.3780: I 3 qu. CAD sv 7b (enemies); AfO 24, 102: 10 (id.); passim in RIs with obj. enemies, warriors, etc. (all pl.), cf. CAD sv *n.* A 7b; AHw sv *n.* I D 1b; also animals, **OB**: Gilg. P III 31 (wolves); **SB**: RIMA 2/I, 291: 90 (ostriches);
2. of doors "to break", **SB**: CT 38, 11: 53 (stat., var. *nuppušū*);
3. of substances: dough ("to break"), **OB**: YOS 11, 26: I 36 ([*līš*]*am*); barley ("to crush"), **OB**: TEBA 56: 11; **SB**: LL VA, said of malt, beerwort and sesame (all pl.) → CAD sv;
4. with abstract obj., **OA**: KUG 8: 13 (accounts: "to clear", stat. pl.).

Naqāru "to tear down, scrape", D not disc., but cf. 6.4.1.2, **OB**: MDP 57, 3: r.5 (fortresses); **SB**: CT 39, 25a: 11 (*qaqqara* (the ground), prot. → 6.6.1.1 sv).

Naqû "to pour out, sacrifice", D mostly + pl. obj. (esp. mass nouns) → 6.4.7.1 sv (group VIIa):
1. variousliquids, **SB**: KAR 16: r.26 (honey+wine+two kinds of beer); Racc. 42: 19; 46: 22 (honey+butter+milk+beer+wine+oil); STT 197: 45 (two kinds of beer); AnBi 12, 286: 98 = (110); BagF. 18, 325: 10 = (114) (beer); KAR 4: r.9 (water); **NA**: *munaqqîtu* "libation bowl" SAA 10, 336: 4 → 6.6.2 with note 18;
2. grain, **SB**: Šurpu V 178. 181; JNES 15, 138: 105. 115. 119; flour: Gilg. V II 48;
3. with obj. *niqû*, **SB**: STT 197: 47;
4. "to shed" (blood), **SB**: CT 41, 22: 20; 40, 46: r.45.

Nasāhu "to tear out, remove", D mostly + pl. obj. → 6.4.1.1 sv (group Ia):

1. "to remove, uproot" persons, **SB**: RIMA 2/I, 148: 20; 157: 9'; CT 40, 42d: 4 +D (Dt); SpTU 4, 145: r.9 (Dt); LKA 77: I 53 acc. to CAD sv lex. sect. (part.);

2. body parts, **OB**: ZA 75, 200: 59 (locks of hair); **SB**: AfO 8, 194: 3 (intestines); SAA 3, 40: 7 (eyes); BWL 190: r.6 (id., restored);

3. other concrete objects, **OB**: AbB 6, 149: r.5' (*hūqī* "steps"?); ARM 13, 18: 6 (*qitmī* "dark spots"?); **MB**: CT 36, 7: II 19 (boundary stones); **SB**: RIMA 2/I, 253: 33 (drain pipes); Sg. 8: 259 (beams); Asb. A VI 60 (ornamental bulls); Gilg. I III 37 (traps); XI 101 (mooring poles, // G, cf. CAD sv 2f); BA 5, 572: 21 (bolts); SBH 4: 105 (roots); **NB**: ABL 1010: 11 (dagger(s); **NA**: ABL 493: r.8 (*sakannu*'s = ?);

4. idiomatic expressions, obj. also sg. and/or abstract), **OB**: AbB 2, 112: 21 (*awātim* "matters"); AbB 9, 52: 27 (silver: "to cash"?); **OA**: CCT 3, 16b: 10 (*šīmam*: "to deduct"); **SB**: "to excerpt" (tablet(s)), both sg. and pl.? JCS 11, 8: 29; DA 35 edge 2; BAM 101: 2; ZA 43, 86: IV 4; and cf. zi.meš-*ha* = *nussuhā* acc. to AHw sv D 7;

5. exceptions with concrete sg. obj. → 6.4.9, **OB**: ARM 27, 36: 37 = (138) (pers.); 18, 6: 19 (*itiqšu* "its tassels"); **SB**: TuL 88: 4 (pers.); JNES 33, 342: 22 (body); Dreams 328: 7 (eye).

Nasāqu "to select, choose", D mostly + pl. obj. → 6.4.7.1 sv (group VIIb):

1. lit., **OB**: AbB 1, 139: 11' (workmen); UET 5, 81: 50 (copper ingots); **OA**: TC 3, 118: 8 (textiles); **MB**: RIMA 1, 183: 42 (young men); **SB**: JCS 11, 8: 30 (days); **NB**: YOS 3, 184: 11 (wool);

2. with sg. obj., **OB**: ARM 13, 44: 9 = (78) (an expert, cf. 6.6.3.2);

3. idiomatic, **OB**: AbB 13, 71: 12 (+ *dabābam* "to look for trouble" (tr. Van Soldt)); **SB**: BSOAS 20, 265: 9 (*ramanka* "yourself"). [AfO 20, 121: 20 *ú-ta-si-ik* is from *esēku*].

Naṣābu "to suck, lick", D **SB**:

1. fingers: SpTU 1, 37: 3 // 2, 44: 3, prot. → 6.6.1.1 sv (versus G + one finger in UET 5, 8: 14. 18 (OB));

2. in **SB** med. (not disc.): AMT 26, 3: 3; BAM 29: 4; 78: 6; BKBM 22: 19 acc. to CAD sv 2, AHw sv D; STT 279: 11; TDP 222: 39; KUB 4, 49: II 2 (medication(s) in honey); AMT 85, 1: II 2 (lard); G usually with object "blood", cf. CAD sv 1a.

Našāku "to bite, gnaw", D is used for pl. obj. (**1.**) → 6.4.2.1 sv (group IIa) and for pl. action (**2.**, **3.**) → 6.6.1.1 sv:

1. outside omen protases, with animate beings and body parts as object, mostly pl., **SB**: BiOr 28, 8: 10; ACh. Sin 34: 28 (people); ACh. Spl. Išt. 37: III 33 +D (people and animals); KAR 298: r. 20 (enemies, part.); Gilg. VI 63 (thighs); AAA 20, 89: 160 (hands (*rittu*)); BWL 190: r.9 (*šī*[*ršu*] "his flesh"); uncert.: BAM 105: 6 (*ṣur-re-e-ki* "your heart" (?), pl. ?);

2. part. → 6.6.2 sv: *munaššiku*, of a dog MSL 8/2, 14: 102; KAR 54: 6; also Gilg. VI 41, qu. in note 11 to Ch. V *sub* B;

3. in prot. → 6.6.1.1 sv, **a)** with a person as subject: TDP 214: 16; 236: 56 (hands); 88: 6 (arms); AfO 11, 223: 52f; TBP 55: 4' (lip); TDP 62: 16; Epilepsy p. 91: 105 = (42); AfO 11, 224: 62 // 222: no. 1: 4'; **b)** with an animal as subject: DA 103: 18 (dogs each other → 9.1.3); CT 40, 33: 9 / TU 8: 8 (a donkey people); CT 40, 34: r.8 // TU 8: r.5 = (50B) (a horse its mate or people); SpTU 3, 94: 90 (a sow, no overt obj.); CT 28, 40: 14 (a mother animal its young); TuL 42: 9 (a sacrificial sheep its tongue); CT 39, 25: 6; ZA 77, 204: 21 (a crow the ground).

Našāpu "to blow away", D not disc., **OB**: ARM 1, 21: r.21' (sesame: "to winnow"); **SB**: BagF. 16, 262: 86 (plaster of a temple wall).

Našāqu "to kiss", D mostly + pl. subj. → 6.5.1 sv:

1. person, **SB**: VAB 2, 357: 86; Ee I 54; SAA 3, 37: 7'f; Akîtu pl. 6: 26 (all sg. obj.);

2. feet, **OB**: Gilg. P I 11. 21; OEC 11, p. 16: 44; Atr. 60: 245; **MB**: BE 17, 5: 18 (knees and feet); **MA**: MVAG 41/3, 12: 38; 14: 3; **SB**: passim, cf. CAD sv 3b-1', AHw sv D 2; **NA**: SAA 1, 133: r.3'. 9';
3. + *qaqqara* "the ground", **SB**: passim in RIs, cf. CAD sv 3b-2', AHw sv D 3.

Našāru "to cut off, reduce", D not disc., cf. 6.8.4:
1. "to set aside", **OB**: YOS 12, 316: 4; 358: 5 (silver); **OA** (→ 6.6.3.1.): BIN 4, 51: 45; CCT 4, 10a: 15 = (62) (silver); Or. 36, 408 note 1 sub d: 3 = (63) (garments);
2. **SB** in various idiomatic meanings: "to cut off" Šurpu V 153. 159 (*māmītu* "curse", part.); CT 16, 14: IV 9a // AfO Beiheft 6, 99: 2 (heaven and earth); "to diminish" CT 16, 14: IV 9b; Lugal 332 (land, part.); KAR 31: r.2 (people); Iraq 38, 90: 8 (offerings); UET 6, 392: 14 // CT 16, 12: I 3 ("everything", part.); "to cut sb off from" HGŠ 96: 13 (pers., non-ag.); "to subtract" LBAT 1495: 8.

Naṭālu "to look at, watch", D → 6.8.1 sv: **OB** Mari ARM 13, 145: 28; 27, 81: 14.

Nêru "to kill, destroy", D not disc., **OB**: Gilg. JCS 8, 92: 14 (a demon); **SB**: SpTU 1, 40: 2 (*ši-pit qaqqadi*, cf. comm. sag.giš.ra = *nu-ú-ú-ru*); mostly part., cf. 6.9.3: RIMA 2/I, 148: 16 (enemies); AGH 116: 14 (demons); St. Reiner 17: 4 (regions of the world); Iraq 38, 91: r.8 ("the evil one", restored, cf. Sum.); without object, **OB** LL: AS 16, 23: 75 *munêrt[um]* "murderess".

P

Pa'āṣu "to crush, smash, hit", D not disc.:
1. lit., **OB**: BagM. 21, 165: 5 (jewelry, Dt); **SB**: AMT 35, 2: 10; SpTU 1, 44: 23 (ingredients), cf. 6.9.2.1;
2. idiomatic: "to steal"?, **NA**: SAA 1, 235: 13; 236: r.6; ABL 992: 21.

Pâdu "to imprison", D mostly + pl. obj. (6.4.4 group IVb): **OB**: AbB 5, 219: r.2' acc. to AHw 1581a sv; ARM 26/2 p. 165 no. 363: 27; **MB**: BE 17, 1: 6; UM 1/2, 22: 13; WZJ 8, 566: 40 (persons); UDBD 116: 6 (ox). For persons D always has a pl. obj., but not in the single case where an ox is object. G + pl. obj. is also common, cf. AHw sv G, and, e.g., AbB 11, 22: 11'; 13, 97: 10'; A.2550: 6' qu. ARM 26/1 p. 282f note 17.

Pakāru "to fetter", D not disc., **SB**: AnSt. 6, 156: 133 (hands+feet+head); **NB**: YOS 3, 67: 13 (persons); 7, 97: 14 (person).

Palāku "to delimit, stake out" (a plot), D **SB**: Sn. 97: 88; 101: 58 = (30) → 6.5.2.

Palāq/ku "to slaughter, massacre", D always + pl. obj. → 6.4.1.1 sv (group Ia):
1. sacrificial animals (mostly sheep, oxen, bulls (*lû*)), **MB**: UM 1/2, 27: 20 (birds?); 50: 18; BE 15, 199: 30 (VA); **SB**: passim, cf. AHw sv D 1, Dt, e.g., VAB 7, 264: 8 = (119) (stat.);
2. enemies "like animals", **MB**: Tn-Ep. IVb: 46 (princes, stat.); RIMA 1, 184: 73; **SB**: KB 1, 186: 43; Sg. Cyl. 18 (part.); Sn. 45: 1.

Palāšu "to pierce, perforate, burgle", D mostly + pl. obj. → 6.4.2.1 sv (group IIa):
1. bodies and body parts, **OB**: AbB 9, 228: 10 (hands, stat.); RA 65, 73: 54' (intestines, stat.); **MA**: KAV 1: V 84. 101; VI 45 (ears); **SB**: Sn. 45: 81 (bodies); TBP 7: 9 (face, stat., pl. t.);
2. other objects, **OB**: MSL 12, 207: 154 (houses, part.); **SB**: BAM 237: IV 40 (blocks); ACh. Išt. 25: 20 (houses); Ee V 58 (water holes); SAA 3, 34: 69 // 35: 41 (holes); **NA**: SAA 2 p. 54f: 595 (id., stat.). 598 (id.);
3. with abstract object, **OB**: ARM 26/2 p. 183 no. 373: 37 (*awātim* "words");
4. idiomatic: + *mātam* "to invade" → 6.4.9, **OB** omen texts: YOS 10, 28: 4; 31: II 22; 42: I 57; 45: 36; 47: 84f // 48: 21f. For the stative *pulluš* in extispicy omens → 10.6.1.1.3.

Paqādu "to entrust, appoint, take care of, inspect", D mostly + pl. obj. → 6.4.7.1 sv (group VIIa):
1. "to entrust to", **OB**: AbB 11, 161: 33 (obj. broken, but pl.); 13, 48: r.5' (animals); NAPR 5, 6: A 32 // B 19' (everything); **OA**: VS 26, 47: 14 (silver); RA 59, 151f: 11. 14. 23. 63; 153: 21 (everything); KTH 18:

38 (id.); **MB**: BE 14, 168: 58 (animals, stat.); **SB**: BWL 134: 128 (everybody, stat.); **NB**: ABL 530: r.10 = (16) (pers., stat.);

2. id. in **MA** with pl. *indirect* obj. → 6.5.2: AfO 10, 38ff no. 78: 13; 88: 12; 102: 9 = (29B); KAJ 185: 15; 213: 13; 214: 23 (sheep to persons, all stat.); MAOG 7, 52a: 12; 49: 19 acc. to Weidner, AfO 10, 45 *ad* no. 40 (id., but not stat.);

3. "to inspect, muster", **OB**: ARM 26/1 p. 287 no. 121: 8 (oracles); **MB**(?): AfO 24, 96: 9 (figurines); **SB**: Erra I 184 (gods); IAsb. 42: 14 (bonds of heaven, part.); CT 16, 5: 184; BiOr 30, 164: 10 (limbs);

4. "to take care of": **MB**: UM 2/2, 51: 19 (houses); **SB**: Ee VI 110 (cf. G in VII 85); PSBA 20, 154: 22; WO 4, 32: VI 1 (sanctuaries); **NA**: SAA 5, 242: 11 (persons, but acc. to Lanfranchi-Parpola to **5**.);

5. "to provide", **SB**: BWL 218: 9 (bribe, logical pl.); **NA**: SAA 10, 353: 18. 22 (sheep (pl.));

6. "to appoint", **SB**: AS 5, 10: 17; Asb. A I 58. 111; SAA 3, 32: 4; **NA**: BagF. 16, 247: 17'; ABL 434: 11 (stat., cf. note 1 to Ch. III); 885: 11 = (15) (stat.); SAA 1, 239: 11 (stat.); 5, 152: 17; 10, 222: r.9 (all persons);

7. with sg. object, **OB**: ARM 27, 1: 4. 7 (palace, possibly an idiomatic usage comparable to those discussed in 6.4.9); **SB**: Maqlû II 50 = (93) (pers., stat.); AfO 18, 298: 34 = (94) (pers.); SAA 3, 3: 17 = (34A) ("my life").

Parāku "to block, obstruct", D not disc., but cf. 6.4.8 and 6.8.4:

1. with pers. obj., **OB**: AbB 11, 193: 19 (Dt); **MA**: KAV 112: 16; **NA**: SAA 3, 33: r.22';

2. of doors and the like, **OB**: ARM 26/2 p. 498 no. 523: 33 (the *pūt nawîm* "front of the steppe"); **MB**: BBS 8: IV 27 (door); **MA**: KAV 215: 10 acc. to Deller, Or. 30, 352 (door, stat.); **SB**: Asb. A IV 82 (streets, stat.);

3. "to lay crosswise" → 6.4.8, **OB**: YOS 10, 42: II 62 (lines on ribs, stat.); **SB**: BagF. 18, 133: 74 (twigs upon braziers); KAR 91: r.20 (poles across a cistern); ArOr 17/1, 196: 29 (spears, stat.); CT 38, 8: 32 (potsherds, stat.); TDP 204: 52/55 (stat.); SpTU 4, 149: II 27' (veins, stat.);

4. with abstract obj., **OB**: AbB 7, 86: 38; 11, 78: 17; 112: 12 (+ *dabābam* "to raise objections"); 3, 48: 18 acc. to AHw sv D 1 and Frankena, SLB IV p. 153 (+ *awāt*[*im*] "to settle affairs"); VAB 6, 207: 10 (*nikkassī* "accounts");

5. without object, **OB**: AbB 1, 135: 25 acc. to AHw sv D 1; TCL 17, 40: 25; VOM 180/1: 6; 12; **MA**: VS 19, 15: 10.

Parāsu "to cut off, cut into pieces, separate, decide", D is often associated with plurality → 6.4.4.1 sv (Ia):

1. animals and body parts (pl.), **OB**: CT 45, 86: 22 (limbs); YOS 11, 26: IV 2 (birds, in food preparation, cf. D + sg. obj. (**4**.) in 25: 47); VAB 7, 330: 8 (limbs); MVAeG 40/2, 64: 9 (toes, stat.);

2. "to separate" people, **OB**: ARM 2, 76: 16; MARI 4, 406: 15; **SB**: SAA 3, 33: r.19 (stat.); **NA**: ABL 85: 7; and animals, **SB**: Asb. A IX 46; VAB 7, 132: 9;

3. with abstract pl. obj., **SB**: SpTU 2, 12: II 12 = (124) (sins, stat.); **NB**: CT 22, 241: 23 (accounts);

4. "to cut or split into many parts", **OB**: YOS 11, 25: 47 (bird, cf. pl. in 26: IV 2); 10, 11: I 15 (the "path" of the liver, stat., qu. as (45) in 10.6.1.1.3); **SB**: CT 17, 5: 53 (animal); AOAT 1, 6: 80 (an *eṭemmu*, VA);

5. + *warka*/*ātu* "to investigate matters/the matter, **OB**: MARI 5, 164f: 20. 25. 41 = (137A); ARM 10, 124: 11; 27, 85: 10; Ét. Garelli 55 M.7322: 25'; **SB**: MSL 1, 80: 33f (cf. note 19).

Parāṣu A "to break an oath", D: "to lie" (not disc.), **SB**: VAB 3, 59: 90. 92; 61: 97; 67: 105 (NB RIs).

Parāṣu B "to perform" rites (*parṣī*), D not disc., but see 8.3.2 and 8.4.2, **SB**: TuL 72: 9; Racc. 89: 5 (Dt).

Parā'u "to cut off, sever", D + pl. obj. → 6.4.1 group Ib): **SB**: Ee IV 131 (veins); SpTU 2, 2: 70 (limbs, Dt); Šurpu V 163 (head+hands+feet); Sn. 45: 3; Asb. A IX 85 (throats (or lives?)); Sn. 46: 15 (belts); Sg. Cyl. 22 (thickets, part.).

G occurs with similar objects, both sg. and pl. (rope, thread, root, body part(s)), cf. AHw sv G. Note G in Sn. 44: 73 (arrow) *pa-ri-i' napšāti*, versus D *ib.* 45: 3 and Asb. A IX 85 *napšātēšunu ú-par-ri-i'*.

Pasāmu "to cover, veil", D not disc., **OB**: AbB 9, 16: 38 (pers., cf. note k to the text); RA 32, 180: 9; 181: 10 // ZA 43, 306: 9 (night, stat.); **SB**: Ét. de Meyer 70: 11 (face); TDP 170: 10 (refl. Dt → 9.1.3 sv).

Pasāsu "to cancel, destroy", D → 5.6.4:

1. concrete objects, **OB**: AbB 3, 34: 14 (door); ARM 14, 18: r.8' (dams, stat.); 26/1 p. 497 no. 241: 27 (head of an *izbu*); RIME 4, 382: 54 (walls, Dt, qu. as (05) in 9.1.1); **SB**: AOTU 1, 295: 18 (pers.); UET 6, 391: 9 (stone, qu. in 3.1.3.1 sv *ṣehheru*); IV R 12: r.22 (part of a wagon); KB 3/1, 192: 30 (stela);

2. tablets, seals, etc., **OB**: RIME 4, 709: 29; 711: 29 (writing); **MB**: MDP 2, 108: 55 (id.); BE 14, 145: 16 (seal, Dt); **SB**: MSL 1, 87: 14 (seal, Dt); 88: 26. 29 (id.); 5, 57f: 90/3 (id., Dt); **NB**: VS 5, 99: 6 (contracts); Cyr. 368: 6 (tablet); Iddin-Marduk 2, 211: 13 (id.);

3. abstract concepts, **OB**: KH XXVI r.28 (judgment); OBRED 1, 54: 20 (*arnam* "penalty"); **SB**: BagF. 18, 468: 14 (part.); IAsb. 42: 13 (bad signs and dreams, part.); JNES 15, 136: 71. 77 (Dt); Asb. A IV 38 (part.); AGH 148: 22; Šurpu II 191; IV 81 (Dt) (sins); YOS 1, 38: II 33 (sin); AnSt. 7, 130: 33 (oracle, *tāmītu*, Dt); CT 23, 2: 14 (the "knot of evil"); BagF. 18, 326: 13' (evil, part.); BHT 87: 17 (deeds, cf. AHw sv D 3).

Paṣādu "to cut into, cleave", D not disc., **MB**: RIMA 1, 267: 7 (mountain rock); 272: 44 (mountains); **NA**: Iraq 4, 186: 16 acc. to AHw sv Dt(t) (temple, intrans. Dt, cf. (05) and (06) in 9.1.1).

Paṣānu "to cover, veil", D not disc., **MA** laws, said of a woman: KAV 1: V 60. 62 (stat.); *ib.* 65f. 88 (Dt); *ib.* 68. 77. 89. 94 (VA); KAV 1 VI 1. 3 (= (03A) in 10.2); *ib.* 7 (= (03B) in 10.2) (stat.); *ib.* 12 (VA).

Pašāru "to untie, release", D not disc., cf. 6.8.4, **SB** unless indicated otherwise:

1. lit.: a knot, 1x **SB**: KB 6/2, 42: 16 (*pitilta*);

2. sorcery, curses, spells, sins, etc: + *kispī* LKA 155: r.17; Maqlû IV 73; V 123; VI 24; K.9666: 3 qu. AHw sv D 2b (part.); RA 18, 165: 21. 23; KAR 165: 16f; cf. also ARM 26/1 p. 532 no. 253: r.14' (stat., OB); + *ruhû* Maqlû V 123; VI 117; K.9666: 3 qu. AHw sv D 2b (part.); SpTU 4, 140: 12; + *šiptu* Maqlû I 134; + *māmītu* Šurpu II 193 Var; III 2; JNES 15, 136: 78 (Dt); + *arnu ib.* 77 (Dt); + *namburbû* BagF. 18, 392; 10'; 469: 16 (part.); ominous signs: BagF. 18, 301: 17 (part.); dreams: JCS 29, 66: 6; MSL 12, 194: 5 (part., OB); part. without genitive: KAR 165: 17 (*šamma mu-pa-še-ru* → 6.6.2 with note 18);

3. with pers. obj.: TCS 2 p. 17 no. 1: 16;

4. other objects: body parts: BAM 248: II 54. 67 (wombs: "to become relaxed", Dt); BWL 343: 2 (clouds: "to dissolve", part.);

5. a process performed on textiles, **OB**: MSL 12, 177: 10 (part. → 6.6.2 with note 18); Syr. 59, p. 130ff, 140f.

Pašāšu "to anoint, smear". D not disc., 1x **OB**: YOS 12, 421: 10 (of straw: "ölen" acc. to AHw sv D 2).

Pašāṭu "to erase", D mostly + pl. obj. → 6.4.1 group Ib):

1. OAk: TIM 9, 35: 13 (designs of a stela); **MB**: BBS 6: II 33 (name(s)); **SB**: Sg. Silber 50+D; Cyl. 76 // Stier 104 (*uṣurātu* "figural representations", part.); VAB 7, 298: 36 (*dabābu* "words" (coll.)); BKBM 32: 51 (spoken words: "to mangle"?, prot. → 6.6.1.1 sv); **NB**: TCL 13, 160: 13 (writing boards);

2. exc. sg. obj, **MB**: KB 4, 80: III 5 (stela).

A case of D + pl. obj. ↔ G + sg. obj. is TIM 9, 35: 13/15 *ša uṣurāt narêja ašar ú-ṣa-ru ú-pa-ša-ṭu* / (...) / [*š*]*a šumī šaṭram ašar šaṭru i-pa-ši-ṭú-ú-ma* "who erases (D) the designs of my stela where I made (!? present!) (them), (...) who erases (G) my written name, where it is written". G occurs passim with obj. "name", cf. AHw sv G 1, but hardly in other contexts, apart from the stative sg. and pl. in omens in an obscure idiomatic meaning, cf. *ib.* sv G 2.

Pâšu "to crush", D 1x + pl. obj. (6.4.1 group Ic): **SB**: BE 31, 26: 10 acc. to AHw sv D (herbs); elsewhere G (rare), cf. AHw sv G.

Patāhu "to perforate, pierce", D + pl. obj. → 6.4.2 group IIb): **SB**: Asb. A VII 37 (persons, reciprocal Dt → 9.1.3); **NB**: ABL 520: r.20; 1000: r.9 (oxen); **NA**: SAA 2 p. 57: 643 (persons). AHw mentions only sg. objects for G (but most instances occur in broken context).

Patālu "to wrap, wind", D → 6.6.2 sv, 1x **OB**: MSL 12, 170: 11 (part.). For *puttulu* in omens → 10.7.1.1.

Patāqu "to cast, build", D not disc., **OB**: ARM 13, 15: 10 (silver); 25, 314: 3. 6 (lead).

Paṭāru "to loosen, release, redeem", D is used with pl. obj. (**1.**-**3.**) → 6.4.3.1 sv (group IIIa), and idiom. (**4.**-**8.**) → 6.4.3.1 and 6.4.9:

1. "to loosen" knots, ties and bonds, *kiṣru*: **OB**: ZA 45, 14: I 45; **SB**: Maqlû I 34; BWL 211: 20; AMT 90, 1: 1; AGH 80: 83 (Dt); *riksu* (concrete, cf. **3b**): BWL 44: 104 (stat.); JNES 17, 138: 19 acc. to AHw sv D 5; OEC 1, 33: 60 (stat.); *ṣimdu*: BWL 114: 38 (all pl.);

2. id. other concrete objects, **OB**: Iraq 25, 183: 9 (hems of a garment); AfO 23, 86a (combs); ARM 18, 3: 7 (mountings); **OA**: kt a/k 98: 7 (textiles: "to unpack"); **MA**: KAJ 310: 4 (hides, stat.); **SB**: BAM 248: II 53. 66 (limbs, Dt); Asb. A I 45; BBS 37: 4; PEA 33: 9 (wells);

3. "to undo" abstract objects: **a**) sins, **OB**: CRRAI 36, 99 Di 614: 07; **MB**: *RA 16, 89 no. 45: 7 (sins, part.); **SB**: BagF. 18, 272: 17'; Maqlû VII 139, cf. AfO 21, 79a; Šurpu IV 93; JNES 33, 282: 137; SpTU 2, 18: 24 (part.); 3, 84: 8 (part.); **b**) ordinances (*riksu*, cf. **1.**), **SB**: BWL 114: 51. 54; **NA**: ABL 733: r.5; **c**) rest: AnSt. 30, 105: 24 (guilt+sin, Dt); BWL 60: 87 (sighs, Dt); AGH 120: 13 (fears, Dt); 36a: 13 (portents, Dt); BagF. 18, 288: 11' (*namburbi*'s, part.); VAB 7, 254: 16 ("to do" calculations);

4. "to release, redeem" of persons (both sg. and pl.), **OB**: AbB 1, 13: 19; 2, 95: 11; 6, 32: 20; 9, 109: 13; 11, 184: 15; 12, 26: 17; 13, 85: 23; Horn Museum p. 125 no. 89: 9; CT 48, 6: 10'; MHET 1, 90: 16; CHJ p. 65 no. 122: 17; ARM 26/1 p. 190 no. 46: 8; **OA**: HUCA 33, 51 note 27: 34; **NA**: SAA 10, 169: r.2; **NB**: ABL 460: r.2; 702: r.2; CT 22, 74: 27; Nbn. 1113: 1. 19 (VA);

5. "to clear, demolish" buildings (both sg. and pl.), **MB**: BE 17, 35: 9 (stat.); RIMA 1, 140: 40; **SB**: BMisc. 4: II 33; **NA**: SAA 1, 77: 15. r.5; RA 60, 62: 10; 63 K.1103: 6'; ABL 1243: 8;

6. intrans. Dt "to decay, disintegrate" → 9.1.1, **SB**: YOS 1, 38: I 21 acc. to AHw sv Dt 1; Iraq 15, 123: 5; VAB 4, 212: 22 (bondings); 98: II 3 (brick wall); BagM 21, 341: 16 (sanctuary, qu. as (06) in 9.1.1);

7. Atypical cases, **SB**: Asb. B V 45 (enemy: "wehrlos machen" acc. to AHw sv D 9);

8. Other cases with sg. obj. → 6.4.3.1 sv, **OB**: AbB 6, 135: r.15' (yoke); 2, 98: 17 (ship); ARM 13, 24: 6, cf. MARI 2, 145 (table: "to remove"?); **SB**: Šurpu II 167 // SpTU 2, 13: 27 = (92) (curse); *AGH 14: 23 (taboo); *ABRT 1, 57: 27 (punishment); Erra I 133. 136. 170 (the "order" (*šipṭu*) of heaven and earth); SpTU 3, 82: I 28 (the structure (*šiknu*) of heaven and earth); MSL 5, 37: 353 (Dt). For *puṭṭur* in omens → 10.6.1.1.3.

Pehû "to lock", D not disc., **SB**: Ee V 56 (nostrils); BRM 4, 13: 21 (doors, non-ag.); **NB**: ABL 327: 19 (doors); 328: r.19 (person: to lock up"?).

Pesēnu "to hide", D not disc., 1x **NB**: TCL 9, 92: 13 acc. to AHw 1583a.

Petû "to open", D mostly + pl. obj. → 6.4.3.1 sv (group IIIa) or it is used idiomatically → 6.4.9:

1. doors, gates, locks, seals, **OB**: ZA 75, 204: 117; Or. 23, 338: 14 (stat.); **SB**: passim, cf. AHw sv *p.* II D 1;

2. houses, rooms, etc., **OB**: AbB 8, 103: r.4' acc. to AHw sv D 3 (houses, stat.); **SB**: Sg. 8: 166. 186. 274. 295 (storerooms); AnSt. 30, 101: 13 (graves, Dt);

3. roads, etc., **OB**: RA 38, 86: 9 // RitDiv. 32: 48 = (02); 35: 107 ("paths" of the liver, stat.); **SB**: passim, cf. AHw sv *p.* II D 6;

4. waterways, **OB**: RIME 4, 603: 27 = (01A); AbB 4, 85: 7; MSL 4, 71: 106; **MB**: UM 1/2, 53: 10; **SB** AMT 45, 5: r.4 // 42, 4: 6; *Iraq 55, 129: I 4' (canals, part.);
5. other concrete objects, **OA**: ICK 1, 183: 19 (messages, stat.); **SB**: Sn. 106: 31; 120: 25 (apertures); CT 39, 32: 25 // 38, 7: 10 (holes in the ground, stat.); IAsb. 74: 11 (bellies: "to slit open"); AfO 19, 61: 6 (wells, part.); Ee VII 60 (wells); RIMA 2/I, 195: 31; 239: 32 (*mahāzī* "cult centres": "to found");
6. with abstract objects, **OB**: RA 86, 5: IV 15 (part.); KH r.XXIV 20 (hardships: "to relieve"); **SB**: BWL 166: 6 (words: "to make known");
7. part. → 6.6.2 sv, **OB**: MSL 12, 165: 238 (*mu-*[*p*]*e-e-t*[*u-ú*]) a person who opens sleuce-gates, cf. CAD sv *mupettû* a and AHw sv *petû* D 9a "Schleusenöffner?"; **SB**: MSL 6, 62: 131f; 76: 62f; 77: 15 *mupattîtum*, a plug for regulating a sluice gate (?) acc. to CAD *l.c.*; also a PN → CAD *l.c.*
8. "to open (sb's ears), inform sb", with *uznu* in plur., **OB**: ARM 26/1 p. 330 no. 165: 6'; **SB/NB/NA**: passim, cf. AHw sv p. II D 11a/b; with *uznu* in sg., **SB**: SAA 3, 1: r.12'; BWL 38: 8; ambiguous: AfO 19, 63: 57 (part.); with ellipse of "ears" **OA**: EL 246: 24; VS 26, 1: 31; 34: 8;
9. "to reclaim" uncultivated land, **OB**: AbB 4, 160: 19'; 10, 52: 13. 17; YOS 12, 440: 10; BBVOT 1, 139: 13; TIM 5, 41: 17; TJAUB 72: 25; VAB 5, 131A: 24; OBRED 4, 549: 25; 553: 16; **SB**: HBA 85: 22 (Dt); KB 6/2, 26: 13 (Dt); **NB**: BIN 1, 125: 8; Camb. 102: 5 acc. to AHw sv D 5 (see NRVGl. p. 124);
10. "to uncover" body parts: **MA** KAV 1: V 64; 67 (head, stat.); AfO 17, 287: 105 (shoulders, stat.);
11. exc. with sg. obj., **OA**: EL 326: 34 (document); **MB**: *Kish I pl. 34b: II 3 (tomb); **SB**: Ee V 54 (well). [NA *petû* D "to remove" is a factitive of *petû* "far away", cf. AHw sv D 15 and *petû* I (adj.) 13; AfO 13, 46: I 3 qu. AHw sv D 6a is an N-stem].

Puāgu "to take away", D 1x VA pl. → 6.4.7 group VIIc): **MA**: KAJ 310: 14 (tablets, VA). Elsewhere only G is found, cf. AHw sv.

Q

Qabû "to say, order", D: "to lament" → 6.8.1 sv *nabû*, **OB**: St. Sjöberg p. 327: 97; mostly as subst. *qubbû* "lamentation", cf. CAD sv *qubbû* s.

Qalāpu "to peel, skin", D mostly + pl. obj. → 6.4.1 (group Ib):
1. **OB** LL: MSL 12, 206: 140 (emblems, part.); **SB**: BKBM 58: 7 acc. to AHw sv D 3 (geckoes, cf. BAM 216: 70 with G + sg. obj.); Gilg. Iraq 28, 110: 26 (feet); CA 88: 16 (figs, VA);
2. part., **OB**: MSL 12, 164: 201 *mu-qá-li-pu-ú* "barley husker" → 6.6.2 sv.
The instances of G in CAD sv 1 have a sg. obj. (plant, animal, body part, metal object, boil), except CT 22, 217: 27 (NB), which, however, may also be a misspelt D form (*li-qé-lu-pu-'*, obj. reeds).

Qalû "to burn, roast, refine", D not disc., **OB**: StMar. 52: 7; ARM 7, 1: 8 (harvest); MDP 57, 11: IV 14 (objects); MSL 12, 193, C1: 4 (*mu-qá-al-lu-ú* "seller of roast barley", part. → 6.6.2 with note 18); **MB**: RIMA 1, 184: 87 (cities); **SB**: Or. 36, 422: 2 (door); CT 40, 46: r.50; 39, 4: 32 = SAA 10, 42: r.5 (something); AGH 100: 20 ((images of) gods); SpTU 4, 153: 3 (alum).

Qamû "to burn" (trans.), D + pl. obj. → 6.4.1 (group Ib): **SB**: BER 4, 152: 27 (roots); Sg. Lie 38: 4 acc. to CAD sv *q.* A 4 (hands); Sg. 8 + AfO 12, 145: 102 (*šīrū* "flesh", Dt); Gilg. EG pl. 42 SP 299: 12 (face, stat.). G occurs passim with sg. and pl. obj., cf. CAD sv *q.* A 1/2, AHw sv *q.* II G.

Qâpu "to believe, entrust", D: "to guarantee", **OAk**: Lewis Coll. 102: 9 qu. CAD sv *q.* A 5 (pers. obj.); part. *muqippu* "guarantor", cf. MAD 3 p. 222; **SB**: LL, cf. CAD sv. → 6.6.2 with note 18.

Qarānu (CAD: *garānu*) "to store, pile up", D + pl. obj. (often coll.) → 6.4.5.1 sv (group Va):
1. possessions, **OB**: KH III 21 (part.); **SB**: CT 37, 5: 11 (part.); Lugal 364; Sn. 138: 47; CT 39, 21: 168 // 22: 1 (Dt) (all obj. *karû* "barley pile(s)"); Or. 36, 116: 31 (*binût karê*, part.); VAB 4, 114: 47; 116: 20; 136:

15 (*makkūru* "property"); BWL 74: 63 (id., stat.); Ash. § 2: VII 3 (*mihirtu* ("produce") of sea and mountains); ZDMG 98, 32: 6 (barley+oil);

2. dead bodies: RIMA 2/I, 15: 22; 18: 54; 20: 19; Sg. Stier 34.

Qâšu "to donate, grant", D mostly + pl. obj. → 6.4.7.1 sv (group VIIa), **SB**:

1. obj. *qīšāti* "presents": Ee V 80; TuL 58: 22; and often in RIs, cf. CAD sv 3; AHw sv *qiāšum* D 2;

2. Dt with sg. (?) subj.: Racc. 26: 25 (subj. broken);

3. rest: MSL 1, 4: 38 (no obj., cf. note 19).

Qatāpu "to pluck, cut off", D mostly + pl. obj. → 6.4.1 (group Ib), **SB**:

1. with obj. *umṣāti* "excrescences" in med.: BAM 168: 66 // 108: 2; STT 97: III 10. 19 // BAM 95: 12; AMT 40, 5: III 5 (Dt); BAM 168: 51 (Dt);

2. exc. with sg. obj.: OEC 6, pl. XX K.4958: 5 acc. to CAD sv lex. sect. (date spadix, context broken).

G usually means "to pluck" (fruit), "to trim" (timber), "to cut off (a branch, a head), both with sg. and pl. obj., cf. CAD sv 1.

Qebēru "to bury, roll, wrap up", D not disc., **OB**: ARM 6, 37: r.5'. r.12'f (corpse); **SB**: Slm.Mon. II 100 (dead enemies); ZA 16, 162: 27 (ropes); BRM 4, 11: 14; BA 5, 617: 6, cf. Landsberger 1967a: 33 (pers.). For the stative *qubbur* in omen protases → 10.7.1.1 sv.

R

Rabāku "to make an infusion", D not disc., but cf. 6.9.2.1, **SB**: BAM 122: r.8 // AMT 68, 1: r.10 = (116); AMT 82, 2: 14 (herbs).

Râbu "to compensate", D not disc., **OA**: TC 1, 29: 25 (losses); **MB**: VS 1, 54: 14 (favour); **SB**: Or. 61, 27: 47 (what sb has lost, // G).

Rakābu "to ride, embark), D not disc., **SB**: Asb. A I 34 (chariots); Ellil 101: 45 (seeder plough). For *rukkubu* "to pollinate" → 8.3.3 and 8.4.2.

Rakāsu "to bind, fix", D mostly + pl. obj. → 6.4.3.1 sv (group IIIa), or it is used idiomatically → 6.4.9:

1. persons, animals and body parts, **SB**: AfO 8, 182: 52 (pers.); Šurpu V 161 (head, hands, feet); Sn. 45: 87; 89: 52; Asb. A II 11. 93; III 92; VS 1, 77: r.18 (hands with rings); CT 17, 21: 83; Iraq 42, 29f: 74'. 144'; *SpTU 2, 2: 86 (limbs); **NA**: ABL 71: r.8 (VA, cf. note 1 to Ch. III). 10; 575: r.6 (horses); SAA 12, 35: r.1 (hands with rings);

2. "to fasten, install" parts of buildings, **SB** RIs, passim, cf. AHw sv D 6, e.g., (120);

3. "to erect" (parts of) buildings, **MB**: JCS 19, 97: 8 (*asuppāti* "outbuildings"); **SB** RIs passim, cf. AHw sv D 6/7;

4. other concrete objects, **OB**: ARM 14, 28: 9 (ships); **OA**: CCT 2, 18: 8; 4, 37a: 30 (*unūtu* "equipment"); **SB**: Gilg. XI 272 (stones); Iraq 42, 31: 200' (the *itātu*, "edges" of an object); Tigl.III 20: 117 acc. to AHw sv D 2 (weapons); Or. 39, 120: 60 (ingredients); note with "everything" (cf. 6.3): BA 5, 533: 19; SBH 4: 37 + 9/10: 35;

5. + *riksātu*, **OB**: SD 5, 32; 15 ("to make a binding agreement"); **SB**: Asb. A I 115; Iraq 27, 5: 26f; TCS 5 p. 158: 3' ("to draw up regulations"); **NB**: CatEdinb. 69: 13;

6. intrans. Dt, **OB**: RA 65, 74: 81' acc. to AHw 1529b sv *zinnu* 1 (rains) → 9.1.5;

7. part., **SB** LL: *murakkisu* "binder of sheaves" MSL 5, 77: 334 → 6.6.2 sv;

8. idiomatic: "to bandage" (obj. sg. and pl.), **OB**: AbB 11, 57: 16; ARM 26/1 p. 575 no. 276: 17 (person); ARM 26/2 p. 25 no. 296: 14 (foot); YOS 11, 19: 3 (no overt obj.); ARM 26/1 p. 290 no. 125: r.8" (id.); **MB**: BE 17, 22: 10 (pers.); **MA**: KAV 1: I 81 (pers.); **NA**: SAA 10, 319: 13 (bandage);

9. idiomatic: "to bind sb by contract" (obj. sg. and pl.): **OB** and **OA** passim, cf. AHw sv D 8/9, also AbB

12, 32: 8; RA 80, 123: 13; VS 26, 17: 28. 33 (all stat.); note refl. Dt VS 26, 64: 16; **MB**: MRWH p. 43 no. 13: 8; **NA**: ABL 896: 22 (no object);

10. exc. with sg. obj., **SB**: Ee V 59 = (38) (tail with ropes) → 6.5.3; TCS 2 p. 33 no. 14: 5f (obj. buck, ram → 6.4.3.1 sv).

Râku "to pour out", D not disc., but cf. 6.9.2.1, **SB**: RA 49, 178: 6 (oil, // G); BAM 140: 13 (oil); TuL 72: 7 (various ingredients); MVAeG 23/1, 41: 51. 53 (bad moods, [...] and sorrows); Bīt Rimki 59: 98 (no overt obj.).

Râmu "to love". D not disc., **OB**: Gilg. P II 4 (recipr. Dt → 9.1.3); **SB**: CT 39, 2: 111 (a dog a man: "to play up to", prot., cf. 6.6.1).

Rapāqu "to nail, trim", D not disc., **OA**: "to put pressure on" KTS 11: 16 (pers.); **SB**: "to fasten" RIMA 2/I, 150: 59 (persons); of a field: MSL 1, 56: 25 "to hoe" (CAD sv **ahzu* lex. sect.).

Rasāb/pu "to strike, cut down", D mostly + pl. obj. → 6.4.1.1 sv (group Ia), all **SB**:

1. persons (pl.), passim in RIs: → AHw sv D 1; note JAOS 88, 126: 20 (recipr. Dt) → 9.1.3;

2. rarely sg., in RIs: Asb. A VII 42; VAB 4, 272: 41; elsewhere: Erra IV 78f; SpTU 2, 8: I 23 // Or. 30, 3: 23;

3. rest: "to beat up": AnSt. 6, 154/6: 103. 134 (limbs); 125 (body?, pl. action?, cf. 6.6.3).

Râs/šu "to hit, strike", D + pl. obj., cf. 6.4.1 (group Ib): **OAk**: AfO 20, 74: II 19 (persons); **OB**: VS 10, 213: 12 (*dadmī* "the inhabited world", part.); **SB**: Ee IV 16 (enemies). There is no exactly parallel use of G, cf. AHw sv G 1.

Rehû "to pour, beget, have intercourse with", D → 6.8.3 sv, **SB**:

1. id.: AnSt. 10, 122: 5'. 21' (person);

2. "to bewitch": Maqlû III 152; VI 57; VII 157 (cf. AfO 21, p. 79b); VIII 9.

Rêṣu "to help, support", D 1x **MB**: BE 17, 52: 23 (reciprocal, cf. 9.1.3).

Retû "to fix", D + pl. obj. → 6.4.3.1 sv (group IIIa): **SB** (but RIME 4 OB):

1. "to fasten" doors: RIMA 2/I, 252: 18 = (120), and passim in RIs → AHw sv D 2;

2. "to fix": RIMA 2/I, 195: 29; 239: 29; 308: 18; WO 2, 226: 154; (corpses on stakes); Ash. p. 62 Ep. 22: VI 27; BagF. 18, 375: 12'; Iraq 42, 31: 198' (pegs); RIME 4, 605: 22 (stelae, part.); MSL 1, 57: 33 (*dulâti*, a hoisting device (pl.)); AnSt. 7, 130: 37 ([*m*]*urdê* = ?); BAM 542: III' 9. 17 qu. AHw sv D 4 (emmer kernels, cf. G in 18); BagF. 18, 133: 85 ("sweet reed" in jars);

3. "to fix" eyes: TDP 40: 23; AfO 11, 223: 19; SpTU 3, 86: 2; AfO 24, 83: 9.

S

Sadāru "to do regularly, to set in a row", D not disc.:

1. "to do regularly" in hendiadys: passim in **OB**, **SB**, cf. CAD sv 4a, 5b, AHw sv D 1, and → 7.4.1; **NB** "to do with care" → CAD sv 7b;

2. "to do/send regularly" (without following verb): passim in **SB**, **MB**, **NB** → CAD sv 5a, AHw sv D 2;

3. "to set in a row, make straight", **SB**: BA 5, 626: I 4 (lines of soldiers, stat.); BMisc. 4: II 31 (reeds); Ash. § 23: 13 acc. to AHw sv D 4 (furrow).

Sahālu "to pierce, stab", D is used for pl. obj. (**1.**) → 6.4.2.1 sv (group IIa) and for pl. action (**2.-3.**) → 6.6.1.2 sv and 6.6.3.3:

1. persons and body parts (pl.), **OB**: Sumer 14, 30: 11 acc. to AHw sv D 2a (kidneys); VS 17, 23: 7 (eyes, part.); **SB**: Gilg XI 269 (obj. broken: [hands]), non-ag.); CT 46, 49: I 12 (limbs); [Tn-Ep. V 40 (Dtn) constr. and meaning obscure];

2. idem (sg.), **SB**: AnSt. 30, 105: 21 = (85) (body, non-ag.); BWL 44: 101 = (86) (pers., non-ag.);

3. "to cause a piercing pain" with pers. obj. and body part(s) as subj., → 6.6.1.2 sv, **SB** med.: BKBM 2: 26; 38: 37 (stomach); BAM 240: 17' (pubic region); 152: IV 16 = (46); 158: III 28; 405: 14 (feet+shins).

Sahāpu "to cover, overwhelm, lay flat", D mostly + pl. obj. → 6.4.3.1 sv (group IIIa):

1. "to overwhelm" enemies, in **SB** RIs: RIMA 2/I, 96: 10; Iraq 37, 12: 7 (part.); BiOr. 27, 148: 4; K.9155: 16 qu. CAD sv 4a; often with subject *melammū*: RIMA 2/I, 13: 41; 17: 2; 33: 15; 214: 24 (all objects pl. or *mātu*); outside RIs, **MB**: Tn-Ep. Ia 12; **SB**: CT 28, 48: r.8 (servants); OEC 6, 32: 13 (mountains, stat.); **NA**: SAA 10, 345: 9 (restored from 346: 8ff) (enemies);

2. "to cover" persons, **SB**: Or. 18, 36: 16 (the dead with dust);

3. part., **SB**: *musahhiptu* "a net for gazelle hunting" MSL 6, 78: 31; 68: 181 → 6.6.2 with note 18;

4. occasionally with sg. obj.: RIMA 2/I, 197: 51; Slm.Mon. II 72 (mountain); Maqlû VIII 41 = (41) (a person with diseases → 6.5.3); IV R 21b: r.19 (sword which overwhelms a demon, part.).

Sahāšu "to catch", D 1x **OB**: Ét. de Meyer 85: 2 (a net (*huhāru*), part. → 6.6.2 with note 18).

Sakāpu "to push away, reject", D not disc., **OB**: persons (sg. and pl.): AbB 1, 29: 22; Mél. Kupper 129: 26; ARM 26/2 p. 324 no. 428: 10; animals: AbB 8, 132: 17; **NB**: YOS 6, 26: 6.

S/zâku "to crush, pound", D: CAD sv 2b "to strain" or the like, AHw sv D "(eingeweichte Drogen) zerdrücken", passim in **SB** med. → *ll. cc.* and cf. 6.9.2.1.

Salāh/'u "to sprinkle, moisten", D not disc., cf. 6.8.4 and 6.9.2.1:

1. with water, **OB**: ARM 3, 79: r.8' (pers., stat.); YOS 11, 26: III 43; IV 5 (ingredients with vinegar); **SB**: BAL 92: Ass. r.30 (// G); BKBM 24: 50 (body part); CT 38, 9: 38 (foundation?, stat.); with beer: Iraq 31, 29: 16 (embers, acc. to CAD sv *šikaru* 1g-2' end); with tears: CT 40, 32: r.16 (ground, prot. → 6.6.1.1 sv); with urine: AMT 51, 4: 6 (pers.); with oil: AfO 23, 86a: r.9 (ground); BagF. 18, 448: 41 (figurines); with cress: BBR 1-20: 34 (lamb); substance unspecified: KADP 1: V 17 (house);

2. with witchcraft, **SB**: Maqlû VII 150;

3. in *šuluhhâ sulluhu* "to perform a sprinkling", cf. 6.9.2.1, **SB**: BagF. 18, 273: 21'; Ištar/Dumuzi 129: 26; BBR 1-20: 99. 155 (// G, and cf. G in 74); BWL 160: r.2;

4. part. *musallihtu*, a vessel used for sprinkling, MB, NB, NA → CAD sv and 6.6.2 with note 18.

Salālu "to flap (wings)", D **SB**: CT 39, 29: 30 = (55A); 30: 58 = (55B); *ib.* 60 (wings) (all prot. → 6.6.1).

Salātu (*šalātu*) "to split off, cut", D mostly + pl. obj. → 6.4.1.1 sv (group Ia):

1. body parts, pl., **OB**: RA 65, 73: 50' (intestines, stat.); **SB**: Lugal 550 (horns); *CT 17, 19: I 8 // SpTU 2, 2: I 8 (sinews); TBP 22: IV 1 (nails, stat.); CT 40, 32: r.23 (su.meš = skin?, prot. → 6.6.1.1 sv *lêku*); **NA**: Or. 22, 44: 3; CA 194: 13' (ribs);

2. other obj., pl., **SB**: BA 5, 572: 19 (bolts); STT 257: 14 (fibers); mass noun: BKBM 46: 39 (wood);

3. "to cut through", **MB**: RIMA 1, 273: 101; 276: 48; 277: 18 (places); 276: 32 (mountains); **SB**: CT 39, 15: 25; 16: 43 (river bank(s), prot., cf. 6.6.1); PSBA 18, 158: 3 (obj. broken but pl.);

4. occasionally with sg. obj. → 6.9.2.2: Ee IV 102 (belly); CT 30, 9: 9 (liver, stat.); TU 1: r.19 (id.); BagF. 18, 301: 18; 469: 16 (cord of evil, part.); Lugal 553 (stone).

Samāšu "to hide" (trans.), D not disc., **OB** Mari: ARM 2, 108: 7 acc. to CAD sv 2; 26/2 p. 294 no. 414: 7; p. 309 no. 420: 51; MARI 6, 40 note 7 A.266: 18 (all pers. pl.); ARM 14, 61: 9 (pers. sg.); 26/1 p. 83 no. 5: 73 (sheep (pl.)); M.5126a qu. AfO 40/1, 10a (metals and precious stones); Ét. Garelli p. 65 M.7595: 4 (matters); M.14913 qu. AfO *l.c.* (id., VA); ARM 26/1 p. 581 no. 281: 10 (no overt object).

Sanāqu "to check, muster, interrogate" (beside intrans. "to arrive"), D → 6.8.1 sv and 6.8.4:

1. "to check" weights and measures: passim, mainly **OB**, **OA** → CAD sv 10a, 14a, AHw sv D 1/4, Dt 1, cf. 6.8.4;

2. "to question, interrogate" persons: passim, **OB**, rarely MB, NB, NA → AHw sv D 5; divided by CAD into "to question, interrogate" (sv 12a) and "to harass, plague" (sv 12b) → 6.8.1 sv;
3. "to transfer" objects, 1x persons, **OB**, **OA**, **NA** → CAD sv 13 (not acknowledged by AHw);
4. "to keep under control, to watch over", **OB**: AbB 7, 138: 21 (person); ARM 3, 18: 20 (persons); KH r.XXI 59 (ox); YOS 10, 24: 29 (palace); 26: I 27 (army, palace); 11: II 25; **SB**: Izbu 124/5: 36'; 43' (country, Dt); SAA 8, 389: r.4; 505: 6 (no overt object);
5. "to close" doors, etc. (all stat.), **OB**: YOS 10, 24: 29; 26: I 26; 29: 3 (the *bāb ekallim*, the *ekallum* and the *abullum* of the liver); **SB**: AnBi. 12, 283: 38 (doors). For adj. *sunnuqu* → 10.3.2 and App. to Ch. X sv.

Sanāšu "to insert", D not disc., but cf. 6.9.2.1, **SB**: Spirits 134: 26'; Racc. 119: 29 = TU 41: 29 (aromatics in a torch, stat.); Maqlû III 20; IX 25. 41 (tallow, wood or reed into body parts of figurines).

Sapāhu "to disperse, scatter, ruin", D mostly + pl. obj. → 6.4.2.1 sv (group IIa):
1. "to disperse" persons and groups, **MB**: UM 1/2, 67: 16 (men); **SB**: Sn. 39: 53; Ash. Nin. A III 59; BL 208: 26 (people); often with coll., such as army VAB 4, 220: 31; 7, 182: 42; land Izbu 208b: I 7; LSS 6/1, 33: 12 // SBH 4: 63; *qinnu* "clan" Šurpu II 53; *puhru* "assembly" Sn. 82: 37; Šurpu II 71; often part. as epithet, **MB/SB**: + *nišī* Ash. B II 27; p. 34: 30; + *ellē/ātu* "hordes" of enemies RIMA 1, 132: 31; 241: 10; 247: 8; 248: 3; 258: 12; 262: 15; 265: 11;
2. "to scatter" animals, objects and substances, **OB**: ARM 27, 145: 8 (*eperī* "earth works"); 26/1 p. 225 no. 86: 18 (sheep, stat.); AbB 7, 82: 20 (barley, Dt (or belonging to **4**.?)); ZA 71, 63: 10' (*kinūnu* "hearth-fire"); **SB**: BA 5, 708: 7 (mountains, part.); BWL 44: 105 (stat.); CT 17, 15: 15; 31: 28 (limbs); MVAeG 40/2, 64: 11 (dust); Asb. A VI 80; IAsb. 34d: III 11; PEA p. 34: V 8 (salt and cress); TuL 46: 10f; SAA 3, 38: 41f (seed); Maqlû V 86 (cloud(s?)); **NB**: Nbn. 293: 1 (date palms, VA); note with abstract obj., **OB**: Ét. Garelli 65 M. 7595: 5 (matter(s): "to divulge");
3. "to sprinkle" water, **SB**: BAM 248: III 27. 29; **NA**: p. 58: 653 ("to spill", stat., cf. note 1 to Ch. III);
4. "to waste, squander" (money, barley, and other commodities, often + *bīta* "the estate"), **OB**, **OA** passim, rarely **SB**, cf. CAD sv 6/7, AHw sv D 1/Dt; also ARM 26/1 p. 503 no. 247: 20 (barley); AbB 10, 164: 15 (silver);
5. "to ruin" a district, **OB** Mari: FM 2 p. 101 no. 60: r.12'; ARM 27, 25: 17;
6. "to thwart, to bring to nought", **OB**: ARM 13, 146: 6 (*ṭêmu* "plan"); **SB**: Ee VII 44 (plans, part.); *ib.* 49 (deeds, part.); I 39 (*alaktu* "activity"); Maqlû VII 6 // V 87; V 5 (sorceries); Šurpu IV 68 (*rikista* "conjuration"); AGH 74: 37 (sin, // G, cf. Iraq 31, 83 *ad* l. 37); IV R 59b: 12 (words); SpTU 1, 12: 23 (advice).

Sarāqu "to strew, sprinkle, scatter", D not disc., but cf. → 6.9.2.1, **SB**: ZA 62, 74: 24; SpTU 2, 17: II 4 (various substances); VS 17, 58: 21 (id., stat.); BagF. 18, 500: 23 (the *turrū* of the house, cf. G in 30); Or. 39, 132: 13 (a herb); BiOr. 30, 179: 39 (*hišihtu* "supplies"); Ash. § 61: 14f; VAB 7, 264: 8; BagF. 16, 244: 12' (*armannu* (an aromatic), all stat.).

Sekēru "to dam, block", D + pl. obj., cf. 6.4.2 (group IIb): **OB**: AbB 9, 227: 13 (canals, stat.); **MB**: BE 17, 12: 5 (*natbaktus*); **SB**: Tn-Ep. IVa 23 (*miṭrēti*, a kind of canals); RA 18, 165: 20 (mouth(s), part.); BWL 52: 18 var. (ears, Dt); TDP 120: 44; 226: 72 (intestines, part.); BE 17, 27: 34 *su-uk-ku-ur* is a stative sg., but the construction is unclear. G mostly has a sg. obj. (water course or body part); G + pl. obj. occurs with obj. *mû* "water" (cf. CAD sv 1a), and a few times elsewhere (KH XLIII 9 (rivers); BER 4, 192: 22 (id.); BWL 42: 85 (lips), CT 17, 25: 26 ([mou]th and nose, acc. to CAD sv lex. sect., but AHw sv G 2: nose)).

Sêru "to rub", D **SB**: AfO 11, 222 no. 2: 5 (head); 213: 12f. 16 (eyes); 222: 3 (temples of the head); TDP 170: 13 (forehead) (all prot., cf. 6.6.1); BiOr 30, 165: I 46. 50 (head, stat.).

Ṣ

Ṣabātu "to seize", D is used with pl. obj. (**1.-9.**) → 6.4.4.1 sv (group IVa) and idiom. (**10.-13.**) → 6.4.9:

1. "to seize, arrest" persons, **OB**: AbB 13, 59: 24; ARM 5, 35: 19; note with coll.: RA 42, 72: 25 (*ṣābani* "our people"); **MB**: BE 17, 55: 14; 58: 11; Tn-Ep. II 5 (stat.); **MA**: Or. 59, 309: 6; **SB** RIs ("to capture" enemies) passim → CAD sv 10b, AHw sv D I 3b; **NA/NB**: passim → CAD *ib.*, AHw sv D I 3a, and the glossaries of SAA 1, 5 and 10;

2. "to bring" persons as witnesses, **OB**: AbB 5, 166: 11; **NB**: ABL 456: 8; **NA**: 550: r.8;

3. "to seize, capture" animals, **OB**: A 3524: 20 qu. CAD sv 10g (cows); **MA**: ZA 73, 77: 8 = (09A) (asses); Assur 3/1, 3: 11 (oxen); **SB**: RIMA 2/I, 26: 73; 103: 8 (elephants); 103: 6 (calves); 135: 72; 154: 125 = (141) (wild bulls); 175: 81f (young of ostriches and deer); 226: 35 (tigers(?));

4. "to seize, occupy" cities and forts, **OB**: RIMA 1, 64: III' 11; **SB**: RIMA 2/I, 133: 25 (cities); **NA**: SAA 5, 2: 15 (forts); 10, 2: r.9 (fortified places);

5. "to seize" produce, merchandise etc., **OB**: AbB 2, 85: 21 (beans); **OA**: TC 2, 39: 13 (*ba'abātīja* "my merchandise"); KTS 30: 8 (*luqūtum* "merchandise"); *ib.* 23 (silver); ATHE 36: 14 (silver); BIN 6, 132: 9 (tin); CCT 4, 25a: 38 (copper); **MA**: MCS 2, 16: 14 (*unūtu* "equipment"; **SB**: Iraq 27, 5: II 10 (field and arable land);

6. "to install, fasten, adorn" parts of buildings, **MB** RIMA 1, 153: 10 (doors); **SB** RIs: 2/I, 320: 29 (beams); KB 3/1, 144: 49 (*šagammī* "door pivots(?)"); **NA**: SAA 11, 15: I 7; r.I 6'; 16: r.I 13' (beams, all stat.); SAA 6, 21: 9 (beams); **NB**: VS 15, 35: 5 (reed and beam); id. with other objects, **MB**(?): AfO 24, 95: 5 (stat.); **SB**: Sg. 8: 386 (garments, stat.);

7. various other idioms with pl. object: **OB**: AbB 13, 5: 8 (stat.). 11 (Dt). r.4'. r.8' (wall and dam, openings in it: "to attend to"); FM 1 p. 94: 8 (canals: "to block"); **SB**: Asb. A II 53 // AAA 20, 84: 82 (roads: id.); **MA**: ZA 82, 224: 6'. 7' (VA) (tablets: "to execute", cf. Postgate, AoF 13, 18ff); **NB**: dates: "to prepare" (CAD sv 10h-3'), "umzäunen" (AHw sv D III 2b); **NA**: SAA 5, 146: 8, qu. in 5.6.4 end (roads, subj. snow (non-ag.)); VA *ṣubbutu* "connected, consecutive" in SB hemerologies, cf. CAD sv *ṣubbutu* 1;

8. stat. with pl. adjunct acc. in *qê ṣubbut* → 5.6.3, omen prot., **OB**: YOS 10, 24: 25; 25: 18; 42: I 36; II 33 = (35A); 46: V 33; RA 65, 73: 27'f; OBE 1: 12ff; **SB**: CT 20, 11: 22 (cf. TU 1: 51f (ideogr.));

9. part. *muṣabbit(t)u*, **SB** LL: a part of a loom; **NB**: an instrument, cf. CAD sv and 6.6.2 sv;

10. "to seize" with sorcery, mostly persons and body parts, pl. and sg., **SB**: passim, cf. CAD sv 10a; AHw sv D I 4, II 1, e.g., CT 39, 46: 46 = (53) (pers., prot. → 6.6.1); Maqlû VI 115 = (10A) (pers., stat.);

11. in **SB** med. "to paralyze": TDP 220: 22 = (11A) (mouth, stat.); "to hurt" *ib.* 214: 21 (pers., prot., cf. 6.6.1); "to hold" SpTU 3, 86: 4 = (13) (breath, prot., cf. 6.6.1); *ib.* 10 (id.); **OB** LL: VA *ṣubbutu(m)* MSL 12, 169: 384; 201: 13 (pers.);

12. + *ṭêmam* "to take action", **OB** Mari: ARM 1, 42: 53; 2, 11: 10; 4, 68: 10; 26/1 p. 108 no. 11: 44; MARI 5, 163ff: 10. 21 (all stat.); *ib.* 165: 69; with ellipse of *ṭêmam*: ARM 26/1 p. 159 no. 27: 37 (stat.);

13. Other idiomatic expressions with sg. obj.: **OB**: JCS 15, 6: 22 = (12) (person); ARM 26/2 p. 227 no. 394: 8 (*rēš awātim* "the essentials", cf. note 23); **OA**: *BIN 4, 72: 1 ("yourself"); **MB**: CT 43, 94: 32 (reciprocal, cf. 9.1.3); **NA**: *ABL 1203: r.4 (stat.: "inlaid");

14. Exc. sg. objects, **MA**: AfO 10, 40 no. 89: 11 (one person, seized by a lion); **SB**: RIMA 2/I, 291: 70 (room: "to adorn", or rooms ?, or cf. 6.5.3 ?); Asb. A III 132 (cf. G in II 26); VAB 7, 328: 41 (both obj. *mūṣû* "exit": "to block"); Or. 61, 24: 25 id., stat.: sg. or pl.?); Dreams 332 c 3 (string).

Ṣamādu "to prepare, harness, bandage", D not disc.:

1. said of water: "to connect", **OB**: AbB 2, 149: 7. 12;

2. "to put on" a crown, **OB**: AbB 13, 145: 21;

3. "to bandage" a person or a wound → 6.4.9, **OB**: ARM 4, 65: 6; 14, 3: 10 = (27); 26/1 p. 578 no. 278:

10. 17; **MB**: UM 1/2, 72: 7; cf. PNs DN-*mu-ṣa-mi-id* UET 5, 245: 2. 6 (**OB**); *ilī-ṣum-mi-id* ZA 82, 184a: 5; 184b: 3 (**OAk**).

4. part. as epithet, **SB**: SpTU 4, 129: V 25 (heaven); BM 33841+: r.3 (gods); cf. Von Weiher, SpTU 4, 40).

Ṣap/bû "to irrigate, moisten", D not disc.:

1. "to irrigate" a field, **OB**: AbB 2, 127: 7. 18; 12, 72: 27; 13, 145: 36;

2. "to moisten" pills with honey, **SB** med.: BAM 159: II 15; AMT 68, 3: II 5 + 50, 2: 3 + 27, 2: 3;

3. a person with blood, **NA**: CT 53, 598: 9;

4. part. *muṣappiu* "dyer", **SB** LL MSL 12, 240: 15; **NA**: SAA 12, 65: 4' → 6.6.2 with note 18.

Ṣarāhu "to heat", D not disc., **MA** "to keep warm" horses, cf. AHw sv *ṣ*. III D, BVW p. 44 sv *salāhu*, and CAD sv *ṣuppu* v.

Ṣarāpu "to burn", D not disc., cf. 6.8.4, **SB** (but **4**. OA):

1. persons and body parts: CT 23, 2: 4 (2x); LSS 1/6, 34 note 10; AfO 18, 293: 60 (all pers. pl.); OEC 6, 41: 55 ("me"); Šurpu VII 10. 28 (body); CT 16, 29: 77 (id.); BWL 36: 110 (cheeks, stat.));

2. other objects: TCS 2 p. 18: 2 (forests); Sn. 47: 31 (urine, interpretation uncert., cf. CAD sv *ṣ*. A 3a-2' vs. AHw sv *ṣ*. I D 2c);

3. med. "to cause a burning pain" (with pers. obj. and *rēš libbi* = epigastrium as subj.) in prot. → 6.6.1.2 sv: AMT 45, 6: 5; 48, 2: 1; 4: r.8; STT 96: 9. 20; 102: 8;

4. "to refine" silver, **OA**: kt 91/k 102: 3; also VA, cf. CAD sv *ṣurrupu* a, AHw sv *ṣ*. 1 → 10.6.1.2.4; 1x **SB**: CT 17, 23: 183 (VA, also of silver (*ṣarpu*)).

Š

Ša'āru "to win, overpower", D not disc., 1x **OB** Mari: MARI 6, 264 M.11009+11010: 12 (person).

Šabāhu "to sprinkle", D not disc., but cf. 6.9.2.1, **OB**: YOS 11, 25: 25. 64 (various ingredients); 26: I 10; II 66 (id. with salt); **SB**: LKA 141: 7 (flour).

Šabāšu "to collect, gather in", D + pl. obj. (6.4.5 group Vb), **SB**: ZA 16, 180: 45 // UM 1/2, 113: III 29 (*la'ûti* "babies"); BWL 170: 34 ([*da*]*dmē* "the inhabited world", acc. to CAD sv 3b); **NA**: SAA 1, 177: 9 (*bītāte* "families"); 7, 108: r.II 1' (textiles, VA); with a mass noun, **MB**: UDBD 136: 2. 6; 137: r.1 (wood). G is found passim with sg. and pl. obj.

Šagāšu "to murder", D 1x with pl. obj., **SB**: LKU 33: 24 (men); 2x as a part. in absolute use: **OB** LL: "murderer" AS 16, 24: 108; 26: 70b → 6.6.2 sv.

Šahātu A "to rinse, clean", D not disc., **SB**: PSBA 40, 108: r.10 (hands+feet → 6.9.2.1.); BagF. 18, 139: 137 (pers., reflexive Dt → 9.1.2 sv, but written with -*ṭu*: from *šahāṭu* "to strip"?); SpTU 2, 12: II 10. 30, cf. also 1, 83: r.25; Sm. 303+: r.30 qu. CAD sv *š*. A 7 (king).

Šahāṭu A "to leap, attack", D not disc., 1x **OB**: RA 36, 10: 5 (person).

Šahāṭu B "to strip, remove", D mostly + pl. obj. (6.4.1 group Ib), **SB** (but **3**. MB):

1. concrete objects: OEC 1, 34: 1 (beams, stat.); IV R 12: r.24 ("all the plating (*ihza*) there is"); BHLT 82: II 4 (swords: "to draw");

2. abstract objects: CT 51, 195: 6 // SpTU 2, 12: II 18 = (125) (evil deeds, stat.);

3. + *ramānu* "oneself": Tn-Ep. IVb 44 ("to take to one's heels, to flee", or something similar).

G occurs far more often with both sg. and pl. obj.

Šakāku "to string, harrow", D not disc., **SB**:

1. "to string", in med. and rit.: BAM 237: IV 41 (blocks); AfO 12, 143: r.I 7 (threads); SpTU 4, 128: 36 (bread crumbs), cf. 6.9.2.1;

2. "to harrow" 1x SB LL: MSL 1, 56: 27 (no overt object).

Šalāḫu "to take out, retrieve", D not disc., 1x **OA**: CCT 2, 3: 35 (silver).

Šalāpu "to draw, tear out", D + pl. obj. (cf. 6.4.1 group Ib): **SB**: UM 1/2, 113: III 19 = (03B); BAL p. 89 Ass. 37 (stat.); **NA**: SAA 2 p. 57: 631 (persons); SAA 11, 144: I 4' (obj. broken but pl., stat.)). G mostly has a sg. obj. (typically weapon or tongue), except Erra IV 94 (husbands), cf. CAD sv 1, AHw sv G. [Cancel WO 2, 406: 5, cf. RIMA 2/I, 305: 31].

Šalāqu "to cut open, slit", D + pl. obj. (6.4.1 group Ib): **SB**: Asb. A IX 36 (camels); Izbu 134: 48 (ears, stat.); **NA**: ABL 419: r.10 (garments); note esp. Izbu 134: 48' with comm. 231: 365j *šu-ul-lu-qa* = *ša ma'diš sal-ta* (from *salātu* "to split", discussed in 6.4.1.1). G is mostly used in the stative (sg. and pl.), cf. CAD sv 1a, but cf. Asb. A IV 69 (obj. mouth, var. tongue). For *šulluqu* adj. → 10.6.1.1.3.

Šalāṭu "to rule, control", only Dt "to reign, exercise dominion" → 9.1.6 sv, **MB/SB** RI: RIMA 1, 240: 7; 2/I, 20: 47. For adj. *šulluṭu* → App. to Ch. X sv.

Šâlu A "to ask", D passim in **OA** → CAD sv *š*. A 6, AHw sv *š*. I D; 2x **OB**: TCL 17, 65: 26 (garment); MHET 1 p. 118 no. 79: r.8' (Dt with subj. *arkatum* "the matter").

Šâlu B "to coat, smear", D 2x + pl. obj. (6.4.3 group IIIc): **OB/MB** RIs: RIMA 1, 23: 29; 32: II 7 (walls with ghee and honey). Cf. G in a similar context: RIMA 1, 49: 48; 185: 145.

Šamāmu "to paralyze", D **SB** med. with pers. object and body parts as subject: CT 23, 46: 27 = (109B) (hands and feet); BAM 56: r.9 (flesh); KAR 80: 4 (arms) (all prot. → 6.6.1.2 sv); other constr.: LKA 85: r.4 ("flesh", // G in KAR 267: 14).

Šamāṭu "to strip off, tear loose", D + pl. obj. (6.4.1 group Ib): **OB**: MCT 82 passim (embankments (*tarahhu*), interpretation uncert.: "to erode"?, thus CAD sv 2b, cf. AHw sv *š*. I D 3); **SB**: ZA 16, 162: 16 // KAR 239: II 12 (unripe dates); JNES 33, 274: 9 (wings). G has sg. and pl. object (dates, forest ("to denude"), body part, metal objects, piece of land, sweat ("to rub away"), cf. CAD sv 1a/d.

Šâmu "to allot, appoint, decree", D not disc., **SB**: Iraq 38, 90: 9 (wisdom to a king); mostly as a divine epithet *mušîm šīmāti* (rarely *šimti*) "who decrees destinies, determines fate" → CAD sv *š*. B 2c-1' (also *šā'im šīmāti* or *šimti* (*ib.* 2c-2')), cf. 6.9.3.

Šapāku "to heap up, pour out", D mainly + pl. obj. (often coll.) → 6.4.5.1 sv (group Va):

1. "to heap up" produce, etc., **SB**: ZA 62, 73: 18 (several kinds of grain); RA 53, 134: 10 (part.); BM 41255a: 3 qu. CAD sv 7a (*karê* "piles of grain", part.); Sg. 8: 263 = (144) (*tabkāni* "piles (of grain)"); Gilg VI 59 (loaves);

2. id., other objects, **MB**: RIMA 1, 235: 36 (heads/corpses "like grain piles"); **SB**: RIMA 2/I, 14: 82 (id.); SBM 52a: 12+D (mountains, part.);

3. "to pour out", **MB**: Tn-Ep. II 10 = (32); **SB**: AnSt. 8, 52: III 39 (oil); CT 46, 49: I 9 (ice); Sn. 97: 84 acc. to CAD sv 7c (bronze: "to cast" pillars, stat.); LL part. *mušappiktu* "pitcher" MSL 7, 84: 164f, cf. 6.6.2 with note 18;

4. a process performed on wool, **OB**: YOS 14, 310: 20 (stat.); BM 16173: 2. 5.

Šapāṣu "to grip, twist", D **SB**, only stative:

1. "paralyzed" TDP 220: 21 acc. to AHw sv D (infant), cf. 10.3.2;

2. in omen prot. *qê šuppuṣ*: TU 3: 9; CT 20, 8: 10f; 17: r.2f → 6.5.3.

Šaqālu "to suspend, weigh, pay", D:

1. "to weigh" (not disc.), **OB**: ARM 18, 4: 6; **OA**: TC 3, 36: 22 (silver); **SB**: LL part. *mušaqqiltu* "balance" CT 41, 39: 7 → 6.6.2 with note 18;

2. "to pay", **OA** passim, cf. CAD sv 7; AHw sv D 1, and cf. (56)-(61) in 6.6.3.1; for D "to make scarce" → 8.4.1 sv; for *šukkulu* "to wipe off, wipe away" → 8.6.

Šaqāru "to pierce (with an arrow)", D + pl. obj. (6.4.2 group IIb), **SB**: ArOr 37, 488: 2 (heart+lungs, part.), Sg. 8: 139 (horses), Sg. Wi. 56: 334 (warriors); Sn. 45: 81 (armies). G is attested only once: CT 17, 26: 47 (obj.: "everything"), qu. CAD sv lex. sect.

Šaqû "to give to drink", D 1x part. → 6.6.2 sv, **OB**: ARM 9, 26: 9 *mušaqqû* "person who gives water to animals".

Šarāmu "to trim"; D 2x + pl. obj. (6.4.1 group Ic), **OB**: KH XXI: r.58 (horns); **NA**: SAA 5, 295: r.3 (beams). G often occurs with sg. and pl. obj., cf. CAD sv.

Šarāpu "to burn", D 2x + pl. obj. (6.4.1 group Ic): **SB**: AMT 5, 1: 11 (several objects, largely broken); BA 5, 708: 11 (*gupnī* "trees", part. (restored: [*mu*-])). G passim with sg. and pl. obj., cf. CAD sv 1.

Šarāṭu "to tear to pieces, shred", D mostly + pl. obj. (6.4.1 group Ib):

1. garments, **OB**: ARM 26/2 p. 175 no. 370: 5'. 14'; **SB**: Sg. 8: 411; AnSt. 6, 154: 100. 108; Fauna 51 c 9; Ash. Nin. A I 56; Sn. 156: 13 (all pl., cf. also 6.3 end)); **NB**: ABL 571: 16;

2. body parts, **SB**: Or. 18, 35: r.3 (wombs of pregnant women);

3. part. **OB** LL [*mu*]-*ša-ar-ri-ṭù* MSL 12, 177: 4 "person who tears garments to shreds", (CAD sv; AHw sv "Zerreisser") → 6.6.2 sv;

4. exc. sg. obj., **OB**: StEb. 2, 49: 5 (a *kirimmu* garment).

Compare **1**. with G for a single garment, cf. CAD sv 1a. The remaining instance of G also has a sg. obj., cf. CAD sv 1b (skin).

Šatāqu "to split, fissure", D only stat., mostly + pl. subj. (cf. 5.1.3) (6.4.1 group Ib), **OB**: AfO 18, 66: 12 // YOS 10, 55: 3 (warts, VA); **SB**: Izbu 134: 47' (ears); TDP 144: 43 (toes); Sg. 8: 326 (torrents of water, "carved" in mountains) (all stat. pl.); stat. sg.: Izbu 161: 31' (hoof), cf. 10.6.1.1.3. G occurs mainly in the stative (CAD sv 1a), rarely in finite forms (*ib.* 1b).

Šatû "to weave", D not disc., **OB** Mari: ARM 13, 10: 6 (garment); **SB** LL only: JAOS 83, 426: 111; MSL 16, 211: 5.

Šaṭāru "to write, register", D + pl. obj. (**1**.-**2**.) → 6.4.8, or idiom. (**3**.) → 6.8.1 sv:

1. "to write", with pl. obj. (for obj. "tablets" see also **3**.), **OB**: ARM 1, 24: 8; 5, 75: r.3; 10, 75: 12 (*awātim*: words or things); **SB**: Sn. 102: 92 (deeds); **NB**: ABL 571: r.5 (words);

2. "to register, record", with pl. obj., **OB**: passim in Mari, examples: a) persons: ARM 5, 51: 17; 10, 123: 16 (stat.); 14, 62: 15; 70: 10 (*ṣābam* "troops"); 26/2 p. 76 no. 314: 33; p. 269 no. 405: r.19' = (106) and (140A); *ib.* r.27' = (140C); p. 274 no. 408: 13; FM 2 p. 112 no. 71: 16; b) rest: ARM 1, 7: 20 = (105) (three lots of wood); outside Mari: AbB 7, 33: 9; 183: 4; JCS 42, 167: edge 8' (stat.) (all persons); **MA**: AfO 10, 42 no. 95: 27 (sheep (pl.));

3. "to write (a letter, report, etc.) to (a person), **OB**: passim in Mari, examples: a) obj. *ṭuppum* ARM 1, 24: 4; 45: 6 (stat.); 48: 7 (stat.); 127: 7 (stat.); 128: 18; 2, 8: 24 (stat.); 10, 166: 3; 167: 3; b) obj. *ṭuppātum* (cf. **1**.) ARM 1, 11: 9 (stat.); 40: 7 (stat.); 3, 19: 20; MARI 5, 183: 7 (stat.); c) obj. *ṭêmum* ARM 26/1, p. 318 no. 153: 17; 26/2 p. 229 no. 395: 8 = (104); 27, 75: 15; d) obj. *meher ṭuppi*- ARM 1, 24: 4; 26/1 p. 155 no. 25: 9; e) *meher ṭêmim* ARM 10, 166: 7; 167: 8; rarely outside Mari: AbB 9, 151: 27; OBTI 21: 22 (both *ṭêmum*); AbB 12, 119: r. 10' (*ṭuppum*);

4. Remainder, **OB**: TCL 18, 88: 15 (field); RitDiv. 30: 17 (*dīnam* "lawsuit"); OBTA 21: 8 (object obscure); all with sg. obj., but atypical or obscure; **NB**: YOS 3, 40: 23 (barley).

Šaṭāṭu "to tear open", D 1x + pl. obj. (6.4.1 group Ic): **SB**: "to cut" burrows (*hersī*) BWL 204 a 9. G also 1x with sg. obj. (belly).

Šâṭu "to pull", D not disc., **SB**: BWL 227: 22 (yoke).

Šebēru "to break, smash", D almost always + pl. obj. → 6.4.1.1 sv (group Ia):
1. body parts, **MB**: RA 77, 20: 22 (teeth, non-ag.); **SB**: KAR 391: 6 (teeth, stat.); FuB 12, 44: 4b (wings of the winds, cf. *ib.* 42: 2b); StWinnett 162: 5 acc. to AHw sv D 7 (idem); **NB**: BIN 1, 94: 27 (ribs); YOS 3, 123: 14 (hands(?));
2. weapons (*kakkū*): passim in **MB/SB** → CAD sv 3a, AHw sv D 1 (all pl.);
3. other concrete objects, **SB**: RIMA 2/I, 253: 32 (beams); IAsb. 78: 11 ("horns" of a ziggurat, cf. *kapāru* B); Sn. 83: 48; 137: 37; Asb. A V 119; PEA p. 34: V 1 (images of gods); CT 38, 11: 48 (doors, stat.); SAA 3, 15: 2 (crossbars of a boat, stat.); **NB**: YOS 6, 81: 7 (spades, VA);
4. substances, **OB**: IM 49239: 16 qu. CAD sv 3e (barley); **OA**: copper: kt n/k 122: 23; 1153: 8;
5. other, **OB**: army (?): *RA 65, 73: 40.

Šêlu "to sharpen, whet", D + pl. obj. → 6.4.2.1 sv (group IIa), **SB** with obj. "weapons": Ee IV 92; RIMA 2/I, 13: 37; Sn. 31: 1; 44: 62; 75: 90; Ash. Nin. A I 71; IAsb. 71: 12; VAB 7, 220: 8; Asb. B V 43; also with "arrows": K.8414: 18 qu. CAD sv 2.

Šepû "to ask", D not disc., 1x **OB**: AbB 3, 53: 23 acc. to AHw sv *š*. IV D (cf. G in 15).

Še'û "to search", D not disc., **MB**: UM 1/2, 59: 16 (witnesses); **SB**: CT 38, 34: 21 var. (a god, // G).

T

Tabāku "to pour out", D usually + pl. obj. (often coll. or mass nouns) → 6.4.5.1 sv (group Va):
1. substances and fluids from the body, **OB**: TCL 18, 86: 34 (*huhhiātim* "vomit"); YOS 10, 47: 24 (*paršam mādam* "a lot of faeces", prot. → 6.6.1.1 sv); MSL 9, 80: 178 (blood); **SB**, often in prot. → 6.6.1: CT 38, 50: 55 (*zê* "faeces", pret. or pres.?); BAM 159: II 50; III 10 (*nīṭa* "bloody excrement"); BAM 578: I 29 ($\underline{\text{sig}}_7$ "yellow (matter)"); 96: III 16; ChDiv. 1, 70: 3 (*rupuštu* "phlegm"); BAM 156: 2 (undigested food); and passim with *dāmu* "blood" → AHw sv D 1b; other contexts: SpTU 1, 44: 13 ("to defecate", no overt object);
2. other substances, **MA**: Or. 18, 413: 24 (aromatics into water); **SB**: BBR 64: 11 acc. to AHw sv D 2b (oil into an incense burner); SAA 3, 10: 17 (oil into containers); BAM 234: 18 (*bahra* "hot (soup)", cf. G in 323: 83); BagF. 18, 130: 19 (three herbs);
3. metaph., **OB**: JRAS CSpl. 71: 14 (*hurbašu* "hoarfrost", part., cf. G in St. Kraus 194: 21); **SB**: ZA 16, 180: 39 acc. to AHw sv D 3 (death); JCS 21, 5: 38 (*epēšu* "evil magic");
4. persons and body parts: "to weaken, render limp", **OB**: AbB 5, 166: 8 (men); **SB**: KAR 80: r. 27 (*piṭ-rīja* "my ....-s" (by means of witchcraft)); cf. *tubbuku* (and *tabku*) → 10.3.2.
5. Rest: **SB**: VAB 4, 254: 22 (Dt: "to crumble", of a building, cf. (05) and (06) in 9.1.1).

Tabālu "to take away, take along", D not disc., **NA**: ABL 1389: r.4 (stolen goods (*tablu*), cf. G in 7).

Tahāhu "to pour", D not disc., **MA**: AfO 17, 273: 37 (pers.); Or. 18, 404f: 3. 23 (liquid: "to shake"?); **SB**: BAM 240: 12f ("to sprinkle" cloth with milk); 510: I 6 (stones with tallow).

Takāpu "to stitch, puncture, cover with dots", D not disc., **OB**: Iraq 25, 183: 5 (textile); **SB**: K.888: 19 qu. AHw sv D 1 (figurines); BAM 515: II 33 (face); for *tukkup* (and *takip*) in omens → 10.7.1.1 sv.

Tamāhu "to seize, control", D + pl. obj. (6.4.4 group IVb): **OB**: KH III 47 (enemies, part.); **SB**: RIMA 2/I, 22: IV 96 (chariots); 26: VII 9; 104: 20 (herds of animals); Asb. A I 131; II 109; III 60; B III 2 (enemies). D is rare, compared to the very common G-stem, both with sg. and pl. obj., cf. AHw sv G. It is undoubtedly not accidental that D is restricted to concrete objects, cf. 5.6.4.

Tarāku "to beat", D not disc., **OB**: of textiles, cf. Lackenbacher, Syria 59 p. 130ff; Iraq 25, 183: 18 acc. to George, Iraq 55, 73; for *turruk* (and *tarik*) in prot. → 10.6.1.1.2 and 10.7.1.1.

Tarāṣu "to direct, stretch, straighten", D mostly + pl. obj. → 6.4.3.1 sv (group IIIa):

1. body parts, **SB**, mostly stat.: Sn. 79: 7; JCS 21, 3: 9; CT 51, 200: 3 (eyes); BHLT 90: 15 (ears); SAA 3, 12: 16 (hands); BWL 34: 80 (fingers (*ú-ba!-na-a-ti*)); RIMA 2/I, 214: 26 (face (*panū*)); prefix forms: WO 4, 32: VI 5 (face (*bunnū*)); KAR 375: III 64 (eyes); ZA 61, 60: 207 (*bunnū*, Dt);

2. id. in prot: → 6.6.1.1 sv: TDP 38: 68 (eyes); CT 41, 10a: 6 (eyes); 10b: 13 // 31, 33: 31 (lips);

3. remainder, **SB**: Tn-Ep. IVa 34 (warriors: "to deploy"); V 10 (*šēp mātika* "the foot of your country", i.e., its boundary?);

4. a process performed on metal, OB Mari: ARM 13, 55: 11 (stat.). 17 = (133); 23 p. 304 no. 387: 5.

Temēru "to bury", D + pl. obj. (6.4.3 group IIIb):

1. lit., **SB**: Or. 40, 148: 51 (various objects); Spirits p. 134: 23' ([statues]); Maqlû II 183 (images); AfO 18, 292: 38 (id.);

2. metaph. "to dissimulate", OB Mari: ARM 26/2 p. 183 no. 373: 3 (words, stat.).

Note esp. D in Or. 40, 148: 51, vs. G in 141: 31. 47, cf. 6.7.2; and also Spirits p. 134: 23' versus G + sg. obj. in 22' (restored); and the indiscriminate use of D and G in Maqlû II 183f acc. to AfO 18, 73b and in AfO 18, 292: 32-51; G is more common, also with pl. obj., cf. AHw sv G.

Ṭ

Ṭabāhu "to slaughter", D mostly + pl. obj. → 6.4.1.1 (group Ia):

1. literally (various animals), **OB**: ARM 14, 7: 7 (sheep); **SB** passim, cf. AHw sv D 1, e.g., Gilg. VI 60 (lambs); VAB 7, 264: 8 = (119) (stat.) (sheep (*aslu*)); **NA**: Iraq 23, 20a: 12 (sheep (pl.), stat.);

2. enemy soldiers and peoples ("like animals"), **SB** passim, cf. AHw sv D 2, e.g., RIMA 2/I, 184: 80; other persons: LKU 43: 6 (girls, stat.); **NA**: ABL 564: 13 (men);

3. exc. sg. obj., **OB**: BM 96996: r.19 (sheep (sg.)); **SB**: MVAeG 21, 80: 11 (pers.).

Ṭapālu "to insult, disparage", D not disc., **OB**: RA 69, 121: 14; ARM 26/2 p. 55 no. 302: 20; p. 203 no. 385: 19' (oath); **SB**: Gilg. VI 159 (pers.); ZA 43, 102: 29 (no overt object, prot. → 6.6.1.1 sv); often part., **OB**: MSL 12, 168: 333; 208: 241; 194a: 16 ("slanderer", cf. CAD sv); **SB**: ZA 43, 104: 17 (prot.); BWL 218: 6 (part. Dt(n)).

Ṭarādu "to drive away, banish, to send", D → 5.6.4 and 6.8.1 sv, **OAk**: RA 35, 48 no. 24b: 2 (Dt); **SB**: AnSt. 6, 152: 60. 63; BWL 86: 270; 216: 23; 218: 56 (rest.) (all person(s)); Gilg. VI 62; BWL 194: 9 (animals, part.); AGH 96a: 6; Šurpu IV 102; BID 131: 80 (demon(s)); BWL 82: 213 (*nēmequ* "wisdom"); **NB**: ABL 1342: 12; BIN 1, 73: 18; TMH 2, 254: 33 (person(s)).

Ṭepû "to spread, plaster", D **SB** med. and rit., cf. 6.9.2.1: AMT 23, 10: 6 (ingredients); BAM 159: IV 21 (powder on the face); SpTU 1, 44: 79 (ingredients on the mouth); BAM 33: 18 (head: "to plaster"); for *ṭuppû* said of fields (OB) → 8.4.2 sv.

W

(W)alādu "to give birth, produce, beget", D mostly + pl. obj. → 6.4.6.1 sv (group VIa):

1. human offspring, **OB**: LE § 59 A IV 29 = (14A) (stat.); APR 96b: 18; Two Elegies p. 70 gloss to line 107 on p. 55: 107 (sons); **SB**: ACh. 2. Spl. 51: 17 (males);

2. referring to the breeding of sheep, **OB** (all with pl. obj.): ARM 26/1 p. 198 no. 55: 20 = (141B); YOS 5, 208: I 6; 212: 8; 217: I 14; TCL 10, 24: 8 (cf. Kraus, *Viehhaltung* 9, 12f, all stat.); Mél. Birot 273: 5; MKT 3, 28: II 17. 19 acc. to AHw sv D 3c;

3. with gods as subject, **SB**: mainly part. → 6.9.3: Ee I 4 (all gods, part.); STC 1, 173: 21; BA 5, 656: 18 (gods); SAA 3, 1: 16 (emending ^{d}<u>ištar</u>.<<u>meš</u>>, cf. CAD sv 2a-2'); with a mass noun as obj.: Or. 36, 116: 30 (grain); 39, 407: 9 (vegetation); ArOr. 37, 487: 8 ("everything"); other forms: Ee I 105 ("the four winds"); AGH 20 b 17 (Dt with subj. *tenēšēti* "mankind"); KAR 80: 22 // RA 26, 40: 11 (id.);

4. metaph., **SB**: BWL 252: 24 (three abstract concepts as subj. and as obj., non-ag.);

5. exc. with sg. obj., **SB**: Lugal 27 (demon). For D "to act as midwife, assist at birth" → 8.3.3 and 8.4.2 sv.

(W)aṣābu "to add, enlarge", D → 6.8.5; unambiguous D forms: **OAk**: OAIC 9: 25 (silver, Dt); **OB**: ARM 26/1 p. 467 no. 226: 13 (chariots, stat.); JRAS Cspl. 71: 13 (offspring, part.); **MB**: SEM 117: III 8 acc. to AHw sv D 1 (abundance); later D passim instead of G, cf. also AHw sv D II and CAD A/2 p. 354b comment on *aṣābu.*

(W)atû "to find, search, select", D → 6.8.1 sv, **SB**: AfO 23, 47 no. 4: 5 (life); Tākultu 126: 166 (the designs (*uṣurātu*) of heaven and earth", stat.); Angim 88: 164 (person); and passim in RI from Adad-nirari III onwards, listed AHw sv *(w)atû* D 3 (and cf. GAG^2 § 106o), CAD sv *atû* v. 2a (interpreted as G).

Z

Zabālu "to carry, transport", D + pl. obj. (6.4.7 group VIIb): **OA**: kt k/k 79: 12 (merchandise); **SB**: CT 39, 27: 20f (young animals, to be understood from the context); 31, 50: 6; KAR 430: r.11 (affairs, Dt). These cases are exceptional, compared to the frequent use of G. With CT 31, 50: 6 *amâtīka ana nakri uz-zab-ba-la-ma* "reports about your affairs will be carried to the enemy", compare, for instance, YOS 10, 33: V 13 with G, and CT 6 pl. 2 case 1 and 20 with Gtn.

Zakāru "to declare, mention, invoke, swear", D not disc., **OB**: MARI 6, 338: 25. 54; ARM 26/2 p. 176 no. 370: 45'. 1" (oath, qu. in 9.1.3 sv, all reciprocal Dt with additional reduplication); **MB**: BBS 3: I 30 (pers.); **SB**: Ee I 8 (gods, stat.); VI 166 (name); VI 108 (*alaktu* "achievement"); VI 97 (curse); IAsb. 36: r.12 ("evil words").

Zamāru "to sing", D not disc., **OB**: JRAS Cspl. 67: 5 (divine power); Atr. 104: 19 (flood).

Zanānu "to provide", D not disc., **SB**: Sg. Cyl. 47 (wisdom, stat.).

Zaqāpu "to erect, plant", D mostly + pl. obj. → 6.4.3.1 sv (group IIIa):

1. "to impale" enemies, **SB**: passim in RIs, cf. CAD sv *z*. A 3c; AHw sv D 4;

2. "to erect" standards (*urigallu*), **SB**, mostly pl.: Racc. 121: 27; ZA 6, 242: 21 (cf. Spirits p. 115) (stat.); AfO 14, 148: 167; BagF. 18, 369: 11'; 370: 25'. 4; 371: 16 (all plur.); AMT 44, 4: 5 (sg., but logical pl.); sometimes sg.: UM 1/2, 121: r.9; AAA 22, 92: 194; KAR 90: 18; IV R 18*: 6. 18, cf. 6.9.2.1;

3. other objects, **SB**: TuL 81: 8 (splinters); BBR 87: II 12 (sticks of cedar wood, stat.); IAsb. 76 c 11 (pillars, part.); 77 c 16 (emblems, part.); BagF. 18, 133: 84 (braziers); 153: 6 (straws); with a mass noun: BBR 26: IV 32 (sweet reed);

4. body parts, **OB**: TuL 43: 2 (eyes); **SB**: a) eyes (all in prot. → 6.6.1.1 sv) CT 41, 10a: 8; Epilepsy p. 71: 21f; TDP 224: 56 (Dtn); KAR 400: r.! 4 (eye); b) hair (mostly stat.) SpTU 1, 84: 29; TDP 30: 101. 108; Syr. 33, 125: 5; KAR 43: r.10 acc. to Streck, ZA 84, 187; other forms: TuL 141: 7 +Var. (Dtn, acc. to AHw sv Dtn); STT 215: III 16; c) penis SpTU 4, 135: II 9;

5. part., **OB**: MSL 12, 164: 205 *mu-za-qi$_4$-[pu]*, CAD sv: an agricultural occupation; AHw sv: "Gartenbinder" → 6.6.2 sv.

Zaqāru "to build high", D not disc., **SB** passim, cf. CAD sv 2a; AHw sv *z*. I D 2.

Zaqātu "to sting, hurt", D **SB**:

1. with body parts as subject and pers. obj.: "to hurt", passim in medical texts → CAD sv 2a, AHw sv D 2/Dtn, all prot. → 6.6.1.2 sv; also SpTU 2, 22: IV 26; 4, 152: 21; Epilepsy p. 69: r.13 = (43);

2. rest: KAR 80: r.26 (pers.); JNES 33, 342: 20 (no overt obj.). For *zuqqut* in omens → 10.7.1.1 sv.

Zarû "to sow, scatter", D **OA**: PennsOATexts no. 13: 9, cf. Veenhof, JESHO 28, 112 and 1987: 46 and 67 note 18 (silver, stat.); "C 18": 33 qu. by Veenhof 1987: 67 note 18 = (31) (tin).

Zâru "to twist", D 2x + pl. obj. (6.4.2 group IIc): **SB**: TDP 98: 51 (fingers, prot., cf. 6.6.1); Or. 24, 256: 7 (feet (partly restored)). G occurs a few times with sg. obj, cf. CAD sv z. A lex. sect and a (I follow AHw in positing one verb *zâru*, rather than two, as in CAD).

Zâzu "to divide, distribute", D → 6.5.2 sv:

1. OB: CDSmith 274: 2 quoted CAD sv 5c (house, stat.); OBTI 14: r.13' ("your silver and PN's silver" → 6.10.2.?). [Cancel AbB 2, 88 (= 13, 60): 12; 2, 159: 13 (cf. AbB 13 p. 55 n. c); ARM 2, 52: 7 (cf. Veenhof, JEOL 27, 65, against AHw sv D 1)];

2. SB: **a)** usually "to distribute, apportion" + *ana*: Ee VI 46; Racc. 129: 14 (part.); ArOr 37, 484: 50 (portions); Ee VI 145; Fs. Bergerhof 177: 5' (station(s)); JNES 26, 203: 39 (ordinances); AfO 17, 89: 4 (courses (*harrānī*)); VAT 13838: 4 qu. CAD sv lex. sect. (food offerings, part.); Ee VII 60 (water); **NA**: SAA 2 p. 46: 430 (*mimmūkun* "all your goods"); exc. with sg. dat.: MSL 1, 4: 39 ("to him", cf. note 19); **b)** rarely "to divide": Ee IV 136 (*kūbu* "monster"); VI 39 (gods); *RA 33, 106: 23 (person, stat.);

3. for later periods, cf. CAD sv 5c, AHw sv D 4 and 6.5.2 sv.

CHAPTER SEVEN

THE FACTITIVE D-STEM

7.0. This chapter discusses the verbs of Types II, III and IV according to the classification of section 5.2. The bulk of the chapter is devoted to Types III and IV, which are valency-extending and comprise verbs that are intransitive in the G-stem (Type III), or else have a low degree of inherent transitivity, in spite of their usually having a direct object (Type IV, e.g., *lamādu* "to know, learn", vs. *lummudu* "to inform, teach"). It was argued in 5.5.2 that the latter type is a subtype of III. In this chapter we will subsume both types under the traditional designation of "factitive" D-stems.

The problems posed by the factitive D-stem are quite different from those of the D-stems of Type I, which were discussed in the previous chapter. Prominent features of the latter are the lack of a clear and consistent differentiation between G and D and the unpredictable nature of their semantic relationship in general. This necessitated a rather detailed description of many individual verbs and the contexts in which they occur.

Factitive D-stems, on the other hand, are characterized by a highly regular and predictable relationship to the G-stem. As a rule, they serve as the transitive counterpart of an intransitive G-stem: G denotes the occurrence of a process, whereas D is used for the corresponding action. Although this regularity is not absolute, we can study them as a category, without a detailed exposition of individual verbs.

The problems posed by the factitive D-stem are of a different kind: first, there is the historical problem of the relationship between the factitive function and the other function(s) of the D-stem, especially the function which is traditionally described as "intensive". This has been a major issue in the controversies concerning the D-stem (cf. 1.4). A second problem is the exact nature of factitivity in contrast to causativity and, accordingly, the relationship of the factitive D-stem to the causative Š-stem.

It is most convenient to treat these problems in reverse order. Thus the latter problem will be discussed first, in sections 7.1 and 7.2. The factitive function itself will be examined in 7.3 and 7.4. Section 7.5 will offer a detailed discussion of those verbs which use both the D- and the Š-stem as factitives. The chapter will end with a discussion of Type II, the marginal type of intransitive G-stems with an intransitive D-stem (7.6).

7.1. Factitive and causative

The factitive D-stem basically serves to underline that an external agent has been added to a (usually) intransitive sentence in which the corresponding adjective or verbal G-stem is used. Whereas the G-stem typically denotes a process or, in the case of an adjective, a state or condition, the D-stem is used for the corresponding action, brought about by an agent. A random example is offered by the following pair of sentences:

(01) AbB 3, 22: 15f (PN tells me that (...)) *qaqqadī kīma šamê tu-ka-ab-bi-tu* "you have honoured (D) me highly" (lit. "you have made my head important like heaven");
(02) *ib.* 31 *eli panānum qaqqadī ka-bi-it* "I am more honoured (G) than before" (lit. "my head is more important than before").

In a prototypical factitive sentence, the subject occurring with the intransitive G-stem can also serve as direct object of the factitive sentence. Thus in the example above *qaqqadī* "my head" is direct object in (01) and subject in (02).

We will consider the use of the D-stem in order to express factitivity more closely in 7.3. Before doing so, we first have to discuss the relationship between factitivity and the closely similar notion of causativity.

7.1.1. Goetze's definition of factitive versus causative

Factitivity, as it was defined in the previous section, is closely related to causativity. In fact, what is called a factitive in Akkadian and in Semitic studies in general, would be described as a causative in general linguistics, and was often described as a causative by Semitists, too, before the appearance of Goetze's epoch-making article *The So-called Intensive of the Semitic Languages* (Goetze 1942), which was discussed in Chapter I.

From a syntactic point of view, there is no difference between causative and factitive: both refer to the same syntactic process: an increase in the number of participants of a predicate by means of the addition of an external agent. In Semitic studies, however, two terms are current for this phenomenon, as a result of the fact that most Semitic languages have two morphological categories with which to express it: first, the verbal stem which is characterized by a sibilant or laryngeal prefix, i.e., the Š-stem in Akkadian and the corresponding stems in other languages (Stem IV in Arabic, the Hiph^c^il in Hebrew, etc.), and, second, the verbal stem with gemination of the second radical, i.e., the D-stem and its equivalents.

Since the appearance of Goetze's article, it has been customary to distinguish the Š-stem as a causative formation from the D-stem as a factitive. Goetze defines the difference as follows (see already 1.7): the function of a causative is "[to] cause someone to act in the way which the basic verb indicates" (*o.c.* 4b); that of the factitive is "[to] make a person or a thing what the adjective indicates", if the D-stem is derived from an adjective (*o.c.* 6b), or "[to] put a person or a thing in the state which the stative describes" for other D-stems (*o.c.* 6a). These definitions have been taken over by GAG for the factitive function of the D-stem (§ 88c), and for the causative function of the Š-stem (§ 89c).

Two objections can be raised against Goetze's definition of the difference between D and Š. In the first place, it makes the semantic nature of the basic verb the decisive factor in determining whether the addition of an external agent will result in a factitive or a causative: if the G-stem expresses a state, the resulting clause expresses the bringing about of a state and is therefore factitive; if it expresses an action or an event, the resulting clause with the additional agent also expresses an action, and is causative. Therefore, the two terms are complementary, and from a syntactic point of view, there is no justification for using two different terms for what is essentially the same phenomenon.

Secondly, as already signalled in GAG § 88c/d/e and § 89d, there are also Š-stems which denote the bringing about of a state, and there are many G-stems which clearly refer to an event rather than to a state, but still have a D-stem. Thus from a semantic point of view there is no one-to-one correspondence between D and factitive on the one hand, and Š and causative on the other.

In spite of this, it will be argued in this chapter that as far as Akkadian is concerned we need two different terms for the process which is generally called causativization, because the D-stem and the Š-stem each represent - at least prototypically - a specific type of relationship between the derived and the basic stem. This relationship is, however, of a different nature than is currently assumed. Therefore, the traditional terms will be retained, but the term "factitive" in particular will be defined in a different way.

We will start with a short discussion of causativity, and subsequently propose a definition of factitivity, concentrating on those aspects in which it contrasts with causativity.

7.1.2. A definition of "causative"

The grammatical category "causative" has the following characteristics.[1] On the syntactic level, a causative involves an increase in valency by one unit vis-à-vis the non-causative verb; this increase is brought about by the addition of an external agent, the "causer". If the non-causative verb is monovalent (intransitive), the causative verb is bivalent (transitive); if it is bivalent, the causative verb is trivalent (doubly transitive).

Semantically, a causative refers to a "causative situation", which consists of two components: the causing situation or the antecedent, and the caused situation or the consequent; the combination of these two results in a causative situation (Nedyalkov-Silnitsky 1973: 1). The causative relation between antecedent and consequent can be expressed in many different ways: with an antecedent *the weather was bad,* and a consequent *we stayed in*, for instance, one can say *we stayed in because of the bad weather*, or *the weather was bad, so that we stayed in*, etc. However, the only form of expression relevant to our purpose is the causative relation expressed by a causative construction, as in *the bad weather forced us to stay in* or *the bad weather made us stay in.*

On the morphological level this causative construction can be realized in three different ways (Nedyalkov-Silnitsky 1973: 2ff; Comrie 1981: 159f), namely, as an *analytical,* a *lexical* or a *morphological* causative. An analytical causative is a periphrastic construction, consisting of a verb meaning "to cause" plus the non-causative verb (as in the sentence *the bad weather made us stay in,* quoted above); this is the normal procedure in Western European languages. In a lexical causative the causative verb is not formally related to the non-causative verb; the stock example is *to kill* as a causative of *to die.* A morphological causative is a verbal form which is derivationally related to the non-causative verb. Since the causative formations of Akkadian come under this type, we will concentrate on the morphological causative.[2]

It is usually either the causative member of the opposition which is marked by a special morpheme (the "causative" morpheme, e.g., the prefix *ša/u-* in the Š-stem), or the non-causative member, which in that case is often called "anti-causative" (Nedyalkov-Silnitsky 1973: 2). In Akkadian the passive/intransitive Št-stem can be considered an anti-causative in so far as it is derived from a causative Š-stem; likewise, the Dt-stem can be used as an "anti-factitive", cf. 9.1.1.

A further distinction relevant to the issue at hand is that between "distant" and "contact" causation (Nedyalkov-Silnitsky 1973: 10f). In distant causation there is a certain time interval between the moment of causing and the moment the act which is caused is performed by the subject of the underlying non-causative verb, the "causee". In contact causation the two moments fall together.

7.1.3. Bivalent versus trivalent causatives

There is an important difference between causatives derived from intransitive verbs and those derived from transitive verbs, i.e., between bivalent and trivalent causatives, respectively. Cross-linguistically, trivalent causatives are used far less frequently than bivalent ones, and there is strong evidence that a trivalent causative formation always develops as a secondary offshoot of a bivalent one. Nedyalkov-Silnitsky (1973: 7ff) offer the following arguments for this. First of all, there are languages which derive morphological causatives exclusively from intransitive verbs, but no languages are known in which only transitive verbs form such causatives (cf. also Comrie 1985: 335f). Second, if a language has more than one causative morpheme, the morphemes which derive causatives from intransitive verbs are more varied than those of transitive verbs. Finally, if the morphemes which derive causatives from transitive verbs differ from those which derive causatives from intransitive verbs, the former are the more complex ones.

Thus the existence of trivalent causatives in a language presupposes the existence of morphologically explicit bivalent causatives, but not vice versa. This strongly suggests that the former are secondary developments of the latter (cf. Kuryłowicz 1964: 87; Jamison 1983: 186ff, who argues the same for the causative in Vedic Sanskrit).

Moreover, trivalent causatives show a predilection for specific semantic classes: if a language has only a few trivalent morphological causatives, these will typically come from verbs of perception, verbs of cognition and the verbs *to eat, to drink* and *to suck* (Nedyalkov-Silnitsky 1973: 16f).[3] These semantic classes comprise verbs which typically have a low degree of transitivity (cf. 5.3 and 5.6.2.1); this suggests that these verbs play an essential role in the spread of causative morphemes from intransitive to transitive verbs (cf. also Kuryłowicz 1964: 87).

Finally, there is a strong tendency among trivalent causatives to leave one of the three participant roles unexpressed, mostly the causee, cf. Nedyalkov-Silnitsky 1973: 31f.

7.1.4. Causatives that are not formally distinguished from non-causatives

A remarkable feature of the causative constructions of some languages is the fact that they have causative verbs which, in contrast to the conditions described above, are not formally distinguished from the corresponding non-causative verb; their causative nature is "determined solely by the environment of the verb" (Nedyalkov-Silnitsky 1973: 3). This phenomenon is especially important if one wishes to appreciate the specific nature of the D-stem in contrast to the Š-stem.

Such causatives are very common in English, which has a large number of verbs used indiscriminately as causatives or as intransitives: *to turn, to move, to break, to grow, to melt, to boil, to open, to burn,* etc., cf. Lyons 1968. According to Nedyalkov-Silnitsky 1973: 4, they were also common in Ancient Chinese, which might suggest that it is typical of languages which use syntactic procedures instead of morphological derivation (i.e., which are predominantly "isolating"). It also has "a limited distribution in different languages and a limited productivity within individual languages" (*ib.* 4). Some examples from European languages are *sortir, descendre, arrêter, rougir* and *grandir* from French, *bewegen* and *brechen* from German, and *koken* "to boil" and *veranderen* "to change" from Dutch. For similar verbs in Semitic, see 11.4.

The verbs displaying this peculiarity can express the verbal concept both as a process and as an action brought about by an external agent. Which of these possibilities applies in a given context is determined by the valency frame: generally speaking, the causative meaning is realized if the sentence contains a constituent which can qualify as an agent. They are typically change-of-state verbs; prominent among them are verbs derived from adjectives, cf. English *to widen, to lengthen, to redden, to worsen, to dry, to empty, to liquefy,* etc. Kuryłowicz 1964: 88, regards such verbs as the starting point for the development of a morphological causative.

The existence of this type of verb in some languages shows that the causative interpretation of a sentence need not depend on the form of the verb, but may also depend on its syntactic structure.[4] For instance, with the verb *to open* and one participant *door*, the only sentence possible (omitting tense differences) is *the door opened*; with an additional participant *John*, the sentence will be *John opened the door*. There is no risk of misunderstanding, the more so because the agent is typically animate and the patient (the object) typically inanimate. To a certain extent, therefore, the morphological distinction between a non-causative verb and the corresponding causative is redundant (Nedyalkov-Silnitsky 1973: 3), and may be absent.

In all likelihood, this morphological redundancy applies only to bivalent causatives, derived from intransitive verbs. If we add a third participant to the sentence which we took as an example above, e.g., *Mary*, its function will be ambiguous: if a sentence as *John opened Mary the door* were possible, the first interpretation of *Mary* would probably be that it is an indirect object: *John opened the door for Mary.* It would never be interpreted as synonymous with *John made Mary open the door.* It seems plausible that, in general, the addition of a third participant to a transitive verb makes the semantic roles in a sentence so complicated that an explicit morpheme is necessary to ensure a causative interpretation. If this claim is correct, it explains why the D-stem of transitive verbs - which is normally bivalent, as we have seen in Chapter VI - is not used as a causative of transitive verbs: if it were used in that function, it would be both bivalent and trivalent, and there would be no formal distinction between the non-causative and the causative verb (see further 7.5.2).

7.1.5. Fixed and alternating valency

Among intransitive verbs, then, we can distinguish between two kinds: verbs which - apart from atypical uses - are always monovalent, and verbs of the kind discussed in the previous section, which can be mono- or bivalent according to the structure of the predicate in which they occur. The former always have the same valency; accordingly, I will refer to them as "fixed valency verbs". The latter will be referred to as "alternating valency verbs".[5]

It should be emphasized that only those valency changes are considered here which involve the addition of an agent and the concomitant demotion of the subject of the basic sentence to the position of direct object. Other possible cases of alternating valency, such as monovalent *to read* or *to drink* versus bivalent *to read a book* or *to drink wine*, are irrelevant in the present context, and are hence ignored.

It seems a plausible assumption that the distinction between fixed and alternating valency verbs correlates with a semantic distinction. To start with the latter kind, the examples mentioned above suggest that the alternating valency verbs will, generally speaking, denote verbal concepts which can be realized both as processes, without intervention from outside, and as actions, brought about by an external agent (cf. Haspelmath 1993: 92ff). If realized as a process, their subject is typically an experiencer rather than an agent. A common characteristic seems to be that they are telic, i.e., they lead to an endpoint, and therefore to a certain result; possibly, they may be characterized as focusing on this result, rather than on the way it came about; according to Haspelmath (1993: 93), they cannot contain "agent-oriented meaning components". This is in particular suggested by verbs of this kind which are derived from adjectives.

Among the typical fixed valency verbs there are two main types: those which are always monovalent, and those which are always bivalent (cf. Berry 1975: 157). The verbs which are always monovalent typically express verbal concepts which in normal circumstances can only be initiated by the intervention of an agent, such as *to dance, to run, to jump, to sleep, to scream, to read, to think, to laugh, to sing, to work,* etc. But also a verb like *to rain,* with zero valency, belongs here.

It follows from the previous section that bivalent verbs are typically fixed valency verbs, since they cannot accommodate an external agent as third participant without a change in form. This applies to the great majority of transitive verbs, especially those which have a high degree of inherent transitivity, because they normally require the presence of a direct object.

The difference between fixed and alternating valency verbs appears most clearly when they are causativized, i.e., when an external agent is added. For the latter type this is a natural process, fully compatible with the semantic nature of the verb. This is presumably the reason why, at least in some languages, it can be realized without any formal change, purely by means of the addition of an agent. The causative use of these verbs is just as natural as the intransitive use, and probably not significantly less frequent.

Causativization of a fixed valency verb, on the other hand, results in a valency which exceeds the "natural" valency of the concept in question. Therefore, it can be expected to be far less frequent than the basic verb, and results in a highly marked verb form, which will generally require an explicit morphological form of expression.

The distinction which is made in this study between causative and factitive is that *the causativization of a fixed valency verb is called a causative, whereas that of an alternating valency verb is called a factitive.*[6]

7.1.6. The difference between causative and factitive

Hence we can describe the difference between a causative and a factitive as follows. A causative usually reflects a clear "causative situation" as described in 7.1.2: the two elements of which a causative situation consists, the external agent and the basic non-causative situation, can be clearly distinguished; the verb can be analysed as consisting of its lexical meaning plus the grammatical feature "causative"; the causee is typically an individualized, often human, participant who may hold a certain degree of control over the action; causation may be either of the "distant" or "contact" type. For most verbs it is a highly marked and relatively rare category.

In a factitive sentence, on the other hand, the typical features of a causative situation are far less easy to identify. The subject of the basic intransitive sentence takes the participant role of patient, just as in any other transitive sentence. More often than not it is inanimate and tends to have no control whatsoever over the action; in fact, the term "causee" is hardly appropriate in a factitive sentence. Causation is always of the "contact" type.

Therefore, a factitive sentence is more or less identical with an ordinary transitive sentence. It is a general feature of highly transitive sentences - including factitive ones - that they refer to situations in which an agentive subject causes a change in a patient object (cf. Lyons 1977: II 488ff).

Compare, for instance, a sentence as *I broke the stick* with *I chopped the stick in two*: the former is a factitive sentence, the latter is not, because we can say *the stick broke*, but not **the stick chopped in two*. This does not lead, however, to any difference in their structure or in the status of the direct object (although it shows the difference between fixed and alternating valency verbs: *to chop in two* cannot be seen as a process, because it requires an agent). The only difference between a factitive verb and an ordinary transitive verb is that the former is derived from the corresponding intransitive verb, either by a zero morpheme (as in English) or by an explicit morpheme (as in Akkadian, see below).

Moreover, since a factitive does not involve an unusual valency, it is not necessarily less frequent and does not represent a highly marked category (if at all morphologically different from the non-factitive verb).

7.1.7. The language-specific nature of alternating valency

The most problematic point of the distinction between fixed and alternating valency verbs, and therefore between causative and factitive, is the fact that there is no clear-cut boundary between them: in fact, we can identify a number of verbs which are typically (or rather prototypically) "alternating valency" (change of state verbs), and verbs which are typically "fixed valency" (intransitive atelic verbs denoting human activities, and most transitive verbs), but a large part of the vocabulary is difficult to classify. Moreover, the occurrence of alternating valency verbs is highly language specific. In English they are very common, as noted in 7.1.4, but many other languages tend to make a consistent formal distinction between actions and processes, so that they have only a few alternating valency verbs or none at all, cf. Haspelmath 1993: 89ff. For instance, in Russian and Spanish the verbs which are semantically comparable to the alternating valency verbs of English tend to be used only as action verbs, whereas the corresponding process verbs are derived from them by means of a reflexive pronoun: Russian *lomát'*, Spanish *romper* "to break" (trans.), versus *lomát'sja* and *romperse* "to break" (intrans.).

7.2. The connection between the D-stem and alternating valency

On the syntactic level, then, we can define a causative as a formation which denotes an increase in valency by one unit through the addition of an agentive subject. On the semantic level we can distinguish "real" causatives from factitives on the basis of whether the verb in question is a fixed or an alternating valency verb. The factitive is a semantic subtype of the causative, restricted to verbs with an alternating valency.

Although the distinction between fixed and alternating valency verbs, and accordingly that between factitive and causative, is not clear-cut and in some respects problematical, it is highly useful in defining the difference between the D- and the Š-stem. Generally speaking, the D-stem is only used for the transitive aspect of alternating valency verbs, i.e., it is exclusively factitive; the Š-stem can also have this function, but mostly serves as a causative, i.e., to indicate an increase in valency which exceeds the natural valency of the verb in question. Thus, on the basis of the definition of fixed and alternating valency we can describe the D-stem as factitive, and the Š-stem as both causative and factitive.

The claim that the D-stem can only serve as a factitive, not as a causative, is based on the following facts: first, the general semantic nature of the non-factitive D-stems of Types I and II (7.2.1); second, the general association of the causative Š-stem with verbs which typically have an animate subject (7.2.2); third, the strong association of the factitive D-stem with adjectives (7.2.3); fourth, the almost complete absence of unambiguously causative D-stems (7.2.4), and, fifth, the occasional occurrence of alternating valency verbs in Akkadian, the "factitive G-stems" (7.2.5.).

7.2.1. Causative, factitive and the four Types of D-stems

In section 5.2 the verbs of Akkadian which have a D-stem were divided into four types, according to whether their D-stem is valency-preserving (Type I with transitive, and Type II with intransitive verbs) or valency-extending (Type III with intransitive verbs, and Type IV with verbs of the type of *lamādu* "to know, learn", versus *lummudu* "to inform, teach", as discussed in 5.5.2). If we apply the terms factitive and causative as defined above to this classification, the situation is as follows: the verbs of Types III and IV extend their valency by means of the D-stem; if the D-stem can only be factitive, not causative, they *must* be alternating valency verbs. On the other hand, we expect those of Types I and II to be typically fixed valency verbs; otherwise they would use the D-stem with valency-extending function. If they are causativized, we expect them to use only the Š-stem.

This is completely borne out by the facts. Type I are transitive verbs with a high degree of inherent transitivity, which in 7.1.5 we argued to be typically fixed valency verbs (i.e., always bivalent). In Chapter VI it was shown that the D-stems of these verbs do not have a higher valency than the G-stems, but are for the most part associated with verbal plurality. In order to causativize them we have to use the Š-stem.

The verbs of Type II, the intransitive G-stems with an intransitive D-stem to be listed and discussed below in 7.6, mostly belong to a few semantically well-defined groups: first, verbs denoting the production of sounds, such as *habābu* "to buzz, low, murmur", and *nabāhu* "to bark"; second, verbs denoting bodily functions (partly overlapping with the preceding group), such as *sa'ālu* "to cough", and *ṣarātu* "to break wind"; third, some atelic verbs denoting various (often mental) activities, for instance *ṣarāmu* "to do one's best". Finally, there is a fourth group with a few miscellaneous verbs; a complete list is included in 7.6. These verbs are typical fixed valency verbs (i.e., always monovalent), since they mostly denote actions performed by animate beings. In the rare cases that they are found in causative sentences, they use the Š-stem; the pertinent instances are quoted in 7.6.

7.2.2. Causative, factitive and the nature of the subject

Whereas the causativization of transitive verbs in Akkadian is the exclusive domain of the Š-stem (see 7.5.2), intransitive verbs can be causativized by means of the D-stem or by means of the Š-stem.[7] The current view, based on Goetze's ideas, and represented, for instance, by GAG § 88c/d/e and 89d, claims that the D-stem is associated with stative verbs, and the Š-stem with fientive verbs (cf. 7.1.1 above).

There is a far stronger correlation, however, between the use of D and Š if they are used to causativize an intransitive verb, and the fixed or alternating valency of that verb. As we argued in 7.1.5, fixed valency verbs, whether monovalent or bivalent, tend to denote actions which can only be initiated by agents, and therefore typically have animate subjects, cf. the examples from English given there, and Berry 1975: 157. Alternating valency verbs, on the other hand, usually refer to processes which can be realized both with and without intervention of an agent.

Accordingly, the intransitive verbs which normally have a Š-stem are for the most part verbs referring to movements which are typically performed by animate beings: *alāku* "to go"; *elû* "to go up" (vs. *elû* "to be high" with D, mainly said of body parts and buildings, cf. 7.5.3 sv); *erēbu* "to enter"; *etēqu* "to pass along, cross"; *hamāṭu* "to hurry" (versus *hamāṭu* "to burn" mainly with D, cf. 7.3.2 and 7.5.5.1 sv); *izuzzu* "to stand up"; *itūlu* and *nâlu* "to lie down"; *kamāsu* "to kneel down"; *lasāmu* "to run", *maqātu* "to fall"; *ra'ābu* "to tremble";[8] *rabāṣu* "to lie down", *rakābu* "to ride"; *tebû* "to stand up"; *(w)arādu* "to descend"; *(w)aṣû* "to go out"; *(w)ašābu* "to sit down". Verbs of other semantic types, but also with animate subject, include *bâtu* "to spend the night"; *mâtu* "to die" and *sapādu* "to mourn".

The factitive D-stem, on the other hand, is typically used with verbs denoting processes which can equally well have animate and inanimate subjects, depending on the nature of the process. This does not only apply to adjectival verbs (see the next section); most fientive verbs with a D-stem can also occur with both inanimate and animate subjects. Some typically have an inanimate subject: *belû* "to go out" (fire); *kabābu* and *hamāṭu* "to burn" (cf. 7.3.2); *parāru* "to fall apart", *qatāru* "to rise, billow" (smoke), *rabû* "to go down" (celestial bodies); *narāṭu, râbu* and *tarāru* "to tremble, shake, quake" (see note 8), and *qatû* "to come to an end". Others occur with both kinds of subject: *halāqu* "to disappear", *qerēbu* and *ṭehû* "to approach"; *târu* "to return"; *sahāru* "to turn"; *pahāru* "to come together"; *emēdu* "to lean against, reach"; *ramāku* "to bathe"; *ṭebû* "to sink".

The tendency for action verbs to use the Š-stem, and for process verbs to use the D-stem for causativization does not hold for all relevant cases. There are some clear counter-examples, but they are not very numerous. Š-stems of verbs which often have an inanimate subject first of all comprise the few adjectival verbs with a factitive Š-stem, which will be mentioned in the next section. Other instances are *bašālu* "to boil", *bašû* "to be, exist" (which is atypical in many respects), and the zero valency verb *zanānu* "to rain".

Factitive D-stems derived from verbs which normally occur only with animate subjects are rare; a rather common example is *namāšu* "to set out, depart". Note that only factitive D-stems are considered here which are typically fientive, not such verbs as *takālu* "to trust", *lamādu* "to know, learn", etc. They belong to the next section.

The majority of intransitive verbs, however, conform to the correlation between action verbs and the Š-stem, on the one hand, and between process verbs and the D-stem on the other.

This leads to the conclusion that the difference between Š and D observed here with regard to the expression of actions and processes, respectively, agrees with the difference between causative and factitive as expounded in 7.1.6. The preference for the Š-stem shown by intransitive verbs which mostly have animate subjects agrees with the fact that causative sentences usually have a clearly individualized causee, which may have some control over the action he is induced to perform, and is therefore typically animate. In a typical factitive sentence the former subject of the intransitive sentence tends to be nothing but a patient who undergoes the action, regardless of his animate or inanimate status.

7.2.3. The factitive D-stem and adjectives

Another argument in favour of the exclusively factitive use of the D-stem is its strong association with adjectives. In 7.1.4 we argued that verbs derived from adjectives have a special affinity with alternating valency, because they are typical change-of-state verbs, and because many qualities, states and conditions can be realized both with and without intervention of an agent.

It is not possible to draw a strict dividing line between D-stems derived from adjectives and those derived from fientive verbs; therefore their numerical proportion is difficult to quantify with precision. However, the list of factitive D-stem in the Appendix to this chapter shows the predominance of verbs which are stative in character and refer to typically adjectival concepts, such as qualities of persons and objects. Accordingly, many of these verbs exist side by side with a common adjective. The precise relationship between the D-stem in general and adjectives will be dealt with in Chapter XI.

Some adjectival verbs, however, have a factitive Š-stem, either as the normal factitive, or as a literary variant of the D-stem. The most prominent cases of the first kind are *mâdu* "to be(come) numerous", *marāṣu* "to be(come) ill, distressed", *nazāqu* "to be(come) worried", *pašāqu* "to be(come) narrow, difficult", *š/sabāsu* "to be(come) angry" and *šarû* "to be(come) rich". The reason why these verbs have a Š-stem is difficult to ascertain. The Š-stems which occur as literary variants of the D-stem, such as *arāku* "to be(come) long", clearly result from a secondary spread of the Š-stem, which, as we have claimed above, can serve both as a causative and as a factitive. In 7.5 we will examine these cases in detail.

A special group is formed by a number of verbs I/w: *(w)apû* "to be(come) visible", *(w)aqāru* "to be(come) scarce, precious, expensive", *(w)asāmu* "to be(come) fitting, suitable", *(w)atāru* "to exceed, surpass"; although most of the latter also occur in the D-stem, Š seems to be their basic factitive stem. The idea, however, that verbs I/w have a Š-stem because of their form or their weak first radical is contradicted by the fact that they also occur in the D-stem, by verbs like *(w)arāqu* "to be(come) green, pale", which mainly uses the D-stem as factitive, and by the frequent D-stems *(w)uššuru* "to let go" and *wu''uru* "to order".

Generally speaking, the Š-stem has a strong association with fientive verbs, for which it is the normal causative formation.

7.2.4. The virtual absence of causative D-stems

A fourth argument for the factitive nature of the D-stem is that it is difficult to find unambiguous fixed valency verbs which use the D-stem as causative. This applies first and foremost to transitive verbs which we have argued to be principally fixed valency. The D-stem is never used to denote a valency increase in transitive verbs, except in Type IV, cf. 7.5.2.

What is more significant is that causative D-stems of intransitive fixed valency verbs are also uncommon. There are a few D-stems derived from typical fixed valency verbs, which we would expect to have a Š-stem instead. Most of these can be explained on the basis of some formal peculiarity. A few come from verbs with a hollow root starting with a sibilant (*s*, *ṣ*, *š* and *z*): *ṣâdu* "to move about, whirl" (often of persons and animals, but also of body parts), D "to cause to turn, make dizzy", *šâbu* "to tremble, sway" (typically with personal subject), D "to make tremble, sway", and *ṣâhu* "to laugh" (factitive D only in *muṣihhu* "clown", i.e., "someone who makes people laugh"), cf. CAD and AHw ssvv.

Verbs with a hollow root starting with a sibilant never appear to have a Š-stem.[9] The reason for this is doubtless phonological: it would cause an apparently undesirable consonant cluster (e.g., **ušṣâh*, **ušṣîh* from *ṣâhu* "to laugh").[10] If such verbs are intransitive, they use the D-stem, regardless of their semantic nature, or else they have neither a D-stem nor a Š-stem. Apart from the three verbs mentioned above, a D-stem (not necessarily factitive, cf. 7.5.2) is attested for *sâmu* "to be(come) red", *sâqu* "to be(come) narrow", *sâru* "to whirl, dance", *ṣâdu* "to melt (intr.)", *ṣâru* "to be illustrious", *šâhu* "to grow", *zâbu* "to dissolve". No D-stem is attested for *ṣâlu* "to quarrel", *ṣêru* "sich verbreitern" (AHw 1588f), *šâbu* "to be(come) gray", *šânu* "to urinate", *šâṣu* "to decline, wane", *šâ'u* "to fly", *šêru* "to rise early", and *zâqu* "to blow" (of the wind).

If the verbs in question are transitive they do not have a causative at all. Apart from some very obscure verbs, this applies to *sâbu* "to draw water", *sâdu* "to slay", *sâku* "to pound, crush", *sêru* "to plaster, rub", *ṣânu* (CAD *zânu*) "to fill, sprinkle", *ṣênu* "to fill, load", *šâlu* "to ask", *šâmu* "to buy", *šâmu* "to establish", *šâṭu* "to drag, pull", *šâṭu* (*šêṭu*) "to despise", *šêlu* "to sharpen", *šênu* "to put on" (shoes), *šêqu* "to smooth out", *šêtu* (*sâtu*) "to leave (over)", *zâzu* "to divide, distribute", *zêru* "to hate".

Thus although semantically *ṣâdu, ṣâhu* and *šâbu* are typical fixed valency verbs, their use of the D-stem can be explained by the fact that verbs of this structure do not form Š-stems.

Another possible case of a causative D-stem is the MA verb *sasû* "to call, summon" (for Bab. *šasû*), the D-stem of which can have the specialized meaning "to make (a herald) proclaim" in MA, cf. CAD sv *šasû* 11, and sv *musassiānu*.[11] The use of the D-stem instead of the causative Š, which we would rather expect here, may be caused by the double sibilant in the root, which makes D and Š very similar in form.[12] It is conceivable that the Š-stem of Assyrian *sasû, *ušassa,* was not recognized as such, reanalysed as a D-stem and assimilated to the rest of the forms as *usassa.* Another possibility is assigning *šasû* to the verbs of Type IV (cf. 5.5.2), because it typically has a low degree of transitivity; semantically however, it does not seem to fit in very well with the other verbs of Type IV.

Finally, an exceptional case is found in the unique D-stem of *ṣalālu* "to sleep" in SKS p. 54: 147 [ka.inim.ma *n*]*a-a'-ra ragga ṣú-ul-lu-li* "Incantation to make a naughty boy fall asleep" (cf. Farber's note on p. 54ff); elsewhere only *ṣalālu* Š is attested.[13]

This leads to the conclusion that typical fixed valency verbs with a causative D-stem instead of the expected Š-stem are hard to find. However, as already stated in 7.1.5, there are many verbs which are difficult to classify on the basis of their meaning.

7.2.5. Factitive G-stems in Akkadian

The relationship between alternating valency and the D-stem is also indicated by the fact that Akkadian has a few verbs which, in the G-stem, can denote both a process and the corresponding action. In so far as they are used to denote an action they will be referred to as "factitive G-stems". The most common of these verbs - which will be discussed in greater detail in 11.4 - is *emēdu* "to lean (intrans.) against, reach", and "to lean (trans.) against, impose"; less common are *dalāpu* "to be or stay awake", and "to keep awake, harass", *kamāsu* "to assemble" (trans. and intrans.) and *ramāku* "to bathe" and "to soak".

These verbs also have a factitive D-stem, so that if they are factitive, both the G- and the D-stem can be used. For most of them D is the usual form, whereas the use of G is restricted to specific contexts (see 11.4.2 for details). This distribution and the generally rare occurrence of the factitive G-stems show that the latter are a residual category, which has largely been replaced by the D-stem. This replacement, which was motivated by a tendency to make the high degree of transitivity inherent in factitive sentences morphologically explicit by means of gemination, has led to the factitive function of the D-stem. Indirectly, it shows the connection between alternating valency and factitivity. In Chapter XI we will discuss the historical development alluded to here in greater detail.

7.2.6. Factitive D versus causative Š

The characteristics of the factitive D-stem enumerated in the preceding sections show that the valency-extending function of D is subject to a number of strict conditions. It is connected with a specific semantic peculiarity of the intransitive basic verb, namely, that it denotes a verbal concept with an alternating valency, i.e., which can be realized both as a process and as an action. It was suggested in 7.1.4 that in such verbs the structure of the predicate is sufficient to indicate a valency increase. This means that the use of an explicit morpheme is redundant. This also applies to the factitive use of the D-stem. In this respect, it is comparable to the use of gemination in other categories, in particular in the pattern *parras* as plural formation of adjectives denoting dimensions (see 3.1.3) and in the D-stems of Type I, discussed in Chapter VI. In both categories the use of D serves to underline rather than indicate a semantic feature which is already implied in the context.[14]

The important difference, however, from these categories is that in the latter the use of a D form is optional, whereas the use of the factitive D-stem is largely obligatory: most of the corresponding G-stems cannot be used as factitives. The reason for this is expounded in Chapter XI.

Apart from the fact that they have an extra participant with agentive function, sentences with a factitive D-stem have none of the semantic features of a typical causative: there is neither a clear causative situation, nor a more or less individualized causee, and distant causation is not possible. They do not differ in any respect from ordinary highly transitive sentences.

Accordingly, there is a clear difference between the D-stem and the causative Š-stem with regard to their relationship to the G-stem. The Š-stem has a clearly derivational status: it is completely predictable in form, and largely predictable in function;[15] it is fully productive in that it can be derived from all kinds of verbs, both transitive and intransitive (with the exception discussed in 7.2.4), but it is usually not very common, especially in transitive verbs. As all causative formations of fixed valency verbs, it is a strongly marked form, because it expresses a valency which is higher than the "natural" valency of the verb in question.

For the verbs with a factitive D-stem the addition of an agentive subject to the intransitive predicate represents a natural configuration, which is compatible with the meaning of the verb. Therefore, the relationship to the corresponding G-stem is different from that of the causative. Many common factitive D-stems are no less frequent than the corresponding G-stems, but there are large variations among individual verbs in the numerical proportion of G to D.

The factitive D-stem is a highly lexicalized category: the derived status of many of its members is etymologically rather than grammatically relevant; such D-stems function as more or less independent verbs, which may be even more common than the basic verb or adjective; prominent examples of this are *wu"uru* "to order" (cf. *(w)âru* "to go"), *(w)uššuru* "to release, let go", etc. (cf. *(w)ašru* "low"), *burru* "to establish sb's guilt" (cf. *bâru* "to stay firm, become certain"), *kunnu* "to establish, to testify" (cf. *kânu* "to be firm, true"), *ukkušu* "to expel" (cf. *akāšu* "to go"). Other examples of lexicalized factitives are *burrû* "to announce, usher in" (cf. *barû* "to see") and *ruddû* "to add" (cf. *redû* "to follow"), which were already mentioned in 5.5.2.

7.2.7. Conclusions

This leads to the conclusion that the distinction between fixed and alternating valency verbs enables us to give a more satisfactory and more comprehensive account of the difference between the D-stem and the Š-stem in their factitive and causative function, respectively, than the current view.

In practice, there is a large overlap between the two approaches: most verbs which are factitive according to Goetze's definition are also factitive according to the definition adopted here. This is caused by the fact that most D-stems are derived from adjectival verbs; as we argued in 7.1.4 and 7.1.5, these are also the most typical alternating valency verbs. It is more specifically in the D-stem associated with fientive verbs, such as *pahāru* "to come together" and *târu* "to return", that the association between the D-stem and alternating valency seems to pay off.

7.3. The nature of factitivity

The actual verbs which have a factitive D-stem fall into two major categories. By far the most frequent category are those which are derived from adjectives. Chapter XI will deal with the importance of this fact for the historical background of the D-stem. For the small group of adjectival verbs with a Š-stem, see 7.2.3.

The second important category are fientive verbs like *pahāru* "to come together" and *târu* "to return". It was argued in 7.2.2 that the fact that they have a factitive D-stem (or rather that they are alternating valency verbs) is related to the fact that they mainly denote processes, as opposed to the intransitive verbs with a Š-stem, which mainly denote activities.

A list of the factitive D-stems of Akkadian is added to this chapter as an Appendix, from which the general nature of the verbs with a factitive D-stem can be elicited. Since it is only in favourable circumstances that we are able to determine whether a verb is basically adjectival or fientive, it is not possible to draw a clear dividing line between the first and the second group. Therefore, they are listed as a single category in the Appendix.

In the following sections we will discuss some factitive D-stems which are particularly interesting, because they cast a clear light on the exact nature of factitivity: in 7.3.1 the verb *malû* "to be(come) full", and in 7.3.2 other verbs which in some respect deviate from the factitive prototype as defined in 7.1. Section 7.3.3 will deal with the relationship between the factitive function of the D-stem and its other functions. In 7.4 we will examine the use of factitive D-stems which are atypical in that they appear in intransitive sentences.

7.3.1. Factitive and agentive: the case of *malû*

The difference between a factitive sentence, which expresses an action, and the corresponding non-factitive, intransitive sentence, which expresses a process, entails two valency changes. The first is quantitative: the addition of an extra participant with the function of agent, which causes the demotion of the original subject to the status of direct object. The second one, which is less obvious, but which may be even more essential to the nature of factitivity in Akkadian than the first one, is qualitative: the change in the nature of the subject from non-agentive in the non-factitive sentence into agentive in the factitive one (cf. Saad and Bolozky 1984: 31).

The importance of the qualitative valency change from non-agentive to agentive is especially clear from the use of the G- and the D-stem of *malû* "to be(come) full, to cover". It shows unambiguously that, at least in this verb, it is the presence of an agentive subject, rather than that of a direct object, which is the decisive criterion for the use of a factitive D-stem. Basically, *malû* is an ordinary Type III verb, with an intransitive G-stem and a factitive D-stem, which, by definition, has an agentive subject (it also has a factitive Š-stem, see 7.5.5.1 sv). Compare the following sentences:

(03) BWL 144: 19 *ša amēli muttaprašsidi ma-li karassu* "the belly of a wandering man is full",
(04) *ib.* 146: 42 *mannu innamdakkāma tu-ma-al-la karaška* "who will give you (something) to fill your belly?").

Both constructions are often extended with an adjunct accusative specifying the substance contained, or the surface covered:

(05) ARM 13, 35: 11 *eleppētum šina šêm li-im-la-a* "let these ships be loaded (lit. become full) with barley",
(06) *ib.* 3, 27: 20ff *elep[pēti]m šināt[i]* (...) *[qē]mam ú-ma-al-la-ši-[na-ti-ma]* "I will load these ships with flour".

However, there is yet a third construction possible, in which the substance is subject and the container object. If we reduce these last sentences to their essentials, we get *the ship is full of barley* for the G-stem and *I fill the ship with barley* for the D-stem. The third construction - which uses the G-stem - would be *barley fills the ship.* To my knowledge, it is not attested in Akkadian with exactly these words, but there are numerous instances with other nouns, cf. CAD sv 5, AHw sv *m.* IV G 10. Consider the following examples:

(07) Atr. 96: 6 *kīma kulīlī im-la-a-nim nāram* "like dragon flies they (the drowned people) have filled the river" (cf. also Gilg. XI 123 discussed in note 17 under (g));

(08) ÖB 2, 66: 64 *šumma* (...) *šulmū mādūtum uṣûnimma kāsam im-ta-lu-ú* "if (...) a lot of bubbles have appeared and have covered (the water in) the cup";

(09) ARM 27, 27: 6ff *ṣarṣar šū* (...) *aqdamāt GN u aharātim ma-li* "those locusts (...) have covered (i.e., "(now) cover") the near and the far banks of the Habur" (see note 17 under (a));

(10) Sg. 8: 143 *sīsêšunu hurri natbak šadê im-lu-ma* "their horses filled the ravines (and) torrents of the mountain";

(11) Maqlû I 23 *maštakal* (ú.in.nu.uš) *libbibanni ša erṣeta* (var. *-tim*) *ma-la-a-ta* "may the *maštakal* which covers the earth purify me" (see note 17 under (b));

(12) Asb. A IV 82 (dead bodies) *ša sūqī purrukū ma-lu-u rebâti* "that keep the streets blocked and fill the squares".

These sentences are transitive, but their subject is clearly not agentive: it represents the substance or the entities with which a container is filled or a locality covered. The non-agentive nature of these subjects is confirmed by the fact that they are often (though not exclusively) inanimate; in so far as they are animate, they are mostly animals. This applies to all examples quoted above, and most of the examples quoted in CAD sv 5.[16] But even if these subjects are human, the contexts clearly show that they are not agentive, since agents must be consciously and volitionally acting beings (cf. Givón's definition quoted in 5.4); they are acting involuntarily, as victims rather than actors. Cf., for instance:

(13) Asb. A I 112 "(I reinstalled the kings and governors who because of the attack of PN) *piqittašun umaššerūma im-lu-u ṣēra* "had abandoned their residences and filled the open country".

The D-stem, on the other hand, is only used if the subject is agentive, i.e., if it consciously and volitionally performs the act of filling or covering. Compare, for instance, (14) with (10), (15) with (07), and (16) with (09):

(14) AKA 339: II (= RIMA 2/I, 211): 115) *pagrīšunu hurru natbaku ša šadê ú-ma-li* "I (...) filled the ravines (and) torrents of the mountain with their corpses" (tr. Grayson) (many cases in CAD sv 8a-2');

(15) ABRT 1, 23: II 23 *damēšunu nāra um-tal-li* "I filled the river with their blood";

(16) AbB 13, 60: 11 *šumma ahi GN gulgullātim lā ú-ma-al-li* "I will certainly cover the bank of the Euphrates with skulls".

The instances of *malû* D quoted in CAD sv 6-9 all have an animate, agentive subject; especially section 7 contains numerous cases which can be contrasted with those of 5. Many instances of this construction have been misunderstood by editors, among which are several of those quoted above.[17]

This leads to the conclusion that in this verb it is not so much the presence of a direct object which motivates the use of the D-stem, but rather is the change from a non-agentive into an agentive subject.

Malû is unique in showing this differentiation between the use of D for transitivity (in the traditional sense) plus agentivity, versus G for transitivity without agentivity. Presumably, this characteristic is bound up with its specific valency frame, which does not only require a subject (in the G-stem), or a subject and a direct object (in the D-stem), but also an additional participant role for the substance or the objects with which something is filled or covered. This may explain why we do not find other clear instances of such a differentiation. A case in point may be the verb *ṣânu* (CAD *zânu*) "to fill, cover, sprinkle", which is normally transitive with an agentive subject, but which occurs a few times with the substance as subject; contrast (17A) with (17B) and (18A) with (18B):

(17A) IV R 26: 15a // SBH 6: 19 // 7: 4 *imat bašme ša amēlu i-ṣa-an-nu* "snake poison which has sprinkled a man";

(17B) CT 16, 49: 295 (ff.) the evil demon *imtu amēla iṣ-ṣa-an* "sprinkles the man with poison";

(18A) Ee IV 99 *ezzūtu šārū karšaša i-ṣa-nu-ma* "furious winds filled her belly".

(18B) BBS 7: II 25f DN (...) *aganutillâ* (...) *li-ṣa-an karassu* "May Marduk fill his belly with dropsy."

However, *ṣânu* differs from *malû* in that it is basically transitive; hence the G forms in the latter two sentences, where *malû* would have a D form.

Note that it is important to make a strict distinction between *malû* and the factitive G-stems which were mentioned in 7.2.5, and are discussed more extensively in 11.4.2. The factitive G-stems remain G-stems in spite of the presence of an agentive subject and a direct object; *malû* can be used in the G-stem with a direct object, but only if it has a non-agentive subject, and it must use the D-stem if its subject is agentive.

7.3.2. Agentivity in other factitive D-stems

The importance of agentivity of the subject is also demonstrated by a few verbs with a factitive D-stem which has an agentive subject, but differs from the prototype (cf. 7.1) in that the correspondence which normally exists between the subject of the intransitive and the object of the factitive sentence, is lacking. The verbs in question are the following:

Hamāṭu G "to burn" mostly has "fire" as subject (spelled *išātu* or ^{d}<u>Girra</u>), or it describes entities as burning or being as hot as fire: roads (BBS 6: I 18), water (CT 39, 14: 16), the arms of a demon (BIN 2, 22: I 38) and, metaphorically, a person in anger (RIMA 2/I, 148: 18), or an angry person's "liver" (*kabattu*, Sg. 8: 413). In this use it can take a direct object, e.g.:

(19) Maqlû II 219 + III 30 ^{d}Girra *ezzu zumurki li-ih-muṭ* "may the fierce Girra (or: fire) burn your body" (also SpTU 3, 74: 168);

(20) AbB 9, 228: 20 *ṣē[tum] a-a ih-mu-ṭa-ni* "may the heat not burn me" (cf. also ARM 26/1 p. 563 no. 261: 13).

The subject of G, then, appears to be non-agentive. The only exception to this are cases where the subject of *hamāṭu* is ^{d}Girra, as in (19). Since *hamāṭu* D in its literal use generally demands an agentive subject, but does not seem to be attested with ^{d}Girra as subject, it seems a plausible assumption that in these cases ^{d}Girra simply stands for *išātu* and is not necessarily deified, even though it is spelled as a divine name and is clearly deified in other circumstances (cf. 5.6.4), for instance with *kabābu*, see below. Another solution is to regard *hamāṭu* as a kind of "factitive D-stem" (cf. 11.4.2).

Hamāṭu D "to burn" (trans.), "to scorch" is not a factitive according to the criterion presented in 7.1, because it does not take "fire" as object, although "fire" is the most common subject of G. The difference with G is that D mostly has an agentive subject, at least outside literary texts: it refers to the heating of oil, the firing of pottery (MA, in CAD listed under *hamāṭu* A 3b "to send quickly"), and the baking of food, cf. CAD sv *h.* B 2c (for Š see 7.5.5.1). Quite atypical is the use of G for the heating of water in an OB recipe (YOS 11, 26: I 51; cf. also N in *ib.* 25: 17). In literary texts the distinction between G and D is somewhat blurred by the frequent metaphorical use of this verb; in medical texts G and D are used indiscriminately for "to cause a burning pain" (CAD sv *h.* B 2d), more or less synonymously with other verbs, cf. 6.6.1.2. Compare, however, (19) with (21), which certainly has an agentive subject:

(21) KAR 333: 6 (The demons) *ú-ha-ma-ṭu zumurka* "burn your body".

Kabābu "to burn" presents about the same situation as *hamāṭu.* It is intransitive in Erra I 33 *kīma* ^{d}Girra *ku/gu-bu-um-ma* "burn like fire" and BBS 6: I 17 *aqqullū i-kab-ba-bu kī išāti* "the *anqullu*'s burn like fire"; it is used metaphorically with a direct object and a non-agentive subject in MAOG 5/3, 42: r.14 *libba lā i-kab-ba-ab-ka* "let (your) heart not burn you" (also SAA 8, 469: 13). D is used for "to char wood", "to set fire to", etc. (CAD sv 2), also in NA *gabbubu* "roasted", cf. AHw sv, CAD sv **gubbubu.* Once, however, D occurs with ^{d}Girra as subject (AfO 18, 283: 61). An isolated instance of G in this meaning is found in Or. 24, 246: 18 (object broken).

Eṣēnu G "to smell" seems to denote an involuntary observation, as against D a conscious act: "to sniff". For D, cf. CT 16, 34: 216 (the demons) *kīma šikkê asurrâ uṣ-ṣa-nu šunu* "sniff the damp course like mongooses" (tr. CAD sv *šikkû*); also AJSL 36, 81: 50; CT 39, 14: 18; Tigl.III 74: 26; KB 6/1, 90: 58. I follow the meaning and interpretations of AHw sv D "beriechen, beschnüffeln" rather than those of CAD sv 2 "to smell bad, to make (something) smell bad".

Šanû "to do for a second time": D is not a pure factitive either, but G is intransitive (mostly used in hendiadys, cf. 7.4.1, and CAD sv *š.* v. A 1a, beside Dt and Št), and D transitive: "to remeasure, repeat, report" (*ib.* sv 2b/c/d). The same relationship between G and D is found in **šalāšu** "to do for a third time" (also mostly in hendiadys, beside D and perhaps Dt (OAk: AfO 20, 40: III 15), cf. CAD sv 1/2), versus D "to triple" (CAD *ib.* 3; for intrans. use of D see 7.4.3.), and in **rebû** "to do fourth" (in hendiadys: BiMes. 19 p. 23: 15), versus D "to multiply by four" (Kisurra 156: 26); cf. Von Soden, St. Reiner 411 note 15.

Sarāru "to be false, criminal", is opposed to D "to deceive, contest", which shows the association of D with an activity and G with a quality, which we also find in *damāqu* D (see 7.4.2) and possibly in several verbs discussed in 7.4.3.

The common feature of these verbs is that their G-stem is intransitive or fluctuates between transitive and intransitive, whereas the D-stem is transitive and agentive, but not factitive in the strict sense of the term. They remind us of the verbs already dealt with in 5.5.3, which show the same characteristic: *dabābu* "to talk, speak" (D "to pester, harass, entreat"), and *kašādu* "to reach, to lay hands on" (D "to drive away, pursue").

For the same reason they also resemble some verbs of Type IV, such as *lamādu* "to know" (D "to inform, teach"), *hasāsu* "to think about" (D "to remind sb of sth"), and *edû* (CAD: *idû*) "to know" (D "to inform sb, mark, identify, assign sth to sb"). Although the D-stems of these verbs can theoretically be analysed as factitives, they function in practice as valency-preserving verbs of the type of *dabābu, kašādu* and *hamāṭu*: they are usually construed with only one direct object, so that they have the same valency as the G-stem.[18] The difference from G is that they denote actions rather than processes, and have an agentive subject and often a personal object.

Slightly different is the case of the intransitive verbs *takālu* "to trust" and *na'ādu* "to pay attention, be concerned" (+ *ana*). Their D-stems are hardly ever used in the meaning "to cause sb to trust sb", and "to cause sb to pay attention to sth", with a personal object and a dative constituent (as *takālu* has in OBTR 150: 19), but normally mean "to inspire confidence to sb, make sb confident", and "to alert, inform sb", respectively, with only a personal object, cf. CAD sv *na'ādu* 5, AHw. ssvv D.

In all these verbs the contrast between G and D seems to be based on the agentive nature of the latter, rather than on a regular factitive relationship as defined in 7.1. They support the claim made in 7.3.1 that an agentive subject is more essential to factitivity than the presence of a direct object.

There are even some cases where a subject performing an (intransitive) activity, rather than being involved in a process, appears to be a sufficient reason for the D-stem to be used. These cases will be discussed extensively in 7.4.

7.3.3. Factitive and intensive

A factitive sentence usually consists of a transitive verb with an agentive subject, a patient object and a telic verb which denotes a change of state. Therefore, it is a prototypical representative of high transitivity, in marked contrast to the corresponding intransitive G-stem. In 5.6.3 it was argued that this sharp contrast in transitivity has caused the highly consistent, predictable and productive nature of the factitive function of D. In Chapter XI we will take a closer look at the process which has led to the situation that we find in the historical stages of Akkadian.

Accordingly, the use of the D-stem in factitive sentences is one aspect of its association with high transitivity, and it is this concept which provides the "missing link" between the two main functions of the D-stem, which are traditionally defined as intensive and causative (cf. 1.1). Both intensives and causatives (which include factitives, see 7.2) involve a high or prototypical degree of transitivity, the former as compared to the corresponding non-intensive transitive verb (cf. 5.6.4), the latter as compared to the corresponding intransitive verb (cf. 5.6.3).

This claim is supported by the fact that a close formal relationship between intensive and causative formations is not specific to the D-stem in Akkadian, but is also found in other languages. Rundgren (1963a: 104ff) points to the striking typological similarity between the D-stem and formations with the suffix *-*eje/o-* in Indo-European languages: both are intensive and iterative in some words, causative in others, and also denominative.[19] The same applies to *-*sk̑e/o-*, which is originally iterative or durative - it still has this function in Hittite and Greek - but can also be causative (in Greek and Tocharian), beside being inchoative in Latin, cf. Kuryłowicz 1964: 106f; Schmidt 1973: 119f; Krause-Thomas 1960: I 209f.

Many parallels are offered by Nedyalkov-Silnitsky 1973: 19f (from Armenian, Ainu, Abkhazian and Georgian, Shoshone and Miwok). Especially interesting are some African languages, where the same verb has intensive or causative meaning depending on the number of participants: in Zulu *enza* is "to work", and *enz-isa* means "to work persistently" if there is no direct object, but "to force to work" with a direct object. In Swahili *chanja* is "to chop" (firewood); *chanjisha* is "to chop energetically" if there is only one complement of the type "firewood', but "to force someone to chop something" if there is a second complement which designates the executor of the action (Nedyalkov-Silnitsky 1973: 20). According to Hopper and Thompson (1980: 264), the Indonesian suffix *-kan* and Chichewa (a Bantu language from Malawi) *-ets-* are both intensive and causative.

Examples of Semitic morphemes which can be both intensive and causative - apart from the D-stem - are the Arabic causative Stem IV *'aqtala* and the "elative" pattern *'aqtalu*, and the Arabic Stem III (*qātala*), which, beside many other functions, also has intensive and causative meaning (Fleisch 1979: 295f; Saad and Bolozky 1984: 37).

These parallels show that there is a relationship between the categories intensive (or whatever name we choose for the phenomenon in question) and causative (or factitive), cf. Haiman (1985: 26): "Recurrent similarity of form must reflect similarity in meaning".

This leads to the conclusion that the factitive function of the D-stem is the outcome of a process of grammaticalization of gemination of the second radical (cf. 2.2.4.2). This process has led to a replacement of the originally iconic function of gemination with a more grammatical, more abstract function, namely, that of underlining the high degree of transitivity of factitive verbs, and of expressing the distinction between intransitive basic verbs and their transitive derivations; in Chapter XI we will examine this process in greater detail.

7.3.4. Concluding remarks

Two final remarks have to be made concerning the factitive D-stem. In the first place, the terms factitive and agentive only refer - strictly speaking - to verb forms in active, transitive sentences. Thus only the prefix forms of the D- and the iterative Dt(n)-stem, plus the imperative, the infinitive and the participle, can be regarded as factitive, not the stative D or Dt(n), nor the passive/intransitive Dt-stem. Here we find the same situation as was described in 5.6.5 with regard to the D-stem of transitive verbs: their association with high transitivity is also restricted to the active forms of the paradigm, and the corresponding statives and Dt forms are only indirectly associated with it, in so far as they are transformations of active sentences.

Likewise, the use of the stative D/Dt(n) or a Dt form of a factitive D-stem is only indirectly related to factitivity. As to the stative, this is shown by the fact that it is often used in a different way from the other forms of the factitive paradigm: to a large extent, the stative D either has a different meaning from the rest of the paradigm, or serves as a stylistic or dialectal variant. Examples of this phenomenon will be given in Chapter X.

As to the Dt-stems, some of them are intransitive counterparts of factitive D-stems; they can be called "anti-factitives", on the model of anti-causatives (cf. Nedyalkov-Silnitsky 1973: 2 and 22ff); other Dt-stems, however, are directly derived from a stative or a *purrus* adjective without the intermediate stage of a factitive D form, cf. 9.1.4.

Accordingly, the Appendix to this chapter, which comprises the most important factitive D-stems, does not contain verbs whose D-stem is found only as a stative, VA and/or Dt-stem. If such verbs are discussed in this study, they can be traced by means of the Index of Akkadian Words.

Secondly, we should comment on two other terms which are often encountered as functions of the D-stem and its equivalents, viz. *declarative* and *estimative*. They are used in Semitic studies to describe the meaning of a few specific D-stems, which express the nuances of "declaring someone to be something" or "regarding someone as something", respectively (cf. section 1.1, and Nedyalkov-Silnitsky 1973: 17f). However, these notions do not represent functions of the D-stem in their own right, on a par with causative and/or factitive, but are realizations of causatives or factitives on the semantic level, dependent on the meaning of the verb and on the specific context in which it occurs (cf. also Goetze 1942: 3; Joüon-Muraoka 1991: 155). Therefore, they are not mentioned here as grammatical functions of the D-stem.

7.4. The intransitive use of factitive D-stems

A number of factitive D-stems can, under certain conditions, be used intransitively. In many of these cases the difference with the G-stem - which is also intransitive - lies in the fact that the latter denotes a process, whereas D denotes an activity and, accordingly, tends to have animate subjects. There are also cases, however, in which it is difficult to detect any motive for the use of D.

They will be discussed in three groups. The first group consists of factitive D-stems without object in hendiadys constructions with another verb (7.4.1). The second group concerns the intransitive use of *damāqu* D (7.4.2). The third group comprises other cases of factitive D-stems used without a direct object (7.4.3).

7.4.1. Factitive D-stems in hendiadys constructions

A number of Akkadian verbs can be used in coordination with a following (main) verb, in order to modify the meaning of the latter; the dictionaries refer to this use as "hendiadys". In translations into English they are usually rendered as adverbs or auxiliary verbs. A well-known instance from the formulaic language of contracts with the verb *târu* "to return" (intrans.) is *lā iturrūma lā iraggamū* "they (the litigating parties) will not complain a second time", lit. "they will not return (and) complain". This construction has been examined in detail by Kraus (1987). Most of the examples adduced here are based on Kraus's study.[20]

The relevance of this phenomenon for the present discussion of the factitive D-stem is based on the fact that there is a striking difference with regard to the use of the G- or the D-stem between fientive verbs and adjectival verbs, if they are used in hendiadys. In the former we find either the G-stem (as in *hamāṭu* "to hurry" (Kraus 1987: 18), *târu* (*ib.* 12 (but D in AbB 9, 40: 18)) and *sahāru* "to do again" (*ib.* 13), *ṣabātu* "to start" (*ib.* 15)) or the D-stem (as in *qatû* D "to do completely" (*ib.* 17) (*qatû* G in hendiadys is uncertain (*ib.* 17)), and in *arāhu* "to go/come quickly" (CAD sv *a.* B 2b); or else we find both G and D without an appreciable difference in meaning (e.g., in *gamāru* "to do, give, pay, etc., completely" (Kraus 1987: 16), *sadāru* "to do regularly, periodically" (*ib.* 10f), *šanû* "to do for the second time" (also Dt, cf. note 13 to Ch. IX, and Št (*ib.* 13)), *šalāšu* "to do for the third time" (*ib.* 13), etc. (for more detailed references see the dictionaries under the respective verbs). For the latter group of verbs it is therefore difficult to judge why G is used in one case and D in another.

In verbs derived from adjectives, on the other hand, we find almost exclusively the D-stem in hendiadys constructions (or the Š-stem for verbs with a factitive Š-stem). The most important of such verbs are the following:

Bunnû "to do sth in a kindly way", from *banû* "to be pleasant, kindly" (Kraus 1987: 26), in AbB 10, 11: 16; 12, 113: 19 (quoted below).

Dummuqu "to do sb a favour, to do sth kindly", from *damāqu* "to be(come) good" (Kraus 1987: 34f); e.g., AbB 2, 86: 35f *šumma bēlī atta tu-da-am-ma-qá-am-ma tušabbalam* "if you, my lord, would be so kind as to send me .....'"; also "to do sth correctly", e.g., SAA 10, 291: 9' *lā ú-dam-mi-iq lā assi* "I did not read correctly", and *ib.* 7'f *lā dam-mu-qu lā sasû šū* (inf.) "it is a matter of not reading correctly" (tr. CAD sv *damāqu* 2d-2').

Dunnunu "to do sth severely, energetically", from *danānu* "to be(come) strong, difficult" (Kraus 1987: 20ff); e.g., AbB 4, 19: 15ff *ana PN_1 u PN_2 ú-da-an-ni-nam-ma aštapram* "I have written to PN_1 and PN_2 in strong words". A remarkable case with the Dt-stem and the letter as subject is AbB 13, 64: 14f (out of two letters) *1 ṭuppu ana PN* (..) *ud-da-an-na-nam-ma illakam* "one letter, in strong words, will come to PN". In a Mari letter we find a few instances of the reverse idiom *ašpur udannin*, cf. Kraus 1987: 29.

Mullû "to do or pay sth completely", from *malû* "to be(come) full" (Kraus 1987: 17), cf. CAD sv 6b end; AHw sv *m.* IV D 12d.

Murruṣu "to do sth severely", from *marāṣu* "to be(come) ill, annoyed" (Kraus 1987: 20); 2x in OB letters (AbB 1, 72: r.2; 112: 14'); this D-stem is hardly attested elsewhere, cf. 7.5.6 sv: *marāṣu* normally uses a factitive Š-stem, also in hendiadys, cf. CAD sv 6a-1'; also ARM 26/1 p. 86f no. 6: 4. 27 (cf. note a); 26/2 p. 184 no. 374: 4; p. 324 no. 428: r.10; p. 342 no. 436: 32, beside the Št-stem (Kraus 1987: 23), cf. CAD sv 8.

Surruru "to act fraudulently", from *sarāru* "to be false, deceitful" (CAD sv 2a); e.g., KH r.XXII: 66 (§ 265) "(if a shepherd) *ú-sa-ar-ri-ir-ma šimtam uttakkir* "has fraudulently altered the mark (on the animals) (and sold them)"; also LE § 33 A III 6 // B II 16.

Šullumu "to do sth completely", from *šalāmu* "to be(come) sound, in a good condition" (Kraus 1987: 17); cf. also CAD sv 12a-2'. A remarkable case of *šalāmu* G in hendiadys (AbB 2, 98: 12) is quoted below.

Tukkulu "to do sth in a reliable way", from *takālu* "to trust, to be(come) reliable"; e.g., AbB 6, 220: 24 *arkatam ú-ta-ak-ki-il aprusma* "I have investigated the matter carefully' (lit. "in a reliable way"); also 218: 29 (cf. *ib.* 15 with *tukkulu* in second position: *warkatam purus tu-uk-ki-il-ma lâtim dannātim lissuhānim* "investigate the matter and make sure that they transfer the strong cattle here", probably not to be regarded as a hendiadys construction (cf. ARM 1, 39: r.10)).

Uddudu "to act quickly", from *edēdu* "to be(come) sharp" (Kraus 1987: 18); e.g., AbB 11, 121: 5 *ud-di-dam-ma sinqam* "arrive here quickly" (also 2, 100: 15; 6, 191: 22; ARM 2, 131: 20). For the meaning, cf. AKT 2, 37: 34 *awīlum e-du-ud* "the man is in a hurry", prob. a stative D of this verb.

Uddušu "to do again", from *edēšu* "to be(come) new" (Kraus 1987: 13); e.g., ARM 2, 51: 10f *nīš ilim ú-di-iš azkurma* "I have sworn a new oath by the god".

Urruku "to do sth at length, to take a long time doing sth", from *arāku* "to be(come) long" (Kraus 1987: 18); e.g., ARM 4, 70: 16 *ú-ra-ka-kum-ma adabbubakkum* "I will speak to you at length" (also in 13).

(W)utturu "to do extra or in addition", from *(w)atāru* "to be superfluous, to exceed" (Kraus 1987: 20); e.g., FM 1 p. 127: 15f (silver) *lu-wa-te-er-ma lulqe* "I want to receive extra". D is rare in this context as compared to Š, cf. CAD sv 2a-2' (D) versus 4c, which is in accordance with the overall prominence of Š over D in this verb, cf. 7.5.6.

Verbs which have a factitive Š-stem instead of a factitive D-stem occur in similar contexts with the Š-stem, such as *mâdu* "to be(come) much" (Kraus 1987: 19) in, for instance, AbB 3, 77: 7 (the slave about whom (...) *awâtim tu-uš-mi-dam-ma tašpuram* "you have written to me at length", and in *marāṣu* and *(w)atāru* mentioned above.

The D- and Š-stems occurring in hendiadys often do not have a direct object. If the main verb has a direct object, it can be argued that the latter also serves as object of the verb in hendiadys, so that it is transitive. This may be the case in, for instance, AbB 12, 113: 19 *ṭup-paka ana awīlim bu-un-ni-a-am-ma šūbilam* "send a carefully worded letter of yours to the gentleman" (tr. Van Soldt). In many other cases, however, there is no object (e.g., in AbB 4, 19: 15ff quoted under *dunnunu,* and in ARM 4, 70: 16 quoted under *urruku*), or the object comes after the verb in hendiadys (as in KH r.XXII 66 (§ 265) quoted under *surruru*), or it is semantically incompatible with the verb in hendiadys, as in AbB 6, 220: 24 quoted under *tuk-kulu* (there is no expression **(w)arkata tukkulu*), and in AbB 10, 205: 13f *kaspam šâti ur-ri-*

ik-ma ana PNF idinši "give that silver to PNF with some delay" (Kraus: "mit Verzögerung").

The reason that adjectival verbs only use the D-stem in hendiadys, whereas other verbs use both G and D depending on the way they use these stems in general, is undoubtedly that verbs in hendiadys do not only have to agree with the main verb in person, number, gender and tense, but also with regard to agentivity of the subject. In most fientive verbs both G and D express an action or an activity, so that there is no incompatibility with the main verb, whichever stem is used. In an adjectival verb, on the other hand, the G-stem only expresses a process, and the subject is strictly non-agentive. This makes it unsuitable to be combined with a verb which denotes an action or an activity. In order to obtain the required agreement in agentivity the D-stem must be used, even though the verb has no direct object. The correctness of this analysis is confirmed by an unusual instance of an adjectival verb in the G-stem in hendiadys, viz. *šalāmu* in AbB 2, 98: 12 *eleppum šī i-ša-al-li-ma-am-ma i̧-[t]u-ur-ra-am* "will that boat return safely?". This G-stem, rather than the expected D-stem, is undoubtedly caused by the inanimate, and therefore non-agentive, subject.

The occurrence of the factitive D-stem without a direct object in these contexts shows that an agentive subject is sufficient to motivate the use of a factitive D-stem, and conversely, that the use of D is necessary if the subject is agentive, whether a direct object is present or not.

7.4.2. The intransitive use of *damāqu* D

The use of a factitive D-stem without object with the function of denoting an action or an activity, as opposed to the use of the G-stem for the corresponding process, is also found in some verbs outside the strict environment of a hendiadys construction. The most common instance is the verb *damāqu* "to be(come) good". Apart from its factitive meaning "to make good, better", "to improve", it can also be used intransitively in the meaning "to do a good deed, to act well, to behave properly or bravely", etc., often with a dative: "to do sb a good turn, a favour", "to be kind to sb", etc. It always has a personal subject, cf. CAD sv 2c-1', 2d-1', AHw sv D 3a/b. A few typical examples are:

(22) ARM 27, 142: 28f (among the soldiers of my lord) *ṣābum mādumma ú-da-mí-iq* "Many soldiers performed well" (also in 26);

(23) AbB 11, 5: 9 *ana bīti abīka ú-da-mi-iq* "I did favors for your family" (tr. Stol);

(24) ARM 26/2 p. 199 no. 384: 23'f *ša ana bēlija ú-[d]a-mi-qú bēlīma ide* "My lord knows what service I have done to him".

If we compare these cases with the use of the prefix forms of the G-stem, there is a clear opposition between the action or activity performed by humans on the one hand, and processes, on the other. The prefix forms of *damāqu* G typically refer to processes, often with inanimate entities as subject (clothing, dreams, name, road, sesame, deeds, cf. CAD sv 1a/b); with personal subject, it means "to prosper, become rich, have good luck" (*ib.* 1a). As such it clearly contrasts with the intransitive use of D for an activity. For the notions expressed by the D-stem, as exemplified above, the G-stem was apparently felt to be unsuitable.

7.4.3. Other factitive D-stems without object

Apart from the cases discussed in the two previous sections, there are some other instances of factitive D-stems used intransitively. We will list them in alphabetical order and offer some more or less tentative suggestions for explaining them. Intransitive cases which can be explained as hendiadys constructions are not included here.[21]

Apālu "to be (too) late": D 1x intrans. "to occur late" (subject Adad, i.e., a thunderstorm) ACh. Ad. 18: 8; cf. Dt "to be done (too) late" (CT 22, 20: 13, subject: sowing); cf. also 9.1.4 sv *uppulu*.

Arāhu "to be quick, go/come quickly": D intrans. "to hurry", cf. CAD sv *a.* A 2a (for KAR 104: 24 see now BagF. 16, 252: 23f with note on p. 254).

Arāku "to be long" (see 7.4.1 sv *urruku*): intrans. D occurs in the apodosis *urrak imât* "he will linger on and die", with an ellipse of "illness"? The complete expression is found in TDP 222: 49 *sili'tašu ú-ra-ak-ma imât*, lit. "he will make his illness long (i.e., "he will have a long illness") and die".

Ebēbu D "to clear oneself" (of an accusation by means of an oath) in OB legal texts (CAD sv 2d; AHw sv D 5b); ellipse of *ramānu* or a similar word ?

Ebû "to be(come) thick", and its synonym **kabāru** have a participle *mumbium* and *mukabbirum* (var. *muktabbirum* with Dt, cf. note 11 to Ch. IX) in LL, which is translated by CAD M/2 ssvv as "boaster, braggart", apparently literally "person who makes himself thick, who inflates himself", AHw ssvv: "der dick aufträgt".

Epēsu "to object" (CAD), "zu schwierig sein" (AHw): D is trans. in AbB 8, 14: r.10'. r.17'; ARM 26/1 p. 134 no. 21: r.18' ("faire des ennuis" acc. to Durand, NABU 90/24); A.7537: 9'. 25' (unpubl., courtesy K.R. Veenhof; in this letter we also find the adj. *uppusu* in *awâtum up-pu-sà-tum* (ib. 7 (rest.) and 39) "oppressive, insulting words"?). Elsewhere it is intrans. "to protest, to raise objections", cf. CAD sv b; AHw sv D: KH § 75+e (UM 5, 93: II 37); KH XIII 65 (§ 47); TCL 18, 147: 18; uncertain: ARM 26/2 p. 362 no. 445: 16, cf. note d.

Labāru "to be(come) old", D "to grant a long life, to live long". G is usually said of periods of time (CAD sv 1a), buildings (*ib.* 1c) and various other non-personal subjects (*ib.* 1d); it is unusual with a personal subject (cf. CAD sv 1b: 1x, apart from PNs). The same applies to the adjective *labiru*, cf. CAD sv *labīru*; if it refers to persons, it means "belonging to the past" or "long-standing" rather than "aged" (CAD sv *labīru* 1a-2' and d). Exceptional instances of *labāru* G with a personal subject are UM 15, 80: II 20 (in AMT 43, 1: 24 quoted CAD sv 1d, the subject is broken off); it is more often found in NA and NB PNs., cf. *ib.* 1b.

Since it is beyond human beings to make somebody or something old, a factitive D-stem of this verb is only possible in a metaphorical sense: it is used with an object in the meaning "to grant a long life", especially in greeting formulae (CAD sv 4b); besides, it is used intransitively in the meaning "to attain a long life, to last long". In this sense it alternates with the Dt-stem *ultabbar* (cf. 9.1.1) and the Š-stem *ušalbar* (cf. 7.5.6 sv) in omen apodoses (CAD sv 3b).

Lemēnu "to be(come) bad, unhappy"; D is normally factitive, but cf. *mulamminat* "she is a woman who has difficulties in giving birth" (cf. CAD sv 5a-5'), opposed to *mušallimat* "she is a woman who brings her pregnancy to term" (cf. CAD sv *mušallimu* adj. 2). The unique expression *lummunu eli* "to become angry with" (?, cf. CAD sv 4) in Ee II 3 looks like a contamination of *lemēnu* with *libbu* as subject "to become angry" (CAD sv 1b) and *lummunu* with *libbu* as object "to make sb angry" (CAD sv 6), on the one hand, and an expression as *šabāsu eli* "to be(come) angry with", on the other.

Mašālu "to be(come) equal, similar" (+ *ana* or *-iš*), D "to make equal, copy", but also "to be equal to, match", with personal subject and an accusative instead of the dative of the G-stem, cf. CAD sv 5 (but Tigl.III 72: 14 has D with *ana*). Thus in this meaning D is more transitive than G, but not factitive, and apparently motivated by its personal subject and its direct object, versus the indirect object of G.

Nakāru "to be(come) hostile, strange; to change" has an intransitive use of D "to move" (CAD sv 7d; AHw sv *n*. I D 9b), alternating with *šubtam nukkuru* (*ib*. 11c and D 9a); this suggests that it is an ellipse.

Namāšu "to depart", D "to make depart, dispatch", but also intrans. "to depart" (common in NA, cf. CAD sv 4).

Nâšu "to shake" (intrans.), "to recede", D "to shake, move" (trans.); D intrans. is found ARM 26/2 p. 166 no. 364: r.5' (with personal subject: cf. *ramû* ?).

Naw/māru "to be(come) brillant, shine"; D is used intrans. in protases of astronomical omens "to clear up" (with an eclipse as subject), beside G and Dt, cf. AHw sv D 1c "hell werden". However, CAD sv *namāru* 3c takes the eclipse as object and understands Sin to be subject. Although in BRM 4, 6: 28 Sin is explicitly mentioned as subject of *naw/māru* D, this interpretation seems unlikely if Sin is not mentioned; cf. also *zakû* below. This intrans. use of D is doubtless comparable to the cases mentioned in note 8 to Ch. V.

Qerēbu "to come to/near", D "to bring to/near, to offer", sometimes intrans. "to come near", cf. CAD sv 13; AHw sv D 2 (also ARM 26/1 p. 276 no. 109: 12; 26/2 p. 298 no. 416: 12. 14).

Ramû "to be(come) loose, relax" (intrans.); its D-stem normally means "to relax" (trans.), "to loosen, untie", but is occasionally found without object in the meaning "to depart", always said of humans, according to AHw sv *r*. III D 4 (OB Mari). These cases of D contrast with intransitive G in denoting an activity of persons, whereas G denotes a process and usually has an inanimate subject (body parts, bandage, foundations, cf. AHw sv *r*. III G/Gtn).[22]

Sahāru "to turn" (intrans.), D "to turn" (trans.), but Tn-Ep. IVb 44 *ú-se-hi-ir-ma* RN "King Kaštiliaš turned (and fled)".

Ṣalāmu "to be(come) black"; D intrans. in ARM 10, 156: 27 *ú-ṣa-al-li-im-ši-im* "I (?) have become angry with her": ellipse of *pānīja* ?, cf. CAD sv 1d-2' and 2b; AHw sv G 1e and D 4a.

Šalāmu "to be(come) sound, in a good condition": D is occasionally used intransitively in *šullumu ina* "to finish doing sth" (ARM 1, 82: 10. 18; OBTR 163: 12), cf. CAD sv 11a-1', doubtless modelled on similar expressions as *gamāru ina* and *kamāsu ina*. For *mušallimat* see under *lemēnu*.

Šalāšu "to do for a third time": D "to do or say for a third time", both in hendiadys (CAD sv 2a/c, cf. 1a/b for G in the same context, cf. 7.4.1) and independently (*ib*. lex. sect. and 2a).

Šapālu "to be(come) low": D (*ušappil(am)ma, uštappil(am)ma* (or pret. Dt?)), is used intrans. in the protases of omens, followed by a stative, presumably "to be situated low(er than is usual)", cf. CAD sv *šapālu* 3d, AHw sv D 3b, 4b/c. It is clearly a hendiadys construction, although not a canonical one, since there is no complete agreement. In astronomical omens we also find an intrans. Dtn (*uštanappal*) "to stay constantly low" (cf. 9.2.2 end), opposed to *ištanaqqu/â*, a Gtn form, cf. CAD sv 7; this suggests that there was felt to be little difference between Gtn and Dtn in this context.

Šaqû "to be high": D is used intransitively as "to go up(stream)": ARM 14, 42: 34f *šumma bēlī adi GN lā ú-ša-qa-am* "if my lord does not go upstream until GN" (elsewhere G, cf. CAD sv *š.* A v. 1b). Also in SpTU 2, 40: r.14, said of a star and apparently referring to a movement, alternating with a stative G in r.13, referring to a fixed position. *Ušaqqīma* is also found in protases followed by a stative in the meaning "to lie high(er than usual)", cf. CAD sv *š.* A v. 2b-2'), as opposite of *uš(t)appil(am)ma.*

Ṭehû "to come to/near", D "to bring to/near", exceptionally intrans.: ARM 26/2 p. 285 no. 411: 31 (scribal error? (but cf. *qerēbu* D)).

(W)arāqu "to be(come) green, pale"; D is intrans. acc. to CAD sv *arāqu* 3 in Asb. B V 69 (parallel to VAB 7, 192: 7) (interpreted as trans. in AHw sv D 1, which seems rather contrived, however: is *urraq* a present G modelled on *ubbal, uṣṣab,* etc.?), and in RA 50, 14: 33, where *iltānu* is doubtless object, not subject, as CAD contends.

(W)atāru "to exceed, be superfluous"; D is used intransitively in omen apodoses, e.g., CT 40, 17: 52 *amēlu ú-wa-at-tar* "the man will become important" (tr. CAD sv *atāru* 2b, also SpTU 1, 69: 15). This can be contrasted with similar apodoses with *(w)atāru* D and a direct object, e.g., *mašrû* "riches" in CT 38, 41: 19, or *mimma* "everything" in 38, 39: 17 and HUCA 40, 91: 19 (OB). Cf. also HGŠ 111: 8 *ina qibītika ut-ta-ra apâti* "mankind prospers upon your command".

Zakû "to be free, clean", D is used without object in astronomical texts with *antalû* "eclipse" as subject: St. Reiner 337: 3; 340: 23, interchanging - without observable difference - with the more frequent G form *iz-ku* (*ib.* passim, also ACh. Sin 33: 10). Compare also SAA 10, 75: 15; 149: 7' (D) with BRM 4, 6: 28 and 41 (G); cf. also *naw/māru* above.

Among these intransitive cases of factitive D-stems we can roughly distinguish four kinds:
(1) G-stems derived from adjectives: they refer to processes, whereas the very rare intransitive use of their D-stems refers to activities: *apālu, arāku, ebēbu* (which might also belong to 3.), *ebû* and *kabāru, epēsu* (?), *lemēnu* and *šaqû* (with personal subject); this also applies to *ramû* D as compared to G. These cases can be compared with *damāqu* D examined in 7.4.2.
(2) Verbs of movement: *arāhu, namāšu, nâšu, qerēbu, ṭehû*; in these verbs both G and D refer to an activity, and it is difficult to establish any clear motive for the use of D.
(3) Verbs whose D-stem is used in highly specialized contexts: *arāku* (medical), *naw/māru, šapālu, šaqû* and *zakû* (astronomical), *ebēbu* (legal; may also belong to 1.).
(4) The remaining verbs, of which only *labāru* occurs more than incidentally.

It is only for the first kind that an explanation for the use of D in these intransitive sentences seems to be at hand. A few others may be explained as ellipses (cf. note 7 to Ch. V). The rare occurrence of almost all these instances makes it clear that they are secondary developments which go back to ordinary factitive verbs. They are interesting in that they show that the boundary between the intransitive G and the factitive D is not quite clear-cut, and that it is possible to deviate from the rule to express certain semantic nuances of the verbs in question.

The intransitive use of the factitive D-stem described here is parallel to a similar use of the Š-stem in factitive Š-stems, such as *anāhu* Š "to have a hard time" (cf. CAD sv *a.* A 5), *pašāqu* Š "to have difficulties" (cf. AHw sv Š 3), and *rabābu* Š "to rest, relax" (cf. AHw sv Š 3). In *labāru* "to be(come) old" both D and Š can be intransitive, cf. also 7.5.6 sv.

7.5. The relationship between the D- and the Š-stem

We will conclude the discussion of the factitive D-stem with a comparison between the use of D and Š in their factitive and causative functions, concentrating on their relationship in those verbs in which both stems serve to express an increase in valency. The forms considered in the following sections do not include the "lexical" Št-stem (cf. GAG § 94c); this stem is basically independent of the Š-stem: it is often derived from verbs which do not have a Š-stem, or has a different meaning which cannot be derived from that of the Š-stem. I have included, however, the (very rare) instances of Št-stems which serve as passive/intransitive forms of factitive Š-stems (cf. GAG § 94b).

7.5.1. Formal aspects of the relationship between D and Š

There is a close formal and functional similarity between the D- and the Š-stem in Akkadian. If we start from a base *parrVs* for the D-stem and *šaprVs* for the Š-stem, they have completely parallel paradigms (cf. GAG Verbalparadigmen 13). This parallelism is confirmed by the development which has taken place in Babylonian: in both the D- and the Š-stem the prefixless forms of the paradigm have replaced the vowel *a* by *u*: in the stative Babylonian *purrus* and *šuprus* for Assyrian *parrus* and *šaprus*; and similarly in the verbal adjective, the infinitive and the imperative (cf. GAG *l.c.* and note 1 to Ch. X).

Syntactically, the factitive D-stem is equivalent to the Š-stem, since both stems serve to increase the valency of a verb by means of the addition of an external agent. The D-stem, however, is restricted to a specific kind of verb, namely, verbs with an alternating valency. As stated in 7.2, it is exclusively factitive, whereas the Š-stem can be both factitive and causative. Therefore, there are situations in which only the Š-stem is available for causativization, and situations in which both D and Š are available. There seem to be no circumstances in which only D is possible, apart from the cases discussed in 7.2.4, the hollow roots starting with a sibilant, where a formal factor is involved.

Otherwise, formal factors seem to play only a minor role in the question of whether a specific verb will choose a D- or a Š-stem for causativization. In some cases a tendency to avoid homonymy may be surmised (cf. GAG § 89d Anm.). A likely example is the fact that *ešēru* "to be(come) right, straight, to go straight toward, to prosper", which we would expect to have a D-stem because it is derived from an adjectival root, actually has a Š-stem *šūšuru*, thus avoiding homonymy with the very frequent D-stem *(w)uššuru* "to release, to let go".

A remarkable and somewhat puzzling case is *abālu* "to be(come) dry"; it mostly uses the

Š-stem in the stative, and the D-stem in the other forms of its paradigm, cf. AHw sv D and Š; CAD sv *a.* B 2 (D) versus 3 (Š), and sv *šābulu.*[23] It is likely that the prefix forms of the Š-stem of this verb are avoided because they can be homonymous with those of the very frequent Š-stem of *(w)abālu* "to bring" (pret. *ušābil* beside *ušēbil*). As for the stative and VA, the change *parrus* > *purrus* which took place in Babylonian would have resulted in a form **šūbul(u)*, coinciding with the stative Š of *(w)abālu* (*šūbul* < **šawbul*). This is doubtless the reason that in *abālu* this change was blocked, and that the original form *šābul(u)* was preserved (unlike, for instance, the stative *šūluk* from *alāku* "to go").

However, the present forms of *abālu* D coincide with the present G of *(w)abālu*: *ubbal* is both "he makes dry" and "he brings". Apparently, this was felt to be less detrimental to communication than the homonymy of both Š-stems. A similar differentiation between Š for the stative and VA, versus D for the rest of the paradigm can be observed for *(w)asāmu* "to be(come) suitable, proper", cf. 7.5.5.1 sv, but in this case there seems to be no obvious reason.

7.5.2. Functional aspects of the relationship between D and Š

Apart from the cases mentioned in 7.5.1, the relationship between D and Š is determined by functional considerations. It is very common for an Akkadian verb to have both a D- and a Š-stem, but often only one of them serves as a causative or factitive. This applies first and foremost to transitive verbs: they use only the Š-stem for causativization, whereas their D-stem preserves the valency of the G-stem, except in the verbs of Type IV (cf. 5.5.2). It was argued above in 7.1.4 that the addition of a third participant to a transitive verb makes the semantic roles of a sentence so complex that an explicit morpheme is necessary to indicate that the sentence should be interpreted as a causative. Since the D-stem of transitive verbs is basically valency-preserving (see 5.2 and Chapter VI), it cannot have the additional function of denoting the causative of these verbs. The Š-stem, which is doubtless in origin the causative of *intransitive* fientive verbs, did not have this disadvantage. It acquired the function of causativizing transitive verbs via its use in transitive verbs of low transitivity and/or verbs which are used both transitively and intransitively, cf. 7.1.3.

Accordingly, we never find the D-stem as causative of transitive verbs in Akkadian,[24] and there is usually a clear difference in use between D and Š of a transitive verb: *ṣabātu* "to seize" and *ṣubbutu* "to seize (many)", versus *šuṣbutu* "to cause to seize", and *petû* "to open" and *puttû* "to open (many)", versus *šuptû* "to cause to open", etc.

Similarly, some intransitive verbs only use the Š-stem as causative or factitive, but also have D forms, which are not factitive. This applies in the first place to the D-stems of Type II, which are intransitive, cf. 7.6 below. But some other verbs, too, have a causative or factitive Š-stem, and in addition a D-stem, which is not used as a factitive, but mostly occurs as a stative, a VA, and/or in the Dt-stem. For instance, *kamāsu* "to kneel, squat" has a Š-stem "to make sb kneel", but also uses the stative D in the meaning "to be in a kneeling or squatting position" (CAD sv *k.* B 3; also RitDiv. 36: 139); this meaning has been lexicalized in NA as "to stay, be stationed" (AHw sv *k.* II D 3 "hält sich auf").[25] In SB a "fientivizing" Dt (see 9.1.4) has been derived from this stative, which we translate as ingressive, e.g., in Gilg. XI 136 *uk-tam-mi-is-ma attašab abakki* "I sat down, crouching, and cried" (tr. CAD sv *k.* B 4).

Another example is *maqātu* "to fall": it has a causative Š-stem beside a stative/VA *muqqutu* "ailing, sick" (cf. 10.7.1.2 sv), but no verbal D-stem (cf. note 6 to Ch. I). This is a rather common situation, which shows the independent position of many *purrus* forms vis-à-vis the verbal D-stem. This issue will be taken up in Chapter X.

However, a considerable number of intransitive verbs have both a factitive D- and a factitive (or causative) Š-stem. In this situation there is no consistent grammatical difference between the two stems. On the one hand, they show a large overlap in meaning, which is apparent from the numerous instances of D and Š forms interchanging in identical or similar contexts (cf., among the examples mentioned below in the presentation of individual verbs, especially *kanāšu* (7.5.3), *pašāhu* (7.5.6), *nesû* (7.5.6), *malû* (7.5.5.1), and *šaqû* (7.5.5.1). In some cases, however, we find a clear stylistic differentiation, in that the factitive Š is restricted to a rather specific type of literary text, whereas D has no such restriction.

On the other hand, the two stems have been differentiated in use in several ways: in a few cases on the basis of dialect, but more often on a semantic basis. This differentiation is, however, rarely consistent, and largely dependent on the meaning of the verb in question: many factitive D- and Š-stems are clear instances of lexicalization.

In the next sections we will discuss the following types of functional differentiation: first, there are some cases in which the differentiation correlates with the causative meaning of Š versus the factitive meaning of D (7.5.3). In some other cases the use of D or Š correlates with a difference in meaning (7.5.4). The most important tendency, however, is to restrict one factitive - typically the Š-stem - to literary texts (7.5.5). Finally, there is a group of verbs in which no consistent difference is observable between their D- and their Š-stem (7.5.6). Section 7.5.7 discusses the general relationship between D and Š with regard to their factitive and/or causative function.

7.5.3. Causative Š versus factitive D of the same verb

In some verbs which have both a Š- and a D-stem the semantic differentiation correlates with the overall causative meaning of Š versus the factitive meaning of D, in the sense that the use of Š displays some of the typical features of a causative as opposed to a factitive, such as an animate causee who has some control over the action to be performed, and a less strict "contact" causation than is typical of a factitive. This is especially clear in verbs which represent borderline cases between fixed and alternating valency, or between transitive and intransitive, such as *elû*, *nakāru* and *sahāru*:

Elû, used in the stative, means "to be high" (rare, cf. CAD sv *elû* A adj., AHw sv *elû* IV G A (the corresponding adjective is more common). Used in other forms of its pardigm, it means "to go up, rise", in a wide range of nuances. It consistently uses the Š-stem for "to cause to go up" (CAD sv 8-12), and the D-stem for "to make high" (CAD sv 5), especially in the expression *rēšī- ullû* "to make high" the head, i.e., the summit of a building (compare RIME 4, 342: 46f with 385: 11f), and figuratively "to make (a person) high", i.e., "to praise, extol".[26]

Nakāru "to be(come) hostile, to rebel, to change, to deny" uses D for a wide range of meanings: "to change (trans.), to remove, expel, transfer", with both animate and inanimate objects, cf. CAD sv 7-11. Š usually means "to incite to rebellion, to instigate", with a personal object (often *māta* "(enemy) land"), *ib.* 14. As a rule, Š serves as causative of "to turn hostile, to rebel" (CAD sv 1a/b), whereas D serves more as factitive of "to change" (*ib.* sv 2).[27]

The differentiation between the D- and Š-stems of these verbs agrees with the distinction made in 7.1.6, between a causative and a factitive. The fientive meanings of *elû* and *nakāru* represent actions which are typically performed by animate beings, viz., "to go up" and "to rebel". Accordingly, they are causativized by Š; they often have a personal causee and allow for the possibility of distant causation. The meanings of G, on the other hand, which refer to processes are made factitive by means of D. This differentiation also agrees with the general association of D with adjectives and Š with fientive verbs.

A similar situation, but rather more complex, is found in *sahāru* "to turn":

Sahāru G has three basic meanings, each with its own construction (cf. CAD sv 1-6): 1. intrans.: "to turn (back/around), return", "to tarry, delay" (OA), with *ana* "to turn to sb" (for help or allegiance), with inanimate subject "to curve, curl"; 2. trans.: "to look for, seek" (things wanted or lost), "to appeal to, beseech" (authorities and gods), "to go around" (a place), "to encircle" (by magic); 3. in the stative: "to surround, be surrounded".

In general, there is a clear correspondence between a specific meaning of G and the use of D or Š. Leaving out some exceptional and atypical instances, we can describe the latter as follows. The use of Š applies to the meanings "to tarry, delay" (OA, *ib.* 14), "to be surrounded" (*ib.* 13a, also Št (*ib.* 15)), "to look for, seek" (*ib.* 12c, rare) and "to encircle" (by magic) (*ib.* 13b). Thus it seems to serve as a causative rather than a factitive (apart from its association with the lexicalized stative): it is associated with the transitive meanings of G, and with "to tarry, delay", which, as a purely human activity, typically seems to involve a fixed valency (cf. 7.1.5).

The most prominent use of D is with body parts, especially *pānī- suhhuru* "to turn one's face (*ib.* 11; 1x *pānī-* + Š: CT 13, 48: 10, doubtless to be explained acc. to 7.5.5, but also 1x *pānī-* + G: Or. 56, 246: 20, versus 247: 30 with D, cf. note 10 to Ch. X). Other typical meanings of D are "to take or lead sb around a place" ((*ib.* 10, vs. G "to go around" a place), and "to do again" in hendiadys ((*ib.* 9b, NA only), vs. G with the same meaning (cf. 7.4.1 above). Thus the use of D correlates with those uses of G which are intransitive or involve a low degree of transitivity (in the case of a locative object, cf. 5.5.1). Thus D mainly seems to function as a factitive.

There is one area in which D and Š interchange, namely, the basic meaning of *sahāru*: "to turn, turn around, turn back, return": cf. CAD sv 8/9a (D) versus 12a/b, 13c (Š). D is the most common form in this meaning, and most Š form are from literary texts (cf. *ib.* 12a), which points to a stylistic differentiation of the type to be discussed in 7.5.5.

A few other verbs are noteworthy because they correlate the use of D or Š with the nature of the object and the concomitant degree of agentivity of the subject, in such a way that Š indicates a higher degree of transitivity than D (and D higher than G):

Qadādu "to bow, incline" is basically intrans., cf. CAD sv 1; e.g., RA 33, 106: 32 *šēpīja issu ishulma adi aq-du-du* "his thorn (lit. "wood", *iṣu*) pierced my feet until I (had to) bow down". It can also be transitive, with a body part as object: *appa qadādu* "to prostrate oneself" and *kišāda qadādu* "to bow the neck" (*ib.* sv 2). These expressions do not involve a high degree of transitivity, since their object is not an independent, strongly affected entity. As such, they contrast with the use of D with a personal object, cf. CAD sv 3a and lex. sect. (also CRRAI 35, 12: r.4'; MSL 17, 20: 288; Emar VI/4 p. 343 no. 735: 13), e.g., VAB 2, 357: 78 *ú-qé-ed-di-da-áš-ši-im-ma ištu kussî* "he pulled her down from the throne".[28] The Š-stem is used if the expression *appa qadādu* is causativized: TuL 71b: 3 and DA 42: 15 *appašu tu-šaq-da(-as)-su* "you make him (the patient) bow down". The other instances of *qadādu* D are not factitive (statives, alternating with statives G, presumably for stylistic reasons, cf. 10.8 with (53)).

Kanāšu "to bend (the knee), to kneel" is semantically related to *qadādu*, but behaves differently. Its G-stem is always intransitive (CAD sv 1/2). With a body part as object, typically *kišāda* "the neck", D or Š is used, but the difference is that D refers to the bending of one's own neck, e.g., VAB 4, 62: 61f *ana DN bēlija kišāda lu ú-ka-an-ni-šu/iš* "I bent (my) neck to my lord Marduk", and Š to the bending of someone else's neck, lit. "to cause sb to bend his neck": BA 5, 385: 13 *kišāda elâ tu-šá-ak-na-aš raggiš* "you mercilessly bend the stiff neck(s of your enemies)" (restored acc. to CAD sv *kanāšu* 7b and sv *elû* A adj. c end), and KAV 171: 13. Thus we find here the same correlation between the use of D versus Š and the degree of transitivity, which in its turn depends on the presence of an external, strongly affected object. It is, however, also possible that these two Š forms are "literary Š-stems", cf. 7.5.5.

Nê'u/ne'û "to turn" (mostly *nê'u* in pret., *ne'û* elsewhere, but many spellings are ambiguous because of the polysemy of the *aleph* sign): unambiguous D forms only occur with object *irta* "to turn (sb else's) breast", i.e., "to make sb flee" (RIMA 2/I, 14: 68; Sg. Wi. 170: 9 [AGH 14: 12 = KAR 25: II 12 is more likely to come from *nâhu* D "to calm down, appease"]. G + *irta* also occurs and can have the same meaning, but can also mean "to turn one's (own) breast", i.e., "to flee", depending on the context, cf. CAD sv 1b. In other contexts G is intrans. (CAD sv 3); unambiguous trans. G forms are found with *idu* "arm" as object (Lugal 41 and 137); all other instances listed as transitive G forms in CAD sv 2 are precatives, in which D and G are indistinguishable in writing, or uncertain for various reasons; it is quite possible that these precatives are D-stems as well. A Š-stem is not attested.

These three verbs, together with *sahāru,* are semantically related, and show basic similarities in the way in which they correlate their G-, D- and Š-stems with increasing degrees of transitivity, but each verb has its own way of dividing the continuous scale of transitivity among the three verbal stems: in their basic meaning of "to turn, bend, bow" they use G without object (e.g., "to bow"), G or D with a body part of the subject as direct object ("to bow the head"), D or Š with a body part of somebody else than the subject as direct object ("to bow sb else's head" or "to make sb bow his head"), and only Š if there is a real causative situation ("to make sb bow his head").

7.5.4. Dialectal and semantic differentiation between D and Š

Dialectal and semantic differentiation play only a minor role in the verbs with two factitives. Clear instances of dialectal differentiation between D and Š are hard to come by. A few possible cases will be mentioned in 7.5.6 among the verbs in which no consistent difference between the use of D and Š is observable. On the other hand, there are a number of verbs with two factitive stems which have been differentiated in meaning in verb-specific, unpredictable ways. Often one of the stems is rare or uncertain. Their common characteristic is a high degree of lexicalization. This concerns the following verbs :

Barû "to look at" has a lexicalized D-stem *burrû* "to announce, usher in", cf. AHw sv *barû* I D/Dt (listed by CAD sv *burrû* v. as a D tantum verb). Š is used as the regular causative "to let see, to show", cf. AHw sv *barû* I Š, CAD sv *barû* A 5. See 5.5.2 for the inclusion of this verb among the factitive Type IV verbs.

Edû "to know" (cf. 5.5.2): D is the most common form and has a wide range of meanings: with a personal object it usually means "to inform, to recognize, to identify"; with an inanimate object "to mark" (tablets, silver, etc.), "to make known" (names, attributes, etc.), "to assign" (+ dative), cf. CAD sv *idû* 4/5. Š is less common and mostly means "to notify, announce, proclaim" (+ acc. or dat.), rarely "to mark" (*ib.* sv 6). Moreover, Š occurs in the expression *abullātim* or *abullam šūdû* "to confine sb within the city gate(s)", paralleled by *bābam wuddûm* in OB Mari (Syr. 50, 279: r.7'; ARM 26/2 p. 84 no. 319: 10f). Thus the differentiation between D and Š seems to be of a purely lexical nature, and is only partial.

Emēdu "to lean against (intrans.), to reach" (cf. 11.4.2 sv) basically has a factitive D "to lean (trans.) against", place, impose", cf. CAD sv 4; Š is sporadically used in several lexicalized meanings: "to support" in PNs, cf. CAD sv 5c (compare the use of G "to look for support" in PNs listed sv 1d-2'); "to accuse" (NB), cf. *ib.* 5b (but AHw sv Š 3 "to impose an *imittu* tax"). A Š form which appears to have the same meaning as D is St. Reiner 192: 32b *kaqqaršu tu-šu-mi-da šēpīja* "you have set my feet on the earth" (tr. Lambert): a literary Š-stem? (cf. 7.5.5). The OAK instances quoted by CAD sv 5a and AHw sv Š 1 are very doubtful.

Erēbu "to enter" normally has a Š-stem, but occurs with a D-stem a few times in the meaning "to enter on a tablet, to registrate", cf. CAD sv 3a, AHw sv D 1, also AbB 6, 144: 14. This reminds one of the use of D in technical contexts, which is also found in a number of D-stems of transitive verbs, discussed in 6.8.3. [Instances from El Amarna are ignored here; ABL 427: r. 3 *ur-ru-bu* may be explained as a stative D with plural subject (cf. 10.6.1), but is more likely to be an error for *irrubū* (3rd p. pl. pres.)].

Halāqu "to disappear, escape"; D "to make disappear, to remove, to ruin, to put an end to, to cause the loss of, to let (a slave) escape", cf. CAD sv 3a/e; Š is restricted to NA/NB with the meaning: "to help to escape" (with a passive Št: ABL 472: r.10).

Maṭû "to be missing" has a D-stem "to diminish" (CAD sv 3/4), of quantities and abstract concepts, versus Š "to treat badly", of persons (*ib.* 7). The differentiation is, however, not quite consistent, since Š is also used in the meaning of D (*ib.* 6): KAR 80: r.33 *diglīja ú-šam-ṭu-u* "they (the demons) diminished my eyesight", probably a literary Š-stem, cf. 7.5.5, and TBP 25: 1 (wealth). The OA instances belong to a separate verb *šamd/tûm* "ermahnen", cf. Landsberger, JNES 8, 27 note § and Hirsch, WZKM 62, 58 note 29.

Palāsu "to watch" (mostly N) uses the Š-stem as causative; D, on the other hand, has the lexicalized meaning of "to apply oneself to" or, negatively, "to keep sb busy, to cause trouble", cf. ARM 26/1 p. 170 note b for discussion. It is also possible, however, that this D-stem comes from a different root.

Rêqu "to go away, depart, recede": AHw distinguishes D "fernhalten" from Š "entfernen" and "sich entfernen lassen".

Redû "to follow, accompany, lead" (cf. 5.5.2): D is lexicalized in the meaning "to add"; Š serves as the regular causative: "to cause to follow/to flow", cf. AHw sv D/Š. See 5.5.2 for the inclusion of this verb among the factitive Type IV verbs.

Šarû "to be(come) rich" normally has a Š-stem (but 1x D: ACh. Ad. 8: 5); in MA D is used with the specialized meaning "to provide plenty (of fodder to horses)" (CAD sv 2); cf. also AHw sv *š*. II D 2 "reichlich geben".

(W)aqāru "to be(come) rare, precious" usually differentiates the Š-stem "to make rare, value, hold in esteem", cf. CAD sv *aqāru* 3, from the D-stem "to finish, use up" (materials, water, etc.), 1x "to ignore", *ib.* sv 2); cf. also Von Soden, Or. 27, 260f.

7.5.5. Stylistic differentiation between D and Š

The next category consists of verbs with two factitive stems, which show no difference in meaning, but have a stylistic difference. This is apparent from the fact that one of them, typically the Š-stem, is found exclusively in literary texts, whereas the corresponding D-stem has no such restriction. In these verbs D and Š alternate in exactly the same contexts, with the same kind of objects. They are often found interchanging in more or less identical sentences or in duplicate versions of the same text (examples will be given in the presentation of the individual verbs below).

In 6.9.2.2 it was pointed out that several verbal stems of Akkadian are used more extensively in literary texts than elsewhere. The use of factitive Š-stems in such texts, instead of the corresponding D-stems, is one of the most striking examples of this phenomenon. This use is largely restricted to a rather small part of the total range of SB texts: in the first place, royal inscriptions (RIs);[29] especially those of the later periods have a striking preference for the literary Š-stem. Secondly, hymns, prayers and laudatory parts of other texts (e.g., of incantations, royal grants and decrees, and the prologue and epilogue of the Codex of Hammurabi). Thirdly, most other religious texts such as those collected by Lambert in BWL; and, finally, the epics of Enuma Eliš and Erra (and occasionally also other epic and mythological texts).[30]

Furthermore, we find occasional instances of literary Š-stems in scholarly literature (omens, medical and astronomical texts). To qualify as a literary Š-stem, a form should not occur in texts which are definitely non-literary, such as letters and legal documents.[31]

The language of these texts is more or less consciously embellished by stylistic devices, such as a special vocabulary, changes in word order and some special morphological forms (cf. GAG § 186e/f; Von Soden 1932/33, esp. 1933: 160ff.

The most convincing evidence for the use of the Š-stem as a stylistic variant of the factitive D-stem is provided by a number of common factitive Š-stems which are attested only in the type of texts enumerated above, with a frequency that rules out chance. They are listed as group I in 7.5.5.1. They are followed by cases with less evidential value: Š-stems which are also restricted to literary texts, but are extremely rare in 7.5.5.2 (group II); Š-stems which are almost restricted to literary texts in 7.5.5.3 (group III). Finally, in 7.5.5.4 a few cases are listed which normally have a factitive Š-stem, but use the D-stem a few times in literary texts (group IV).

7.5.5.1. GROUP I: Factitive Š-stems which only occur in literary texts.

Arāku "to be(come) long": D is found in all kinds of texts, with spatial and temporal concepts as object (also in hendiadys, cf. 7.4.1 and intrans., cf. 7.4.3). Š, on the other hand, is restricted to the following texts: RIs (VAB 4, 190: I 8; 224: 35; 280: VII 25; VIII 10' (*mu-ša-rik*! acc. to AHw sv Š); CT 34, 27: 39; 30: 26, all of NB kings; BagM. 21, 358: 14; 360: 12f (coupled with *rapāšu* D!), of the provincial governor of Suhu); a poetic text about Naram-Sin (BiOr 30, 361: 28); the epilogue of the Codex of Hammurabi (KH r.XXVI 103), and two prayers (ZDMG 98, 36: 11; AGH 34: 29). Especially striking is the alternation of D and Š of *arāku* with *ūmu* "day" and *palû* "reign" as object, without any observable difference (for D cf. CAD sv 3b), e.g., in the same text in BagF. 18, 413: 29 (Š), versus 411: 12 (D) with object "days".

Ezēzu "to be(come) angry": factitive D is rare (cf. note 21); Š occurs in a myth (Or. 30, 3: 16'. 22'); in Ludlul bēl nēmeqi (BWL 343: 2. 4. acc. to AHw 1555b sv), and as an adjective *šē/ūzuzu* in RIs and prayers (listed in CAD sv *šēzuzu*).

Galātu "to be(come) nervous, afraid": D is common in all kinds of texts; Š only occurs in RIs (Sg. Cyl. 11; Sg. Wi. 98: 15; Ash. § 53: r. 38; VAB 7, 292: 19); hymns (ArOr. 37, 484: 32; OEC 6, 87 K.5158: r.15); a prayer (K.9514: 8), and a bilingual magic text (CT 17, 22: 128 // SpTU 2, 2: IV 136).

Hamāṭu "to burn" (trans. and intr.): for G and D cf. 7.3.2. In literary texts D is occasionally replaced by Š/Št(n), always in its literal meaning "to burn, scorch", mostly in the participle *muš(t)ahmiṭu*: in a RI (Ash. 97: r.14); in a prayer (AfO 19, 63: 47); in hymns (SAA 3, 2: 33; BWL 126: 18; 136: 179 [128: 42 is read *tu-šah-bat* by AHw 1557b sv *habātu* III]); in an epic (Ee IV 40); in Ludlul bēl nēmeqi (AnSt. 30, 106: 115).

For the synonymity of D and Š cf. especially Ee IV 40 *nabla muš-tah-me-ṭu* "a scorching arrow", versus LKU 33: 20 *nablī mu-ha-am-me-ṭu-ti* (id., plur.), and SAA 3, 2: 33 [DN] *mu-šah-miṭ zā'irī* "who scorches the enemies", versus OEC 6, 19: 3 (a torch) *mu-ha-am-me-eṭ ajjābī* "that scorches the enemies".

Helû "to shine, be brillant" rarely has a factitive D (only part., also as PN); Š only occurs in the following texts: RIs (Sg. Silber r.4 (read *ú-šah-li* by AHw sv *h.* II Š 2); Sn. 107: 38; 120: 28); prayers (AfO 19, 54: 201); and hymns (BWL 126: 2. 4; 136: 178; KB 6/2, 112: 35; JRAS Cspl. 34: 2; ZA 4, 240: 3).

Lamādu "to know", D "to inform, teach": its very common D-stem is replaced by a Š-stem in the following texts: RIs (Sg. 8: 210; Ash. § 53: r.50); a hymn (STT 70: 1); a hymnal part of an incantation (BA 10/1, 2: r.16f acc. to CAD sv lex. sect.); a diviner's manual (BBR 1-20: 10); and Ludlul bēl nēmeqi (BWL 38: 18; 40: 32 and AnSt. 30, 105: 39).[32]

Malû "to be(come) full" is found in the Š-stem, beside the normal factitive D-stem (cf. 7.3.1), in RIs (KB 3/1, 144: 6; Slm.Mon. II 99; Ash. 83: r.32; OEC 1, 34: 3; HS 1885: 9, qu. AHw sv Š 1 (RI ?)); in the closely related epic of Tukulti-Ninurta (AfO 18, 44: r.13 = Tn-Ep. VIb: 13); in hymns and prayers (IV R 20: 4; St. Reiner 192: 34); and in "divine love lyrics" (MIO 12, 48: 7f). [The obscure OAk. instance MDP 14, 90: 14f is not considered here].

For the synonymity of D and Š cf. especially Slm.Mon. II 99 *šal[mātē]šunu pān namê ú-šam-li* "he covered the entire surrounding (area) with their bodies", versus RIMA 1, 184: 103f *šalmāt qurādīšunu ṣēra rapša lū ú-me-el-li* "I covered the wide plain with the bodies of their warriors"; and IV R 20: 4 *ṣēru bāmâti šaqummatu ú-šam-li* "he filled the plain, the open country with silence" (tr. CAD sv lex. sect.), versus VAB 7, 182: 43 [...] *šaqummati ú-mal-li* "I filled [...] with silence".

Marāru "to be bitter" has a Š-stem which only occurs in RIs with *kakkū* "weapons" as object, cf. CAD sv *m.* A 4 ("to make prevail", corresponding to G "to prevail" with weapons as subject, *ib.* 2); but AHw sv Š "bitter machen"; in a commentary this use of *marāru* is equated with *danānu* "to be(come) strong" (Izbu 218: 212f); cf. also OB *kakkī mar-ru-tim* Syr. 33, 67: 32f), and ŠI.IR-ni_5 *i nu-ma-ri-ir* in ARM 26/2 p. 419 no. 483: 25, cf. Lackenbacher, NABU 87/82: "... pour rendre nos forces plus solides".

Masāku "to be bad, inferior", D "to spoil, revile", seems to use Š in the meaning of D a few times: in an epic (Erra I 53, V 50); in a prayer (AfO 25, 42: 67); and in BWL 218: 7 (a collection of popular sayings). Obscure and not considered are Erra IIb 21 and Or. 18, 35: 16. However, Š is so similar in form and meaning to the very common Š-stem *šussuku* "to remove, reject, abolish" (CAD sv *nasāku* 5/6), that one or more of the instances quoted here may belong to that verb (AHw sv *nasāku* Š 3c, for instance, assigns Erra V 50 to *šussuku*).

Palāhu "to be(come) afraid, have respect" has a Š-stem instead of the usual D-stem in RIs (Ash. p. 4: 39; 20: A 14); in an epic (Erra IV 56) and in an incantation (ZDMG 69, 96: 11).

Qatāru "to smoke, billow" has a factitive D which frequently occurs in omens and medical texts, occasionally also in literary texts, cf. CAD sv 3-6. Š only rarely occurs: in epics (Ee V 51; Tn-Ep. V 26 (but the text has *ú-ša-AG-mi* rather than *ú-ša-aq-tar*)), in a Kassite votive inscription (JAOS 88, 193: 24), and in a literary royal letter (Iraq 56, 138: r.6').

Qatû "to come to an end", usually with a factitive D, has a Š-stem in the epilogue of the Codex of Hammurabi (KH r.XXVII 56), in the "Descent of Ištar" (ZA 58, 193: 131), and in a RI: RIMA 2/I, 25: 67 (with object *napištu*, an expression which everywhere else has the D-stem, cf. CAD sv 6b).

Rabû "to be(come) big, great" is the textbook example of a semantic differentiation between D and Š: its D-stem is reported to mean "to raise, rear" (children, animals, plants), whereas the general meaning "to make big(ger), enlarge" is assigned to the Š-stem, cf. AHw sv D and Š, and GAG § 89d. Two facts, however, raise serious doubt that this semantic opposition captures the basic nature of the difference between D and Š. First, the differentiation between the two meanings is not consistent: there are counterexamples in both directions.[33] On the one hand, D is used, firstly, in RIs for the enlargement of buildings (AHw sv D 7, e.g., RIMA 1, 192: 33 (but *ib.* 30 and Sn. 100: 55 have Š in the same expression; cf. also AHw sv Š 5)) and Ash. Nin. A VI 32); secondly, with a personal object in the meaning "to promote" (AHw sv D 4, e.g., YOS 10, 42: II 61; Sg. Lie 40: 255; ArOr 37, 485: 62 (reflexive Dt, cf. 9.1.2); and, thirdly, in the meaning "to increase" silver (SAA 6, 293: r.3; ADD 235: r.8).

On the other hand, Š is occasionally used in the meaning "to raise (a son)":

(25) AOAT 2, 323: 3 (RN) *ša* DN_1 DN_2 (...) *kīma abi u ummi ú-šar-bu-u-šu* "(the king) whom DN_1 and DN_2 (...) raised as a father and a mother";

(26) AfO 18, 50: 20 (= Tn-Ep. I 20) *ú-šar-bi-šu-ma DN kīma abi ālidi arki māri bukrišu* "like a physical father, Enlil raised him second to his firstborn son".[34]

Second, all instances of the Š-stem listed in AHw sv Š are found in literary texts. We can classify them as follows:

A) Royal inscriptions: AfO 20, 74: 32 (OAk.); LIH 97/9: 52/4 (= RIME 4, 382: 42); AOB 128: 18 (= RIMA 1, 189: 18); 130: 21 (= *ib.* 190: 21); 132: 6 (= *ib.* 190: 31); 136: 2 (= *ib.* 192: 30); 140 no. 6: 9 (= *ib.* 210: 9); TP I 17 (= RIMA 2/I, 13: 17). 46 (= *ib.* 13: 46); KAH 2, 84: 78 (= *ib.* 151: 78); AKA 248: 49 (= *ib.* 253: 49); Sg. 8: 60. 161; Sg. Lie 42: 271; Sg. Cyl. 30; Sn. 48: 4; 56: 4; 100: 55; 133: 85; 135: 5. 9; Ash. § 2: III 6; Ash. p. 21: 23; 96: 8; 97: 9; 98: 32; PEA 29: 13; Asb. B I 10; IAsb. 80: r.6; 87: 27; VAB 4, 108: 45; 180: 40; Sumer 13, 191: 29; CT 36, 21/2: 26. 33; 37, 15: 65 // UM 15, 79: II 65; JNES 17, 137: 4; further related texts such as the prologue and epilogue of the Codex of Hammurabi (KH I 15; II 5; IV 19; r.XXVI 57), royal grants (SVAT 3: 4; NARG p. 63 no. 32: 29 (= SAA 12, 19: 29')), and a *kudurru* (BBS 36: II 27).
B) hymns and prayers: HGŠ 121: 9; Or. 23, 346f: 2. 4. 8. 14. 19; 36, 120: 63; KB 6/1, 48: 30; KAR 73: 27; AGH 134: 101; AOS 53 (= JAOS 88), 130: 4; WO 1, 477: 2; BA 5, 565: IV 14; 595: 13; ZA 4, 241: 43. 45 (= ZA 61, 60: 221. 223); ZA 5, 68: 27 (= AfO 25, 42: 83); KB 6/2, 108: 12 (= SAA 3, 2: 12); PSBA 20, 158: 5; AK 1, 21: 9 (= St. Kraus 198: 60). Additional instances not found in AHw: BagF. 18, 393: 25'; 301: 3; 307: 29"; AfO 18, 294: 84.
C) myths and epics: Ee I 153. 155; Erra I 62; V 51. 61; RA 46, 88: 10 (Št); AfO 18, 50: 20, quoted above as (25); UET 6, 398: 18; JCS 21, 128: 5.
D) laudatory parts of incantations: AGH 24: 3; 130: 18; 134: 101.
E) colophons: AOAT 2, 323: 3, quoted above as (24).
F) Other: CRRAI 35, 10: 18 (bilingual letter to a king, not in AHw).

Consequently, the literary character of *rabû* Š is more consistent than the semantic difference between "to raise, rear" and "to enlarge". This suggests that the difference between D and Š is stylistic rather than semantic. For the "elative" *šurbû* see also note 39.

Râšu "to be(come) jubilant": D and Š "to make jubilant", cf. AHw sv D/Š: D occurs in a RI (YOS 9, 45: II 7), in the prologue of the Codex of Hammurabi (KH III 11), and in prayers (AGH 16: 8; 64: 3; 66: 34 acc. to AHw sv *riāšu(m)*); Š in a hymn (BA 5, 572: 4) and in an epic (Ee VI 111).

Šapālu "to be)come) low" uses the Š-stem only in the infinitive, in the expression *šušqû u šušpulu* "to exalt and to abase": in a hymn (ArOr 37, 489: 24), in an epic (Ee IV 8, quoted in a NB letter: CT 54, 22: r.30) and in an unpublished literary text qu. CAD sv 8; without *šušqû* in a hymn (Or. 23, 214: 8 acc. to AHw 1589b sv).

Šaqû "to be(come) high, go up", normally with a factitive D, has Š in an epic (Ee I 92. 148. 159; IV 8 (cf. *šapālu* above); VI 105. 140; VII 13 (i.e., 7 out of 16 instances: it was obviously a favourite form of the author of Enuma Eliš); in RIs (Sn. 100: 54; Sumer 13, 190: 16); in hymns (SAA 3, 2: 25; 3: 1; ArOr 37, 489: 24); in a prayer (JCS 21, 260: 19); in the laudatory part of an incantation (AGH 24: 21); in the "Babylonian Theodicee" (BWL 86: 267); and in a poetic text about Naram-Sin (BiOr 30, 361: 28).

The interchangeability of D and Š is apparent from a comparison of CAD sv *š.* A v. 2e/f (D) with 4b/c (Š). Note especially the use of D and Š in the same sentence in Sn. 100: 54 *arkānu šú-uš-qu-ú tamlî kabitti ublamma 20 tibkī ṣēr mahrî uṣṣibma 180 tibkī ú-šaq-qi elāniš* "later my heart urged me to make the terrace higher (Š), so I added 20 layers to the former altitude and made it 180 layers high (D)" (cf. Luckenbill *ad. l.*). For the "elative" *šušqû* see note 39.

Šarāhu "to be(come) proud, glorious" is generally a literary verb with a very common factitive D. Non-literary forms include PNs (CAD sv 3a, 4 and 5) and a Dt-stem in OB letters, see 9.1.1. The use of Š is strongly restricted: it is only found in hymns and prayers (BA 5, 596: 14; SAA 3, 2: 6. 29; 3: 1. 18; AfO 25, 39: 29), in an epic (Erra IV 40) and in a RI (AfO 20, 94: 109). For the use of D and Š in the same contexts, compare CAD sv 3 (D) with 6 (Š).

(W)asāmu "to be fitting, proper": D and Š are both largely restricted to literary texts, more specifically, to the description of buildings in RIs, cf. CAD sv *asāmu* lex. sect. and 2/3. The only observable difference is that Š is normally used as stative/VA, and D for the rest of the paradigm (cf. *abālu* in 7.5.1). Exceptions are: stative D in VAB 4, 76: 17. 21 and Wedg. 16: r. 14; prefix forms of Š in RA 15, 181: 22 and VAB 4, 64: 30 (*ú-ša-as-sí-im-šu*, a contamination of D and Š?). However, a VA D *wussum(t)um* is attested as a PN in OAk, cf. 10.6.3.2. Obscure and not considered is BIN 1, 79: 9 (NB).

The same coexistence of D and Š with no observable difference, but with Š restricted to literary texts is found in the D tantum verb *kullumu* "to show" (cf. 8.6 sv). Its Š-stem (+Štn) is found only in RIs, cf. CAD sv 7, AHw sv Š/Štn (for ŠD see 9.3). [Gilg. Y VI 289 is uncertain; Craig ABRT 2, 16: 20 = JRAS 1929, 12: 23 is read *mu-šak-li-lat* by AHw sv *šuklulu* II Š 2].[35]

7.5.5.2. GROUP II: verbs with a factitive D-stem (except for *agāgu,* of which only a *purrus* adjective and stative is attested), which is very rarely (one or two attestations) replaced by a "literary" Š-stem:

Agāgu "to be(come) angry", Š 1x in an epic (Erra I 123).

Damāqu "to be(come) good", Š 2x in a bilingual royal letter (MDP 57, 15: 9) and a prayer (AfO 19, 63: 48). [Cancel RA 21, 130 note 32, cf. BagF. 18, 390: 12 with note 16].

Enēšu "to be(come) weak", Š 1x in a hymn (MVAG 13, 216: 28 acc. to AHw sv *ṣīlēhtu* 1).

Hadû "to be(come) glad", Š 1x in RI (IAsb. 82a: 13).

Kabātu "to be(come) heavy", Š 1x in RIs (VAB 4, 164: 22). [AbB 1, 117: 6 read *šu-uṣ$_4$-bu-tim*?].

Karû "to be(come) short", Š 1x in a prayer (AfO 19, 63: 58).

Lemēnu "to be(come) bad, unhappy", Š 1x in an epical fragment (SpTU 1, 4: 20').

Nâhu "to rest, subside": D "to appease, pacify, extinguish, satisfy", Š 2x in prayers (SBH 44: 11; AGH 124: 3 (part. Št(n)? or contamination with *anāhu*? (cf. CAD note sv *anāhu* A)). [ARM 4, 26: 40 is very doubtful].

Nakālu "to be(come) clever, to cheat", Š 1x in RI (Ash. p. 22 a 16 + BiOr. 21, 146: 53).

Nêšu "to stay alive, recover", Š 2x in a myth (HSAO 186: I 5) and an epic (Ee VI 151).

Pahāru "to come together", Š 1x in a myth (JNES 14, 15: 14 (OB, // SB *u-pa-hir* JNES 17, 56: 54)).

Parādu "to be(come) afraid", Š 2x in RIs (RIMA 1, 310: 5; 316: 3, both partially restored).

Parāru "to fall apart", Š 1x in a hymn (SBH p. 37 no. 18: r.9 (*tu-ša[p-ri-ir]* // BRM 4, 9: 52 *tu-par-ri-ir*)).

Qerēbu "to come near, approach", 1x in an epic (Ee IV 44). [All other alleged instances of Š are either Št-stems, or are more likely to belong to *karābu* Š (also AbB 12, 99: 22, cf. 13, 85: 26)].

Râbu "to tremble", 1x in a RI (RIMA 2/I, 41: 9).

Ramāku "to bathe", 1x in a prayer (AfO 19, 59: 163).

Rapāšu "to be(come) broad, wide", 1x in a poetic text about Naram-Sin (BiOr 30, 361: 28).

Sabā'u "to toss, roll" (waves), 1x in RI (OEC 6, 71: 9). [The other instances listed CAD sv 4 and AHw sv Š are of uncertain interpretation].

Ṣalāmu "to be(come) black, dark", 2x in a RI (Ash. § 80: I 5) and a prayer (STT 68: 11).

Ṣamû "to be(come) thirsty", 1x in the epilogue of the Codex of Hammurabi (KH r.XXVII 40).

Zenû "to be(come) angry", 2x in SAA 2, p. 39: 265 (NA vassal treaty) and in a commentary on Maqlû and Šurpu (KAR 94: 42).

7.5.5.3. GROUP III: literary Š-stems which occur exceptionally also in non-literary texts:

Kanāšu "to submit, bend down" has both a factitive D and a factitive Š. The latter occurs in the following texts: RIs (passim, cf. CAD sv 7a-1'); hymns and prayers (OEC 11 p. 16: 45; RA 22, 173: 49; HGŠ 33: 54; LSS 1/6, 50: 5; AGH 124: 19; SAA 3, 3: r.6. r.18; an epic (Tn-Ep. VIa: 14); a mythical fragment (HSAO 186: 16. 19); for D and Š with object *kišāda* "neck" see 7.5.3.

Non-literary instances of Š include its use as an abbreviated PN *mu-šèk-niš* (CAD sv 7a-3'), and in NA letters (2x, but in typically literary phrases, cf. CAD *l.c.*).

Labāšu "to wear" (clothes) has a frequent factitive D-stem which is basically used in three ways: 1."to dress sb in a garment, to provide sb with clothing"; 2. figuratively "to cover sb with an illness" (mostly leprosy), and 3. "to cover, coat" (a building with metals or bricks). For 3. we often find Š in RIs, cf. CAD sv 5c-1' (alternating with D, cf. especially RA 82, 143: 37' (Š), versus D in 144: 13'; 147: 23 and 149: 28). For meaning 2. we occasionally find Š in other literary texts: hymns (PSBA 20, 157: r.10; Or. 36, 124: 132); a prayer (AfO 19, 62: 39 acc. to AHw sv Š 2); in Ee I 137 and in a curse formula (AfO 16, 43: 31 (NB)), which everywhere else has D (cf. Nougayrol, JCS 2, 205ff).

The literary character of *labāšu* Š is contradicted, however, by a single instance in an OB letter: AbB 4, 144: 20f (you said to me) *ṣubātam šu-ul-bi-iš-šu ṣ[ub]ātam ú-ša-al-bi-šu-ma* "provide him with a garment!"; (so) I provided him with a garment." This is also the only instance in which Š is used in meaning 1.

Ṭâbu "to be(come) good, pleasant", with a frequent factitive D, also has a frequent factitive Š, which only occurs in literary texts, with one possible exception. The literary texts in question are: RIs (IV R 12: 22; Sg. Wi. 168: 6 acc. to AHw sv Š 1b; Sn. 99: 48; Ash. § 2: VI 19; Asb. B V 32; VAB 7, 190: 17; VAB 4, 124: 6; 256: 5; OEC 1, 35: 15; cf. also ÉR 351; colophons (AOAT 2, 326: 5); hymns (ArOr 37, 485: 86; KAR 16: r.22; Wedg. 16: 3); and some other literary texts (UFBG 473: 8 (a prayer), SAA 3, 28: 2' (a "literary letter to a king"), AOTU 1, 279: 38 (= Lugal 19), AR 17: 7 (= VAB 7, 394: 17, a royal dedication to a goddess), BWL 54: 31 (Ludlul bēl nēmeqi), SpTU 1, 136: 8 (epithet of a temple). Less clearly literary is CT 17, 25: 7 (a bilingual magic text).[36]

For the synonymity of D and Š see especially the expression *libba* (sometimes *kabatta*) *ṭubbu* "to please, satisfy someone", lit. "to make the heart glad", in which D can be replaced by Š (*šuṭubbu* or *šuṭūbu*) in literary texts, cf. AHw sv D 4b/c and Š 4), and cf. the divine epithets ÉR 350f (DN) *ša* (..) *rē'ussu* (...) *eli nišē GN ú-ṭi-bu* "DN who made his (the king's) sovereignty pleasing to the people of GN", versus *ib.* 351 (DN) *ša* (...) *šarrussu* (...) *uš-ṭib-bu eli nišē* (id., with "kingship").

The only non-literary instance is found in an OB letter: BagM. 2, 59: 23ff *ana anniātim kīma bītum annûm libbam / gamram ittika ītawû u zikir šumika / irammu šu-ú!-ṭù-ba-ši-na tele"i* "Dem gemäß, daß dieses "Haus" offen mit dir spricht und deinen Ruf (zu erhalten) liebt, kannst du diese (Mißhelligkeiten) zum Guten bringen." (tr. Falkenstein, and cf. AHw sv Š 3 "freundlich machen"). The passage is, however, not quite unequivocal.

7.5.5.4. GROUP IV: a few verbs are listed here in which the reverse is found of the situation described so far: they have a Š-stem as their normal factitive, but occasionally use the D-stem in literary texts. This applies to:

Ew/mû "to turn/change into, etc.: normally Š as factitive, D is twice found instead of Š in RIs (RIMA 2/I, 52: 12; Sg. 8: 230); these instances have been separated from OB *uwwû* (SD 5, 30: 40) "to alter (fraudulently)", which is used in a quite different context (for *uwwû* see 8.4.2).

Nâlu "to lie (down): normally Š, cf. CAD sv 4, AHw sv *niālu(m)* Š. D twice occurs in RIs (RIMA 1, 192: 13; WO 1, 57: 18) in combination with *kī(ma) šūbe* "to lay (enemies) flat like reeds (cf. CAD sv *šūbu*); elsewhere Š is used in this expression (RIMA 2/I, 15: 20; 16: 80; 24: V 94; VI 5). Probably the D form *tu-ut-ti-il* HS "175": II 8 qu. AHw sv *itūlu* D (OB lit.) also belongs here.

Ra'ābu "to tremble" normally uses a Š-stem (cf. note 8), cf. AHw sv Š/Št, but 1x Dt // Št: FuB 12, 42: 2b *uš-tar-'i-i-ba* (var. *uš-tar-i-bi*) // *ur-ta-'i-[ba]* (bilingual description of a demon).

Rabābu "to be(come) weak, yield" normally has a Š-stem, which is mostly intransitive, however: "to rest, relax", cf. AHw sv Š 3 (cf. also SpTU 3, 120: I 48 *šur-bu-bu* = *ú-tu-lu*). Factitive Š ("to weaken, to subdue") only occurs RIMA 2/I, 23: 65. D is only found in an epic (Ee III 32 (// ŠD)); a prayer (OECT 6 pl. 24 K.3021: 4 (coll. Lambert)), and an incantation (LKU 24: 1-19 passim). [For JRAS 1932, 559: 13 (object trees) cf. CAD sv *mēsu* A lex. sect. (derived from *râbu* D "to shake")].

7.5.6. D- and Š-stems with no apparent difference in use

In the intransitive verbs whose Š-stem is not differentiated in meaning from the D-stem, and which are not restricted to literary texts either, it is usually difficult to detect any difference in use between D and Š. There are a few cases in which dialectal differentiation is or may be involved.[37] The following verbs can be mentioned here:

Adāru "to be(come) dark, worried": Š is the usual factitive, factitive D is rare (JCS 9, 8: A 12 (? *uh-ta-di-<ir>*); UET 5, 44: r.6), but stative D and Dt forms are common (cf. 9.1.4), cf. CAD sv *a.* A 3/4.

Anāhu "to exert oneself" may be a case of dialectal differentiation: it has a Š-stem in Bab., but a D-stem in Ass., cf. AHw sv. The suggestion of CAD sv *anāhu* A (note on p. 105b) to derive *anāhu* D from another verb (**wanāhum*) is rejected by Veenhof 1972: 114.

Arāhu "to be quick, go/come quickly": D "to send quickly", "to hurry" (intrans.) and "to do quickly" in hendiadys, cf. CAD sv *a.* A 2/3; Š is also used in hendiadys (ARM 26/1, p. 414 no. 192: 22; Hém. 80: 11).

Bâšu "to come to shame": normally D "to put to shame"; Š in AbB 4, 152: 16. 19 (uncertain).

Dalāpu "to be or stay awake": D "to keep awake, harass", mainly in RIs, cf. AHw sv D; Š has about the same meaning, and is found in SB and NA.

Ebēbu "to be(come) clean, pure": normally D, Š 1x BIN 1, 42: 22f (NB letter). [Cancel Ash. § 53 p. 79: 8, cf. Borger's note on p. 46 *ad* II 30].

Ekēlu "to be(come) dark": normally D, Š in TuL 21: II 4; III 7 (uncertain: from *ekēlu* or from *šaqālu* "to weigh"? cf. AHw sv *mušeqqilum*).

Elēṣu "to swell, rejoice": D occurs as a factitive in CT 37, 22a: 11 (context broken); elsewhere as an infinitive (verbal noun) followed by *libbi* or *kabatti*. Otherwise Š is used for the finite forms, cf. CAD sv 3; Dt only occurs as infin. in LL.

Hasāsu "to think about, to heed": D "to remind", "to study" (intrans.); Š is occasionally used in similar meanings: "to remind, to inform", cf. AHw sv D 2/3, CAD sv 11/12. An atypical instance is BA 5, 596: 11 *li-šah-sis TN* "let him (a god) pay attention to TN" (AHw sv Š 1 "sich lernen lassen"); all instances are SB, NB and NA.

Labāku "to be(come) soft, steeped": D "to steep, macerate"; Š 1x RA 60, 31: r.3' (recipe).

Labāru "to be(come) old": D occurs from OB onwards in all kinds of texts, both trans. and intrans., cf. 7.5.3. sv. Š is post-OB, and particularly common in RIs (intr. and trans., cf. CAD sv 6/7); other instances are found in hymns (KAR 3: 16; SAA 3, 4: r.II 21'), in a "literary letter" (SAA 3, 26: r.4'), in hemerologies (CAD sv 6a end), and 2x in NA letters, once in a greeting formula (ABL 716: 5), and once (ABL 7 = LAS 123 = SAA 10, 197: r.16) in a letter which wholly consists of blessings in a clearly literary style (cf. *labāru* G in r.15). Generally speaking, then, Š seems to have a more literary character than D, although it is not restricted to the typically literary texts enumerated in 7.5.5. For the synonymity of D and Š cf. the names of the city walls of Dur-Šarrukin quoted CAD sv 4a and 7 with *mu-lab-bir* in Sg. Cyl. 71, versus *mu-šal-bir* in Sg. Stier 90f (both with object *palê šarri*).

Magāru "to agree with, obey, grant": D and Š seem to be differentiated on the basis of dialect in that OA uses only D, and OB only Š in the meaning "to get to agree, bring about an agreement". In SB D acquires the meaning "to reconcile" (+ *itti* "with"), 1x "to force to obey, to subdue" (Sn. 135: 10), with a personal object, and Š "to cause to find acceptance" (prayers, good deeds, etc.), cf. CAD sv 7/8.

Marāṣu "to be ill, distressed" has Š as its usual factitive, cf. CAD sv 6-8; AHw sv Š; factitive D is rare; it is occasionally found in OB letters in hendiadys, cf. 7.4.1 sv; as an independent verb perhaps in ARM 26/1 p. 309 no. 145: 17 (restored), and a few times later: BE 17, 67: 9; BWL 194: r.23; MSL 14, 467: 65.

Mašālu "to be(come) equal, similar", D "to make equal, to copy, to be equal to, to match"; Š (rare) seems to mean "to make equal": in hendiadys with *zâzu* "to divide (fields) equally" CT 34, 38: I 22 (= TCS 5, 160: 22'); and in Iraq 36, 202: 37. 39 (persons: "to share equally").

Nabāṭu "to shine brightly": normally Š, cf. CAD sv 4/5, AHw sv Š/Št; D is exceptional: BBS 5: II 16; CT 12, 6: I 26 (LL); ACh. Išt. 26: 28 (= (12) in 9.1.1 (Dt)).

Naw/māru "to shine, be(come) bright": D is the most common factitive; Š duplicates most of its uses, compare CAD sv 8a with 5 (e.g., AOTU 1, 120: 35 (Š) with SAA 3, 39: 32 (D) in almost identical contexts), 8b with 3b, 8c with 3b, 8e with 2a-2'; only 8d (*īnam šuwwurum* "to look sharp" is not (yet) atttested with D. However, Š is mainly restricted to literary OB (St. Reiner 190: 27; 192: 46; ZA 44, 32: 22; Gilg. Y VI 250. 256, but 1x in a letter (OBTR 309: 12, with *īnum*)), and to NA (AOTU 1, 120: 35; SAA 3, 37: 11'; MVAeG 41/3, 64: 38. 40; SVAT 24: II 18; CA 130: V 27' acc. to CAD sv 8a; Or. 22, 39: r.7; cf. also NA *mušanmirtu*, a lighting device, CA 126: II 11'). The remaining instances are RIMA 1, 10: 13' (OA votive inscription), Or. 17, 418: 3 (SB hymn, but from an Assyrian environment) and AfO 24, 95: 6 (*li-ša-ap-pi-ru*) from Elam. Thus the difference between D and Š seems to be at least partially dialectal.

Nesû "to withdraw, go away": D and Š (+ŠD) "to remove, keep away, drive away". The contexts in which D and Š occur largely overlap, esp. in the meaning "to keep away or "to drive away" evil, guilt, disease, etc. from the body, cf. CAD sv 3c (D) and 4b (Š), and Ee II 105 (D // Š acc. to CAD sv 3c); but both stems are also used in the more concrete sense of removing objects and persons, cf. *ib.* 3a/b (D) and 4a (Š).

Pašāhu "to cool down, calm down": D and Š idem, but trans. There seems to be no difference whatsoever between them; the most prominent parallels concern the use of D and Š with *libba* or *kabatta* "to calm down sb's heart, to set at ease", and with body parts. Note D and Š as variants in CT 17, 26: 77 and Maqlû VII 42. With personal object Š is mostly used, with diseases only D, cf. AHw sv D 5. *Pašāhu* is mainly found in SB.

Râhu "to be left over", D and Š "to leave over", both rare, no difference observable, cf. AHw sv *riāhu(m)* D and Š.

Râqu "to be(come) empty, unemployed", D and Š "to make empty, to leave unemployed", no difference observable, cf. AHw sv *riāqu(m)* D and Š.

Salāmu "to be(come) friendly, make peace": D "to reconcile, bring about peace", Š 1x CT 54, 186: r.3 acc. to AHw 1587a sv (NB).

Ṣalālu "to sleep, fall asleep": normally Š, but 1x D: SKS p. 54: 147, cf. 7.2.4.

Šanû "to change" seems to use the D-stem mainly in Bab., whereas Ass. (and western peripheral areas) replace it by the Š-stem, especially in contracts, cf. CAD sv *š.* B v. 7. However, Š is also used in literary texts, in accordance with the tendency discussed in 7.5.5, e.g., Tn-Ep. V 32 DN *ša qurādīšunu ú-še-eš-ni ṭē-ma* "Ištar confused the judgment of their warriors", a rare variant of the very common idiom *ṭēma šunnû*, cf. CAD sv *š.* B v. 5a-2'.

(W)atāru "to be superfluous, in excess": both D and Š are frequently used; D is found in OB, OA and NB letters, in OB and MA laws, and in RIs, interchanging with Š, cf. for instance, RIMA 1, 189: 18 (D) with 258: 36 (Š). Acc. to AHw sv Š, Š is "meist lit[erarisch]". This is always true of the "elative" *šūturu* (cf. note 39), but the other forms of *(w)atāru* Š are also used in non-literary (mostly NA and NB) texts: AJSL 38, 184: 20 (astronomical text); BIN 1, 55: 22 (NB letter), Or. 35, 313 sv *biltu* 2b (NA legal doc.), ABL 923 = LAS 117 = SAA 10, 174: 9 (NA letter), and some NB PNs (quoted CAD sv 4a end).

7.5.7. Conclusions on the relationship between D and Š

The detailed comparison of D- and Š-stems of the same verb which both have a valency-extending function leads to the following conclusions.

First of all, the fundamental difference between these stems is that the factitive D-stem can only underline a valency extension which is compatible with the "natural" valency of the concept expressed by the verb, whereas the Š-stem can indicate a valency exceeding the "natural" valency inherent in the verbal concept (cf. 7.2.6). Therefore, D can only be used for valency extension if the verb in question has an alternating valency, whereas Š has no such restriction.

Conclusive evidence for this claim is offered by the overall distribution of the valency-extending use of D and Š over the various types of verb (cf. 7.2.1 and 7.2.2), and in particular by the verbs discussed in 7.5.3. As noted there, the verbs *qadādu, kanāšu, nê'u* and *sahāru* use the D-stem for the first step of valency extension, from intransitive to transitive, or from lowly transitive to highly transitive (e.g., the former with a body part of the subject as direct object, the latter with a personal direct object). With the exception of *nê'u*, they use the Š-stem for the next step, typically involving another person, and representing a real causative situation. In these verbs the Š-stem takes over when the D-stem has reached its maximum valency of two (bivalent) (cf. 7.1.4).[38]

The other verbs discussed in 7.5.3, *elû* and *nakāru*, exemplify the correlation of D with processes which can be realized with or without intervention of an agent ("to be high", "to be(come) hostile", and that of Š with actions that are typically performed by agents ("to go up", "to rebel").

The exemplary relationship between D and Š which is found in the verbs of 7.6.3 can only be realized in verbs of a specific semantic nature, namely those which represent borderline cases between transitive and intransitive (such as *qadādu*, etc.), or which can be both adjectival and fientive (such as *elû* and *nakāru*). Therefore, this kind of relationship between D and Š of the same verb is restricted to only a few verbs.

In other verbs the coexistence of two valency-extending stems has been exploited for other ends, namely a semantic or a stylistic differentiation. The semantic differentiation involved is realized in a more or less unpredictable way, so that the contrast between the factitive nature of D and the causative nature of Š is less prominent. If there is stylistic differentiation, this contrast is completely neutralized, and D and Š both serve as factitives.[39]

The second conclusion is that the difference between D and Š which Goetze and GAG claim to exist (cf. 7.1.1), namely, that the D-stem indicates the bringing about of a state or a condition, and the Š-stem the causing of an event or an action, and that the former is therefore more nominal in character and the latter more verbal, is no more than a consequence of the distinction between causative and factitive as defined in 7.1.6. Since verbs which denote the realization of a state or a condition typically have an alternating valency (cf. 7.1.5), there is a natural connection between D and such verbs. On the other hand, basic verbs which denote actions typically have a fixed valency, which associates them with the Š-stem in a natural way.

The view that the D-stem is more nominal, and the Š-stem more verbal in character is based on the denominative origin of the former (cf. 11.1) and its association with adjectives, whereas the Š-stem is associated with fientive verbs. This difference is reflected in the way in which D and Š forms of the same verb are rendered into German in AHw: D-stems tend to be glossed by more nominal expressions, Š-stems by more verbal ones. Typical examples are *malû* D "anfüllen", Š "voll werden lassen"; *ṣamû* D "durstig machen", Š "dürsten lassen", *qatāru* "zu Rauch machen", Š "rauchen lassen", *magāru* D "zur Zustimmung bringen", Š "zur zustimmen bringen", *qatû* D "zu Ende bringen", Š "beenden", and *riāšum* D "zum Jauchzen bringen", Š "jauchzen lassen". Another kind of distinction often made by AHw between D- and Š-stems of the same verb can be exemplified by *ezēzu*: D "erzürnen", Š "zürnen lassen", and *lamādu*: D "unterrichten, lehren", Š "lernen lassen" (cf. also AHw sv. *hadû, nakālu, šapālu* and *zenû*).

Two points of criticism can be raised against this. First, the semantic differences claimed to exist between D and Š are generally too subtle to be verifiable from the actual use of the forms in question, and, second, most of the verbs involved have a Š-stem which is more or less restricted to literary texts and is often used in precisely the same contexts as the D-stem (cf. 7.5), which makes the existence of a semantic difference unlikely.

Finally, we can define the factitive D-stem as the unmarked way for valency extension, and the Š-stem as the marked way, in accordance with the marked nature of real causatives as against factitives (cf. 7.2.6). This agrees with other differences between D and Š. First of all, the Š-stem has a more uniform function: with an insignificant number of exceptions (cf. note 15), all Š-stems are valency-extending (either causative or factitive), whereas only a part of the D-stem is valency-extending (only Types III and IV, cf. 5.2). Second, the Š-stem has a wider use: it can extend the valency of all verbs, whereas the use of D is restricted to a specific type of verb. Third, the morpheme of the Š-stem, the prefix *ša/u-*, is an external addition to the basic stem; the resulting verb form is therefore more transparent and easier to analyse than the geminate second radical characterizing the D-stem, which is an internal modification of the stem.

All these factors add up to making the Š-stem the more "powerful" of the two valency-extending devices of Akkadian. It is not surprising, then, that the Š-stem is also more productive than the D-stem. This explains the rise of the "literary Š-stems" discussed in 7.5.5, which encroach on the domain of the D-stem, doubtless because of the advantages that the Š-stem has over the D-stem.

7.6. Non-factitive D-stems of intransitive verbs: the D-stems of Type II

We will conclude this chapter by listing and discussing the D-stems of Type II, which comprises the intransitive verbs whose D-stem is valency-preserving, i.e., also intransitive. A number of these verbs, however, also occur with a direct object, both in the G-stem and in the D-stem; this object is typically an "inner object", specifying the nature of the action (as in English *to sing* versus *to sing a song*, and cf. *dabābu* "to speak (words)" in 5.5.3), and does not lead to a sentence with high transitivity. However, D forms occur relatively more often with such objects than G forms. The basic difference between Type II and Type III, which are both intransitive, is that in Type II the use of D does not correlate with the presence of an external agent, whereas it does in Type III.

It was argued in 7.2.1, that these verbs provide important evidence for the nature of the D-stem as factitive rather than causative, because they are typical fixed valency verbs. Accordingly, if they are causativized, they generally use the Š-stem. There are, however, a few problematical cases (cf. *halālu* and *nasāsu*).

Type II comprises only a small number of verbs, most of which are very rare. Moreover, most of them belong to three rather well-defined semantic groups. The largest one (group I) consists of verbs denoting sounds; next comes a small group (II) of verbs denoting more or less involuntary sounds which are related to bodily functions ("to cough, belch, vomit, fart", etc.), and some other bodily activities. Group III comprises a few verbs referring to activities of the mind which are atelic ("to think, plan, remember", etc.), and some other cases which do not fit in with the preceding groups.

7.6.1. Group I

Anāhu "to produce a moaning (?) sound", acc. to CAD sv *a.* B 3 (Dt only); very uncertain, only occurring in CT 42, 41b: 7 *ú-ta-na-ah* (which Von Soden, BiOr 18, 71f, emends to *ú-<uš>-ta-na-ah* or *uš!-ta-na-ah*, from *anāhu* Š), and STT 52: 52 *ut-ta-na-ah*: from this verb?

Habābu G denotes various sounds: that of flowing water, of birds and insects, and of bulls (in the Š-stem: SBH p. 121 no. 69: 20 *[al]pīka ina tarbaṣu lu-šá-ah-bi-ib* "I will make your bulls low in the cattle pen". Š is also common in the meaning "to cause (water) to murmur" in RIs, cf. CAD sv *h.* A (1), AHw sv Š 1. D is said of insects: AfO 8, 200: 66 bugs *ú-ha-am-ba-bu.*

With a personal subject, G and D have an erotic or sexual connotation, cf. Gröneberg, RA 80, 188ff; it is combined with *eli* (in G), or with an object (in G and D); D occurs TCS 2, p. 31 no. 13: 46 *hu(-ub)-bi-ban/ba-an-ni* "make love to me" (with G as variant: *hu-ub-ba-an-ni* TCS 2, p. 33 no. 14: 8 (emended by Biggs to *hu-ub-<bi>-ba-an-ni*)). Difficult is KAR 386: 8 *šumma ṣēru amēla ú-hab-ba-ab*: "if a snake hisses at a man" (thus AHw sv D 1, but CAD sv *h.* B (b) "to caress").

Habāru "to make a noise": no D attested, Dt 1x BWL 40: 40 *surriš uštādir zamar uh-ta-bar* "one moment he is dejected, the next he cries out with joy", cf. 9.1.6 sv. A causative Š occurs 2x, cf. CAD sv *h.* A (c).

Halālu "to wheeze, to murmur": D takes a direct object in Racc. 140: 343 (the exorcist ...) níg.kala.ga. urudu *ina libbi bīti ú-hal-lal* "will sound the copper ....-bell in the temple" (also JCS 43/5, 96: 76; 97: 81). A Dt form is perhaps found in St. Sjöberg 326: 92 (context broken).

***Lahāšu** "to whisper" (Gt, no G attested); for D, cf. CAD sv 2 (also UET 7, 156: r.I 4'); for Dt, cf. CAD sv 3: AfO 11, 224: 83 *šumma ul-tah-ha-aš* "if he whispers" (contrasting with *ib.* 81f *š. rigma kabar/qatan* "if he speaks loud/soft"); for the use of Dt here, see below and 9.1.6 sv; there is no reason to translate "to whisper to oneself" (CAD sv 3) nor "sich einflüstern lassen" (AHw sv Dt). A similar case is JCS 29, 66: 21 *[šumma] mu-ul-tah-hi-iš* "if he is a whisperer".

Na'āru "to roar": G occurs only as a part. *nā'i/eru* (the stative *na-'-[a-rat]* mentioned CAD sv should rather be restored to a part.: *na-'i-[rat]*), and once as an infin. (in a commentary qu. CAD sv lex. sect.). D once occurs in the stative (ZA 16, 180: 41, see note 4 to Ch. X)) and as part. in the epithet *nā'iru kibrāti* "who roars against the four quarters" (unless this is from *nêru* "to kill", cf. App. to Ch. VI sv). For the finite forms of this verb Dt is used, cf. CAD sv, AHw sv Dt.

Nabāhu "to bark": both G and D (1x Gtn); AHw distinguishes G "bellen" from D "kläffen".

Nahāsu "to wail, lament": G 1x AfO 19, 52: 148; usually Dt, cf. CAD sv *n.* B d (also St. Sjöberg 327: 100), occasionally D, cf. *ib.* c. There is considerable uncertainty about the meaning and classification of many forms of this verb and its possible homonyms, cf. CAD sv *n.* A and B, the remarks on p. 132f, and AHw sv *nahāsu* D and *duhhusu.*

Nasāsu "to complain, lament" (with human beings or a god as subject): G is mostly used without object, cf. CAD sv lex. sect. and a (with a cognate object (*nissatu*) in RA 33, 105: 11 and an inner object in TuM NF 3, 25: 17 (cf. AfO 23, 86a Z. 17) *qubbêša ṭābūtim i-na-as-sà-as* "sie singt ihre angenehmen Klagelieder" (tr. Wilcke in AfO *l.c.*)); D twice occurs with an direct object: AGH 132: 49 a house that *ú-na-as-sa-su bikâti* "moans with sorrow" (tr. CAD sv b); and ACh. Ad. 4: 47 (*šumma*) DN *rigimšu kīma immeri ú-na-sis* "if Adad has made his thunder sound like a (bleating) sheep" (cf. AHw sv *n.* I D, but CAD quotes this instance sv *nazāzu* 3). In these sentences *bikâti* and *rigimšu* can best be explained as inner objects. The third instance, however, KAR 339: 14 *pāšu kabta tu-na-si-is* (in broken context), can hardly mean anything but "you made his venerable mouth resound", which makes the D-stem valency-extending and thus incongruent with Type II.[40]

It is difficult to distinguish this verb from *nazāzu*, which is said of animals and trees, cf. CAD sv (where also ACh. Ad. 4: 47 is listed, sv 3); in addition, CAD and AHw assume a D tantum verb *nussusu* "to shake, wave, flap, rock", and "schütteln", respectively.

Na'û G "to shout", D "to lament", acc. to CAD sv (all instances very uncertain; AHw lists most forms under *nahû* "etwa "seufzen"" (to be cancelled acc. to CAD sv ***nahû*).

Nazāmu "to complain" (G only OA, Gtn 1x MB): D is found in CT 40, 11: 69, Šurpu II 76, cf. CAD sv 3a, and TCL 1, 25 (= VAB 6, 139): 13 *tu-na-za-mi-in-n*[*i*]: this is translated as a causative in CAD sv 3a "you will make me complain", but a translation "you are complaining about me" is more satisfactory, cf. line 4 and 15 in the same letter *tazzimtaki* "your complaint", and cf. ARM 4, 70: 6ff with a comparable situation. The most frequent form is the Dt-stem, cf. CAD sv 4, AHw sv Dt. A causative Š-stem is attested once (RA 34, 7: 28).

Raṣānu "to make a loud noise, to acclaim" (G uncertain, but cf. Gtn in ZA 62, 226: 16, with GAG § 35c): D only occurs as a stative/VA (see 10.7.2); for the fientive forms Dt is used, cf. AHw sv Dt.

To this small group of verbs we can add some other verbs already discussed in earlier chapters which are semantically related to the verbs denoting sounds. In the first place, *dabābu* "to talk, speak", whose D-stem - as we saw in 5.5.3 - can also be intransitive: "to grumble, complain" (CAD sv 8a); further, *nabû* and *qabû*, discussed in 6.8.1, with their D-stems *nubbû* and *qubbû* "to wail, complain" (but *nabû* G can also have this meaning, cf. CAD sv *n*. B a). It was argued in 6.8.1 that, etymologically, these verbs denote sounds, and that the actual meaning of G results from the weakening of such an older meaning. If this is correct, there is no reason to assume that there are two different verbs *nabû*, as CAD does. Finally, *napāhu* "to light, set fire to, rise" (of the sun), whose D-stem - apart from its transitive use discussed in 6.4.8 - is also used without object in the meaning "to hiss, snort, rattle", cf. CAD sv 5b; possibly also "to blow" of the wind, *ib.* 5a (but AHw sv D 3 "wegblasen" (trans.). For an explanation of the fact that so many of these verbs are I/n verbs, see GAG § 102b.

A remarkable aspect of the verbs denoting sounds is that they frequently occur in the Dt-stem. It is possible that this is a consequence of the association of D with high transitivity: this association may have caused a reluctance to use the D-stem without object, and a tendency to use the Dt-stem instead, with its general detransitivizing function which is usually realized as passive, intransitive, reflexive, etc., cf. 9.1.[41] Alternatively, it may be a reflex of the contextual durative meaning of the infix *-ta-* which was posited in 4.1.2.1, and which, in the present tense, has largely been replaced by *-tana-*.

Many other verbs denoting sounds do not have a D-stem, but for some of them other forms with gemination of the second radical are attested: *bakû* "to cry, wail" has the agent nouns *bakkā'u* and *bakkû*, fem. *bakkîtu* "wailing, wailer, mourner"; *ṣarāhu* "to lament" (intr., or with inner object) has *ṣarrihtu* "wailing woman" (RA 70, 112: G 27, variant *muṣarrihtu*, *ib.* M 16); *šagāmu* "to roar, resound" has a derivation with gemination of the second radical of an unusual pattern, in the idiom *šaggumūta* + *alāku* Š "to reduce (cities) to wailing", acc. to CAD sv *šaggumūta*. All these verbs use the Š-stem as causative.

7.6.2. Group II

Ganāhu G and D "to cough"; AHw sv distinguishes G "husten" from D "husten und würgen", and CAD sv remarks that "the contexts from SB texts and the Aram. etymology (*g^enaḫ* "to vomit") suggest that *gunnuhu* (possibly against *ganāhu*) does not refer simply to coughing but rather to fits of coughing and retching, etc."

Ganāṣu "to sniff, wrinkle (one's nose)" (CAD), "(Nase, Lippen) hochziehen" (AHw). G only LL, D has nose or nostrils as object (CAD sv a, AHw sv D), and occurs without object in the part. *muganniṣu* "sneering, arrogant person" (CAD M sv; also *gunnuṣu*, cf. note 4 to Ch. X). Elsewhere Dt is used if there is no object (BWL 100: 58; AfO 19, 116: 23, beside *hanāṣu* Dt in 24, see below).

Gešû "to belch": G is intrans., or has wind, slime or water (?) as object, cf. CAD sv a, AHw sv G. D is intrans. (TDP 66: 67' (coordinated with a Gtn form); K.3273: 9 (qu. AHw sv D), or has blood or wind as object (AMT 27, 2: 16; TDP 234: 37). Of special interest is RA 17, 176: I 9'f (the Ardat-lilî demon) *ša eṭemmaša ina pî lā ku-teš-šu-u* "whose ghost cannot be belched forth from the mouth" (tr. CAD sv b), where it is doubtless the presence of a real (not inner) direct object (grammatically subject here) which has caused the use of D.

Hanāṣu is semantically difficult. G once occurs in broken context; D is used, first, with animals as subject and *ana* ("to rub oneself against" (said of male animals, as part of the sexual act), acc. to CAD sv 2a, but AHw sv D 2 "die Zähne zeigen"); and, second, with body parts (lips, teeth) as direct object and a personal subject (CAD sv 2b "to rub", AHw sv D 1 "(Nase, Lippen) hochziehen)". The rarity of G does not allow to establish any difference in meaning or use between G and D. *Hanāṣu* is semantically related to *ganāṣu* (cf. AfO 19, 116: 23f), which is the main reason for including it here.

Na'āšu G and D, of uncertain meaning, cf. CAD sv: "The occ[urrence]s refer to the symptoms of a sick person", AHw "in Atemnot geraten?".

Našāhu G and D "to have diarrhea": D only LL: MSL 9, 128: 178f KU = *na-ša-h*[*u*], *nu-šu-*[*hu*].

Nešû G and D "to vomit" (G only LL): D 1x IV R 18 no. 6: 7; further LL: KUB 16, 87: r.14ff *nu-uš-šu* (but in CAD sv *nušû* A listed under the substantive "vomit".

Sa'ālu G (rare) and D "to cough": AHw distinguishes G "husten" from D "lange husten"; this is indicated by cases as: AMT 83, 1: r.17 *amēlu šū ana maldariš ú-sa-al* "that man expectorates continually" (tr. CAD sv b), and *ib.* 51, 1: 10 *šumma amēlu irassu paṭratma ú-sa-'a-a*[*l*] "if a man's chest is not congested and still he expectorates" (tr. CAD *l.c.*; or rather "keeps coughing", cf. 6.6.1), and *ib.* 51, 2: 4 (*šumma*) [*ha*]*hha* dib.meš-*su* (*iṣṣanabbassu*) *ú-sa-al* "(if) coughing fits keep attacking him and he keeps coughing", with D and Gtn in coordination. D also occurs with a direct object (*tābīlu* "dry phlegm", cf. CAD *l.c.* The existence of a causative Š is shown by the occurrence of a passive Št: AMT 54, 1: 9. 12 *uš-ta-áš-'a-al* "he will be made to cough").

Ṣarātu G and D "to break wind"; both CAD and AHw sv assign a durative meaning to D: "to break wind repeatedly", and "dauernd furzen", respectively.

The D-stems of these verbs are paralleled by a small number of D tantum verbs which also denote sounds and bodily functions: *guhhubu* "to cough", *gu''ušu* "to vomit" (AHw sv *gâšu*, but no G attested), and *nuhhuṭu* "to chuckle, hiccup(?)" acc. to CAD, AHw "schnaufen?". In addition, there are a few verbs whose D-stem is used intransitively for some bodily function, with no apparent connection to the meaning of G: *ruppudu* "sich aufbäumen o.ä." (AHw sv *rapādu* II D 3); *ṣubburu* "to have diarrhea" (CAD sv *ṣabāru* A 4a), "Koliken bekommen" (AHw sv *ṣabāru* I D 2), and *šurruhu* "Mund, Maul aufsperren, Gier zeigen" (AHw sv *šarāhu* II D), but CAD sv *šurruhu* "meaning uncertain" (but "to drool" or "to dribble" are suggested in the glosses).

No doubt the larger and much better attested group of D tantum verbs meaning "to pray" (cf. 8.7) are also semantically related to these verbs. They all have a durative nuance in common.

In so far as the verbs of groups I and II are sufficiently frequent to allow conclusions, it seems plausible that the D forms express various nuances of verbal plurality, such as a repetition, a longer duration, or a greater intensity, and that they more or less take the place of Gtn forms in other verbs. It is difficult to prove this for each individual instance, and in some verbs the difference between G and D may have become blurred, but it is suggested by the semantic nature of these verbs, which makes them especially susceptible to such notions as iterative and intensive, and by most of the contexts in which they are used, cf., for instance, the coordination of *sa'ālu* D with Gtn forms and its use in *šumma* clauses (cf. 6.6.1).

7.6.3. Group III

Haṭû "to fail, err, sin": D id. in OB Mari: ARM 13, 24: r.3'; 26/2 p. 254 no. 402: 19; p. 365 no. 449: 13. 26 (2x); Probably to be distinguished from NB *huṭṭû* "to damage, impair", cf. CAD sv 4.

Kapādu "to think, plan" (with inner acc. ("whatever ....", battle, evil, etc.) or *ana*, cf. 5.5.1) is almost always G; D is rare (AbB 5, 172: 20 ("to take care of"?); JNES 17, 137: 5' ([*lemn*]*ēti* "evil")); for the difference with G, cf. perhaps MSL 16, 81: 112f ir^pa-ag^pag = *ka-pa-du* / ir.pag.ag.ag = *kup-pu-du*.

Kaṣāpu (CAD *keṣēpu*) "to account(?), think, plan", D "to plan, devise".

Sâru "to whirl, dance" uses the D-stem in the expression *surta surru* "to make a circle", cf. CAD sv 2.

Ṣarāmu G and D "to strive for, be concerned with"; G is the usual form, D mainly occurs with an object in expressions as LSC 114a: 9 *ēma ú-ṣa-ar-ra-mu lukšud* "may I achieve whatever I strive for" (reading acc. to CAD sv 2; AHw sv D 1/2); in this expression CAD sv (p. 102a) plausibly suggests a contamination of *ṣarāmu* D with *ṣummuru* "to strive for, to plot". D is also attested as a stative *ṣurrum* (ARM 3, 75: 6), beside *ṣarim* "concerned" (esp. OB Mari).

Šadāhu "to march, move in procession" twice occurs in the D-stem with the road as object: VS 1, 36: I 11 DNF *mu-šad-di-hat harrānu*; STT 69: 4 (The Pleiades) *mu-šad-di-hu ṣuṣē* "who walk over the reeds".

The use of *hasāsu* D (normally "to remind") without object in the meaning "to study, think up, investigate" (CAD sv (9)) should also be mentioned here; with object it is found in TDP 182: 42f (*šumma* (...) egir.meš-*šú ú-ha-as-sa-as* "if he (....) (constantly) thinks about his .... ("inheritance"? "future"?)".

In conclusion, the verbs of Type II are exceptional in that their D-stem is intransitive; they go against the general association of the D-stem with high transitivity. On the other hand, most of them are extremely rare, and/or highly specialized in meaning.

Notes to Chapter Seven

1 The following account is primarily based on Nedyalkov-Silnitsky 1973; Comrie 1981: 158ff; 1985. For the concept of valency, see Lyons 1977: 486ff; Comrie 1981: 51ff.

2 Akkadian has also lexical causatives, such as *dâku* "to kill" versus *mâtu* "to die" (beside *mâtu* Š "to cause to die"), and occasionally forms analytical causatives by means of *nadānu* "to give". These are "permissive" causatives, cf. CAD sv 11 "to permit"; see for this term Nedyalkov-Silnitzky 1973: 10ff.

3 For Modern Arabic, for instance, Saad 1982: 69f, lists four groups of transitive verbs which have a causative (expressed by Stem II or IV): 1. physical perception inchoative verbs; 2. cognitive inchoative verbs; 3. cognitive active verbs; 4. *akala* "to eat" and *šariba* "to drink". In Classical Arabic the range was somewhat wider (*o.c.* 71). Cf. also Saad and Bolozky 1984: 33 for Arabic, 34 for Hebrew. The much wider use of trivalent causatives in Akkadian (cf. 7.2.6) seems to be rather atypical.

4 This is in accordance with the current view in general linguistics which claims that syntax is a higher level of grammar than morphology, and that "the forms of words are specified with respect to syntactic concepts, not the other way around" (Fillmore 1968: 3).

5 Cf. Berry 1975: I 156f; she distinguishes between *unrestricted* processes ("the type of process which combines equally well with either one or two participants"), e.g., *to open, break, warm,* and *restricted* processes ("the type of process which is associated with a relatively fixed number of participants"); this fixed number can be two, e.g., *to hit, throw, kick*, or one, e.g., *to run, walk, dance.*

6 The term factitive has the disadvantage that in general linguistics it is employed in a variety of meanings. One can speak of a "factitive" causative as opposed to a "permissive" causative, to indicate the difference between "to cause or force", and "to let or allow" someone to do something; cf., for instance, Nedyalkov-Silnitsky 1973: 10. Lyons (1977: II 491ff) defines factitive verbs as verbs denoting "a process or event whereby a cause produces an effect (or result)", as opposed to "operative" verbs, which concentrate on how an action is performed upon, or affects, the patient. On the other hand, the term factitive is well established in Semitic studies, and although it is defined here in a different way than elsewhere, there is in practice a considerable overlap between verbs which are factitive according to the usual definition, and those which are factitive according to the definition adopted here. Therefore, it seems preferable to adhere to it rather than to coin some new term.

7 There is also a large group which can use both stems; in most of these cases one of them is clearly the usual form, whereas the other one is either very rare or restricted to specific contexts. Thus even in that case we can usually establish one basic causative stem. The verbs which use both D and Š to express an increase in valency are discussed in 7.5.

8 There is a clear correlation between *ra'ābu,* which typically has an animate subject and a Š-stem (cf. AHw sv), and the (etymologically related?) verb *râbu* "to shake, tremble", which typically has an inanimate subject (usually heaven, earth, and *rību* "earthquake", cf. AHw sv *r.* I G) and a D-stem. The other verbs for "to tremble, shake, quake, etc." also tend to have inanimate subjects and a D-stem, but usually with less consistency (see the dictionaries ssvv *narāṭu, nâšu* and *tarāru*; for *šâbu* see 7.2.4).

9 Only one of the verbs of this type is reported to have a Š-stem by AHw, viz. *šêtu* "to leave (over)"; the two instances mentioned are, however, very doubtful. CAD does not list a Š-stem of any of the relevant verbs. The fact that two verbs have a Št-stem (*ṣâlu* "to quarrel" (1x, emended, cf. AHw sv)) and *šâmu* "to establish") does not contradict the rule, because this stem often exists independently of the Š-stem, and the formal reason which motivates the non-existence of a Š-stem does not apply to it.

10 All the same, *izuzzu* "to stand" has a Š-stem *ušzaz, ušziz* (beside *ušazza/iz*), cf. GAG § 107f/g.

11 AHw sv D inconsistently translates the D-stem as "ausrufen" (not causative!), but the participle *musassianu* as "der den Ausruf veranlaßt" (677b sv).

12 In OB, for instance, we find the forms *uš-ta-as-sí-ši* (AbB 3, 2: 25, acc. to AHw sv Š 1b and CAD sv 12) and *tu-uš-ta-ÁŠ-si* (UET 5, 26: 25), which are interpreted by the dictionaries as Š-stems, presumably correctly, but which - from a formal point of view - could also be D-stems. The later form *ušalsa* is unequivocally a Š-stem.

13 An uncertain case which is reputed to be a causative D-stem is that of *raqādu* "to dance" in KAR 158: II 40 *enūma tu-ra-aq-qi-du anta*, for which AHw sv D proposes "zum Tanzen bringen?". However, the passage is completely obscure.

14 Several scholars who advocated the traditional view concerning the D-stem outlined in Chapter I, have expressed the feeling that only the Š-stem is a real causative, whereas the D-stem, in spite of its causative function, is not. Wright, for instance, states (1896/98: 31) that "the causative or factitive signification is common to the second and fourth forms [i.e. the D-stem and the Š-stem], the apparent difference being that it is original in the latter, but derived in the former." A similar idea is expressed by Ryder 1974: 91, and by Porges 1875: 45 (as quoted by Ryder 1974: 162).

15 There are very few Š-stems which have an unpredictable non-causative meaning. They comprise a few lexicalized forms such as *šulputu* "to destroy", from *lapātu* "to touch, smear, affect", *šūzubu* "to rescue", from *ezēbu* "to leave, abandon", and *šurbubu* "to rest, relax" (intrans.!) from *rabābu* "to be(come) weak, soft", and a few denominative verbs, such as *šuklulu* "to make complete, perfect" from *kullatu* "totality", cf. 8.3.2 and GAG § 89e.

16 The relevant instances included in CAD sv 5 comprise the following inanimate subjects, apart from the ones mentioned in (07) - (12): in 5a: threads (see Excursus (c)) and spun material; in 5b: oil, splendour, words, lichen, roots, moles, scars, warts; in lex. sect: greatness. The animals include snakes+scorpions, ants and wild pigs. The human(like) subjects are gods, soldiers, kings+governors (quoted as (13)) and demons (4 cases in total).

17 A selection of illustrative cases of *malû* G with a direct object which are interpreted incorrectly in text editions and in CAD is :

(a) ARM 27, 27: 6ff quoted as (09) above: Birot's translation "Les deux rives du Habur en sont pleines" is ungrammatical (no agreement between subject and predicate).

(b) Maqlû I 23 quoted as (11); The translation given here (cf. also CAD sv *maštakal* c) is preferable to that of Von Soden *apud* Meyer, AfO 21, 71a *ad* Z. 23 "wovon die Erde voll ist" (*maštakal* is fem. acc. to AMT 85, 1: II 16, cf. CAD sv b-1').

(c) Maqlû I 9 *qû im-ta-na-al-lu-ú pīja*: as it stands, this can only mean "threads fill/cover my mouth repeatedly" (or "completely"?, cf. 4.2.3); the translation of CAD sv 5a, with "they" (i.e., the sorcerers) as subject requires an emendation of *im* to *um*, cf. also Von Soden, AfO 21, 71a *ad* Z. 9.

(d) TDP 178: 16 *šumma* (...) *ahhāzu pānīšu* si.a.meš "if jaundice covers his face time and again" (or:

"completely"?, cf. 4.2.3): si.a.meš should be interpreted as *imtanalla*, not *umtanalli*, as Labat does.

(e) CT 39, 16: 49 *šumma* (...) *mūša ahāt* [*nāri*] *im-lu-ma* "if its water has covered the banks [of the river]" is quoted by CAD erroneously under 1b instead of 5.

(f) Ash. 106: 20 *ummānī māt GN ana sihirtiša kīma išpati ú-mal-li* is quoted by CAD sv 7h with "my army" as subject; however, "I" must be the subject, in accordance with Borger's translation.

(g) Gilg. XI 123 "(Did I give birth to my people) *kî mārī nūnī ú-ma-al-la-a tâmtamma* "(only) to fill the sea (with them) as with fish-spawn?" This translation makes the clause far more dramatic than the usual translation with *nišū'a* (line 122) as subject of *umallâ* (e.g., CAD sv *malû* 7h). The ending *-â* does not pose a difficult problem, since it is often used vacuously in the SB version of Gilgameš (e.g., I III 35).

There are, however, some problematical cases:

(h) CT 39, 50b: r.14 *šumma lū murašû lū šikkû qaqqara ú-mál-<lu>-ú* "if wild cats or mongooses cover the area" (*imallû* expected).

(i) AbB 13, 5: r.5'f *apparātim ša GN mê li-im-lu-ú*: as the text stands, *malû* serves here as a factitive G-stem: "let them fill the marshes of GN with water", which is highly unusual (but see (m) below and 11.4.2). Alternatively, we could emend the verb to *li-ma-lu-ú*, or *mê* to *mû* (as in line 12): "let water fill the marshes of GN". Restore [*ap-pa-ra-ti*]*m* in 12?

(j) Asb. A IX 45 (and elsewhere) "prisoners of war and cattle *naphar mātija* (...) *um-dal/da-al-lu-ú/u* "filled my entire country", where we expect a G-stem: although it may be a Dt with plural subject (cf. 9.1.5), rather than a factitive perfect (note that the rest of the passage uses the preterite), it is more likely to be an error for "I filled"; the parallel passage Asb. B 82: 15 with *un-ta(-na)-al-lu-u* seems to have "my troops" (line 6) as subject, cf. Piepkorn's translation (AS 5, 83).

(k) BagM. 21, 344: 15f *gulgullātīšunu kima* na_4.meš *šadî* kur.meš *u nahal um-tal-lu* "Ihre Schädel, wie Bergsteine, füllten Berge und Wadis" (tr. Cavigneaux/Ismail): this translation requires a G-stem; it seems best to regard *um-tal-lu* as a bad spelling for a first p. sg. perfect *um-tal-li* (just as in the parallel sentence 360: 37); the alternative solution, to regard it as a passive Dt with "mountains and wadis" as subject, is stylistically improbable.

(l) Šurpu VII 32 *ru'tu rupuštu pīšu im-ta-li* (var. *um-tal-li*) "spittle and foam has filled his mouth": the D form represents an inferior variant.

(m) RA 15, 181: 8 *ta-am-ta-le-e qātišša* "you have handed over to her" (in obscure context); it looks like a factitive G-stem, cf. 11.4.2; this idiom normally has a D form, cf. CAD sv 9c-1'.

18 *Lamādu* D "to inform, teach" is normally construed with a personal object (the person informed or taught), whereas the contents of the information is added by means of *aššum*, cf. CAD sv 7a, *pace* AHw sv D 1. The double object we would expect if it were a pure factitive of G "to know, learn" is unusual, except in OA for the meaning "to inform", cf. CAD sv 7a and "to charge a price to sb", cf. Veenhof 1972: 418ff, and in Nuzi and LB for "to teach", interchanging with *ana*, *ib.* 7b). This state of affairs is also found in the more or less synonymous verb *edû* (CAD: *idû*) "to know". Its D-stem *(w)uddû* is regularly combined with only one object, either personal ("to inform sb"), or inanimate ("to mark, identify, to assign"); in the latter case an additional person is introduced by *ana* (CAD sv 4e). The expected double object occurs only exceptionally (RA 75, 111: VII 16 (unless *-ši* stands for *-šim*)). Likewise, *hasāsu* "to mention, think about, remember" usually has only a personal object in the D-stem ("to remind sb"), rather than a double object, cf. CAD sv 8 (a rare instance with a double accusative is PennsOATexts 9: 18ff (OA)).

19 Indo-European scholars who advocate a unitary origin for all verbs of this type generally derive the causative meaning from the intensive, just as it is done in Semitic with the D-stem, cf. Jamison 1983: 9ff

(Jamison herself dissents from this view and argues them to be of different origin); cf. also Kuryłowicz 1964: 85ff. Verbs with the suffix *-jan* in Germanic also share intensive and causative meaning, cf. Von Kienle 1960: 261.

20 Kraus speaks of "Koppelung" instead of hendiadys (1987: 3ff). We will not go into the many problems associated with this construction. It seems, however, that if we want to define it as a syntactic phenomenon in its own right, we have to impose much stricter conditions on it than Kraus does. Perhaps the most important of these is that there must be a semantic relation of subordination: i.e., the meaning of the main verb must be noticeably modified by that of the preceding verb, and the meaning of the two verbs together must be different from that of the verbs individually. Without such conditions, cases of "Koppelung" can hardly be distinguished from cases of ordinary coordination.

21 Uncertain or spurious cases of factitive D-stems used intransitively are the D-stems of *ezēzu* "to be(come) furious", *berû* "to be(come) hungry" and *ṣamû* "to be(come) thirsty". *Ezēzu* D "to make furious", is reported by CAD sv 2 to be intransitive: "to become furious". However, in none of the instances mentioned this meaning is indisputable: VS 10, 214: IV 15 *kî uz-za-zu rigimša* is transitive: "if she makes her crying furious" (if the reading is correct: Gröneberg, RA 75, 109 *ad l.* reads *uz-za-šu*); BWL 146: 6 *bēlū dīnika* UZ-*za-zu ina muhhika* is doubtless from *izuzzu* "to stand up, rise", rather than from *ezēzu* D; cf. AoF 10, 59f: no. 7: 6' *ummiānum ina muhhika lā iz-za-a-az* "laß der Glaübiger nicht gegen dich auftreten" (tr. Kraus, and cf. Kraus's note *ad* l. 6'; cf. also AbB 2, 141: 14, Landsberger, ZDMG 69, 510, and the expression *izuzzu eli* "to prevail over" (Izbu 206: 29). This suggests that VS 10, 214: VIII 26f [D]N UZ-*zi-iz išnû* [*pa*]*nūša palhiš* is also from *izuzzu*: "she (Ṣaltu) rose, her face fearsomely distorted (with anger)" (we can either read UZ as IZ_x, or regard *uzzaz* as a variant of *izzaz*, cf. the infinitives *izuzzu* and *uzuzzu* (GAG § 107d)). The forms [*u*]*z-za-ta* and *uz-za-at* mentioned CAD sv 2 cannot be derived from *ezēzu* D.

Berû and *ṣamû* seem to have an intransitive D in BWL 144: 16 *bur-ru-ú akālu ṣu-um-mu-ú šatû eli amēli illak*, if we follow the translation of Lambert ("Hunger and eating, thirst and drinking, come upon a man") or CAD sv *akālu* 1a-5' (A/1 p. 249b): "to eat when one is hungry, to drink when one is thirsty (only this) is befitting to a person". The interpretation is difficult, but *burrû* and *ṣummû* seem to be verbal adjectives rather than infinitives: "for a hungry one to eat, and a thirsty one to drink fits a man" (which agrees with CAD's translation). For the infinitive construction, cf. AbB 1, 124: 31ff (compared with 23f). If this is correct, these verbs do not have an intransitive D-stem.

22 The semantic change "to loosen" → "to depart" is paralleled by other verbs as *paṭāru* and *nasāhu*; the act of loosening and the concomitant separation of the objects involved is metaphorically extended to the act of loosening oneself from a place, i.e., to departing; English *to leave* (originally transitive: "to leave behind") and French *partir* (originally "to divide") show a similar metaphorical extension.

23 The following exceptions can be noted: prefix forms of Š are AbB 3, 31: 14; Or. 17, 307: 17; Erra IV 121; AMT 64, 1: 7 (glossed as uncertain by CAD sv *a.* B 3); the VA D occurs St. Reiner 192: 62 and SAA 10, 226: r. 2 (the latter is probably a plural form of *ablu,* cf. 10.6.1). Other forms quoted AHw sv *ubbulu* are obscure, cf. *uppulu.*

24 This claim is not invalidated by the fact that such D forms, just as other transitive verbs, can be used in contexts which imply that the subject does not perform the action himself, but lets someone else do it. For example, *šaṭāru* D "to write" is regularly translated as "faire écrire" in French publications, especially those of Mari documents (e.g., by Birot in ARM 14, 62: 15 and 70: 10, and passim). This is not incorrect, since it is likely that most senders did not write their letters themselves, but the causative meaning is purely contextual in such cases, and not expressed by the D form in question; for the meaning of *šaṭāru* D

see 6.4.8 and 6.8.1, and for this type of "pseudo-causatives" see Rundgren 1966: 133f.

25 CAD sv. *k*. A 4c assigns this expression to the homonymous verb *kamāsu* "to assemble", which is very improbable, since *kamāsu* "to assemble" implies a plurality of people, whereas the NA stative *kammus* is often said of a single person. The semantic development "to kneel, squat" > "to stay, dwell" seems perfectly natural, cf. the same polysemy in *(w)ašābu* "to sit (down), to reside" (cf. CAD sv *ašābu* 2).

26 Besides, in NA D has a lexicalized meaning "to set aside, remove" (CAD sv 6); *ullû* is also used as a literary variant of *elû* "high", comparable to the cases mentioned in 10.7.2, cf. App. to Ch. X sv. AbB 1, 123: 10 *še'am lu-li-am* is doubtless a scribal error for *lu-<še>-li-am* (with haplography of the first part (ŠE) of LI).

27 CAD sv 14c ascribes a further meaning to *nakāru* Š, viz. "to instigate sb to remove (an inscription)", in VS 5, 143: 7 *ša dibbī annûtu ú-[nak-kar ú]-šam-kar* "who removes these words or incites someone to remove (them)". If restoration and interpretation are correct, this is perhaps a unique instance of Š as a causative of D. However, it is clearly secondary: it is modelled on similar idioms with G versus Š (cf. the dictionaries ssvv *pašāṭu, šaṭāru, dabābu*, etc.), and occurs in a LB contract from the Achaemenid period. For RA 70, 111: M 7 *[appātīš]unu ú-ša-ag-li-ib* (cf. *gullubu* "to shave") see note 35.

28 An exception is RIMA 2/I, 257: 11 RN *qa-di-id kal malkī* "subduer of all princes" (tr. Grayson); it is attractive to accept Von Soden's emendation *<mu>-qa-di-id* (AHw sv G 6), but not absolutely necessary: since we have to do with tendencies, not rules, occasional deviations are to be expected, in particular as a result of stylistic considerations. Grayson's note disregards the difference between *qadādu* G and D.

29 Von Soden 1932/33: I 166ff) does not include royal inscriptions in his corpus of texts, but states (174 note 3) that they have taken over many elements from the literary language he describes. With respect to the use of the "literary Š-stem", they do not differ at all from the other texts which he defines as literary.

30 There is a striking difference between Enuma Eliš and Erra, on the one hand, and other epic texts, such as Gilgameš, Atrahasis, Anzû, Etana and Adapa, on the other, in their use of the "literary Š-stems". In the latter texts hardly any literary Š-stems are found. This contrast correlates with the period in which they are believed to have been created: they date from the OB period, whereas Enuma Eliš and Erra date from MB times or later. For a general discussion and characterization of literary texts, see Oppenheim 1964: 250ff; Kraus 1973: 32f; GAG § 186 and 191.

31 Although we occasionally find phrases which are clearly influenced by literary diction, especially in NA and NB letters, which are mostly written by scholars, cf. Parpola 1970/83: II 442f for an enumeration of blessings and greeting formulae with literary phraseology.

32 CAD sv 8 translates *lamādu* Š as "to cause to teach", making it a causative of D. This is quite unusual, cf. GAG § 89c Anm. (but see note 27). In order to prove that this is correct, we need instances in which all three participants supposed to be present in such a causative sentence are explicitly mentioned. However, in none of the instances of *lamādu* Š the causee (the one who does the actual teaching) is mentioned. Therefore, BWL 40: 32 *puluhti ekalli ummān ú-šal-mid* means "I taught the populace reverence for the palace", as correctly translated by Lambert, not "I had the people taught ...", as claimed by CAD.

33 Instances from peripheral dialects and some obscure or broken cases (KAR 4: r.7 and St. Reiner 190: 28) are not taken into account here.

34 The translation is Lambert's *ad l.*, except that Lambert translates "exalted" for "raised". An unbiased translation seems to require "to raise" rather than "to exalt", which fits the context less well, since the

subject is the father (although it cannot be quite excluded).

35 Similar cases (but very uncertain) may be Ee V 63 *ú-šá-aZ-bi-i'*, which is tentatively derived from *ṣubbû* "to inspect, devise" by CAD note sv *sabā'u*, and Tn-Ep. V 21 *ú-še-eg-[li-l]a gillātīšu* "he committed many sins against me" (reading and tr. CAD sv *gullulu* v. d), with a Š form instead of the usual D-stem *gullulu* (cf. 8.4.2 sv) in a paronomastic construction. The two texts in which they occur belong to the ones which abound in literary Š-stems; this supports the view that the exceptional Š forms should be explained in the same way as the other forms discussed in this section and the next ones. A third case may be RA 70, 111: M 7 (the king) *[appātīš]unu ú-ša-ag-li-ib* // G 19 *appātīšunu ú-ga-al-li-i[b]* "shaved off their *abbuttu*" (cf. CAD sv *appatu* A end) with Š and D as variants. It stems from an OB historical epic, a literary text which, however, does not show any other literary Š-stems. Another possibility that suggests itself is that the Š form is a causative of the D tantum verb *gullubu*. This might theoretically seem conceivable, but causative Š-stems of D stems cannot be demonstrated with certainty for Akkadian, cf. note 27.

36 Spurious or doubtful instances are *ú-šá-da-ba* (ABL 1419: 9, qu. AHw sv Š 1a), which is derived from *tebû* by Lanfranchi and Parpola, SAA 5, 58: 9 (cf. glossary p. 239b sv), and MARI 7, 178: r.7' *uš-te-*TI*-ib-šu*: error for *uš-te-ri-ib-šu* ?

37 Note that we do not take into account cases of deviating dialectal use of D or Š which are only attested in peripheral areas of Akkadian: *balāṭu* Š (1x, cf. CAD sv 12), *târu* Š (cf. AHw sv Š), and *hamāṭu* D "to hurry" (cf. CAD sv *h.* A 3a (for 3b (MA) see *h.* B in 7.4.2.)) in El Amarna; *tebû* D (1x, cf. AHw sv D) in Ugarit (intransitive, probably a scribal error).

38 This does not imply that a D-stem cannot be trivalent: there are some trivalent D-stems such as *kullumu* "to show sth to sb", with a double accusative. However, they are not derived from a bivalent form of the same verb (there is no verb **kalāmu* "to see", or something similar). They are parallel to trivalent basic verbs, such as *paqādu* "to provide sb with sth" and *râmu* "to donate", both with a double accusative.

39 The use of the Š-stem as a literary variant of the factitive D-stem also has a bearing on the problem of the "elative" in Akkadian. Speiser (1967: 465ff) claims that a number of Akkadian words of the pattern *šuprus* are not derived from the causative Š-stem, but are adjectives - going back to Proto-Semitic - with "elative" function, i.e., they denote "some intensification of the basic meaning" (1967: 473), and that the causative is "a specialized, and hence later, application of the morpheme used for the elative." (1967: 493). Examples of elatives adduced by Speiser (1967: 473ff) include *šurbû* "supreme", *šūturu* "surpassing", *šušqû* "exalted", *šūquru* "most precious", *šupšuqu* "most difficult" and *šumruṣu* "sorely afflicted, painful" (Speiser's translations).

However, most of the forms quoted by him as elatives belong to verbs which use either the Š-stem or both D and Š as factitives, but not just the D-stem, in spite of the fact that they are typical stative verbs associated with adjectives. As we saw in 7.2.2, such verbs have a strong predilection for the D-stem, rather than the Š-stem, as factitive. This also applies to other "elatives" which are not mentioned by Speiser, such as *šūpû* "brillant, famous", *šūsumu* "fitting, proper", *šū/ēzuzu* "furious, raging" and *šušruhu* "glorified" (cf. CAD ssvv). This strongly suggests that they are ordinary derivatives of the corresponding Š-stems with the same status as other statives and verbal adjectives, and have the same secondary, literary origin as those Š-stems.

Whether they are real elatives, i.e., whether they denote an "intensification", as compared to the normal adjective or stative of the G-stem, is very difficult to establish (cf. 10.8). The most obvious difference with the corresponding simple adjectives is a stylistic one: they are highly restricted in use: they occur only in a small number of literary texts, mostly as epithets of gods, kings, or highly esteemed, often religious, objects, acts and institutions. The only exception to this is *šumruṣu*, from *marāṣu* "to be(come) ill, annoyed", which normally has a factitive Š-stem (cf. 7.2.3); *šumruṣu* serves as the ordinary stative or verbal adjective of *marāṣu* and is not restricted to literary texts, cf. CAD sv *marāṣu* 6 and *šumruṣu* adj. Its use is parallel to that of *purrus* forms of verbs which have a factitive D-stem (cf. Chapter X).

40 An alternative explanation is to regard these three instances as factitives or causatives. In that case these sentences are transformations of intransitive sentences with *bikâtu, rigimšu* and *pāšu* as subject (cf. 7.1). This is unprobable, however, at least for the first two, because *nasāsu* is only attested with animate subjects (*pāšu* could be regarded as such in a metonymical sense).

41 This may provide an explanation for an exceptional form such as [*u*]*d-da-ab-*[*b*]*a-*[*a*]*b* in FM 1 p. 82: 16, for which the context suggests "he is complaining all the time" (Joannès: "il a multiplié les plaintes"), but which can only be a present Dt (Joannès's transcription [*u*]*d-da-ab-bi-ib* is inconsistent with the copy). Furthermore, it suggests that the very frequent *-t-* forms of the verb *nâdu* "to praise" are not Dtn forms, as is assumed by the dictionaries (e.g., CAD sv 4/5), but Dt forms. The dictionaries do not list an unambiguous Dtn form (i.e., with the infix *-tan-*); the only present forms attested are KAR 119: r.11 = BWL 120: 11 *ut-ta-'a-a-ḍ*[*a*], which is emended to *ut-ta-<na>-'a-a-*[*da*] by CAD sv lex. sect. and by AHw sv Dtn (with *du* for *da*), and SBH p. 22 no. 10: 65 *ut-ta-'a-ad*, which may be a passive Dt, however (cf. AHw sv Dt).

APPENDIX TO CHAPTER SEVEN: List of factitive D-stems.

The following points should be noted. First of all, for a D-stem to qualify as factitive, it should be attested in an unambiguously factitive sentence, i.e., normally in a sentence with an object, or at least an agentive subject (see 7.3.4). Statives and VAs have an ambiguous status (cf. note 2 to Ch. V): if they are derived from a common factitive D-stem and show the expected resultative meaning, they are included here among the factitive D-stems (although strictly speaking they are not factitive themselves, cf. 7.3.4). However, D-stems which *only* occur as statives or (verbal) adjectives are not listed here, but in Chapter X, which deals with the pattern *purrus*. *Purrus* adjectives are also listed in Chapter X, whereas the corresponding factitive D-stem is listed here; the verb *burrumu* "to weave, twine", for instance, lit. "to make multicoloured" is listed below, but the adjective *burrumu* is to be found in the Appendix to Chapter X.

The status of Dt forms is also ambiguous: in so far as they are passive/intransitive derivations of a factitive D-stem, they have been included in the list. If such a Dt-stem is discussed in Chapter IX, which deals with the secondary stems derived from the D-stem, this is indicated by a reference to the relevant section. Many Dt forms, however, are directly derived from a *purrus* adjective, without the intermediate stage of a factitive D-stem (see 9.1.4), and a few may be direct derivations of a Gt-stem (see 9.1.5), so that the existence of a Dt-stem is not sufficient to prove the existence of a factitive D-stem. If, therefore, a verb has a Dt-stem without a D-stem being attested, it is not listed in this Appendix. If such a verb is discussed elsewhere, it can be traced by means of the Index of Akkadian Words. Factitive Dtn and ŠD forms are listed and discussed in 9.2 and 9.3 respectively.

References are added only for instances which cannot or cannot easily be found in the dictionaries, and for verbs which occur only a few times. In some cases, additional references from texts which have appeared since the publication of the dictionaries, have been included, especially in the case of very rare or otherwise interesting verbs. If no meaning of the D-stem is given, it simply serves as the factitive counterpart of G (cf. 7.1). If a verb also has a factitive Š-stem, this is indicated by means of "+Š", with a reference to the section in which Š-stem in question is discussed. Note that forms belonging to the "lexical" Št-stem have not been included in this list. Pu refers to a *purrus* stative or (verbal) adjective, Dt to a Dt-stem.

If the meaning of the G-stem of an adjectival verb is glossed with "to be", this G-stem is only attested as a stative or an adjective (and sometimes as an infinitive as the citation form in a lexical list, cf. note 2 to Ch. V); with "to be(come)" it is indicated that also prefix forms are found. Since it is impossible to draw a clear dividing line between D-stems derived from adjectives and those derived from fientive verbs, they are presented here as one category.

A

Abālu "to be(come) dry", D fact. (also ARM 26/2 p. 260 no. 404: 43); +Š → 7.5.1; for Dt → 9.1.1.

Adāru "to be dark, worried": mostly factitive Š, rarely D → 7.5.6 (more often stative D and Dt → 9.1.4); for Dt → 9.1.1. This *adāru* (≈ *a.* B in CAD), often spelled with *h*, is an adjectival verb, to be separated from *adāru* "to fear", not spelled with *h*, which is basically a fientive verb. However, the meaning of the two verbs is so similar that in many contexts it is difficult to determine which of them is meant.

Akāšu "to go to": D/Dtn "to drive out, displace" (same verb?); for G, cf. comment of CAD A/1 265 sv.

Anāhu "to be(come) tired, exert oneself": D uncertain, mainly OA → 7.5.6; for Dt → 7.6.1 (same verb?).

Apālu "to be (too) late": D → 7.4.3 (intrans.); for Dt → 9.1.4.

Arāhu "to be quick, go/come quickly": D "to send quickly" (also ARM 26/1 p. 32 note 132 A.2057: 37), "to do quickly" in hendiadys (also Š) → 7.4.1, and intrans. → 7.4.3. This verb is to be distinguished from *arāhu* "to devour, destroy" (also D, cf. AHw sv *a.* II D, CAD sv *a.* B (with a different arrangement of some forms), and from *urruhu* "to frighten" (AHw sv *a.* I D 4, CAD sv *a.* A lex. sect.). [For AbB 9, 66: 11 see *šarāhu* Dt].

Arāku "to be(come) long": D fact., also in hendiadys → 7.4.1; +Š lit. → 7.5.5.1.

Arāru "to fear, be agitated" (but AHw: "zittern, flackern"): D "to cause fear, panic" (AHw "aufstören, aufscheuchen") Angim p. 70: 89 (gods); also TCL 18, 90: 34 (town); for Dt → 9.1.1.

Ašāšu "to be(come) worried": D/Dt "to cause distress, mistreat" (mostly stative → App. to Ch. X sv); for Dt → 9.1.1.

B

Ba'ālu "to be(come) abnormally large": D/Dtn fact. AK 1, 21: II 1 (= St. Kraus 198: 52), but assigned to *bêlu* by CAD sv *bêlu* 2 ("to make sb a ruler"); also AbB 3, 15: 13. 23 (losses).

Ba'āšu "to be(come) bad, smell bad": D "to cause to smell bad, besmirch".

Bahāru (CAD: *buhhuru*) "to be hot, cooked": D/Dtn fact. → 8.4.1.

Bahû "to be thin, emaciated": D fact. 1x AMT 45, 5: 14 (body).

Balāṣu "to stare, protrude" (eyes or anus): D "to set in a fixed stare, to make protrude"

Balāṭu "to be(come) well, be alive": D "to keep alive, in good health, heal, provide with food"; Dt → 9.1.1.

Banû "to be beautiful, pleasant": D "to adorn, beautify, provide with", also AbB 12, 168: 12; also in hendiadys → 7.4.1.

Barāmu "to be multicoloured": D fact., also "to weave, twine", also SpTU 1, 1: II 9'; 3, 80: 11 → 8.4.1.

Barû "to see" (cf. 5.5.2): D "to announce, usher in"; +Š "to let see" → 7.5.4.

Bâru "to stay firm, become certain": D "to establish (in court), to prove sb's guilt or liability".

Bâšu (CAD *ba'āšu* B) "to come to shame": D "to put to shame"; +Š ? → 7.5.6.

Belû "to go out" (fire): D "to extinguish".

Berû "to be(come) hungry": D fact.; for BWL 144: 16 *bur-ru-ú* see note 21. [The Š forms mentioned in AHw sv *b.* II Š (TP I 8 = RIMA 2/I, 12: 8 *mu-še-eb-ru ṣēnī* (DN) "who exposes the wicked"; also VS 1, 71: 8) probably belong to *barû* Š "to show"].

D

Da'āmu "to be(come) dark": D fact. → 8.4.1 (if KAR 80: r.32 // RA 26, 41: r.9 *ú-da-i-mu* (obj. *liptīja* "my ...-s") belongs here, as claimed by AHw sv D, but acc. to CAD sv *dâmu* it belongs to *dâmu* "to be giddy, to stagger").

Dalālu "to be inferior": D "to oppress" (only infin.).

Dalāpu "to be or stay awake" (G also factitive → 11.4.2): D "to keep awake, harass"; +Š → 7.5.6.

Dâlu "to wander around, be restless": D "to make restless, anxious" ? (AHw sv D "in Unruhe versetzen", but CAD sv 2 "to show indifference") AbB 6, 190: r.10'; ARM 1, 61: 9 (cf. Š in 38); OEC 6, 13: 2; cf. also stative in AbB 8, 102: 12. 37; all from the same verb? (cf. note CAD sv p. 59).

Damāqu "to be(come) good": D/Dt(n) (?); in hendiadys → 7.4.1; also intrans. → 7.4.2; +Š lit. → 7.5.5.2.

Damû "to have convulsions": D "to cause convulsions", acc. to CAD sv, but AHw sv *dummû* translates D as "weinend halten" (denominative of *dimtu* "tear").

Danānu "to be(come) strong": D/ŠD fact.; D also in hendiadys → 7.4.1; for Dt → 9.1.1.

Dašāpu "to be sweet": D fact. ZA 61, 58: 178; BWL 172: IV 9 → 8.4.1.

Dešû "to be abundant": D/Dt(n) "to make abundant, to provide lavishly" → 8.4.1; for Dt → 9.1.1.

E

Ebēbu "to be(come) pure": D fact.; also intrans. → 7.4.3; +Š → 7.5.6; for Dt → 9.1.1 and 9.1.2.

Ebēṭu "to be tied, have cramps", D "to cause cramps", acc. to CAD, but AHw: etwa "unter Krämpfen anschwellen?", D "zum Schwellen bringen" (obj. feet, tongue); its precise meaning and relation with other verb(s) *ebēṭu* and *ubbuṭu* are unclear.

Ebû "to be(come) thick" (G precative in ZA 75, 200: 35): D fact. YOS 11, 26: I 26 (*tu-ú-ba*); intrans. as part. AS 16, 24: 95 *mu-um-bi-[u]m* "boaster, braggart" (LL, equated with *mukabbirum* and *muktabbirum*, cf. *kabāru* below, → 7.4.3.

Edēdu "to be(come) pointed": D "to act quickly" in hendiadys → 7.4.1.

Edēšu "to be(come) new": D/Dtn fact.; D also in hendiadys → 7.4.1; for Dt → 9.1.2. For *uššušu* → 8.4.1 and 11.2.2.

Edû (CAD *idû*) and *wa/edû* "to know": D (*(w)uddû*)/Dt/ŠD "to inform, to mark, identify, to assign"; +Š → 7.5.4.

Ekēlu "to be(come) dark": D fact.; +Š ? → 7.5.6; for Dt → 9.1.1.

Ekû (CAD *akû* A adj.) "to be poor, orphaned": D fact. RIME 4, 604: 69.

Elēlu "to be(come) pure": D fact.; for Dt → 9.1.1 and 9.1.2.

Elēpu "to sprout, grow, stretch forth": D 1x uncertain (BBS 6: I 24 "to lengthen"?); 1x Dt(n) "to produce" (fruit) KB 3/1, 150: 27 acc. to AHw sv Dtn; VAB 4, 190: II 6 // YOS 9, 85: 29 *li-te-el-li-pu* (subject offspring) may be Gtn or Dt; +Š ? (obscure, cf. CAD sv 1c end); for Dt → 9.1.1.

Elēṣu "to swell, rejoice": D fact. only CT 37, 22a: 11; elsewhere D in *ulluṣ libbi* or *kabatti*; otherwise Š is used, cf. CAD sv 3.

Elû "to be high, go up": D/Dt(n) "to make high, raise", versus Š "to cause to go up" → 7.5.3.

Emēdu "to lean against (intrans.), to reach" (G also factitive → 11.4.2): D "to lean against" (trans.), to place, impose", cf. CAD sv 4; + Š → 7.5.4.

Emēmu "to be(come) hot": D fact.

Emēṣu "to be(come) hungry": D fact. CTMMA 78: a 31 acc. to Hecker, NABU 90/139.

Enēšu "to be(come) weak": D fact.; +Š lit. → 7.5.5.2; for Dt → 9.1.1.

Epēqu "to be massive, solid" (but trans. acc. to AHw sv): D "to solidify, to concentrate" (troops), cf. CAD sv *e.* A 2 (also AfO 19, 63: 43 acc. to AHw sv D 3 (qu. as ZA 4, 228: 15)); for Dt → 9.1.4.

Epēsu "to object, be difficult" (?): D "to protest, raise objections" (also intrans.) → 7.4.3.

Erēbu "to enter" has a causative Š, but D occasionally in specialized meaning "to enter" (into a document) in OB → 7.5.4: TCL 11, 200: 21'; AbB 3, 3: 21; 6, 144: 14.

Erēru "to be(come) dry" (G present in BAM 22: 34): D fact. (cf. Köcher, AS 16, 323ff).

Erû "to be naked": D "to bare, strip" (skull, ground).

Êru "to be(come) awake": factitive D uncertain: JCS 8, 89a: 13a (or from *(w)âru* "to go"?).

Ešēbu "to grow luxuriantly": D 1x "to plant" AbB 10, 42: 7 acc. to Von Soden, BiOr 43, 734. [For TP VII 27 *lu-uš-šib* read *lu-uš-me-li* (*malû* ŠD), cf. RIMA 2/I, 27: 27].

Etēku (AHw *etāku*) "to be on the alert" (CAD), "sich beeilen" (AHw): D "to alert" and "zu Eile antreiben", respectively, 2x NA: ABL 170: r.14; 641: 6.

Etēqu (AHw *atāku*) "bend, twist": D UM 1/1, 14: 7; LKA 153: r.18; BWL 42: 65 acc. to AHw sv *ubānu* 1a; cf. Landsberger 1967a: 12f note 32.

Eṭēlu "to be(come) mature, adult": D "to raise to adulthood" 1x MSL 1, 101: 20.

Eṭû "to be(come) dark": D fact.; cf. also AHw 1555b sv; also SpTU 2, 1: I 15; for Dt → 9.1.1.

Ew/mû "to become": D "to turn, change" (into: *kīma* or *-iš*); normally fact. Š → 7.5.5.4; for OB *uwwû* → 8.4.2.

Ezēzu "to be(come) angry": D fact. (but see note xx); +Š lit. → 7.5.5.1.

G

Galātu "to twitch, start": D/Dtn/ŠD "to frighten, scare away"; +Š lit. → 7.5.5.1.

Gapāru (CAD *gubburu*) "to be powerful": D 1x "to overpower" (?) UM 1/2, 113: I 15.

Gapāšu "to be(come) huge, massive": D SB "to gather" (?) Atr. 118: 22; 120: 38 (obj. fish); for Dt → 9.1.1.

Gašāru "to be(come) powerful": D 1x NB "to concentrate" RA 27, 18: 15 (troops, but AHw sv D: "überlegen machen"); for Dt → 9.1.1, 9.1.3 and 9.1.7.

H

Habālu "to become indebted to sb (for an amount): D/Dt "to make sb indebted to" → 5.5.2.

Habāru "quitter sa résidence", D "déplacer" acc. to Durand, Ét. Garelli p. 24 note 27.

Hadû "to be(come) glad, pleased": D fact.; +Š lit. → 7.5.5.2.

Halāpu (only stative) "to be dressed in": D "to dress, cover" (cf. *labāšu*); probably to be separated from *halāpu* "to slip in", used in prefix forms, which has a Š-stem (YOS 11, 19: 14).

Halāqu "to disappear, escape": D/ŠD fact.; +Š (NA/NB) "to help to escape" → 7.5.4.

Hâlu "to dissolve": D fact. 1x AMT 62, 3: 10 (herbs) acc. to AHw sv D.

Hamāṭu "to burn" (trans. and intrans. → 7.3.2): D fact. → 7.3.2; +Š lit. → 7.5.5.1; for Dt → 9.1.1.

Hamû "to trust, rely" (+ dat.): D "to make confident" (cf. *takālu*).

Harāpu "to do/come early" (often in hendiadys): D 1x in hendiadys ABL 302: 13 (also Š, cf. CAD sv *h.* A c/d).

Hasāsu "to think about, heed" (cf. 5.5.2): D "to remind"; D also intrans. "to study" → 7.6.3; +Š → 7.5.6.

Hašāšu "to rejoice": D "to make rejoice" KAR 333: r.11.

Hâšu "to worry" (lit. "to choke" acc. to Heimpel, NABU 96/46): D fact. TI pl. II: II 32 acc. to AHw sv *h.* I D (but CAD: *hâṭu* (5) "to trace"); ARM 14, 103: 8' acc. to AHw 1560b sv; also ARM 27, 27: 22.

Helû "to shine, be brillant": D only part. (also as PN, cf. CAD sv *muhellû*); +Š lit. → 7.5.5.1.

K

Kabābu "to burn" (trans. and intr. → 7.3.2): D "to burn (trans.), to char" → 7.3.2.

Kabāru "to be(come) thick": D fact.; also intrans. as part. AS 16, 24: 95 *mu-ka-bi-rum* (var. *mu-uk-tab-bi-rum*, cf. note 11 to Ch. IX) "boaster, braggart", cf. *ebû* above, and → 7.4.3 sv *ebû*.

Kabātu "to be(come) heavy, important": D fact.; also "to honour" → 10.4.2; +Š lit. → 7.5.5.2; for Dt → 9.1.7.

Kamālu "to be(come) angry": D fact. (?) AfO 19, 64: 77 (context broken).

Kanāšu "to bend, submit": D/ŠD "to bend" (trans.), "to force into submission"; for D and Š with obj. *kišāda* → 7.5.3; +Š lit. → 7.5.5.3; for Dt → 9.1.1.

Kanû "to be honoured, cherished" (for G see AHw 1566a sv (doubtful)): D "to honour, cherish, gladden", cf. AHw sv *kanû*, CAD sv *kunnû* v., and Berger, ZA 60, 130ff.

Kânu "to be(come) firm, true": D/Dtn "to establish, set up, testify", etc.; for Dt → 9.1.3.

Kap/bāṣ/su "to curl, droop" (CAD), "etwa 'sich zusammenziehen, einknicken'" (AHw): D fact. AfO 11, 223: 14f.

Karû "to be(come) short": D "to make short, to cause hardship"; +Š lit. → 7.5.5.2.

Kaṣû "to be(come) cold": D "to let cool off, allow to cool".

Kašû "to become profitable" (subject *takšītu*): D/ŠD "to make profitable" (object *takšītu*); "to enlarge" (temple); also intrans.; also Ét. Garelli 18 A.1499 = M.9046+: 22f; ARM 27, 26: 22.

Kâšu "to be late, delayed": D "to delay".

L

Labāku "to be(come) soft, steeped": D/Dtn "to steep, macerate"; +Š → 7.5.6.

Labāru "to be(come) old": D "to grant old age, to prolong"; D also intrans. → 7.4.3; +Š lit. → 7.5.6; for Dt → 9.1.1.

Labāšu "to wear" (clothes) (cf. 5.5.2): D "to dress sb, to provide sb with clothes"; +Š lit. → 7.5.5.3; for Dt → 9.1.1, esp. note 5 to Ch. IX.

Lakû (CAD *lukkû* "mng. uncert.") "to be(come) weak" (?): D fact. TC 3, 93: 14; RIMA 1, 192: 8. [*Lakkû* listed in AHw sv (OA) is from *leqû*, cf. App. to Chapter VI sv].

Lamādu "to know, learn" (cf. 5.5.2): D "to teach, to inform" → 7.3.2; +Š lit. → 7.5.5.1 sv.

Lapānu "to be(come) poor": D fact. Racc. 135: 259 acc. to AHw sv D; SpTU 4, 149: II 27'. 30'.

Lemēnu "to be(come) bad, unhappy": D fact.; also intrans. → 7.4.3; +Š lit. → 7.5.5.2; for Dt → 9.1.3.

M

Magāru "to agree with, obey, grant" (cf. 5.5.2): D "to get to agree, to reconcile"; +Š → 7.5.6.

Malû "to be(come) full" (for trans. G → 7.3.1): D/Dtn/ŠD fact.; +Š lit. → 7.5.5.1.

Marāru "to be(come) bitter": D fact.; +Š lit. (with object "weapons") → 7.5.5.1.

Marāṣu "to be ill, distressed": D/ŠD fact., mainly in hendiadys → 7.4.1, but very rare → 7.5.6; Š is the usual factitive, cf. CAD sv 6-8; AHw sv Š.

Masāhu (CAD: *mussuhu*) "to be bad, inferior": D "to treat with contempt (OA, also OB AbB 8, 149: 22?) → 8.4.1.

Masāku "to be(come) bad, evil": D "to spoil, revile"; +Š lit. → 7.5.5.1.

Maṣû "to be(come) equal, sufficient": D is uncertain because of its homonymy with *(w/m)uṣṣû* "to spread, open wide" (cf. 8.6); possibly, all cases listed under CAD sv *maṣû* 4 and AHw sv D belong to this verb (cf. also CAD M/1 note on p. 350a). The regular factitive of *maṣû* is Š, cf. CAD sv 6/7, compare esp. the idiom *mala (ammar) libbi* + G "to have full discretion" (*ib.* sv 2), vs. + Š "to give full discretion" (*ib.* sv 7). The OA Dt forms listed CAD sv 5, AHw sv Dt, certainly belong to *maṣû*, since they interchange with G forms in the same context (in hendiadys, cf. Kraus 1987: 40) → 9.1.7.

Mašālu "to be(come) similar, equal": D fact.; D also intrans. → 7.4.3; +Š → 7.5.6.

Mašû "to forget": D "to make forget" acc. to CAD and AHw, but no unambiguous factitives are attested, cf. 5.5.2.

Matāqu "to be(come) sweet": D fact. STT 68: 6 (part.).

Maṭû "to be(come) missing, inferior": D/ŠD fact.; +Š → 7.5.4; for Dt → 9.1.1.

Medû "to be known" (secondary stative derived from *idû* "to know"): D "to observe, watch".

N

Na'ādu "to pay attention, be concerned" (+ dat.); D/Dt(n)) "to alert, inform" → 7.3.2; +Š (with different meaning) acc. to AHw sv Š, corresponding to *šahātu* D in CAD, cf. sv *šahātu* A 6 (cf. 8 for Š).

Nabāṭu "to shine brightly": D fact., rare for the usual factitive Š → 7.5.6; for Dt → 9.1.1.

Nagālu "gleißen, glühen" acc. to AHw (CAD: mng. uncert.): D fact. LS 1/6, 34: 24.

Nahāru "etwa "verdorrt sein?"" acc. to AHw (CAD: mng. uncert.): D fact. Maqlû V 38; VI 127.

Nahāšu "to be(come) prosperous": D fact.

Nâhu "to rest, subside": D "to appease, pacify, extinguish, satisfy"; +Š lit. → 7.5.5.2.

Nakālu "to act cleverly, be(come) artistic": D "to execute sth artistically"; +Š → 7.5.5.2. In the expression *nikilta nakālu* "to play a trick, deceive" versus *niklāti nukkulu* (ABL 416: r.6) *nakālu* is transitive and D belongs to the D-stems with a plural object discussed in 6.4.

Nakāru "to be(come) hostile, change, rebel, deny": D/Dtn "to change (trans.), to remove, expel, transfer"; D also intrans. → 7.4.3; +Š → 7.5.3.

Nâlu "to lie down": factitive D rarely instead of factitive Š → 7.5.5.4.

Namāšu "to set out, depart": D "to dispatch"; D also intrans. in NA → 7.4.3.

Napāšu "to relax, expand": D "weit machen, aufatmen lassen" acc. to AHw sv D; CAD: "to air(?), to put in good repair, to clean out(?), often with object *libba* "to set sb's mind at ease"; for Dt → 9.1.1.

Naqādu (CAD *nakādu*) "to be in a difficult position": D only CT 51, 147: r.22, cf. Reiner, St. Kraus 287. AHw differentiates *naqādu* (stative only) from *nakādu* (no stative) "Herzklopfen bekommen", CAD assigns all cases to *nakādu*. [AbB 3, 22: 14 *ú-na-qí!?-du!?-šu* acc. to AHw sv D, very doubtful].

Narābu "to be moist, soft" [cancel present G CT 29, 49: 28, cf. CAD sv]: D UET 6, 391: 10; also YOS 11, 26: I 18 (infin.).

Narāṭu "to shake, tremble": D/ŠD "to shake (trans.), cause to tremble".

Nâšu "to shake, recede": D "to move, shake, dislodge"; D also intrans. → 7.4.3.

Natāku "to drip, drop" (intrans.): D/Dtn "to drop, let dribble" (trans.) [The alleged Štn *uš-ta-nat-tak* in TDP 162: 59 is more likely to be a "lexical" Št because of its different meaning].

Naw/māru "to shine, be(come) bright": D/ŠD fact.; D also intrans. → 7.4.3; +Š → 7.5.6; for Dt → 9.1.1.

Nesû "to withdraw, go away": D/ŠD "to remove, keep away, drive away"; +Š → 7.5.6.

Nêšu "to stay alive, recover": D only in *muna''išu* "veterinarian", cf. CAD M sv; +Š lit. → 7.5.5.2.

Nê'u/ne'û "to turn" (trans. and intr. → 7.5.3): D fact. → 7.5.3.

P

Pahāru "to come together": D "to bring together"; +Š lit. → 7.5.5.2; for Dt → 9.1.1.

Palāhu "to fear, respect, honour": D/Dtn "to frighten"; +Š lit. → 7.5.5.1; for Dt → 9.1.3.

Palāsu "to watch" (mostly N): D "to apply oneself to, to keep sb busy, to cause trouble" (mostly stative), versus Š "to cause to see" → 7.5.4.

Panû "to turn to, to precede": D "to deliver quickly" (OA).

Pâqu (AHw *piāqum*) "to be(come) narrow": D fact. ZA 36, 188: 29 (uncertain: rather from *epēqu*?).

Parādu "to be(come) frightened": D/Dtn/ŠD "to startle, frighten"; +Š lit. → 7.5.5.2.

Parāru "to fall apart": D "to disperse, shatter"; +Š lit. → 7.5.5.2.

Pašāhu "to cool down, calm down": D/ŠD; +Š → 7.5.6.

Patānu "to be(come) strong", D fact.

Pazāru "to hide (intr.), to go secretly" (for G see ARM 27, 65: 13. 17 with note b): D/ŠD "to hide (trans.), transport secretly, smuggle".

Peṣû "to be(come) white", D fact.

Q

Qadādu "to bow" (trans. and intrans. → 7.5.3): D fact.; +Š → 7.5.3.

Qadāšu "to be clean": D "to make ritually clean, purify"→ 8.4.1; for Dt → 9.1.2.

Qalālu "to be(come) light, weak, unimportant": D/Dtn fact., also "to reduce, discredit" → 10.4.2; also AbB 13, 57: 12 (oil); ARM 27, 57: 7; 133: 37 (person).

Qâlu "to fall" (AHw *qiālum*): D acc. to AHw "zum Fall bringen" ARM 2, 25: r.16'; CCEBK 37: 9 (both uncertain), cf CAD sv *q.* B 2.

Qarādu (CAD: *qurrudu*) "to be a hero": D "to make into a hero" BWL 166: 5; AGH 50: 16? → 8.4.1.

Qarāru "to (over)flow": D "to spray, sprinkle", cf. CAD sv 3. [To be separated from *g/qarāru* "to roll, be curved" (with its quadriliteral derivations *nagarruru* and *šugarruru*), and *garāru* "to become afraid, shy away", with a factitive Š (CAD: *garāru* A and B)].

Qašādu (CAD: *quššudu*) "to be pure, holy": D "to purify"→ 8.4.1.

Qatānu "to be(come) thin, narrow": D Sg. 8: 332 "to form into single file" [For ARM 1, 83: 24 and Maqlû V 163 see CAD note sv].

Qatāru "to rise" (smoke, fog), "to become gloomy": D/Dtn "to cause to smoke, fumigate, make gloomy"; +Š lit. → 7.5.5.1; for Dt → 9.1.1 and 9.1.2.

Qatû "to come to an end, perish": D "to finish, use up, destroy"; +Š lit. → 7.5.5.1.

Qerēbu "to come near, approach": D/Dtn "to bring near, offer"; +Š lit. → 7.5.5.2.

R

Rabābu "to be(come) weak, yield": D/ŠD "to weaken, subdue", rare, more often Š → 7.5.5.4.

Rabû A "to be(come) big, great": D/ŠD "to make big, great, enlarge, promote, bring up, raise"; +Š lit. → 7.5.5.1.

Rabû B "to go under, to set": D "to submerge, soak, extinguish".

Râbu "to tremble": D "to cause to tremble"; +Š lit. → 7.5.5.2.

Râhu "to be left, to remain": D "to leave over"; +Š → 7.5.6.

Ramāku "to bathe" (intrans., + acc.: "in", G rarely factitive → 11.4.2): D/Dtn "to bathe" (trans.), "to prune" (FM 1 p. 108: 11); +Š lit. → 7.5.5.2.

Ramû "to be(come) weak, loose": D/Dtn/ŠD fact., but also "to leave" (trans.) (NA), and intrans. "to depart" → 7.4.3.

Rapāšu "to be(come) wide": D/ŠD; +Š lit. → 7.5.5.2; for Dt → 9.1.1.

Raqāqu "to be(come) thin": D "fein auswalzen" (AHw sv D); also YOS 11, 26: I 27.

Râqu (AHw *riāqu(m)*) "to be(come) empty, unemployed": D "to empty, to leave unemployed"; +Š → 7.5.6.

Râšu (AHw *riāšu(m)*) "to be jubilant, exult": D "to make jubilant"; +Š lit. → 7.5.5.1.

Raṭābu "to be moist": D also "to irrigate"; also AbB 10, 170: 15.

Rebû "to do fourth": D "to multiply by four" → 7.3.2 sv *šanû.*

Redû "to follow, accompany, lead" (cf. 5.5.2): D/Dtn/ŠD "to add"; +Š "to cause to follow/to flow" → 7.5.4.

Rêqu (Ass. *ruāqu*) "to go away, depart, recede": D "to keep away, remove"; +Š → 7.5.4.

Rešû "to be harsh, unjust" (only adj. in LL): D/Dt(n) "to wrong, treat unjustly" → 8.4.1.

S

Sabā'u "to toss, bound, roil": D (only part.) "to make (the sea) roil"; +Š lit. → 7.5.5.2.

Sahāmu "to be or come under pressure" [G not attested; N: ARM 6, 37: r. 13']: D "to put under pressure" KH r.XIII: 18 (§ 172); RA 46, 92: 57 (restored); in OB MARI with *ana* "to speak defiantly to" MARI 7, 199: 38 with note on p. 201f (Charpin: "narguer").

Sahāru "to turn, to tarry, to seek, to surround": D "to turn" (trans.), "to lead around, to do again" (in hendiadys); +Š → 7.5.3.

Sakānu "to dwell, be stationed" (stative only, OB Mari, cf. Charpin, AfO 40/1, 5f): D "to settle" (trans.), "to make inhabit" ARM 26/1 p. 168 no. 35: 12; 26/2 p. 80 no. 316: 16'.

Sakātu "to be(come) silent": D "to silence".

Salāmu "to be(come) friendly, make peace": D "to reconcile, bring about peace"; +Š → 7.5.6.

Samû "to be(come) anxious, troubled": D "to hamper, interfere, harass" (CAD; AHw: "etwa 'lahmlegen'").

Sâmu (AHw *siāmum*) "to be(come) red": D fact. (see esp. CAD sv 2).

Sâqu (AHw *siāqum*) "to be(come) narrow": D also "to constrict, put in a tight spot".

Sarāru "to be false, criminal": D "to deceive, contest", cf. 7.3.2.

Sehû "to be(come) rebellious": D "to disturb, make unrecognizable". [Cancel Š, for AHw sv Š cf. CAD sv *sahāpu* 5].

Ṣ

Ṣadāru "etwa "schief werden, liegen"?", D "Augen verdrehen?" → 8.4.1, acc. to AHw, but CAD sv *ṣudduru* "to twitch the eyes or the nose": TuL 141: 8 var.; TDP 54: 13; usually occurring as *purrus* adj. → 10.6.2 and App. to Ch. X sv.

Ṣâdu A "to move or turn around": D/Dtn "to cause to turn, make dizzy" → 7.2.4.

Ṣâdu B "to melt" (intrans.): D "to melt" (trans.).

Ṣâhu (AHw *ṣiāhu(m)*) "to laugh": D only part. *muṣihhu* "clown" → 7.2.4.

Ṣalālu "to sleep, fall asleep": D 1x SKS p. 54: 147; elsewhere Š → 7.2.4 and 7.5.6.

Ṣalāmu "to be(come) black, dark": D/Dtn fact., also "to calumniate" ARM 26/2 p. 288 no. 412: 5; perhaps also 10, 156: 27; intrans.? → 7.4.3; +Š lit. → 7.5.5.2.

Ṣamû "to be(come) thirsty": D fact. (for BWL 144: 16 see note 21); +Š lit. → 7.5.5.2.

Ṣarāru "to flow, drip": D "to let drip, to libate"; also part. *muṣarrirtu* "ein Tropfgefäß" (AHw sv).

Ṣâru (AHw *ṣiāru(m)*, CAD *ṣīru* adj.) "to be illustrious, outstanding": D fact. RIME 4, 382: 61; KH II 29 → 8.4.1.

Ṣehēru "to be(come) be small, young": D fact.

Š

Šâbu "to tremble, sway": D "to make tremble, sway" → 7.2.4.

Šadālu "to be(come)broad, wide": D fact.; also ARM 2, 30: 11 acc. to ARM 27, p. 153 note 5; for Dt → 9.1.1.

Šahāhu "to crumble, come loose": D "to loosen, cause to waste away"; also SpTU 2, 2: I 10.

Šahānu "to be(come) warm": D fact.; for Dt → 9.1.1.

Šahātu "to fear" (cf. 5.5.2): D "to frighten"; for Dt → 9.1.1.

Šâhu (AHw *siāhum*) "to grow": D only part. *mušihhu* (part of a clepsydra: "lengthener" acc. to CAD sv *mušihhu*, and CT 41, 27: 6 (obscure)).

Šakāru "to be (come) drunk": D fact. BAM 260: 1.

Šalāmu "to be(come) sound, in a good condition": D/Dtn "to keep well, complete, give in full, etc.; for D intrans. → 7.4.3; in hendiadys → 7.4.1.

Šalāšu "to do for a third time": D "to triple" → 7.3.2; also intrans. → 7.4.3; in hendiadys → 7.4.1.

Šamāhu "to be(come) abundant, flourish, thrive": D/Dtn fact.

Šanû A "to do for the second time": D/Dt(n) "to repeat, report, double" → 7.3.2.

Šanû B "to change, be different": D fact.; +Š → 7.5.6.

Šapālu "to be(come) low, to go down": D/Dtn fact.; also intrans. → 7.4.3; +Š lit. → 7.5.5.1.

Šapû A "to be(come) loud, thick": D in *rigma šuppû* "to call out loudly", cf. CAD sv *š.* A v. 2.

Šapû B "to be(come) silent" (prob. only Gt, cf. CAD sv *š.* B 1, versus AHw sv *š.* III G): D "to silence, subdue".

Šaqālu "to be scarce": D fact. → 8.4.1; Atr. 72: 11; AbB 7, 158: 6; see also *šuqqulu* in App. to Ch. X.
Šaqû "to be(come) high, to go up": D/Dtn "to raise, elevate, extol"; also intrans. → 7.4.3; +Š lit. → 7.5.5.1.
Šarāhu "to be proud, glorious"; D/Dt(n) "to glorify, to make magnificent, plentiful"; +Š lit. → 7.5.5.1; for Dt → 9.1.1.
Šarû "to be(come) rich": D "to provide plentifully", 1x "to make rich" (normally Š) → 7.5.4.
Šasû "to shout, call": D "to make (a herold) proclaim" → 7.2.4 (MA, elsewhere Š).
Šatāhu "to be(come) long, elongated": D fact. KB 6/2, 136: 12.
Šaw/mû "to become roasted": D "to roast" MDP 23, 318: 6; G also factitive → 11.4.2.
Šebû "to be(come) satiated": D/Dt(n) "to satiate, satisfy".
Šemû "to hear, listen: D fact. 1x "to inform" → 5.5.2; elsewhere causative Š.

T

Takālu "to trust"(with *ana*): D/Dtn "to encourage, give confidence" → 7.3.2.
Tamû "to swear": D "to make sb swear, administer an oath" → 5.5.2 (also Š acc. to AHw sv *t*. II Š: ARM 13, 145: edge 1, uncertain).
Taqānu "to be(come) orderly, secure": D/Dt(n) fact.
Tarāru "to tremble, quake, sway": D "to make tremble".
Tarāṣu "to be(come) right, correct, fitting": D fact.
Târu "to return, to change into": D/Dtn fact.; Š only EA, cf. AHw sv Š.
Tebû "to rise, stand up": D 1x Ugarit: PRU 3, 70: 24 (intrans., doubtless incorrect); elsewhere Š.

Ṭ

Ṭâbu (AHw *ṭiābum*) "to be(come) good, beautiful, glad, satisfactory": D/Dtn fact.; +Š lit. → 7.5.5.3.
Ṭahādu "to be(come) luxuriant": D "to make luxuriant, to provide abundantly with".
Ṭanāpu "to be(come) dirty": D fact.
Ṭebû "to sink": D "to submerge".
Ṭehû "to come near, approach": D "to bring near".

W

Wa/edû → *edû*.
(W)apû "to be(come) visible": D uncertain, cf. AHw sv D: the origin and interpretation of the idiom *uppu laqe* in MA, of *u₄/ú-pi-* in OAk PNs, and of *uppû* mentioned sv D 1c, all remain obscure; in RA 35, 181f note 5: 7 read *nu-up-pí-ih*. The regular factitive is Š, cf. CAD sv *apû* A 4/5; AHw sv *(w)apû(m)* Š.
(W)aqāru "to be(come) scarce, precious, expensive": D "to make scarce, use up" (rare); +Š → 7.5.4.
(W)arāqu "to be(come) green, pale": D fact.; also intrans.? → 7.4.3. [ABL 452 (= SAA 1, 66): 8. 13 qu. AHw sv Š "vergolden" is from *šurruqu* "to cast", acc. to Oppenheim *et al.* 1970: 94 note 122].
(W)âru "to go, advance": D/Dtn *wu"uru* "to order, command", same verb? → 7.2.6.
(W)asāmu "to be(come?) suitable, proper" [pref. G uncert.]: D fact. → 7.5.1; +Š lit. → 7.5.5.1.
(W)ašāru "to be low, humble" (only LL and *ašru* adj.): D/Dtn *(w)uššuru* "to let go, release" → 7.2.6.
(W)ašāṭu (CAD: *uššuṭu*) "to be stiff, stubborn": D VAB 4, 84 no. 5: II 10.
(W)atāru "to exceed, surpass": D "to augment"; also intrans. → 7.4.3; in hendiadys → 7.4.1; +Š → 7.5.6.

Z

Za'ānu (CAD sv *zânu* a 1'-b') "to be provided, adorned with": D "to provide, adorn with", cf. AHw sv D.
Zâbu "to flow": D only in part. *muzibbu* "water clock", lit. "letting (water) flow", cf. AHw and CAD sv.
Zakû "to be free, clean": D fact. [Cancel Š, mentioned CAD sv 8: in RA 35, 4: 7 read *uš-ta-na-sà-qú* from *nasāqu* Št, cf. AHw sv].
Zenû "to be(come) angry": D fact.; +Š → 7.5.5.2.

CHAPTER EIGHT

D TANTUM VERBS and DENOMINATIVE D-STEMS

8.0. The final group of verbal D-stems which remain to be discussed according to the classification adopted in 5.1 are the D-stems which are independent of the G-stem. They comprise two kinds: D-stems which do not have a corresponding G-stem, the D tantum verbs, and denominative D-stems, i.e., D-stems which are directly derived from an adjective or a substantive. If this noun is itself deverbal, the D-stem has a corresponding G-stem, from which it is indirectly derived via this noun. Many denominative D-stems, however, do not have a corresponding G-stem and are therefore also D tantum verbs.

Since the relationship to the G-stem is the decisive factor in classification (cf. 5.1), these two kinds of D-stems have the same status in that they are relatively independent of the G-stem (if any). Accordingly, they are discussed in one chapter, which thus deals with all verbal D-stems which have not been discussed in Chapter VI (viz., those derived from transitive G-stems, designated as Type I in 5.2), and Chapter VII (those derived from intransitive verbs or low transitivity verbs: Types II, III and IV).

8.1. Problems of classification

The distinctions made in the previous section raise a number of problems. In the first place it should be determined what exactly is a D tantum verb. The definition adopted here is that a D tantum verb is a verbal D-stem for which no corresponding verbal G-stem with a sufficiently similar meaning is attested.

Apart from the terms "verbal D-stem" and "verbal G-stem", which were already defined in 5.1.1 and note 2 to Ch. V, several aspects of this definition are problematical.

The first problem is the term "sufficiently similar". It is often largely subjective whether we regard specific G- and D-stems as belonging to the same root or to different but homonymous roots. Some illustrative cases (already mentioned in 6.0) are *lupputu* "to tarry, be delayed" and *zubbulu* "to linger, to keep waiting". The dictionaries list these verbs under *lapātu* "to touch, smear, affect" and *zabālu* "to carry", although it is not obvious how the meanings of the D-stems could have developed out of those of the G-stems. Therefore, they are listed here as D tantum verbs, see 8.6.

Other ambiguous cases include *burrû* "to usher in, announce" (CAD sv *burrû*, but in AHw sv *barû* I "to see" D); *hussû* "to crush" (herbs) (CAD sv *hussû*, but AHw sv *hesû* "to press" D 2); *qubbû* "to lament" (CAD sv *qubbû*, AHw sv *qabû* II "to speak" II D); *marāqu* "to clear from claims" (CAD sv *murruqu,* AHw sv *marāqu* "to crush" D 2b), and *murruru* "to check" (CAD sv *murruru,* AHw sv *marāru* I "to be(come) bitter").

None of these verbs are regarded here as D tantum verbs, because the differences in meaning between G and D do not seem to be unbridgeable. *Burrû* can be explained as a lexicalized factitive of *barû,* cf. 5.5.2 and 7.5.4; *hussû* and *hesû* are actually quite similar in meaning (cf. 6.8.3 sv); it was argued in 6.8.1 sv *nabû* that *qubbû* represents the original meaning of the root, and that *qabû* "to speak" results from a weakening of this meaning; *murruqu* and *murruru* seem to be plausible cases of lexicalized D-stems (for *murruru* via the meaning "*to taste (whether sth is bitter)".

This situation also holds for verbs such as *wu''uru* "to command, send" versus *(w)âru* "to go", *ukkušu* "to expel, drive away" versus *akāšu* "to go", and *(w)uššuru* "to let go, release" versus *(w)ašru* "low, humble". They are lexicalized to such an extent that their relationship to the G-stem has lost its grammatical relevance and is mainly etymological. In practice they serve as independent verbs with the same status as D tantum verbs. However, since their semantic relationship to the G-stem is regular (they are normal factitives), they are not included in this chapter.

A second problem is posed by verbs that normally occur in the D-stem, but also show more or less uncertain instances of G forms by way of exception. For instance, the verb *buzzu'u* "to treat unjustly, put under pressure" is listed by AHw sv as a D tantum verb. CAD, on the other hand, lists it under *bazā'u,* on the basis of the OA forms *ba-za-ša* and *ba-za-am,* which are interpreted as infinitives of the G-stem. This interpretation has been disproved by a new occurrence of this word in the nominative: *ba-ZU-um.*[1] Therefore, *buzzu'u* should be classified as a D tantum verb in accordance with AHw.

Another case is the rather common D-stem *ṣummuru* "to strive for, to wish, to plot". There is a single instance of an infinitive G *ṣa*$^{!}$*-ma-r*[*i*?] in Lugal 117, cf. CAD sv *ṣamāru* lex. sect. (cf. the remark on p. 93b), and AHw sv *ṣamāru* I G. For the dictionaries, this is reason to list this verb under the G-stem. Two objections can be raised against this. First, the reading of the infinitive G is not established beyond all doubt; second, the literary and rather contrived style of Lugal suggests that this unique infinitive, if it is read correctly, is an artificial backformation on the basis of the D-stem. It seems to be preferable, therefore, to classify *ṣummuru* as a D tantum verb, too.

A comparable problem concerns *ṣubbû* "to look into, to examine" (1x a very doubtful G form, cf. CAD sv note on p. 227b) and *nuhhutu* "to trim, to clip" (1x *na-hu-uD* ARM 3, 8: 12, interpretation obscure, but probably a different word). All these cases are classified as D tantum verbs here.

These cases may suffice to show the number of subjective judgments involved in the classification of the D-stems under discussion. The same subjectivity is involved in determining whether a given D-stem is directly derived from the corresponding G-stem, or via a deverbal noun; in other words, whether it is denominative or not. This problem will be addressed in the discussion of the denominative function of D in 8.3.3.

8.2. General features

What D tantum verbs and denominative D-stems have in common is that they do not contrast grammatically with corresponding forms of the basic verbal stem, the G-stem. They are themselves the (relatively) basic stem from which other verbal stems may be derived; in practice this only applies to the secondary stems Dt, Dtn and ŠD, for which see Chapter IX; a few also have a Š-stem. Therefore, they do not have a grammatical function, but they represent a purely lexical category of verbs. In this respect they differ from the D-stems discussed in Chapters VI and VII, the use of which is largely determined by their opposition to the G-stem (although for those of Chapter VI this is only true to a limited extent, see 5.6.4 and 6.1).

The question confronting us, therefore, is not what their grammatical function is, but why they take the D-stem as their basic stem rather than the G-stem, like most other verbs. It is only rarely possible to answer this question. It seems arguable, for instance, that the verb *puhhu* "to replace, exchange" is restricted to the D-stem because it is derived from *pūhu* "replacement", a noun with a rather unusual pattern. The reverse derivation, *pūhu* as a deverbal noun of *puhhu*, is also theoretically possible, but it leaves unexplained why *puhhu* is a D tantum verb.

Another noteworthy case is *gullubu* "to shave". Nominal derivations of the root *G-L-B*, such as *gallābu* "barber", *naglabu* "razor" and *gulībātu* "hair cuttings", show that once a G-stem **galābu* was in use (cf. 3.4). The occurrence of a *purrus* name *Gullubu*, which doubtless means "bald" (cf. 10.6.3), suggests that parallel to this G-stem a *purrus* adjective existed of the type discussed in 10.3.2, e.g., *buqqumu* "with scarce hair" beside *baqāmu* "to pluck" and *huššulu* "crippled" beside *hašālu* "to crush". These forms belong to the group of *purrus* forms for salient bodily characteristics listed in 10.6.2, many of which refer to a condition of the hair. It seems a plausible assumption that the D tantum verb *gullubu* is a denominative of this adjective with factitive meaning: "to make bald" → "to shave", which has replaced the simple verb.

Similar processes have doubtless been operative in some other verbs, too, but it is usually difficult to find conclusive evidence for this. As to the denominative D-stems in general, they turn out to be rather homogeneous in meaning, and their selection of the D-stem can be plausibly related to their semantic nature (see 8.5). For the other D tantum verbs the situation is more complicated, and it often does not seem possible to determine why a specific verb occurs in the D-stem rather than in the G-stem.

We will first deal with the denominative D-stems in 8.3 - 8.5, and subsequently with the D tantum verbs (in so far as they are not denominative) in 8.6 - 8.7.

8.3. Denominative D-stems

Denominative (or denominal) verbs are verbs which are directly derived from a substantive or an adjective. The concept of denominative verbs in general is a difficult and elusive one. Before presenting the verbs in question, therefore, we have to make some preliminary remarks.

8.3.1. The term "denominative"

The term denominative is used in Semitic studies in two different ways which should be carefully distinguished: on the one hand, it is used to describe a specific feature of a verbal category as a whole; on the other hand, it can refer to the etymological background of an individual verb.

Used in the first way, it refers to claims that a specific verbal (morphological) category as a whole is derived from a nominal category. In this sense it is applied to the D-stem, for instance, by Christian (see 1.4) and by Goetze, who claims (1942: 6b) that the D-stem is denominative because it is derived from the stative, which in Goetze's view is a nominal formation, and that its denominative function is "the primary force of the form" (see also 1.6).

Claims of this type are often quite plausible, as can be illustrated on the basis of many Semitic verbal categories. For instance, the suffix conjugation of West Semitic (Arabic *qatala,* Hebrew *qāṭal*, etc.) doubtless goes back to a category similar to the Akkadian stative (cf. 2.2.2 and 4.1.2.1), and therefore has a nominal origin, just like the latter. The same may be true of the Akkadian present *iparras*, which can be explained as derived from agent nouns with gemination such as those discussed in 3.2 and 3.3; if this hypothesis is correct, the Akkadian present is also denominative.

In fact, if we consider the development of the verbal systems of some Semitic languages, e.g., Hebrew and Aramaic, over periods which are historically attested, we see that the renewal of the verbal system mainly takes place by means of constructions which are based on participles and verbal adjectives, i.e., on nominal forms (cf., in general, Hodge 1975). This is especially evident in the Neo-Aramaic dialects, which have developed an intricate system of verbal categories by means of such periphrastic constructions consisting of participles and verbal adjectives combined with pronominal elements (cf., among others, D. Cohen 1984: 458ff). There is no reason to assume that a similar process was not already operative in the prehistoric phase of Semitic. The Akkadian stative is an obvious example of a formation with a clearly nominal origin which has been incorporated into the verbal paradigm since the earliest period of attestation. It is quite possible that also the Semitic prefix conjugation has such an origin, only going back much further in time.

Many verbal categories, then, can plausibly be argued to be denominative in origin. However, this fact only refers to their etymological background and seems to be hardly relevant for the way they perform their actual (synchronic) grammatical function. A grammatical function can only be established on the basis of syntactic arguments, not on the basis of historical ones. This is also true of the D-stem: Goetze's claim that the D-stem is denominative in origin (*l.c.*) is doubtless correct (cf. 11.1), but it does not follow from this that it has a factitive function, as Goetze seems to imply.

In Chapter XI, where the background of the D-stem and its historical development are examined, we will discuss the widespread view that its origin is denominative in the sense just referred to. In this chapter, however, the term will be used exclusively in its second meaning, in which it concerns individual verbs which are directly derived from a substantive or an adjective. In this meaning the term is often encountered in grammars and handbooks of Semitic, too. Thus denominative, as it is used in this chapter, refers to an etymological feature of an individual verb.

8.3.2. The denominative function of the D-stem

In the traditional accounts of the D-stem the denominative function is usually ranked among its most important functions, beside the intensive and the causative function, and illustrated with a number of examples that look fairly convincing (e.g., Brockelmann 1908: 509; Moscati 1969: 124; Wright 1896/98: 32; Gesenius-Kautzsch 1985: 138f; Bauer-Leander 1922: 291; Joüon-Muraoka 1991: 155f; for Akkadian see, for instance, GAG § 88g and Ungnad-Matouš 1964: 75.

However, a few qualifications need to be made in this context. First of all, the function "denominative" cannot be put on a par with the other functions of the D-stem as described in previous chapters, nor with their traditional counterparts, the causative and the intensive. The latter are grammatical functions, i.e., they specify the grammatical relationship of the D-stem to other categories which are in opposition to it (in this case chiefly the G-stem). As we saw in the previous section, the term denominative only refers to the etymological origin of the D-stem in question, not to its grammatical function.

Most denominative D-stems do not have a grammatical function, since they are not in opposition to another verbal stem. In the few cases where they do, i.e., where they contrast with a denominative G-stem, they do not fall under the definition of denominatives, because they are not derived directly from a noun, but via the basic G-stem (see 11.2). The clearest cases are the D-stems *šunnû* "to repeat, report", *šullušu* "to triple, do or say for a third time" and *rubbu'u* "to multiply by four". They are derived from the numerals *šinā* "two", *šalāš* "three" and *erbe* "four" via the denominative G-stems *šanû* "to do again, for a second time", *šalāšu* "to do for a third time" and *rebû* "to do for a fourth time" (cf. 7.3.2 sv *šanû*). These D-stems are basically (but not consistently) used as factitives of the G-stems; in other words, D has the function which is normal for D-stems of intransitive verbs.

A few transitive verbs which are likely to be denominatives show a similar state of affairs. *Kadāru* "to establish" (a boundary (from *kudurru* "boundary stone"))" and *parāṣu* "to perform" (a rite (*parṣu*)) are used both in the G- and in the D-stem; in so far as the few instances attested allow us to judge, D and G of these two verbs are used indiscriminately, just as many other D- and G-stems of transitive verbs (cf. especially 6.8.4). Consequently, if denominative D-stems are in opposition to G-stems, they tend to behave like ordinary D-stems.

Second, other verbal stems than the D-stem can be denominative, too, in particular the G-stem, the Š-stem and the "lexical" Št-stem.

As for denominative G-stems, AHw characterizes more than 50 G-stem verbs as denominative (cf. also GAG § 73e). For most of them there are no cogent arguments why they should be regarded as such, but a sufficient number remains to prove the existence of such G-stems. Apart from *šanû, šalāšu* (not designated as denominative in AHw), and *rebû* (not in AHw), plausible examples are the following (but see below 8.3.3):

Bâtu "to spend the night" (from *bītu* "house").
Hamāšu II "to do sth for a fifth time" (there are no convincing instances of a corresponding D-stem, *pace* AHw sv).
Haṣāṣu II "to build" (a reed hut (*huṣṣu*)).
Kadāru "to establish a border" (also D, see above).
Kapārum II "to pour bitumen (*kupru*) on sb".
Kasāpu II "to present a *kispu*-offering".
Panû "to turn to" or "to go in front" (from *pānū* "face, front side").
Parāṣu II "to perform a rite" (also G, see above).
Qanānu I "to build a nest" (*qinnu*).
Šalāgu "to snow" (not in AHw; cf. CAD sv, from *šalgu* "snow", *pace* Landsberger 1967a: 15b note 42, and 1926: 363).
Šamātu I "to mark" (from *šimtu* "mark, branding iron").
Šênu "to put on shoes" (*šēnu*).[2]

Denominative Š-stems are not very common:

Šuklulu "to make complete, perfect" (cf. *kullatu* "totality").
Šūlulu II "to acclaim, exult" from *alāla*, an exclamation of joy (also Gt, cf. note 2).
Šumṣulu "to spend the day" (cf. *muṣlālu* "midday, siesta time").
Šumšû "to spend the night" (cf. *mūšu* "night").
Šutlumu "to bestow, grant" (if related to *(a)tulimānu* "both hands" and *talīmu* "favourite brother (?)").

Moreover, many "lexical" Št-stems (cf. GAG § 94c and Streck 1994, esp. 179ff) are doubtless denominatives of nouns with the pattern *taprist* or *taprīs*; among the most convincing cases are:

Šutanūdu "to praise" from *tanīdu* or *tanittu* "praise".
Šutēmuqu "to entreat, implore" from *tēmī/ēqu* "prayer, supplication".
Šutersû "to prepare" from *tersîtu* "preparation, equipment".
Šutēṣû "to quarrel, vie" from *tēṣî/êtu* "quarrel, argument" (in the dictionaries listed under *(w)aṣû*, in spite of the totally different meaning (AHw sv *waṣû* Št^2, CAD sv *aṣû* v. 11 (but see the note on p. 383b)).

A denominative Št-stem from a noun with another pattern is *šutāhû* "to join, to conspire", which is doubtless based on *athû* "mutual partners".[3]

This situation is also found in other Semitic languages. In Hebrew, for instance, denominative verbs occur not only in the Picel, but also in the Qal, the Hifcil and the Nifcal (Bauer-Leander 1922: 289ff). Especially illuminating is the use of denominative verbs in Arabic, as described by Fleisch 1979: 263ff. He gives a long list of denominatives in the basic stem (264ff), and states that they are also numerous in Stems II, III and IV, fairly ("assez") numerous in Stems V and X, that there are a small number of them in Stems VI, VIII and IX and only two in Stem VII (*o.c.* 322). He further explains (*ib.*) the frequent use of Stems II and IV from the fact that many denominatives mean "to cause" or "to produce" the noun from which they are derived, which agrees well with the grammatical function of these stems described by him as causative or factitive.

He concludes (1979: 328ff) that denominative verbs are normally formed according to Stem II or IV, and that if another stem is used, this is due to some semantic property of the verb in question; e.g., if Stem V, VIII or X is used, it is intended to convey a reflexive or "middle" interpretation of the agent.

This suggests that if a verb is derived from a noun, the selection of a specific verbal stem depends on the intended meaning of the verb and on the function that the verbal stems have in general. It further suggests that the reason why the D-stem is often used for the purpose of forming denominative verbs is that there is a certain affinity between the way in which it is generally used and the meaning of these verbs; there can be little doubt that this affinity concerns the degree of transitivity inherent in them. We will return to this question in 8.5, after the presentation of the denominative D-stems of Akkadian.

8.3.3. How to distinguish denominatives from ordinary verbs

One of the most difficult problems with regard to denominative verbs is how to distinguish them from ordinary verbs (cf. Kuryłowicz 1972: 155f). Since most nouns are deverbal in Semitic, a verb derived from such a noun will often show a rather close semantic relationship to the basic verb, which makes it difficult to judge whether it is directly derived from the verb or not.

The meaning of a denominative verb is closely associated with that of the source noun. Generally speaking, if X is the basic noun, the verb will mean "to be X", "to resemble X", "to behave like X", etc., if it is intransitive, and "to make X", "to produce X", "to use X", "to desire X", etc., if it is transitive, cf. Kuryłowicz 1972: 155; Comrie 1985: 346ff.

A special kind which deserves to be mentioned since it is sometimes claimed to be a separate function of the D-stem are denominative D-stems with a "privative" meaning, which denote the removal of the source noun, such as Arabic *qarrada* "to clean an animal of ticks" (*qurād*), cf. Wright 1896/98: 32, and Hebrew *zinnẹḇ* "to attack the rearguard of an army", lit.

"to cut off the tail" (*zānāḇ*). The only Akkadian instance seems to be *uppulu* "to delouse" (LL) from *uplu* "louse".

Thus the meaning of a denominative verb is not predictable from that of the source noun. Which of the possible nuances enumerated above is realized depends on the situation for which the word is created. Therefore, denominative verbs can have contradictory meanings, such as Arabic *jallada*, from *jild* "skin", which can be "privative" ("to skin sb"), but also means "to bind" (a book), i.e., "to wrap it in a skin", and Hebrew *siqqẹl* (source noun not attested), which can mean "to stone", i.e., "to kill sb with stones", but can also be "privative": "to remove stones from a field" (Gesenius-Kautzsch 1985: 149; many examples in Nöldeke 1910: 101ff).

A denominative verb is easier to identify as the meaning of the source noun is more divergent from that of the verb. A clear case of such a situation is *rukkubu* "to pollinate" (a date palm) versus *rakābu* "to ride". The meaning of this D-stem is clearly related to *rikbu* in the highly specialized meaning of "male efflorescence (of a date palm)", cf. Landsberger 1967: 19b. This makes it virtually certain that *rukkubu* is a denominative of *rikbu*. Comparable cases are *uhhuzu* "to mount (an object) in precious materials", which is clearly more closely connected with *ihzū* "mountings" than with *ahāzu* "to take", from which both words are ultimately derived, and *kurruṣu* "to slander", which is derived from *karṣu* "slander, calumny", which in its turn is likely to be a specialized derivation of *karāṣu* "to pinch off, break".

Rather less certain is the claim made in 1.8 that *wulludu* in the meaning "to act as midwife" is a denominative rather than a direct derivation of *(w)alādu* "to give birth to", because it would seem possible to interpret it as meaning basically "to cause to give birth" or "to make born" (cf. Goetze 1942: 6). The most cogent argument against this claim is that D-stems of transitive verbs cannot have a causative meaning for the reasons expounded in 7.2. It seems more likely, therefore, that it is derived from a noun such as *wildu* "child" or *(w)ālittu* "woman in labour"; that it is denominative is also suggested by its technical meaning.

An ambiguous case is *rukkusu* in the meaning "to bind sb by contract" (cf. App. to Ch. VI sv **9**). On the one hand, it seems possible to explain this simply as a metaphorical use; on the other hand, it could be viewed as a denominative of *riksu* "contract, agreement", which is closely associated in meaning with *rukkusu*, cf. AHw sv *riksu* C.

An important criterion, then, for identifying denominative verbs and distinguishing them from ordinary verbs is whether the meaning of the source noun and the denominative verb are rather specific and closely similar, in the sense that they form the nominal and the verbal expression of a single action and are found in the same contexts.

The more specialized this meaning is, the more certain we can be about the denominative character of the verb in question. This also explains why so many of the instances listed below are very rare: a specialized word can only be used in a small number of contexts.

Moreover, the more specific the meaning is, the more relevant it is for the nature of the verb that it is a denominative. The case of *šanû* "to do for a second time" is illustrative in this context. It is doubtless a denominative of *šinā* "two", but it is so common and general that this fact can hardly be seen as a relevant aspect of its meaning. For a "real" denominative verb the fact that it is denominative and that it is closely associated with its source noun is an essential and indispensible part of its meaning.

8.4. List of denominative D-stems

On the basis of the preceding considerations and the criteria adopted above, we will now present a list of D-stems which are likely to be denominative in the sense defined above. They will be divided into two groups, first those which are derived from adjectives (8.4.1), then those derived from substantives (8.4.2).

8.4.1. Denominative D-stems derived from adjectives

It will be argued in Chapter XI that the verbal D-stem as a category is historically derived from adjectives with gemination; thus it is denominative in the first of the two meanings assigned to the term in 8.3.1. Some D-stems derived from adjectives can be argued to be denominative also in the second meaning of the term, i.e., they are directly derived from the adjective, without the intermediate stage of a verbal G-stem. This applies to all simple adjectives which do not have a corresponding G-stem and to a number of *purrus* adjectives.

To start with the former kind, the definition of a D tantum verb adopted in 8.1 implies that a D-stem derived from an adjective which does not have a verbal G-stem is a D tantum verb, and since it must be derived from the adjective it is also denominative. In some cases we can actually prove that the D-stem is directly and synchronically derived from the adjective, not from another form of the simple stem (see 11.2.2).

The D-stems which meet these requirements are the following (for references see the dictionaries):[4]

Buhhuru "to make hot, cook" (D/Dtn), from *bahru* "hot".

Burrumu "to make multicoloured, weave, twine", from *barmu* "multicoloured".

Duqququ "to shatter", is derived from *daqqu* "very small", acc. to CAD sv and AHw sv *daqāqu*; it is said of enemy countries and walls, always with *haṣbattiš* or *kīma haṣbatti* "like a pot(sherd)". CAD also assigns to this verb cases in which it is said of herbs in medical texts; AHw derives these from a different verb *dakāku* (G only LL) "zerstoßen, zerreiben", a root variant of *dâku* "to kill".

Duššû "to provide abundantly with" (D/Dt/Dt(n)), from *dešû* "abundant".

Duššupu "to make sweet", from *dašpu* "sweet".

Du''umu "to make dark", from *da'mu* "dark".

Kuzzubu "to flatter, fawn", from *kazbu* "charming, attractive" (PN only); the semantic relationship between *kuzzubu* and *kazbu* is irregular.

Mussuhu "to treat with contempt" (D/Dt (? AbB 8, 149: 22)), from *mashu* "inferior".

Quddušu and **quššudu** "to purify, consecrate" (D/Dt pass. or reflexive → 9.1.2), from **qadšu* "holy, pure" (only fem. *qadištu* attested, cf. CAD sv *qadištu* and 11.2.2.

Qurrudu "to make into a hero", from *qardu* "heroic".

Ruššû "to wrong, treat unjustly" (D/Dt(n)), from *rešû* "rücksichtslos?" acc. to AHw sv (LL only).

***Sukkuku** "to become deaf" (only Dt attested, cf. 9.1.4), from *sakku* "deaf".

Ṣudduru "to twitch the eyes or the nose" (?), from *ṣad(i)ru* (TBP 20: 4'f *ṣa-di-ra*, and GAG § 12b Anm.); elsewhere always *ṣudduru* "squinting, crooked", cf. 10.6.2.

Ṣurru "to make famous", from *ṣīru* "famous".

Šuqqulu "to make scarce", from *šaqlu* "scarce".

Tubbuku "to render limp", from *tabku* "limp", a lexicalized VA of *tabāku* "to pour out".

Ukkû "to make destitute", from *ekû* "poor".

Uššušu "to renew", from *eššu* "new", cf. 11.2.2.

For none of these adjectives a verbal paradigm is attested. However, the derivation of verbal forms from adjectives is doubtless a productive procedure, so that this may be merely accidental. Since the D-stems, with the exception of *kuzzubu*, are regular factitives, they are included in the Appendix to Chapter VII.

There are also a few D-stems which can be argued to be denominative verbs directly derived from *purrus* adjectives. This applies to cases for which no simple adjective is attested, such as the *purrus* forms which denote salient bodily characteristics (cf. 10.6.2):

Gullubu "to shave", see 8.2 (D/Dt (ARM 26/1 p. 282 no. 115: r.5')); also Š (RA 70, 111: M 7: causative (cf. note 35 to Ch. VII)? or same meaning?).

Ḫuppudu "to make blind", from *ḫuppudu* "blind", cf. 10.6.2.

***Ḫuzzû** "to become lame" (only Dt attested), from **ḫuzzû* (*ḫunzû*) "lame", cf. 10.6.2.

***Kubbulu** "to become paralyzed" (only Dt attested, cf. 9.1.4), from *kubbulu* "lame, paralyzed", cf. 10.6.2.

Kupputu A "to make compact, lump-shaped" (D/Dt), from *kupputu*, cf. CAD sv *kupputu* A v., AHw sv *kapātu* D; often stative in omens, cf. App. to Ch. X sv. For *kupputu* B see 8.6 sv.

Lu''û "to make dirty, to defile" (D/Dt), from *lu''û* "dirty".

Tu''umu "to double" (?), from *tu''umu* "double", only in SAA 10, 95: 10 (uncertain, context broken, AHw sv *t.* II D 1 "überlegen ??"). [The LB instances quoted AHw *ib.* D 2 rather belong to *ṭêmu* "to take care of, to rule"].

***Ṭummumu** "to become deaf" (only Dt attested), from *ṭummumu* "deaf", cf. 10.6.2.

These *purrus* forms do not have parallel simple adjectives and - with the exception of *gullubu*, which underwent its own semantic development - denote typically adjectival qualities, i.e., those which are stable and more or less permanent. This suggests that the adjectives are basic and that the occasional verbal forms are secondarily derived from them, as happened with *gullubu* according to 8.2.

8.4.2. Denominative verbs derived from substantives

These are the verbs which are denominative in the proper sense of the word: they are closely associated with and arguably derived from a substantive.

Gullulu A "to act unjustly towards, commit (a sin)" (D/Dt(n)), with *ana*; a denominative of *gillatu* "sin" acc. to AHw sv. For *gullulu* B see 8.6.

Hubbulu "to damage", denominative of *hibiltu* "damage" acc. to CAD sv *habālu* A 2a (MB), beside *hubbulu* "to destroy" and "to do wrong"; cf. *habālu* "to wrong, oppress".

Huttupu "to present as a *hitpu*-sacrifice" (D/Dt (LKU 51: r.22, restored)), cf. AHw sv *hatāpu* D; G only occurs as infin. in LL and in Elam (MDP 10), cf. AHw and CAD sv *hatāpu*.

Kuddunu "to ask for protection", acc. to AHw 1569a sv, from *kidinnu* "divine protection" (only SpTU 2, 22: IV 34 dingir.meš *ú-ka-da-an* "I ask the gods for protection").

(**Kudduru** "to establish a border", also G, see 8.3.2 above).

Kullulu "to crown, veil" (D/Dt), from *kulūlu* "crown" (also SpTU 1, 83: 2; BiOr. 28, 11: 17').

Kurruṣu "to accuse, slander", from *karṣu* "slander, calumny" (only KH r.X: 66 (§ 161)), ultimately derived from *karāṣu* "to pinch off, break".

Lullû "to provide abundantly with", from *lalû* "desire, charm, luxury" (also TIM 9, 54: 14; RIMA 2/I, 290: 51).

Muhhuru "to send or go upstream" (D/Dt (→ 9.1.6)), from *māhirtu* "(boat moving in) upstream direction" (mainly OB Mari), cf. CAD sv *mahāru* 7b and *māhiru* 2; AHw sv *m.* D 2 and *māhirtu*; see also 6.8.3 sv.

Mujjuru "to plough with a *majāru*-plough", only ARM 27, 3: 13 *mu-jú*(PI)-*úr* (infin.), cf. note c.

Muṣṣuru "to fix a boundary", from *miṣru* or *miṣirtu* "boundary" (Ee V 3 var.; VI 43 var.); doubtful, possibly from *eṣēru* "to draw, to design", cf. AHw sv *maṣāru* D 2. [Cancel ARM 1, 71: 9, cf. ARM 26/2 p. 435 no. 498: 12 with note a].

Nukkusu "to balance an account", from *nikkassu* (OAk *u-na-ki-is*, 3x, cf. Foster, NABU 89/115).

Puhhu "to exchange, replace" (D/Dt reciprocal → 9.1.3 sv, also Š in the same meaning in Bo.), from *pūhu* "replacement".

(**Purruṣu** "to perform" (rites), from *parṣu* "rite", also G, see 8.3.2).

Ruggubu "to provide with an attic (*rugbu*)".

Rukkubu "to pollinate" (a date palm), from *rikbu* "male efflorescence" (of a date palm), cf. 8.3.3.

Ruqqû "to make perfume"; AHw sv suggests that it is a denominative of *rīqu* or *riqqu* "perfume, fragrant wood".

Ruttû "to trap, ensnare", acc. to Durand *apud* Lafont, ARM 26/2 p. 505 note c, denominative of *rutû* "trap, snare" (cf. AHw sv *rutu*); only *ib.* p. 504 no. 526: 13.

Summulu "to form a stairway" (LL), acc. to CAD sv, from *simmiltu* "ladder, stairway".

Ṣubbû "to form an army", from *ṣābu* "troops, workers, army" (BrockmonT. p. 20: 12', acc. to Kutscher, *ib.* p. 31 (OAk)).

Ṣuddû "to provide with food, provision", from *ṣidītu* "provisions" (also NAPR 5, 5: C 12 // D 06'; A 16 // C 17 // D 12' (VA *ṣú-ud-du-tam*); A 44 // D 12'; AbB 13, 104: 7'. 14').

Ṣullulu "to cover with a roof, put on top", from *ṣulūlu, ṣulultu* "roof", ultimately from *ṣillu* "shade"; cf. *ṣalālu* "to sleep" (different root? or did *ṣalālu* originally mean "to lie in the shade"?).

Šubbutu "to lodge", from *šubtu* "seat, dwelling" (only YOS 7, 5: 8f, NB).

Šukkunu "to appoint sb *šaknu* (governor, commander)" (cf. *wukkulu* below) (only CT 34, 41: 24 (= TCS 5, 169: 24), doubtful, cf. Grayson *ad l.*, CAD sv *šakānu* 9; AHw sv *š.* D).

***Šummunu** "to anoint with oil" (only passive Dt), from *šamnu* "oil" (only SAA 10, 226: r.2, NA).

***Šuttupu** (only reciprocal Dt *šutattupu*, cf. 9.1.3) "to form a partnership", from *šutāpu* "partner".

Šuwwuru "to surround" (ARM 26/1 p. 295 no. 129: 22), denom. of *šewēru* "ring", acc. to Durand, *l.c.* note c (doubtful, cf. Gröneberg 1989: 30 note 6). [Or. 41, 344: 15 read *li-še*$_{20}$*-ši*$^{!}$*-ra-nim*, cf. Moran, RA 77, 189].

Tullulu "to equip, fit out", from *tillu/û* "outfit, equipment, trappings".
***Tuppû** (only OA *tappû*) "gemeinsame Sache machen mit (+ acc.)", acc. to AHw sv *tappûm* II, from *tappû* "partner, companion" (CCT 3, 20: 30f).
Ṭuppû "to register" (on a tablet (*ṭuppu*)), cf. AHw sv *ṭepû* D 1.
Uhhuzu "to mount in precious materials" (D/Dt), from *ihzū* "mountings".
Uppulu A "to appoint sb one's heir", from *aplu* "heir, oldest son" (only KH r.XV (= § 178): 17, and perhaps CT 4, 37c: 11, cf. Kraus, SD 9, 51 note 124).
Uppulu B "to delouse" (LL), from *uplu* "louse", cf. 8.3.3.
Uppuqu "to make a compact load" (for an *upqum*-donkey) (OA), cf. Veenhof 1972: 3 note 9; also CCT 6, 11a: 10.
Urrunu "to consider guilty, incriminate", from *arnu* "guilt, punishment" (ARM 26/1 p. 175 no. 39: 45; 26/2 p. 70f no. 312: 12'. 15') (in EA also stative G, cf. AHw sv *arānu* II).
Ussuqu "to apportion", from *isqu* "lot, destiny, share", especially in *isqēti ussuqu* "to apportion lots", cf. CAD sv *esēqu* 2; AHw sv *esēqu* D 1.
Uwwû "to alter (fraudulently)", from *iwîtu* "fraud"; RA 63, 49: 50 (*ú-wi-i*); *ib.* 54 (*ú-wu-ú*); SD 5, 30: 40 (*ú-wu-ú*), object "tablet" or *tā'ītu* (paronomastic), cf. Finkelstein, RA 63, 52, *pace* Kraus RA 73, 135ff.
Wukkulu "to appoint sb *waklu* (overseer)", acc. to AHw sv *wakālu* D, cf. *šukkunu* above (AbB 3, 11: 15; VS 18, 114: 9).
Wulludu "to act as midwife", i.e., "to deliver" (a woman in labour), or "to help (the child) being born"; possibly denominative of *wildu* "child", or *(w)ālittu* "woman in labour", cf. 8.3.3.
Wuššupu "to conjure", denom. of *(w)āšipu* "conjurer, exorcist" ? (cf. AHw sv *(w)ašāpu*).
(*Wu''ûm* AHw → *uwwû*).
***Wuzzunu** (only OA *wazzunum*) "to lend one's ear, listen", from *uznu* "ear" (ATHE 64: 43; AKT 2, 32: 23), cf. AHw sv *wazzunum*.

8.5. Conclusions

This enumeration shows that the denominative D-stems are typically transitive, and that most of them conform to the definition of high transitivity given in 5.3 and 5.4, because they tend to denote a telic action with an agentive subject and an affected object. Apart from *gullulu* "to act unjustly towards, commit a sin", which has an indirect object, and *kuzzubu* "to flatter, fawn", which has a quite irregular relationship to *kazbu* "charming, attractive", the only exceptions to this general situation are rare and more or less doubtful words (*nukkusu, summulu, ṣubbû* and **wuzzunu*).

This suggests that these verbs appear in the D-stem because their meaning is congruent with the overall association of the D-stem with a high degree of transitivity, and not primarily because it has a denominative function. In a few individual cases, such as *puhhu* "to replace" and *ṭuppû* "to register", formal factors may also have played a part.

8.6. D tantum verbs

Apart from the D tantum verbs which can be explained as denominative there are also D-stems without corresponding G-stem which cannot be so explained. These are listed in this section. It also includes a few D-stems of which a G-stem is attested, but with a meaning so divergent that they are unlikely to belong to the same root. D tantum verbs of which the meaning cannot be established with a reasonable degree of certainty have been omitted. This applies in particular to the verbs which only occur in V R 45, a lexical text which lists a large number of D forms without any further details as to their meaning or the verb from which they are derived.

As noted in 8.2, there are no obvious reasons why most of these verbs do not occur in the G-stem as well. A few speculations on this point will be found in 8.7.

Bubbulu "to parade, carry a standard", cf. Villard, FM 1 p. 147f, often as participle *mubabbilu* "standard-bearer", mostly in OB Mari; for references (not for the meaning) see also CAD/AHw sv *mubabbilu*. It is possible that *bubbulu* is related to *w/babālu* "to carry"; in that case it is comparable to the lexicalized D-stems of 6.8.3.

***Buddudu** "to squander", cf. CAD/AHw sv (NA).

Buhhusu "prüfen", acc. to Von Soden, Or. 46, 185 and AHw 1549a sv (Aramaic loanword, only in AOAT 2, 299: 6).

Bullu "hinwerfen" acc. to AHw 1549a sv, correcting 137a sv, in STC 1, 220: 6. 8 [*ṣehru*] *u rabû ú-ba-al-lu dulla* "young and old lay down (their) work", acc. to Von Soden *apud* Reschid and Wilcke, ZA 65, 61. The other instances quoted AHw sv 137a rather belong to *abālu* "to bring, carry". They all represent the euphemistic expression *šimtu PN ubil* "Fate carried PN away", i.e., "PN died". CAD sv *abālu* A 4b is doubtless correct in listing this idiom under *abālu* "to bring, carry": all forms can be derived from *abālu*, except *ub-bil* (BabLaws 340: 17), which is doubtless a bad spelling, and *ub-til* (Erra IV 101; BWL 70: 9). As Lambert, BWL 303 *ad* line 9, suggests, this form owes its existence to a reanalysis of *ubil* as coming from *bullu*, on the model of, for instance, *ukīl* from *kullu* "to hold". The correctness of Lambert's view is confirmed by the occurrence of *ub-til* in another idiomatic expression which normally has *abālu*: ZA 65, 56: 51 (whoever) *ana mimma epšet marušti u gullulti qāssu ub-til* "has intended (lit. has brought his hand to) any deed of evil and wickedness".

Buqquru "untersuchen", acc. to Von Soden, Or. 37, 270 and AHw 1549a sv (Aramaic loanword, only ABL 295: 7 acc. to Von Soden *l.c.*).

Bussumu "erfreuen", acc. to Von Soden, StBoT. 7, 21 *ad* IV 12 and AHw 1592a sv (AbB 8, 69: 8); also adj. *bussumu* "angenehm".

Bussuru "to bring good news, to praise", cf. CAD/AHw sv (also ARM 26/2 p. 432 no. 494: 14).

Butturu "verstümmeln" acc. to AHw sv (not in CAD), only in *mubattiru*, a pernicious insect, cf. AHw/CAD sv, and in *Butturu*, a MB horse name, cf. 10.6.3.2.

Bu"û "to look for, examine, strive" (D/Dt/Dtn), cf. CAD/AHw sv.

Buzzu'u "to treat unjustly, put under pressure", cf. AHw sv, CAD sv *bazā'u* (cf. 8.1); also AbB 12, 90: 11; acc. to Joannès also "to rob, plunder" in OB Mari: ARM 26/2 p. 339 no. 435: 14 (city); FM 2 p. 149 no. 82: 21' (ice).

Duhhusu "to harass", cf. CAD/AHw sv. [The Dt forms mentioned AHw sv Dt 1/2 have been assigned to *nahāsu* Dt in 7.6.1; those under Dt 3 (said of stars) are unclear, cf. CAD sv *nahāsu* A 10].

Dummû "?", cf. CAD/AHw sv; byform of *damāmu* "to mourn"? (the translation of AHw "weinend halten" (as a denominative of *dimtu* "tear") seems very unlikely, cf. Landsberger, WO 3, 52 note 27c).

Duppuru "to remove, go away" (D/Dt) [Dtn ARM 10, 154; 7' uncert.], cf. Moran, JCS 33, 44ff, and CAD/AHw sv, AHw sv *ṭapāru* D/Dtn/Dt); also ZA 68, 115: 60; ARM 27, 131: 18; JCS 42, 174: 17.

Durruku "to thresh", cf. AHw 1550a sv *darāku* III D and 1575b sv *mudarriktu* (NA loanword from Aramaic).

Guhhubu "to cough", cf. CAD/AHw.

Gullulu B "to make blind", cf. AHw 1555b sv *galālu* II D, CAD sv *qullulu* v. a-1'/b [a-2' obscure]; for *gullulu* A see 8.4.2.

Gu"ušu (*guššu*) "to vomit", cf. AHw sv *gâšu* II (no G forms attested), not in CAD (also BAM 90: 16 acc. to AHw 1556a sv *gâšu* II; SpTU 3, 88: II 10).

***Guzzû** "to hide" (intrans.) (only Dt, only LL).

Huddušu "to rejoice" (also Dt, only LL), cf. CAD sv, AHw sv *hadāšu*.

Huttutu "to be infested with vermin" (CAD), "mit Ungeziefer verseuchen" (AHw) (only LL).

Kubbû "to patch, sew", cf. CAD/AHw sv.

Kullu "to hold, offer" (D/Dt/Dtn), cf. CAD/AHw sv.

Kullumu "to show, instruct" (D/Dt pass./recipr. → 9.1.3/Dtn/ŠD), cf. CAD/AHw sv; also Š in the same meaning, see 7.5.5.1 end.

Kunnušu "einsammeln" acc. to AHw sv *kanāšu* II D (no G forms), only SAA 5, 3: r.20.

Kupputu B "to gather, collect" acc. to CAD sv *k*. B; possibly the same word as A, cf. AHw *l.c.* For *kupputu* A see 8.4.1.

Kuṣṣudu "to delay" acc. to CAD sv, AHw sv *kaṣādu* "festhalten", D id (also Dt pass.), but also N attested, so that the non-occurrence of G is probably accidental.

Lummu "auflösen" acc. to AHw sv *l*. III, CAD sv *l*. v.: mng. uncert.; only *tu-lam* and *tu-la-am* in medical texts, in the same contexts as *tulammam* from *lamāmu* "to chew": errors or a root variant?

Lupputu "to be delayed" (D/Dt, cf. 9.1.6), cf. CAD sv *lapātu* 4k, AHw sv *lapātu* D 3, and cf. 8.1.

***Lu"upu** "in ein Tuch hüllen", acc. to AHw sv *la"upum* II, CAD sv **luhhupu* v. "to treat textiles in a particular way"; cf. also Veenhof 1972: 96 note 158; OA only, with VA *la"upum*.

Muggušu "to neglect?" acc. to CAD sv; AHw sv: "?"; only CT 45, 52: 16.

Muqqu "to do slowly, hesitate" (D/Dt, cf. 9.1.6), stat. "to be slow, sluggish", cf. CAD/AHw sv (also AbB 12, 68: 26; ARM 26/2 p. 285 no. 411: 44; often with *ana* + infin., but in ARM 26/2 p. 298 no. 416: 7 + acc.

Murrû "to be silent" acc. to CAD sv (not in AHw); only LL and KAR 92: r.20.

Muššu'u "to rub, anoint" (D/Dtn), cf. CAD/AHw sv.

Mu"û "to praise, adore", cf. CAD sv *mu'û* A, AHw 1576b sv *mu"û* "(Gott) anrufen".

***Muzzu** (only Dt) "to refuse", cf. CAD/AHw sv *mâzu*.

***Nuddudu** "to search", cf. CAD sv, *pace* AHw sv *nadādu* D 1/2.

Nugguru "to denounce", cf. CAD sv; AHw sv *nagāru* II D.

Nuhhutu "to trim, clip", cf. CAD sv; AHw sv *nahātu* D, and cf. 8.1.

Nuhhuṭu "to chuckle, hiccup" acc. to CAD sv, "etwa "schnaufen" ?" acc. to AHw sv.

Nuppuqu A "sich verstopfen, sich verhärten" acc. to AHw sv *napāqu* D; acc. to CAD sv *napāqu* mng. unkn. (G in LL).

Nuppuqu B "to pay attention", cf. CAD sv (only LL and PN).

Nussusu "to shake, wave, flap" acc. to CAD sv; "schütteln" acc. to AHw sv. Cf. also *nasāsu* in 7.6.1 sv and *nazāzu* in CAD/AHw.

Pullusu "to engage sb's attention, disturb" (D/Dt), stative "to be busy, occupied", cf. AHw sv *palāsu* D/Dt, and Durand, ARM 26/1 p. 170 note b.

Puqqu "to heed, pay attention" (D/Dt stative → 9.1.6), cf. AHw sv (+ acc. or *ana*).

***Pussuku** "to remove, clear away", cf. AHw sv *passuku* (NA).

Qubbulu "to accept", cf. CAD sv *qubbulu* A, AHw sv *qubbal* (Aramaic loanword).

Qu"û "to wait, wait for, trust", cf. CAD/AHw sv (+ acc. or *ana*).

Ruggû "to wrong, claim sth fraudulently", cf. AHw sv (+ acc. or *ana*).

Ruppudu "?", cf. AHw sv *rapādu* II D 3: "v[on] Krampfbewegungen Todkranker" in the medical texts of TDP, translated "er bäumt sich auf". Related to *rapādu* "to walk around"?

Russû "etwa '(durch Wasser) aufweichen'" acc. to AHw sv.

Ru"umu "to cut off", cf. AHw sv.

Subbusu "to assemble" (trans.), cf. CAD/AHw sv, and Von Soden, Or. 37, 266 and 46, 194 (Aramaic loanword).

Suddudu "to take care of, care for" (+ acc.), cf. CAD sv, AHw sv *sadādu* D. Since the meaning of G is unknown, it is difficult to determine whether D and G belong together.

Sullû (SB/NB/NA often replaced by *ṣullû*) "to pray, appeal" (D/Dtn), cf. CAD/AHw sv (+ acc. or *ana*).

Suppû A "to pray" (D/Dtn), CAD/AHw sv (+ acc. or *ana*).

Suppû B "to abduct, take away, seduce" (D/Dt), cf. CAD sv *suppû* B, AHw sv *sepû* III; mostly said of slaves, slave girls and comparable persons (also ARM 21 p. 556 no. 410: XI 20'; ARM 26/2 p. 379 no. 453: 23. 28), but also of kings (Mél. Kupper 129: 31: same word?).

Surrû "überprüfen" acc. to AHw sv *surrûm* II; CAD sv *surrû*: mng. uncert.

Ṣubbû "to watch from afar, examine" (D/Dt), cf. CAD/AHw sv; also Št "to execute according to plan".

Ṣullû → *sullû*.

Ṣummuru "to strive for, wish, plot", cf. CAD sv *ṣamāru* v., AHw sv *ṣ*. I (+ acc. or *ana*); cf. 8.1.

Ṣuppu "to rub, rub down a horse" acc. to CAD sv *ṣ*. v., "über-, abdecken" acc. to AHw sv *ṣ*. II.

***Ṣ/suwwû** "reden?" acc. to AHw sv *ṣawwûm*; CAD sv **suwwû*: mng. uncert.; only KTS 15: 20 (OA).

Šuddû → *tuddû*.

Šugguru "to lie, cheat", cf. CAD sv *šugguru*, AHw sv *šuqquru* (also AbB 6, 188: 31').

Šuhhû A "to have (illicit) sexual intercourse" (D/Dt) acc. to CAD sv *š*. A v.; "schwängern" acc. to AHw sv *š*. III (with acc. or *itti*).

Šuhhû B "to remove, abolish, destroy", cf. CAD sv *š*. B and C, which corresponds to AHw sv *š*. II "unkenntlich machen".

Šukkulu "to wipe away, polish" (D/Dt/Dtn), cf. Deller and Watanabe, ZA 70, 198ff, with NABU 1990/3 (Von Soden, NABU 1991/55 unlikely, cf. *šaqālu* "to make scarce"), and CAD sv (also ShT p. 81: 60 (*zūt bēlišu* "the sweat of his master"); SpTU 3, 67: IV 20).

Šummu "to reflect, deliberate", cf. CAD/AHw sv; also Št with the same meaning? (only in PNs).

Šurru "to bend down, lean, go down" (D/Dtn), cf. CAD/AHw sv.

Šurrû "to begin, inaugurate", cf. CAD/AHw sv.

***Šu"û** (only Dt *šuta"û*) "to be negligent, treat sth lightly", from the root *Š-'-I* acc. to Landsberger, WZKM 56, 120 note 30.

Tuddû and **šuddû** are secondary formations built on the stative D *uddu* (and *šuddû* on the stative Š ?) of *(w)uddû* "to inform, mark, identify" in the NB and LB expression *ṣupur PN kīma kunukkišu tuddât/šuddât* "PN's fingernail is marked (on the tablet) instead of his seal"; cf. AHw sv *tuddû*, CAD sv *idû* 4a.

Tullû "to adorn, drape", cf. AHw sv.

Ubburu "to accuse, bind (by magic)", cf. AHw sv *abāru* III D (also SpTU 2, 19: 10).

Uhhuru "to be delayed, be in arrears", cf. AHw sv *ahāru* D.

Ukkudu "to slander" (only LL), cf. AHw sv *ekēdu* D.

Unnutu (D intrans./Dt → 9.1.4) "to become dim, faint, weak" (mainly of stars), cf. AHw sv *enētu* D/Dt; more often used in the stative in the same contexts, cf. App. to Ch. X sv *unnutu*.

Urruhu "to frighten", cf. CAD sv *arāhu* A lex. sect., AHw sv *arāhu* I D 4.
Uṣṣuru A "to listen attentively", cf. AHw sv *uṣṣurum* II.
Uṣṣuru B "to sever, cut off", only in Angim 140 acc. to AHw 1591b sv *u.* III D (part.).
(W)urrû (*murrû*) "to cut off" (D/Dt), cf. AHw sv *(w)urrû*, CAD sv *arû* C "to cut branches" (G only LL).
(W)ussû (*mussû*) "to identify, distinguish" (D/Dt), cf. AHw sv.
(W)uṣṣû (*muṣṣû*) "to spread, open wide", cf. AHw sv.
(W)uṣṣuṣu "to interrogate" (D/Dt), cf. AHw sv.
Zubbulu "to keep sb waiting (trans.), linger" (intrans.), cf. CAD sv *zabālu* 3/4, AHw sv *zabālu* D; cf. 8.1.
Zummû "to be deprived of sth" (+ adjunct acc.), deprive sb of sth" (+ double acc.), cf. CAD/AHw sv.

8.7. Some final observations on the D tantum verbs

As indicated in 8.2, it is usually not possible to determine the reason for the absence of a G-stem in these D tantum verbs. They are no less diverse in meaning than the G-stem is, and the semantic homogeneity which we observe in the denominative D-stems discussed in 8.4, most of which imply a high degree of transitivity, is conspicuously lacking. We will restrict ourselves to pointing out one fact which may have influenced the absence of a G-stem in some of these verbs.

Both among the D tantum verbs which are transitive, but imply a low degree of transitivity according to the criteria discussed in 5.3 and 5.4, and among those which are intransitive, we find a considerable number of verbs which denote atelic activities that imply a certain duration. They can be divided into clusters of verbs which semantically belong together:

1. verbs of waiting, lingering, delaying, etc.: *kuṣṣudu* (?), *lupputu, qu''û, uhhuru, zubbulu,* possibly also *muqqu*;
2. verbs denoting sounds and bodily functions: *guhhubu, gu''ušu, nuhhuṭu, nuppuqu* A, and *ruppudu.*
3. verbs of praying: *s/ṣullû, suppû, mu''û*;
4. verbs of observing and reflecting: *ṣubbû, šummu, uṣṣuru* A;
5. verbs for other atelic activities: *bu''û, puqqu, ṣummuru.*
6. A special case is the very frequent D tantum verb *kullu* "to hold, to offer", which is transitive but basically stative, and therefore also a low transitivity verb.

These verbs are either intransitive or have a low degree of transitivity; for many of the latter this is indicated by the fact that they tend to be construed interchangeably with a direct object and with *ana* (cf. 5.5.1), for instance, *qu''û, s/ṣullû, suppû, puqqu* and *ṣummuru.*

Some of them can be related to other groups of D-stems, especially those of Type II, listed in 7.6: compare the verbs of sound and bodily functions mentioned here with those listed in 7.6.1 and 7.6.2 (Groups I and II), and, for instance, *ṣummuru* with *kapādu, kaṣāpu* and *ṣarāmu* from Group III in 7.6.3. They are all typically intransitive fixed valency verbs whose D-stem is not factitive.

It is possible that the absence of a G-stem is related to the atelic durative notion inherent in the meaning of these verbs. This is suggested by GAG § 88h with regard to some of them. It is, however, clear that this is not a sufficient reason, since we find numerous verbs of the same semantic nature which are common in the G-stem; it is, at the most, one factor among many others which together are responsible for the absence of a G-stem.

Notes to Chapter Eight

1 The text in question is kt u/k 4 (= Kültepe-kaniş 2 pl. 50 no. 2a): 9f *ba-ZU-um u šillatum ibašši*, cf. CAD sv *šillatu* 2a.

2 As "Denom." AHw further characterizes the G-stems *ahû* II, *arādu* II (EA), *arānu* II (EA), *dašāpu, derû, *enēbu, halābu* (from Semitic *ḥala/īb* "milk"), *kabāšu* I, *kanāzu, labānu* II, *labātu, nalāšu, nawûm* II, *parā'u* II, *qadû* III, *râ'u, rêtu, ṣe'ārum, ša'āru* I, *šarāku* II and *šêru*; as "wohl Denom." it characterizes *abāru* III, *awûm, baqālu, bêlu* and *erēpu*, and as "Denom. ?" *bakāru, dalû* II, *dešû, ebēlu, hadāšu, hahû* II, *katāru, nâpu* II, *panāku, pasāmu, qemûm, šêpu, ṭêmu* and *za'û* II. For *zaqānu* "to have a beard" (only inf.), which AHw - doubtless correctly - claims to be a denominative of *ziqnu* "beard", see note 2 to Ch. V.

3 Apart from the "lexical" Št-stem, in which the infix *-ta-* is clearly a reflex of the prefix *ta-* of the source noun, the verbal stems with infixed *-ta-* (Gt, Dt) hardly seem to be used as denominatives, if at all. Cases which have been claimed as such are *alālu* Gt "to shout *alāla*" (cf. AHw sv *alālu* III "ein Freudenlied singen"), *paqādu* Dt "sich bemühen", acc. to AHw sv *paqādu* Dt (LB), which is a denominative of *pitqudu* "umsichtig" acc. to GAG § 93d, and *qabālu* Gt "to fight" (cf. AHw sv *qitbulu*, rejected by CAD sv *qubbulu* B). Of these cases only the first two have anything to say for them; the third one is probably spurious. In *šutattupu* "to form a partnership", a denominative of *šutāpu* "partner", the Dt form is doubtless due to the reciprocal nuance inherent in its meaning, cf. 9.1.3.

4 The dictionaries handle these verbs differently. CAD generally regards them as D tantum verbs and lists them accordingly under the same form as is used here, but if an infinitive G is attested as a citation form in LL - which is ignored here, cf. note 2 to Ch. V - the verb is listed as a G-stem (cf. *barāmu, dašāpu, dešû, qadāšu* and *sakāku*). AHw generally lists them under the corresponding G-stems, except *uššušu*, for which see 11.2.2.

CHAPTER NINE

THE SECONDARY STEMS OF THE D-STEM

9.0. This chapter deals with the secondary stems derived from the D-stem: the Dt-stem, the Dtn-stem and the ŠD-stem. These are not the only secondary derivations of the D-stem; in NA we find a passive Dtt-stem (GAG § 93e), which has been treated here as part of the Dt-stem, but deserves a fuller discussion in a NA context (cf. Von Soden, Or. 19, 385ff; Parpola, StOr. 55, 199f); moreover, especially in OB and SB, there are some forms which show not only gemination but also reduplication of the second radical. Whiting (1981: 18ff) refers to them as DR-, DRt- and DRtn-stems. Many of these forms are controversial as to how they should be analysed and do not seem to have a well-defined function. Some of them, however, can be plausibly explained as extensions of Dt-stems with reciprocal or pluralizing meaning, and are mentioned as such in sections 9.1.3 and 9.1.5, respectively. Other controversial instances are not discussed.[1]

9.1. The Dt-stem

The basic function of the Dt-stem is to serve as the intransitive counterpart of the D-stem. It is based on the general detransitivizing function of the morpheme *-ta-* (cf. 4.1.2.1), and in actual contexts it can be realized in various ways, depending on the meaning of the verb in question and on the context. They all have in common that they involve a reduction in the degree of transitivity. Moreover, the Dt-stem is occasionally used to underline plurality of the subject, not only in cases in which the corresponding D-stem underlines plurality of the object (for such cases see Chapter VI), but also in some other verbs.

Six different realizations of these basic functions can be roughly distinguished. First of all, the Dt-stem is used as a general passive/intransitive derivation of the D-stem (9.1.1); second and third, two special manifestations of this use in a specific class of verbs are the reflexive and reciprocal functions (9.1.2 and 9.1.3 respectively); fourth, the Dt-stem also serves to fientivize *purrus* forms, even in cases where no (factitive) D-stem is attested (9.1.4); fifth, it can also be used in contrast to the Gt-stem in order to underline plurality of the subject (9.1.5), and finally, it can be used to underline the intransitive nature of some D-stems, most of them belonging to Type II (9.1.6). Section 9.1.7 discusses some difficult but interesting cases which do not clearly belong to one of the six previous groups. Forms which are formally Dt-stems but in fact part of the paradigm of the Dt(n)-stem (cf. 4.1.2.2) are discussed in 9.2.

This survey does not contain an exhaustive enumeration of attested Dt forms, but intends to give a survey of the possible translations of the Dt-stem.

9.1.1. The general passive/intransitive use of the Dt-stem

The most common use of the Dt-stem is to serve as passive/intransitive derivation of the D-stem. In this construction the direct object of the transitive sentence with the D-stem is promoted to subject. There are no convincing examples in which the original agent of the transitive sentence is retained as an oblique constituent; this does not only hold for the Dt-stem, but for all passive categories of Akkadian, and also for statives which require a passive translation.

Just as the N-stem, the Dt-stem can refer both to actions performed by an agent which is not overtly expressed, and to processes which come about without the intervention of an agent. It depends on the meaning of the verb and on the context which of the two possibilities applies. However, many contexts are ambiguous in this respect.

Generally speaking, the passive/intransitive Dt-stem is not particularly frequent; even for very common transitive verbs we hardly ever find more than a few instances in the dictionaries. This is doubtless related to the relatively restricted use that Akkadian makes of passive verb forms in general - such as the passive N-stem and the passive Št-stem - but possibly also to the fact noted in 5.6.5 that the use of the D-stem is largely motivated by high transitivity, so that the use of the Dt-stem is basically restricted to sentences which are felt as derivations of an active sentence.

A few random examples of Dt-stems requiring a passive translation are the following:

(01) AbB 6, 191: 20f *ina muhhi udêma qātu lā ú-tam-ma-ad-ma* "let no hand be laid on the utensils" (passive of the common idiom *qāta ummudu* "to lay hand(s) on");

(02) Maqlû V ll. 15 (reading acc. to Geller apud Mayer, Or. 61, 382 n. 9) *mannu pû iptil uṭṭatu ú-kaṣ-ṣir* (...) *kīma pû lā ippattil uṭṭatu lā uk-ta-aṣ-ṣa-ru* "who has ever twined (G) chaff and knotted (D) barley? (...) just as chaff cannot be twined (N), (and) barley cannot be knotted (Dt)";

(03) UET 5, 75: 4f *ṣalam PN hurāṣam ú-ta-ah-ha-az* "the statue of PN will be inlaid with gold";

(04) RA 40, 82: 15 *bīt awīlim us-sà-pa-ah* "the man's estate will be squandered".

The clearest instances showing omission of an implied agent, where a passive translation is usually most appropriate, are found in the Dt-stems of the transitive verbs which generally have a high degree of transitivity, especially those discussed in Chapter VI and many transitive D tantum verbs. Common examples of the former kind are the Dt-stems of the following verbs in the Appendix to Chapter VI (which includes references): *abātu* "to destroy, ruin", *balālu* "to mix" and "to pollute", *esēru* B "to shut in, enclose", *gamāru* "to finish, to use up", or, said of persons, "to assemble" (trans.) (but see below), *hepû* "to break, demolish" (see also below), *kamāsu* "to finish, collect, bring in", *kasû* "to bind", *katāmu* "to cover, close", *pasāsu* "to cancel, destroy", *pašāru* "to untie, release", *paṭāru* "to loosen, redeem" (see also below), *petû* "to open", and *sanāqu* "to check, keep under control, harass".

Examples of Dt-stems of transitive D tantum verbs (see 8.4 and 8.6) for which a passive translation is most appropriate are those of the following verbs: *bu''û* "to look for" (cf. CAD sv 6, AHw sv Dt), *duppuru* "to remove" (cf. CAD sv 3, AHw sv *ṭapāru* Dt), *kullulu* "to veil, crown" (with subject "bride" or "wife" BiOr. 28, 11: 17'; SpTU 1, 83: 2), *kullumu* "to show, instruct" (cf. CAD sv 6, AHw sv Dt 1) and *lu''û* "to make dirty, defile" (OEC 6, 28: 8; BRM 4, 9: 13), and see also (03) above.

However, for some Dt forms of these transitive verbs it is difficult to decide whether a passive or an intransitive or still another translation is most suitable; this applies, for instance, to *abātu* Dt, if it said of buildings and mountains: "to be destroyed" or "to collapse" (cf. App. to Ch. VI sv **1.**/**2.**), to *gamāru* Dt "to be finished, used up" or "to run out" (of supplies, cf. *ib.* sv **1.**), or, if it is said of persons, "to be assembled" or "to assemble" (intrans.) (cf. *ib.* sv **9.**), and to *paṭāru* Dt "to be loosened" or "to come loose". For *paṣānu* Dt one may hesitate between a passive and a reflexive translation in KAV 1: V 66 *harimtu lā tu-up-ta-aṣ-ṣa-an* "a prostitute shall not veil herself" or "shall not be veiled" (cf. 9.1.2).

In other contexts some of these Dt-stems clearly require an intransitive translation. Some verbs with basic meanings such as "to destroy" or "to untie" are said of buildings in the Dt-stem and then mean "to decay, fall into ruin", e.g.:

(05) RIME 4, 382: 52f (Six great forts ...) *in* [*l*]*a*[*b*]*irūtišunu in r*[*a*]*mānišunu up-ta-as-sí-sú-ma* "in their old age they had fallen into ruin on their own accord" (tr. Frayne);

(06) BagM. 21, 341: 14ff *akītum* (...) *labāriš illikma up-te-eṭ-ṭir* "Das Akîtu (...) war alt geworden und fing an zu zerbröckeln" (tr. Cavigneaux-Ismail) (see further App. to Ch. VI sv *paṭāru* **6.**).

Similar idioms are found for the Dt-stems of *hepû* "to break, destroy" (BWL 146: 38, qu. as (23) in 6.4.9), *paṣādu* (Iraq 4, 186: 16 acc. to AHw sv Dt(t)), *sarāhu* D "to ruin, destroy" (YOS 1, 38: I 22), and *tabāku* "to pour out" (VAB 4, 254: 22).

Other cases of the intransitive use of a Dt-stem of the transitive verbs of Chapter VI are *kaṣāru* Dt "to gather, join forces" and "to gather" (of clouds), and *rakāsu* Dt "to gather", also said of clouds, which are discussed in 9.1.5.

With regard to Dt-stems derived from D-stems of intransitive verbs, which normally have factitive meaning (cf. Chapter VII), the same indeterminacy exists as to whether an agent is implied or not, and, accordingly, whether we should prefer a passive or an intransitive translation.

Generally speaking, a passive translation seems to be most appropriate for Dt forms of D-stems which are more or less lexicalized; this applies, for instance, to the following instances: *akāšu* Dt "to be driven away, expelled", *balāṭu* Dt "to be provided with food" (esp. in *ana butalluṭi*, cf. CAD sv 11, but cf. also *ana bu-tal-lu-ṭi-šú* "in order to be healed" Iraq 55, 66: 4), *bâru* Dt "to be convicted", *emēdu* Dt "to be imposed" (cf. (01) above and see 11.4.2 sv), *kabātu* Dt "to be honoured", *kânu* Dt "to be established, assigned", *labāšu* Dt "to be provided with clothing" (also Iraq 41, 93: 8, see note 5), *nakāru* Dt "to be changed, removed", *parāru* Dt "to be dispersed, shattered", *qalālu* Dt "to be despised", *qatû* Dt "to be finished, paid in full", *šalāmu* Dt "to be compensated", *šanû* Dt "to be remeasured", *târu* Dt "to be returned", *ṭehû* Dt "to be offered" and *wedû* Dt "to be identified, assigned" (see the dictionaries ssvv).

The conditions under which Dt forms of factitive D-stems are used, resemble those under which their stative D is used. This issue is discussed in 10.4.2, where it will be argued that the stative D mostly occurs if the verb in question is to some extent lexicalized, because a lexicalized verb tends to develop a complete paradigm. In other cases, there is a tendency to use suppletive forms of the G-stem for those forms which do not occur in sentences with a high degree of transitivity, such as stative and Dt forms, cf., for instance, (15) - (17) below.

For Dt-stems of factitive D-stems which have not been lexicalized, it is often difficult to determine which translation is preferable. Usually the context leaves both possibilities open. Consider the following sentences:

(07) BAM 323: 24 var. *ṣētukka uš-tah-ha-na kala abrātum* "by your glow all people are warmed / become warm" (or even "warm themselves", cf. CAD sv *šahānu* 2; note also Gt *iš-tah-ha-na* in the same context in HGŠ 118: 4);

(08) VAB 4, 94: 30 *ašar kadrūti uk-ta-an-na-šú* "where (even) the mighty ones are made submissive" (tr. CAD sv *kanāšu* 6), or "submit";

(09) RA 40, 90: 11 *mātum ú-ta-wa* "the land will turn / be turned into a wasteland";

(10) RA 44, 30: 49 *ēnum uš-ta-ah-ha* "the high priestess will become / be made pregnant";

(11) ARM 2, 28: 7 (Since last year I have been in control of the water of GN, but now the man of Ešnunna has appeared) *ut-ta-az-zi-iq-ma ṣabāt īnim šâti ul ele"i* "I have become / have been made anxious that I may not be able to hold on to that well".[2]

Other instances are *ašāšu* Dt "to become or be made anxious (BWL 40: 47), *napāšu* Dt "to expand or be expanded" (CT 39, 11: 40), *qatāru* Dt "to become or be made dejected" (CT 39, 46: 55), *sakāku* Dt "to become or be made deaf" (BWL 52: 18), *šahātu* Dt "to become or be made fearful" (Erra I 25) and *šakāsu* Dt "to become or be made dry" (Iraq 25, 184: 23, cf. Livingstone, Fs. Deller 178). This kind of ambiguity is structural in verbs such as *edēšu* Dt "to become new" or "to be made new" (or even "to renew oneself", cf. 10.1.2.), and in the Dt-stems of *ebēbu, elēlu* and *quddušu* "to become pure", "to be purified" (or "to purify oneself", cf. 9.1.2).

In most cases, however, its seems more natural to translate such Dt forms as ingressives (inchoatives) ("to become"), rather than as passives; in the following instances this seems to be the obvious way:

(12) ACh. Išt. 26: 28f *šumma* ^{mul}AŠ-<u>iku</u> *innamirma ut-tab-baṭ / ú-tak-kal* "If Pegasus has appeared and becomes bright / dark";

(13) CBSM p. 90 § 31: 1 *amēlu šū ul-tab-bar* "this man will grow old" (or perhaps: "will live long", as (18) - (24) below), see further CAD sv *labāru* 5);

(14) AMT 48, 1: 8. 11 + 78, 3: 5. 8 *inib irrî adi lā uk-tap-pi-tu tubbal tasâk* "you dry and bray the fruit of the *irrû*-plant before it becomes compact" (reading and tr. acc. to CAD sv *kupputu* A v. 3).

Similar instances can be quoted from *abālu* Dt "to become dry" (RA 85, 19: 16 (*pace* Anbar and Stol)), *(h)adāru* Dt "to become perturbed" (STT 23: 31 // 25: 31 acc. to CAD sv *a.* A 4), *danānu* Dt "to become strong" (DA 7: 24; Gilg. Bo. 15), *dešû* Dt "to become abundant" (cf. CAD sv *dešû* v. 3), *ekēlu* Dt "to become dark" (RA 46, 96: 76), *enēšu* Dt "to become weak" (financially: TC 1, 29: 17 (OA)), *eṭû* Dt "to become dark" (cf. CAD sv *eṭû* v. 3), *habāṣu* Dt "to become elated" (Erra V 21 (but *habāṣu* Dt in Or. 17, 418: 19 apparently refers to a sound, cf. perhaps 7.6.1)), *maṭû* Dt "to become less, to decrease" (Gilg. I IV 28; SAA 10, 294: r.32), *na-w/māru* Dt "to become bright" (ACh. Ad. 17: 19), *pahāru* Dt "to come together" (cf. AHw sv Dt), *rapāšu* Dt "to become wide" (BAM 168: 52), and *rašû* Dt "to become red" (EAK 1, 101: 17). Further instances are the Dt forms without corresponding D-stem enumerated in 9.1.4.

This state of affairs raises the question what the difference is between these Dt-stems and the corresponding G-stems, which, especially in the case of adjectival verbs, usually require an ingressive translation as well; for instance, the G-stems of *danānu* and *rapāšu* also mean "to become strong" and "to become wide" respectively. In addition, some adjectival verbs also use the N-stem with ingressive meaning, cf. GAG § 90g.

In such cases, G and Dt seem to be largely interchangeable; this can be inferred from instances such as the following, where Dt and G (in (17) perhaps N) occur side by side:

(15) AGH 80: 81ff *kīma šamê lūlil* (...) *kīma erṣeti lūbib* (...) *kīma qereb šamê lu-ut-ta-mir* "may I become pure as the sky (...), clean as the earth (...), bright as the middle of heaven";

(16) *ib.* 134: 90 *tarbaṣī lirpiš liš-tam-di-lu supūrī* "may my cattle pen become large, may my fold become vast" (tr. CAD sv *šadālu* 3);

(17) RA 46, 96: 76 [*ūm*]*ūšu ú-te-ek-ki-lu šamû id-da-*[*a'-mu*] "his [day]s have darkened, the sky has turned dark" (where *idda*[*'mū*] may be a perfect G, but is more probably a pret. N).

For some verbs, however, the Dt-stem is used to express a nuance different from the G-stem: whereas G basically denotes a process, some Dt-stems are more likely to refer to an activity. They have an animate subject, and instead of "to become" they rather express the notion of "to act, to behave in a particular way". These activities are similar to the ones expressed by some factitive D-stems used without object, which were discussed in 7.4.3. Cf. the following instances of the Dt-stems of *gašāru, gapāru* and *napāšu*:

(18) Gilg. I IV 38f (in Uruk) *ašar Gilgameš* (...) *kī rīmi ug-da-aš-šá-ru eli nišī* "where Gilgameš, like a wild bull, acts overbearingly towards the people " (also *ib.* 46);

(19) SAA 8, 255: r.7 *kabtu ug-da-ap-pa-šá-am-ma lemutti ippuš* "a mighty person will act haughtily and commit evil." (perhaps also AMT 78, 8: 9 acc. to AHw sv *gapāšu* Dt 2);

(20) FM 1 p. 115: 18 (If I have been sitting in my house for only one day) *adi ana kīdim uṣṣûma ut-ta-ap-pa-šu napištī iššuš* "I feel heavy-hearted until I can go outside and breathe freely".

The most common instance of this kind of Dt-stem is *šarāhu* Dt "to boast, glory in, act arrogantly", from *šarhu* "proud", cf. CAD sv *šarāhu* A 4., e.g.:[3]

(21) RA 45, 172: 30f *kīma* (...) *tu-uš-ta-ra-hu ina qereb ekalli* "when you act haughtily in the midst of (your) palace" (tr. CAD *l.c.*);

(22) RA 75, 111: VII 39 *uš-ta-ar-ra-ah elki* "she behaves arrogantly towards you".

Some other interesting cases are:

(23) AMT 86, 1: II 14 (if the patient is now flushed, now pale, and then his face becomes darker and darker and) *ú-ta-ad-da-ar lā inâh* "he acts with agitation and he cannot rest" (perhaps also SAA 10, 196: r.6 (Parpola: "to keep in the dark", but cf. *adāru* G in 19 and r.2));

(24) ZA 43, 96: 14 *šumma arir ú-tar-ra-ar* "if he is fearful (of nature), he will act with trepidation" (?).

Other instances of Dt forms which might be explained in the same way are *duhhusu* Dt in ZA 43, 104: IV 18), *ešû* Dt in ACh. 2. Spl. 14: 50, *eṭēlu* Dt in KB 6/2, 44: 21 +D, *lemēnu* Dt in CT 38, 17: 105 (*ul-te/tam-man* "he will behave badly" ? or: "he will become unhappy" ?), and *nakāru* Dt in ZA 44, 122: 23.

An intermediate position between the ingressive instances (12) - (14) and the Dt forms (18) - (24), which denote activities performed by agentive subjects, is taken by the Dt-stem of *hamāṭu* "to burn" in:

(25) CT 17, 19: 22 *kīma ša ina išāti nadû uh-tam-maṭ* (// *ú-tam-maṭ* SpTU 2, 2: I 19) "he will burn like one who has been thrown into the fire".[4]

This also applies to several verbs expressing the concepts of blooming and flourishing, which have a remarkable preference for the Dt-stem: *elēpu, enēbu, hanābu* (which are doubtless derived from the same root) and *hanāmu,* both with personal and non-personal subjects:

(26) VAB 4, 190 no. 23: II 5f // YOS 9, 85: 28f *līpū'a ina šarrūti li-te-el-li-pu* "may my descendants flourish in (their) kingship";

(27) Or. 36, 124: 125 *ana gašru mā[r bē]l ilāni ú-tan-nab-šú* "to the mighty son of the lord of the gods I am blooming (with beauty)" (Lambert: "I am seductive"; cf. note on p. 132: *enēbu* Dt "to make oneself *unnubu*"); cf. also in the same context UnDiv. 120 B 17 *tu-uh-tan-nab tu-uh-ta[š-šá-áš]*;

(28) ZA 44, 32: 5f *[uh]-ta-an-na-mu eluššu [ha]-na-bu mašrahu duššupu kuzbu* "blooming splendour (and) sweet charm flourish upon her" (cf. CAD sv *nannabu* end); also Or. 46, 201: 7 *tu-úh-da-na-ma* "you are blooming" (OAk);

(29) Gilg. I II 37 *itiq pertišu uh-tan-na-ba kīma Nisaba* "the locks of his hair grow abundantly like barley" (cf. also Atr. 72: 16 of clouds).

Since verbal D-stems of these verbs are hardly attested (only *elēpu* and *enēbu* in LL), these Dt-stems are related to the ones discussed in 9.1.4, which are directly derived from the corresponding *purrus* forms rather than from the (factitive) verbal D-stems.

Which of the possible translations mentioned in this section is selected in a particular case is purely dependent on the context and the meaning of the verb; the Dt-stem itself denotes no more than a reduction in transitivity. In the following sections some more specialized manifestations of this function are discussed.

9.1.2. Dt forms with a reflexive translation

Some Dt-stems can be translated as reflexives. In a prototypical reflexive sentence the subject acts on himself or herself, and thus performs also a second participant role in the sentence, usually the direct object, see Lichtenberk 1994: 3504ff (cf. also Lyons 1968: 361ff; Givón 1990: 628ff). Lichtenberk distinguishes nominal, verbal and possessive reflexive markers, of which the first two are relevant to Akkadian.

Nominal markers for expressing reflexivity in Akkadian are the nouns *ramānu* (Ass. **ramănu*) or *pagru* with the appropriate personal suffix, cf. GAG § 43a and AHw ssvv. In accordance with Lyons (1968: 362), who distinguishes between "explicitly reflexive", e.g., English *to kill oneself* and "implicitly reflexive", e.g., *to dress, to shave* (in their reflexive interpretation), sentences with the objects *ramānu* and *pagru* can be called "explicitly reflexive". In a small number of verbs, however, reflexivity can also be expressed by means of the affixes *-ta-* and *-na-*; this can be compared to the implicitly reflexive verbs of English, with the difference that in these verbs reflexivity is not coded on the verb at all, whereas in Akkadian it normally requires one of the aforementioned affixes, in other words, the use of the Gt-, the Dt- or the N-stem, cf. GAG^3 § 92h, 93c and 90f, respectively. An exception to this rule, mentioned in 7.4.3 sv, is *ebēbu* D in the meaning "to purify oneself" in OB contracts.

However, these affixes are not specifically reflexive (cf. 9.1), and whether they should be interpreted as reflexive or otherwise in a given case can only be determined on the basis of the context. It turns out to be extremely difficult to distinguish the reflexive use of the Dt-stem from its intransitive and passive use. In the previous section we touched on the Dt-stems of *ebēbu, elēlu* and *quddušu* (*quššudu*). They are often translated as "to purify oneself", "to cleanse oneself", etc., but in many contexts a translation "to be purified" or "to become pure" is equally possible. A striking case in point is the fact that CAD gives some instances of *elēlu* and *ebēbu* Dt a reflexive translation in one place, but a passive translation in another: KAR 177: r.I 35 (*šarru*) *li-te-lil li-te-bi-ib* is translated as "(the king) should purify himself, cleanse himself" by CAD sv *elēlu* 3a, but as "the king shall be purified, be cleansed" sv *ebēbu* 3 (cf. also KAV 218 A II 22 and 32 sv *ebēbu* 3 (= HBA 86: 31f), vs. *ib.* 18 and 20 sv *elēlu* 3a (= HBA 86: 20f). A similar case is *paṣānu* Dt in KAV 1: V 66, mentioned in the preceding section).

The situation illustrated by these verbs is symptomatic of most verbs which are claimed to be reflexive. With the necessary reserves, however, the following Dt-stems seem to be used as implicit reflexives in some contexts at least:

Ebēbu and **elēlu** Dt "to purify oneself", cf. CAD *llcc.*; AHw ssvv Dt.
Edēqu Dt "to dress (oneself)" (Ee I 68).
Edēšu Dt "to renew oneself", cf. CAD sv 3, but AHw sv Dt "erneuert werden".
Eqû Dt "to anoint oneself" (cf. AHw sv *tuqqû*) (AnSt. 10, 112: 32ff // SpTU 1, 1: II 8; BBR 1-20: 29; 79: 4).
Lapātu Dt "to anoint oneself" (BWL 58: 26).

Mesû Dt "to wash (oneself)", cf. CAD sv 6; AHw sv *mesû* II Dt 2 (unambiguously passive instances are Šurpu VII 28 and CT 16, 11: 35 *kīma pūr(i) šikkati lim-te-es-si* "may he be cleaned like a pot for oil" (tr. CAD sv lex. sect.)).

Pasāmu Dt "to veil oneself": TDP 170: 10 [If a patient .....] *libbī qaqqadī iqabbi up-ta-sa-am* "keeps (cf. 6.6.1) saying "my belly, my head!" and keeps veiling himself".

Paṣānu Dt "to veil oneself" (KAV 1: V 65f, see above).

Qatāru Dt "to fumigate oneself", acc. to CAD sv 5, but AHw sv Dt 2 "beräuchert werden".

Quddušu (*quššudu*) Dt "to purify oneself", cf. CAD sv *qadāšu* 5; AHw sv *qadāšu* Dt.

Rakāsu Dt "to bind oneself" in OA: VS 26, 64: 16 *ru-ta-ki-is* (imp.), reflexive of *rakāsu* D "binden, für Zahlungen verantwortlich machen" (AHw sv D 8).

Šahātu Dt "to wash (oneself)", cf. CAD sv *š.* A 7, AHw sv *š.* IV Dt "sich abspülen mit". Note that BBR 26: III 4 is listed in CAD sv *šahāṭu* B 7 "to strip (oneself)"; cf. BagF. 18, 139: 137 where the verb is written with *ṭ* (*tuš-tah-ha-ṭu*); see also the note in CAD Š/1 p. 86b.

The instance of *pasāmu* from TDP quoted in full is one of the most convincing cases of a reflexive Dt, since - in contrast to most other passages - a passive interpretation seems to be excluded here. Many other Dt forms which are claimed to be reflexive in the dictionaries and in GAG are not mentioned here because there seems to be insufficient reason to regard them as reflexive rather than as passive or intransitive.[5]

9.1.3. Reciprocal Dt forms

Some Dt-stems can be used to express reciprocity. In a prototypical reciprocal sentence "there are two participants that play identical pairs of roles vis-à-vis each other" (Lichtenberk 1994: 3506), cf. also Givón 1990: 628ff). The subject of a reciprocal sentence is always (at least logically) plural and usually animate. Just as in the previous section we can distinguish between nominal and verbal markers of reciprocity (Lichtenberk, *l.c.*); the former are explicit, the latter implicit, in the sense given to these terms in the previous section.

The usual way of expressing reciprocity in Akkadian is by means of an explicit nominal marker, in older periods mostly *ahum aham, ahum ana ahim,* etc., lit. "brother (to) brother" (cf. CAD sv *ahu* A 3), later *ahāmeš* and various related forms (cf. *ib.* sv, and GAG § 43b and 120e). In Chapter VI several D-stems were mentioned which are accompanied by *ahāmeš*: *rasāb/pu* **1.** (JAOS 88, 126: 20), *rêṣu* (BE 17, 52: 23) and *ṣabātu* **13.** (CT 43, 94: 32). It is possible that the plurality which is inherent in a reciprocal construction causes the use of these D-stems. If in Asb. A VII 37 *up-ta-at-ti/te-hu ahāmeš* "they pierced each other" the verb form is a perfect, it also belongs here, but it might also be a preterite Dt; in that case the explicit indication of reciprocity by means of *ahāmeš* is underlined by the reciprocal Dt form (cf. KTH 19: 32 quoted below sv *kabāsu*). Occasionally other expressions are used, such as *birīt birīt* (cf. CAD sv), or a repetition of the noun involved, e.g., DA 103: 18 *šumma kalbu kalba ú-na-šak* "if dog bites dog", i.e., "if dogs bite each other", and SAA 8, 109: 4 *šumma* (...)

qarnu qarnu i-dir "if the horns (of the moon) have met" (lit. embraced), and cf. also AMT 9, 1: II 26f qu. in 6.4.2.1 sv *k/qanānu.*

In addition, it seems that reciprocity can also be expressed by means of A *itti* B followed by a reciprocal verb form, usually a Gt-stem. Compare, for instance, CHJ p. 42 no. 124: 8 PN_1 *u* PN_2 *iṣ-ṣa-ab-tu-ma* "PN_1 and PN_2 fell out (with one another)" with TCL 18, 86: 43 *it-tišu ti-iṣ-bu-ta-ku* "I have a quarrel with him" (cf. also ARM 27, 36: 24f), and, with the same verb in a different context, RA 38, 81: r.26 *šumma kakkum u danānum ti-iṣ-bu-tu* "if the 'weapon mark' and the 'fortress' are joined to each other" with YOS 10, 40: 3 [*šumma ubā*]*n hašî qablîtum itti ša pāni hurhudim ti-iṣ-bu-ta-at* "If the middle finger of the lung is joined to the front of the trachea" (both trs. CAD sv *ṣabātu* 9a-2' a'). The two expressions seem to be semantically equivalent. The construction A *itti* B can be regarded as intermediate between explicit and implicit reciprocity.

Implicit reciprocity is expressed by no more than a specific verbal stem, either the Gt-stem (GAG § 92d), the N-stem (*ib.* 90f), the Št-stem (*ib.* § 94d) or the Dt-stem. The following Dt-stems with reciprocal meaning can be quoted:

Gašāru "to be(come) powerful", D "to concentrate" (troops, 1x, cf. App. to Ch. VII sv) is once used in the Dt in a context which suggests a reciprocal use: AGH 6: 8 *šarhā<tu> nišū ug-da-šá-ra ana amāri kâ*[*ta*] "proud people vie with each other to see you".

Kabāsu "to step upon, to trample" occurs once in the Dt-stem in OA in the idiomatic meaning "to put pressure on each other": KTH 19: 32 *šīm ṣubātīja* (...) *ina barīkunu lā tù-uk-tá-ba-sà* "do not exert pressure on each other among yourselves concerning the price of my garments" (tr. CAD sv 6). Here, too, we see that reciprocity is made explicit by means of *ina barīkunu.*

Kânu Dt "to confirm or establish mutually", cf. CAD sv 5 (OA).

Kullumu Dt usually has a passive meaning, but occurs with a reciprocal meaning (and additional reduplication of the second radical, see below) in AbB 9, 204: 5ff (the canal ....) *ša anāku u atta nu-uk-ta-la-al-li-mu* "which you and I showed each other" (but note Gröneberg's reservations (1989: 31)).

Lemēnu Dt is found in BWL 100: 41 *itti bēl ṣaltika ē* [*t*]*ul*/*t*[*u-ul*]*-tam-mì-in* "do not exchange bad treatment with your adversary" (tr. CAD sv 7); cf. GAG^3 § 93d.

Palāhu Dt "to frighten each other" occurs in RA 53, 38: r.5 *ištu atta u šū tu-up-ta-al-la-ha* "depuis que toi et lui vous vous faites peur mutuellement" (tr. Kupper).

Puhhu "to exchange" offers a few highly interesting reciprocal forms in OB contracts:

(30) OBRED 3 p. 138 no. 455: 19ff (PN_1 and PN_2) ^{19}*imtagrūma ina ṭú!-ba-ti-šu-nu* (*ṭú!*: Dekiere *li-*) ^{20}*u mitgurtišunu* ^{21}*eqlam kīma eqlim up-te-eh-ú* ^{22}*pu-uh-hu leqû šurdû* "PN_1 and PN_2 came to an agreement: of their own free will and with (their) mutual consent they exchanged fields (lit. field like field) with one another. They have exchanged and received it and passed it on";

(31) *ib.* p. 100 no. 426: 30ff (PN_1 gave a field in exchange for a field (*id-di-in* (*in*: Dekiere *x*) *ú-pi-ih*) to PN_2) ^{30}*ina mitgurtišunu* ^{31}*ahum ana ahim ú-pi-ih* ^{32}*pu-uh-hu šurdû le!-q*[*ú-ú*] ^{33}[*li*]*bbašunu ṭāb* "with (their) mutual consent one exchanged with the other; they have exchanged it, passed it on and received it; they are satisfied." (cf. also VAB 5, 116: 10ff with the same clauses referring to the exchange of slave girls);

(32) OBRED 2, p. 112 no. 216: 16'ff (Two *nadîtus* have exchanged fields) 16'PNF$_1$ 17'*ana* PNF$_2$ 18'*ú-pi-ih-ši-im* 19'*pu-tu-uh-ha libbašina ṭāb* "PNF$_1$ gave it (her field) to her (PNF$_2$) in exchange; they have exchanged with each other (stative Dt); they are satisfied".

In (30) the reciprocity is implicit according to the distinction made above: it is only expressed by the verb form *uptehhū*; it is left unexpressed in the following clause, which describes the condition of the participants resulting from the transaction (*puhhū*, etc.). The corresponding clause in (31) has an explicit expression of reciprocity: *ahum ana ahim*, showing the interchangeability of the two expressions. The importance of (32) lies in the fact that here the reciprocity is (also) expressed in the final clause, with the stative Dt *putuhhā*. These three instances illustrate the various possibilities of expressing reciprocity and demonstrate that they are to a certain extent interchangeable.

Râmu Dt "to love each other" in Gilg. P II 4 *úr-[ta]-'a$_4$-mu kilallūn* "they loved each other"; cf. also the use of Gt in MVAeG 40/2, 86: 114f (man and wife) *(ul) ir-tam-mu* "will (not) love each other".

Samāhu Dt "to join forces with each other" in Iraq 17, 26: 9 acc. to CAD sv 5 *issahejiši lā nu-s[a-t]a-mah* "we cannot join forces with each other" (tr. CAD sv *samāhu* 5, cf. also line 16 in the same text).

Šanānu Dt "to quarrel with" in ARM 26/2 p. 192 no. 380: 8 PN$_1$ *itti* PN$_2$ *uš-ta-an-na-an* "PN$_1$ and PN$_2$ are quarrelling" (cf. also *ib.* p. 193 no. 380: 22'). The Gt-stem of *šanānu* is far more frequent in this meaning, cf. CAD sv 3.

***Šuttupu** "to form a partnership" (only Dt) is listed in 8.4.2 as a denominative D-stem derived from *šutāpu* "partner"; the Dt form can be explained from the inherent reciprocity of the verb. In meaning and structure it resembles *šutāhû* "to join, to conspire", which was mentioned in 8.3.2 as a denominative Š-stem of *athû* "mutual partners", where, however, the reciprocal meaning seems to lie primarily in the source noun.

Tamû Dt "to swear to one another": instances are mentioned and discussed in Whiting 1981: 2ff; apart from gemination, they also have reduplication of the second radical, cf., for instance, OBTA 23: 22f *[an]āku ú šūt [n]u-ta-ma-am-ma* "he and I will swear an oath to each other", see below. Whiting also mentions a Gt form (his no. 6), which parallels the interchange of Dt and Gt observable in *râmu* and *šanānu.*

Zakāru Dt "to swear to each other" in ARM 26/2 p. 176 no. 370: 45' (kings) *nīš ilī uz-za-ka-ak-ki-r[u]* "swore an oath by the god to each other" (also *ib.* 1"); also MARI 6, 338: 24f RN$_1$ *itti* RN$_2$ *u* RN$_3$ *nīš ilim uz-za-ka-ki-ir* (also *ib.* 54 with *ú-za-ka-ak-ki-ir*); these forms also have additional reduplication of the second radical, see below.[6]

In those cases in which the use of Dt is not caused by other factors - for instance, because the verb is a D tantum verb (*puhhu, kullumu, *šuttupu*) or based on a factitive D-stem (*kânu, pulluhu* and perhaps *guššuru* and *lummunu*) - it may be explained as motivated by the inherent plurality of the subject of a reciprocal sentence. This could in particular apply to the transitive verbs *kabāsu, râmu, samāhu, šanānu, tamû* and *zakāru.*

If this claim is correct, Dt is an optional alternative to the Gt-stem, which is far more common for expressing reciprocity, in the same way as the D-stem of transitive verbs is an optional alternative to the G-stem in sentences with a plural object. This would explain the alternation of Dt and Gt in *šanānu* and *tamû* without an observable difference in meaning. It also seems to be supported by the remarkable Dt forms that are extended with reduplication of the second radical: *kullumu, tamû* and *zakāru.* It is likely that these cases of reduplication also serve to underline the inherently plural nature of reciprocity. The same phenomenon is observable in some intransitive Dt forms of *kaṣāru* and *pahāru* with plural subject, which will be presented in 9.1.5.

9.1.4. Dt forms contrasting with *purrus* forms

A number of Dt-stems, especially those which are derived from verbs denoting adjectival concepts (states and qualities), are more closely associated with the *purrus* form of the same root than with the (factitive) D-stem. They serve to derive fientive forms from the *purrus* form, in the same way as the N-stem is used to derive fientive forms from simple adjectives and statives of the G-stem, the so-called "ingressive" function of the N-stem (cf. GAG § 90g).

This relationship between *purrus* and the Dt-stem is best observable in verbs of which a D-stem with the appropriate meaning is not attested. A case in point was mentioned in 7.5.2: the stative *kummus* "to be in a kneeling or squatting position", from which a Dt-stem can be derived to denote the corresponding action of kneeling or squatting, although no factitive D forms of this verb are in use. Other instances of this kind of relationship include the following verbs:

U"ulū (stative plural) occurs in omen protases with water as subject, alternating with the corresponding Dt form *uta"alū*: "to coagulate (?)" acc. to CAD sv 3 and 4c, "zusammenlaufen" and "zusammengelaufen sein" acc. to AHw sv Dt and D 3; apparently a lexicalized use of the normal meaning of *e'ēlu* "to hang up, to bind" (see 6.4.3.1 sv).

Ṣuhhutu "?" (describing some defect of the eye) (cf. 10.6.2) alternates with a Dt form in CT 41, 27: edge 3, cf. CAD sv *ṣahātu* 2 and *ṣuhhutu* adj.

Šummuṭu "pointed, tapering", said of the three surfaces of the "finger" in CT 30, 22b: 5, alternates with Dt in CT 28, 50: r.19 *uš-te-mi-ṭu*, with the same subject.

Ummulu "faint, scintillating", said of stars (cf. 10.7.1.3 sv and App. to Ch. X sv), alternates with Dt forms in the same contexts, cf. AHw sv *ummulu* I 3 and *(w)amālu* D 3 and Dt 2; compare also, in a different context, BWL 54 k *dūtum um-mul-tum* "my gloomy appearance" with *ib.* 32: 47 *dūtī ú-tam-mil* "my appearance has become gloomy" (trs. Lambert).

Unnutu "dim, faint, weak", said of stars (cf. 10.7.1.3 sv and App. to Ch. X sv), alternates with Dt forms in the same contexts, cf. AHw sv *enētu* D 3 and Dt and *unnutu.*

Uppulu "late" (cf. App. to Ch. X sv) versus CT 22, 20: 13 (sowing) *lā ú-ta-ap-pal* (D is also used intransitively, cf. 7.4.3 sv *apālu*).

Uppuqu "massive, solid" (see 10.7.1.1 sv and App. to Ch. X sv), alternating with the precative Dt in RA 38, 85: 12 // RitDiv. 31: 32 and 34: 89 *li-te(-ep)-pi-iq* (said of the lung),

Ussulu "constipated" occurs in AMT 58, 1: 2 *us-su-ul*, versus *ú-ta-as-sal* in *ib.* 56, 1: 8 in the same context, acc. to CAD sv *esēlu* c.

In most of these cases the absence of a D-stem is related to the meaning of the adjectives involved; they denote states which can generally not be brought about by the intervention of a human agent; therefore, these Dt forms are independent of the D-stem. Their importance lies in the fact that they show that a Dt-stem need not always be derived fom a D-stem, but can be derived directly from a *purrus* form, skipping the intermediate stage of the D-stem.

Further instances of Dt forms without corresponding D-stem which are ingressives of *purrus* forms are *kubbulu* Dt in Asb. B V 11 *šapassu uk-tam-bil-ma īnu iṣhirma* "his lip was paralyzed and (his) eye became small", from *kubbulu* "lame, paralyzed" (cf. 10.6.2); *ṭummumu* Dt and *sukkuku* Dt in BWL 52: 18 *uznāja ša uṭ-ṭa-am-mi-ma us-sak-ki-ka hašikkiš* "my ears which had become deaf and clogged like those of a deaf man", from *ṭummumu* and *sukkuku* "deaf" (cf. 10.6.2). Possibly also *uttazziq* versus *nuzzuq* quoted as (11) in 9.1.1, and the interchanging *purrus* statives and Dt forms of *ebēṭu* in MSL 4, 72: 151ff (meaning obscure) represent the same phenomenon.

These Dt forms are unambiguous instances of verbs which must be translated by means of "to become", rather than "to be made", cf. the discussion in 9.1.1. However, the same relationship between *purrus* and Dt is doubtless also operative in other cases where a factitive D-stem does exist. In such cases, however, it cannot be proved whether the relationship between *purrus* and Dt is direct, as in the cases listed above, or indirect via the D-stem. Cases in point may be the stative D and the Dt-stem of *adāru* "to be(come) disturbed, restless" (D very rare), of *ašāšu* "to be(come) worried" (D rare), and of *ekēlu* "to be(come) dark" (D rare).

9.1.5. Dt versus Gt.

There are also some Dt-stems which primarily seem to stand in opposition to the Gt-stem, rather than being dependent upon the corresponding D-stem. This aspect of the Dt-stem was first noted by Edzard (1962: 116f). Edzard points to the similarity in meaning between *kaṣāru* Dt: "sich zusammenrotten, -ballen" (said of people and clouds) and *kaṣāru* Gt "ineinander fügen", "verflechten", which is said of body parts (fingers, tails, cf. CAD sv 5b), mostly in the stative, and tentatively suggests (117a) that Dt indicates here "eine zahlen-, bzw. mengenmässige Steigerung von Gt".

Edzard's suggestion is corroborated by the occurrence of some parallel cases of verbs with meanings that are similar to *kaṣāru* in the meaning under discussion. They are all verbs which are inherently plural, since they refer to the notion of bringing together or uniting. A remarkable thing is that the Gt forms involved are mostly verbal adjectives, and only rarely finite verbal forms. Apart from *kaṣāru,* the verbs in question are *kapālu* "to roll up, coil, entwine", *kamāru* "to heap up" and *rakāsu* "to bind".

Kaṣāru "to bind together, join, collect, organize" (cf. 6.4.3.1 sv for D): the relevant Gt forms are all statives and VAs,[7] which apparently have the meaning "entwined":[8] stative in MVAeG 40/2, 62: 3 *šumma ubānātūšu ki-iṣ-ṣu-ra* "if his fingers are entwined" (also CT 40, 29a: 5 (tails)); VA in AfO 14, 150: 202 2 *ṣalam māšī ki-iṣ-ṣu-ru-ti* "two figures of linked twins", and similar cases mentioned in CAD sv *kiṣṣuru.* An instance of unclear metaphorical use is LKA 22: 15 *kalû ki-iṣ-ṣu-ru* "the *kalû*-singers sing in unison (?)" (tr. CAD sv *kaṣāru* lex. sect). These cases contrast with the use of *kaṣāru* Dt with people and clouds as subject, for which see App. to Ch. VI sv **4**. Compare especially:

(33) ARM 6, 58: 15ff 30 Sutaeans (...) *ana šahāṭim uk-t[a]-a[ṣ]-ṣí-ra-am* "have banded together for making a raid";

(34) *ib.* 26/1 p. 287 no. 121: 11f The Benjaminites with their troops and [...] *uk-ta-ṣa-ṣa-ra-am* "are banding together (to lay siege to GN)" (similar form in 3, 16: 12);

(35) SAA 8, 41: 2f im.diri.[meš] (with gloss *ur-pa-a-ti*) *uk-ta-ṣa-ra* "clouds will gather".

In (34), note especially the reduplication of the second radical, which, in addition to gemination, presumably serves to underline the plural subject, just as in the cases of *kullumu, tamû* and *zakāru* Dt quoted in 9.1.3.[9]

Admittedly, the D-stem of *kaṣāru* is often used with people as object: "to collect, prepare", especially in military contexts, cf. App. to Ch. VI sv **3**.; therefore, these Dt forms can also be considered instances of the intransitive use of Dt which was illustrated in 9.1.1. However, the parallelism with the verbs to be mentioned next suggests that under specific semantic circumstances a direct association between Gt and Dt is plausible for the expression of the meanings in question.

Kapālu Dt "to gather" (intrans.) is used of persons in RIME 4, 603: 15ff *7 šarrāni (...) ša uk-ta-ap-pí-lu-nim akmīšunūti* "I defeated 7 kings who had gathered against me", and YOS 10, 48: 30 // 49: 2 *mātum ana bēliša // šarriša uk-ta-pa-al* "the land will gather against its lord // king". In addition, it is said of water with an uncertain meaning: CT 39, 14: 24 *šumma nāru kīma ṣēri uk-tap-pa-lu-ma* "if the (water of the) river .... like a snake", and Or. 58, 91: 16'b *šumma (rumīkātu) uk-tap-pa-lu* "if the washing water ...." ("Wenn es sich zu Spiralen? bildet" (tr. Farber)), *Kapālu* Gt is mostly used of animals (snakes, lizards and birds) "to be or become entwined", both in finite forms and in the stative, cf. CAD sv 2, and also in the VA, cf. CAD sv *kitpulu*. An instance referring to humans is Ugar. 5, 278: II 10 ("to wrestle"), cf. CAD sv *qubbulu* B. *Kapālu* D is hardly attested; the only certain instance is the participle D in *mu-qa-pil zê* "who rolls excrement" (a dung beetle), cf. App. to Ch. VI sv.

Rakāsu "to bind" is used in the Dt-stem with rain as subject: RA 65, 74: 81' *zinnū ina šamê úr-ta-ak-ka-s[u]* "rain clouds will gather in the sky". This can be contrasted with *zunnu rit-ku-su* "continuous rain (clouds)" in ACh. Spl. 4: 10 and *mehû rit-ku-su* "a continuous storm" in CBSM p. 158 § 78: 11. A remarkable intransitive use of G is FM 2 p. 104 no. 62: 7 *zunnū ir-ku-su-ma* "Les pluies ont été continues" (tr. Durand), cf. the similar use of *kaṣāru.*

Kamāru "to heap, pile up" is used in one instance in the Dt-stem with persons as subject (normally it is said of property and concrete objects, cf. App. to Ch. VI sv **1./2.**): Gilg. I v 34 + II II 41 *eṭlūtu uk-tam-ma-ru elīšu* "the men gathered around him". This can be compared with the use of the Gt, which is said of poison (Ee I 162, etc., infin.), snow (Sg. 8: 101, stative) and of a headache, which *kīma zunni mūši kit-mu-ru* "has accumulated like nightly rain" (CT 17, 26: 79).[10] The VA is used to qualify *išittu* "storehouse, treasures" (Sg. 8: 257. 316. 351); a finite form occurs in AbB 1, 37: r.8' with possessions as subject (*ša mahrika*), all in the meaning "to accumulate" (intrans.).

Although the evidence is scanty and inconclusive, and most of these uses of Dt can be explained as intransitive counterparts to the D-stem, the semantic parallelism between Dt and Gt seems to be sufficiently strong to suggest a special relationship of the kind suggested by Edzard 1962: 117a. It seems, therefore, a plausible assumption that the use of the Dt forms is related to the inherent plurality of the subjects of these verbs, and then especially if people are concerned: all instances of Dt are plural (including the collective *mātu* "the people") and have a personal subject, and all instances with a personal subject use the Dt-stem (except *kitpulu* in the specialized meaning "to wrestle" in a text from Ugarit). With clouds, both Dt and Gt are found; with other subjects only Gt, except in the obscure expression of *kapālu* Dt with water as subject. This situation agrees with the general association of the D-stem with salient categories as outlined in 5.6.4.

9.1.6. Dt to underline low transitivity

A number of intransitive D-stems, in particular those of Type II listed in 7.6, also occur in the Dt-stem without observable difference in meaning from the D-stem. This phenomenon was noted in 7.6.1, where it was shown that many verbs denoting sounds and some others are attested even more frequently in the Dt-stem than in the D-stem, in contrast to the relative rarity of Dt-stems of other types. Such verbs include *na'āru* "to roar", *nazāmu* "to complain", *lahāšu* "to whisper", *nahāsu* "to wail, lament" and *raṣānu* "to make a loud noise, acclaim". It was argued in note 41 to Ch. VII that also *nâdu* "to praise" is often Dt, rather than Dtn, as claimed by the dictionaries (beside being used as a passive Dt).

There are still other Dt-stems which do not seem to differ in meaning from the D-stem, if the latter is intransitive. This applies to the following instances (a few cases have been included which look similar although no D-stem is attested):

Ganāṣu "to sniff, wrinkle" (one's nose) (?), cf. 7.6.2 sv.

Hanāṣu (meaning obscure, cf. 7.6.2 sv) in AfO 19, 116: 24 (demons) *ša ana mahar marṣi* [*t*]*u-uh-ta-an-na-ṣa* "who always ..... in the presence of a sick man" (cf. *ganāṣu* in 23).

Lupputu "to be delayed" (cf. 8.6 sv) is once used in the Dt-stem in the same meaning: YOS 13, 413: 6 *lā ul-ta-ap-pá-at* "let him not be delayed" (perhaps to be explained acc. to 9.1.4.) [the unique transitive instance CCT 2, 26b: 14 *tu*-[*l*]*a*?-BI-*ta-ni*, mentioned in AHw sv *lapātu* D 3a, is obscure; perhaps something like "you charged me" (K.R. Veenhof, personal communication)].

Mahāru D "to send or go upstream" (cf. CAD sv 9b and 8.4.2) is once attested in the Dt-stem: ARM 26/1 p. 155 no. 25: 5f (the army will set out and) *an*[*a*] *pān*[*īk*]*a um-ta-ah-ha*-[*r*]*a-am* "will go upstream to meet you".

Mekû "to be negligent, disregard" (no D attested) is once found in the Dt-stem in LL: MSL 4, 125: 32 *lā tu-um-te-k*[*i*].

Muqqu "to do slowly, hesitate" (cf. 8.6 sv), is once used in the Dt in ARM 26/2 p. 285 no. 411: 44 *šū ana alākim um-ta-a*[*q*] "he is slow in setting out, he hesitates to set out".

Puqqu "to heed, pay attention to" (cf. AHw sv and 8.6 sv) has a stative Dt which is translated by AHw sv Dt as "er achtet immer auf", apparently as a kind of durative counterpart to the D-stem (see below).

Šalāṭu Dt "to reign, exercise or acquire authority", cf. CAD sv *š*. A 6 (but no D attested, except as *purrus* adj., cf. App. to Ch. X sv): ARM 26/2 p. 113 no. 342: 19 GN_1 *kalūšu ina* GN_2*-ma uš-ta*-[*a*]*l-la-aṭ* "The whole of Assur reigns in GN_2", and RIMA 1, 240: 7 (RN *ša* ...) *ina kibrāti ul-te-li-ṭu-ma* "who has acquired dominion over the entire world" (also *ib.* 2/I, 20: 47).

Šapālu "to become low, to go down" has a Dt-stem "to move downstream", cf. CAD sv 6 (SAA 1, 82: r.5; FM 1 p. 119 note 2: 8). It is possible that the use of *uštappil(am)ma* (beside *ušappil(am)ma*) in omen protases in hendiadys with a following stative (cf. CAD sv 3d) also belongs here, cf. 7.4.3.

(W)aqû "to wait" (G and D) probably has a Dt-stem with an idiomatic meaning: *utaqqû* "to wait, to watch, to heed", cf. AHw sv *(w)aqû* Dt.

Two explanations seem to be possible for this parallel use of D and Dt with the same valency and no apparent difference in meaning. The first is that the use of the Dt-stem is indirectly related to the association of the D-stem with high transitivity. This may have caused a tendency to replace it with the Dt-stem in cases where this association is absent. In that case these Dt forms have their usual meaning of indicating a reduction in transitivity (cf. 9.1.1). The fact that intransitive D-stems are found in similar contexts (cf. especially 7.4.3 and 7.6), shows that this replacement is not obligatory.

The second explanation is that these Dt forms have a durative nuance as compared to the D-stem. This possibility is suggested by the contextually determined durative function of the infix *-ta-*, which was discussed in 4.1.2.1, and is parallel to a similar use of some Gt-stems (cf. GAG § 92f), and of the Št-stem of *ešēru* "to be(come) straight, to prosper": *ešēru* Š and Št are differentiated as "to bring in order" and "to keep in order" respectively by GAG § 94f. However, this contrast is difficult to verify on the basis of the respective contexts.

9.1.7. Varia

Many Dt forms have not been included in the previous sections, because they do not belong to any of the types discussed so far, or because they are in some respect uncertain and problematic. In so far as they are interesting enough to deserve to be mentioned, they are discussed in this section. This applies to the following cases:

Ekēku (or *akāku*?) Dt occurs in three different contexts, all quite obscure: first, in AbB 7, 167: 28 *ana kurummat DN lā nu-ta-ak-ka-ak* (Kraus: from *ekēku* "to scratch"; AHw sv *takāku*: "unklar"); second, in AfO 19, 52: 148 *urra ú-tak-ka-ak mūša inahhi[s]* "by day he scratches himself, by night he sheds tears" (tr. Lambert); the context, however, rather suggests that a verb of sound is required; third, in Izbu 181: 14' (if a mare bears twins and their bodies) *ú-tak-ka-a-ka* "..." (with a comm. (*ib.* 226: 500) *ú-tak-ka-ku* = *mi-ṣu*). Leichty offers no translation; the context suggests some reciprocal Dt form.

Gašāru Dt in RIMA 2/I, 290: 48f *nārtu iš[tu] elēna ana kirî tu-ug-da-ša-ra*: probably "the (water of the) canal gains in strength/speed (on its way down) from above into the gardens", cf. Kinnier Wilson, Iraq 50, 80. Dt is also found with other meanings: Gilg. I IV 39 (= (18)), cf. 9.1.1, and AGH 6: 8 quoted in 9.1.3 sv (reciprocal).

Kabātu Dt is used in OA in hendiadys with a following verb, e.g., in BIN 4, 9: 21f *ku-ta-bi$_4$-it-ma alkamma* "komm doch gefälligst!" acc. to AHw sv *kabātu* Dtn 2, CAD sv *k.* 10 "make an effort (?) and come here"; also *ib.* 6, 7: 6; RA 59, 158: 7 ("Fais-(nous) l'honneur de venir" (Garelli)). This Dt form can be explained from the intransitive nature of the sentence, although in similar hendiadys constructions the use of D is far more common, cf. 7.4.1. There is no reason to regard these forms as Dtn, as AHw sv Dtn and Hecker (1968: 146 § 87b) do.

Maṣāru Dt is found in Or. 58, 90: 15'b (subject: water, cf. 9.1.5 sv *kapālu*), and in SpTU 2, 34: r.15 (subject unclear); both instances are obscure.

Maṣû Dt interchanges in OA with the G-stem in hendiadys with a following verb: "to do sth on one's own authority", cf. AHw sv Dt and G 7c α "(es) in die Hand nehmen, sich einschalten".

Na'āpu (or *nâpu*) Dt is said of the sky in ACh. Ad. 20: 20 *šumma birqu ibriqma šamû ut-ta-a-pu* "if lightning has flashed and the sky keeps (cf. 6.6.1) ......-ing" (CAD sv *nâpu* B: mng. uncert., AHw sv *nâpu* I Dt "(etwas?) bewegt werden") and CT 40, 3: 64 (If the beams of a man's house) *ut-ta-a-pu* "..." (AHw same translation, CAD sv *na'āpu* b "to dry out"). The interpretations of CAD and AHw do not seem very plausible. If both instances come from the same verb, it would seem more likely that this Dt-stem also refers to the emitting of some sound, cf. SpTU 3, 100: 16 *na-a-pu* = *šasû*.

Nagāšu "to go", mostly Gtn "to walk around", is found twice in the Dt-stem in the same meaning as Gtn: BWL 100: 32 *ē tu-ut-tag-ge-eš* "do not walk around" and Gilg. X I 5 PN *ut-tag-gi-šam-ma* [....]. They are classified in the dictionaries as Dtn-stems, but since the Dtn-stem is associated with the D-stem, which is usually transitive, we expect the Dtn-stem to be transitive as well ("to make walk around"). Although this argument is not quite decisive (cf., for instance, *šadāhu* in 7.6.3), it seems more likely that these forms are Dt-stems of the type discussed in 9.1.6, cf. AHw sv Dt, *pace* CAD sv 3.

Napāṣu Dt is once used in a meaning comparable to the intransitive use of G: "to kick, strike, flop about, thrash around(?)", acc. to CAD sv 1, namely in Sem. 3, 11: 5 (If a man in his bed) *ut-tap-pa-aṣ* "thrashes about" (cf. CAD sv *napāṣu* 9). This use can be compared to the Dt forms referring to activities quoted as (18) - (24) in 9.1.1.

Paqādu Dt is used in LB in the meaning "sich bemühen", acc. to AHw sv Dt, and may be a denominative of *pitqudu* "umsichtig" acc. to GAG § 93d, cf. note 3 to Ch. VIII.

Šerû "to go into hiding" (cf. CAD sv *š*. B) may offer an additional instance of Dt as plural of Gt (? or perfect?), cf. 9.1.5. This claim is based on the parallelism between ASJ 7, 26: 259 *kīma suttinnu mutta-priši ina nigiṣṣi eš-te-ri* "like a bat on the wing I hid in a crevice" (tr. CAD sv lex. sect.), and Angim 127 acc. to CAD sv *š*. B lex. sect. (the Anunnaki) *kīma humṣīrī ina nigiṣṣāte uš-tar-r*[*u-u*] "hid in crevices like mice". Besides, there is one instance with the stative Dt (or Dt(n), cf. 9.2): SpTU 2, 28: 14 (the Anunnaki) *ikmesūma šu-ta-ru-ú na-*[... "knelt down, hiding [....]", cf. CAD *l.c.*

Finally, a problematic case: a verb which is used in omen protases to denote the sound made by a bird, the *aribu*, a crow or a raven, e.g., SpTU 2, 32: 7 *šumma aribu ana pān amēli uh-ta-niq* "if a crow/raven has croaked in front of a man"; also Sumer 34 Arab. sect. 43: 8 (*i/uh-ta-naq*), CT 39, 25a: 8 (*uh-ta-niq*) and *ib.* 10 (*i/uh-ta-na-qu* with plural subject). The dictionaries only know the CT forms; CAD analyses them as Dtn forms of a verb *huqqu* "to croak, to caw", which necessitates the reading NAQ_x for NIQ, for which no parallels are available; AHw assigns them to *hanāqu* Dt and Gt respectively: "ersticken". Since the form *i/uh-ta-niq*, as it stands, cannot be a present form, it is unlikely to be a *-tan-* form either, since, as we saw in 6.6.1, *-tan-* forms usually occur in the present in omen protases. So AHw is correct in deriving these forms from *hanāqu* "to strangle". On the other hand, the context clearly suggests a verb of sound; therefore, it seems plausible that *hanāqu* is used intransitively here in the meaning "to make a choking sound", which seems to be a suitable designation for the sound produced by these birds. The only stem which fits all four forms is the Dt-stem: in two cases a present Dt for a durative activity, in the other two a preterite Dt for a once-only event (cf. 6.6.1). The predilection of verbs denoting sounds for the Dt-stem was pointed out in 7.6.1 and 9.1.6.

9.2. The Dtn-stem

9.2.1. How to distinguish the Dtn-stem from the Dt-stem

It follows from the analysis of the Gtn-stem as proposed in 4.1 that strictly speaking the Dtn-stem only exists in the present tense, and that the other forms of its verbal paradigm have not been differentiated from, and are thus suppleted by, the Dt-stem. Such forms are indicated here as Dt(n) forms.

This situation causes a considerable formal ambiguity as to whether a specific form is a Dt or a Dt(n) form. This ambiguity is, however, largely resolved by their difference in function: because the Dtn-stem is the iterative formation of the D-stem, it has the same valency, i.e., it is usually transitive; the Dt-stem, on the other hand, is usually passive/intransitive. Thus in most cases it is possible to distinguish them on the basis of the context.

Moreover, as a passive/intransitive category, the Dt-stem does not have a complete verbal paradigm. In the first place, it has no participle, because the Akkadian participles are primarily agent nouns and are therefore not normally formed from derived passive or intransitive forms; thus participles of the pattern *muptarris* can be assigned to the Dt(n)-stem.[11] Secondly, for similar reasons, the imperative, the infinitive, the stative and the VA of the Dt-stem are unusual, too; they tend to be formed only from Dt-stems which do not have a passive meaning.[12] Thus the non-finite forms of the Dt paradigm can generally be regarded as Dt(n) forms.

There is also ambiguity between the preterite of the Dtn-stem and the perfect of the D-stem: both have the pattern *uptarris*. Since the use of the perfect and the preterite, especially in literary texts, from which most relevant forms stem, largely overlaps, it is hardly ever possible to decide on the basis of the context whether a given *uptarris* form is a perfect or a preterite, and, accordingly, whether it is a D or a Dt(n) form. Since the Dtn-stem is in general a rather rare category, and since iterativity can also be expressed just by the context, such forms are mostly regarded here as perfects of the D-stem rather than as preterites of the Dt(n)-stem. There are, however, a few cases which might be Dt(n), such as:

(32) ARM 2, 103: 12f *ālišam sugāgī u laputtê ut-ta-hi-id* "I alerted the sheikhs and the officials in all the cities" (tr. CAD sv *na'ādu* 6);

(33) KTH 12: 17 *ṭuppē mimma ana ālim ul-ta-pì-tù* "all the letters that I have written to the city".

The distributive adjective *ālišam* and the indefinite pronoun *mimma* show the plurality of the actions, which may be reflected in the verb form; on the other hand, precisely because it is clear from the context, it need not be expressly indicated by the use of an iterative form.

Consequently, a considerable number of verbs which are listed in the dictionaries (especially in AHw) as having a Dtn-stem, are not presumed to have one here.[13]

9.2.2. The use of the Dtn-stem

The Dtn-stem is a relatively rare form; according to the statistics presented in note 1 to Chapter V, 86 verbs are listed in AHw as having a Dtn-stem, more than half of them hapax legomena. Some of these have to be cancelled according to the previous section (see note 13), and others are spurious or doubtful, so that only about 50 verbs remain.

The use of the Dtn-stem is completely parallel to that of the Gtn-stem. It is basically the iterative formation of the D-stem, just as the Gtn-stem is that of the G-stem. This is most evident from the fact that a considerable part of the occurring Dt(n) forms come from D tantum verbs, for which it is the only possible iterative form: from *bu''û* "to look for" (Maqlû II 206; VII 89; AfO 11, 367: 3), *gullulu* "to act unjustly towards" (UET 6, 395: r.19), *kullu* "to hold, offer" (cf. AHw sv Dtn), *kullumu* "to show, instruct" (cf. AHw sv Dtn, also 1569b sv), *muššu'u* "ro rub, anoint" (LKU 62: r.8), *ruššû* "to wrong" (TCL 18, 135: 14; ZA 9, 160: 25. 28, cf. CAD sv *murtaššû*); *sullû* "to pray" (JCS 15, 6: 24); *suppû* id. (BRM 4, 12: 37 // DA 221: 15), *ṣullû* id. (cf. AHw sv *ṣ*. III Dtn), *šukkulu* "to wipe away, polish" (Or. 17, 301: 3; 302: 20; 18, 409: 16) and *šurru* "to bend down, lean, go down" (cf. AHw sv *š*. I Dtn). The Dtn-stems of the highly lexicalized D-stems *wu''uru* "to order, command" (cf. AHw sv *(w)âru* Dtn) and *(w)uššuru* "to let go, release" (TMH 1, 1c: 18; TC 3, 73: 38) can also be added to this group.

A second important group of Dtn-stems consists of those derived from factitive D-stems, for which the Dtn-stem is also the only available iterative formation; they include the Dt(n)-stems of *akāšu* D "to drive out, displace" (AbB 1, 115: r.3' (cf. D in r.5'); AfO 14, 144: 58), *ba'ālu* D "to make (abnormally) large" (AbB 3, 15: 23 (cf. 13)), *bahāru* D "make hot, cook" (LKU 57: 9; AMT 26, 2: 4 + 25, 6: I 10), *damāqu* D "to make good" (AbB 11, 61: 4), *dešû* D "to provide abundantly" (only KAR 80: 17 // RA 26, 40: 6 part. *mu-ud-de-šu-u/ú māhāzī*, which probably shows a confusion between *muddišu* "renewing" (*edēšu* D) and *mudeššû* "abundantly providing (*dešû* D), as suggested by CAD sv *edēšu* 2a-1'), *edēšu* D "to renew" (cf. AHw sv Dtn), *galātu* D "to frighten, scare away" (often, cf. AHw sv Dtn), *kânu* D "to establish, set up, testify" (common, cf. AHw sv Dtn), *labāku* D "to steep, macerate" (Or. 18, 416: 17), *na'ādu* D "to alert, inform" (AbB 6, 154: 5' acc. to AHw 1577a sv), *nakāru* D "to remove, change" (often, cf. AHw sv *n*. I Dtn), *napāšu* D "to expand" (IAsb. 74: r.10), *natāku* D "to let drip" (BAM 66: 25; 111: II 21), *palāhu* and *parādu* D "to frighten" (common, cf. AHw ssvv Dtn), *qalālu* D "to despise" (ZA 43, 94: 44;[14] ICK 1, 183: 7), *qatāru* D "to fumigate" (AMT 70, 3: 2), *qerēbu* D "to offer" (LKA 159: 17; MVAeG 41/3, 14: 5 (qu. as (12) in Ch. IV), *ramāku* D "to bath" (trans.) (AMT 70, 3: 6), *ramû* D "to loosen, weaken" (CT 40, 49: 22), *šaqû* D "to lift" (TBP 23: r.7), *šarāhu* D "to praise" (cf. AHw sv *š*. I Dtn), *takālu* D "to make sb confident" (AbB 7, 19: 7); *taqānu* D "to make orderly" (SBH 69: 12) and *târu* D "to return" (trans.) (passim, cf. AHw sv Dtn). To this group we may also add the Dtn-stem of *ṣâdu* D "to make dizzy" (cf. 7.2.4) in medical texts, cf. AHw sv *ṣ*. I Dtn.

Dtn-stems of transitive verbs are very rare; this is not surprising in the light of what was said in 6.7.3: transitive verbs that do not have a D-stem evidently do not have a Dtn-stem either, and transitive verbs that do have a D-stem mostly do not have other verbal stems which are associated with verbal plurality, not even a Gtn-stem. The attested Dt(n) forms come from *gerû* "to proceed against" (Maqlû III 140; UnDiv. 104 BM 41005: III 11), *kašādu* "to chase away" (SAA 2 p. 49: 478) and "to join" (WO 5, 34: 22 acc. to AHw 1567a sv), *katāmu* (AbB 9, 113: 13), *mahāru* "to appeal to" (LKA 29e: I 2), *sahālu* "to pierce" (Tn-Ep. V 40, obscure), *šasû* "to call" (ARM 14, 48: 27), and *zaqāpu* "to erect, plant" (TDP 224: 56; BMS 53: 9; LKA 155: r.6).

A rare but noteworthy phenomenon is the use of intransitive Dtn forms in protases of astronomical omens in clauses where we would expect Gtn forms: *ṣalāmu* Dtn "to become ever darker" in StOr. 1, 356: 23 // ACh. 2. Spl. 84: 9 (of the *zīmū* of a star); *šapālu* Dtn "to stay constantly low" (of a planet) acc. to CAD sv 7 (contrasting with *šaqû* Gtn!); *mahāru* Dtn "to gain elevation" (of the sun) acc. to CAD sv 9 in Mul-apin p. 75: I 18 (versus *šapālu* Dtn *ib.* p. 73: I 12).

9.3. The ŠD-stem

The ŠD-stem as a purely literary category distinct from the Š-stem was first identified by Von Soden (1932/33: II 151ff). It comprises only a small number of verbs and is restricted to a specific range of texts, namely, those which belong to what Von Soden calls "der hymnisch-epische Dialekt" (cf. 6.9.2.2). The few instances occurring elsewhere are probably to be explained in a different way, although they have the same form, and to be kept apart from the literary ones, the more so because some of them come from peripheral dialects.[15]

The following list comprises the instances of ŠD forms known to me, arranged according to verb and accompanied by a survey of the texts in which they occur. They are SB, unless indicated otherwise.

Danānu ŠD "to strengthen", 1x in a LB royal epic (BHLT 72: 22).

Edû (*wedû*) ŠD "to assign", 1x in JCS 31, 103: 49 (epic of Anzu).

Halāqu ŠD "to destroy", 2x in Ee (I 39. 45).

Kalû ŠD "?" (cf. *kalû* "to detain, withhold"), 1x in AfO 19, 65a: II 11 (*tuš-kal-l*[*i* in broken context) (prayer).

Kanāšu ŠD "to subjugate", 1x in BWL 174c: 2.

Kašû ŠD "to make successful" (cf. CAD sv *kašû* B) in AnSt. 30, 105: 23 *iqabbīma killata uš-kaš-ši* "if he speaks, he makes everything successful" (Ludlul bēl nēmeqi).

Kullumu "to show, instruct", 1x in AfO 19, 57: 108 (prayer).

Malû ŠD "to fill, cover" is common in the following texts (cf. CAD sv 13, AHw sv *m.* IV ŠD): RIs from Tiglatpileser I (1100 BC) to Nabonidus (passim); Ee (I 86. 136. 154; II 22; III 26. 84. 102); hymns and prayers (AfO 19, 62: 41 (rest.); AGH 102: 9; PSBA 20, 159: 9); rest: ZA 43, 14: 10 = SAA 3, 32: 10 ("The

Under-world Vision of an Assyrian Prince"); BRM 4, 9: 42 (lamentation); AAA 22, 78: 40 (*Utukkū lemnūtu*).

Manû ŠD "to count" (?) 1x in Ee VI 151 (see JCS 46, 132 *ad* line 151: *muš-man-ni* variant to *muš-neš-šu*).

Maṭû ŠD "to diminish", 1x in AnSt. 30, 105: 27 (*muš-man-ṭi*) (Ludlul bēl nēmeqi).

Mesû ŠD "to wash, wipe off", 1x in AfO 19, 65: III middle 7 (prayer, cf. CAD sv *nahāsu* B d).

Naprušu ŠD "to cause to fly", 1x in RA 27, 18: 16 (inscription of an Assyrian dignitary from the time of Shalmaneser IV).

Narāṭu ŠD "to cause to tremble", 2x in RA 75, 109: IV 14 (OB); Lugal 45.

Nasāqu ŠD "to select", 1x in AfO 19, 63: 48 (prayer).

Naw/māru ŠD "to brighten, illuminate" is by far the most common ŠD-stem and has a wider distribution than the other ones; it is used in RIs of Sennacherib (Sn. 107: 39; 120: 28; 155 no. 21: 6) and Nabonidus (VAB 4, 232: 30; 258: 20); in Ee (V 82); in hymns (BWL 126: 1. 3; 126: 17; 136: 176f); and in hymnal parts of incantations and rituals (Or. 42, 503: 9 (OB); 36, 275: 15 (= BagF. 18, 241: 69); Maqlû II 21f (cf. AfO 21, 72b); II 78; AGH 78: 35; 126: 10; 128: 5; 152c: 5; BBR 60: 29; KAR 32: 31; BA 10, 1: 4). The rest includes AfO 19, 60: 208 (prayer); BWL 172: 14 (fable); KAR 158: VII 45 (incipit of a love song); in broken context: BWL 175a: 6; KAR 158: IV 4. It is especially frequent as participle (*mušnammeru*), as an epithet mostly of gods.

Nesû ŠD "to remove", 1x in PSBA 17, 139: 11 (hymn (*tuš-na-as-si hi-ṭù*)).

Parādu ŠD "to scare away", 1x in St. Kraus 194: 9 (hymn).

Pašāhu ŠD "to cool down, calm down", 6x in MIO 12, 53: 6 (OB), KAR 321: r.5 (literary, but further unspecifiable); AfO 19, 60: 196. 198; 64: 68f (prayer).

Pašāṭu ŠD "to erase", 1x in AfO 19, 64: 93 (prayer).

Paṭāru ŠD "to loosen" (*ašgāgu* "battle line"), 1x in AfO 19, 64: 89 (prayer).

Pazāru ŠD "to hide", 1x in KH IV 11 (OB: prologue of KH).

Petû ŠD "to open", 3x in BWL 134: 149. 153 (ears) and in Erra IIIc: 41 (ears).

Rabābu ŠD "to weaken, subdue", 3x in Ee (I 162; II 48; III 52 (with variant D)).

Rabû ŠD "to bring up, enlarge, extend", in Ee II 34 and elsewhere, and in RIs of Sennacherib (Sn. 79: 5; 101: 61; 113: 13; 130: 71; 132: 68; 153: 15; AfO 20, 94: 118).

Ramû "to cause to inhabit", 1x in Ee IV 146.

Rapāšu "to widen", 1x in Sn. 153: 19 (RI of Sennacherib).

Redû "to add", 7x in Ee I 134; II 20; III 24. 82; and in RIs of Sennacherib (Sn. 128: 48 var.; OIP 24 pl. 18: 6 (cf. p. 20); JCS 5, 29: 5).

[**Taqānu** ŠD, mentioned by Von Soden, 1932/33: II 153, is to be cancelled: the form in question (*mu-uš-ta-aq-qí-in*) should be read *muštakkin*, from *šakānu* "to place" Gtn, cf. Von Soden, ArOr. 17/2, 360f].

The restricted occurrence of this verbal stem which was alluded to above concerns the following points. First of all, almost all instances stem from SB literary texts; these texts are roughly the same as those mentioned in 6.9.2.2, which also show a specific, more extended use of some D-stems of transitive verbs, and those of 7.5.5, which typically contain instances of literary factitive Š-stems. Four of them, however, come from OB literary texts (*narāṭu, naw/māru, pašāhu, pazāru*).

Second, it is clear from this enumeration that some texts have a special predilection for the ŠD-stem, especially Enūma Eliš, the RIs of Sennacherib and the two "literary prayers" to Marduk edited by Lambert in AfO 19, 55ff, in particular the second one (p. 61ff, cf. Lambert's comment on p. 49), which contains five ŠD forms that are attested nowhere else and which - a fact that is even more significant - come from transitive verbs (see below).

Third, the ŠD-stem also has an incomplete paradigm. It only comprises the present *ušparras*, the preterite *ušparris* and the participle *mušparris*.[16] It is remarkable that in the verbs with a weak third radical the forms ending with *-i*, which are preterites according to the normal vocalization rules of the derived stems, are also used for the present, for instance *uš-kaš-ši* in AnSt. 30, 105: 23, *tuš-na-as-si* in PSBA 17, 139: 11, *tuš-mas-si* in AfO 19, 65: III middle 7, and all three instances of *petû* ŠD mentioned in the list. A possible explanation of this phenomenon may be that the geminate of these forms was felt to mark the present tense rather than factitivity, as in the D-stem, i.e., that a form such as *tušpatti* was interpreted as a present of the regular (non-literary) preterite *tušapti*.

The fourth restriction concerns the types of root that can have a ŠD-stem: apart from two instances that come from verbs II/gem. (*danānu* and *rabābu*), ŠD-stems are only formed from strong roots and roots with a weak third radical. They are apparently not derived from roots with a weak first radical, and roots starting with a sibilant; the latter doubtless for the same phonetic reason which also blocks the formation of Š-stems of hollow roots starting with a sibilant, cf. 7.2.4. ŠD-stems of hollow roots are not found either; they would presumably coincide in form with the corresponding forms of the Š-stem (e.g., present *ušmât*, preterite *ušmît*), and thus be interpreted as Š-stems, since the Š-stem is a far more common and productive verbal stem than the ŠD-stem.

Most of the verbs taking a ŠD-stem are intransitive, and normally have a factitive D-stem.[17] With four exceptions, however (*danānu, kašû, narāṭu* and *pazāru*), the verbs to which this applies also have a factitive Š-stem. Some of these Š-stems belong to the group of literary Š-stems discussed in 7.5.5 (*kullumu, malû, parādu, rabû, rapāšu*); others belong to the Š-stems which seem to be completely interchangeable with the D-stem (cf. 7.5.6): *na-w/māru, nesû, pašāhu*; still others to the Š-stems which are more or less differentiated in meaning from the D-stem: *kanāšu* (cf. 7.5.3), *edû, halāqu, maṭû* (cf. 7.5.4); for *rabābu* see 7.5.5.4.

In so far as D and Š are differentiated in meaning, the ŠD-stem agrees with the D-stem. This applies to the third of the three groups just mentioned, and also to the four exceptions mentioned above, which have a ŠD-stem but no Š-stem. It is most evident in the rare ŠD-stems derived from transitive verbs: they do not share the causative meaning of the Š-stem; this may be inferred from the use of *mesû, nasāqu* and *petû*; the other cases occur in a broken or otherwise obscure context (*pašāṭu, paṭāru, kalû, manû*). Finally, the ŠD-stem of *redû* clearly sides with the idiomatic D-stem *ruddû* "to add", not with the Š-stem *šurdû* "to cause to bring, follow or flow". In only two cases does the ŠD-stem agree with the Š-stem in meaning: in *naprušu* and *ramû*, neither of which has a D-stem.

The contexts of these ŠD-stems do not suggest that they differ significantly in meaning from the corresponding D- or Š-stems (cf. Von Soden 1932/33: II 152). Goetze's claim (JNES 4, 248 note 13) that a form such as *urabbi* means "make great, grown up", *ušarbi* "cause (someone/something) to become great", but *ušrabbi* "cause (someone/something) to be made great(er), larg(er), enlarged" is not supported by the actual use of these forms (for *rabû* D versus Š see 7.5.5.1). This also applies to Speiser's claim (1967: 485f) that the ŠD-stem is the factitive of "elative" forms such as *šurbû* (cf. note 39 to Ch. VII). Speiser bases this claim on a comparison of Ee I 147 *ušašqi DN ina berīšunu šâšu uš-rab-bi-iš* "She [Tiāmat] exalted Kingu, made him the greatest among them", with *ib.* 154 *lū šur-ba-ta-ma hā'irī ēdû atta* "thou [Kingu] art indeed chief, my only spouse art thou" (Speiser's translations), where the ŠD and the "elative" of the same root are used side by side to refer to the same god. This is open to the following objections. First, it was argued in note 39 to Ch. VII that a form like *šurbû* is not so much an elative as a literary byform of *rabû,* based upon a "literary Š-stem"; second, the correlation between Speiser's elatives (1967: 473ff, cf. note 39 to Ch. VII) and the ŠD-stems listed here is very weak: only two verbs have both an elative and a ŠD-stem (*rabû* and *pašāhu*). Finally, concepts such as "greatest", which correspond to the degrees of comparison, are expressed purely by the context in Akkadian, both in adjectives (cf. 10.9) and in verbs. The connection between the "elative" and the ŠD-stem lies in the fact that both categories are typical representatives of a specific literary style.

To sum up, the majority of ŠD-stems occur in a relatively late stage of the language, they are restricted to a small number of literary texts, they have an incomplete paradigm, they are only derived from a small range of root types, and they have the same function as the D-stem or, in a few cases, the Š-stem. Thus they are a redundant category, whose function can be equally well performed by other verbal stems. This suggests that they are more or less artificial forms which were apparently created by Babylonian scholars with the purpose of enhancing the literary nature of a text by means of forms which are not found in ordinary language; in this respect they offer an exact parallel to the literary Š-stems discussed in 7.5.5. The reverse claim, made by Speiser (1967: 487), that "[t]he evidence clearly precludes a late development" and that it has "a common Semitic origin" is very unlikely. The fact that the ŠD-stem is completely absent in the enormous and varied corpus of OB and OA letters strongly suggests that it simply did not exist in everyday language.

Notes to Chapter Nine

1 Most of these forms are discussed by Whiting 1981, see especially the survey on p. 18f; see also Kienast 1957b and 1961, Durand and Charpin, NABU 88/17 and Gröneberg 1989. Other controversial forms which may be based on D forms are not discussed either. This applies to *šu-ut-ra(-aq)-qú-du* (RA

75, 109: III 8. 12, cf. GAG § 95c and Von Soden 1932/33: II 154 note 5), *šu-ta-aw-we-er-šu* (ARM 1, 10: 18, cf. NABU 88/17 sub 10, but note that this form does not have reduplication, cf. Gröneberg 1989: 30; it rather looks like an imperative Št of *nawāru*), the verb *utlellû* "to rise (above)" (cf. Von Soden, ZA 50, 179ff; Rundgren 1959b), and the forms listed in CAD sv *danānu* 4 as Dt forms with reduplication of the third radical, meaning "to become of even thickness, to contend for superiority" (versus AHw sv *danānu* III "Vertretung übernehmen" (but differently in GAG[3] § 101f)).

2 For the D-stem of *nazāqu* "to be worried", cf. *nuzzuq* AbB 7, 22: 11 (quoted as (57) in 10.8), and the nominal derivation *tazzīqu* "vexation" (cf. George, NABU 94/27). There is no need to posit an otherwise unattested verb *nasāqu* C, as in CAD. It is also unlikely that this is a form of *nasāqu* "to choose", as claimed by AHw sv D 1.

3 No doubt AbB 9, 66: 10f *ina muhhij[a] šu-ta-ar-ri-ih* "use your authority on my behalf", also belongs to this verb, rather than to an otherwise unattested *arāhu* Št "to hurry", as assumed by Stol and the dictionaries.

4 A difficult case is AfO 19, 58: 130 *kabtassu nangullatma u/ih-[ta]m-maṭ-ka* "his mind is ablaze and is burning (or: he is burning) (with sorrow) because of (??) you" (parallel to *ibakkīka* "he is weeping to you"); Dt or Gt ?.

5 Only a few of the Dt forms mentioned in GAG[3] § 93c can actually be regarded as reflexive: for *šarāhu* Dt, *habāṣu* Dt and *paṭāru* Dt see 9.1.1; for *kaṣāru* Dt see 9.1.5; for *e'ēlu* Dt and *kamāsu* Dt ("to kneel") see 9.1.4. *Labāšu* Dt does not mean "sich bekleiden" (thus also in AHw sv Dt), but "to be provided with clothing" (BE 17, 34: 36; HSS 19, 11: 23; Iraq 41, 93: 8); the other instances quoted AHw sv Dt are rather Gt-stems meaning "to put on" (clothes)). It is difficult to avoid the impression that in AHw and GAG many forms are considered to be reflexive mainly because in German they are best translated by means of "sich".

6 An uncertain case of a reciprocal Dt-stem is RA 75, 109: III 1 *gapāru* Dt (reciprocal acc. to CAD sv *gubburu* 2, but its form is irregular and the context unclear; Gröneberg *ad l.* reads *uktapparu* from *kapāru* "to purify"). The form *uk-ta-ṣa-ṣa-rū* (ARM 3, 16: 12), designated as reciprocal in GAG § 93c is rather intransitive, see 9.1.5.

7 The finite forms listed by CAD sv 5a as Gt-stems could also be forms of the perfect G used intransitively, cf. AHw sv G 4b/c, where they are regarded as "elliptic" G forms. Unambiguous intransitive G forms are VAB 7, 184: r.1 *eli GN da'ummatum ik-ṣu-ru* "darkness gathered over GN", and RSO 41, 319: 29/32 (said of incense).

8 Gt statives with other meanings are not considered here: first, *kiṣṣur* in the meaning "girt with" (cf. CAD sv lex. sect. and 5b) is probably a literary variant of *kaṣir* in this meaning (cf. AHw sv G 8); second, Ee I 6 *ki-iṣ-ṣu-ru/ra* seems to be an inferior variant of *kuṣṣurū* (cf. App. to Ch. VI sv 5.).

9 Cf. note 1 for the literature on these forms; the doubts expressed by Gröneberg 1991: 29f about the correctness of *uktaṣaṣṣaram* seem unwarranted, because the form recurs several times, is paralleled by the forms quoted in 9.1.3, and can be assigned a specific function (although the use of reduplication is clearly optional).

10 In Iraq 5, 56: r.7 (Babylon is the city) *ša nišāšu mešrâ kit-mu-ru-ú* "whose inhabitants have amassed wealth" the stative has a direct object and requires an active translation. Therefore, it should be kept apart from the other instances. It is one of the many examples of the literary use of the stative Gt, cf. GAG § 92f and 4.1.2.1.

11 A possible exception is *muktabbiru* "boaster, braggart", which is lexically equated with *mukabbiru* (cf. 7.4.3 sv *ebû*), and may belong to the type of Dt-stems discussed in 9.1.6. Note, however, that *muptarrisu* is also the pattern of the participle of the Gtn-stem, so that instances derived from verbs in which the meanings of D and G, and thus also of Dtn and Gtn, are very similar, are ambiguous, such as the epithets *muštappik karê* "who piles up grain stacks" from *šapāku* "to heap up, to pour out" (cf. 6.4.5.1 sv), and *muttakkip šadê* "who butts the mountains" from *nakāpu* "to butt, to gore" (CAD sv *n.* A 2a), cf. 6.7.3.

12 Instances of Dt imperatives are *mu-te*$_9$*-si* "wash (yourself)" (JCS 22, 26: 21. 23), *ru-tab-bi* "elevate yourself" (ArOr. 37, 485: 62), *ru-ta-ki-is* "bind yourself" (VS 26, 64: 16), (*kasapka*) *šutabbi* "satisfy yourself with (i.e., recoup) your silver", cf. CAD sv *šebû* v. 3, which can all be regarded as reflexive. *Ku-ta-i-na* (CCT 4, 21b: 12) is reciprocal (cf. *kânu* Dt in 9.1.3 sv); for *šu-ta-ar-ri-ih* (AbB 9, 66: 11) see 9.1.1 with note 3. An instance of a Dt infinitive is that of *balāṭu* Dt (Iraq 55, 66: 4) quoted in 9.1.1. Statives Dt include the "durative" stative Dt of *puqqu* (cf. 9.1.6 sv), the reciprocal stative *putuhhā* (qu. as (32) in 9.1.3), and the pluralizing one *šutarrû* (if correctly interpreted, cf. 9.1.7 sv *šerû*). A unique instance of an abstract noun built on a stative/VA of the Dt-stem (or Dt(n)-stem?) is *šutarruhūtu* in RIMA 2/I, 151: 75); its interpretation is obscure.

13 This applies to *ašāšu* (CT 17, 10: 71), *hepû* (Iraq 27, 5: II 10), *herû* (Gilg. VI 52), *lemēnu* (AbB 7, 61: 20), *pahāru* (HSS 5, 99: 11), *sapāhu* (CT 17, 31: 28), *ṣabātu* (Iraq 27, 5: II 10), *ṣarāpu* (CT 23, 2b: 4; ZA 61, 56: 153), *šamāhu* (VAB 4, 112: 26), *ṭabāhu* (Gilg. XI 70). Other cases listed as Dtn in the dictionaries but regarded as Dt forms here are *nâdu* (see note 41 to Ch. VII), *kabātu* (see 9.1.7 sv), *lahāšu* (see 7.6.1 sv and 9.1.6), *nagāšu* (see 9.1.7 sv), *huqqu* (CAD) see 9.1.7 end, and *šanû* Dt in hendiadys, cf. 7.4.1.

14 This omen apodosis reads [...] *uq-ta-na-la-al ina têrtišu innassah*, which is translated in CAD sv *qalālu* 5 "he will be discredited and removed from his office". If this translation is correct, it is a unique instance of a Dtn form with passive meaning, serving as iterative to a passive Dt-stem. It seems preferable, therefore, to follow Kraus in assuming that a direct object has to be restored in the break: "[Wenn] er [...] herabzusetzen pflegt, ...".

15 The ŠD forms in question are those of *marāṣu* in VAB 2, 170: 9. 40 (Amarna), of *rakābu* in Emar VI/3 p. 356 no. 373: 180', of *palāku* in CT 22, 221: 6. 14 (NB) and of *katāmu* in CT 19, 45a: r.8 (a lexical list of diseases, no context). For *galātu* ŠD in a Šumma ālu omen see note 16.

16 A unique form which looks like a perfect of the ŠD-stem, but is from a Šumma ālu omen, not from a literary text, is CT 41, 31: r.29 (if a pig.........) *amēla uš-ta-ga-lit* "has scared a man". Comparison with CT 38, 47: 46 (if a pig has entered a man's house and) *amēla uš-gal-lit* "has scared the man" suggests that these forms are perfect and preterite respectively of a factitive verbal stem of *galātu* "to start". This may be a ŠD-stem, but a quadriliteral variant **šugallutu* would also lead to these forms, cf. GAG Verbalpar. 37.

17 Von Soden's claim that most ŠD-stems come from adjectival verbs ("Adjektivwurzeln") is not borne out by the facts. Among the verbs listed above only *danānu, maṭû, naw/māru, rabû* and *rapāšu* can - with varying degrees of certainty - be classified as such. It is, however, very difficult to establish definite criteria for establishing which verbs are adjectival and which are not. As to *malû*, the fact that it is used as a (lowly) transitive verb and as an intransitive verb with an adjunct accusative (cf. 7.3.1) suggests that it is a fientive change-of-state verb, rather than an adjectival verb.

CHAPTER TEN

THE PATTERN *PURRUS*

10.0. The pattern *purrus*[1] takes a crucial position in the discussion of the D-stem, first, because it is the form from which the D-stem as a verbal category is derived, and second, because it shows the various stages through which gemination of the second radical has developed from an iconic device with an expressive meaning to a grammatical morpheme which is part of the D-stem. These two issues will be discussed in detail in Chapter XI.

This chapter presents a detailed account of the use of *purrus*. In order to clarify the exact nature of this pattern two fundamental distinctions should be made. The first of these is between *purrus* as an inflectional category and *purrus* as a lexical category, in other words, between the inflectional and the lexical function of *purrus*; the *purrus* forms in question will be designated in short as inflectional and lexical *purrus* forms.[2] The former kind comprises those which are used as statives and verbal adjectives of the D-stem, the latter those used as adjectives, independently of any verbal paradigm.

The second distinction to be made is that between those uses of *purrus* which agree with other categories with gemination of the second radical in being based on the iconic nature of gemination, and those for which no association with iconicity can be established.

Both distinctions are problematic: the one between the inflectional and the lexical function, because only in favourable circumstances is it possible to identify a given *purrus* form as belonging to one or the other kind; the distinction between iconic and non-iconic uses is problematic, because the borderline between what constitutes iconic use and what does not, is extremely fuzzy, not only in general, but in particular also in this case. Nevertheless, they are necessary in order to enable a satisfactory description of *purrus* as a unified category.

Since inflectional *purrus* forms belong to the D-stem from which they are derived, they are in principle discussed under that D-stem, i.e., in Chapters VI, VII and VIII, according to whether they come from a transitive, an intransitive or a D tantum verb, respectively. However, since there is no clear-cut distinction between the two types, this principle will not be adhered to rigorously. The main concern of this chapter is the lexical function of *purrus*. We will concentrate on its general characteristics, in particular on the following issues: the basic function of *purrus* as a nominal category (10.1), the relationship between the inflectional and the lexical function (10.2 - 10.5) and the various situations in which lexical *purrus* forms are used (10.6 - 10.7). Section 10.8 examines the merits of the widespread view that *purrus* has an intensive function; 10.9 attempts a general characterization of the nature of *purrus*, followed in 10.10 by some concluding remarks.

In the course of this discussion many *purrus* forms are studied more or less extensively in appropriate places, but no attempt is made to give an exhaustive account of all attested *purrus* forms and their various meanings. The Appendix contains a list of most *purrus* forms mentioned in the dictionaries and some others, but many of these are not discussed any further.

A final remark should be made concerning *purrusu* as the infinitive of the D-stem. This chapter will not deal with *purrus* in this function. From a historical point of view, the (verbal) adjective and stative *purrus(u)* and the infinitive *purrusu* are doubtless the same form.[3] The infinitive, however, which expresses the action of the verb without regard to person, number, tense and diathesis (GAG § 85b), is an inflectional member of the verbal paradigm. Accordingly, its meaning and use is dependent on that paradigm, and completely predictable. Thus *purrus* infinitives are discussed as part of the D-stem to which they belong.

10.1. *Purrus* as a nominal pattern

Purrus is basically a nominal pattern, on a par with the nominal patterns discussed in Chapter III: *parras, parris* and *parrās*, a fact which is perhaps more evident from its Assyrian form *parrus*. It is most similar to *parras*, because both *parras* in its main functions (discussed in 3.1.2 and 3.1.3) and *purrus* denote states and qualities, and as such contrast with *parris, parrās* and some other *parras* forms (cf. 3.1.1, 3.2 and 3.3), which are basically agent nouns referring to activities rather than qualities. Therefore, *parras* and *purrus* are opposed to the simple adjective *parVs*, whereas the other patterns are opposed to the agent noun and present participle *pāris* (cf. 3.4).[4]

On the other hand, *purrus* differs from these nominal patterns in two important points. First, in its productivity: whereas *parras, parris* and *parrās* amount to only a few dozen instances each, there are about 550 roots of which a *purrus* form is attested. The second difference concerns the fact that *purrus* is not a purely nominal category. It has, at least partially, been incorporated into the verbal paradigm of the D-stem, in order to serve as its stative and verbal adjective. This development is doubtless responsible for its enormous productivity.

In the following sections we will elaborate on the exact kind of states and qualities expressed by *purrus*, and on the way it is related to other forms of the same root, such as the corresponding verbal D-stem and/or the simple adjective.

10.2. The inflectional function of *purrus*

The basic character of *purrus* as a category denoting states and qualities manifests itself in two functions: first, in the use of *purrus* as stative and VA of the D-stem, and, second, in its use for adjectives denoting more or less permanent qualities which do not (necessarily) result from a preceding action.

The former represents the inflectional function of *purrus*. An inflectional *purrus* form serves as the stative and VA of the D-stem, in order to denote the result of the action in question, in the same way as *paris* serves as stative/VA of the G-stem. In this function, *purrus* typically denotes states which result from a preceding action; it is an inflectional member of the verbal paradigm, predictable in meaning and fully productive: it can be derived from any D-stem which meets the general conditions for having a stative.[5] In general these *purrus* forms occur more often as statives than as VAs, unless the latter have acquired some specialized meaning.

Since inflectional *purrus* forms are dependent upon the verbal D-stem, there is no point in presenting a complete list of *purrus* forms of this type; they are discussed as part of the D-stem to which they belong. Instead, I will limit myself to quoting a few illustrative examples. They concern *purrus* forms derived from fientive verbs, both transitive and intransitive, and from D tantum verbs. Since the distinction between the lexical and the inflectional function of *purrus* is problematic for those forms which are derived from adjectives, the discussion of this type will be deferred to a separate section (10.4).

A few random examples of *purrus* statives with resultative meaning are the following:

(01A) ARM 26/1 p. 127 no. 17: 20ff (The god is raging (*ulappat*) in the upper district (...); the inhabitants of whatever towns have been affected should not enter the towns which have not been affected) *assurri māta*[*m*] *kal*[*ā*]*ša ú-la-ap-pa-tu* "lest they affect (D) the whole area";
(01B) *ib.* 30 *mātum lu-up-pu-ta-at* "the (whole) area has been affected (D)." (Also quoted in Chapter VI as (70) and (72), cf. the discussion in 6.6.3.2);

(02A) KH r.XIX 36ff (§ 226) *šumma gallābum balum bēl wardim abbutti wardim lā šêm ú-gal-li-ib* "if a barber has shaved off the *abbuttu* of a slave who is not his property without permission of the slave's owner";
(02B) VAB 5, 37: 12f *ellēta abbuttaka gu-ul-lu-ba-at* "you are free; your *abbuttu* is shaved off";

(03A) KAV 1: VI 1ff *šumma a'īlu esirtušu ú-pa-ṣa-an / 5 6 tappā'ēšu ušeššab / ana pānīšunu ú-pa-ṣa-an-ši* "if a man intends to veil his concubine, he will invite 5 or 6 of his associates and veil her in their presence";

(03B) *ib.* 6ff *esirtu ša ana pānī ṣābē lā pa-ṣu-nu-tu-ú-ni* (...) *esirtumma šīt* "a concubine who has not been veiled in the presence of people (...) remains a concubine";

(04) ARM 26/1 p. 267 no. 101: 25ff [25]PN [*ú*]-*sà-hi-ra-an-né-ti* (...) [28](...) *kīma 1* lú.gal.ku$_5$ [29]*ina šubtim sú-uh-hu-ra-nu* "PN has evicted us. (...) As the nearest petty officer, we have been evicted from (our) post. (Let my lord (...) send him a letter that he may not evict us" (*lā usahharannêti*).

Example (01) is a D-stem of the transitive verb *lapātu* "to touch, smear, affect" (cf. also (132) and (133) in 6.9.5 for similar clauses with *nakāsu* and *tarāṣu*); (02) is a D tantum verb; (03) is an intermediate case: a G-stem *paṣānu* is attested once (cf. AHw sv G), but in a different context, and for the act of veiling a woman D forms are mostly used, cf., apart from this verb, *pasāmu* D, and especially the VAs *pussum/ntu, kullultu* and *kuttumtu,* which can all refer to a veiled bride, see App. ssvv. Finally, (04) is from a basically intransitive verb. Examples of such statives and VAs of transitive D-stems could be multiplied at will.

Generally speaking, the conditions determining the use of the stative and VA are the same as those which determine the use of the D-stem in question itself (but see 5.6.5). Thus, if the D-stem is regularly found with a plural object, the *purrus* form tends to qualify a noun in the plural; this can be exemplified by means of many verbs in the Appendix to Chapter VI, where the occurrence of a stative/VA is indicated by "stat." or "VA"; see in particular *edēlu, (h)arāmu, hepû, nakāsu, palāq/ku, palāšu, ṣabātu, šatāqu, tarāṣu* and *ṭabāhu*. If the D-stem has some idiomatic or lexicalized meaning, this is also shared by the stative/VA *purrus(u)*; see, for instance, the same Appendix under the verbs *balālu* **2.**, *epēšu* **1.**, *hamāṣu* **2.** and **3.**, *kasû* **2.**, *ṣabātu* **10.** and *šaṭāru* **3.**

However, two qualifications need to be made with regard to this statement. The first of these concerns the difference in transitivity between the stative and most other members of the verbal D-stem. As argued in 5.6.4 and in Chapter VI, the use of the verbal D-stem is largely determined by the high degree of transitivity inherent in most transitive verbs. The stative/VA, however, denotes a state and, therefore, the absence of action or change, so that it has zero transitivity. That we still find many cases of D statives and VAs is due to two factors. First, as already noted in 5.6.5, a sentence with a stative/VA is a transformation of an active sentence; second, it is a general function of *purrus*, both inflectional and lexical, to underline plurality of the entity it refers to (see 10.6.1 for details). Thus the tendency to preserve in the stative/VA the verbal stem used in the basic active sentence, together with the tendency to use a *purrus* form to qualify a plural noun, leads to a rather frequent use of the stative and VA D in this situation.

The use of *purrus* statives and VAs in D-stems with an idiomatic and lexicalized meaning is caused by the fact that such meanings make a D-stem into a verb which is to some extent independent of the G-stem, so that its use is not determined any more by high transitivity, but simply by its specialized meaning. In this respect such D-stems behave in the same way as D tantum verbs.

The second qualification concerns the fact that also some *purrus* forms have a tendency to become lexicalized, i.e., to develop their own semantic peculiarities and thus to become independent of the verbal D-stem. This process is comparable to that occurring in Western European languages with past participles, which also have a tendency to develop into adjectives, more or less independent of the corresponding verb. Examples from English are *crowded, delighted, tired, engaged* (to be married), *sacred,* etc., cf. Matthews 1991: 55f.

The process of lexicalization of *purrus* forms is facilitated by the fact that the stative and the VA, especially those of fientive verbs, stand somewhat apart from the other members of the verbal paradigm of Akkadian, because of their nominal background. This makes it sometimes difficult to make a clear-cut distinction between the lexicalized use of *purrus* and its regular use as stative or VA of a verbal D-stem.

Lexicalization of statives and VAs leads to a more or less specialized meaning, and often to a use which differs from that of the verbal paradigm. As already noted in 6.4, we find a considerable number of VAs in the singular derived from D-stems, which normally occur with a plural object. Some typical examples of this phenomenon are *uṣṣuru* said of a slave: "branded" (Camb. 290: 3; Dar. 492: 2), from *eṣēru* "to draw, design"; *diqāru kas-su-pat* "chipped cooking pot" (SAA 7, 88: r.6) from *kasāpu* "to chip, to break off", and 1(?) *kussû ṣarbatu šu-bu-ur-tum* "one broken poplar chair" (BE 14, 163: 16, cf. *ib.* 18 chairs) from *šebēru* "to break, smash". Other instances are found in lexical texts: *eṣṣû uṣṣurtu* "a marked gecko" (MSL 8/2, 62: 235a) from *eṣēru* "to draw, design"; *qaqqadu húp-pu-ú* "a broken head" (MSL 14, 282: 365) from *hepû* "to break, destroy", and *daltu ru-ku-uš-tu* "a solid door" (MSL 6, 24: 225) from *rakāsu* "to bind". Two parallel cases are found in OB letters from Mari:

(05) ARM 2, 130: 4f *awīlum šū kīma saparrim šu-ub-bu-ur-tim ina bītišu ul uṣṣi* "that man does not leave his house just like a broken wagon";

(06) ARM 27, 12: 10 [*ina*]*nna kuṣṣū ikšudūnim u elep*[*pum*] *hu-up-pa-at* "now the winter has set in and the ship is broken" ("hors d'usage", acc. to Durand apud Birot *ad l.*).

The semantic nature of these word groups and the general function of *purrus* (cf. 10.9) suggest that these *purrus* forms serve to underline the permanence of the condition involved.

Other common instances of statives and VAs that show specialized uses which are unpredictable from the meaning of the D-stem are *puṭṭuru* "frayed" (said of liver parts) from *paṭāru* "to loosen, untie", *turruku* "bruised" or "dark" (opposed to *namru* "light") from *tarāku* "to beat", and *lupputu* "anomalous, unfavourable" from *lapātu* "to touch, affect" (for all references not given here, see the Appendix). Since this occurs on a rather large scale in the technical language of omens, these cases will be discussed in a separate section (10.7.1).

10.3. The lexical function of *purrus*

The lexical function of *purrus* concerns its use as a nominal pattern for the formation of adjectives. In many respects, lexical *purrus* forms are diametrically opposed to inflectional ones.

First of all, the inflectional *purrus* forms denote states which result from a preceding action and therefore have a verbal background. The lexical ones typically denote "pure" states which do not presuppose a preceding action. Usually, they denote stable, more or less permanent qualities which are unlikely to be derived from verbs. Accordingly, the corresponding D-stem of such *purrus* forms is often rare or non-occurring, or it has a different meaning from the *purrus* form. In some cases it can plausibly be argued that it is a denominative of the *purrus* form (see 10.3.1 on *huppudu*).

Secondly, an inflectional *purrus* form is basically a verbal form, since it belongs to a verbal paradigm; it can secondarily be nominalized as a VA. A lexical *purrus* form is basically a noun, either an adjective or a substantive, which can secondarily be used in the stative, just as any other adjective. Accordingly, inflectional *purrus* forms are typically used as statives, and less often as VAs. Lexical ones are typically used as adjectives and substantives, as qualities or designations of persons (for instance as proper names), and less often as statives. The relationship between the stative and the (verbal) adjective of a lexical *purrus* form is the reverse of that existing in an inflectional *purrus* form.

Thirdly, whereas inflectional *purrus* forms are productive derivations of the verbal D-stem with inflectional status, the lexical function of *purrus* is clearly a derivational category, which is productive only to a limited extent. It will be shown in the course of this chapter that most lexical *purrus* forms are rare, and tend to have a highly restricted, specialized meaning.

Since lexical *purrus* forms are not derived from the D-stem, the question is where they do come from; in other words, what their relationship is to other forms of the same root. On the basis of this relationship, we can distinguish four types which will be discussed one by one: first, lexical *purrus* forms which are isolated, in the sense that no forms without gemination are attested of the same root (10.3.1); second, *purrus* forms which are loosely connected with a transitive G-stem without being a regular (semantically predictable) derivation (10.3.2); third, *purrus* forms which are derived from intransitive verbs, which do not have other D forms (10.3.3). The fourth type are *purrus* forms which are derived from basic adjectives; as already stated in 10.2, they will be discussed separately in 10.4.

There are no clear-cut boundaries between these four types, and it is only in favourable circumstances that we can establish with some degree of certainty what the background of a given *purrus* form is. Therefore, the following classification is not exhaustive, but is only intended to illustrate each type, in order to show what kinds of relationship we can expect to find.

There is still a fifth kind that is theoretically possible, namely, *purrus* forms directly derived from substantives. There are no unambiguous instances of this in Akkadian; a possible case is *uzzubu,* which, according to Landsberger (1934: 103) and CAD sv *izbu*, means "malformed", and is associated with the substantive *izbu* "malformed newborn baby or young". However, AHw sv *uzzubu* translates "etwa 'vernachlässigt, verkommen'", and relates it to *ezēbu* "to abandon, neglect, leave". Unfortunately, *uzzubu* is only attested in lexical lists, which makes it difficult to establish its precise meaning. Its Sumerian equivalents, as quoted by AHw sv, partly resemble those of *izbu* as quoted in AHw and CAD sv; this seems to make Landsberger's interpretation preferable to that of AHw.

10.3.1. Isolated lexical *purrus* forms

Purrus forms of which the root is not attested in forms without gemination include a number of words which represent the most typical function of *purrus*, namely, denoting salient bodily characteristics (they will be listed and discussed in 10.6.2), for instance *gubbuhu* "bald", *huppudu* "blind", *ṭummumu* "deaf", *kubbulu* "lame, paralyzed", and many nouns which are only found in lexical texts, such as *uqqup/bu, uqquru* and *uṣṣudu*, all referring to some physical defect ("crippled"). A prominent subgroup is formed by *purrus* forms which are only attested as proper names. Many of them come from roots not recurring in other words, so that we do not know their precise meaning, but they are important evidence of the nature of the pattern *purrus*; see further 10.6.3.

Some of these *purrus* forms have a corresponding verbal D-stem, such as *huppudu* "to make blind", or a Dt-stem (*tuṭammumu* "to become deaf", *kutabbulu* "to become lame, cf. 9.1.4). The proportional frequency of adjective and verb, and the semantic nature of the *purrus* forms (stable qualities) suggest that such D-stems are occasional denominative derivations of the *purrus* forms (see further 8.4.1). This particular relationship is more clearly evidenced by some *purrus* forms derived from adjectives, such as *burrumu* "multicoloured" and *duššupu* "sweet", and by the "pseudo-*purrus* form" (cf. 10.7.1.2) *du'ummu/du'ūmu* "dark", with the rare D-stems *burrumu* "to make multicoloured, weave, twine", *duššupu* "to make sweet" and *du''umu* "to make dark" (see AHw and CAD ssvv).

If the difference in frequency between the *purrus* form and the D-stem is less pronounced, the derivational relationship between them is ambiguous, and we cannot establish whether the *purrus* form in question is inflectional or lexical (or both). This applies especially to D tantum verbs which denote qualities and adjectival concepts, such as *lu''û* "to defile, make dirty", *kupputu* "to make compact" and *muqqu* "to be(come) weak". For the verb *gullubu* "to shave" (cf. 8.2) it can be demonstrated that its *purrus* form can mean both "bald" (lexical, as a PN, cf. 10.6.3.2) and "shaven" (inflectional, e.g., in (02B) and as a designation of a type of priest, cf. CAD sv *gullubu* adj. b).

10.3.2. Lexical *purrus* forms related to transitive verbs

Many lexical *purrus* forms are loosely connected with a transitive G-stem without being a regular (semantically predictable) derivation, e.g., *buqqumu* "with scarce hair" (cf. *baqāmu* "to pluck"), *hummuṣu* "baldheaded" (cf. *hamāṣu* "to strip, skin, tear off"); *huššulu* "crippled" (cf. *hašālu* "to crush"); *kuṣṣuṣu* "crippled" (cf. *kaṣāṣu* "to trim, cut, mutilate"), *ṣubbutu* "paralyzed" (cf. *ṣabātu* "to seize") and *tubbuku* "limp" (cf. *tabāku* "to pour out").

Such *purrus* forms belong to the ones listed and discussed below in 10.6.2. and 10.6.3. They typically refer to qualities which can be viewed as resulting from the action expressed by the verb, just as the normal VA (*baqmu* "plucked, shaven", *hamṣu* "stripped", *ṣabtu* "seized", etc.). However, they have the additional nuance of describing that quality as more or less permanent and salient, and underlining its more or less pathological, or at least undesirable nature. Moreover, they typically refer to animate beings. The verb *hašālu* "to crush", for instance, is normally only used for objects and foodstuffs, cf. CAD sv., but its *purrus* derivation *huššulu* "crippled" typically refers to humans. The fact that *huššulu* is also used as plural of *hašlu* "crushed" in OA *mu-ha-lu ha-šu-lu-tum* "crushed *muhālus*" (kt z/k 14: 2f) illustrates the multifunctionality of *purrus* (see 10.6.1 for the use of *purrus* for plurality).

Less certain instances of the same semantic relationship between a *purrus* form and a transitive verb are *hummuru* "crippled" (from *hemēru* "to break, smash"?), and *hubbušu*, which refers to an unidentified physical defect (from *habāšu* "to break into pieces"? (AHw differently, cf. App. sv)). A further case is *sukkuku* "deaf, stupid" from *sakāku* "to clog, stop up" (cf. AHw sv *sakāku*), but *sakāku* may also be intransitive, as CAD sv contends; in that case it belongs to the next section.

Sometimes the difference in meaning between the *purrus* form and the verb is such that it is questionable whether they are related at all. This applies, for instance, to *ṣuhhutu*, which refers to a bodily defect, and *ṣahātu* "auspressen" (AHw), "to extract sesame oil, to process wine and juices" (CAD), and to *kuṣṣudu* "crippled" and the verb *kuṣṣudu* "to delay" (CAD), "festhalten" (AHw). It seems more likely that these words are derived from different roots.

Apart from this rather homogeneous group of adjectives denoting striking characteristics, there are some other *purrus* forms which are etymologically related to transitive verbs, but are semantically of a different nature, such as *sunnuqu* "closed, fastened" (of doors and bolts) versus *sanāqu* "to check, interrogate" (but also intransitive "to arrive"), and *kuṣṣuru* "having a hard soil", versus *kaṣāru* "to join, bind together".

There is no clear-cut borderline between the *purrus* forms mentioned here, and some others which in 10.2 were claimed to be lexicalized, such as *puṭṭuru* "frayed" and *turruku* "bruised, dark-blue". The latter represent a specialized use of the verbal adjective of the D-stem; the *purrus* forms mentioned in this section are formations which are independent of the D-stem, and are directly derived from the root (or from the G-stem). In practice, the two categories are often hard to distinguish. This applies in particular to many of the *purrus* forms which belong to the technical language of omens (cf. 10.7.1).

10.3.3. Lexical *purrus* forms related to intransitive verbs

A third important source of lexical *purrus* forms are intransitive verbs which do not have other D forms. Examples are *burruqu* "with reddish face and red hair" from *barāqu* "to flash" (of lightning), *burruru* "shining"(?), cf. *barāru* "to shine, sparkle"; *bu''utu* "staying overnight" (of the moon and herbs) from *bâtu* "to spend the night", *kummusu* "kneeling, squatting" from *kamāsu* "to kneel down, to squat" (cf. also 7.5.2), *muhhû* "ecstatic" from *mahû* "to become frenzied",[6] *muqqutu* "collapsed" (CAD), "(krankhaft) verfallen" (AHw), which is said of body parts in medical texts, from *maqātu* "to fall" (for the verbal D-stem *muqqutu* registered in the dictionaries, see note 6 to Ch. I), *muṭṭuru* "soggy, oozing moisture" from *maṭir* (id., only stative attested), *pussulu* "bent, twisted" from *pasālu* "to bend, twist" (intrans.), *quppu* "buckled" (of walls (*igāru*)) from *qâpu* "to buckle, cave in",[7] *rubbuṣu* "crouching" (of a dog) from *rabāṣu* "to lie down", *šulluṭu* "masterful" from *šalāṭu* "to rule, control" (no D-stem attested, only Dt, cf. 9.1.6), *uggû* from *egû* "to be(come) careless, neglectful", *uggumu* "angry" from *agāmu* "to become angry" (G also ARM 18, 38: 7; an adjective **agmu* is not attested), and *urrupu* "dark, cloudy" from *erēpu* "to become dark".

Purrus forms of verbs with a D-stem in another meaning include *kuššu* "abundant" (of hair) (cf. *kuššû* "to make profitable, enlarge"), *quddudu* "sunken, sagging" (cf. *quddudu* "to make sb bow" (see also 7.5.3)), *suhhuru* "curly" (of hair) (cf. *suhhuru* "to turn" (trans.), *ṣuhhu* "laughing, smiling" (cf. *ṣuhhu* "to make laugh", only in *muṣihhu* "clown", cf. 7.2.4), *uddupu* "windy" from *edēpu* "to blow" and *ṣu"udu* "whirling" (cf. *ṣuddu* "to cause to turn", cf. 7.2.4).

What was said in the previous section about the relationship of these *purrus* forms to the corresponding verb is basically applicable to these cases, too, but less conspicuously so, because we also find *purrus* forms here which do not obviously imply any permanence or salience (*kummusu, bu"utu, uggumu*).

Purrus forms from intransitive verbs which do have a D-stem are mostly used in their inflectional function, because these D-stems are regularly transitive (factitive) verbs which use *purrus* as stative/VA; an example is *suhhurānu* in (04), quoted in 10.2. In many cases, however, the status of such *purrus* forms is ambiguous; in this respect they resemble the *purrus* forms of adjectives, to be discussed next, which show the same problem to a much larger extent.

10.4. *Purrus* forms derived from adjectives

In the discussion of the inflectional and lexical functions of *purrus* so far, *purrus* forms derived from adjectives have been left out of account, because the criteria we have laid down to distinguish between them (cf. 10.3) are often insufficient to determine to which type a given *purrus* form that is derived from an adjective belongs. The main reason for this is that in many contexts it is difficult to judge whether the state in question is envisaged as dependent on a preceding verbal action or as a pure state that does not result from a preceding action.

This does not apply to all cases, however. On the one hand, we find *purrus* forms of adjectives which clearly have an inflectional function, because they denote the result of the action expressed by the D-stem, e.g.:

(07) TCL 17, 4: 6ff *2 gur še'um zu-uk-ku* (...) [8]*šumman šārum* [9]*išširam še'am kalā[šū]man* [10]*uz-za-ak-ki* "only two gur of barley have been winnowed, (...); were the wind right, I would have had all the barley winnowed" (tr. CAD sv *zakû* v. 4d);

(08A) ARM 9, 17: 9ff *52 karpāt karānim ṭābim ana 40 karpāt karānim sīmim ru-uq-qa* "52 jars of good wine have been emptied into 40 jars of red wine";
(08B) *ib.* 15 *248* (?) [*karpāt karānim*] *ú-ri-qú* "they have emptied 248 (?) jars of wine";

(09) ARM 1, 42: 15ff *ṣābum ša halṣika ištu ūmī mādūtim* [16]*ul ub-bu-ub-ma ūm tēbibtim* [17]*ītarkū u ina kīma inanna* [18]*ub-bu-ub ṣābim ul tele"i* [19]*ina tajjartikāma ṣābam* [20]*tu-ub-ba-ab* "the people of your district have not been cleared for a long time; the time for the clearing has passed, and (because) at the moment your cannot clear the people, you must clear them immediately on your return";

(10) VAB 5, 27 (= CT 8, 48a): 5ff "(PN is the son of PNF) [5]*ummašu ú-li-il-šu* [6]*ana ṣīt šamši pānīšu iškun* (...) [14]*ul-lu-ul* "His mother freed him and turned his face towards the east (...). He is free";

(11A) Gilg. XI 242 *lū ud-du-uš parsīgu ša qaqqadišu* "let the headband of his head be renewed";
(11B) *ib.* 251 *ú-te-ed-*[*diš parsīgu ša*] *qaqqadišu* "the headband of his head was renewed".

Since in these cases the action which has led to the state expressed by the stative is explicitly mentioned, the context leaves no doubt that these *purrus* forms are resultative. Therefore, they are instances of unambiguously inflectional *purrus* forms.

On the other hand, there are also some *purrus* forms which are unambiguously lexical, because there is no corresponding D-stem: *puggulu* "strong", *šu"uru* "hairy", *(w)urrušu* "dirty", *zuqqunu* "bearded". Also *uddudu* "sharp, pointed" (of the "horns" of the moon) is more likely to be derived from *eddu* than from the verb *uddudu*, because *uddudu* always means "to act quickly", cf. 7.4.1 - although there can be little doubt that it could also be used for "to sharpen" if the need arises. Only a small number of such *purrus* forms is unambiguously lexical, because the enormous productivity of the verbal D-stem has led to its being derived from almost all *purrus* forms. The largest group of *purrus* forms without a corresponding D-stem is that of salient bodily characteristics and proper names to be discussed in 10.6.2 and 10.6.3.

In many other cases it is difficult to determine whether a given *purrus* form is used in its inflectional or lexical function, because of the difficulty of distinguishing "pure" from resultative states (see 10.4.1). The situation is further complicated by the indiscriminate use of G and D forms to denote the result of the action expressed by a factitive D-stem (see 10.4.2).

10.4.1. "Pure" versus resultative states

From a theoretical point of view, the contrast between the lexical and the inflectional function of *purrus* reflects the difference between states which are, and states which are not the result of a preceding action. In many contexts, however, it is irrelevant whether a state is resultative or not: an object that has been cleaned is clean, and a person who has been freed, is free. If there is no explicit reference to the preceding action, as in (07) - (11) above, it is often impossible to infer from the context which kind of state is envisaged by the speaker. Consider, for instance, the following sentences:

(12) Gilg. M III 10 *lū ub-bu-bu ṣubātūka qaqqadka lū mesi mê lū ramkāta* "your clothes should be clean (?, or cleaned?), your hair (lit. head) washed, (yourself) bathed in water";

(13) AbB 1, 2: 16 *maṣṣārātum lū du-un-nu-na* "Die Wachen sollen verstärkt sein" (tr. Kraus; also 6, 107: 7f; 7, 49: 2'; 50: 10'; 10, 150: 18; CTMMA p. 87 no. 69: 8).

In (12) it seems impossible to decide which of the two translations is more appropriate, and thus whether *ubbubū* should be regarded as an inflectional or a lexical *purrus* form. In (13) "strengthened" seems to be more appropriate than "strong", since these letters, with the exception of AbB 6, 107: 7f, concern a state of emergency because of the approach of enemy troops; thus they suggest that *dunnunā* is an inflectional *purrus* form used as stative of *dunnunu* "to strengthen". This is supported by a factitive sentence such as *maṣṣartam* [...] *ud-da-an-ni-in* "he has strengthened the guard" (ARM 10, 74: 26f; cf. also 14, 127: 9f). However, a translation "the guards should be strong" is not quite excluded. This also seems to be the best interpretation of:

(14) ARM 3, 12: 6f *ālum GN u halṣum ša*[*lim*] *bazhātūja du-un-nu-na* "la ville de Terqa et le district vont bien. Mes forces de gendarmerie sont solides" (tr. Kupper),

where the coordination with *šalim* speaks against a resultative interpretation.[8] It is completely parallel to:

(15) ARM 26/2 p. 119 no. 346: 4f *ālum GN šalim maṣṣārātūja da-an-na* (cf. also AbB 5, 158: 5f).

An additional argument against regarding *dunnunu* as an inflectional *purrus* form in this context is the fact that, whereas the verb *dunnunu* is a regular factitive D-stem which has no association with plurality whatsoever, the adjective and stative almost exclusively occur in the plural, see 10.6.1.2.1 sv.

The use of a *purrus* form such as *dunnunā* in combination with *maṣṣārātu*, etc., and of other *purrus* forms to be discussed in the next section strongly suggests that in Akkadian the logical distinction between pure and resultative states is only expressed by the context, and that therefore only the context decides (or does not make it possible to decide) whether we translate *ubbubū* in (12) as "clean" or "cleaned", and *dunnunā* as "strong" or "strengthened". This implies that the use of the stative G versus D in such cases does not correlate with the distinction between a pure and a resultative state, but is dependent upon other factors. These will be discussed in the next section.

10.4.2. Stative D versus stative G

It was argued in Chapter VII (see especially 7.3.4) that a stative cannot be factitive, because an essential feature of factitivity is the presence of an agentive subject. Since the stative expresses states and conditions, whereas an agentive subject presupposes an action, a stative cannot have an agentive subject. Even if the stative has a direct object, it still expresses a state or condition of the subject, not an action performed by the subject. Accordingly, it is always non-agentive and has zero transitivity according to the criteria for transitivity discussed in 5.3 and 5.4 (cf. also Binnick 1991: 187).

Therefore, the *purrus* statives presented in the preceding section are not used because they are factitive, but because the sentence in which they occur is a transformation of a factitive sentence (cf. 5.6.5 and 10.2). It is, however, also possible to use the stative G to denote the result of an action expressed by a factitive D-stem, apparently without difference in meaning. Compare especially (16), already quoted in 10.4 as (10), with (17):

(16) VAB 5, 27 (= CT 8, 48a): 5ff "(PN is the son of PNF) [5]*ummašu ú-li-il-šu* [6]*ana ṣīt šamši pānīšu iškun* (...) [14]*ul-lu-ul* "His mother freed him and turned his face towards the east (...). He is free";

(17) VAB 5, 29 (= BE 6/1, 96): 6ff (PNF_1 is the daughter of PNF_2) [6]PNF_2 (...) [7]*[ú]-ul-li-il-ši [pānī]ša ana ṣīt šamši iškun* (...) [14]*el-le-et ša ramāniša šī* "PNF_2 (...) freed her and turned her face towards the east." (...) PNF_1 is free (G) to dispose of herself",

where the stative G *ellet* occurs in exactly the same phrase as the stative D *ullul*.

This semantic equivalence of stative G and D can be illustrated by means of a number of frequent expressions which use both forms without a noticeable difference in meaning. The most prominent example of this phenomenon is the expression found in OB legal texts *libbi PN ṭāb* "PN is satisfied" (because he has been paid the amount due), cf. AHw sv *ṭiābu(m)* G I 4c α. It also occurs in the less common form *libbi PN ṭūb*, with a stative D instead of G (cf. *ib.* D 4b ε). A detailed discussion is found in Muffs 1973: 69ff. As to the difference between *ṭāb* and *ṭūb* in this context, Muffs claims (1973: 103) that if *ṭūb* is used,

> "the satisfaction of the heart is not an independent state of mind, but a condition induced by some preceding activity or, more specifically, by some preceding performance. The stative form *libbašu ṭūb* implies the existence of the active - and primary - form **libbašu uṭīb* "he (the buyer) satisfied his (the seller's) heart"."

This account is quite correct, not only with regard to the meaning of the phrase under discussion, but also with regard to the resultative function of the stative of a fientive verb in general. The implication of this statement, however, that the phrase *libbi PN ṭāb*, with the stative G, does denote "an independent state of mind" (1973: 103), is incorrect. The contexts in which the two expressions are used do not suggest any difference in meaning; this also follows from Muffs's own conclusion (1973: 101ff) that the difference is chronological.[9]

With the stative G the satisfaction is no less dependent on the preceding transaction than with the stative D. This is shown by instances such as the following, where the transaction is explicitly mentioned as the cause of the satisfaction:

(18) Horn Museum p. 136 no. 99: 5ff <u>še</u> *sabûtim* (...) *libbi PN ṭa-a-ab* "PN has been satisfied by means of barley for brewing" (i.e., he has received payment in the form of barley);

(19) AbB 10, 193: 10 *še'am u šamaššammī libbašu ṭa-a-ab* "mit Gerste und Sesam ist er befriedigt" (tr. Kraus); also CT 8, 26b: 11ff.

It is, however, more common to use the stative D of *ṭâbu* if an adjunct accusative is added, cf., for instance, CT 45, 117: 16f; CT 48, 42a: 11; VAB 5, 86: 23f; 95: 17f; UM 8/2, 205: 10f;

JCS 9, 59:1ff. This is caused by the fact that the presence of an adjunct accusative makes the sentence more clearly a derivation of an active sentence, such as:

(20) JCS 9, 99a no. 87: 5f (PN_1 bought a slave named PN_2 from PN_3 (and) PN_4) *šīmam gamram libbašu ù-ṭì-ib* "(and) satisfied him with the full price."

In other words, it enhances the verbal nature of the derived sentence with the stative.

A similar use of the stative G in expressions which include a factitive D-stem is found in the expressions *qaqqad PN kubbutu* "to honour sb", lit. "to make sb's head heavy (important)", and its antonym *qaqqad PN qullulu* "to despise, dishonour sb", lit. "to make sb's head light" (CAD sv *kabātu* 5, *qaqqadu* 8a 3'-a', and *qalālu* 4b). When these expressions are used in the stative, we usually find the G-stem (*ib.* sv 3b and 2b, respectively); cf. especially:

(21A) (= (01) in Ch. VII) AbB 3, 22: 15f (PN tells me that (...)) *qaqqadī kīma šamê tu-ka-ab-bi-tu* "you have honoured (D) me highly" (lit. "you have made my head important like heaven") (cf. also 28.);

(21B) (= (02) in Ch. VII) *ib.* 31 *eli panānum qaqqadī ka-bi-it* "I am more honoured (G) than before" (lit. "my head is more important than before");

(22) OBTR 150: 30f (Do you not know that) *awīlum ša bītānūšu lā taklū qaqqassu ina ekallišu qá-al-lu* "a man whose own personnel is unreliable is despised (G) in his palace?" (lit. "his head is light").

These statives in the G-stem, then, do not only denote the result of the processes involved (such as in AbB 2, 86: 26 *kaqqadī lā i-qá-al-li-il* "let me not be dishonoured" (lit. "let my head not become light"), but also that of the corresponding actions. On the other hand, it is also possible to use the D-stem in such contexts, as appears from the VA D in:

(23) AbB 3, 11: 12 *bītam ku-ub-bu-tam u bītam qú-lu-[lam t]apâd* "you want to put into fetters the honored and the despised household alike" (tr. CAD sv *qullulu* adj.).[10]

It could be argued that in these cases the stative G denotes the result of the process involved, and the stative D that of the action; that, for instance, *ēl* means "he has become (and therefore is now) pure" and *ullul* "he has been made (and therefore is now) pure". Although this may theoretically be correct, it is meaningless because it cannot be proved or disproved; in practice these two forms are used in exactly the same contexts. Moreover, it seems to be contradicted by instances such as the MB PN (quoted in CAD sv *ellu* 1d) *Ina-nāri-el-le-et* "She-was-Cleared-(of Guilt)-by-the-River-(Ordeal)" (tr. CAD *l.c.*).

A more likely explanation for this fluctuation between the use of the stative G and D in order to denote the result of the action expressed by a factitive D-stem is that it is due to the influence of two contrasting tendencies. On the one hand, there is a tendency to use the D-stem because the sentence is a transformation of a factitive sentence with a D form; on the other hand, there is a tendency to use the G-stem, because G, as the unmarked form, is appropriate in a sentence with zero transitivity.

Generally speaking, the first tendency will tend to be stronger, as the D-stem is more independent of the G-stem, i.e., as it is more lexicalized and therefore less predictable in meaning. This tendency can be exemplified by means of lexicalized factitive D-stems such as *kunnu* "to establish, confirm, verify", *(w)uššuru* "to let go, release" and *šunnû* "to repeat, report". They regularly have a stative D rather than G: *kūn* "it has been established, etc.", *(w)uššur* "he has been released" and *šunnu* "it has been repeated or reported" (more examples are given below). As a result of the lexicalization of these verbs, these statives have a quite different meaning from the corresponding simple statives and adjectives (*kīnu* "firm, true, loyal", etc., *wašru* "low, humble" and *šanû* "second, different"). This makes it undesirable to use them interchangeably. Moreover, whereas purely factitive D-stems can dispense with a stative and other non-factitive forms (such as a Dt-stem), lexicalized verbs tend to develop a complete paradigm of their own, which also includes a stative, a VA and a Dt-stem.

Typical examples of the use of *purrus* statives (and rarely VAs) which can be explained on the basis of this tendency include the following types:

1. Statives of more or less lexicalized factitive D-stems, such as *qurrub* "presented" from *qurrubu* "to present, offer" (see 10.10), *nukkur* "changed, removed" from *nukkuru* "to change, remove", *lubbuš* "provided with clothing" from *lubbušu* "to provide with clothing" (see below). Many of them have specialized meanings and belong to some kind of technical language: *zukku* "winnowed" (of barley) from *zukkû* "to winnow" is an agricultural term (cf. (07) and note 10). Two statives from the commercial language of OA merchants which deserve to be mentioned here are those of *ṣahhuru* "to deduct", and of *šabbu'u* "to satisfy", both good examples of lexicalized D-stems (instances are listed by Veenhof 1972: 430 for *ṣahhur*, and CAD sv *šebû* 2c/3 for *šabbu*). A third OA case is *balluṭ* "credited", which is discussed below.

2. Statives accompanied by an adjunct accusative, a construction which unambiguously points to a verbal background, e.g., *bunnu* "provided with", *duššu* and *ṭuhhud* "abundantly provided with", *tiqna tuqqun* "adorned with ornaments", and individual cases as *mê ruṭṭub* "soaked with water", i.e., "irrigated".

3. *Purrus* forms which are transformations of fixed, more or less idiomatic expressions with a factitive D-stem: the OB idioms *libba ṭubbu* "to satisfy", *qaqqada kubbutu* and *qullulu* "to honour" and "to despise", respectively (see above). Similar cases are *libba lummunu* "to make the heart bad", i.e., "to anger" and *pānī* or *zīmī nummuru* and *ukkulu* "to make the face radiant", i.e., "glad, happy", and "to make the face dark", i.e., "somber", respectively.

4. Apart from such more or less fixed expressions, there are also some individual cases where the context shows unambiguously that the *purrus* form is used to denote the result of an action, such as (07) - (11) quoted above.

On the other hand, the second tendency, viz., to use the stative G, tends to prevail if the D-stem, instead of being lexicalized, is a purely factitive counterpart of the G-stem, with a precise parallelism in meaning. This explains the fact that a number of statives and VAs of factitive D-stems are very rare or non-occurring, even though the factitive D-stem itself and the G-stem are very common.

The most striking instance is the stative D of *malû* "to be(come) full", *mullu*. It is very rare as compared to the frequent occurrence of both the G- and the factitive D-stem of *malû* (cf. 7.3.1). Only seven instances are known to me.[11] It is significant that in all five OB instances *mullû* does not have its literal meaning of "to fill or cover sth or sb with sth", but a more or less idiomatic meaning; in other words, it is to some extent lexicalized:

(24/25) ARM 10, 124: 20f/23 *nakrum ana qāt bēlija mu-ul-*[*lu*] (...) *nakrum ana qātija mu-ul-lu* "the enemy has been delivered into my lord's hand / my hand(s)";

(26) RA 86, 79: 11 *uṣurātum mu-ul-la-a qātiššu* "the "designs" have been delivered into his (Marduk's) hand(s)";

(27) ARM 14, 54: 22f [*ištēn*] *mārī ana epinnātim ša GN mu-u*[*l*]*-lu* "one son of mine has been assigned to the "ploughs";

(28) *ib.* 50: 19 *ul ana behrim mu-ul-<<lu>>la-a-ku* "I have not been assigned to the elite troops."

These sentences are resultatives of sentences such as the following:

(29) ARM 10, 8 (= 26/1, 214): 14 *nakrīka ana qātika ú-ma-al-la* "I will deliver your enemies into your hand(s)";

(30) ARM 6, 40: 8 PN (...) *sugāgšu ana behrim ú-ma-al-li-šu-ma* "as to PN (...), his sheikh assigned him to the elite troops".

It can hardly be accidental that this very rare stative is almost exclusively found in cases in which *malû* D does not have a quite literal meaning, but is slightly lexicalized, and therefore more independent from the G-stem than in its literal meaning.

Similar cases are the statives D of *balāṭu* "to live, be(come) healthy", etc., and *qatû* "to come to an end". Apart from its occasional use in NB PNs (see 10.6.3.3), the stative D of *balāṭu* is only used in the idiomatic, highly specialized meanings "to credit" (an amount) in OA, cf. Veenhof 1987: 52ff, and "ventiler" in OB, cf. Durand, MARI 3, 260ff. The stative and VA D of *qatû* are occasionally found in contexts which suggest a lexicalized meaning "perfect", rather than simply "finished", most clearly in:

(31) RIME 4, 607: 100f (the temple) *ša ipištam šuklulūma ummênūtam qú-ut-tu-ú* "that is perfect of construction and consummate as to (its) workmanship" (AHw sv *qatû* D 5: "meisterlich vollkommen").

This meaning also seems to offer the best interpretation in Ugar. 5, 313: 28 [*m*]*akût šinni qú-ut-tù-tù* "un panneau d'ivoire parfait" (Nougayrol), and STT 28: II 35 *epšēti qu-ut-ta-ti* "perfectly executed work" (on a throne).[12]

Other common factitive D-stems with a stative which is very rare are *hulluqu* "to make disappear, remove, destroy" (1x, see 10.6.1.2.2), and *šullumu* "to complete, compensate, safeguard, etc." (see 10.6.1.2.3).

Finally, a remarkable case of the statives G and D of the same verb (*labāšu*) in the same sentence is:

(32) ARM 6, 39: 8ff (I have investigated the case of the menials: from the 400 menials) [8]1 me *ṣābum ṣubātī la-bi-iš* [9]*u* 3 me *ul lu-ub-bu-úš* [10]*u aššum ṣābim ša ul la-*[*ab-šu*] [11]PN_1 [12][*u*] PN_2 *asniqma* (...) "one hundred (already) have clothing (G), and three hundred have not (yet) been

provided (D) with it; concerning the menials that do not have (or: have not been provided with) clothing (G) I have questioned PN_1 and PN_2, (...)"

The use of the stative D *lubbuš* in 9 is caused by the fact that *lubbušu*, lit. "to make sb wear or put on sth" has acquired the slightly lexicalized meaning "to provide sb with clothing" (CAD sv *labāšu* 3b-1'). *Labiš* in 8 is ambiguous: it may be explained as the unmarked form with the same meaning ("have already been provided with"), but it is more likely that the use of G implies that the one hundred menials had clothing from the outset, and did not need to be provided with it. The stative G in 10 - assuming that the restoration is correct - is doubtless an example of the use of G as the unmarked form, referring to the same situation as the preceding marked D form.[13]

10.4.3. Conclusions about *purrus* forms of adjectives

The various tendencies which determine whether in a given context the stative G or the stative D of an adjective will be used can be summarized as follows. First of all, the tendency to opt for the stative D is stronger as the verbal D-stem in question is more lexicalized, i.e., has a meaning which is more or less unpredictable from the regular meaning of the corresponding G-stem or adjective (cf. *kūn, (w)uššur, šunnu*, etc.). Second, if there is no lexicalization, and the D-stem is a pure factitive of the G-stem, both the stative D and the stative G are possible (cf. *ṭāb/ṭūb*, etc.). Third, in this situation the choice between G and D is based on the same criteria which also determine the use of lexical *purrus* forms, i.e., D is preferred if the subject is plural (cf. *dunnunā*) and/or has a high degree of salience; these functions of *purrus* in its lexical function will be discussed in 10.6.

This means that a *purrus* form derived from an adjectival verb is motivated either by its being derived from a verbal D-stem (in that case it is inflectional), or by the semantic nature of the sentence in which it occurs (in that case it is lexical). Which of the two applies in a given case, will generally be difficult to determine (cf. *ubbubū* in (11)).

A consequence of this state of affairs is that any stative can denote the result of a process or an action, also the stative G. This is shown by the cases discussed in 10.4.2, especially by *libbi PN ṭāb*, and by an individual instance such as the PN *Ina-nāri-el-le-et* quoted in 10.4.2. It is also the reason for the rare occurrence of the stative D of some frequent factitive D-stems, such as *mullu*.

10.5. General conclusions about the lexical and inflectional functions of *purrus*

The general conclusion which can be drawn from the discussion of the lexical and inflectional functions of *purrus* is that we can distinguish a number of unambiguous inflectional *purrus* forms (those derived from fientive verbs and some others which for semantic reasons can be regarded as dependent on the verbal D-stem), and a number of unambiguously lexical *purrus* forms (those for which a corresponding verbal D-stem does not seem to be in use). These cases are the prototypes of both categories. In many other cases it is difficult to classify a given *purrus* form as belonging to either category, especially in the case of *purrus* forms derived from adjectives.

An alternative to distinguishing inflectional and lexical *purrus* forms would be to regard all *purrus* forms as inflectional, i.e., as derivations of a verbal D-stem, even though this is not actually attested. This approach seems to be implied in a formulation such as the one adopted in GAG § 55n, where *purrus* is simply defined as the pattern of "Verbaladjektive des D-Stammes" (similarly in Ungnad-Matouš 1964: 42 § 36e). In this view, lexical *purrus* forms should be regarded as analogical to other *purrus* forms which do have a verbal D-stem in the appropriate meaning. For instance, on the model of a possible derivation *dannu* "strong" → *dunnunu* "to strengthen" → *dunnunu* "(strengthened with the result that he/it is) strong", we might derive the lexical *purrus* form *puggulu* from a sequence *paglu* "strong" → **puggulu* "to strengthen" → *puggulu* "(strengthened with the result that he/it is) strong", with the omission of the intermediate stage which is so typical of derivational processes, cf. Kuryłowicz 1972: 7.

Two major objections can be raised against this approach. First of all, the number of lexical *purrus* is far too large to make this explanation acceptable, and many of them denote qualities which can hardly be envisaged as derived from a verbal paradigm; this is especially true of the *purrus* forms to be discussed in the next sections, which denote salient bodily characteristics.

Second, not only the meaning of these *purrus* forms, but also the parallelism between *purrus* (originally *parrus*, see note 1) and the other nominal patterns *parras, parrās* and *parris* strongly suggests that *purrus* has a nominal background, and that its verbal function results from a secondary development.

Third, the distinction between the inflectional and the lexical function of *purrus* enables us to explain the historical background of the D-stem. It will be argued in Chapter XI that the D-stem as a verbal category is a denominative formation of *purrus* adjectives, i.e., of lexical *purrus* forms, and that subsequently the *purrus* form was also used as the stative/VA of the D-stem; this relationship can be expressed as follows: *purrusu* (adj.) → *uparras* → *purrusu* (stat./VA), where *uparras* symbolizes the verbal D-stem.

This double use of *purrus* is based on the model of the situation existing in the G-stem, where the corresponding simple pattern *parVs* has the same double function: in fientive verbs *parVs* (in fact always *paris*) serves as the stative/VA derived from the verbal paradigm (e.g., *iṣabbat* "he seizes" → *ṣabit* "he has (been) seized"). This corresponds to the inflectional function of *purrus*. In adjectival verbs *parVs* is the adjective on which the verbal paradigm is based (e.g., *dannu* "strong" → *idannin* "he becomes strong"), which is parallel to the lexical function of *purrus*.

There are some indications that as a result of the high productivity of the D-stem as a verbal category, there is a gradual shift in the nature of *purrus* from mainly lexical in the older stages of Akkadian to predominantly inflectional in later stages. This issue will be taken up in 10.10, after the discussion of the actual use of *purrus.*

10.6. The lexical use of *purrus*

The use of *purrus* in Akkadian is extremely varied, and even if we restrict ourselves to its lexical function, it is difficult to give a definition which encompasses all its possibilities. There are, however, two uses which stand out as the most typical domain of lexical *purrus* forms, namely that of denoting salient bodily characteristics, and that of underlining plurality. These uses are manifestations of the original iconic nature of gemination, because they represent semantic extensions in comparison to the corresponding forms without gemination (cf. 2.2.4).

In this respect there is a close similarity between the lexical *purrus* forms and the D-stems of transitive verbs discussed in Chapter VI: in both categories plurality and salience are important factors in determining the use of forms with gemination.

However, the association of *purrus* with plurality and salience is more complex and less consistent than that of the D-stems of transitive verbs. This is firstly caused by the fact that *purrus* also has the inflectional function discussed in 10.2, which causes the use of *purrus* forms on the basis of the corresponding verbal D-stem, without any relation to such notions as plurality and salience. Secondly, it is caused by the extensive lexicalization of *purrus* forms. This has led to a conventional and stereotyped use, especially in the technical language of omens, and ultimately to the disappearance of the contrast with the simple form. Thus we find many *purrus* and *parVs* forms without appreciable difference in meaning in similar contexts. Such cases will be dealt with in 10.7.

First of all, we will discuss the two functions which are based upon the iconic nature of gemination: that of underlining plurality in 10.6.1, that of denoting salient bodily characteristics in 10.6.2.

10.6.1. *Purrus* for plurality

The first typical aspect of *purrus* to be discussed is its association with plurality. This function concerns both inflectional and lexical *purrus* forms. The inflectional *purrus* forms associated with plurality are the statives and VAs derived from transitive verbs with a D-stem that normally has a plural object; they were discussed extensively in 6.4. Frequently occurring instances of this use are statives and/or VAs such as ***huppû*** "broken" from ***hepû*** "to break" (6.4.1), ***nukkusu*** "cut off" from ***nakāsu*** "to cut off" (6.4.1), ***rukkusu*** "bound" from ***rakāsu*** "to bind" (6.4.3) and ***ṣubbutu*** "seized" from ***ṣabātu*** "to seize" (6.4.4). These *purrus* forms are motivated by both the corresponding use of the verbal D-stem with a plural object and the general association of *purrus* with plurality (see below).

The association of *purrus* with plurality is not restricted to *purrus* forms which are used as statives or VAs of D-stems with a plural object. Other *purrus* forms are found with this function, too. Since their use is independent of a verbal paradigm, they fall under the lexical function of *purrus*. They are parallel to the use of *parras*, also a purely nominal category, as the plural of adjectives denoting dimensions, cf. 3.1.3; as noted in 3.1.3.3, the two patterns are complementary in this respect.

In practice, there is no difference between lexical and inflectional *purrus* forms as regards their association with plurality, and therefore *purrus* forms and the D-stems of transitive verbs show no difference on this point either (cf. 6.3 for the latter). First of all, the criteria for what constitutes plurality are the same: it does not only comprise grammatical, but also semantic plurality, namely, collectives and mass nouns (the latter especially in OA, see 10.6.1.2.4); secondly, it concerns the same entities: primarily persons and animals, body parts and large concrete objects (cf. 6.4.9); finally, the same conditions apply with regard to the redundant and optional character of the forms with gemination.

Thus for all practical reasons the two kinds of *purrus* forms merge into a single category of *purrus* for plurality. Accordingly, it is often fruitless to speculate on whether a given *purrus* form with a plural subject is dependent upon a verbal D-stem, or whether it is used independently. Especially in omens there are many borderline cases of *purrus* forms which can be regarded as D statives of transitive verbs, but also as more or less lexicalized, independent adjectives. Examples are *ṣurrupu* "(coloured) red" and *tukkupu* "speckled", quoted below in 10.6.1.1.1 as (34). There is no significant difference between these *purrus* forms and others which have been assigned to Chapter VI, such as *udduhu* "covered with patches", discussed in 6.5.3. The reason for treating the latter in Chapter VI and the former in this chapter is a matter of convenience rather than of principle.

There are a few cases from which it transpires that the behaviour of the corresponding verbal D-stem may be an important factor in the use (or non-use) of *purrus* as a plural of the simple adjective, even if it is lexicalized. This concerns *lupputu* and *turruku* in omens.

In OB Mari texts, the result of an extispicy (*têrētum*) is expressed with the stative *šalmā* if it is favourable, and with *laptā* or *lupputā* if it is unfavourable. It is plausible that the use of *lupputā* is caused by the plural subject *têrētum* (although it is difficult to prove, since to my knowledge the singular *têrtum* is not attested in this context in Mari texts), and that it is an optional alternative to *laptā* (the contexts do not seem to point to a difference in meaning between them).[14] However, we never find *šullumā* as predicate of *têrētum*; even side by side with *lupputā*, only *šalmā* is used, cf. especially:

(33) MARI 6, 338: 60ff (I will have an extispicy performed here) *šumma têrētūja ša-al-ma* [61]*kakkī itti awīl GN eppeš ulāšūma têrēt[ū]ja* [62]*lu-up-pu-ta ka[kk]ī ul eppeš* "if my extispicy is favourable,

I will give battle with the man of Ešnunna; if, on the other hand, my extispicy is unfavourable, I will not give battle." (A similar case is FM 2 p. 112 no. 71: 5ff).

The reason why *laptā* can be replaced by *lupputā,* whereas *šalmā* is never replaced by *šullumā* is doubtless that the D-stem of *lapātu* "to touch, smear, affect", is usually associated with plurality (cf. 6.4.8 sv and 6.6.3.2), whereas that of the intransitive verb *šalāmu* is not, since it is a factitive D-stem (but see 10.6.1.2.3 for a possible counter-example).

A similar case is that of *tarik* "bruised, dark" (or something similar) and its antonym *naw/mir* "light", which, also in extispicy omens, are used in opposition to qualify various organs of the sacrificial animal. In the plural *tarkū/ā* alternates with *turrukū/ā* (see 10.6.1.1.2 below), but for its antonym we only find the simple stative *naw/mrū/ā,* cf. CAD sv *namāru* 1e (the stative *nuww/mmur* mainly occurs with *pānū* and *zīmū* "face", cf. 10.4.2).

In this case, too, the explanation is doubtless that *naw/mir* is derived from *naw/māru,* which has a factitive D-stem unconnected to plurality, whereas *tarik* is a lexicalized stative of *tarāku* "to beat". The association of this verb with plurality is not very clear (cf. App. to Ch. VI sv), but semantically it belongs to the kind of verbs which usually have a D-stem with plural object (group III in 6.4.3). In this case, too, then, it seems to be the D-stem on the background which bears on whether a stative G or D will be used.

The evidence for plurality as the motivating factor for the use of *purrus* instead of the simple adjective is twofold. In the first place, it consists of contrasting pairs of the kind presented in Chapter VI, in which a *parVs* and a *purrus* form are directly opposed with a concomitant difference in the nature of the subject, usually singular versus plural (10.6.1.1.1) or partly versus totally affected (10.6.1.1.2). Most of such pairs come from omen protases. Other *purrus* forms underline a kind of plurality which is the result of the action, or is inherent in their meaning (10.6.1.1.3).

The second type of evidence for the association of *purrus* with plurality consists of *purrus* forms which are always or practically always combined with a plural subject or substantive. These will be discussed in 10.6.1.2.

10.6.1.1. Contrasting pairs of *purrus* and *parVs*

10.6.1.1.1. *Purrus* and *parVs* correlating with plural versus singular subject.

In omen texts we find cases in which a singular subject, accompanied by a stative of the G-stem, is contrasted with the same subject in the plural, accompanied by a *purrus* form:

(34A) YOS 10, 31: IX 7ff *šumma martum būdāša tu-ku-pa-a-ma ṣú-ur-ru-pa* "if the shoulders of the gall bladder are full (D) of specks and red" (i.e., "full of red specks", cf. 10.7.1.1 sv) (cf. *ib.* 24);
(34B) ib. 13ff *šumma martum muhhaša ta-ki-im-ma ṣa-ri-ip* "if the top of the gall bladder is full (G) of red specks." (cf. also *ib.* 1ff);

(35) Izbu 54: 8ff (If a woman has given birth and) *uzun imittišu ha-az-mat / uzun šumēlišu ha-az-mat*

/ *uznāšu hu-uz-zu-ma* "the right ear (of the child) is shrivelled (G) (...) / the left ear (of the child) is shrivelled (G) (...) / (both) ears (of the child) are shrivelled (D) (...)";

(36) TDP 130: 47ff [*šumma*] *qinnat imittišu nap-hat* (...) / [*šumma qinnat šumēlišu nap-hat* (...)] / [*šumma*] *qinnātūšu nu-up-pu-hu* (...) "if his (the patient's) right buttock is bloated (or inflamed) (G) (...), [if his left buttock is bloated (...)] / [if] (both) his buttocks are bloated (D) (...)".

The last instance is especially informative. Many omen texts are built on the principle of such "triplets", in which paired parts of the body are first mentioned separately (right and left) and then together. The D-stem used for the third clause underlines either the plurality of the subject or the notion of completeness, in contrast to the partial affectedness of the subject in the first two clauses (see the next section); most probably, both notions influence the tendency to use the D-stem here.

On the other hand, such triplets also show the optional nature of its use. In fact, among the many triplets occurring in the medical diagnostic omens of TDP, it is only here that a D-stem is used; in all similar triplets found in TDP *paris* is also used in its third member, cf. TDP 86: 46f; 102: III 1ff (both *napāhu*); 46: 12ff; 68: 1ff; 86: 45f; 102: 13f (all *tarāku*); 46: 6ff (*pa'āṣu*); 68: 6ff (*paṭāru*); 102: 7ff (*hesû*). Of these verbs, *napāhu, tarāku* and *paṭāru* are attested with a D-stem for plurality in other texts (see the App. to Ch. VI under the respective verbs; for *tarāku* also the next section and 10.7.1.1, and for *napāhu* 10.6.1.2.1).

10.6.1.1.2. Partial versus complete affectedness of the subject

In other contrasting pairs the opposition between stative G and D does not refer to singular versus plural but rather to partial versus complete affectedness: G is used if the quality refers to only a part of the subject, *purrus* underlines that the whole of the subject is involved:

(37) YOS 10, 36: I 7f [*šumma im*]*itti hašîm ta-ar-*[*k*]*a-at* (...) / *šumma imitti hašîm u šumēl hašîm tu-ur-ru-k*[*a*]*-at* "If the right of the lung is dark (G), (...) / if the right and the left of the lung are dark (D), (...)";

(38) ib. 48: 41f // 49: 13f *šumma bamtum imittam la-ap-ta-at-ma lipissa rabi* (...) / *šumma bamtum imittam u šumēlam lu(-up)-pu-ta-at* (...) "if the thorax(?) is affected (G) on the right side and the spot is large, (...) / if the thorax(?) is affected (D) on the right and the left side (...)." (tr. CAD sv *liptu* A 3b);

(39A) ARM 26/1 p. 276 no. 109: 11ff *dūr libbim* (..) *ṣulmam kīma hudušším ta-ri-ik* "the *dūr libbim* (cf. *l.c.* note c) is darkened (G) by a black spot like a *hudušsu*(-stone?)";

(39B) *ib.* 6ff šà.har *imittam u šumēlam ṣulmam tu-ur-ru-ka* "the šà.har is, both on the right and the left side, darkened (D) by a black spot" (where, however, the subjects are not identical).

Cf. also YOS 10, 42: II 62 *pu-ru-ku* (subject: 6 lines (*tallu*)), vs. III 21 *pa-ri-ik* (1 line), which are, however, not contiguous, and Emar VI/4 p. 305 no. 682: 9'f with *hamšu* vs. *hu-u*[*m-mu-šu*], which is partly broken; for a similar use of *lapātu* D, see (69) - (72) in 6.6.3.2. It is possible that the following case belongs here, too:

(40A) YOS 10, 53: 3/4 *šumma* kuš mušen *ana 2 / ana 3 ta-ri-ik* "if the skin of the "bird" has two / three bruises" (G) (tr. CAD sv *mašku* 1b);
(40B) *ib.* 4 *šumma* kuš mušen *tu-ur-ru-uk* "if the skin of the "bird" is (completely?) bruised (D)".

The optional and highly unpredictable nature of the use of *purrus* is shown by the fact that, beside the preceding instance, we find in the same text:

(41) YOS 10, 53: 9/10/11 *šumma* si mušen zi / gùb / zi *u* gùb *ta-ri-ik* "if the "horn" of the "bird" is dark (all G) on the right side / left side / right and left side" (also 15ff, 26ff).

where *tarik* is used for all three members of the triplet. This is the usual state of affairs in TDP (see above), and is also found in YOS 10, 36: IV 10/12/14. In another OB omen text, on the other hand, we find three times *turruk* in a similar triplet (YOS 10, 45: 66ff). Thus the use of *tarik* and *turruk* varies according to the text. This would seem to point to a semantic difference, such as "dark" versus "very dark" (cf. 10.8), but this is difficult to reconcile with the cases where the contrast G vs. D correlates with the contrast singular versus plural.

10.6.1.1.3. *Purrus* for "inherent" plurality

In other cases the plural element is inherent in the meaning of the *purrus* form (cf. 6.4.1.1 sv *parāsu*). Several types can be distinguished. The first one concerns verbs with meanings such as "to divide, to split"; consider the following cases:

(42A) SSAW 120/3, 17: 16f *šumma šumēl martim adi 2 / 3 pa-ṭe$_4$-er* "if the gall bladder is split (G) in two / three" (cf. also *ib.* 19: 3ff);
(42B) *ib.* 18 *šumma šumēl martim piṭrum 4 5 6 adi mādūti pu-uṭ-ṭú-úr* "if the gall bladder (has) a *piṭrum* and is split into 4, 5, 6 or many (parts) (D)";
(43A) RA 44, 30: 44 *šumma išissa ip-ṭù-ur* "if its base (i.e., of the *naplastum*) is split (G)";
(43B) *ib.* 47 *šumma naplastum ana 4 pu-uṭ-ṭù-ra-at* "if the *naplastum* is split in four" (D) (or: "the *naplastum* (as a whole)", like (37) - (40) above?);
(44A) YOS 10, 33: V 22/24/26 *šumma ṣēr ubānim šalaštūšunu šulūšā / rubū'ā / šinā ip-ṭù-ru* "if the surfaces (?) of the "finger", all three of them, are split (G) in three / four / two";
(44B) *ib.* 28/31/34 *šumma ṣēr ubānim šalaštūšunu šulūšā / rubū'ā / šinā pu-ṭù-ru* "if the surfaces (?) of the "finger", all three of them, are split (D) in three / four / two" (also 37 and 39).

The last instance is somewhat enigmatic. First of all, instead of a stative (44A) contains a preterite form of the G-stem used intransitively (also in (43A)), but in other protases the stative G is used.[15] Second, in (44B) the protases of lines 28 and 37, and also those of lines 31 and 39, are completely identical, but their apodoses are different. Third, it is unclear to me what the difference in meaning between (44A) and (44B) is.

It is likely that cases where *puṭṭuru* is not accompanied by a numeral are to be explained in the same way, cf. 10.7.1.1 sv. Another *purrus* stative used in the same circumstances is:

(45) YOS 10, 11: I 14f *šumma padānum adi šalāšīšu pu-ru-us* "if the "path" is split (D) in three" (rather than "severed three times", as CAD has sv *šalāšīšu* b).[16]

The second type are verbs meaning "to perforate", in which *purrus* forms are apparently used to underline the notion of "perforated with many holes"; cf. the following contrasting pair:

(46A) OBE 16: 15'/16' *šumma kalīt imittim* (zag) / *šumēlim* (gùb) *pa-al-ša-at* (...) "If the right / left kidney is perforated (G) (i.e., has a hole) (...);
(46B) *ib.* 17' *šumma kalītum imittam* (zag) *pu-ul-lu-ša-at* "if the kidney is perforated (D) (i.e., has many holes) on the right".[17]

If this claim is correct, it may explain other singular instances of *purrus* forms which are normally associated with plurality; most of such cases concern *purrus* forms derived from D-stems which normally have a plural object. This applies, first of all, to the unique use of *pullušu* with singular subject in the omen protasis YOS 10, 45: 24 (see 6.4.2.1 sv for *palāšu* D with plural object), and, second, to the same form in MSL 7, 87: 210 *pu-lu-uš-[tum]* and 90: 262 *pu-ul-lu-šu*, which qualify or designate a kind of jar. It may also apply to the use of the VA D of *patāhu* "to perforate" in *nappû pu-ut-tu-hu* and *quppatum pu-ut-tu-úh-tum* "a sieve with many holes", and "a basket with many holes", respectively (CT 4, 30a: 6f). However, it is also conceivable that these instances are to be explained in the same way as those mentioned in 10.2 end, i.e., that *purrus* underlines the permanence of the condition involved.

Some other statives of *purrus* forms may also be interpreted as representing inherent plurality. *Hurruru*, from *harāru* "to dig, groove", is translated by CAD sv *harāru* A 2b as "has many grooves", opposed to *harir* "has a groove" (they are not attested in contrasting pairs); *šuttuqu*, from *šatāqu* "to split", as "split in many places" *ib.* sv *šatāqu* 2a; *sullutu* as "split into many parts" *ib.* sv *salātu* 3a-2', and *šulluqu* "slit in many places" *ib.* sv *šalāqu* 2 in the translation of Izbu 134: 48. This interpretation of *šulluqu* is supported by the gloss *šu-ul-lu-qa* = *ša ma'diš sal-ta* (Izbu 231: 365j): "*šulluqā* means "much split"".

A third case of inherent plurality concerns the use of *purrus* in words which denote colours or combinations of colours. Just as *pulluš* and *puttuh* are likely to imply a plurality of perforations, *tukkup* "speckled", which occurs in SB with a singular subject, may be interpreted as "having many specks", and *turrup* "dotted" as "covered with many coloured dots".

The most striking instance of this phenomenon is *udduh* "covered with patches", discussed in 6.5.3. The passage STT 108: 15/18 and 22, quoted there as (37), shows that in that instance at least a plural adjunct accusative involving a single colour ("two white patches") does not lead to the use of a *purrus* form, but that one involving a combination of three colours does. It is possible that the high frequency of *burrumu* "multicoloured", which is much more common than the simple adjective *barmu*, is also related to the fact that it inherently denotes a plurality of colours.

10.6.1.2. Other indications for the association of *purrus* with plurality

The second indication that one of the functions of *purrus* is to underline the plurality of the word qualified, is that many *purrus* forms are predominantly attested in the plural. However, it is only rarely that we find relatively common *purrus* forms used exclusively in the plural, because most of them are also used for the other functions of *purrus,* namely, for its inflectional function and to express salient bodily characteristics, in which they occur indiscriminately with singular and plural subjects.

Generally speaking, the association of *purrus* with plurality is less consistent than that of the D-stems of transitive verbs. Therefore, it is often uncertain whether in a given context it is plurality or some other factor which is the actual motive for the use of *purrus.* This problem is especially acute in the case of the numerous stereotyped and lexicalized *purrus* forms used in omens and literary texts. Thus many claims in the following sections are made with some reservation.

Four groups of *purrus* forms will be distinguished: first, a group of common *purrus* forms which are predominantly used in the plural, at least in a part of their meanings (10.6.1.2.1); second, a group of very rare *purrus* forms only attested in the plural (10.6.1.2.2), third, a few instances of *purrus* forms which are apparently used for plurality, but normally have another function (10.6.1.2.3), and, fourth, a few mainly OA *purrus* forms which are used to qualify mass nouns, especially metals (10.6.1.2.4).

10.6.1.2.1. *Purrus* forms occurring predominantly in the plural

A large number of the more common lexical *purrus* forms tend to occur far more often in the plural than in the singular. It is, however, unusual to find cases which are consistently restricted to plurality. The only instance which comes to mind is *uddud* "sharp, pointed", but this is only said of the horns of the moon in astronomical omens, so that it exemplifies the stereotyped use of many *purrus* forms (see 10.7) rather than their association with plurality. Most other *purrus* forms which only occur in the plural are so rare that this is probably accidental. In almost all other cases the link with plurality is inconsistent.

A very typical use of *purrus* in the plural (or rather dual), to which we will return in 10.9, is its occurrence with paired body parts, in expressions such as BWL 44: 98 *muq-qu-ta šēpā-ja* "my feet are limp" (tr. Lambert), and MSL 4, 75: 284f *īnān pu-ur-ru-da-tum* "frightened eyes".

The following list presents the *purrus* forms which show an association with plurality that, although not consistent, is unlikely to be accidental (for references concerning the *purrus* form see the Appendix).

Dunnunu "strong" is only attested in OB and SB and is usually plural. Most instances are from OB, where we find it in the following cases (cf. App. **A. 1./2.**):

1. Combined with *maṣṣārātu* "guards" and some other words of related meaning (*baz(a)hātu* "military posts", *sakbū* "guard troops") in the expression already discussed in 10.4.1, most often in Mari letters, always in the plural. *Dannu* occurs in the same combinations, both in sg. (OBTA no. 9: 7; UM 1/2, 43: 12

and pl. (e.g., AbB 5, 158: 6; ARM 26/1 p. 445 no. 216: r.7'; 26/2 p. 119 no. 346: 5 = (15)), and is the only form outside OB as far as these subjects are concerned.

2. In combination with *awātum* "matters" and *ṭuppu* "tablet, letter" in OB letters. In this and similar contexts the G-stem is far more common in OB (e.g., AbB 9, 83: 26; Sumer 23 pl. 15: 15; ARM 14, 118: 16). Outside OB it is the only form attested (often in OA: cf. CAD sv *dannu* 2e).

3. In liver omens *dunnunu* qualifies the *tallu* ("diaphragm" acc. to Jeyes 1989: 77ff) and the *nimšū* (sinews, acc. to CAD sv), the latter in opposition to *šaknū* "lax (?)" (acc. to CAD sv *šakānu* 7h). The *tallu* is also attested with the simple adjective *dannu* (JCS 11, 101b: 20. 31).

4. Finally, in two other instances: AbB 12, 32: 20 = (64), discussed in 10.9; and Atr. 88: 32f *lū du-un-nu-na uniātum* / *kupru lū da-a-an* "The tackle should be very strong, let the pitch be tough" (tr. Lambert), where *dunnunā* and *dān* correlate with a pl. and sg. subject.

After the OB period (cf. App. **B. 1./2.**) *dunnunu* survives only in SB, in a small number of contexts: in RIs, qualifying walls, thresholds, foundations, poles, cities, troops (*kiṣrū*); exceptionally sg. (citadel). In other literary texts, it is said of roots and of power (*emūqā*, dual); in omens it qualifies the *zihhu* (cf. note 22) in the meaning "hard", versus *nurrubu* "soft". In one case it is said of a seam (k̲é̲š̲ = *riksu*: possibly a plural is meant). In LL *dunnunu* is equated with *puggulu* "strong".

The number of sg. instances amounts to 5 in OB (AbB 9, 237: 19; 12, 32: 20; YOS 10, 42: III 5. 8. 16) and 4 in SB (Sg. 8: 299; DA 217: 4; TU 2: r.11 // CT 28, 44a: r.6; SpTU 4, 129: VI 22). Although *dunnunu* is thus predominantly associated with plurality, other factors play a part, too, in particular the stereotyped use of *purrus* in omens and literary texts to be discussed in 10.7.1.

Duššû "abundant, numerous" is said of domestic animals, water, meals, produce, offerings and incense in literary texts, cf. CAD and AHw sv (also RA 82, 160: 41 (offerings)); therefore it also belongs to the literary *purrus* forms discussed in 10.7.2.

Because of the notion of plurality which is inherent in its meaning, *duššû* is mostly plural, or refers to a collective, such as *ṣēnu* "flock" and *hiṣbu* "abundance", cf. CAD sv.[18] Moreover, it is far more common than the simple form *dešû*, which is usually said of people, except in VAB 4, 160: 11 (and elsewhere in this text) *arqū de-šu-tu* "abundant vegetables" (which may also stand for /*deššūtu*/, a literary *parras* form (cf. 3.1.2), and BWL 60: 98 [*ina mākāl*]*ē de-eš-šu-ti* "with abundant meals" (with which compare UM 12, 6: 7 *ina mākālē du-uš-šú-tú*).

K/Qunnunu "coiled, curled" is said of hair(s), feet, lines on the forehead and the horns of the moon in various kinds of omens; of hair and intestines in LL, and of gods in Gilg. ("curled up like dogs"). The stative G *kanin* is only found in TDP 104: 32 (sg. subj.). In the sg. *K/Qunnunu* only occurs as a PN, see 10.6.3.2. For *k/qanānu* D with pl. object, see 6.4.2.1 sv.

Kubbutu "heavy" is occasionally used with various objects in the plural (loops, shields, balls, etc.); it is, however, possible that some instances assigned in the App. to *kupputu* "compacted, lump-shaped" also belong to *kubbutu*. The simple plural *kabtūtu*, etc., is far more common, cf. CAD sv *kabtu*. In addition, *kubbutu* is also used as stative/VA of *kubbutu* "to honour" (cf. 10.4.2), and as a PN, see 10.6.3.2.

Kuppupu "bent, curved" (feet, fingers, veins of the eye); note esp. TDP 50: IV 9 with *kup-pu-*[*pu*], vs. Syr. 33, 125: 7 with *kap-pu*, in the same protasis). The sg. occurs as a PN (see 10.6.3.2) and in LL.

Lupputu "unfavourable", said of *têrētum* "extispicies" in OB Mari (App. **2.**), was already discussed above in 10.6. In OB extispicy texts from other sources, however, *lupputu* is used differently, see 10.7.1.1 sv.

Nuppuhu frequently alternates with *naphu* in medical diagnostic texts (in other texts it is rarely found and does not have a clear association with plurality, cf. App. **2b**). It is very common, for instance, in TDP.

Its meaning is variously given as "bloated, swollen" (CAD sv 7) and "inflamed" (AHw sv *napāhu* D 5 "entzündet"). Because the ideographic writings of *nuppuhu* are ambiguous, we will restrict ourselves initially to instances which are written syllabically. These are mostly used with plural subjects: the dictionaries record 13 instances (cf. App. **2a**: eyes, feet, buttocks, borders of the eye, feet+ankles, intestines, head+face+lips, veins, exta (*têrētu*) and the face (pl. t.)). It is found once with a sg. subject (head). The stative G *napih* is common in the same contexts and qualifies both singular and plural body parts, but more often singular ones, cf. CAD sv *napāhu* 3b: belly (*libbu*, BAM 393: r.11; KAR 151: 38 (of a sheep)), epigastrium (TDP 112: 17', KUB 37, 31: 8; KBo 9, 49: r.9), eye (sg.) (TDP 36: 31f; CT 23, 43: 8; 44: r.III 1; AMT 18, 3: 6), breast (TDP 102: 17), buttock (130: 47 = (36)), groin (*rebîtu*, 236: 52f), pelvis (*rapaštu*, 108: 12), penis (134: 28) and flesh (*šīru*, YOS 10, 47: 9; RA 63, 155: 10, both OB). Plural cases include the intestines (*qerbū*, e.g., TDP 120: 45ff, and passim), hands (220: 29) and testicles (136: 65). G forms in triplets with sg. and pl. side by side (cf. 10.6.1.1.1) are TDP 86: 46f = (58A) (side(s) of the throat (*kirru*)) and 102: III 1ff (kidney(s)). Note that plural instances spelled sar.me(š) are ambiguous, see 10.8.

As to the ideographic spellings with sar, which are common in SB, it will be argued in 10.8 that only sar.meš with a singular subject may be relevant in this context: it is likely to stand for *nuppuh*, and it qualifies the epigastrium (TDP 112: 18'), the side of the throat (86: 47f = (58B)) and the ear (AMT 105, 1: IV 7). These cases should be added to the exception with a singular subject mentioned above. An ambiguous and atypical case is BAM 23: 3 *īnīšu* sar-AH "he has bloated (or: inflamed) eyes", with the patient as subject, and a pl. adjunct acc. (cf. 6.5.3); it may be interpreted as sar-IH (*napih*) or sar-UH (*nuppuh*).

This enumeration suggests that an important reason to use *nuppuhu* instead of *naphu* is plurality of the subject: only five cases of *nuppuhu* have a sg. subject. This is also shown by the contrasting pair (36) quoted in 10.6.1.1.1. *Napih* is used predominantly in the sg. but, as the unmarked form, it can also be used in the plural.

Purruku "lying crosswise" qualifies lines on the diaphragm (*tallu*, YOS 10, 42: II 62, vs. G with sg. subject in III 21), veins, potsherds and the face in various kinds of omens (all pl.). The stative/VA G is far more frequently used in such contexts, cf. AHw sv *parāku* G 1a/b.

Pussulu "bent, twisted" is usually said of the feet, interchanging with *paslu*, cf. AHw sv *pasālu* G 1. The sg. is found as PN and in LL.

Šuddudu "distended" is used 5x in TDP to qualify veins and intestines (1x subj. br.). Elsewhere only the stative G occurs, cf. CAD sv *šadādu* 5b-1'.

Uddudu "pointed" is only used with with the horns (*qarnā-*) of the moon as subject, alternating with the stative G *eddā* (cf. 10.8). The stative G fem. *eddet* or *eddat* occurs with *qarnu* in the sg. in SAA 8, 263: 6; 384: 10, and passim, cf. CAD sv *edēdu* 1, AHw sv *edēdu* sv G 2.

Zu"uru "twisted" is also said of the horns of the moon (5x). The stative G *zīr* is more common, both in sg. and pl., cf. AHw sv *zâru* I G 2, CAD sv *zâru* B a/b/c, but is not said of the horns of the moon (in one instance it refers to the horn of a goat in a simile (CT 20, 32: 72)).

10.6.1.2.2. Rare *purrus* forms occurring only in the plural

Some other *purrus* forms which are only attested in the plural are so rare that their restriction to plurality may be accidental. It is only by their multitude that they have evidential value. The following enumeration comprises those which occur three times or less. Almost all of them are mainly found as statives in omen texts. They are SB unless indicated otherwise.

For references concerning the *purrus* forms see the Appendix; for those of the corresponding G forms see the dictionaries. For the exceptional use of *mullû, ummudu, kunnu* and *šullumu* motivated by a plural subject see 10.6.1.2.3.

Bullulu "variegated" (arms), 1x, elsewhere stative G, cf. CAD sv *balālu* 1e.
Bulluṣu "staring, protruding" (eyes); 1x, elsewhere stative/VA G.
Bu"uru "?" (subj. broken); possibly pl. of *bēru* "scarce" like *zu"ur*, pl. of *zīru* "twisted".
Gullutu "frightened" (animals); 1x, elsewhere stative/VA G.
Hullû "shining" (toes); 1x, the stative G is also found 1x qualifying a body part (ZA 43, 98: 24 (heart)).
Hulluqu "destroyed" (witchcraft); 1x, elsewhere stative/VA (passim).
(H)ummuru (D) "red" or "inflamed" (eyes); 2x, cf. *hamru* said of the eyes (CT 17, 19: 24 // SpTU 2, 2: I 21).
Hummuṭu "hot, scorching" (destinies); 1x, elsewhere G.
Hunnuqu "constricted" (intestines), 1x, elsewhere *haniq*, cf. CAD sv *hanāqu* 2; AHw sv *hanāqu* G 1/2.
Huṭṭû "faulty, portending evil" (omens); 1x, elsewhere *haṭû*, cf. AHw sv *haṭû* I (but CAD sv *hāṭû* adj.).
Kummudu "?" (lines of the hand, fingers), 2x, no stative/VA G in comparable contexts.
Kummulu "angry" (gods), 3x, normally stative/VA G.
Nullušu "covered with dew" (subj. *pānātū'a* = ?), 1x, no stative/VA G attested.
Nurruṭu "quivering" (lances), 1x (cf. note 4); stative G also 1x (SEM 117: II 19 (mountains)).
Puššuqu "narrow, difficult" (water, the "path" of the liver), 2x, elsewhere stative/VA G (passim).
***Pu"ugu** "taken, seized" (tablets), 1x, elsewhere stative G, cf. AHw sv *puāgu* G.
Ṣummuru "bloated" (intestines); 1x, elsewhere stative G, cf. AHw sv *ṣemēru* G.
Šuhhu "long" (planks); 1x, elsewhere *šīhu*, cf. CAD sv *šīhu* adj.
Šummuṭu "tapering, pointed" (AHw), or "sunken, flattened" (CAD) (nostrils, the *ṣēr ubāni* of the lung); 3x, elsewhere *šamiṭ* passim.
Uttuk/qu "bent, curved" (palm trees; 1x subj. broken but pl.); VA G *etqu* only LL, cf. CAD sv.
Uṭṭû "dark" (eyes); 1x (Iraq 31, 31: 41 *ú*[!]*-ṭa-a* acc. to AHw 1555b sv (but Lambert and CAD sv **šumṭû* read *šam-ṭa-a* "weakened")), elsewhere the stative and VA G is used.
Zuqqunu "bearded" (persons); 1x (OAk), elsewhere *zaqnu*, passim.

10.6.1.2.3. Some additional cases of interest

Finally, a few cases will be considered of *purrus* forms which seem to be motivated by plurality of the subject by way of exception, whereas they normally have some other function. This concerns in the first place at least two cases from literary texts:

(47) Sg. 8: 387 (objects) *ša kakkabī hurāṣi mul-lu-ma* "which are covered with gold stars";

(48) *ib.* 96 + AfO 12, 144: 96 (a high mountain) *ša* (...) *ina qereb šadê um-mu-da rēšāšu* "whose peaks reach into the middle of the sky" (tr. CAD sv *qerbu* 1f-1').

(47) and (48) represent a unique use of these *purrus* forms. The stative *mullu* was discussed in 10.4.2, where it was established that it is very rare and only used for some more or less lexicalized meanings of *malû* D "to fill, cover". It seems most plausible to explain this instance as resulting from an occasional association of *mullu* with plurality. This is supported by (47). Usually, *ummud* is the stative of *ummudu* "to impose" (cf. 11.4.2), which is clearly un-

suitable here, and the usual expression for reaching the sky is the stative G of *emēdu* with *šamû* in the acc., cf. CAD sv *emēdu* 1c; cf., for instance, in the same text:

(49) Sg. 8: 19 (a mountain) *ša eliš rēšāša šamāmi en-da-ma* "whose peak reaches the sky above".

In (48), then, the use of the stative D seems to be motivated by the formally dual nature of *rēšā* "head, peak". These two exceptional cases are doubtless modelled on other *purrus* forms, and probably an attempt on the part of the scribe to attain a literary flavour by using a form which is unusual elsewhere.

Two other cases, now from omens, which may be explained in the same way, are:

(50) SAA 8, 304: r.4 *qarnāšu kun-na* "its (the moon's) horns are normal";

(51) CT 38, 11: 47 *šumma bītu bābātūšu šu-ul-lu-mu* "if the doors of the house are sound".

Usually, *kūn* serves as stative of the common D-stem *kunnu* "to establish, set up, testify" (cf. 10.4.2); here it seems to be used as a plural of the simple adjective *kīnu* "firm, true, normal", etc., doubtless modelled on such plural forms as *turrukā, uddudā* and *zu''urā,* which are common qualifications of the horns of the moon. In so far as the *purrus* form *šullumu* is used at all, it serves as stative of *šullumu* "to keep well, make complete, give in full", etc. (cf. 10.6.1); here it seems to be used as plural of *šalmu* (parallel to *šabburā* "broken" in the preceding line, cf. 6.4.1.1 sv), although a translation "repaired" (i.e., as stative of *šullumu* "to repair", cf. CAD sv *šalāmu* 12b) cannot be excluded.

10.6.1.2.4. *Purrus* for mass nouns

A special aspect of the association of *purrus* with plurality is its use for qualifying mass nouns. It was pointed out in 3.1.3.2 and 6.3 that some apparent exceptions to the use of verbal D-stems of transitive verbs with a plural object can be explained by assuming that mass nouns can behave in the same way as plurals.

The most evident manifestation of this is the use of *purrus* with metals in OA. This refers to the following cases:

Dammuqum "of fine quality", always said of copper, cf. CAD sv b (no unambiguous cases of *damqum*); OB uses both *damqum* and *dummuqum* with copper. For the meaning given here, rather than "refined", cf. Dercksen 1996: 35f.

Hassu'um "crushed"? is once said of copper (CCT 1, 42a: 22), cf. Dercksen 1996: 39f.

Lammunum "of bad quality", always said of copper, cf. CAD sv 2b and Dercksen 1996: 37; not found outside OA; the simple adjective *lamnu* is not attested in OA as a qualification of copper.

Massuhum "of inferior quality", said of silver, copper and tin, cf. CAD sv **mussuhu* adj. 2 and **mussuhu* v. 2, and Dercksen 1996: 37. No **mashum* attested. Not found outside OA.

Massu'um "refined", lit. "washed" (*mesû* to wash) occurs once as a qualification of copper (ICK 1, 85: 8); everywhere else the simple VA *masi'um* is used, qualifying copper and silver, cf. CAD sv *mesû* adj. 2a/b, and Dercksen 1996: 34f.

Ṣarrupum "refined", always said of silver, cf. CAD sv *ṣurrupu* a. Other dialects, OB in particular, only use *ṣarpu* to qualify silver (except CT 17, 23: 183 *kīma ṣarpi ṣur-ru-pi* "like refined silver" (SB)), cf. CAD ssvv. For the process of refining, however, OA can use the G-stem *ṣarāpu*, cf. CAD sv *ṣ*. A 1a, but also D (kt 91/k 102: 3) and cf. the verbal noun *ṣarrupūtum* "refining procedure" (cf. Veenhof 1972: 46f).

Šabburum "broken", always said of copper, cf. CAD sv c and Dercksen 1996: 40f; not found outside OA; no *šabru* attested in OA.

Šahhuhum "corroded" is said of tin, also only in OA.[19]

The consistency with which OA uses *purrus* forms to qualify metals is remarkable, because it contrasts with other dialects which have the same idiom only in a few cases, and because the words in question are hardly attested in any other context in OA. On the other hand, it agrees with the fact that the use of D-stems of transitive verbs is also more common in OA than in other dialects, if the object is a mass noun; see, for instance, *ṣabātu* **5.** in 6.4.4.1 sv, *laqātu* **1.** in 6.4.5.1 sv, and *paqādu* **1.** in 6.4.7.1 sv.

With other mass nouns than metals, such as food stuffs, we occasionally find *purrus* forms, too, in OA, but too rarely to draw meaningful conclusions. A noteworthy instance is St. Güterbock 39 note 34 kt g/k 18: 12 š̲e̲-*um kà-lu-ṣú-um* "shrivelled wheat" (see below). A substantivized *purrus* form may be *ma-ru-ru-um*/*ma-ru-ra-am* "bitter (oil?)" (CCT 1, 42b: 7. 14) from *marru* "bitter", if this spelling represents *marrurum*, cf. CAD sv **murruru* A.

In other dialects the situation is the same: we find *purrus* forms to qualify mass nouns, but this is too incidental to conclude that there is a causal relationship. A word as *še'u* "barley" is often qualified by a *purrus* form: apart from **kulluṣu*, by *hummušu* "?", *hunnuṭu* "?", **qullû* "roasted", *šuqqulu* "scarce", *tubbuku* "stored", *uppulu* "late" (but **aplu* is apparently never used). Similarly, we find *šamaššammū* (pl.) "sesame" with *bunnû* "of fine quality" and *nuppuṣu* "crushed" (but always *halṣūtu* "pressed"). Seed and flour are qualified by *ubbulu* "dry" (or *uppulu* ?); wine by *hubburu* (meaning uncertain), *hurrupu* "early", *uppulu* "late", *duššupu* "sweet" and *ṭuhhudu* "abundant"; beer by *hummuru* (meaning unknown) and *duššupu* "sweet".

For metals we find *purrus* forms such as *hussuru* "broken", said of copper (OB), *ummuru* of bronze (SB LL), *kubburu* "thick" of iron, *nuhhutu* "inferior?" and *murruqu* "of good quality" of silver (NB), *hummuṣu* of copper "stripped" of impurities acc. to CAD sv *hammuṣu*, but AHw sv *hammuṣu*: "Bez. einer geringen Kupferqualität" (MA), and *puṣṣû* "white" as a qualification of gold in ARM 7, 4: 17 *hurāṣum pu-ṣú-ú* (OB), but it is uncertain whether this is a *purrus* form, cf. AHw sv *puṣû*.

Consequently, outside OA there is too little consistency in the relationship between mass nouns and the use of *purrus* to prove or disprove that there is a causal relationship. Most of these expressions, especially those of the later periods, seem to be more or less stereotyped.

10.6.1.3. Conclusions

The following conclusions can be drawn with regard to the association of *purrus* with plurality. First of all, the contrasting pairs quoted in 10.6.1.1 show that the use of *purrus* can be caused by plurality (in a broad sense), and suggest that, apart from grammatical plurality, it is also used to convey related nuances such as completeness, total affectedness and inherent plurality.

Second, in this function *purrus* is an optional alternative to the normal plural of the adjective without gemination (*parsūtu/parsātu*). Gemination is a redundant morpheme added to the basic plural morpheme, the ending *-ūtu/ātu*. It is actually unpredictable when it will be used and when it will not be used. In fact, the number of *purrus* forms which can arguably be connected with plurality is small in comparison to the use of forms without gemination in the same circumstances. In this respect the use of *purrus* is exactly parallel to that of the pattern *parras* discussed in 3.1.3, and to the verbal D-stem of transitive verbs discussed in Chapter VI.

The relationship between *purrus* and the simple adjective, as described here, raises the question what the difference is between forms with and without gemination when they occur in the plural. This problem will be examined in 8.10 after the discussion of the other functions of *purrus*.

Finally, the association of *purrus* with plurality represents only a small part of its total use; conversely, only a part of the plural *purrus* forms found in omen protases can be explained as being motivated by this association. Many of such *purrus* forms are also used in the singular and alternate with simple forms without any noticeable difference. This enhances the importance of the contrasting pairs of 10.6.1.1, and necessitates some reservation as to the causal relationship between plurality and the use of *purrus* in omen protases in general (see further 10.7.1).

10.6.2. *Purrus* forms for salient bodily characteristics

The second function of lexical *purrus* forms which can be connected with the iconic nature of gemination is to denote salient characteristics of animate beings, mostly persons. Since these characteristics tend to be of a more or less pathological nature, they are often subsumed under the term "bodily defects". These *purrus* forms first were studied as a group by Holma, who defined their common semantic element as "Körperfehler bzw. körperliche Auffälligkeiten" (1914: 8); cf. also GAG § 55n: "zur Bezeichnung krankhafter Zustände und von Körperfehlern gebraucht".

The common feature of these words is that their meaning implies a high degree of salience, which is due to the fact that bodily defects immediately catch the eye of an observer, and provoke a strong emotional response. This causes the use of patterns which are extended by a formal device such as gemination (cf. 2.2.3). Similar categories of adjectives occur in other Semitic languages, e.g., *qiṭṭēl* in Hebrew and *'aqtal* in Arabic (cf. Joüon-Muraoka 1991: 253; Fisher 1965: 11ff).

For the expression of such meanings *purrus* is the most common pattern. Most of them, however, can also be expressed by the simple adjective, which, as the unmarked form, is applicable in all circumstances. Generally speaking, however, the forms without gemination are much less common than the *purrus* forms. This is a major difference between the *purrus* forms discussed here and those which are associated with plurality. The list below includes examples of such simple adjectives interchanging with *purrus* forms.

Occasionally we find still other patterns for the expression of salient bodily characteristics, sometimes with a geminate second radical, such as *z/sarriqu* "with speckled eyes" (CAD sv), or "etwa 'schillernd'" (AHw sv), which is related to Arabic *'azraq* "blue" according to Landsberger (1967b: 139), *passalu* "crippled" (cf. 3.1.2), and *pessû* "lame, limping", or exceptionally with reduplication, such as *hašhašu* "etwa 'humpelnd'" according to AHw sv.

Another feature of most *purrus* forms discussed here is that they are very infrequent; many only occur in lexical texts. This is due to the fact that they denote characteristics that are very specific and therefore only rarely applicable. This also causes considerable uncertainty as to their exact meaning. Often we have to content ourselves with vague definitions as "a kind of cripple" or "a characteristic bodily trait". This problem is even more acute for the numerous *purrus* forms used as proper names, which will be dealt with separately in 10.6.3.

The following list presents the most typical instances of the use of *purrus* for the expression of bodily defects. It comprises the form itself, its (probable) meaning, and the period in which it is attested in this function; if LL is added, the form only occurs in lexical texts; if a parallel simple adjective is attested, this is stated, too, but only if it is used in the same meaning as the *purrus* form; see CAD and AHw for references. For all other references, see the Appendix to this chapter.

Buqqumu "person losing his hair(?) (OB LL); (lamb) ready for plucking" (SB LL); also *baqmu* LL.

Burruqu "with reddish face and red hair" (CAD), "mit blitzenden Augen" (AHw) (SB); also PN → 10.6.3.2.

Burrus/šu "with hair growing in patches" (CAD), "kahlköpfig ?" (AHw) (OB LL); also *baršu* LL; also PN → 10.6.3.2.

Gubbuhu "bald" (MB, SB); also PN → 10.6.3.2.

Gurrudu "with hair falling out in tufts" (CAD), "mit schütterm Haar" (AHw), or simply "bald" (Deller, NABU 92/79) (OB, SB); also PN → 10.6.3.2.

Gurruṣu "leprous" (NA); also *garṣu* LL; also PN → 10.6.3.2.

Hubbuṣu "sehr geschwollen, üppig" (AHw); "a characteristic bodily trait" (CAD) (OB LL); also *habṣu*; also PN → 10.6.3.2.

Hubbušu "hart geschwollen" (AHw sv); "a characteristic bodily trait", "defective" (CAD) (OB, SB); also PN → 10.6.3.2.

Hummuru "crippled" (OB, MA, SB); also PN → 10.6.3.2.

Hummuṣu "bald" (OB); also *hamṣu* LL; also PN → 10.6.3.2.

Hummušu "lame, paralyzed" (MB, SB).

Huppudu "blind" (OB, SB); also PN → 10.6.3.2.

Huššulu "schwerverletzt?" (AHw), "a characteristic bodily trait" (CAD) (SB); also PN → 10.6.3.2.

***Huzzû** "lame, limping" (always *hunzû*) (MB, NB LL); also PN → 10.6.3.2.
Kubbulu "paralyzed" (OB, SB); also PN → 10.6.3.2.
Kuṣṣudu "crippled" (SB).
Kuṣṣuṣu "having a maimed hand" (OB, SB LL).
Luhhumu "long-haired" (SB LL); also *lahmu.*
Pussulu "bent, twisted" (OB, SB); also *paslu*; also PN → 10.6.3.2.
Sukkuku "deaf" (OB, MB, SB, NA); also *sakku*; also PN → 10.6.3.2.
Ṣubbutu "paralyzed" (OB, SB); also *ṣabtu* LL, cf. 6.6.3 sv *ṣabātu.*
Ṣudduru (*ṣunduru*) "crooked", "squinting", or a similar defect (SB); also *ṣadiru* (cf. GAG § 12b Anm.); also PN → 10.6.3.2.
Ṣuhhutu (describing some defect of the eye) (OB, SB); also PN → 10.6.3.2.
Šuppuṣu "seized, paralyzed" (SB).
Šu''uru "hairy" (OB, SB); also *še'ru.*
Tubbuku "limp, lame" (OB LL), also *tabku.*
Ṭummumu "deaf" (OB, SB; also as adverb *ṭummumiš*).
Ukkudu "crippled" (OB, SB LL); also PN → 10.6.3.2.
Upputu "blind" (OB, SB, Nuzi).
Uqqup/bu "crippled" (OB LL).
Uqququ "dumb, paralyzed" (SB LL).
Uqquru "crippled" (OB LL).
Ussulu/uṣṣulu "lame" (OB, SB); also *eṣlu.*
Uṣṣudu "crippled" (SB LL).

Similar words of which the meaning is unknown, but which are described by CAD as denoting a "characteristic bodily trait", include *huggulu* (SB), *hunnunu* (OB, SB), and *mulluṭu* (SB LL). There can be little doubt that many of the *purrus* forms listed in the next section, which are only attested as proper names, also belong to this group, see 10.6.3. Some of the *purrus* forms mentioned in note 4 resemble this group, too, although they tend to express mainly non-physical characteristics.

There are many other adjectives which agree with the ones listed above in occurring more often in the *purrus* form than in the simple form, but which do not so much express defects as other kinds of salient characteristics. Some common cases are *burrumu* "multicoloured" (see also 10.6.1.1.3), *kupputu* "compacted, lump-shaped", *muhhû* "ecstatic" (see 10.3.3 with note 6), *ruššû* "red"[20], *uppuqu* "massive, solid", and the "pseudo-*purrus* form" (see 10.7.1.2 sv) *du'ummu* or *du'ūmu* "dark".

In contrast to the cases listed above, there are also *purrus* forms which express positive salient characteristics, such as *duššupu* "sweet", *kuzzubu* "charming, attractive" (also *kazbu*) and *unnubu* "fruitful, luxuriant" (SB, probably from the same root as the common OB proper name *Hunnubu*, see 10.6.3.2).

These words show that the use of *purrus* for the expression of bodily defects is not an isolated phenomenon, but only the most outspoken manifestation of a general association of *purrus* with salience. In fact, salience is an essential feature of the semantics of the entire category of lexical *purrus* forms. This will be further examined and illustrated in 10.9.

As to their derivational background, these *purrus* forms come from any of the four types distinguished in 10.3: many of the examples quoted there are taken from the list presented above, since the *purrus* forms it contains are in general unambiguously lexical.

10.6.3. *Purrus* names

10.6.3.1. Introductory remarks

A corollary of the use of *purrus* for the expression of salient bodily characteristics is its use for proper names which describe a characteristic feature of their bearer (henceforth "*purrus* names"), cf. Stamm 1939: 264f; Holma 1914; Ranke 1905: 20ff.

It is needless to say that establishing the meaning of a *purrus* form used as a proper name is mere speculation. Only if it is also attested as an ordinary noun, or has a root which recurs in other words and can be argued to have a meaning that is appropriate for describing a person, can we tentatively derive the name from that root and assign a meaning to it. There can be little doubt, for instance, that the *purrus* names *Gullubu, Kubburu* and *Sukkuku* mean "bald", "fat", and "deaf", respectively, and that the women's names *Duššuptum, Kuzzubtum* and *Hunnubtum* have meanings as "sweet", "charming" and "blooming", respectively.

In some cases a tentative etymology may be provided by comparison with other Semitic languages, e.g., *Duššumum,* which has no related words in Akkadian, but is connected with a West Semitic root meaning "to be fat" by Von Soden 19932/33: II 166 note 1, and AHw sv.

Some other *purrus* names can be associated with a root that recurs in other words, but has a meaning which is difficult to reconcile with the description of persons. Instances are *G/Qurruru* and *garāru* "to roll" or *qarāru* "to flow", *Pullusum* and the D tantum verb *pullusu* "to keep sb busy", and *Sulluhu* and *salāh/'u* "to sprinkle". Their meanings should be regarded as uncertain.

Finally, there are many *purrus* names which cannot be connected with a known root. Their meaning remains completely unknown. It is only on the basis of the overall use of *purrus,* that we can hypothesize that they denote some bodily characteristic of their bearer. The difficulty of identifying the etymology of such names is enhanced by the polysemy of many cuneiform signs, which do not or only partly distinguish between different consonants with the same basis of articulation (dentals, labials, gutturals and sibilants).

It is not the aim of this section to offer a detailed study of *purrus* names. Rather, it intends to highlight some specific points which are relevant for the general nature of *purrus* and for the study of the D-stem as a whole. Therefore, no attempt will be made at an exhaustive listing, nor at a detailed discussion of all possible meanings which could be assigned to a *purrus* name.

The following lists present a substantial number of *purrus* names, for the most part culled from the dictionaries, to illustrate their overall nature, and especially the period(s) in which they are attested. The importance of this latter point will be explained below. The list is divided into three parts. List I contains *purrus* names which are known to denote salient bodily characteristics and were also listed in the preceding section; List II contains further *purrus* names which - with the reservations expressed above - have plausible etymologies; List III consists of *purrus* names without such an etymology. If no source is given, the word is listed in both dictionaries (for CAD, in so far as it is available, i.e., up to and including Š/3). All names are quoted in their masculine form. If no translation of the name itself is given, its meaning can be derived directly from that of the corresponding verb or adjective.

10.6.3.2. Lists of *purrus* names

List I: *Purrus* names denoting salient bodily characteristics.

For the meaning of these *purrus* names see the previous section; the following of the *purrus* forms listed there also occur as proper names: **Burruqu** (MB, NA), **Burrus/šu** (OAk, OA), **Gubbuhu** (OB, MB), **Gurrudu** (OB), **Gurruṣu** (MA, NA), **Hubbuṣu** (OB, NB), **Hubbušu** (OB, NB), **Hummuru** (OB, MB, NB), **Hummuṣu** (OB), **Huppudu** (OB), **Huššulu** (OB), ***Hunzû** (*Huzzû*) (OB (YOS 12, 80: 5), MB, NB), **Kubbulu** (OB), **Kuzzubu** (OB, MB, NB), **Pussulu** (OB, MB), **Sukkuku** (OAk, OB, OA (LB 1209: 11; kt a/k 478: 50), MB, NA), **Ṣudduru** (OB, MB, NA), **Ṣuhhutu** (OAk, OB, MB), **Ukkudu** (OB).

List II: Other *purrus* names with a plausible etymology.

Bulluṭu (*balāṭu* "to be(come) well, alive"); AHw: "zum Leben erweckt"; CAD (sv *balāṭu* v. 6a-4'): abbreviated name (NB, see below).

Buqqušu (*baqāšu* "to be wide"); AHw: "sehr breit"; CAD: bodily trait (OAk, OB).

Burruru (*barāru* "to shine, sparkle"); CAD: "with filmy eyes"; AHw: -- (OA).

Butturu (*butturu* "verstümmeln" acc. to AHw sv *b.* II): AHw: "mit verstümmeltem Bein"; CAD: "bodily trait" (horse name) (MB).

Dullupu (*dalāpu* "to be or keep awake"); CAD: "heavy-eyed (for lack of sleep)"; AHw: "sehr ruhelos" (MB, NB).

Dummuqu (*damāqu* "to be(come) good") (NB).

Duššupu (*dašpu* "sweet") (OB).

Gullubu (*gullubu* "to shave"); "bald" (OB).

Gunnuṣu "constantly wrinkling the nose" (OB LL); cf. note 4 and *ganāṣu* in 7.6.2.

Guppušu (*gapšu* "huge, massive"): AHw "sehr massig"; CAD: -- (OB).

Huddudu (*Hundudu*) (*huddudu* "to make a deep incision" (CAD), AHw sv *hadādu* "tief einschneiden"): CAD G 157a (no transl.); AHw: -- (OAk).

Hunnubu (*hanābu* "to grow abundantly, be luxuriant"); AHw: "sehr üppig"; CAD: "mng. uncert." (OB, MB).

Hurruru (*harāru* "to dig, groove"); AHw: "mit tiefer Narbe(?)"; CAD: -- (OB).

Hurruṣu (*harāṣu* "to cut, incise"); AHw: "mit Narben oder Furchen"; CAD: "bodily trait" (OB, NB).

Hurrušu (*harāšu* "to be dumb, mute"); cf. Dossin, RA 62, 75f; Bottéro, Or. 34, 377, *pace* CAD and AHw sv (MB).

Huṣṣubu (*haṣābu* "to cut, break off" ?); CAD: "bodily trait"; AHw: -- (OB).

Huššulu (*hašālu* "to crush, shatter"); AHw: "schwerverletzt?"; CAD: "bodily trait" (OB).

Huzzumu (*hazāmu* "to be shrivelled"); CAD: "stupid (lit.: a person with a shriveled(?) ear)"; AHw: "beschnitten an ...") (OB).

Kubburu (*kabru* "thick, fat) (OB).

Kubbutu (*kabtu* "heavy, honoured"); CAD (sv 2a): "thick, squat"; AHw (sv 1b): "sehr schwer" (OAk, OB, NB, MA (Farber, ZA 75, 219f)).

Kuppupu (*kapāpu* "to bend, curve"); AHw: "sehr krumm, gebeugt"; CAD: "bent, bowed" (OB, MB).

Mullušu (*malāšu* "to pluck out); CAD: "with torn-out hair"; AHw: "mit ausgerupftem Haar" (OAk).

Muššulu (*mašālu* "to be(come) similar, equal"); AHw/CAD: no meaning; cf. also MAD 3, 186 (OAk).

Nuhhulu (*nahālu* "to sift" ?); AHw: "etwa "voller Narben"?"; CAD: "mng. unkn." (NB).

Nuhhuru (*nahāru* "to snore", acc. to CAD, *nahāru* etwa "verdorrt sein?", acc. to AHw sv *n.* I); AHw: "etwa "abgemagert"?"; CAD: "mng. uncert.", horse name (MB).

Nummuru (*naw/māru* "to shine, to be(come) bright") (NB, see below).

Nurrubu (*narbu* "soft, moist") (OB).

Puhhuru (*pahāru* "to come together") (NB, see below).

Pussunu (*pasām/nu* "to veil, cover"); cf. MAD 3, 218 (OAk).

Puzzuru (*pazāru* "to hide" (intrans.)); AHw: no meaning given (OB, MB).

Qunnunu (*k/qanānu* "to coil, twist"); AHw: "lockenhaarig?"; CAD: "uncert. mng." (OAk, MB, MA).

Quttunu (*qatnu* "thin, fine"); AHw: "sehr schlank"; CAD: "very thin" (OB, MB).

Sukkulu (*sakālu* "to appropriate fraudulently"); AHw: "wegraffend"; CAD: "mng. unkn." (name of a dog of Marduk) (SB), see note 4.

***Sullumu** (only fem. *Sulluntu*), cf. *salāmu* "to be(come) friendly, to make peace" ? or cf. *sullunu* "to be luxuriant?" (cf. AHw and CAD sv)) (MB).

Šullumu (*šalāmu* "to be(come) sound, in a good condition") (NB, see below).

Šummuhu (*šamhu* "luxuriant") (OB, MB).

Šuppulu (*šaplu* "low, deep"); CAD: "short (of stature)"; AHw: -- (OAk).

Tukkulu (*takālu* "to trust"); AHw: "ermutigt" (NB, see below).

Ṭuppušu (*ṭapšu* "fat?") (NB, see below).

Ukkumu (*ekēmu* "to take away"); AHw: "raüberisch" (name of a dog of Marduk) (SB), see note 4. [*Ukkumu* NB perhaps from Aramaic *ukkāmā* "black", acc. to AHw sv].

Unnubu (**enēbu* "to bear fruit, to bloom"); AHw: "fruchtbar gemacht, sehr fruchtbar" (OB, MB).

***Wuqquru** (*(w)aqru* "precious") in *Waqqurtum* (OA), cf. Veenhof 1972: 103 with note 178.

Wurruqu (*(w)arqu* "green, yellow"); AHw: "sehr gelb" (OB).

Wussumu (*(w)asāmu* "to be(come?) suitable, proper"; AHw: "besonders angemessen (gestaltet)" (OAk, OB).

(W)uššuru (*(w)uššuru* "to let go, release"); AHw sv 4a: "herunterhangend" (of hair) (MB, MA).

***Zu"unu** (only fem. *Zu"untum*) (*za'ānu* "to be adorned"); AHw: "geschmückt"; CAD: "adorned, decorated, beautiful" (OB).

List III: *Purrus* names without a plausible etymology.

Buhhusum (OAk).

Dulluqu (OB).

Duššumu (OAk, OB).

***Gullulu** (NA)

G/Qurruru (OB, MA).

Huddulu (OB, Elam).

***Huggulu** (OB, MB).

***Hunnunu** (in *Hunninānu*, *purrus* form?) (OB).

***Huzzuh/'u** (*Hunzuhu*) (MB, NB, see below) (same as *Hunzû* ?).

Huzzulu (OAk, OB).

Mulluqu (OB).

Nuṭṭupu (OB).

Pullusu (cf. *pullusu* "to keep busy, to disturb" ??) (OAk).

Rupp/bbuk/qu (OB).

Suhhumu (OB).
Sukkumu (SB) (variant of *sukkulu* in List I).
Sulluhu (*salāhu* "to sprinkle, moisten" ??) (OB).
Su"ulu (OB: FM 1 p. 140: 51. 54. 57).
***Ṣuppuru** (only fem. *Ṣuppurti*) (OB Elam).
Tunnuhu (OB: AbB 12, 80: case 1; tablet 4).
Unnunu (OB, MB).
Upp/bburu (MB).
UrruZu (MB).

10.6.3.3. Conclusions about the *purrus* names

The relevance of these *purrus* names for the subject at hand is based on the following points. First, in so far as their meaning can be established, they offer additional evidence for what seems to be one of the basic functions of *purrus,* namely, to denote salient characteristics of animate beings. Moreover, they support the originally expressive nature of the geminate contained in *purrus.* Beside onomatopoetics, descriptions of persons, both as adjectives (epithets) and as names, belong to the categories which are most susceptible to expressive extensions (cf. Kuryłowicz 1973: 260; Martinet 1937: 178f).

Secondly, in particular those *purrus* names which do not have a plausible etymology provide additional support for the basically nominal character of the pattern *purrus.* They have no corresponding verbal D-stem from which they can be derived, and it seems unlikely that in all these cases such a D-stem existed but accidentally is not attested.

Finally, an important motive for presenting a survey of attested *purrus* names is to show their distribution over the successive periods of Akkadian. It is evident from the lists in the preceding section that they were especially popular in OAk and OB; in OAk their number is surprisingly large in comparison to the rather limited number of texts extant from that period. They occur less frequently in OA and MB.

However, in NB and LB texts we find a certain revival of *purrus* names. The following cases are attested in these periods: *Bulluṭu, Dullupu, Dummuqu, Hubbuṣu, Hubbušu, Hummuru, Hurruṣu, Huzzû, Kubbutu, Kuzzubu, Nuhhulu, Nummuru, Puhhuru, Šullumu, Tukkulu* and *Ṭuppušu.*

Some of these late names are apparently survivals from earlier periods that continue to be used (*Dullupu, Hubbuṣu, Hubbušu, Hummuru, Hurruṣu, Huzzû, Kubbutu, Kuzzubu*). Several others are new. Most of the new ones have a different character from the older ones: apart from *Ṭuppušu* (see List II) and *Nuhhulu,* which has no etymology, they do not refer to salient bodily characteristics. This applies to *Bulluṭu, Dummuqu, Nummuru, Puhhuru, Šullumu* and *Tukkulu.* The dictionaries suggest in various places[21] that they are abbreviations of the kind of theophoric names which are typical of the later periods of Akkadian, for instance, *Bulluṭu* from a name as *Bulluṭsa-rabi* (Stamm 1939: 116). This is suggested by the fact that they coexist with longer names in which the same D-stem appears as a finite form or a participle (*DN-uballiṭ, DN-mudammiq, Mutakkil-DN,* etc.). Another NB *purrus* name is *Bu"ītu* "the desired one" (fem.), which does not refer to a bodily characteristic, either, but is a VA of *bu''û* "to look for", cf. CAD sv **bu'û* adj. Thus the typical nature of the OB and OAk *purrus* names seems to be partly lost in NB and LB.

It is possible that the decline in popularity of *purrus* names after the OB period is connected with an overall decline in the use of lexical *purrus* forms in this period; this will be further discussed in 10.10.

10.6.4. Conclusions about *purrus* for salient bodily characteristics

The semantic range of the characteristics enumerated in 10.6.2 and 10.6.3, which are more commonly expressed by *purrus* forms than by forms without gemination, and in particular the predominance of bodily defects strongly suggest that this preference for *purrus* is related to the salience of these qualities, and that the pattern ultimately has an expressive origin.

If this claim is correct, the use of *purrus* to denote salient bodily characteristics and its function of underlining plurality are two parallel manifestations of the basically iconic nature of *purrus*, and of gemination in general. Just as the *purrus* forms discussed in 10.6.1 underline plurality, those of 10.6.2 and 10.6.3 underline the salience which is inherent in the meaning of the adjective (and also in that of the substantive which it qualifies). Salience and plurality can be seen as semantic extensions vis-à-vis the basic forms, which are iconically reflected in the formal extension contained in the geminate.

In section 10.9 we will attempt to give a general definition of the nature of *purrus* in its iconic functions, and to establish what the difference is between corresponding forms with and without gemination.

10.7. Lexicalized *purrus* forms in omens and literary texts

Apart from the two kinds of *purrus* forms discussed in 10.6, which can be explained on the basis of the iconic background of gemination, there are many other *purrus* forms, which are used in various circumstances without showing any clear trace of iconicity. This applies by definition to the inflectional *purrus* forms, but also to many others which cannot be regarded as statives or VAs of a verbal D-stem.

Generally speaking, the clearest cases of iconically motivated *purrus* forms (those for plurality and salient characteristics) are found in the oldest periods of Akkadian. They consist of the adjectives discussed in 10.6.2, among which OB forms are prominent, the *purrus* names discussed in 10.6.3 (mostly OAk and OB), some of the *purrus* forms for mass nouns in OA (*dammuqum*, *lammunum* and *massuhum,* cf. 10.6.1.2.4), and the use of *purrus* for plurality, as it appears especially in the contrasting pairs quoted in 10.6.1.1, which mostly come from OB omens.

It is certainly true that most of these cases have counterparts in later periods of Akkadian, that many individual lexical *purrus* forms continue to be used, and that in particular the use of *purrus* to underline plurality remains productive (cf. especially 10.6.1.2.3). However, the impression gained from the overall use of *purrus*, especially in the vast amount of extant SB texts, is that the iconically motivated uses of *purrus* are in decline.

The most striking feature we observe in these texts with regard to the use of *purrus* is large scale lexicalization. Many *purrus* forms have acquired a specialized meaning (in particular in the technical language of various types of omens), are only used in specific contexts, or have only survived in stereotyped expressions and/or in a small set of literary texts.

Traces of a similar situation are already found in earlier periods; for instance, *lammunum* is only attested as a qualification of copper in OA, not in other contexts, and copper is only qualified by *lammunum*, never by the simple form *lamnum*. The same is likely to apply to *dammuqum*; at least no syllabic spellings of (*werium*) *damqum* are found, but it is often spelled ideographically with $\underline{\text{sig}}_5$, cf. 10.6.1.2.4 and CAD sv *dummuqu* b. This shows that these are fixed combinations in which the use of a *purrus* form is conventional, and suggests that the actual motive behind the preference for forms with gemination (the fact that copper is a mass noun) is no longer operative. In SB such stereotyped and conventional *purrus* forms seem to form the majority.

Such a process of lexicalization leads to the disappearance of the contrastive relationship to the simple form, and thus to the loss of the iconic nature of gemination. As noted in sections 2.2.4.2 and 2.2.4.3, it is a general feature of expressive and iconic categories to lose their special character in the course of time.

The consequences of this widespread process of lexicalization can be seen in all dialects and periods of Akkadian, but they are especially clear in SB omens and literary texts, two genres that are generally characterized by a stereotyped and conventional style. In order to illustrate this phenomenon we will discuss the most important of such *purrus* forms in the following sections; first, in 10.7.1 those which occur in omen texts, and in 10.7.2 those which are typically literary.

10.7.1. Lexicalized *purrus* forms in omen texts

Omen texts played an important role in previous sections, providing the bulk of the evidence for the association of *purrus* with plurality (cf. 10.6.1.1). The cases mentioned there, however, constitute only a very small part of the total occurrence of *purrus* forms in omen texts. In these texts the relationship between *purrus* and *parVs* is far more often erratic and unpredictable, and it is often quite unclear why in a specific instance a *purrus* form is used.

The language of omens is a highly technical jargon, in which many words have their own, probably very precise, meaning. Accordingly, the adjectives used to describe the various ominous phenomena are often not used in their usual sense, but are lexicalized and stereotyped in some very specific context; cf., for instance, the expressions discussed in 6.5.3 *qê ṣubbut* "held by filaments", *lipiam* (or *lipâ*) *kussu* "enveloped in fat", and *zihhī hullul* "hung with pustules".

This is also illustrated by the fact that many *purrus* forms occurring in such texts are highly restricted in use and combined with only a few different subjects. Some *purrus* forms are even restricted to a single expression, e.g., *hussuru* "blunted" (only said of the breastbone (*kaskasu*) of a sheep), *uddudu* "pointed" (only in the plural of the horns of the moon), *zuqquru* "elevated" (only of the *manzāzu* of the liver), *šuppulu* "low" (only found in hendiadys with a following stative, cf. 7.4.3), and **šubbu* (only fem. *šubbat*, of unknown meaning, describing a quality of the gall bladder). Almost restricted to a single expression is *puttulu* "coiled", which is mostly said of the *kakku*, the "weapon" mark.

I will illustrate the main characteristics of the use of *purrus* in omen texts by examining some prominent cases, arranged according to the type of omen text: extispicy omens in 10.7.1.1; medical and physiognomic omens in 10.7.1.2, and astronomical omens in 10.7.1.3. The discussion will be limited to a number of rather common or interesting words; instances stemming from other types of text are not considered here.

10.7.1.1. Typical *purrus* forms from extispicy omens

Of all types of omen, extispicy omens have the most technical and specialized vocabulary to describe features of the ominous organs of the sacrificial animal and of the animal itself. The precise meaning of many of the terms used is difficult to establish. This also applies to the numerous *purrus* forms found in extispicy omens. Many of them are used in a very restricted context with some precise technical meaning and do not seem to stand in opposition to the corresponding simple adjectives. Their use seems to be largely stereotyped and conventional. The following list illustrates these features by means of some rather common *purrus* forms found in extispicy omens.

Guppušu "huge, massive" is used in OB liver omens to qualify the *nīru*, probably the omasal impression (cf. CAD sv *nīru* A 4; Jeyes 1989: 71); in MB it once qualifies the "foot" mark. This represents a strong degree of specialization vis-à-vis the simple adjective *gapšu*, which is mostly a literary word, especially popular in RIs, qualifying floods and rivers, armies, cedars (?), a bull ("huge"), a hand ("strong"), and gods and persons ("proud, overbearing"), cf. CAD sv *gapšu* and *gapāšu* a.

Hurruru "deeply incised" is said of various parts of the liver and of the sacrificial animal, from OB onwards. The stative G *harir* is used with similar, but not with the same subjects, cf. CAD sv *harāru* A 2a. For a possible "inherent plurality" in *hurruru*, see 10.6.1.1.3.

Hussuru "blunted" is only used in SB for the breastbone (*kaskasu*) of a sheep; in one text we find *hesir* in this combination (ChDiv. 1, 95: 17f), with no apparent difference.

Kupp/bbuṣ/su "curled" occasionally replaces the very common stative *kap/biṣ/s* to qualify parts of the liver or the lung, for reasons difficult to establish.

Lupputu "abnormal, anomalous" qualifies various parts of the exta in OB: the "flesh" (*šīrum*), the "yoke" (*nīru*) and the thorax of a sheep. The stative G *lapit* is only found in YOS 10, 48: 41 // 49: 13, which was quoted as (38) in 10.6.1.1.2 to demonstrate the association of *lupputu* with plurality. This meaning should be kept apart from the expression *damam lapit/lupput* "smeared with blood", which seems to have no correlation with plurality, cf. esp. YOS 10, 47: 86ff // 48: 23ff) with 3x *lupput* in a triplet with right, left and right+left (cf. also App. to Ch. VI sv **3b**).

In SB *laptu* and *lupputu* always seem to be written ideographically. *Lapit* (masc. tag-*it*, fem. tag-*at*) is rare as a qualification of specific parts of the exta, but common with general words such as *têrtu* "extispicy" (cf. CAD sv *lapātu* 1m). On the other hand, the spelling tag.meš, which - at least if it has a sg. subject - is likely to stand for *lupput(at)* is common in SB, cf. CAD *ib.* 4f. Tag-*it* and tag.meš are found side by side in the fragmentary omen text CT 31, 45: 7/12, cf. note 27.

Muṭṭuru "soggy, oozing moisture" occurs in OB qualifying the bladder, a part of the "finger", and once with the subject broken off. In SB it is replaced by *mundurat*, which once qualifies the liver and more often the gall bladder. The corresponding G form *maṭir* is always preceded by a colour noun in the acc. (except in the atypical instance from a medical text AMT 18, 10: 9 *šumma amēlu īnāšu ma-ṭi-ra* "if the eyes of a man are moist"): in OB by *tirka* or *terka* "a dark spot" (YOS 10, 39: 24; OBE 16: 22f); in SB by *urqa* (sig_7) "a yellow or green spot", but mostly by *pūṣa* (babbar) "a white spot" (cf. CAD sv *matāru*, also JCS 37, 144 no. 14: 3, MB).

Because *maṭru* only occurs with a preceding colour noun, and *muṭṭuru* and *mundurat* do not, they apparently differ in meaning; possibly *muṭṭuru* refers to a moist condition of the organ as a whole (cf. 10.6.1.2.2), e.g., CT 28, 48a: 5 *šumma martu kīma imgurri mun-du-rat-ma mûša ṣalmū DN irahhiṣ* "if the gall bladder is soggy like the clay envelope (freshly put on around a tablet), and its bile is black (tr. CAD sv *imgurru*), Adad will cause an inundation", and *maṭru* only to an oozing spot on it.

Nurrubu "soft, moist" is practically only used with *zihhu*, cf. CAD sv a.[22] Slightly different is KAR 153: 11 *dīhu duqququmma mûšu nu-ru-bu* "(if on the middle "finger" of the lung is) a minute pustule whose fluid is soft". The only exceptions are YOS 10, 55: 5 (// AfO 18, 66: 13) *umṣātim nu-úr-ru-ba-tim* "moist warts" (OB) and TU 2: 10 // CT 28, 48c: 4 *rikbu nu-úr-ru-bu* "a soft crust" (SB).

In OB only *nurrubu* occurs; in later texts it is occasionally replaced by the simple form *narbu* (cf. CAD sv *narbu* d). Interesting is TU 2: 55 *šumma ina rēš marti dīhu nadīma nu-úr-ru-bu* (for /*nurrub*/, stative 3 sg. masc.) "if a *zihhu* lies on the top of the gall bladder and it is soft", which is equated with *dīhu nàr-bu* in a commentary (CT 20, 40: I 24). *Nurrubu* is a typical example of a specialized *purrus* form.

Puttulu "coiled" is mostly said of the *kakku*, the "weapon" mark, in one text of the filaments, in SB. The stative G is found in OB and SB referring to a range of other parts of the exta (intestines, gall bladder, the *ṣibtu*), cf. AHw sv *patālu* G 2/3.

Puṭṭuru is rather common in extispicy omens in the meaning "split" or "frayed", or something similar, alternating with *paṭru*. The basic meaning of *paṭru* is "loose", cf. *paṭāru* "to loosen, untie", which is doubtless appropriate in many cases. That it can also mean "split" is suggested by qualifications such as *ana/adi N(-šu)* "into two, three, etc., parts", which is occasionally found with *paṭru* (e.g., YOS 10, 26: III 21/32; 47: 57ff; RA 38, 82: 6ff), but which is common with *puṭṭuru* (SSAW 120/3, 17: 18; YOS 10, 33: V 28. 31. 34. 37. 39; 39: 29. 31; RA 44, 30: 47). The meaning "frayed" is based on the comparison with *mušṭu* "comb" (e.g., Iraq 54, 106: 5 *šumma* kaskal *panūšu kīma mušṭi pu-ṭú-ru* "if the front of the "path" is frayed like a comb", also RA 44, 13: 3f; CT 30, 29a: 6 (ideogr.)), and with the mouth of a saw (St. Reiner 150 b 1f *šumma manzāzu kīma pî šaršari pu-ṭur* "if the *manzāzu* is frayed like the "mouth" of a saw.").

The association of *puṭṭuru* with plurality is shown by (42) - (44), quoted in 10.6.1.1.3. Its (optional) use in the meaning "split" (into many parts) suggests that it is motivated by the plurality inherent in this meaning, and that it can also mean "split" if there is no explicit indication of the type *ana/adi N(-šu)*, for instance, in RA 67, 44: 71', OBE 14: 21 and TDP 108: 15. If the quality expressed is compared to a comb or a saw, only *puṭṭuru* is found (see above). This may be accidental, but it is also conceivable that the many splits or frays implied cause a strong preference for *puṭṭuru*, rather than *paṭru*. Thus *puṭṭuru* combines a certain degree of semantic differentiation with an association with plurality.

Qubburu "buried" (acc. to AHw sv *qebēru* D 4b and Richter, NABU 92/24, but CAD sv *qubburu* "mng. uncert.") is said in SB of the crucible and the middle finger of the lung, cf. CAD *l.c.*, a clear case of specialized use of *purrus*. There is no stative G attested in a corresponding meaning.

Ruššuku "dried out, withered" is mostly said of the *zihhu* in OB and SB omens (cf. note 22), once of the *ṣibtu* (the "processus papillaris", cf. Jeyes 1989: 72), and the "finger" of the lung; no G forms are attested.

***Šubbu** (only fem. *šubbat*) describes an unknown quality of the gall bladder; the instances are listed in CAD sv *šâbu* A 2b. It is not found in other contexts, nor is a stative G attested.

Šukkusu "dried out" is only used to qualify the top of a *zihhu* (cf. note 24) and pock marks (*ziqtu*) on the diaphragm. No G forms are attested in omens.

Šuppulu "low" is only used in hendiadys with a following stative, e.g., RA 40, 58: 29 *šumma danānu šu-pu-ul-ma šakin* "if the "fortress" lies lower than usual", interchanging with *uš(t)appil(am)ma*, cf. CAD sv *šapālu* 3d. The same applies (with a few exceptions) to **šuqqû** "high", cf. CAD sv *šaqû* A 2b-2'.

Tukkupu and *takip* "speckled, covered with (coloured) specks", are always combined with a colour indication in OB extispicy omens, either in the form of a preceding adjunct accusative (e.g., YOS 10, 25: 24 (if a *zihhu* lies on the palace gate and) *pūṣam tu-uk-ku-up* "it is covered with white (specks)"), or by means of a following stative in hendiadys (e.g., in (34A) quoted in 10.6.1.1.1). In SB *tukkupu* and *takpu* are widespread, not only qualifying the exta, but also stones, celestial bodies, human body parts, etc., cf. AHw sv *takāpu* D 3. They seem to be always preceded by a colour name, as in OB, but *takpu* can also be preceded by *tikpu* "dot" (AHw sv: "Tüpfelung").

It was shown in 10.6.1.1.1 that the use of *tukkupu* can be motivated by plurality of the subject, but *tukkupu* has a sg. subject in other places (such as YOS 10, 25: 24 and 36: I 1 just mentioned). It seems plausible that in this word the use of a form with gemination is also related to the inherent plurality of colours that it denotes, cf. 10.6.1.1.3. There is one passage in which G and D alternate in duplicate texts: STT 108/9: 7 with *tak-pat*, versus BAM 378: II' 6' *tuk-ku-pat* (cf. Horowitz, ZA 82, 113: 7) (said of a stone).

Turruku presumably denotes a dark colour which results from beating (? cf. *tarāku* "to beat"); in OB it is used differently from SB. In OB it is only found in extispicy omens; its use is rare compared to the ubiquitous *tarku*, which qualifies the same entities much more frequently. It was shown in 10.6.1.1.2 that if *turruku* and *tarku* are in opposition, the former may be motivated by some nuance of plurality, see (37), (39) and (40), but that this does not apply to other cases.

In SB, on the other hand, *tarku* seems to be the only surviving form in extispicy omens and medical texts, cf. AHw sv *tarāku* G 7, and, for instance, TDP passim (often spelled ideographically with $\underline{\text{gi}}_6$, cf. Nougayrol, RA 40, 72). In astronomical texts, however, *turruku* is consistently used of the horns of the moon (always dual). This shows that the use of *turruku* is purely conventional, and that there was not a productive opposition between the G and the D forms in question.

Ulluṣu "swollen, hypertrophic" is only common as a qualification of parts of the exta in OB, MB and SB.

This use represents a specialized aspect of *elēṣu* "to swell, be jubilant"; no other forms of this verb are used in comparable contexts.

Uppuqu "massive, solid, without openings" is common both in extispicy omens and in Šumma izbu. In the former kind it qualifies various parts of the sacrificial animal and the exta, interchanging with *epqu*, for which cf. CAD sv *epēqu* A 1a. In Šumma izbu it is said of the various parts of an *izbu*, also beside *epqu*; cf. esp. Izbu 134: 46' *šumma izbu uznāšu up-pu-qá* "if an anomaly's ears are solid" with CT 40, 30b: 13 *šumma alpu uznāšu ep-qá* "if an ox's ears are solid". For Izbu 95: 69'/70' with *uppuq* versus *epqu* see note 27. In spite of this contrasting pair, there seems to be no significant difference in meaning between *up-puq* and *epiq*. The greater frequency of the former is doubtless related to the salient and pathological nature of the quality expressed; typologically it belongs to the words treated in 10.6.2.

Urruru "dried out" is said of various parts of the liver in extispicy omens and a few times in physiognomic omens. There are no instances of *erru* in comparable contexts.

Zuqquru "elevated, raised" is only used to qualify the "station" (*manzāzu*) of the liver. *Zaqru* occasionally occurs with other parts of the exta (the *tīrānū* and the *šulmu*), but is more common in other kinds of o-mens to qualify human body parts (nose, head, fore-arm (?), epigastrium), cf. CAD sv *zaqru* e. *Zuqquru* is a good example of the highly specialized use of some *purrus* forms.

Zuqqutu "pointed" qualifies several of the "fortuitous marks" on the liver (cf. Jeyes 1989: 81ff). There is no corresponding use of *zaqtu*.

10.7.1.2. *Purrus* forms in medical and physiognomic omens

Another large corpus of omens comprises medical (diagnostic) and physiognomic omens, in which *purrus* typically qualifies body parts of persons. Interesting *purrus* forms typical of these omens are the following:

Du"umu "dark" is only once attested with certainty, in the adverb *du"umiš*, cf. 10.7.2. Elsewhere the spellings that are found point to a form **du'ummu** or **du'ūmu**: the stative 3rd p. sg. fem. *du-'-ú-mat* or *du-'-um-mat*, 3rd p. pl. masc/fem. *du-'-ú-mu/ma* or *du-'-um-mu/ma*.[23] This indicates that the 3rd p. masc., usually spelled *du-'-um* (but *du-um* in CT 28, 29: r.3), is to be interpreted as */du'umm/* or */du'ūm/* rather than */du"um/*, which is theoretically also possible. In this way we can derive all forms from either *du'ummu* or *du'ūmu*.[24] Since they are used in the same way as the *purrus* forms of other adjectives, they are discussed here as if they were *purrus* forms. Both forms will be subsumed under the form *du'ummu*

Du'ummu mainly occurs in two kinds of texts: medical and astronomical omens (all SB, but 1x OB *du'ummatum* "darkness" ARM 26/1 p. 433 no. 205: 5'). In the former, they are more or less restricted to the medical texts of TDP (passim, cf. CAD sv a); other instances are CT 28, 29: r.3, TBP 38a: r.20' and SpTU 4, 149: III 14f (all physiognomic omens; note esp. TBP 38a: r.20' (D) // BRM 4, 23: 15 (G)). Other texts of the same kind mainly use *da'mu*, cf. CAD sv *da'mu* a/b/d.

If in TDP different colours of diseased organs are enumerated, it is in a fixed order and a fixed form: *sāmu* "red", *(w)arqu* "green", *ṣalmu* "black", *tarku* "bruised" and *du'ummu*.[25] This suggests that *du'ummu* was the neutral form of the adjective. Interestingly, other texts use *da'mu* in such enumerations, e.g., KAR 472: II 10 // TBP 11b: VII 15' (white, yellow, black, *da-a'-mu*); CT 28, 27: 37 (*da-a'-mu*, red, black, white); 33: 6/10 (*namru* "shining", *da-a'-mu*, white (*peṣû*), white (*pelû*), green); *ib.* 11/14 (*namru, da-a'-mu*, red, green). For the authors of these texts *da'mu* was apparently the neutral form.

In astronomical omens *da'mu* and *du'ummu* interchange without observable difference in meaning; it is usually said of the rising (ud.da = *ṣītu*) of celestial bodies, cf. CAD sv *da'mu* f and *du'ummu* b; for instance in the following passage:

> (52) ACh. Spl. 8: 20ff [20]*šumma ṣīt Sin magal eklet* [...] [21]*š. ṣīt Sin magal du-'-ú-mat* (...[...]) [22](erased) [23]*š. ṣīt Sin eli ša ginâ da-a'-mat* ([...]) (...) [25][*š. Sin u Šam*]*aš ṣīssunu du-'-ú-mat* (...) "If the rising of the moon is very dark (*eklu*), (...) / If the rising of the moon is very dark (*du'ūmu*) (...) / (erased) / If the rising of the moon is darker (*da'mu*) than normal (...) / If the rising of the moon and the sun is dark (*du'ūmu*) (...)".

Compare especially 23 with ACh. 2. Spl. 3: 40 *šumma ṣīt Sin eli ša ginâ du-'u-mat* (both apodoses are broken off); see also 10.9 for *da'mu* or *du'ummu eli.*

In conclusion, it appears that the use of *du'ummu* is restricted to the technical language of medical, physiognomic and astronomical omens. There are no indications that it differs semantically from *da'mu.* For some speakers it is the neutral form of the adjective, interchangeable with *da'mu.* This may be compared to the similar state of affairs in *burrumu* "multicoloured", which is also more frequent than the simple form *barmu.* The prominence of marked forms in these adjectives is doubtless related to the fact that they refer to colours - *burrumu* even to a plurality of colours, cf. 10.6.1.1.3 - and thus have a high degree of inherent salience.

Muqqutu is used mainly in the diagnostic omens of TDP to describe parts of the body (for other cases, see App. sv): kidneys (sg/pl), pelvis, buttocks (sg/pl), penis, testicles, thighs (sg/pl.); once with broken subject. In other texts it is hardly found (cf. App.).

The stative G *maqit* is also said of parts of the body, but different ones: in TDP temples (dual) (38: 68 and 218: 5), the tip of the nose (56: 25), the *girru* (dual) (86: 53) and the face (pl.) (74: 37f). In other texts it is said of the neck (TBP 25: 4), breasts (*ib.* 11b: VII 8'), the navel (BRM 4, 22: 9) and the rectum (BAM 240: 29). The dictionaries give the same translation for *maqit* and *muqqut*: CAD sv *maqātu* 2 and 6 translates "to collapse", AHw sv G II 12 and D 2 "(krankhaft) verfallen". If this is correct, it is unclear what the difference between them might be. They are never found in direct opposition; they do not even occur side by side in the same text. The fact that they occur with different subjects, however, suggests that they do not have exactly the same meaning; it would be in keeping with other *purrus* form to assume that *muqqut* has some specialized technical meaning.

Muṭṭû "having a reduced appetite or capacity" is common in medical texts and is said of persons, with an adjunct acc. specifying the inadequacy, cf. CAD sv *maṭû* v. 4c; e.g., BAM 234: 9 *akala u šikara muṭ-ṭu* "he has no desire to eat and drink beer", or TDP 230: 119 *šumma šerru* (...) *tulâ muṭ-ṭú* "if a baby (...) has no desire (to take) the breast" (trs. CAD *l.c.*). In the case of diminished eyesight both *muṭṭu* and *maṭi* are used, cf. CAD *l.c.* and sv 2b, respectively. The use of *muṭṭu* is a specialized medical idiom, which is doubtless ultimately motivated by the fact that it specifically refers to persons.

Nuppuhu "bloated" or "inflamed" was discussed in 10.6.1.1.1 and 10.6.1.2.1 because of its association with plurality, and will again be discussed in 10.8 in relation to the alleged intensive nature of *purrus.* It is a typical example of a word used in a specialized medical meaning.[26]

Suhhuru "curved, curly", when used in the protases of omens, qualifies external parts of the body (hair, neck, mouth, foot and the dome of the skull, several parts of the liver, and a few fortuitous marks on it.

The stative G *sahir* is used in exactly the same contexts (and in many more). Often, however, the preterite *ishur* and the present *isahhur* are used in the same circumstances, apparently without difference in meaning. A more common meaning of *sahir* in omen texts and elsewhere is "surrounded with" (+ acc.), or, with a direct object, "surrounding" (CAD sv *sahāru* 3c).

It is hard to detect any differences between *suhhur* and *sahir* in the protases of omen texts. They never seem to be in opposition in the same passage. There is one instance of two omens differing only in that one has *sahir* and the other *suhhur*, but they come from different texts: TDP 20: 23 *šumma kalli qaqqadišu sa-hir* (Var. *i-sah-hur*) *imât* "if the dome of his (the patient's) skull is round (??), he will die", versus Syr. 33, 123: r.6 [*šumma mar*]*ṣu kalli qaqqadišu su-uh-hur* (apodosis broken).

Šuhhuṭu only occurs in the medical texts of TDP and qualifies external organs of the human body; its meaning is unknown; no corresponding G forms are attested.

Turrupu "dotted, speckled" is mostly said of external body parts (face, ears, eyes, fingers, nails); no G forms referring to body parts are attested in omens (but CT 39, 16: 43 of water (Šumma ālu), and OBTR 124: 5 acc. to Von Soden, NABU 91/54 and 94/75 (OB letter). It was argued in 10.6.1.1.3. that the use of *turrup* may be motivated by the plural notion inherent in its meaning.

Uppuqu "massive, solid, without openings", which is common in extispicy and Šumma izbu omens, was discussed in the previous section, q.v.

Urrupu "cloudy, dark" is mostly used in SB medical texts, qualifying the eyes, the face and the nose. It is only rarely used in its literal sense, referring to meteorological phenomena: Emar VI/4 p. 255 no. 651: 44 (day, MB); MSL 12, 108: 163 ([sky], rest.), SAA 8, 435: 5 (subj. broken). The G-stem is generally used in such contexts, for instance, with *ūmu* as subject, cf. CAD sv *erēpu* a; but cf., on the one hand, Gilg. I II 48 *panūšu ar-pu* "his face was dark"), and on the other hand Emar VI/4 p. 255 no. 651: 44 *ūmu ur-ru-up*, which contrasts with *ūmu na-me-er*. *Urrupu* clearly represents a specialized medical term.

Zuqqupu "erect, standing on end" is said only of hair in SB physiognomic omens. Other texts use *zaqpu* without noticeable difference, cf. CAD sv *zaqāpu* 1e-2'.

10.7.1.3. *Purrus* forms from astronomical omens:

In these omens celestial bodies and their attributes are described. Some typical *purrus* forms in these texts which merit discussion are the following:

Du"umu "dark" was already discussed in 10.7.1.2.

Lummunu "bad, evil, unfortunate" is used in SB astronomical omens with the specialized meaning "dim, obscured", cf. App. sc **2b**. *Lemnu* is not attested in this meaning.

Mulluhu is a SB technical term of unknown meaning referring to stars (CAD sv *malāhu* 3b: "to flicker?", AHw sv *m.* D 2b "zerfasern"). No other forms of this root are used in comparable contexts.

Uddudu "pointed, sharp" is only used to qualify the horns of the moon (always pl.), alternating with the stative G without noticeable difference, cf. 10.8. In the rare instances where the subject is a single horn of the moon, the stative G is used: ACh. 2. Spl. 1: I 8. 10; SAA 8, 263: 6 (*ed-de-et*); *ib.* 384: 10 (*ed-da-at*). Cf. also AfO 14, pl. IV II 17. 19, etc., with a preterite *e-du-ud* instead of a stative.

Turruku "dark" is only said of the horns of the moon in SB, at least in so far as syllabic spellings are concerned; this is in marked contrast to its use in OB extispicy omens, cf. 10.6.1.1.2. The corresponding use of the stative G is not attested (compare this with the indiscriminate use of *eddā* and *uddudā* with the horns of the moon).

Ummulu "faint, scintillating" and **unnutu** "dim, faint, weak" occur in SB with stars; no corresponding G forms are found.

10.7.2. Lexicalized *purrus* forms in literary texts

The second kind of text in which *purrus* forms and simple forms are used indiscriminately are literary texts. It was argued in 6.9.2.2 and especially in 7.5.5 that Akkadian literary texts differ from ordinary texts in the extensive use they make of forms and grammatical categories which are not used, or used in a far more restricted way, in other genres. This seems to apply to the use of *purrus* as well, although in this case the differences are not very pronounced. There are a small number of *purrus* forms which do not seem to be used outside literary texts.

The following list contains a number of *purrus* forms which are mainly (but not necessarily exclusively) found in literary texts.

Duššupu "sweet, pleasing" only occurs in literary texts (RIs, hymns and prayers, love songs, epics and religious poetry); it is used both in its literal meaning "sweet" (of beer and wine), and metaphorically, of songs, persons and parts of the body. The simple form *dašpu* is less common, and used only literally, of beer, wine and fruit (cf. CAD sv).

Nukkulu "artful, ingenious" is very restricted in use: it is said of buildings and artefacts in SB RIs and epics. In exactly the same contexts we also find *naklu*, cf., for instance, Sn. 128: 43 (a building) *lā nu-ku-lat epištaš*, with *ib.* 103: 45 (a palace) *epištaš lā nak-lat-ma* "its construction was not ingenious". Cf. CAD sv *naklu* b/c for other examples. *Naklu* differs from *nukkulu* in that it has a wider use: it is also said of persons, thoughts and acts, cf. CAD sv a/b and d.

Nussuqu "choice, well-chosen" is used in SB to qualify utterances, a person, artefacts and materials, cf. CAD sv. Its use is restricted to RIs, wisdom literature (the "Babylonian Theodicy" in BWL 70ff), and a prayer. *Nasqu* is mainly used in non-literary texts, cf. CAD sv. (often in Nuzi), but RIs use both forms. If persons are qualified, *nasqu* is more common than *nussuqu* in all kinds of texts (*nussuqu* refers to a person only in BWL 74: 68).

Puggulu "strong" is used in SB RIs, hymns, prayers and epics, mainly as an epithet of gods and words for "power"; a non-literary instance is AfO Beiheft 17, 13b top (date palm). The simple adjective *paglu* is mostly found in the combination *ina ašūhī/erēnī paglūti* "with strong (beams of) firs/cedars", but is also said of arms, bulls and river banks. This is a remarkable reversal of the tendency to use adjectives with gemination preferably in combination with concrete entities.

Šuddulu "broad, spacious, abundant" is common in SB RIs, hymns, prayers and epics, as an epithet of the earth and other localities, buildings, offerings, mind ("far-reaching"), cf. CAD sv *šadālu* 2a/b and *šuddulu*. *Šadlu* is used in practically the same contexts, cf. CAD sv *šadlu*: beams, gates, earth and sea, temples, persons, offerings, and also of the heart. Noteworthy instances are KB 1, 176: 22 *ṣurru šum-du-lu*, versus VS 1, 37: II 49f *ṣurru šad-lu* "a far-reaching mind", and BiOr. 9, 89: 4 *erṣetu šá-dil-ta* versus BWL 126: 28 [*š*]*u-um-dul-ta erṣetu* "the vast earth".

Šummuhu "abundant, flourishing" is said of vegetation and offerings in RIs, once of a person in an elegy (but often as a PN, cf. 10.6.3.2); *šamhu* is also typically literary (apart from its use as a PN, cf. CAD sv 2b), and mainly used of people, rarely of vegetation, cf. CAD sv 1/2.

Šurruhu "supreme" (of gods, kings, words), "abundant" (of gifts and offerings), "arrogant" (of enemies).

Šarhu is also often used of gods and kings (translated "proud, noble" by CAD sv a/b, also in a negative sense, cf. CAD sv b); less often of celestial bodies, animals, utterances and a few concrete objects.

Some other literary *purrus* forms which are less common, but show the same interchangeability of G and D in the same contexts are *guššuru* and *gašru* "powerful", *uzzuzu* and *ezzu* "angry, raging" (beside the "elative" *šū/ēzuzu*) and *ruṣṣunu* and *raṣmu* (sic) "acclaimed, honoured". Typical terms from SB building inscriptions are *ṣuhhuru* "(too) small" and *quppu* "buckled", the latter always said of *igāru* "wall", mostly in the plural (but there is no simple adjective **qīpu* attested of this verb, cf. note 7).

A certain differentiation is observable in *uggugu* and *aggu* "angry": *uggugu* is always said of gods, whereas the simple adjective *aggu* only occurs with *libbu* "heart", cf. CAD sv; also literary is *duššû* "abundant, numerous", already discussed in 10.6.1.2.1, because it is mostly used in the plural.

Some other *purrus* forms are common in non-literary texts in OB, but survive predominantly in literary contexts later on; this applies to *dunnunu* "strong" (cf. 10.6.1.2.1), *dummuqu* "good" (cf. 10.10), and *qurrubu* "close" (cf. 10.10).

The popularity of *purrus* as a literary form is also demonstrated by the fact that it is mainly in literary texts that we find adverbs with the ending *-iš* derived from them:

Du"umiš "darkly" (*du-u'-'u$_5$-mi-iš*, late copy of an OB text).
Dulluhiš "in a hurried or perturbed way" (SB).
Dunnuniš "strongly" (SB).
Hummuṭiš "hotly" (qualifying *nubbû* "to lament" (OB) and *bakû* "to cry" (SB)).
Purrušiš "in a flattering way" (OB).
Ṣuhhiš "merrily" (OB).
Ukkuliš "dark" (construed with *emû* Š "to make", SB).
Urruhiš "quickly" (passim in RIs, cf. AHw sv, MB/SB).
Uššušiš "in a distressed way" (SB).

There are also a few non-literary adverbs of the pattern *purrusiš* attested in omens, but these are derived from *purrus* forms which do not normally have a corresponding simple adjective: *ukkupiš* "close, in a compact way" (?), *ummuliš* "scintillating", and possibly *šullušiš* "in three parts" (emended, text *ullušiš*).

10.7.3. Conclusions on *purrus* forms in omens and literary texts

The words discussed in the previous sections may suffice to show that the *purrus* forms found in omens and literary texts are mainly a lexicalized category of individual adjectives which share a common pattern but which in other respects all show their own specific behaviour. Their use is not determined by a grammatical rule, and their relationship with the simple adjective is accordingly erratic and unpredictable.

Of the *purrus* forms from omen texts, some do not have a corresponding simple adjective (e.g., *ruššuku, šuhhuṭu, mulluhu, ummulu, unnutu*), or do not use it in the context in question (*ulluṣu, urruru, zuqqutu*), others have been differentiated from it on the basis of their meaning or the kind of subject with which they are combined (e.g., *guppušu, muṭṭû, muṭṭuru, puṭṭuru, zuqquru*). Still others alternate with the simple adjective in the same contexts without an observable difference in meaning. In some of these cases *purrus* is used for plurality (see 10.6.1.2.1 and 10.6.1.2.2); in others it is unclear what the motive is for the use of *purrus* rather than the simple form (*hussuru, kupp/bbuṣ/su, suhhuru, tukkupu, zuqqupu*).

The use of the literary *purrus* forms of 10.7.2 is largely conventional and stereotyped, too. They typically occur in more or less fixed expressions, in which *purrus* and *parVs* seem to be used interchangeably. These contexts do not seem to support the view that they have a significant difference in meaning.

If there is any difference between these *purrus* forms and the simple forms at all, it is doubtless stylistic. The iconic background of *purrus*, its longer form, and the fact that it was less used and thus more special, make it into a more expressive counterpart of the simple adjective. Therefore, these *purrus* forms are comparable to the "elative" briefly discussed in note 39 to Ch. VII, and to the "literary" *parras* forms mentioned in 3.1.2, such as *šammahu* "luxuriant", *šarrahu* "proud, noble", *š/sabbasu/û* "angry", etc., which are used beside the simple adjective in the same kind of text without an observable difference.

10.8. The alleged intensive function of *purrus*

It is often claimed that the pattern *purrus* serves to form adjectives with an intensive meaning, i.e., that they are used to denote a higher degree of the quality in question than the corresponding simple adjective. For instance, GAG § 55n describes *purrus* as comprising "Verbaladjektive des D-Stammes (...), oft mit einer gegenüber dem einfachen Adj. gesteigerten Bedeutung". Similar statements are found in Ungnad/Matouš 1964: 42 and Moscati 1969: 79. In GAG, this statement is followed by a few instances of *purrus* forms glossed with an "intensive" translation: *šubburum* "ganz zerbrochen", *nussuqu* "sehr erlesen", *kurrûm* "sehr kurz". In the same vein, AHw tends to translate *purrus* adjectives with "sehr" oder "ganz", e.g., *lummunu* "sehr schlecht, ganz schlimm", *dunnunu* "sehr fest", *puggulu* "sehr stark", etc. It is, however, not explicitly stated what kind of evidence there is that, for instance, *puggulu* means "very strong", rather than simply "strong". This suggests that it is not so much based on textual evidence, as on the consideration that *purrus*, as part of the D-stem, shares the intensive meaning which is traditionally ascribed to some D-stems (cf. 1.5).

At first sight, such an intensive meaning seems to be in accordance with the general function of gemination in Akkadian. It was argued in 2.1.5 that, in so far as it is not grammaticalized, gemination in Akkadian is associated with notions such as plurality (in the case of some substantives and adjectives), habituality (in agent nouns), durativity (in the present tense forms of D-stems of transitive verbs, cf. 6.6.1), etc. Therefore, it would seem plausible that in the case of adjectives the semantic extension expressed by the geminate can be realized as an increase in intensity. Dressler 1968: 78ff explicitly mentions intensity as one of the possible realizations of verbal plurality (cf. 2.1.5).

Moreover, as already noted in 6.4.9, 6.8.1 and 6.8.2, some D-stems of transitive verbs can be used to denote actions which are in some respect more intensive than the actions denoted by the G-stem, because they require more energy, more time, or have a more drastic effect on the object, than the corresponding G-stem. Alhough their number is small, and although there are no indications that the D-stem has a regular and productive intensive function (cf. 6.8.2), they show that the concept of intensity is not foreign to the forms under discussion.

However, it is difficult to find any positive evidence in favour of the claim that *purrus* has the regular function of denoting intensive adjectives. In part, this is due to a methodological problem. In an ancient language like Akkadian, for which we have no native speakers, it is difficult to distinguish different degrees of intensity (cf. Dressler1968: 188). We can only recover those differences between contrasting categories which result in an observable difference in context. This is not the case with differences in degrees of intensity. The choice between neutral and intensive is entirely subjective: it depends on the state of mind of the speaker whether he chooses to represent a given situation as "dangerous" or "very dangerous", or a person as "good" or "very good". Therefore, the context will usually not provide us with reliable clues to decide whether a given form has an intensive meaning or not.

There are some circumstances, however, which could suggest that a form has an intensive meaning. One of these applies if a form is consistently used in contexts which can be argued on independent grounds to be susceptible to intensive ways of expression, e.g., because of their contents, style, vocabulary, etc. For *purrus* adjectives, this approach is ineffective: most *purrus* forms are far too rare, and those which are not, show a high degree of inconsistency in their use, as may be clear from the discussion in this chapter.

A second circumstance which could prompt us to assume that a category has an intensive meaning applies if the neutral and the alleged intensive form are used side by side in the same context in a specific relationship to one another. For instance, if we find a statement such as "A is X, but B is XX" (in which X is a quality expressed by a neutral adjective, and XX the same quality expressed by a corresponding intensive adjective), in a context which makes it clear that XX is definitely not ascribed to A (e.g., if a contrast is intended), or if we find sentences of the type "A is not X, but XX", we are justified in concluding that X and XX differ in meaning and that XX is likely to be an intensive counterpart of X.

Such statements are, however, not attested in Akkadian. In the relatively rare instances in which we find a simple adjective and a *purrus* form in direct contrast, a relationship as described above does not seem to apply. Some instances of this situation in which statives of transitive verbs are involved were quoted in 6.9.4 as (124) - (128). It was argued there that the reason for juxtaposing a G- and a D-stem is stylistic, and that there is no significant difference in meaning between them. Some cases with *purrus* forms which are more adjectival in nature than the statives quoted in 6.9.4 are:

(53) KAR 125: r.11 *qàd-da lētāšu qù-ud-du-du pānū-*[*šu*] "its (of the *igirû* bird) cheeks are sunken, sunken is its face" (tr. CAD sv *qadādu* 2b-2') (cf. also *ib.* 17);

(54) HGŠ 105: 24 *dal-ha-ku dul-lu-ha-ku* "I am disturbed and restless";

(55) SAA 3, 7: 2 *šar-hat šu-ru!-hat*) "it (a palm tree) is glorious, most glorious" (tr. Livingstone).

Neither these cases, nor the ones quoted in 6.9.4, meet the conditions stipulated above for establishing an intensive meaning, since there is no contrast between different subjects (we should not interpret (53) as containing an opposition of the type "A is X, but B is XX"), nor between different degrees of intensity (in (55) it is not denied that the palm tree is glorious).

It is much more likely that, just as the cases quoted in 6.9.4, these instances are motivated by stylistic variation. They belong to the genre of hymns and prayers which are characterized by a highly repetitive style, with long enumerations of synonyms. The use of the stative G and D of the same verb has the same function as the juxtaposition of (near-)synonymous words. It is illustrative here to quote the wider context of (54):

(56) HGŠ 105: 24ff [24]*dal-ha-ku dul-lu-ha-ku la'šāku pardāku za-*[...] [25]*marṣāku abkāku nadâku nas*[*sāku*] [26]*attana'batu u uzabbalu e-*[...] [27]*attanaktamu ina kišpī ruhî rusî up*[*šašī*] [28]*lu"ubāku lupputāku* "I am disturbed, restless, depressed, fearful and [...]; I am ill, upset, downcast and wretched; I am ruined time and again, I linger on [...]; I am constantly overwhelmed by sorcery, (magic) spittle, dirt and witch[craft]; I am afflicted and unclean."

The coordinated pairs of statives G and D in (53) - (55) can best be explained as instances of this kind of stylistic variation. Accordingly, they offer no evidence for the alleged intensive function of *purrus*. They rather suggest some degree of interchangeability between them; this impression is fully confirmed by the way many *purrus* forms are used in literary texts in general, cf. 10.7.2.

In non-literary texts such cases are hardly found. An instance from an OB letter, which to my knowledge is unique, is:

(57) AbB 7, 22: 9ff *kīma tešmê* (sic) *na-az-qá-ku u PN ana awātim nu-uz-zu-uq* "Wie du gehört hast, bin ich verärgert (or "bekümmert", cf. note b on p. 19), auch PN ist wegen der Sache sehr verärgert." (tr. Kraus).

Kraus obviously regards *nuzzuq* as an intensive form, but his translation is slightly awkward because "auch" combines two different concepts ("annoyed" and "very annoyed"). The context does not point to a contrast between the two statives ("I am annoyed but PN is (not annoyed but) *very* annoyed"), and therefore does not force us to interpret *nuzzuq* as an intensive. On the other hand, it is difficult to imagine what the difference could be (assuming that there should be any difference at all).

A type of text which seems to be especially relevant for establishing the difference between contrasting *parVs* and *purrus* forms, is the extensive omen literature which is extant in Akkadian. As already noted in 6.6.1, omens and omen-like texts have the stereotyped structure of a conditional sentence introduced by *šumma* (the protasis), followed by an apodosis which states the prediction (or the prescription in some medical texts), in case the protasis is realized. In the protases, features of the entrails of the sacrificial animal, the behaviour of celestial bodies, (abnormal) features of new-born babies and animals, symptoms of diseased persons and many other phenomena which were regarded as ominous are enumerated in a more or less systematic way (Oppenheim 1964: 206ff; Bottéro 1987: 133ff).

Because of their stereotyped character and systematic organization, such protases come as close to being minimal pairs as we can possibly hope to achieve for Akkadian. In 6.6.1 we made use of omens to establish the durative character of D present forms of transitive verbs, and in 10.6.1.1 we did so for the association of *purrus* with plurality. On the other hand, omen texts have the disadvantage that they are highly stereotyped (see 10.7), and that many words have a specialized meaning which is difficult to identify with precision.

The question is whether there are contrasting pairs in omen protases - similar to the ones presented in 10.6.1.1 - that provide evidence for an intensive meaning of *purrus*. These would have to consist of consecutive or at least neighbouring protases which are identical except for having a *purrus* form in the one case and the corresponding *parVs* form in the other, and a different apodosis. Such a contrast would demonstrate that *purrus* and *parVs* differ in meaning, and a likely difference would seem to be a difference in intensity.

Actually, instances which meet these requirements are very hard to find. If *purrus* and *parVs* interchange in the same text, in consecutive or neighbouring omens, this interchange almost always correlates with a difference in the nature of the subject: *purrus* is used if the subject is plural or totally affected, as against *parVs* if the subject is singular or partly affected; or else the *purrus* form in question can be argued to be inherently plural ("split into many parts", etc.). In other words, if *purrus* and *parVs* are in direct contrast, this regularly correlates with the contrast between singular and plural, which is one of the most important functions of *purrus*, as we saw in 10.6.1.

There is a very small number of cases in which *purrus* and *parVs* are contrasted in the same passage without a concomitant difference in subject. This concerns the pairs *nuppuh/napih* and *uddudā/eddā*.[27]

Nuppuh/napih. There are a few cases of *nuppuh* and *napih* in consecutive sentences with the same subject, but they are marred by uncertainty about the correct interpretation of ideographic spellings and the precise nuance expressed by *nuppuh*. Consider the following omens from TDP:

(58A) TDP 86: 46f *šumma kirri imittišu nap-hat iballuṭ - šumma kirri šumēlišu nap-hat imât / šumma kirrāšu nap-ha ušannahma imât* "if the right side of his throat is bloated (or: inflamed), he will recover; if the left side of his throat is b., he will die; if (both) sides of his throat are b., he will die after having a hard time."

(58B) ib. 47f *šumma kirri im*[*ittišu* s]ar.me *murrussu* [..] KI.MIN *imât / šumma kirri šumēlišu* sar.me *murrussu kabit - šumma kirrāšu* sar.me *imât* "if the right side of his throat is (very?) b., his illness

[..] ditto, he will die; if the left side of his throat is (very?) b., his illness is serious; if both sides of his throat are (very?) b., he will die";

(59) TDP 112: 17bf (*šumma*) *rēš libbišu na-pi-ih nakid* / *šumma rēš libbišu* sar.meš *ṣibit eṭemmi* "if his epigastrium is bloated, he is in a dangerous situation; if his epigastrium is (very?) bloated: seizure by a ghost."

In these cases the stative G of *napāhu* "bloated" (or "inflamed", but this is irrelevant here), contrasts with verb form which is spelled ideographically. The interpretation of the ideographic spellings of *napāhu*, sar.me or sar.meš (and also sar.sar(-*hu*)), is uncertain, cf. CAD sv (p. 270a): they may represent the stative D *nuppuh(ū/ā)*, but also the common Ntn-stem *ittananpah(ū/ā)*, or even the stative G in the plural *naphū/ā*.

In (58B), however, sar.me is likely to represent a stative form (either G or D), because all predicates qualifying the *kirru* in this section (TDP 84/6: 41ff) are in the stative. If it is the stative G, the two triplets have the same protasis, but different apodoses, which seems unlikely. If sar.me stands for the stative D *nuppuhā*, this is one of the very rare cases where we find a *purrus* and a *parVs* form in direct opposition without a concomitant difference in subject. This would point to a difference in meaning. The exact nature of this difference remains uncertain, however: it is conceivable that *nuppuh* expresses intensity ("very bloated"), but it may also express nuances such as completeness ("bloated entirely or all over", cf. 10.6.1.1.2) or permanence ("bloated all the time").

The same applies to (59), if sar.meš also stands for *nuppuh*. This is less certain, however, since the *rēš libbi* can also be qualified by the Ntn-stem of *napāhu*, cf. CAD sv 12 (written syllabically, for instance, in KUB 37, 190: 5 *it-ta-na-an-pa-ah*), so that sar.meš may also stand for this form.

In conclusion, the evidence provided by these contrasting pairs for a possible difference in intensity between *napih* and *nuppuh* is inconclusive. It may be significant that the only instance in which *napih* and *nuppuh* are in direct opposition and both spelled syllabically is (36) quoted in 10.6.1.1.1, in which the use of G versus D correlates with a singular and a plural object, respectively.

Eddā/uddudā. A case of *purrus* and *parVs* in direct contrast is found in the astronomical omens edited in SAA 8, where the statives G and D of *edēdu* "to be sharp, pointed" are often used to qualify the "horns" of the moon. The following passage is especially noteworthy:

(60A) SAA 8, 105: 3f [*šumma Sîn ina tāmartišu*] *qarnāšu ed-da mahīru iz*-[xx] / [xxx] *ina māti ibašš*[*i*] "[If at its appearance the moon's] horns are pointed, business will ..[..]; there will b[e ...] in the land." (tr. Hunger);

(60B) *ib.* 5f [*šumma Sîn ina tāmarti*]*šu qarnāšu ud-du-da šar Akkadi ē*[*ma panūšu*] / *šaknū māta unnaš* : *ēma panūšu šaknū* [*māta ibêl*] "[If at] its [appearance the moon's] horns are very pointed, the king of Akkad will weaken [the land wherever he turns]; wherever he turns [he will rule the land.]" (tr. Hunger).

At first sight, these are two successive omens whose protases only differ in having *eddā* versus *uddudā*. This would prove that *eddā* and *uddudā* must differ in meaning; the assumption, then, that *uddudā* means "very pointed" (cf. Hunger's translation) seems to be near at hand. The case is, however, more complicated. We find the same protasis, but now with *eddā*, and practically the same apodosis in:

(61) SAA 8, 329: 2ff [*šumma Sîn*] *ina tāmartišu qarnāšu ed-da* / *šar Akkadi ēma illaku māta ibêl* : *šar Akkadi ēma panūšu šaknū māta unnaš*.

The comparison of (61) with (60B) suggests that they are variants of the same omen. This is confirmed by the comparison of (62A) with (62B) and of (63A) with (63B), two pairs which are identical but for *eddā* in one protasis and *uddudā* in the other:

(62A) SAA 8, 9: 6 *šumma Sîn ina tāmartišu qarnāšu ú-du-[da] / šar Akkadi ēma panūš[u šaknū] māta ibê[l]*;
(62B) SAA 8, 318: 3f *š. Sîn ina tāmartišu qarnāšu ed-da šar Akkadi ašar panūšu šaknū māti ibêl*;

(63A) SAA 8, 331: 4f [*šumma Sîn*] *ina tāmartišu qarnāšu ed-da / šarru māt nakrišu unak*[*kap*] "[if] at its appearance the [moon]'s horns are pointed: the king will strike d[own] the land of his enemy." (tr. Hunger);
(63B) SAA 8, 362: 1ff *šumma Sîn ina tāmartišu / qarnāšu ud-du-da / šarru māt nakrišu unakkap*.[28]

This suggests that, even though they occur side by side in (60A/B), omens with *eddā* and *uddudā* are not in contrast but are variants of a single omen, possibly stemming from different traditions. This does not necessarily entail that both statives have exactly the same meaning, but it shows that this passage cannot be used as evidence that they differ in meaning or that *uddudā* is an intensive of *eddā*.

This leads to the conclusion that the evidence offered by the use of *purrus* in contrast to *parVs* in omens lends no support to the claim that *purrus* has an intensive function. On the other hand, there is positive evidence that *purrus* and *parVs* do *not* differ in intensity. This is provided by all cases where *purrus* stands in opposition to *parVs* and is used to underline plurality. In these cases, there can be no difference in intensity at the same time (cf. also (33) in 10.6.1 with note 14). It might be theoretically possible that *purrus* does have an intensive meaning in other contexts, for instance, in (some of) the passages (53) - (59), where the direct contrast between *purrus* and *parVs* may have been interpreted by a speaker of Akkadian as a contrast in intensity. However, there seems to be no positive evidence for this either. In the next section it will be argued that the overall function of *purrus* does not support such a claim.

The strongest argument for an intensive function of *purrus* turns out to be an indirect one, namely, the fact that other forms with gemination are used to express various aspects of verbal plurality and that it is therefore probable that *purrus* should have a similar function. However, iconicity can be realized in many other ways than intensity, such as permanence, an increase in salience, completeness, etc. It will be argued in 10.9 that *purrus* is more likely to express these notions than intensity.

10.9. A general characterization of *purrus*.

In this section we will attempt to define those features which can be regarded as typical of the category of lexical *purrus* forms as a whole. They are more conspicuous in the *purrus* forms used for salient characteristics and for plurality than in those occurring in the stereotyped language of omens and literary texts, but in general they appear to be valid for the latter category, too.

Purrus is basically a nominal pattern which has two clearly identifiable functions, namely, to underline plurality and to denote salient bodily characteristics. These functions suggest that it has an iconic, expressive background, which is caused by its geminate second radical and its contrast with the simple adjective.

It is especially the association of gemination with plurality which may help us to clarify the relationship between *purrus* and the corresponding simple form. If *purrus* underlines plurality it must have a parallel *parVs* form, from which it does not differ in meaning, but only in its restriction to plurality. Because the primary plural morpheme is the ending, the added geminate is redundant and optional. This raises the question why it is sometimes used at all, and what the difference is between *purrus* and *parVs* in plural contexts, where both forms are allowed.

The solution is to be found in the corresponding use of the *parras* forms derived from adjectives denoting dimensions, which were studied in 3.1.3. Such adjectives, used in their literal sense, have a high degree of inherent salience, because they refer primarily to the size of concrete objects. As was shown in 3.1.3.2, the use of the *parras* plurals of these adjectives is usually restricted to situations where the adjective refers to a plural entity which is also salient itself: persons, animals, body parts and large concrete objects. This suggests that the function of gemination can be defined as underlining the salience which is inherent in the meaning of the word group as a whole.

This implies that the forms with and without gemination refer to the same situation; by using the former the speaker underlines the plural and salient character of the word group; by using the latter, he leaves it implicit. Therefore, the forms with gemination do not express some specific semantic notion which is added to the qualified word (such as intensity, for example) and which is absent if the form without gemination is used.

It was stated in 3.1.3.3, that the patterns *parras* and *purrus* are complementary in their association with plurality. Although *purrus* is semantically a far less homogeneous category, it seems that its use can be related to the same factors and that its function of underlining plurality can be described in the same terms as the corresponding function of *parras*.

The difference between *parras* and *purrus* is that the latter form can also be used to underline a high degree of salience without plurality. This is most evident in its function of denoting salient bodily characteristics. This function of *purrus*, and its predominance over the simple adjective in such contexts, is also motivated by the salient nature of the qualities involved. On the basis of this, we can explain the two functions of *purrus* as different manifestations of a single function, namely, to underline the salience which is inherent in the meaning of the adjective in combination with that of the substantive which it qualifies. Just as in the case of *parras*, the difference between *purrus* and *parVs* lies in the fact that *purrus* makes these aspects explicit, whereas *parVs* leaves them unexpressed. Therefore, the use of *purrus* is redundant and optional and does not add any notion which is extrinsic to the meaning of the word group.

The following characteristics of *purrus* can be accounted for on the basis of this description. First of all, it explains the range of entities that are typically qualified by *purrus* forms. These include first and foremost animate, mostly human, beings. They occupy the top position in the salience hierarchy, cf. Comrie 1981: 178ff; Wallace 1982: 211ff. It does not seem to make much difference whether they are singular or plural. The clearest instances of this tendency are the *purrus* forms for salient characteristics and proper names discussed in 10.6.2 and 10.6.3, which by definition refer to animate beings.

The second kind of entity which is often qualified by *purrus* forms are body parts, especially those which normally occur in pairs. Since body parts rank high in the salience hierarchy, the combination of salience and plurality enhances the tendency to use a *purrus* form in such a context. Moreover, the borderline between qualifications of persons and of body parts is blurred by the fact that most words referring to bodily aspects of people can also be used to refer to a specific part of the body to which the characteristic in question applies. For instance, "blind" can be said of the eyes, but also of the person in question; if a person's feet are crippled, he can be called "crippled" himself, too, etc.

In *purrus* forms which qualify body parts occurring in pairs (eyes, ears, hands, feet, etc.) or regularly in the plural (fingers and toes) plurality (or duality) and salience go hand in hand. This makes such word groups into the most frequent ones to contain *purrus* forms. The same words are also often qualified by the *parras* forms of 3.1.3. The following list is a selection of examples, which could easily be added to:

A. Dual body parts:

Buttocks (*qinnu*): *nuppuhu* "bloated" or "inflamed", *šuhhutu* "?";

Cheeks (*lētu*): *quddudu* "sunken", *turrupu* "dotted, speckled", (*usukku*): *nuššu* "shaken" (?), *ṣurrupu* "red";

Ears (*uznu*): *huzzumu* "shrivelled", *kuppuṣu* "curled", *sukkuku* "deaf", *šuttuqu* "split", *uppuqu* "massive";

Eyes (*īnu*): *bulluṣu* "staring", *(h)ummuru* "inflamed" (?), *nuppuhu* "bloated" or "inflamed", *puhhuru* "close together", *purrudu* "frightened", *ṣuhhutu* "?", *ṣudduru* "squinting?", *ubbuṭu* "blind", *uppû* "dim", *uppuqu* "massive", *urrupu* "dark", *(w)uššuru* "loose";

Feet (*šēpu*): *hummuru* "crippled", *kubbulu* "lame", *kunnunu* "twisted", *kuppupu* "bent, curved", *muqqutu* "limp", *nuppuhu* "bloated" or "inflamed", *pussulu* "twisted", *tubbuku* "limp", *ubbuṭu* "paralyzed", *ussulu* "lame";

Forearms (*ammatu*): *bullulu* "variegated";

Hands (*qātu*): *ussulu* "lame";

Horns (of the moon) (*qarnu*): *kunnu* "stable", *turruku* "dark", *uddudu* "pointed", *zu"uru* "twisted";

Jaws (*isu*): *nuššu* "shaken" (?), *surru* "loose" (?);

Kidneys (*kalîtu*): *tukkupu* "speckled";

Knees (*birku*): *(w)uššuru* "loose";

Nostrils (*nahīru*): *šummuṭu* "pointed".

B. Body parts occurring in greater number than two (usually dual in form, cf. GAG § 61c):

Fingers (or finger tips) and toes (*ubānu*): *huddudu* "incised", *hullû* "shining", *kummudu* "?", *kuppupu* "bent, curved", *quddumu* "?", *šummuṭu* "pointed", *šuttuqu* "split", *urruru* "withered";

Nails (*ṣupru*): *quddumu* "?", *sullutu* "split", *tukkupu* "speckled", *turrupu* "dotted, speckled", *urruru* "withered";
Teeth (*šinnu*): *nuššu* "shaken" (or: "loose"?), *unnušu* "weak".

C. The words for "face", which are pluralia tantum:

Face (*pānū* or *zīmū*): *quddudu* "sunken"; *ṣurrupu* "red"; *ukkulu* "dark"; *urrupu* "dark".

Other *purrus* forms which qualify body parts in the plural or dual come from D-stems associated with plurality, cf. App. to Chapter VI sv *hamāṣu* **2.** (eyes), *kasû* **1./2.** (arms), *kaṣāru* **2.** (hands, feet), *letû* **1.** (heels), *mesû* **1.** (arms), *palāšu* **1.** (hands) and *šebēru* **1.** (teeth).

Thirdly, other entities than animate beings and body parts are more rarely qualified by lexical *purrus* forms, unless they are plural.

The salience of the quality itself is also an important factor which influences the use or non-use of a *purrus* form. There is a correlation between the proportional frequency of the *purrus* form and the salience of the quality that it expresses: salient qualities, i.e., those which can be observed directly by the senses, especially the eyes, are more often expressed by *purrus* than qualities of a more abstract nature.

This is most evident in the *purrus* forms for salient bodily characteristics, in which the tendency to use a *purrus* form is so strong that the corresponding simple adjectives are much more infrequent than the *purrus* form. But other adjectives, which denote less striking, more "normal", but still salient qualities, are also relatively frequently expressed by *purrus* forms; cf. such forms as *burrumu* "multicoloured", *duššupu* "sweet", *kupputu* "compact", *ukkulu* "dark", *dunnunu* "strong" and the "pseudo-*purrus* form" (cf. 10.7.1.2 sv) *du'ummu* or *du'ūmu* "dark". Another group of salient adjectives are those which denote dimensions; as noted in 3.1.3, they use *parras* instead of *purrus*, and therefore are not mentioned here.

On the other hand, many of the more abstract adjectives are only rarely used in the *purrus* form, cf., for instance, *eššu* "new", *kīnu* "true, firm, etc.", *šalmu* "in good condition", *ṭābu* "good", *(w)atru* "additional, superfluous". They are mainly or only used as inflectional *purrus* forms. The *purrus* forms *dummuqu* "good" and *lummunu* "bad" are rather common, but still rare as compared to the extremely frequent simple forms *damqu* and *lemnu*, and restricted to a small number of uses (cf. 10.10). An exception to this correlation between the salience of the quality and the frequency of *purrus* is *qurrubu* "near, close", which is atypical in many respects (cf. 10.10).

The second phenomenon which can be explained on the basis of the description of the function of *purrus* given above is that we only find contrasting pairs of *purrus* and *parVs* which also differ in some other respect (typically a singular versus a plural subject), and no contrasting pairs which are otherwise identical: such pairs would be semantically equivalent instead of contrastive. The same state of affairs was found in contrasting pairs of D-stems of transitive verbs, cf. 6.7.1.

Thirdly, the semantic extension of which the geminate is an iconic reflection is immanent, not contingent on the view of the speaker. Therefore, it is not possible to differentiate by means of *purrus* between degrees of the quality expressed; in other words, it cannot be used to indicate a higher degree than the simple adjective. In order to convey such a notion Akkadian has recourse to adverbs such as *mādiš* and *magal* "very". This explains why we also find these adverbs with *purrus* forms, apparently without causing a pleonasm, for instance *mādiš lupput*, said of the extispicies (ARM 27, 112: 9), *mādiš dummuq*, said of a message (*ib.* 26/1 p. 536 no. 256: 13), *mādiš dunnun*, said of a letter (AbB 9, 237: 19), *magal du'ūmat* (ACh. Spl. 8: 21 = (52)), etc. It also explains why Akkadian does not consistently use the *purrus* form for the expression of the comparative "stronger than": we find both *purrus* forms and simple adjectives before *eli*; cf., for instance, the use of *da'mu eli* in ACh. Spl. 8: 23 = (52), but *du'ummu eli* in the same protasis in ACh. 2. Spl. 3: 40 (cf. 10.7.1.2 sv); *guššur e[li* in SAA 3, 2: 24, versus RA 75, 111: VII 14 *ga-aš-ra-at el kala ilātim šī* "she (Ištar) is the most powerful of all goddesses."[29] The presence of *eli* in a clause seems to have no influence on whether a form with or without gemination is preferred.

Thus the relationship between *purrus* and *parVs* is fundamentally different from relationships which at first sight may seem similar to it, such as the grades of comparison in Indo-European languages, in which most adjectives have a comparative and a superlative, the latter often with "elative" meaning, e.g., Latin *altus* - *altior* - *altissimus* "high - higher - highest or very high". Such grades of comparison are inflectional categories with a regular semantic relationship. In Latin, for instance, if it is possible to say *vir notus* "a famous man", it is normally also possible to say *vir notissimus* "a very famous man". Whether a speaker of Latin prefers to call someone *notus* or *notissimus*, depends on his subjective assessment of that person's fame, but if he uses *notissimus*, he refers to a larger amount of fame, on average, than if he uses *notus*.

The situation in Akkadian is quite different. For some adjectives a speaker of Akkadian can also choose between a simple form and a *purrus* form, but his choice is determined by some inherent quality of the adjective, the substantive which is qualified, or both: if these belong to a certain semantic class, and/or are plural, he can use the *purrus* form to underline the semantic nature of the word group in question, or he can omit this and prefer the simple form. In both cases the situation referred to is essentially the same. Therefore he has a different kind of choice to make. This choice is in general only applicable for a specific class of adjectives, basically those which have a more or less concrete, salient meaning.

An illustration of the typical situation in Akkadian is offered by the use of the adjective *dannu* "strong, powerful, severe, difficult" in the expression *šarru dannu* "mighty king", a ubiquitous epithet of kings in RIs from OAk onwards (cf. CAD sv *dannu* 3b). If there were a regular relationship between an intensive category *purrus* and a neutral category *parVs*, we would expect to find at least some instances of **šarru dunnunu* "very mighty king". This expression, however, is never used.[30] The only explanation can be that *dunnunu* does not simply denote a high degree of *dannu*, but that it has its own individual range of uses, which does not necessarily coincide with that of *dannu*. This is confirmed by the actual use of *dunnunu*, as presented in 10.6.1.2.1.

In this particular case, we may venture an explanation for the absence of **šarru dunnunu*: the adjective *dannu* presumably refers to the political power of the king, not to his physical strength. It would be quite in accordance with the general meaning of *purrus* to claim that *dunnunu*, said of persons, refers to a salient, i.e., visible feature of the person qualified, such as his physical strength or the impression of strength he makes. The evidence available is far too meagre for any definite conclusion, but it may be significant that the only OB instance of *dunnunu* referring to a single person seems to convey precisely this nuance:

(64) AbB 12, 32: 20 sag.geme$_2$ *šubarîta ša du-un-nu-na-at u ṣehret ša ubbalū šāmam* "buy me a Subarian slave girl - one that is *dunnunat* and young - that they have available" (lit. "bring").

Dunnunat clearly refers to physical strength here, but it would seem that an intensive translation "very strong" is inappropriate, since it is somewhat contradictory with "young"; the appropriate nuance seems to be rather "that is visibly strong", "that strikes one as being strong".

10.10. The shift from lexical to inflectional

A final point to be discussed is the historical development which is observable in the use of *purrus* between the older periods of Akkadian on the one hand (OAk, OB, OA), and the later periods (from MB and MA onwards) on the other. There are a number of indications which suggest that in the course of the attested history of Akkadian the lexical function of *purrus* gradually declines in favour of its inflectional function. In other words, from a nominal, adjectival category, it becomes more and more a deverbal category, whose use is dependent on the corresponding verbal D-stem.

These indications are the following. As already stated in 10.7, the most typical and most unambiguous representatives of the lexical function of *purrus* are found in OAk, OB and OA. These include first of all the *purrus* names discussed in 10.6.3. It was shown there that they are especially common in OAk and OB and become far less frequent in later periods, although some of them continue to be used.

Second, some of the *purrus* forms which qualify metals in OA (cf. 10.6.1.2.4) are also typically lexical, especially *dammuqum* "of fine quality", and *lammunum* and *massuhum* "of bad quality", all referring to copper. They cannot be explained as inflectional, i.e., as VAs of the D-stem, as is sometimes claimed: *dammuqum* cannot mean "refined" since it is opposed to *lammunum*, cf. 10.6.1.2.4 sv and Dercksen 1996: 35ff.

The third indication is the fact that some common *purrus* forms appear in OB in contexts which suggest that they represent the lexical function of *purrus*, whereas later on they are found as clear instances of its inflectional function. The clearest case is that of *qurrubu* "near, close". Other *purrus* forms which merit discussion in this context are *dummuqu* "good", *dunnunu* "strong", *lummunu* "bad" and *ṣuhhuru* "small":

Qurrubu "near, close" is a highly atypical *purrus* form in that it does not denote a salient or inherent characteristic of the entity it qualifies, but its spatial or temporal relation to another entity. It is mainly found in OB and MA letters. In the latter period it clearly serves as a resultative stative of *qurrubu* "to bring near, to present", cf., for instance:

(65) KAV 108: 12f (textiles) *ša ana šarri qar-ru-bu-ú-ni* "which have been presented to the king";

(66) MVAeG 41/3, 66: 49 *naptunu qar-ru-ub* "the meal has been served".[31]

This use contrasts with the use of *qurrubu* in OB letters, where it is rather common (the dictionaries do not list any OA instances). Its usual meaning is "near, close", without the implication of a verbal action of "bringing near" or "presenting". A few typical examples are:

(67) AbB 2, 151: 10 *ipiš nikkas namriātim qú-ur-ru-ub* "the accounting for the fattened animals is near" (tr. CAD sv *namriātu* 2) (cf. *ib.* 179: 10 (same sender and receiver) *nikkas namriātim qé-ru-ub*);

(68) *ib.* 13, 153: 16 *šumma kaspum lā qú-ur-ru-ba-ak-ku* "if the silver is not available to you";

(69) *ib.* 3, 18: 17 *bīssa ana bītija qú-ru-ub* "her household is close to my household";

(70) JCS 42, 144: 15ff [*m*]*ātkāma kīl u ana GN lū qú-ur-ru-ba-at* "Keep just your militia and stay close to GN" (tr. Eidem), cf. also *ib.* 140: 14'f;

(71) AbB 7, 64: 9 *alākī qù-ru-ub* "my departure is imminent".[32]

In these cases an interpretation as a pure state, and therefore a lexical *purrus* form seems preferable, although it cannot be decided with certainty. Ambiguous cases are:

(72) AbB 7, 60: 10 *še'um ša* ugula mar.tu *ana mahriki qù-ru-ub* "the barley of the general has been forwarded to you", or "is available to you";

(73) AbB 11, 94: 9 *kanīku lū qú-ur-ru-um-ma* "even if a sealed document is submitted", or: "available"); cf. also YOS 8, 71: 13.

None of these cases is as convincing as the MA ones quoted above. The usual meaning of *qurrub* in OB seems to be simply "near, close". After OB, this use of *qurrub* is rare: the dictionaries list only three SB instances, probably stereotyped survivals of OB usage:

(74) AfO 17, 85: 9 *attalû qur-ru-ub* (beside *qit-ru-ub* in the same line) "an eclipse is imminent";

(75) *ib.* 12 *halāqšu qur-ru-ub* "its (Babylon's) destruction is imminent";

(76) BBS 3: IV 22ff PN_1 (..) *ana ahhūti ana* PN_2 *ul qu-ur-ru-ub* "PN_1 was not in a brotherhood relation to PN_2" (tr. CAD sv *qerēbu* 12).

Although the evidence is too meagre to be conclusive, these examples may suggest that there was a shift in the use of the stative *qurrub* after the OB period.

Dummuqu "good", although very rare as compared to the ubiquitous *damqu,* is also rather common in OB letters, usually in stock phrases, one of which (77) is clearly ironic:

(77) AbB 12, 121: 5 *ša tēpušanni du-um-mu-qá-at* "what you have done to me is just fine" (tr. Van Soldt); cf. the same phrase with G in 164: 5 and 166: 5;

(78) AbB 6, 220: 36 *epēška du-um-mu-qá-am lušme* "may I hear your good action(s)";

(79) AbB 7, 167: 25 *dabābam du-um-mu-qá-am ittišu dubub* "have a friendly talk with him"; also *ib.* 8 and 10, 181: 18; cf. the same phrase with G in 9, 169: 13.

On the basis of the context these *purrus* forms can be regarded as pure adjectives rather than as VAs of *dummuqu* "to make good". As was stated above, this also applies to *dammuqum* in OA. After OB *dummuqu* becomes very rare: three instances are known from literary texts, two of which are plural (see App.), to be explained according to 10.7.2 and/or 10.6.1.2.1?

Dunnunu "strong" is also a typically OB *purrus* form. It was discussed in 10.6.1.2.1. Its use in SB is largely restricted to a small range of use: in RIs it is said of (parts of) buildings, in extispicy omens of parts of the liver. These instances can also be explained as stereotyped survivals from OB usage.

Lummunu "bad, evil, unfortunate" occurs as a lexical *purrus* form in OA qualifying copper, cf. 10.6.1.2.4. Apart from the combination with *libbu,* based on the expression *libba lummunu* "to make sb angry or worried" (cf. 10.4.2), it is found almost exclusively in SB in a few fixed meanings: "unfortunate, miserable" (of persons, perhaps also "ill-tempered"), "dim, obscured" of celestial bodies in astronomical omens, and "unpropitious" of signs, omens and similar phenomena. The simple form *lemnu* is mostly said of enemies, other dangerous persons and entities, and of abstract nouns, meaning "evil, dangerous" etc., cf. CAD sv 1a/b/d; it only interchanges with *lummunu,* if it is said of omens (*ib.* 1c). Thus there is a large degree of differentiation between the two forms, and *lummunu* is restricted to a few specific contexts.

Ṣuhhuru "small" is even more remarkable in the degree to which it is stereotyped in SB. In OB and OA it is only attested as stative of *ṣuhhuru* in its technical meaning of "to deduct", cf. 10.4.2. In these dialects it is the *parras* form of this adjective which has the function normally performed by *purrus* forms, cf. 3.1.3.1 sv and 3.1.3.3. After the OB and OA period, *ṣuhhuru* also appears in other meanings, but with a very restricted range of subjects: it is said of (parts of) buildings in RIs ("(too) small"), and of celestial bodies in astronomical omens ("small(er than usual")), apart from a single instance in which it qualifies a pustule (*zihhu*) on the liver (cf. note 22). It is never used in the most common meaning of *ṣehru,* i.e., "young", said of animate beings.

The impression gained from the very frequent use of *purrus* in SB, and its use in other texts from MB and MA onwards, is that it can mostly be explained as inflectional, or else it is found in those kinds of texts which were examined in 10.7, viz., omens and literary texts. The relatively unpredictable and stereotyped nature of the *purrus* forms found in these texts suggests that they form an unproductive category of residual cases, which have survived because of their more or less technical meaning. Unambiguous instances of lexical *purrus* forms, such as those found in OAk, OB and OA, are difficult to find in SB.

Although the evidence gathered here is by no means conclusive, one may venture the hypothesis that in later Akkadian *purrus* is more dependent on the verbal D-stem than in the early period. If this is correct, it shows the gradual incorporation of *purrus* into the verbal paradigm of the D-stem, and therefore its continuous grammaticalization: starting as a purely nominal form with an expressive origin, it ends up as a mainly grammatical form whose use is dependent on the verbal D-stem.[33]

This process runs parallel to the one noted in 10.7, the lexicalization of originally iconic *purrus* forms. Just as some *purrus* forms are grammaticalized, others are lexicalized: they acquire a specialized meaning, no longer contrast with the simple adjective, and lose their iconic character.

Whether this claim about the historical development of *purrus* is correct or not, the attested *purrus* forms cover the whole range from clearly expressive in those used to refer to salient bodily characteristics (cf. 10.6.2 and 10.6.3) to grammatical in those which have become statives and VAs of the D-stem.

10.11. Conclusions

In order to describe the overall use of the pattern *purrus,* two distinctions have been made in the course of this chapter, first, that between inflectional and lexical *purrus* forms, and, second, that between lexical *purrus* forms which are "typical" in that their use can be explained on the basis of the iconic nature of gemination, and those which cannot be so explained. It was also claimed that the former category represents the most original kind, whereas the latter kind has been subject to a process of lexicalization and the concomitant erosion of its iconic nature.

Both distinctions are rather problematic, the first one, because only in favourable circumstances is it possible to classify a given *purrus* form as inflectional or lexical; the second one, because it is based on criteria which are conflicting and subjective, and because the two kinds involved cannot be defined rigorously. Therefore, they often do not allow us to decide to which kind a given *purrus* form belongs, either. It could be objected, then, that they raise as many problems as they are meant to solve.

However, it should be emphasized that these distinctions are not aimed at a practical classification of every individual *purrus* form that is found in Akkadian. Their purpose is only to bring at least some order in the extremely varied use of *purrus* and to demonstrate that among the members of the pattern *purrus* three different types are discernible: *purrus* forms which are inflectional, and those which are not inflectional, and among the latter type some which can and some which cannot be plausibly explained on the basis of the iconic nature of gemination. To which type a specific *purrus* form belongs is of secondary importance. Therefore, the fact that only a small part of them can be classified with certainty does not detract from the importance and the theoretical basis of these distinctions.

Moreover, they are based on the historical development which is observable in the use of *purrus* in the course of the history of Akkadian. The problematical nature of this pattern is caused by the fact that it takes an intermediate position between an inflectional category, the use of which is determined by a grammatical rule, and a derivational category which comprises a number of more or less independent words, of which the meanings and the ways in which they are used are unpredictable.

Ultimately, it is only in a historical perspective that we can see the unity of the pattern as a whole: only the processes of grammaticalization and lexicalization enable us to find the common element in the various uses of *purrus*.

Notes to Chapter Ten

1 Strictly speaking the designation *purrus* only applies to Babylonian; Assyrian has *parrus* instead, which is generally assumed to be the older form (Kuryłowicz 1972: 50; Moscati 1969: 156; Kienast 1957a: 108; Reiner 1966: 75). In accordance with general usage, and because Babylonian offers far more *purrus* forms than Assyrian, I will refer to the pattern as a whole as *purrus*; forms which occur only in Assyrian will be preceded by an asterisk, as in CAD.

2 The use of the term "lexical" here, rather than the more common term "derivational", as opposed to "inflectional", follows Matthews 1991, Chapter IV: "Lexical Derivation".

3 The infinitive *purrusu* is basically an abstract verbal noun with a specialized function; this verbal noun is a substantivation of *purrus* used as a (verbal) adjective. The use of adjectives as abstract nouns without any formal change is a widespread phenomenon in Semitic, cf. Kuryłowicz 1972: 94.

4 In contrast to the basic function of *purrus*, i.e., denoting states and qualities, there is a small number of *purrus* forms which seem to denote activities rather than states. This concerns the following words (for references and other uses of the forms quoted here, see the Appendix to this chapter): *dubbubu* "talking (nonsense)"; *gunnuṣu* "constantly wrinkling the nose"; *hussusu* "worrying"; *nurruṭu* "quivering"; *nu''uru* "roaring"; *nuzzumu* "constantly complaining"; *ruttutu* "trembling"; *sukkulu* "ravening" (name of a dog of Marduk); *ṣuhhu* "laughing, smiling"; *ṣu''udu* "whirling", *turruru* "trembling" and *ukkumu* "rapacious" (name of a dog of Marduk). They are all extremely rare and some of the translations given are by no means certain. The adjectives *dubbubu* and *hussusu* must be distinguished from the statives *dubbub* and *hussus* of the common D-stems *dubbubu* "to complain, harass" and *hussusu* "to remind" (of which *hussus* is not attested according to the dictionaries, but this is doubtless accidental).

Most of these *purrus* forms come from verbs which are basically atelic and do not have a stative of the G-stem, such as those of Type II, listed in 7.6. Instead of these *purrus* forms we would rather expect the agentive pattern of the D-stem (*muparris*) for the expression of these notions; in some cases this is actually attested alongside the *purrus* form: beside *gunnuṣu* and *nu''uru* we also find *mugannisu* and *muna''iru*, cf. 7.6.2 and 7.6.1 ssvv. On the other hand, they are typical *purrus* forms in that they refer to rather salient activities, and that some of them have the negative connotation which is characteristic of some types of *purrus* forms (cf. 10.6.2).

The fact that the usual function of *purrus* is to denote states and qualities suggests that these words denote habitual activities which are viewed as characteristic properties; for instance, the nuance expressed by *nuzzumu* is perhaps comparable to that of English *querulous* as opposed to "(constantly) complaining".

5 I.e., that it denotes an event which is telic (bound, terminative). Atelic verbs, which denote processes or actions without a natural endpoint (cf. Binnick 1991: 189f), e.g., Akkadian *ṣullû* "to pray" and *qu''û* "to wait for", usually lack a stative.

6 *Muhhû* "ecstatic" refers to a kind of priest, cf. CAD sv. This form and its fem. *muhhūtu* occur only in OB, beside the simple form *mahû* (MSL 12, 194 C 3: 14 *ma-hu-ú-um* and TCS 1, 369: 5 *mah-im* (i.e. */mah'im/*, an OAk form which proves that there is no geminate in this word)). *Muhhû* is later replaced by *mahhû*, fem. *mahhītu*. This replacement is motivated by the fact that *muhhû* is semantically irregular with-

in the category of *purrus* forms, because it came to denote a profession, i.e., an activity, whereas *purrus* normally denotes salient bodily characteristics, i.e., qualities (see 10.6.2). The introduction of *mahhû*, fem. *mahhîtu* is caused by a tendency to remove this irregularity, because *parrû* represents the normal pattern for agent nouns of roots with a weak third radical. This process has left a clear trace in the fem. form *mahhūtu* (cf. CAD sv *muhhūtu*), which is a blend of the old and the new form. It is possible that the general decline which is observable in the lexical function of *purrus* after the OB period (cf. 10.10) also plays a role in this replacement.

7 It is remarkable that in this verb the stative/VA is always D, wheras no other D forms are attested, cf. CAD sv *qâpu* B. Possibly, this is caused by a wish to avoid homonymy with the VA *qīpu* "trustworthy" of the verb *qâpu* "to believe, to entrust", with its frequent derivation *qīpu* "official".

8 Kupper's translation seems to be more natural than Durand's of almost the same phrase in ARM 26/1 p. 580 no. 280: 17 "La ville va bien, mes gens d'armes ont été renforcés." A completely ambiguous context is *ib.* p. 426 no. 199: 27f *maṣṣārātūki eli ša panānum lū du-un-nu-na* "Les gardes que tu as à monter doivent être plus fortes qu'auparavant." (Durand).

9 This chronological difference between *libbi* PN *ṭāb* and *libbi* PN *ṭūb* can also be deduced from a perusal of the OB contracts from Sippar which are being published in chronological order by L. Dekiere, of which the first four parts are available so far (OBRED 1-4). *Libbi* PN *ṭūb* is the older expression: its earliest occurrence is in OBRED 1, 3: 10, a document dating from the reign of Iluma-ila of Sippar, who is, according to Edzard 1957: 129, a contemporary of Sumu-abum (1894-1881) or Sumu-la-el (1880-1845) of the First Dynasty of Babylon (dates according to Brinkman *apud* Oppenheim 1964: 337). Its latest occurrence (OBRED 1, 104: 7) is from an undated document from the reign of Sin-muballiṭ (1812-1793). The earliest case of *libbi* PN *ṭāb* is OBRED 1, 46: 9 from the 13th year of Sabium (1844-1831); the latest dated one in OBRED 1-4 is OBRED 3, 449: 18 from the 28th year of Samsuiluna (1749-1712), but there can be little doubt that it continues in use as the current form. This shows that in Sippar only *ṭūb* was used in this expression initially, that it came to be rivalled by *ṭāb* sometime in the middle of the 18th century BC, and was ultimately replaced by it.

10 A verb which shows a similar behaviour is *zakû*, which is used in the same context as *elēlu* in (16) and (17), cf. CAD sv *zakû* v. 2c-3' (from Ugarit: = PRU 3, 110a: 1ff; 107b: 1ff; 111a: 9ff). Compare also the use of the stative D *zukku* in (07), quoted in 10.4, and TCL 17, 1: 18, on the one hand, and the use of the stative and adjective *zaku/zakû* with barley, on the other (TCL 17, 2: 28; ARM 6, 37: 4; OBTR 88: 9; MSL 1, 88: 38). A comparable case is also the alternation of Or. 56, 246: 20 *pānūša sa-ah-ru* and *ib.* 247: 30 *pānūša su-uh-hu-ru*, cf. 7.5.3 sv.

11 Five of them are OB; they are all quoted in this section; the only SB instance (Sg. 8: 387) is quoted as (47) in 10.6.1.2.3. The last one (OA: ICK 1, 65: 6, quoted in CAD sv *malû* v. 9b) is problematic and will not be discussed here.

12 Unclear to me is Or. 40, 140: 10' *guhšâ lā qu-ut-ta-a*. On the other hand, in CT 38, 12: 72 *šumma epēš bīti qú-ut-tu-ma* "if the building of the house is finished", *quttu* does not seem to differ from *qati*.

13 The claim of CAD sv *labāšu* 3b-1' (p. 20a) that this instance of *lubbuš* has to do with plurality is very unlikely; first of all, nowhere else is *labāšu* D associated with plurality (see, however, 10.6.1.2.3 for some other unique instances), and, second, both subjects are completely equivalent in being grammatically singular (collective), but logically plural. It seems unlikely that this would lead to a differentiation in the verb forms on the basis of plurality.

14 The translations of the editors of Mari texts waver between "mauvais" (e.g., ARM 10, 87: 7 (Dossin), 14, 86: 34 (Birot), 26/2 p. 416 no. 479: 28 (Lackenbacher)), "très mauvais" (e.g., 26/1 p. 316 no. 152: 11 (Durand), 27, 22: 8 (Birot)) and "trop mauvais" (26/1 p. 323 no. 156: 32 (Durand)), but this seems rather based on the traditional view that *purrus* is intensive, than on indications inferred from the context. In the passage quoted here as (33) *lupputā* is contrasted with *šalmā* in such a way that at least in this case an intensive meaning seems excluded. See 10.8 on this problem in general.

15 The intransitive use of normally transitive verbs is not uncommon in the technical language of omen texts, cf. note 8 to Ch. V.

16 Cf. also KUB 4, 73b: 2 *šumma manzāzu adi 4-šu pu-uš-šu-uṭ*, where the meaning of *puššuṭ* is, however, unclear (lit. "erased", cf. App. to Ch. VI sv). Elsewhere only the stative G is attested in omen protases (AHw sv G 2a/b: "ist eingeschnürt und unsichtbar?").

17 Jeyes translates *palšat* and *pullušat* with "exposed" and "thoroughly exposed", respectively (from *palāsu* "to see" ?), apparently regarding the latter form as intensive, about which see 10.8. Her emendation *kalītum* <*ša*> zag in 17' is superfluous, since *ša* is also absent in lines 20/23 (for *imittam* as an adverb of place, see CAD sv *imitta*); the tablet is, however, written rather carelessly. Since the expected omen for the left side corresponding to 17' is lacking, an alternative might be to emend to *šumma kalītum* zag <*u* gùb> *pullušat* "if the kidney is perforated on the right and the left side", so that lines 15'ff form a triplet similar to those discussed in 10.6.1.1.1 and 10.6.1.1.2.

18 This does not apply, however, to the use of *duššu* as stative of *duššû* "to provide abundantly with", e.g., CT 16, 14: IV 31 and SBH p. 60 no. 31: 8 (CAD lists these two instances under *duššû* adj., but they doubtless belong to the comparable expressions listed under *dešû* v. 2 (correctly AHw sv *dešû* D 3)).

19 Another instance may be *ammurum* which is said of silver, and is derived by AHw sv from *amāru* D "(Metall) prüfen?": "etwa 'geprüft'", together with the verb form *ú-mì-ru-ú* (CCT 4, 34c: 11); cf. also Dercksen 1996: 164 note 512 and Sturm, Ugarit-Forschungen 27, 487ff. The verb form is derived from another verb *amāru* "to pile up" by Veenhof 1972: 391. AHw also lists *lakkû* "eine geringe Silberqualität", but this is rather a VA of *leqû* "to take, receive", cf. App. to Ch. VI sv.

20 Unless *ruššû* is a byform of *huššû* "red" which is a Sumerian loanword (huš). Lieberman (1977: 317 no. 334) regards both *ruššû* and *huššû* as going back to Sumerian huš. However, the evidence for Sumerian *r* interchanging with *h* is weak, cf. Sjöberg, ZA 65, 218 *ad* l. 50 (cf. also šu.hu.uz and šu.ru.uz, cf. CAD sv *šabābu* A lex. sect., which is, however, a loan from Akkadian ((*išāta*) *šūhuzu* "to kindle a fire".

21 Cf. CAD sv *balāṭu* v. 6a-4'; AHw sv *bulluṭu* ("z(um T(eil) Kurzn(ahme)?"), *puhhuru* 1, *šullumu* and *tukkulu* (with a question mark).

22 For some reason, this small mark on the liver has a striking preference for being qualified by *purrus* forms, some of which are hardly attested anywhere else; apart from *nurrubu*, this applies to *duqququ* "tiny", *ruqququ* "thin", *ṣullumu* "black" and *ṣurrušu* "branching". Less uncommon are *dunnunu* "hard", *ṣuhhuru* "small" and *zuqqutu* "pointed". Some other *purrus* forms with which it is also combined include *ruššuku* "dry", *šukkusu* "dry", *lu''û* "dirty" and *ṣullulu* "covered", but these do not occur as simple adjectives.

23 Ambiguous spellings without *-um-* or *-ú-* are ACh. 2. Spl. 3: 36. 39f *du-'u-mat*, TDP 138: 11 *du-'u-mat* (but *ib.* 12f *du-'-ú-mat/mu*), TBP 38a: r.20 *du-'u-mu-ti*, Proto-Diri 44b/45 $^{ku.uk.ku}$MI.MI = *du-hu-mu-um, da-a'-mu-um* (cf. Diri I 257 *du-'-ú-m[u]*) (quoted CAD sv lex. sect.).

24 There is still a third form of the same root: *da'ummu* in LL: sa = *da-hum-mu*, quoted CAD sv. More frequent are the derived adverb *da'ummiš* and the substantive *da'ummatu* "darkness" (cf. CAD and AHw ssvv). Whether *da'ummu* is a "Steigerungsadj. mit numinosem Bedeutungsgehalt" and means "unheimlich dunkel", as GAG § 55p claims on the basis of the meaning of other members of the pattern *paruss*, remains unverifiable.

25 Cf. TDP 100/2: 9ff; 104: 25ff; 108: 7ff; 120: 35ff; 136: 54ff; 138: 72f/1ff; slightly different is 54: 1f [*peṣi*], *ṣalim*, [...], *du-'-um*. There are no syllabic writings of *da'mu* in TDP, but occasionally its ideogram mud occurs (114: 40f; 118: 20; 120: 32, qualifying *damu* "blood").

26 It is implicit in the discussion of *nuppuh* in 10.6.1.2.1, that the spelling NE-ÚH, mostly found in the medical texts of TDP, and interpreted as *nuppuh* by CAD sv *napāhu* 7, represents a word or expression different from *nuppuhu*. This follows from the following considerations. First, in some texts it is found beside the normal ideogram for *napāhu*, sar (cf. TDP 24: 61f vs. 26: 68 (both from MLC 2639, published in JCS 2, 305/8), 112: 18'f and 30' vs. 116: 2 (both from A.3506), and 156: 10 vs. 162: 58 (both from K.3962); this suggests that they stand for different words. A second and more important reason is that NE-ÚH is generally used with other subjects than *nuppuhu* and *naphu*. The latter words usually have body parts as subjects (see 10.6.1.2.1 and CAD sv *napāhu* 3, 7 and 12); NE-ÚH, on the other hand, usually qualifies the patient himself (TDP 96: 23/7; 96: 36 + 234: 26; 156: 10; 232: 15; SpTU 1, 34: 26; 37: 18), sometimes with an adjunct accusative specifying a body part, or consisting of the word "body" (TDP 26: 67; 24: 61f); in 212: 8 "body" itself seems to be subject. Assuming that it is possible to use ÚH as a phonetic complement, a possible reading of NE-ÚH would be *ṣurruh* "hot, feverish" from *ṣarāhu* "to heat, scorch", cf. CAD sv *ṣ*. A, which in the stative G and the N-stem is used for "to be(come) hot, feverish", cf. *ib.* 2 and 4, and has NE as an ideogram, cf. *ib.* lex. sect. To my knowledge, however, syllabic spellings of *ṣurruh* have not been found so far.

27 A number of other instances look promising at first sight, but turn out to fail to meet the condition that the two contrasting protases should differ only in having *purrus* versus *parVs*. In some of these one of the protases has an additional stipulation (e.g., SAA 8, 257: 6f vs. 8f; Izbu 95: 69'f; 134: 47' and 49'; TDP 122: 2/6 vs. 7; 136: 65f) or contains an ambiguous ideographic spelling (e.g., TDP same instances). For the absence of TDP 96: 36 + 234: 26 with NE-ÚH and *na-pi-ih* side by side, see note 26. In CT 31, 45: 7/12 we find tag-*it* (= *lapit*) and tag.meš (= *lupput*) side by side qualifying the *kunukku*, but the apodoses are broken off. There are also some instances which meet all the conditions required but occur in different texts (e.g., YOS 10, 41: 26 vs. RA 67, 44: 71' (*paṭer* and *puṭṭur*), TDP 50: IV 9 vs. Syria 33, 125: 7 (*kuppup* and *kapip*), *ib.* 6 and TDP 20: 23 (*suhhur* and *sahir*, quoted in 10.7.1.2 sv *suhhuru*).

28 The other omens with *eddā* and *uddudā* of SAA 8 (see the glossary sv *edēdu*) also have very similar apodoses: compare 389: r.1 with (62A/B), and compare 505: 5f with (63A/B). Cf. also 257: 6f (same protasis with *ud-du-da*) and 8f (idem with *ed-da*, but with the addition of zalág.meš to *eddā*, which destroys the parallelism, see note 27. The precise contents of the apodosis seem to be of little importance, as long as it is unambiguously favourable or unfavourable.

29 Since Akkadian does not have a grammatical category for the grades of comparison (cf. GAG § 68a), *gašrat eli* should be translated "the most powerful of" or "more powerful than", depending on whether we regard the subject as being one of the set of entities with which it is compared, or as being placed outside this set.

30 The fact that sometimes a need was felt to reinforce and thereby renew this stock phrase is demon-

strated by the occasional use of the reduplicated variant of *dannu* in, for instance, *šar Aššur dan-dannu* (Sn. 127 f 3), *rubû dan-dan-nu* (Ash. § 65: 23), and *dan-na-ku dan-dan-na-ku* (RIMA 2/I, 147: 14).

31 Further KAJ 223: 4; MVAeG 41/3, 64: III 43. Occasionally, it is found in other dialects: LB (CT 49, 156: 12) and SB (SpTU 2, 12: II 8). The NB VA *qu-ru-bé-e-tu*$_4$ (CT 22, 82: 25) is obscure, but possibly motivated by plurality, cf. 10.6.1 and CAD sv *qurrubītu*.

32 Cf. CAD sv *qerēbu* 12. Other OB instances are AbB 6, 212: 12 (subj. *šakān awīlē*); 8, 96: 17 (subj. *šiprum*); 10, 120: 2 (subj. *elūlu*, a festival); 174: 24 (subj. unknown); 12, 182: r.6' (subj. ugula mar.tu); BagM 2, 58: III 17 (subj. *ummānātūka*); ShT p. 81: 70 (subj. *ṣābum*); MHET 1 p. 136 no. 91: 10' (subj. person). In all these expressions the simple stative *qerub* is more common than *qurrub*; in Mari, *qurrub* seems to occur only in ARM 3, 41: 12 (restored), whereas *qerub* is quite common.

33 It is possible that the change in meaning of *gullubu* from "bald", only in OB PNs, to "shaven", elsewhere from OB onwards - for instance in (02B) quoted in 10.2, and as a kind of priest in NB, cf. CAD sv *gullubu* adj. b - and the replacement of *muhhû* "ecstatic" by *mahhû* after the OB period (cf. note 6) are also symptoms of this shift.

APPENDIX TO CHAPTER TEN: List of *purrus* forms

The purpose of this Appendix is twofold. First, it contains the references for all *purrus* forms which have been quoted and discussed in Chapter Ten. Second, it presents a list of *purrus* forms attested in Akkadian, in so far as they are included in the dictionaries. Additional cases that have come to light since the publication of the dictionaries have also been included, but no pretense at completeness is made. The criteria for inclusion and the indications of dialect and period are the same as those followed in Chapter Six, q.v.

In the entries the lexical and inflectional functions of *purrus* have been distinguished as far as this is possible. Usually the inflectional use of a *purrus* form is mentioned first, followed by the verbal D-stem from which it is derived and the section where this D-stem is discussed (if it is discussed at all). Further references are only given, if the *purrus* form is mentioned somewhere in this chapter, if it is not mentioned in the dictionaries, or if it is very rare. Subsequently, the lexical use of a *purrus* form is mentioned, with full references, indications of dialect and period, and related form of the same root, unless the word is so common, and used so uniformly that a general reference to the dictionaries seems to be sufficient. Most *purrus* forms are used in both functions; if a more or less clear-cut distinction can be made, this is indicated by means of **1.** for the inflectional, and **2.** for the lexical function. In most cases, however, such a distinction is not possible, and the various uses have not been strictly separated. All words are listed as (verbal) adjectives, even if only stative forms are attested. LL designates instances only found in lexical lists; note, however, that LL is omitted for instances from the lexical series MSL.

B

***Buddudu** st. of *buddudu* "to waste, squander" → 8.6 sv (NA: ABL 415: r.3).

Buhhusu PN → 10.6.3.2.

Bullû "?" (CAD: mng. uncert.; AHw "zersetzt"), cf. *belû* "to go out" (fire)? **OB**: YOS 10, 31: IX 31. 48 (blood).

Bullulu **1.** st. D of *balālu* "to mix, pollute" → 6.4.5 and 6.8.1 sv; **2.** "spotted, variegated", cf. *ballu* id. (CAD sv 1e) → 10.6.1.2.2, **OB**: Or. 23, 338: 5 (forearms).

Bulluṣu "staring" (eyes), cf. *balāṣu* "to stare, protrude" → 10.6.1.2.2, **SB**: AfO 18, 74a: 27.

Bulluṭu st. of *bulluṭu* "to credit an amount" (OA), cf. *balāṭu* "to live", etc. → 10.4.2. Also PN → 10.6.3.2.

Bunnû 1. "beautiful, of good quality", cf. *banû* id.; **SB**: SpTU 4, 149: III 7f (a woman's breast); BAM 409: 21' (sesame); Racc. 119: 16 (appearance, interpr. uncert.); **2.**: st. of *bunnû* "to adorn, provide" → 10.4.2.

Buqqumu CAD: "person losing his hair(?)", cf. *baqāmu* "to pluck" (wool) → 10.3.2 and 10.6.2, **OB**: MSL 12, 169: 395; "(lamb) ready for plucking" (tr. CAD sv), **SB**: MSL 8/1, 38: C 256f.

Buqquru st. D of *b/paqāru* "to claim, vindicate" (e.g., AbB 1, 58: 16).

Buqqušu PN → 10.6.3.2.

Burru st. D of *bâru* "to stay firm, become certain".

Burrû "hungry", cf. *berû* "to be(come) hungry"; **SB**: BWL 144: 16 (person, cf. note 21 to Ch. VII).

Burrumu "multicoloured", cf. *barmu* id. → 10.3.1, 10.6.2, 10.9, passim, see CAD and AHw sv.

Burruqu CAD: "with reddish face and red hair"; AHw "mit blitzenden Augen", cf. *barāqu* "to flash" (of lightning) → 10.3.3, 10.6.2; **SB**: KUB 37, 31: 3 (face); TBP 25: r. 3 (woman); 6: 41 (subj. broken); BagF. 18, 360: 62 (goat); MSL 12, 229: 11' (person). Also PN → 10.6.3.2.

Burruru "shining"? (but CAD: "with filmy eyes"), cf. *barāru* "to shine, sparkle" → 10.3.3; **OB**: MSL 12, 183: 50 (eyes); **SB**: BRM 4, 23: 16 (spots (on the body), var. of *burrumu* (error?)). Also PN → 10.6.3.2.

Burrus/šu LL CAD: "with hair growing in patches"; AHw: "kahlköpfig?", cf. *barāšu* "to pluck" (LL only) → 10.6.2, **OB**, cf. CAD sv. Also PN → 10.6.3.2.

Bussumu "angenehm", cf. *bussumu* "erfreuen", acc. to AHw 1592a sv. → 8.6 sv.

Buttuqu st. D of *batāqu* "to cut off, pierce, break".

Butturu PN of horses (MB), AHw: "mit verstümmeltem Bein", cf. AOS 37, 29 → 10.6.3.2.

***Bu"û** VA of *bu"û* "to look for" → 8.6, only occurring as a PNF *Bu"ītu*, cf. AHw sv *bu"û* I → 10.6.3.3.

Bu"uru "?" → 10.6.1.2.2; **SB**: TDP 54: 12 (subj. broken), cf. CAD sv *bu'uru* B and *bēru* C adj. [TDP 60: 39 → *puhhuru*].

***Bu"ušu** "?", **OA**: BIN 6, 201: 20 (persons).

Bu"utu "staying overnight", cf. *bâtu* "to spend the night" → 10.3.3; **SB**: SAA 8, 346: r.3 (moon, cf. G in r.6f); TCS 2 p. 54b: 10 (herbs, cf. Biggs's comm. on p. 58b).

Buzzu'u st. of *buzzu'u* "to treat unjustly, put under pressure" → 8.6.

D

Dubbubu 1. "talking (nonsense)" (see note 4), **SB**: ZA 65, 56: 47; **2.**: st. of *dubbubu* "to complain, harass" → 5.5.3.

Dukkušu "pierced" ?, cf. *dakāšu* "to pierce, sting" (CAD), or "etwa 'auftreiben, ausbeulen'" (AHw); **OB**: RA 65, 71: 10' (intestines); **SB**: RA 73, 67: 17 (gall bladder).

Dullu st. of *dullu* "in Unruhe versetzen" (AHw sv *dâlu* D); "to show indifference" (CAD sv *dâlu* A) (AbB 8, 102: 12. 37).

Dulluhu st. D of *dalāhu* "to disturb", e.g., HGŠ 105: 24 // LKA 155: r.13 = (54) and (56); also adverb *dulluhiš*, **SB**: "worriedly" Ee I 119; SBH 70: 17; or "hurriedly" KAR 111: r.10 → 10.7.2.

Dullulu VA of *dullulu* "to oppress" (only inf. attested) (Ash. Bab. Ep. 37a: 13).

Dullupu and **Dulluqu** PNs → 10.6.3.2.

Dummû st. D of *damû* "to have convulsions" (CAD) or of *dummû* "weinend halten" acc. to AHw sv *dummû*, cf. App. to Ch. VII sv *damû*.

Dummuqu "good, beautiful", cf. *damqu* id.

1a) OA/OB: said of copper, see CAD sv b → 10.6.1.2.4;

1b) OB → 10.10: AbB 7, 167: 8. 25 = (79); 10, 181: 18; CRRAI 36, 102 Di. 460: 20 (words (*dabābum*)); AbB 6, 220: 36 = (78); 12, 121: 5 = (77) (action); 1, 16: left edge 2 (ploughing team); 3, 34: 43 (door); ARM 26/1 p. 536 no. 256: 13 (message); p. 362 no. 179: 27 (a god (?), interpretation difficult, cf.

Durand *ad l.* and CAD sv *dummuqu* a). Cf. also *dummuqtu* "good deed, favour" in OB, related to the intransitive use of the verb *dummuqu* discussed in 7.4.2, cf. AHw sv (also ARM 26/2 p. 365f no. 449: 44. 47; 27, 125: 3; AbB 13, 158: 5. 7, etc.);

1c) **SB** → 10.10: CT 37, 21a: r.4 (*šipru* "construction"); Asb. A X 70 (dreams); BWL 177: 25 (omens), JNES 4, 158: 47 (sheep, LL, partly restored);

2.: st. D of *damāqu* "to be(come) good", mostly in hendiadys (cf. 7.4.1): RA 53, 177: 17 (OB); SAA 10, 352: 14 (NA) [291: 7' infinitive, cf. CAD sv *damāqu* 2d-2']. Also PN → 10.6.3.2.

Dunnunu "strong", cf. *dannu* id. → 10.6.1.2.1;

A) **OB**: **1.** + *maṣṣarātum* "guards", *baz(a)hātum* "military posts" and *sakbū* "guard troops" → 10.4.1, in Mari: RA 35, 178: 24; ARM 3, 12: 7 = (14); 17: 21; 13, 117: 8; 14, 75: 29; ARM 26/1 p. 426 no. 199: 28 (qu. in note 8); p. 580 no. 280: 17; 26/2 p. 412 no. 475: 5; p. 428 no. 491: 40; p. 446 no. 505: 18 (rest.); p. 449 no. 509: r. 9'; elsewhere: AbB 1, 2: 16 = (13); 6, 107: 8; 7, 49: 2'; 50: 10'; 150b: 18;

2. other cases: AbB 4, 111: 30; 11, 137: 11 (matters (*awātum*)), AbB 9, 237: 19 (tablet); 12, 32: 20 = (64) (slave girl); YOS 10, 47: 35 (the *nimšū* (flanks ?) of a sheep); 42: III 5. 8. 16 (the *tallu* of the liver); Atr. 88: 32 (tackle (*uniātum*));

B) **SB**: **1.** in RIs, mostly pl.: Sg. 8: 165. 190. 240 (walls). 278 (cities); BSOAS 30, 495: 12' (troops); VAB 4, 216: 15 (joints); JAOS 38, 167: 20 (poles); AAA 19, 103: 6; Sg. Wi. 170: 14 (foundations); rarely sg.: Sg. 8: 299 (citadel);

2. elsewhere: BWL 165: 11 (roots); Gilg. I III 4 and elsewhere (*emūqā* "power"); DA 217: 4; TU 2: r.11 // CT 28, 44a: r.6 (pustule (*zihhu*), cf. note 22); SpTU 4, 129: VI 22 (seam). LL: cf. CAD sv lex. sect. Adv. *dunnuniš*, **SB**: Sn. 118: 16 → 10.7.2. [Obscure and not discussed: AbB 9, 90: 7 and FM 1 p. 76: 7 (reading very uncertain)].

Duppuru st. of *duppuru* "to remove, go away" → 8.6 sv.

Duqququ "tiny", cf. *daqqu* id. and *daqqaqu* in 3.1.3.1; **OB**, cf. CAD sv lex. sect. (LL); **SB**: KAR 153: 11 (pustule (*zihhu*), cf. note 22).

Durrû st. of *durrû* (meaning unknown, cf. CAD sv).

Duššu st. D of *dâšu* "to thresh, trample" (only FM 2 p. 35 no. 10: 42).

Duššû **1.** "abundant", cf. *dešû* id. → 10.6.1.2.1, **SB**, cf. CAD and AHw sv (also RA 82, 160: 41); **2.**: st. of *duššû* "to provide abundantly with" (+ acc.) → 10.4.2 and note 18.

Duššumu PN → 10.6.3.2.

Duššupu "sweet, pleasing", cf. *dašpu* id. → 10.3.1, 10.6.2, 10.9: **OB**: RA 22, 172: 9; MIO 12, 48: 1 acc. to AHw sv *šaptu(m)* A 1a (lips); MIO 12, 48: 9f (*dādū* "love-making"); 50: 13 (subject unclear); ZA 44, 32: 6 (attractiveness (*kuzbu*)); OEC 4, 152: I 43 (LL). **SB**: AGH 26: 29; BWL 60: 95; Erra I 58 (beer); Sn. 116: 76; 125: 51; SAA 3, 7: 15; RIMA 2/I, 151: 75 (wine); SAA 3, 28: 11' (lips); KAR 158: r.II 18 (*lahannatu*, a female person, G or D?); St. Kraus 202: 36. 38 (songs); VAB 7, 240: no. 6: 14; YOS 1, 42: 11 // UCP 9, 385: 11 (*rē'ûtu*, the "shepherdship" of the king). Also PN → 10.6.3.2.

Du''umu "dark", cf. *da'mu* id.; attested with certainty only as an adverb *du''umiš* (LKU 106: 7 *du-ÚH-HU-mi-iš*, cf. also 15) → 10.7.2. Elsewhere *du'ūmu* or *du'ummu* → 10.7.1.2, 10.6.2, 10.9, **SB** passim in medical, physiognomic and astronomical omens, cf. CAD sv *du'ummu*, AHw sv *da'āmu* D, e.g., ACh. Spl. 8: 21. 25 = (52).

G

Gubbuhu "bald" → 10.3.1, 10.6.2, **MB**: VAB 2, 357: 32; **SB**: AnSt. 10, 124: 38'. 41'; KAR 202: I 54. Also PN → 10.6.3.2. [BWL 190: r.10 obscure].

Gullubu **1.** PN "bald" → 10.6.3.2; **2.**: st. of *gullubu* "to shave" → 8.2 and 8.4.1, e.g., VAB 5, 37: 13 = (02B).

***Gullulu** PN → 10.6.3.2.

Gullutu "frightened", cf. *galātu* "to twitch, start" → 10.6.1.2.2, **SB**: LKU 46: 3 (animals).

Gummuru st. D of *gamāru* "to bring to an end, use up, control".

Gummutu "angry" acc. to AHw sv, **NB**: CT 22, 10: 18, cf. Von Soden, AfO 19, 149.

Gunnunu st. D of *ganānu* "to confine" (UM 1/2, 57: 11. 20. 28).

Gunnuṣu LL "constantly wrinkling the nose", cf. note 4 and *ganāṣu* in 7.6.2, **OB**: MSL 12, 181: 50. Also PN → 10.6.3.2.

Guppušu "huge, massive", cf. *gapšu* id. → 10.7.1.1, **OB**: YOS 10, 46: V 26; RA 38, 86: 16; 41, 52: 11'; Or. 56, 247: 36; **MB**: JCS 37, 149: 28 (parts of the liver). **SB**: AfO 9, 119: 5 (sheep); CT 27, 23: 16f (hair, paw); SAA 8, 357: 3 (star). Also PN → 10.6.3.2.

Gurrudu CAD: "with hair falling out in tufts"; AHw sv *qurrudu*: "mit schütterm Haar", or "bald" acc. to Deller, NABU 92/79 → 10.6.2, **OB**: MSL 12, 109: 170; **SB**: BAM 3: II 32 (head); MVAeG 40/2, 84: 106 (hair); MSL 7, 101: 433 (clay? (same word?)). Also PN → 10.6.3.2.

G/Qurruru A "leaky", cf. *qarāru* "to (over)flow", **NB**: VS 6, 73: 3; CT 4, 21a: 3 (vats).

G/Qurruru B PN → 10.6.3.2.

Gurruṣu "leprous", cf. *garṣu* LL id., and *gi/erriṣānu* "sheep affected with scab" (CAD sv) → 10.6.2, **NA**: SAA 10, 160: 3 (skull). Also PN → 10.6.3.2.

Guššuru "powerful", cf. *gašru* id. → 10.7.2, **SB**: Ee I 19 (god); SAA 3, 2: 24 (a god's greatness (*narbû*)).

H

Hubbulu st. D of *habālu* "to be(come) endebted to".

Hubburu "?" (CAD: mng. uncert.; AHw sv *habāru* II D 2 "dick machen" (= *kabāru*)); **SB**: CT 20, 27a: 14 (part of the liver); KAR 395: V 5 ([body part]); **NA**: a qualification of wine, cf. SAA 7, glossary sv *habburu* (same word?) → 10.6.1.2.4.

Hubbuṣu AHw: "sehr geschwollen, üppig"; CAD: "a characteristic bodily trait", cf. *habāṣu* "etwa 'schwellen'" acc. to AHw sv *h.* I, → 10.6.2; **OB**: MSL 4, 117: 13. Also PN → 10.6.3.2.

Hubbušu "?" (CAD: "a characteristic bodily trait", "defective", cf. *habšu* "brittle, wrinkled or cleft" and *habāšu* "to break into pieces"; but AHw sv *h.* I: "hart geschwollen", from *habāšu* "hart werden, anschwellen") → 10.3.2, 10.6.2; **OB**: MSL 12, 109: 171; **SB**: JCS 1, 242: 31 (man); Izbu 37: 66 (child); 68: 25 (head); SpTU 4, 149: II 39' (woman's breast); AOS 37, 20b: 8 (horse). Also PN → 10.6.3.2.

Hubbutu st. D of *habātu* "to be(come) indebted" (CatRyl. 19: 9; BIN 8, 141: 12).

Hubbuṭu "fastened" acc. to AHw sv, in UM 8, 194: III 15, cf. *ebēṭu* "to gird"? (CAD *sv* ***hubbû*** v. reads *hu-ub-bu-ma* ("mng. uncert.")).

Huddudu "deeply incised, indented", cf. *haṭāṭu* "to dig" ?; **OB**: YOS 10, 25: 74 (flesh); **SB**: TBP 22: III 8 (finger tips); AMT 30, 2: 9 (mouth); SpTU 3, 152: 40 (skull (*muhhu*) of a patient); Sg. 8: 21 (wadi); OIP 24, 20: 8 (ravines). Also PN → 10.6.3.2.

Huddulu PN → 10.6.3.2.

***Huggulu** (always *hungulu*) LL "?" (CAD: "a characteristic bodily trait"); **SB**: SpTU 1, 83: r.20 (*hu-un-gu-la* = *la-ma-a*$_4$). Also PN → 10.6.3.2.

Hukkumu st. D of *hakāmu* "to know, understand" (ARM 23, 100: 3; 26/2 p. 81 no. 316: 14").

Hullû "shining", cf. *helû* "to shine, be brillant" → 10.6.1.2.2, **SB**: TDP 180: 23 (toes).

(H)ullulu st. D of *(h)alālu* "to hang" (trans.) → 6.5.3 and 10.7.1.

Hullupu st. D of *halāpu* "to be dressed in" (only stative).

Hulluqu "removed", cf. *halāqu* "to disappear, escape" → 10.4.2, 10.6.1.2.2, **SB**: Maqlû I 34 (magic deeds).

Hummû st. of *hamû* "to paralyze".

Hummuru A "crippled", cf. *hemēru* "to break, smash" (AHw 1560b sv) ?, → 10.3.2, 10.6.2; **OB**: ARM 26/2 p. 491 no. 519: 14; MSL 12, 201: 9ff (person); 13, 230: 316 (feet); **MA**: AfO 18, 304/6: II 27. III 13. IV 8 (statuettes of animals, same word?); **SB**: passim, cf. CAD and AHw sv (persons and animals), also SpTU 3, 67: III 30 (person). Also PN → 10.6.3.2.

Hummuru B "shrivelled, shrunk", cf. *hamru* "dried out, shrunk" (CAD sv *hamru* adj., AHw sv *hamāru*); **SB**: Izbu 216: 136 *kelṣu* = *hum/hu-um-mu-ru*, cf. *kalāṣu* "to shrivel" (same word as **A**?).

Hummuru C (a qualification of beer, always substantive), **NA**, cf. SAA 7 gloss. sv *hammurtu* → 10.6.1.2.4.

(H)ummuru D "red" or "inflamed" (eyes), cf. AHw sv *emēru* I → 10.6.1.2.2; **SB**: Ee I 121; TDP 74: 35; SpTU 4, 152: 43 (subj. br., this word?).

Hummuṣu 1. "baldheaded" (CAD) → 10.3.2, 10.6.2, **OB**: MSL SS 1, 32: 135 (cf. G in 136); **MA**: a qualification of copper → 10.6.1.2.4; **2**.: st. D of *hamāṣu* "to tear off, strip" → 6.4.8, 6.8.1. Also PN → 10.6.3.2.

Hummušu A LL "lame, paralyzed" → 10.6.2, **SB**: BM 37059: 1 qu. CAD sv *kabālu* lex. sect. (*hum-mu-šat* = *ku-ub-bu-la-*[*at*]); also Emar IV/4 p. 305 no. 682: 10' ? → 10.6.1.1.2.

Hummušu B (a qualification of barley, AHw: "aus abgeknickten Ähren"; CAD: mng. unkn.), cf. *hamāšu* (? see the note CAD sv *h.* A (p. 61a)) → 10.6.1.2.4, **SB**: MSL 11, 83: 165.

Hummušu C "one fifth (of a shekel)", cf. *hamiš* "five", acc. to AHw sv *hummušu* I (NB).

Hummuṭu A "early (bearing)", cf. *hamāṭu* "to be quick, to haste"; YOS 3, 200: 5 (date palms).

Hummuṭu B 1. "hot, scorching", → 10.6.1.2.2, **SB**: SBH 54: 59 acc. to AHw sv (destinies). Also adverb *hummuṭiš* → 10.7.2, **OB**: MIO 12, 53: 8; **SB**: STC pl. 74: III 14; **2**.: st. D of *hamāṭu* "to burn" → 7.3.2.

Hunnubu PN → 10.6.3.2.

Hunnunu "?" (CAD: "a characteristic bodily trait") → 10.6.2, **OB**: MSL 12, 168: 343; **SB**: AfO 11, 223: 35 (nose); TIM 9, 87: 7 (LL); **NA**: ABL 285: 9 (subj. broken). Also PN → 10.6.3.2.

Hunnuqu "constricted", cf. *haniq* id. (CAD sv *hanāqu* 2) → 10.6.1.2.2, **SB**: ChDiv. 1, 92: 7 (intestines).

Hunnuṭu (a qualification of barley) → 10.6.1.2.4., **SB**: LL, cf. CAD sv.

Huppû st. D of *hepû* "to break" → 6.4.1.1; also sg. → 10.2, **OB**: ARM 27, 12: 10 = (06) (ship); **SB**: MSL 14, 282: 365 (head).

Huppudu "blind" → 10.3.1, 10.6.2, **OB/SB**, cf. Farber, ZA 75, 211ff; also ARM 26/2 p. 428 no. 491: 15; p. 502 no. 525: 11; SpTU 3, 94: 8. Also PN → 10.6.3.2.

Huppupu "cracked" (?) (door, acc. to CAD sv *huppupu* v. 1).

***Hurrudu** st. D of *harādu* "?" (AHw sv *h.* III "etwa "zusammenfügen""; CAD sv *h.* C "mng. uncert.").

Hurrumu st./VA D of *harāmu* "to cover, enclose" → 6.4.3.1 sv.

***Hurrupu** "early", cf. *harāpu* "to be early"; **NA**: AfO 18, 340: IIb 13 (wine) → 10.6.1.2.4.

Hurruru "deeply incised", cf. *harāru* "to dig, groove" → 10.6.1.1.3, 10.7.1.1, **OB**: YOS 10, 14: 10; 36: I 13; 42: III 53; **MB**: JCS 37, 136: 60; Emar VI/4 p. 305 no. 682: 5'f; **SB**: CT 20, 41: VI 10 (all body parts in extispicy omens). Also PN → 10.6.3.2.

Hurruṣu 1. PN → 10.6.3.2; **2**. st. D of *harāṣu* "to cut off, reduce, confiscate".

Hurrušu 1. PN → 10.6.3.2; **2**. st. D of *harāšu* "to bind; D "to plant" (trees) (same verb ?).

***Hussû** (only OA *hassu'u*) → 10.6.1.2.4, OA: CCT 1, 42a: 22 (copper, VA D of *hesû* "to crush").

Hussuru "blunted, broken"; **OB**: + copper, see AHw sv 2 ("Kupfer-Schrott ?") → 10.6.1.2.4; MSL 13, 246 section 6: 8' (tooth, cf. G in 7); **SB**: KAR 423: I 21; ChDiv. 94b: 6; 95: 18; CT 20, 16b: r.7; (all + *kaskasu* "breastbone") → 10.7.1.1; MSL 13, 159: 90 (oven).

Hussusu "worrying" (AHw sv *h.* D 2 "ist nachdenklich"), cf. *hasāsu* "to think", see note 4, **MB**: Tn-Ep. fr. E 23 (person); cf. also 7.6.3.

Huṣṣubu PN → 10.6.3.2.

Huṣṣuṣu st./VA D of *haṣāṣu* "to break" (reed).

Huššuhu st. D of *hašāhu* "to need, require".

Huššulu 1. "crippled", cf. *hašālu* "to crush, shatter" → 10.3.2, 10.6.2, **SB**: Izbu 37: 65 (child); **2.** "crushed" → 10.6.1.2.4, **OA**: kt z/k 14: 3 (*mu-ha-lu*). Also PN → 10.6.3.2. [KAR 350: 14 *huš-šu-lu* obscure].

Hušušu st. in CT 38, 15: 54 (wall with clay): "bulging" (CAD sv *hašāšu* B), "beschmieren" (AHw sv *h.* II).

Huttupu st. D of *hatāpu* "to slaughter".

Huṭṭû 1. "faulty, portending evil", cf. *haṭû* id. → 10.6.1.2.2, **SB**: BagF. 18, 495: 2 (omens); **2.**: st. of *huṭṭû* "to damage, ruin" (ABL 530: r.5').

Huṭṭupu st. D of *haṭāpu* "to wipe off" ?, cf. AHw 1560b sv (only UET 6, 396: 23 (tears)).

***Huzzû** (always *hunzû*) "lame, limping" → 10.6.2, **SB**: STT 403: 2 (LL). Also PN → 10.6.3.2.

***Huzzuhu** (always *hunzuh/'u*, prob. same word as *huzzû*) PN → 10.6.3.2.

Huzzulu PN → 10.6.3.2.

Huzzumu "shrivelled"?, cf. *hazmu* id. → 10.6.1.1.1; **SB**: Izbu 54: 10 = (35) (ears), TBP 27a: II 4' (person, uncert.); **NB**: ABL 462: r.9 (persons, CAD sv: "stupid", AHw sv "beschnitten an ...". Also PN → 10.6.3.2.

K

Kubbû st./VA of *kubbû* "to patch, sew" → 8.6 sv.

***Kubbubu** (*gabbubu*) "roasted", cf. *kabābu* "to burn" → 7.3.2; **NA**: SAA 7, 154: II' 10'; 159: I 6; Or. 17 pl. 22: 15. 18 (sheep (sg.)).

Kubbulu "lame, paralyzed" → 10.6.2, **OB**: VAB 6, 176: 28 (person); MSL 13, 230: 314 (feet); **SB**: Izbu 37: 62 (child); 178: 19' (calf); 62: 83f (foot); AMT 24, 1: 3. 9 (mouth); BRM 4, 22: 19 ([penis]); for LL see further CAD sv lex. sect. and BM 37059: 1 qu. CAD sv *kabālu* lex. sect. Also PN → 10.6.3.2.

Kubburu "thick, fat", cf. *kabru* id. and *kabbaru* in 3.1.3.1, → 3.1.3.3, **OB**: AbB 3, 55: 25 (measuring rope); RitDiv. 32: 53 (parts of the liver); **SB**: LKU 16: 12 (= (16B) in Ch. III) (limbs of a bull); BWL 255: 4 (person); TU 1: 33 (liver); KAR 395: V 3 (subj. broken); LTBA 2, 1: XIII 80 (LL); **NB**: Nbn. 530: 2 (iron → 10.6.1.2.4); NA said of sheep "fattened", cf. SAA 7 glossary sv *kabāru*. Some instances may also be interpreted as *kuppuru* or *qubburu* (q.v.). Also PN → 10.6.3.2.

Kubbusu st./VA D of *kabāsu* "to step or walk upon, trample".

Kubbutu 1. "heavy", cf. *kabtu* id. → 10.6.1.2.1, **OA**: CCT 2, 36a: 12 (metal objects); **MA**: AfO 18, 308: IV 18 (bronze loops); AfO Beiheft 6 no. 53: 13 (shields); **SB**: SBH p. 108: 46 acc. to Landsberger, WZKM 57, 23 (*pukkī* "balls", Landsberger: "Reifen"); said of objects *kubbutu* is difficult to distinguish from *kupputu*, q.v.; **2.**: st/VA of *kubbutu* "to honour, respect", e.g., AbB 3, 11: 12 = (23) → 10.4.2. Also PN → 10.6.3.2.

Kullu st. of *kullu* "to hold, offer" (mainly NB/LB, cf. CAD sv 1e-5', 3b-3', 3c, 3g-4').

Kullulu st./VA of *kullulu* "to crown, veil", esp. *kullultu* of a bride, cf. CAD sv lex. sect and a → 10.2.

Kullumu st. of *kullumu* "to show" → 8.6 sv.

***Kulluṣu** "shrivelled", cf. *kalāṣu* "to shrivel"; **OA**: St. Güterbock 39 note 34 kt g/k 18: 12 (barley) → 10.6.1.2.4.

Kummudu "?", cf. *kamādu* "to weave, process linen"? → 10.6.1.2.2, **SB**: TBP 11c: VI 23' (lines of the hand); 28: 7' (fingers).

Kummulu "angry", cf. *kamālu* "to be(come) angry" → 10.6.1.2.2, **MB**: Tn-Ep. Ib: 46 (rest.); **SB**: AGH 22: 11; 46: 67.

Kummuru st. D of *kamāru* "to heap, pile up".

Kummusu A st. D of *kamāsu* "to finish, collect, bring in".

Kummusu B "kneeling, squatting", cf. *kamāsu* "to kneel down, squat" → 7.5.2, 10.3.3, **OB**: RitDiv. 36: 139 (sheep (sg.)); **MA**: MVAeG 41/3, 14: 4; AnSt. 8, 46: 19; VAB 4, 290: I 5 (person); **NA**: Iraq 20, 183: 59 (persons), and passim in the meaning "to stay, be stationed", see CAD sv *k.* A (sic) 4c.

Kummusu C LL "awe-inspiring" ?; **SB**: BAW 1, 71: 18 (equated with *rašbu*, LL).

Kunnu 1. st. of *kunnu* "to establish, set up, testify" → 10.4.2; 2. "normal", cf. *kīnu* "true, regular, normal", **SB**: SAA 8, 304: r. 4 = (50) (horns of the moon) → 10.6.1.2.3.

Kunnû st./VA D of *kanû* "to be honoured, cherished", D "to honour, cherish, treat with care".

Kunnuku st. D of *kanāku* "to seal, put under seal".

K/Qunnunu "coiled, curled", cf. *kanānu* "to coil, twist" → 10.6.1.2.1, **OB**: AfO 18, 63: 21 (hair); MSL 12, 105: 33 ((hair of a) person; **SB**: TBP 12c: III 19 (id.); *ib.* 2a: 12 (lines on the forehead); AMT 68, 1: 14 (feet); ACh. 2. Spl. 6: 2 (horns of the moon); MSL 16, 193: 87 (intestines; Gilg. XI 115 (gods). Also PN → 10.6.3.2.

Kunnušu 1. st. D of *kanāšu* "to bend, submit" (note esp. Iraq 20, 183: 59 (persons, NA)). 2. "bent", **OB**: YOS 10, 11: V 1 (liver part); **SB**: KAR 395: V 6 (nose).

Kuppû "bent, blunted", cf. *kepû* "to bend, blunt"; **SB**: ACh. Spl. 7: 22 (*ku-pi* (horn, gloss on *ka-pí*).

Kuppupu "bent, curved", cf. *kapāpu* "to bend, curve" → 10.6.1.2.1, **SB**: TBP 19: III 6 (feet); MVAeG 40/2, 62: 2 (fingers); TDP 50: IV 9 acc. to AHw sv *kapāpu* D 1 (veins of the eye); CT 41, 29: r.12 (LL). Also PN → 10.6.3.2.

Kupp/bbuṣ/su "curled", cf. *kap/bāṣ/su* "to bend over, curl, droop" → 10.7.1.1, **OB**: YOS 10, 36: I 29. 34; **SB**: TU 6: II 15; SAA 4, 285: 4; AfO 26, 47: 6; CT 30, 48a: 9 (all: parts of the liver); Izbu 56: 22 (ears).

Kupputu "compacted, lump-shaped" (CAD sv *kupputu* adj. and *k.* A v. 2), or "ist gehäuft, wuchert" (AHw sv *kapātu* D 4b/c) → 10.6.2 and 8.4.1, **OB/SB**: passim of parts of the liver, see CAD/AHw *ll.cc.* (also OBE 16: 36' (bladder); SpTU 4, 149: III 33 (a woman's navel, cf. TBP 11c: VII 14); other uses, **SB**: MVAeG 40/2, 68: 9 (hair); TU 36: r.49 (stone); **NB**: BE 8, 154: 28 (stone). Difficult to distinguish from *kubbutu* "heavy".

Kurru "?" (Ee I 66), cf. CAD sv *kâru* B, AHw sv *kâru* II.

Kurrû "short" (pl. of *kurû*), see note 3 to Ch. III (not a *purrus* form).

Kussû st. D of *kasû* "to bind, paralyze" → 10.7.1.

***Kussupu** st./VA D of *kasāpu* "to chip, break off", VA also sg. → 10.2 (SAA 7, 88: r.6. 8 (cooking pot, NA)).

Kussusu VA D of *kasāsu* "to gnaw, consume" (MSL 7, 24: 257a (reed)).

Kuṣṣudu A "crippled" → 10.3.2, 10.6.2, **SB**, cf. CAD sv lex. sect. for LL (see MSL 13, 219: 49ff); **SB**: BWL 76: 76; RA 53, 135: 22.

***Kuṣṣudu B** st. of *kaṣṣudu* "to delay" (OA).

Kuṣṣupu st. D of *kaṣāpu* (CAD: *keṣēpu*) "to think, plan".

Kuṣṣuru 1. st./VA D of *kaṣāru* "to bind together, etc." 2. "having a hard soil" → 10.3.2, **OB**: VAB 5, 131: 14 (field).

Kuṣṣuṣu "crippled" (AHw: "ein Krüppel ohne Hand?"), cf. *kaṣāṣu* (CAD: *gaṣāṣu*) "to trim, cut, mutilate" → 10.3.2, 10.6.2, **OB**: MSL 12, 201: 7; **SB**: MSL 16, 164: 329.

Kuššû "abundant (of hair)", cf. *kašû* "to be profitable, yield profit" → 10.3.3, **SB**: MVAeG 40/2, 74: 57f; 76: 59ff (*kuššî*); 82: 96; 84/6: 112ff.

Kuššudu st./VA of *kuššudu* "to chase away, pursue" → 5.5.3 sv.

Kuššupu st./VA D of *kašāpu* "to bewitch".

Kuttumu st./VA D of *katāmu* "to cover, close"; note esp. **SB**: + *kallatu* "bride", cf. CAD sv b → 10.2; AOAT 1, 6: 83 (an *eṭemmu*); Sg. 8: 210 (land: "remote(?)" (CAD), "unzugänglich" (AHw); **NB**: BR 6, 28: 1 (ship: "covered").

Kuzzubu "charming, luxuriant", cf. *kazbu* id. → 10.6.2, **MB**: RA 16, 79 no. 24: 2 (goddess); **SB**: MVAeG 41/3, 58: 2 (stone); KADP 22: I 15 (illness, same word?). Also PN → 10.6.3.2.

L

Lubbuku st./VA D of *labāku* "to be(come) soft, steeped"; esp. **OB**: YOS 10, 31: VI 24 (gall bladder).

***Lubbunu** st. of *lubbunu* "to reinforce" (AfO 17, 146: 4; KAR 6: II 24).

Lubbušu st./VA D of *labāšu* "to wear" (clothes) → 10.4.2, e.g., ARM 6, 39: 9 = (32). **2. NB**: "(still) having its fleece" (sheep), cf. CAD sv.

Luhhumu LL "with long hair", cf. *lahmu* id. → 10.6.2, **SB**: MSL 8/1, 45: 307 (ox).

Luhhušu → *lu"ušu*

Lullû st. of *lullû* "to provide lavishly" (Iraq 24, 94: 37) → 8.4.2 sv.

Lummû st. D of *law/mû* "to wrap, surround" (ZA 16, 172: 48).

Lummudu 1. st./VA D of *lamādu* "to know, learn". **2.** LL, of a plough and a calf, cf. CAD sv.

Lummunu 1. st./VA D of *lemēnu* "to be(come) bad, unhappy" → 10.4.2, 10.10;
2. "bad, evil, unfortunate", cf. *lemnu*: **a) OA**: + copper → 10.6.1.2.4, passim, cf. CAD sv 2b; **b)** otherwise, **OB**: TBP 62: 8' (road); **SB**, of persons ("unfortunate, miserable; also "ill-tempered"?): CT 41, 21: 27; AnSt. 6, 150: 2; SpTU 4, 149: IV 13f. 26; of omens and ominous signs ("unfavourable"): CT 31, 39: II 22; RA 61, 35: 15; LKA 139: 21 // 140: 11 // JRAS 1929, 281: 4; 282: 6; SpTU 3, 80: 33; of celestial phenomena ("dim, obscured") → 10.7.1.3: ACh. 2. Spl. 78: I 9; 84: 8; 119: 50; SpTU 1, 84: 14; K.230: 14 and K. 3780: I 9 qu. CAD sv 2c; rest: AnSt. 6, 150: 8 (features); Ash. Bab. Ep. 32: 13 (ruinous state of a building).

Lummuṣu "?"; **SB**: Izbu 213: 41 (eyes, possibly a misinterpretation of *hummuṣu*, cf. CAD sv).

Luppunu LL "poor", cf. *lapnu*; **OB**: MSL 12, 201: 3 (person).

Lupputu 1. st./VA of *lapātu* "to touch, smear, affect" → 6.6.3.2, e.g., ARM 26/1 p. 127 no. 17: 30 = (01B); for *damam lupput* see App. to Ch. VI sv *lapātu* 3b;
2. a) "anomalous" → 10.7.1.1, **OB**: said of parts of the liver YOS 10, 17: 42; 48: 42 // 49: 14 = (38); RA 44, 13: 4; **SB**: passim, always written tag.meš, cf. CAD sv *lapātu* 4f; **b)** "unfavourable"; OB Mari + *têrētum* passim (always pl.) → 10.6.1, cf. CAD sv 4f (also ARM 14, 86: 34; 26/1 p. 316 no. 152: 11; p. 323 no. 156: 32; p. 372 no. 189: 3'; 26/2 p. 416 no. 479: 28; MARI 6, 338: 62 = (33); FM 2 p. 112: no. 71: 7, etc.); **c)** rest: "damaged, soiled" said of a container, a boat and a rag (*ulāpu*), cf. CAD sv.

***Luqqû** st./VA D of *leqû* "to take, receive" (BIN 4, 79: 8'. 14'. 18' (OA)) → 5.6.2.1 and App. to Ch. VI sv.

Luqqutu st./VA D of *laqātu* "to pick up, collect, take away" (VA: AOAT 1, 6: 80 (*eṭemmu*)).

Luttû st. D of *letû* "to split, divide" → 5.6.4.

Lu"û st/VA of *lu"û* "to make dirty, pollute" → 8.4.1 sv.

Lu"ubu st. D of *la'ābu* "to affect with the *li'bu*-disease" (metaphorically: HGŠ 105: 28; AGH 78: 56).

***Lu"upu** st./VA of *la"upu* "to wrap up, envelop" (ATHE 62: 8, OA) → 8.6 sv

Lu"ušu (*luhhušu*) st. D of *la'āšu* "to bother" (AbB 13, 120: 9).

***Lu"uṭu** "?", cf. *lâṭu* "to confine, keep in check" ? (JNES 13, 212: 26 // 213: 25).

***Luwwû** → *lummû*.

Luzzuzu "?"; **OB**: UET 7, 93: r.34 (person, LL).

M

Muddudu st. D of *madādu* "to measure, deliver" (BWL 211: 13).

Muddulu "salted, pickled", cf. *madālu* "to salt, pickle" (meat); OAk/SB, cf. CAD sv.

Muhhû "ecstatic", cf. *mahû* "to become frenzied", **OB**, cf. CAD sv *mahhû* → 10.3.3, 10.6.2 and note 6.

Muhhuru st. D of *mahāru* "to receive, approach, confront" (only MDP 57, 184 passim (mng. unkn.)).

Muhhuṣu 1. st. D of *mahāṣu* "to hit, smash, weave"; **2.** LL (qualifies persons and reed or wood objects ("mit Beschlägen versehen?" (AHw)), **OB**: MSL 12, 161: 105 + 181: 33 (person); **SB**: MSL 5, 165: 161; 170: 238; 7, 46: 217 (object).

Mukkulu "?", cf. *mekēlu* (mng. unkn., both said of hair, cf. AHw 1574b sv); **OB**: RA 75, 110: V 7 (?, rest.).

Mullû "handed over, assigned": stative of *mullû* "to fill" (24)-(28) → 10.4.2; otherwise: Sg. 8: 387 = (47) (ornaments) → 10.6.1.2.3.

Mulluhu "?" (said of stars, CAD sv *malāhu* 3b: "to flicker?", AHw sv *m.* D 2b "zerfasern") → 10.7.1.3, **SB**: SAA 8, 158: r.7; ACh. Išt. 21: 47; ACh. 2. Spl. 64: 9; VAT 7830: 18 qu. CAD and AHw *l.c.*

Mulluqu and **Mullušu** PNs → 10.6.3.2.

Munnû st. D of *manû* "to count, recite, entrust".

Mulluṭu "?"; **SB**: MSL 12, 229: IV 10' (person) → 10.6.2.

Muqqu "weak, feeble", cf. *muqqu* "to do slowly, hesitate" → 8.6; **OB/SB**: cf. CAD sv *muqqu* adj. (person); *ib.* sv *muqqu* v. (person, body parts, troops); **OA**: CCT 2, 31a: 14 (person).

Muqqutu "collapsed" (CAD), "(krankhaft) verfallen" (AHw), cf. *maqātu* "to fall" → 10.3.3, 10.7.1.2, **OB**: MSL 12, 181: 53; MSL SS 1, 20: 25 (person); **SB**: BWL 44: 98 (feet); TDP 102: 4ff; 108: 13; 132: 51; 136: 59; 138: 18f (body parts, sg. or pl.); 242: D 2 (subject broken).

Murruhu "?"; **OB**: MSL 12, 160: 87 (person).

Murruqu A "of good quality"; **NB**: cf. CAD sv (silver (but AHw sv *murruqu* "gereinigt") → 10.6.1.2.4); tunic, coat of mail, donkey (but AHw *ib.* "von Ansprüchen befreit").

Murruqu B "clear, intelligible" (of texts) (CAD sv, but acc. to AHw sv *marāqu* D 2a stative of *murruqu* "reinigen"); **SB**, cf. CAD sv.

Murruru A "bitter", cf. *marru* id.; **OA**: CCT 1, 42b: 7. 14 (oil? → 10.6.1.2.4); **SB**: SpTU 3, 76: 15 (bread or food *mur-ru-r[a(-am)]* "is bitter for me").

Murruru B st./VA of *murruru* "to check, castrate".

Mussû st./VA D of *mesû* "to wash"; also **OA** VA *massu'um* "refined" (copper) (ICK 1, 85: 8) → 10.6.1.2.4.

***Mussuhu** "of bad quality"; OA: of metals, cf. CAD sv **mussuhu* v. and adj. → 10.6.1.2.4.

Mussuku "bad, ugly", cf. *masku*; **SB**: Izbu 38: 70 (child); BWL 40: 35 (abstract subj.); Gilg. XI 216 (bread, spelled *muš-šu-kàt*: same word?). The MA PN *Massuku* (OMA I 321f) is probably a *parras* form, cf. note 2 to Ch. III.

Muṣṣû → *w/muṣṣû*.

***Muššuhu** "?"; **OA**: CCT 2, 13: 33 (words or matters, same word as **mussuhu* ? (q.v.)).

Muššulu st. D of *mašālu* "to be(come) similar, equal". Also PN → 10.6.3.2.

***Muttuqu** "sweet", cf. *matqu* id.; **MB**: only in *mattuqtu*, a kind of cake (Emar VI/3 p. 385 no. 387: 20).

Muṭṭû "having a reduced appetite or capacity", cf. *maṭû* "to be(come) missing, inferior" → 10.7.1.2; **SB**, cf. CAD sv *maṭû* v. 4c.

Muṭṭuru (SB *mundurat*) "soggy, oozing moisture", cf. *maṭir* (stat.) id. (for *-ṭ-*, cf. Kraus, JCS 37, 144 note 42; 169 note 93; for the meaning, cf. Jeyes 1989: 133f, against AHw/CAD sv *madāru*) → 10.7.1.1, **OB**: OBE 8: 34 ("finger" of the liver, restored); 16: 34'f (bladder); YOS 10, 36: I 4 (subject broken); TU 1: 7 (liver); CT 20, 41: IV 20 (rest.); 28, 48: 5; 30, 33a: 13; 41b: 13 (gall bladder).

***Muzzuhu** (*munzuhu*) "?"; **OB**: MSL 12, 181: 29 (person).

***Muzzu'u** "narrow, difficult", cf. *mazā'u* "to squeeze"; **NA**: SAA 1, 63: 13" (road); 97: 10 (river).

N

Nuhhu st./VA D of *nâhu* "to rest, subside". Note esp. **OB**: ARM 26/2 p. 221 no. 391: 65 (words, rest.); **SB**: JNES 33, 278: 94 var. (water, // G).

Nuhhub/pu "insolent" ?, **SB**: BWL 216: 21 (fox).

Nuhhudu "alerted", st. D of *na'ādu* (*nahādu*) "to pay attention, be concerned" (AbB 6, 145: 14).

Nuhhulu PN → 10.6.3.2.

Nuhhuru "?", cf. *nahru* "dry" ?; **SB**: BAM 124: III 19; AMT 75, 1: III 31 (foot); *ib.* 28 (subj. broken). Also name of horses (MB) → 10.6.3.2, cf. AOS 37, 12: 4 and CAD sv *nuhhuru* B.

Nuhhušu 1. st. D of *nahāšu* "to prosper" (AbB 3, 52: 30). **2.** "prosperous", CT 40, 42: 16 (slaves); ZA 43, 96: 7 (subj. broken).

Nuhhutu A "stunted, trimmed", st. of *nuhhutu* "to trim, clip", cf. CAD sv, AHw sv *nahātu* D 1/2.

Nuhhutu B (a qualification of silver and linen) → 10.6.1.2.4, **NB**, cf. CAD sv *nuhhutu* adj.

Nukkulu "artful, sophisticated", cf. *nakālu* "to act cleverly, to cheat" → 10.7.2; **SB**: IV R 12: 24; Sg. 8: 299; Sn. 128: 43 (construction (*epištu* or *epšētu*)); Tigl.III: 76: 29 (bull colossi); Ee VI 84 (bough); I 93 (shape). [CAD sv c: uncertain].

Nukkumu st. D of *nakāmu* "to stock, heap up".

Nukkupu "perforated"(?) (cf. *nakāpu* "to butt, gore" ? (acc. to CAD sv *nakāpu* B another verb)), **SB**: Izbu 171: 77' (womb of an *izbu*); 197 K.12754: 6 (heads, rest.).

Nukkuru 1. "strange, unusual, anomalous", cf. *nakru* "strange, foreign, hostile"; **OB**: RA 75, 110: VI 9 (person); 108: I 12; 111: VI 24 (deeds (*sipru*)); ZA 53, 216: 11; Gilg. Bo. 22f (everything); Tn.-Ep. IIIa 22 (mind (*qerbu*)); **MB/SB**: of parts of the liver in extispicy omens, cf. CAD sv *nakāru* 7c (also JCS 37, 133: 10); **2.** st./VA of *nukkuru* "to change, remove", etc. → 10.4.2.

Nukkusu st./VA D of *nakāsu* "to cut off, fell".

Nullušu "covered with dew", cf. *nalāšu* "to dew" → 10.6.1.2.2, **SB**: TCS 2 p. 39 no. 20: 5 (*pānātū'a* = ?).

Nummuru → *nuwwlmmuru*

Nuppuhu 1. "bloated" or "inflamed", cf. *naphu* id. → 10.6.1.2.1, 10.8: **a)** in **OB/SB** medical texts, mostly pl.: **OB**: RA 65, 73: 34' (intestines); **SB**: TDP 34: 17 (eyes); 56: 18; 240: 18 (feet); 130: 49 = (36) (buttocks); 144: 52' (borders of the eye); 206: 71 (feet+ankles); 234: 34 (face); STT 89: 203; CT 23, 44: r.5 (eyes); BAM 3: I 27 (head+face+lips); BWL 44: 94 (veins (*šer'ānū*)); 32: 51 (exta (*têrētu*)); exc. sg.: CT 23, 33: 17 (head). For additional cases spelled sar.me(š), see 10.6.1.2.1 and 10.8. For the spelling NE-ÚH see note 26; **b)** other texts, **OB**: TCL 17, 57: 11. 26 (ewe); MSL 4, 72: 160ff (obscure); **SB**: MSL 9, 95: 147 ([feet] ?, LL); **NB**: UET 4, 178: 1 (windpipe); **2.** st. D of *napāhu* "to light". [MSL 4, 172: 60f unclear].

Nuppulu "blind(ed)" (AHw sv; CAD: "mng. uncert."), cf. *napālu* "to tear out, to blind"; **SB**: STT 323: 73; KAR 382: r. 64; CT 41, 27: 11 (all said of a gecko).

Nuppuṣu 1. st./VA D of *napāṣu* "to strike, smite"; **2.** "crushed", a qualification of malt, beerwort and sesame → 10.6.1.2.4, cf. CAD sv (LL).

Nuppušu "?", cf. *napāšu* "to relax, expand" ?; **OB**: AbB 6, 21: 20 (house: "in good repair" (CAD sv *napāšu* A 5b)); **SB**: SpTU 4, 149: II 38'; III 16 ((tip of) a woman's breast).

Nuqqû st. D of *naqû* "to pour out, sacrifice" (CT 41, 22: 20; 40, 46: r.45).

Nuqqudu "concerned", cf. *naqādu* "to be in a difficult position"; **OB**: AbB 1, 2: 24; 7, 47: 10'; 50: 21.

***Nuqquru** "mit Einkerbungen versehen" acc. to AHw sv *naqquru*: **OA**: TC 3, 113: 8 (tablet).

Nurrubu "moist, soft", cf. *narbu* id. → 10.7.1.1; **OB**: YOS 10, 55: 5 // AfO 18, 66: III 13 (warts); **SB**: of the *zihhu* passim in liver omens, cf. CAD sv a; otherwise: TU 2: 10 // CT 28, 48c: 4 (crust (*rikbu*)); MSL 14, 265: 8'. Also PN → 10.6.3.2.

Nurruṭu "quivering", cf. *narāṭu* "to tremble, quiver" → 10.6.1.2.2 + note 4, **SB**: VAB 7, 256: 22 (lances).

Nussuhu st. D of *nasāhu* "to tear out, remove".

Nussuqu 1. "choice, well-chosen" → 10.7.2, **SB**: said of utterances, persons, artefacts and materials, cf. CAD sv; **2.**: st. D of *nasāqu* "to select, choose".

Nuššu "shaking, loose", cf. *nâšu* "to shake, recede"; **SB**: Epilepsy p. 59: 9 (cheeks); SpTU 1, 31: 8; STT 89: 208 (jaws); 279: 1 (teeth); TDP 48: E I 5 (subj. broken).

Nutturu "?", cf. *natāru* "to break up" ?; **OB**: RA 65, 73: 51' (intestines); MSL 12, 160: 78 (person); **SB**: TBP 13: 25 (jaws of a person). Also PN → 10.6.3.2.

Nuṭṭupu "?", cf. *naṭāpu* "to tear out" ?; **OB**: ARM 10, 32: r.8' (obscure); MSL 4, 72: 164ff (person, emended). Also PN → 10.6.3.2.

Nu''udu st. D of *nâdu* "to praise".

Nu''uru "roaring', cf. *na'āru* "to roar", see note 4, **SB**: ZA 16, 180: 41 (Lamaštu).

Nuww/mmuru st./VA D of *naw/māru* "to shine, be brillant" → 10.4.2, 10.6.1. Also PN → 10.6.3.2.

Nuzzumu "querulous", cf. *nazāmu* "to complain", see note 4, **OB**: ARM 10, 124: 13. 16 (context broken).

Nuzzuqu "worried" or "annoyed", cf. *nazāqu* "to be worried, annoyed" → 10.8; **OB**: AbB 7, 22: 11 = (57).

P

Puggulu "strong", cf. *paglu* id. → 10.4, 10.7.2, **SB**: Or. 36, 120: 74; Iraq 31, 85: 22 (god); SBH 10: r.22 // 9: r.39; 18: 29; VAB 4, 220: 25; Ee I 18; BA 10/1 p. 8: 14; OEC 6 pl. 24 K.3031: r.6; JCS 6, 66: 31 (all: power (*emūqu*)); PKOM 2, 8: 2 (power (*kubukku*)); SKT 2, 1: 11 (chapel (*kiṣṣu*)); VAB 4, 164 B: VI 21 (limbs of a dog); SpTU 4, 149: IV 19 ([body parts]); AfO Beiheft 17, 13b top (date palm); STT 180: 13 (context broken); also LL, cf. AHw sv.

Puhhu st. of *puhhu* "to replace, exchange" → 8.4.2 and 9.1.3 sv.

Puhhuru 1. "contracted, close together": **OB**: YOS 10, 28: 8 (gall bladder); 42: I 30 (heart); **SB**: TU 2: r.20 // CT 28, 44a: 17 (gall bladder); TDP 60: 39' (teeth, emended); MVAeG 40/2, 68: 7f (convolutions of the intestines); Izbu 125: 43' (eyes); **2**.: st./VA D of *pahāru* "to come together". Also PN → 10.6.3.2.

Pulluhu "fearful", cf. *palāhu* "to fear, respect", **OB**: TCL 18, 95: 25 (person).

Pulluq/ku "slaughtered", st./VA D of *palāq/ku* "to slaughter".

Pullusu "engaged in, busy", cf. *pullusu* "to engage sb's attention, to trouble" → 8.6. Also PN → 10.6.3.2.

Pullušu st./VA D of *palāšu* "to pierce, perforate, burgle"; in omens also with sg. subj. → 10.6.1.1.3: **OB**: YOS 10, 45: 24 (rib); OBE 16: 17' = (46B) (kidney); VA sg. → 10.2, **SB**: MSL 7, 87: 210; 90: 262 (a kind of jar).

Puqqu st. of *puqqu* "to pay attention to" → 9.1.6 (BWL 86: 270; Ash. 80: 32).

Puqqudu st. D of *paqādu* "to entrust, appoint, take care of, inspect".

Purru "?", **SB**: CT 28, 29: 5 (face), cf. AHw sv *pâru* II D.

Purrudu "fearful", cf *parādu* "to be(come) frightened", **OB**: MSL 4, 75: 285 (eyes) → 10.6.1.2.1; **OA**: CCT 4, 10a: 17 (person); **SB**: TDP 222: 42 (intestines, same word?).

Purruku "lying crosswise", cf. *parāku* "to block, obstruct" → 10.6.1.2.1, **OB**: YOS 10, 42: II 62 (lines); **SB**: TDP 204: 52/5; SpTU 4, 149: II 27' (veins); KUB 37, 31: 3 (face); CT 38, 8: 32 (potsherds).

Purruru st./VA D of *parāru* "to dissolve, fall apart". Note esp. in omens: **OB**: ÖB 2, 114: 3 (oil); AfO 18, 65: 17 (mind (*ṭēmu*)); **SB**: AMT 75: IV 17 (heel(s)); TDP 78: 71f (*talammu* "torso"?); ChDiv. 1, 89: 11 ((part of) intestines); ACh. Sin 5: 7; ACh. Spl. 12: 24 (moon); ACh. 2. Spl. 117: 7 ("torch").

Purrusu st./VA D of *parāsu* "to cut off, separate, decide"; special cases: **OB**: YOS 10, 11: I 15 = (45) (the "path" of the liver → 10.6.1.1.3); **SB**: MVAeG 40/2, 64: 9 (toes); AOAT 1, 6: 80 (*eṭemmu*); ACh. 2. Spl. 14: 13 (moon).

Purrušu "flattering", cf. *parāšu* "to flatter", **SB**: MSL 17, 161: 289 (mouth, LL); also adverb [*pu*]-*ru-ši-iš*, **OB**: SEM 90: III 5 → 10.7.2. [SpTU 1, 36: 16 (excrements) unclear].

***Pussuku** st. of *passuku* "to clear away, to remove" (NA) → 8.6.

Pussulu "bent, twisted", cf. *pasālu* "to bend, twist" (intrans.) → 10.3.3, 10.6.2, **OB**: MSL 4, 72: 168 (person); 13, 230: 309 (feet); **SB**: AnSt. 10, 124: 38'. 41'; Izbu 185: 9; 223: 415; SpTU 1, 71: 9; 3, 94: 9ff (feet); 4, 149: IV 20 ([body parts]); MSL 13, 219: 51ff. Cf. also ARM 26/2 p. 285 no. 411: 45 and p. 292 no. 413: 5 (*ṭēmu*): same word? Also PN → 10.6.3.2.

Pussum/nu st./VA D of *pasāmu* "to cover, veil" (esp. *pussum/ntu* "the veiled one" = "bride", cf. AHw sv *pussum/nu* 3b). Also PN → 10.6.3.2.

Pussuqu "?", cf. *pasāqu* ? (mng. also unknown), **SB**: MSL 13, 175: 6'.

Pussusu st./VA D of *pasāsu* "to cancel, destroy" → 5.6.4 (VA: MSL 7, 24: 260f; 101: 423 (reed, clay)).

Puṣṣû "white", cf. *peṣû* id.; **OB**: ARM 7, 4: 17 *hurāṣum pu-ṣú-ú* "white gold" → 10.6.1.2.4, and note 19 to Ch. II.

Puṣṣudu "?", **SB**: MSL 14, 265: 7a' (beside *nurrubu* and *ruṭṭubu*).

***Puṣṣunu** "veiled", st./VA D of *paṣānu* "to veil", **MA**, e.g., KAV 1: VI 7 = (03B) → 10.2.

Puššuhu st. D of *pašāhu* "to cool down, calm down".

Puššuqu "narrow, difficult", cf. *pašqu* id. → 10.6.1.2.2; **OB**: AbB 1, 37: 6 (water); RitDiv. 32: 48 (the "path" of the liver).

Puššuru st. D of *pašāru* "to untie, release".

Puššuṭu "effaced" ?, cf. *pašāṭu* "to erase"; **OB**: MDP 57, 184 passim (obscure, opp. *muhhur*); **SB**: KUB 4, 73b: 2 (part of the liver), see note 16.

Puttû "open(ed)", st./VA of *petû* "to open"; for VA cf. AHw sv *puttû* (most instances unclear) (also YOS 12, 157: 6. 8f).

Puttuhu "perforated", VA D of *patāhu* "to perforate", **OB**: CT 4, 30a: 6 (sieve); *ib.* 7 (basket) → 10.6.1.1.3.

Puttulu "coiled", VA D of *patālu* "to wrap, wind" → 10.7.1.1, **SB**: DA 218: 16 // SpTU 1, 80: 56; CT 31, 10a: 14 (rest.) (*kakku*, the "weapon" mark); TU 1: 56. r.1 (filaments).

Puttuqu "cast, moulded", VA D of *patāqu* "to cast, mould"; **OB**: MSL SS 1, 29: 32f (cf. G in 31).

Puṭṭuru **1.** in omens "split, frayed" → 10.7.1.1, **OB**: + *ana/adi N(-šu)*: SSAW 120/3: 18 = (42B); YOS 10, 33: V 28. 31. 34 = (44B). 37. 39; 39: 29. 31; RA 44, 30: 47 = (43B); other cases: RA 44, 13: 3f; 67, 44: 71'; OBE 14: 21; **SB**: Iraq 54, 106: 5; CT 30, 29a: 6; St. Reiner 150 b 1f (all: liver parts); TDP 108: 15 (pelvis); spelled ideogr. (duh.meš): *ib.* 100: 2 (breast); SpTU 1, 80: 82f (parts of the "palace gate"); **2.** st./VA D of *paṭāru* "to loosen, untie".

***Pu''ugu** VA D of *puāgu* "to take away" (KAJ 310: 14 (tablets, MA)) → 10.6.1.2.2.

Puzzuru "hidden", st./VA of *pazāru* "to hide" (intrans.) (also ZA 71, 62: 10' ?). Also PN → 10.6.3.2.

Q

Qubburu "buried" acc. to AHw sv *qebēru* D 4b, but CAD sv *qubburu* "mng. uncert." → 10.7.1.1, **SB**: said of parts of the liver and the "finger" of the lung, cf. CAD *l.c.*

Quddudu "sunken sagging", cf. *qadādu* "to bow" → 10.3.3, **OB**: TCL 18, 123: 6 (cheeks); **SB**: Gilg. EG pl. 42 SP 299: 8; KAR 125: 17. r.11 = (53) (face); BAL II 90: Nin. 81; STT 341: 4 (nose).

Quddumu "?"; **SB**: SpTU 4, 149: II 31' (nails); IV 25 (toes); IV 30 (toe nails).

Quddušu **1.** st. of *quddušu* "to purify, consecrate". **2.** "pure, holy" (temples, offerings, ritual appurtenances, person, river, mountain, water), cf. CAD sv *quddušu* adj., and cf. *quššudu*. For *quddušu* and its secondary form *quššudu* (q.v.) instead of **qadšu*, see 11.2.2.

***Qullû** (only fem. *qullîtu*) VA D of *qalû* "to burn, roast", **NB**: barley, ghee, cf. CAD sv → 10.6.1.2.4.

Qullulu st./VA *qullulu* "to discredit, to despise" → 10.4.2, 3.1.3.3, e.g., AbB 3, 11: 12 = (23).

Qullupu VA D of *qalāpu* "to peel, skin" (NA: CA 88: 16 (figs)).

Qummû st. D of *qamû* "to burn" (Gilg. X I 44 (face)).

Qunnunu → *kunnunu.*

Quppu "buckled", cf. *qâpu* "to buckle, cave in" → 10.3.3, **SB**: said of wall(s), cf. CAD sv.

Qurrubu **1.** st. of *qurrubu* "to bring near, offer, present" → 10.10, e.g., KAV 108: 13 = (65), MVAeG 43/1, 66: 49 = (66); perhaps also AbB 7, 60: 10 = (72) and 11, 94: 9 = (73).
2. "near, imminent, present, available" → 10.10, mainly OB, cf. CAD sv *qerēbu* 12, e.g., AbB 2, 151: 10

= (67); 3, 18: 17 = (69); 7, 64: 9 = (71); 13, 153: 16 = (68); JCS 42, 144: 17 = (70); also AbB 12, 182: r.6'; MHET 1 p. 136 no. 91: x+10 (all: person); RA 85, 17 no. 5: 6 (tablet); **SB**: AfO 17, 85: 9 = (74); *ib.* 12 = (75); BBS 3: IV 26 = (76).

Qurrudu → *gurrudu.*

Q/gurrunu st. D of *qarānu* "to store, pile up" (BWL 74: 63 (property)).

Quššudu 1. st./VA of *quššudu* "to consecrate" (e.g., RIMA 2/I, 45: 83. 89 (palace)); **2. SB**: (in MA RIs) "holy" (temple, person, offerings), cf. CAD sv *q.* adj. → 11.2.2.

Quttû 1. st./VA D of *qatû* "to come to an end"; **2.** "perfect", **OB**: RIME 4, 607: 101 = (31) (temple); **SB** → 10.4.2 and note 12.

Qutturu "smoke-blackened, smoky", cf. *qatāru* "to rise (smoke, fog), **OB**: Ét. de Meyer 82: 35 (face); MIO 12, 54: r.18 (door jambs); Atr. 72: 21 (subj. broken); **SB**: CT 39, 35: 36 (lamp).

Quttunu "thin, fine", cf. *qatnu* id. and *qattanu* in 3.1.3.1, and → 3.1.3.3, **OB**: MSL 12, 160: 85 (person, cf. G in 86). Also PN → 10.6.3.2.

R

Rubbû 1. "big, great", cf. *rabû* id. and *rabbû* in 3.1.3.1, and → 3.1.3.3, **OB**: St. Reiner 190: 28 (misfortune); **2.** VA of *rubbû* "to bring up, raise, grow" (only BR 8/7, 47: 15).

Rubbu'u st. of *rubbu'u* "to multiply by four" → 7.3.2 (only Kisurra 156: 26).

Rubbuṣu "crouching", cf. *rabāṣu* "to lie down" → 10.3.3, **OB**: ZA 71, 62: r.14' (dog).

Ruddû st./VA of *ruddû* "to add" (VA only BBS 36: V 29).

Ruggubu "provided with a *rugbu*" ("attic"?) → 8.4.2, mostly said of *bītu* "house, cf. AHw sv; also of the wind, cf. CAD sv *ziqziqqu* lex. sect. (meaning: ?, same word ?).

Ruggugu "evil, wicked", cf. *raggu* id.; **SB**: BWL 134: 127 (person); MSL 17, 62: 111; CT 18, 38b: r.[13] +D (LL).

Ruhhu VA D of *râhu* "to be left, to remain", acc. to AHw sv.

Rukkubu VA of *rukkubu* "to pollinate" → 8.3.3 and 8.4.2.

Rukkusu st./VA D of *rakāsu* "to bind, fix"; note also VA sg. in LL: MSL 6, 24: 226 (door); 13, 149b: 5 (house) → 10.2.

Rummû st./VA D of *ramû* "to be(come) weak, loose".

Rummuku st./VA D of *ramāku* "to bathe".

***Ruppudu** "?"; **OA**, cf. AHw sv *rapādu* II D 1.

Rupp/bbuhu "?"; **OB**: MSL 13, 120: 190 (hand).

Rupp/bbuk/qu PN → 10.6.3.2.

Ruppušu "broad", cf. *rapšu* id. and *rappašu* in 3.1.3.1, and → 3.1.3.3; **SB**: Izbu 149: 97'f (tongue); TBP 11c: VII 15 (a woman's navel); SpTU 4, 149: III 33f (id., 33 is a gloss on *kupputat*); AfO 19, 56: 22. 24 (the *milku* of a god); MSL 13, 213: 25. [SBH 69: r.9 obscure].

Ruqqu st. D of *râqu* "to be(come) empty" (ARM 9, 17: 11 = (08A)).

Ruqququ LL "thin, small", cf. *raqqu* id. and *raqqaqu* in 3.1.3.1 and → 3.1.3.3, **OB**: RitDiv. 35: 105 (pustule (*zihhu*), cf. note 22); **SB**: MSL 13, 213: 26; 7, 101: 424, cf. 9, 194.

Ruṣṣunu "acclaimed, honoured" (?), cf. *raṣānu* "to make a loud noise, acclaim" → 7.6.1 and 10.7.2; **OB**: OEC 11 p. 16: 23f; **SB**: SAA 3, 4: r.II 14'; Or. 36, 122: 118; BWL 252: 11 (all: person); JAOS 83, 425: 20 (LL).

Ruššû "red", cf. *rasû* "to be(come) red", passim, cf. AHw sv *ruššû* I → 10.6.2 with note 20.

Ruššuku "dried out, withered"; **OB/SB** said of exta → 10.7.1.1: YOS 10, 18: 52; 22: 18; DA 217: 14; CT 30, 6: 19 // TU 2: 51. r.8f (all: pustule (*zihhu*), cf. note 22); YOS 10, 35: 17 (*ṣibtu*); CT 31, 40: IV 18 ("finger" of the lung); other cases: **SB**: Izbu 148: 89' (tongue); 231: 377c (comm.: *ru-uš-šu-kát = ab-la-at*). Also ARM 18, 2: 6 (*ihzū* "mountings", OB): same word? [RitDiv. 35: 105 read *ru-uq-qú-uq*].

Ruššušu "?", cf. *rašāšu* "to become red-hot" ?; **SB**: KAR 367: r.8 +D (cont. br.).

Ruttutu "trembling", cf. *ratātu* "to tremble, shake", see note 4; **OB**: AS 16, 24: 108 (LL).

Ruṭṭubu st./VA D of *raṭābu* "to be moist" (e.g., TCL 17, 6: 6; VA also MSL 14, 265: 10') → 10.4.2.

Ru''umu st. D of *râmu* "to love"; **SB**: Or. 36, 118: 37; St. Kraus 202: 29; cf. also OB PNF [f]*ru-ú-ma-tum/tim* ARM 26/1 p. 599 sv [f]*Rûmatum*.

S

Subbuku st. of *subbuku* "to plait?".

Subbulu "?", **SB**: ACh. Išt. 7: 67 (planet, cf. AHw sv *zabālu* D 4).

Subbusu VA of *subbusu* "to assemble" → 8.6 (only ABL 774: 7).

Sudduru st./VA D of *sadāru* "to do regularly, to set in a row".

Suhhû st. of *suhhû* "to disturb, confuse" (unclear: ArOr 17/1, 192: r.19 (fingers); KAR 71: r.7 (mouth)).

***Suhhumu** (only fem. *Suhhuntum, Suhuttum*) → PN 10.6.3.2.

Suhhupu st. D of *sahāpu* "to cover, overwhelm, lay flat".

Suhhuru 1. "curved, curly" → 10.3.3, **OB/SB** passim of hair, parts of the liver, and body parts, cf. CAD sv. (also RitDiv. 32: 52; 34: 96; JCS 37, 148f no. 18: 10. 27; Epilepsy p. 61: 20); **2.** st./VA of *suhhuru* "to turn" (trans.) → 7.5.3, e.g., ARM 26/1 p. 267 no. 101: 29 = (04) and see note 10.

Sukkuku "deaf", cf. *sakāku* "to clog" → 10.3.2, 10.6.2, passim, cf. CAD sv (also ARM 26/2 p. 140 note 7; ARM 24 p. 169; MDP 57, 246: 7; SKS p. 94: 14). Also PN → 10.6.3.2.

Sukkulu (name of a dog of Marduk): "wegraffend" acc. to AHw sv, cf. *sakālu* I "to appropriate", but CAD sv "mng. unkn." (but refers to *sakālu* "to balk, to get stuck"), see note 4; var.: *sukkumu*; cf. *ukkumu* below.

Sukkupu st. D of *sakāpu* "to lie down, to rest". [*Sú-ku-up* AbB 6, 13: 9 unclear].

Sukkuru st. D of *sekēru* "to dam, block".

Sulluhu st. D of *salāh/'u* "to sprinkle". Also PN → 10.6.3.2.

Sullulu "?"; **SB**: CT 38, 13: 82 (house).

Sullumu st. of *sullumu* "to forfeit a pledge" (OB Elam) (CAD sv, but AHw sv *šalāmu* D 9 "restituieren"). Also PN → 10.6.3.2.

Sullunu "luxuriant"; **SB**: VAB 4, 168: 27 acc. to AHw sv *sullunu* I.

Sullutu st. D of *salātu* "to split" → 10.6.1.1.3.

Sullu'u "ill", cf. *salā'u* "to become ill"; **OB**: ARM 26/2 p. 425 no. 489: 19. 25 (person).

Summu "red", cf. *sâmu* id.; **OB**: YOS 10, 47: 22 (blood), cf. note 19 to Ch. II.

Summuhu st./VA of *summuhu* "to mix, include, decorate".

Summunu "one eighth part", cf. *samāne* "eight", acc. to AHw sv (CAD different) (LB).

Sunnup/bu st. D of *sanāp/bu* "to tie" (AGH 42: 6 (context broken)).

Sunnuqu 1. "closed" → 10.3.2, **OB**: YOS 10, 24: 29; 26: I 26; 29: 3 (the "palace gate", the "palace" (or "palace <gate>"?) and the "gate" of the liver, resp.); **SB**: AnBi. 12, 283: 38 (doors); "scarce, restricted", **OB**: OBTR 120: 13. 24 (rations); "dense, narrow", **OB**: ARM 27, 25: 33 ([city]?: "densely built"); **SB**: ArOr 37, 485: 58 (furrows: "closely aligned", acc. to Civil 1994: 82); MSL 13, 181: 15 (alley); **2.** st./VA D of *sanāqu* "to check, interrogate, harass".

Sunnušu "?", cf. *sanāšu* "to insert"? **MB/SB**, cf. CAD sv (qualifies *lubuštu* "garment").

Suppuhu 1. st./VA D of *sapāhu* "to scatter, disperse"; **2.** "sparse" (hair), **SB**: TBP 4c: II 14'.

Surru "?", cf. *sâru* "to whirl, circle"?; **SB**: Izbu 93: 50' (jaws, Leichty: "loose").

Surrudu "packed, loaded", cf. *sarādu* "to load, pack"; **MB**: ZA 45, 200: 15 (asses); **SB**: STT 71: 36 (wagon); MSL 8/1, 51: 361 (ass).

Surruhu st. of *surruhu* "to destroy" (UM 1/2, 48: 7).

Surruqu st. D of *sarāqu* "to strew, sprinkle, scatter".

Surruru "mendacious", cf. *sarāru* "to cheat, to be criminal"; **SB**: ZA 43, 96: 15 (person).

Su"ulu PN → 10.6.3.2.

Su"uqu (?) "narrow", cf. *sīqu* id.; **SB**: Sg. 8: 330 *mēteqa su-ú-qa* "a narrow path" (but cf. CAD sv *sūqu* adj., AHw sv *sūqu* 5b: standing for *sīqu* ?).

Ṣ

Ṣubbû "perfect", cf. *ṣubbû* "to observe, to plan" ?, **SB**: JAOS 103, 217: 6 (features of a god).

Ṣubbubu st. D of *ṣabābu* "to spread" (wings).

Ṣubbutu **1.** "lame, paralyzed" → 10.3.2, 10.6.2, **OB**: MSL 12, 201: 13; 169: 384 (person); **SB**: TDP 220: 22 (mouth), also *ib.* 64: 41'f (person, ideogr.). **2.** st./VA D of *ṣabātu* "to seize".

***Ṣuddu** (only fem. *ṣuddat*) st. D of *ṣâdu* "to turn or move around" (CT 31, 25a: 14).

Ṣuddû st./VA of *ṣuddû* "to provision" → 8.4.2 (VA: NAPR 5, 5: A 16 = C 17 = D 12' (read *ṣú-ud-du-tam*)).

Ṣudduru (referring to a bodily defect, CAD sv "to twitch", AHw sv *ṣadāru* "etwa "schief werden, liegen"") → 10.6.2, **SB**: CT 40, 38a: 16; SpTU 2, 35: 18 (eyes); TDP 142: 3'; 238: 4 (nose or mouth); LKA 35: 17 (teeth); Izbu 38: 72; AnSt. 10, 120: 32'; 124: 38'. 41' (person). Also PN → 10.6.3.2.

Ṣuhhu (*ṣu"uhu*) "laughing, smiling", cf. *ṣâhu* "to laugh" → 10.3.3, **OB**: ARM 1, 52: 33 (meal: "fancy" acc. to CAD sv; "lächerlich, unsolide" acc. to AHw sv *ṣ.* I); **SB**: BWL 216: 30 (face); CT 38, 14: 3. 21 (appearance of a house and a roof: "pleasant", acc. to CAD sv *ṣâhu* b); also adverb *ṣuhhiš* → 10.7.2, **OB**: YOS 11, 24: 22; ZA 44, 32: 21 acc. to Wasserman, NABU 92/80.

Ṣuhhuru **1.** "small", cf. *ṣehru* id. and *ṣehheru* in 3.1.3.1 and → 3.1.3.3, **SB**: **a**) DA 217: 12 (pustule (*zihhu*), cf. note 22); **b**) of celestial bodies: SAA 8, 114: 8; 10, 100: 20; ACh. Išt. 17: 14; **c**) of (parts of) buildings: Sn. 103: 44; 104: 60; 128: 42; 131: 57; Ash. § 43: 22; VAB 4, 236: 53.
2. st. of *ṣuhhuru* "to deduct" (OA, rarely OB, cf. Veenhof 1972: 430f) → 10.4.2.

Ṣuhhutu (describing a defect of the eyes) → 10.6.2, **OB**: MSL 12, 162: 135; 183: 41; 216: 18'; **SB**: AMT 13, 3: 4; Izbu 213: 39 (*ṣi-ih-hu-tú*); CT 18, 31: 22 + STT 394: 37 (LL). Also PN → 10.6.3.2.

Ṣullulu st./VA of *ṣullulu* "to cover with a roof, put on top" → 8.4.2 (VA only YOS 13, 323; 2); note esp. of liver parts in omens, cf. CAD sv *ṣ.* A v. 1b, and metaphorically "obscure, difficult" VAB 7, 256: 17 (text). [MSL 1, 93: 35 (+ *dīnu*) obscure].

Ṣullumu "black", cf. *ṣalmu* id.; **OB**: CT 44, 37: 9; OBE 14: 23 (pustule (*zihhu*), cf. note 22); *ib.* 1: 17 (filament (*qû*)); see also note 19 to Ch. II. [AfO 18, 306: IV 6 uncertain].

Ṣullupu st./VA D of *ṣalāpu* "to cross out, cancel". [VAB 16 (= AbB 6), 13 : 9 unclear, cf. *sukkup*].

Ṣummû "thirsty", cf. *ṣamû* "to be(come) thirsty"; **SB**: BWL 144: 16 (person), see note 21 to Ch. VII.

Ṣummudu VA D of *ṣamādu* "to prepare, harness, bandage" (LL, said of wagon and plough), cf. CAD sv.

Ṣummuru A st. of *ṣummuru* "to strive for, to plan" → 8.6.

Ṣummuru B "distended", cf. *ṣemēru* "to distend" → 10.6.1.2.2., **SB**: STT 89: 129 (intestines).

Ṣummutu st. D of *ṣamātu* "to transfer" (only PRU 3, 63b: 12).

Ṣuppu (Ass. *ṣa"upu*) st./VA of *ṣuppu* "über-, abdecken" acc. to AHw sv *ṣ.* II, but CAD sv *ṣ.* adj. "solid, massive (objects), thick, compacted (textile) → 8.6.

Ṣuppû VA D of *ṣap/bû* "to irrigate, moisten" (Dar. 382: 22, uncert.).

Ṣuppuru "?"; **OB**: RA 38, 87: 3 (fleece of a sheep). Also PN → 10.6.3.2. [BWL 204 b 6; TBP 9d: r.14' unclear].

Ṣurrû "split" (palm spathes), cf. CAD/AHw sv (Aramaic ?).

Ṣurruhu "high", **SB**: JAOS 83, 429: 265; 443: 118 (house, LL, cf. Durand, CRRAI 38 p. 119 n. e).

Ṣurrumu "concerned", cf. *ṣarāmu* "to strive for"; **OB**: ARM 3, 75: 6 (person) → 7.6.3.

Ṣurrupu st. D of *ṣarāpu* "to burn" (trans.), "to make red" (BWL 36: 110; AfO 19, 52: 150); of silver "to refine", **OA**: passim, cf. CAD sv a, → 10.6.1.2.4; **SB**: CT 17, 23: 183; in omens "red", **OB**: YOS 10, 31: IX 10 = (34A); *ib.* 24 ((parts of the) gall bladder); TBP 13: 15 (face); CT 28, 27: 41 (iris); 39, 14: 22 (water of the river); 41, 22: 21 (earth).

***Ṣurruru** st. of *ṣurruru* "to libate" (NA) (only CA 88: 22).

Ṣurrušu "branching", cf. *ṣurrušu* "to branch"; **OB**: ÖB 2, 20: 42; 48: 150; 62: 9 (oil on water); YOS 10, 22: 23 (pustule (*zihhu*), cf. note 22).

Ṣu"udu "whirling", cf. *ṣâdu* "to whirl, turn about" → 10.3.3, **OB**: JRAS Cspl. 70: 8 (storm).

Ṣu"uhu → *ṣuhhu*

Š

***Šubbu** (only fem. *šubbat*) "?" (describing the gall bladder), cf. *šâbu* "to tremble" ? → 10.7.1.1, cf. CAD sv *šâbu* A 2b.

***Šubbû** st. D of *šebû* "to be(come) satiated, satisfied", **OA** → 10.4.2.

Šubburu st./VA D of *šebēru* "to break, smash"; note esp. VA: **OA** said of copper → 10.6.1.2.4; VA also sg. (ARM 2, 130: 4 (wagon, OB); BE 14, 163: 16 (chair, MB) → 10.2.

***Šubbušu** VA D of *šabāšu* "to collect, gather in" (SAA 7, 108: r.II' 1').

Šuddû → *tuddû*.

Šuddudu "distended" (?), cf. *šadādu* "to stretch, pull" → 10.6.1.2.1, **SB**: TDP 120: 38. 46f; 234: 37 (muscles); 126: 46 (?, rest., subject broken).

Šuddulu "broad, spacious, abundant", cf. *šadlu* id. → 10.7.2, **SB**: passim, cf. CAD sv *šadālu* 2a/b and *šuddulu* (the earth and other localities, buildings, offerings and the mind) (also SpTU 2, 1: I 10; 5: r.52).

Šugguru st. of *šugguru* "to cheat, lie", cf. CAD sv → 8.6.

Šuhhu "long", cf. *šīhu* id. → 10.6.1.2.2, **SB**: Ash. Nin. A V 74 (planks).

Šuhhû A st. of *šuhhû* "to remove, abolish" (CAD sv *š.* B v. a), or "unkenntlich machen" (AHw sv *š.* II D 1) → 8.6.

Šuhhû B VA of *šuhhû* "to ruin, destroy" (CAD sv *š.* adj.; acc. to AHw same verb as *š.* B).

Šuhhû C st. of *šuhhû* "to have (illicit) intercourse" (CAD sv *š.* A v. 1), or "schwängern" (AHw sv *š.* III D) → 8.6.

Šuhhû D "?", **OB**: ARM 26/1 p. 82 no. 5: 45 (person, Durand: "hostile", cf. note r on p. 85).

***Šuhhuhu** st. D of *šahāhu* "to crumble, come loose"; note esp. OA of metal: "loosened" (CAD sv *šahāhu* 2c), "Metall korrodieren" (AHw sv *šahāhu* D 2) → 10.6.1.2.4.

Šuhhuru "?", **OB/SB**: MSL 12, 195: 23; 102: 199 (person, AHw sv: *šu"uru* from *šu"uru* "hairy" q.v.).

Šuhhutu "afraid", cf. *šahātu* "to fear", **OB**: AbB 2, 157: 8; ARM 2, 22: 12 acc. to AHw sv *šahātu* III D.

Šuhhuṭu A st. D of *šahāṭu* "to take off, strip, remove".

Šuhhuṭu B "?", cf. the preceding verb? → 10.7.1.2; **SB**: said of external body parts (side of the throat (*kirru*), spine, buttocks, penis, testicles, pelvis, crotch (*sūnu*)), all in TDP, cf. CAD sv *šahāṭu* B 6.

***Šukkulu** st. of *šukkulu* "to wipe away, polish" → 8.6 (only Or. 17, pl. 36: I 11, context broken, MA).

Šukkusu st. D of *šakāsu* "to dry out" (only of exta: YOS 10, 26: IV 25 (top of a pustule (*zihhu*), cf. note 22); OBE 14: 22f. 25 (pock marks (*ziqtu*)) → 10.7.1.1.

Šukkuṣu "wild" (or sth similar), cf. *šakṣu* id., **SB**, cf. CAD sv (LL) (or read *šūkuṣu*, "elative" of *akṣu* ?).

Šullumu st. of *šullumu* "to keep in good condition, guard, repair, finish, etc." → 10.4.2 (ARM 1, 22: 10f); for CT 38, 11: 47 = (51) → 10.6.1.2.3. Also PN → 10.6.3.2.

***Šullupu** st. D of *šalāpu* "to draw, tear out".

Šulluqu 1. describing a horse, **MB**: AOS 37, 20 no. 11: 12; **2**.: st. D of *šalāqu* "to cut open, split" → 10.6.1.1.3.

Šullušu 1. st./VA D of *šalāšu* "to prepare the soil for the third time"; **2**. "threefold, tripled", **OB/SB**, cf. CAD sv *šullušu* A adj. (also OBE 16: 38'f). Adv. *šullušiš* "in three parts", MVAeG 40/2, 80: 79 (<*šu*>*-ul-lu-ši-iš*, cf. AHw and CAD sv); cf. also CAD sv *šullultu* and *šullul*.

Šulluṭu "masterful", cf. *šalāṭu* "to rule, control" → 10.3.3, **SB**: RIMA 2/I, 194: 6 (god).

Šummu A st. of *šummu* "to think, reflect" (only St. Sjöberg 326: 64, uncert.).

Šummu B st. D of *šâmu* "to allot, appoint, decree" (only Iraq 42, 28: 24', uncert.).

***Šummû** st. D of *šemû* "to hear" (only NA: ABL 896: 13 → 5.5.2).

***Šummudu** st. D of *šamādu* "to apply" (ornaments) (MA).

Šummuhu (*šummuku*) "luxuriant, lavish", cf. *šamhu* id. → 10.7.2, **SB**: passim, cf. CAD sv *šamāhu* 3a/c, *šummuhu* and *šummuku* (gods, offerings, forest, orchard). Also PN → 10.6.3.2.

Šummuṭu A "pointed, tapering", (cf. AHw sv *šamāṭu* II G 2 "spitz zulaufen", *pace* CAD sv *š*. 1e and 2c) → 10.6.1.2.2, **SB**: CT 30, 22b: 5 (parts of the exta); TBP 23: 15 (nostrils); SpTU 4, 149: II 19' (fingers). [VS 17, 4: 3 is a noun rather than a *purrus* form; AbB 6, 8: 24 read *šú-úh-mu-ṭú* acc. to AHw sv *hamāṭu* II Š 1].

Šummuṭu B VA of *šamāṭu* "to strip off, tear loose" (only LL, cf. Landsberger 1967a: 4, 18).

Šunnû A st./VA of *šunnû* "to repeat, report, remeasure; to double" → 10.4.2 (VA only NESA 345: 5).

Šunnû B 1. "different, unusual": **OB**: RA 75, 110: V 36. 40 (appearance); **SB**: Erra I 23 (divine power); BWL 128: 49; IV R 20: 24; IM 67692: 300 (qu. CAD sv *š*. B v. 4d (p. 407a)) (tongue, i.e., language); ND 5502: IV 13 (qu. CAD *ib*. (p. 407b)) (ice); **2**.: st. D of *šanû* "to be(come) different, to change".

Šunnu'u st. D of *šanā'u* "to suffuse" (eyes with blood).

Šuppuku st. D of *šapāku* "to heap up, pour out".

Šuppulu st./VA D of *šapālu* "to be(come) low, go down", in omen protases in hendiadys with another stative, cf. CAD sv *šapālu* 3d → 7.4.3, and in Sg. 8: 190. 242 (*hiriṣṣu* "moat", cf. CAD sv *šapālu* 3b. Also PN → 10.6.3.2. [SpTU 4, 149: III 34 read *ru-pu-šat*].

Šuppuṣu "seized, paralyzed", cf. *šapāṣu* "to seize, grip" → 10.3.1 and 10.6.2, **SB**: (replacing *ṣubbutu*, cf. 6.5.3) TDP 220: 21 (child); CT 20, 8: 10f; 17: r.2f; TU 3: 9 (parts of the liver).

Šuqqû st. D of *šaqû* "to be(come) high, go up" (Ash. § 61: 18, also in omen protases, cf. CAD sv *šaqû* A v. 2b-2' → 7.4.3).

Šuqqulu 1. "scarce", cf. *šaqlu* id., **OB**: ARM 27, 25: 11 (barley → 10.6.1.2.4); AbB 10, 69: 21 (people, *pace* Von Soden, BiOr. 43, 734b); **2**.: st. D of *šaqālu* "to pay" (**OA** only) → 6.6.3.1.

Šurru st. of *šurru* "to bend down, lean, go down" → 8.6 (BBR 1-20: 3 // 75: 20; CT 41, 21: 29).

Šurrû A st. of *šurrû* "to begin, inaugurate" → 8.6 (UVB 15, 37: r.4). [CT 8, 6a: 18 unclear].

Šurrû B st. D of *šerû* "to lean" (intrans.) (CT 20, 7a: 8; Sn. 156 no. 24: 4).

Šurruhu "supreme, abundant, arrogant", cf. *šarhu* id. → 10.7.2, **SB**: passim, cf. CAD sv *šarāhu* A 3 and *šurruhu* adj. (said of gods and kings, of gifts and offerings, of utterances, and of deeds ("arrogant")), e.g., SAA 3, 7: 2 = (55); also SpTU 3, 75: 9 (rites (*sakkū*).

Šurruru "?", cf. *šarāru* (mng. unknown), **SB**: BRM 4, 15: 15 // 16: 13 (the "weapon" mark on the exta).

Šurruṭu VA D of *šarāṭu* "to tear to pieces, to shred"; VA also sg.: MSL 10, 133: 203.

***Šussû** (only MA: *sassu*) st. D of *šasû* "to shout, call" → 7.2.4.

Šuttuhu "elongated", cf. *šatāhu* "to be(come) long, elongated", **OB**: CBS 7005: 1 qu. CAD sv *šatāhu* 2 (snake); **SB**: Ee I 100 (limbs).

Šuttuqu st./VA D of *šatāqu* "to split": "furrowed", **OB**: YOS 10, 55; 3 // AfO 18, 66: 12 (warts); "split into many parts" → 10.6.1.1.3, **SB**: TDP 144: 43' (toes); Izbu 134: 47' (ears); 161: 31' (hoof); Sg. 8: 326 (mountains by torrents).

Šuṭṭuru st. D of *šaṭāru* "to write, register".

Šu"uru A "hairy", cf. *še'ru* id. → 10.4 and 10.6.2, **OB/SB**: said of persons and sheep, cf. CAD sv *š.* A.

Šu"uru B "dirty" acc. to CAD sv *š.* B (same word as A?).

T

Tubbuku 1. st./VA of *tabāku* "to pour out" (MDP 14, 83 no. 26: 11 (barley → 10.6.1.2.4); BAM 222: 15 (textiles ?)). **2.** "limp, lame" → 10.3.2, 10.6.2, **OB**: MSL 12, 169: 385; 201: 12 (person); 13, 230: 315 (feet); **SB**: SpTU 3, 77: 5 (person).

Tuddû (also *šuddû*) st. of *tuddû* "kenntlich machen", cf. AHw sv *tuddû* (secondary formation derived from (*w)adû* D (and Š?)).

Tukkulu "full of confidence, reliable", cf. *takālu* "to trust", **OB**: RA 75, 110: V 3 (goddess); AbB 6, 134: 13 (utensils); **SB**: JAOS 83, 435: 135 (LL: *t.* = *dunnunu*); **NA**: "relying on" (+ *ana muhhi*) SAA 10, 354: r.18; ABL 555: r.8f; 992: r.11 (all: person). Also PN → 10.6.3.2.

Tukkupu st. D of *takāpu* "to pierce, cover with (coloured) specks" → 10.6.1.1.1 and 10.7.1.1, said of the exta in **OB/SB** omens: passim, cf. AHw sv *takāpu* D 3a/b; e.g., YOS 10, 31: IX 9 = (34A); other cases, **SB**: ZA 16, 170: 37; SpTU 1, 27: 27' (flanks of a panther).

Tullû st./VA of *tullû* "to deck out, to drape" → 8.6.

Tulluku "?", **OB**: MSL 12, 160: 91 (person).

Tullulu st. of *tullulu* "to fit out" (UnDiv. 114: 21; CatEdinb. 77: I 5; SAA 7, 166: 3; 165: r.I 6'; 174: 9') → 8.4.2.

Tummû st. D of *tamû* "to swear".

Tummuru st. D of *temēru* "to bury".

Tunnuhu PN → 10.6.3.2.

Tuqqunu st./VA of *tuqqunu* "to sort out, decorate" (mostly with *tiqna*) → 10.4.2.

Turru st./VA of *turru* "to return, report, change into" (trans.); note esp.: in omens "turned around", cf. AHw sv *târu* D 15; "closed" (doors): AbB 7, 50: 9'; AnBi 12, 283: 38.

Turruku "dark, bruised", cf. *tarku* id., and *tarāku* "to beat" → 10.6.1.1.2, 10.7.1.1, **OB**: + exta (YOS 10, 33: IV 39; 36: I 8 = (37); 45: 23. 66ff; 51: IV 21 // 52: IV 22; 53: 5 = (40B); RA 65, 71: 3'. 6'. 11'; ARM 26/1 p. 276 no. 109: 8 = (39B)); **SB**: CT 39, 16: 46 (water); elsewhere in SB said of horns of the moon, cf. SAA 8 glossary sv *tarāku*, and of the exta (but always spelled ideogr. MI.meš).

Turrupu "dotted, speckled", cf. *tarāpu* "mit Farbe überzogen sein ?" (AHw sv, and cf. Von Soden, NABU 91/54) → 10.7.1.2, **SB**: CT 28, 29: 4; TBP 50: r.32 (face); TDP 68: 4ff (ear(s)); 98: 56 (part of the fingers); 208: 80 (eyes); SpTU 4, 149: II 33' (nails); CT 38, 15: 49f (walls).

Turruru "trembling"?, cf. *tarāru* "to tremble", see note 4, **SB**: TDP 20: 16 (base of the skull); 144: 55 (heart).

Turruṣu st/VA D of *tarāṣu* "to stretch, direct" (VA uncert. cf. Landsberger, WO 3, 77 n. 114).

Tu"umu "double, twin", **NB**: BAW 2, 54: 14; HMB 54: 30; **NA**: SAA 1, 203: 3. 5; Or. 17 pl. 23: 3.

Ṭ

Ṭubbu 1. st. D of *ṭâbu* "to be(come) good, beautiful, etc., mostly with *libbu*, → 10.4.2 (OB), and of *ṭubbu* "to refine" (metal) (LB), cf. AHw sv *ṭiābu(m)* D 1b; **2. SB**: Gilg. V I 5; KAR 104: 26 (way (*gerru*)).

Ṭubbû VA D of *ṭebû* "to sink" (only of herbs: "soaked" AMT 4: 28; BBR 1-20: 34). [Erra I 144 unclear].

Ṭubbuhu st. D of *ṭabāhu* "to slaughter".

Ṭuhhû st./VA D of *ṭehû* "to come near, approach" (note esp. OA stat. "to have a claim to", cf. AHw sv *ṭehû* I D I 2).

Ṭuhhudu st./VA of *ṭuhhudu* "to provide or equip abundantly" → 10.4.2.

Ṭummumu "deaf" → 10.3.1 and 10.6.2, **OB/SB**: MSL 9, 129: 274; 14, 125: 718; 534: 6; 17, 196: 45; AS 16, 23: 75; 37: 35; 39: 2 (LL). Also adverb *ṭummumi/eš* → 10.7.2 (AOAT 2, 192: 5; RA 53, 133: [10] +D acc. to AHw sv.).

Ṭuppû st. of *ṭuppû* "to register" (AHw sv *ṭepû* D 1 "in ein Verzeichnis eintragen") → 8.4.2.

Ṭuppušu PN → 10.6.3.2.

Ṭurrudu st. D of *ṭarādu* "to drive away, banish" → 5.6.4 and 6.8.1 (AbB 11, 112: 17 (persons, uncert.)).

U

Ubbubu st./VA D of *ebēbu* "to be(come) clean" → 10.4.2, e.g., ARM 1, 42: 16 = (09), Gilg. M III 10' = (12) (VA only LL: AS 16, 23: 83; KUB 1, 35: 9).

Ubbuhu st. D of *ebēhu* "to gird" (Iraq 31, 31: 37/9, LKA 1: II 21. 37. [Ee V 90 unclear].

Ubbulu "dry", cf. *ablu* id., and *abālu* in 7.5.2; **OB**: St. Reiner 192: 62 (person); **SB**: BRM 4, 32: 8 (flour → 8.7.1.2.4.); **NA**: SAA 6, 288: 15 (seed → 10.6.1.2.4); SAA 10, 226: r.2 (persons).

Ubburu st. of *ubburu* "to accuse" (only MAOG 2/3, 26: 16) → 8.6. [RA 53, 135: 33 unclear].

Ubbutu st. D of *abātu* "to destroy" (VAB 4, 254: 18 and (metaphorically) KAR 350: 19 → 6.4.1.1 sv).

Ubbuṭu A describes one or more bodily defects: "swollen" (cf. *ebēṭu* "to swell", also FM 1 p. 94: 8), or "bound" → "paralyzed" (cf. *ubbuṭu* B and *hubbuṭu*), or "contorted" of eyes or feet (cf. Šurpu VII 24, and *ubbuṭu* "hunger" ?), **OB**: MSL 12, 160: 84; 4, 72: 151f (same verb??); **SB**: Izbu 68: 26 (all: person); MSL 9, 95: 146 (feet); Izbu 47: 19; 123: 28' (eyes, acc. to Farber, ZA 75, 213ff: "blind"); see also *uppuṭu*.

Ubbuṭu B st. of *ubbuṭu* "als Sicherheit nehmen?", acc. to AHw sv *u*. IV (only Iddin-Marduk 28: 9, LB), lit. "to bind" ? (cf. *hubbuṭ* and *ubbuṭu* A). [Cancel AHw's *ubbuṭu* III, acc. to Farber, ZA 75, 216 + note 18].

Uddudu "pointed", cf. *eddu* "sharp, pointed" → 10.4, 10.6.1.2.1, 10.7.1.3, 10.8, **SB**: + horns of the moon: TU 17: 12, SAA 8 passim, cf. glossary sv *edēdu* (= (60B) - (63)); **OA**: "pressed, in a hurry", cf. 7.4.1 sv *ud-dudu*.

Udduhu st. D of *edēhu* "to cover with patches", **OB/SB** → 6.5.3.

Uddulu st. D of *edēlu* "to close".

Uddupu 1. st. D of *edēpu* "to blow into, inflate"; **2**. "windy", see note 4, **SB**: MSL 12, 108: 162 (sky).

Udduru "dark, worried, annoyed", cf. *adāru* "to be dark, worried", **OB**: MARI 5, 167: 11 (heart); MSL 12, 160: 82 (person); **SB**: CT 39, 17: 52 (god); 40, 5: 33f (persons); TuL 58: II 4 ("face" of trees); MSL 16, 159: 179 (person).

Uddušu st. D of *edēšu* "to be(come) new" (e.g., Gilg. XI 242 = (11A); ARM 1, 50: 14; BWL 48: 10; KAR 104: 26).

Uggû "neglectful", cf. *egû* "to be(come) careless, neglectful" → 10.3.3, **OB**: FM 2 p. 12 no. 1: 6 (person).

Uggugu A "angry", cf. *aggu* id., **OB**: MSL 12, 159: 55; 178: 11; **SB**: Ee I 43; IV 60; Gilg. VI 81; Asb. B V 76 (all: person or god).

Uggugu B → *uqququ*

Uggumu "angry", cf. *agāmu* "to be(come) angry" → 10.3.3, **MB**: Tn-Ep. IVb 29; **SB**: Ee II 92 (rest.) (person).

Uhhuru st./VA of *uhhuru* "to come late, be delayed" → 8.6.

Uhhuzu st./VA of *uhhuzu* "to mount" (an object in precious material) → 8.3.3 and 8.4.2; also 1x st. D of *ahāzu* "to marry" → App. to Ch. VI sv.

Ukkudu "crippled" → 10.6.2, **OB**: MSL 9, 80: 176; **SB**: MSL 14, 438: 109; CT 11, 35d: r.15. r.22 (LL) Also PN → 10.6.3.2.

Ukkulu "dark, sombre", cf. *eklu* id. → 10.4.2, **SB**: Ash. p. 23 no. 32: 14; 82-5-22, 559 qu. CAD sv *zīmu* 1b-2' (appearance (*zīmū*)); ACh. 2. Spl. 105: 4 (*zīmū* of the day); Gilg. VII IV 17; CT 28, 29: 3 (face (*pānū*)); ACh. 2. Spl. 105: 5 (the rising (*ṣītu*) of the day); AGH 134: 72 (days); AAA 22, 76: 32 ((shadow of a?)

demon); SpTU 3, 80: 33 (dreams); SAA 8, 502: 14 (sides (*idātu*) of Scorpius). Also adverb *ukkuliš* BWL 70: 15 → 10.7.2.

Ukkumu "rapacious" (name of a dog of Marduk), see note 4, cf. *ekēmu* "to take away" (AHw sv, cf. *sukkulu*). Also PN (dog) → 10.6.3.2.

Ukkup/bu "near, imminent", cf. *ekēp/bu* "to come near, be at hand", **OB**: ARM 26/1, p. 563 no. 261: 8 (expedition); **SB**: AfO 11, 224: 78 (word); ACh. 2. Spl. 103: 11 (rain); LKA 137: 9. 20. 24 (judgment); **NB**: CT 22, 107: 6 ((time for) service). Also adverb *ukkupiš* → 10.7.2, **SB**: CT 38, 50: 55; BWL 82: 208, restored acc. to CAD sv *kīša* b.

Ukkušu st./VA of *ukkušu* "to expel, drive away"; note esp. in extispicy omens: "displaced", cf. CAD sv *akāšu* 3c.

Ullû 1. st./VA D of *elû* "to be high, to go up" → 7.5.3; **2.** "raised", MB/SB, said of parts of the exta (JCS 37, 130: 17; 148: 19; CT 20, 7a: 28f; SAA 4, 283: 4; 308: 3; 326: 2), and "lofty", said of gods (HS 1880: III 13; St. Kraus 202: 35; SAA 3, 2: 34).

Ulluhu st./VA D of *elēhu* "to sprinkle, to decorate".

Ullulu st/VA D of *elēlu* "to be(come) pure" → 10.4.2, e.g., VAB 5, 27: 14 = (16); Gilg. I IV 26.

Ullupu st. D of *elēpu* "to stretch forth", acc. to CAD sv *elēpu* 1b (only CT 41, 26: 2).

Ulluṣu "swollen, hypertrophic", cf. *elēṣu* "to swell, be jubilant", said of parts of the exta → 10.7.1.1, **OB**: JCS 11, 99b: 14 ("split" (*piṭru*)); **MB**: JCS 37, 136: 54; 146: 14 ("fortress" (*danānu*)); 143: 10'; 148: 11 (*nīši rēši*); **SB**: TU 1: 3 (liver); ChDiv. 1, 104: 7; SAA 4, 348: 3' (*danānu*); CT 31, 48b: 11. 13; 30, 35a: r.4 (vertebra (*kunukku*)); KAR 434: r.10 (flesh (*šīru*)).

Ummudu **1.** st. D of *emēdu* "to lean against, to reach" → 11.4.2; **2.** Sg. 8: 387 = (47) → 10.6.1.2.3.

Ummulu "faint, scintillating"; **SB**: of stars → 10.7.1.3, cf AHw sv *u.* I 3 and *(w)amālu* D 3, Dt 2; rest: BWL 54 k (appearance (*dūtu*)); LL of a bed, cf. AHw *ib.* 2. Also adverb *ummuliš* SAA 8, 114: 6; 10, 100: 18 → 10.7.2.

Ummuqu "wise", cf. *emqu* id., **OB**: St. Sjöberg 326: 54; RA 16, 166: II 3f // CT 51, 163: 4f (LL). [TIM 2, 121: 21 qu. AHw sv is read *e!-mu-qá-tum* in AbB 8, 121: 21].

Ummuru "checked, inspected", cf. *amāru* "to see" → 10.6.1.2.4. with note 19, **OA**: cf. AHw sv *ammuru*; **SB**: MSL 9, 202: 359 (bronze); see also *(h)ummuru*.

Unnubu "fruitful, luxuriant", cf. **enēbu* "to grow luxuriantly" → 10.6.2; **SB**: IV R 30 no. 2: 37; MSL 14, 326: 41; CT 18, 31: 13f + STT 394: 29 (LL, cf. AHw sv). Also PN → 10.6.3.2.

Unnunu PN → 10.6.3.2.

Unnuqu LL "narrow" ?, **SB**: MSL 13, 181: 16 (beside *sunnuqu* and *ussuru*).

Unnušu st./VA of *enēšu* "to be(come)weak" (BAM 1: I 11/4 // CT 14, 23b: 11/4 (teeth); VAB 4, 60: 35 (building); CT 11, 36d: 25 (LL, pl.? or abstract?); MSL 14, 269: 13' (abstract?); SAA 1, 223: r.11' (army)).

Unnutu "dim, faint, weak" (cf. also AHw 1553b sv *enētu* D) → 10.7.1.3, **SB**: of celestial bodies, passim, cf. AHw sv *u.* and *enētu* D 3; other cases: Izbu 208b: II 2 acc. to AHw 1553b sv D (belly of a child); BAM 396: I 14 // 159: I 15.

Uppû A st. D of *(w)apû* "to become visible" (?), only in MA formula *uppu laqe* "is acquired and taken (into possession)" (CAD sv *apû* A 2), "ist vorgezeigt und übernommen" (AHw sv *(w)apû* D 2).

Uppû B "cloudy, dim", cf. *apû* "to be(come) cloudy" (of eyes) (but AHw sv *apû* III "zudecken"), **SB**: CT 16, 13: 66 (days); 17, 25: 11 (sky).

Uppulu "late" (in the season), **OA**: Or. 25, 142: 2 (demon, same word?); **OB**: AbB 10, 96: 2' (ploughing); VAB 6, 320: 6 (furrows); **SB**: BWL 244: 38 (barley → 10.6.1.2.4); ACh. Išt. 20: 86 (rain); CT 39, 21: 154 (flood); MSL 8/1, 11: 51 (sheep); 46: 320 (ox). Also as a substantive "late barley", cf. AHw sv 1, and *uppultu*, cf. AHw sv.

Uppuqu "massive, solid, without openings", cf. *epēqu* and *epqu* → 10.7.1.1, 10.6.2, **OB**: YOS 10, 47: 83 // 48: 9 (neck of the sacrificial animal); Izbu 202: 15; 203: 40 (neck of an *izbu*); **SB**: Izbu 51: 62' (eyes); 79: 66f (mouth); 95: 69' (neck); 97: 96' (spine); 134: 46' (ears); 137: 79' (head); KAR 151: 37. 39; CT 20, 39: III 13; ChDiv 1, 128: 7 (all: (part of the) lung); CT 30, 20: 11 (gall bladder); KAR 440: r.3 ("path"); 423: II 43; DA 209: 14 ("palace gate"); CT 31, 25b: r.1f (rib); 20, 37: 17f; 32: 77ff (crucible). [Atr. 94: 26 unclear].

Uppuru st. D of *apāru* "to be covered, to wear on the head", **OB**: Atr. 62: 284 acc. to AHw sv D; **SB**: SKS p. 102: 2 (qu. as (128) in Ch. VI); KAR 395: r.I: 3.

Upp/bburu PN → 10.6.3.2.

Uppusu A "oppressive, insulting" ?, cf. *uppusu* "to protest" → 7.4.3 sv *epēsu*, **OB**: A.7535: 7. 39 (words).

Upp/bbusu B st. of *upp/bbusu* "to hem" → 8.6 (only MKJ 34).

Uppušu st./VA of *uppušu* "to calculate" (mainly OB) or "to copy" (a tablet) (SB). Note also Gilg. I II 36 ("provided with"); VA only CT 18, 2: I 70 (other verb acc. to Landsberger 1967a: 25 note 71.

Upputu "blind" (cf. Farber, ZA 75, 212ff) → 10.6.2; also RA 75, 22: 3 + note on p. 23/5 (OB); SKS p. 94: 14 (OB); see also *ubbuṭu*.

Uqqû A st./VA D of *equ* "to paint, smear" (SpTU 2, 8: I 30; 3, 69 III passim).

Uqqû B "withered"; **SB**: Izbu 54f: 14f; 215: 114f (ear).

Uqqup/bu "crippled" → 10.3.1, 10.6.2, **OB**: MSL 12, 201: 1.

Uqququ "paralyzed, dumb", cf. *eqēqu* "to be tied, paralyzed" → 10.6.2, **SB**: MSL 12, 229: 13 (person); **SB**: AfO 11, 224: 67 (tongue); TU 14: r.32 (LL). [AOTU 1, 283: 10 obscure].

Uqquru A "crippled" → 10.3.1, 10.6.2, **OB**: MSL 12, 160: 79; 179: 37; 205: 30.

Uqquru B "engraved" ?, only in Qatna: RA 43, 148: 116; 150: 127; 156: 190; 160: 222; 176: 30; from which verb? (not *naqāru* D, as CAD sv 4 claims, unless it is an incorrect form).

Urrubu st. D of *erēbu* "to enter" (cf. 7.5.4 sv *erēbu*.

Urruhu "quick", cf. *arhu* id., **SB**: BM 93078: 7' qu. Spirits p. 35: 7' (lion (demon)). Also adverb *urruhiš* passim in lit. texts → 10.7.2, cf. AHw sv.

Urruku "long", cf. *arku* id. and *arraku* in 3.1.3.1, also → 3.1.3.3, **OB**: BiOr. 11, 82a: 7 (qu. as (15B) in Ch. III) (knees of a dog); **OA**: CCT 4, 6c: 19 (unidentified objects, cf. note 7 to Ch. III); **SB**: Izbu 98: 117' (subj. broken).

Urrupu "cloudy, dark", cf. *erēpu* "to be(come) cloudy" → 10.3.3, in literal sense, **MB**: Emar VI/4 p. 255 no. 651: 44 (day); **SB**: MSL 12, 108: 163 ([sky], rest.), SAA 8, 435: 5 (subj. broken); metaph., **SB**: TDP 26: 75; 76: 55; 108: 21f; 244: E 8; BAM 174: 36' // 175: 1 (eyes); TDP 54: 5 (nose); TDP 244: E 9 (face); SpTU 4, 149: I 32 (part of the face); AAA 22, 76: 32 (demon).

Urruru "dried out", cf. *erēru* "to dry out" (cf. Köcher, AS 16, 323ff) → 10.7.1.1, **OB**: YOS 10, 42: III 52; RA 44, 13: 12 (the *nīru* ("yoke") of the liver); **SB**: SpTU 1, 80: 81 (part of the "palace gate"); CT 28, 48: 12; 30, 49b: 16 (gall bladder); TBP 28: 14 (buttocks?); SpTU 4, 149: II 28'; IV 27 (nails).

Urruṣu "?", **SB**: MSL 12, 109: 173a + OIP 97, p. 90 no. 40: 3 (LL). Also PN → 10.6.3.2.

Ussuhu "?", cf. *esēhu* "to assign" ?; **OB**: ARM 9, 97: 20 (garment, cf. AHw sv *halû*); **SB**: CT 38, 8: 35 (potsherds, same word?).

Ussuku A st. D of *esēku* "to assign" (ARM 1, 42: 25).

Ussuku B "?"; **OB**: YOS 10, 55: 4 (warts). [BWL 44: 93; ACh. Spl. 61: 12; BiOr. 14, 193b: 5 unclear].

Ussulu "constipated", cf. *esēlu* "to be constipated", **SB**: AMT 58, 1: 2 + 56, 5: 2 (patient), cf. also CAD sv *eṣēlu* lex. sect.

Ussuru "enclosed, narrow", cf. *esēru* "to shut in, enclose", **SB**: CT 31, 26: 4 (gall bladder); 38, 11: 50 (doors); MSL 13, 181: 14' (alley).

Uṣṣudu "crippled" → 10.3.1, 10.6.2, **SB**: MSL 13, 219: 54.

Uṣṣulu (sometimes *ussulu*) "paralyzed" → 10.6.2, **OB**: ARM 1, 89: 8 acc. to MARI 5, 184; MSL 12, 201: 6; 13, 118: 123 (person); **SB**: TDP 92: 42 ([feet]); 144: 42 (toes, rest.); ROM 991: 18ff qu. CAD sv *eṣēlu* lex. sect. (hands+feet); Izbu 158b: j (limbs of a sheep); 183: 40' (legs of a foal); further LL: MSL 12, 143: 24f; 13, 219: 50 (person); MSL 17, 210: 10' (hands+feet).

Uṣṣuru st./VA of *eṣēru* "to draw, design"; VA also sg. → 10.2: "branded" (slave) Camb. 290: 3; Dar. 492: 2; "marked" (gecko) MSL 8/2, 62: 235a.

Uššubu "blooming, abundant", cf. *ešēbu* "to grow luxuriantly", **SB**: MSL 13, 161: 40 (laments); SBH 37: 2f // IV R 30 no. 2: 38 (person).

Uššuqu "?", **OB**: MSL SS 1, 23: 25 (teeth).

Uššušu "worried, distressed", cf. *ašāšu* "to be(come) worried", **OB**: ARM 26/1 p. 136 no. 22: 5; MSL 12, 168: 336; **SB**: OEC 6, 42: 4; 44: 5; SAA 3, 47: 6f; AnSt. 6, 156: 140; MSL 17, 224: 137f.

Uttuku A "bent, curved", cf. CAD sv *etēqu* B (AHw: *atāku*) "to bend, twist" → 10.6.1.2.2, **SB**: CT 41, 16: 19 // 17b: 6 // 18: r.4 (date palms); KUB 37, 31: 6 (subj. broken); CT 41, 29: r.12 (LL).

Uttuku B st. D of *etāku* "to alert" (only NA: ABL 170: r.14; SAA 8, 94: 4).

Uṭṭû "dark", cf. *eṭû* "to be(come) dark" → 10.6.1.2.2, **SB**: Iraq 31, 31: 41 acc. to AHw 1555b sv *eṭû* II D (eyes).

Uṭṭulu st. D of *eṭēlu* "to be(come) mature, adult" (Ee I 88: the *ṣītu* "birth" of a god, cf. CAD sv *ṣītu* 2a).

Uṭṭuru st. D of *eṭēru* "to pay", cf. CAD sv *eṭēru* B 2a.

U''ulu st. of *u''ulu* said of water: "to coagulate" (CAD sv *e'ēlu* 4c), "zusammenlaufen" (AHw sv D 3) →9.1.4.

Uzzubu "malformed", cf. *izbu* "malformed baby or young" → 10.3, **OB**: MSL 12, 169: 391/3; 195: 25; 13, 118: 42; **SB**: 8/1, 24: 173; 49: 339r; 8/2, 21, 180d. [MSL SS 1, 22: 36 from *ezēbu*?].

Uzzuhu st. D of *ezēhu* "to gird" (Gilg. I v 7).

Uzzuzu "raging, furious", cf. *ezēzu* "to be furious", **OB**: Atr. 92: 54 (wind); **SB**: AGH 118: 6. 8 (god); 134: 94 (mind (*kabattu*)).

W

(W)uddû st. of *(w)uddû* "to inform, mark, identify, assign".

Wulludu st. D of *(w)alādu* "to give birth, produce, beget".

(W)uqquru: cf. *(w)aqru* "scarce, precious, expensive", only in OA *waqqurtum* or *uqqurtum*, a PN or a kind of priestess → 10.6.3.2.

(W)urrû VA of *(w)urrû* "to cut off" (CAD: *arû* C) → 8.6 sv (MSL 5, 119: 309).

(W)urruqu "green, yellow", cf. *(w)arqu* id., **OB**: ÖB 2, 15: 11 (oil, *ú-ru-uq* // PI-*ru-uq*), **SB**: TBP 50: r.30' (mole). Also PN → 10.6.3.2.

(W)urrušu "dirty", cf. *(w)aršu* id. → 10.4, **OB**: MSL 12, 195: 24 (person); **SB**: RA 53, 135: 32 (people); BHLT 64: 14 (clothes); ACh. Šam. 2: 8 (brilliance (*šarūrū*) of a star); MSL 4, 35: 92; MSL 16, 85: 223, and passim in *urruštu* "unclean woman", cf. AHw sv *(w)urrušu*.

(W)ussumu "suitable, proper", cf. *(w)asmu* id., **OA**: HUCA 39, 23: 26; **SB**: VAB 4, 76: 17. 21 (temple); Wedg. 16: r.14 (deeds). Also PN → 10.6.3.2.

W/muṣṣû st. of *w/muṣṣû* "to spread, open wide" (only BA 5, 339: 2) → 8.6.

(W)uṣṣubu st. D of *(w)aṣābu* "to add" → 6.8.5 (only ARM 26/1 p. 467 no. 226: 13).

(W/m)uššuru st./VA of *(w/m)uššuru* "to let go, release" → 10.4.2; **2.** "loose" of parts of the liver, cf. AHw sv *wašāru* D 9b (also RitDiv. 32: 45; JCS 37, 130: 9; 150 : 54); of the eyes of an *izbu* (Izbu 95: 72'); of knees (MSL 13, 230: 324); "flowing" of hair (Gilg. II IV 6; RA 18, 166: 15; UnDiv. 108: 10. 14). Also PN → 10.6.3.2.

(W)uššuṭu "fierce, obstinate", cf. *(w)asṭu* id., **MB**: UM 2/2, 20: 11 (horses); **SB**: SpTU 4, 100: 1 (neck of a man).

(W)uttû st. of *(w)atû* "to find, search, select" → 6.8.1 sv (Tākultu 126: 166).

(W/m)utturu st./VA of *(w)atāru* "to exceed, surpass" (mainly **OA** versus *batqum* or *batiq* "deficient", cf. Veenhof 1972: 405ff). Other cases, **OAk**: in PN *Wu-túr-bēlī* OIP 14, no. 79: 4; **OB**: FM 2 p. 221 no. 119: 15 (persons: "too many"); in PN: *Wu-tu-ur-dunnī* AbB 9, 238: 3; 266: 1; **SB**: AS 16, 285: 20 (a cow *šiknātemu-tu-rat* "of imposing figure" (tr. CAD sv *šikittu* A 1b)); BWL 158: 7 (person *uttur pîšu* "boastful"); 160: 18 (person: "superior"); MVAeG 40/2, 80: 87 (of hair: "excessive").

W/mu"uru st. of *w/mu"uru* "to order, send, command".

Z

Zukkû st./VA of *zukkû* "to clean, to free, to winnow" → 10.4.2 and note 10, e.g., TCL 17, 4: 6 = (07).

Zukkuru st. D of *zakāru* "to declare, mention, invoke, swear".

Zummû st./VA of *zummû* "to deprive, miss, be deprived of" → 8.6 (VA only KAR 26: 27, uncert.).

Zunnû "angry", cf. *zenû* id., **SB**: MSL 17, 47: 12; ZA 19, 382 K.3597: 5 (the sun and the moon).

Zunnunu st. D of *zanānu* "to provide with" (Sg. Cyl. 47).

Zuqqunu "bearded", cf. *zaqnu* id. → 10.4, 10.6.1.2.2, **OAk**: WO 9, 211: 10 (persons).

Zuqqupu "standing on end" (hair), cf. *zaqāpu* "to erect, plant", **SB**: TDP 30, 101. 108f; Syr. 33, 125: r.5; SpTU 1, 84: 29.

Zuqquru "elevated, raised", cf. *zuqquru* "to build high, to raise" → 10.7.1.1, **OB/MB/SB**: only in liver omens said of the *manzāzu* or parts of it, cf. CAD sv *zaqāru* 2b (but AHw interprets *sukkur* from *sekēru* "to block, dam", cf. sv *sekēru* D 2b); also JCS 37, 130ff passim. [JCS 11, 102a (= 37, 147): 17 uncertain].

Zuqqutu "pointed", cf. *zaqātu* "to sting", **OB**: YOS 10, 18: 60 ("weapon" mark); 44: 58 ("foot" mark, text *zu-qú*-QÁ-*at*); RitDiv 32: 51; 35: 109 (several marks on the liver); **SB**: CT 30, 44a: 6 (top of the "weapon" mark); MSL 4, 72: 169. [RA 41, 32: 10 unclear].

***Zurrû** st. D of *zarû* "to sow, scatter" (only OA: PennsOATexts no. 13: 9, cf. Veenhof 1987: 67 note 18).

Zu"unu st./VA D of *za'ānu* "to be provided, adorned with". Also PN → 8.7.3.

Zu"uru "twisted", cf. *zâru* "to twist" → 10.6.1.2.1., **SB**: SAA 8, 218: 2; 547: 1'; LKU 120: 8; ACh. Išt. 28: 6; Spl. 48: 6 ("horns" of celestial bodies).

Zuzzu (also *zu"uz*) st. D of *zâzu* "to divide, distribute" → 6.5.2 sv.

CHAPTER ELEVEN

THE DEVELOPMENT OF THE D-STEM

11.0. This chapter shows how the various ways in which the D-stem is used - as described in the Chapters V to X - are interrelated, and how these uses have developed out of the original nature of gemination as an iconic device used to underline the expressive character of certain words.

In principle, it is a matter of conjecture how the D-stem has evolved into the extraordinarily productive category with the variety of functions that we find in Akkadian. It is precisely this productivity which has obscured many of the processes that have been operative. Therefore, this chapter is necessarily more speculative than the preceding ones, but it is so only to a limited extent, because almost all stages in the functional development of the D-stem have left observable traces in the language, and because other languages provide typological parallels to the developments that I assume to have taken place. This enables us to reconstruct these developments with a reasonable degree of certainty.

11.1. The rise of the D-stem

It seems a plausible assumption that the verbal D-stem is a denominative formation originating from adjectives with gemination of the second radical. This has been maintained by several scholars (Wright 1890: 198; Rundgren 1964: 76f; Ryder 1974: 165; Kuryłowicz 1972; 7 and 154) and is indicated by the following points.

First of all, many D-stems, not only in Akkadian, but also in other Semitic languages, are demonstrably derived from nouns (cf. 8.3). This shows that the D-stem is a common and productive device for the formation of denominative verbs, although it is not the only verbal stem with this function (cf. 8.3.2).

Secondly, cross-linguistically, verbs derived from adjectives with the meanings "to be", "to become", "to make" or "to cause" the quality expressed by the adjective are among the most common types of derived verbs, cf. Comrie 1985: 345f. Many languages have such verbs, even though they do not have other morphological causatives. This is true of most Western European languages; English, for instance, has many verbs derived from adjectives, such as *to cool, to lengthen, to equalize,* etc. (cf. 7.1.4), but no real causative verbs, apart from a few lexicalized relics, such as *to lie* : *to lay, to sit* : *to set, to fall* : *to fell, to drink* : *to drench.* Kuryłowicz (1964: 88) considers verbs derived from adjectives to be the starting point for the development of morphological causatives.

Third, as already claimed in various places in this study (e.g., 7.2.3), there is a strong association between the D-stem and adjectives. This can easily be deduced from a perusal of the Appendix to Chapter VII, where verbs predominate which denote typical adjectival concepts, such as states, conditions and qualities.

Almost all common simple adjectives have a derived *purrus* adjective, and most of them also have a verbal D-stem with factitive function. Rather than listing them all, it is more economical to concentrate on the exceptions, i.e., those adjectives which do not have a corresponding *purrus* adjective and/or a factitive D-stem.

There are two types of such adjectives, first, those which use the Š-stem instead of the D-stem, and, second, those which do not have any derived adjective or verb with gemination or another kind of extension. The first type was discussed in 7.2.3. It is a small group and it cannot normally be established why its members use Š instead of D.

The second type is more relevant in this context. If we leave out a number of extremely rare and uncertain cases, we can list the following adjectives belonging to it:

A/ekṣu	dangerous, overbearing	**naṭû**	fitting, appropriate[f]
akû	crippled[a]	**ne/abû**	bright
dabru	fierce, mighty	**pelû**	red
dapnu	heroic, martial[b]	**pîqu**	narrow[g]
emṣu	sour	**saklu**	stupid, barbarous
erhu	aggressive[c]	**ṣēnu**	evil, wicked
eršu	wise	**šaggu**	stiff (CAD), kraftlos (AHw)
gaṣṣu	ferocious	**šegû**	wild, raging
kaššu	powerful (flood)	**šēru**	terrible, fierce
katû	poor, destitute	**šību**	gray, old[h]
laššu	absent[d]	**šūru**	black, grey[i]
la'û	weak, small[e]	**ṭarru**	bearded
nadru	raging, furious	**(w)ēdu**	single, alone[j]

Notes: a) mainly used as subst. b) also *dăpinu* (or *dāpinu*), *dappinu*, *dappānu* (cf. 3.3.2). c) acc. to AHw sv, but byform of *arhu* "quick" acc. to CAD sv. d) rarely as a noun, usually stative "(there) is/are not". e) mostly as subst. "small child, baby" (*la'û* beside *šerru la'û*). f) stative only. g) unless *tu-pa-aq* ZA 36, 188: 29 belongs to this verb rather than to *epēqu*. h) mainly used as subst. "old man/woman, witness". i) acc. to AHw, but CAD sv *š.* adj. "mng. uncert.". j) mainly used as subst.

Most of these words typically occur as epithets in rather stereotyped literary contexts (*a/ekṣu, dabru, dapnu, erhu, eršu, katû, nadru, ne/abû, pīqu, ṣēnu, šēru*); some others are mainly found in lexical texts (*šegû, ṭarru*). Only a few of them have a wider currency and are also attested outside literary texts (*la'û, naṭû, pelû, šību, šūru, (w)ēdu*). *Laššu* is a secondary formation, built upon *lā išû* "have-not", cf. AHw sv. In the case of *la'û* the derivation of a form with gemination was doubtless blocked because of the homonymous *purrus* adjective *lu''û* "dirty" and its verbal D-stem "to make dirty, defile"; this may also apply to other cases such as *ne/abû* (cf. *nubbû* "to lament"), *šēru* (cf. *šurru* "to descend, to lean"), and *šību* (cf. *šubbu* "to cause to sway or tremble").

For the rest, the main reason why these adjectives do not have a derived form with gemination is doubtless that there was felt to be no need for them, because they were only used in conventional and stereotyped expressions. This applies most clearly to those used as epithets in literary texts.

Apart from the D-stems derived from adjectives, there is a second large class of D-stems, namely those derived from transitive verbs, which were discussed in Chapter VI. As noted there, it mainly concerns verbs with a high degree of inherent transitivity. There is a correlation between the degree of transitivity of a verb and the frequency of its verbal adjective. It is typical of highly transitive verbs to have a VA that is relatively frequent as compared to the VAs of low transitivity verbs. This is caused by the fact that, generally speaking, the frequency of a VA is related to the extent to which the state it denotes is relevant for the entity that has undergone the action expressed by the verb, the patient. If this action entails a drastic, permanent, or generally salient change in the patient, the resulting state will be highly relevant, and speakers will often find occasion to express this state as an attribute of the patient (cf. GAG § 77g). Accordingly, VAs of the highly transitive verbs discussed in Chapter VI are fairly common, such as *edlu* "closed", *hablu* "wronged", *halṣu* "pressed" (of oil), *hepû* and *šebru* "broken", *kanku* "sealed", *kaṣru* "joined, organized", *mahṣu* "beaten", *mesû* "washed", *naksu* "cut", *parsu* "severed", *paṭru* "loosened", *petû* "open(ed)", *raksu* "bound", *saphu* "scattered", *ṣabtu* "seized", etc. (see the dictionaries ssvv).

On the other hand, an important criterion for low transitivity is that the actions involved do not entail a salient change in the patient himself, but in the location or position of the patient (cf. 5.6.2.1). Therefore, the resulting state will generally not describe a very relevant characteristic of the patient. The situation is aptly described by Landsberger (1926: 362), who qualifies the verbs which are here characterized as highly transitive as "resultatbildend", and summarizes the difference as follows "[H]ole ich ein Brot vom Bäcker, so ist dieses für die Zukunft kein geholtes, aber ein zerbrochener Gegenstand bleibt zerbrochen."

Accordingly, the VAs of lowly transitive verbs tend to be conspicuously more infrequent than those of highly transitive verbs. As to Akkadian, VAs of the lowly transitive verbs, such as those mentioned in 5.6.2.1, are, generally speaking, very rare. For instance, those of the very frequent verbs *ahāzu* "to take", *leqû* and *mahāru* "to receive", *nadānu* "to give", *našû* "to carry", *rašû* "to acquire", *šakānu* "to place", *šâmu* "to buy", *šapāru* "to send", *(w)abālu* "to bring", *zabālu* "to carry" are rare, some of them even virtually unattested, at least in their primary function of attributive adjectives; if they are found, it is mainly in idiomatic expressions (*našû* in *našia(m)/našâ rēši(m)* "with raised head"), in lexicalized meanings (*nadû* "abandoned, uncultivated, fallow"), and then most of all as substantives: *šaknu* "governor, commander", *šapru* "envoy"; *leqû* "adopted child"; *kalû* "captive", from *kalû* "to detain, hold back", etc. (see the dictionaries ssvv). As a real VA in its basic attributive function with a literal meaning, it is very rare.

Consequently, the frequency of the use of the D-stem of transitive verbs correlates with the frequency of the corresponding (verbal) adjective. This suggests that the nucleus of the D-stems of transitive verbs came into being via the verbal adjective, from which a VA with gemination was derived. The model of *damqu* "good" → *dummuqu* (adj.) gave rise to a derivation *ṣabtu* "seized" → *ṣubbutu* (VA), which was subsequently expanded with a denominative verbal D-stem: *damqu* → *dummuqu* (adj.) → *dummuqu* (verb), *ṣabtu* → *ṣubbutu* (VA) → *ṣubbutu* (verb). In the case of lowly transitive verbs, for instance *nadānu* "to give", a process *nadnu* → **nuddunu* did not occur because of the rarity of *nadnu,* in combination with the fact that the meaning "to give" did not promote the use of forms with gemination, given the association of the latter with salient and more or less stable qualities. Occasionally, however, such forms could arise by analogy with highly transitive verbs, e.g., OA *laqqu'u* from *leqû* (OA *laqā'u*) "to receive", cf. App. to Ch. VI sv. We may conclude that the VA has played an important role in the spread of D-stems of transitive verbs, on a par with the role of the adjective in the factitive D-stems.

There can be little doubt, however, that the actual derivation of the D-stems of transitive verbs is not based on the VA, but on the G paradigm as a whole: synchronically, *ṣubbutu* "to seize" is not derived from *ṣabtu,* but from *ṣabātu* (see 11.2.4), because *ṣabtu* itself is a derived form dependent on the paradigm of the G-stem. The important point here is that the frequency of D-stems of transitive verbs, which are not derived from adjectives, cannot be adduced as an argument against the original association of D with adjectives.

The conclusion seems to be justified, then, that the nucleus of the D-stem as a verbal category is to be found in adjectives with gemination of the second radical. Akkadian has two adjectival patterns with gemination of the second radical: *purrus* and *parras* (cf. 3.1); it is likely that, at least originally, they were in complementary distribution: *parras* for adjectives denoting dimensions, *purrus* for other adjectives, cf. 3.1.3.3. Of these two patterns, *purrus* is by far the most productive. Therefore, I will speak of *purrus* as the pattern from which the verbal D-stem is derived, leaving the possibility open that for the adjectives with a *parras* form the verbal D-stem is derived from this *parras* adjective.

11.2. The spread of the D-stem

In historical Akkadian there seem to be no restrictions on the derivation of D-stems from any particular kind of G-stem; all differences which may have existed in earlier periods in this respect between various classes of G-stems have been obliterated by the productivity of the D-stem. This makes it difficult to reconstruct in detail how the D-stem has spread.

However, starting from the hypothesis that the verbal D-stem is a denominative of *purrus* adjectives we can distinguish a number of stages in the derivational process which has led to this spread. We may hypothesize that generally speaking the beginning of an earlier stage is likely to have preceded the beginning of the next one, but for the rest older stages remained productive, so that in practice they occurred largely simultaneously.

11.2.1. D-stems from *purrus* adjectives

The first stage is - *ex hypothesi* - the derivation of verbal D-stems from *purrus* adjectives. It has remained productive throughout the history of Akkadian. This can be deduced from the existence of rare verbal D-stems such as *huppudu* "to blind", *duššupu* "to make sweet", *burrumu* "to weave, to twine", which are derived from the adjectives *huppudu* "blind", *duššupu* "sweet", and *burrumu* "multicoloured". The fact that these adjectives are much more common than the corresponding verbs and denote typically adjectival concepts (stable, inherent qualities), suggests that the verbs are denominated from the adjectives (cf. 8.4.1).

11.2.2. D-stems from simple adjectives

However, since most *purrus* forms have a simple adjective existing alongside, which is the basic form of the paradigm of adjectival verbs, the derivation *dummuqu* (adj.) → *dummuqu* (verb) is equivalent to (*damqu* →) *dummuqu* (adj.) → *dummuqu* (verb), which has been reanalysed as *damqu* (→ *dummuqu* (adj.)) → *dummuqu* (verb). In this way a direct association has developed between the simple adjective and the verbal D-stem. Such a shift in the source of a derived category is common in the history of languages: a form built upon another form which is itself not basic, can be associated directly with the basic form, in this case the simple adjective (cf. Kuryłowicz 1972: 7, 154, and see 11.2.4 below). Thus the dominating and most productive procedure for deriving verbal D-stems is directly from the simple adjective.

In normal circumstances it is hardly possible to reconstruct the precise background of a derivational structure. For most verbs, for instance, we have no direct evidence to establish whether a D-stem such as *dummuqu* "to make good, improve" is ultimately derived from *damqu* "good", from *dummuqu* "good" or from the G-stem *damāqu* "to become good".

In some cases, however, phonetic peculiarities of the forms involved can reveal the exact relationship between such forms. For the case at hand it concerns the adjectives *qašdu* "holy" and *eššu* "new". They come from the roots QDŠ and 'DŠ, so that the expected adjectival forms are **qadšu* and **edšu*. The cluster *-dš-*, however, is avoided in Akkadian (GAG § 29d, Reiner 1966: 50f): it is either assimilated to *-šš-*, as in *šeššu* < **šedšu* "sixth", and in *eššu*, or it undergoes metathesis: *qašdu* instead of **qadšu* (GAG § 36b); on a morpheme boundary it is realized as *-ss-* (GAG § 84b).[1]

The regular D forms of these roots are *quddušu* (adj. and verb) and *uddušu* (verb), based on the underlying forms **qadšu* and **edšu*. They remain in use throughout the attested history of Akkadian, cf. CAD sv *qadāšu* 3/4/5, *edēšu* 2/3. However, in RIs from the MA period and other SB texts from Assyrian sources, *quddušu* is replaced by *quššudu* (adj. and verb).

The metathesis in this form can only be explained if we derive *quššudu* directly from the adjective *qašdu,* in which *-šd-* is phonologically motivated; *quššudu* cannot arise from the other possible source of the D-stem, the G-stem *qadāšu* (which is actually only attested as an infinitive in LL and probably did not exist as a real form in normal language, cf. note 2 to Ch. V).

Likewise, *uddušu* "to renew" is rivalled, in OB Susa and SB/LB, by an alternative *uššušu* (cf. AHw sv *u.* III), which can only be based upon the adjective *eššu,* just as *ullulu* "to purify" is based upon *ellu* "pure", etc. It cannot be based upon the G-stem *edēšu* "to become new".

This change in the relationship between adjective and D-stem is also indicated by the fact that for some very common factitive D-stems the corresponding *purrus* form is extremely rare or demonstrably secondary, e.g., for *mullû* "to fill, to cover", *(libba) ṭubbu* "to satisfy", *bulluṭu* "to keep alive", *šullumu* "to keep well, to complete", etc., cf. 10.4.2.

11.2.3. D-stems from verbal adjectives

Beginning as a derivation of adjectives the D-stem could easily spread to verbs via VAs. There is no clear-cut distinction between basic and verbal adjectives. Although we can distinguish in Akkadian a large group of typical basic adjectives (which denote stable, inherent qualities, use the patterns *paris, paras* or *parus,* and occur far more frequently than the corresponding adjectival verb) and an even larger group of VAs (which are derived from fientive verbs, only use the pattern *paris,* typically denote the result of the action denoted by the verb, and are generally speaking less frequent than the verbal forms of the paradigm), there is an intermediate group with the pattern *paris,* of which it is difficult to establish to which category a specific adjective belongs. It consists especially of intransitive change-of-state verbs, such as *berû* "to be(come) hungry" and *abālu* "to be(come) dry".

The existence of such an intermediate group whose members are ambiguous as to whether they are basic or verbal adjectives is likely to have facilitated the spread of the verbal D-stem from basic to verbal adjectives, as described in 11.1. The derivation of D-stems from VAs led in particular to the creation of D-stems of transitive verbs. For intransitive verbs, a derivation *pahāru* "to come together" → *pahru* "assembled, being together" → *puhhuru* (VA) → *puhhuru* (verb) "to bring together" gave rise to *pahāru* "to come together" → *puhhuru* (verb) "to bring together", through the same process.

11.2.4. D-stems derived from all kinds of verbs

This eventually led to a situation in which a D-stem could be derived from any G-stem, even without the existence of a VA or stative, through a direct association between the G-stem and the D-stem. This development is another example of the process mentioned in 11.2.2: in this case the relationship 1. basic verb → 2. deverbative noun → 3. denominative verb changed into 1. basic verb → 2. deverbative verb, by skipping the intermediate stage (cf. Kuryłowicz 1972: 7, 154). It allowed the creation of D-stems of intransitive atelic verbs (Type II), which do not have a stative or VA, such as *nabāhu* "to bark" → *nubbuhu* "to bark (loudly?)". It is also conceivable, however, that purely verbal forms with gemination have existed from the outset, independent of those which were derived from adjectives, and were subsequently incorporated into the D-stem.

In this way the D-stem has become a true "derived verbal stem" in the sense in which this term is generally used in Semitic studies. Etymologically, therefore, the D-stem is denominative (cf. 8.3.1), since it was originally used for deriving verbs from adjectives and nouns, but synchronically it is also deverbative: it serves to derive verbs from other (simple) verbs.

The function which these different types of D-stems acquired is determined by the contrast with other verbal forms of the same root, notably the G-stem, and is therefore not necessarily uniform. This will be elaborated in the following sections.

11.3. The functional differentiation of the D-stem

The next issue to address is the functional differentiation within the D-stem. The main form this differentiation assumes on the grammatical level is the distinction between the valency-extending and the valency-preserving functions (cf. 5.2). The question is: how do we account for the fact that in intransitive verbs the D-stem normally denotes a valency increase (*pahāru* "to come together" versus *puhhuru* "to bring together"), whereas in transitive verbs it preserves the same valency as the G-stem, so that *ṣabātu* and *ṣubbutu* both mean "to seize")?

The association of gemination of the second radical with high transitivity, which applies both to transitive verbs with a D-stem (cf. 5.6.4) and to factitive D-stems (cf. 5.6.1), offers a straightforward explanation for the rise of this functional differentiation and makes it possible to reconstruct how the historical situation found in Akkadian has come about. In order to clarify this process we will use a partly hypothetical example, namely some forms of the root RPŠ "to be wide, broad".

The starting point is the existence of a basic adjective **rapašum* "wide" (historically *rapšu(m)*). From this adjective a G-stem verb was derived: *rapāšu(m)*. Verbs derived from adjectives generally have a very small range of possible meanings. A verb derived from the adjective "good", for instance, will typically have one or more of the following meanings: "to be good, become good, make good/better, do good (to), behave well, regard as good". For most other adjectives the range is even more restricted: in general, a verb derived from an adjective X will mean "to be/become/make X" (cf. 8.3.3 and Comrie 1985: 345f). Thus we may posit as possible meanings for *rapāšu(m)* "to be/become/*make wide".

In many cases an adjective with gemination existed side by side with the simple adjective, in this case *rappašum* (cf. 3.1.3); the semantic relationship between *rapšum* and *rappašum* conformed to the general relationship between neutral and iconic adjectives and could take various forms (in this case *rappašum* came to be used as a plural to the simple adjective, cf. 3.1.3.2). From *rappašum* a verb could be derived, too: *ruppušum* (or *rappušum* in its older Assyrian form), which basically had the same meaning as *rapāšum* ("*to be/become/make wide"), but was restricted in use in a way parallel to that of its source noun *rappašum* (i.e., associated with plurality?).

The simple verb and the verb with gemination could coexist more or less independently, each with its own semantic range. This accounts for the idiomatic and lexicalized D-stems mentioned in 6.8.1 and 6.8.3, for individual cases such as *kuššudu* "to chase away, pursue" versus *kašādu* "to reach, arrive" and *dubbubu* "to harass, entreat" versus *dabābu* "to speak" (cf. 5.5.3), and probably also for at least some of the D tantum verbs (cf. 8.6).

In many cases, however, the two verbs remained closely associated with one another because of their formal and semantic similarity (identity of root consonants and lexical meaning). This state of affairs provided an ideal starting point for a functional differentiation: speakers of Akkadian tended to prefer the form with gemination in transitive sentences, i.e., to express "to make wide", because of the high degree of transitivity inherent in such sentences, which denote a telic action and have an agentive subject and a patient object (cf. 5.3 and 5.4). This led to a restriction of the simple verb to sentences which do not have these characteristics, i.e., to intransitive sentences denoting a process.

The association of gemination with high (rather than low) transitivity is based upon the fact that an increase in transitivity is equivalent to an increase in notions such as duration, intensity and number: it is one of the possible semantic extensions which, as argued in 2.1.5 and elsewhere, are often iconically underlined by gemination in Akkadian. The general connection between high transitivity and intensity was already pointed out by Hopper and Thompson (1980: 264, cf. 7.3.3).

Through this process *ruppušum* acquired its factitive meaning "to make wide", whereas *rapāšum* was restricted to the meaning "to be(come) wide". Thus starting from the following hypothetical situation (for the sake of the argument we render the iconic meaning of *rappašum* and *ruppušum* with "very", in spite of 10.8):

(01)	process	*irappiš* he/it becomes wide	*urappaš* *he/it becomes (very) wide
	action	*irappiš* *he makes wide	*urappaš* he makes (very) wide,

we end up with the situation which is historically attested in Akkadian:

(02)	process	*irappiš* he/it becomes wide	---------
	action	----------	*urappaš* he makes wide

Once the tendency to associate the D-stem with actions and to restrict the G-stem to processes has set in, it will soon become obligatory, because it is in two respects a development towards greater isomorphism (cf. 2.1). First, it offers the possibility to match the semantic difference in transitivity, and the concomitant syntactic difference between transitive and intransitive (in the traditional sense of the word) with a morphological difference.[2] Second, it leads to a consistent association of the most common types of verbal D-stems (the factitive D-stems of Types III and IV and the D-stems derived from transitive verbs of Type I), with high transitivity.

As we argued in 5.6.3, this development filled a gap in the system: cross-linguistically, the tendency to make a morphological distinction between actions and processes is a widespread phenomenon; according to Nedjalkov-Silnitsky 1973: 4, and Haspelmath 1993: 100ff, only a few languages share the peculiarity of English that it frequently uses the same form for intransitives and causatives as in *to open* and *to break* (cf. also 7.1.7).

On the other hand, this process caused the loss of another distinction: that between the neutral meaning of the G-stem and the original iconic meaning - for instance, their association with plurality, etc. - of the forms with gemination. Since *urappaš* did not contrast any longer with *irappiš* in the meaning *"he makes wide", its original meaning was lost and only the factitive meaning survived. The empty slot beside *irappiš* was filled by the Gtn-stem and that beside *urappaš* by the Dtn-stem (neither stem is attested for this verb, but this is doubtless accidental: Gtn-stems of adjectival verbs are generally uncommon, cf. 6.7.3). This explains the peculiarity noted in 6.7.3. that the Gtn-stem is rare in transitive verbs with a valency-preserving D-stem: in these verbs the function of D did not shift from an iconic to a valency-related one, so that no empty slot occurred for the Gtn-stem to fill.[3]

This model also explains the relationship between the D- and the G-stems of the transitive verbs of Type I and the intransitive verbs of Type II. These D-stems are valency-preserving and have a considerably less predictable relationship to the corresponding G-stem than the factitive D-stems. As argued in 5.6.3, this is caused by the fact that there is no significant difference in the typical degree of transitivity with which they are associated. Therefore, the development outlined above, which is made possible by the sharp contrast in transitivity between actions and processes, did not take place in transitive verbs, in which the G-stem is highly transitive, too. Thus, the transitive verbs with a D-stem preserved the original contrast between neutral and iconic, the latter of which was realized in various more or less unpredictable ways, such as plurality, lexical differentiation, etc.

The intransitive verbs of Type II are typical fixed-valency verbs, because they denote activities which cannot come about without an agent; therefore, their D-stems cannot have a factitive function. Instead, they preserve the intransitive nature of the G-stem. It is possible - but difficult to prove on the basis of the contexts in which they occur - that their meaning is intensive or durative as compared to that of the G-stem, cf. 7.6.2.

Consequently, the association with high transitivity explains not only the fact that D-stems of intransitive verbs are factitive (valency-extending) in function, but also the fact that those of transitive verbs are not factitive, but valency-preserving.[4]

11.4. Additional evidence: the "factitive G-stems"

It cannot be proved that a G-stem such as *rapāšum* could also be used for "to make wide", i.e., that it could be factitive, in a prehistoric stage of Akkadian, nor that the D-stem *ruppušum* ever meant "to become (very) wide".[5] However, there are a number of indications that point in this direction. First of all, there are typological parallels, such as the fact that verbs derived from adjectives in English and other languages are often alternating valency verbs, cf. 7.1.4. Second, a more important argument is the fact that some Semitic languages, including Akkadian, have preserved remnants of a situation in which the intransitive and the factitive use of a verb are both expressed by forms of the G-stem, either with different vocalizations or without any formal distinction. These are the "factitive G-stems", which were mentioned in 7.2.5. In 11.4.1 we will discuss such cases in so far as they occur in other Semitic languages than Akkadian (mainly from Arabic), and in 11.4.2 the evidence from Akkadian itself.

11.4.1. Evidence from Semitic.

Arabic instances of factitive G-stems are *waqafa* "to stop" (trans. and intrans.), *fatana* "to charm" and "to be charmed", *ᶜadala* "to be equal" and "to make equal", *ḫabara* "to perish" and "to destroy" (cf. Brockelmann 1913: 139f; Saad 1982: 66). They represent real alternating valency verbs, comparable to the English verbs mentioned in 7.1.4.

Apart from these cases, there are also traces of a different way of formalizing the distinction between intransitive and factitive, namely by means of vowel alternation (apophony). Arabic, for instance, has - beside the factitive G-stems mentioned above - verb pairs such as *ḥazina* "to be sad" versus *ḥazana* "to make sad", *xafiya* "to be hidden" versus *xafā* "to hide" (cf. Brockelmann 1913: 139f; Saad 1982: 66; Fleisch 1979: 280ff note 1; Kuryłowicz 1972: 67f; D. Cohen 1984: 148f). Hebrew has *mālā* "to fill" beside *mālẹ* "to be(come) full". Such cases are residual, cf. Fleisch and Saad, *ll.cc.*: in Arabic, factitives are productively derived by means of Stems II and IV, and in Hebrew by means of the Piᶜel. This suggests that the latter process has replaced the factitive G-stems with and without apophony, cf. also Rundgren 1966: 136f; 1980: 58ff.

11.4.2. Evidence from Akkadian: factitive G-stems in Akkadian

In Akkadian we find a very small number of factitive G-stems. They suggest that the rather strict separation between intransitive G-stems and factitive D-stems is not original, and that at an earlier stage of the language G-stems were also used in factitive sentences, just as in the Arabic and Hebrew instances quoted above. Apart from a few unique cases (see below), only four such verbs are attested in the older stages of the language (OB and OA); the rest does not occur before SB.[6] These four verbs are:

Emēdu G in its intransitive use means "to lean (intrans.) against, reach, come into contact", cf. CAD sv 1, AHw sv G 1/2; note that its complement can take an accusative, but also *ana*, cf. 5.5.1 sv. The D-stem has the usual factitive meaning: "to lean" (trans.), place on", cf. CAD sv 4, AHw sv D. However, the G-stem can have the same meaning: "to place, lean, impose, inflict", cf. CAD sv 2/3, AHw sv G 3/4/5. The difference between D and G is that the former is mainly used with concrete objects: body parts (usually the hand, sometimes *idu* "arm", *pūtu* "forehead", *qaqqadu* "head" or *zuqtu* "chin"), beams, merchandise, a ship ("to moor"), a river ("to flank" (with embankments)), a field ("to provide" (with water)), etc., rarely with other kinds of objects (fire) (for Sg. 8: 96 = (48) in Ch. X, see 10.6.1.2.3; Erra I 17 *um-mì-da tubqāti* "go into hiding!" (CAD sv 4c-5') is an idiomatic expression of obscure origin).

The G-stem, on the other hand, is predominantly used in fixed idioms with abstract objects, in particular with the meaning "to impose" labour, punishment, fines, taxes and disease (CAD sv 2/3, AHw sv G 4). In addition, G is found in many other contexts, also with concrete objects, for instance, "to load" (donkeys with barley, people with objects (also FM 2 p. 146 no. 80: 11. 17)), "to support" (parts of buildings with columns, esp. in RIs), "to serve" food (YOS 11, 26: II 16), "to impose" a yoke (*apšānu* and *nīru*, but note the metaphorical meaning), etc., cf. CAD sv 2a, 3a, 3l.

The difference between G in its transitive use and D can be summarized as follows. D is restricted to concrete objects, which imply a higher transtivity than abstract ones, because concrete is more salient than abstract (cf. 5.6.4). In accordance with its unmarked status, G has a wider range of use, but is largely stereotyped in fixed expressions. In the present context, the important fact is that G is both intransitive and factitive, and in the latter use interchanges with D.

Dalāpu "to wake up, awake" (intrans.), and "to wake up" (trans.), OB, e.g., in Ét. Garelli 416: 6 *i-da-al-li-ip rē'û ul(i) iṣallal* "the shepherd stays awake, he cannot sleep", versus *ib.* 11 [*e*]*zzum* (...) *i-da-al-li-pa-an-ni* "the goat (...) keeps me awake". D is also trans.: "to keep awake, harass" (cf. CAD sv 3), "feindlich bedrängen, in Unruhe halten" (AHw sv D), but only attested in SB. Possibly, D has a stronger meaning than G in its transitive use.

Kamāsu "to assemble" (people, life stock, harvest) is normally transitive and uses both G and D in this meaning; therefore, it was assigned to Chapter VI and treated in 6.4.5.1 sv. However, there are a few cases in OB where it is intransitive: ARM 26/2 p. 347 no. 437: 29f *mātum kalūša ana dannātim ik-mi-ìs* "the whole region has gathered into the fortresses" (cf. also *ib.* p. 166 no. 364: r.9', partly restored and not quite certain); OBTR 305: 13f *kalūšu ana dunnišu li-ik-mi-ìs* "each man should gather into his stronghold"; YOS 10, 36: I 37 *māt ik-mi-sú ana aburri* *uṣ*$_x$(IZ)-*ṣi-a-am* "the people of the country who had assembled (in the fortress for protection) will be able to go (again) to the outside fields" (tr. CAD sv *aburru* 2a).

These three instances of the G-stem have an animate subject; as we saw in 6.4.5.1 sv, *kamāsu* D is mainly used if the direct object is animate. Thus in this particular use *kamāsu* G can be regarded as a factitive G-stem if it is transitive. We see here the same situation as in *emēdu*: G can be transitive and intransitive, D only transitive; moreover, D is mostly used with animate objects, G both for animate and inanimate objects (barley, the harvest, etc.); the latter are less salient than animate beings.

There are a few more instances of intransitive *kamāsu* with an animate subject, but they are ambiguous because they can also be interpreted as N-stems: YOS 10, 36: I 35 *nawûka ana āl dūri i-ka-mi-is* "your herds will come together into a fortified city" (tr. CAD sv *namû* A 1b-2', note that the following apodosis has the intransitive instance of *ikmisu* quoted above), and ARM 3, 14: 16 and 13, 103: 31 (troops) *i-ka-am-mi-sa-am*. However, all unambiguous instances of *kamāsu* N quoted in the dictionaries have an inanimate subject (barley, silver, (the harvest of) a field, a legal case ("to settle"), sheep plucking ("to finish")). This suggests that the ambiguous cases with an animate subject are G-stems.

If these claims are correct, *kamāsu* is construed in two different ways: if animate beings are subject, the G-stem can be intransitive and factitive, so that *kamāsu* belongs to the factitive G-stems; otherwise it is an ordinary transitive verb, which can only be made intransitive or passive by means of the N-stem. This difference is doubtless caused by the fact that inanimate beings cannot come together of their own accord; therefore, *kamāsu* cannot be factitive if it refers to inanimate beings, cf. 7.1.5.

Šêtu (*sêtu*) intrans. "to be left over, remain, escape", trans. "to leave", mainly OA, cf. CAD sv, AHw sv *š*. II (D uncertain, cf. CAD sv 3).

Three similar cases from OB, which are unique, are the agentive use of *hamāṭu* G "to burn", which is normally non-agentive (cf. 7.3.2, versus D "to burn" (trans.), scorch"), in YOS 11, 26: I 51 *mê ta-ha-ma-aṭ* "you heat the water", that of *mašālu* "to be(come) similar, equal, half", D "to make equal" (also intrans., cf. 7.4.3) in YOS 11, 26: I 19 *līška ta-a-ma-aš-ša-al* "you divide your dough into halves", and that of *šaw/mû* "to burn, to roast", which is transitive in TIM 9, 88: 6 *buqlam ši-wi-i* "roast the malt", but intransitive in ARM 14, 2: 17f *nēšum šū išātam iš-wi-ma* "that lion was roasted in the fire", both OB (cf. also *šamû* G "to roast" in Lugal 94 (SB)). It is possible that these factitive G forms are survivals that are typically preserved in specific kinds of technical language, such as recipes.

Other cases of the factitive use of otherwise intransitive G-stems come from SB. Most of them are very rare; it is, therefore, difficult to judge whether they can be considered instances of the phenomenon under discussion, or whether they represent idiosyncratic secondary developments, or even errors or misreadings. This concerns the following verbs:

Apāru "to put on one's head" (in the stative: "to have/wear on the head") has a factitive D "to put on sb else's head, provide sb with a head dress", just as *labāšu* G "to put on/wear" (clothes) versus D "to dress sb else, provide sb with clothes", with which it is often coordinated (cf. 5.5.2). However, in RIs we find G with the meaning of D: RIMA 1, 234: I 28; 2/I, 147: 9; Sumer 13, 191 // VAB 4, 234: I 23; Sg. 8: 342 + AfO 12, 146: 342; MLVS 3, 34: 5. They might be real archaisms, but also cases of an artificial literary usage. Other instances of G in this meaning are STT 251: 11' and SpTU 1, 12: 10'. MVAeG 41/3, 12: 31 *li-t[ep-pi]-ru-ka* (reading acc. to AHw sv Gtn) is Dt(n) rather than Gtn, *pace* AHw sv Gtn and CAD sv 1c; LKU 32: 12 (= SKS p. 102: 2) is quoted as (128) in 6.9.4.

Arāru "to fear" is used as a factitive in UET 6, 392: 5 (demons) *amēlu muttalliku i-ru-ru-ma* "frightened the suffering man" (tr. CAD sv *a*. B lex. sect.); normally D (TCL 18, 90: 34; Angim 89).

Bašālu "to boil" (intrans.) can be transitive according to CAD sv 3 "to keep boiling" (*ta-ba-ši-il* in glass texts, ZA 36, 194 note 3), sv 4 "to boil (objects) in a liquid" (*i-ba-šu-lu*$_4$ SAA 12, 68: 37), and sv 5 "to bake" (bricks) (only Nuzi HSS 9, 150: 10). However, the first instance is uncertain: AHw sv G 2 interprets it as a stative *bašil* (*bašālu* belongs to the *a/a* vowel class).

Ešû "to trouble, to blur (eyes)" is usually transitive, but is found a few times in OB and SB with the troubled or blurred object as subject: KAR 97: 11 *šamû iš-šu-ú* "the sky becomes dull" (also ZA 43, 309: 1

(rest.), and ZA 47, 92: 25 *namrāti iš-šá-a* "bright things will become dull". D is also transitive, cf. AHw sv D.

Nesû "to go away, to depart", D "to remove, to take far away" (also Š, cf. 7.5.6 sv). A few times G appears in the meaning of D, all SB: Šurpu IV 72 (sin, cf. 87 intrans.!); AnSt. 8, 60: 31 (fear); Or. 36, 120: 80 (illness; Lambert emends to a D form, although both extant manuscripts show a G form), cf. CAD sv 2.

Patānu means "stark werden" and "stärken" according to AHw sv *p.* II G, but the transitive use is only attested in NB, LB and NA PNs, such as DN-*pít-na-an-ni,* which makes it rather doubtful.

Ramāku "to bathe", is normally intransitive, but takes an acc. of the substance bathed in, usually water, cf. AHw sv G 1. D is the normal form for "to bath sb" (people or animals, cf. *ib.* D, 1x Š, cf. 7.5.5.2 sv). However, in medical prescriptions we find a transitive use G with herbs as object: "(Drogen) wässern", *ib.* G 5. The use of G rather than D in this context may be connected with the inanimate nature of the object, cf. 5.6.4.

In comparison to the great mass of regular factitive D-stems, the evidence for the factitive use of the G-stem is extremely scarce in Akkadian. Apparently, the impact of the D-stem on the transitive use of alternating valency verbs was so strong, that they have been almost completely replaced by D forms.

11.5. Conclusions

The following conclusions concerning the verbal D-stem can be drawn from the preceding account.

First of all, in 5.2 and elsewhere we established that the various uses of the D-stem can be reduced to two grammatical functions, namely a valency-preserving and a valency-extending one. The difference between these functions is directly related to a difference between the corresponding G-stems, namely, whether these are transitive or intransitive or, more accurately, whether they typically have a high or a low degree of transitivity.

One of the basic principles of modern linguistics is that the function of a grammatical category depends on its opposition to other categories (cf. Rundgren 1963a: 109ff). If we apply this to the D-stem, we observe that the functional diversity which is so often claimed to be its most typical feature, is largely apparent: it only reflects a difference in the basic category, at least, in so far as the D-stem is not lexicalized; in that case, however, it does not have a grammatical function.

In this respect the D-stem does not differ essentially from other verbal stems, such as the Š-stem and the N-stem. The basic function of the Š-stem is causative, but it can denote both a bivalent and a trivalent causative, depending on whether the G-stem is monovalent (intransitive) or bivalent (transitive). The basic function of the N-stem is the derivation of fientive forms from non-fientive forms such as statives and adjectives. If an N form is derived from an adjective or from the stative of an intransitive verb, it is translated as an ingressive (inchoative) (GAG § 90g) and the N-stem is valency-preserving; if it is derived from the stative of a transitive verb, it is translated as a passive (GAG § 90e), first, because most statives of transitive verbs are "objective resultative" (cf. Nedjalkov-Jaxontov 1988: 8f), i.e., they have the direct object of the basic active sentence as subject and therefore require a passive translation, and, second, because they are in contrast with the G-stem in this respect. In this case the N-stem is valency-reducing. Thus these verbal stems have a uniform function, but the way this function is realized varies depending upon the verb in question (and the context).

All D-stems, then, which are in opposition to corresponding G-stems ultimately have the same function: they denote an increase in transitivity vis-à-vis the G-stem. The difference with the Š- and the N-stem, however, is that the use of the latter two is to a large extent regular and predictable, whereas that of the D-stem is strongly lexicalized.

The second conclusion also concerns an important principle of modern linguistics, namely, that the relationship between form and function - in this context between the form of a morpheme and its grammatical function - is arbitrary. This applies without any doubt to the vast majority of morphemes, including, for instance, the prefixes of the verbal stems just mentioned: *ša-* of the Š-stem and *na-* of the N-stem. In the case of gemination, however, it seems that this principle should be qualified to some extent.

On the one hand, it is obvious that there is no direct relationship between gemination and high transitivity. On the other hand, in the light of the general use of gemination, it is doubtless not accidental - and therefore not arbitrary - that, in a situation in which parallel forms with and without gemination existed side by side, a functional differentiation arose on the basis of the degree of transitivity, in such a way that the forms with gemination were associated with high transitivity, and the corresponding forms without gemination restricted to contexts in which a high degree of transitivity is absent or irrelevant, rather than the other way around. Of the two theoretical possibilites, the association between gemination and high transitivity prevailed because it created a more iconic situation than the reverse one.

Thirdly, it was claimed on several occasions that gemination has the typical function of making a semantic feature which is already present in the context explicit, rather than that of independently expressing a feature that would not be there if it had not been explicitly indicated. This claim was made in particular with regard to *parras* as a plural formation of adjectives denoting dimensions in 3.1.3.2, to *purrus* with the function of indicating plurality and salience in 10.9, and to the D-stems of transitive verbs in 6.4.9 and 6.7.1. In these cases gemination is optional.

Basically, this state of affairs also applies to factitive D-stems. The actual contrast between a factitive verb and its intransitive counterpart can also be expressed - and is doubtless primarily expressed - by a difference in the valency frame (more specifically, the presence of an agent in the former), cf. 7.1.4. and Nedyalkov-Silnitsky 1973: 3. In this case, therefore, the D-stem can also be argued to underline a feature already present in the context. However, the difference with the other categories is that, with the exception of the factitive G-stems, the use of D in factitive sentences is obligatory, doubtless as a result of a gradual spread of the D-stem, furthered by the cross-linguistically strong tendency to differentiate formally between actions and processes (cf. 11.3).

One could therefore argue that the most typical feature of the D-stem is not so much the fact that it seems to have a variety of functions, as the fact that by itself it does not perform any grammatical function at all. Its main function seems to be that of underlining or emphasizing a feature which is already present in the context.

The final conclusion to be drawn with regard to the D-stem is that the "traditional" view about its nature, as held by scholars at the end of the nineteenth and the beginning of the twentieth century (cf. Chapter I), is basically correct. To summarize, their view is that the D-stem is semantically homogeneous, since it is also morphologically uniform, that the original function is the intensive, because the geminate second radical symbolizes the intensification of the action expressed by the G-stem, and that the causative is derived from the intensive, since intensity can imply that the agent makes someone else perform the action (cf. section 1.4 and the quotation from Brockelmann's *Grundriß* on p. 4f).

On all essential points, the results of the present study agree with this traditional view. It turns out that the scholars in question were right in their intuitions about the basically iconic nature of gemination, about the "intensive" meaning that follows from it, and about the priority of the intensive over the causative meaning. However, they did not have the necessary linguistic apparatus at their disposal to give these intuitions a convincing scientific basis.

In this respect, the objections raised by Goetze against the "traditional" view are justified, but in the end they turn out to be unfounded. Especially the fact that Goetze disparages the relationship between gemination and intensity as a "romantic notion", rather than a correct intuition about the nature of language, led him to a vision which has obscured rather than clarified the real nature of the D-stem.

Notes to Chapter Eleven

1 Of **qadšu* we only find the fem. *qadištu* (a kind of woman, cf. CAD sv), in which *d* and *š* are not contiguous so that it is not against the rule. Beside *qašdu* we also find **qaššu* (in OB Mari *qaššatum*, a type of consecrated woman, cf. CAD sv). In their literal use as adjectives, **qaššu* and *qašdu* are almost completely replaced by the *purrus* form *quddušu* and its secondary form *quššudu*, which also serve as basis for the factitive verbs *quddušu* and *quššudu* "to purify, consecrate", cf. App. to Ch. X ssvv, AHw and CAD ssvv, and Hirsch, AfO Beiheft 13, 57f note 298.

2 This process is an example of Kuryłowicz's fifth "law" of analogy: "Pour rétablir une différence d'ordre central la langue abandonne une différence d'ordre plus marginal" (1973: 80). In this case the semantic (and largely redundant) difference between G and D is abandoned in favour of a syntactic difference. Another matter is whether we should speak of *rétablir* or perhaps of *établir* for this Akkadian process; see 11.4.1 below.

3 This explanation of the factitive function of the D-stem was anticipated by Rundgren (1963a: 104ff; 1964: 77; 1966: 135f), who based himself on Kuryłowicz's explanation (1956: 86ff) of the causative function of the IE suffix **-eje/o-*. Rundgren points to the similarity between the development of **-eje/o-* from iterative/denominative to causative and that of the D-stem. However, Rundgren's insistence on the fact that the iterative function must have become unproductive for the factitive function to develop (1963a: 105, 109, 111, 114), seems to be contradicted by Akkadian: the use of the D-stem for plurality, durativity, etc., does not become lost, but is restricted to transitive verbs, for which a factitive function does not develop. This suggests that in factitive verbs the association with plurality, durativity, etc., seems to have been abandoned only as a result of the rise of the factitive function, not vice versa.

4 According to Kuryłowicz 1956: 88 (quoted by Rundgren 1966: 135) "Les exposants formels du mode d'action deviennent des morphèmes indiquant la diathèse (voix) ou se lexicalisent." The former happened to the factitive D-stems, the latter to many D-stems of transitive verbs and of intransitive verbs of Type II.

5 I assume that the intransitive use of factitive D-stems illustrated in 7.4.3 is a secondary phenomenon that is not directly connected with the development discussed here.

6 Note that the transitive and intransitive use of the G-stem of *malû* "to be(come) full" and "to fill, to cover" represents a different phenomenon, cf. 7.3.1 end.

CHAPTER TWELVE

GEMINATION: FROM ICONIC TO GRAMMATICAL

12.1. In Chapter II (2.1.5) those categories of Akkadian were listed that show gemination of the second radical, with an outline of the functions which are generally ascribed to them. Now that we have established these functions more accurately, we are in a position to sketch an overall picture of the role of gemination in Akkadian and its development from iconic to grammatical. The categories in question are repeated here, with a short description of their function(s) based on the results of the present study:

1. The present tense gemination, which - as argued in 2.2.4.2 - can be explained as resulting from the grammaticalization of an originally iconically motivated category which probably expressed durativity, iterativity or a similar notion.

2. The D-stem (including the secondary stems (Dt, Dtn, ŠD) derived from it, which were described in Chapter IX). With the exception of the marginal group of intransitive D-stems discussed in 7.6, and a number of D tantum verbs listed in 8.6, the basic function of the D-stem is that of underlining an increase in transitivity vis-à-vis the corresponding G-stem. In intransitive verbs this is usually realized as the factitive function (Chapter VII); in transitive verbs the D-stem is associated with plurality and salience, mostly plurality of the direct object and the action itself, sometimes of other constituents, cf. Chapters VI and XI.

3. The Gtn-stem, which serves to denote various aspects of verbal plurality, cf. Chapter IV and 6.7.3;

4. The pattern *parras*, whose main function is that of underlining plurality and salience in adjectives denoting dimensions, cf. 3.1.3;

5. The patterns *parris* and *parrās*, which denote agent nouns; the geminate underlines the more nominal character of these words, which correlates with the more permanent nature of the activities expressed, cf. 3.2, 3.3 and 3.4;

6. The pattern *purrus*, which is partly nominal, serving to underline salience and plurality, cf. 10.6, and partly verbal, as stative and VA of the D-stem, cf. 10.2;

7. A few substantives which form their plural by means of gemination, cf. 2.1.5.

12.2. In order to explain the functional relations between these categories three claims were made in Chapter II concerning the general nature of gemination, in so far as it is motivated and contrasts with a corresponding form without gemination. First, the functions performed by the majority of the categories enumerated in 12.1 show a striking degree of similarity: they have to do with nominal or verbal plurality. This suggests that there is a relationship between gemination and the expression of plurality, and that gemination can therefore be explained as an iconic phenomenon: the formal extension (gemination) corresponds to a semantic extension (plurality). Second, gemination has an expressive origin since it plays an important role in the formation of expressive words, comparable to that of reduplication and some other formal extensions. Third, gemination is involved in a process of grammaticalization which has partly eroded its iconic nature and made it into a grammatical device to perform various grammatical functions.

12.3. On the basis of these three claims we can describe the nominal and verbal categories of Akkadian that show gemination of the second radical as representing different stages in this process of grammaticalization.

The starting point is the use of gemination as an expressive device. It is found in individual words which belong to the semantic classes defined in 2.2.3 as being especially susceptible to expressive extensions, i.e., those which refer to highly salient entities or qualities. They differ from the contrasting simple words in that they contain, apart from their referential meaning, an additional nuance expressing the emotional involvement of the speaker, which is iconically reflected in a formal extension. They typically belong to sporadic, unproductive patterns. In this category, gemination is still closely related to reduplication and other formal extensions. Instances from Akkadian and other Semitic languages were mentioned in 2.2.4.1.

Only a small number of the motivated words with gemination can be regarded as expressive in the strict sense of the word. The great majority of them belong to productive patterns and tend to show a rather consistent semantic relationship to the basic category, i.e., they tend to be predictable in meaning. This is also the case in Akkadian: the sporadic patterns referred to above are hardly found here (cf. 2.2.4.1); almost all Akkadian words which can be considered expressive on the basis of the semantic criteria just mentioned belong to a single pattern: *purrus* (cf. 10.6.2 and 10.6.3). This shows that in Akkadian the grammaticalization of these words is already on its way.

12.4. Among the productive patterns with gemination we can distinguish several types on the basis of the extent to which they show grammaticalization.

The first type consists of three categories, which can be taken together because they are more or less equivalent in this respect: the pattern *parras* in its most common function of underlining plurality in adjectives denoting dimensions (3.1.3), the pattern *purrus,* mainly in its lexical function (cf. especially 10.3, 10.6 and 10.9), and the D-stems of transitive verbs (cf. 6.4.9 and 6.7.1).

In these categories the forms with and without gemination seem to alternate without any observable difference. However, the forms with gemination are more restricted, in that their use is dependent upon the presence of two semantic features in the context: a relatively high degree of salience and (often) some aspect of plurality. Gemination makes these features explicit. In contexts which meet the conditions of salience and plurality, a speaker of Akkadian can choose whether he will use a simple form or a form with gemination. If he chooses the simple form, he leaves the salience involved unexpressed and implicit in the context; if he chooses the form with gemination, he makes it explicit.

The relevance of salience here provides the link between this use of gemination and its use for expressivity. The factors determining which form the speaker chooses are similar to those which determine whether he chooses a real expressive form as defined in the previous section, or the corresponding neutral form.

Thus the use of these categories with gemination is optional. This makes the relationship between forms with and without gemination a classic instance of that between a marked and an unmarked category, cf. the account of Comrie (1976: 112):

> One of the most decisive criteria [of markedness] is that, in many cases, the meaning of the unmarked category can encompass that of its marked counterpart. The clearest example of this situation is where overt expression of the meaning of the marked category is always optional, i.e. where the unmarked category can always be used, even in a situation where the marked category would also be appropriate."

Gemination of this type is functionally non-contrastive, in the sense that we do not find cases where forms with and without gemination are used in opposition to each other; if they are used side by side, they are either alternative forms referring to the same situation or quality, or else they accompany and underline another difference between the clauses in which they occur, typically the contrast between singular and plural.

12.5. The second type comprises the patterns for agent nouns, of which only *parris* and *parrās* will be considered here (cf. 3.2 and 3.3). It resembles the previous group in that these patterns have the same function as the corresponding simple category *pāris*. In this type gemination underlines the more nominal character of the word in question, which correlates with the expression of a more permanent activity, as is natural in words denoting professions and habitual activities.

In principle *parris* and *parrās* forms can interchange with *pāris* forms, and it seems likely that they are non-contrastive, just as the previous type. However, the widespread alternation of forms with and without gemination in the same contexts which is so typical of the words of the previous type, is largely absent here. This shows that in practice these agent nouns are lexicalized to such an extent that for many specific cases only one pattern is available, whereas the other possible patterns have been differentiated in meaning or are not used at all (cf. 3.4).

Moreover, this type differs from the previous one in that it shows no association with salience (apart from the trivial fact that agent nouns are primarily persons). Its productivity suggests that the actual creation of *parris* and *parrās* forms is a purely analogical process in which the iconic nature of the geminate has become conventional.

12.6. The third type comprises the Gtn-stem. Just as the two previous types it is clearly iconic in that it denotes verbal plurality. On the other hand, it differs from them in being contrastive: we find contexts in which G and Gtn are directly in opposition to each other (cf. 4.3 end). Therefore, it can denote verbal plurality independently of the context; in this respect it is not optional in the sense in which the first and second type are optional. However, such notions as iterativity and habituality are often indicated by the context as well; this is actually how the function of Gtn evolved: from a form which could express contextually determined durativity, cf. 4.1.2.1.

The Gtn-stem denotes verbal plurality in general, without any connection with salience. This is due to the fact that this connection is only possible if a corresponding non-salient (or less salient) category is available. However, as noted in 4.1.2.1, the category with which the Gtn-stem originally contrasted, the form *iptaras,* lost its contextually determined durative function when it shifted to a perfect; in this way the Gtn-stem became the only category available for the expression of verbal plurality.

12.7. The fourth type is the factitive D-stem, discussed in Chapter VII. Gemination is contrastive and obligatory here, with the proviso mentioned in 11.5 about the factitive G-stems and the primary nature of the *syntactic* difference between intransitive and factitive. The actual use of the factitive D-stem has no association with salience or plurality for the reasons expounded in 11.3: the contrast between geminate and simple forms shifted from iconic versus neutral to factitive versus intransitive, which resulted in the loss of the iconic aspects of its meaning. However, the rise of the factitive function as described in 11.3 was made possible by the association of gemination with salience, which is a basic ingredient of high transitivity (cf. 5.4).

Factitivity is one of the most important ways in which gemination of the second radical has been grammaticalized in Akkadian. As a result, the iconic nature of the geminate, which is readily observable in the meaning of the first three types, where the presence of the geminate correlates with a clear extension in the meaning of the form, is less evident in the factitive D-stem. In those types the contrast between the geminate and the simple form can be described as quantitative: gemination correlates with an increase in number, duration or frequency. In the factitive D-stem gemination has acquired a more abstract value: instead of a concrete, "quantitative" difference, we find a difference between geminate and neutral which can be called "qualitative", namely a difference in transitivity.

The pluralizing function of the first three types implies a lower degree of grammaticalization than the valency-changing function of the fourth type. The usual development is from expressing notions such as plurality to performing valency-related functions, and not vice versa, cf. Kuryłowicz 1956: 88. Therefore, D-stems denoting plural action represent a more original stratum of D-stems, at least functionally, than those which denote an increase in valency, cf. 11.3.

12.8. The fifth type is the geminate of the present tense (*iparras*). It represents an advanced stage of grammaticalization (see 2.2.4.2). It has a purely grammatical function, although its basic function of expressing non-completed actions is doubtless related to its original durative character, cf. the relationship which generally exists between imperfective aspect and durative Aktionsart (Comrie 1976: 25ff).

This also applies to the sixth type, the pattern *purrus* in its function as the stative and verbal adjective of the D-stem, cf. 10.2. This function is purely grammatical and is only indirectly connected with the originally iconic nature of gemination, namely, in so far as the verbal D-stem from which the *purrus* form is derived is connected with it.

12.9. Beside the process of grammaticalization described in the previous sections, which has led to the rise of various grammatical categories with a specific function, there is also a continuous process of lexicalization through which individual words develop their own idiosyncratic and unpredictable meanings, and thus become more or less independent of the category to which they formally belong, cf. 2.2.4.3.

Especially many D-stems of transitive verbs (cf. in particular 6.8.3 and 6.9.3) and many *purrus* adjectives (cf. 10.7) have been lexicalized to a large extent. They are stereotyped in meaning and use, do not contrast any more with the corresponding simple form, and thus have not preserved many traces of their original iconic character.

12.10. This leads us to the following conclusions. First of all, the impact of grammaticalization on the role of gemination in Akkadian can be demonstrated by means of a comparison between the functions of the various nominal and verbal categories with gemination. The combined evidence which they provide supports the claim that in motivated categories with gemination which contrast with simple categories gemination has, or originally had, an iconic function, even though this may not be obvious in each of these categories individually.

Second, the two most important verbal functions of gemination in Akkadian are that of indicating the present tense and of underlining high transitivity; both result from the grammaticalization of the former iconic function of gemination. The third function is that of underlining plurality and salience, both in verbal and in nominal categories.

Third, grammaticalization has led to a functional diversification of the categories with gemination, so that the connection between them was obscured. Each of the types distinguished above represents a different stage in this process. But also within a single category the status of gemination may vary widely. This is most evident in the pattern *purrus*. On the one hand, it has largely preserved the expressive character of gemination in the adjectives for salient bodily characteristics (12.3) and belongs to the first type (12.4) because of its association with plurality. On the other hand, it also belongs to the sixth type (12.8), in so far as it serves as the stative and verbal adjective of the D-stem (cf. 10.2). Therefore, *purrus* is a prime example of a formally uniform category which has fallen apart through grammaticalization.

Fourth, in this way not only the D-stem but all motivated categories with gemination can be associated with each other, since they have a common background, although they differ in the extent to which they have been grammaticalized and in the concrete function that they perform as a result of this process.

ABBREVIATIONS and BIBLIOGRAPHY

GENERAL ABBREVIATIONS

acc. = accusative
act. = active
adj. = adjective
apod. = apodosis
App. = Appendix
approx. = approximate(ly)
Ass. = Assyrian
Bab. = Babylonian
Bo = Boğazköy
coll. = collective
constr. = construction
D (in +D) = duplicate
disc. = discussed
DN(F) = divine name (fem.)
EA = El-Amarna
esp. = especially
exc. = exception(ally)
fem. = feminine
GN = geographical name
ideogr. = ideographic(ally)
idiom. = idiomatic(ally)
imp. = imperative
inf. = infinitive
intrans. = intransitive
lex. sect. = lexical section (CAD)
LB = Late Babylonian
lit. = literal(ly)
LL = lexical list(s)/text(s)
MA = Middle Assyrian
masc. = masculine
MB = Middle Babylonian
med. = medical (text(s))
metaph. = metaphorical(ly)
MN = month name
NA = Neo-Assyrian
NB = Neo-Babylonian
non-ag. = non-agentive
OA = Old Assyrian
OAk = Old Akkadian
OB = Old Babylonian
obj. = object
part. = participle
pass. = passive
pers. = person(al object)
pl. = plural
pl. t. = plurale tantum
PN(F) = personal name (fem.)
pres. = present
pret. = preterite
prob. = probably
prot. = protasis
refl. = reflexive
rest. = restored/restoration
RI = royal inscription
rit. = ritual (text(s))
RN = royal name
qu. = quoted
sb = somebody
sg. = singular
stat./st. = stative
sth = something
subj. = subject
subst. = substantive
tr. = translation
trans. = transitive
Ug. = Ugarit
uncert. = uncertain
unident. = unidentified
VA = verbal adjective

ABBREVIATIONS OF SERIES AND PERIODICALS

AfO	Archiv für Orientforschung
AOAT	Alter Orient und Altes Testament
ArOr	Archív Orientální
AS	Assyriological Studies (Chicago)
BA	Beiträge zur Assyriologie und semitischen Sprachwissenschaft
BiOr	Bibliotheca Orientalis
HUCA	Hebrew Union College Annual
JA	Journal Asiatique
JAOS	Journal of the American Oriental Society
JCS	Journal of Cuneiform Studies
JEOL	Jaarbericht van het Vooraziatisch-Egyptisch Genootschap Ex Oriente Lux (Leiden)
JESHO	Journal of the Economic and Social History of the Orient (Leiden)

JNES	Journal of Near Eastern Studies
JNSL	Journal of Northwest Semitic Languages
MSS	Münchener Studien zur Sprachwissenschaft
MUSJ	Mélanges de l'Université Saint-Joseph (Beyrouth)
Or.	Orientalia (Rome)
OrSuec	Orientalia Suecana
RA	Revue d'assyriologie et d'archéologie orientale
StOr.	Studia Orientalia (Societas Orientalis Fennica)
WdO	Die Welt des Orients
WZKM	Wiener Zeitschrift für die Kunde des Morgenlandes
ZA	Zeitschrift für Assyriologie und vorderasiatische Archäologie
ZDMG	Zeitschrift der Deutschen Morgenländischen Gesellschaft
ZS	Zeitschrift für Semitistik und verwandte Gebiete

ABBREVIATIONS OF TEXT EDITIONS

Editions of Akkadian texts are quoted with the abbreviations enumerated in AHw III p. IXff, with the following additions:

Akîtu	S.A. Pallis, *The Babylonian Akîtu Festival*, Copenhagen 1926.
AKT	Ankara Kültepe Tabletleri / Ankaraner Kültepe-Texte (1/2: E. Bilgiç *et al.*, Ankara 1990, 1995; 3: E. Bilgiç and C. Günbattı, Stuttgart 1995).
AMM	Anadolu Medeniyetleri Müzesi. Yıllığı, Ankara
Angim	J.S. Cooper, *The Return of Ninurta to Nippur* (an-gim dím-ma), Analecta Orientalia 52, Rome 1978.
AoF	Altorientalische Forschungen (Berlin).
ASJ	Acta Sumerologica (Japonica).
Assur	Assur, Monographic Journals of the Near East (Malibu).
BagF.	Baghdader Forschungen (16 = B. Pongratz-Leisten, *Ina šulmi īrub*; 18 = S. M. Maul, *Zukunftsbewältigung*).
BBVOT	Berliner Beiträge zum vorderen Orient, Texte (Berlin).
Berytus	Berytus, Archaeological Studies Published by the Museum of Archeology of the American University of Beirut.
BrockmonT.	R. Kutscher, *The Brockmon Tablets at the University of Haifa: Royal Inscriptions*, The Shay Series of the Zinman Institute of Archaeology, Haifa 1989.
CTMMA	Cuneiform Texts in the Metropolitan Museum of Art, Vol. I, ed. by I. Spar, New York, 1987
Dumuzi	B. Alster, *Dumuzi's Dream, Aspects of Oral Poetry in a Sumerian Myth*, Mesopotamia, Copenhagen Studies in Assyriology, vol. 1, Copenhagen 1972.
Emar	D. Arnaud, *Recherches au pays d'Aštata, Emar VI. 1-4*, Paris 1985-87.
Epilepsy	M. Stol, *Epilepsy in Babylonia*, Cuneiform Monographs 2, Groningen 1993.
Ét. de Meyer	*Cinquante-deux réflexions sur le Proche-Orient ancien*, offertes en hommage à Léon De Meyer, ed. H. Gasche *et al.*, Mesopotamian History and Environment, Occasional Publications II, Louvain 1994.

Ét. Garelli — *Marchands, Diplomates et Empereurs*, Études sur la civilisation mésopotamienne offertes à Paul Garelli, ed. D. Charpin and F. Joannès, Paris 1991

FLAN — *Figurative Language in the Ancient Near East*, ed. M. Mindlin, M.J. Geller, J.E. Wansbrough, London 1987.

FM — Florilegium Marianum, Paris 1992-

Fs. Bergerhof — *Mesopotamica - Ugaritica - Biblica*, Festschrift für Kurt Bergerhof zur Vollendung seines 70. Lebensjahres am 7. Mai 1992, ed. M. Dietrich and O. Loretz, AOAT 232, Neukirchen-Vluyn 1993.

Fs. Deller — *Ad bene et fideliter seminandum*, Festgabe für Karlheinz Deller zum 21. Februar 1987, ed. G. Mauer and U. Magen, AOAT 220, Neukirchen-Vluyn 1988.

FuB — Forschungen und Berichte, herausgegeben von den Staatlichen Museen zu Berlin.

Horn Museum — M. Sigrist, *Old Babylonian Account Texts in the Horn Archaeology Museum*, Andrews University Cuneiform Texts, vol. IV, Berrien Springs 1990.

Iddin-Marduk — C. Wunsch, *Die Urkunden des babylonischen Geschäftsmannes Iddin-Marduk*, Cuneiform Monographs 3a/b, Groningen 1993.

Ištar/Dumuzi — W. Farber, *Beschwörungsrituale an Ištar und Dumuzi*, Wiesbaden 1977.

kt — Siglum of unpublished tablets from Kültepe (Kaniš).

Kültepe-Kaniṣ — T. Özgüç, Eski Yakındoğu'nun Ticaret Merkezinde Yeni Araştırmalar (New Researches at the Trading Center of the Ancient Near East), Ankara 1986.

LB — Siglum of unpublished tablets in the de Liagre Böhl Collection, Leiden.

Lugal — J. van Dijk, LUGAL UD ME-LÁM-bi NIR-ĜÁL, Leiden 1983.

MARI — MARI, Annales de Recherches Interdisciplinaires, Paris 1982-.

MBTexts — O.R. Gurney, *The Middle Babylonian Legal and Economic Texts from Ur*, British School of Archaeology in Iraq, 1983.

Mél. Birot — *Miscellanea Babylonica*, Mélanges offerts à Maurice Birot, ed. J.-M. Durand and J.-R. Kupper, Paris 1985.

Mél. Kupper — *De la Babylonie à la Syrie, en passant par Mari*, Mélanges offerts à Monsieur J.-R. Kupper à l'occasion de son 70e anniversaire, ed. Ö. Tunca, Liège, 1990.

MHET — Mesopotamian History and Environment, Texts, I-, Ghent 1991-.

MSL SS — Materials for the Sumerian Lexicon, Supplementary Series, Rome 1986-.

Mul-apin — H. Hunger and D. Pingree, Mul.apin: *An Astronomical Compendium in Cuneiform*, AfO Beiheft 24, Horn 1989.

NABU — Nouvelles Assyriologiques Brèves et Utilitaires, Paris, 1987-.

NAPR — Northern Akkad Project Reports, Mesopotamian History and Environment, Series I, Ghent, 1987-.

OBE — U. Jeyes, *Old Babylonian Extispicy, Omen Texts in the British Museum*, Leiden 1989.

OBRED — L. Dekiere, *Old Babylonian Real Estate Documents from Sippar in the British Museum*, Mesopotamian History and Environment, Series III, vol. II, 1-4, Ghent, 1994-.

OBTA — R.M. Whiting Jr., *Old Babylonian Letters from Tell-Asmar*, Assyriological Studies 22, Chicago 1987.

PennsOATexts — W.C. Gwaltney Jr., *The Pennsylvania Old Assyrian Texts*, Hebrew Union College Annual Supplements, Number 3, Cincinnati 1983.

RIMA — Royal Inscriptions of Mesopotamia, Assyrian Periods, Toronto 1987-.

RIME — Royal Inscriptions of Mesopotamia, Early Periods, Toronto 1990-.

RitDiv. — I. Starr, *The Rituals of the Diviner*, Bibliotheca Mesopotamica 12, Malibu 1983.

SAA	State Archives of Assyria, Helsinki 1987-.
SKS	W. Farber, *Schlaf, Kindchen, Schlaf!, Mesopotamische Baby-Beschwörungen und -Rituale,* Mesopotamian Civilisations 2, Winona Lake 1989.
Spirits	F.A.M. Wiggermann, *Mesopotamian Protective Spirits, The Ritual Texts,* Cuneiform Monographs 1, Groningen 1992.
SSAW	Sitzungsberichte der sächsischen Akademie der Wissenschaften zu Leipzig (120/3 = Scharf, J.-H., *Anfänge von systematischer Anatomie und Teratologie im alten Babylon,* 1988).
St.Eb.	Studi Eblaiti (Rome)
St. Güterbock	*Anatolian Studies Presented to Hans Gustav Güterbock on the Occasion of his 65th Birthday,* ed. K. Bittel, Ph.H.J. Houwink ten Cate and E. Reiner, Istanbul 1974.
St. Hallo	*The Tablet and the Scroll,* Near Eastern Studies in Honor of William W. Hallo, ed. by M.E. Cohen, D.C. Snell and D.B. Weisburg, Bethesda Md, 1993.
St. Kraus	*Zikir Šumim,* Assyriological Studies Presented to F.R. Kraus on the Occasion of his Seventieth Birthday, ed. G. van Driel, Th.J.H. Krispijn, M. Stol and K.R. Veenhof, Leiden 1982.
St. Reiner	*Language, Literature, and History*: Philological and Historical Studies Presented to Erica Reiner, ed. F. Rochberg-Halton, American Oriental Series 67, New Haven 1987.
St. Sjöberg	DUMU-E_2-DUB-BA-A, Studies in Honor of Åke W. Sjöberg, Occasional Publications of the Samuel Noah Kramer Fund 11, ed. H. Behrens, D. Loding and M.T. Roth, Phila-delphia 1989.
TTK	X. Türk Tarih Kongresi, Ankara: 22-26 Eylül 1986, Kongreye Sunulan Bildiriler, II. Cilt, Ankara 1990.
Two Elegies	S.N. Kramer, *Two Elegies on a Pushkin Museum Tablet,* Moscow 1960.
Udug-hul	M.J. Geller, *Forerunners to Udug-hul, Sumerian Exorcistic Incantations,* Freiburger Altorientalische Studien, Band 12, Stuttgart, 1985.
Viehhaltung	F.R. Kraus, *Staatliche Viehhaltung im altbabylonischen Lande Larsa,* Mededelingen der Koninklijke Nederlandse Akademie van Wetenschappen, Afd. Letterkunde, Nieuwe Reeks, deel 29 No. 5, Amsterdam 1966.

ABBREVIATIONS OF HANDBOOKS

Three important works on Akkadian are quoted by means of an abbreviation:

AHw	W. von Soden, *Akkadisches Handwörterbuch,* Wiesbaden, 1959/81.
CAD	A.L. Oppenheim, E. Reiner, *et al. The Assyrian Dictionary of the Oriental Institute of the University of Chicago,* Chicago/Glückstadt, 1956-.
GAG	W. von Soden, *Grundriß der akkadischen Grammatik,* Analecta Orientalia 33/47, Rome 1952 (GAG^2 refers to additions included in the Ergänzungsheft of 1969; GAG^3 to additions first included in the third edition of 1995).

BIBLIOGRAPHY

Aartun, K. 1975. Über die Grundstruktur der Nominalbildungen vom Typus *qaṭṭāl/qaṭṭōl* im Althebräischen, *JNSL* 4, 1-8.

Ambros, A.A. 1969. Zur Bedeutungsgeschichte der arabischen Nominalform *fa^{cc}āl(at)*, *WZKM* 62, 87-104.

Anttila, R. 1989. *Historical and Comparative Linguistics*, 2nd ed., Current Issues in Linguistic Theory 6, Amsterdam/Philadelphia.

Balkan, K. 1974: Cancellation of Debts in Cappadocian Tablets from Kültepe, in: K. Bittel, Ph.H.J. Houwink ten Cate, E. Reiner (eds.), *Anatolian Studies Presented to Hans Gustav Güterbock on the Occasion of his 65th Birthday*, Istanbul, 29-41.

Barth, J. 1894. *Die Nominalbildung in den semitischen Sprachen*, 2. Aufl., Leipzig.

Bauer, H. 1910. Die Tempora im Semitischen, *BA* 8/1, 1-53.

---. and Leander, P. 1922. *Historische Grammatik der hebräischen Sprache des Alten Testamentes*, Halle.

Beeston, A.F.L. 1970. *The Arabic Language Today*, London.

Berry, M. 1975. *An Introduction to Systemic Linguistics*, London/Sydney.

Binnick, R.I. 1991. *Time and the Verb, a Guide to Tense and Aspect*, New York/Oxford.

Black, J.A. and Al-Rawi, F.N.H. 1987. A Contribution to the Study of Akkadian Bird Names, *ZA* 77, 117-126.

Blake, B.J., 1994. *Case*, Cambridge Textbooks in Linguistics, Cambridge.

Borger, R. 1979. *Babylonisch-assyrische Lesestücke*, 2., neubearbeite Auflage, Analecta Orientalia 54, Rome.

Bottéro, J. 1987. *Mésopotamie, L'écriture, la raison et les dieux*, Bibliothèque des histoires, Paris.

Botterweck, G.J. 1952. *Der Triliterismus im Semitischen*, Bonn.

Brockelmann, C. 1908. *Grundriß der vergleichenden Grammatik der semitischen Sprachen*, I. Band: Laut- und Formenlehre, Berlin.

---. 1913. *Grundriß der vergleichenden Grammatik der semitischen Sprachen*, II. Band: Syntax, Berlin.

---. 1928. Deminutiv und Augmentativ im Semitischen, *ZS* 6, 109-134.

Buccellati, G. 1968. An Interpretation of the Akkadian Stative as a Nominal Sentence, *JNES* 27, 1-12.

---. 1988. The State of the "Stative", in: Y. L. Arbeitman (ed.), *FUCUS, A Semitic/Afrasian Gathering in Remembrance of Albert Ehrman*, Current Issues in Linguistic Theory no. 58, Amsterdam/Philadelphia, 153-189.

Bybee, J.L. 1985. *Morphology. A Study of the Relation between Meaning and Form*, Typological Studies in Language 9, Amsterdam/Philadelphia.

---, and Dahl, Ö. 1989. The Creation of Tense and Aspect Systems in the Languages of the World, *Studies in Language* 13-1, 51-103.

---, Perkins, R. and Pagliuca, W. 1994. *The Evolution of Grammar*, Chicago/London.

Cantineau, J. 1950. La notion de "schème" et son altération dans diverses langues sémitiques, *Semitica* 3, 73-83.

Caplice, R. 1980. *Introduction to Akkadian*, Studia Pohl, Series Maior 9, Rome.

Castellino, G.R. 1962. *The Akkadian Personal Pronouns and Verbal System in the Light of Semitic and Hamitic*, Leiden.

Catford, J.C. 1977. *Fundamental Problems in Phonetics*, Edinburgh.

Christian, V. 1929. Bemerkungen zu Bergsträssers "Einführung in die semitischen Sprachen", *WZKM* 36, 203-219.

---. 1935. Die kausative Bedeutung des semitischen Steigerungsstammes, in: *Miscellanea Orientalia dedicata Antonio Deimel annos LXX complenti*, Analecta Orientalia 12, Rome, 41-45.

Civil, M. 1994. *The Farmer's Instructions, a Sumerian Agricultural Manual*, Aula Orientalis - Supplementa 5, Barcelona

Cohen, D. 1970. *Études de linguistique sémitique et arabe*, Janua Linguarum, Series Practica 81, The Hague/Paris.

---. 1984. *La phrase nominale et l'évolution du système verbal en sémitique. Études de syntaxe historique*, Collection linguistique publiée par la Société de Linguistique de Paris LXXII, Paris.

Cohen, M. 1936. *Traité de langue amharique*, Paris.

Comrie, B. 1976. *Aspect*, Cambridge Textbooks in Linguistics, Cambridge.

---. 1981. *Language Universals and Linguistic Typology*, Oxford.

---. 1985. Causative Verb Formation and Other Verb-Deriving Morphology, in: T. Shopen (ed.), *Language Typology and Syntactic Description* III, Cambridge, 309-348.

Croft, W. 1990. *Typology and Universals*, Cambridge Textbooks in Linguistics, Cambridge.

Delitzsch, F. 1889. *Assyrische Grammatik*, Berlin.

Deller, K. 1959. *Lautlehre des Neuassyrischen*, diss. Vienna.

Dercksen, J.G. 1996. *The Old Assyrian Copper Trade in Anatolia*, Uitgaven van het Nederlands Historisch-Archaeologisch Instituut te Istanbul, no. 75, Istanbul.

Diem, W. 1970. Die Nominalform *fuᶜāl* im klassischen Arabisch, *ZDMG* 120, 43-68.

---. 1982. Die Entwicklung des Derivationsmorphems der *t*-Stämme im Semitischen, *ZDMG* 132, 29-84.

Dillmann, A. and Bezold, C. 1907. *Ethiopic Grammar*, 2nd ed., translated by J.A. Crichton, London.

Dressler, W. 1968. *Studien zur verbalen Pluralität: Iterativum, Distributivum, Intensivum in der allgemeinen Grammatik, im Lateinischen und Hethitischen*, Sitzungsberichte der Oesterreichischen Akademie der Wissenschaften. Philosophisch-historische Klasse, Band 259, Abh. 1, Vienna.

---. 1985. *Morphonology: the Dynamics of Derivation*, Linguistica Extranea. Studia 12, Ann Arbor.

Driver, G.R. and Miles, J.C. 1935. *The Assyrian Laws*, Oxford.

Edzard, D.O. 1957. *Die "zweite Zwischenzeit" Babyloniens*, Wiesbaden.

---. 1962. Die Stämme des altbabylonischen Verbums in ihrem Oppositionssystem, in H.G. Güterbock *et al.* (eds.), *Studies in Honor of Benno Landsberger on his Seventy-Fifth Birthday, April 21*, AS 16, 111-120.

---. 1982. Zu den akkadischen Nominalformen *parsat-*, *pirsat-* und *pursat-*, *ZA* 72, 68-88.

Eilers, W. 1964/66. Zur Funktion von Nominalformen, *WdO* 3, 80-145.

Fillmore, C.J. 1968. The Case for Case, in: E. Bach, R.T. Harms (eds.), *Universals in Linguistic Theory*, London/New York, 1-88.

Fischer, W. 1965. *Farb- und Formbezeichnungen in der Sprache der altarabischen Dichtung*, Wiesbaden.

---, and Jastrow, O. 1980. *Handbuch der arabischen Dialekte*, Porta Linguarum Orientalium, neue Serie XVI, Wiesbaden.

Fleisch, H. 1955. Le nom d'agent *faᶜal*, *MUSJ* 32, 167-172

---. 1961. *Traité de philologie arabe*, vol. I: Préliminaires, Phonétique, Morphologie Nominale, Beyrouth.

---. 1968. *L'arabe classique. Esquisse d'une structure linguistique*, 2ème éd., Beyrouth.

---, 1979. *Traité de philologie arabe*, vol. II: Pronoms, Morphologie Verbale, Particules, Beyrouth.

Furlani, G. 1949. *Grammatica babilonese e assira*, Pubblicazioni dell'Istituto per l'Oriente 46, Rome.

Gelb, I.J. 1955. Review of Soden, W. von, *Grundriß der akkadischen Grammatik*, BiOr. 12, 93-111.

Gesenius, W. and Buhl, F. 1915. *Hebräisches und aramäisches Handwörterbuch über das Alte Testament*, 17. Aufl., Berlin/Göttingen/Heidelberg.

Gesenius, W. and Kautzsch, E. 1985. *Hebräische Grammatik*, Hildesheim/Zürich/New York (repr. of 1909).

Givón, T. 1976. On the SOV Origin of the Suffixal Agreement Conjugation in Indo-European and Semitic, in A. Juilland (ed.), *Linguistic Studies Offered to Joseph Greenberg* (Studia Linguistica et Philologica 4), Saratoga, vol. III, 481-503.

Givón, T. 1979. *On Understanding Grammar*, Orlando.

---. 1984. *Syntax. A Functional-typological Introduction*, vol. I, Amsterdam/Philadelphia.

---. 1990. *Syntax. A Functional-typological Introduction*, vol. II, Amsterdam/Philadelphia.

Goetze, A. 1942. The So-called Intensive of the Semitic Languages, *JAOS* 62, 1-8.

Goshen-Gottstein, M.H. 1969. The System of Verbal Stems in the Classical Semitic Languages, in *Proceedings of the International Conference on Semitic Studies held in Jerusalem 19-23 july 1965*, Publications of the Israel Academy of Sciences and Humanities. Section of Humanities, Jerusalem 1969, 70-91.

---. 1985. Review of F. Leemhuis, *The D and H Stems in Koranic Arabic*, *BiOr*. 42, 278-283.

Greenberg, J.H. 1966. *Language Universals: with Special Reference to Feature Hierarchies*, Ianua Linguarum, Series Minor 59, The Hague.

Greenstein, E.L. 1984. The Phonology of Akkadian Syllable Structure, *Afroasiatic Linguistics* 9/1, 1-71.

Gröneberg, B. 1989. Reduplications of Consonants and "R"-stems, *RA* 83, 27-34.

Haiman, J. 1985. *Natural Syntax: Iconicity and Erosion*, Cambridge Studies in Linguistics 44, Cambridge.

Haspelmath, M. 1993. More on the Typology of Inchoative/Causative Verb Alternations, in: B. Comrie, M. Polinsky (eds.), *Causatives and Transitivity*, Studies in Language Companion Series 23, Amsterdam/Philadelphia 1993, 87-111.

Hecker, K. 1968. *Grammatik der Kültepe-Texte*, Analecta Orientalia 44, Rome.

Hirsch, H. 1969. Zur Frage der *t*-Formen in den keilschriftlichen Gesetzestexten, in W. Röllig (ed.), *Lišān Mithurti, Festschrift Wolfram Freiherr von Soden zum 19. VI. 1968 gewidmet von Schülern und Mitarbeitern*, AOAT 1, Neukirchen-Vluyn, 119-131.

Hodge, C.T. 1975. The Nominal Sentence in Semitic, *Afroasiatic Linguistics* 2/4, 69-75.

Holma, H. 1914. *Die assyrisch-babylonischen Personennamen der Form* quttulu, Annales Academiae Scientiarum Fennicae B XIII/2, Helsinki.

Hopper, P.J. and Thompson, S.A. 1980. Transitivity in Grammar and Discourse, *Language* 56, 251-299.

---. and ---. 1982. *Studies in Transitivity*, Syntax and Semantics 15, New York.

---. and Traugott, E.C. 1993. *Grammaticalization*, Cambridge Textbooks in Linguistics, Cambridge.

Huehnergard, J. 1987. "Stative," Predicative Form, Pseudo-verb, *JNES* 46, 215-232.

Illingworth, N.J.J. 1990. *Studies in the Syntax of Old Babylonian Letters*, diss. Birmingham.

Jakobson, R. 1990. *On Language*, Cambridge Mass./London.

---, and Waugh, L.R. 1987. *The Sound Shape of Language*, 2nd ed., Berlin/New York/Amsterdam.

Jamison, S.W. 1983. *Function and Form in the* -áya-*formations of the Rig Veda and Atharva Veda*, Ergänzungshefte zur Zeitschrift für vergleichende Sprachforschung Nr. 31, Göttingen.

Jenni, E. 1968. *Das hebräische Pi*ᶜ*el. Syntaktisch-semasiologische Untersuchung einer Verbalform im Alten Testament*, Zürich.

Jespersen, O. 1924. *The Philosophy of Grammar*, London/New York.

Jeyes, U. 1989. *Old Babylonian Extispicy, Omen Texts in the British Museum*, Uitgaven van het Nederlands Historisch-Archaeologisch Instituut te Istanbul, no. 64, Istanbul.

Joly, A. 1907. Quelques mots sur les dérivations du trilitère et les origines du quadrilitère en arabe, *Actes du XIVe Congrès International des Orientalistes* (Alger 1905), 3ème parti, 3ème section, Paris, 394-436.

Jongen, R. 1985. Polysemy, Tropes and Cognition, in W. Paprotté and R. Dirven (eds.), *The Ubiquity of Metaphor, Metaphor in Language and Thought*, Current Issues in Linguistic Theory 29, Amsterdam/Philadelphia, 121-139.

Joüon, P. 1926. Études de sémantique arabe, *MUSJ* 11/1, 3-36.

Joüon, P. and Muraoka, T. 1991. *A Grammar of Biblical Hebrew*, Subsidia Biblica 14, Rome.

Justice, D. 1987. *The Semantics of Form in Arabic, in the Mirror of European Languages*, Studies in Language Companion Series 15, Amsterdam/Philadelphia.

Kamil, M. 1956. Zur Bildung der vierradikaligen Verben in den lebenden semitischen Sprachen, in *Studi Orientalistici in Onore di Giorgio Levi della Vida* I, Pubblicazioni dell'Istituto per l'Oriente 52, 459-483, Rome.

Key, H. 1965. Some Semantic Functions of Reduplication in Various Languages, *Anthropological Linguistics* 7.3, 88-102.

Kienast, B. 1957a. Der Präfixvokal *u* im Kausativ und im D-Stamm des Semitischen, *MSS* 11, 104-108.

---. 1957b. Verbalformen mit Reduplikation im Akkadischen, *Or.* 26, 44-50.

---. 1961. Weiteres zum R-Stamm des Akkadischen, *JCS* 15, 59-61.

---. 1967. Zu den Vokalklassen beim akkadischen Verbum, in: D.O. Edzard (ed.), *Heidelberger Studien zum alten Orient*, Adam Falkenstein zum 17. September 1966, 63-85.

Kienle, R. von. 1960. *Historische Laut- und Formenlehre des Deutschen*, Sammlung kurzer Grammatiken germanischer Dialekte, Hauptreihe Nr. 11, Tübingen.

Knudsen, E.E. 1980. Stress in Akkadian, *JCS* 32, 3-16.

---. 1982. An Analysis of Amorite, *JCS* 34, 1-18.

---. 1984/86. Innovation in the Akkadian Present, *OrSuec.* 23/25, 231-239.

Kraus, F.R. 1973. *Vom mesopotamischen Menschen der altbabylonischen Zeit und seiner Welt*, Mededelingen der Koninklijke Nederlandse Akademie van Wetenschappen, Afd. Letterkunde, Nieuwe Reeks, deel 36 No. 6, Amsterdam/Londen.

---. 1984. *Nominalsätze in altbabylonischen Briefen und der Stativ*, Mededelingen der Koninklijke Nederlandse Akademie van Wetenschappen, Afd. Letterkunde, Nieuwe Reeks, deel 47 No. 2, Amsterdam/Oxford/New York.

---. 1987. *Sonderformen akkadischer Parataxe: die Koppelungen*, Mededelingen der Koninklijke Nederlandse Akademie van Wetenschappen, Afd. Letterkunde, Nieuwe Reeks, deel 50 No. 1, Amsterdam/Oxford/New York.

Krause, W. and Thomas, W. 1960. *Tocharisches Elementarbuch* I, Heidelberg

Kuryłowicz, J. 1956. *L'apophonie en indo-européen*, Prace Językoznawcze 9, Wrocław.

---. 1961. *L'apophonie en sémitique*, Prace Językoznawcze 24, Wrocław/The Hague.

---. 1964. *The Inflectional Categories of Indo-European*, Heidelberg.

---. 1972. *Studies in Semitic Grammar and Metrics*, Prace Językoznawcze 67, Wrocław/Warszawa/Kraków/Gdańsk.

---. 1973. *Esquisses linguistiques* I, Internationale Bibliothek für allgemeine Linguistik 16/I, München.

---. 1975. *Esquisses linguistiques* II, Internationale Bibliothek für allgemeine Linguistik 37, München.

---. 1977. *Problèmes de linguistique indo-européenne*, Prace Językoznawcze 90, Wrocław/Warszawa/Kraków/Gdańsk.

Lambert, W.G. 1992. Prostitution, in V. Haas (ed.), *Außenseiter und Randgruppen*, Beiträge zu einer Sozialgeschichte des alten Orients, Xenia (Konstanzer althistorische Vorträge und Forschungen) 32, Konstanz, 127-157.

Lancellotti, A. 1962. *Grammatica della lingua accadica*, Analecta Hierosolymitana 1, Jerusalem.

Landsberger, B. 1926. Die Eigenbegrifflichkeit der babylonischen Welt, *Islamica* 2, 355-372.

---. 1934. *Die Fauna des alten Mesopotamien nach der 14. Tafel der Serie HAR-RA = hubullu*, Abhandlungen der philologisch-historischen Klasse der sächsischen Akademie der Wissenschaften 42/6, Leipzig.

Landsberger, B. 1967a. *The Date Palm and its By-products according to the Cuneiform Sources*, AfO Beiheft 17, Graz.

---. 1967b. Über Farben im Sumerisch-Akkadischen, *JCS* 21 (published 1969), 139-173.

Larsen, M.T. 1967. *Old Assyrian Caravan Procedures*, Uitgaven van het Nederlands Historisch-Archaeologisch Instituut te Istanbul, no. 22, Istanbul.

Leemhuis, F. 1977. *The D and H stems in Koranic Arabic*, Publications of the Netherlands Institute of Archaeology and Arabic Studies in Cairo 2, Leiden.

Lehmann, C. 1985. Grammaticalization: Synchronic Variation and Diachronic Change, *Lingua e Stile* 20/3, 303-318.

Lichtenberk, F. 1994. Reflexives and Reciprocals, in: R.E. Asher and J.M.Y. Simpson (eds.), *The Encyclopedia of Language and Linguistics*, Oxford/New York, vol. 7, 3504-3509.

Lieberman, S.J. 1977. *The Sumerian Loanwords in Old-Babylonian Akkadian*, vol. I: *Prolegomena and Evidence*, Harvard Semitic Studies no. 22, Missoula.

Lipin, L.A. 1964. *Akkadskij jazyk*, Moscow.

Loprieno, A. 1986. *Das Verbalsystem im Ägyptischen und im Semitischen*, Göttinger Orientforschungen, IV. Reihe, Band 17, Wiesbaden.

Loretz, O. 1960. Die Hebräische Nominalform *qattāl*, *Biblica* 41, 411-416.

Lühr, Rosemarie. 1988. *Expressivität und Lautgesetz im Germanischen*, Monographien zur Sprachwissenschaft 15, Heidelberg.

Lyons, J. 1968. *Introduction to Theoretical Linguistics*, Cambridge.

---. 1977. *Semantics*, I-II, Cambridge.

Martinet, A. 1937. *La gémination consonantique d'origine expressive dans les langues germaniques*, Copenhagen.

Matthews, P.H. 1991. *Morphology*, 2nd ed., Cambridge Textbooks in Linguistics, Cambridge.

Mayerthaler, W. 1988. *Morphological Naturalness*, Linguistica Extranea. Studia 17, Ann Arbor.

McMahon, A.M.S. 1994. *Understanding Language Change*, Cambridge.

Meillet, A. 1912. L'évolution des formes grammaticales, *Scientia* (*Rivista di Scienza*) vol. 12, no. XXVI/6, 130-148.

---. 1931. *Esquisse d'une histoire de la langue latine*, 2ème éd., Paris.

Moravcsik, E.A. 1978. Reduplicative Constructions, in J.H. Greenberg (ed.), *Universals of Human Language*, Vol. 3, Word Structure, Stanford Ca., 298-334.

Moscati, S. (ed.). 1969. *An Introduction to the Comparative Grammar of the Semitic Languages*, Porta Linguarum Orientalium, Neue Serie VI, Wiesbaden.

Muffs, Y. 1973. *Studies in the Aramaic Legal Papyri from Elephantine*, Studia et Documenta ad Iuris Antiqui Pertinentia 8, New York.

Nedjalkov, V.P. and Jaxontov, S. Je. 1988. The Typology of Resultative Constructions, in: V.P. Nedjalkov (ed.), *Typology of Resultative Constructions*, Typological Studies in Language 12, Amsterdam/Philadelphia, 3-62.

Nedyalkov (sic), V.P. and Silnitsky, G.G. 1973. The Typology of Morphological and Lexical Causatives, in: F. Kiefer, (ed.), *Trends in Soviet Theoretical Linguistics*, Foundations of Language, Supplementary Series 18, Dordrecht, 1-32.

Nöldeke, Th. 1875. *Mandäische Grammatik*, Halle.

---. 1904. *Beiträge zur semitischen Sprachwissenschaft*, Strassburg.

---. 1910. *Neue Beiträge zur semitischen Sprachwissenschaft*, Strassburg.

Nyberg, H.S. 1954. Zur Entwicklung der mehr als dreikonsonantischen Stämme in den semitischen Sprachen, in F. Meier (ed.), *Westöstliche Abhandlungen Rudolf Tschudi.....überreicht*, Wiesbaden, 128-136.

Oppenheim, A.L. 1964. *Ancient Mesopotamia, Portrait of a Dead Civilization*, Chicago/London.

---, *et al.* 1970. *Glass and Glassmaking in Ancient Mesopotamia*, The Corning Museum of Glass Monographs, vol. 3, New York.

---, Reiner, E., *et al.* 1956-. *The Assyrian Dictionary of the Oriental Institute of the University of Chicago*, Chicago (= CAD).

Palmer, L.R. 1972. *Descriptive and Comparative Linguistics, A Critical Introduction*, London.

Panagl, O. 1975. Kasustheorie und Nomina agentis, in H. Rix (ed.), *Flexion und Wortbildung*, Akten der V. Fachtagung der Indogermanischen Gesellschaft Regensburg, 9. - 14. September 1973, Wiesbaden, 232-246.

Parpola, S. 1970/83. *Letters from Assyrian Scholars to the Kings Esarhaddon and Assurbanipal*, I-II, AOAT 5/1-2, Neukirchen-Vluyn.

Peirce, C.S. 1960. *Collected Papers*, 3 vols, Cambridge Ma.

Pfister, R. 1969. Methodologisches zu *fluere* - *fließen* u.ä., *MSS* 25, 75-94.

Poebel, A. 1939. *Studies in Akkadian Grammar*, AS 9, Chicago.

Porges, N. 1875. *Über die Verbalstammbildung in den semitischen Sprachen*, Vienna.

Procházka, S. 1995. Semantische Funktionen der reduplizierten Wurzeln im Arabischen, *ArOr* 63/1, 39-70.

Ranke, H. 1905. *Early Babylonian Personal Names*, The Babylonian Expedition of the University of Pennsylvania, Series D: Researches and Treatises, vol. III, Philadelphia.

Ravn, O.E. 1949. Babylonian Permansive and Status indeterminatus, *ArOr*. 17/2, 300-306.

Reckendorf, H. 1967. *Die syntaktischen Verhältnisse des Arabischen*, Leiden (repr. of 1895).

Reiner, E. 1966. *A Linguistic Analysis of Akkadian*, Janua Linguarum, Series Practica 21, The Hague/Paris.

---, and Renger, J. 1974/77. The Case of the Secret Lover, *AfO* 25, 184-185.

Rowton, M.B. 1962. The Use of the Permansive in Classic Babylonian, *JNES* 21, 233-303.

Rundgren, F. 1955. *Über Bildungen mit* š- *und* n-t-*Demonstrativen im Semitischen. Beiträgen zur vergleichenden Grammatik der semitischen Sprachen*, Uppsala Universitets årsskrift, Uppsala.

---. 1959a. *Intensiv und Aspektkorrelation, Studien zur äthiopischen und akkadischen Verbalstammbildung*, Uppsala/Wiesbaden.

---. 1959b. Akkadisch *utlellūm* "sich erheben", *Or.* 28, 364-369.

---. 1963a. Das Verbalpräfix *yu-* im Semitischen und die Entstehung der faktitiv-kausativischen Bedeutung des D-Stammes, *OrSuec.* 12, 99-114.

---. 1963b. Erneuerung des Verbalaspekts im Semitischen, *Acta Universitatis Upsaliensis*, N.S. 1: 3, 49-108, Uppsala.

---. 1964. Ablaut und Apothematismus im Semitischen, *OrSuec.* 13, 48-83.

---, 1966. Kausativ und Diathese, ein Beitrag zur allgemeinen Sprachwissenschaft, *Die Sprache* 12, 133-143.

---. 1980. Principia Linguistica Semitica, *OrSuec.* 29, 32-102.

Ryckmans, G. 1938. *Grammaire accadienne*, Louvain.

Ryder, S.A. 1974. *The D-stem in Western Semitic*, Janua Linguarum, Series Practica 131, The Hague/Paris.

Saad, G.N. 1982. *Transitivity, Causation and Passivization, A Semantic-syntactic Study of the Verb in Classical Arabic*, Library of Arabic Linguistics, Monograph No. 4, London/Boston/Melbourne.

---, and Bolozky, Sh. 1984. Causativization and Transitivization in Arabic and Modern Hebrew, *Afroasiatic Linguistics* 9/2, 29-38.

Sapir, E. 1921. *Language*, New York.

Saussure, F. de. 1964. *Cours de linguistique générale*, 3ème éd., Paris.

Schaefer, Chr. 1994. *Das Intensivum im Vedischen*, Historische Sprachforschung, Ergänzungsheft 37, Göttingen.

Scheil, V. and Fossey, C. 1901. *Grammaire assyrienne*, Paris.

Schmidt, K.H. 1973. Transitiv und Intransitiv, in: G. Redard (ed.), *Indogermanische und allgemeine Sprachwissenschaft*, Akten der IV. Fachtagung der Indogermanischen Gesellschaft Bern, 28. Juli - 1. August 1969, Wiesbaden, 107-124.

Segert, S. 1975. *Altaramäische Grammatik*, Leipzig.

Shapiro, M. 1991. *The Sense of Change: Language as History*, Bloomington/Indianapolis.

Siebesma, P.A. 1991. *The Function of the Niph^{c}al in Biblical Hebrew*, Assen.

Soden, W. von. 1932/33. Der hymnisch-epische Dialekt des Akkadischen I-II, *ZA* 40, 163-227; 41, 90-183.

---. 1962. Das akkadische *t*-Perfekt in Haupt- und Nebensätzen und sumerische Verbalformen mit den Präfixen *ba-*, *imma-* und *u-*, in H.G. Güterbock *et al.* (eds.), *Studies in Honor of Benno Landsberger on his Seventy-Fifth Birthday, April 21*, *AS* 16, 103-110.

---. 1965/81. *Akkadisches Handwörterbuch*, Wiesbaden (= AHw).

---. 1973. Iterativa im Akkadischen und Hethitischen, in E. Neu and C. Rüster (eds.), *Festschrift Heinrich Otten*, Wiesbaden 1973, 311-319.

---. 1989. *Aus Sprache, Geschichte und Religion Babyloniens*, Gesammelte Aufsätze herausgegeben von Luigi Cagni und Hans-Peter Müller, Istituto Universitario Orientale, Dipartimento di Studi Asiatici, Series Minor XXXII, Naples.

---. 1995. *Grundriß der akkadischen Grammatik*, 3., ergänzte Auflage, Analecta Orientalia 33/47, Rome (= GAG).

---. and Röllig, W. 1991. *Das akkadische Syllabar*, 4., durchgesehene und erweiterte Aufl., Analecta Orientalia 42, Rome.

Speiser, E.A. 1967. *Oriental and Biblical Studies*, Collected Writings of E.A. Speiser, edited and with an Introduction by J.J. Finkelstein and M. Greenberg, Philadelphia.

Stamm, J.J. 1939. *Die akkadische Namengebung*, Mitteilungen der vorderasiatisch-ägyptischen Gesellschaft 44, Leipzig.

Stankiewicz, 1954. Expressive Derivation of Substantives in Contemporary Russian and Polish, *Word* 10, 457-468.

Steiner, G. 1981. Die sog. *tan*-Stämme des akkadischen Verbums und ihre semitischen Grundlagen, *ZDMG* 131, 9-27.

Streck, M. P. 1994. Funktionsanalyse des akkadischen $Št_2$-Stamms, *ZA* 84, 161-197.

---. 1995. *Zahl und Zeit, Grammatik der Numeralia und des Verbalsystems im Spätbabylonischen*, Cuneiform Monographs 5, Groningen.

Taylor, J. 1995. *Linguistic Categorization, Prototypes in Linguistic Theory*, 2nd ed., Oxford.

Tischler, J. 1976. *Zur Reduplikation im Indogermanischen*, Innsbrucker Beiträge zur Sprachwissenschaft, Vorträge 16, Innsbruck.

Ullendorff, E. 1955. *The Semitic Languages of Ethiopia: A Comparative Phonology*, London.

Ullmann, S. 1962. *Semantics, An Introduction to the Science of Meaning*, Oxford.

---. 1973. *Meaning and Style: Collected Papers*, Language and Style Series 14, Oxford.

Ungnad, A. 1926. *Babylonisch-Assyrische Grammatik*, 2nd ed., München.

---, and Matouš, V. 1964. *Grammatik des Akkadischen*, München.

Veenhof, K.R. 1972. *Aspects of Old Assyrian Trade and its Terminology*, Studia et Documenta ad Iura Orientis Antiqui Pertinentia 10, Leiden.

---. 1987. "Dying Tablets" and "Hungry Silver", Elements of Figurative Language in Akkadian Commercial Terminology, in M. Mindlin, M.J. Geller and J.E. Wansbrough (eds.), *Figurative Language in the Ancient Near East*, London, 41-75.

---. 1995. Old Assurian *iṣurtum*, Akkadian *eṣērum* and Hittite GIŠ.HUR, in Th.P.J. van den Hout and J. de Roos (eds.), *Studio Historiae Ardens*, Ancient Near Eastern Studies Presented to Philo H.J. Houwink ten Cate on the Occasion of his 65th Birthday, Istanbul, 311-332.

Voigt, R.M. 1987a. Derivatives und flektives T im Semitohamitischen, in H. Jungraithmayr and W.W. Müller (eds.), *Proceedings of the Fourth International Hamito-Semitic Congress*, Current Issues in Linguistic Theory 44, Amsterdam/Philadelphia 1987, 85-107.

---. 1987b. Die *tan*-Stämme und das System der Verbalformen im Akkadischen, *ZDMG* 137/2, 246-265.

Wallace, S. 1982. Figure and Ground: The Interrelationships of Linguistic Categories, in: P.J. Hopper (ed.), *Tense-Aspect: Between Semantics and Pragmatics*, Typological Studies in Language 1, Amsterdam/ Philadelphia, 201-223.

Wehr, H. 1952. *Der arabische Elativ*, Akademie der Wissenschaften und der Literatur in Mainz, Abh. der Geistes- und Sozialwissenschaftlichen Klasse, Nr. 7, Wiesbaden.

---. and Cowan, J.M. 1966. *A Dictionary of Modern Written Arabic*, Wiesbaden.

Whiting, R.M. 1981. The R Stem(s) in Akkadian, *Or.* 50, 1-39.

Wissmann, W. 1932. *Nomina postverbalia in den altgermanischen Sprachen, nebst einer Voruntersuchung über deverbative ō-Verba*, Göttingen.

Worth, D.S. 1967. The Notion of "Stem" in Russian Flexion and Derivation, in: *To Honor Roman Jakobson*, Essays on the Occasion of his Seventieth Birthday, 11 October 1966, Janua Linguarum, Series Maior 31-33, The Hague/Paris 1967, vol. III, 2269-2288.

Wright, W. 1890. *Lectures on the Comparative Grammar of the Semitic Languages*, Cambridge.

---. 1896/98. *A Grammar of the Arabic Language*, 3rd ed., Cambridge: Cambridge University Press.

Yannay, I. 1974. Augmented Verbs in Biblical Hebrew, *HUCA* 45, 71-95.

Zaborski, A. 1994. Archaic Semitic in the Light of Hamito-Semitic, *Zeitschrift für Althebraistik* 7, 234-244.

Index of Akkadian words

This index includes the Akkadian words discussed in the course of this study. Verbal entries are arranged according to verbal stems. Unless indicated otherwise, D-stems are mentioned under the corresponding G-stem, also if they are discussed separately. References to passages in which two or more verbal stems are compared or contrasted are included under the stem with the most specific meaning; for instance, if the G and the D-stem of a verb are compared, the passage is referred to under the D-stem. *Purrus* forms are indexed separately if they are discussed separately in Chapter X; otherwise they are referred to under the verbal D-stem.

Nominal and verbal forms of the same root are distinguished by means of n. and v. respectively, wherever necessary. All *purrus* forms are characterized as nouns (n.) to distinguish them from the verbal D-stem. D/Š refers to the comparison of the D- and Š-stems of intransitive verbs discussed in Chapter VII. The glosses added in the case of homonyms are for ease of identification only. Bold numbers refer to detailed discussions of important words.

A

abāku (send) 103; D 201
abāku (uproot) D 112[11], 122, 201
abālu D 293; Dt 322; D/Š 265f, 289[23]
abāru 317[2]
abātu 178; D 112[11], **122f**, 127f, 143, 188, 190, 202; Dt 319f
abb(ā')ū 25
abbalu (?) 67[6]
abnu 54, 84
abullu 96
adāru 98f; D 293, 424; Dt 322f, 329; D/Š 277
agāgu D 424; D/Š 275
agāmu 350; D 424
agāru D 185, 202
aggagû 51
aggu 387
ahāmeš 325
ahāzu 17[6], 65, 103, 431; D 12f, 140, 202; Štn 71; → also *uhhuzu*
ahhātu 25
ahhāzu 64f
ahhū 25
ahû v. 317[2]
akāku Dt 332
akālu 102, 160; Gtn 81
akāšu 17[8], 302; D 251, 293, 302; Dtn 335
ākil karṣī- 61
ākilu 60
akkilu 59, 65
akṣu 430
akû n. 430
alaktu 42
alāku 96ff, 246; Gtn 80, 97f, 172; Gt 86[7]
alālu (jubilate) Gt 317[3]; Štn 85[2]
alālu (hang) → *(h)alālu*
alātu D 122, 126f, 167, 186, 202
āliku 65, 67[11]
alkakātu 42
allaku 50, 64
allāku 50. 64f
amāru 99, 102, 112[7]; Gtn 83f, 172
ammāru 64
anāhu (exert o.s.) D 293; D/Š 277; Š 265
anāhu (sing) D 202, 282
apālu (pay) 103; D 140f, 183, 194, 202; Gtn 83, 156, 172
apālu (be late) D 262, 264, 293; Dt 328
apāru 98, 440; D 192, 426
arādu 317[2]
arāhu 259; D 262, 264, 293; D/Š 277; [Štn] 85[2]
arāku D 260ff, 264, 293; D/Š 272
arāmu → *(h)arāmu*
arānu 317[2]
arāru 40, 98, 440; D 293; Dt 323
arhu 430
arku 56
arraku 52f, 56, 61, 67[9]
ašāru 103
ašāšu D 293; Dt 321, 329; Ntn 47[17]
asīru 62
aššaru 50
athū 307
aw/mīlūtu 118, 197[2]
awû 317[2]

B

ba'ālu 99; D 293; Dtn 335
ba'āšu D 293
babbanû 41
babbilu 59f
bābilu 60
bābu 96
bahāru D 111[2], 293, 309; Dtn 335
bahû v. D 293
bajjašu/û 51
bakāru 317[2]
bakkā'u 63f, 283
bakkarū 46[5]

bakkû 63, 283
bakru 46[5]
bakû v. 283; Gtn 81, 156, 172
balālu D 137, 176, 192, 194, 202, 406; Dt 319
balāṣu D 293
balāṭu D 355f, 293; Dt 341[12]; Š 291[37]
banû n. 41
banû v. (be beautiful) D 259f, 293, 355
baqālu 317[2]
baqāmu 348; D 157, 198[9], 203
baqāru D 203, 406
baqbaqqu 40
baqmu 348, 372
baqqu 40
barāmu (be multicoloured) D 293, 309, 348
barāmu (to seal) D 131, 203
barāqu 349
barāru 40, 349
barbaru 43
baršu 372
barû v. 99, 251; D 251, 293, 301f; D/Š 270
bâru (stay firm) 251; D 251, 293; Dt 320
bâru (hunt) D 203
barmu 35, 42
baṣāru D 203
baṣāṣu 40
bašālu 247, 440
bašāmu D 139, 203
bašû 247
bâšu D 293; D/Š 277
batāqu 106; D 108, 122, **123**, 126f, 147, 183, 203
bâtu 246, 306, 349
bâ'u 103
be'āšu D 187, 203
belû v. 246; D 293
bêlu v. 99, 103, 317[2]
berû v. Gtn 83; D 289[21]; 293
bêru 102
birbirrū 40
bītu 96
bubbulu v. 313
bubūtu 43
**buddudu* v. 313
buhhusu n. 376, 406
bu''îtu 377f, 407
bullu v. 313
bullû n. 406
bullulu n. 368, 406
bulluṣu n. 368, 406
bulluṭu n. 375, 377, 407
bun(n)annû 42
bunnû n. 370, 407
buqāqu 40
buqāšu 31
buqqumu n. 303, 348, 372, 407
buqquru v. 313
buqqušu n. 31, 375, 407
buqūmu 47[16]
burmāmu 42
burrû n. 407
burrumu n. 48[19], 348, 364, 373, 396, 407
burruqu n. 349, 372, 375, 407
burruru n. 349, 375, 407
burrus/šu n. 372, 375, 407
burummu/ū 35
bussumu n. 407
bussumu v. 313
bussuru v. 313
bušû 139
butturu n. 375, 407
butturu v. 313
bu''û v. 313, 316; Dtn 335; Dt 320
bu''uru n. 368, 407
bu''utu n. 349f, 407
buzzu'u v. 90, 302, 313

D

da'āmu D 294, 309, 348; N 322
da'āpu D 203
da'mu 35
da'ummu 35, 46[4]
dababābu 41f
dabābu 24, 40, 96, 256, 281; D 23, **100**, 283; Dt 292[41]
dabbibu 59
dagālu 102; Gtn 81
dajjālu 63
dajjānu 63
dakāku 41
dakāšu D 203, 407
dâku 41, 104, 286[2]; D 116, 126, 203
dalāhu D 203f, 407
dalālu D 294
dalāpu 249, 439; D 294; D/Š 277
dallapiš 51
dalû v. 317[2]
dâlu D 294, 407
damāmu 40; Gtn 81
damāqu D 259, 261f, 294; Dtn 335; D/Š 275
damdammu 40
damû v. 294
danānu (be strong) 105; D 259f, 294, 352; Dt 322; ŠD 336, 338
danānu (mng. uncert.) 340[1]
dandannu 41, 405f[30]
dannu 41
dânu D 204
dapānu 68[20]
dap(i)nu 68[20], 430
dappānu 64, 67[10], 430
dappinu 67[10], 68[20], 430
daqāqu 40
daqqaqu 52f
daqqiqu 67[10]
darāsu D 179, 183, 204
dâṣu D 204
dašāpu 317[2]; D 294, 309, 348
dašpu 111[2]
dâšu D 128, 130, 183, 190, 204, 408
da'ummatu 405[24]
da'ummiš 405[24]
da'ummu 405[24]
dekû v. D 179, 204
derderru 43

derû v. 317[2]
deššû 52
dešû v. 317[2]; D 294, 309, 355, 404[18]; Dtn 335; Dt 322
diqdiqqu 40
dubbubtu 23f
dubbubu n. 402[4], 407
duhhusu v. 313; Dt 323
dukkušu n. 407
dulluhiš 387
dullupu n. 375, 377, 407
dulluqu n. 376, 407
dummû v. 313
dummuqu n. 369, 375, 377ff, 387, 396, 398ff, 407f
dunnuniš 387
dunnunu n. **365f**, 387f, 396ff, 400, 404[22], 408
duppuru v. 92, 313; Dt 320
duqduqqu 40
duqququ n. 58, 404[22], 408
duqququ v. 309
durduru 42
durruku v. 314
duššû n. **366**, 387, 408
duššû v. 309
duššumu n. 374, 376, 408
duššupu n. 348, 370, 373ff, 386, 396, 408
du''umiš 387
du'ummu/du'ūmu 35, 48[19], 348, 373, **383f**, 396, 408
du''umu v. 309, 348

E

ebēbu D 262, 264, 294, 351f, 424; Dt 321, 324; D/Š 277
ebēlu 317[2]
ebēru 103
ebēṭu D 294; Dt 329
**ebbû* 66[3]
e/ibru 46[5]
ebû v. 294; D 262, 264
e/iṣṣū 25
ebbarūtum 46[5]
ebberu 50
ebēru Gtn 83
ebû v. 66[3]
eddešû 52
eddu 351, 392f
edēdu D 294, 260
edēhu D **151f**, 190, 204, 364
edēlu D **131**, 183, 188, 192, 204
edēpu D 108, 171, 176, 204
edēqu D 204; Dt 324
edēšu D 260, 294, 424; Dtn 335; Dt 324
edlu 431
edû 98, 256; D 288[18], 294; D/Š 270; ŠD 336, 338; N 99
e'ēlu D **131**, 172, 184, 204f, 328; Dt 328
egēru Gtn 172; D 128, 205
egû v. 350
ekēku Gtn 156, 175, 204; D 157, 175; Dt 332
ekēlu D 294, 355, 424; Dt 322, 324, 329; D/Š 277
ekēmu 103; D 135, 205
ekēp/bu D 425; Nt(n) 110[1]
ekkēmu 63
ekkimu 63
ekṣu 430
ekû v. D 294, 310
elēhu D 171, 180, 205
elēlu D 294, 353; Dt 321
elēpu D 294; Dt 323
elēṣu D 294; D/Š 277
elû v. 246; Gtn 172; D 290[26], 294; D/Š 268, 279f
emēdu 96f, 108, 247, 249, 439; D 108, 112[7], 294, 368f; Dt 320; D/Š 270
emēmu D 294
emēṣu (be hungry) D 294
emṣu (sour) 430
emūqu 118, 197[2]
**enēbu* 317[2]; Dt 323
enēšu D 294; Dt 322; D/Š 275
enû v. 104
enūtu 118, 197[2]
epēqu D 294; Dt 328
epēsu D 262, 264, 294
epēšu 42; D 142, 148, 170, 180, 183, 195f, 200[20], 205, 426; Gtn 172
equ v. Dt 324
erbe 305
erbīšu 81
erēbu 96, 246; Gtn 172; D 295; D/Š 270
erēpu 317[2], 350
erēru D 295
erēšu (ask) Gtn 172
erēšu (cultivate) D 205
erhu 430
ēribu 67[11]
ērišu 63
errēšu 63
eršu 430
erû v. D 295
êru D 295
esēhu D 140, 205
esēku 103; D 205
esēlu Dt 328
esēpu D 205
esēru (put under pressure) D 181, 183, 206
esēru (enclose) D 62, 181, 206; Dt 319
eṣēlu D 128, 206
eṣēnu D 206, 255
eṣēru D **139**, 153, 167, 206
ešēbu 42; D 295
ešēru Š 265, 332; Št 112[7]; 332
ešrīšu 81
eššu 396, 433f
ešû v. 440f; D 128; Dt 323
etāku D 295, 427
etēqu (bend) D 295, 427
etēqu (cross) 103, 246; Gtn 83, 172
eṭēlu D 295; Dt 323
eṭēru (take away) 102
eṭēru (pay) 103

eṭṭēru 63
eṭû v. D 295; Dt 322
ew/mû v. D 295; D/Š 277
ezēbu 103, 206; Š 287[15]
ezēzu D 289[21], 295; D/Š 272, 280
ezzu 387

G

gabgabu 43
galātu 98; Gtn 156, 172; D 295; Dtn 335; D/Š 272; ŠD 341[16]
galgal(la)tu 43
galgaltu 43
gallābu 63, 65, 303
gallābūtu 63
gamālu 103; Gtn 85
gamāru 112[7]; D 112[11], 117, 142, 180, **181**, 183, 206f; Dt 319f
gamgammu 43
gammalu/û 50
ganāhu D 284
ganāṣu D 284; Dt 331
gapāru D 295; Dt 340[6]
gapāšu D 295; Dt 322
gapšu 380
garānu → *qarānu*
garṣu 372
gaṣāṣu → *kaṣāṣu*
gaṣṣu 430
gašāru D 295; Dt 322, 326f, 332
gašru 387
gâšu 284
gerru 96
gerû v. D 207; Dtn 336
gešû v. D 284
gimillu 47[16]
ginâ 81
gubbuhu n. 90, 348, 372, 375, 408
gubgubu 43
guhhubu v. 284, 314, 316
gulgul(la)tu 43
gulībātu 303
gullubu n. 35, 303, 348, 374f, 406[33], 408
gullubu v. 348; Š 290[27], 291[35], 310
**gullulu* n. 376, 408
gullulu v. (act unjustly) 311f; Dtn 335; Š 291[35]
gullulu v. (make blind) 314
gullutu n. 368, 409
gummutu n. 409
gunnuṣu n. 375, 402[4], 409
guppušu n. 375, 380, 388, 409
gurgurru 43
gurrudu n. 372, 375, 409, 409
g/qurruru n. 374, 376, 409
gurruṣu n. 372, 375, 409
guššuru n. 387, 409
gu''ušu v. 284, 314, 316
**guzzû* v. Dt 314

H

habābu 17[8], 42, D **282**
habālu (become indebted) 98; D 295; N 99
habālu (oppress) D 180
habāru (be noisy) Dt 282
habāru (migrate) D 295
habāṣu (break) D 207
habāṣu (be elated) Dt 322
habāšu 349; D 207
habātu (rob) D 135, 207
habbātu 63
habbilu 59
habbūbu 34
hablu 431
habṣu 372
habû v. D 207
hâb/pu D 187, 207
hadāšu 317[2]
hadû v. D 295; D/Š 275, 280
hahû 317[2]
hā'iṭu 161
hakāmu D 183, 207, 409
halābu 317[2]
halālu (wheeze) 40; D 281f
(h)alālu (hang) 112[8]; D 91, **151**, 190, 207, 380
halāpu D 295
halāqu 14, 247; D 295, 356; D/Š 270; ŠD 336, 338
halāšu D 186f, 207
halhallatu 40
halṣu 431
hâlu D 295
hamāmu D 137, 207
hamāṣu 348, D 126, **142**, 146, 176, 183, 208
hamāšu (be fifth) 306; D 362
hamāṭu (burn) 96, 160, 246, **254f**f, 440; D 295; Dt 323, 340[4]; D/Š 272
hamāṭu (hurry) 246, 259; D 291[37]
hamṣu 348, 372
hamšīšu 81
hamû v. (paralyze) D 208
hamû v. (trust) D 295
hanābu 42; Dt 323
hanāmu Dt 323
hananābu 42
hanāqu 51; Gtn 172; D 122, 126, 183, 208; Dt 333
hanāṣu D 284; Dt 331
hannabu 66n2
hannamu 51
hannaqu 51, 64
hannāqu 64
hapāpu 40; D 208
haphappu 40
(h)apû v. D 131, 184, 208
harādu 98; N 99
(h)arāmu D **132**, 172, 184, 208
harāpu D 295
harāru 41; D 208
harāṣu D 208
harāšu D 180, 208
harharu 42
harrānu 96, 112[11]
hâru 102
hasāpu D 208
hasāru D 208
hasāsu 98; Gtn 47[17]; D 256, 285, 288[18], 295; D/Š 277
hassā'u 64, 68[17, 20]
hassûm 68[20]

hasû n. 68[20]
haṣābu D 122, 208
haṣāṣu (break) D 112[11], 122, 127, 208f
haṣāṣu (build a hut) 306
haṣṣaṣu 66[1]
haṣṣīnu 24
haṣṣuṣu 66[1]
hašāhu 99
hašālu 348f
hašāšu D 295
hašhašu 42, 372
haššа'u 51
hašû D 112[11], 209
hâšu D 295
hatāpu D 209
hattītu 34
hatû v. D 108, 171, 209
haṭāmu D 128, 209
haṭṭā'u 59
haṭṭi'u 59
haṭṭû 59
haṭû v. D 285
hâṭu 103; D 209
hazāju 68[20]
hegallu 139
helû v. D 295; D/Š 272
hemēru 349
hepû n. 431
hepû v. 112[8]; D 84, **123**, 127, 143, 146, 183, 193, 209; Dt 319f
herû v. 41; D 209
hesû v. 362; D 180, 209, 301f
hibabîtu 42
hibibātu 42
hinhinu 43
hiṣbu 139
hubbulu v. 311
hubburu n. 370, 409
hubbuṣu n. 372, 375, 377, 409
hubbušu n. 349, 372, 375, 377, 409
hubbuṭu n. 409
hubšāšû 42
hubullu 47[16]
hubūru 47[16]
huddudu n. 375, 409
huddulu n. 376, 409
huddušu v. 314
huggulu n. 373, 376, 409
hullû n. 368, 409
hulluqu n. 368, 409
hummuru n. (crippled) 349, 375, 377, 409f
hummuru n. (shrivelled) 410
hummuru n. (of beer and barley) 370, 410
hummuru n. (red) 368, 410
hummuṣu n. 348f, 375, 410
hummušu n. (lame) 372, 410
hummušu n. (of barley) 370, 410
hummušu n. (one fifth) 410
hummuṭiš 387
hummuṭu n. (hot) 368
hummuṭu n. (early) 410
hunābu 31
hunnubu n. 31, 66[2], 373ff, 410
hunnunu n. 373, 376, 410
hunnuqu n. 368, 410
hunnuṭu n. 370, 410
huppû n. 346, 359, 410
huppudu n. 35, 348, 372, 375, 410
huppudu v. 310
huppupu n. 410
huqqu v. 333
**hurrupu* n. 370, 410
hurruru n. 364, 375, 380, 410
hurruṣu n. 375, 377, 410
hurrušu n. 375, 410
**hussû* n. 369, 410
hussû v. 301f
hussuru n. 370, 380, 388, 410
hussusu n. 402[4], 410
huṣṣubu n. 375, 410
huššû n. 48[19], 404[20]
huššulu n. 303, 348f, 372, 375, 411
huššušu n. 411
huttupu v. 311
huttutu v. 314
huṭṭû n. 368, 411
huzālu 31
huzzû n. 373, 375, 377, 411
**huzzû* (*hunzû*) v. 310
**huzzuh/'u* n. 376, 411
huzzulu n. 31, 376, 411
huzzumu n. 376, 411

I

idû v. → *edû*
ihzū 13, 114, 308
ilkakātu 42
immeru 24
inbu 51
innabātum 51, 66[2]
innabu 51, 66[2]
išbabtu 42
itūlu 246
izbu 347
izuzzu 246, 289[21]; Gtn 172

K

kabābu 96, 246; D **255**, 295, 411
kabāru D 262, 264, 295
kabāsu 106; D 121, **129**f, 144, 164ff, 167, 176, 184f, 188, 190f, 209f; Dt 325ff
kabāšu 317[2]
kabātu D 295, 354f; Dt 320, 332; D/Š 275
kabbaru 23, 52f, 55f, 61, 67[8, 9]
kabru 23
kadāru 306; D 210
kajjānu 64, 68[19]
kalbu 42
kalkaltu 43
kalû n. 431
kalû v. G 14, 103, 431; [D] 103; ŠD 336, 338
kamālu 51; D 295
kamāru Gt 330; D 112[11], **137f**f, 190, 210; Dt 330, 340[10]
kamāsu (collect) 249, 290[25], 439f; D **138**, 183, 210; Dt 319; N 439f
kamāsu (kneel) 246; 290[25]; D 411; Dt 328; D/Š 266f

kammalu 51
kamû v. D 210
kanāku 62; D **132**, 135, 146, 183f, 189, 193f, 210f
k/qanānu D **129**, 157, 186f, 211
kanāšu (bend) D 296; Dt 321; D/Š 267, 269, 276, 279; ŠD 336, 338
kanāzu 317[2]
kanīku 62
kanku 431
kanû v. D 296
kânu 61, 251; D 296, 355; Dtn 335; Dt 320, 326f, 341[12]
kapādu 97, 316; D 211, 285
k/qapālu Gt 330f; D 211; Dt 330f
kapāpu 41
kapāru (clean) D 157, 181, 187, 211
kapāru (uproot) D 112[11], 122, 127, 165f, 172, 211
kapāru (pour bitumen) 306
kap/bāṣ/su D 296
karābu 97; Gtn 172; D 150, 171, 211
karāku D 211
karāru 102
karāṣu 65, 308; D 157, 198[9], 211
karātu D 122, 126f, 157, 159, 211
karrištu 65
karṣu 308
karû D 296; D/Š 275
kâru D 187, 211
kasāmu 126
kasāpu (break off) D 122, 211f
kasāpu (offer) 306
kasāsu D 122, 160, 212
kaskasu 43
kasû D 135, 151, **181**, 183, 185, 189ff, 212, 380; Gtn 173
kaṣāpu 316; D 285
kaṣāru 112[8], 340[7]; D **132**, 135, 145f, 157, 159, 183, 189, 192f, 212; Gt 86[8], 329f, 340[8], 340[9]; Dt 110, 320, 329f, 340[6]
kaṣāṣu 348; D 122, 172, 212
kāṣiru 63, 67[11]
kaṣru 431
kaṣṣaru (?) 66f[6]
kaṣṣāru 63
kaṣû v. D 296
kâṣu D 122, 213
kašādu 96f, 256; D **100**, 112[10], 213; Dtn 336
kašāpu D 213
kašāru D 181, 183, 213
kašāšu 47[17], 103
kašāṭu 126; D 213
kaškaššu 41
kaššaptu 62
kaššāpu 64
kaššu 41, 430
kašû v. D 296, 350; ŠD 336, 338
kâšu D 296
katāmu 109; D 112f[11], 117, 135, 157, **181**, 184, 191, 213, 412; Dtn 336; Dt 319
katāru 317[2]
katā'u D 140, 213
katû n. 430
kaw/mû v. D 213
kazbu 312, 373
kepû v. 41; D 412
kimkimmu 43
kīnu 355, 396
kipkippu 43
kiskīsu 43
kubbû v. 314
kubbulu n. 35, 348, 373, 375, 411
kubbulu v. Dt 310, 329, 348
kubburu n. 58, 67[8], 370, 374, 376, 411
kubbutu n. 366, 376f, 411
kuddunu v. 311
kudkudu 43
kudurru 306
kulbābu 42
kullu v. 103, 314, 316; Dtn 87[13]; 335
kullulu n. 345f, 411
kullulu v. 311; Dt 320
kullumu v. 275, 314; Dtn 335; Dt 320, 326f; D/Š 275; ŠD 336, 338
**kulluṣu* n. 370, 411
kummudu n. 368, 411
kummulu n. 368, 411
kummusu n. (kneeling) 349f, 411
kummusu n. (awe-inspiring?) 411
k/qunnunu n. 366, 376, 412
kunnušu n. 412
kunnušu v. 314
kunukku 47[16]
kuppû n. 412
kuppupu n. 366, 376, 412
kupp/bbuṣ/su n. 380, 388, 412
kupputu n. 373, 396, 412
kupputu v. (make compact) 310, 348; Dt 321
kupputu v. (collect) 314
kurkurru 43
kurru n. 412
**kurrû* 66[3], 388, 412
kurruṣu v. 65, 311
kurû 66[3]
kuṣṣu/kūṣu 61
kussupu n. 346, 412
kuṣṣudu n. 349, 373, 412
kuṣṣudu v. 314, 316
kuṣṣuru n. 349, 412
kuṣṣuṣu n. 348, 373, 412
kuššû n. 350, 412
kuttumu n. 345f, 412
kuzābu 31
kuzzubu n. 31, 373ff, 377, 412
kuzzubu v. 309f, 312

L

la'ābu D 213f
la'ātu D 214
labāku D 296; Dtn 335; D/Š 278
labānu (beg) D 157, 214
labānu (make bricks) 317[2]
labāru D 262, 264f, 296; Dt 321; D/Š 278

labāšu 92, 98f; D 296, 355ff, 403[13]; Dt 320, 340[5]; D/Š 276; N 99
labātu 317[2]
labbabu 51
labbašu 66n1
labbu 51
**lahāšu* Gt 282; Dt 331
lahmu 373
lakkû 404[19]
lakû v. D 296
lamādu 91, 98f, 247; Gtn 84; D 256, 288[18], 296; D/Š 272, 280; Š 290[32]; N 99
lamāmu D 214
lapānu D 296
lapātu 114; D 142, 148, 158, 160, 164ff, 167, 173, 185, 200[22], 214; Dt 324; Š 287[15]; → also *lupputu* v.
laplaptu 43
lappanu 51
laptu 44
laqātu D **138**, 144, 146, 164, 178, 184, 192f, 214f
laqlaqqu 40
lasāmu 246; Gtn 80
lassamu 50
lašlašu 41
laššu 41, 430
latāku D 183, 215
lâṭu D 112[11], **136**, 172, 188ff, 215
la'û n. 430
law/mû v. D 178, 215
lêku D 158f, 215
lemēnu D 263f, 296, 355; Dt 323, 326f; D/Š 275
lemmenu 52
lemû/lêmu 102
leqû n. 431
leqû v. 103, 431; Gtn 81ff, 172; D 164, 215
letû D 107, 112[11], 126, 215
lubūšu 47[16]
luhhumu n. 373, 413
lullû v. 311
lummu v. 314
lummunu n. 369, 378f, 385, 388, 396, 398, 400, 413
lummuṣu n. 413
luppunu n. 413
lupputu n. 346, 360f, 366, **381**, 413
lupputu v. 13, 114, 301, 314, 316; Dt 331
luqūtu 118, 197[2]
lu''û n. 404[22], 413
lu''û v. 310, 348; Dt 320
**lu''upu* v. 314
lu''ušu n. 413
lu''uṭu n. 413
luzzuzu n. 413

M

madādu D149, 164, 180f, 194, 215
mādiš 397
mādu 164
mâdu 248; Š 260
magāgu D 128, 215
magal 397
magāru 98f; D 296; D/Š 278, 280; N 99
mahāru 97, 103, 431; D 17[7], 114, 180, 183, 215f, 413; Gtn 83, 172; Dtn 336; Dt 331
mahāṣu 106; D 86[8], 142, 153, 158f, 165f, **176**, 190, 216; Gtn 173
mahhî/ûtu 402f[6]
mahhû 402f[6]
mahhūru 45[3]
māhirtu 114
māhiṣu 65, 67[11]
mahru 17[7]
mahṣu 431
mahû n. 402f[6]
mahû v. 349
makāru D 128, 216
[*makkāru*] 63
makkūru 118, 139, 197[2]
mala 81, 118, 197[5]
māliku 67n11
malû v. 96, 252ff, 287f[17]; D 260, 296, 355f, 368f; ŠD 336ff; D/Š 267, 272f, 280
mamītu 97
manû v. D 171, 181, 216; ŠD 337f
maqātu 17[6], 246, 349f; Gtn 82, 84f, 156, 172; [D] 17[6]; D/Š 267
marāqu D 122, 171, 180, 187, 216
marāru D 296; D/Š 273
marāṣu 248; D 260, 296; D/Š 278; Š 260
marāṭu D 158, 216
marraṣu 51
marru 370
masāhu D 296
masāku D 296; D/Š 273
**massaku* 66[2]
maṣāru Dt 333
maṣṣartu 352;
maṣû v. D 296; Dt 333
mašādu D 180, 216
mašālu 440; D 263, 296 D/Š 278
mašāru Gtn 80
mašāšu 40; D 217
mašā'u 68[17]; D 217
mašmaš(š)u 40
maššī'u 59
maššû 50
mašû v. 98f; D 296
matāqu D 296
matqu 34
mātu 118, 143, 197[2]
mâtu 246, 286[2]
maṭru 350
maṭû v. D 296; Dt 322; D/Š 270; ŠD 337f
mazāqu D 217
mazā'u D 128, 176, 217
medû v. D 296
mekû v. Dt 331
mesû n. 431
mesû v. D 112[11], 178, 182, 217; Dt 325, 341[12]; ŠD 337f

mêšu D 217
mihhūru 45[3]
mimma 81, 118, 164
mû 118
mubannû 161
muddulu n. 413
muganniṣu 402[4]
muggušu v. 314
muha''iṭu 161
muhhû n. 349, 373, 402f[6], 406[33], 413
muhhuru v. 114, 311
muhhuṣu n. 413
mujjuru v. 311
mukkulu n. 414
muk(t)abbiru 341[11]
muktaššaššu 47[17]
mullû n. 355f, 368f, 414
mulluhu n. 385, 388, 414
mulluqu n. 376, 414
mullušu n. 376, 414
mulluṭu n. 373, 414
muma''iru 161
mummirtu 99
munappilu 127, 160
munaggiru 161
muna''iru 402[4]
munaššik(t)u 160
mundah(hi)ṣu 74
mupattilu 161
mupettû 160
muqallipu 127, 160
muqerribu 161
muqqu n. 414
muqqu v. 314, 316, 348; Dt 331
muqqutu n. 17[6], 349f, **384**, 414
murakkisu 160
murrû v. 314
murruhu n. 414
murruqu n. (good) 370, 414
murruqu n. (clear) 414
murruqu v. 301f
murruru n. 370, 414
murruru v. 302
murtap(pi)du 74
musassiānu 249, 287[11]
mussû n. 369
mussuhu n. 369, 378f, 414
mussuhu v. 309
mussuku n. 66[2], 414
muṣabbit(t)u 160
muṣarrihtu 283
muṣihhu 248
muṣṣuru v. 311
mušaggišu 127, 160
mušahhinu 161
mušaqqû 161
mušarriṭu 127, 160
**muššuhu* n. 414
muššulu n. 376, 414
muššu'u v. 314; Dtn 335
muštabbabbu 47[17]
muštap(pi)tu 74
muštar(ri)hu 74
muštar(ri)qu 74
mūtap(pi)lu 74
muttak(ki)pu 74f
muttāqu 34
muttuqu n. 414
muṭṭû n. 384, 388, 414
muṭṭuru n. 350, **381**, 388, 414
mu''û v. 314, 316
muzaqqipu 160
**muzzu* v. Dt 314
**muzzuhu* n. 414
**muzzu'u* n. 414

N

na'ādu D 256, 297, 414; Dtn 335
na'āpu Dt 333
na'āru D 282; Dt 331
na'āsu D 187, 217
na'āšu D 284
nabāhu 17[8]; D 282
nabāṭu D 297; Dt 321; D/Š 278
nabû v. D 178, 217, 283, 430
nadānu 87[15], 102, 286[2], 431; Gtn 82, 172; Š 73
nadru 430
nadû n. 431
nadû v. 95, 102, 111f[7]; Gtn 81, 83f, 172f
nâdu D 184, 217; Dtn 87[13]; Dt 292[41], 331
nagālu D 297
nagāšu Gtn 80; Dt 333
naggāru 68[16]
naglabu 303
nahāru D 297
nahāsu D 282; Dt 331
nahāšu D 297
nahnahatu 43
nâhu D 297, 414; D/Š 275
najjālu 63, 65
nakālu D 297; D/Š 275, 280
nakāmu D **138**f, 190, 195f, 217
nakāpu D 86[8], **129**f, 146, 158, 165ff, 172, 217
nakāru Gtn 172; D 263, 297, 355, 415; Dtn 87[13], 335; Dt 320, 323; D/Š 268, 279f; Š 290[27]
nakāsu D **123f**, 127, 158, 172, 188, 190, 193, 217f; Dt 110
nakkapû 50
nakkaru 51
naklu 386
naksu 431
nâku Gtn 82
nalāšu 317[2]
nâlu 246; D 297; D/Š 277
nam(m)ušīšu 42
namāšu 17[8], 42, 247; D 263f, 297
namrirrū/namrīrū 42
namurru 35
napāhu 40, 95, 362; Gtn 173; D **142**, 218, 283; Ntn 82, 391
napālu D 112[7], **124**, 127, 158, 190, 218
napāṣu D 107, **124**, 126ff, 172, 184f, 218; Dt 332
napāšu D 297; Dtn 335; Dt 321f
napharu 118
nāpilu 160
nappāhu 63
naprušu ŠD 337ff

nâpu (pay) 317[2]
nâpu ("?") Dt 333
naqādu D 297
naqāru D 126, 158, 198[9], 218
naqû D 140, **141**, 171f, 186f, 218
narābu D 297
narāṭu 17[8], 246, 286[8]; D 297; ŠD 337f
nasāhu 107, 111[7]; D **124**, 127, 146, 172, 183ff, 194, 219
nasāku 104
nasāqu D 140, **141**, 166, 172, 184, 219; ŠD 337f
nasāsu D 281ff
nasqu 386
naṣābu D 158f, 219
naṣāru 102f
naṣnāṣu 43
našāhu D 284
našāku D 112[11], 121, **129**f, 154f, 159, 219
našāpu D 112[11], 157, 219
našāqu D **149**, 166, 173, 190, 219f
našāru D 108, 112[11], 163f, 181, 220
našû n. 431
našû v. 17[6], 95, 102, 111[7], 431; Gtn 84, 172
nâšu 286[8]; D 263f, 297
natāku D 297; Dtn 335
naṭālu 97, 103; Gtn 83, 172; D 176, 220
naṭû n. 430
na'û v. D 283
naw/māru 42, 361; D 263f, 297; Dt 322; D/Š 278; Št 340[1]; ŠD 337f
naw/mû 317[2]; Dt 321
nazāmu D 283; Dt 331
nazāqu 248; D 329, 340[2], 390; Dt 321, 329
nazāzu D 283
ne/abû n. 430
nêru D 220
nesû v. 441; D 297; D/Š 267, 278; ŠD 337f
nešû v. D 284
nêšu D 297; D/Š 275
ne'û/nê'u D 297; D/Š 269, 279
nikkassu 170
nuddudu v. 314
nugguru v. 314
nuhhup/bu n. 414
nuhhulu n. 376f, 414
nuhhuru n. 376, 415
nuhhušu n. 415
nuhhutu n. (of silver) 370, 415
nuhhutu v. 302, 314
nuhhuṭu v. 284, 314, 316
nuhšu 139
nukkulu n. 386, 415
nukkupu n. 415
nukkuru n. 415
nukkusu n. 359
nukkusu v. (balance an account) 311f
nullušu n. 368, 415
nummuru n. 376f, 416
nuppuhu n. **366f**, 384, 390f, 415
nuppulu n. 415
nuppuqu v. (be constipated?) 314, 316
nuppuqu v. (pay attention) 314
nuppuṣu n. 370, 415
nuppušu n. 415
nuqqudu n. 415
**nuqquru* n. 415
nurrubu n. 376, **381**, 404[22], 415
nurruṭu n. 368, 402[4], 415
nussuqu n. 386, 388, 415
nussusu v. 314
nuššu n. 415
nutturu n. 416
nuṭṭupu n. 376, 416
nu''uru n. 402[4], 416
nuzzumu n. 402[4], 416

P

pa'āṣu 362; D 187, 220
pâdu D 135, 172, 220
paglu 386
pagru 324
pahāru 91, 105, 247, 251; D 297; Dt 322; D/Š 275
pakāru D 220
palāhu 98f; D 297; Dtn 335; Dt 326f; D/Š 273; N 99
palāku (delimit) 150f, 220
palāq/ku (slaughter) D **124f**, 126, 128, 172, 189, 220
palāsu D 297; D/Š 270
palāšu D **129**f, 146, 183, 220
palhu 51
pallahû 51
panāku 317[2]
panû n. 118
panû v. 306; D 297
paqādu 103, 291[38]; D 140, **141**, 149, 151, 164, 170, 172, 183, 191, 220f; Dt 110, 317[2]; 333
pâqu D 297
parādu D 297; Dtn 87[13], 335; D/Š 275; ŠD 337f
parāku Gtn 173; D 143, 181, 183, 221, 362, 416
parāru 246; D 297; Dt 320; D/Š 275
parāsu 106, 112[8]; D **125**, 127, 149, 172, 192, 194, 199f[19], 221, 362
parāṣu (break an oath) D 221
parāṣu (perform rites) 306; D 221
parā'u (sever) D 122, 221f
parā'u (sprout) 317[2]
parriku 59
parriṣu 59
parsu 431
pasālu 350
pasāmu 317[2]; D 222; Dt 325
pasāsu D 107, 112[11], 126, 144, 222; Dt 319f
paslu 373
paspasu 40
passalu 51, 66[2], 372
paṣādu D 222; Dt 320
paṣānu 344; D 222; Dt 320, 324f

pašāhu D 297; D/Š 267, 278; ŠD 337ff

pašāqu 248; Š 265

pašāru D 112[11], 135, 144, 157, **182**, 184, 222; Dt 319

pašāšu 62; D 222

pašāṭu 122, 126f, 159, 222; ŠD 337f

pašīšu 62

pâšu D 122, 187, 223

patāhu D 128, 223; Dt 325

patālu D 223

patānu (eat) 102

patānu (be strong) 441; D 297

patāqu D 184, 223

patru 97

paṭāru 95, 106, 111[7], 112[8], 362; Gtn 172; D 112[11], **132ff**, 144ff, 149, 170, 183f, 198[11], 223; Dt 319f; ŠD 337f

paṭru 431

pazāru D 297; ŠD 337f

pehû D 108, 135, 223

pelû n. 430

pesēnu D 223

pessû 372

peṣû v. D 297

pettenu (?) 67[6]

petû n. 431

petû v. 91, 112[8]; Gtn 81, 172, 174; D 112[7], **133**, 135, 145f, 183f, 188, 191, 195f, 223f; Dt 319; D/Š 266; ŠD 337f

pētû 160

p/bilp/billu 40

pilpilû 42

pīqu 430

puāgu 91; D 140, 224

puggulu n. 351, 358, 386, 388, 416

puhhu v. 311; Dt 326f, 341[12]

puhhuru n. 376f, 416

puhpuhhu/ū 40

puhpuhu 43

puhru 118, 197[2]

pulluhu n. 416

pullusu n. 374, 376, 416

pullusu v. 314

pullušu n. 364, 404[17], 416

puqqu v. 314, 316; Dt 331, 341[12]

purru n. 416

purrudu n. 416

purruku n. 367, 416

purrusu n. 416

purrušiš 387

purrušu n. 416

purussā'u 47[16]

**pussuku* v. 314

pussulu n. 66[2], 350, 367, 373, 375, 416

pussum/nu n. 345f, 376, 417

pussuqu n. 417

puṣṣû n. 48[19], 370, 417

puṣṣudu n. 417

puššuqu n. 368, 417

puššuṭu n. 404[16], 417

puttuhu n. 364, 417

puttulu n. 380f, 417

puṭṭuru n. 346, **381f**, 388, 417

**pu''ugu* n. 368, 417

puzzuru n. 376, 417

Q

qabālu Gt 317[2]

qabbā'u 64

qabû Gtn 81, 172; D 13, 178, 224, 283, 301f

qadādu D 290[28], 298; D/Š 269, 279f

qadāšu D 298

qadištu 443[1]

qadû v. 317[2]

qajjalu 51

qajjašu 51

qalālu 354; D 58, 67[9], 298, 354f; Dtn 335, 341[14]; Dt 320

qalāpu D 108, 122, 126, 186, 224

qallalu 52, 54

qalû v. D 157, 224

qâlu D 298

qamû D 122, 224

qanānu (build a nest) 306

qanû n. 118, 197[3]

qâpu (entrust) D 224

qâpu (buckle) 350

qaqqadu 43

qaqqaru 149

qarādu D 298, 310

qarānu D **138**f, 144, 190, 224f

qarāru D 298

qarrādu 64, 68[20]

qašādu D 298

qašdu 433

qaššatum 443[1]

qâšu 103; D **141**, 172, 190, 199f[19], 225

qatānu D 298

qatāpu D 122, 225

qatāru 246; D 298; Dtn 335; Dt 321, 325; D/Š 273, 280

qatnu 68[20]

qattanu 52, 54f, 61, 67[9]

qatû v. 246; D 259, 298, 356, 403[12]; Dt 320; D/Š 273, 280

qebēru D 110, 181, 225

qemû 317[2]

qerēbu 247; D 263f, 298, 355, 399, 417f; Dtn 82, 335; D/Š 275

qīpu 403[7]

qû "thread" 151f, 198[13]

qubbû v. 13, 301f

qubbulu v. 315

qubburu n. 382, 417

quddudu n. 350, 417

quddumu n. 417

quddušu n. 417, 433f

quddušu v. 111[2], 310, 433f; Dt 321, 325

qullû n. 370, 417

qullulu n. 67[9]

qumqummatu 42

qunnunu → *kunnunu*

quppu n. 350, 387, 417

qurrubu n. 387, 396, 399, 417f

qurrudu n. → *gurrudu*

quššudu n. 418, 433f

quššudu v. 310, 433f; Dt 325

quttû n. 356, 418
quttunu n. 58, 68[20], 376, 418
qutturu n. 418
qu''û v. 97, 315f

R

ra'ābu 246, 286[8]; D/Š 277
rabābu D 298; D/Š 277; Š 265, 287[15]; ŠD 337f
rabāku D 187, 225
rabāṣu 246, 350
rabbû 52, 54, 66[3], 84
rābiṣu 65, 67[11]
rabû v. (be big) 88[17]; D 298, 418; Dt 341[12]; D/Š 273f; ŠD 337ff
rabû v. (go down) 246; D 298
râbu (compensate) D 225
râbu (tremble) 246; 286[8]; D 298; D/Š 275
radādu 41
raggimu 59
rahhiṣu 59
râhu D 298; D/Š 278
rakābu 65, 246; D 225; → also *rukkubu*
rakāsu Gt 330; D 112[11], **133f**f, 145f, 153, 172, 183ff, 189f, 225f, 308; Dt 110, 320, 325, 330, 341[12]
rākibu 65
rakkābu 64f
rakkasu 66[1]
raksu 431
râku D 187, 226
ramāku 247, 249, 441; D 298; Dtn 335; D/Š 275
ramānu n. 324
ramû (loosen) D 263f, 298; Dtn 335
ramû (throw) ŠD 337ff
râmu (love) 103; D 226, 419; Dt 327
râmu (bestow) 102, 291[38]
rapādu 17[8], 86[8]; Gtn 80, 172
rapāqu D 226
rapāšu D 298; Dt 322; D/Š 275; ŠD 337f
rappašu 52, 54, 67[9]
raqādu Gtn 80; D 13, 287[13]; ŠDt 339f[1]
raqāqu D 298
raqqaqu 52, 54f
raqqu 68[20]
raqqû 65
raqraqqu 40
râqu D 298; D/Š 279
rasāb/pu D **125**, 127f, 188f, 226, 325
râs/šu D 112[11], 122, 226
raṣānu D 283; Dt 331
raṣmu 387
rašāšu 41
rašû (get) 103, 431; Gtn 172
rašû (be red) 41; Dt 322
râšu 298; D/Š 274, 280
rašubbu 35
raṭābu D 298, 355
râ'u 317[2]
rebû v. 305; D 255, 298
redû 41, 99; Gtn 172; D 99, 251, 298; D/Š 271; ŠD 337f
rehû D 180, 226
rêmu 103
rêqu D 298; D/Š 271
rêṣu D 226, 325
rešû v. D 298, 310; Dtn 335
retû Gtn 172ff; D **134**, 189f, 226
rêtu 317[2]
re'û v. 103
riksu 308
rīqa rīqa 40
rubbû n. 58, 418
rubbuṣu n. 350, 418
ruggû v. 315
ruggubu v. 311, 418
ruggugu n. 418
rukkubu v. 65, 308, 311
rukkusu n. 346, 359, 418
rukūbu 47[16]
**ruppudu* n. 418
ruppudu v. 285, 315f
rupp/bbuhu n. 418
rupp/bbuk/qu n. 376, 418
ruppušu n. 58, 418
ruqqû v. 311
ruqququ n. 58, 68[20], 404[22], 418
russû v. 315
ruṣṣunu n. 387, 418
rušruššu 43
ruššû n. 48[19], 373, 404[20], 418
ruššuku n. 382, 388, 404[22], 418f
ruššušu n. 419
ruttû v. 311
ruttutu n. 402[4], 419
ruṭṭubu n. 419
ru''umu n. 419
ru''umu v. 315

S

sa'ālu 17[8], 91; D 284
sabā'u D 298; D/Š 275
sâbu 249
sadāru 112[9], 259; D 183, 226
sâdu 249
sahālu D 108, 121, **130**, 154f, 159, 167, 190, 226f; Dtn 336
sahāmu D 298
sahāpu D 109, 112[11], **134**, 143f, 153, 172, 188, 190, 227
sahāru 65, 97, 112[9], 247, 259; Gtn 172; D 65, 263, 298, 403[10]; D/Š 268f, 279
sahāšu D 112[11], 227
sahharu 50
sahhiru 59, 65
sahlû 118
sakāku 349; Dt 310, 321, 329
sakālu Gtn 85
sakānu D 299
sakāpu "to reject" D 183, 227
sakātu D 299
sakku 373
saklu 430
s/zâku D 227, 249

salā'/hu D 159, 181, 187, 227
salālu D 157, 227
salāmu D 299; D/Š 279
salātu D **125**, 127, 188, 227
samāhu Dt 327
samāšu D 227
samû v. D 299
sâmu 248; D 299
sanāqu 112[9]; D 166, **178**, 182f, 185, 227f; Dt 319
sanāšu D 187, 228
sapādu 246
sapāhu D 110, **130**, 135, 146, 172, 184, 228; N 110
sapānu 126
saphu 431
sapsapu 43
sâqu 248; D 299
sarādu D 420
sarāhu Dt 320
sarāqu D 181, 187, 228
sarāru D 255, 260, 299
sarrāru 63
sarriqu → *zarriqu*
sâru 248; D 285, 419
sâtu 249
sehû v. D 299
sekēru D 112[11], 128, 228
sêru 249; D 228
sikkūru 45[3]
simmu 59
sīqu 420
subbulu n. 419
subbusu v. 315
suddudu v. 315
suhhumu n. 377, 419
suhhuru n. 350, 384f, 388, 419
sukkuku n. 349, 373ff, 419
sukkulu n. 376, 402[4], 419
sukkumu n. 377
sullû v. 97, 315f; Dtn 335
sulluhu n. 374, 377
sullulu n. 419
*_sullumu_ n. 376
sullunu n. 419
sullutu n. 364
sullu'u n. 419
summu n. 48[19], 419
summulu v. 311f
summunu n. 419
sunnuqu n. 349, 419
sunnušu n. 419
suppû v. (pray) 97, 315f; Dtn 335
suppû v. (abduct) 315
sūqāqû 42
sūqu 42, 96
surru n. 419
surrû v. 315
surruru n. 420
surruru v. 97
su''ulu n. 377, 420
su''uqu n. 420

Ṣ

ṣabābu 40
ṣabātu 73, 106, 259, 348; Gtn 172, 174; Gt 326; D 83, 108f, 112[7], 135, **136f**, 144ff, 151, 156, 166, 183f, 195f, 229, 325, 379f; Dt 110; D/Š 266
ṣabtu 348f, 373, 431
ṣābu 118, 143, 197[1], 197[2]
ṣadāru D 299, 310, 420
ṣadiru 373
ṣâdu (whirl) 248f; Gtn 80, 172; D 299, 350, 420; Dtn 335
ṣâdu (melt) 248; D 299
ṣahātu Dt 328
ṣahharu 52, 61, 67[9]
ṣâhu 248f; D 299
ṣajjadu 51
ṣajjahu 51
ṣalālu 17[6]; D 17[6], 249, 299; D/Š 279
ṣalāmu D 263, 299; Dtn 336; D/Š 275
ṣalā'u 102
ṣallamu 51
ṣallāmu 51, 64
ṣâlu 249; Št 287[9]
ṣamādu D 135, 146, 148, 229f
ṣamāru → *ṣummuru* v.
ṣamû v. D 289[21], 299; D/Š 275
ṣânu 249, 254
ṣap/bû v. D 181, 230
ṣarāhu (heat) D 230
ṣarāhu (lament) D 283
ṣarāmu D 285
ṣarāpu D 112[11], 160, 181, 230
ṣarāru (flash) 42
ṣarāru (flow) D 299
ṣarātu D 284
ṣarraru 50
ṣarrihtu 283
ṣarrišu 59
ṣarritu 59
ṣarrupūtum 370
ṣarṣar 40
ṣâru 248; D 299
ṣe'ārum 317[2]
ṣehēru D 58, 299, 355
ṣehheru 52, 54f, 61, 66[5]
ṣehru 66[5]
ṣēnu (evil) 430
ṣênu 102, 249
ṣēru 96f
ṣêru 249
ṣubbû n. 420
ṣubbû v. (examine) 302, 315f, 420
ṣubbû v. (form an army) 311f
ṣubburu v. 285
ṣubbutu n. 348, 359, 373, 420
ṣuddû v. 311
ṣudduru n. 373, 375, 420
ṣuhhiš 387
ṣuhhu n. 350, 402[4], 420
ṣuhhuru n. 58, 387, 400, 404[22], 420
ṣuhhutu n. 328, 373, 375, 420
ṣullû v. 97; Dtn 335
ṣullulu n. 404[22]
ṣullulu v. 311, 420
ṣullumu 48[19], 404[22], 420
ṣumāmītu 42f
ṣumāmu 42f
ṣummû n. 420

ṣummuru n. 368, 420
ṣummuru v. 302, 315f
ṣūmu 43
ṣuppu v. 315
ṣuppuru n. 377, 420
ṣurarû 42
ṣurru v. 310
ṣurruhu n. (?) (feverish) 405[26]
ṣurruhu n. (high) 421
ṣurrumu n. 421
ṣurrupu n. 360, 370, 421
ṣurrušu n. 404[22], 421
**ṣ/suwwû* v. 315
ṣu''udu n. 350, 402[4], 421

Š

ša 118, 197[5]
ša'āru (win) D 230
ša'āru (be hairy) 317[2]
šabābu 47[17]
šabāhu D 187, 230
š/sabāsu 248
šabāšu D 137, 230
š/sabbasû 51, 388
šâbu 248f, 430; D 299, 421
šadāhu D 285
šadālu D 299; Dt 322
šaddidu 59
šaddihu 59
šādidu 60
šadlu 386
šagāmu 283f
šagāšu 104; D 126, 198[9], 230
šaggašû 50
šaggāšu 59, 63, 160
šaggišu 23, 59, 67[12], 160
šaggu 430
šaggumūta 284
šāgišu 23, 60
šahāhu D 299
šahānu D 299; Dt 321
šahātu (rinse) D 187, 230; Dt 325
šahātu (fear) 98f; D 299; Dt 321
šahāṭu (leap) Gtn 80, 172; D 230
šahāṭu (strip) D 122, 127, 192, 230
šâhu 248; D 299
šahurru 35
šakāku D 187, 230
šakānu 17[6], 102, 431; Gtn 81, 83, 172
šakāru D 299
šakāsu Dt 321
šakkarānû 51
šakkarû 51
šakkinu 59
šakkūru 34, 52
šaknu 431
šalāgu 306
šalāhu D 231
šalāmu D 260f, 263, 299, 356, 360f, 369; Dt 321
šalāpu D 122, 126, 231
šalāqu D 122, 231
šalāš 305
šalāšīšu 81
šalāšu 255, 259; D 263, 299, 305, 422
šalāṭu 97, 350; Dt 231, 331
šallaṭu 50
šalmu 396
šâlu (ask) 249; D 185, 231
šâlu (to coat) 131; G 231
šamāhu D 299
šamāmu D 160, 186, 231; Ntn 47[17]
šamaššammū 118
šamātu 306
šamāṭu (strip off) D 122, 231
šamāṭu (be pointed) Dt 328
šamhu 386
šammahu 51, 66[2], 388
šammaru 51, 62
šâmu (buy) 102, 249, 431; Gtn 70, 83
šâmu (decree) 249; D 190, 231; Št 287[9]
šanānu Gt 47[17]; Dt 327
šanassu 81
šanû v. (do again) 255, 259; D 299, 305, 355; Dtn 87[13]; Dt 321
šanû v. (change) D 299, 422; D/Š 279
šânu 249
šapāku Gtn 172, 174; D **138**f, 150f, 184, 190, 195f, 231
šapālu D 263f, 299; Dtn 336; Dt 332; D/Š 274, 280
šapāru 102, 431; Gtn 81f, 172
šapāṣu 91; D 151, 231
šapātu 86[8]
šāpiru 67[11]
šappalu 51
šapru 431
šapû (be loud) D 299
šapû (be silent) D 299
šaqālu (weigh) 42, 103; Gtn 82; D 162ff, 185, 231
šaqālu (be scarce) D 300, 310
šaqāru D 112[11], 128, 232
šaqû v. (be high) Gtn 336; D 264, 300; Dtn 335; D/Š 267, 274
šaqû v. (to water) D 232
šāqû 161
šaqummu 35
šarāhu D 86[8], 300; Dtn 87[13], 335; Dt 85[2], 322f, 340[3], 341[12]; D/Š 274
šarāku (give) 102
šarāku (suppurate) 317[2]
šarāmu D 122, 156, 232
šarāpu D 122, 126, 232
šarāqu 102
šarāṭu D 118, 122, 126, 232
šarhu 322, 387
šarrahu 51, 62, 388
šarrāqu 62f, 65
šarruqum 50, 62, 65
šarruttu/šarrūtu 61
šarû v. D 249; D/Š 271
šassā'u 64, 68[17]
šasû Gtn 81, 84, 156, 172; D 249; Dtn 336; Š 287[12]
šâṣu 249
šatāhu D 300

šatāqu 91; D 122, 127, 232
šattišam 81
šatû v. (drink) 102; Gtn 172
šatû v. (weave) D 232
šaṭāru D 143, **176f**, 195, 200[22], 200[23], 232, 289f[24]
šaṭāṭu D 122, 232
šâṭu D 232, 249
ša'ûlšā'u 249; Gtn 80
šaw/mû 440; D 300
šebēru D 108, **126**, 128, 184, 189, 233
šebû v. D 300, 355; Dt 341[12]
šegû n. 430
šêlu 249; D **130**, 189f, 233
šemû 103; Gtn 83f, 172; D 99
šênu 249, 306
šepû v. "to ask" D 233
šēpu 149, 198[12]
šêpu 317[2]
šêqu 249
šeršerratu 40
šeršerru 40
šertu 40
šerû v. D 422; Dt 333, 341[12]
še'ru 373
šēru 430
šêru 249, 317[2]
šeššu 433
šeššīšu 81
šêtu 249, 287[9], 440
še'u 118, 197[3]
še'û Gtn 81, 172; D 233
šēzuzu 291f[39], 387
šību 430
šina 305
šinīšu 81
šīru/ū 118, 197[4]
**šubbu* n. 380, 382, 421
šubburu n. 346, 370, 388, 421
šubbutu v. 311
šuddû v. 315
šuddudu n. 367, 421
šuddulu n. 386, 421
šugguru v. 315
šuharruru 42
šuhhu n. 368, 421
šuhhû n. 421
šuhhû v. (make pregnant) 315; Dt 321
šuhhû v. (abolish) 315
**šuhhuhu* n. 370, 421
šuhhuru n. 421
šuhhutu n. 421
šuhhuṭu n. 385, 388, 421
šukkulu v. 315; Dtn 335
šukkunu v. 311
šukkusu n. 382, 404[22], 421
šukkuṣu n. 421
šuklulu v. 287[15], 306
šullumu n. 376f, 421
šulluqu n. 364, 422
šullušiš 387, 422
šullušu n. 422
šulluṭu n. 350, 422
šūlulu v. 306
šumma 154ff
šummu v. 315f
šummuhu n. 66[2], 376, 386, 422
šummunu v. 311
šummuṭu n. 368, 422
šumruṣu n. 291f[39]
šumṣulu v. 306
šumšû v. 306
šūmū 118
šunnû n. 422
šuppulu n. 376, 380, 382, 422
šuppuṣu n. 373, 422
šupšuqu n. 291f[39]
šūpû n. 291f[39]
šuqallulu 42
šuqammumu 42
šuqqulu n. 370, 422
šūquru n. 291f[39]
šurbû n. 291f[39]; 339
šurru v. 92, 315, 430; Dtn 87[13]; 335
šurrû v. 315
šurruhu n. 386f, 422
šurruhu v. 285
šurruru n. 422
šūru 430
šūsumu n. 291f[39]
šušqû n. 291f[39]
šušruhu n. 291f[39]
šutāhû v. 307
šutanūdu v. 306
šutarruhūtu 341[12]
šutēmuqu v. 306
šutersû v. 306
šutēṣû v. 306
šutlumu v. 306
šuttuhu n. 422
šuttupu v. Dt 311, 317[2]; 327
šuttuqu n. 422f
šūturu n. 291f[39]
**šu''û* v. Dt 315
šu''uru n. (hairy) 90, 351, 373, 423
šu''uru n. (dirty) 423
šuwwuru v. 311
šūzuzu n. 291f[39], 387

T

tabāku 106, 348; Gtn 172; D 112[7], **138f**f, 159, 186f, 233, 310; Dt 320
tabālu 86[7], 95, 103, 111[7]; D 233
tabku 373
tadānu 86[7]
tahāhu D 233
tajjāru 64, 68[19]
takālu D 256, 260, 300; Dtn 335
takāpu D 233
tamāhu D 135, 172, 233
tammāmītu 42
tammamû 42, 50
tamû v. 86[7], 97ff, D 300; Dt 327
taqānu D 300, 355; Dtn 335; [ŠD] 337
tarāku D 233, 361f, 423
tarāpu D 423
tarāru 246, 286[8]; D 300, 423
tarāṣu (stretch) Gtn 156, 175; D 108, **134**, 159, 172, 184, 193f, 234

tarāṣu (be right) D 300
tarû v. 102
târu 247, 259; D 300, 423; Dtn 87[13], 335; Dt 321; Š 291[37]
**taṣû* 86[7]
**tašābu* 86[7]
tebû v. 246; D 300, 291[37]
temēru D 131, 171f, 234
terterru 43
tubbuku n. 348, 370, 373, 423
tuddû v. 315
tukkulu n. 376f, 423
tukkupu n. 360, 364, **382**, 388, 423
tullû v. 315
tulluku n. 423
tullulu v. 312
tumāmîtu 42
tunnuhu n. 377, 423
**tuppû* v. 312
turruku n. 48[19], 346, 361f, **382**, 385, 423
turrupu n. 364, 385, 423
turruru n. 402[4], 423
tu''umu n. 423
tu''umu v. 310

Ṭ

ṭabāhu D 116, **126**, 128, 172, 188f, 234
ṭabbihu 59
ṭābu 396
ṭâbu D 300, 353ff, 403[9], 423; D/Š 276
ṭahādu D 300, 355
ṭanāpu D 300
ṭapālu D 159, 181, 234
ṭarādu 62, 103; D 107f, **178**, 234
ṭarīdu 62
ṭarru 430
ṭebû v. 247; D 300
ṭehû v. 247; D 264, 300, 423; Dt 321
ṭêmu 317[2]
ṭepû v. D 187, 234
ṭubbu n. 423
ṭuhdu 139
ṭuhhudu n. 370
ṭummumiš 373, 424
ṭummumu n. 348, 373
ṭummumu v. Dt 310, 329, 348, 424
ṭuppû v. 312
ṭuppušu n. 376f, 424

U

ubbulu n. 370, 424
ubburu v. 315
ubbuṭu n. 424
uddudu n. 351, 367, 380, 385, 392f, 424
uddupu n. 350, 424
udduru n. 424
uggû n. 350, 424
uggugu n. 387, 424
uggumu n. 350, 424
uhhuru v. 13, 92, 315f
uhhuzu v. 12f, 65, 308, 312
ukkû v. 310
ukkudu n. 373, 375, 424
ukkudu v. 315
ukkuliš 387
ukkulu n. 48[19], 396, 424f
ukkumu n. 376, 402[4], 425
ukkupiš 387
ukkup/bu n. 425
ullû n. 425
ulluṣu n. 382f, 388, 425
ullušiš (?) 387
ūmišam 81
ummānu 118, 143, 197[2]
ummuliš 387
ummulu n. 328, 385, 388, 425
ummulu v. Dt 328
ummuqu n. 425
**ummuru* n. 370, 404[19], 425
unnubu n. 51, 66[2], 373, 376, 425
unnunu n. 377, 425
unnuqu n. 425
unnušu n. 425
unnutu v. 315, 385, 388, 425
unūtu 118, 197[2]
uppû n. (cloudy) 425
uppulu n. 370, 425
uppulu v. (appoint heir) 312
uppulu v. (delouse) 308, 312
uppuqu n. 373, 383, 385, 426
uppuqu v. (make a compact load) 312
upp/bburu n. 377, 426
uppusu n. 426
uppuṭu n. 373, 426
upšašū 42
uqqû n. (withered) 426
uqqup/bu n. 348, 373, 426
uqququ n. 373, 426
uqquru n. 348, 373, 426
urruhiš 387
urruhu n. 426
urruhu v. 316
urruku n. 58, 67[7], 426
urrunu v. 312
urrupu n. 48[19], 350, 385, 426
urruru n. 383, 388, 426
urruṣu n. 377, 426
ussuhu n. 426
ussuku n. 426
uss/ṣṣulu n. 373, 426f
ussuqu v. 312
ussuru n. 426
uṣṣudu n. 348, 373, 427
uṣṣuru n. 345
uṣṣuru v. (listen) 316
uṣṣuru v. (sever) 316
uššubu n. 427
uššuqu n. 427
uššušu n. 427
uššušiš 387
uššušu v. 310, 434
utlellû 340[1]
uttuk/qu n. 368, 427
uṭṭû n. 368, 427
uwwû v. 312
uzzubu n. 347, 427
uzzuzu n. 387, 427

W

(w)abālu 102, 266, 431; Gtn 172; Š 266; Štn 87[13]
wa/edû G → *edû*; D 294; Dt 321
(w)alādu Gtn 83, 172; D 108, **139f**, 183f, 188, 190, 195, 234f, 308; → also *wulludu*
(w)ālittu 308
wamā'um 86[7]
(w)apû 248; D 300
(w)aqāru 248; D 300; D/Š 271
(w)aqqaru 51
(w)aqû 97; Dt 332
(w)arādu 246
(w)arāqu 248; D 264, 300
(w)arhišam 81
(w)arqu 34
(w)arraqu 51
(w)arû 102; Gtn 172
(w)âru 251; D 248, 300, 302; Dtn 87[13]; 335
(w)asāmu 248; D 265, 300; D/Š 275
(w)aṣābu D **182**, 235
(w)aṣû 96, 246; Gtn 85, 156; Štn 87[13]
(w)ašābu 17[6], 96, 246
(w)ašāru D 90, 248, 251, 300, 302, 355; Dtn 335
(w)ašāṭu D 300
(w)ašru 251, 302, 355
(w)aššābu 63
(w)atāru 248; D 260, 264, 300; Š 260
(w)attaru 51f
(w)atû D **177**, 235
wazwazu 40
(w)ēdu 430
wildu 308
wukkulu v. 312
wulludu v. 12f, 308, 312
**wuqquru* n. 376, 427
(w)urrīqu 34
(w)urrû v. 316
(w)urruqu n. 48[19], 376, 427
(w)urrušu n. 351, 427
(w)ussû v. 316
wussumu n. 376, 427
(w)uṣṣû v. 316
(w)uṣṣuṣu v. 316
wuššupu v. 312
(w)uššuru n. 376, 427
wuššuṭu n. 428
**wuzzunu* v. 312

Z

za'ānu D 300
zabālu 65, 114, 431; Gtn 81, 172; D 140, 156f, 235, 301; → also *zubbulu* v.
zabbilu 59f, 65
zābilu 60
zâbu 248; D 300
zajjāru 65
zakāru Gtn 82; D 235; Dt 327
zakû v. D 264, 355, 300, 403[10]
zamāru D 235
zammāru 59, 63
zammeru 59
zanānu (provide) D 235
zanānu (to rain) 247
zaqānu 111[2], 317[2]
zaqāpu 41, 62; Gtn 156, 159, 175; D **134**, 172, 190, 235; Dtn 336
zaqāru 34; D 235
zaqātu D 112[11], 154f, 160, 186, 235
zāqipānu 160
zaqīpu 62
zaqīqu 42
zaqnu 89, 111[2]
zaqqinu 67[10]
zâqu 41f, 249
z/ṣarāpu 102
zarriqu 59, 372
zarû v. D 150f, 171, 235
zâru D 128, 236
za'û 317[2]
zâzu 249; D 12f, 112[8], **150**, 199f[19], 236
zenne'u 52
zenû v. D 300; D/Š 276, 280
zêru 103, 249
zikkarū 46[5]
zikru 46[5]
zīmū 355
zimzimmu 43
ziqīqu 42
ziqnu 317[2]
ziqqurratu 34
ziqziqqu 41
zīru 40
ziruziru 40
zizru 40
zubbulu v. 65, 114, 301, 316
zummû v. 316
zunnû n. 428
zunzunu 40
zuqaqīpu 41, 48[22]
zuqqunu n. 351, 368, 428
zuqqupu n. 385, 388, 428
zuqquru n. 380, 383, 388, 428
zuqqutu n. 383, 388, 404[22], 428
**zu''unu* n. 376
zu''uru n. 367, 428

Index of Akkadian texts

This index includes all references to Akkadian texts which are quoted in the course of this study, with the exception of the following sections: the Appendices to Chapters VI, VII and X, the enumeration of literary Š-stems in 7.5.5, and the list of ŠD forms in 9.3. From these sections only those references have been included which are noteworthy for some reason. Bold-faced numbers refer to numbered passages (00).

A. (Chicago)
7537: 7. 9'. 25'. 39 262

AbB
1, 2: 16 **352**
1, 13: 19 198[11]
1, 27: 2ff 108
1, 27: 20 123, 127
1, 27: 20ff **147**
1, 27: 28 123, 127
1, 37: r.8' 330
1, 51: 26 198[11]
1, 72: r.2 260
1, 112: 14' 260
1, 115: r.3'ff 335
1, 117: 6 275
1, 123: 10 290
1, 124: 23f. 31ff 289
1, 130: 27 177
1, 132: 10 14
2, 46: 12. 18 198[11]
2, 86: 15 99
2, 86: 26 354
2, 86: 35f 259
2, 88: 12 236
2, 98: 12 260f
2, 98: 17 133
2, 100: 15 260
2, 141: 14 289
2, 151: 10 **399**
2, 159: 13 236
2, 162: 7 123
2, 169: 12. 16 111f[7]
2, 170: 15 198[11]
2, 179: 10 399
3, 2: 25 287
3, 3: 21 295
3, 11: 12 **354**
3, 11: 15 312
3, 15: 10f 81
3, 15: 13. 23 335
3, 16/7: 13 55
3, 18: 17 **399**
3, 22: 14 297
3, 22: 15f/31 **238 354**
3, 34: 14 112[11]
3, 77: 7 260
4, 19: 15ff 259f
4, 20: 10/21ff **193**
4, 144: 20f 276
4, 152: 16. 19 277
5, 158: 5f 352
5, 158: 6 366
5, 172: 20 285
5, 232: 9 96
6, 8: 24 422
6, 13 : 9 419
6, 22: 6 **148**
6, 107: 7f 352
6, 135: r.15' 133
6, 144: 14 295
6, 154: 5' 335
6, 188: 31' 315
6, 191: 20f **319**
6, 191: 22 260
6, 212: 12 406[32]
6, 218: 15. 29 260
6, 220: 24 260
6, 220: 36 **399**
7, 19: 7 335
7, 22: 9ff **390**
7, 22: 11 340[2]
7, 42: 13 96
7, 49: 2' 352
7, 50: 10' 352
7, 60: 10 **399**
7, 61: 20 341[13]
7, 64: 9 **399**
7, 153: 8f/36ff/47ff 123, **193**
7, 167: 8. 25 **400**
7, 167: 28 332
8, 14: r.10'. r.17' 262
8, 18: 8 68[17]
8, 69: 8 313
8, 96: 17 406[32]
8, 121: 21 425
8, 149: 22 296, 309
9, 32: 10 198[11]
9, 40: 18 259
9, 66: 10f 340[3]
9, 66: 11 85[2], 293, 341[12]
9, 83: 26 366
9, 90: 7 408
9, 104: 20 90
9, 113: 9ff **174**
9, 113: 13 336
9, 169: 13 400
9, 190: 16. 18 63
9, 204: 5ff 326
9, 216: 10f 97
9, 228: 20 **255**
9, 237: 19 366, 397
10, 11: 16 259
10, 42: 7 295
10, 77: 10f 81
10, 120: 2 406[32]
10, 144: 16 198[11]
10, 150: 18 352
10, 174: 24 406[32]
10, 176: 6 198[11]
10, 181: 18 400
10, 193: 10 **353**
10, 205: 13f 260f
11, 5: 9 **261**
11, 61: 4 335
11, 72: 31 112[7]
11, 94: 9 **399**
11, 119: 8 198[11]
11, 121: 5 260
11, 130: 16' 198[11]
12, 32: 20 366, 398
12, 65: 29 **165**f
12, 68: 26 314
12, 80: case 1/tablet 4 377
12, 90: 11 313
12, 99: 22 275
12, 113: 19 259f
12, 121: 5 **399**
12, 164: 5 399
12, 166: 5 399
12, 182: r.6' 406[32]
13, 5: 12. r.5'f 288
13, 8: 5ff **82**
13, 9: 11 82
13, 49: 11 124
13, 56: 9' 177
13, 60: 11 **253**
13, 60: 12 236
13, 60: 69 119
13, 64: 14f 259
13, 85: 26 275
13, 104: 7'. 14' 311

13, 104: 7'. 14' 311
13, 149: 25f 85
13, 153: 16 **399**
13, 155: 6 **81**

ABL (cf. SAA)

113: 13 **151**
210: 17 125 125
283: r.17 149
347: 10 200[20]
416: r.6 297
427: r. 3 270
435: 19 182
452: 8. 13 300
460: r.2 133
467: 28 54
494: r.2 54
511: 18 **148**
530: r.9'/13' **141**
702: r.2 133
793: r.19 149
885: 10f **141**
892: r.24f **147**
892: r.25 123
896: 13 99
1009: 11 66[1]
1022: 8 129
1132: 7 54, 67[9]
1203: r.4 137
1389: 19 213
1419: 9 291

ABRT

1, 4: I 12f **83**
1, 23: II 23 **253**
1, 57: 27 133
2, 16: 20 275

ACh.

Ad. 4: 47 282f
Ad. 8: 5 271
Ad. 9: 4 **81**
Ad. 17: 19 322
Ad. 18: 8 262
Ad. 20: 20 333
Išt. 26: 28f **321**
Sin 33: 10 264
Šam. 1: III 35 176
Spl. 4: 10 330
Spl. 8: 20ff **384**, 397
Spl. 61: 12 426
2. Spl. 1: I 8. 10 385
2. Spl. 3: 36. 39f 404[23]
2. Spl. 3: 40 384, 397
2. Spl. 14: 50 323
2. Spl. 20: 39 139
2. Spl. 51: 17 140
2. Spl. 84: 9 336

ADD (cf. SAA)

235: r.8 273

AfK

1, 28: II 1 99

AfO

8, 28: 9 **127**
8, 182: 52 133
8, 200: 66 282
10, 34ff passim **149**
10, 35 no. 61: 7 63
10, 40 no. 89: 11 137
10, 43 no. 102: 9 **149**
11, 222 no. 1: 6 157
11, 222 no. 1: 8 **174**
11, 222 no. 2: 8 157
11, 224: 81ff 282
11, 367: 3 335
12, 144: 96 **368**
12, 146: 342 440
13, 46: I 3 224
14, 144: 58 335
14, 146: 120 96
14, 150: 202 329
14, pl. IV II 17ff 385
17, 85: 9. 12 **399**
17, 146: 3/6/7f **53**
17, 146: 6. 11 67[9]
17, 272: 22 202
17, 273: 36 124
17, 285: 94 181
17, 287: 105 181
18, 50: 20 **273**
18, 64: 23 66[3]
18, 66: 13 381
18, 67: 28. 31f **84**
18, 283: 61 255
18, 290: 18 **120**, **191**
18, 292: 32-51 234
18, 298: 29ff 149, **170**f
18, 298: 34 141
18, 306: IV 6 420
18, 306: IV 13' 54, 67[9]
18, 349: 11 68[20]
19, 52: 148 282, 332
19, 58: 130 340[4]
19, 63: 43 294
19, 65: III middle 7 337f
19, 116: 23f 284, 331
20, 40: III 15 255
20, 121: 20 219
23, 47 no. 4: 5 177
23, 86a Z. 17 282
25, 39: 12 **83**
27, 70: 20f **80**
Beiheft 17, 13b top 386

AGH

6: 8 326, 332
14: 12 269
14: 23 133, 149
48: 107 133
74: 37 130
80: 81ff **322**
80: 83 119
96: 19 136
132: 49 282
134: 90 **322**
142a: 3 149

AIPO

14, 135: 17. 20ff 148

AJSL

36, 81: 50 255

Akkadica

25, 3: 6. 9 178

AK

1, 21: II 1 293

AKA (→ RIMA)

251: 85 122
339: II 115 **253**

AKT

2, 32: 23 312
2, 37: 34 260
3, 38: 15. 27 132

AMM

p. 152 kt k/k 108: 10 217

AMT

9, 1: II 26f 129, 326
15, 3: IV 5 158
18, 3: 6 367
18, 10: 9 381
25, 6: I 10 335
25, 6: II 7 54, 67[9]
26, 2: 4 335
27, 2: 16 284
43, 1: 24 262
44, 4: 5 198[5]
48, 1: 8. 11 **321**
51, 1: 10 284
51, 2: 4 284
54, 1: 9. 12 284
56, 1: 8 328
58, 1: 2 328
63, 5: IV 3 159
66, 2: 7f 159
67, 1: IV 23 **144**
68, 1: r.10 **187**
70, 3: 2. 6 335
74: II 19 **187**
75: 1, IV 19 107
75, 1: IV 26 158
78, 3: 5. 8 **321**
78, 8: 9 322
80, 1: 12 202
83, 1: r.17 284
85, 1: II 16 287
85, 1: II g 53
86, 1: II 3 **174**
86, 1: II 14 **323**

105, 1: IV 7 367
105: 15/19 123
105: 19 198[10]

AnBi.

12, 286: 98ff **186**

AND

120: 8 52

Angim

89 440
90f 141
127 333
140 316
165 112[11]

AnSt.

5, 102: 71 130
6, 156: 132 134
8, 50: 10 138
8, 52: III 39 150
8, 60: 31 441
10, 112: 32ff 324
10, 122: 4' 66[5]
10, 122: 4'. 20' 55
20, 112: 8 40
30, 105: 21 108, **167**
30, 105: 23 336
30, 105: 27 337f
33, 148: 13. 15. 18 149, 198[12]

AoF

10, 59f: no. 7: 6' 289

AOAT

2, 299: 6 313
2, 323: 3 **273**

AOTU

1, 283: 10 426

Arkeol. Dergisi

4, 7: 24f 163

ARM

1, 7: 19ff **177**
1, 10: 18 340[1]
1, 39: r.10 260
1, 42: 9. 24 177
1, 42: 15ff **351**
1, 42: 26ff **192**f
1, 42: 33 138
1, 71: 9 311
1, 82: 10. 18 263
1, 83: 24 298
1, 89: 6 14
2, 20: 7 96
2, 24: 12f 100
2, 25: r.16' 298
2, 28: 7 **321**
2, 34: 36 208
2, 51: 10f 260
2, 52: 7 236
2, 100: r.5' 96
2, 103: 12f **334**
2, 130: 4f **346**
2, 131: 20 260
2, 133: 10 14
2, 138: 7 96
3, 8: 12 302
3, 12: 6f **352**
3, 14: 16 440
3, 16: 12 330, 340[6]
3, 17: 17ff **150**
3, 17: 20 171
3, 18: 13 176
3, 20: 5. 11 177
3, 22: 22ff **166**
3, 27: 20ff **252**
3, 41: 12 406[32]
3, 75: 6 285
4, 24: 24f **83**
4, 26: 40 275
4, 70: 6ff 283
4, 70: 16 260
5, 54: 5ff 81
5, 34: 7. 11 177
6, 5: 5 54
6, 5: 12f 84, **143**
6, 5: 13 123
6, 37: 4 403[10]
6, 37: r.4'-14' 110
6, 39: 8ff **356**
6, 40: 8 **356**
6, 43: 25ff **166**
6, 43: 27 200[24]
6, 57: r.15' 138
6, 58: 15ff **330**
7, 4: 17 370
7, 23: 2 134
8, 1: 27 67[12]
8, 77: 5. 9 198[11]
9, 17: 9ff. 15 **351**
9, 26: 9 161
10, 8: 14 **356**
10, 74: 26f
10, 87: 7 404[14]
10, 97: 12 177
10, 119: 5 177
10, 124: 10f 125
10, 124: 20f/23 **356**
10, 129: 20 71
10, 146: 4 66[3]
10, 146: 4/7 **54**
10, 154: 7' 313
10, 156: 27 263
10, 173: 13 81
13, 13: 5f 55
13, 22: 12 177
13, 24: 6 133
13, 24: r.3' 285
13, 35: 11 **252**
13, 44: 7ff **166**
13, 44: 9 141, 200[24]
13, 55: 9ff/17 **193**f
13, 103: 31 440
13, 141: 10 177
13, 145: edge 1 300
14, 2: 17f 440
14, 2: 20 **59**
14, 3: 10/19 **148**
14, 7: 5 144
14, 7: 6 **54**, **84**
14, 42: 34f 264
14, 48: 27 336
14, 50: 19 **356**
14, 54: 22f **356**
14, 62: 6 177, 197[1]
14, 62: 15 197f[5], 289
14, 70: 10 289
14, 79: 30 126
14, 86: 34 404[14]
14, 103: 8' 295
14, 118: 16 366
14, 121: 29 82
14, 127: 9f 352
18, 38: 7 350
18, 8: 6 **81**
21, 410: XI 20' 315
23, 9: 80 177
23, 581: 7. 9. 10f. 24 54
23, 581: 29 55
26/1, 6: 4. 27 260
26/1, 17: 20ff **165**
26/1, 17: 20ff/30 **344**
26/1, 17: 30 **165**
26/1, 21: r.18' 262
26/1, 25: 5f 331
26/1, 27: 37 112[7]
26/1, 39: 45 312
26/1, 40: 25 142
26/1, 55: 4ff/19f **195**
26/1, 101: 25ff **344**
26/1, 109: 12 263
26/1, 109: 6ff/11ff **362**
26/1, 115: r.5' 310
26/1, 121: 11f **330**
26/1, 129: 22 311
26/1, 144: 16' 197[1]
26/1, 152: 11 404[14]
26/1, 156: 32 404[14]
26/1, 192: 23 142
26/1, 197: 15 132
26/1, 199: 27f 403[8]
26/1, 201: 13 177
26/1, 205: 5' 383
26/1, 214: 14 **356**
26/1, 216: r.7' 366
26/1, 236: 6f 112[7]
26/1, 261: 13 255
26/1, 261: 17ff **165**
26/1, 276: 22ff **165**

26/1, 280: 17 403[8]
26/1 p. 159 note a
A.2821: 9 142
26/2, 312: 12'. 15' 312
26/2, 319: 10f 270
26/2, 329: 18'/21' **194**
26/2, 342: 19 331
26/2, 346: 4f **352**
26/2, 346: 5 366
26/2, 364: r.5' 263
26/2, 364: r.9' 439
26/2, 370: 45' 327
26/2, 374: 4 260
26/2, 380: 8. 22' 327
26/2, 380: 11 178
26/2, 380: r.5' 54
26/2, 384: 23'f **261**
26/2, 394: 6ff 200[23]
26/2, 394: 8 137
26/2, 395: 5ff **177**
26/2, 402: 19 285
26/2, 405: 24'ff/r.19'f **195, 177**
26/2, 408: 6. 13. 39 177, 200[25]
26/2, 411: 31 264
26/2, 411: 44 314, 331
26/2, 416: 7 314
26/2, 416: 12. 14 263
26/2, 428: r.10 260
26/2, 435: 14 313
26/2, 436: 32 260
26/2, 437: 29f 439
26/2, 445: 16 262
26/2, 448: 10 177
26/2, 449: 13. 26 285
26/2, 453: 23. 28 315
26/2, 468: 16 177
26/2, 468: 19 177
26/2, 469: 7 134
26/2, 471: r.4' 67[12]
26/2, 479: 28 404[14]
26/2, 483: 25 273
26/2, 483: 38 132
26/2, 483: 38f 200[23]
26/2, 494: 14 313
26/2, 498: 12 311
26/2, 526: 13 311
26/2 p. 462: 5" 54
27, 1: 4. 7 141
27, 3: 13 311
27, 12: 10 123, **346**
27, 22: 8 404[14]
27, 27: 6 40
27, 27: 6ff **253**, 287
27, 27: 22 295
27, 36: 24f 326
27, 36: 35ff **194**
27, 36: 37 124, 127
27, 57: 4f 81
27, 57: 28f 178
27, 59: 22. 29 84
27, 61: 10 64
27, 65: 13. 17 297
27, 75: 15 177
27, 80: 23 177
27, 85: 9f 125
27, 89: 20ff **83**
27, 100: 22f **170**
27, 107: 6ff/11ff **82**
27, 112: 9 397
27, 131: 18 313
27, 142: 26ff **261**
27, 161: 4ff **166**
27, 163: 3 178

ArOr

37, 484: 50 150
37, 485: 62 273, 341[12]
37, 488: 2 112[11]

AS

16, 193: 15 177
16, 24: 95 294f

Asb.

A I 111/113 141
A I 112 **253**
A II 26 137
A II 117 97
A III 132 137
A IV 82 **253**
A VII 37 325
A VIII 12 133
A IX 45 288
A IX 85 222
B V 11 329
B V 69 264
B 82: 15 288

Ash.

p. 106: 20 288
§ 53 p. 79: 8 277
§ 65: 23 405f[30]
Nin. A I 56 118
Nin. A VI 32 273

ASJ

7, 26: 259 333

ASKT

p. 127: 34 112[11]

ATHE

41: 12 163
58: 15 163
64: 43 312

Atr.

58: 211. 226. 231 **194**
60: 5 + Add. p. XII 211
60: 243 133
60: 256 211
72: 16 323
80: V 19 133
84: 28 133
88: 32f 366
90: 44 178
92: 55 133
94: 26 201, 426
96: 6 **253**
108: 51 132
110: 61 132
112: 6 96
124: 22 201

BA

5, 385: 13 269
5, 533: 17 124
5, 618: 26 123

BabLaws

340: 17 313

BagF.

16, 252: 23f 262
16, 261: 65f 85
16, 262: 86 112[11], 157
18, 130: 16ff **186**
18, 133: 82ff 186
18, 139: 137 325
18, 272: 17' 112[11]
18, 305: 19 139
18, 325: 10 **187**
18, 357: 19 **186**
18, 358: 29f. 47f 186
18, 359: 60f 186
18, 361: 87 **186**

BagM.

2, 58: III 17 406[32]
2, 59: 23ff 276
2, 78: 13 67[12]
21, 341: 14ff **320**
21, 344: 15f 288
21, 360: 37 288

BAL

II 86: Ass. 3 68[19]
II 89: 42, 45, etc. 96

BAM

22: 34 295
23: 3 367
26: 1 **155**
66: 25 335
74: IV 3 150
90: 16 314
105: 6 219
111: II 21 335
122: r.7'f **187**
124: II 46 **187**
152: IV 16 **155**
168: 52 322
234: 9 384
237: IV 39 132
240: 29 384
248: III 55 **167**

248: IV 30 **144**
323: 24 **321**
378: II' 6' 382
393: r.11 367

BBR

1-20: 29 324
26: III 4 325
26: III 19 96
79: 4 324

BBS

3: IV 22ff **399**
6: I 17 255
6: I 18 254
6: II 52 47[17]
7: II 25f **254**
34: 9ff 122

BDHP

66: 6 141

BE

6/1, 96: 6ff **353**
14, 128a: 19 66[5]
14, 163: 16ff 346
15, 7: 1f **82**
15, 48: 3 82
17, 5: 18 149
17, 27: 34 228
17, 34: 36 340[5]
17, 52: 23 325

BiMes.

19 p. 16: 4 **165**f
19 p. 23: 15 255

BIN

1, 79: 9 275
1, 124: 2 53
2, 22: I 38 254
4, 9: 21f 332
4, 10: 14 67[9]
4, 33: 6. 8 163
4, 51: 45 163
4, 65: 39.50 163
4, 67: 7 174
4, 72: 1 137
4, 157: 9. 23 126
6, 7: 6 332
6, 20: 22 63
6, 24: 3 55
6, 54: r.9' 132
7, 75: 14 123

BiOr.

9, 89: 4 386
11, 82a: 7 **58**
14, 193b: 5 426
18, 71f: 1. 21 178
18, 71: 8 134
28, 11: 17' 311, 320
28, 11f: 22'f 123

BKBM

2: 26 108
30: 43 **127**, **167**, 202
32: 51 159

BM

41255a: 3 138
96996: r.19 198[10]

BMS

53: 9 336

BRM

4, 6: 28. 41 263f
4, 9: 13 320
4, 9: 40 96
4, 12: 27 63
4, 12: 37 335
4, 13: 21 108
4, 16: 16 47[17]
4, 22: 9 384
4, 23: 15 383
4, 23: 16 66f[6]
4, 32: 12 55

BrockmonT.

p. 20: 12' 311

BSOAS

20, 264: r.3 141
20, 265: 9 141

BW

15: 16b 112[11]

BWL

32: 47 328
32: 56 52
34: 74 53
34: 80 234
38: 3 182
40: 32 290
40: 40 282
40: 47 321
42: 65 295
42: 72 112[11]
44: 93 426
44: 98 365
44: 101 108, **167**
52: 18 321, 329
54 k 328
58: 26 324
60: 98 52, 366
70: 9 313
74: 52 182
78: 136 124, 198[10]
80: 167 50
82: 213 107
100: 32 333
100: 39 112[11]
100: 41 326
100: 58 284
120: 11 292
126: 28 386
134: 139 50
144: 16 289
144: 19 **252**
144: 26 126
146: 6 289
146: 38 123, **147**, 320
146: 42 **252**
190: r.10 408
192: 25 62f
242: 21 50
252: 19ff 108

"C 18": 33 **150**
"C 18": 33 171

Camb.

273: 7 66[5]
290: 3 346

CBSM

p. 64 § 7: 1 158
p. 90 § 31: 1 **321**
p. 158 § 78: 11 330

CCEBK

37: 9 298

CCT

1, 42a: 22 369
1, 42b: 7. 14 370
2, 14: 7 174
2, 26b: 14 331
2, 31a: 14 414
2, 42: 8 17[6]
3, 8b: 30. 32 163
3, 11: 11 174
3, 14: 11 132
3, 16b: 10 127
3, 20: 17f. 38f 88[17]
4, 6c: 18ff 67[7]
4, 10a: 13ff **163**
4, 21b: 12 341[12]
4, 34c: 11 404[19]
5, 2a: 20 132
5, 6a: 7/19f **163**
5, 32b: 3 63
6, 11a: 10 312

ChDiv.

1, 95: 17f 380

CHJ

122: 17 198[11]
124: 8 326

CRRAI

35, 12: r.4' 269

CT

4, 30a: 6f 364
4, 37c: 11 312

6, 2: case 1 **81**
8, 6a: 18 422
8, 26b: 11ff 353
8, 48a: 5ff **351**, **353**
13, 48: 10 268
16, 11: 35 325
16, 12: I 3 112[11]
16, 13: III 17 **59**
16, 14: IV 31 404[18]
16, 23: 334 129
16, 34: 216 255
16, 37: 15 96
16, 49: 295 **254**
17, 10: 71 341[13]
17, 19: 6 112[11], 127
17, 19: 8 **125**
17, 19: 22 **323**
17, 19: 24 368
17, 23: 183 370
17, 25: 31 **125**
17, 26: 79 330
17, 31: 28 341[13]
19, 45a: r.8 341[15]
20, 32: 72 367
20, 40: I 24 381
22, 20: 13 262, 328
22, 74: 27 133
22, 82: 25 406[31]
22, 221: 6. 14 341[15]
23, 2b: 4 341[13]
23, 43: 8 367
23, 44: r.III 1 367
23, 46: III 26f **186**
27, 3: 10 99
27, 14: 31 99
28, 27: 37 383
28, 29: 8 157
28, 29: r.3 383
28, 33: 6-14 383
28, 44a: r.6 366
28, 48a: 5 381
28, 48c: 4 381
28, 50: r.19 328
29, 49: 28 297
30, 22b: 5 328
30, 29a: 6 381
30, 30b: 11 158
31, 33: 31 108
31, 33: r. 17/18 157
31, 45: 7/12 381, 405[27]
31, 50: 6 235
34, 29: 13 174
34, 41: 24 102, 311
37, 10: 2 174
38, 1: 15ff 85
38, 1: 18 **84**
38, 11: 47 **369**
38, 12: 72 403[12]
38, 17: 105 323
38, 39: 17 264
38, 41: 19 264
38, 44a: 7 160
38, 45/6: 18 157
38, 47: 42 158
38, 47: 46 341[16]
38, 50: 50f 158
39, 4: 32 157
39, 7b: r.5 158
39, 11: 40 321
39, 14: 16 254
39, 14: 18 255
39, 14: 24 330
39, 16: 43 385
39, 16: 49 288
39, 18: 74 123
39, 25a: 8. 10 333
39, 25a: 11 158
39, 27: 20 **156f**
39, 29: 30 **157**
39, 30: 58 **157**
39, 33: 51 96
39, 38: r.7 158
39, 41: 17/23 **156**
39, 44: 10 199[17]
39, 44: 10f 85
39, 44: 15 99
39, 46: 46 **156**
39, 46: 55 321
39, 48b: 10 159
39, 50b: r.14 288
40, 3: 64 333
40, 8c: 11 158
40, 11: 69 283
40, 12: 7/8 **85**
40, 17: 52 264
40, 26: 14 158
40, 29a: 5 329
40, 30b: 13 383
40, 31a: 11 159
40, 32: r.16 159
40, 32: r.23 158
40, 34: r.8/r.16 **155**
40, 34: r.17 158
40, 41a: 8 158
40, 43a: 3 157
40, 43a: 4 158
40, 46: 11 96
40, 46: r.50 157
40, 49: 12 157
40, 49: 22 335
41, 9a: 1 **53**, **58**
41, 10b: 13 108
41, 27: edge 3 328
41, 31: r.29 341[16]
42, 41b: 7 282
43, 94: 32 325
45, 52: 16 314
45, 117: 16f 353
48, 42a: 11 353
49, 156: 12 406[31]
51, 142: 6 63
51, 147: r.22 297
51, 195: 6 **192**

CTMMA

78: a 31 294
87 no. 69: 8 352

DA

7: 24 322
42: 15 269
103: 18 325
217: 4 366
221: 15 335

Dar.

492: 2 346

Dreams

310 b 13/19 159
311 a 2 159
328: 7 198[10]
329 a 62 **155**
330: 56f 85
332 c 3 137

EAK

1, 101: 17 322

Ee

I 6 340[8]
I 54 149
I 66 51
I 68 324
I 87 50
I 147 339
I 154 339
I 162 330
II 3 263
II 105 278
IV 16 112[11]
IV 40 272
IV 99 **254**
IV 136 150
V 1 198[5]
V 3 311
V 54 133
V 59 134, **153**
V 63 291
V 90 424
VI 39 150
VI 43 311
VI 151 337
VII 46 85[2]
VII 60 150
VII 63 139, **167**
VII 90 123, 190
VII 125 50

EL

7: 8 96
245: 7f **163**
286: 1 96
290: 15' 67[9]

326: 34 133

Emar (no.)

VI/3, 373: 180' 341[15]
VI/3, 446: 41 126
VI/4, 651: 23 54
VI/4, 651: 23/24 **56f**
VI/4, 651: 44 385
VI/4, 682: 9'f 362
VI/4, 735: 13 269

Epilepsy

p. 69: r.13 **154**
p. 69: r.13 160
p. 91: 104f **154**

Erra

I 17 439
I 25 321
I 33 255
I 133 133
I 136 133
I 144 423
I 170 133
IIId: 10 98
IV 101 313
IV 111 66[5]
IV 122 66[5]
V 21 322

Ét. de Meyer

70: 33 198[10]
85: 2 112[11]
85: 15 178

Ét. Garelli

55 M.7322: 25'
153: 40f **81**
416: 6. 11 439

FM

1 p. 63: 32ff **83**
1 p. 76: 7 408
1 p. 82: 16 292
1 p. 108: 11 298
1 p. 115: 18 **322**
1 p. 119 note 2: 8 332
1 p. 127: 15f 260
2 no. 1: 6 424
2 no. 10: 5 96
2 no. 46: 15 177
2 no. 62: 7 330
2 no. 66: 8f 80
2 no. 71: 5ff 361
2 no. 80: 11. 17 439
2 no. 82: 21' 313
2 no. 130: 6ff/18ff **193**f

FuB

12, 42: 2b 277

GC

1, 388: 16 53

Gilg.

I II 37 **323**
I II 48 385
I III 35 288
I IV 28 322
I IV 38f **322**
I IV 39 332
I V 34 330
II II 41 330
VI 41 112[11]
VI 52 341[13]
VI 59 138
VI 85. 90 171
X I 5 333
X I 16. 21 131
X V 26f **83**
XI 70 341[13]
XI 122f 288
XI 123 253
XI 136 267
XI 211 **83**
XI 212 139
XI 242 **351**
XI 251 **351**
XI 269 108
XI 274 130
XII 21 98
Bo. 15 322
Iraq 28, 110: 26 108
M I 10 96
M III 10 **351**
P II 4 327
Y VI 289 275

Glass

p. 32: A 10 53
p. 32: B 17 53
p. 63 § III 18 171

Gol.

20: 24 63

HBA

86: 20f. 31f 324

HGŠ

96: 13 108
105: 24ff **390**
111: 8 264
114: 17 108, 171
118: 4 321

Horn Museum

p. 125 no. 89: 8 198[11]
p. 127 no. 91: 4 198[11]
p. 136 no. 99: 5ff **353**

HSS

HSS 5, 99: 11 341[13]
HSS 9, 150: 10 440
HSS 19, 11: 23 340[5]

HUCA

40, 91: 19 264

IAsb.

42: 14 191
71: 13 176
74: r.10 335

ICK

1, 65: 6 403[11]
1, 85: 8 369
1, 183: 7 335

Iraq

4, 186: 16 320
5, 56: r.7 340[10]
17, 26: 9 327
17, 40 no. 9: 18 68[20]
21, 52: 42 96
25, 184: 23 321
27, 5: II 10 341[13]
28, 110: 26 108
30, 101: 17 129
30, 159: 16 68[20]
30, 230 right: 14 158
31, 31: 41 368
31, 87: 50 112[11]
41, 93: 8 320, 340[5]
50, 85: 6ff **181**
54, 106: 5 381
55, 66: 4 320, 341[12]
55, 129: I 4' 133

Izbu

54: 8ff **361f**
95: 69'/70' 383, 405[27]
124: 35'/36' **56**
124: 36' 55
134: 46' 383
134: 47'. 49' 405[27]
134: 48' 364
149: 93' 157
172: 100'f 85
181: 14' 332
206: 29 289
223: 416 51
226: 500 332
231: 365j 364

JAOS

88, 126: 20 325

JCS

8, 89a: 13a 295
9, 8: A 12 277
9, 59: 1ff 354
9, 99a no. 87: 5f **354**
11, 101b: 20. 31 366
11, 102a: 17 428
15, 6: 22 **137**
15, 6: 24 335
15, 7: 20 **148**
22, 26: 21. 23 341[12]
29, 66: 6 157
29, 66: 8 51f
29, 66: 21 282

37, 144 no. 14: 3 381
37, 147: 17 428
42, 140: 14'f 399
42, 144: 15ff **399**
42, 174: 17 313
43/5, 96: 76 282
43/5, 97: 81 282

JNES

13, 212: 26 215
13, 213: 25 215
17, 137: 5' 285
33, 342: 20 112[11]

JRAS

1929, 12: 23 275
CSpl. 71: 14 138

K. (Kouyunjik)

K.3273: 9 284
K.11716+: 5 157

kt

a/k 478: 50 375
b/k 176: 17ff **162**
g/k 18: 12 370
n/k 404: 4 55
u/k 4: 9f 317[1]
z/k 14: 2f 349
86/k 98: 14 162
91/k 102: 3 370
91/k 158: 17f **164**
92/k 1050: 9 163

KADP

11: II 69 66[1]
12: I 13 66[1]

KAJ

104: 4 205
160: 7 63
162: 4 63
223: 4 406[31]

KAR

4: r.7 290
4: r.12 **82**
16: r.26 141, 171
25: II 12 269
80: 17 335
80: r.32 294
80: r.33 270
92: r.20 314
97: 11 440
104: 24 262
107: 37 177
119: r.11 292
125: r.11. 17 **390**
151: 38 367
153: 11 381
157: r.30 **155**, 160
158: II 40 287
165: 17 112[11], 222
177: r.I 35 324
202: I 27 171
226: I 6 181
267: 14 160
333: 6 **255**
339: 14 282
350: 14 411
350: 19 123, 127
368: 3 **125**
386: 8 282
392: obv.! 23 159
472: II 10 383

KAV

1: I 50ff. 65 124
1: I 80. 92. 96 124
1: II 53 124
1: II 67f **82**
1: III 57. 79 124
1: V 65f 325
1: V 66 320, 324
1: V 92 124
1: VI 1ff/6ff **344**
1: VI 74f 202
1: VII 1ff **195**f
2: IV 17 124
98: 37 132
99: 24 177
104: 22 177
108: 12f **399**
171: 13 269
218 A II 18-32 324

KB

1, 176: 22 386
3/1, 150: 27 294
4, 80: III 5 198[10]
6/1, 90: 58 255
6/2, 44: 21+D 323

KBo

9, 49: r.9 367

KH

XI 18 198[11]
XIII 65 262
r.IV 3 198[11]
r.VII 33ff 199[16]
r.VIII 47. 52. 61 140
r.VIII 6f 199[16]
r.IX 71 96
r.X 24ff 140
r.X: 66 311
r.XII 39. 41. 44 140
r.XIII 18 199[16]
r.XV: 4 63
r.XV 17 312
r.XVII 78. 85. 90 158
r.XVIII 1. 6 158
r.XVIII 11. 25. 46 158
r.XIX 36ff **344**
r.XXI: 57f **156**
r.XXII 66 260
r.XXIII 96 198[11]
r.XXVI 34 159
§ 75+e 262

Kish

I pl. 34b: II 3 133

Kisurra

153: 24 96
156: 26 255

KTH

12: 17 **334**
19: 32 325f

KTS

15: 20 315
57c: 11 142

KUB

4, 73b: 2 404[16]
16, 87: r.14ff 284
37, 31: 8 367
37, 139: 6f 68[20]
37, 168: III 8' 47[17]
37, 190: 5 392

KUG

19: 7. 13 163
26: 11ff **163**
27: 23 163

Kültepe-kaniş

2 pl. 50 no. 2a: 9f 317[1]

LB

1201: 9 174
1209: 11 375

LE

A III 6 // B II 16 260
A IV 11 // B IV 15 96
A IV 13f // B IV 17 158
A IV 20ff **155**
A IV 29f 140

LKA

22: 15 329f
29e: I 2 336
73: r.9 141
136: r.4 202
141: 18 131
153: r.18 295
155: r.6 336
159: 17 335

LKU

16: 12 **58**
32: 12 440
33: 15 139
33: 20 272

51: r.22 311
57: 9 335
62: r.8 335
85: r.4 160

LSC

110f 200[21]
114a: 9 285

LSS

1/6, 34 note 10 112[11]
3/4, 25: 14 138

LTBA

2, 1: VI 39 68[20]

Lugal

94 440
117 302
257 112[11]

MAOG

5/3, 17: 14 112[11]
5/3, 42: r.14 255

Maqlû

I 9 287
I 23 **253**, 287
II 33f 50
II 37ff 149, **170**
II 50 141
II 119 63
II 164. 175 191
II 172-179 191
II 174 123
II 183f 234
II 206 335
II 219 **255**
III 30 **255**
III 94-98 191
III 96f 50
III 104ff **189**
III 109 132
III 110 123
III 140 336
III 151ff **167**
III 162/4 **191**
III 181 139, 153
III 186 **59**
IV 36 **167**
IV 117-130 191
V 11. 15 **319**
V 35 112[11]
V 125-131 191
V 135 96
V 163 298
V 166-180 191
VI 115 **136**
VII 2 **144**
VII 2. 6 **195**f
VII 89 335
VII 154 96
VIII 41 **153**

MARI

3, 46: 17 207
5, 164: 20. 25 194
5, 164: 24f 125
5, 165: 39ff **82**, 125, **194**
5, 165: 64 **194**
5, 258: 7f 174
6, 338: 24f. 54 327
6, 338: 60ff **360f**
7, 45: 12'. 15' 96
7, 178: r.7' 291
7, 199: 38 298
7, 199: 39 47[17]

MDP

14, 51: 12 200
14, 56: 20 200
57, 167: 30 152

Mél. Kupper

129: 31 315

MHET

1 p. 136 no. 91: 10' 406[32]

MLVS

3, 34: 5 440

MSL

1, 3f: 35-39 141, 150, 199f[19]
1, 19: 45 182
1, 80f: 33-38 125, 199f[19]
1, 88: 38 403[10]
1, 93: 35 420
1, 93: 36f 125, 199f[19]
4, 72: 151ff 329
4, 72: 171f **60**
4, 75: 284f 365
4, 119: 19f **148**
4, 125: 32 331
4, 172: 60f 415
5, 37: 353 133
5, 116: 272 55
6, 24: 225 346
7, 13: 82 53
7, 87: 210 364
7, 90: 262 364
7, 112: 112 55
7, 161: 49 **153**
8/2, 62: 235a 346
9, 10: 109 50
9, 128: 178f 284
11, 28: 10'f 85
12, 108: 163 385
12, 160: 85f 68[20]
12, 160: 89 51
12, 161: 129 63
12, 162: 138 68[20]
12, 162: 139 64
12, 162: 155 51
12, 164: 221f 160
12, 169: 394 68[20]
12, 183: 8 68[20]
12, 183: 9 64
12, 185: 47f 51
12, 194 C 3: 14 402[6]
12, 197: 20 52
12, 209: 313 64
12, 230: IV 28' 161
13, 213: 26 68[20]
14, 282: 365 346
16, 81: 112f 285
16, 156: 90 63
16, 159: 178 63
16, 275: 21'ff 176
17, 20: 288 269

Mul-apin

p. 73: I 12 336
p. 75: I 18 336

MVA(e)G

21, 80: 11 198[10]
23, 59: 37 177
40/2, 62: 3 329
40/2, 64: 9 125
40/2, 80: 79 422
40/2, 82: 90 53
40/2, 82: 91 54
40/2, 86: 114f 327
41/3, 12: 31 440
41/3, 14: 4ff **82**
41/3, 14: 5 335
41/3, 64: III 43 406[31]
41/3, 66: 49 **399**

NABU

88/17 nos. 13-15 47[17]
88/17 no. 34 44

NAPR

5, 5: A 44+D 311
5, 5: C 12+D 311

Nbn

163: 2 53
164: 12 53
441: 5f 67[6]
1113: 1. 19 133

NESA

345: r.2 123

ÖB

2, 65: 52 **85**
2, 65/6 passim 199[17]
2, 66: 61 **85**, 199[17]
2, 66: 64 **253**

OBE (no.)

1: 12ff 151
14: 21 382
14: 30ff **173**
16: 15'ff **364**

16: 15'ff. 20ff 404[17]
16: 22f 381

OBRED (no.)

1, 3: 10 403[9]
1, 46: 9 403[9]
1, 104: 7 403[9]
2, 216: 16'ff **327**
2, 260: 17 51
3, 426: 30ff **326**
3, 449: 18 403[9]
3, 455: 19ff **326**

OBTA (no.)

9: 7 365
23: 22f 327
31: 9 99

OBTR (no.)

88: 9 403[10]
124: 5 385
147: 28 47[17]
150: 19 256
150: 30f **354**
163: 12 263
305: 13f 439

OEC

OEC 1, 33: 60 119
OEC 6, 7: 20 **53, 58**
OEC 6, 19: 3 272
OEC 6, 28: 8 320

OIP

27, 57: 25 163

Or.

17, 301: 3 335
17, 302: 20 335
17, 418: 19 322
17, pl. 22: 4. 9 149
18, 409: 16 335
18, 416: 17 335
23, 338: 3ff **53**
24, 246: 18 255
36, 120: 80 441
36, 124: 125 **323**
36, 403 no. 20: 11f **164**
36, 403 no. 21: 4f **164**
36, 408 note 1 sub d 2ff **163**
40, 140: 10' 403[12]
40, 141: 31'. 47' 171
40, 148: 51 171
41, 344: 15 311
46, 201: 7 323
56, 246: 20 268, 403[10]
56, 247: 30 268, 403[10]
58, 90: 15'b 333
58, 91: 16'b 330
61, 24: 25 137

PennsOATexts

9: 18ff 288

PR

437: 26 51

PRU

3, 70: 24 300
3, 107b: 1ff 403[10]
3, 110a: 1ff 403[10]
3, 111a: 9ff 403[10]
4, 226 b 9 200[21]

PSBA

17, 139: 11 337f

RA

8, 67: II 7/9 96
15, 181: 8 288
16, 89 no. 45: 7 133
17, 176: I 9'f 284
18, 165: 20 112[11]
18, 198: 3 107, 112[11]
21, 130 note 32 275
26, 40: 6 335
26, 41: r.9 294
28, 161: 30 130
33, 105: 11 282
33, 106: 23 150
33, 106: 24 96
33, 106: 32 130, 269
34, 7: 28 283
35, 4: 7 300
35, 46 no. 18: 3 **57**
35, 48 no. 24b: 2 178
35, 49 no. 28: 2 55, **57**
35, 181f note 5: 7 300
35, 183 note 2: 7 142
38, 81: r.26 326
38, 82: 6ff 381
38, 85: 12 328
40, 58: 29 382
40, 82: 15 **319**
40, 90: 11 **321**
41, 32: 10 428
41, 41: 7 112[11], 123
42, 72: 28f **165**f
44, 13: 3f 381
44, 30: 44ff **363**
44, 30: 47 381
44, 30: 49 **321**
45, 172: 30f **323**
46, 90: 42 149
46, 96: 76 **322**
48, 146: 109 149
48, 180: 14 96
49, 178: 6 **187**
50, 14: 33 264
53, 38: r.5 326
53, 135: 33 424
58, 127 Sch. 22: 39 162
59, 151ff: 11. 14. 23. 63 141
59, 152: 37 141
59, 158: 7 332
63, 49: 50. 54 312
63, 155: 10 367
65, 71: 16'f **57**
65, 71: 19' 68[17]
65, 73: 40' 126
65, 74: 68' **82**
65, 74: 74' 123
65, 74: 81' 330
67, 42: 17' 53
67, 44: 71' 382, 405[27]
70, 111: G 19 291
70, 111: M 7 290f, 310
70, 112: G 27 283
70, 112: M 16 283
74, 117: 10ff **82**
75, 109: III 1 340[5]
75, 109: III 8. 12 339f[1]
75 109: III 24 68[19]
75, 111: VII 14 397
75, 111: VII 39 **323**
75, 112: VIII 26f 289
77, 20: 22 108
82, 160: 41 366
85, 19: 16 322
86, 79: 11 **356**

Racc.

Racc. 26: 25 141
Racc. 28: 21 139
Racc. 42: 19 141, 171
Racc. 46: 22 141, 171
Racc. 92: r.9 131
Racc. 93: 14 131
Racc. 119: 13 131
Racc. 129: 14 150
Racc. 140: 343 282

RIMA (p.)

1, 51: 131 126
1, 64f: III' 7ff **83**
1, 101f: 5ff **148**
1, 183: 23. 44 177
1, 184: 103f 273
1, 189: 18 279
1, 192: 33 273
1, 234: I 22 177
1, 234: I 28 440
1, 240: 7 331
1, 310: 5 136
2/I, 12: 8 293
2/I, 13: 20 177
2/I, 14: 68 269
2/I, 20: 47 331
2/I, 27: 27 295
2/I, 135: 70 50
2/I, 147: 9 440
2/I, 147: 14 405f[30]
2/I, 148: 18 254
2/I, 151: 75 341[12]

2/I, 154: 124 50
2/I, 154: 124ff **195**f
2/I, 178: 130 215
2/I, 195: 29 119
2/I, 201: 118 131
2/I, 207: 71 131
2/I, 211: 115 **253**
2/I, 226: 33ff 195f
2/I, 245: 13 131
2/I, 248: 86 131
2/I, 252: 16ff **190**
2/I, 254: 85 122
2/I, 257: 11 290
2/1, 282: 63f **174**
2/I, 290: 48f 332
2/I, 290: 51 311
2/I, 291: 70 137
2/I, 305: 31 231
2/I, 308: 18 119

RIME

4, 342: 46 268
4, 382: 52f **320**
4, 385: 11f 268
4, 603: 15ff 330
4, 603: 26f. 47 **120**
4, 603: 47 133
4, 604: 67 126
4, 604: 69 294
4, 607: 100f **356**
4, 607: 128 177
4, 700: 8 134

RitDiv.

30: 9 133
31: 32 328
32: 47f **120**
34: 89 328
35: 105 418f
36: 139 267

RSO

41, 319: 29/32 340[7]

SAA

1, 66: 8. 13 300
1, 77: r.1/r.7 211
1, 77: r.7 66[1]
1, 82: r.5 332
1, 110: 12ff 123
1, 133: r.3' 149
1, 190: 10 97
1, 229: 10 123
2 p. 49: 478 336
3, 2: 24 397
3, 3: 17 141, **151**
3, 7: 2 **390**
3, 10: 29 53
3, 29: r.4 59
3, 29: r.10' 54
3, 30: 2 59
3, 32: r.20f 108
3, 32: r. 21' 171
3, 37: 8' 149
3, 39: 32 278
3, 39: r.13f 211, 213
4, 45: r.11' 152
5, 58: 9 291
5, 105: 17 63
5, 146: 7f 108f
5, 294: 12'f/14'f **53**
5, 294: 16'f **56**
5, 295: 28 54
6, 293: r.3 273
7, 88: r.6 346
8, 9: 6 **393**
8, 41: 2f **330**
8, 105: 3ff **392**
8, 109: 4 325f
8, 255: r.7 **322**
8, 257: 6ff 405[27], 405[28]
8, 263: 6 367, 385
8, 304: r.4 **369**
8, 318: 3f **393**
8, 329: 2ff **392**
8, 331: 4f **393**
8, 362: 1ff **393**
8, 384: 10 367, 385
8, 389: r.1 405[28]
8, 435: 5 385
8, 469: 13 255
8, 505: 5f 405[28]
10, 21: r.8' 55
10, 26: r.7' **167**
10, 42: r.5 157
10, 72: 9 54
10, 75: 15 264
10, 95: 10 310
10, 100: 29 **167**
10, 149: 7' 264
10, 196: 19. r.2. r.6 323
10, 198: 19 182
10, 226: r.2 289, 311
10, 291: 7'ff 259
10, 294: r.4 137f
10, 294: r.32 322
11, 219: II 28' 66[1]
12, 68: 37 440

SBH (no.)

4: 37 112[11]
6: 19 **254**
7: 4 **254**
9/10: 35 112[11]
10: 65 292
18: r.9 275
31: 8 404[18]
39: r. 14 182
69: 12 335
69: 20 282
69: r.9 418

SBM

52a: 12+D 138

SD

5, 30: 40 312

Sem.

3, 11: 5 333

SEM

117: II 19 368
117: III 8 182

Sg.

8: 17 98
8: 19 **369**
8: 27 132
8: 90 112[11]
8: 96 **368**, 439
8: 101 330
8: 143 **253**
8: 254 132
8: 257 330
8: 262f **195**f
8: 299 366
8: 316 330
8: 330 420
8: 342 440
8: 351 330
8: 387 **368**, 403[11]
8: 413 254
Cyl. 10 **196**
Cyl. 22 136
Cyl. 71 278
Cyl. 76 139
Lie 40: 255 273
Lie 42: 270 177
Lie 52: 15 134
Wi. 98: 14 **123**
Wi. 98: 14f **195**f
Wi. 112: 80 **123**
Wi. 168: 2 177
Wi. 170: 9 269

ShT (p.)

81: 60 315
81: 70 406[32]

SKS (p.)

42: 45 **120**, 131, **192**
54: 147 17[6], 249, 279, 299
78: 293f **186**
102: 2 **192**, 440
104: 14f 197[5]

Slm.Mon.

II 73 **82**
II 99 273

Sn.

23: 8f 136
30: 60 149
44: 73 222
45: 3 222

46: 12 124, **144**
97: 88 **150**
99: 46 112[11]
100: 54 274
101: 58 **150**
103: 45 386
109: 17 174
123: 29 174
127 f 3 405f[30]
128: 43 386 386
133: 79 174

Spirits

p. 10: 96 152

SpTU (no.)

1, 1: II 8 324
1, 8: 1-10 **189**
1, 12: 10' 440
1, 34: 26 405[26]
1, 36: 16 416
1, 37: 3 158
1, 37: 18 405[26]
1, 44: 13 112[7]
1, 69: 15 264
1, 72: 17 63
1, 82: 11'. 17'. 41' 51
1, 83: 2 311, 320
1, 83: r.4 53
2, 2: I 6 112[11], 127
2, 2: I 8 **125**
2, 2: I 19 323
2, 2: I 21 368
2, 2: I/II 44. 46 133
2, 2: II 82ff/86 133
2, 12: II 8 406[31]
2, 12: II 12 **192**
2, 12: II 18 **192**
2, 12: II 26ff **191**
2, 13: 26f **170**
2, 18: 24 133
2, 19: 10 315
2, 22: IV 26 160
2, 22: IV 34 311
2, 24: 2 127
2, 28: 14 333
2, 32: 7 333
2, 34: r.15 333
2, 40: r.13f 264
2, 44: 3 158
3, 67: IV 20 315
3, 74: 104ff 189
3, 74: 112 132
3, 74: 181 139, **153**
3, 76: 15 414
3, 76: 18 176, **192**
3, 80: 32 **83**
3, 82: I 28 133
3, 86: 4 **137**
3, 88: II 10 314
3, 94: 150 158
3, 100: 16 333
4, 129: VI 22 366
4, 149: II 20' 50
4, 149: II 24'-33' 67[8]
4, 149: III 14f 383
4, 149: III 34 422

SSAW

120/3, 17: 16ff **363**
120/3, 17: 18 381
120/3, 19: 3ff **363**

StEb.

2, 49: 5 198[10]

St. Güterbock

35, 1A: 14f **164**
39 note 34 kt g/k 18: 12 370
40 kt c/k 1645: 7ff **164**

St. Kraus

194: 21 138f
198: 52 99, 293

StOr.

1, 356: 23 336

St. Reiner

150 b 1f 381
190: 28 290
192: 32b 270
192: 62 289
337: 3 264
340: 23 264

St. Sjöberg

326: 92 282
327: 100 282

STC

1, 220: 6. 8 313

STT

23: 31 322
25: 31 322
28: II 35 356
28: V 4' 66[5]
52: 52 282
65: 16 51
66: 35 50
69: 4 285
87: 29 53
89: 58 160
108: 15/18. 22 152, 364
108/9: 7 382
251: 11' 440

Sumer

13, 191: I 23 440
14, p. 31: 27 178
15, pl. 8: 23f 97
23, pl. 15: 15 366
34 Arab. sect. 42: 5 199[17]
34 Arab. sect. 43: 7 199[17]
34 Arab. sect. 43: 8 333

Šurpu

II 76 283
II 166f **170**
II 167 133, 149
III 86 **59**
IV 72. 87 441
V-VI 30 182
VII 28 325
VII 32 288

Syr.

19, 109: 28 141
33, 123: r.6 385
33, 125: 6f 405[27]
33, 125: 7 366
50, 279: r.7' 270

Takultu

126: 166 177

TBP (no.)

11b: VII 8' 384
11b: VII 15' 383
11c: VI 37' 131
20: 4'f 310
21: 27 54
23: 3f 205
23: r.7 335
25: 1 270
25: 4 384
38a: r.20' 383, 404[23]
38a: r.21 66f[6]
55: 5 129

TC

1, 29: 17 322
2, 34: 16f **174**
2, 44: 31ff **80**
3, 62: 23 132
3, 63: 31ff **163**
3, 73: 38 335
3, 79: 19. 21 163
3, 107: 17 163
3, 137: 3 17[6]

TCL

1, 25: 4. 13. 15 283
1, 195: 4ff **194**
1, 195: 14 141
9, 121: 10f **56**
11, 200: 21' 295
11, 245: 1ff/34 142
17, 1: 18 403[10]
17, 2: 28 403[10]
17, 4: 6ff **350**
17, 7: 10 63
17, 59: 20 200[24]
18, 86: 43 326
18, 90: 34 440

18, 135: 14 335
18, 147: 18 262

TCS

1, 369: 5 402[6]
2 p. 31 no. 13: 46 282
2 p. 33 no. 14: 5f 134
2 p. 33 no. 14: 8 282
5, 80: 21 **137**
5, 169: 24 102, 311

TDP

4: 31 **155**
8: 20f **85**
10: 31f 85
20: 23 385, 405[27]
20: 26f 129, 157
24: 61f 405[26]
26: 67f 405[26]
36: 31f 367
38: 68 384
42: 39 **186**
46: 6ff 362
46: 12ff 362
48 C II: 6ff 85
50: III 11 159
50: IV 9 366, 405[27]
54: 1ff 405[25]
56: 25 384
60: 39 407
66: 67’ 284
68: 1ff 362
68: 6ff 362
74: 37f 384
84/6: 41ff **392**
86: 45ff 362
86: 46ff 367, **391f**
86: 53 384
96: 23/7 405[26]
96: 36 405[26], 405[27]
100/2: 9ff 405[25]
102: 7ff 362
102: 13f 362
102: 17 367
102: III 1ff 362, 367
104: 25ff 405[25]
104: 32 366
108: 7ff 405[25]
108: 12 367
108: 15 382
112: 17’ 367
112: 17’bf **392**
112: 18’ 367
112: 18’f. 30’ 405[26]
114: 40f 405[25]
116: 2 405[26]
118: 20 405[25]
120: 32 405[25]
120: 35ff 405[25]
120: 45ff 367
122: 2/7 405[27]
130: 47 367
130: 47ff 362
134: 28 367
136: 54ff 405[25]
136: 65 367
136: 65f 405[27]
138: 11ff 404[23]
138: 72f/1ff 405[25]
144: 56’ 157
144: 57’ 159
156: 10 405[26]
162: 58 405[26]
162: 59 297
170: 10 325
170: 20 176
178: 16 287f
182: 42f 285
182: 44f 124, 158
188: 6 157
190: 20 159
192: 34 157
192: 35 159
212: 8 405[26]
216: 1 159
218: 5 384
218: 11 159
220: 22f **137**
220: 29 367
222: 49 262
224: 55 156
224: 56 159, 336
230: 119 384
232: 15 405[26]
234: 26 405[26], 405[27]
234: 37 284
236: 52f 367

TI

pl. II: II 32 295

Tigl.III

72: 14 263
74: 26 255

TIM

2, 121: 21 425
2, 129: 23f 97
9, 35: 13/15 222
9, 54: 14 311
9, 88: 6 440

TLB

2, 21: 10 63

TMH

1, 1c: 18 335

Tn-Ep.

I 20 **273**
II 10 **150**
IIIa 7. 45 68[19]
IV 25 50
IVb 44 263
V 19 68[19]
V 21 291
V 26 273
V 32 279
V 40 226, 336
VIa 21 123

Tn.II (→ RIMA 2/I)

r.48 215

TP (→ RIMA 2/I)

I 8 293
VII 27 295

TSifr.

37a: 10f 141

TTK 2

pl. 290: 6ff **162**
pl. 291: 7ff 162

TU

2: 10 381
2: 55 381
2: r.11 366
8: r.5 **155**
9: 15 157
17: r.12 54

TuL

43: r.11 158
71b: 3 269
74: 7 123, 198[10]
88: 4 124, 127

TuM

1, 22a: 12 163
NF 3, 25: 17 282

Udug-hul

34: 254 54

UET

5, 8: 14. 18 158
5, 26: 25 287
5, 75: 4f **319**
6, 391: 9 55
6, 391: 10 **54**, 297
6, 392: 5 98, 440
6, 392: 14 112[11]
6, 395: r.19 335
7, 156: r.I 4’ 282

Ugar.

5, 278: II 10 330
5, 313: 28 356

UM

1/1, 14: 7 295
1/2, 43: 12 365
1/2, 56: 8 123
1/2, 58: 11 200[21]
1/2, 63: 18 205
1/2, 72: 26 200[21]
1/2, 113: III 18f **120**

2/2, 69: 3/16/26 53
5, 93: II 37 262
8, 194: III 15 409
8/2, 205: 10f 353
12, 6: 7 366
12/1, 6: r.13 **54**
15, 79: I 65 174
15, 80: II 20 262

UnDiv.

104 BM 41005: III 11 336
120 B 17 323

VAB

2, 14: I 77 54
2, 170: 9. 40 341[15]
2, 357: 78 269
2, 357: 86 149
4, 62: 61f 269
4, 68: 29 174
4, 76: 13 66[5]
4, 84 no. 5: I 24 174
4, 84 no. 5: II 2 63
4, 94: 30 **321**
4, 102: II 29 63
4, 112: 26 341[13]
4, 116: 17f **174**
4, 118: 10 174
4, 132: 15 174
4, 134: 38 174
4, 134: 47ff **174**
4, 136: 9 174
4, 138: 16 174
4, 160: 11 366
4, 174: 34 123
4, 190 no. 23: II 5f **323**
4, 190 no. 23: II 6 294
4, 216: 1 136
4, 216: 25 134
4, 222: 12 174
4, 234: I 23 440
4, 254: 22 320
4, 256: 6 174
5, 23a: 47 123
5, 27: 5ff **351**, **353f**
5, 29: 6ff **353**
5, 37: 12f **344**
5, 86: 23f 353
5, 95: 17f 353
5, 116: 10ff 326
6, 139: 4. 13. 15 283
6, 207: 19 123
7, 182: 43 273
7, 184: 53 123
7, 184: r.1 340[7]
7, 192: 7 264
7, 264: 8 **189**
7, 328: 41 137
7, 348: 1 97

VAT

14051: 4 138

VS

1, 36: I 11 285
1, 37: II 49f 386
1, 37: III 34 141
1, 71: 8 293
5, 11: 9f 67[6]
5, 143: 7 290
8, 71: 8f 96
10, 213: 14 140
10, 214: IV 15 289
17, 4: 3 422
18, 114: 9 312
19, 7: 1. 6 53
26, 55: 25 163
26, 64: 16 325, 341[12]

WO

2, 150: 83 141
2, 406: 5 231
5, 34: 22 336

YOS

1, 38: I 22 320
6, 154: 8 66[5]
7, 5: 8f 311
8, 71: 13 399
9, 85: 28f **323**
9, 85: 29 294
10, 11: I 14f 125, **363**
10, 24: 33ff 152
10, 25: 24 382
10, 26: I 35 **136**
10, 26: III 21/32 381
10, 26: III 29 123
10, 31: IX 7ff/13ff/24 **361**
10, 31: IX 51ff **82**
10, 33: V 22/39 **363**
10, 33: V 28. 31. 34. 37. 39 381
10, 33: V 29 51
10, 36: I 1 382
10, 36: I 7f **362**
10, 36: I 35ff 439f
10, 36: IV 10ff 363
10, 39: 24 381
10, 39: 29. 31 381
10, 40: 3 326
10, 41: 26 405[27]
10, 41: 55f **81**
10, 42: II 33ff **151**
10, 42: II 61 273
10, 42: II 62 362, 367
10, 42: III 5. 8. 16 366
10, 42: III 21 362, 367
10, 45: 24 364
10, 45: 66ff 363
10, 47: 9 367
10, 47: 24 139, 159
10, 47: 26 159
10, 47: 40f 158
10, 47: 47 55, **57**
10, 47: 57ff 381
10, 47: 86ff 381
10, 48: 23ff 381
10, 48: 30 330
10, 48: 41 381
10, 48: 41f 165, **362**
10, 49: 2 330
10, 49: 13 381
10, 49: 13f 165, **362**
10, 50: 14 198[13]
10, 51: IV 3ff **173**
10, 52: IV 20f 198f[14]
10, 52: IV 23 198f[14]
10, 53: 3f **363**
10, 53: 9/10/11 **363**
10, 55: 5 381
11, 20: 10f 200[24]
11, 25: 17 255
11, 25: 26 182
11, 25: 54 138
11, 25: 63. 66. 70 138
11, 26: I 10. 66 138
11, 26: I 16 182
11, 26: I 19 440
11, 26: I 26 294
11, 26: I 51 255, 440
11, 26: II 16 439
11, 26: IV 19 138
11, 27: 6. 15 182
11, 27: 47 138
13, 413: 6 331
14, 42: 4 67[12]

ZA

4, 228: 15 294
9, 160: 25. 28 335
16, 154: 3 107
16, 176: 58 129
16, 180: 31 51
16, 180: 33f **120**
16, 180: 41 282
16, 184/6: 25f **187**
16, 186: 26 129
36, 188: 29 297, 430
43, 92: 42 159
43, 94: 44 335
43, 96: 14 **323**
43, 98: 24 368
43, 102: 29 159
43, 104: IV 18 323
43, 309: 1 440
44, 32: 5f **323**
44, 32: 21 420
44, 122: 23 323

47, 92: 25 441
52, 248: 62 158
53, 216: 5 107
61, 56: 153 341[13]
62, 226: 16 283
65, 56: 51 313
68, 115: 60 313
71, 61: 2'f 199[18]
73, 77: 6ff **136**
73, 78: 18 **136**
75, 200: 35 294
75, 202/4: 96f **165**f
82, 113: 7 382
82, 205: 35ff **181**
83, 5: 22ff **165**f
83, 5: 24 112[11]

II R

47: I 13 **59**

IV R

18 no. 6: 7 284
20: 4 273
21b: r.19 112[11]
25: II 22 124, 198[10]
26: 15a **254**

Published in the series STUDIA SEMITICA NEERLANDICA

1. *C. van Leeuwen*, Le développement du sens social en Israel*
2. *M. Reisel*, The mysterious Name of Y.H.W.H.*
3. *A.S. van der Woude*, Die messianischen Vorstellungen der Gemeinde von Qumrân*
4. *B. Jongeling*, Le rouleau de la guerre des manuscrits de Qumrân*
5. *N.A. van Uchelen*, Abraham de hebreeër*
6. *H.J.W. Drijvers*, Bardaan of Edessa*
7. *J.H. Meesters*, Op zoek naar de oorsprong van de Sabbat*
8. *A.G. van Daalen*, Simson*
9. *Leon A. Feldman*, R. Abraham, b. Isaac ha-LEVI TaMaKh. Commentary on the Song of Songs*
10. *W.A.M. Beuken*, Hagai-Sacharja 2-8
11. *Curt Leviant*, King Artus, a Hebrew Arthurian Romance of 1279*
12. *Gabriel H. Cohn*, Das Buch Joan*
13. *G. van Driel*, The Cult of Aššur*
14. *Wilhelm Th. In der Smitten*, Esra. Quellen, Überlieferung und Geschichte*
15. Travels in the world of the Old Testament. Studies presented to prof. M.A. Beek, on the occasion of his 65th birthday*
16. *J.P. Fokkelman*, Narrative art in Genesis. Specimens of stylistic and structural analysis*
17. *M.D. Koster*, The Peshitta of Exodus. The Development of its Text in the Course of Fifteen Centuries
18. *C.H.J. de Geus*, The Tribes of Israel*
19. *J.P. Fokkelman*, Narrative Art and Poetry in the Books of Samuel. A full interpretation based on stylistic and structural analyses. Volume I: King David (II Sam. 9-20 & 1 Kings, 1-2)
20. *J. Hoftijzer*, The Function and Use of the Imperfect Forms with Nun Paragogicum in Classical Hebrew
21. *K. van der Toorn*, Sin and Sanction in Israel and Mesopotamia*
22. *J.P. Fokkelman*, Narrative Art and Poetry in the Books of Samuel. A full interpretation based on stylistic and structural analyses. Volume II: The Crossing Fates (1 Sam. 13-31 & II Sam. 1)
23. *L.J. de Regt*, A Parametric Model for Syntactic Studies of a Textual Corpus, Demonstrated on the Hebrew of Deuteronomy 1-30
24. *E.J. van Wolde*, A Semiotic Analysis of Genesis 2-3. A Semiotic Theory and Method of Analysis Applied to the Story of the Garden of Eden
25. *T.A.M. Fontaine*, In Defence of Judaism: Abraham Ibn Daud. Sources and Structures of ha-Emunah ha-Ramah
26. *J.P. Fokkelman*, Narrative Art and Poetry in the Books of Samuel. A full interpretation based on stylistic and structural analyses. Volume III: Throne and City (II Sam. 2-8 & 21-24)
27. *A.J.C. Verheij*, Verbs and Numbers. A Study of the Frequencies of the Hebrew Verbal Tense Forms in the Books of Samuel, Kings, and Chronicles
28. *P. Siebesma*, The Function of the niph'al in Biblical Hebrew in relationship to other passive-reflexive verbal stems and to the pu'al and hoph'al in particular
29. *Y. Gitay*, Isaiah and His Audience. The Structure and Meaning of Isaiah 1-12
30. *J.P. Fokkelman*, Narrative Art and Poetry in the Books of Samuel. A full interpretation based on stylistic and structural analyses. Volume IV: Vow and Desire (1 Sam. 1-12)
31. *Y. Endo*, The Verbal System of Classical Hebrew in the Joseph Story. An Approach from Discourse Analysis
32. *N.J.C. Kouwenberg*, The Gemination in the Akkadian Verb

* out of stock